Music in the USA

A Documentary Companion

D1560648

Music in the USA

A DOCUMENTARY COMPANION

JUDITH TICK

EDITOR

WITH PAUL BEAUDOIN

ASSISTANT EDITOR

OXFORD

UNIVERSITY PRESS

2008

OXFORD
UNIVERSITY PRESS

Oxford University Press, Inc., publishes works that further
Oxford University's objective of excellence
in research, scholarship, and education.

Oxford   New York
Auckland   Cape Town   Dar es Salaam   Hong Kong   Karachi
Kuala Lumpur   Madrid   Melbourne   Mexico City   Nairobi
New Delhi   Shanghai   Taipei   Toronto

With offices in
Argentina   Austria   Brazil   Chile   Czech Republic   France   Greece
Guatemala   Hungary   Italy   Japan   Poland   Portugal   Singapore
South Korea   Switzerland   Thailand   Turkey   Ukraine   Vietnam

Copyright © 2008 by Oxford University Press, Inc.

Published by Oxford University Press, Inc.
198 Madison Avenue, New York, New York 10016

www.oup.com

Oxford is a registered trademark of Oxford University Press

Library of Congress Cataloging-in-Publication Data
Music in the USA : a documentary companion /
[compiled by] Judith Tick with Paul Beaudoin.
p.   cm.
ISBN 978-0-19-513987-7; 978-0-19-513988-4
1. Music—United States—History and criticism—Sources.
I. Tick, Judith. II. Beaudoin, Paul E., 1960–
ML200.M89 2007
780.973—dc22   2007012017

*Publication of this book was supported in part by a grant from the
H. Earle Johnson Fund of the Society for American Music.*

*This volume is published with generous support from the
Lloyd Hibbert Publication Endowment Fund of the American Musicological Society.*

Printed in the United States of America
on acid-free paper

To Stephen Howes Oleskey

Preface

TO THE "MIND-TRAVELLING READER"

As I have assembled the selections in this book, I have come to hear the sources talk to one another in imaginary conversations which could never have been predicted. Samuel Sewall, a seventeenth-century judge officiating as psalm leader at the Old North Church in Boston, communes with Pete Seeger, a twentieth-century singer-songwriter: both are determined to get their respective congregations to sing. Two ordinary people at the battlefront, one a Revolutionary War soldier and the other a Southern girl behind Confederate lines, experience unexpected moments of empathy with the enemy through music. The nineteenth-century critic John Sullivan Dwight has faith in music's power to serve humanity; so does the composer Pauline Oliveros. Jimi Hendrix and George Crumb join the Electric Church.

I was "talked to" as well by William Wood, an obscure English tourist, who came to New England in 1634. This may have been long ago, but he turned out to be a kindred spirit. Wood wrote a short travelogue for the folks back in London about the "exotic" Indians in the New World and the only slightly less exotic colonials. He defined his purpose as "Laying downe that which may both enrich the knowledge of the mind-travelling Reader, or benefit the future Voyager." How modern he sounds! Here was a clear statement of my quest: to harness the formidable energy of primary sources in a collection of documents so that my students, other teachers, and curious music lovers and readers might "mind-travel" into the many worlds of American music.

Acknowledgments

An anthology of this sort, covering a daunting time-span of music and culture, is indebted to the scholarship of others. Over several years I have received excellent advice and support from a community of fellow music historians, colleagues, students, and friends.

I would especially like to thank the following colleagues for sharing their expertise with me: Ray Allen, Amy Beal, Martha Bayles, Ed Berlin, Adrienne Fried Block, E. Douglas Bomberger, Jim Briscoe, Martin Brody, J. Peter Burkholder, Tara Browner, Raoul Camus, Eric Chasalow, Dale Cockrell, Norm Cohen, Nym Cooke, Mary Jane Corry, Richard Crawford, Daniel Kingman, Scott DeVeaux, Melissa de Graaf, Daniel Goldmark, Sandra Graham, John Graziano, Andrew Homzy, Joseph Horowitz, Mark Eden Horowitz, Harlan Jennings, John Koegel, Karl Kroeger, Allan Lott, Victoria Levine, Leta Miller, Judith McCulloh, Anne Dhu McLucas, Nancy Newman, Kevin E. Mooney, Kay Norton, Tom Owens, Jann Pasler, Ruth Perry, Ron Pen, Lewis Porter, Katherine Preston, Guthrie Ramsey, Ronald Radano, Brenda Romero, Deane Root, Christopher Schiff, Lawrence Schenbeck, Mike Seeger, Peggy Seeger, Kay Shelemay, Larry Starr, William Summers, Steve Swayne, Vivian Perlis, Paul Wells, and Josephine Wright. I am especially grateful to John Koegel.

To Thomas Riis and Denise Von Glahn, I owe a special debt. Both of them generously read through the first complete draft of this manuscript and provided substantive critiques and encouragement.

My colleagues in the Department of Music at Northeastern University contributed their special expertise and resources to this book. A special thank you to James Anderson, Leonard Brown, Anthony De Ritis, Virginia Eskin, Joshua Jacobson, Leon Janikian, Junauro Landgrebe, Ava Lawrence, Jan McMorrow, Dennis Miller, Emmett Price, Ron Smith, and Richard Strasser. Also at Northeastern, within the College of Arts and Sciences and the Women's Studies Program, I would like to thank Inez Hedges and Debra Kaufman; at Snell Library, Debra Mandel, Carol Pouilotte, Laura Stokes, and Will Wakeling. Other curators, librarians, and archivists, and expert musicians helped with documents, including Virgil Blackwell; Carol Bonomo Albright; Bridget Carr, archivist of the Boston Symphony Orchestra; Marie Carter at the Leonard Bernstein Office; Darwin Scott, Brandeis University; James W. Campbell, New Haven Colony Historical Society; Deborah Foley at Random House; Katherine Fox, Harvard Business School; Eumie Imm-Stroukoff, librarian, archivist, and assistant director, Research Center, Georgia O'Keeffe Museum; Ellen Highstein; James Kendrick and Wes Clarke for the Charles Ives Foundation and the Virgil Thomson Foundation; Erin Mayhood at Boston University; Mark Moss at *Sing Out!*; Suzanne Mrozak of the Folk Song Society, Greater Boston; Carissa Rosenberg, *Seventeen* magazine; David Tick, jazz musician; and Kathleen Tunney, the Museum of Modern Art.

Many students (former and current) at Northeastern University and other colleges and universities in Boston and New York helped this project in a variety of ways, including background research, scanning, typing, proofreading, and fact-checking. I would like to acknowledge the assistance of the following: Cara Behan, Ari Bessendorf, Kim Campbell, Davide Ceriani, Elizabeth Craft, Gordon Dale, Glenda Goodman, Mary Greitzer, Andrew Goldschmidt, Katrina Goldschmidt, Melissa de Graaf, Rachel Gillett, Jody Graham, Jasmine Hagans, Sarah Heile, Jennifer Jones-Wilson, Amareena J. Leone, Drew Massey, Tim Pezzoli, Megan Southwick, Megan Tarquinio, Matt Temkin, Jill Van Nostrand, Peter Vasconcellos, Scott Verastro, Sarah Wardrop, and Kristy Williams.

My former student Anna Kijas is in a class all by herself. I am deeply indebted to her brilliant archival skills. She also contributed expert help with licensing and permission problems. Her commitment to this book, especially in the winter and spring of 2006 and the fall of 2007, made it possible to meet a deadline.

I regularly teach a course in American music, which is a requirement for music majors in the Department of Music, and I have been using selections from this anthology for the past few years. In the spring 2006 I asked a group of students to critique many readings, and I benefited from the insights of the following undergraduate music majors: Marcus Castrillon, Jason Coffman, Christopher Dobbins, Nicole Fenton, Michael Halloran, Meghan Holcomb, Jessica Kaminski, Peter Mancuso, Nicole Massey, Jonathan Miller, Adam Partridge, and Christopher Saunders.

I also would like to thank editors (former and present) at Oxford University Press. Maribeth Payne initially acquired this book and I benefited from her comments as well as those of Tom Owens. Kim Robinson watched over the project for two years. Norman Hirschy, assistant music editor, has been very helpful and knowledgeable about many aspects of the production process. Working with production editors Stacey Hamilton and Sara Needles was my good fortune. Lora Dunn also contributed her editorial support. To OUP's music editor, Suzanne Ryan, I owe a special debt of gratitude. Not only did she provide detailed editing, but she sustained a total commitment to this project through its many travails. Thank you also to independent editors Leah Goodwin and Marilyn Bliss for production help.

Over the years many friends have provided common sense, kindness, and enthusiasm for this project. I would like to thank Sandra Buechler, Adrienne Fried Block, Martin Brody, Robert Cogan, Pozzi Escot, Virginia Eskin, Ellen Golde, Roger Golde, Judith Rosen, Ron Rosen, Barbara Schectman, Joseph Steinfield, Mae Rockland Tupa, Eleanor Weiss, and Herbert Weiss. I want to acknowledge my gratitude in particular to Carol J. Oja and Kay Shelemay. One could not ask for friends and colleagues with better hearts and minds. Kay and I, along with Jane Bernstein, Ellen Harris, and Jessie Ann Owen, used to meet regularly as a "Gang of Five," and they cheerfully listened to sometimes overly detailed accounts of my latest enthusiasm. To the members of my biography group, Joyce Antler, Megan Marshall, Frances Malino, Lois Rudnick, Susan Quinn, and Roberta Wollons, who heard so much about the challenges of this project, thank you so very much for your unfailing loving criticism and collective wisdom.

To the daughters, Erica and Allison, thank you for sharing your musical taste, your files, and your iPod play lists—even if neither of you learned music as a feminine accomplishment. To my husband, Stephen Oleskey: without you, nothing happens.

***

Paul E. Beaudoin's separate acknowledgments are as follows:

For their various assistance, advice, materials, and support, I wish to acknowledge the following: Amherst College Music Library, Amherst, MA: Milton Babbitt; Ed Berlin; Benjamin Boretz from *Perspectives of New Music* and Bard College; Martin Boykan; Martin Brody; Raoul Camus; Gene Caprioglio of C. F. Peters; Stephanie Chaileau of *Musical America;* Eric Chasalow; Sedgwick Clark; Stephen Drury; Cornelia Eisenkraemer; Wilma Cozart Fine; Thomas Goldsmith from *The News & Observer* in Raleigh, NC; the Howard A. Gottleib Archival Research Center at Boston University; Sarah Gregory; Yves Hyacinthe and the Interlibrary Loan Staff of Snell Library, Northeastern University; Marissa Iacobucci of *MUSICWORKS* magazine; Tom Johnson; Tammy Kernodle; Richard Kostelanetz; Bryan Koza; Laura Kuhn and the John Cage Trust; Peter Lesser of W. W. Norton; Dennis Miller; Holly Mocavek and staff at the Mugar Library, Boston University; Meredith Monk; Barbara Monk-Feldman; Del Moore, librarian at the Colonial Williamsburg Foundation; Jean Morrow; Jean and Maryalice Mohr, from the library at the New England Conservatory of Music, Boston; the Pauline Oliveros Foundation; Devin Phillips; Christopher Pouliot; Bruce Raeburn of Tulane University; Rezwan Razani, from Warner Bros.; Michael Rodriguez; Deane L. Root; the Salem Public Library, Salem, MA; Aaron Silverstein, LLD; Constance Stallard, from the Music Library at University of Colorado at Boulder; Joseph Straus; Aaron Tachovsky; Joseph Weiss and the Frank Loesser Foundation; Jason Wisuri and Sheila Mullowney; and the *Newport Daily News,* Newport, RI.

Credits

TEXTS

Gonzalo Solís de Merás, *Pedro Menéndez de Avilés: Memorial,* trans. Jeannette Thurber Connor (Gainesville: University of Florida Press, 1964). Used by permission.

The Diary of Samuel Sewall: 1674–1729, ed. M. Halsey Thomas. Copyright © 1973 by Farrar, Straus and Giroux, Inc. Reprinted by permission of Farrar, Straus and Giroux, LLC.

Excerpts from *Papers of Benjamin Franklin,* ed. Leonard W. Labaree with Helen C. Boatfield and James H. Hutson, assistant eds. (New Haven, Conn., and London: Yale University Press, 1967). Reprinted by permission.

Excerpts from *The Performing Arts in Colonial Newspapers, 1690–1783,* ed. Mary Jane Corry, Kate Van Winkle Keller, and Robert Keller (New York: University Music Editions, 1997). A CD-ROM publication. Used by permission.

J. W. Molnar, "A Collection of Music in Colonial Virginia: The Ogle Inventory," *Musical Quarterly* 49, no. 2 (April 1963): 150–62. Copyright © 1963. Used by permission of Oxford University Press.

Excerpts from *The Diary and Autobiography of John Adams.* Reprinted by permission of the publisher from *The Adams Papers: Diary and Autobiography of John Adams,* Vol. 1. Ed. L. H. Butterfield (Cambridge, Mass.: The Belknap Press of Harvard University Press, 1961). Copyright © 1961 by the Massachusetts Historical Society.

William S. Powell, "A Connecticut Soldier under Washington: Elisha Bostwick's Memoirs of the First Years of the Revolution," *William and Mary Quarterly,* 3rd ser., 6, no. 1 (January 1949): 103–4. Copyright © 1949. Reprinted by permission of the Omohundro Institute of Early American History and Culture.

Daniel Read Papers, Manuscript Collection no. 27, Whitney Library, New Haven Colony Historical Society, Connecticut. Used by permission.

Excerpts from W. C. Reichel, *Something about Trombones* and *Memoirs of Jedidiah West, Charles F. Beckel and Jacob C. Till, Trombonists* (Bethlehem, Pa.: Moravian Publication Office, 1884). Reprinted with the permission of the Bethlehem Digital History Project.

"The Original Jim Crow" (New York: E. Riley, ca. 1832), reproduced in W. T. Lhamon, *Jump Jim Crow: Lost Plays, Lyrics and Street Prose of the First Atlantic*

Agnes de Mille, *Dance to the Piper* (Boston: Little, Brown, 1951). Used by permission of Harold Ober Associates.

The Duke Ellington Reader, ed. Mark Tucker (New York: Oxford University Press, 1993). Copyright © 1993. Reprinted by permission of Oxford University Press.

Jump for Joy. Music by Duke Ellington. Lyrics by Sid Kuller and Paul Francis Webster. Copyright © 1941 (renewed) by EMI Robbins Catalog, Inc. Lyrics reprinted by permission of Alfred Publishing Co., Inc. All rights reserved.

Excerpts from *The Autobiography of Malcolm X* (New York: Ballantine, 1964). Copyright © 1964 by Alex Haley and Malcolm X. Copyright © 1965 by Alex Haley and Betty Shabazz. Used by permission of Random House, Inc.

Excerpts from Billie Holiday with William Dufty, *Lady Sings the Blues* (New York: Penguin, 1956). Copyright © 1956 by Eleanora Fagan and William F. Dufty. Used by permission of Doubleday, a division of Random House, Inc.

Excerpts from "Lady Day," in Teddy Wilson with Arie Ligthart and Humphrey Van Loo, *Teddy Wilson Talks Jazz* (New York and London: Continuum, 1996). Copyright © 1996. Reprinted with the permission of Continuum International Publishing Group.

Oscar Peterson, *A Jazz Odyssey: An Autobiography* (New York: Continuum International, 2002). Used by permission of Continuum International Publishing Group. Copyright © 2002.

Leonard Bernstein Correspondence. © Amberson Holdings LLC. Used by permission of the Leonard Bernstein Office, Inc.

Howard Taubman, "Bernstein as Composer. Maestro Contemplates Stage Synthesis of Vernacular and Music of Our Time," *New York Times,* January 13, 1967. Copyright © 1967 by the New York Times Co. Reprinted with permission.

Excerpts from Stephen Sondheim's work. Used by permission of Stephen Sondheim.

Alfred Duckett, "'Got a Right to Sing Blues'—Muddy Waters: Something That Troubles Gets Needed Airing," *Chicago Defender,* March 26, 1955. Used with permission of *Chicago Defender.*

Jack Gould, "Elvis Presley: Lack of Responsibility Is Shown by TV in Exploiting Teenagers," *New York Times,* September 16, 1956. Copyright © 2002. Reprinted by permission of University of Texas Press.

Kays Gary, "Elvis Defends Low-Down Style," *Charlotte Observer,* June 26, 1956. Reprinted with permission of the *Charlotte Observer.* Copyright © by the *Charlotte Observer.*

Excerpts from Charles Reich, *The Greening of America* (New York: Random House, 1970). Copyright © 1970. Reprinted by permission of Charles Reich.

David Wild, "The Jubilant Experience of the Classic Quartet: Interview with McCoy Tyner," *Down Beat* 46, no. 13 (July 12, 1979). Reprinted with the permission of David Wild.

Excerpts from Miles Davis with Quincy Troupe, *Miles: The Autobiography* (New York: Simon and Schuster, 1989). Copyright © 1989. Reprinted by permission of Simon & Schuster.

Michael W. Rodriguez, "Vietnam & Rock and Roll." Used by permission of Michael W. Rodriguez.

George Crumb, *Black Angels (Thirteen Images from the Dark Land) for Electric String Quartet*. Used by permission of New World Records. CRI SD 283, ℗ 2006. Copyright © 2006 by Recorded Anthology of American Music, Inc. www.new worldrecords.org.

Milton Babbitt, "Electronic Music: The Revolution in Sound," *Columbia University Magazine* (Spring 1960). Reprinted by permission of Princeton University Press.

Edward T. Cone, "A Budding Grove," *Perspectives of New Music* 3, no. 2 (Spring–Summer 1965). Reprinted with the permission of *Perspectives of New Music*.

Eric Chasalow, "Mario Davidovsky: An Introduction," *AGNI Magazine* 50 (1999). Used by permission of Eric Chasalow.

Elliott Carter, liner notes for *String Quartets No. 1* (1951) and *No. 2* (1959). Reprinted by permission of Nonesuch Records.

John Cage, "Composition as Process," in *Silence* (Middletown, Conn.: Wesleyan University Press, 1962). Copyright © 1962 by John Cage. Reprinted by permission of Wesleyan University Press.

Harold Schonberg, "Art and Bunk, Matter and Anti-Matter," *New York Times*, September 24, 1967. Copyright © 1967.

Pauline Oliveros, "Sonic Meditations," *Source: Music of the Avant-Garde* 5, no. 2 (1971). Reprinted by permission of Pauline Oliveros and Larry Austin.

Steve Reich, "Music as a Gradual Process," in *Anti-Illusion: Procedures/Materials*, ed. Marcia Tucker and James Monte (New York: Whitney Museum of American Art, 1969). Reprinted by permission of Steve Reich.

Richard Dyer, "Making Star Wars Sing Again," *The Boston Globe*, March 28, 1999. Copyright, *The Boston Globe*.

ILLUSTRATIONS

Title page for *The Analytical Instructor for the Pianoforte in Three Parts* Op. 15 by Benjamin Carr, 1826. Reprinted by permission of the Music Department, The Free Library of Philadelphia.

Photograph of Banjo Clown in Black Face, ca. 1860s, by R. A. Lord, from *America's Instrument. The Banjo in the Nineteenth Century*. Jim Bollman Collection. Reprinted by permission.

"The Band of 'Zouaves,'" 114th Pennsylvania Infantry in front of Petersburg, Virginia, August, 1864. Courtesy of Library of Congress, Prints & Photographs Division.

"Picture of Jenny Lind Dolls and Locket holding an albumen photograph of Louis Moreau Gottschalk." Reprinted by permission of the *New York Times*.

"Francis Densmore and Mountain Chief (Blackfoot), March 1916 at a recording session" from the Smithsonian Institution.

Amy Beach concert program and photograph. Used by courtesy of Adrienne Fried Block.

"Time, Gentlemen, Please!" and "Le Cake Walk" from the editor's private collection.

"Duke Ellington and His Orchestra." Used by permission of the Archives Center, National Museum of American History, Smithsonian Institutions.

"Professional Lindy Dancers in the 1940s." Used by permission of Simon & Schuster.

Photograph of bluesmen in Memphis. Copyright Ernest C. Withers. Used by permission of Panopticon Gallery.

"Milton Babbitt and RCA Mark II Synthesizer." Copyright © 2006. Reprinted by permission of EMF Institute.

The Residency Composers at Midpoint. Used by permission of Meet the Composer.

"The First Tejano Conjunto Festival en San Antonio 1982" by Marcelino F. Villanueva, Jr. in *Puro Conjunto*. Copyright © 2001. Reprinted by permission of the Center for Mexican-American Studies, University of Texas and Austin.

Wes Wilson, Psychedelic Poster. Reprinted by permission of Wes Wilson and Wolfgang's Vault.

MUSIC

"Bonyparte." Tro-© Copyright 1941 (Renewed) Ludlow Music, Inc., New York. Used by permission.

Contents

1880–1920

1920–1950

1950–1975

1975–2000

List of Illustrations

Introduction

Music in the USA: A Documentary Companion is an anthology of historical primary-source documents about music and musical life in the United States from around 1540 to 2000, ranging from psalmody to hip-hop. The documents were chosen with a few questions in mind. What should one listen for in American music?[1] What words will expand our musical imaginations? What have composers, performers, critics, and ordinary people told us about music as social practice?

Many new voices speak to us from these pages. One of the book's primary goals is to represent the unruliness that defines American musical traditions and to offer a broader spectrum of musicians and peoples than has commonly been the case. At the same time, the selections register the combined influence of the survey texts now in circulation for courses in the field. Thus, *Music in the USA* also takes advantage of an auspicious moment in scholarship about the history of its subject. Compared to, say, a mere 25 years ago, there is simply so much more attention being paid to American music of all colors, shapes, sizes, stars, and stripes. An area of study once relegated to the backwaters of historical musicology now commands an equal place within it.

This is a book in which words summon sound. We will "hear" music through autobiographical narratives written by some of the people who make it (composers and performers). Many excerpts connect either directly or indirectly to specific musical compositions or more generally to various aspects of the craft.

Words also travel through sound to experience. As the ethnomusicologist Carol Robertson has written, "Music is one of the most important footprints left by the passage of time."[2] We will trace these footprints through such diverse sources as newspaper advertisements, professional reviews, record company catalogs, letters, and diaries. What was it like to be there? To remember your mother singing "Barbara Allen" as a love song in the 1770s? To be one of the first Americans to hear Beethoven's Fifth in 1841? To be part of the Marxist Composers Collective? To be in the studio at Muscle Shoals when Aretha Franklin "handcrafted her grooves"?

Finally, words about sound lead to ideas. What is American music? As the sources in this book demonstrate, there has never been a single answer to that question, any more than there has been a single answer to the question: who is an American?[3] And the efforts to reflect on answers past and present keep tensions intact, showing how music acts as a magnet for the pressures and conflicts around national identity—and our humanity.

"Nowhere is a greater range of musical traditions more prominently represented than in North America" with "an increasingly multi-ethnic population that has sustained and transformed the tradition of its homelands," writes another ethnomusicologist, Kay Kaufman Shelemay.[4] In a country built on immigration, how do artists grapple with the idea of a "national voice" or "national character" in music? Need they? How do we reconcile pluralism with this statement from the American philosopher John Dewey? "Every culture has its own collective individuality. Like the individuality of the person from whom a work of art issues, this collective individuality leaves its indelible imprint upon the art that is produced."[5]

Another recurrent theme in this volume is the classic American debate over the roles and responsibilities of art in a democracy. "No other single aspect of twentieth-century music seems so central as the celebrated and oft-trotted-out gap between composer and audience. . . . It is our defining neurosis," writes the classical-music critic Kyle Gann.[6] In fact, as soon as American composers thought of themselves as "artists," they thought about their responsibilities as citizens. What obligations do musicians carry in relation to their democratic values? Does a democracy have reciprocal responsibilities to its artists?

Race pervades all three of these categories of craft, experience, and ideas. From the earliest encounters between Native Americans and European colonizers to the still-evolving impact of Latino culture on Norte America, American music marks the stages of our nation's cultural change. Sometimes, music is ahead of the curve; sometimes not. The central importance of African-American music within American music as a whole deserves special mention, bringing with it this enduring question: how and why did the musical practices of an oppressed and alienated people for too long characterized as "primitive" and "inferior" become so vital to the American musical imagination?[7]

ORGANIZATION

The book is divided into chronological units that reflect important moments, trends, and themes within American music history.

The first part, "1540–1770," covers the colonial period, beginning with the early encounters between indigenous peoples and Europeans. While this section emphasizes foundational texts related to Protestant psalmody, it also touches on secular music, aided by source scholarship from research in colonial newspapers.

Part 2, "1770–1830," is dominated by progressive trends within the genre of music composed for social worship, as it developed from "ritual to art" in churches and singing schools.[8] A few "celebrities" among theater singers endorsed enough hit songs to reach the colonial parlors in a few cities. And a niche market for learning music as a social accomplishment reached out to American girls.

The next part, "1830–1880," marks the arrival of American popular music. Blackface minstrelsy, the songs of Stephen Foster, the "melodies Louisianne" of Gottschalk, and African-American "jubilee songs," which embodied American "otherness"—from working-class humor to exotic hybridity to enslavement and the moral issues of emancipation and freedom—all reached transatlantic audiences.

Part 4, "1880–1920," establishes an intellectual, artistic, and economic infrastructure for a wide range of American musical genres and styles. Pop music hopefuls went to Tin Pan Alley in lower Manhattan as movie hopefuls go to Los Angeles today. Folk music gained some establishment prestige. Classical composers launched a national symphonic music. By 1900, the construction of major concert halls and even a few opera houses stabilized a classical-music tradition previously built mainly on touring opera troupes and traveling orchestras.

Next, "1920–1950" marks a high point of American musical achievement, when the synergy between democracy and pluralism produced enduring music across the spectrum of styles. Various kinds of classic American sound ideals emerged in this era, shaped by such composers as Ellington, Gershwin, and Copland and by new styles, such as bluegrass. Today, we recognize this era through such trademark phrases as the "great American songbook," the "classic musical theater," Hollywood's "golden age" of film musicals, and "classic country."

Part 6, "1950–1975," shows the intersections of social change, media, and technology and the mark they left on these years. The rise of rock and roll depended upon radio; the evolution of rock shaped a counterculture. In the 1960s, with the civil rights movement and the Black Arts movement, came soul and new directions for jazz. With the women's movement came performance art and extended vocal techniques. Electronic music was practiced by a small, influential, intellectual, urban elite, often but not exclusively based in universities, even though the serial style no longer dominated composition after 1968.

Finally, in "1975–2000," postmodernism, as both a reigning attitude and an aesthetic, redefines the meaning of tradition and cultural canons. The many contradictions of these decades defy easy categorization. The ethnic musical enthusiasms of minorities coexisted with an equally powerful sense of globalization. Landmark works such as *Einstein on the Beach* (1976) recalibrated opera and dispensed with storytelling at the same time that hip-hop ushered in new forms of social realist art. Technology crossed genre boundaries, bringing with it "sampling" and digitized sound. New audio and video technology empowered the privatized musical experience, beginning with portable players (e.g., the Walkman) in 1979, at the same time that the Internet expanded the notion of a "public."

A NOTE ABOUT SOURCES

While the chronology outlined above guides this book, on occasion the sources step out beyond it. The chapters' titled sidebars, which fast-forward from one era to another, highlight the impact of older styles on contemporary musical habits and the predominance of revival movements in the twentieth century as a whole.

A book of this sort stands on the foundation of scholarship in the field. In most cases, the original document has been retrieved in order to confirm and supplement the text selection. A word about the Internet is in order to suggest the depth of the intellectual revolution at hand. Many primary-source data banks are online; to offer a few examples among many—all American music imprints before 1800 and vast collections of American sheet music through the *American Memory* sites of the Library of Congress are now digitized; sound files and video clips are increasingly online; as are all books published in English before 1700. Sometimes, this has led to revisionist thinking about sources—and equally to a sense of gratitude for the technology that made the work for this book mostly easier, even if sometimes harder because of the vast quantity of what is "out there" in Internet space.

In the end, *Music in the USA: A Documentary Companion* is just that, a guide through thickets of styles and ideas offering choices that seem right but not the only kind of right. That it has been difficult to select from the varieties of American musical experiences—that there are many important trends, people, ideas, and values not covered—needs to be said even if it sounds a familiar note from an optimistic anthology maker, who reluctantly stopped writing *da capo* on her e-mails, accepting that there was no *finé*, only "time out."

A NOTE ABOUT EDITORIAL POLICIES

The editorial policies applied here reflect the need to balance scholarly practices with the demands of a textbook. Given the diverse nature of these documents, I have leaned toward flexibility rather than consistency.

With respect to issues of language, problems vary over time. Before 1830, antiquated spellings have been retained to convey shifting practices. In the interest of historical accuracy, racial epithets (whose wounding power seems both to increase and decrease with time) and other offensive words have been left undisturbed. Obvious misprints of words unrelated to musical concerns have been corrected silently.

Practices of annotations have similarly received a flexible approach. In general, lesser-known people mentioned in my introductions to sources have been supplied with birth and death dates, as have names in endnotes. Given the numbers of musicians or musical titles sometimes named in a single source, this was a practical compromise. Occasional footnotes (as opposed to endnotes) record the work of another editor of a source being used here. My own editorial annotations are limited to those that improve the overall comprehensibility and functionality of the document. With respect to the process of finding sources, the scholarship which provided the initial reference for the material at hand has been listed in the source citation at the end of the document.

~~~~~~

NOTES

1. This phrase is indebted to Aaron Copland, *What to Listen for in Music* (New York: McGraw Hill, Inc., 1939).

2. Carol E. Robertson, ed., *Musical Repercussions of 1492: Encounters in Text and Performance* (Washington, D.C.: Smithsonian Institution Press, 1992): 2.

3. Eric Foner, "Who Is an American?" in *Who Owns History? Rethinking the Past in a Changing World* (New York: Hill and Wang, 2002): 150.

4. Kay Kaufman Shelemay, *Soundscapes: Exploring Music in a Changing World,* 2nd ed. (New York: Norton, 2006): xiii.

5. John Dewey, *Art as Experience* (New York: Minton, Balch, 1934): 330.

6. Kyle Gann, *American Music in the Twentieth Century* (New York: Schirmer, 1997): 184.

7. This question is indebted to one asked by Wilfrid Mellers in his book review of Christopher Small's *Music of the Common Tongue:* "why is it that the music of an alienated, oppressed, often persecuted black minority should have made so powerful an impact on the entire industrialized world, whatever the colour of its skin and economic status?" Wilfrid Mellers, "Musickings and Musicology," *Musical Times* 129, no. 1739 (January 1988): 19.

8. Richard Crawford, *America's Musical Life: A History* (New York: Norton, 2001): 29.

1540–1770

1

$\mathcal{E}$ARLY ENCOUNTERS BETWEEN INDIGENOUS

PEOPLES AND EUROPEAN EXPLORERS

(Castañeda, Drake, de Meras, Smith, Wood)

These selections come from reports of encounters between Europeans and indigenous peoples on the American continent, when explorers looking for gold landed on both coasts of what is now the United States. As conquest and colonization expanded, the literature of observation grew. Narratives written about those expeditions sometimes include details of musical moments filled with cultural confusion. This sampling includes a descriptive fragment of a work song in a genre still alive today; two longer accounts of ceremonial meetings where violence lies just below the surface of the festivities; sections from the writings of Captain John Smith, famous today as the man whose life the legendary princess Pocahontas saved; and a softer comment from a tourist to seventeenth-century New England.

The "conquistador" Francisco Vásquez de Coronado (1510–1554), traveling from Mexico City northward in search of gold, arrived at a Zuni village in present-day

New Mexico around 1540–1541. On a subsidiary expedition, one of Coronado's sol-
diers described the sight of women grinding corn to make tortillas, singing along with
a flutist whose music lightened their labor. While the songs remain a mystery, record-
ings made in the late twentieth century of corn-grinding songs from southwestern
Navajos from the Canyon de Chelly echo this account.

They keep the separate houses where they prepare the food for eating and where they grind the meal, very clean. This is a separate room or closet, where they have a trough with three stones fixed in stiff clay. Three women go in here, each one having a stone, with which one of them breaks the corn, the next grinds it, and the third grinds it again. They take off their shoes, do up their hair, shake their clothes, and cover their heads before they enter the door. A man sits at the door playing on a fife while they grind, moving the stones to the music and singing to-gether. They grind a large quantity at one time, because they make all their bread of meal soaked in warm water, like wafers.

SOURCE: George Parker Winship, *The Coronado Expedition 1540–1542* (Chicago: Rio Grande Press, 1964): XII:270, cited as "From the Second Part, which treats of the high villages and provinces and of their habits and customs, as collected by Pedro de Cas-tañeda, native of the city of Najara. Chapter 4, of how they live at Tiguex, and of the province of Tiguex and its neighborhood." Tiguex was located on the Rio Grande not far from Acoma, New Mexico.

~~~~~~~~~

Sir Francis Drake (ca. 1543–1596), famous as the first Englishman to sail around the
world, left enough notes and memories among his fellow passengers on his ship The
Golden Hinde to enable narratives of his exploits to be reconstructed and published
after his death. The following excerpts, which treat encounters of Drake and his crew
among Indians in the San Francisco Bay area in 1579, spill over with cultural con-
fusions. The Indians dance and sing to men they believe to be gods; the Englishmen
pray and sing to their God and recoil from the mutilation ceremonies designed to ap-
pease them. In the midst of this drama, the Indians hear Protestant psalm singing—
and they like it. They coin a word to indicate to these strangers that they wish to hear
more. "Gnaah," they say, imitating the nasal qualities of the English voices.

The next day after our coming to anchor in the aforesaid harbor, the people of the country shewed themselves; sending off a man with great expedition to us in a canow. Who being yet but a little from the shore, and a great way from our ship, spake to us continually as he came rowing on. And at last at a reasonable distance staying himself, he began more solemnly a long and tedious oration, after his manner; using in the delivery thereof, many gestures and signs; moving his hands, turning his head and body many wayes; and after his oration ended with great shew of reverence and submission, returned back to shoar again. He shortly came again the second time in like manner, and so the third time when he brought with him (as a present from the rest) a bunch of *Feathers,* much like the feathers *of a black crow,* very neatly and artificially gathered upon a string, and drawn together in a round bundle, being very clean and finely cut, and bearing in length an equall proportion one with another; a speciall cognizance (as we afterwards observed) which they that guard their Kings person, weare on their heads. . . .

The 3rd day following, viz. the 21, our ship having received a leake at sea, was brought to anchor neer the shoar, that her goods being landed, she might be repaired: but for that we were to prevent any danger that might chance against our safety, our generall first of all landed his men, with all necessary provision to build tents and make a fort for the defence of ourselves and goods: and that we might under the shelter of it, with more safety whatever should befall, end our business; which when the people of the country perceived us doing, as men set on fire to war, in defence of their country, in great hast and companies, with such weapons as they had, they came down unto us, yet with no hostile meaning, or intent to hurt us: standing when they drew neere, as men ravished in their mindes, with the sight of such things as they never had seen, or heard off before that time: their errand being rather with submission and feare to worship us as gods, then to have any war with us as with mortal men.

[Drake and his men, after urging the natives to cover their nakedness, eat a meal in front of them to demonstrate their mortality.] . . . Notwithstanding nothing could perswade them, nor remove that opinion which they had conceived of us, that we should be gods. . . .

As soon as they were returned to their houses, they began amongst themselves a kind of most lamentable weeping and crying out; which they continued also a great while together, in such sort, that in the place where they left us (being neer about 3. quarters or an English mile distant from them) we very plainly, with wonder and admiration did heare the same: the women especially, extending their voices, in a most miserable and doleful manner of shreeking. . . . [After two days, the natives performed more ceremonies of submission, including flailing their bodies.] . . . This bloudy sacrifice (against our wils) being thus performed, our generall with his company in the presence of those strangers fell to prayers: and by signes in lifting up our eyes & hands to heaven, signified unto them, that God whom we did serve, and whom they ought to worship, was above: beseeching God if it were his good pleasure to open by some means their blinded eyes; that they might in due time be called to the knowledge of him the true and ever-living God, and of Jesus Christ whom he hath sent, the salvation of the Gentiles. In the time of which prayers, singing of psalms, and reading of certain chapters in the Bible, they sate very attentively; and observing the end of every pause, with one voyce still cryed, oh, greatly rejoycing in our exercises. Yea they took such pleasure in our singing of psalmes, that whensoever they resorted to us, their first request was commonly this, *Gnaah,* by which they intreated that we should sing. . . . [Additional ceremonies of submission and spiritual acceptance of these "gods" followed, signified by more singing and dancing amid self-flagellations.] . . . And being now come to the foot of the hill and neere our fort, the Scepter-bearer with a composed countenance and stately carriage, began a song, and answerable thereunto, observed a kind of measures in a danc[e]: whom the Ki[ng] with his guard, and every sort of person following, did in like manner sing and daunce, saving only the woman who danced but kept silence. As they daunced, they still came on: and our Generall perceiving their plain and simple meaning, gave order that they might freely enter without interruption within our bulwark: where after they had entred, they yet continued their song, and daunce a reasonable time: their women also following them with their wassaile boales in their hands, their bodies bruised, their faces torn, their dugs, breast, and other parts bespotted with bloud, trickling down from the wounds, which with their nailes they had made before their coming.

SOURCE: *Sir Francis Drake Revived. Who is or may be a Pattern to stirre up all Heroicke and active SPIRITS of these Times, to benefit their Countrey and eternize their Names by like Noble ATTEMPTS: Being a Summary and true Relation of foure severall VOYAGES made by the Said Sir Francis DRAKE to the WEST-INDIES . . . Collected out of the Notes of the said Sir Francis Drake; Master Philip Nichols, Master Francis Fletcher, Preachers; and the Notes of divers other Gentlemen (who went in the said Voyages) carefully compared together* (London: Nicholas Bourne, 1653): 67–76.

～～～～～

This memoir written by a crew member, Gonzalo Solís de Merás, describes encounters in 1565 between Florida Indians and the conquistador Pedro Menéndez de Avilés (1519–1574), an early warrior from Spain who made claims for Nueva España and is both infamous for the massacre of French Huguenots, who had arrived there first— thus dislodging French claims to the territory—and famous for ensuring and developing the settlement as a Spanish colony, San Augustín. (Now called St. Augustine, the city describes itself as the oldest permanent settlement within the United States.) Here, Menéndez, who is referred to as the adelantado, or military commander, encounters the Indian cacique, or chief, Carlos, who already had experience with the French. A music lover, Menéndez crossed the Atlantic with an entourage of musicians on board. The description of his banquet of conquest, written by a soldier on the scene, includes references to both Spanish and native music making and cultural rivalry.

And the day following that on which Cacique Carlos departed from the brigantines, the Adelantado went to dine with him, taking 200 arquebusiers with him and a flag, 2 fifers and drummers, 3 trumpeters, one harp, one vihuela de arco,* and one psaltery, and a very small dwarf, a great singer and dancer, whom he brought with him. The cacique's house was about two arquebuse shots from where he landed, and 2,000 men might gather therein without being very crowded: the Adelantado's people marched in order to that house and he did not allow them to enter it, but stationed them outside, ready for any emergency, with their fuses lighted.

He [the *Adelantado*] entered the cacique's house alone, with about 20 gentlemen, and stood where there were some large windows, through which he could see his men: the cacique was in a large room, alone on a [raised] seat with a great show of authority, and with an Indian woman also seated, a little apart from him, on an elevation half an *estado*** from the ground; and there were about 500 principal Indian men and 500 Indian women: the men were near him, and the women near her, below them.

When the Adelantado mounted to that place, the cacique yielded his seat to him, and drew quite a distance apart.

The Adelantado placed him near him, and then the cacique rose, and went toward the Adelantado to take his hands, according to their custom; going through a certain ceremony

*A *vihuela de arco*, a sort of primitive violin. A *vihuela* is a guitar.

**A length measure of 1.85 yards.

which is like kissing the King's hand here; no greater mark of deference can be given among them. . . . And more than 500 Indian girls, from 10 to about 15 years, who were seated outside the window, began to sing, and other Indians danced and whirled: then the principal Indian men and women who were near the cacique sang, and they said, according to what was afterward found out, that this was the greatest demonstration of rejoicing, for a ceremony of allegiance, that that cacique or any other of that country, could give the Adelantado.
. . .

After the cacique's principal Indians had finished dancing and singing, the Indian women who were outside, at no time left off doing so, until the Adelantado departed, and they sang with much order: they were seated in groups of 100, and 50 of them would sing a little and stop, then another 50 would sing. The cacique asked the Adelantado, after his principal Indians had danced, whether he wished that they should bring the food for him and his Christians.
. . .

When the repast was being carried in, the Spaniards blew the trumpets which were outside, and while the Adelantado was eating, they played the instruments very well and the dwarf danced: 4 or 6 gentlemen who were there, who had very good voices, began to sing in excellent order, for the Adelantado was very fond of music and always tried to take with him the best he could; when the Indians heard it they were strangely pleased. The cacique told the young girls to stop singing, for they knew little and the Christians knew much: their music ceased: the cacique prayed that until the Adelantado should depart, his men should always keep on singing and playing the instruments: the Adelantado commanded that it be so.

SOURCE: Gonzalo Solís de Merás, *Pedro Menéndez de Avilés: Memorial*, trans. Jeannette Thurber Connor (Gainesville: University of Florida Press, 1964): 145–46, 148–49.

~~~~~~~~~

In 1606, the soldier and adventurer John Smith (1580–1631) joined the Virginia Company's expedition to search for gold and ended up as an administrator of a makeshift colony. He stayed in what the English named Jamestown until 1609 and left a detailed record of the culture of the Powhatan confederacy, in what we now call the Virginias and Maryland. His survival skills have become legend: book 3 of the Generall Historie *recounts his capture by the king of the Powhatans, whose warriors were "ready with their clubs to beate out his braines [when] Pocahontas, the King's dearest daughter, when no intreaty could prevaile, got his head in her armes, and laid her owne upon his to save him from death." As one might expect, Smith's veracity in this instance has been questioned by some contemporary historians, but his skill as a reporter has been recognized. In book 2, Smith recounts ceremonial music for war and for burials with instruments.*

For their Musicke they use a thicke Cane, on which they pipe as on a Recorder. For their warres they have a great deepe platter of wood. They cover the mouth thereof with a skin, at each corner they tie a walnut, which meeting on the backside neere the bottome, with a small rope they twitch them together till it be so tought and stiffe, that they may beat upon it as upon a drumme. But their chiefe instruments are Rattles made of small gourds, or Pumpcons shels. Of these they have Base, Tenor, Countertenor, Meane, and Treble. These mingled with their voyces sometimes twenty or thirtie together, make such a terrible noise as would rather affright, than delight any man. If any great commander arrive at the habitation of a Werowance [chief], they spread a Mat as the Turkes doe a Carpet for him to sit upon. Upon another right opposite they sit themselves. Then doe all with a tunable voice of shouting bid him welcome. After this doe two or more of their chiefest men make an Oration, testifying their love. Which they doe with such vehemency, and so great passions, that they sweat till they drop, and are so out of breath they can scarce speake. So that a man would take them to be exceeding angry, or stark mad. Such victuall as they have, they spend freely, and at night where his lodging is appointed, they set a woman fresh painted red with *Pocones* [a root made into a red powder] and oyle, to be his bed fellow.

OF THEIR RELIGION

There is yet in *Virginia* no place discovered to be so Savage, in which they have not a Religion, Deere, and Bow, and Arrowes. All things that are able to doe them hurt beyond their prevention, they adore with their kinde of divine worship; as the fire, water, lightning, thunder, our Ordnance, peeces, horses &c. But their chiefe God they worship is the Devill. Him they call *Okee*, and serve him more of feare then love. They say they have conference with him, and fashion themselves as neare to his shape as they can imagine. In their Temples they have his image evill favouredly carved, and then painted and adorned with chaines of copper, and beads, and covered with a skin, in such manner as the deformitie may well suit with such a God.

For their ordinary burials, they dig a deepe hole in the earth with sharpe stakes, and the corpse being lapped in skins and mats with their jewels, they lay them upon stickes in the ground, and so cover them with earth. The buriall ended, the women being painted all their faces with blacke cole and oyle, doe sit twenty-foure houres in the houses mourning and lamenting by turnes, with such yelling and howling, as may expresse their great passions.

In this place commonly are resident seaven Priests. The chiefe differed from the rest in his ornaments, but inferior Priests could hardly be knowne from the common people, but that they had not so many holes in their eares to hang their jewels at. The ornaments of the chiefe Priest were certaine attires for his head made thus. They tooke a dosen, or 16, or more snakes skins and stuffed them with mosse, and of Weesels and other Vermines skins a good many. All these they tie by their tailes, so as all their tailes meete in the toppe of their head like a great Tassell. Round about this Tassell is as it were a crowne of feathers, the skins hang round about his head, necke, and shoulders, and in a manner cover his face. The faces of all their Priests are painted as ugly as they can devise, in their hands they had every one his Rattle, some base, some smaller. Their devotion was most in songs, which the chiefe Priest beginneth and the rest followed him, sometimes he maketh invocations with broken sentences by starts and strange passions, and at every pause, the rest give a short groane.

> *Thus seeke they in deepe foolishnesse,*
>
> *To climbe the height of happinesse.*

It could not be perceived that they keepe any day as more holy then other; But onely in some great distresse of want, feare of enemies, times of triumph and gathering together their fruits, the whole Country of men, women, and children came together to solemnities. The manner of their devotion is, sometimes to make a great fire, in the house or fields, and all to sing and daunce about it with Rattles and shouts together, foure or five houres. Sometimes they set a man in their midst, and about him they dance and sing, he all the while clapping his hands, as if he would keepe time, and after their songs and dauncings ended they goe to their Feasts.

> SOURCE: Captain John Smith, *The Generall Historie of Virginia, New-England, and the Summer Isles, with the names of the Adventurers, Planters, and Governours from their first beginning An. 1584 to this present 1624 . . . Divided into Six Bookes by Captaine JOHN SMITH, Sometymes Governour in those Countryes & Admirall of New England* (London: Printed by I. D. and I. H. for Michael Sparkes, 1624): 34–36.

～～～～～

Little is known about the travel writer William Wood (ca. 1580–1639), who wrote one of the earliest and fullest accounts of indigenous peoples in the Massachusetts Bay colony. Alden Vaughan, the editor of a modern edition (1977), praises Wood's reliability and places him in New England between 1629 and 1633. Upon returning to England, Wood published this volume, which went through two other editions by 1639. From his perspective as a tourist, Wood noticed details about domestic life that include a rare observation about lullabies.

CHAP. XIX. *OF THEIR WOMEN, THEIR DISPOSITIONS, EMPLOYMENTS, USAGE BY THEIR HUSBANDS, THEIR APPAREL, AND MODESTY*

To satisfie the curious eye of women-readers, who otherwise might thinke their sex forgotten, or not worthy [of] a record, let them peruse these few lines, wherein they may see their owne happinesse, if weighed in the womans ballance of these ruder *Indians,* who scorne the tutorings of their wives, or to admit them as their equals, though their qualities and industrious deservings may justly claime the preheminence, and command better usage and more conjugall esteeme, their persons and features being every way correspondent, their qualifications more excellent, being more loving, pittiful, and modest, milde, provident, and laborious than their lazie husbands.

[There is a long discussion of women's duties, including building houses, planting corn, trapping lobsters by hand, cooking, and weaving.] They likewise sew their husbands' shooes, and weave coates of Turkie feathers; besides all their ordinary household drudgery which dayly lies upon them, so that a bigge bellie hinders no businesse, nor a childbirth takes much time, but the young infant being greased and sooted, wrapt in a Beaver skin, bound to his good behaviour with his feete up to his bumme, upon a board two foot long and one foot broade, his face exposed to all nipping weather, this little *Pappouse* travels about with his bare footed mother to paddle in the Icie Clammbanks after three or four daies of age have sealed his passeboard and his mothers recoverie. For their carriage it is very civill, smiles being the greatest grace of their mirth; their musicke is lullabies to quiet their children, who generally are as quiet as if they had neither spleene or lungs. To heare one of these *Indians* unseene, a good eare might easily mistake their untaught voyce for the warbling of a well tuned instrument. Such command have they of their voices.

> SOURCE: William Wood, *New England's Prospect: A true, lively, and experimentall descrip-tion of that part of America, commonly called New England: discovering the State of that Countrie, both as it stands to our new-come English Planters; and to the old Native Inhab-itents. Laying downe that which may both enrich the knowledge of the mind-travelling Reader, or benefit the future Voyager* (London: Tho. Cotes for John Bellammie, 1634): 94, 96.

2

FROM THE PREFACE TO THE FIRST EDITION OF THE

BAY PSALM BOOK

The *Bay Psalm Book* (1640), the first book printed in the English-speaking colonies, belongs to a long tradition in Protestant worship. In contrast to Catholic practice, where the classic psalms from the Bible were chanted in Latin, Protestant reformers considered psalms to be community songs. They turned the free verse of the 150 psalms of David into rhymed poetry with four-line verses. Different "meters," or syllable counts per line, controlled the verse patterns. Thus "versified" and "metered," to use the old terms, the psalms were then sung to a few popular tunes everybody knew. Making proper and useful translations from the Old Testament concerned Puritan authorities—around thirty of whom worked on the *Bay Psalm Book*—far more than did the music itself. One of the points of controversy between the Catholic church and Protestant Reformers had involved the right to use the Hebrew Bible rather than the prescribed Latin translations made of it. Thus, like earlier Protestant translators such as Henry Ainsworth, the *Bay Psalm Book*'s authors went back to the Hebrew sources, proudly claiming that they wrote "close fitting" translations of the original Hebrew texts. This selection from the preface reproduces three Hebrew words, which were loosely translated to parallel the New Testament categories of psalms, hymns, and spiritual songs—categories which defined sacred-song publication for two centuries.

The *Bay Psalm Book* follows what has been called the "scriptural principle"; this rule, following the teachings of John Calvin, allowed only psalms and no other poetry to be sung at Puritan church services.[1] But over the course of the next century, this rule was broken and the spread of freely composed devotional hymnody competed with psalmody.

In this first excerpt from the preface, which most scholars attribute to John Cotton and less frequently to Richard Mather, complex learned arguments justify the practice of versified or metric psalmody.

The singing of Psalmes, though it breathe forth nothing but holy harmony, and melody: yet such is the subtilty of the enemie, and the enmity of our nature against the Lord, & his wayes, that our hearts can finde matter of discord in his harmony, and crotchets of division in this holy melody.—for—There have been three questiōs especially stirrīg cōcerning singing. First—what psalmes are to be sung in churches? Whether Davids and other scripture psalmes, or the psalmes invented by the gifts of godly men in every age of the church. Secondly, if scripture psalmes, whether in their owne words, or in such meter as english poetry is wont to run in? Thirdly—by whom are they to be sung? whether by the whole churches together with their voices? or by one man singing alōe and the rest joynīg in siléce, & in the close sayīg amen.

Touching the first, certainly the singing of Davids psalmes was an acceptable worship of God, not only in his owne, but in succeeding times. as in Solomons time *2 Chron. 5.13.* in Iehosaphats time *2 chron. 20.21.* in Ezra his time *Ezra 3.10, 11.* and the text is evident in Hezekiahs time they are commanded to sing praise in the words of David and Asaph, *2 chron. 29, 30.* which one place may serve to resolve two of the questions (the first and the last) at once, for this commandement was it cerimoniall or morall? some things in it indeed were cerimoniall, as their musicall instruments &c but what cerimony was there in singing prayse with the words of David and Asaph? what if David was a type of Christ, was Asaph also? was every thing of David typicall? are his words (which are of morall, universall, and perpetuall authority in all nations and ages) are they typicall? what type can be imagined in making use of his songs to prayse the Lord? If they were typicall because the cerimony of musicall instruments was joyned with them, then their prayers were also typicall, because they had that ceremony of incense admixt with them: but wee know that prayer then was a morall duty, notwithstanding the incense; and soe singing those psalmes notwithstanding their musical instruments. Beside, that which was typicall (as that they were sung with musicall instruments, by the twenty-four orders of Priests and Levites. *1 chron 25.9.*) must have the morall and spirituall accomplishment in the new Testament, in all the Churches of the Saints principally, who are made kings & priests *Reu. 1.6.* and are the first fruits unto God. *Reu. 14.4.* as the Levites were *Num. 3.45.* with hearts & lippes, instead of musicall instruments, to prayse the Lord; who are set forth (as some judiciously thinke) *Reu. 4.4.* by twēty foure Elders, in the ripe age of the Church, *Gal. 4.1, 2, 3.* answering to the twenty foure orders of Priests and Levites *1 chron. 25.9.* Therefore not some select members, but the whole Church is commaunded to teach one another in all the severall sorts of Davids psalmes, some

being called by himselfe מזמורים psalms, some תהילים: Hymns some: שידים: spirituall songs.[2]
Soe that if the singing Davids psalmes be a morall duty & therefore perpetuall; then wee under
the new Testamēt are bound to sing them as well as they under the old: and if wee are expresly
commanded to sing Psalmes, Hymnes, and spirituall songs, then either wee must sing Davids
psalmes, or else may affirm they are not spirituall songs: which being penned by an extraordīary
gift of the Spirit, for the sake especially of Gods spir[i]tuall Israell; not to be read and preached
only (as other parts of holy writ) but to be sung also, they are therefore most spirituall, and still
to be sung of all the Israell of God: and verily as their sin is exceeding great, who will allow
Davids psalmes (as other scriptures) to be read in churches (which is one end) but not to be
preached also, (which is another end) soe their sin is crying before God, who will allow them to
be read and preached, but seeke to deprive the Lord of the glory of the third end of them, which
is to sing them in Christian churches.

〜〜〜〜〜

*Then follows an extended argument in the form of a series of hypothetical objections
to the idea of psalm singing, followed by refutations of the objections. This excerpt
discusses issues more directly involved with literary and therefore musical practice.
Note how the preface takes a quick swipe at a rival volume of psalms by Ainsworth,
in use at the Puritans' rival, the Plymouth Colony of Pilgrims.*

As for the scruple that some take at the translatiō of the book of psalmes into meeter, because
Davids psalmes were sung in his owne words without meeter: wee answer— First—There
are many verses together in several psalmes of David which run in rithmes [rhythms] (as those
that know the hebrew and as Buxtorf shews *Thesau. pa. 629*.)[3] which shews at least the lawfull-
ness of singing psalmes in english rithmes.

Secondly. The psalmes are penned in such verses as are sutable to the poetry of the hebrew language, and not in the common style of such other bookes of the old Testament as are not
poeticall; now no protestant doubteth but that all the bookes of the scripture should by Gods ordinance be extant in the mother tongue of each nation, that they may be understood of all, hence the
psalmes are to be translated into our english tongue; and if in our english tongue wee are to sing
them, then as all our english songs (according to the course of our english poetry) do run in metre,
soe ought Davids psalmes to be translated into meeter, that soe wee may sing the Lords songs, as
in our english tongue soe in such verses as are famil[i]ar to an english eare which are commonly
metricall: and as it can be no just offence to any good conscience, to sing Davids hebrew songs
in english words, soe neither to sing his poeticall verses in english poeticall metre: men might
as well stumble at singing the hebrew psalmes in our english tunes (and not in the hebrew tunes)
as at singing them in english meeter, (which are our verses) and not in such verses as are generally used by David according to the poetry of the hebrew language: but the truth is, as the Lord
hath hid from us the hebrew tunes, lest wee should think our selves bound to imitate them; soe
also the course and frame (for the most part) of their hebrew poetry, that wee might not think our
selves bound to imitate that, but that every nation without scruple might follow as the grave sort
of tunes of their owne country songs, soe the graver sort of verses of their owne country poetry.

Neither let any think, that for the meetre sake wee have taken liberty or poeticall licence to depart from the true and proper sence of Davids words in the hebrew verses, noe; but it hath beene one part of our religious care and faithfull indeavour, to keepe close to the originall text.

As for other objections taken from the difficulty of *Ainsworths* tunes, and the corruptions in our common psalme books, wee hope they are answered in this new edition of psalmes which wee here present to God and his Churches. For although wee have cause to blesse God in many respects for the religious indeavours of the translaters of the psalmes into meetre usually annexed to our Bibles, yet it is not unknowne to the godly learned that they have rather presented a paraphrase then the words of David translated according to the rule *2 chron. 29.30.* and that their addition to the words, detractions from the words are not seldome and rare, but very frequent and many times needles[s], (which we suppose would not be approved of if the psalmes were so translated into prose) and that their variations of the sense, and alterations of the sacred text too frequently, may justly minister matter of offence to them that are able to compare the translation with the text; of which failings, some judicious have oft complained, others have been grieved, wherupon it hath bin generally desired, that as wee doe injoye other, soe (if it were the Lords will) wee might injoye this ordinance also in its native purity: wee have therefore done our indeavour to make a plaine and familiar translation of the psalmes and words of David into english metre, and have not soe much as presumed to paraphrase to give the sense of his meaning in other words; we have therefore attended heerin as our chief guide the originall, shūning all additions, except such as even the best translators of them in prose supply, avoiding all materiall detractions from words or sence. The word ⸵ which wee translate *and* as it is redundant sometime in the Hebrew, soe somtime (though not very often) it hath been left out, and yet not then, if the sence were not faire without it.

As for our translations, wee have with our english Bibles (to which next to the Originall wee have had respect) used the Idioms of our owne tongue instead of Hebraismes, lest they might seeme english barbarismes.

~~~~~~~~

Then follows more discussion of synonyms and points of translation about particular words. The famous conclusion and its memorable sentence about conscience and piety triumphing over aesthetics demonstrates the literary power of the Puritan Divines. Their rhetorical style (including their penchant for run-on sentences) would influence American readers (and therefore writers and composers) and become part of our national literary imagination.

A s for all other changes of numbers, tenses, and characters of speech, they are such as either the hebrew will unforcedly beare, or our english forceably calls for, or they no way change the sence; and such are printed usually in an other character.

If therefore the verses are not alwayes so smooth and elegant as some may desire or expect; let them consider that Gods Altar needs not our pollishings: *Ex. 20.* for wee have respected rather a plaine translation, then to smooth our verses with the sweetnes of any paraphrase, and soe have attended Conscience rather then Elegance, fidelity rather then poetry, in translating the hebrew words into english language, and Davids poetry into english meetre;

> *that soe wee may sing in Sion the Lords*
>
> *songs of prayse according to his owne*
>
> *will; untill hee take us from hence,*
>
> *and wipe away all our teares, &*
>
> *bid us enter into our masters*
>
> *joye to sing eternall*
>
> *Halleluiahs.*

SOURCE: *The Whole Booke of Psalmes: Faithfully Translated into English Metre; Whereunto is prefixed a discourse declaring not only the lawfullnes, but also the necessity of the heavenly Ordinance of singing Scripture Psalmes in the churches of God*, trans. Richard Mather, John Eliot, and Thomas Weld (Cambridge, Mass.: Stephen Daye, 1640). These excerpts are taken from a facsimile edition (Chicago: University of Chicago Press, 1956). Archaic spellings have been retained, except for modernized printings of the letters s and i.

~~~~~~~~

NOTES

1. On the "scriptural principle" and also for an excellent overview of psalm texts, see From Psalm Book to Hymnal. Selections from the Lowell Mason Collection. Excerpts from an exhibition at the Yale Divinity School Library, January 18–March 30, 2000. http://www.library.yale.edu/div/hymnexh.htm.

2. The transliterations of the Hebrew are *mizmorim* for psalms, *tehilim* for hymns, and *shirim* for spiritual songs. The literal translations are "psalms," "praises," and "songs," but the translations here are reasonable interpretations for Christian purposes. The second Hebrew word is misspelled in the original and has an extra "lamed" in it. It should read תהילים.

3. This probably refers to the work of a prominent Christian Hebraist, Johannes Buxtorf (1564–1629) and his *Thesaurus grammaticus linguae sanctae hebraeae*.

3

Four Translations of Psalm 100

(*Tehilim, Bay Psalm Book,* 1640 and 1698, Watts)

These different translations of Psalm 100 show process at work and interpretation at play. The translation from the original Hebrew is in biblical poetry, that is to say, free verse with a strong sense of antiphonal call and response built into the text. The *Bay Psalm Book* translations are plain and direct. Decades later, the famous British poet Isaac Watts (1674–1748) impressed his own personality upon Psalm 100, as shown in the excerpts from his translations from 1719.

The character of poetry affects music: the robust tunes of seventeenth-century psalmody yielded to the more complex fuguing tunes, anthems, and hymn settings of late eighteenth-century American composers, such as William Billings, Daniel Read, and Justin Morgan, all of whom set Watts's texts.

Psalm 100 is a sacred song from Tehilim, *the Hebrew word meaning songs of praise and referring to the 150 psalms. Tradition ascribes the origin of these sacred songs to David, the musician-king of ancient Israel (ca. 1000 BCE). However, scholars now*

Facsimile of Psalm 100 from *Bay Psalm Book*, 1698, p. 428. The tune for "Old Hundred" published in the *Bay Psalm Book*, 1698, with solmization syllables for two parts. The top part contains the melody (written in the G clef) and the bottom part written in the F clef, suits an instrument more than a voice. Words are not included partly because the tune could be used for several psalms in "first meeter" or long meter of 8 8 8 8.

date various elements of the psalm collection to a wider period of time, from roughly 950 to 300 BCE.

PSALM 100 תהלים ק׳

1
A psalm for praise.
Raise a shout for the LORD, all the earth;

2
worship the LORD in gladness;
come into His presence with shouts of joy.

3
Acknowledge that the LORD is God;
He made us and we are His,
His people, the flock He tends.

4
Enter His gates with praise,
His courts with acclamation.
Praise Him! Bless His name!

5
For the LORD is good;
His steadfast love is eternal;
His faithfulness is for all generations.

SOURCE: *The Book of Psalms: A New Translation according to the Traditional Hebrew Text* (Philadelphia: Jewish Publication Society, 1997): 1216–1217.

PSALM 100 FROM THE *BAY PSALM BOOK* (1640)

PSALME 100

A Psalme of prayse
Make yee a joyfull sounding noyse
unto Jehovah, all the earth:

2
Serve yee Jehovah with gladness:
before his presence come with mirth.

3
Know, that Jehovah he is God,
who hath formed it is hee,
& not ourselves: his owne people
& sheepe of his pasture are wee.

4
Enter into his gates with prayse,
into his Courts with thankfullness:
make yee consession unto him,
& his name reverently blesse.

5
Because Jehovah he is good,
for evermore is his mercy:
& unto generations all
continue doth his verity.

SOURCE: *The Whole Booke of Psalmes* (Cambridge, Mass.: Stephen Daye, 1640): 205.

~~~~~~~

This later translation from the Bay Psalm Book *(1698) was set to one of the three "first meeter" tunes (with eight syllables to each line, now known as "long meter"). Its robust tune, which appeared in the* Genevan Psalter *in 1561, helped to make Psalm 100 into an iconic song, known to this day as "Old Hundred."*

A PSALM OF DAVID
FIRST MEETER

[1–2]
Shout to Jehovah all the earth.
With joyfulness the Lord serve ye:
Before his presence come with mirth.

3
Know, that Jehovah God is he,
It's he that made us and not we,
His folk his pastures sheep also

4
Into his gates with thanks come ye
With praises to his Court-yards go.

5
Give thanks to him, bless ye his Name
Because Jehovah he is good:
His mercy ever is the same:
His truth throughout all ages stood.

SOURCE: The Psalms, Hymns and Spiritual Songs of the Old and New Testament: Faithfully Translated into English Meetre For the use, Edification and Comfort of the Saints in publick and private, especially in New-England, 9th ed. (Boston: Printed by B. Green and J. Allen for Michael Perry, 1698): 246–247, with the tune on p. 428.

~~~~~~~

ISAAC WATTS'S TRANSLATIONS AND PARAPHRASES

Isaac Watts "Christianized" the psalms by inserting the name of Jesus into some texts—to take one example—and also by poeticizing the language through his own powerful gifts. He provided plain and fancy translations, the latter called "paraphrases," and sometimes he even supplied free additions to the psalms. In this selection, excerpts from Watts's translations show these varieties of approach at work. Verse 1 is a plain translation in long meter; it is followed by a paraphrase, also in long meter, in which one verse of the original inspires three verses by Watts. Following that is a stanza 6, which is a free addition.

PSALM 100. 1ST PART. LONG METRE.
PRAISE TO OUR CREATOR.
"A PLAIN TRANSLATION" OF VERSES 1 AND 2

1

Ye nations of the earth, rejoice
Before the Lord, your sov'reign King;
Serve him with cheerful heart and voice,
With all your tongues his glory sing.

2

The Lord is God; 'tis he alone
Doth life, and breath, and being give;
We are his work, and not our own;
The sheep that on his pastures live.

PSALM 100. 2D PART. LONG METRE.
A PARAPHRASE OF VERSES 1 AND 2

1

Sing to the Lord with joyful voice;
Let ev'ry land his name adore;
The northern isles shall send the noise
Across the ocean, to the shore.

2

Nations attend before his throne
With solemn fear, with sacred joy;
Know that the Lord is God alone:
He can create, and he destroy.

3

His sov'reign pow'r, without our aid
Made us of clay, and form'd us men;
And when like wand'ring sheep we stray'd;
He brought us to his fold again.

4

We are his people, we his care,
Our souls and all our mortal frame:

What lasting honours shall we rear,
Almighty Maker, to thy name?

5
We'll crowd thy gates with thankful songs,
High as the heav'ns our voices raise;
And earth, with her ten thousand tongues,
Shall fill thy courts with sounding praise.

Verse 6 [an addition to the original]
Wide as the world is thy command,
Vast as eternity thy love
Firm as a rock thy truth must stand,
When rolling years shall cease to move.

SOURCE: Isaac Watts, *The Psalms of David: Imitated in the Language of the New Testament and Applied to the Christian State and Worship* (1719). Excerpts taken from a later edition (Cooperstown, N.Y.: H. & E. Phinney, 1843): 196–97.

4

FROM THE DIARIES OF SAMUEL SEWALL

Samuel Sewall (1652–1730), a lawyer and Superior Court justice for the Massachusetts Bay colony, left diaries that illuminate colonial culture between 1674 and 1729. Many entries convey the pervasiveness of psalm singing in and out of church, from services to private crises at home to dinners with friends.

Sewall is remembered for a life of darkness and light. As one of several judges in the Salem Witch trials of 1692, he sentenced twenty people to death. Five years later he recanted in a public apology which inaugurated a public period of repentance. He was the only judge to do so. Did this act of conscience change his life? On the much smaller public arena of his local church, Sewall displays mindfulness of his actions that suggest a conscience forever heightened. As a "preceptor" (or "praecentor") at the Old South Church in Boston for about 24 years, he "set the tune," or gave the starting pitch, for congregational singing. He took this job very seriously, and if the congregation strayed off improperly from one tune or another— thereby threatening the experience of musical community—he blamed himself.

Friday May 22d. 1685. had a private Fast: the Magistrates of this town with their Wives here. Mr. Eliot prayed, Mr. Willard preached. I am afraid of Thy judgments—Text Mother gave.

Mr. Allen prayed; cessation half an hour. Mr. Cotton Mather prayed; Mr. Mather preached Ps. 79, 9. Mr. Moodey prayed about an hour and half; Sung the 79th Psalm from the 8th to the End: distributed some Biskits, and Beer, Cider, Wine. The Lord hear in Heaven his dwelling place.

Thorsday, Novr 11. [1686]. I deliver'd my Commission to the Council, desiring them to appoint a Captain for the South-Company; left it with them to put 'em in mind on't. As was coming home Capt. Hill invited me to his House where unexpectedly I found a good Supper. Capt. Hutchinson, Townsend, Savage, Wing and sundry others to the number of 14 or 15, were there. After Supper sung the 46th Ps.

Febr. 2 [1718]. *Lord's Day*. In the Morning I set York Tune, and in the 2d going over, the Gallery carried it irresistibly to St. David's, which discouraged me very much. I spake earnestly to Mr. White to set it in the Afternoon, but he declines it. p.m. The Tune went well. Madam Winthrop went out before the Admissions.

Lord's Day, Feb. 23. [1718]. Mr. Foxcroft preaches. I set York Tune, and the Congregation went out of it into St. David's in the very 2[n]d going over. They did the same 3 weeks before. This is the 2[n]d Sign.* I think they began in the last Line of the first going over. This seems to me an intimation and call for me to resign the Praecentor's Place to a better Voice. I have through the divine Long-suffering and Favour done it for 24 years, and now God by his Providence seems to call me off: my voice being enfeebled. I spake to Mr. White earnestly to set it in the Afternoon; but he declin'd it. After the Exercises, I went to Mr. Sewall's, Thank'd Mr. Prince for his very good Discourse: and laid this matter before them, told them how long I had set the Tune; Mr. Prince said, Do it Six years longer. I persisted and said that Mr. White or Franklin might do it very well. The Return of the Gallery where Mr. Franklin sat was a place very Convenient for it.

Feb. 27. [1718]. I told Mr. White Next Sabbath was in a Spring Moneth, he must then set the Tune. I set now Litchfield Tune to a good Key.

Octobr 29. [1719]. Thanks-giving-day: between 6 and 7. Brother Moodey and I went to Mrs. Tilley's; and about 7, or 8, were married by Mr. J. Sewall, in the best room below stairs. Mr. Prince pray'd the 2d time; Mr. Adams the Minister of Newington was there, Mr. Oliver and Mr. Tim Clark Justices, and many more. Sang the 12, 13, 14, 15, and 16. verses of the 90th Psalm. Cous. S. Sewall set a Low-dutch Tune in a very good Key, which made the Singing with a good number of Voices very agreeable. Distributed Cake. Mrs. Armitage introduced me into my Bride's Chamber after she was a-bed. I thank'd her that she had left her room in that Chamber to make way for me, and pray'd God to provide for her a better Lodging: So none saw us after I went to bed. Quickly after our being a-bed my Bride grew so very bad she was fain to sit up in her bed; I rose to get her Petit-Coats about her. I was exceedingly amaz'd, fearing lest she should have dy'd. Through the favor of God she recover'd in some considerable time of her Fit of the Tissick, spitting, partly blood. She her self was under great Consternation.

May 26. [1720]. Din'd with the Churches at the Dragon. Between 4 and 5. The Govr adjourn'd to Ten a-clock Satterday morning, and presently rose up and went away. NB. Went to Bed after Ten: about 11 or before, my dear Wife was oppress'd with a rising of Flegm that obstructed her Breathing. I arose and lighted a Candle, made Scipio give me a Bason of Water (he

---

*Sewall seems to imply that this is the second intimation he had had of the failure of his musical gift, to be interpreted by him as a hint that the congregation would welcome his successor. (M.H.S.EDS.) Percy A. Scholes deals at length with Sewall's musical interests in his book, *The Puritans and Music in England and New England* (London, 1934).

was asleep by the Fire) Call'd Philadelphia, Mr. Cooper, Mayhew. About midnight my dear wife expired to our great astonishment, especially mine. May the Sovereign Lord pardon my Sin, and Sanctify to me this very Extraordinary, awfull Dispensation. Major Epes, Dr. Cotton Mather, Mr. Williams of Hatfield, of Derefield, Mr. Prince, Mr. Whiting of Concord, visit me in a very friendly and Christian manner. Before Supper I sung the 130th Psalm, and a staff out of the 46. Mr. Williams of Hatfield, sympathising with me, said twas what befell the Prophet Ezekiel.

SOURCE: M. Halsey Thomas, ed., *The Diary of Samuel Sewall*, vol. 1: 1674–1708, vol. 2: 1709–1729 (New York: Farrar, Straus, and Giroux, 1973): 1:63, 125; 2:881, 885–86, 887, 932, 950.

5

THE MINISTERS RALLY FOR MUSICAL LITERACY

(Mather, Walter, Symmes)

After 1700, a decline in the quality of psalm singing in church led to calls for reform among Puritan and Congregational ministers. The issue attracted some of the most prominent church authorities in Boston, who not only delivered but published sermons on this topic. As they argued for musical literacy, they encouraged an increase in local singing schools, which were typically held in the evenings after work. The schools were run by itinerant musicians who went on the road from town to town, holding short-term courses and getting paid by the locals. In due course, a musically literate population emerged in New England, which in turn laid the groundwork for new American composition after 1770. Minister-reformers like John Tufts (1689–1750) and Thomas Walter (1696–1725) published the first tune books for social worship in the colonies.

The reformers called their approach "regular singing" or singing "by rule," and they intended to supplant the "old way" of "lining out" the psalms, which, at least according to its strongest critics, produced vocal chaos. The practices of "oral tradition" —this modern phrase was actually used by Walter—are criticized so vehemently that we can hear what they heard: the heterophonic results of the old way and a lack of uniformity in practice, just what modern folklorists prize today. The selections here preserve the variety of devices that printers used to evoke the dynamics of speech, with uppercase and italicized words capturing the flavor of their didactic voices.

~~~~~~~~~
~~~~~~~~~
~~~~~~~~~

The most famous—if not infamous because of his role in the Salem witch trials—among Boston ministers, the Reverend Cotton Mather (1663–1728) entered early into the debate. Mather sanctioned the use of other kinds of scripture to be turned into metric song and therefore foreshadowed the popularity of the English hymn writer Isaac Watts.

HERE is our PSALTER! And were we enriched with no more Treasures than These, wherein the Holy SPIRIT of GOD has thus provided for the *songs* of His People, what a precious Article in, *The Unsearchable Riches of* CHRIST, have we therein to be exceedingly Thankful for?

BUT supposing that we have no *other* Portions of the Inspired Writings exhibited in the *Tuneable Poetry* of the Ancients, must we thence conclude, that we are forbidden to put any other *Portions* of them into such a *Metre*, as may render them capable of being *Sung* among the People of GOD? Surely, the Servants of GOD may take other *Paragraphs* of our BIBLE, especially such as have the most Illustrious *Mysteries of the Gospel*, so plainly Contained and Revealed in them, that in *Singing* thereof, we shall *shew forth the Salvation of GOD*, and they may with the *Singing* thereof, *Give Thanks unto the Lord*, as it becomes *the Redeemed of the Lord*.

~~~~~~~~~

In this longer excerpt, Mather marshals his arguments to justify "regular singing," challenging American musicians to write new tunes for worship. A few choice phrases demolish any notion that good congregational singing was typical.

IT is Remarkable, That when the *Kingdom* of GOD has been making any *New Appearance*, a mighty Zeal for the *singing* of PSALMS, has attended it, and assisted it. And may we see our People grow more *Zealous* of this *Good Work*, what an hopeful *Sign of the Times* would be seen in it. That *the Time of Singing is come, and the Voice of the Turtle is to be heard in the Land?*

BUT in the pursuance of this Holy Intention, it would be very desirable, that People (and especially our YOUNG PEOPLE, who are most in the Years of Discipline,) would more generally *Learn to SING* and become able to Sing by RULE, and keep to the NOTES of the TUNES, which our *Spiritual Songs* are set unto; which would be to *Sing*, as *Origen* expresses it, Ἐμμελῶς καὶ συμφότως; *Agreeably and Melodiously.*[1] In Early Days a Famous Council condemned it; in that there were β—— α—— [unintelligible Greek], *Disorderly Clamours*, with which the *Psalmody* was then sometimes disturbed. In Later Days, *Cassander* upbraided it, *Ad feritatem quandum barbaricum composito Sono, Boant, Latrant, mugiunt, frendunt, rudunt, et quidvis potius quam canunt.— Tarttaricos quosdam clamores Exprimunt.* In plain English, *They made sad and wild Work on't.* It has been found accordingly in some of our Congregations, that in length of Time, their *singing* has degenerated, into an *Odd Noise*, that has had more of what we want a Name for, than any *Regular Singing* in it; whereby the *Celestial Exercise* is dishonoured; and indeed the *Third Commandment* is trespass'd on. To take notice of the *Ridiculous Pleas*, wherewith some very weak People, go to confirm this Degeneracy, would indeed be to pay too much Respect unto them. And they must have strange Notions of the Divine SPIRIT, and of His Operations, who shall imagine, that the Delight which their *Untuned Ears* take in an *Uncouth Noise*, more than in a *Regular singing*, is any *Communion* with Him. The Skill of *Regular Singing*, is among the *Gifts* of GOD unto the Children of Men, and by no means unthankfully to be Neglected or Despised. For the Congregations, wherein 'tis wanting, to recover a *Regular Singing*, would be really a *Reformation*, and a Recovery out of *Apostacy*, and what we may judge that Heaven would be pleased withal. We ought certainly to serve our GOD with our *Best*, and *Regular Singing* must needs be *Better* than the confused Noise of a Wilderness.

   GOD is not for Confusion in the Churches of the Saints; but requires, *Let all things be done decently.* 'Tis a Great Mistake of some weak People, That the *Tunes* regulated with the *Notes* used in the *Regular Singing* of our Churches are the same that are used in the Church of *Rome.* And what if they were? Our *Psalms* too are used there. But the *Tunes* used in the *French Psalmody*, and from Them in the *Dutch* also, were set buy a famous Martyr of JESUS CHRIST; and when *Sternhold* and *Hopkins* illuminated England, with their Version of the *Psalms*, the *Tunes* have been set by such as a Good Protestant may be willing to hold Communion withal. The *Tunes* commonly used in our Churches, are *Few*; T'were well if there were *more.* But they are also *Grave*, and such as well *become the Oracles of GOD*, and such as do Steer clear of the Two Shelves, which *Austin* was afraid of; when he did, *In cantu Sacro fluctuare, inter Periculum Voluptatis, et Experimentum Salubritatis;* in danger of too much *Delicacy* on the one side, and *Asperity* on the other.

   The *Musick* of the Ancient Hebrews, an Adjustment whereto seems to be all the *Measure* of their *Poetry*, (after all the Attempts of *Gomarus*, and other Learned Men otherwise to *Measure* it,) being utterly Lost; and, as *Aben. Ezra* observes, of the *Musical Instruments* in the *Hundred and Fifteth* Psalm, wholly Irrecoverable; we have no way Left us now, but with *Tunes* composed by the *Chief Musicians* for us, to *do as well as we can.*

   IT is to be desired, that we may see in the Rising Generation, a fresh and Strong Disposition to *Learn* the proper *Tunes;* that GOD may be Glorified, and Religion beautified, with a *Regular Singing* among us; And that, *To them that are his Servants, He may let His mov'e be seen;* His Glory also unto those that are their Children here: And that the Lovely Brightness of the Lord who is our GOD, may with Conspicuous Lustre be seen shining *upon us.*

   SOURCE: Cotton Mather, *The Accomplished SINGER* (Boston: B. Green, 1721): 5, 21–24.

〜〜〜〜〜

The Reverend Thomas Walter (1696–1725) compiled one of the first American tune books. In this preface, Walter approaches the problem of congregational singing more as a musician than as a minister.

SOME BRIEF AND VERY PLAIN INSTRUCTIONS FOR SINGING BY NOTE

WHAT a Recommendation is this then to the following Essay, that our Instructions will give you that knowledge in Vocal Musick, whereby you will be able to sing all the Tunes in the World, without hearing of them sung by another, and being constrained to get them by heart from any other Voice than your own?

THESE Rules then will be serviceable upon a *Threefold* Account. *First,* they will instruct us in the right and true singing of the Tunes that are already in use in our Churches; which, when they first came out of the Hands of the Composers of them, were sung according to the Rules of the *Scale of Musick,* but are now miserably tortured, and twisted, and quavered, in some Churches, into an horrid Medly of confused and disorderly Noises. This must necessarily create a most disagreeable Jar in the Ears of all that can judge better of Singing than these Men, who please themselves with their own ill-founding *Echoes.* For to compare small things with great, our *Psalmody* has suffered the like Inconveniences which our *Faith* had laboured under, in case it had been committed and trusted to the uncertain and doubtful conveyance of *Oral Tradition.* Our Tunes are, for want of a Standard to appeal to in all our Singing, left to the Mercy of every unskilful Throat to chop and alter, twist and change, according to their infinitely divers and no less odd Humours and Fancies. That this is most true, I appeal to the Experience of those who have happened to be present in many of our Congregations, who will grant me, that there are no two Churches that sing alike. Yea, I have my self heard (for Instance) *Oxford* Tune sung in *three* Churches (which I purposely forbear to mention) with as much difference as there can possibly be between *York* and *Oxford,* or any two other different Tunes. Therefore any man that pleads with me for what they call the *Old Way,* I can confute him only by making this Demand, *What is the* OLD WAY? Which I am sure they cannot tell. For, one Town says, theirs is the true *Old Way,* another Town thinks the same of theirs, and so does a third of their Way of Tuning it. But let such men know from the Writer of this Pamphlet (who can sing all the various Twistings of the old Way, and that too according to the *Genius* of most of the Congregations as well as they can any one Way; which must therefore make him a better Judge than they are or can be;) affirms, that the Notes sung according to the *Scale and Rules of Musick,* are the true *old Way.* For some body or other did compose our Tunes, and did they (think ye) compose them by Rule or by Rote? If the latter, how came they pricked down in our *Psalm Books?* And this, I am sure of, we sing them as they are there pricked down, and I am as sure the Country people do not. Judge ye then, who is in the right. Nay, I am sure, if you would once be at the pains to learn our Way of Singing, you could not but be convinced of what I now affirm. But our Tunes have passed thro' strange *Metamorphoses* (beyond those of *Ovid*) since their first Introduction into the World.

AGAIN, it will serve for the Introduction of more Tunes into the Divine Service; and by these, Tunes of no small Pleasancy and Variety, which will in a great Measure render this Part of Worship more delightfull to us. For at present we are confined to *eight or ten Tunes,* and in some Congregations to little more than half that Number, which being so often sung over, are too apt, if not to create a Distaste, yet at least mightily to lessen the Relish of them.

THERE is one more Advantage which will accrue from the Instructions of this little Book; and that is this, that by the just and equal *Timeing* of the Notes, our Singing will be reduc'd to an exact length, so as not to fatigue the Singer with a tedious Protraction of the Notes beyond the compass of a Man's Breath, and the Power of his Spirit: A Fault very frequent in the Country, where I my self have twice in one Note paused to take Breath. This *keeping of Time* in Singing will have this Natural effect also upon us, that the whole Assembly shall begin and end every single Note, and every Line exactly together, to an Instant, which is a wonderful Beauty in Singing, when a great Number of Voices are together sounding forth the Divine Praises. But for want of this, I have observed in many Places, one Man is upon this Note, while another is a Note before him, which produces something so hideous and disorderly, as is beyond Expression bad. And then the even, unaffected, and smooth sounding the Notes, and the Omission of those un-natural Quaverings and Tunings, will serve to prevent all the Discord and lengthy Tediousness which is so much a Fault in our singing of Psalms. For much time is taken up in shaking out these Turns and Quavers; and besides, no two Men in the Congregation quaver alike, or to-gether; which sounds in the Ears of a good Judge, like *Five Hundred* different Tunes roared out at the same time, whose perpetual interferings with one another, perplexed Jars, and unmea-sured Periods, would make a Man wonder at the false Pleasure, which they conceive in that which good Judges of Musick and Sounds, cannot bear to hear.

> SOURCE: Reverend Thomas Walter, *The Grounds and Rules of Musick Explained; or, An In-troduction to the Art of Singing by Note. Fitted to the Meanest Capacities* (Boston: J. Franklin, 1721): 2–5.

~~~~~~~

The Reverend Thomas Symmes (1677–1725) argued persuasively for the founding of singing schools, using as his rhetorical style the time-honored mode of interrogating himself. His comment about the popularity of "pernicious songs and ballads" refers to the popular music of the day, generally sold by street musicians and peddlers hawk-ing broadsides.

Q. 9. *WOULD it not greatly tend to the promoting [of] Singing Psalms, if* Singing Schools *were promoted?* Would not this be a Conforming to *Scripture Pattern?* Have we not as much need of them as GOD's People of Old? Have we any Reason to expect to be inspired with the Gift of *Singing,* any more than that of *Reading?* or to attain it without the use of suitable Means, any more than they of Old, when *Miracles, Inspirations,* &c. were common? Where would be the *Dif-ficulty,* or what the *Disadvantages,* if People that want *Skill* in *Singing,* would procure a *Skilfull Per-son to Instruct* them, and meet *Two or Three* Evenings in the Week, from *Five or six* a Clock, to *Eight,* and spend the Time in Learning to Sing? Would not this be an innocent and profitable *Recreation,* and would it not have a Tendency (if prudently managed) to prevent the unprofitable *Expence* of Time on *other Occasions?* Has it not a Tendency to divert Young People (who are most proper to learn) from Learning *Idle, Foolish,* yea, *pernicious Songs and Ballads,* and banish all such *Trash* from their Minds? Experience proves this. Would it not be proper for *School Masters* in *Country Parishes* to teach their *Scholars?* Are not they very unwise who plead against Learning to Sing by Rule, when they can't learn to Sing at all, unless they learn by Rule? Has not the grand *Enemy of Souls* a hand in this, who prejudices them against the best Means of Singing?

SOURCE: Thomas Symmes, *The Reasonableness of Regular Singing, or Singing by Note. In an Essay to Revive the True and Ancient Mode of Singing Psalm-Tunes according to the Pattern of our New England Psalm Books; the Knowledge and Practice of which, is greatly decay'd in most Congregations. Writ by a Minister of the Gospel. Perused by Several Ministers in the Town and Country; and Published with the Approbation of all who have Read it* (Boston: B. Green, 1720): 20.

~~~~~~~~

NOTE

1.   The proper translation of the last Greek word is "harmoniously."

6

$\mathcal{B}$ENJAMIN FRANKLIN ADVISES HIS BROTHER

ON HOW TO WRITE A BALLAD AND

HOW NOT TO WRITE LIKE HANDEL

A founding father of the United States, signer of the American Constitution, states-man, inventor, social critic, and aphorist ("He that lies down with Dogs shall rise up with fleas"), Benjamin Franklin (1706–1790) was also an avid musician, who played the harp and guitar and invented a mechanism to improve the "musical glasses," which he called the "armonica." Sometime before 1764, Franklin received a request for advice from his brother Peter, who had written a poem in ballad form and sought a composer to set it.

Franklin's response underscores the popularity of Anglo-American ballads in this era, for he named well-known titles from oral tradition and ballad opera, in-cluding "Chevy Chase" (also called "The Battle of the Cheviot"). He advised his brother not to set texts as if they were opera numbers, using examples from Han-del's work as what not to do. A child of the Enlightenment, Franklin used arguments based on "nature" in ways that also evoke the ideas of the French philosopher Jean-Jacques Rousseau.

~~~~~~
~~~~~~

Dear Brother,

I like your ballad, and think it well adapted for your purpose of discountenancing expensive foppery, and encouraging industry and frugality. If you can get it generally sung in your country, it may probably have a good deal of the effect you hope and expect from it. But as you aimed at making it general, I wonder you chose so uncommon a measure in poetry, that none of the tunes in common use will suit it. Had you fitted it to an old one, well known, it must have spread much faster than I doubt it will do from the best new tune we can get compos'd for it. I think too, that if you had given it to some country girl in the heart of Massachusetts, who has never heard any other than psalm tunes, or Chevy Chace [sic], the Children in the Wood, the Spanish Lady, and such old simple ditties, but has naturally a good ear, she might more probably have made a pleasing popular tune for you, than any of our masters here, and more proper for your purpose, which would best be answered, if every word could as it is sung be understood by all that hear it, and if the emphasis you intend for particular words could be given by the singer as well as by the reader; much of the force and impression of the song depending on those circumstances. I will however get it as well done for you as I can.

Do not imagine that I mean to depreciate the skill of our composers of music here; they are admirable at pleasing practised ears, and know how to delight one another; but, in composing for songs, the reigning taste seems to be quite out of nature, or rather the reverse of nature, and yet like a torrent, hurries them all away with it; one or two perhaps only excepted.

You, in the spirit of some ancient legislators, would influence the manners of your country by the united powers of poetry and music. By what I can learn of their songs, the music was simple, conformed itself to the usual pronunciation of words, as to measure, cadence or emphasis, &c. never disguised and confounded the language by making a long syllable short or a short one long, when sung; their singing was only a more pleasing, because a melodious manner of speaking; it was capable of all the graces of prose oratory, while it added the pleasure of harmony. A modern song, on the contrary, neglects all the proprieties and beauties of common speech, and in their place introduces its defects and absurdities as so many graces. I am afraid you will hardly take my word for this, and therefore I must endeavour to support it by proof. Here is the first song I lay my hand on. It happens to be a composition of one of our greatest masters, the ever famous Handel. It is not one of his juvenile performances, before his taste could be improved and formed: It appeared when his reputation was at the highest, is greatly admired by all his admirers, and is really excellent in its kind. It is called, The additional FAVOURITE *Song in* Judas Maccabeus *[the aria "Wise men flatt'ring may deceive us" from act II].*

Now I reckon among the defects and improprieties of common speech, the following, viz.

1.   Wrong placing the accent or emphasis, *by laying it on words of no importance, or on wrong syllables.*

2. Drawling; *or extending the sound of words or syllables beyond their natural length.*

3. Stuttering; *or making many syllables of one.*

4. Unintelligibleness; *the result of the three foregoing united.*

5. Tautology; *and*

6. Screaming, *without cause.*

For the wrong placing of the accent, or emphasis, *see it on the word* their *instead of being on the word* vain.

And on the word from, *and the wrong syllable* like.

For the Drawling, *see the last syllable of the word* wounded.

And in the syllable wis, *and the word* from, *and syllable* bove.

For the Stuttering, *see the word* ne'er relieve, in

Here are four syllables made of one, and eight of three; but this is moderate. I have
seen in another song, that I cannot now find, seventeen syllables made of three, and
sixteen of one; the latter I remember was the word charms; viz. Cha, a, a, a, a, a, a, a,
a, a, a, a, a, a, a, arms. *Stammering with a witness!*

For the Unintelligibleness; *given this whole song to any taught singer, and let her*
sing it to any company that have never heard it; you shall find they will not understand
three words in ten. It is therefore that at the oratorio's and operas one sees with books
in their hands all those who desire to understand what they hear sung by even our best
performers.

For the Tautology; *you have, with their vain mysterious art,* twice repeated;
Magic charms can ne-er relieve you, *three times.* Nor can heal the wounded heart,
three times. Godlike wisdom from above, *twice; and,* this alone can ne'er deceive
you, *two or three times. But this is reasonable when compared with* the Monster
Polypheme, the Monster Polypheme, *a hundred times over and over, in his admired*
Acis and Galatea *[Chorus, "Wretched Lovers," act II].*

As to the screaming; *perhaps I cannot find a fair instance in this song; but who-*
ever has frequented our operas will remember many. And yet here methinks the words
no *and* e'er, *when sung to these notes, have a little of the air of* screaming, *and would*
actually be scream'd by some singers.

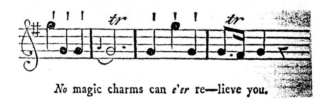

No magic charms can *e'er* re—lieve you.

I send you enclosed the song with its music at length. Read the words without the
repetitions. Observe how few they are, and what a shower of notes attend them: You
will then perhaps be inclined to think with me, that though the words might be the
principal part of an ancient song, they are of small importance in a modern one; they
are in short only a pretence *for singing.*

I am, as ever,
Your affectionate brother,
B. F.[ranklin]

P.S. I might have mentioned Inarticulation *among the defects in common speech that*
are assumed as beauties in modern singing. But as that seems more the fault of the
singer than of the composer, I omitted it in what related merely to the composition.
The fine singer in the present mode, stifles all the hard consonants, and polishes away
all the rougher parts of words that serve to distinguish them one from another; so that
you hear nothing but an admirable pipe, and understand no more of the song, than
you would from its tune played on any other instrument. If ever it was the ambition of
musicians to make instruments that should imitate the human voice, that ambition
seems now reversed, the voice aiming to be like an instrument. Thus wigs were first

made to imitate a good natural head of hair; but when they became fashionable, though in unnatural forms, we have seen natural hair dressed to look like wigs.

SOURCE: Leonard W. Labaree, ed., and Helen C. Boatfield and James H. Hutson, assistant eds., *Papers of Benjamin Franklin,* vol. 11: *January 1 through December 31, 1764–65* (New Haven, Conn.: Yale University Press, 1967): 538–43. Also quoted in Carleton Sprague Smith, "Broadsides and Their Music in Colonial America," in *Music in Colonial Massachusetts 1630–1820:* vol. 1: *Music in Public Places,* ed. Barbara Lambert (Boston: Colonial Society of Massachusetts, 1980): 171–74.

7

Social music for the elite in

COLONIAL WILLIAMSBURG

Williamsburg, the capital of Virginia, the largest British colony, enjoyed influence and wealth from its plantation economy and offered a relatively sophisticated cultural life to its small but powerful elite class. Now famous as a site of historic restoration, the city today includes Colonial Williamsburg, which opened as a national park in 1932 and describes itself as "the world's largest living-history museum." Costumed history interpreters reenact daily life between 1699 and 1780, and music plays an important role in their activities.

The modern-day Williamsburg musicians strive for historically informed performance, using original eighteenth-century instruments such as a double-manual harpsichord, a small chamber organ, and a square pianoforte. Performers adopt the eighteenth-century personas of local musicians, such as the town organist (and town jailer) Peter Pelham (1721–1805). Liner notes often reproduce comments from letters and diaries of citizens like Anne Blair, who in 1769 wrote that she heard "performances of Felton's [sonatas or concertos], Handel's, Vivally's [Vivaldi's] &c every night." No Williamsburg musical amateur is as celebrated as its favorite son, Thomas Jefferson, who played the violin and amassed an impressive library of music books and scores.

Enough concert music was performed by both professionals and accomplished amateurs and heard in concerts and in elegant plantation homes in Williamsburg in the mid-eighteenth century to encourage an entrepreneurial London concert manager and keyboardist—Cuthbert Ogle (d. 1755)—to emigrate there in 1754. His advertisement in the *Virginia Gazette*, reprinted below, shows his target market: gentlemen and lady amateurs. Upon his death, the York County Records of Virginia recorded an inventory of Ogle's estate, which began with his "plad night gown," and contained an important list of musical compositions that has since become Ogle's toehold in history. The inventory, compiled partly by Pelham, documents the taste of the times: Italian chamber concertos, Italian opera selections, popular ballads, songs and instrumental music by contemporary English composers, and of course, Handel, whose works outnumbered those of any other single composer. Thus the suave ornamentations and soothing melodies of an internationally viable late Baroque and early classical style seeped into the musical experiences of colonial America. The inventory's scant musical information is supplemented here in notes adapted from a scholarly study by John Molnar. Several CD anthologies, which include music from Ogle's inventory, are produced and sold through the Colonial Williamsburg museum.

VIRGINIA GAZETTE (WILLIAMSBURG), MARCH 28, 1755, P. 41

The subscriber living at Mr. Nicholson's in Williamsburg, proposes to teach Gentlemen and Ladies to play on the Organ, Harpsichord or Spinet; and to instruct those gentlemen that play on other instruments, so as to enable them to play in concert. Upon encouragement I will fix in any part of the country. [signed] Cuthbert Ogle.

INVENTORY OF ESTATE OF CUTHBERT OGLE, SEPTEMBER 15, 1755

LVIII. APPRAISEMENT[S] OF THE ESTATE OF MR CUTHBERT OGLE DEC'D APRIL 23, 1755

	£.s.d.
1 plad-night gown	0..7..6
1 new cloth Coat & Green Waistcoat	2..10..
1 old Brown Coat & 2 pair Breeches	1..
1 French grey Coat & breeches & black, silk Waistcoat	3..
New market coat	1..6..0
Old cloak 10s, 11 shirts 40s, 6 cravats 7s. 6d	2..17..6
5 p stockins 20s, 6 Towils 3s.	
9, 4 Linnen Handkerchiefs 5s	1..8..9

1 silk handerchief 3s. 2 Wiggs 10 s. 2 pair shoes 10s	1..3..0
1 pr Boots 5s. 1 Hair Trunk 15s. 1 Old hatt 5s	1..5..0
1 Plain Gold Watch £15. 1 Spy Glass 10s. 9	15..10..9
½ lb Green Tea 4s. some Fiddle Strings 4s.	0..8..0
2 p Temple Spectacles 5s.	
2 sets shoe & knee Buckles 2s. 6	0..7..6
a Fiddle & Case 21s. 6, Harpsichord	
and 2 Hammers &c 22£11.6	23..13..
Musick: 2 sets Pasquatis *Overtures* 4s each[1]	0..8..
10 Books Handels songs[2]	1..10..0
4 large sets Italian songs[3]	1
6 Sonatas by Schickard	0..4..
4 books of Symp. to Handels oratorios	0..10..
The Musical entertainment[4]	0..5..
Lamps Songs[5]	0..5..
Apollos Feast by Handel[6]	0..5..
Nares *Lessons* 6s,[7] Avisons *Concertos* 4s[8]	0..10..
6 *Concertos* by Burgess & 6 by Hasse in one book[9]	0..7..6
4 small books of Stanley	0..8..0
6 Sonatas Degeardino[10]	0..5..0
Lamps thorough Bass 7s. 6,[11] Albertis 8 Sonatas 5s[12]	0..12..6
5 Concertos by Ramesa 4s,[13] 2 concertos by Avison 1s. 6	0..5..6
6 concertos by Hebden in 7 parts[14]	0..8..
1 Concerto in 7 parts by Avison[15]	0..1..4
12 English songs by Pasquati[16]	0..5..
1 large Book of songs Palma	0..5..
Songs in Acis and Galatea, Handel	0..5..
Alcocks *Lessons* 4s.[17] Grannoms *Songs* 4s.	0..8..
1 Vol Feltons Concertos	0..4..6
8 Concertos Avisons	0..6..0
Feltons Lessons	0..4..0
Correlli's Sonatas in Score manu[script]	2..0..0
No. 13	0..2..6
Leveridges Songs in small[18]	0..4..
Songs by Hasse	0..4..
Catches by Purchet & Blow[19]	0..2..
Ballards by Grannom[20]	0..3..6
An unbound book of Italian Songs	0..4..
5 large Books of Concertos manu[script]	1..0..
Harlequin Ranger[21]	0..2..
Loose Music	0..0..6
	69..3..4

Peter Pelham, Charles Jones, John Low. Returned into York County Court 15th Sept. 1755 ordered to be recorded

SOURCES: *York County Wills & Inventories:* vol. 20, 1745–1759: 373–74. Available at http://www.pastportal.com/Archive/Probates/Html/PI0349.htm; also printed in "Libraries," *William and Mary College Historical Quarterly Magazine* 3, no. 4 (April 1895): 251–53. John W. Molnar, "A Collection of Music in Colonial Virginia: The Ogle Inventory," *Musical Quarterly* 49, no. 2 (April 1963): 150–62. Molnar includes other probable and possible compositions related to this inventory.

~~~~~~~~

NOTES

The notes below are adapted from Molnar's inventory.

1. Nicolo Pasquali, *Raccolta di Overture, e symphonie, per due Violini e un Basso con un alto Viola, Tromba, Coroi di caccia, e tymbali di rinforzo*, nella I, III, V, IX, XI . . . (London, 1750).

2. George Frideric Handel, *Handel's Songs selected from his latest Oratorios for the Harpsichord, Voice, Hoboy, or German Flute*, 6 parts (London, 1749, 1751).

3. *Farinelli's Celebrated Songs collected from Sig. Hasse, Porpora, Vinci, and Veracini's Operas (Galuppi, Lampugnani, and Pescetti's Chamber Airs). Set for German Flute, Violin, or Harpsichord*, 14 parts (London, 1736–1755).

4. Charles Corbett, ed., *Biekham's Musical Entertainment in 2 volumes, with figured basses by John F. Lampe; the musick by Purcell, Handell, Corelli, Green, and other Eminent Masters* (London, 1740).

5. Johann Friedrich Lampe, *Lyra Britannica: A collection of favourite English Songs, set to Musick by Mr. John Friedrich Lampe* (London, ca. 1745).

6. G. F. Handel, *Apollo's Feast; or, the Harmony of ye Opera Stage. Being a well-chosen Collection of the favourite and most celebrated Songs out of the latest Opera's compos'd by Mr. Handel done in a plain and intelligible Character with the Symphonies for Voices and Instruments, etc.* (London, 1738?), vol. 5.

7. James Nares, *Eight Setts of Lessons for the Harpsichord compos'd by Mr. James Nares, Organist of York-Minster* (London, 1747).

8. Charles Avison, *Two Concertos, the first for Organ or Harpsichord in 8 Parts, the second for Violins in 7 Parts* (Newcastle: Joseph Barber, 1742).

9. Henry Burgess, Jr., *Six Concertos for Organ or Harpsichord, also for Violins and other instruments in 5 Parts* (London, 1740–1741). Johann Adolph Hasse, *Six Concertos Set for the Harpsichord or Organ* (London, 1741).

10. Felice Giardini, *Six Sonatas for a Violino Solo e Basso: Opera Prima* (London, 1751?).

11. Johann Friedrich Lampe, *A Plain and Compendious Method of Teaching Thorough-Bass* (London: J. Wilcox, 1737).

12. Domenico Alberti, *VIII Sonata per Cembalo: Opera Primo, da Domenico Alberti* (London, 1748? possibly somewhat earlier).

13. Jean Phillippe Rameau, *Five Concertos for the Harpsichord compos'd by Mr. Rameau, accompanied with a Violin or German Flute or 2 Violins and a Viola with some Select Pieces for the Harpsichord alone* (London: Printed for J. Walsh, ca. 1750).

14. John Hebden, *Six Concertos in 7 Parts for 4 Violins, a Tenor, a Violoncello, and a Thorough Bass for Harpsichord: Opera Secunda* . . . (London, not later than 1748).

15. Charles Avison, *Six Concertos in Seven Parts: Opera Terza* (London, 1751).

16. Nicolo Pasquali, *XII English Songs in Score, collected from several Masques and other Entertainments* (London, 1750).

17. John Alcock, *Six Suites of Easy Lessons for the Harpsichord or Spinnet, with a Trumpet Pierce* (London, 1741).

18. Richard Leveridge, *A Collection of Songs in Two Volumes* (London, 1727).

19. Henry Purcell, *The Catch Club; or, Merry Companions for 3 and 4 Voices (London: J. Walsh, 1720?).*

20. *Lewis Christian Austin Grannom,* 12 New Songs and Ballads with their Symphonies for German Flute or Violin: Opera Quarta (London: R. Bennett, 1752).

21. Henry Woodward, *The Musick in Harlequin Ranger: As it is perform'd at the Theatre Royal in Drury Lane, set for the Violin, German Flute, or Hautboy with a Thorough Bass for the Harpsichord* (London: J. Oswald, 1752 [1751?]).

ADVERTISEMENTS AND NOTICES

FROM COLONIAL NEWSPAPERS

Advertisements from colonial newspapers offer colorful snapshots of colonial daily life and the various roles music played in it. These few items have been selected from a huge database of around 54,000 items from 1690 to 1783. Some mark historically significant events, such as early public concerts of secular music, the first recorded performance of a ballad opera, and the first libretto for an American ballad opera. Others name prominent performers or performing organizations. A rebellious congregation refusing to sing "by rule" brings to life the controversial reform movement discussed in chapter 5. One man searches for exactly the right versions of his favorite popular songs, among them "Chevy Chase." Other notices offer rewards for the capture of runaway slave-musicians. Teachers who depended upon music being considered a fashionable accomplishment advertise lessons on some kinds of instruments for men, and others for women. Musicians then as now scrambled to make a living. The final advertisement in this chapter could furnish the plot of a transatlantic novel.

BOSTON NEWS LETTER, APRIL 16–23, 1716, P. 22

This is to give notice that there is lately sent over from London a choice collection of musickal instruments, consisting of flaguelets, flutes, haut-boys [oboes], bass-viols, violins, bows, strings, reeds for haut-boys, books of instructions for all these instruments, books of ruled paper. To be sold at the dancing school of Mr. Enstone in Sudbury-Street near the Orange-Tree Boston. Note. Any person may have all instruments of musick mended, or virgenalls and spinnets strung and tuned at a reasonable rate, and likewise may be taught to play on any of these instruments above-mention'd; dancing taught by a true and easier method than has been heretofore.

NEW ENGLAND COURANT, SEPTEMBER 9–16, 1723, PP. 21, 22

Last week a Council of Churches was held at the south part of Brantrey, to regulate the disorders occasion'd by regular singing in that place, Mr. Niles the minister having suspended seven or eight of the church for persisting in their singing by rule, contrary (as he apprehended) to the result of a former council; but by this council the suspended brethren are restor'd to communion, their suspension declar'd unjust, and the congregation order'd to sing by rote and by rule alternately, for the satisfaction of both parties.

BOSTON GAZETTE, FEBRUARY 3–10, 1729, P. 22[1]

This is to give notice, that there will be a consort of musick performed on sundry instruments, at the dancing school in King-Street, on Tuesday the 18th instant, at six a clock in the evening, and that tickets for the same will be delivered out at seven shillings and six pence each ticket, at the places following, viz. at Mr. Luke Vardy's at the Royal Exchange, at Mrs. Meer's at the Sun Tavern near the dock, and at the place of performance. N.B. No person to be admitted after six.

PENNSYLVANIA GAZETTE (PHILADELPHIA), MARCH 5–13, 1730, P. 41

At the house formerly Thomas Chalkley's in Laetitia court, near Blackhorse alley, are taught writing, arithmetick, with the true grounds of the French tongue, at twenty shillings per quarter, by [signed] Thomas Ball. N.B. His wife teaches writing and French. Likewise singing, playing on the spinet, dancing, and all forms of needle-work are taught by his sister, lately arrived from London.

BOSTON GAZETTE, DECEMBER 20–27, 1731, P. 22

On Thursday the 30th of this instant December, there will be performed a concert of musick on sundry instruments at Mr. Pelham's great room being the house of the late Doctor Noyes near the Sun Tavern. Tickets to be delivered at the place of performance at five shillings each the concert to begin exactly at six a clock, and no tickets will be delivered after five the day of performance. N.B. There will be no admittance after six.

SOUTH CAROLINA GAZETTE, JUNE 17–24, 1732, P. 42

For the benefit of Henry Campbell. The 1st of next month, at the Council Chamber, will be performed a Consort of Vocal and Instrumental Musick: To begin at 7 o'clock. N.B. Country Dances for diversion of the ladies.

SOUTH CAROLINA GAZETTE, NOVEMBER 4–11, 1732, P. 42

To be sold by the printer hereof, bonds, bonds and judgments . . . Barclay's Apology for the Quakers, Watt's Psalms, the Honour of the Gout, Bowman's Sermon, Beggars Opera, Village Opera, Robinhood's Opera, the Fatal Extravagant, a tragedy.[2]

SOUTH CAROLINA GAZETTE, FEBRUARY 8–15, 1735, P. 32[3]

On Tuesday the 18th inst[ant] will be presented at the Court-Room, the opera of Flora, or Hob in the Well, with the Dance of the two Pierrots, and a new Pantomime Entertainment in grotesque characters, called The Adventures of Harlequin & Scaramouche, with the Burgo-master Trick'd. Tickets to be had at Mr. Shepheard's in Broad-street at 40 s. each. To begin at 6 o'clock precisely.

NEW YORK WEEKLY JOURNAL, JANUARY 12, 1736, P. 32

On Wednesday the 21st of January instant, there will be a consort of musick, vocal and instrumental, for the benefit of Mr. Pachelbel.[4] The harpsicord part perform'd by him self. The songs, violins and German flute by private hands. The concert will begin precisely at: 6 o'clock. In the house of Robert Todd Vintner. Tickets to be had at the Coffee-House, and at Mr. Todd's at 4 shillings.

VIRGINIA GAZETTE (WILLIAMSBURG), NOVEMBER 17–24, 1738, PP. 11, 12, 21

A letter from John Ray, of New York, to Peter Ennis, of Colraine, in Ireland, pedler. New York, December 16, 1737. Dear Comrad, and Loving Brether in Adversity, I received twa letters fre you, beth in october last, and written by a Quakar, or some other blockhead, neither written or subscribed by yer sel, and written wee yer ane han, wharein ye compleen in for want of monies. . . . [The remainder of this paragraph and seven more discuss John Ray's desire that Peter Ennis and his family receive help from him and come to America] [signed] John Ray.

Postscript. . . . [There follows a description of what Ennis should buy to bring with him, including] Buy sax quire of ballads, aw ald yens, as the Bab[e]s in the Wood, Chevy Chase, but see the last lines be, The English fleed. The Blackmoor, Montross's Lines, Oft have I vow'd to Loove, nor dar Loove, Regard my Grief, Mineful Melpomeny, Young Filander, Macaferson, and sindry other ald songs.[5] . . . [The sentence finishes with a list of books to be bought.] Ye must enquire in Dublin of a printer that will sell the ballads at 6d the quire, for Mrs. Lawrence will not sell them se cheap.

BOSTON EVENING POST, OCTOBER 17, 1743, P. 22

Whereas Cambridge, a Negro man belonging to James Oliver of Boston, doth absent himself sometimes from his master; Said Negro plays well upon a flute, and not so well on a violin. This is to desire all masters and heads of families not to suffer said Negro to come into their houses to teach their prentices or servants to play, nor on any other accounts. All masters of vessels are also forbid to have any thing to do with him on any account, as they may answer it in the law.

N.B. Said Negro is to be sold: Enquire of said Oliver.

NEW YORK GAZETTE & WEEKLY POST BOY, DECEMBER 3, 1750, P. 23[6]

This evening will be presented, a comedy, called, The Beggar's Opera: with a farce, called, The Mock Doctor.

VIRGINIA GAZETTE (WILLIAMSBURG), JUNE 12, 1752, P. 22

This is to inform the public, that Mr. Hallam,[7] from the new theatre in Goodmansfields, London, is daily expected here with a select Company of Comedians; the scenes, cloaths, and decorations are all entirely new, extremely rich, and finished in the highest taste, the scenes being painted by the best hands in London, are excell'd by none in beauty and elegance, so that the ladies and gentlemen may depend on being entertain'd in as polite a manner as at the theatres in London, the company being perfect in all the best plays, opera's, farces, and pantomimes, that have been exhibited in any of the theatres for these ten years past.

MARYLAND GAZETTE (ANNAPOLIS), SEPTEMBER 29, 1757, P. 33

Ran away from the subscriber, at Stratford, in Westmoreland County, on Sunday the 28th of August, Charles Love, a tall thin man, about sixty years of age; he professes music, dancing, fencing, and plays extremely well on the violin, and all wind instruments; he stole when he went away a very good bassoon, made by Schuchart, which he carried with him, as also a Dutch or German fiddle, with an old hautboy and German flute, which are his own; he rode a small white horse, with a Virginia made saddle, and a coarse blue cloth housing: it is supposed he will make towards Charles-Town in South-Carolina.

      Whoever apprehends the said Love, and brings him to me, in Stratford, shall have eight pounds reward, if taken in Virginia; nine pounds if taken in Maryland or North-Carolina, and ten pounds if taken any where else on the continent. [signed] Philip Ludwell Lee.

NEW HAMPSHIRE GAZETTE (PORTSMOUTH), NOVEMBER 23, 1759, P. 33

This day is published, sold at the Printing-Office in this town, printed on a large . . . paper, (Price 12/Old Tenor) A NEW SONG on the successes of the year past, against the French, more particularly in America. An earnest address on the death of General Wolfe. Also A NEW THANKS-GIVING SONG. Together with another on the reduction of Quebeck, Ticonderoga, Niagara, Crown Point, &c. The above are also sold by Samuel Evans Post Rider.

PENSYLVANISCHE BERICHTE, NOVEMBER 23, 1759, P. 41

Es ist eine Orgel zu verkauffen, so dem verstorbenen Mattheis Gensel gehoeret hat. Sie stehet aufgesetzt in der Lutherischen Kirch um obern End Germanton: Bemeldte Orgel hat 8 Register mit dem Pedal. Wan einige Kirchgemeine willens ist Eine zu kauffen, so koennen die selbige Orgel in besagter Kirche besehen, weil sie allda [missing text] noch aufgesetzet steht. Es wird Credit vor ein theil der Bezahlung gegeben werden bey des bemeldten verstorbenen seinen Executoren, Jacob Weyne in Philadelphia, und Christoph Meng u. Catharina Meng in Germanton.

[An organ is offered for sale, that belonged to the deceased Mattheis Gensel. It is installed in the Lutheran church at the upper end of Germantown. The above-mentioned organ has eight registers with the pedal. If any church community wants to buy one, they can see the self-same organ in the above-mentioned church, since it is still set up there. The executors of the afore-mentioned deceased will give credit for a portion of the payment, Jacob Weyne in Philadelphia, and Christoph Meng and Catharine Meng in Germantown.]

PENNSYLVANIA GAZETTE (PHILADELPHIA), DECEMBER 1, 1763, P. 32

Mr. Bremner begs leave to acquaint the public, that he intends to open his music school, on Monday, the 11th inst[ant] at Mr. Glover Hunt's, near the Coffee-house, in Market-street, where young ladies may be taught the harpsicord, or guittar, on Mondays Wednesdays and Fridays, from 10 o'clock in the morning till 12, at twenty shillings per month, and forty shillings entrance money: Likewise young gentlemen may be taught the violin, German flute, harpsicord, or guittar, from 6 o'clock in the evening till 8, on Mondays, Wednesdays and Fridays, for the same price and entrance money.

VIRGINIA GAZETTE (WILLIAMSBURG), MARCH 28, 1766, P. 41

To be sold, a young healthy Negro fellow, who has been used to wait on a gentleman, and plays extremely well on the French horn. For further particulars apply to the printer.

PENNSYLVANIA CHRONICLE, MARCH 30–APRIL 6, 1767, P. 433

Just published, and to be sold at Samuel Taylor's, book-binder, at the corner of Market and Water Streets, price one shilling and sixpence, a new American Comic Opera, of two acts, called The Disappointment: or, the Force of Credulity.
by Andrew Barton, Esq.[8]

SOUTH CAROLINA & AMER GENL GAZETTE, APRIL 10–17, 1771, P. 11

Charlestown, South Carolina, April 11th, 1771. The St. Caecilia Society[9] gives notice that they will engage with and give suitable encouragement to musicians properly qualified to perform at their concert provided they apply on or before the first day of October next. The performers they are in want of are a first and second violin, two hautboys, and a bassoon, whom they are willing to agree with for one, two or three years. John Gordon, President. Thomas Ln. Smith, Vice President.

RIVINGTON'S NEW YORK GAZETTE, FEBRUARY 3, 1774, P. 12

A Young Gentleman, who writes a fair copy, and a legible running hand, who speaks Latin elegantly, reads and construes Greek and Hebrew, teaches the principles of the mathematics, geography, astronomy, eloquence, and most of the classic studies; understands musick, strings, quills and tunes harpsichords and spinnets, writes musick in the best manner, and who is a compleat master of singing, as it relates either to the church or theatre. Such a person would be glad to serve any gentleman's family or school, in one or all [of] the above branches. He has presided as a clerk in a very large book and stationary-store, has likewise officiated as tutor (in musick, dancing, and dramatic oratory) in several gentlemen's families of the first rank and distinction in New-England, and has recommendations from each. Perhaps the candid public will not reckon it a deed of vanity to observe that the above young person is son to a deceased gentleman, formerly a London merchant, who has been justly celebrated for his benevolence, hospitality, and charitable donations, which he was then enabled to execute by the most immense interest in America, without exception. But has since by repeated insults of rapacious fortune, died insolvent, just after his youngest son had compleated an early and fine education. From such prospects, behold him an orphan, reduced to the wretched necessity of using these accomplishments (which were meant merely to befit his birth & adorn social life) as the means of his subsistence; obliged to solicit public employment, with nothing to recommend him but his education and an unblemished character. For these and other reasons he wishes the tuition of a private gentleman's family, as he was brought up in one which regarded the strictest decorum; with respect to manners & principle, who never learnt to measure their fate by popular prejudice, or the caprices of the vulgar. Inquire of the Printer.

> SOURCE: Adapted from Mary Jane Corry, Kate Van Winkle Keller, and Robert Keller, eds., *The Performing Arts in Colonial Newspapers, 1690–1783* (New York: University Music Editions, 1997), a CD-ROM publication. Some notes for this chapter were researched by Anna Kijas.

~~~~~~~~~

NOTES

1. This ad predates that of the concert given on December 30, 1731, conventionally credited as the "earliest recorded public concert of secular music in the New World," by which is meant the English-speaking colonies. See H. Joseph Butler, "Peter Pelham," in *Grove Music Online*, ed. L. Macy (available at http://www.grovemusic.com).

2. Robert Barclay was a Quaker theologian whose *Apology for the True Christian Divinity* (1678) is referred to here. Watts's *Psalms* are discussed in chapter 3; "The Honour of the Gout" was a medical treatise printed by Benjamin Franklin in 1732. The advertisement indicates early interest in ballad operas; the revolutionary ballad opera *The Beggar's Opera* by John Gay premiered in London in 1728 and in the colonies in 1750. The anonymous ballad opera *Robin Hood* dates from 1730. Joseph Mitchell's play *The Fatal Extravagance* was written in 1726.

3. This ad documents the first recorded performance of an opera in the English-speaking colonies, the ballad opera *Flora*.

4. Charles Pachelbel (1690–1750), a German émigré and son of Johann Pachelbel (1653–1706), was a prominent colonial musician, active church organist, and friend and teacher of Peter Pelham.

5. "Sax quire" refers to six choirs, or printed folios. Named here are broadside ballads and theater songs.

6. This advertises the first American performance of Gay's famous opera.

7. Lewis Hallam (1714–1756) founded a company which, under the name of the American Company, and later the Old American Company, pioneered theater in the colonies.

8. It is not definitively known if "Andrew Barton" was a stage pseudonym for Thomas Forrest, who is often cited as the author of the opera. The performance was canceled because of the work's controversial political and social commentary. It received its premiere about two centuries later, in 1976.

9. The St. Caecilia (Cecilia) Society, founded in 1762, was the first musical society to be founded in the English-speaking colonies.

1770–1830

"CHRISTOPHER CROTCHET,

SINGING MASTER FROM QUAVERTOWN"

After 1770, the popularity of singing schools in New England exploded, soon spreading to other parts of the country to remain a staple of rural life into the twentieth century. With singing schools came singing masters, a whole class of musicians who made their way into American literature as a particular social type and class. In this satire of an itinerant singing master, the author creates the cartoonish character of Christopher Crotchet from Quavertown, the punning title constructed from English musical terms. The story includes the titles of some classic church hymns from a then-by-gone era.

The precedent for using the figure of the singing master as a satirical stereotype had already been set most famously by Washington Irving in *The Legend of Sleepy Hollow* (1820), where the unfortunate schoolteacher Ichabod Crane meets up with the headless horseman. In that classic, psalm singing plays but a small role. But here, it supplies the frame for a story of wry observations about Yankee manners through a domestic plot: the outsider singing master coming to a small town and seeking contributions for his singing school, a resistant father fretting about the cost, local girls vying for the new man in town, and the rich man's daughter losing out to an underestimated rival.

The author, Seba Smith (1792–1868), a journalist and one of the first American humorists, wrote as a literary persona he called Major Jack Downing. This story comes from one of Smith's last books.

Your New England country singing-master is a peculiar character; who shall venture to describe him? During his stay in a country village, he is the most important personage in it. The common school-master, to be sure, is a man of dignity and importance. Children never pass him on the road without turning square round, pulling off their hats, and making one of their best and most profound bows. He is looked up to with universal deference both by young and old, and is often invited out to tea. Or, if he "boards round," great is the parade, and great the preparation, by each family, when their "week for boarding the master" draws near. Then not unfrequently a well fatted porker is killed, and the spare-ribs are duly hung around the pantry in readiness for roasting. A half bushel of sausages are made up into "links," and suspended on a pole near the ceiling from one end of the kitchen to the other. And the Saturday beforehand, if the school-master is to come on Monday, the work of preparation reaches its crisis. Then it is, that the old oven, if it be not "heaten seven times hotter than it is wont to be," is at least heated seven times; and apple-pies, and pumpkin-pies, and mince-pies are turned out by dozens, and packed away in closet and cellar for the coming week. And the "fore room," which has not had a fire in it for the winter, is now duly washed and scrubbed and put to rights, and wood is heaped on the fire with a liberal hand, till the room itself becomes almost another oven. George is up betimes on Monday morning to go with his hand-sled and bring the master's trunk; Betsy and Sally are rigged out in their best calico gowns, the little ones have their faces washed and their hair combed with more than ordinary care, and the mother's cap has an extra crimp. And all this stir and preparation for the common school-master. And yet he is but an every-day planet, that moves in a regular orbit, and comes round at least every winter.

But the *singing-master* is your true comet. Appearing at no regular intervals, he comes suddenly, and often unexpected. Brilliant, mysterious, and erratic, no wonder that he attracts all eyes, and produces a tremendous sensation. Not only the children, but the whole family, flock to the windows when he passes, and a face may be seen at every pane of glass, eagerly peering out to catch a glimpse of the singing-master. Even the very dogs seem to partake of the awe he inspires, and bark with uncommon fierceness whenever they meet him.

"O, father," said little Jimmy Brown, as he came running into the house on a cold December night, with eyes staring wide open, and panting for breath. "O father, Mr. Christopher Crotchet from Quavertown, is over to Mr. Gibbs' tavern, come to see about keeping singing-school; and Mr. Gibbs, and a whole parcel more of 'em wants you to come right over there, cause they're goin' to have a meeting this evening to see about hiring of him."

Squire Brown and his family, all except Jimmy, were seated round the supper table when this interesting piece of intelligence was announced. Every one save Squire Brown himself, gave a sudden start, and at once suspended operations; but the Squire, who was a very moderate man, and never did anything from impulse, ate on without turning his head, or changing his position. After a short pause, however, which was a moment of intense anxiety to some members of the family, he replied to Jimmy as follows:

"I shan't do no sich thing; if they want a singing-school, they may get it themselves. A singing-school won't do us no good, and I've ways enough to spend my money without paying it for singing." Turning his head round and casting a severe look upon Jimmy, he proceeded with increasing energy.

The cover of *Father Kemp's Old Folks Concert Tunes*, 1860. A revival troupe that
sang the "good old tunes" of New England psalmody dressed in period costumes.
On the cover is the stereotype of the New England Singing School Master, an
image that later appeared in Harry Smith's record set, *Anthology of American Folk
Music* (see chapter 97).

"Now, sir, hang your hat up and set down and eat your supper; I should like to know
what sent you off over to the tavern without leave."

"I wanted to see the singing-master," said Jimmy. "Sam Gibbs said there was a singing-
master over to their house, and so I wanted to see him."

"Well, I'll singing-master you," said the Squire, "if I catch you to go off so again without leave. Come, don't stand there; set down and eat your supper, or I'll trounce you in two
minutes."

"Now, pa," said Miss Jerusha Brown, "you *will* go over and see about having a singing-school, won't you? I want to go dreadfully!"

"Oh, I can't do anything about that," said the Squire; "it'll cost a good deal of money, and I can't afford it. And besides, there's no use at all in it. You can sing enough now, any of you; you are singing half your time."

"There," said Mrs. Brown, "that's just the way. Our children will never have a chance to be anything as long as they live. Other folks' children have a chance to go to singing-schools, and to see young company, and to be something in the world. Here's our Jerusha has got to be in her twenty-fifth year now, and if she's ever going to have young company, and have a chance to be anything, she must have it soon; for she'll be past the time bime-by for sich things. 'Tisn't as if we was poor and couldn't afford it; for you know, Mr. Brown, you pay the largest tax of anybody in the town, and can afford to give the children a chance to be something in the world, as well as not. And as for living in this kind way any longer, I've no notion on't."

"How delightful it will be to have a singing school," said Miss Jerusha: "Jimmy, what sort of a looking man is Mr. Crotchet?"

"Oh, he is a slick kind of a looking man," said Jimmy.

"Is he a young man, or a married man?" inquired Miss Jerusha.

"Ho! Married? No; I guess he isn't," said Jimmy, "I don't believe he's more than twenty years old."

"Poh; I don't believe that story," said Jerusha, "a singing-master must be as much as twenty-five years old, I know! How is he dressed? Isn't he dressed quite genteel?"

"Oh, he's dressed pretty slick," said Jimmy.

"Well, that's what makes him look so young," said Miss Jerusha. "I dare say he's as much as twenty-five years old; don't you think he is, mother?"

"Well, I think it's pretty likely he is," said Mrs. Brown; "singing-masters are generally about that age."

"Well, Jimmy," said Miss Jerusha, "when he stands up, take him altogether, isn't he a good-looking young man?"

"I don't know anything about that," said Jimmy; "he looks the most like the tongs in the riddle, of anything I can think of:

'Long legs and crooked things,'

Little head and no eyes.'"

"There, Jim, you little plague," said Miss Jerusha, "you shall go right off to bed if you don't leave off your nonsense. I won't hear another word of it."

"I don't care if you won't," said Jimmy, "it's all true, every word of it."

"What! then the singing-master hasn't got no eyes, has he?" said Miss Jerusha; "that's a pretty story."

"I don't mean he hasn't got no eyes at all," said Jimmy, "only his eyes are dreadful little, and you can't see but one of 'em to time neither, they're twisted round so."

"A little cross-eyed, I s'pose," said Mrs. Brown, "that's all; I don't think that hurts the looks of a man a bit; it only makes him look a little sharper."

While those things were transpiring at Mr. Brown's, matters of weight and importance were being discussed at the tavern. About a dozen of the neighbors had collected there early in the evening, and every one, as soon as he found that Mr. Christopher Crotchet from Quavertown was in the village, was for having a singing-school forthwith, cost what it would. They accordingly proceeded at once to ascertain Mr. Crotchet's terms. His proposals were, to keep twenty evenings for twenty dollars and "found," or for thirty and board himself. The school to be kept three evenings in the week. A subscription-paper was opened, and the sum of fifteen dollars was at last made up. But that was the extent to which they could go; not another dollar could be raised. Much anxiety was now felt for the arrival of Squire Brown; for the question of school or no depended entirely on him.

"Squire Brown's got money enough," said Mr. Gibbs, "and if he only has the will, we shall have a school."

"Not exactly," said Mr. Jones; "if *Mrs.* Brown has the will, we shall have a school, let the Squire's will be what it may."

Before the laugh occasioned by this last remark had fully subsided, Squire Brown entered, much to the joy of the whole company.

"Squire Brown, I'm glad to see you," said Mr. Gibbs; "shall I introduce you to Mr. Christopher Crotchet, singing-master from Quavertown?"

When the ceremony of introduction was over, Mr. Gibbs laid the whole matter before Mr. Brown, showed him the subscription-paper and told him they were all depending upon him to decide whether they should have a singing-school or not. Squire Brown put on his spectacles and read the subscription-paper over two or three times, till he fully understood the terms, and the deficiency in the amount subscribed. Then without saying a word he took a pen and deliberately subscribed five dollars. That settled the business; the desired sum was raised, and the school was to go ahead. It was agreed that it should commence on the following evening, and that Mr. Crotchet should board with Mr. Gibbs one week, with the Squire the next, and so go round through the neighborhood.

On the following day there was no small commotion among the young folks of the village, in making preparation for the evening school. New singing-books were purchased, dresses were prepared, curling-tongs and crimping-irons were put in requisition, and early in the evening the long chamber in Gibbs' tavern, which was called by way of eminence "the hall," was well filled by youth of both sexes, the old folks not being allowed to attend that evening, lest the "boys and gals" should be diffident about "sounding the notes." A range of long narrow tables was placed round three sides of the hall, with benches behind them, upon which the youth were seated. A singing-book and a candle were shared by two, all round the room, till you came to Miss Jerusha Brown, who had taken the uppermost seat, and monopolized a whole book and a whole candle to her own use.

After a while the door opened, and Mr. Christopher Crotchet entered. He bent his body slightly, as he passed the door, to prevent a concussion of his head against the lintel, and then walked very erect into the middle of the floor, and made a short speech to his class. His grotesque appearance caused a slight tittering around the room, and Miss Betsy was even guilty of an incipient audible laugh, which, however, she had the tact so far to turn into a cough as to save appearances. Still it was observed by Miss Jerusha, who told her again in a low whisper that she ought to be ashamed, and added that "Mr. Crotchet was a most splendid man; a beautiful man."

After Mr. Crotchet had made his introductory speech, he proceeded to try the voices of his pupils, making each one alone follow him in rising and falling the notes.

When the process of sounding the voices separately had been gone through with, they were called upon to sound together; and before the close of the evening they were allowed to commence the notes of some easy tunes. It is unnecessary here to give a detailed account of the progress that was made, or to attempt to describe the jargon of strange sounds, with which Gibbs' hall echoed that night. Suffice it to say, that the proficiency of the pupils was so great, that on the tenth evening, or when the school was half through, the parents were permitted to be present, and were delighted to hear their children sing Old Hundred, Mear, St. Martin's, Northfield, and Hallowell, with so much accuracy, that those who knew the tunes, could readily tell, every time, which one was being performed. Mrs. Brown was almost in ecstasies at the performance, and sat the whole evening and looked at Jerusha, who sung with great earnestness and with a voice far above all the rest. Even Squire Brown himself was so much softened that evening, that his face wore a sort of smile, and he told his wife, "he didn't grudge his five dollars a bit."

SOURCE: Seba Smith (aka "the original Major Jack Downing), 'Way Down East; or, Portraitures of Yankee Life (Philadelphia: John E. Potter, 1854): 76–79, 80–81, 82–83, 84–89, 90–91. Cited and partially quoted in Nicholas E. Tawa, High-Minded and Low-Down: Music in the Lives of Americans, 1800–1861 (Boston: Northeastern University Press, 2000): 95.

$\mathcal{S}$INGING THE REVOLUTION

(Adams, Dickinson, Greeley)

The political turmoil leading up to the American Revolution is captured in the ballads and songs that colonial militants sang. As abuses from England accumulated, and resentments hardened, one and then another outrage or cause turned into a topical song. Old or popular tunes got new words and these in turn were printed in newspapers and on broadsides. The many verses of these ballads—they could number twenty-five or more—did not prove an obstacle to a public used to memorizing and singing "Chevy Chase." These selections describe a few topical ballads that survive today in different forms and sometimes for different reasons.

In the first excerpt, John Adams, who would become the second president of the United States, is already a sophisticated and determined political leader. He describes a social gathering of self-identified Sons of Liberty—fighters for the revolutionary cause. Could they control their rivalries and jealousies? How shrewdly the intellectual Adams analyzes the power of music "to tinge the mind"—to make individuals stop thinking about their ambitions and behave like a "chorus," singing themselves into a group that could act as one.

MONDAY AUGUST 14, [1769]

Dined with 350 Sons of Liberty at Robinsons, the Sign of Liberty Tree in Dorchester. We had two Tables laid in the open Field by the Barn, with between 300 and 400 Plates, and an Arning of Sail Cloth overhead, and should have spent a most agreable Day had not the Rain made some Abatement in our Pleasures. Mr. Dickinson the Farmers Brother, and Mr. Reed the Secretary of New Jersey were there, both cool, reserved and guarded all day. After Dinner was over and the Toasts drank we were diverted with Mr. Balch's Mimickry. He gave Us, the Lawyers Head, and the Hunting of a Bitch fox. We had also the Liberty Song—that by the Farmer, and that by Dr. Ch[urc]h, and the whole Company joined in the Chorus. This is cultivating the Sensations of Freedom. There was a large Collection of good Company. Otis and Adams are politick, in promoting these Festivals, for they tinge the Minds of the People, they impregnate them with the sentiments of Liberty. They render the People fond of their Leaders in the Cause, and averse and bitter against all opposers.

To the Honour of the Sons, I did not see one Person intoxicated, or near it.

Between 4 and 5 O clock, the Carriages were all got ready and the Company rode off in Procession, Mr. Hancock first in his Charriot and another Charriot bringing up the Rear. I took my Leave of the Gentlemen and turned off for Taunton, oated at Doty's and arrived, long after Dark, at Noices. There I put up. I should have been at Taunton if I had not turned back in the Morning from Roxbury—but I felt as if I ought not to loose this feast, as if it was my Duty to be there. I am not able to conjecture, of what Consequence it was whether I was there or not.

Jealousies arise from little Causes, and many might suspect, that I was not hearty in the Cause, if I had been absent whereas none of them are more sincere, and stedfast than I am.

SOURCE: *Diary and Autobiography of John Adams*, ed. L. H. Butterfield (Cambridge, Mass.: Belknap, 1962): 1:341–42.

~~~~~~~

"The Farmer" referred to by Adams was the pen name of John Dickinson (1732–1808), a sophisticated lawyer from Maryland and a founding father, who wrote essays protesting unfair tax laws. Dickinson's protest ballad "The Liberty Song" fit new words to a popular march, "Heart of Oak" by the English composer William Boyce (1711–1779). "Heart of Oak" survives today as the official march for both the British navy and the Canadian navy. According to the cultural historian Kenneth Silverman, Dickinson's "Liberty Song" is "probably the first set of verses by an American to be learned by heart by a larger, intercolonial audience." [1]

JOHN DICKINSON'S "THE LIBERTY SONG," AS PUBLISHED IN THE *BOSTON GAZETTE*, JULY 18, 1768

COME, join Hand in Hand, brave AMERICANS all,
And rouse your bold Hearts at fair LIBERTY's Call;

No tyrannous Acts *shall suppress your* just Claim,
Or stain with Dishonor *AMERICA's Name.*

CHORUS: In Freedom we're BORN, and in FREEDOM we'll LIVE,
Our Purses are ready,
Steady, Friends, Steady,
Not as SLAVES, but as FREEMEN our Money we'll give.

Our worthy Forefathers—*let's give them a Cheer—*
To Climates unknown *did courageously steer;*
Thro' Oceans *to* Deserts *for* Freedom *they came,*
And dying bequeath'd us their Freedom *and* Fame—

(Chorus)

The TREE their own Hands had to LIBERTY rear'd,
They liv'd to behold growing strong and rever'd;
With Transport then cry'd, "now our Wishes we gain,
For our Children shall gather the Fruits of our Pain,"

(Chorus)

Then join Hand in Hand brave AMERICANS all,
By uniting *we stand, by* dividing *we fall;*
IN SO RIGHTEOUS A CAUSE let us hope to succeed,
For Heaven approves of each generous Deed.—

(Chorus)

This Bumper I crown for our SOVEREIGN's Health,
And this for BRITANNIA's Glory and Wealth;
That Wealth and that Glory immortal may be,
If she *is but* just—*and if* we *are but* free.—

(Chorus)

SOURCE: Adapted from Mary Jane Corry, Kate Van Winkle Keller, and Robert Keller, eds., *The Performing Arts in Colonial Newspapers, 1690–1783* (New York: University Music Editions, 1997), a CD-ROM publication.

~~~~~~~

Some ballads from the colonial era had a longer life than one might expect. Horace Greeley (1811–1872) was the famous newspaper publisher of the New York Tribune *and a presidential candidate in 1872, who remembers his New Hampshire neighbors singing many of the fifty stanzas of "American Taxation." Other songs mentioned by Greeley offer evidence about oral tradition. His mother, Mrs. Greeley, also sang "The Taking of Quebec" about the famous battle of 1759 during the British, French, and Indian War as well as the classic Anglo-American ballad "Cruel Barbara Allen,"*

which is referred to as a "love-lorn ditty." A century later, ballad revivalists from both
England and the United States would encounter the term "love songs" for "Barbara
Allen" and similar songs among mountain singers in Tennessee and Kentucky.

Let me revert for a little to our New Hampshire life, ere I bid it a final adieu.

I have already said that Amherst and Bedford are in the main poor towns, whose hard, rocky soil yields grudgingly, save of wood. Except in the villages, if even there, there were very few who could be called forehanded in my early boyhood. Poor as we were, no richer family lived within sight of our humble homestead, though our western prospect was only bounded by the "Chestnut Hills," two or three miles away. On the east, our range of vision was barred by the hill on the side of which we lived. The leading man of our neighborhood was Captain Nathan Barnes, a Calvinist deacon, after whom my brother was named, and who was a farmer of decided probity and sound judgment,—worth perhaps, $3,000. Though an ardent Federalist, as were a majority of his townsmen, he commanded a company of "exempts," raised to defend the country in case of British invasion, during the war of 1812.

The Revolutionary War was not yet thirty years bygone when I was born, and its passions, its prejudices, and its ballads were still current throughout that intensely Whig region. When neighbors and neighbors' wives drew together at the house of one of their number for an evening visit, there were often interspersed with "Cruel Barbara Allen," and other love-lorn ditties then in vogue, such reminiscences of the preceding age as "American Taxation," a screed of some fifty prosaic verses, opening thus:—

> *While I relate my story,*
> *   Americans, give ear;*
> *Of Britain's fading glory*
> *   You presently shall hear.*
> *I'll give a true relation,*
> *   (Attend to what I say,)*
> *Concerning the taxation*
> *   Of North America.*

The last throes of expiring loyalty are visible in this long-drawn ballad,—Bute and North, and even Fox, being soundly berated for acts of tyranny whereof their royal master, George III, was sole author, and they but reluctant, hesitating, apprehensive instruments.

The ballads of the late war with Great Britain were not so popular in our immediate neighborhood, though my mother had good store of these also, and sang them with spirit and effect, along with "Boyne Water," "The Taking of Quebec," by Wolfe, and even "Wearing of the Green," which, though dating from Ireland's '98, has been revived and adopted in our day, with so vast and deserved an Irish popularity.

We were, in the truest sense, democrats, we Scotch-Irish Federalists from Londonderry, where Jefferson received but two votes in the memorable struggle of 1800.[2] When, for a single year at the "Beard Farm," our house echoed to the tread of a female "help," whose natural abilities were humble, and whose literary acquirements were inferior even to ours, that servant always ate with the family, even when we had the neighbors as "company"; and, though her wages were but fifty cents a week, she had her party, and invited the girls of the neighborhood to be her guests at tea, precisely as if she had been a daughter of the house. Nowhere were manners ever simpler, or society freer from pretension or exclusiveness, than in those farmers' homes.

SOURCE: Horace Greeley, *Recollections of a Busy Life* (New York: J. B. Ford, 1868): 50–52. Partially quoted in Nicholas Tawa, *High-Minded and Low-Down: Music in the Lives of Americans, 1800–1861* (Boston: Northeastern University Press, 2000): 162–63.

~~~~~~~~

NOTES

1. Kenneth Silverman, *A Cultural History of the Revolution* (New York: Thomas Y. Crowell Co., 1976): 112. A sound file of this tune is available at http://www.collectionscanada.ca/gramophone/m2-3001.1-e.html.
2. Greeley is referring to the tumultuous presidential contest between the Federalist John Adams and Thomas Jefferson in 1800, which was won by Jefferson.

ELISHA BOSTWICK HEARS A SCOTS PRISONER

SING "GYPSIE LADDIE"

In this account, Elisha Bostwick (1748–1834), a colonial soldier fighting during the Revolutionary War among General George Washington's troops, describes how he learned the still-famous Anglo-American ballad "Gypsie Laddie" from a Scottish soldier captured in battle near Princeton, New Jersey, in 1777. The ballad, which Bostwick thought "must die with me," has had a long life. Bob Dylan recorded an American variant, "Black Jack Davey," in 1992.[1]

A]n alarm was made [and] our army cross'd the bridge & form'd on the South side of the Creek South of the town where in the evening & through the night fires were kept continually burning while at the same time our army by a circuetous night march arrived at sun rise the next morning at Princeton attacked those of the enemy who were left there kill'd about one hundred & took about three hundred prisoners (the talk was that his excellency had been too much exposed to the fire of the enemy)[.] N.B. the body of a British Capt by the name of [William] Leslie was found among the dead which was taken along with us in a waggon & the next morning was buried with the honers of War he was said to be a Nobleman. I did not See the Corps & was not at the funeral for my feet were so sore I was glad to be still and only heard the firing. Genl. [Hugh] Mercer was kill'd in this Battle and some highlanders with their Scotch plaid dress were Conducted to Peekshill under a guard which was composed of those of us who belong'd to Col. Webbs Reg[imen]t. and here Col Webb discharged the Supernumerary officers of his Regt. & they went home[.] [H]e gave me that command together with Lt. Ball & Ensn. Hulbert where-upon we immediately recrossed the Hudson March'd back to head quarters at Morristown— Before I go further I will mention one Simple Circumstance while on our March with the pris-oners a part of whom while under my immediate care were Spreading their blankets upon the floor for the nights lodging [when] I saw a women or two with them. I enquired into it & was told that it was sometimes allow'd a Sergt. to have his wife with him who drew rations the Same as a Soldier[,] were very Serviceable & Supported virtuous characters & about Midnight when all was Still one of the Prisoners arose up & Sung what he Call'd the Gypsie laddy, Some of the lines I always retain'd in memory among which were these.

> Will you leave your houses, will you leave your lands,
> And will you leave your little children a-a-h
> Will you leave your true wedded Lord & lying with a Gypsie Laddy
>   a-a-h
> Will you leave your true wedded lord & lying with a Gypsie Laddy
>   a-a-h
> Yes I will leave my houses I will leave my lands
> And I will leave my little children a-a-h
> I will leave for you my true wedded Lord & lying with a Gypsie
>   Laddy a-a-h
> I will leave for you my true wedded Lord & lying with a Gypsie
>   Laddy a-a-h
> Last night I slept on a Silken bed of down
> Alongside my lawful & true wedded Lord
> But now I sleep in an ashy corner happy with my Gypsie Laddy a-a-h
> But now I sleep in an ashy corner happy with my Gypsie Laddy a-a-h
>   And then lay down again.

The tune was of a Plaintive Cast & I always retain'd it & Sung it to my Children but that must die with me.

SOURCE: William S. Powell, "A Connecticut Soldier under Washington: Elisha Bostwick's Memoirs of the First Years of the Revolution," *William and Mary Quarterly*, 3rd ser., 6, no. 1 (January 1949): 103–4. Cited and partially quoted in Carleton Sprague Smith, "Broad-sides and Their Music in Colonial America," in *Music in Colonial Massachusetts 1630–1820*, ed. Frederick S. Allis, Jr. (Boston: Colonial Society of Massachusetts, 1980): I:315–16.

~~~~~~

NOTE

1.   Bob Dylan, "Blackjack Davey," *Good As I Been To You*. Sony, 1992.

12

A SIDEBAR INTO BALLAD SCHOLARSHIP

The Wanderings of the "Gypsy Laddie"

(Child, Sharp, Coffin, Bronson)

Anglo-American ballads have benefited from generations of scholarly devotion, partly because of the influence of an American literary scholar, Francis J. Child (1825–1896), who established a canon of English and Scottish ballads with such authority that they still bear the numbers he assigned them. "Gypsy Laddie" is thus "Child 200." Child reviewed English and Scottish literary sources and also collected material from ordinary folks, some of whom are named here. His first source for this ballad names an obscure Johnny Faa, whom Child thought was a fictional character, but we now think it likely that he lived in Scotland in the 1600s.[1]

In the early 1910s, ballad scholarship shifted from texts to tunes, as a new generation of collectors discovered that people living in the American Appalachian Mountains still sang Child ballads. From England came Cecil Sharp (1859–1924), whose research was prompted and aided by Olive Dame Campbell (1882–1954), a settlement school teacher from Massachusetts. Many of their informants, like many of Child's, were women, who have thus become associated with preserving this genre in oral tradition. Aunt Lize Pace remembered Sharp years later: "Years ago when that funny old Englishman come over the mountains and wrote down these old love songs that I know, I could sing like a mockingbird and wasn't no step that I couldn't put my foot to in a dance."[2]

Later American scholars traced the texts and tunes of Child ballads, sometimes using nineteenth-century songsters (collections of texts only). The titles collected by Tristram Coffin (1892–1955) read like the children's game of "telephone." Bertrand Bronson (1902–1986) listed 128 text sources for the "Gypsie Laddie," and reprinted 93 tune variants. He also added references to field recordings in the Archive of American Folk Song, some by famous musicians, including Bascom Lunsford, Woody Guthrie, Jean Ritchie, and Texas Gladden; recordings by the last three are available on CD.

This list is intended to convey the links in the chain of survival documented by scholarship. No two people named here sang "Gypsie Laddie" in quite the same way. (For an example of variants of another well-known song, see chapter 24.) Even without examples of the text and tune variants, the roster suggests the humanity of the process through which ballads enter into tradition.

FROM FRANCIS J. CHILD'S SOURCE LIST FOR "GYPSY LADDIE" BETWEEN 1740 AND 1840 (CHILD NO. 200)

A. "Johny Faa, the Gypsy Laddie," Ramsay's *Tea-Table Miscellany*, vol. iv, 1740.

B. a. *The Edinburgh Magazine and Literary Miscellany* (vol. lxxx of the Scots Magazine), November 1817, p. 309. b. A fragment recited by Miss Fanny Walker, of Mount Pleasant, near Newburgh-on-Tay.

C. "Davie Faw," Motherwell's MS., p. 381; from the recitation of Agnes Lyle, Kilbarchan, 27 July 1825, "Gypsie Davy," *Motherwell's Minstrelsy*, 1827, p. 360.

D. "The Egyptian Laddy," Kinloch MSS, v, 331, in the handwriting of John Hill Burton, from a reciter who came from the vicinity of Craigievar.

E. "The Gypsie Laddie," Mactaggart's *Scottish Gallovidian Encyclopedia*, 1824, p. 284.

F. "Johnny Faa, the Gypsey Laddie," *The Songs of England and Scotland*, [P. Cunningham], London, 1835, II, 346, taken down, as current in the north of England, from the recitation of John Martin, the painter.

G. a. "The Gypsie Loddy," a broadside, *Roxburghe Ballads*, III, 685. b. A recent stall-copy, Catnach, 2 Monmouth Court, Seven Dials.

H. "The Gipsy Laddie," *Shropshire Folk-Lore*, edited by Charlotte Sophia Burne, p. 550.

I. Communicated by Miss Margaret Reburn, as sung in County Meath, Ireland, about 1860.

J.   a. "The Gipsey Davy," from Stockbridge, Massachusetts. Written down
      by Newton Pepoun, as learned from a boy with whom he went to school
      in Stockbridge, Mass. b. From the singing of Mrs. Farmer, born in
      Maine, learned by her daughter about 1840.
K.   "Lord Garrick," a, b, communicated by ladies of New York. From Mrs.
      Helene Titus Brown of New York. b. from Miss Emma A. Clinch of New
      York. Derived, 1820, or a little later (a) directly (b) indirectly from the sing-
      ing of Miss Phoebe Wood, Huntington, Long Island, and perhaps learned
      from English soldiers there stationed during the Revolutionary War.

SOURCE: Francis J. Child's sources for "Child no. 200," in *The English and Scottish Popular Ballads, 1882–1898* (1886; reprint, New York: Dover, 2003): IV:61–73.

CECIL J. SHARP'S INFORMANTS FOR "GYPSY LADDIE" COLLECTED IN 1916 IN THE UNITED STATES FROM FIELD WORK IN THE APPALACHIAN MOUNTAINS

A.   Sung by Mrs. J. Gabriel Coates at Flag Pond, Tenn., Sept. 1, 1916.
B.   Sung by Mrs. Mary Norton at Rocky Fork, Tenn., Sept. 2, 1916.
C.   Sung by Mrs. Hester House at Hot Springs, N.C., Sept. 15, 1916.
D.   Sung by Mrs. Jane Gentry at Hot Springs, N.C., Sept. 14, 1916.
E.   Sung by Mrs. Kitty Gwynne at Rocky Fork, Tenn., Sept. 5, 1916.
F.   Sung by Mrs. Sarah Buckner at Black Mountain, N.C., Sept. 16, 1916.
G.   Sung by Mr. N. B. Chisholm at Woodridge, Va., Sept. 27, 1916.
H.   Sung by Mrs. Franklin at Barbourville, Knox Co., Ky., May 9, 1917.
I.   Sung by Mrs. Lizzie Gibson at Crozet, Va., April 26, 1918.
J.   Sung by Mrs. Delie Hughes at Cane River, Burnsville, N.C., Oct. 5, 1918.

SOURCE: Cecil J. Sharp, collector, *English Folk Songs from the Southern Appalachians:
Comprising two hundred and seventy-four Songs and Ballads with nine hundred and sixty-
eight Tunes. Including thirty-nine Tunes contributed by Olive Dame Campbell*, ed. Maud
Karpeles (Oxford: Oxford University Press, 1932): 233–39.

TRISTRAM COFFIN'S LIST OF VARIANT "LOCAL TITLES" ASSOCIATED WITH "GYPSIE LADDIE"

"Bill Harman," "Black-eyed Davy," "Black-jack Davy" (David, Daley), "Cross-eyed David,"
"Egyptian Davy O," "Gay Little Davy," "Georgia Daisy," "Gypsea Song," "Gypsie (Gypsen,

Gypso) Davy," "Gypsy Daisy," "It Was Late in the Night When Johnny Came Home," "Oh Come and Go Back My Pretty Fair Miss," "Seven Gypsies in a Row," "The Dark-clothes Gypsy," "The Gypsies," "The Gypsy (Gyptian) Laddie," "The Gypsy Lover," "The Heartless Lady," "The Lady's Disgrace," "The Three Gypsies," "When Carnal First Came to Arkansas," "When the Squire Came Home."

SOURCE: Tristram P. Coffin, *The British Traditional Ballad in North America* (Philadelphia: American Folklore Society, 1950): 121.

~~~~~~~

BERTRAND BRONSON'S LIST OF RECORDINGS OF CHILD NO. 200, 1941–1961

As found in the archive of American Folk Song (AAFS) at the Library of Congress (LC) and a few other commercial recordings, with numbers from his larger list of variants and with places and dates of recordings added.

No. 4, "Black Jack Davy," Bascom Lamar Lunsford, AAFS no. 9474 (A1) [LC, 1949]

No. 8, "The Davy," Mrs. Carrie Grover, AAFS no. 4454 (B1) [April 1941]

No. 17b, "The Gypsy Davy," Woody Guthrie, AAFS [LC, 1941]

No. 27, "Gypsie Laddie," Mrs. Mary Bird McAllister, AAFS no. 11866 (A1) [Brown's Cove, Virginia, 1958–1959]

No. 29, "Gypsie Laddie [Untitled]," Mrs. Texas Gladden, AAFS no. 5233 (A1) [Salem, Virginia, 1941]

No. 38, "Gypsie Laddie," Jean Ritchie, Folkways LP-FA 2301 (A1) [1961]

No. 49, "The Gypsie Laddie," Ewan MacColl, Riverside no. RLP 12-637 (A5) [1957]

No. 81, "The Gypsie Laddie," Florence Shiflett, AAFS no. 12006 (B24) [Brown's Cove, Virginia, July 13, 1962]

No. 82, "Gypsie Laddie," David Morris, AAFS no. 12007 (A7) [July 13, 1962]

No. 83, "Gypsie Laddie," Robert Shiflett, AAFS no. 12004 (A2) [Brown's Cove, Virginia, July 1961]

No. 96, "Gypsie Laddie," Arthur Keefe, AAFS no. 10501 (A16) [June 28, 1949]

No. 101, "Black Jack Davy," Mrs. T. M. Davis, AAFS no. 11894 (B18) [n.a.]

No. 102, "Gipsy Draly," Mrs. Oleava Houser, AAFS no. 11908 (B34) [September 28, 1958; listed as "Black Jack Davy" at LC]

No. 105, "Gypsum Davy," Mrs. Donald (Emma) Shelton, AAFS no. 10008 (A9).

No. 113, "David," Mrs. Wayne (Claudia) Roberts, AAFS no. 10007 (A16) [September 28, 1950; listed as "Gypsy Laddie" at LC]

No. 116, "Black Jack Davy," Buck Buttery, AAFS no. 11909 (B24) [August 19, 1958; listed as "Black-Jack Davey" at LC]

No. 117, "Black Jack David," John Pennington, AAFS no. 11894 (B7) [July 1954; listed as "Black Jack Davy" at LC]

No. 123, "Gypsy Davy," Mrs. May Kennedy McCord, AAFS no. 5303 (A1) [Springfield, Missouri, October 21, 1941]

SOURCE: Bertrand H. Bronson, *The Traditional Tunes of the Child Ballads* (Princeton, N.J.: Princeton University Press, 1959–1972), 3:198–201.

~~~~~~~

NOTES

1. Sigrid Rieuwerts, "The Historical Moorings of "The Gypsy Laddie": Johnny Faa and Lady Cassillis," in Joseph Harris, ed. *The Ballad and Oral Literature* (Cambridge: Harvard University Press, 1991): 78–96.
2. Aunt Lize Pace, quoted in John Lomax and Alan Lomax, eds., *Our Singing Country* (New York: Macmillan, 1941): 151.

13

WILLIAM BILLINGS AND THE NEW SACRED MUSIC

(Billings, Gould)

William Billings (1746–1800) inaugurated the great wave of home-grown newly composed sacred music with the publication of his *The New England Psalm Singer*, a landmark for many reasons. As the historian Nicholas Temperley writes, "At one stroke [Billings] published 127 new compositions. We know now, for certain, that this was more than three times the entire corpus of American compositions published before that time. . . . Although he had not fully mastered his medium, he was laying the foundations of a new style of composition."[1]

One of the most vivid writers among American composers, Billings crafted entertaining as well as informative introductions to his tunebooks. With values that appeal to our fondness for mavericks, Billings conveyed a skepticism about orthodoxy and authority in vivid language that still appeals to our sense of American individualism. The Preface to *The New England Psalm Singer*, reprinted here, includes his now-famous statement that he thinks it best for "every *Composer* to be his own *Carver*." Yet Billings could admit mistakes and avowed more humility in *The Singing Master's Assistant* (1778), whose Preface is reprinted here as well. That book, which became known as "Billings' Best," includes "Chester," "Jargon," and "I Am the Rose of Sharon."

In his last collection, *The Continental Harmony* (1794), Billings wrote an explanation of music fundamentals, with a long section in the form of a dialogue between master and student. Billings's comments about performance practice, an excerpt of which is reprinted here, remind us of "experiments in sonority."[2] Billings ends with one of his inimitable poems praising the fuging tune, a genre he inaugurated in his first book of compositions and which has since defined the New England Singing School of composers.

Apparently, Billings lived as he composed, flouting his enemies and irritating his friends, as the concluding selection by a writer close to his time makes clear.

FROM *THE NEW-ENGLAND PSALM-SINGER* (1770)

To all Musical Practitioners.

PERHAPS it may be expected by some, that I should say something concerning Rules for Composition; to these I answer that *Nature is the best Dictator,* for all the hard dry studied Rules that ever was prescribed, will not enable any Person to form an Air any more than the bare Knowledge of the four and twenty Letters, and strict Grammatical Rules will qualify a Scholar for composing a Piece of Poetry, or properly adjusting a Tragedy, without a Genius. It must be Nature, Nature must lay the Foundation, Nature must inspire the Thought. But perhaps some may think I mean and intend to throw Art intirely out of the Question, I answer by no Means, for the more Art is display'd, the more Nature is decorated. And in some sorts of Composition there is dry Study requir'd, and Art very requisite. For instance, in a *Fuge,* where the Parts come in after each other, with the same Notes; but even there, Art is subservient to Genius, for Fancy goes first, and strikes out the Work roughly, and Art comes after, and polishes it over. But to return to my Text; I have read several Author's Rules on Composition, and find the strictest of them make some Exceptions, as thus, they say that two Eighths or two Fifths may not be taken together rising or falling, unless one be Major and the other Minor; but rather than spoil the Air, they will allow that Breach to be made, and this allowance gives great Latitude to young Composers, for they may always make that Plea, and say, if I am not allow'd to transgress the Rules of Composition, I shall certainly spoil the Air, and Cross the Strain, that fancy dictated: And indeed this is without dispute, a very just Plea, for I am sure I have often and sensibly felt the disagreeable and slavish Effects of such a restraint as is here pointed out, and so I believe has every Composer of Poetry, as well as Musick, for I presume there are as strict Rules for Poetry, as for Musick. But as I have often heard of a Poetical Licence, I don't see why with the same Propriety there may not be a Musical Licence, for Poetry and Music are in close Connection, and nearly allied, besides they are often assistants to each other; and like true friends often hide each others failings: For I have known a Piece of Poetry that had neither *"Rhime nor Reason"** in it, pass for

---

*A simple Fellow bro't a Piece of Prose to Sir *Thomas Moore* [More] for his Inspection; Sir *Thomas* told him to put it into Rhime, accordingly he did; upon which Sir *Thomas* said to him, now it is *Rhime;* but before it was neither *Rhime nor Reason.*

tolerable good Sense, because it happened to be set to an excellent Piece of Musick, and so get respect rather for its good fortune in falling into such respectable Company than for any Merit in itself; so likewise I have known and heard a very indifferent Tune often sung, and much caress'd, only because it was set to a fine Piece of Poetry, without which recommendation, perhaps it would not be sung twice over by one Person, and would be deem'd to be dearly bo't only at the expence of Breath requisite to perform it—for my own Part, as I don't think myself confin'd to any Rules for Composition laid down by any that went before me, neither should I think (were I to pretend to lay down Rules) that any who came after me were any ways obligated to adhere to them, any further than they should think proper: So in fact, I think it is best for every *Composer* to be his own *Carver*. Therefore, upon this Consideration, for me to dictate, or pretend to prescribe Rules of this Nature for others, would not only be very unnecessary, but also a great Piece of Vanity.

<p style="text-align:center">~~~~~~~</p>

Billings's view on the sound ideal for performing his compositions weights the distribution of voice parts in favor of the bass line.

"THOUGHTS ON MUSIC" FROM CHAPTER IX

In order to make good Music, there is great Judgment required in dividing the Parts properly, so that one shall not over-power the other. In most Singing Companies I ever heard, the greatest Failure was in the Bass, for let the Three upper Parts be Sung by the Best Voices upon Earth, and after the Best Manner, yet without a sufficient Quantity of Bass, they are no better than a Scream, because the Bass is the Foundation, and if it be well laid, you may build upon it at Pleasure. Therefore in order to have good Music, there must be Three Bass to one of the upper Parts. So that for Instance, suppose a Company of Forty People, Twenty of them should sing the Bass, the other Twenty should be divided according to the Discretion of the Company into the upper Parts, six or seven of the deepest Voices should sing the Ground Bass, which I have set to most of the Tunes in the following Work, and have taken Care to set it chiefly in the compass of the Human Voice, which if well sung together with the upper Parts, is most Majestic, and so exceeding Grand as to cause the Floor to tremble, as I myself have often experienced. Great Care should also be taken to Pitch a Tune on or near the Letter it is set, though sometimes it will bear to be set a little above and sometimes a little below the Key, according to the Discretion of the Performer; but I would recommend a Pitch Pipe, which will give the Sound even to the nicety of a half a Tone.

SOURCE: William Billings, *The New-England psalm-singer; or, American chorister. Containing a number of psalm-tunes, anthems and canons. In four and five parts. (Never before published.) Composed by William Billings, a native of Boston, New-England* (Boston, New-England: Printed by Edes and Gill, 1770): 18–20.

~~~~~~

FROM *THE SINGING MASTER'S ASSISTANT* (1778)

PREFACE

KIND READER,

NO doubt you (do, or ought to) remember, that about eight years ago, I published a Book entitled, *The New England Psalm Singer*, &c. And truly a most masterly and inimitable Performance, I then thought it to be. Oh! how did my foolish heart throb and beat with tumultuous joy! With what impatience did I wait on the Book-Binder, while stitching the sheets and puting on the covers, with what extacy, did I snatch the yet unfinished Book out of his hands, and pressing it to my bosom, with rapturous delight, how lavish was I, in encomiums on this infant production of my own Numbskull? Welcome; thrice welcome; thou legitimate offspring of my brain, go forth my little Book, go forth and immortalize the tune of your Author; may your sale be rapid and may you speedily run through ten thousand Editions, may you be a welcome guest in all companies and what will add tenfold to thy dignity, may you find your way into the Libraries of the Learned. Thou art my Reuben,[3] my first born, the beginning of my strength, the excellency of my dignity, and the excellency of my power. But to my great mortification, I soon discovered it was Reuben in the sequel, and Reuben all over; for unstable as water, it did not excell: But since I have began to play the Critic, I will go through with my Criticisms, and endeavour to point out its beauties as well as deformities, and it must be acknowledged, that many of the pieces are not so ostentatious, as to sound forth their own praises; for it has been judiciously observed, that the oftener they are sounded, the more they are abased. After impartial examination, I have discovered that many of the pieces in that Book were never worth my printing, or your inspection; therefore in order to make you amends for my former intrusion, I have selected and corrected some of the Tunes which were most approved of in that book, and have added several new pieces which I think to be very good ones; for if I thought otherwise, I should not have presented them to you. But however, I am not so tenacious of my own opinion, as to desire you to take my word for it; but rather advise you to all purchase a Book and satisfy yourselves in that particular, and then, I make no doubt, but you will readily concur with me in this sentiment, the *Singing Master's Assistant*, is a much better Book, than the *New England Psalm Singer*.

> SOURCE: *The Singing Master's Assistant; or, Key to practical music*, 3rd ed. (Boston, 1781). Text from *The Complete Works of William Billings*, ed. Hans Nathan (Charlottesville: University of Virginia Press, 1977): 3–4.

~~~~~~

FROM *THE CONTINENTAL HARMONY* (1794)

SCHOLAR.   Pray sir, what is the difference between the *Medius* and *Treble?*

MASTER.   When a piece of music is set in four parts, if a woman sings the upper part, it is called a *Treble,* because it is threefold, or the third octave from the Bass, but if a man sings it, it is called a *Medius,* or *Cantus,* because he sings it an octave below a Treble.

SCHOLAR.   Which is the best of these two?

MASTER.   It is sometimes set so, as for one part to be best, and sometimes the other; but in general they are best sung together, viz. if a man sings it as a Medius, and a woman as a Treble, it is then in effect as two parts; so like-wise, if a man sing[s] a Tenor with a masculine and a woman with a feminine voice, the Tenor is as full as two parts, and a tune so sung, (although it has but four parts), is in effect the same as six. Such a conjunction of masculine and feminine voices is beyond expression, sweet and ravishing, and is esteemed by all good judges to be vastly preferable to any instrument whatever, framed by human invention. It is an old maxim, and I think a very just one, viz. *that variety is always pleasing,* and it is well known that there is more variety in one piece of fug[u]ing music, than in twenty pieces of plain song, for while the tones do most sweetly coincide and agree, the words are seemingly engaged in a musical warfare; and excuse the paradox if I further add, that each part seems determined by dint of harmony and strength of accent, to drown his competitor in an ocean of harmony, and while each part is thus mutually striving for mastery, and sweetly contending for victory, the audience are most luxuriously entertained, and exceedingly delighted; in the mean time, their minds are surprisingly agitated, and extremely fluctuated; sometimes declaring in favour of one part, and sometimes another—Now the solumn bass demands their attention, now the manly tenor, now the lofty counter, now the volatile treble, now here, now there, now here again—O inchanting! O ecstatic! Push on, push on ye sons of harmony, and

        Discharge your deep mouth'd canon, full fraught with Diapasons;[4]

        May you with Maestoso, rush on to Choro-Grando,

        And then with Vigoroso, let fly your Diapentes[5]

        About our nervous system.

SOURCE: "The Continental Harmony, containing a number of anthems, fuges, and cho-russes, in several parts." Composed by William Billings. (Boston: Isaiah Thomas and Ebenezer T. Andrews, 1794): xv, xviii.

~~~~~~~

We have heard the late Rev. Dr. Pierce, of Brookline, relate many incidents in regard to the life and character of Billings, he being personally acquainted with him, and having so frequently sung with him. He said Billings had a stentorian voice, and when he stood by him to sing, he could not hear his own voice; and every one that ever heard Dr. Pierce sing, especially at Commencement dinners, at Cambridge, knows that his voice was not wanting in power.

Billings was somewhat deformed in person, blind with one eye, one leg shorter than the other, one arm somewhat withered, with a mind as eccentric as his person was deformed. To say nothing of the deformity of his habits, suffice it to say, he had a propensity for taking snuff that may seem almost incredible, when in these days those that use it are not very much inclined to expose the article. He used to carry it in his coat-pocket, which was made of leather; and every few minutes, instead of taking it in the usual manner, with thumb and finger, would take out a handful and snuff it from between his thumb and clenched hand. We might infer, from this circumstance, that his voice could not have been very pleasant and delicate.

He for many years kept a music-store in Boston, and was once in a while annoyed by the tricks of boys. Having a sign projecting from his door over the sidewalk, with the words "Billings' Music" on each side, one evening a couple of cats, with their hind legs tied together, were thrown unceremoniously across the sign; and when their faces came together below, their music was not of the sweetest kind, and rather grating to the tenant's ear. A multitude of hearers soon assembled, and had an opportunity of reading the sign, and hearing their music, such as it was, a long time before they could be released.

> SOURCE: Nathaniel D. Gould, *History of Church Music in America* (Boston: Gould and Lincoln, 1853): 46.

NOTES

1. Nicholas Temperley, "First Forty: The Earliest American Compositions," *American Music* 15/1 (Spring 1997): 21.
2. Temperley, "First Forty": 21.
3. "Reuben" means "Behold my son" in Hebrew, as found in *Genesis* 29:32.
4. "Diapason" is an octave.
5. "Diapente" is a fifth.

14

$\mathcal{D}$ANIEL READ ON PIRATING AND "SCIENTIFIC MUSIC"

Daniel Read (1857–1836), a major figure among early American composers of sacred music, confronted issues of a burgeoning musical marketplace, in which the growing supply of tunebooks were meeting the demands of singing schools, singing societies, and church choirs. Read's collection of his own compositions, *The American Singing Book,* went through five editions between 1785 and 1796 and was pirated by other authors during his lifetime. The letter of 1793 reproduced below shows the problems of survival in a marketplace without copyright protection.

Read lived long enough to witness a change of taste in the settings of hymn tunes. In the post-1800 generation, the "scientific" musician set the standards. Witnessing the success of Lowell Mason's *The Boston Handel and Haydn Society Collection of Church Music* (1822), Read had to defend his music from increasingly harsh criticism. No more parallel fifths, fewer dance rhythms, less open twangy sounds; the same qualities prized now were those most suspect then. Read, who named his eldest son George Frederick Handel Read, nevertheless resisted encroachments on his artistic authority from church officials. The second letter shows his adaptability and his sense of loss. Ironically, the "pirating," or unauthorized borrowing by other tunebook publishers, made it possible for Read's music to survive. "Greenwich" was published 82 times in Read's own era.[1] "Calvary," "Sherburne," and "Lisbon" remain favorites at Sacred Harp singing conventions in the Southern states even today.

~~~~~~
~~~~~~

LETTER FROM DANIEL READ TO MR. JACOB FRENCH, NEW HAVEN, JUNE 10, 1793

Sir

Your favour of the 22d April I did not receive until the 7th just.—It is not only ungenerous but unjust to publish the works of any author without his consent.—Irritated beyond measure at the unprovoked robbery committed upon the American Singing Book by the Editor of the Worcester Collection and having no redress but by retaliation there being then no law in existance to prevent such abuses I availed myself of that opportunity to publish some peices [sic] from the Worcester Collection to which I had no right. But since the Statute of the United States made for the purpose of securing to Authors the Copyright of their work, I ~~am determined to~~ do not mean to give any person cause to be offended in that way, on the other hand. I think it my duty to prosecute any person who prints my music without my consent, as much as if he were a common Theif or Housebreaker. Your proposal to exchange music is doubtless a good one and provided we can accommodate each other I shall have no objection, but I have never had the pleasure of seeing The New American Melody and consequently know nothing about the Music contained in it and besides, the Law requires an agreement in writing signed in the presence of two credible Witnesses.—There are some Tunes I have seen which I should like to print provided I publish any more music particularly one called All Saints, I do not know but you are the proprietor of it.—I wish it was convenient for you to take a ~~ride~~ tour this way and call on me, and tis very probable we could form a contract agreable to your mind and if it is a matter of much consequence to you I make no doubt but ~~it will be agreable to~~ you will be willing to take that Trouble. I wish for an harmonious agreement with all professors of music and particularly with Authors and publishers, and should be peculiarly happy to make acquaintance with you.—There has an A[n]them entitled The farewell by French been published here by one Asael Benham of Wallingford. I give you this information because I think it my duty to do as I would be done by[.] I am Sir your humble ~~and devoted~~ servant and sincier [sincere] friend.

Daniel Read

Mr. Jacob French
Uxbridge

~~~~~

This draft of a complete letter, responding to an attack from Read's nemesis, one Mr. Hart, names the musical authorities from Europe circulating in the newly formed United States at the time, including theorists and composers (where Beethoven's name is struck out).

New Haven, May 7th 1829

Dear Sir,

Your favor of the 1st Inst[ant] has been received, together with Professor Fitch's answers to several questions ~~offered~~ proposed to you by me some time ago, and a letter to
you from the Rev. Luther Hart of Plymouth. ~~I hardly know how to express my gratitude
to you for the interest you are taking in the work in which I have been for a considerable time engaged.~~

Mr. Fitch's communication requires no remarks from me; but Mr. Hart's Letter
demands a particular consideration. I agree with Mr. H. in the general principles laid
down in his letter. Viz. That the kind of music which has prevailed in New England till
within a few years, is not good, and that music of a more solid and more solemn kind
ought to be introduced into our churches.—That ~~number of~~ there are but few scientific
musicians in our country ~~is~~ who have a familer and thorough acquaintance with the
principles of harmony, and that a book which will not bear the critical examination of
those few ought not to be published. These, I think, are the leading principles in Mr.
H's letter. There are however some ~~other~~ ideas in the letter which, I think, it is my duty
to notice. Mr. Hart seems to have imbibed a wrong idea of ~~the work~~ the plan I have
adopted in the work I have undertaken. He ~~seems to~~ speaks as if I were making a collection to please myself and ~~were~~ making alterations in tunes to ~~suit~~ please my own
individual taste without being ~~being~~ guided by established principles or, ~~(if you please)~~
by the laws of harmony. I think Mr. H could not have got this idea from my letter; I believe I have said no such thing, and I am sure I never intended any such thing, but exactly the reverse. My object ~~is~~ is and has been from the first to be wholly guided by settled
principles, and to make just such a book as Mr. H. says he wants, 'A book that rests on
the broad ground of settled principles rather than on the narrow one of individual taste.'
But it may be asked, if Mr. H. did not get his ideas from my letter where did he get them?
I answer they have probably originated in a ~~want of confidence in my~~ preconceived opinion that ~~I am deficient in my knowledge in or the science of harmony, or my judgement
or my taste are ind~~ my talents are inadequate to the undertaking. This Idea seems to run
through the whole of the letter. He is fearful I shall do more evil than good. He probably
thinks my knowledge in the abstruse science of harmony is deficient, and therefore if I
make a book at all, it will abound with errors and unnecessary alterations, that I shall
aim to please my own uncultivated taste without being guided at all by settled principles.
On this subject, perhaps I ought to be silent. ~~And so I certainly would be if no other
question were involved in it but that of my knowledge~~ It is unimportant as it respects
myself, what opinion Mr. H. or any other gentleman has respecting my knowledge of
music; I have no ambition to appear knowing on that or any other subject any farther
than will be of use to my neighbours or to the publick. But as it respects the work
which I have undertaken I think it important that the truth should be known both
by my friends and by myself. If I have made a mistake and undertaken a work which
I am incapable of executing, the sooner I know it and relinquish it the better. On the
other hand if I am capable of finishing the work in such a manner as to merit the
approbation of the critic as well as subserve the interest of the christian publick, it is
important that those whose pattronage I seek should have some well grounded confidence in my abilities. I ask to be indulged in making a few remarks. With this view of
the subject I [illegible] and my prayer is that I may be enabled to do it with humility.

I very well know the strong prejudices against ~~the talents of~~ an author or compiler ~~is~~ are calculated to prevent his work becoming useful. For this reason I wish ~~to remove~~ all existing prejudices in the present instance, if any there be, may be removed. ~~Bear the criticism meet the approbation of the few scientific musicians in our country and at the same time furnish the american churches with a valuable collection of church music as well as to subserve the cause of interest of religion and promote the glory of God.~~

It is probable that Mr. Hart has formed his opinion of my skill in the science of music from the books which I published from 25 to 40 years ago. He may say, 'I have examined Mr. R's books, and I find nothing in them which warrants the conclusion that he is a "scientific musician." If he makes another book it may not be any better than those he has already made.' This reasoning may be correct, or, rather ~~at least~~ it might have been so twenty years ago: But since the publication of my last book, about twenty years ago—since my first acquaintance with Professor Fisher, in whose lamented death ~~has taken from bloted out one of the brightest stars~~ in the constellation of scientific musicians, has lost one of its brightest Stars,—since studying the writings of such men as D'Alambert, ~~Calcutt~~cutt, Jones, Hollman, Gieb, and Hastings,—since carefully examining the system of harmony practically exhibited in Handel's Messiah, Hayd'n's Creation and other similar works,—since having an opportunity of trying and comparing different progressions of harmony, both allowed and forbidden, on the organ, I say, since these things have taken place, my ideas on the subject of music have been considerably altered; I will not say improved. Mr. Hart speaks of altering tunes etc., as being adventurous and producing evil. There is something in those two words altering tunes which is very disagreable in the ears of some good men who are lovers of the good old tunes; but not so with Messrs Hastings an Mason, both of whom have made many alterations in the old tunes, (if indeed, correcting errors in old copies can be called altering tunes. ~~If I send a writing to a literary friend to correct for the press and he should correct the bad grammar~~ [sic!] ~~he finds in it, would it be proper to charge him with altering my writing?~~ If I am to make a book which will stand the test of a critical examination by scientific musicians, it is my business to see that the harmony is altogether correct ~~what ever the copies~~ whether it agrees with the copies in other books or not. My object is to put everything note within the rule and to leave nothing without. I do not however expect my work will be perfect, but it shall be my endeavor to make it as nearly so as my feeble abilities will permit. Mr. H. proposes that I should take the best copies of the tunes in common use and adopt them without alteration. This may be good advice with respect to some tunes, but it cannot be adopted as a general rule without frustrating my plan of furnishing the churches with a collection of Church music which shall be correct and agreable to the established rules of harmony. Mr. H. farther proposes that I should bring forward much foreign music. I have ~~by me~~ several valuable foreign ~~valuable~~ collection[s] of church music from which I shall select all the tunes that appear to be worthy of a place in the collection I am making. Perhaps Mr. Hart does not know that many, ~~perhaps most~~ of the tunes which appear in American publications under ~~with~~ the names of Handel, Hayd'n, Mozart, ~~Bethoven,~~ etc., are scraps cut out of the ~~large~~ oratorios of those authors, patched up and altered to make metre of them; like cut[t]ing scraps out of West's or Trumbull's historical paintings, as if, because the whole peice is beautiful, it must also be beautiful in its parts separately.

Those great master[s,] I have been told, ~~stoop low enough~~ think it beneath their dignity to become composers of plain psalm tunes.*

It has ever been, and still is my intention to have my work ~~submitted to an examination~~ examined by some one or more scientific musician[s] before it goes to the press, provided any such can be found who are not interested in any other work of the kind. I have thought of Professor Fitch, Mr. G. Whiting of Cheshire and Mr. L. Hart of Plymouth, knowing them all to be lovers of good music but not knowing how deeply versed they are ~~were~~ in the science of Harmony. Mr. Hastings, if he was not interested in a work of the kind, would be just such a man as I should choose. I once proposed to him that the publishers of Church music should come together and agree upon a standard copy for every tune in common use and let all the compilers conform to that standard; but he said it could never be done—there were obsticles in the way which could never be overcome; for, said he, I am interested in one publication to a large amount, and my good friend Mr. Mason in another, etc.

I should be pleased to have an interview with Mr. Hart: I hope he will call on me when he happens to be in town. Perhaps I ought to apologize for troubling you so much with this business, but I feel ~~that~~ as if you, being a minister of the gospel, must ~~feel~~ take an interest in every thing which concerns the churches.

If you think it will be for the interest of the cause to communicate the ideas contained in this letter to Mr. Hart, I have no objection, and perhaps he will be able to name some person well qualified to examine my work that I have not thought of. I am dear Sir with ~~sentiments~~ of esteem and respect ~~one of~~ your ~~parishioners~~ sincere friend[s]

Daniel Read

P.S. ~~There are two reasons for my taking~~ I have taken this method to communicate my thoughts to you on this subject, because I think I can make myself better understood in this way than in a verbal communication and that it will take up less of your valuable time.

SOURCE: Manuscript Collection no. 27, Daniel Read Papers, Whitney Library, New Haven Colony Historical Society, Connecticut. Cited and partially quoted in Irving Lowens, "Daniel Read's World: The Letters of an Early American Composer," in his *Music and Musicians in Early America* (New York: Norton, 1964): 159–77.

~~~~~~~~~

NOTE

1.   Richard Crawford, ed., *The Core Repertory of Early American Psalmody* (Madison, WI: A-R Editions, Inc., 1984): xxxvi.

*Most of the European music which finds its way into this country under the denomination of Sacred Music, is composed for, and adapted to a particular set of words, and although much of it is very excellent and may with propriety be used on particular ocasions; yet, as it cannot be sung in the psalms and hymns commonly used in our churches, very little of it, ~~ought not~~ in my humble opinion, ought to be ~~incorporated~~ introduced into a book designed to contain a body of Church music ~~only~~. Very valuable collections of this kind of music have been published in Massechusetts under the titles of Old Colony Collection and H[andel] & H[aydn] Society's Collection.

15

TURN-OF-THE-CENTURY THEATER SONGS
FROM REINAGLE, ROWSON, AND CARR
"America, Commerce, and Freedom"
and "The Little Sailor Boy"

Entertainment—watching plays and dances, enjoying a favorite song sung by professionals, laughing at the antics of Harlequin clowns, hearing political gossip
about the new nation—was found by Americans at the theater, which after the Revolution was over, and bans against public performances were lifted, flourished in
cities such as New York, Charleston, Baltimore, and particularly Philadelphia. As the
theater flourished, so did popular music. New songs were composed and printed in
larger quantities than ever before. Then (as now) famous performers could make a
song popular; even if no great American songwriter emerged in the late 1700s or
early 1800s, some songs rose to the top and stayed around longer than one might
expect. Two noteworthy examples are "America, Commerce, and Freedom"—a patriotic ballad with political overtones—and "The Little Sailor Boy," the latter named
as "the most successful song written in the United States before 1800."[1] Like the
theater itself, these songs were indebted to English taste and English artists coming to the United States to make their fortunes. The songs' makers—composers Alexander Reinagle (1756–1809) and Benjamin Carr (1768–1831) and lyricist Susanna

Rowson (1762–1824)—all knew one another and collaborated mainly in Philadelphia, which they helped to establish as an important center for ballad opera and dance. These excerpts, part music, part illustration, show their theatrical world along with their music.

The most sophisticated composer of his time, Reinagle managed the New Theatre Company, also known as the Chestnut Street Theatre Company. The company opened in 1791, and Reinagle conducted its orchestra and produced his own ballad operas. Already nationally famous as the author of the bestselling novel *Charlotte Temple* (1791), Rowson was Reinagle's librettist of choice. She later moved to Boston and owned a fashionable boarding school for girls, hiring outstanding musicians as teachers. Carr was active as a teacher, composer, and music publisher.

The broadside reprinted here of "America, Commerce, and Freedom" has only Rowson's words. Somehow this sailor's drinking song, typically sung by a male singer, ended up as a patriotic favorite sung on the Fourth of July. Today, the words seem like a capitalist mantra, linking the country, its economic system, and its sense of democracy. "America, Commerce, and Freedom" originated in a theatrical dance piece, or "pantomimical dance," known as *The Sailor's Landlady* or *Poor Jack*. In the playbill reprinted here, the lead role of Poor Jack was danced by John Durang (1768–1822), who made the hornpipe famous and whose name still graces a traditional fiddle tune.

"The Little Sailor Boy" (words, Rowson; music, Carr) presents a miniature melodrama—a prayer for the safety of a young boy at sea includes a fortissimo passage to express the heroine's worry and the dangers at sea. The fermatas encourage vocal display and, especially in the repeated refrain, improvised ornamentation. Many leading actress-singers famously performed this solo display piece, and their names are listed in the sheet music of this song, reprinted here.

SOURCE: http://www.library.upenn.edu/collections/rbm/keffer/b2n5.html.

NOTE

1.   Charles Hamm, *Yesterdays: Popular Song in America* (New York: Norton, 1979): 29.

NEW SONG,

Sung by Mr. Darley, jun. in the Pantomimical Dance, called

The Sailor's Landlady.

WORDS BY MRS. ROWSON: MUSIC BY MR. REINAGLE.

HOW blest the life a sailor leads,
    From clime to clime still ranging,
For as the calm the storm succeeds,
    The scene delights by changing.
When tempests howl along the main,
    Some object will remind us,
And cheer, with hopes to meet again,
    The friends we left behind us.

CHORUS.

For, under snug sail, we laugh at the gale ;
    And, tho' landsmen look pale, never heed 'em ;
But toss off the glass, to a favourite lass,
    To America, commerce, and freedom.

And when arriv'd in sight of land,
    Or safe in port rejoicing,
Our ship we moor, our sails we hand,
    Whilst out the boat is hoisting.
With chearful hearts the shore we reach ;
    Our friends, delighted, greet us ;
And tripping lightly o'er the beach,
    The pretty lasses meet us.

CHORUS.

When the full flowing bowl enlivens the soul,
    To foot it we merrily lead 'em ;
And each bonny lass will drink off her glass,
    To America, commerce, and freedom.

Our prizes sold, the chink we share,
    And gladly we receive it ;
And when we meet a brother tar
    That wants, we freely give it :
No free-born sailor yet had store,
    But chearfully would lend it :
And when 'tis gone, to sea for more ;
    We earn it, but to spend it.

CHORUS.

Then drink round, my boys ; 'tis the first of our joys
    To relieve the distress'd, clothe, and feed 'em ;
'Tis a duty we share, with the brave and the fair,
    In this land of commerce and freedom.

(Price three cents.)   *M. Carey, Printer.*

A broadside for "America, Commerce, and Freedom," described above as "New Song from *The Sailor's Landlady*," words by Mrs. Rowson; music by Mr. Reinagle.

Mr. CARR's Night,
1795

On WEDNESDAY EVENING, the 22d of *April*, will be prefented,

A COMIC OPERA, called, The

HIGHLAND REEL.

Shelty,	(the Piper)	Mr. H O D G K I N S O N,
Sandy,		Mr. C A R R,
Serjeant Jack,		Mr. K I N G,
Charley,		Mr. M A R T I N,
Captain Dafh,		Mr. M U N T O,
Laird of Coll,		Mr. A S H T O N,
Laird of Raafay,		Mr. R I C H A R D S,
Croudy,		Mr. L E E,
Benin,		Mr. D U R A N G,
And, M'Gilpin,		Mr. P R I G M O R E.
Lads and Laffes,		Meffrs. Miller, Leonard, M'Knight, &c.
		Mrs. Wilfon, Mrs. Miller, Mrs. Durang, &c.
Jenny,		Mrs. H A L L A M,
And, Moggy,		Mrs. H O D G K I N S O N.

To conclude with a **HIGHLAND REEL**, by the Characters.
End of the Opera, a Song, by Mrs. POWNALL.
After which, a PANTOMIMIC INTERLUDE, called,

POOR JACK, or, *The Sailor's Landlady.*

With new Mufic, and a compil'd *Naval Overture*, called,

The SAILOR's MEDLEY,

By Mr. C A R R.

Poor Jack,	(with a Hornpipe)	Mr. D U R A N G,
Ben Bobftay,	with a SONG, called, (*American Commerce and Freedom,*)	Mr. M U N T O,
Joe Tackle,		Mr. M I L L E R,
Will Forecaftle,		Mr. B A R W I C K,
Sam Stern,		Mr. W O O L L S,
And, Ned Haulyard,		Mr. M A R T I N.
Landlady,		Mr. L E E,
Laffes,		Mrs. Wilfon Mifs Chaucer, Mrs. Durang, Mrs. King, &c.
And, Orange Girl,		Madame G A R D I E.

To which will be added, a Mufical After-Piece, called, The

CHILDREN in the WOOD.

The Mufic by Dr. Arnold, with Accompanyments and additional Songs, by Mr. Carr.

Walter,	Mr. H O D G K I N S O N
Sir Rowland,	Mr. M A R R I O T T,
Apathy,	Mr. P R I G'M O R E,
Gabriel,	Mr. M A R T I N,
Oliver,	Mr. L E E,
Ruffians,	Meffrs. Leonard, M'Knight, &c.
Domeftics,	Meffrs. Durang, Miller, &c.
Conftables,	Meffrs. Woolls, Barwick, &c.
And, Lord Alford,	Mr. K I N G.
Jofephine,	Mrs. H O D G K I N S O N,
Children,	Mifs Harding, and a young Child,
Winnefred,	Mrs. H A M I L T O N,
And, Lady Alford,	Mrs. M E L M O T H.

Vivat Refpubli :.

Playbill, Mr. Carr's Night. An evening presented by the Old American Company as a benefit for Benjamin Carr included a performance of "America, Commerce, and Freedom" in the pantomime "Poor Jack, or, *The Sailor's Landlady.*"

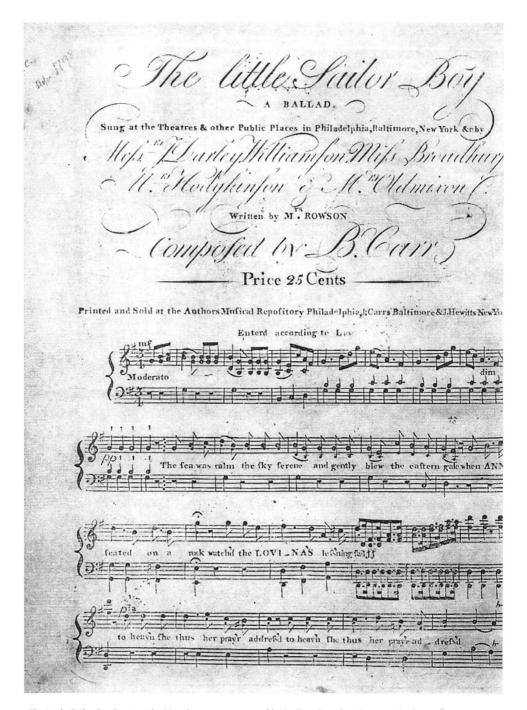

"The Little Sailor Boy," written by Mrs. Rowson, composed by B. Carr. Sung by Messrs. J. Darley, Williamson, Miss Broadhurst, Mrs. Hodgkinson, and Mrs. Oldmixon, 1798.

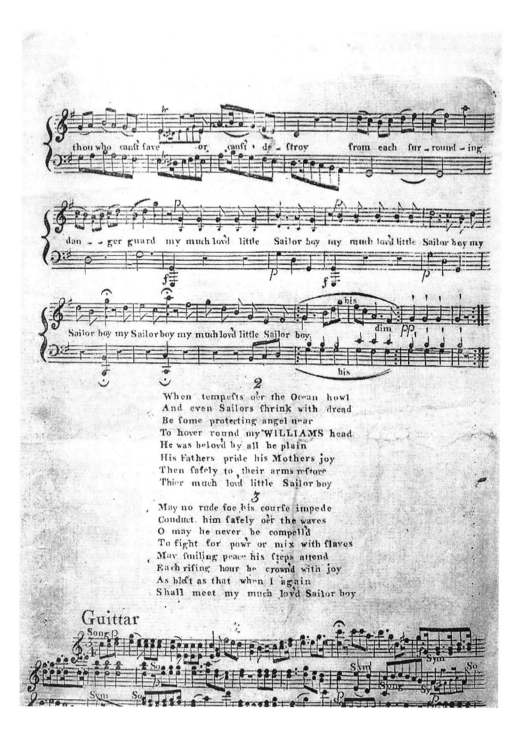

thou who canst save or canst de stroy from each sur round ing

dan - - ger guard my much lov'd little Sailor boy my much lov'd little Sailor boy my

Sailor boy my Sailor boy my much lov'd little Sailor boy, bis

dim bis

2

When tempests o'er the Ocean howl
And even Sailors shrink with dread
Be some protecting angel near
To hover round my WILLIAMS head
He was belov'd by all he plain
His Fathers pride his Mothers joy
Then safely to their arms restore
Thier much lov'd little Sailor boy

3

May no rude foe his course impede
Conduct. him safely o'er the waves
O may he never be compell'd
To fight for pow'r or mix with slaves
May smiling peace his steps attend
Each rising hour be crown'd with joy
As blest as that when I again
Shall meet my much lov'd Sailor boy

Guittar

Song

The cover of Benjamin Carr's *The Analytical Instructor for the Piano Forte in Three Parts*. Op. 15, Philadelphia, 1826, depicts his target market.

16

$\mathcal{P}$ADRE NARCISO DURÁN DESCRIBES
MUSICAL TRAINING AT THE MISSION SAN JOSE

Music and the performance of liturgy and polyphonic sacred music played an important role at many Franciscan missions, the first of which was founded in 1769 at San Diego. By 1823, 21 missions had been established in Alta California, as part of New Spain (Nueva España). At its major musical center, Mexico City, a grand cathedral offered colonial Spanish composers opportunities to compose polyphonic liturgical music, which traveled north into what is now the United States. In 1991, manuscripts of the colonial Mexican Baroque composer Ignacio de Jerusalem (1707–1769) were discovered at the San Fernando Mission, and his compositions were soon after recorded by professional musicians to critical acclaim.[1]

Who sang this music and played the instruments still extant at some Franciscan missions? Many were Native Americans, who were often pressed into forced labor at the missions and at the same time received some education, including musical training. Padre Narciso Durán (1776–1846) was among the most successful friar-musicians, and he left important historical accounts of his efforts to instruct Native American boys in music. After leaving his homeland of Catalonia (northern Spain) for Alta California in 1806, he worked at Mission San Jose for the next 27 years, acquiring a reputation as one of the best musicians in the mission system. He managed to organize an orchestra and a boys' choir and even compiled the *Libro de Coro* (1813), or choir book, for his own use. Also known as the *Mission*

Music Book, the *Libro de Coro* is a major document of this era. Its 156 parchment pages are filled with the black-and-red notation that scholar William Summers describes as a "pan–Spanish Empire phenomenon." In the preface, excerpts from which are reprinted here, Durán demonstrates his own innovation—a simplified approach to sight-singing. Summers describes it as justifying "both his abandonment of the requirements of teaching the modal system and the very practical move to reduce drastically the number of melodies learned by his choristers for the proper[s] of the Mass."

Durán's somewhat pessimistic views of Indians' aptitude for musical training come through in his responses to a questionnaire sent by an administrative colonial functionary to 18 missions. Preceding the selection from the *Libro de Coro,* the questionnaire and Durán's responses show his prejudice, which, as Summers notes, "Durán himself definitely re-thought and transcended in his performances."[2]

Question 33: Have they any inclination towards music? With what musical instruments are they acquainted? With string or wind instruments? Are these the same they have always used? Are they acquainted with our instruments and do they use them? Do they have any songs in their own languages? Are they sweet, lively and in tenor? Are they more inclined to music of a sad and melodious kind or to that which is warlike? In case they have their own songs which tones do they use? If possible describe these and give the notes.

[Answers from] Mission San Jose. We have observed in them no inclination towards music which has any resemblance to ours. Nor do they have or know anything about string or wind instruments. They have some songs which they sing at their dances but they are hardly composed of complete human words but are rather some outrageous shouts and the yells of animals. Wherefore it is impossible to reduce them to musical tones and notes. At the mission the singers and musicians who are youths learn rather readily both the plain chant and figured music as well as playing any kind of instrument. At this mission there are fifteen violinists and three celloists. They perform at church functions in a becoming and splendid manner in excess of what could have been expected when we first came here.

SOURCE: *As the Padres Saw Them: California Indian Life and Customs as Reported by the Franciscan Missionaries, 1813–1815,* trans. Maynard Geiger (Santa Barbara, Calif.: Santa Barbara Mission Archive Library, 1976): 133, 136–137.

FROM THE *LIBRO DE CORO*

Dear Reader: I here offer you this book that you may use it, if you wish, as a guide during the course or cycle of the principal feasts of the year.

When we arrived at this Mission the Ecclesiastical Chant was so faulty that the one song the boys knew, the *Asperges,* had neither feet nor head, and seemed a howl rather than a song. And let us not speak of the masses, for in telling you, scarcely with-out exaggeration, that they did not know how to answer *Amen,* you can judge the rest for yourself. It is true that singing was being organized at some of the Missions, but as I did not deem it necessary to send the boys elsewhere to learn, and as I did not hasten to teach them myself, things remained the same. All this was due to the conviction, which, thanks be to God, has proven very false, that the boys did not possess the ability to take up singing.

At this time some musical instruments had already come to the Mission, and I, observing that the boys of the neighboring Missions managed them easily enough, began to interest myself in sending some of the boys of this Mission to Santa Clara to learn the rudiments of music, convinced that they would later perfect themselves here. The results exceeded my first hopes; and now that music was somewhat under way, with names given to all the melodies, and the melodies assigned to their proper tones, in order to identify them among the tones found in music, the sacred functions were carried out with a fitness more than mediocre. But this promised to last only as long as there should be some Father who knew music; a fact that some of the Missions are experiencing.

By this time I was convinced that the boys were able to learn two or three entire masses, and render them quite well, but I also realized that among eight or ten boys only two or three really knew the masses, so that if these were missing there could be no High Mass. It seems to me that this point is borne out by experience, and the reason may well be because the boys learn the masses entirely by memory, and not by rule and principle; and since the Indians are so short on memory that out of ten or twelve hardly two remember the following day what they learned the day before, it follows that if these two or three, whom we say excel, fall sick, or their voices change, or they are missing for any other reason, the others, who sing only by being towed and following the rest, are stranded, and one must teach them again. And if in this case there be no Father who knows music, *quid faciendum?* Behold a Mission in this plight! Because music and the choir depended on two or three, now that they are gone, the rest, instead of performing a devout and solemn service, fall into a jargon and create a clamor so ridiculous that it certainly belies the majesty and sanctity of the religious worship that we render to God in His churches.

Therefore what is most necessary at a Mission is to teach the boys the Sacred Chant according to rules or principles so that they will not have to trust everything to memory, but will be able to read notes and sing by themselves whatever is plainly written; and this not only two or three among ten or twelve, but all, or the greater number of them, with the inequality that must always be taken for granted. But what rules or principles are within the grasp of some Indians, that is to say of some —!? Not being able to convince myself of their ability to learn music according to the rules laid down by the masters of the art, and not being able to teach them these rules because I myself do not know them, I decided to attain the same end with some arbitrary rules, which make up the system or method that I am about to explain.

As [a] basic principle I ordained that there should never be a distinction between musicians and singers, but that both hands and mouth should perform their respective functions; that is to say the same men both sing and play. At first they were confused, but now they do it without the least difficulty. I also deemed it advisable that instruments should always accompany the singing, even having the Requiem accompanied by the two violins. This for two reasons! First, to firmly sustain the voices of the boys, not permitting them to go flat or sharp, as regularly happens without this precaution. Secondly, that, seeing the distances between notes on the instruments, due to the various finger positions, the boys might gain some idea of the same intervals in singing, modulating their voices accordingly.

Then I gave them what I call the scale of natural notes, making them sing and play it at one and the same time. Afterwards I gave them the scale of half-notes, denoted by sharps and flats, as given below. But I did not burden them with that which is most difficult and complicated about music and singing; which seems to be the diversity of clefs, according to which the musical notes Ut, re, mi, etc., change their domicile or position on the staff. This seemed to me to be beyond the grasp of Indians, especially since the Chant must always be accompanied by instruments, which have set positions for the notes. It struck me, I say, incomprehensible to call, for example, the lowest space of the *Ffaut clef Ut,* and then with another clef to have to say *Re* or *Mi* at the same place. Accordingly I decided to do away with the diversity of clefs and use solely the clef of *Ffaut.*

But how did we cope with all the tones found in a choir book? How could one single clef with the same fixed and unchangeable position of the musical notes accommodate itself to all the melodies, when *Fa,* for example, must sound like *Mi,* or *Mi* like *Fa?* Here is the focal point of the difficulty, and I am going to tell you how I solved it. On several occasions I have asked the masters if it were possible to sing all tones using only the *Ffaut* clef with the aid of flats and sharps, and they have always answered in the affirmative, but that it was against the rule, and that the experts would disagree, not understanding the case. But as I did not have to write for masters, nor even for students, but for these poor Indians, and bearing in mind that some of the masters also make rules of their own which others contradict, and that the present prologue is an attempted explanation of the system of this book, very easy, that the masters may understand it, I finally determined, not with the authority of a master, but due to the need of the Indians, to attempt an arbitrary method of using only the *Ffaut* clef, and consequently of placing the musical notes of all tones in a single domicile or position in such a way that they spell all the scales, effecting changes of tones and chant by use of flats and sharps.

[After describing further simplifications of psalm tones for the propers of the mass, Fr. Durán concludes.] Moreover, I want to tell you, not without some certainty, that if anyone should attempt to change this system and introduce the ordinary rules, making the boys learn them, no matter how good a teacher he may be, if his work be not lost, it will last only as long as he lasts; for when he leaves all music and singing will come to naught. But on the contrary if he keeps things as they are now, he will have to do nothing more than introduce boys as novices, permitting them to grow up at the side of the older singers, and when they marry let him give them domestic employment, such as weaving, shoemaking or blacksmithing, in order to have them always on hand when there is singing or playing to be done. In this way I am convinced that music and singing will not degenerate, even if I am absent, contrary to the opinion of some who think that all will die out when I am gone.

Here, then, my Friend, you have the explanation of the method and purpose of this book, written for this Church of St. Joseph. I know beforehand that if you are a master, improvements and objections will occur to you which I do not foresee, but which if I did I would meet to the best of my ability. In general, however, I respond that you should bear in mind the slowness of the Indians. Take away, add or correct whatever seems advisable, but if you do not really know music, for the love of God and St. Joseph, conform yourself to this method. And may the Lord, who rewards each one according to the measure of one's work in upbuilding the Church, repay your labor and humility abundantly if you do whatsoever you are able to preserve the dignity and the holiness of the Chant. *Vale, et ora pro me.* The year 1813.

SOURCE: Owen Francis da Silva, *Mission Music of California* (Santa Barbara, Calif.: Schauer Printing Studio, 1941): 29, 30–31, 33.

NOTES

1. See the liner notes by Craig H. Russell for the recording *Mexican Baroque* by the male vocal group Chanticleer (Teldec 96353), which includes some of Russell's scholarship on this topic.
2. The quotations from Professor William Summers are from an e-mail communication to the author, April 23, 2000.

17

Moravian Musical Life at Bethlehem

(Henry, Till, Bowne)

Many German-speaking Slavic immigrants came to the colonies in the eighteenth century, searching for religious tolerance. The Moravians, who came from a southern section of what we now call the Czech Republic, brought with them their extraordinary love of music. At their colonies in Bethlehem and Lititz, Pennsylvania, and Salem, North Carolina, which they founded in the 1740s and 1750s, music flourished in their churches, schools, and homes. Much of it came from Europe, and they performed Haydn's symphonies; his oratorio, *The Creation;* and works of Handel and Mozart much earlier than did the rest of the United States. Moravian composers such as Jeremiah Dencke (1725–1795), John Antes (1740–1811), Johann Friedrich Peter (1746–1813), and Johannes Herbst (1735–1812) composed music in the international classical style of these European masters, and their solo songs, duets, hymn settings, and organ compositions are still performed in Moravian churches today. The Moravian legacy loosely belongs to that of the Pennsylvania "Dutch" country ("Dutch" as in *Deutsch,* for German). The Moravians have preserved their culture in meticulously kept archives, and their lyrical compositions have been revived and studied by scholars and performance groups devoted to early American music.

The way that the Moravians organized their society invited music in. The first excerpt, by James Henry, one of the first historians of Moravian society, explains how members lived in separate residences known as "choir houses," according to age, sex, and marital status. (In this context, the term "choir" has no musical meaning.) A choir house participated as a unit in services of sacred worship, including special annual festivals and "love feasts" (Liebesmahlen), during which music played a major ceremonial role. The best singers among them performed concerted songs, typically written for solo or two sopranos, strings, and organ; mixed choirs of men and women sang anthems and hymns.

FROM JAMES HENRY'S CHRONICLE OF MORAVIAN LIFE AND RELIGION (1859): CHAPTER VI, "THE MORAVIAN CULTUS"

The origin of the Choir Festival generally attached itself to some bright point of history, where, in the past annals of the Church, a remarkable awakening had taken place in the earlier epochs of Herrnhut [a town in Moravia]. Out of this origin some sacred feeling emanated, and, although the Festival was a matter of joy, the happiness of the day was always imbued with solemnity. On the opening of the Festival, in the morning, the event was announced from the belfry of the church by chorales, performed on wind instruments, and as the "Choir," in whose honor the day was celebrated, entered the hall of worship, these strains of solemn melody sounded impressively upon the ears of all. Within the precincts of the Sisters' House it was usual for the Sisters, on their own Festival, to receive the salutation of a choir of female voices, greeting them at daylight, before they rose, with anthems of joy. . . .

As to the services of the church during the Festival, they consisted in the usual forms of devotion, preaching and singing; the introduction and close, as well as that of the Love-Feast, always characterized by orchestral music, selected from the old and best masters of cathedral composition. This species of music received no small degree of cultivation; and, as it was expressive of the Moravian love of music in general, found a useful application in all solemn church celebrations. At an earlier period of Moravian history, the Festival of the single Sisters was accompanied by a multitude of ceremonials and church services, yet these were so blended with vocal and instrumental music as to render the scene highly picturesque, viewed by a mere spectator, aside from its spiritual character.

. . .

Up to a recent date, the Sisters' Festival was sustained in our villages with all its unique observances. The early salutation at the doors of the sleeping apartments; the procession to and from the place of worship, of girls in white apparel, with the characteristic head-dress and pink ribbon, and the whole of the front seats of the church presenting a uniform picture of the maiden's choir; the absorbing music of the orchestra; the promenades in the open air in the garden, with music in the intervals from an amateur company of musicians; the chorales on the trombones on the opening of the Love-Feast, as in the days of Marienborn and Herrnhaag; the congratulations extended by the old to the young, indicating their wishes for happiness now and solicitude for a life's peace in future,—all these demonstrations of a refined, cultivated, and deeply-devoted Christian life, were witnessed in our Moravian villages.

The Festival of the Single Brethren, too, had its marked features, and they passed through many of the solemnities that honored the Single Sisters, such as anthems and chorales on wind instruments in the morning, the harbinger of the Festival, the procession into the church, the enjoyment of Love-Feast and collations during the day, the final close at evening with some beautiful and stirring performance of the orchestra, introductory to the liturgy,—all these festivities constituted the round of a Christian Moravian's life and lent to the aspect of his creed the realization of a heaven on this side of eternity.

We might term the Festival the great embodiment of the strongest characteristics of Moravianism, a perfect blending of profound religion with earthly pleasure. It is not often that we discover such a phenomenon in the social world that admits and exercises Christianity. There is a feeling of stern duty in its religion that too often blunts the pleasure of ordinary life, and the line drawn between the two is so strongly marked that one must be sacrificed to the other.

SOURCE: James Henry, *Sketches of Moravian Life and Character* (Philadelphia: Lippincott, 1859): 128–129, 133–34. Available at http://www.hti.umich.edu/cgi/t/text/text-idx?c=moa ;idno=AJK2796.0001.001.

~~~~~~~

Trombone quartet choirs—another famous feature of Moravian music—played hymns from the church tower to open festival days. The following obituary for the trombone player Jacob Till shows how valued he was.

Jacob C. Till was born in the Moravian town of Hope, N.J., June 15, 1799, and removed to Bethlehem with his parents while still a child. For a time he assisted his father in the manufacture of pianos, but having a taste and fondness for music, adopted it professionally. Becoming a thorough musician he could perform on several wind and stringed instruments as occasion required.

Mr. Till, besides filling for a time the position of organist of the Moravian Church in Bethlehem, and for fifty years or more a member of its Trombone Choir, was an active member of the Philharmonic Society and the once celebrated "Bethlehem Band." While a member of the latter organization, he performed principally on the clarionet. He was instructor of the first military band formed in Mauch Chunk. Many years ago Mr Till became a resident of Easton, Pa., and was appointed organist of St. John's Church; but he seldom failed to visit Bethlehem, to attend and participate in the impressive services of Passion Week. On Easter morn, April 9, 1882, about the hour when the beautiful Litany of the Resurrection, to which he loved to listen, was being read in the Church of his fathers at Bethlehem, the spirit of "Puppy" Till (as he was familiarly called by his Moravian associates) passed from earth to join the Heavenly Choirs. Four days subsequently, the remains of the last of the old Bethlehem Quartette of Trombonists were brought from Easton and interred on Nisky Hill Cemetery.

> SOURCE: "Something about Trombones," *Bethlehem Digital History Project*, available at http://bdhp.moravian.edu/music/trombones.html. Taken from W. C. Reichel, *Something about Trombones and the Old Mill at Bethlehem* (Bethlehem, Pa.: Moravian Publication Office, 1884).

<center>~~~~~~~</center>

Many non-Moravian Americans knew about these colonies and came to visit them as tourists, including the famous, like Benjamin Franklin, John Adams, and George Washington, and the ordinary, like Eliza Southgate Bowne (1783–1809) from Maine. In the selection, she comments on music making partly because of its prevalence and partly because she was an amateur musician herself. From the ages of 14 to 17, she lived at Susanna Rowson's boarding school in Medford, Massachusetts (see chapter 20) and took piano lessons there. At 21, she was a married woman traveling with her husband. Her letter describes a chamber concert performed by the Moravian Collegium Musicum, a chamber music society founded around 1744.

LETTER FROM ELIZA BOWNE TO HER SISTER (1803)

Bethlehem, August 9, 1803

I intended writing before I left New York, but was so much engaged in preparing for our journey, I had no time. My great wish to see this famous Bethlehem is at length gratified. You can scarcely imagine any thing more novel and delightful than every thing about here, so entirely different from any place in New England. Indeed, in travelling thro' the State of Pennsylvania, the cultivation, buildings, and every thing are entirely different from ours,—highly cultivated country, looks like excellent farmers. Barns twice as large as the houses, all built of stone; no white painted houses, as in New England. We crossed the famous Delaware at Easton. It separates New Jersey and Pennsylvania. We saw some beautiful little towns in New Jersey likewise, but in Pennsylvania the villages look so many clusters of jails, and the public buildings like the Bastille, or, to come nearer home, like the New York State prison,—all of stone, so strong, heavy, and gloomy, I could not bear them; the inhabitants most all Dutch, and such jargon as you hear in every entry or corner makes you fancy yourself in a foreign country. These Bethlehemites are all Germans, and retain many of the peculiarities of their country—such as their great fondness for music. It is delightful: there is scarcely a house in the place without a Piano-forte; the Post Master has an elegant grand Piano. The Barber plays on almost every kind of music[al instrument]. Sunday afternoon we went to the Young Men's house to hear some sacred music. We went into a hall, which was hung round with Musical Instruments, and about 20 musicians of the Brethren were playing in concert,—

an organ, 2 bass viols, 4 violins, two flutes, two French horns, two clarionets, bassoon, and an Instrument I never heard before, made up the Band; they all seemed animated and interested. It was delightful to see these men, who are accustomed to laborious employments, all kinds of mechanics, and so perfect in so refined an art as music. One man appeared to take the lead and played on several different instruments, and to my great astonishment I saw the famous musician enter the breakfast room this morning with the razor-box in his hand to shave some of the gentlemen. . . . We went to the Schools,—first was merely a sewing school, *little children, and a pretty single sister about 30, with her white skirt, white, short, tight waistcoat, nice handkerchief pinned outside, a muslin apron and a close cambric cap, of the most singular form you can imagine. I can't describe it; the hair is all put out of sight, turned back before, and no border to the cap, very unbecoming but very singular, tied under the chin with a pink ribbon,—blue for the married, white for the widows. Here was a Piano-forte, and another sister teaching a little girl music. We went thro' all the different schoolrooms— some misses of 16,—their teachers were very agreeable and easy, and in every room was a Piano. . . . At the single Sisters' house we were conducted round by a fine lady-like woman, who answered our questions with great intelligence and affability. I think there were 130 in this house; [it] altogether seemed more like a nunnery than any thing I had seen. . . . My husband is so fond of roving, I don't know but he'll spoil me. We both enjoy travelling very much, and surely it is never so delightful as in company with those we love. Only think, 'tis just a year to-day since we first saw each other, and here we are, Married, happy, and enjoying ourselves in Bethlehem. . . .*
Affectionately,
Eliza S. Bowne

SOURCE: Eliza Southgate Bowne, *A Girl's Life Eighty Years Ago: Selections from the Letters of Eliza Southgate Bowne*, ed. and with an introduction by Clarence Cook (New York: Scribner's, 1887): 172–177. Editor's annotations not included in the text above.

18

REVEREND BURKITT BRINGS
CAMP MEETING HYMNS FROM KENTUCKY
TO NORTH CAROLINA IN 1803

American folk hymnody embraces several different kinds of songs—folk hymns, religious ballads, and revival hymns—all used for social worship. One stream for this repertoire comes out of populist Christian evangelical movements, especially the Second Great Awakening of religious revivalism around 1800. This spawned a largely but not exclusively rural phenomenon known as the "camp meeting." Famous accounts—some sympathetic, some not—tell of thousands of people camping out in forests and meadows for several days to sing and pray in born-again ecstatic conversion experiences. These accounts locate the beginnings of the movement in Kentucky and southern Ohio in the early 1800s. In this selection, we witness how the music spread to other parts of the country. Lemuel Burkitt (1750–1807) a Baptist preacher who was at the famous revival meeting at Cane Ridge, Kentucky, in 1801, brought its music back to his congregation in Kehukee, North Carolina. He experienced firsthand the conversionary power of music and soon after published a small collection of spiritual songs, which he claims achieved almost instant popularity.

There was a small appearance of the beginning of the work [of conversions] in Camden, and the Flat-Swamp and Connoho church, in 1800—32 this year were baptized in Camden, 22 in the Flat-Swamp church, and 24 at Connoho. But at the Association at Great-Swamp in 1801, Elder Burkitt, just returning from Tennessee and Kentuckey, brought the news to this Association, and proclaimed it from the stage, than in about eight months six thousand had given a rational account of a work of grace on their souls, and had been baptized in the state of Kentuckey and that a general stir had taken place amongst all ranks and societies of people, and that the work was still going on.

The Lord was pleased to make use of weak and simple means to effect great purposes, that it might be manifest that the work was *his* and not *man's. Singing* was attended with a great blessing: Elder Burkitt published two or three different pamphlets, which contained a small collection of spiritual songs, some of which he had brought from the western countries. They were in very great demand. As many as 6000 books were disposed of in two years. We might truly say, *the time of singing of birds had come, and the voice of the turtle was heard in our land.*[1] At every meeting, before the minister began to preach, the congregation was melodiously entertained with numbers singing delightfully, while all the congregation seemed in lively exercises. Nothing seemed to engage the attention of the people more; and the children and servants at every house were singing these melodious songs. From experience, we think, we can assure our readers, that we have reason to hope, that this, with other means, proved a blessing in this revival. *Shaking hands* while singing, was a means (though simple in itself) for to further the work. The ministers used frequently, at the close of worship, to sing a spiritual song suited to the occasion, and go through the congregation, and shake hands with the people while singing; and several when relating their experience, at the time of their admission into church fellowship, declared that this was the first means of their conviction. The act seemed so friendly, the ministers appeared so loving, that the part with whom the minister shook hands, would often be melted in tears. The Hymn

> *I long to see the happy time,*
>
> *When sinners all come flocking home*
>
> *To taste the riches of his love,*
>
> *And to enjoy the realms above.*

And especially that part of it,

> *Take your companion by the hand;*
>
> *And all your children in the band,*

—many times had a powerful effect. *Giving the people an invitation to come up to be prayed for,* was also blessed.

SOURCE: Lemuel Burkitt and Jesse Read, *A Concise History of the Kehukee Baptist Association* (Halifax, Va.: A. Hodge, 1803): 140–41, 144–45.

〰〰〰〰〰

NOTE

1.   Here, Burkitt is probably quoting a verse from the Song of Solomon, as it was translated in the King James version of the Bible: "The flowers appear on the earth; / the time of the singing of birds is come, / and the voice of the turtle is heard in our land." Other translations replace "turtle" with "turtle-dove."

John Fanning Watson and
Errors in Methodist Worship

John Fanning Watson (1779–1860), the first important local historian of Philadelphia and Pennsylvania, wrote a polemical tract related to religious disputes and debates among various Protestant sects in the early 1800s. His critique of the Methodist church coincides with its growth in the early 1800s. He targeted in particular what he considered to be the undisciplined hymn singing associated with revivals and camp meetings. Like many educated religious leaders, Fanning fought the losing battle of trying to control musical enthusiasm. He singled out blacks in particular, thus documenting for future historians the survival of West African cultural traits in African-American Protestantism.

PREFACE

Methodist Reader.

This little book is written *specially* for *your* benefit. The author has no pecuniary interest in its sale, nor any *party* end to answer. He is one of your brethren of long and approved standing among you; and his *sole* motive in the present work is to do good: to point out the *way of error,* that you may shun it; and to show the *way of God,* that you may walk therein.

He has seen with much pain and regret some signs of *enthusiasm* and *error* crept into our church, which *should* have been checked by those who were our *overseers* in the Lord. He verily believes that *they* should have *restrained* and *not fostered* the unprofitable emotions of *screaming, hallowing* and *jumping,* and the *stepping and singing* of *senseless,* merry airs. These have often prejudiced true and vital religion.

. . .

We have too, a growing evil, in the practice of singing in our places of public and society worship, *merry* airs, adapted from old *songs,* to hymns of our composing: often miserable as poetry, and senseless as matter,* and most frequently composed and first sung by the illiterate *blacks* of the society. Thus instead of inculcating sober christianity in them who have least wisdom to govern themselves; lifting them into spiritual pride and to an undue estimation of their usefulness: overlooking too the counsel of Mr. Wesley, who has solemnly expressed his opinion in his book of hymns, as already amply sufficient for all our purposes of rational devotion: not at all regarding his condemnation of this very practice, for which among other things he actually expelled three ministers . . . for singing *poor, bald, flat, disjointed hymns:* and like the people in Wales, singing the same verse over and over again with all their might 30 or 40 times, "to the utter discredit of all sober christianity;" neglecting too, the counsel of Dr. Clarke in this matter, "never to sing hymns of your own composing in public, (these are also the very words of injunction of our own Discipline . . .), unless you be a first rate poet, such as can only occur in every ten or twenty *millions* of men; for it argues incurable vanity." Such singing as has been described, has we know, been ordinarily sung in most of our prayer and camp meetings: sometimes two or three at a time in succession. In the meantime, one and another of musical feelings, and consonant animal spirits, has been heard stepping the merry strains with all the precission of an avowed *dancer.* Here ought to be considered too, a most exceptionable error, which has the tolerance at least of the rulers of our camp meetings. In the *blacks'* quarter, the coloured people get together, and sing for hours together, short scraps of disjointed affirmations, pledges, or prayers, lengthened out with long repetition *choruses.* These are all sung in the merry chorus-manner of the southern harvest field, or husking-frolic method, of the slave blacks; and also very greatly like the Indian dances. With every word so sung, they have a sinking of one or other leg of the body alternately; producing an audible sound of the feet at every step, and as manifest as the steps of actual negro dancing in Virginia, &c. If some, in the meantime sit, they strike the sounds alternately on each thigh. What in the name of religion, can countenance or tolerate such gross perversions of true religion! but the evil is only occasionally condemned, and the example has already visibly affected the religious manners of some whites. From this cause, I have known in some camp meetings, from 50 to 60 people croud into one tent, after the public

---

*"Touch but one string, 'twill make heaven ring," is of this character. What string is that which can effect this! Who can give any sense to it? Take another case: "Go shouting all your days," in connexion with "glory, glory, glory," in which go shouting is repeated six times in succession. Is there one particle of sense in its connexion with the general matter of the hymn? and are they not mere idle expletives, filled in to eke out the tunes? They are just exactly parallel to "go *screaming, jumping,* (or any other participle) *all your days! O splendour, splendour."* Do those who are delighted with such things, consider what delights them? Some times too, they are from such impure sources, as I am actually ashamed to name in this place.

devotions had closed, and there continue the whole night, singing tune after tune, (though with occasial episodes of prayer) scarce one of which were in our hymn books.* Some of these from their nature, (having very long repetition choruses and short scraps of matter) are actually composed as sung, and are indeed almost endless. But our Discipline has some rule on this matter, . . . speaking of cautions in singing, says, "they must be chosen suitable, not too much at once, and seldom more than five or six verses." The English conference has resolved "that no singing be allowed in any of our churches after the public service, as we think,["] say they, ["]singing at such times tends to extinguish the spirit of devotion, and to destroy those serious impressions, which may have been made by the previous ministry. Let our preachers take care to examine the hymns which are to be sung on special occasions; and let them reject all those which are not decidedly unobjectionable in in point of sentiment and poetry, and we earnestly recommend that our own authorized hymns be generally preferred for all such purposes." Are those who sing so long, and so incessantly, (frequently they are very young and inexperienced persons) quite sure they continue to sing with the spirit and the understanding; and are they able to discriminate how little of it is of mere animal spirits?** Are they sure they have not afterwards felt no undue weariness of the flesh, and incompetency to engage with life and animation, in the subsequent public devotions? These are sober questions which their consciences should answer in the fear of God, for all things are to done to his glory, and most especially in worship.

If it be just and right for one, two or three, to jump and scream, to clap their hands, and thump and pat the floor, either by stamping or by *stepping* the music, or to see-saw their bodies to and fro, then it is right for all; and if all should once do it, we cease at once to be a "church of peace, and order as becometh the saints," and become the house of "confusion," which God has said he will not own! Indeed, what edification, or decency, or order could be expected in such an assembly? We may thank God, hitherto, such general emotion has not been permitted; or we should ere now have ceased to have had churches.

SOURCE: [John Fanning Watson], *Methodist Error; or, Friendly, Christian Advice, To those Methodists, Who indulge in extravagant emotions and bodily exercises. By a Wesleyan Methodist* (Trenton, N.J.: D. & E. Fenton, 1819): preface, 28–34. Selected passages are also in Eileen Southern, *Readings in Black American Music*, 2nd ed. (New York: Norton, 1983): 62–64.

*It is worthy of remark, that not one of our appointed hymns under the article "rejoicing and praise," nor among the "new hymns," have any hymns of this character, therefore they who want them most, have to forsake that standard.

**We will not be willingly censorious, but we cannot forbear to hint at an important fact in the history of sound; musical tones are capable of infusing themselves into our nerves with the most pleasurable emotion: Scotch soldiers can be excited to deeds of the most extravagant daring, by the mere tones of their bagpipe; our Indians are so sensible to the spell of their rude music, that they affect their bodies to its sounds, much like our blacks, until they actually fall senseless to the ground; most men have felt the influence of the violin, or of martial music on the feet; and we all have seen many of the irrational creation strangely affected by the sounds of instruments. These facts are worth the thoughtful consideration, of the young and unreflecting convert: let such test their devotion, by trying for a time, if they have equal pleasure in solemn, silent prayer and meditation. It they have not this test, I should greatly fear that their fervour is in part adventitious and animal.

20

REVEREND JAMES B. FINLEY AND MONONCUE SING "COME THOU FOUNT OF EVERY BLESSING"

The Reverend James B. Finley (1781–1856) was a Methodist preacher "civilizing" Indian tribes in the Northwest of the early 1800s—from Kentucky to Michigan. A brief excerpt from the preface to his memoirs sets the stage for his tales from 70 years of experience. To "civilize" meant to convert; to convert meant to sing. The second excerpt describes his singing a hymn with his Christian Indian friend Mononcue. Finley translates "Come Thou Fount" into Mononcue's language of the Wyandot Indians, a tribe better known by the name of Huron today. "Come Thou Fount" first appeared in print as "Hallelujah," in John Wyeth's *Repository of Sacred Music: Part Second* (1813), published in Pennsylvania. It is still sung by many Protestant denominations today. Finley cites a verse that does not appear in this printed source, and thus his version documents folk process at work.

PREFACE

No living man, probably, has seen and known more of the Indians in the north-west than my-self. During almost seventy years I have been among them, as it were—have been acquainted with their principal men, studied their history, character, and manner of life. With me it has not been, as with most who have written about them, a mere matter of theory; for I have been among them, hunted and fished with them, ate and lodged in their wigwams, and been subjected to all the labors, excitements, perils, and privations of life among them. In this long experience and observation, I have gathered up many things which I thought worthy of record. Some of them occurred in my experience as a missionary among them.

Kentucky, Ohio, Indiana, and Michigan, were the great battle-fields between barbarism and civilization in the west. My acquaintance extended over all these states; and there is scarcely a spot celebrated in Indian warfare which I have not visited again and again. Tales of Indian life and warfare were the entertainments of my childhood; the realities of these things were among the experiences of my manhood. Now, when the scene is nearly over with me on earth, I have gathered up these reminiscences of the past, to amuse and instruct the generations of a later age. Those who enjoy so goodly a heritage in this vast region, ought to know through what trials and perils their forefathers obtained it for them.

FROM THE CHAPTER "REFLECTIONS IN THE FOREST"

Having made arrangements for our journey to the north, we started December 10, 1823. Our company consisted of Mononcue, Squire Gray-Eyes, and Jonathan Pointer, for interpreter. Mononcue and Jonathan went by Stewart's to take their farewell of him—the rest of us having done it previously—and were to meet us at the Big reservation. Gray-Eyes and myself took the packs and horses, and went a nearer route across the plains. This day was cold—the wind blow-ing from the north, and the snow driving in our faces. After traveling several miles, we stopped at a cottage, warmed ourselves, and made a repast on bread and meat. We then started, and en-tered a gloomy forest. The snow hanging on the bushes across our path, and the dark, lowering clouds suspended over us, led us to serious reflections on death and the grave. While solemn meditations were passing through our minds, the clouds were dispersed, and the cheerful sun shone brilliantly upon us. The thought of the second advent of Christ, in all his splendor, and a redemption from the grave, followed; and we felt a prelibation of the raptures of that day when clouds and storms should cease forever, and the light of God's countenance shine upon us all.
    The great contrast between the darkness and the light, made us remember the poor, be-nighted Indians we were going to visit. They were living in the gloom of death, while the hate-ful superstition of past and present delusions had buried all their comforts. Crime of all de-scriptions, as the fruit of the intoxicating draught, had polluted every fountain of happiness; and witchcraft, with its midnight enchantments, girded all the other evils, and fastened them firmly on the poor Indian's soul. No cheerful ray of hope, breaking through the darkness of the future, came to bless or comfort him. All was a dark and dreary uncertainty; but the darkness will soon give way before the glorious light of the Gospel of Christ. We are his embassadors, and bring good news and glad tidings of great joy. "How beautiful upon the mountains are the feet of him that bringeth good tidings!"

After traveling several miles, and the shades of night had began to inclose us, we came to some Indian houses, the inhabitants of which were wandering in the forest in quest of game. Here we concluded to stay for the night. After making a good fire, feeding and securing our horses, my comrade made search for, and procured a root of sassafras, of which we made tea, which, after riding in the cold, was very refreshing. After having supped, we commended ourselves to God, by prayer and thanksgiving, imploring his blessing on our journey and its objects, and spread our blankets, and lay down to rest. The night being cold, we had frequently to rise and renew our fire. In the morning we had prayer, fed our horses, and while eating our breakfast, our two friends, Mononcue and Pointer, joined us. We set out through a thick forest, and traveled a small Indian trail, our way being often obstructed by logs and swamps.

We had translated a hymn into Wyandott, and employed ourselves in learning to sing together,

> *Hail thou blest morn, when the great Mediator*
>
> *Down from the regions of glory descends, etc.*

This day my two companions and Pointer learned to sing the translation tolerably well, and we made the swamps and the surrounding forest vocal with our songs.

. . .

This day was dark and cold. Sometimes the snow fell so fast that we could hardly discern the trace. Late in the evening we reached the Lower Rapids of the Maumee river, and forded it just above the principal rapid. The ford was seemingly dangerous, on account of the fissures in the rocks, some of which were deep and narrow. The swiftness of the stream was such, that it seemed almost impossible, should the horses stumble and fall, that we could escape drowning; but we had no other way to get across, and, protected by a kind Providence, we passed in safety. That night we rode ten miles, and put up at a public house kept by a man who had made a profession of religion.

As the snow was deep, and the day unfavorable, we were the only travelers, and were permitted to occupy the bar-room. After we had partaken of some refreshments—the first we had received since morning—we were invited to have prayers with the family; and in this we enjoyed ourselves well. I asked Mononcue to sing, who was aided by the other Indians, and, after singing, to join in prayer. They sang in the sweetest strains, in Indian, the following hymn:

> *Come thou Fount of every blessing,*
>
> *Tune my heart to sing thy grace, etc.,*

and I sang with them in the English, which seemed to have a powerful effect on the man of the house and his family, it being a strange thing to them to hear Indians thus sing and pray. My old friend's soul was fired with his theme, and he prayed as if the heavens and the earth were coming together. When we arose from our knees, he and Squire Gray-Eyes went and shook hands with all in the house, weeping and exhorting them, in Indian, to turn to God, believe and live. We had a good meeting, for many of the family wept. Here I will give a few verses of the hymn before mentioned, in the Wyandott language:

Yar-ro-tawsa shre-wan daros

    Du-saw-shaw-taw-tra-war-ta

Di-da-sha-hoo-saw-ma-gawrah

    Dow-ta-ta ya-tu-haw-shu.

CHORUS: Durah-ma-yah! durah-ma-yah!

    Ded-so-mah-ras qui-hun-ca.

ENGLISH: Halleluiah! halleluiah!

    We are on our journey home.

Yar-ro-tawsa shre-wan daros

    Shasus tatot di cuarta

Scar tre hoo tar share wan daro

    Sha yar ne tshar see sentra.

Durah-ma-yah! durah-ma-yah! etc.

On-on-ti zo-hot si caw-quor

    Sheat un taw ruh de Shasus so

You yo dashar san de has lo

    Dishee cuw quar, na ha ha.

Durah-ma-yah! durah-ma-yah! etc.

After we retired, brother Mononcue asked me, "Is this man religious?" I said, "Yes, I believe so." "How can that be," said he, "while he keeps and sells the fire-waters? [meaning ardent spirits.] I thought that religious men were to love God and all men, and not do any evil; and can there be a worse evil than the keeping and measuring out this destructive thing, which makes men crazy, and leads them to commit any crime, even murder?" I told him it was a great evil and sin, and I could not see how any man could be good and practice it; that it never did any good, but was always productive of the worst crimes. He then replied that all such ought to be kept out of the Church, or turned out if they were in and would not quit it. I agreed with him in sentiment; so, after prayer, we spread our blankets, and committed ourselves to sleep.

SOURCE: Rev. James B. Finley, *Life among the Indians; or, Personal Reminiscences and Historical Incidents. Illustrative of Indian Life and Character* (Cincinnati, Ohio: Curtis & Jennings, [1857]): 3–4, 380–82, 385–87.

1830–1880

21

THOMAS D. RICE ACTS OUT

JIM CROW AND CUFF

Blackface minstrelsy is now acknowledged as the first original American contribution to Western theater and as the wellspring of such later genres as American vaudeville and musical comedy. It stands as a permanent reminder to our collective cultural conscience of unexpected consequences, including that our national entertainment has roots in our national disgrace. The solo or duo song-and-dance acts of the late 1820s led to theatrical skits and parody operas from the 1830s on, and then to complete evenings' entertainments in the 1840s and 1850s of song, dance, recitations, and theatrical skits. Blackface performance dominated American entertainment for most of the nineteenth century, and memories of the tradition were evoked in popular films through the 1950s without much self-consciousness. Thus, in the wake of Thomas Dartmouth Rice (1808–1860) and his success in conquering high-society London in 1836, came what the theatrical scholar W. T. Lhamon describes as the first Atlantic popular culture.

Rice created the famous stage character Jim Crow. According to myth, his song "Jump Jim Crow" (1830) was based on a caricature of an African beggar or stable hand, or a street performer even, somewhere in Ohio or Kentucky or Virginia. Although we don't know for sure by whom or where, "Jim Crow" was born. After the Civil War, segregation laws were called Jim Crow laws. Ironically, the "Jim Crow" song as it evolved through the decades of the mid-1800s occasionally expressed sensitive views about racial inequalities in and among its attacks on class privilege.

SELECTED LYRICS FROM "THE ORIGINAL JIM CROW"*

1
Come listen all you galls and boys
*I's jist from Tuckyhoe,***
I'm goin to sing a little song,
My name is Jim Crow.

Chorus:
Weel about and turn about and do jis so,
Eb'ry time I weel about and jump Jim Crow.

2
Oh I'm a roarer on de Fiddle,
And down in old Virginny,
They say I play de skyentific
*Like Massa Pagannini.****

7
I wip my weight in wildcats
I eat an Alligator,
And tear up more ground
Dan kifer 50 load of tater.

17
I met a Philadelphia niggar
Dress'd up quite nice & clean
But de way he 'bused de Yorkers
I thought was berry mean.

18
So I knocked down dis Sambo
And shut up his light,
For I'm jist about as sassy,
As if I was half white.

*"The Original Jim Crow" as published by E. Riley in New York at Chatham Street, probably 1832.

**There are many Tuckahoe place names. Perhaps the most famous, and patent for many others, is the plantation where Thomas Jefferson grew up because his father managed the estate. . . .

***Nicolo Paganini (1788–1840), Italian violin virtuoso, was the proverbial model of excellence.

21

Now my brodder niggars,
I do not think it right,
Dat you should laugh at dem
Who happen to be white.

22

Kase it dar misfortune,
And dey'd spend ebery dollar,
If dey only could be
Gentlemen ob colour.

37

Should dey get to fighting,
Perhaps de blacks will rise,
For deir wish for freedom,
Is shining in deir eyes.

42

Its berry common 'mong de white
To marry and get divorced
But dat I'll nebber do
Unless I'm really forced.

44

An I caution all white dandies,
Not to come my way,
For if dey insult me,
Dey'll in de gutter lay.

SOURCE: "The Original Jim Crow" (New York: E. Riley, ca. 1832), reproduced in W. T. Lhamon, *Jump Jim Crow: Lost Plays, Lyrics and Street Prose of the First Atlantic Popular Culture* (Cambridge, Mass.: Harvard University Press, 2003): 95–96, 98–99, 101–102.

〜〜〜〜〜〜

Other aspects of blackface minstrelsy concern the popularity of opera burlesques
among minstrel troupes, which by implication bears witness to the widespread dis-
semination of opera among all classes. Here are a few scenes from the most popu-
lar stage vehicle before the Civil War—Rice's burlesque or operatic olio Oh! Hush!
or, The Virginny Cupids! (1833). In addition to the stock characters of Cuff and
Rosa, it satirizes Italian opera, just beginning to be known in American cities.
W. T. Lhamon, Jr., writes how the text indentations "preserve differences among
spoken, recitative, and sung parts. Low blackface characters in drag performing
recitative furthered the burlesque on so-called Italian opera that high audiences
favored."[3]

OH! HUSH! OR, THE VIRGINNY CUPIDS!
AN OPERATIC OLIO

ACT 1

Scene 1. Exterior, Street. The characters discovered blacking boots. Some sitting down. Sam Johnson sits on a chair, R., his feet resting on a barrel. He is reading a newspaper, which he holds upside down. All laugh and begin to get up as the curtain rises.

CUFF: Pete, I hab been round to all the hotels today, an' I got so many boots to black by four o'clock dat I don't tink I can do it. Now, den, boys, if you polish dem by dat time, I'll gib you a holiday dis ebenin'.

PETE: Ah! dat's right, Cuff, we'll gib 'em de shine ob de best Day and Martin*—but, Cuff, gib us a song.

CUFF [*sings*]: *Come, all you Virginny gals, and listen to my noise,*
    Neber do you wed wid de Carolina boys;
For if dat you do, your portion will be:
    Cowheel and sugarcane, wid shangolango tea.

Full Chorus
    Mamzel ze marrel—ze bunkum sa!
    Mamzel ze marrel—ze bunkum sa!
When you go a-courting, de pretty gals to see
    You kiss 'em and you hug 'em like de double rule ob free.
De fust ting dey ax you when you are sitting down,
    Is, "Fetch along de Johnny-cake—it's gitting rader brown."

Chorus
    Mamzel ze marrel, &c.

Before you are married, potatoes dey am cheap,
    Money am so plenty dat you find it in de street.
But arter you git married, I tell you how it is—
    Potatoes dey am berry high, and sassengers is riz.

Chorus
    Mamzel ze marrel, &c.

CUFF [*turning round after the song, discovers* Johnson]: I say, Pete, who is dat comsumquencial darkey ober dar, dat is puttin' on so many airs?

PETE: I don't know, Cuff. He stopped here a few minutes arter you went away, an' he's been reading dar eber since. Speak to him.

CUFF [*approaching* Johnson, *scrutinizes his person*]: Why, it am Sam Johnson!

*boot polish

ALL: Sam Johnson!

CUFF: Yes, to be sure it am.

JOHNSON [*looking through his eyeglass*]: Gemblem, is you distressing your conversation to me?

CUFF: Yes, sar, I is distressing my observation to you inderwidually, collectively, skientifically and alone. [*Seats himself on the barrel.*]

JOHNSON [*rising*]: Well, sar, den I would hab you to know dat my name, sar, is Mr. Samuel Johnson, Exquire, an' I don't wish to be addressed by such—[*pointing to crowd*]—low, common, vulgar trash! You had better mind your business and brack your filthy boots. [*He sits down again.*]

CUFF [*gets off the barrel*]: I say, Pete, I'll tell you whar I seed dat darkey. He used to work in de same shop wid me for old Jake Simmons, but he drawed a high prize in de lottery, and retired from de 'spectable profession of bracking boots. De last time I seed him he was down in old Virginny on a coon hunt. I'll tell you suffin' 'bout it. [*He sings:*]

> 'Way down in old Virginny, 'twas in de arternoon
>   Oh! Roley, boley!
> Wid de gun dat Massa gib me, I went to shoot the coon.

~~~~~~~~~~

The rest of the scene finds Johnson set upon by the crowd, and he flees after they tear up his newspaper and throw boots and shoes at him. Johnson then goes to the house of Rose to court her. The parody of manners includes a guitar serenade with fancy references to the Roman god of wine, Bacchus. The situation is classic comic theater: the love triangle of two men and a woman, with one suitor ending up in the closet. The first song, "Lubly Rosa," parodies George Washington Dixon's minstrel classic "Coal Black Rose" (1828). In Dixon's original text, the suitor is a lower-class black playing a banjo. Rice substitutes a guitar to satirize the pretentious bourgeois Sam Johnson.

Scene 2. Exterior of Rose's House—*Dark Stage. Staccato music.*

JOHNSON [*enters with guitar to serenade*]: Tank heaben! I hab got clar ob dem ruffian darkies at last. I neber was so grossly insulted in all my life. Dey nearly spiled my best clothes, and—but let me see, I promised to gib my lubly Rosa a serenade dis ebenin', and if I can only find de house. [*Goes up to house.*] Yes, here is de house—I know it from a tack in de door. [*Sings:*]*

----

*Much of the humor depends upon our noticing that from here until the end of the play, despite all the capers and interruptions, nearly all the dialogue is sung now.

SONG: "LUBLY ROSA"

Oh! lubly Rosa, Sambo has cum
*   To salute his lub wid his tum, tum, tum.*
So open de door, Rose, and luff me in,
*   For de way I lub you am a sin.*

ROSE [*appears at Window and sings*]:
*   Oh, who's dat knocking at my door,*
*   Making such a noise wid his saucy jaw,*
*   Ise looking down upon de stoop,*
*   Like a henhawk on a chicken-coop.*
*   So clar de kitchen.*

JOHNSON:
*   'Tis Sambo Johnson, dearest dove,*
*   Come like Bacchus, God of Love;*
*   To tell his lubly Rosa how*
*   He's quit his old perfersion now*
*   So clar de kitchen.*

ROSE:
*   Oh, hold yer hat and cotch de key,*
*   Come into de little backroom wid me;*
*   Sit by de fire and warm your shin,*
*   And on de shelf you'll find some gin.*
*   So clar de kitchen.*

[*She drops the key.* Johnson *catches it in his hat and exits into the House.*]

Scene 3. Interior of Rose's House. Table set—cups and saucers for two and two chairs.

CUFF [*enters L. and sings*]:

SONG: "COAL BLACK ROSE!"

I wonder whar de debil my lubly Rosa's gone,
She's luff me half an hour sittin' all alone.
If she don't come back an' tell me why she didn't stay wid me,
I'll drink all de sassengers and eat up all de tea.

Chorus
Oh, Rose! you coal black Rose!
I neber lub a gal like I lub dat Rose.

ROSE   [*enters R., and sings*]:
Now, get up, you Cuffy, an' gib me up dat chair,
*   Mr. Johnson'll play de dickens if he cotch you sitting dar.*

CUFF: *I doesn't fear de devil, Rose, luff alone dat Sam,*
If dat nigger fool his time wid me, I'll hit him . . . I'll be . . . [breaks a plate].

Chorus
Oh, Rose &c.

ROSE: *Now, get you in de cupboard, Cuff, a little while to stay.*
             I'll give you plenty applejack when Sambo's gone away.

CUFF: *I'll keep my eye upon him—if he 'tempts to kiss or hug,*
             I'll be down upon him like a duck upon a bug.

[Rose *conducts* Cuff *to the closet, puts him in and closes the door.*]

SOURCE: *Oh! Hush! or, The Virginny Cupids,* in W. T. Lhamon, *Jump Jim Crow: Lost Plays, Lyrics and Street Prose of the First Atlantic Popular Culture* (Cambridge, Mass.: Harvard University Press, 2003): 148–49, 152–54.

Carte de visite by R. A. Lord, 158 Chatham Street, NY ca. 1860s, of minstrel in clown outfit with banjo. Source: Philip F. Gura and James F. Bollman, *America's Instrument. The Banjo in the Nineteenth Century* (Chapel Hill: University of North Carolina Press, 1999): 21.

22

WILLIAM M. WHITLOCK, BANJO PLAYER FOR

THE VIRGINIA MINSTRELS

In 1843, the Virginia Minstrels—a quartet of stage musicians—contrived a whole evening's entertainment out of their blackface song-and-dance routines and their band of fiddle, banjo, bones, and tambourine. No one from the band, including its most prominent member, Dan Emmett (1815–1904; the composer of "I Wish I Was in Dixie's Land," aka "Dixie," 1860), later remembered in exactly the same way how it happened. But they all remembered their success. In New York, the Virginia Minstrels launched the national craze for the blackface minstrel show in 1843.

One selection here, a memoir-obituary of a founding member of the Virginia Minstrels, William "Billy" Whitlock (1813–1878), gives Whitlock's account of the first performance, and a second selection by another on-the-spot observer is also included. Whitlock was an experienced blackface entertainer, and his background reminds us of the circus roots of blackface. More important, Billy played the banjo, and this selection also includes his memory of learning the instrument from the famed Irish-American banjo virtuoso Joe Sweeney (1810–1860), who is credited with introducing its fifth drone string.

The aged minstrel whose death was recorded in last week's issue [of the *New York Clipper*] was born in this city in 1813. Until 1840 he "worked at case" in printing-offices, and it was while he was employed as a compositor on a religious journal that he made his first appearance on any stage. This was in 1835, as Cuff in the negro sketch of "Oh Hush," which T. D. Rice had already rendered popular. It was as part of a rather unpretentious show that Mr. Whitlock thus appeared, and Dan Gardner, who married Whitlock's sister, and who is now residing in Philadelphia, was its wench-dancer.

. . .

After having traveled through Georgia and both Carolinas, the company reached Lynchburg, Va., and there Whitlock was introduced to Joe Sweeney, the father of all the banjo-players. Up to that time Whitlock had never seen a banjo. During his four days' stay in Lynchburg Sweeney had one made for him, and taught him a tune—"Settin' on a Rail," which was then very popular. He now devoted his spare time to mastering the banjo. Every night during his journey South, when he was not playing, he would quietly steal off to some negro hut to hear the darkies sing and see them dance, taking with him a jug of whiskey to make them all the merrier. Thus he got his accurate knowledge of the peculiarities of plantation and cornfield negroes. Reaching this city [New York] on July 6, 1838, he at first performed with Gardner in Hester street, and then went with Henry Rockwell the circus-manager to the Richmond Hill Theatre. There, singing "The Raccoon Hunt," he played the banjo for the first time in public. Although in his autobiography he specifically sets up no such claim, yet he seems to have been the first person to play that instrument in this city. Billed as "Billy Whitlock, the Celebrated Ethiopian Singer and Original Banjoist," he had the metropolitan field all to himself until 1839, when Joe Sweeney came to town.

It was Whitlock's habit to travel with circuses in the Summer, and to "work at case" in the Winter. In the Winter of 1839–40 he abandoned type-setting to enter into an engagement with P. T. Barnum, under whom he visited all the chief cities of the Union, playing the banjo while Master John Diamond danced. For a time Billy Williams the comedian was with the party. Whitlock and Diamond first performed under Barnum's management at Welsh's Circus, under canvas in Broadway, between Broome and Spring streets. This was almost the first of Barnum as a showman, and before he had a Museum [exhibition hall]. Whitlock traveled with him for several years, and played the banjo for the new Master John Diamond (Frank Lynch) after the original had left P. T. B. It was during his journeyings with the original Diamond that an incident occurred which has an important bearing upon the origin of negro minstrelsy. We reproduce Mr. Whitlock's own words:

> While Diamond and myself were performing at the Walnut-street Theatre, Philadelphia, I practiced with Dick Myers the violinist; and on our benefit night we played the fiddle and the banjo together for the first time in public. I retained this novel idea in my memory for future reference. The origination of the Minstrels I claim as my own idea, and it cannot be blotted out. One day I asked Old Dan Emmett, who was in New York at the time, to practice the fiddle and the banjo with me at his boarding-house, in Catherine street. We went down there, and when we had practiced two or three tunes Frank Brower called in (by accident). He listened to our music, charmed to the soul. I told him to join us with the bones, which he did. Presently Dick Pelham came in (also by accident), and looked amazed. I asked him to procure a tambourine and make one of the party, and he went and got one. After practicing for a while, we went

to the old resort of the circus crowd—the "Branch," in the Bowery—with our instruments, and in Bartlett's Billiard room performed for the first time as the Virginia Minstrels. A programme was made out, and the first time we appeared upon a stage, before an audience, was for the benefit of Pelham, at the Chatham Theatre. The house was rammed-jammed with our friends, and Dick, of course, put dollars in his purse.

The banjo then used by Whitlock, which had been made in 1840, and which he played in Great Britain with the Virginia Minstrels, was presented by him to his daughter Mrs. Edwin Adams, who probably has it yet.

Through the medium of the obituary of Richard W. Pelham, and later through the history of the troupe published among these "Annals" from data furnished by Dan Emmett last year, our readers are nearly all familiar with the movements of the pioneer band of negro minstrels—William Whitlock, banjo; Richard Pelham, tambourine; Dan Emmett, violin; and Frank Brower, bones. Their first performance in public was given in early 1843, and in the following April they sailed for England in the packet-ship New York, with the late George B. Wooldridge (afterwards "Tom Quick" of *The New York Leader*) as their agent. It may not be amiss to give Wooldridge's account of their origin in the Catherine-street boarding-house:

> The four together in one room, and the banjo, bones, violin and tambourine lying around loose, as if by an accident, each one picked up his tools and joined in a chorus of "Old Dan Tucker" while Emmett was playing and singing. It went well, and they repeated it without saying a word. Each did his best and such a rattling of the principal and original instruments in a minstrel band was never heard before. Frank Brower was the first to open his chin-music as they came to a rest, by saying: "Boys, we've got it—it's a novelty—it is something new!" Says Whitlock: "Let's go in together as a band of minstrels." "Agreed!" was the response from all hands. "Let's try it again," says Pelham; and they did, going through all of Dan's choruses and songs.

The band broke up in England.

SOURCE: "Amusement Annals—Clipper Series, No. LXII. William M. Whitlock. The Origin of Negro Minstrelsy." *New York Clipper*, vol. 26, no. 3, p. 21, April 13, 1878. Also reprinted in Bob Flesher and Rita Flesher, eds., *Historical Reprints of the Origin of Negro Minstrelsy* (Moreno Valley, Calif.: Dr. Horsehair Music, 1999): 14–17. Also partially quoted in Charles Hamm, *Yesterdays: Popular Song in America* (New York: Norton, 1979): 127.

23

EDWIN P. CHRISTY, STEPHEN FOSTER, AND "ETHIOPIAN MINSTRELSY"

Edwin P. Christy (1815–1862) made a fortune in the blackface world, as the sums at the end of this chapter prove. In 1842, Christy formed the Christy Minstrels, and they sang Stephen Foster's (1826–1864) "Ethiopian," or blackface, minstrel songs on tour. Wary of public disapproval of blackface music, Foster initially kept his name off some of his blackface songs, making a deal with Christy to have Christy rather than Foster listed as the author of "Old Folks at Home." A few years later, Foster tried to change the terms, but the letter reprinted here as the first selection accomplished nothing. Thus, "Old Folks at Home" initially appeared as "sung by Christy's Minstrels, written and composed by E. P. Christy." By 1852, this song had sold approximately 40,000 copies at a time when 3,000 to 5,000 copies of a song made a hit. The music-industry historian Russell Sanjek writes, "Only after renewal of the copyright in his most successful work, in 1879, did Foster's name appear on its cover as author and composer."[1] Foster died a penniless alcoholic in New York City.

Christy, on the other hand, made sure he got as much credit as he could. Repeatedly, Christy pressed his claims to be named the "originator" of blackface minstrelsy in print and in court. He won a lawsuit in New York State supporting this claim on the narrow grounds that—as even his rival Dan Emmett acknowledged—Christy contributed "the singing in harmony and introducing the various acts, together with wench-dancing and solo playing."[2]

These "various acts" formed the staple of the stage entertainments Christy produced at his own opera house in New York City. Christy's Opera House is mentioned in the second selection, which reprints for the first time the preface to volume 4 of Christy's *Plantation Melodies*. Each volume of *Plantation Melodies* (1851–1856) included lyrics (but not music) for about sixty songs as well as scripts for farces and skits. The anonymous author of the preface writes genteel hype, as if Christy were the deliverer of American cultural independence. He emphasizes in particular the popularity of Christy's sophisticated operatic burlesques. Despite years of glory and enough fame to inspire a folk revival band in the 1960s to call themselves the New Christy Minstrels, Christy did not survive changes in his luck. When his own income declined along with the stage and theater during the Civil War years, Christy committed suicide.

May 25, 1852
E. P. Christy, Esq.
Dear Sir
    As I once intimated to you, I had the intention of omitting my name on my Ethiopian songs, owing to the prejudice against them by some, which might injure my reputation as a writer of another style of music, but I find that by my efforts I have done a great deal to build up a taste for the Ethiopian songs among refined people by making the words suitable to their taste, instead of the trashy and really offensive words which belong to some songs of that order. Therefore I have concluded to re-instate my name on my songs and to pursue the Ethiopian business without fear or shame and lend all my energies to making the business live, at the same time that I will wish to establish my name as the best Ethiopian song-writer. But I am not encour-aged in undertaking this so long as "Old folks at home" stares me in the face with an-other's name on it. As it was at my own solicitation that you allowed your name to be placed on the song, I hope that the above reasons will be sufficient explanation for my desire to place my own name on it as author and composer, while at the same time I wish to leave the name of your band on the title page. This is a little matter of pride in myself which it will certainly be to your interest to encourage. On the receipt of your free consent to this proposition, I will if you wish, willingly refund you the money which you paid me on that song, though it may have been sent me for other considerations than the one in question, and I promise in addition to write you an opening chorus in my best style, free of charge, and in any other way in my power to advance your inter-ests hereafter. I find I cannot write at all unless I write for the public approbation and get credit for what I write. As we may probably have a good deal of business with each other in our lives, it is best to proceed on a sure basis of confidence and good under-standing, therefore I hope you will appreciate an author's feelings in the case and deal with me with your usual fairness. Please answer immediately.
Very respectfully yours,

Stephen C. Foster

SOURCE: Stephen Collins Foster, "Letters to E. P. Christy," in *The American Composer Speaks: A Historical Anthology, 1770–1965*, ed. Gilbert Chase (Baton Rouge: Louisiana State University Press, 1966): 56–57.

~~~~~~~~~

THE PREFACE TO CHRISTY'S *PLANTATION MELODIES*, VOLUME 4 (1854)

EDWIN P. CHRISTY, ESQ., THE ORIGINATOR OF ETHIOPIAN MINSTRELSY.

"Our native music, beyond comparing, Is sweetest, far, on the ear that falls."

Thus sings the sweet lyric poet, Samuel Lover, and the sentiment finds a ready responsive echo in every heart and in every nation which is alive to truth, patriotism and feeling. Whether the *native* strains are awakened by the voice, the viol, the guitar, harp, bag-pipe, or the *banjo,* they each alike exercise the same perpetual and eternal charm upon the soul; whilst their *authors,* or those who have the honor of developing and diffusing their inspiring power, are justly hailed as the benefactors of mankind!

After our countrymen had, by the force of *native genius* in arts, arms, science, philosophy and poetry, &c., &c., confuted the stale cant of our European detractors, that nothing original could emanate from Americans—the next cry was, that we had no NATIVE MUSIC; which exclamation was tauntingly reiterated, until our countrymen found a triumphant, vindicating APOLLO in the genius of E. P. CHRISTY, who, possessing a soul responsive to

"A concord of sweet sounds,"

and combining the talents of musician, vocalist and poet, was the *first* to catch our *native airs* as they floated wildly, or hummed in the balmy breezes of the sunny south, turn them to shape, and give them

"A local habitation, and a name,"

until the air of our broad, blest land, and even that of Europe, became vocal with the thousand native melodies called into existence by his inexhaustible powers; and millions have been elevated to wealth and happiness through the sole medium of his original school of minstrelsy.

EDWIN P. CHRISTY was born in the fair city of Philadelphia, in the year 1815, his parents ranking amongst the most respectable residents of the famed city of "Brotherly Love." At the age of ten years, the state of his health rendered a change of air necessary; and his parents, at the suggestion of some friends who were in business at New Orleans, consented to his removal to that city, where, recovering his health, and possessing a remarkable proficiency in education for a youth of his years, he was placed as a clerk in a mercantile house: but a youth of his romantic temperament was, very naturally, more fond of the book of *nature* than the day-book of the counting house; and being permitted to pay frequent visits to the Menagerie of Messrs. Purdy & Welch, he became infatuated with a desire to see a little more of "the animal," and after wringing a slow leave, he was suffered to engage with those gentlemen, under whose protection he made a tour through all the Southern States, adding no little to his stature, as well as to his knowledge of music, men and things.

Immediately on his return to New Orleans, he was again received into the house of his former employers. Our hero now assumed the new position of superintendent of *a ropewalk,*[3] one of the duties of which was to overlook the operations of a number of slaves engaged in it; and it was in this capacity that he acquired his superior knowledge of the *negro characteristics,* traits, humor and melody which his observant genius has since turned to such golden account.

At this time it was the custom of the "darkies" to hold their holiday meetings at a spot known as "CONGO GREEN," where, amid their mirth, music, dance and festivity, he, with the soul of an artist, and the tact of a student of nature's eccentricities, amassed those rich stores of entertainment which have long stamped him as the most truthful and pleasing delineator of Ethiopian humor and melody.

In 1832, Mr. Christy's love of varying the phases of life placed him in the extensive Circus Caravan of MESSRS. PURDY, WELCH & DELAVAN, with whom he travelled and performed for a number of years, and proved a great card, being celebrated as a NEGRO MELODIST, punster and singer; and subsequently his genius soared from the glimpses of the *sawdust* to the *legitimate* boards of THESPIS, and he became a member of the Eagle Street Theatre, Buffalo, under the management of Messrs. DEAN & MCKINNEY, in which he acquired immense popularity as a BUFFO VOCALIST, and made rapid advances as an ACTOR.

But his passionate love for music, and his thorough appreciation of the beauties of Ethiopian melody, turned his talents again to that subject; and in 1841 he conceived his glorious plan of organising the FIRST BAND of ETHIOPIAN MINSTRELS, the members of which, independent of their proficiency on their several instruments, should possess sufficient science and practical skill in music to enable them to harmonise and SCORE systematically the original NEGRO SOLOS, quartettes, chorus and concerted pieces, and play and sing them with true precision and effect.

Every person at all versed in musical matters will acknowledge this to be such an undertaking as would *try* the powers of any Director of a *Grand Opera*—a task as *original* as difficult, demanding a correct taste, true musical science, inexhaustible patience, and no inconsiderable expenditure; yet, by our friend Christy, this great plan was accomplished, and with what results, thousands, ay, millions of admiring auditors have TOLD throughout the land.

Subsequently Mr. Christy, the pioneer in NEGRO MINSTRELSY, with his unrivalled Band, visited almost every city in the United States and the Canadas, eliciting everywhere the spontaneous praise of the public and the press, while his deportment and talent as a *business man,* vocalist or *gentleman,* have invariably made him welcome in the best circles.

In 1846, Mr. Christy established himself in the great city of New York, and opened at Palmo's Opera House, now Burton's Theatre, with a series of his matchless Ethiopian performances; and since that period he has rendered various other edifices *noted* "TO A CHARM," and realized a fame and fortune unequalled in the annals of the WORLD'S MINSTRELSY. Who has not heard of CHRISTY'S OPERA HOUSE? Whilst the numerous and stupendous *Italian Opera* enterprises have successively burst like bubbles on the tide of the times, and various *Ethiopian* organizations, with their innumerable appellations, have expired like so many *ephemera,* CHRISTY'S OPERA has maintained its onward and upward course, prospering and to prosper.

Although our hero forsook the counting-house for the more congenial pursuit of Minstrelsy, he did not forget his *clerkship;* and whilst he *noted* up, he also carefully *noted down,* on the proper *ledger lines,* a *scale* of his receipts and expenses. If further proof is needed of his progressive prosperity, here are the FACTS in FIGURES, showing the *moderate* receipts of the first year, and comparing them with the *enormous increase* in the last:—

Year.	No. of Concerts.	Receipts.
1842,	69	$1,847[.]52
1853,	312	47,971[.]75

His first year's *profits,* in 1842, were less than $300, while, in others, they have been over $25,000.

One saw so much of E. P. Christy, "in public, on the stage," and so little of him socially and in private life, that we know but little of his private character. His purse, now well lined, is known to be ever open to the calls of the distressed.

Besides all this, he has set half of the world singing and merry. From Canada to California the air is vocal with his varied melodies. In the drawing-room, counting-house, cottage and camp—in the plantation and palace—in the street, saloon, and sabbath-school—his *airs* are the preludes or finales to all operations; and so long as a heart beats time, responsive to "OLD FOLKS AT HOME," the name of E. P. CHRISTY will endure as THE SOLE FOUNDER OF AMERICAN MINSTRELSY.

SOURCE: Edwin P. Christy, Christy's Plantation Melodies, no. 4: The Only Authorized Edition of Genuine Christy's Songs. Published under the authority of Edwin P. Christy, Originator of Ethiopian Minstrelsy, And the first to Harmonize Negro Melodies (Philadelphia, New York, Boston, Baltimore: Fisher & Brother, 1854): v–vii.

~~~~~~~

NOTES

1. Russell Sanjek, *American Popular Music and Its Business: The First Four Hundred Years, from 1790 to 1909* (New York: Oxford University Press, 1988): II:75–76.
2. From a letter by Dan Emmett (1815–1904) on the First Negro Minstrel Band, published in the *New York Clipper,* May 19, 1877, reprinted in Hans Nathan, *Dan Emmett and the Rise of Early Negro Minstrelsy* (Norman: University of Oklahoma Press, 1962): 285–86.
3. A "ropewalk" typically referred to that section of a hemp factory, or perhaps also the building itself, where rope was made from hemp. It took hard factory labor—typically, slave labor in New Orleans at this time—to process hemp.

24

Stephen Foster's Legacy

(Foster, Gordon, Robb, Simpson, Willis, Galli-Curci, Ellington, Charles)

A broad multicultural public heard itself in the songs written by Stephen Foster (1826–1864), who forged a synthesis among a variety of styles—from Thomas Moore's Irish parlor songs and bel canto Italian opera to blackface minstrelsy and revival hymns. Gold Rush miners in California put their own words to "Oh! Susanna." Black abolitionists, subverting its racist lyrics, used the tune for freedom songs. Foster's mega-success "Old Folks at Home" appeared in stage versions of Harriet Beecher Stowe's novel *Uncle Tom's Cabin*. In John Robb's monumental collection of Hispanic folk music of the American Southwest, a delightful "Susanita" appears. Foster's songs were as common as bread on the table.

The relationship between Foster's music and issues around race remains controversial. His nostalgic plantation laments camouflage racism at the same time that some of his musical portraits of African Americans have courtly dignity. Many singers from many races perform his songs in their own way, sometimes transgressing the Foster tradition with irony and wit.

TWO VERSES AND THE CHORUS FROM
FOSTER'S "OH! SUSANNA" (1848)

I come from Alabama
With my Banjo on my knee
I'se gwine to Lou'siana
My true lub for to see.
It rain'd all night de day I left,
De wedder it was dry;
The sun so hot I froze to def
Susanna, dont you cry.

Chorus:
Oh! Susanna, do not cry for me;
I come from Alabama
Wid my Banjo on my knee.

I jumped aboard de telegraph,
And trabbelled down de riber,
De Lectric fluid magnified,
And Killed five Hundred Nigger
De bullgine¹ buste, de horse run off,
I really thought I'd die;
I shut my eyes to hold my breath,
Susanna, don't you cry.

SOURCE: "Oh! Susanna," with the cover sheet attribution to *Music of the Original Christy Minstrels* (New York: C. Holt, Jr., 1848). Lyrics and music are available under the song title as Item 15 in *Music for the Nation: American Sheet Music, 1820–1860* on line through *American Memory*, Library of Congress. [http://memory.loc.gov]

～～～～

During the height of the California Gold Rush in 1848 and '49, companies of adventurers boarded ships to sail around Cape Horn, South America to get to the fabled land of instant wealth. The ship Eliza left Salem, Massachusetts in 1848, according to the historian Octavius Howe, who chronicled its rites of passage and the music made by its sailors on route to find their fortunes.

I came from Salem City,
With my wash bowl on my knee,
I'm going to California
The gold dust for to see.
It seemed all night, the day I left,
The weather it was dry,

The sun so hot I froze to death,
Oh! brothers, don't you cry.

Chorus:
Oh! California,
That's the land for me,
I'm going to Sacramento
With my wash bowl on my knee.

I jumped aboard the Liza ship
And traveled on the sea,
And every time I thought of home,
I wished it wasn't me.
The vessel reared like any horse,
That had of oats a wealth,
It found it couldn't throw me, so,
I thought I'd throw myself.

I thought of all the pleasant times
We've had together here,
I thought I ought to cry a bit,
But couldn't find a tear.
The pilot bread was in my mouth,
The gold dust in my eye,
And, though I'm going far away,
Dear brothers, don't you cry

I soon shall be in Francisco,
And then I'll look around,
And when I see the gold lumps there,
I'll pick them off the ground.
I'll scrape the mountains clean,
I'll drain the rivers dry,
A pocket full of rocks bring home,
So, brothers, don't you cry.

SOURCE: Octavius Thorndike Howe, *Argonauts of '49: History and Adventures of the Emigrant Companies from Massachusetts, 1849–1850* (Cambridge, MA: Harvard University Press, 1923): 77, 79. Partially reprinted in R. W. Gordon, "American Folksongs: In Pioneer Days," *New York Times*, January 15, 1928; included in *Folk Songs of America* (New York: Federal Theater Project, 1938) and Gordon's excerpts on line in "California Gold: Northern California Folk Music from the Thirties. Collected by Sidney Robertson Cowell." Available at http://memory.loc.gov/ammem/afcchtml/cowhome.html.

John Robb collected this version with some shared text from Julianita Trujillo in Chimayó, New Mexico, in 1949. The verse is in 6/8 and the refrain returns to 2/4.

Susanita se embarcó
en un buque de vapor,
y sospirando decía,
—¿por qué se me fué mi amor?—

Refrán
¡Ay, Susana!
no llores por mí
que me voy para Alta California
a traer oro para ti.

[Suzanita went a-traveling
On a steamship one fine day,
But with sadness she was sighing,
"Why has my love gone away?"

Refrain:
Oh, Suzanna!
Don't you cry for me
For I'm off to Upper California
To bring back gold to thee.]

SOURCE: John Donald Robb, *Hispanic Folk Music of New Mexico and the Southwest: A Self-Portrait of a People* (Norman: University of Oklahoma Press, 1980): 588–89.

"Oh! Susanna" was adapted as a freedom song in the songster The Emancipation Car *by J. Mc. C[arter] Simpson (1820?–1877). He wrote eight new stanzas, and his preface explains his strategy.*

PREFACE

As soon as I could write, which was not until I was past twenty-one years old, a spirit of poetry, (which was always in me,) became revived, and seemed to waft before my mind horrid pictures of the condition of my people, and something seemed to say, "Write and sing about it—you can sing what would be death to speak." So I began to write and sing.

. . .

In my selections of "Airs," I have gathered such as are popular, and extensively known. Many superstitious persons, and perhaps, many good conscientious, well-meaning Christians, will denounce and reject the work on account of the "Tunes," but my object has been to change the flow of those sweet melodies (so often disgraced by Comic Negro Songs, and sung by our own people,) into a more appropriate and useful channel; and I hope that my motives may be duly appreciated; and that this little work, (the *first* of the kind in the United States,) may find a resting place and a hearty welcome in every State, community and family in the Union, and as far as a friend to the slave may be found.

. . .

J. Mc. C. SIMPSON
Elder in Charge of the Zion Baptist Church, Zanesville, Ohio.

"AWAY TO CANADA":
ADAPTED TO THE CASE OF MR. S, FUGITIVE FROM TENNESSEE

1
I'm on my way to Canada,
*   That cold and dreary land;*
The dire effects of slavery,
*   I can no longer stand.*
My soul is vexed within me so,
*   To think that I'm a slave;*
I've now resolved to strike the blow
*   For freedom or the grave.*

[Chorus:]
O righteous Father,
*   Wilt thou not pity me?*
And aid me on to Canada,
*   Where colored men are free.*

4
Grieve not, my wife—grieve not for me,
*   O! do not break my heart,*

For nought but cruel slavery
    Would cause me to depart.
If I should stay to quell your grief,
    Your grief I would augment;
For no one knows the day that we
    Asunder might be rent.

[Chorus:]
O! Susannah,
    Don't you cry for me—
I'm going up to Canada,
    Where colored men are free.

SOURCE: J. Mc. C. Simpson, *The Emancipation Car: Being an Original Composition of Anti-Slavery Ballads, composed exclusively for the Under-Ground Rail Road* (Zanesville, Ohio, 1852): iv, vi, 63–67.

This little squib by Richard Storrs Willis (1819–1900), the editor of the magazine The Musical World and New York Musical Times, *reproaches Foster for writing Ethiopian songs.*

MISCELLA

We were recently visited by a celebrated Pittsburgher, namely, Stephen C. Foster, Esq., the author of the most popular Ethiopian melodies now afloat—such, for example, as *Nelly Bly; Oh! Boys, carry me 'long; Uncle Ned; The Old Folks at Home,* and many others. Mr. Foster possesses more than ordinary abilities as a composer; and we hope he will soon realize enough from his Ethiopian melodies to enable him to *afford* to drop them and turn his attention to the production of a higher kind of music. Much of his *music* is now excellent, but being wedded to negro idioms it is, of course, discarded, by many who would otherwise gladly welcome it to their pianos. We were glad to learn from Mr. F. that he intends principally to devote himself hereafter to the production of "White men's music."*

SOURCE: Richard Storrs Willis, "Miscellaneous Musical News," *New York Musical World,* January 29, 1853, 75.

---

*Firth, Pond & Co., have just published Mr. Foster's last song—*My Old Kentucky Home, Good Night*—which he thinks will be more popular than any of his previous compositions.

As if demonstrating anew the affinities between Foster and Italian bel canto singing, the Italian opera singer Amelita Galli-Curci (1882–1963) routinely included "Old Folks at Home" in her concert recitals and on her acoustic recordings. Galli-Curci became an American citizen in 1921, and perhaps she wished to validate her affinities for her new homeland by providing an extensive technical analysis of a revered song.

MME. GALLI-CURCI'S INTERPRETATION

For the interpretation of the song we sought out Mme. Galli-Curci, who has probably made the greatest success of it of any singer.

"Yes, I sing this song in all my concerts," began Mme. Galli-Curci. "People love it, and so do I. Even the staid Englishman likes the song, and I featured it throughout my recent tour of England. I never get tired of it, and that is the real test of any song.

"If art is an attempt to express itself in terms of real life, simplicity and sincerity, then this song must be recorded as one of the greatest achievements in the entire realm of art. Consider it first from the standpoint of simplicity. Most of the words used are of one syllable. There are no modulations into other keys, and only three primary chords are used throughout—the tonic, the dominant and the subdominant. In the verse a four bar phrase is repeated four times, twice with semi-cadence (dominant seventh) and twice with tonic cadence. The song would be great if judged only by its abiding simplicity.

"But then it is also sincere. It strikes a universal chord. Everyone experiences a longing for dear ones at one time or another. This feeling is as old as life itself, and is one of the reasons as well why the song will go on forever.

NOT EASY TO SING

"Do not think that this is an easy song to sing—I mean artistically. It is, on the contrary, extremely difficult. It is slow in tempo and the notes are sustained. The very first sentence takes a drop at the end and leaves you suspended on a high note with fast diminishing breath supply.

"But every singer should have this song in his or her repertoire. It will 'go well,' as they say, with any audience if sung capably. When giving a concert, the moment my accompanist strikes the opening chords of this song, an undercurrent of satisfaction sweeps over the house which manifests itself in 'ohs,' 'ahs,' sighs and more voluble demonstrations. The audience recognizes an old friend. Yet the very fact that everyone knows the song makes it all the more difficult to sing. How to sing it in an individual way is the question. The first thing I would say to do then is to be absolutely sincere—to do otherwise is to have recourse to cheap melodramatics. There should be no hair-pulling or shedding of glycerine tears. There should only be a straightforward, sympathetic expression that reflects its true character. The real feeling for the song must come from within, and who has not felt this same longing and nostalgia?

THREE IMPORTANT POINTS

"The three important points in singing *Old Folks at Home* are simplicity, directness and pathos. Simple longing is the keynote, and one should not digress or elaborate. There should also be a directness of appeal. The pathos in the song is expressed by the color timbre of the voice, and this is, perhaps, the most important element. In fact, tone in this song is everything—purity, warmth, roundness. The high notes in particular should be round and velvety.

"Those phrases in which I strive particularly for varying tonal colors are, in the first verse, *sadly I roam* and *longing,* and in the refrain, *All de world* and *Oh! darkies!* Tone color or timbre is difficult to explain. First the singer must have a mental concept of just the shade of tone he wishes to produce. With this concept in mind, the larynx will tend to mold the tone. It is the function of the singing organ to be obedient and elastic.

"In the chorus, I take the phrase *All de world* in whole voice. And then there is a deal of pathos that can be expressed in *Oh! darkies,* pausing slightly after darkies. I also make a significant pause at the end of *folks* in the last line of the refrain."

Mme. Galli-Curci added as well a few hints on practicing.

"I am a great believer," she said, "in staccato scale practice. I am convinced that it is productive of unusually good results, and that it makes for a healthy condition of the throat and vocal chords. In the whole matter of practice, I favor the old Garcia method; the high notes round, soft and velvety—in other words, beautiful singing without strain. *Old Folks at Home* should be sung that way. It is a perfect jewel and worthy of one's best efforts."

Note.—The music as contained in the music supplement is secured exclusively for THE MUSICAL OBSERVER as sung by Mme. Galli-Curci, and shows just how she sings the number. Mme. Galli-Curci sings the first and second verses only in concert. Where to breathe is indicated by commas (,).

SOURCE: Stephen Kemp, "Mme. Galli-Curci Tells How to Sing Foster's Most Famous Song," *Musical Observer* 24, no. 4 (April 1925): 9–10.

~~~~~~~

Edward "Duke" Ellington (1899–1974) in collaboration with the screenwriter Sid Kuller (1910–1993) and songwriter Paul Francis Webster (1907–1984), wrote the stage musical revue Jump for Joy *in 1941 as a protest against theatrical stereotypes of black life and culture. In the prologue to the show, the "Sun Tanned Tenth of the Nation" went into action. From the pit, Duke Ellington spoke a verse (more or less in ballad meter) that used Foster as the punch line.*

Now, every Broadway colored show,
According to tradition,
Must be a carbon copy
Of the previous edition,
With the truth discreetly muted,
And the accent on the brasses.
The punch that should be present
In a colored show, alas, is

Disinfected with magnolia
And dripping with molasses.
In other words,
We're shown to you
Through Stephen Foster's glasses.

SOURCE: Edward "Duke" Ellington, *Jump for Joy*, ed. Martin Williams and Patricia Willard (Washington, D.C.: Smithsonian Collection of Recordings, 1988): 13.

~~~~~~~

Ray Charles (1930–2004) scored his first big hit by turning "Old Folks at Home" into "Swanee River Rock" (1957). Charles changed the words to eliminate what Ellington called the "magnolia" and the "molasses," and Charles gospelizes it. This text transcription, which includes the back-up interpolations of the Raylets, a female quartet, suggests the vitality of Charles's reinterpretation of Foster's tune into a "rock-and-soul" song.

SWANEE RIVER ROCK

Do you know? Way down [way down]
down upon the Swanee [Swanee]
Talk'n 'bout the river [river] yeah
You know I'm so far [so far] so far away [so far away].
Oh yeah
Do you know that's where [that's where]
Where my heart is a turning [turnin'] oh, ever [ever]
That's where [that's where]
That's a-where the old folks stay
Ah—All the world is sad and lonely now
Everywhere I roam [roam, roam, roam].
Keep a telling you my darlin' [darlin']
How my heart is growin' sad [so sad] and lonely [lonely]
Because I'm so far [so far]
I'm far from my folks back home [the folks back home].

All the world is sad and lonely now
Everywhere I roam
Keep a telling you my darling
How my heart is growin sad
So sad and lonely
Because I'm so far
So far from my folks back home
Yeah

I'm far from my folks back home
Yeah
So far from my folks back home
Yeah
Oh far from my folks back home
Yeah

SOURCE: Ray Charles, "Swanee River Rock," from *The Birth of Soul: The Complete Atlantic Rhythm & Blues Recordings, 1952–1959* (Atlantic & Atco Remasters Series, 1991): CD 3. Text transcription by Anna Kijas, following the precedent in William Austin, *"Susannah," "Jeannie," and "The Old Folks at Home": The Songs of Stephen C. Foster from His Times to Ours* (New York: Macmillan, 1975): 339–40. This version differs in a few details.

~~~~~~~

NOTE

1.   A "bullgine" is a steam locomotive.

25

THE FASOLA FOLK, *THE SOUTHERN HARMONY,*

AND *THE SACRED HARP*

(Walker, White and King)

During the mid-1800s, new musical styles for Christian hymnody emerged from the fervor of evangelical movements in "the West" (Ohio and Kentucky) and in the South (particularly Alabama and Georgia). Folk spirituals still treasured for their beauty today, among them "Idumea," "Wayfaring Stranger," "Zion's Walls," and "Wondrous Love," found their way into new anthologies for social worship. In two classic publications, *The Southern Harmony* and *The Sacred Harp,* this music is linked to a unique performance practice tradition called "shape-note" singing. Shape-note notation reduces the seven-note-scale syllabic pattern to four syllables—fa, sol, la, mi—and accompanies each syllable with its own distinctive shape: triangle, circle, square, diamond. It is intended to simplify sight-singing and thereby improve congregational singing. While the term "fasola singers" comes from this solmization, such technical details do not capture the sense of community that accompanies the whole tradition nor the understated power of the singing style.

In *The Southern Harmony* (1835), editor William "Singing Billy" Walker claimed that almost 100 of his songs had "never before been published." Among them was "New Britain," known today as "Amazing Grace," set as a three-voiced contrapuntal hymn in archaic elegance, and reprinted here as the first selection. By 1866, with two more editions of *The Southern Harmony* to his credit, Walker estimated he had sold approximately 600,000 copies. Acknowledging its historical importance, the Federal Writers' Project of the Works Progress Administration (WPA) reproduced a facsimile of the first edition of *The Southern Harmony* in 1939. Annual "big singings" of music from *The Southern Harmony*, held in Benton, Kentucky, still honor Walker's legacy, with the beautiful hymn "Holy Manna" traditionally opening the festivities.

When settings in *The Sacred Harp* (1844) moved from three voices to four, the repertoire embraced a wider variety of songs, including standards from New England singing-school composers, camp meeting revival hymns, and new material by its two editors, B. F. White and E. J. King. The book launched a publications dynasty within the fasola tradition, and White issued four editions of *The Sacred Harp* in his lifetime.

White and King actually borrowed the text for their "General Observations" from their rival William Walker in their second edition of *The Sacred Harp*. Aimed at amateur singers, their work documented choral practices which differ from today's conventions. Women doubled the tenor part, men doubled the treble (soprano) part, changes in dynamics were encouraged, and even improvised ornamentation was practiced. And tunes took priority over words, as rule 18 suggests.

"NEW BRITAIN" AS FOUND IN *THE SOUTHERN HARMONY*

Shape note facsimile of "New Britain," now better known as "Amazing Grace" from *The Southern Harmony*, 1854: 8.

SOURCE: William Walker, *The Southern Harmony, and Musical Companion*, 2nd ed., ed. Glenn C. Wilcox (Philadelphia, 1854; reprint, Lexington: University Press of Kentucky, 1987): xxvii–xxix. Also available in score with midi versions of tunes at http://www.ccel .org/w/walker/sharm.

FROM THE SECOND EDITION OF *THE SACRED HARP*

A person or persons may be well acquainted with all the various characters in psalmody, (or music;) they may also be able to sing their part in true time, and yet their performance be far from pleasing; if it is devoid of necessary embellishments, their manner and bad expression may conspire to render it disagreeable. A few plain hints, and also a few general and friendly observations, we hope will tend to correct these errors in practising of vocal music.

GENERAL OBSERVATIONS

I. CARE should be taken that all the parts (when singing together) begin upon their proper pitch. If they are too high, difficulty and perhaps discords will be the consequence; if too low, dulness and languor. If the parts are not united by their corresponding degrees, the whole piece may be run into confusion and jargon before it ends; and perhaps the whole occasioned by an error in the pitch of one or more of the parts of only one semitone.

2. It is by no means necessary to constitute good singers that they should sing very loud. Each one should sing so soft as not to drown the teacher's voice, and each part so soft as will admit the other parts to be distinctly heard. If the teacher's voice cannot be heard it cannot be imitated, (as that is the best way to modulate the voice and make it harmonious,) and if the singers of any one are so loud that they cannot hear the other parts because of their own noise, the parts are surely not rightly proportioned, and ought to be altered.

3. When singing in concert the bass should be sounded full, bold, and majestic but not harsh; the tenor regular, firm, and distinct; the counter clear and plain, and the treble soft and mild, but not faint. The tenor and treble may consider the German flute; the sound of which they may endeavour to imitate, if they wish to improve the voice.

4. Flat keyed tunes should be sung softer than sharp keyed ones, and may be proportioned with a lighter bass; but for sharp keyed tunes let the bass be full and strong, but never harsh.

5. The high notes, quick notes, and slurred notes, of each part, should be sung softer than the low notes, long notes, and single notes, of the same parts. All the notes included by one slur should be sung at one breath if possible.

6. Learners should sing all parts of music somewhat softer than their leaders do, as it tends to cultivate the voice and give them an opportunity of following in a piece with which they are not well acquainted; but a good voice may be soon much injured by singing too loud.

7. When notes of the tenor fall below those of the bass, the tenor should be sounded strong, and the bass soft.

8. While first learning a tune it may be sung somewhat slower than the true time or mood of time requires, until the notes can be named and truly sounded without looking on the book.

9. Learners are apt to give the first note where a fuge [fuguing tune] begins nearly double the time it ought to have, sounding a crotchet almost as long as a minim in any other part of the tune, which puts the parts in confusion by losing time; whereas the fuges ought to be moved off lively, the time decreasing (or the notes sung quicker) and the sound of the engaged part or parts increasing in sound as the others fall in. All solos or fuges should be sung somewhat faster than when all the parts are moving together.

10. There are but few long notes in any tune but what might be swelled with propriety. The swell is one of the greatest ornaments to vocal music if rightly performed. All long notes of the bass should be swelled if the other parts are singing short or quick notes at the same time. The swell should be struck plain upon the first part of the note, increase to the middle, and then decrease softly like an echo, or die away like the sound of a bell.

11. All notes (except some in syncopation) should be called plain by their proper names, and fairly articulated; and in applying the words great care should be taken that they be properly pronounced and not torn to pieces between the teeth, nor forced through the nose. Let the mouth be freely opened, but not too wide, the teeth a little asunder, and let the sound come from the lungs and be entirely formed where they should be only distinguished, viz. on the end of the tongue. The superiority of vocal to instrumental music, is that while one only pleases the ear, the other informs the understanding.

12. When notes occur one directly above another, (called choosing notes,) and there are several singers on the part where they are, let two sing the lower note while one does the upper note, and in the same proportion to any other number.

13. Your singers should not join in concert until each class can sing their own part correctly.

14. Learners should beat time by a pendulum, or with their teacher, until they can beat regular time, before they attempt to beat and sing both at once, because it perplexes them to beat, name time, and sound the notes at the same time, until they have acquired a knowledge of each by itself.

15. Too long singing at a time injures the lungs.*

*A cold or cough, all kind of spirituous liquors, violent exercise, too much bile on the stomach, long fasting, the veins overcharged with impure blood, &c. &c. are destructive to the voice of one who is much in the habit of singing. An excessive use of ardent spirits will speedily ruin the best voice. A frequent use of some acid drink, such as purified cider, vinegar, and water mixed and sweetened a little with honey, or sugar with a little black or cayenne pepper, wine, and loaf sugar, &c. if used sparingly, are very strengthening to the lungs

16. Some teachers are in the habit of singing too long at a time with their pupils. It is better to sing but only eight or ten tunes at a lesson, or at one time, and inform the learners the nature of the pieces and the manner in which they should be performed, and continue at them until they are understood, than to shun over forty or fifty in one evening, and at the end of a quarter of schooling perhaps few beside the teacher know a flat keyed tune from a sharp keyed one, what part of the anthem, &c requires emphasis, or how to give the pitch of any tune which they have been learning unless some one inform them. It is easy to name the notes of a tune, but it requires attention and practice to sing them correctly.

17. Learners should not be confined too long to the parts that suit their voices best, but should try occasionally the different parts, as it tends greatly to improve the voice and give them a knowledge of the connexion of the parts and of harmony as well as melody.* The gentlemen can change from bass to tenor, or from tenor to bass, and the ladies from treble to tenor, &c.

18. Learners should understand the tunes well by note before they attempt to sing them to verses of poetry.

19. If different verses are applied to a piece of music while learning, it will give the learners a more complete knowledge of the tune than they can have by confining it always to the same words. Likewise applying different tunes to the same words will have a great tendency to remove the embarrassment created by considering every short tune as a set piece to certain words or hymns.

20. When the key is transposed, there are flats or sharps placed on the stave, and when the mood of time is changed, the requisite characters are placed upon the stave.

21. There should not be any noise indulged while singing, (except the music,) as it destroys entirely the beauty of harmony, and renders the performance very difficult, (especially to new beginners;) and if it is designedly promoted is nothing less than a proof of disrespect in the singers to the exercise, to themselves who occasion it, and to the Author of our existence.

22. The apogiatura [sic] is placed in some tunes which may be used with propriety by a good voice; also the trill over some notes; but neither should be attempted by any one until he can perform the tune well by plain notes, (as they add nothing to the time.) Indeed no one can add much to the beauty of a piece by using what are generally termed graces, unless they are in a manner natural to their voice.

23. When learning to sing, we should endeavour to cultivate the voice so as to make it soft, smooth, and round, so that when numbers are performing in

---

*Melody is the agreeable effect which arises from the performance of a single part of music only. Harmony is the pleasing union of several sounds, or the performance of the several parts of music together.

concert, there may on each part (as near as possible) appear to be but one uniform voice. Then, instead of confused jargon, it will be more like the smooth vibrations of the violin, or the soft breathings of the German flute. Yet how hard it is to make some believe soft singing is the most melodious, when at the same time loud singing is more like the hootings of the midnight bird than refined music.

24. The most important ornament in singing is strict decorum, with a heart deeply impressed with the great truth we utter while singing the lines, aiming at the glory of God and the edification of one another.

25. All affectation should be banished, for it is disgusting in the performance of sacred music, and contrary to that solemnity which should accompany an exercise so near akin to that which will through all eternity engage the attention of those who walk in climes of bliss.

26. The nearest perfection in singing we arrive at, is to pronounce the words* and make the sounds as feeling as if the sentiments and sounds were our own. If singers when performing a piece of music could be as much captivated with the words and sounds as the author of the music is when composing it, the foregoing directions would be almost useless; they would pronounce, accent, swell, sing loud and soft where the words require it, make suitable gestures, and add every other necessary grace.

27. The great Jehovah, who implanted in our nature the noble faculty of vocal performance, is jealous of the use to which we apply our talents in that particular, lest we use them in a way which does not tend to glorify his name. We should therefore endeavour to improve the talent given us, and try to sing with the spirit and with the understanding, making melody in our hearts to the Lord.

SOURCE: "The Sacred Harp," 2 ed. By B. F. White & E. J. King. (Philadelphia: S. C. Collins, N. E. Corner Sixth and Minor Streets, 1860): 23–24. Also see: http://digital.lib.msu.edu/ projects/ssb/display.cfm?TitleID=610&Format=jpg&Pagenum=001. "Shaping the Values of Youth: Sunday School Books in 19th Century America."

*In singing there are a few words which should vary a little from common pronunciation, such as end in i and y; and these should vary two ways. The following method has been generally recommended: In singing it is right to pronounce majesty, mighty, lofty, &c. something like majestee, mightee, loftee, &c.; but the sense of some other words will be destroyed by this mode of expressing them; such as sanctify, justify, glorify, &c. These should partake of the vowel O, rather than EE, and be sounded somewhat like sanctifay, justifay, glorifay, &c. It would indeed be difficult to describe this exactly; however, the extreme should be avoided on both sides.

26

𝓐 SIDEBAR INTO THE DISCOVERY OF

SHAPE-NOTE MUSIC BY A NATIONAL AUDIENCE

(Jackson, *The Sacred Harp,* 1991)

Fasola singing came to the attention of a national audience after George Pullen Jackson (1874–1953) published his classic study *White Spirituals in the Southern Uplands* (1933). A professor of German at Vanderbilt University, Jackson directed a choral group that performed shape-note hymns in concert, and he even issued a few recordings.

Jackson's book stirred up unexpected admiration among contemporary urban composers. Aaron Copland and Ruth Crawford Seeger, for example, read modernism into the spare quartal harmonies of shape-note settings, and they made inventive arrangements of some of the hymns. In a column on "America's Musical Autonomy," for the *New York Herald Tribune* on March 12, 1944, Virgil Thomson championed Jackson's work within the field of "United States musical folklore" as "full of sensational discoveries," and the impact of these discoveries on Thomson's unique musical idiom has been frequently acknowledged.

In the first excerpt, Jackson discusses regional differences between the North and South, typically reproaching Yankees for what he regards as unduly formal musical habits. Jackson would later generate much scholarly controversy through his insistence that black spirituals arose from and were dependent upon white spirituals, ignoring their performance practice as a crucial element of history.

SOUTHERNIZING OF SONGS

From what has been said above in connection with *Sacred Harp* singing in conventions, it may be inferred that vocal practice and the printed or notated page differ. This is true. It is also true that the fasola folk sing in a manner quite different from any present-day vocalism I have ever heard in any other section. I have already mentioned one of these differences—their more rapid tempo, or their penchant for singing more notes to the minute. I have also touched upon their unwillingness to tolerate, in any one of the four harmonic parts, long sequences of the same note repeated for successive text syllables and words. A third difference is their bent for melodic ornamentation.

When a song was made in the South, especially in the South Carolina–Georgia section, it was almost sure to show those earmarks. When it originated elsewhere—in the North or the East and was subsequently sung in the South and incorporated in southern song books—the local peculiarities were often grafted upon it, a practice which our Georgia musician, William Hauser, rightly called "southernizing." In Hauser's *Hesperian Harp*, page 347, is a song called "Prescott." And at the top right of this song we read, "Composed originally by Geo. Oates; but here *Southernized* by Wm. Hauser." I found the song which was subjected to the southernizing process in the *Christian Minstrel* (page 283), a song book which was made in Philadelphia (1846) by a Pennsylvanian and aimed at northern buyers and singers. The melody of this song has the same note sequence in both northern and southern versions. It is in the bass and the middle parts that the difference between northern and southern arrangements appears, as the following samples will show:

It will be noticed that the servile and eventless northern alto has become southernized into a sequence that sounds like a fairly good independent tune. What violence such changes may have done to the harmony seems to have been looked upon as a secondary matter. The first rule was to make each part melodically interesting. And in this the fasola productions remind us strikingly of fifteenth-century polyphonic practice.

On the preceding pages we have given many illustrations of the fasola leaning toward the more-notes-to-the-minute style of delivery. Their fondness for dance tunes was one clear indication of this bent. I have found no such songs in northern-used books. When Pennsylvania's Jesse Aiken accepted the moderately lively and enormously popular "Greenfields" ("How tedious and tasteless the hours") for use in his *Christian Minstrel,* he was careful to preserve his

professional dignity by explaining at the top right that the tune was "inserted by particular request." The southern fasola folk had no dignity to preserve, no draggy church traditions to up-
hold. Hence they all used "Greenfields" without apology. They hurried their borrowed songs as
is seen in "Prescott," where the 3/2 tempo is changed to 3/4. And they made new tunes with perfect freedom to indulge their sectional tendency.

ORNAMENTATION

The third feature of southern fasola singing, ornamentation, seldom gets into the notation. Watch
closely a singer of *Sacred Harp* or *Southern Harmony* tunes and you will realize that the page before him shows only a fraction of what he sings. Like old-timey handwriting, his vocal production
is full of stylistic flourishes. One of these flourishes, noticeable especially in closing cadences,
is that in which the voice, usually a man's voice, flips up momentarily, on its transition from one
long tone to another lower one, to a falsetto grace note much higher than either of the notes in the
melody proper and then returns, equally momentarily, to the original note before proceeding to
the closing one.

. . .

The striking difference between the song tastes of northern and southern singers in the
first half of the nineteenth century is emphasized by the 1840 edition of Timothy and Lowell
Mason's *Sacred Harp* (Cincinnati). I find in that comprehensive collection *only one* of the eighty
tunes which are listed above as the most widely popular in the South. That one song was the "Go
Tell Aunt Rhody" tune, called "Greenville," MPT 80.[1] But, after all, this difference may not be so
much a matter of singers' tastes as a matter of compilers' tastes, the southern compilers allowing the singers to sing what they like; the northern compilers providing the public with what they
should sing.

> SOURCE: George Pullen Jackson, *White Spirituals in the Southern Uplands* (Chapel Hill:
> University of North Carolina Press, 1933; reprint, New York: Dover, 1965): 209–13.

*Jackson did not live long enough to witness a historical irony. As the big singing con-
ventions of* The Sacred Harp *declined in the South, interest in shape-note music
moved northward. In New England—so hospitable to folk revivals in general and to
early music as well—a regional preservationist renaissance of sorts has taken root.
There a small but loyal following of musicians, often based in universities, organizes
singings and contributes new music to the repertoire. In a new edition of* The Sacred
Harp *in 1991, the preface sustain the optimism of commitment. Most important,
the section on "Rudiments"—from which we have taken only a few key passages—
relishes the now-venerated deviations from conventional harmony.*

PREFACE: *THE SACRED HARP,* 1991 EDITION

Since the *Sacred Harp* was first compiled in 1844 by Benjamin Franklin White, it has been revised only four times: 1869, 1911, 1936 and 1991. However, an appendix was added in 1850, 1859, 1960, 1967, and 1971. So, you see, the *Sacred Harp* has been left alone for most of its life.

Each revision and each appendix was done to put new life in the books, each time adding new or present-day authors. This is the main reason it has lasted so long and will continue to survive.

We bless and revere the memory of those venerable patriarchs who dedicated their lives to the support of *Sacred Harp* music and through whose efforts and leadership the book was improved at various times. Today the book is more popular and is used throughout the United States of America.

In conclusion, we the music committee appointed by the President of the Sacred Harp Publishing Company, Inc., in 1985 thank all who have spoken words of encouragement or helped us in any way. We respectfully submit the work performed by us, and we hope and pray that it will satisfy the great demand of the music people throughout this country.

        Respectfully submitted,
        The Music Committee

RUDIMENTS OF MUSIC

Author's Note. The *Sacred Harp* tradition is separate and distinct from other musical traditions. Accordingly, these rudiments are based on those of previous editions of the *Sacred Harp* by Paine Denson (*Original Sacred Harp, Denson Revision*, 1936), Joe S. James (*Original Sacred Harp,* 1911), and B. F. White and E. J. King (*Sacred Harp,* 1844) except where these are incomplete or where they conflict with actual practice.

Chapter I: Introduction

. . .

5.   The *Sacred Harp* uses **four-part harmony**. The parts, in order of increasing pitch, are **bass** (sung by men), **tenor** (men and women), **alto** (usually women), and **treble** (men and women). The doubling of the tenor and treble (and sometimes the alto) in the vocal ranges of men and women creates an effect of six- (or seven-)part harmony.

. . .

Chapter VI: Mechanics of Singing

. . .

4.   The voice should be natural and unpretentious. The ideals of popular, art, concert, and opera singing do not apply to the *Sacred Harp*. In particular, few traditional *Sacred Harp* singers produce a conscious **vibrato**, or pulsation of the voice. In group singing, vibrato can create undesired harmonic effects.

. . .

Chapter VIII: Harmony and Composition

. . .

3. Late 18th-century New England composers (represented in the *Sacred Harp* by Billings, Read, Swan, Morgan, and others) used harmony that is basically **tertian**, that is, based on intervals of thirds. In contrast, the harmony used by the early 19th-century compilers of singing-school manuals (such as the *Sacred Harp*) is basically **quartal**, that is, based on intervals of fourths, and their close relatives, fifths. In the early 20th century alto parts were added to the three-part pieces in the *Sacred Harp,* resulting in a hybrid harmony, part quartal and part tertian.

. . .

12. One rule of conventional harmony that is frequently violated in the *Sacred Harp* states that chords should be complete triads (or triads augmented with another note). In fact, most of the chords in 19th-century compositions are dyads. Even when alto parts were supplied in the 20th century, many of the chords were left as dyads by having the alto double a note in the existing harmony. This is especially true of minor pieces.

13. Another rule of conventional harmony prohibits the motion of parts in parallel (or consecutive) fifths and octaves, where two voices maintain a constant interval over several notes. Parallel octaves are built into *Sacred Harp* singing when men and women sing the same part. In addition, parallel fifths between parts are a natural part of quartal harmony, and they abound in the *Sacred Harp.*

. . .

Chapter XI: Organization and Conduct of Singings and Conventions

1. An **annual singing** lasts one day and a **convention** two days or more. In another sense, a convention is an organization that sponsors singings. A **special singing** occurs only once, has a frequency other than annual, or occurs irregularly. Most **all-day singings** last from 9 or 10 a.m. to 3 or 4 p.m. Conventions, churches, or other groups sponsor **singing schools,** where one can learn to read music and sing from the *Sacred Harp.*

2. Although the proceedings at singings tend to be informal, there is a formal structure of officers and committees, and the minutes of singings are usually published.

SOURCE: The Sacred Harp: The Best Collection of Sacred Songs, Hymns, Odes, and Anthems Ever Offered the Singing Public for General Use, rev. ed. (Carrollton, Ga.: Sacred Harp Publishing, 1991): 13, 21, 22, 25. Excerpts from "Rudiments of Music" revised by John Garst.

~~~~~~~~~

NOTE

1.   No explanation of MPT is found in Jackson's list of abbreviations.

27

THE BOSTON PUBLIC SCHOOLS SET A NATIONAL

PRECEDENT FOR MUSIC EDUCATION

In 1837, the Boston School Committee accepted the arguments of petitioners Lowell Mason (1792–1872) and his colleagues to incorporate the teaching of vocal music
into the public-school curriculum. Their report established a precedent for publicly
funded music education across the country. Unlike the authors of the *Bay Psalm
Book,* they offered mainly secular rationales. American enterprise stands behind
their official position. Mason helped to found a music school known as the Boston
Academy of Music in 1833. To secure the approval of the Boston bureaucracy, Mason
taught vocal music as an experiment in the city's public schools free of charge for
one year.

REPORT ON MEMORIAL OF
THE BOSTON ACADEMY OF MUSIC,

And on petitions signed by sundry citizens, praying that music may be
introduced into the public schools of the city.

School Committee, August 24, 1837.

The select Committee of this Board, to whom was referred the memorial of the Boston Academy of Music, together with two petitions signed by sundry respectable citizens, praying that instruction in vocal Music may be introduced into the Public schools of this City, having had the matter under consideration, ask leave to present the following

Report:

The Committee have given to the subject that attention which its importance required. They have afforded the memorialists [petitioners] a hearing, and availed themselves of such means of information as it was in their power to obtain. After mature deliberation and a careful scrutiny of arguments and evidence, the Committee are unanimously of opinion that it is expedient to comply with the request of the petitioners. As, however, the subject is one but recently presented to this community, and one therefore upon which much honest difference of opinion, and perhaps some prejudice, may be supposed very naturally to exist, the Committee are desirous to spread before the Board the reasons which have led to their conclusion. If there be weight or value in these reasons, the conclusion grounded on them will not probably be denied; if on the other hand, they be fallacious or unsound, the weakness and the fallacy will both here and elsewhere be exposed. The Committee invite the Board to a dispassionate examination of the question. When viewed in all its bearings, it is one, in their opinion, of great public interest. At the same time, it must be admitted, there are peculiar difficulties in the way of its discussion. Music has, in popular language, too generally been regarded as belonging solely to the upper air of poetry and fiction. When, however, it is made the grave subject of legislative enactment, it is necessary to summon it from this elevation, and checking the discursive wanderings of the imagination, consider it in connection with the serious concerns of real life. The Committee will endeavor to discuss the question with the sobriety which the occasion demands. They are well aware that the cause which they support can find no favor from a Board like this, except so far as it reaches the convictions through the doors, not of the fancy, but of the understanding.

There are two general divisions which seem, in the opinion of the Committee, to exhaust the question. The *first* is, the intrinsic effect of the study of vocal Music, as a branch of instruction in the schools, and on them; and *secondly*, its extrinsic effect as a branch of knowledge without them. Under these two divisions we propose to treat the subject.

There is a threefold standard, a sort of chemical test, by which education itself and every branch of education may be tried. Is it intellectual—is it moral—is it physical? Let vocal Music be examined by this standard.

Try it *intellectually*. Music is an intellectual art. Among the seven liberal arts, which scholastic ages regarded as pertaining to humanity, Music had its place. Arithmetic, Geometry, Astronomy and Music, these formed the *quadrivium*. Separate degrees in Music, it is believed, are still conferred by the University of Oxford. Memory, comparison, attention, intellectual faculties all of them, are quickened by the study of its principles. It is not ornamental merely. It is not an accomplishment alone. It has high intellectual affinities. It may be made, to some extent, an intellectual discipline.

Try Music *morally*. There is,—who has not felt it,—a mysterious connection, ordained undoubtedly for wise purposes, between certain sounds and the moral sentiments of man. This is not to be gainsaid, neither is it to be explained. It is an ultimate law of man's nature. "In Music,["] says Hooker, ["]the very image of virtue and vice is perceived."[1] Now it is a curious fact, that the natural scale of musical sound can only produce good, virtuous, and kindly feelings. You must reverse the scale, if you would call forth the sentiments of a corrupt, degraded, and degenerate character. Has not the finger of the Almighty written here an indication too plain to be mistaken? And if such be the case, if there be this necessary concordance between certain sounds and certain trains of moral feeling, is it unphilosophical to say that exercises in vocal Music may be so directed and arranged as to produce those habits of feeling of which these sounds are the types? Besides, happiness, contentment, cheerfulness, tranquility,—these are the natural effects of Music. These qualities are connected intimately with the moral government of the individual. Why should they not, under proper management, be rendered equally efficient in the moral government of the school?

And now try music *physically*. "A fact,["] says an American physician, ["]has been suggested to me by my profession, which is, that the exercise of the organs of the breast by singing contributes very much to defend them from those diseases to which the climate and other causes expose them." A musical writer in England after quoting this remark, says, "the Music Master of our Academy has furnished me with an observation still more in favor of this opinion. He informs me that he had known several persons strongly disposed to consumption restored to health, by the exercise of the lungs in singing." But why cite medical or other authorities to a point so plain? It appears self-evident that exercises in vocal Music, when not carried to an unreasonable excess, must expand the chest, and thereby strengthen the lungs and vital organs.

Judged then by this triple standard, intellectually, morally, and physically, vocal Music seems to have a natural place in every system of instruction which aspires, as should every system, to develope man's whole nature.

. . .

To those, then, not acquainted with the subject, it may be necessary to state that the Pestalozzian system, as it has been called, has been applied to Music. The works of Nägeli and Pfeiffer, now in general use upon the continent of Europe, are founded on this system.[2] These works were introduced into this country by Mr. William C. Woodbridge, of whose early services in this cause, it is here fitting to make honorable mention. They led soon afterwards to the formation of the Boston Academy of Music, an institution destined, it is believed, to achieve great good in this community. One of the objects in forming the Academy was to carry vocal Music, by the aid of its Professors, into the schools, and they have since published a Manual of vocal Music, constructed upon the basis of the works just mentioned. Of this Manual, an eminent musical writer in England says "it is the best work on the subject in the English language, and it is highly creditable to the new world to have set such a pattern to the old." According to the principles of the Manual, a lesson in vocal Music, as given by the Professors of the Academy, is not unlike a lesson in Arithmetic.[3] Musical takes the place of numerical notation. The blackboard, not the book, is before the pupil, and by the use of his own faculties and senses he goes from principle to principle, till the whole science is evolved. How then can an exercise of this kind be adverse to discipline? On the contrary, it is itself a discipline of the highest order, a subordination of mind, eye, and ear, unitedly tending to one object; while any deviation from that object is at once made known. Melody is concerted action, and is discipline aught else? "Where Music is not, the Devil enters," is a familiar German proverb in regard to schools; and after witnessing the lessons in Music as given according to the Pestalozzian system, the Committee do not hesitate to say, that if any want of discipline follow the introduction of vocal Music into a school, the fault must be with the Master of that school,—it is not in the system.

. . .

SOURCE: "Report [of the select committee, to whom was referred the memorial of the Boston academy of music, together with two petitions signed by sundry respectable citizens, praying that instruction in vocal music may be introduced into the public schools of this city]," in *City Documents: Consisting of Miscellaneous Reports Made to the City Council, by Committees, Boards, and Other Departments of the City Government with an Index.* Com. Council Document no. 19, Boston Public Library, Government Documents no. 3 in 7594.10 (Boston: John H. Eastburn, 1838): 1–4, 9–10.

~~~~~~~

NOTES

1. Edward William Hooker (1794–1875) was a minister in the Boston area who frequently lectured on the importance of sacred music.
2. Michael Traugott Pfeiffer and Hans Georg Nägeli, *Aussug aus der Gesangbildungslehre nach Pestalozzischen Grundsätzen, von Pfeiffer und Nägeli zunachst für Volksschulen bestimmt* (Zürich: H. G. Nägeli, 1810).
3. Lowell Mason published *The Manual of the Boston Academy of Music for Instruction in the Elements of Vocal Music on the System of Pestalozzi* in 1834. This was the official text for the academy's music-teacher training course.

28

LORENZO DA PONTE RECRUITS AN
ITALIAN OPERA COMPANY FOR NEW YORK

Lorenzo Da Ponte (1749–1838), the librettist of Mozart's three great comic operas, moved in 1805 to New York (where he would die), tenaciously importing the culture of his homeland. At eighty, he produced a season of Italian opera, four years after the success of Manuel García's company, the first to perform authentic Italian opera in the United States. After he helped García (1775–1832) with the American premiere of *Don Giovanni* (1826), Da Ponte wondered if that success could be repeated. He recruited Giacomo Montresor, an opera impresario from Bologna, to mount some new productions. Unfortunately, the troupe suffered financial disaster on a grand scale. This letter, published in full in English for the first time, contains many astute observations on American musical taste and the challenges of importing foreign-language opera. Occasional flashes of Da Ponte's wit illuminate his persuasive powers; his injunction to Montresor to "hope and dare" evokes the bravura of his own personality.

New York, August 1st, 1831.

Most esteemed Mr. Giacomo,

Your letter unfortunately arrived a bit too late so it is not possible for me to answer you today as the ship for Havre had already departed when I received it. Now, however, I do not want to lose any time in answering you. Please pay close attention and keep in mind that it is an 83 year-old man who is writing to you, a man who has dedicated more than half his life to the glory of his country and knows well the affairs of the theater. Also, after 26 years of observations and experience, I can as well say without arrogance that I know the character of the Americans with whom I live. This said, and with my generally recognized honesty as a guarantee, I have the daring to tell you with the greatest frankness in the world that a good and well-organized company of Italian singers would make a fortune in America. I have said a good company, but I should have said a very good, magnificent, excellent company, so that it could compete with and possibly win over that of Garzia [sic]. I think this will be difficult, but not impossible, nor very complex. It will be barely possible to replace Garzia's daughter and, for some roles, Garzia himself. However, if the entire company proves to be of good quality, this would compensate for the lack of perfection for [the absence of] those two [Manuel García and his daughter, the future Maria Malibran] and would be enough to ensure the reputation of the company. Before giving you a precise answer to what you ask concerning me and this country, I will tell you my opinion on this very important point [having a company of good quality], upon which depends the success of this most noble enterprise. If you can provide a prima donna *singer, a skilful* prima buffa *or, as people say, one good for the billboard, an excellent* primo basso *singer, an excellent comic character, a good tenor, a second tenor who if not a great singer is at least a good-looking one, a young woman able to perform the parts of man-woman and woman-man, for example in the role of the page in the Figaro, please bravely come to America and your destiny as well as that of your fellows will be bright. Aside from what I have outlined for you, I am the first to advise you to remain in Italy, even if I am eager to see a good opera in New York. Supposing that you will be able to do what I have asked you, I will answer your letter point by point.*

I will see the owner of the best theater of this city as soon as possible and I will try to obtain a written agreement of his wants and conditions. In the meantime I will gather all my friends and pupils (I have had no less than 1,800 in this city) and I will see if it will be possible to convince them to construct a theater—they had wanted to do so, with my intermediation, for Garzia, but Garzia foolishly refused to accept. For the moment I can tell you something that will be useful to you as a reference. There are two theaters which have had major success in this city. One costs 6,000 colonnati, the other costs 14,000 [colonnati] in rent.[1] However, it would not be difficult to obtain [this theater] for this amount, since, other than drama, hosts the comedy and the national tragedies. The fact that this [theater] is in a better situation than the other does not mean that it is more necessary or useful. To convince you of this you only need to know that when Garzia left from New York, his daughter sang alone with a pack of dogs for several nights, and the impresario paid her 600 colonnati, still having high profits. Before I will send this letter, I will see what [conditions] can be obtained and I will inform you about this.

Regarding the permission of the government and of the certainty to have the pos-sibility to sing without taxes or additional fees, please be absolutely calm. The govern-ment does not deal with such business at all. There is no theater that belongs to it, and it does not pay for or ask for payments on the entertainments of the citizens. As long as there is order, decency, observance of the laws and public peace, everyone can do what-ever he or she prefers: stay, come, and go wherever he or she likes, and having amuse-ment where, how and when he or she enjoys. If my word is not enough, to absolve you of any doubt you simply need to know that every year a company of cats, I mean cocks (it was a[n] error of pen)[2] comes from New Orleans to New York and then moves to Philadelphia, Boston, Baltimore and to some other cities in America. After a tour of two or three months, they go back to New Orleans with their pockets filled by silver and with the applause of all who enjoy French screaming and caterwauling of the cats in measure. I would bang my head against the walls every time I read the praise those venal hacks or long-eared Midases (there are many in America, too) give to these guastan mestieri.[3] In the meantime, however, they laugh and enjoy it, saying joyously before leaving [to go back to New Orleans] to their compatriots and friends: "See you next August!" So one says: "Have all the Italians lost their courage?" If they only had one fourth of [the courage that] these French (that we in Italy would receive with whis-tles and rotten tomatoes, and are applauded here in America) have, the success ob-tained by Garzia as well as the things that I myself have said and said again, it would have been enough to spread the wings of the Italians and fly without hesitation to America. This way, they would have passed from the hell (that is today the whole Europe) to the terrestrial paradise of the America[s], securely accumulating earnings, and coming back to Italy to enjoy them in more tranquil times.

I cannot give you a precise answer concerning what you ask about the upper-circle boxes, since there are no upper-circle boxes in these theaters. There is a first, a second and a third order in addition to that of the gallery. However, separations are not made to divide spectator from spectator. At a glance, the effect is perhaps even better [than in European theaters] since everyone can talk with his neighbors, having only a division made by low tables that are distinguished by doors and exterior numbers. The space of these almost-cells is much larger than our balconies, both in breadth and in depth. Each of them easily contain[s] eighteen to twenty people seated on small stairs. I think the first three levels contain more than 1,200 people, more than 400 in the parterre, and at least 300 in the fourth level. One night the theater was sold-out and yielded 1,600 piastre despite rumors of possible theft. For the first three levels, one pays one colonnato, three quarters for the parterre, and one quarter for the galleria. The sub-scribers (for one year or just one trimester) do not have any decrease in price. The only advantage is the possibility to choose a preferred place. There are three or four reserved upper-circle boxes, and these have a higher cost. Giuseppe Bonaparte[4] had one in the time of Garzia. This is everything I know regarding this point. I will, however, speak with the owner to learn more, particularly if there are any privileged places that do not have to belong to a new impresario. I know that the owner of the theater has one, but I think all others are free. Rumors are that expenses per night are 200 piastre but I would know how to decrease them by one third. From Italy you should bring an excel-lent first violin, a good oboe, a master for the harpsichord, and a prompter. It would be a good thing to bring a theatrical painter too, since the local ones ask for sixty times more than they need. Do not bring a copyist but make sure that all the operas you wish to perform will have all the single parts for all instruments, since here copies cost six times that which it costs in Italy. If paints, as I believe, are not expensive in Italy, it will be better [to bring] a supply of it, as well as strings for violins and [contra]bass, and reams of music paper for anything that could happen. [Here] there is enough cloth but I do not know the different prices: I will inquire about it. Concerning the choir singers I do not know what to say. We have a lot of them, and they are usually better than the Italians. However, when they sing our words, they excoriate the ears of the listeners. If you could bring over six to eight singers who would be able to perform a rudimentary ballet in addition to singing in the choir, I think this could make an excellent impression in a country that has never seen one [a ballet] before.

Now I will tell you something about the choice of operas. Mozart and Rossini are undoubtedly the two masters who curry the most favor in America. So, you should bring along with you Mozart's Le nozze di Figaro *and* Il Don Giovanni, *and Rossini's* Il Barbiere di Siviglia *and* La gazza ladra *(in addition to some of his other* opere buffe*) which have been appreciated and will be appreciated at any time. Also bring some of the more popular operas of the most renowned modern [composers]. I think, however, that many operas of the past would greatly please local audiences, and I would advise you to have in your collection Paisiello's dramas* Il re Teodoro, La molinara *and* I zingari, *Sarti's* Le gelosie villane *and* I litiganti, *Martini's* Cosa rara, L'arbore di Diana *and* La capricciosa corretta, *Cimarosa's* L'impresario in angustie *and* Il matrimonio segreto, *Guglielmi's* La pastorella nobile *and Salieri's* L'Assur re d'Ormus.[5] *If your company does not own these dramas, you will be able to have them for almost nothing, since in Italy everyone fell asleep. Here, however, they will not sleep, and they will not let anyone sleep in the theater. Tastes have changed in Italy but not for the better and [what has happened] to the great Mozart is a testament to this. I also advise you to have with you a great quantity of separate arias, duets, trios, and quartets, and I will take care of fitting them with the parts of the actors. I know every singer has his or her own strong points: please bring them with you and I will make them gallop, flying in the sky as Ruggiero on the hippogriff.[6] I am old and I have one foot and a half in the grave but, if a good Italian opera [company] comes to America, I think I will be rejuvenated in a moment and I will become more robust than Hercules. You cannot imagine, dear Mr. Giacomo, how much I care about this matter; I, that created myself the taste for the Italian language and literature in the whole America; I, that taught more than 1,800 people to speak and to write the language of Petrarch and Boccaccio, introducing their immense beauty; I, that brought 18,000 volumes of chosen works only in this city [New York], defending them against our envious rivals, placing them in various libraries and, at my expense, in the colleges that previously did not know of them and could not appreciate them; I, poor as all poets, old, without friends or help, I have accomplished and I keep accomplishing all [these] things; I anticipate that the enchantment of our music would give almost generally a new impulse to the love and study of our [suave/ gentle] language. This is only the scope of my goals and the sweetest desire of my honored heart. Everything I say, however, is nothing more than a drop of water compared to the whole ocean if confronted with the things made by me to honor my poor, wretched, and sacrificed homeland. Please come and you will see.*

Concerning the gift you are expecting or that at least you would have from the 50,000 piastre of subscription which you talked about with my brother, or the pecuniary disbursement, or the stocks,[7] or similar things that are usual in Europe, we should not even talk about it. The Americans are almost all merchants: they make business of everything, even of the entertainment. Come, do everything possible to please [the audience], awaken the enthusiasm for pleasure in some people and the hope for profit in others, and then hope and dare. And, if you become disillusioned with this, call me a buffoon if you want or stupid. Some leading people of the city offered 100,000 piastre of subscription to Garzia, with my intermediation a few days before he left. I repeat this to you and I ask you to say it in my name to everyone who wants to understand and has courageous heart.

I will do whatever is in my power, and I will do it with the strength of [my] soul, now and forever for you and all you[r] followers. I will see the amateurs as soon as possible, all friends or pupils of mine, and I will try to persuade them to obtain in your name a fair contract from the owner of one of the best theaters. I will also try to arrange the payments and to receive a certain number of boxes or tickets for several nights as a compensation for the company that will come. Unfortunately, during this season almost everyone is in his countryside home. However, I will make sure to organize everything well, I will write, request, I will stimulate desires, and at the right time I will write you to describe the effect of my actions which will be like the results of a good lawyer, and an honest, impartial, and sincere friend.

I say again that all will depend upon the merit of the singers. Four excellent, two good, and two or three not bad. This is what is needed, and there you will be. I have some other things to tell you, but I do not have any more space in this letter. Please read it to your friends, and if this will not be enough, it will be their fault. If Mombelli is still alive and you can see him, talk to him about me. He knows me and he knows that everything I say is gold. Give him my respects and work it so that he will give you his daughter.[8] You cannot bring less to make a good impression. We have here a German female singer who has good voice and good taste, and we also have two Italians who can play roles if necessary. You know Rosich and Dorigo and you know how good they are. We also have Ferron, who is very good as well and could be useful.[9] I will not miss writing to Havana, and I will write you soon to tell you everything that could be useful and what can be hoped [from this enterprise]. I will not send a copy of this letter to Maestro Centroni but I will inform him of everything. Please write me back immediately.

Cordially your friend,

Lorenzo Da Ponte

SOURCE: Lorenzo Da Ponte, *Storia incredibile ma vera, della compagnia dell'opera italiana, condotta da Giacomo Montresor in America, in Agosto dell'anno 1832* [*An Incredible Story but a True One: A History of the Italian Opera Company Brought to America by Giacomo Montresor in August of the Year 1832*] (1833); republished in Cesare Pagnini, *Memorie e altri scritti di Lorenzo Da Ponte* (Milan: Longanesi, 1971): 784–91. Translated and edited with annotations for this book by Davide Ceriani.

~~~~~~~~~

NOTES BY DAVIDE CERIANI

1. It is not clear how to translate *colonnati* into American currency. Aleramo Lanopoppi, in *Lorenzo Da Ponte: Realta e leggenda nella vita del librettista di Mozart* (Venice: Marsilio, 1992), translates the term as "dollars."

2. Here, Da Ponte is punning on the Italian words *gatti* (cats) and *galli* (Gauls, or the French).

3. Literally, "saboteurs of professions," or "wreckers of professions."

4. Joseph Bonaparte (1768–1844), older brother of Napoleon Bonaparte, lived in New Jersey and Philadelphia from 1816 to 1839.

5. Most of these operas were either fashionable in Vienna when Da Ponte worked there as a court poet or they included him as a librettist. "Martini" refers to Martín de Sóler.

6. *Ippogrifo* in Italian, after the mythical animal created by Ludovico Ariosto in his *Orlando Furioso.*

7. Da Ponte literally says *carato*, meaning the stocks one owns in a company, firm, or enterprise.

8. Mombelli's daughter Ester was at that time a well-known soprano and an esteemed interpreter of Rossini's operas.

9. Paolo Rosich and Elisabetta Ferron came to America with García's company.

29

MUSIC EDUCATION FOR AMERICAN GIRLS

Before the Civil War, the numerous private schools for girls, known at the time as "female academies" or "female seminaries," offered musical training and lessons in voice and some instruments. Many popular cantatas by American composers [e.g., George Root's *The Flower Queen* (1852), and William Bradbury's *Esther* (1856)] were written with this student population in mind. Root also published an anthology, *The Young Ladies' Choir* (1846). Mid-nineteenth-century taste is displayed in the account and program for a "soirée musicale" at Cherry Valley Female Seminary in New York, which demonstrates the standard concert taste of the period as well as the level of achievement of the students in some institutions which made music a speciality. The concert includes opera arrangements, pieces composed by visiting piano virtuosi, and even one composition by Beethoven.

The selection "Mems for Musical Misses," which appeared in one of the leading culturally sophisticated magazines of the period, combines musical advice with a set of social values that gives us the context for training women to be "accomplished." These values encouraged women to become reasonably skilled amateurs, to learn to sing in their social circles, to play piano music for dancing—and not to take themselves too seriously as artists. But of course many did (see chapter 40).

MUSICAL PROGRESS

The programme of a *Soirée Musicale* to be given by Mr. J. A. Fowler and his pupils at the Female Academy at Cherry Valley, a beautiful and picturesque village in the center of this State [New York], is given below, omitting the names of the performers which we are not at liberty to insert. For many years foreigners only were considered qualified to assume the *baton* or direct the studies of those aiming at a high standard in music, but of late years intelligent and educated Americans are beginning to take the field, and every day brings us the gratifying intelligence of their enterprise and success in this vocation.

Twenty-five years ago such an entertainment as the one inserted below could only have been given by the best artists in the country. Now, in a Female Seminary, remote from the great Emporium of Art, some of the most difficult and elaborate compositions are rendered in a style, (judging from Fowler's former entertainments,) rarely excelled by the most skillful artists. We notice in the programme over thirty different performers, and only regret that we cannot be in their midst to witness the triumph of well directed native talent in the most divine of arts.

When Mr. Fowler first came to Cherry Valley, about twelve years since, there were only six pianos in the place. Now there are over one hundred besides the instruments used in the institution. A large Female Institution has been built up, not by a stock company, but by subscription, and Mr. Fowler has had during the last term over sixty pupils in the musical department. So much for musical progress in a little town of only nine hundred inhabitants.

PROGRAMME—PART FIRST

1—OVERTURE—Il Pirata—arranged for two pianos, eight hands. (Bellini.)

2—MARCHE ITALIENE—arranged for two pianos[,] eight hands. (Donizetti.)

3—SOLO—Favorite Air, with variations, piano. (Grobe.)

4—POLKA BRILLIANTE—Arranged for two pianos, eight hands, and harp. (Strauss.)

5—DUO CONCERTANTE—Variations and Rondeau Brilliant,—O! Dolce Concerto—two pianos. (Herz.)

6—SOLO—Le Palais d'hiver, Mazurka Caprice, piano. (Goria.)

7—POLKA BRILLIANTE—Arranged for two pianos, 12 hands. (Jullien.)

8—SOLO—Variations Brilliantes—Somnambula, Piano. (Beyer.)

9—REVIEW MARCH—Arranged for two pianos, eight hands. (Glover.)

10—SOLO—La Fille du Regiment, Grande Fantasie, Piano. (Strakosch.)

11—GRAND DIVERTISSMENT—Two pianos. (Greulich.)

12—SOLO AND CHOURUS—Bird of the North. (Root.)

PART SECOND

1—OVERTURE—Egmont—arranged for two pianos, eight hands. (Beethoven.)

2—GRAND MARCH—Arranged for two pianos, eight hands. (Blessner.)

3—GRAND DUO CONCERTANTE—Two pianos, Op. 15. (Herz.)

4—MARCH FROM THE PROPHET—Arranged for two pianos, eight hands. (Meyerbeer.)

5—SOLO—Comin' Thro' the Rye, Piano. (Jaell.)

6—KATY-DID POLKA—Arranged for two pianos, eight hands, flute, violoncello, and harp. (Jullien.)

7—SOLO—Variations Brilliantes—Lucia di Lammermoor, piano. (Mocker.)

8—CHORUS—The Comparison. (German.)

9—SOLO—La Sylphide—Fantasie Romantique, piano. (Strakosch.)

10—SOLO—March from Norma, harp. (Bochsa.)

11—SOLO—Duke of Reichstadt's Waltz—with variations, piano. (Le Carpentier.)

12—PRIMA DONNA WALTZ—Arranged for two pianos, eight hands, flute and violoncello. (Jullien.)

SOURCE: "Musical Progress," unsigned column in *Musical World and Times* 9, no. 14 (August 5, 1854): 161.

~~~~~~~

MEMS FOR MUSICAL MISSES

S IT in a simple, graceful, unconstrained posture. Never turn up the eyes, or swing about the body: the expression you mean to give, if not heard and felt, will never be understood by those foolish motions which are rarely resorted to but by those who do not really feel what they play. Brilliancy is a natural gift, but great execution may be acquired: let it be always distinct, and however loud you wish to be, never thump. *Practice* in private music far more difficult than that you play in general society, and aim more at pleasing than astonishing. Never bore people with ugly music merely because it is the work of some famous composer, and do not let the pieces you perform before people not professedly scientific be too long. If you mean to play at all, do so at once when requested: those who require much pressing are generally more severely criticised than others who good-humoredly and unaffectedly try to amuse the company by being promptly obliging. Never carry books about with you unasked; learn by heart a variety of different kinds of music to please all tastes. Be above the vulgar folly of pretending that you can not play for dancing; for it proves only that if not disobliging, you are stupid. The chief rule in performing this species of music is to be strictly accurate as to time, loud enough to be heard amid the dancers' feet, and always particularly distinct—*marking* the time: the more expression you give, the more life and spirit, the better will your performance be liked: good dancers can not dance to bad music. In waltzes the first note in the bass of every bar must be strongly accented. In quadrilles the playing, like the dancing, must be gliding. In reels and strathspeys the bass must *never* be running—always octaves—struck with a strong staccato touch; and beware of playing too quick. In performing simple airs, which very few people can do fit to be listened to, study the *style* of the different nations to which the tunes belong. Let any little grace be clearly and neatly executed, which is never done brilliantly or well by indifferent performers of a higher style of merit. Make proper pauses; and although you must be strictly accurate as to time, generally speaking, it should sometimes be relaxed to favor the expression of Irish and Scotch airs. Beware of being too sudden and abrupt in your *nationalities*—caricaturing them as it were—which ignorant and sometimes indeed scientific performers often do, totally spoiling by those "quips and cranks" what would otherwise be pleasing, and which sounds also to those who really understand the matter very ridiculous. Do not *alter* national airs; play them simply, but as *full* as you please, and vary the bass. In duets, communicate your several ideas of the proper expression to your fellow-performer, so that you may play into one another's hands—give and take, if I may so express myself; and should a mistake occur, do not pursue your own track, leaving your unfortunate companion in difficulties which will soon involve yourself; but cover it as well as you can, and the generality of listeners will perhaps never discover that one was made, while the more sapient few will give you the credit you deserve.

As regards singing, practice two or three times a day, but at first not longer than ten minutes at a time, and let one of these times be before breakfast. Exercise the extremities of the voice, but do not dwell long upon those notes you touch with difficulty. Open the mouth at all times, in the higher notes especially, open it to the ears, as if smiling. Never dwell upon consonants. Be distinct from one note to another, yet carry them on glidingly. Never sing with the slightest cold or sore throat. Vocalize always upon A, and be careful to put no B's before it. Never take breath audibly. Begin to shake *slowly* and steadily. Practice most where the *voce di petto* (chest voice) and the *voce di gola* (throat voice) join, so as to attain the art of making the one glide imperceptibly into the other. The greatest sin a singer can commit is to sing out of tune. Be clear, but not shrill; deep, but not coarse.

When you intend to sing, read the words, and see that you understand them, so as to give the proper expression. Let all your words be heard: it is a great and a common fault in English singers to be indistinct. Study flexibility. Practice both higher, louder, and lower than you sing in public; and when practicing, open your mouth wider than it would be graceful to do in company. Do not change the sound of the letters; sing as like speaking as you can. It is better to sing *quite plain* than to make too many turns and trills: these, when attempted at all, should be executed very neatly. Study simplicity: it is better to give no expression than false expression. Never appear to sing with effort or grimace; avoid affectation and every peculiarity. Never sit when you sing, if you can possibly help it, but stand *upright*. Give more strength in ascending than in descending. Do not suffer yourself to be persuaded to sing soon after eating. Accidental sharps ought to be sung with more emphasis than accidental flats. The Italian vowels *a* and *i* have always the same sound, but *e* has two different ones: the first like the *ai* in *pain*; the other like *ea* in *tear, wear*, or *swear*. *O* has also two sounds: one like *o* in *tone*; the other like the *au* in *gaudy*. Articulate strongly your *double* consonants when singing French or Italian. The voice is said to be at its best at eight-and-twenty, and to begin to decline soon after forty, when the more you strain and try to reach the higher notes that are beginning to fail you, the quicker you hasten the decay of your powers. Children should never be allowed to sing much, or to strain their voices: fifteen or sixteen is soon enough to begin to practice constantly and steadily the two extremities of the voice; before that age, the middle notes only should be dwelt upon, or you run the risk of *cracking*, as it is termed, the tones. Never force the voice in damp weather, or when in the least degree unwell; many often sing out of tune at these times who do so at no other. Take nothing to clear the voice but a glass of cold water; and always avoid pastry, rich cream, coffee, and cake, when you intend to sing.

SOURCE: "Mems for Musical Misses," *Harper's New Monthly Magazine* (September 1851): 488–89.

30

CARLY EXPRESSIONS OF CULTURAL NATIONALISM

(Hopkins, Fry, *Putnam's Monthly*)

In the young United States, expressions of cultural nationalism took (and still do take) many forms. In the 1840s and 1850s, American composers, trying to scale the magic mountain of concert music, often felt oppressed by the European patriarchs on the summit. With so few orchestral resources available to them, they believed American-based orchestras had a special obligation to let their music be heard and American audiences had a special obligation to listen.

Making room for fledgling efforts required the kind of determination shown by the midcentury writer and composer Charles Jerome Hopkins (1836–1898), who stated his case for a New York–based American Musical Union in 1855.

THE CAUSE OF AMERICAN MUSIC

[Letter to the] Ed. of The Musical World—*I am glad to see the interest for American music has at last begun to exhibit itself in the proposed organization of an association to be called the* "N.Y. American Musical Union," *for the purpose of encouraging the efforts of young American composers and having their productions performed in a suitable manner—of course, provided they are considered sufficiently meritorious by a competent committee.*

The Association is to consist of an instrumental quartet (to be increased to an octet, if considered expedient), a vocal quartet (to be increased to a sextet under the same condition), and good amateur vocalists, and performers on the different instruments, the desire being to give all kinds of compositions a fair trial, and a chance of being properly performed, except those requiring a full Orchestra and Chorus.

It is the intention of the gentlemen already interested in this new idea, to give a Soirée every month or two months, as may be the more acceptable, during the winter season, on which occasions nothing but American compositions will be presented.

This idea has already received the sanction of many of our most accomplished and respectable musical amateurs, among whom is Mr. Pell, the able conductor of the 'Euterpean Orchestral Society.'

It has not been "considered necessary to confine" the privilege of membership to native Americans, but to allow foreigners to belong thereto, provided only their principles are Republican, and their aim be in common with us, the production of native art. One of this latter description is Mr. Fritz Mollenhauer, the celebrated violinist under whose able direction, the instrumental Quartet party belonging to the new association expects to flourish.

It is the opinion of many, and it has been often asserted, more especially by foreigners, that America can boast of no classical music.

Now such an assertion only shows the ignorance of the perpetrator thereof, for, as our efforts thus far in collecting American musical compositions have proved, it does exist, and to a greater extent than many imagine. But heretofore there has been no chance for a native composer to place his music before the public in such a manner as to have it fairly tried and impartially judged. We speak now more particularly with regard to classical chamber music.

For example, how often has it been ironically asked, where are your American quartets, quintets, etc.? We are glad we can answer such questions, and inform the inquirer where he can find not only quartets and quintets, but overtures and symphonies for full score of orchestra, all the works of native Americans who have never been out of the country.

But, it may be asked, "Is all this music good for anything? Is it classic and original?" Suffice it to say, that in Philadelphia, where a party has been in the habit of performing some of this "American music," and that party consisting in a great measure of German professors of music, some of the quartets have been pronounced equal to Onslow or Spaeth!

Some of your readers may have a little curiosity to know who this composer might be. We answer that it is Mr. Charles Homman [sic],[1] now living in Brooklyn, a gentleman whose retiring disposition and native modesty, have been the principal barriers to his having become long ere this, one of the most celebrated, if not the most so, of American composers.

We have already in our possession three instrumental pieces from the pens of Mr. Hommann, and Mr. George F. Bristow, the talented conductor of the New York Harmonic Society. And we have in prospect many other kinds of compositions from different composers.

We think it will only be necessary for it to be generally known that there is now a chance for all young Americans who desire to distinguish themselves by musical composition to have their labors rewarded by a fair trial and impartial criticism to secure the good will and coöperation of many individuals who otherwise would be disposed to throw a bucket of cold water upon the embryo idea of such a thing.

But to all those who object to it on the ground that American music is not good music, it is un-classical, plagiaristic, or unfit to be compared with German productions, we would say, "Give it a fair trial." If Americans do not know how to compose now, it does not follow that they never will know how. Let them try it.
[signed] Justitia[2]

SOURCE: [Charles Jerome Hopkins], letter, *Musical World* 12, no. 7 (June 16, 1855): 79; Cited and quoted in Vera Brodsky Lawrence, ed., *Strong on Music: The New York Music Scene in the Days of George Templeton Strong:* vol. 2, *Reverberations, 1850–1856* (Chicago: University of Chicago Press, 1995): 749–50.

~~~~~~~

Perhaps no American musical figure gained so much publicity—good and bad—for his advocacy of American classical music than William Henry Fry (1813–1864), composer of the opera Leonora. Fry served as music critic for Horace Greeley's newspaper, the New York Tribune, in that city from 1852 on, and in November of that year, he gave a series of public lectures on the history and aesthetics of music. Fry also loved a good fight, and his eleventh lecture, he lambasted the American public for its indifference to the plight of American artists. It is not useful to chronicle every punch Fry threw or received in return when discussing emerging classical composition in this era. Still, occasionally, Fry rose above himself and waved the flag with such powerful sweeps that his polemic packed a wallop. Here is a short paragraph of Fry at his most eloquent from his eleventh lecture, the full text being lost, but sections from which were quoted in newspapers.

It is time we had a Declaration of Independence in Art, and laid the foundation for an American School of Painting, Sculpture, and Music. Until this Declaration of Independence in Art shall be made—until American composers shall discard their foreign liveries and found an American School—and until the American public shall learn to support American artists, Art will not become indigenous to this country, but will only exist as a feeble exotic, and we shall continue to be provincial in Art. The American composer should not allow the name of Beethoven, or Handel or Mozart to prove an eternal bugbear to him, nor should he pay them reverence; he should only reverence his Art, and strike out manfully and independently into untrodden realms, just as his nature and inspirations may invite him, else he can never achieve lasting renown.

SOURCE: William Henry Fry as quoted in Irving Lowens, *Music and Musicians in Early America* (New York: Norton, 1970): 217–18.

~~~~~~~~~

Fry and his colleague, composer George Frederick Bristow (1825–1898) both partic-ipated in a famous critical brawl around this time, recounted here in Putnam's Monthly Magazine. *The argument concerned the lack of American music performed in the concert programs of the New York Philharmonic Society. Bristow felt so strongly about this that he resigned his post in the orchestra for a while. The editor gives the relevant details while also making the case for art as a transnational, in-deed, universal language. The issues discussed here are still argued today.*

FROM THE COLUMN TITLED "EDITORIAL NOTES—MUSIC"

Among civilized nations there is, probably, none so little musical as the American. In any company of a score of men the chance is that not one sings. It may be assumed that a glee is impossible among them. In Italy, Germany, France, Spain, in all the northern nations, and, perhaps, England, the chances are precisely the reverse. We do not regard the Ethiopian opera and the popularity of *Old Folks at Home* as proof of a general musical taste. At the concerts of the Philharmonic Society at least half of the audience is German, and at the Opera, if the number of those who go in obedience to fashion and from other unmusical notions, is deducted, there is not a large audience left. But we do not wish to decide too soon. The experiment of the best artists with low prices is yet to be tried. We are sure of one thing, as we have been from the be-ginning, that it will be a sad failure if it be attempted to base the success of the undertaking upon any sympathy or support other than musical. The structure of society in this country is really so different from that of other countries, that any such effort must fail, as it deserves to fail.

If, however, we have not heard much music during the winter, there has been a musi-cal correspondence as bitter and fierce as the doings of musicians are so sure to be. It com-menced by a notice, by Mr. Willis, Editor of the *Musical World and Times,* of Mr. Fry's music. That gentleman responded in defence of his music, and, in the course of the correspondence claimed a position as a composer, which Mr. Willis would by no means allow. Assertions were made to the effect that the Philharmonic Society gave no countenance to American productions, which drew Mr. Bristow and the Society into the correspondence. The Editor of *Dwight's Journal of Music,* published in Boston, had a word to say, in the most good-humored manner; but Messrs. Fry and Bristow, who pursued the subject with great ardor, took every thing in sad seriousness, and the latter gentleman, as we understand, resigned his connection with the Philharmonic Society. Whether Mr. Fry succeeded in establishing the point that his music is as good as anybody's music, we are unable to say. It seems to us, however, that he mistook the means of doing so. If a man can compose as well as Mozart and Beethoven, let him do it. If a man can paint as Titian painted,—let him paint and not talk about his painting. If he has composed and painted, and insists that the result is as good as Titian's and Mozart's, but that, of course, we are so prejudiced in favor of the old and foreign that we will not recognize the excellence,—then, equally, it is foolish to argue the matter, for the very objection proposed, proves the want of that critical candor which can alone justly decide the question. If we like music because it is old and foreign, it is clear that we do not like it for its essential excellence. But Mr. Fry claims to compose fine music,—why, then, should he heed the opinion of those who do not determine according to the intrinsic value, but by some accidents of place and time? Why does he not go on composing, and leave his works to appeal to the discriminating and thoughtful both of this and of all ages? Burke advised Barry to prove that he was a great painter by his pencil and not by his pen. It was good advice, we think, because it was common sense.

We are glad to state that the Philharmonic was never more flourishing than it is now. It is unfortunate that their concerts were given in the Tabernacle, that most dingy and dreary of public halls. But the music performed was of the best. It was German music, most of it, it is true,—but then, German music comprises so much of the best of all instrumental compositions, that it was almost unavoidable. Has Mr. Fry, and those who complain of over-much German in the selections of this Society, yet to learn that art is not, in any limited sense, national? Raphael's *Transfiguration* is as much American as Italian. A devout Catholic of the western hemisphere feels its meaning and enjoys its beauty as much as the Pope. Homer celebrates events occurring before America was discovered, but he is much dearer to a thoughtful American than Joel Barlow. In the realm of art it is not possible to introduce distinctions so invidious. The best of every great performance in art is human and universal. It is not what is local and temporary which makes the fame of a great artist, but it is that which the world recognizes and loves, and there is nothing more pernicious to the cause of real culture than this effort to institute a mean nationality in art. Mr. Fry may be very sure that we shall prefer Shakespeare, and Mozart, and Michel Angelo, whether they were born in Greenland or Guinea, to any American who does not do as well as they. . . .

SOURCE: *Putnam's Monthly Magazine of American Literature, Science, and Art* 3, no. 17 (1854): 564–65.

~~~~~~~~

NOTES

1. Charles Hommann (1803–after 1866), primarily active in Philadelphia, was a composer of symphonic and chamber compositions.
2. Vera Brodsky Lawrence identifies the writer as the American composer Charles Jerome Hopkins in Lawrence, ed., *Strong on Music: The New York Music Scene in the Days of George Templeton Strong: vol. 2, Reverberations 1850–1856* (Chicago: University of Chicago Press, 1995): 749.

31

JOHN S. DWIGHT REMEMBERS HOW HE AND HIS CIRCLE "WERE BUT BABES IN MUSIC"

John Sullivan Dwight (1813–1893) was the most influential music critic in nineteenth-century America. He was the first writer to make a living at the perilous trade of music criticism and his *Journal of Music* (1852–1881) gave him a national platform for his views. "Dwight's" had everything in it: reports from around the country and from Europe by his correspondents, letters from readers, reviews of concerts and books, and of course, lots of Dwight's opinions. As Dwight settled into prominence, his views hardened into dogma and snobbery. But the younger Dwight had developed his aesthetics in the context of one of the liveliest progressive intellectual movements of the nineteenth century. In this selection, Dwight remembers the thrill of the discovery of "great music" for himself and his New England friends.

And such friends! Dwight's circle included the leaders of transcendentalism. Dwight began his work life as a Unitarian preacher, but became an avid transcendentalist in the 1840s. He joined the Transcendental Club (a group which began in 1836 and included Emerson, Margaret Fuller, and Thoreau) and wrote articles for the *Harbinger* and the *Dial* (both transcendentalist magazines). His first extended treatise on music was published by another important transcendentalist, Elizabeth Peabody. He lived at the utopian arts colony Brook Farm near Concord, Massachusetts, for several years. More aesthete than theologian, Dwight became a minister of and to art, so to speak, transferring his sense of the divine to his philosophy of music. One transcendentalist belief maintained that music had the innate spirituality to override religious sectarianism. Dwight's "mass clubs," which he proudly recalls here, are cases in point: the glory of music enabled Protestants—and even non-Christians— to sing the words of the Catholic mass and experience God.

Dwight avoided the term "Romantic" to describe his aesthetics, though he was influenced by German idealism and the transformative power of classical music as a social force for the good. His ideas influenced Henry Lee Higginson, the founder of the Boston Symphony Orchestra (see chapter 54). Further, Dwight's equation of Emerson and Beethoven found echoes in Charles Ives (see chapter 63).

MUSIC A MEANS OF CULTURE

Our musical history has been peculiar. We were in no sense a musical people forty years ago. Nothing could be further from the old New England character and "bringing up,"—we will not call it culture. But, strangely (and not much in accordance with the common theory that the way to elevate the taste is to begin with what is light and popular), the first real and deep interest in music awakened here in Boston was an interest in the greatest kind of music. Handel, and then more irresistibly Beethoven, were the first to take deep hold on thoughtful, earnest, influential souls. This was when the new spirit of culture, in the fullest, freest, highest sense, became in various ways so rife in this community. So that it is scarcely paradoxical to say, that music in this country, or at least this portion of the country, "came in with the Conqueror." That is to say, the love for the highest kind of music (for it is only the love of it, not the creative gift as yet), which has for some time been imputed to this once Puritanical Boston and the regions spiritually watered from it, came in with the conquering *ideas,*—with the ideas of spiritual freedom, of self-reliance, of the dignity of human nature, of the insignificance of creeds compared with life and practice, of social justice, equal opportunities to all, a common birthright in the beautiful,— ideas which from the time of Channing[1] began to quicken the whole thought and conscience of the young Republic, and which were glowing with fresh fervor of conviction in the light of that ideal philosophy which, where it made one mystic, made a dozen practical and sound reformers, —ideas fitly summed up in the one idea of CULTURE, in the nobler sense in which it then began to haunt the mind, as something distinct from, and superior to, the barren routine of a narrow, utilitarian, provincial, and timid education; culture in the sense of free unfolding of intrinsic germs of character, of conscious, quick, sincere relationship and sympathy with all the beauty and the order of the universe, instead of in the old sense of a mere makeshift clothing upon from without with approved special knowledges, conventional beliefs and maxims, and time-honored prejudices. Intimately implied in this idea of culture is the aesthetic principle. For what is culture without art?—art, the type and mirror of ideal, complete life, the one free mode of man's activity, wherein he may become partaker in the Divine creative energy? And what form of art, what ministry to the aesthetic instinct, was so peculiarly the need and product of our age, so widely, easily available, as music? It was not strange that it should come in with the conquering ideas, as we have said.

At all events, it is a fact of some significance that the interest here felt in Beethoven began at the same moment with the interest in Emerson,[2] and notably in the same minds who found such quickening in his free and bracing utterance. It was to a great extent the young souls drawn to "Transcendentalism" (as it was nicknamed), to escape spiritual starvation, who were most drawn also to the great, deep music which we began to hear at that time. For, be it re-membered, the first great awakening of the musical instinct here was when the C Minor Sym-phony of Beethoven was played, thirty years ago or more, in that old theatre long since vanished from the heart of the dry-goods part of Boston, which had been converted into an "Odeon," where an "Academy of Music" gave us some first glimpses of the glories of great orchestral music.[3] Some may yet remember how young men and women of the most cultured circles, whom the new intellectual dayspring had made thoughtful and at the same time open and im-pressible to all appeals of art and beauty, used to sit there through the concert in that far-off upper gallery or sky-parlor, secluded in the shade, and give themselves up completely to the in-fluence of the sublime harmonies that sank into their souls, enlarging and coloring thenceforth the whole horizon of their life. Then came the Brook Farm experiment; and it is equally a curi-ous fact, that music, and of the best kind, the Beethoven Sonatas, the Masses of Mozart and Haydn, got at, indeed, in a very humble, home-made, and imperfect way, was one of the chief interests and refreshments of those halcyon days. Nay, it was among the singing portion of those plain farmers, teachers, and (but for such cheer) domestic drudges, that the first example sprang up of the so-called "Mass Clubs," once so much in vogue among small knots of amateurs. They met to practise music which to them seemed heavenly, after the old hackneyed glees and psalm-tunes, though little many of them thought or cared about the creed embodied in the Latin words that formed the convenient vehicle for tones so thrilling; the *music* was quite innocent of creed, except that of the heart and of the common deepest wants and aspirations of all souls, darkly locked up in formulas, till set free by the subtile solvent of the delicious harmonies. And our genial friend who sits in Harper's "Easy Chair"[4] has lately told the world what parties from "the Farm" (and he was "one of them") would come to town to drink in the symphonies, and then walk back the whole way, seven miles, at night, elated and unconscious of fatigue, carrying home with them a new good genius, beautiful and strong, to help them through the next day's labors. Then, too, and among the same class of minds (the same "Transcendental set"), began the writ-ing and the lecturing on music and its great masters, treating it from a high spiritual point of view, and seeking (too imaginatively, no doubt) the key and meaning to the symphony, but any-how establishing a vital, true affinity between the great tone-poems and all great ideals of the human mind. In the "Harbinger," for years printed at Brook Farm, in the "Dial," which told the time of days so far ahead, in the writings of Margaret Fuller[5] and others, these became fa-vorite and glowing topics of discourse; and such discussion did at least contribute much to make music more respected, to lift it in the esteem of thoughtful persons to a level with the rest of the "humanities" of culture, and especially to turn attention to the nobler compositions, and away from that which is but idle, sensual, and vulgar.

The kind reader will grant plenary indulgence to these gossiping memories, and must not for a moment think it is intended by them to claim for any one class the exclusive credit of the impulse given in those days to music. Cecilia[6] had her ardent friends and votaries among conservatives as well. But is it not significant as well as curious, that the free-thinking and ide-alistic class referred to (call them "Transcendental dreamers" if you will, they can afford to bear the title now!) were so largely engaged in the movement,—that among the "select few," constant to all opportunities of hearing the great music in its days of small things here, so many of this class were found? The ideas of those enthusiasts, if we look around us now, have leavened the whole thought and culture of this people; have melted icy creeds, and opened genial communion between sects; have set the whole breast of the nation heaving, till it has cast off the vampire of at least one of its great established crimes and curses; have set all men thinking of the elevation of mankind. These are the conquering ideas, and with them came in the respect for music, which now in its way, too, is leavening, refining, humanizing our too crude and swaggering young democratic civilization. A short pedigree! but great ideas, by their transforming power, work centuries of change in a few years.

The great music came in then because it was in full affinity with the best thoughts stirring in fresh, earnest souls. The same unsatisfied, deep want that shrank from the old Puritanic creed and practice; that sought a positive soul's joy instead of abnegation; that yearned for the "*beauty* of holiness," and for communion with the Father in some sincere way of one's own without profession; that kindled with ideals of a heaven on earth and of a reign of love in harmony with Nature's beauty and the prophecies of art,—found just then and here unwonted comfort, courage, and expression in the strains of the divine composers, of which we were then getting the first visitations. It was as if our social globe, charged with the electricity of new divine ideas and longings, germs of a new era, were beginning to be haunted by auroral gleams and flashes of strange melody and harmony. Young souls, resolved to keep their youth and be true to themselves, felt a mysterious attraction to all this, though without culture musically. Persons not technically musical at all would feel the music as they felt the rhythm of the ocean rolling in upon the beach. They understood as little of the laws of one as of the other fascinating and prophetic mystery. Beethoven, above all, struck the key-note of the age; in his deep music, so profoundly human, one heard, as in a sea-shell, the murmur of a grander future. Beethoven, Handel, Mozart, found no more eager audience than among these "disciples of the newness"[7] (as some sneeringly called them), these believing ones, who would not have belief imposed upon them, who cared more for life than doctrine, and to whom it was a prime necessity of heart and soul to make life *genial*. This was to them "music of the future," in a more deep and real sense than any Wagner of these later times has been inspired to write.

All this, to be sure, does not prove us to be a "musical people." It does prove that the great music, into which great, earnest men like Beethoven breathed the secret of their lives, has a magnetic, quick affinity with the great thoughts and impulses beginning at that time to renew religion, politics, society, and the whole spirit and complexion of the age.

. . .

We were but babes in music, doubtless, and capable of little scientific understanding of the works we heard with rapture. Shall it be said, then, that this love was mostly affectation, or illusion? What was the so great need of understanding? Are great poems written, are great pictures painted, were the old cathedrals planned and reared, only for those who have themselves the knowledge and the power to do the like? The picture in the window which all passers stop to see was not made solely or mainly for professional enjoyment, but for mere laymen also, ignorant of the art that made it, yet open, it may be, to the full influence and beauty of the thing made. Is nature spread out only for astronomers and physicists and chemists, or to rejoice and raise, refine and harmonize, the unscientific heart and soul of you and me? The least instructed of us may like the greatest kind of music, for the same reason that he likes the greatest kind of man; for the same reason that we enjoy real poetry more than that which is weak and commonplace, or find ourselves happier with Shakespeare than with Tupper.[8] May not a community which prefers an Emerson for its lecturer be credited with all sincerity in choosing to sit under the influence of Beethoven rather than of Verdi, finding itself more warmed thereby? And if you are personally attracted to a fine, deep, genial nature, rather than to a shallow creature of convention, why should you not be to the music into which some finer, deeper natures put their very lives? It is not our own fault, surely, if we find that we love Mozart, as we love Raphael or Shakespeare, and turn to such when we most need strengthening refreshment, while we should be simply bored by miscellaneous concerts, pot-pourris of the hackneyed sentimentalities or flash fancies of third and tenth rate composers. And if a man insist that this is all sheer self-illusion, and that we really do not like the thing we think we do, of what use can it be to argue with him? Friend, be you true to your love, as we too would be true to ours! We will not quarrel.

Our point is simply: The great music has been so much followed and admired here, not by reason of any great musical knowledge in said followers[,] not because we have any technical musicianship or proper musicality, but purely because the music was *great,* deep, true, making itself felt as such; we love the music for the great life that is in it. Let the emphasis fall on the word *great,*—*great* music,—if you still find it hard to credit our capacity of pleasure in mere music pure and simple.

From such beginnings, by degrees, and for a long time through the medium of very poor means of performance,—which only confirms our theory, that it was some inkling of the divine ideas, the life within the symphony, that first caught the imagination of listeners not very musical, it might be,—there grew up here a pretty deep and general love of noble music; until, at length, for better or for worse (we think for better), music occupies this people's time and thought quite largely, yet not so largely as it will and must do. What may be called a "musical movement" is making headway. Much froth about it, no doubt, there is; much vainglory, splurge, and sounding advertisement; too much passion for excitement, for the extraordinary, for "big things." Our great choral societies, for example, may shrink from the real great work, from the sincere, quiet, outwardly unrewarding tasks, which build up the artistic character, which are the true tests of sufficiency in art, in favor of the easier enterprise that carries with it more *éclat* and advertisement. They may postpone solid everyday excellence to exhibition splendors, festivals, and jubilees on some unprecedented scale. But all this implies a genuine heart-life in music somewhere. Where there is smoke there must be fire. Fuss and feathers make the greater show and catch the vulgar; but it is because heroes have been and will be again when God and a great crisis call. Do not charge all the egotism and vanity of musical artists, their catering to low tastes by cheap display, their grandiloquent announcements, their jealousies of one another, to music, or even wholly to themselves. It is the speculating, sordid, money-getting fever of the whole world around them that does the mischief, sets the singers at loggerheads, lowers the standard of composers and performers, and tempts the artist soul to sell its birthright and become a travelling thaumaturgic virtuoso. Music would make all this better, could she become ten times the public mistress that she is.

SOURCE: John S. Dwight, "Music a Means of Culture," *Atlantic Monthly* 26, no. 155 (September 1870): 321–25.

~~~~~~~~

NOTES

1. William Ellery Channing (1780–1842) was the religious leader of Unitarianism, a movement centered in Boston in the 1830s and 1840s.

2.   Ralph Waldo Emerson (1803–1882), a philosopher of transcendentalism, rose to public prominence in Boston in the late 1830s and 1840s. By the time Dwight wrote this memoir, Emerson was revered as the "Seer of Concord" and enjoyed a national reputation as a great American writer and thinker.

3.   The orchestra of the Boston Academy of Music performed three movements of Beethoven's Symphony no. 5 (excluding the third movement) on April 3, 1841, at the Odeon Theater on Washington Street. Dwight did not attend this performance, but he did hear the Academy's orchestra perform the complete Symphony no. 5 the following year.

4.   George William Curtis (1824–1892), a journalist, contributed to *Harper's Monthly* widely read essays in a column called "The Easy Chair" during the 1860s. A friend of Dwight, Curtis also lived at Brook Farm.

5.   Margaret Fuller (1810–1850), a major feminist and transcendentalist writer, published some of the earliest essays on classical music and classical composers in the United States.

6.   Cecilia, or St. Cecilia, is the patron saint of church music, in particular, and music in general.

7.   This phrase was used in the 1840s to disparage followers of Unitarianism.

8.   The English moralist Martin Farquhar Tupper (1810–1889) authored in the mid-1800s widely read books of didactic poetry, but they are now considered banal and superficial.

32

GEORGE TEMPLETON STRONG HEARS

THE AMERICAN PREMIERE OF BEETHOVEN'S FIFTH

What was it like to be one of the first Americans to hear Beethoven? His music is so familiar today that it is difficult to imagine an era when such famous works as his Fifth Symphony were barely known—and could not be known—by most Americans. How did interpretations of the work's meaning compare with those current today? The famous diaries of the snobbish, opinionated, and witty George Templeton Strong (1820–1875) offer some perspectives.

Strong was a New York lawyer and a musical amateur. As one of the original subscribers in 1842 to the New York Philharmonic Society—the first symphony orchestra to be founded in the United States—(and later serving as its president from 1870 to 1874), Strong heard Beethoven's Fifth not only once, but several times. He was 21 years old when he attended its premiere by a pick-up orchestra in 1841, and he heard it again at the first concert of the newly formed New York Philharmonic. Over the next 14 years, Strong heard the work a few more times. His comments reveal a deepening appreciation and, in the last excerpt, a growing skepticism about his own typically Romantic approach in imposing philosophical rhapsodies on instrumental music. Strong filled his life with music. How extraordinary that when his own son insisted on becoming a composer, Strong disowned him.

FEBRUARY 11 [1841]

Went to the German charitable concert at the Tabernacle, which was jammed with Dutchmen like a barrel of Dutch herrings. I scarcely saw an Anglo-Saxon physiognomy in the whole gallery. The music was good, very well selected and excellently well performed, so far as I could judge. The crack piece, though, was the last, Beethoven's *Sinfonia* in C minor. It was generally unintelligible to me, except the Andante.*

DECEMBER 8 [1842]

Heard the first Philharmonic concert last night. The instrumental part of it was glorious. . . . Beethoven's Symphony in C minor was splendidly played, and the Overture to *Oberon* still better, if possible. I never knew before half the grace and delicacy of this composition. An orchestra of over sixty, most perfectly drilled, and composed of all the available talent in the city, gave an effect to it very different from what I've heard on former occasions when it's been performed. But what put it into the heads of the Society to bring forward Madame Otto and Mr. Charles E. Horn as the vocal performers? Both were poor enough—the former sings like a hand organ—in the progress of human ingenuity automatons will doubtless be made at some future day to sing with just as much expression—and the latter can't sing at all. In the very first note he gave, in his duet from—something—his voice broke most horribly.

MAY 19 [1844]

Feel today particularly happy—or particularly unhappy—I can't certainly determine which—for did I not hear the Symphony in C minor by one Ludwig van Beethoven, opus 67, played *ad unguem* [to exactness] by the Philharmonic? Haven't I been fairly tingling all day with the remembrance of that most glorious piece of instrumental music extant, the second movement? (Twice played, by the by—the first *encored* symphony on record.) Haven't I been alternately exulting in the accurate possession of *this* relic and lamenting the fruitlessness of my efforts to get hold of *that*, all day long?

I expected to enjoy that Symphony, but I did not suppose it possible that it could be the transcendent affair it is. I've heard it twice before, and how I could have passed by unnoticed so many magnificent points—appreciated the spirit of the composition so feebly and unworthily—I can't conceive.

It is—unspeakable!

*Strong was not alone in finding Beethoven's music "unintelligible"—or, at least, unusual—on first hearing. In 1831, still early days for Beethoven in America, a critic wrote of *The Mount of Olives*, part of which was performed by the Sacred Music Society at St. Paul's on February 24: "Beethoven is an author of great originality,—his compositions are truly energetic, and filled with uncommon passages,—his modulation is abstruse, and every listener feels, at the *first bar*, that he is about to hear something new; his discords attract our attention . . ." (*Euterpeiad*, March 1, 1831, p. 211).

The first movement, with its abrupt opening, and the complicated entanglement of harmonies that makes up the rest of it, is not very satisfactory or intelligible to me as a whole, though it abounds in exquisite little scraps of melody that come sparkling out like stars through a cloudy sky. But the second and fourth movements (the third isn't much) are enough to put Beethoven at the head of all instrumental composers if he'd never written another note. They're just one succession of *points,* and yet each is *perfect;* each seems as if it had been a single effort of the composer's genius that gave them birth.* There's nothing in them like the mere aggregation of distinct though original and beautiful passages that one notes in Rossini's music, for example.

The introduction of the subject of the second movement by the violins and its instantaneous ringing repetition by the full orchestra is matchless—so is the stately opening of the fourth.

But it's idle to write about it. If I were asked for an explanation of the Symphony, and to tell the exact train of thought that produced it, I should be at a loss; but the first general purport of its story would seem to be, for the first movement, weariness, sorrow, and perplexity—energies preying on themselves—the want of an object for life—and the disheartening sense that earnest minds feel, at a certain stage of their development, of the worthlessness of all that they're doing and living for, and their need of something that may wake them up to real and energetic existence.** Then, in the second, is the glorious birth of the new principle—of love, ambition, or some yet higher element, and its exulting and triumphant progress, in freshness and vigor, on to the victory and full fruition of its end and aim, which seems to be the subject of the Finale.

There's a specimen. Probably a good many other solutions would meet the problem, but Beethoven didn't write without meaning, and something like that the Symphony in C Minor, Number 5 (opus 67), may well mean.

MAY 26 [1855]

[At the Philharmonic]

. . .

—and for . . . the C-minor Symphony, for the existence whereof all should be profoundly thankful who are happy enough to be impressable by music. Not because it is most transcendent as a work of art, but because it embodies, conveys, teaches a lesson of Truth and Right which no extant poem, essay, or sermon speaks out with as much clearness and vigor.

Whoever can translate into *articulate* song its glorious message of Hope and Love and Effort blossoming out from chaos, uncertainty, indolence, and coldness of heart, leaving doubt and loneliness and desolation far behind them—a joy and glory in themselves, but triumphant at last in consummate victory over all things—whoever can put this into poetry as *truly* as Beethoven has pictured it in music, can do what this uneasy self-conscious age wants, and will place him, the Poet, far up on the slopes of Olympus.

Twaddle, rhapsody, rigmarole, and hyper-flutinated bosh. Transcendental German gas. Artificial ecstasy over a piece of very nice music. Ridiculous pretense of something grand,

*Next to "light and shade," the most crucial attribute of music, according to nineteenth-century standards, seems to have been "points."

**Strong seems to have been superimposing his own frustrations and repressions upon imaginary parallels in a Fifth Symphony of his own devising.

gloomy, significant, profound, and mysterious in a very pleasing composition. My "criticism" of the symphony is an easy thing to criticize. To set forth what I mean—fully, accurately, and without apparent exaggeration and *real* slip-slop would require two pages of very careful writing. So subtle and intangible and evanescent a subject as the significance of a musical work can't be fairly defined or discussed, except in words the most precise and carefully chosen. Offhand scribbling about it in one's journal can't be much more than fustian or flummery. But probably the most studied and eloquent recital and argument would convey no meaning, save to one who saw with the same eyes as its writer.

Probably no two people hear the same music exactly in the same way. Beethoven (e.g.) addresses the better part of every man, but the precise meaning of his message differs with the personality of each. Each fits the music with a different story. It means one thing to *A* and another to *B*. But the true meaning—the real actual intent of the composer? Very like, he had none. . . .

Certainly a great musical thought is something more than the mere imagining of a composer. It could not so stir the hearts of men if it were merely the cunning collocation of sound. That language which speaks to us so vaguely, yet with an expression so much keener and deeper than that of any other, must convey Truth and Reality, or something of the relations of Truth toward our own being.

How shall we learn its real meaning? How learn what it tells us? Would Beethoven's own commentary be reliable on one of his own works? I suppose not. . . .

So do three lines of bosh call sometimes for thirty more—of apology and explanation—which only carry one deeper still into a ravine of fog.

SOURCE: Vera Brodsky Lawrence, ed., *Strong on Music: The New York Music Scene in the Days of George Templeton Strong*: vol. 1, *Resonances 1836–1849*; vol. 2, *Reverberations, 1850–1856* (Chicago: University of Chicago Press, 1988, 1995): 1:111, 157–58, 243–44; 2:571–73.

33

GERMAN AMERICANS ADAPTING AND
CONTRIBUTING TO MUSICAL LIFE

The selections in this chapter all concern the influence of German music and musical life in the United States in the middle decades of the nineteenth century. The
1850s in particular saw the onset of large-scale immigration from Germany in the
aftermath of the failed German Revolution of 1848. The celebrated tours of the Germania Society Orchestra in the early 1850s were one by-product. Singing societies
and a developing audience for European classical music were another. The relative
lack of support for classical European music was noticed by many German newcomers, and it fueled their sense of separateness from American mainstream culture and their sense of mission to improve it.

In time, German-American communities founded their own musical institutions,
particularly male choral societies, which flourished in every major center of German
population. The *Bund,* or cooperative society, made up of member choruses from
different cities began with an annual meeting in 1849 at Cincinnati. The number of
societies in attendance grew from 5 in that year to 32 in 1877. A description of the
festival in 1878, which is reprinted here, gives the flavor of the event.

The impact of such sustained support for music making spilled over into musical life at large. Cincinnati's Music Hall was constructed along the lines of the
Saengerbund Exposition Hall. The German love of oratorios and symphonic music
yielded important performances of choral works by eighteenth- and nineteenth-

century German masters, including many premieres in cities from Milwaukee to New Orleans.

~~~~~~~~

A GERMAN-AMERICAN NEWSPAPER FROM CLEVELAND DESCRIBES MAINSTREAM AMERICAN TASTE (1852)

Nach langer klangloser Zeit die erste Musik und zwar klassische Musik. Wir lebten wieder in Deutschland, wo wir so oft jene herrliche Quartette für Streichinstrumente hörten. Auch das Publikum war europäisch, Franzosen, Deutsche und Engländer, und gar selten nur dazwischen ein amerikanische Gesicht. Europäer weisen was sie hören werden, wenn Quartette von Haydn und Beethoven auf dem Programm stehen. Es war ein nicht zahlreiches Publikum da und das scheint zu beweisen dass das amerikanische Publikum noch die Minstrels der klassischen Quartett Soireen vorzieht, denn diese fanden immer ein volles Haus. Das kleine Publikum war um so dankbarer und aufmerksamer, applaudierte jeden Satz.

After a long time without sound, [we now have] the first music and actually classical music. We once more lived in Germany, where we so often heard those wonderful quartets for strings. Even the public was European—French, German, and English, and rarely an American face in the midst. Europeans know what they will hear if quartets by Haydn and Beethoven are on the program. It was not a numerous public there and that seemed to show that the American public prefer minstrels to the classical quartet evening. The small public was very thankful and attentive, they applauded each movement.

> SOURCE: "Erster Soiree des klassischen Quartetts unter Direction des Hrn. C. Vaillant,"
> *Wächter am Erie*, November 24, 1852.

~~~~~~~~

The historian Mary Jane Corry, who contributed this selection and the preceding section, writes of the following, "This paper claim[ed] to have readers in Germany such as Franz Liszt, Lachner and Moscheles."

A NEW GERMAN-AMERICAN MUSIC NEWSPAPER DESCRIBES ITS OBJECTIVES

Deutsche Musik Zeitung, Philadelphia, October 1, 1859

1. Hebung der Musik in den Vereinigten Staaten.

2. Fortbildung der dieser Aufgabe berufene Musiker.

3. Anregung zu einem ernsten, der wahren Kunst forderlichen Streben.

4. Vermittelung einer näheren Bekanntschaft der Leistungen und Fahigkeiten der in Amerika zerstreut lebenden Musiker.

5. Erziehung angehender und Amerkennung volenditer Künstler.

6. Reichhaltigkeit des Inhalts, um die Leser mit den wichtigsten Ereignissen in der musikalischen Welt in Verbindung zu halten.

7. Gediegenheit der zur Fortbildung bestimmten Abhandlungen; durch die Bi-ographien der jenigen Künstler und musker, die ihre Kunst in den Verei-nigten Staaten durch ein ernstes Streben u. Handeln Nutzen gebracht, dem Verdienste ein bliebendes Denkmal zu setzen.

8. Sowie durch eine gerechte und ganzlich parteifreie Kritiken ausubenden Künstlern nutlich zu sein.

1. Improvement of music in the United States.

2. Development of this duty by professional musicians.

3. Encouragement of effective efforts towards a serious, true art.

4. Communication of a closer acquaintance of accomplishments and abilities of musicians living throughout America.

5. Education of incipient and recognition of accomplished artists.

6. Richness of content, in order for the reader to be in contact with the most important events in the musical world.

7. Reliability of certain procedures for development through biographies of those artists and musicians who brought their art to the United States who profited through serious striving and transactions, setting a lasting memorial [example].

8. Thus through a just and entirely party-free [unprejudiced] critique to be use-ful to working artists.

A NEWSPAPER FEATURE ON THE *SAENGERFEST* IN CINCINNATI IN 1879

THE *SAENGERFEST*

On the Eve of the Great Festival

The Decorations, Arrival of the Singers and Preparations for the Event

A Pleasant Sketch of Mendelssohn and His Sister—Concert Regulations—Press Representatives

Festival Notes

The nearness of the great German Musical Festival was apparent on every hand yesterday. Under the stimulus of what the Germans call "die Feststimmung," the city blossomed like a rose. It is a question of whether on any of the preceding festivals, whether under the auspices of the German Bund or the local May Festival Association, there has been such general and generous decorations. In the business portions, but especially along the line of march of the monster procession, which will be the first formal demonstration, there is hardly a building that does not display a show of bunting, some pictures, mottoes, or waving garlands of evergreens. A glance down Fourth street is thrilling, its colors being profuse and varied enough to arouse patriotism in every heart that feels a sentiment concerning the land of its birth or adoption. The inhabitants of the German districts prefer greens to bunting. At the northern end of the canal bridge on Vine street four arches span the street and sidewalks. They are wound with cedar, and form the portals to the trans-Rhenish precincts. Small saplings have been set up in front of many buildings, and though they make a small show of shade, they relieve the dull prospects of bricks, flagstones, and mortar.

The decorations have an intrinsic beauty, but they are also indicative of a spirit of interest in the festival, which lends to them an additional charm. Today, not the Germans alone, but all our citizens will cull out a holiday and devote it to recreation and enjoyment. In the case of thousands it will end in attendance upon what will be a magnificent performance of a magnificent work, the oratorio of [Mendelssohn's] "St. Paul." It matters not whether the listener have a cultured taste and a critical judgment or not. Touched by the events and sights of the day, he will be more than usually sensitive to the music, and its beauties will make him more liberal, more generous, more kindly toward his neighbors. These festivals promote this spirit. The Germans are full of gratitude because of the hearty interest and willingness to co-operate in the work of preparation by the American born citizens. The attention bestowed upon it by the English newspapers has challenged the surprise and praise of their German contemporaries who were wont in the past to look upon the Saengerfeste as their exclusive domain. The Volksblatt, which has led the local German press, sees [missing text; perhaps a program in the English newspapers] of all the concerts and the words of the vocal compositions, full lists of all the committees that have made the preparations for the festival, a historical sketch of the North American Saengerbund, biographical notices of the conductors, soloists, and composers, brief historical sketches of the principal works to be rendered, and complete lists of all the members in the Maennerchor [male choruses] and mixed chorus[es], arranged under the heads of the societies to which they belong. All the matter except their names is printed in English and German. The book will be given gratis to all the singers and the members of the various committees. To the public the cost is twenty-five cents.

SOURCE: "The Saengerfest." *Cincinnati Daily Gazette*, June 11, 1879, 8.

Writing some years after the establishment of the Saengerfests, the critic Henry Krehbiel linked the German singing societies explicitly to the foundations of classical music in Cincinnati, and by implication to other cities as well. He repeats in a most genteel manner the observation that Germans like beer with their music.

EXPOSITION HALL 1873

Cincinnati's Saengerbund Exposition Hall, a whitewashed wooden building constructed in 1867 to hold choral concerts with ca. 2000 singers for regional meetings of German men's choruses from Louisville, Columbus, Cleveland, St. Louis, and Detroit.

The North American Sängerbund aims to hold a festival biennially. Popular interest has died out in these great gatherings to some extent, but festivals have been held in which as many as three thousand singers participated. Candor compels the confession that at most of these festivals the worship of Gambrinus was more industriously cultivated than the worship of Apollo, but they have, nevertheless, done great service in spreading musical culture throughout the country. Indirectly, Cincinnati, where the German festivals started, and which now enjoys the reputation of being pre-eminently the festival city of America, through the merit of her great biennial music festivals, established by Theodore Thomas in 1873, owes her Music Hall, Festival Association, Exposition Buildings, College of Music, and Art Museum to the influence of the German Sängerfests. A hall built for one of the Sängerfests proved to be so useful a structure that it was preserved. The Expositions were called into being to occupy the hall. Then Mr. Thomas developed the festival idea, and after two festivals had been given, with great success, the public spirit of Cincinnati's citizens brought forth the fine fruit of the permanent buildings which are now one of the chief ornaments of the city. And so the good work went on.

SOURCE: Henry Krehbiel, "Appendix," in his *Review of the New York Musical Season, 1889–90* (New York and London: Novello, Ewer, 1890): 169.

34

$\mathcal{E}$MIL KLAUPRECHT'S GERMAN-AMERICAN NOVEL

CINCINNATI; ODER, DIE GEHEIMNISSE DES WESTENS

In 1854, Emil Klauprecht (1815–1896), a prominent writer and political leader in Cincinnati, published the most important German-American novel of the nineteenth century, *Cincinnati; oder, die Geheimnisse des Westens* (*Cincinnati; or, The Mysteries of the West*). Klauprecht wrote a convoluted plot not easily summarized in a few sentences, but the young city of Cincinnati, a crossroads between East and West, gave him the perfect background to dramatize cultural differences. He wrote this novel at the time when Stephen Foster's popularity was at its height and the Germania Orchestra had completed several national tours. Klauprecht's characters reflect topical issues, such as the cultural inferiority of the New World, as opposed to the Old, and the derivative nature of American classical music. This excerpt opens with an ill-fated parlor performance of Beethoven's song "Adelaide," in front of "pork aristocrats" who wake up only for "Yankee Doodle." Beethoven's song was already widely known in the United States.

Johanna had never appeared more beautiful or more attractive as on that evening. The inner joy that she felt over the termination of the irritating trial, the accusations which she had made against him for his rare visits, filled his heart with happiness. And to spend this evening at the side of the lovely girl, whose magic filled him up, had brought him this invitation which he could not refuse without seeming crude. He followed the old man, who had presented his arm to Johanna, at Günther's side, not without sensing the ill feeling which he would encounter in a place where John Stevens was to be found.

The appearance of the host with his guests naturally led once more to the inevitable, endless process of presentations with hand-shaking. Johanna, her father and Filson were each given the name of every single guest in turn, and then the company, suitably satisfied that the goddess of decency had been paid sufficient tribute, reformed in its semi-circle.

"Miss Johanna," old Zacharias began, "our ladies and gentlemen look forward with true longing to your beautiful voice. Will you satisfy our universal desire and give us occasion to marvel at your wonderful talent."

As Johanna expressed her regret that she did not know many English songs, *Mistress* Morrell, a lady who had studied German *Lieder* for five dollars an hour and who was generally regarded as an extraordinary learned lady, began:

"We ask you, Miss, for a German song, a song full of spirit and depth, a song by Beethoven."

"By Beethoven, that's right, by the great Beethoven," several of the neighboring ladies joined in applause.

Johanna complied with the request with the most lovable willingness.

She set herself down at the piano and began Beethoven's "Adelaide."

Filson listened to the sweet tones of the charming singer, captivated as she sensually ennobled Melanchthon's poem like blustering evening breezes, like the lilies of the valley of May, or as the flute of the nightingale plays to the heart.

"*Beautiful!*" was whispered here and there by beautiful lips, and a "*Charming*" emerged from the men in the applause.

The singer had barely reached the enchanting verse:

Einst o Wunder erblüht auf meinem Grabe

Eine Blume der Äsche meines Herzens.

[Once, oh miracle, upon my grave bloomed

A flower from the ashes of my heart.]

Then there was a yawn here and there in the place of the earlier rustles of applause, and this involuntary expression of boredom had soon won the entire company with its sympathetic power.

Mistress Morrell, the enthusiast for the great master, was the first to close her eyes, *Mistress* Prescott with her two daughters, and *Mistress* Hopkins, *Mistress* Shaw, *Miss* Taylor, *Miss* Peabody, *Mistress* Noodle and the entire row of feminine idols soon followed her example. Naturally the gentlemen were gallant enough to follow the ladies in general relaxation and enthusiastic sleep. One eyelid after another gradually closed, and as the last verse of the song, "Deutlich schimmert auf jeden Purpurblättchen" [Clearly shimmers on every purple leaf] with its repeated echo, "Adelaide—Adelaide . . ." had ended, Beethoven's melody had done the work of Oberon's lily-rod. The entire company was in *deep* slumber, as the sonorous snoring of old Zacharias and his neighbor indicated. Filson surveyed the tossing group with a smile.

"Go immediately to 'Yankee Doodle,' *Fraulein* Johanna," he whispered to the singer, who had been so immersed in her playing that she had not observed the marvelous impact which her splendid portrayal of this masterwork had made. The fun-loving girl followed his suggestion with panache; the wild notes of the national hymn sounded out, and like the trumpet of the Last Judgment it jolted through the souls of the sleepers. All eyes opened at once; the flat, sleepy looks of the ladies were enlivened with new fire; the men's legs were seized with a patriotic, victorious enthusiasm which seemed to want to pound the dead to pieces with their stomping.

"Splendid! Magnificent!" old Zacharias cried when Johanna was finished and all the gentlemen clapped their approval so that the walls shook. "Our Yankee Doodle beats all of Beethoven, Mozart and other whatsits from the field with bells. Such a lamenting tone is good for church and camp meetings, but I myself prefer a healthy *nigger*-song."

"A Negro song preferred to the great Beethoven?" *Mistress* Morrell responded, crinkling her nose. "Would it be possible that your ear is so closed to understanding this noble world of melody? I was seized, enchanted by these charming notes. The play and song of Miss Steigerwald were both entirely worthy of the great master, admirable."

"Unique!" *Mistress* Prescott remarked.

"Not to be outdone!" *Miss* Taylor stammered.

"Charming!" declared *Mistress* Hopkins.

"Enthusing!" called *Mistress* Peabody.

"Seraphic! Heavenly!" rejoiced *Mistress* Noodle.

"I have not yet shown your own enthusiasm, *ladies,*" the baleful Zacharias purred, "but I appeal to our young friend, Mr. Filson. He will be the arbitrator in our struggle between Yankee Doodle and Beethoven, between American music and German classical music, *ladies.*"

"Forgive me, Mr. Stevens," Filson answered with a smile, "that I place myself on the side of the ladies. What Moore once heard proclaimed in Rome, I'll apply to Beethoven: the composer deserves to lead all the angelic choirs as chapel-master of heaven! Unfortunately, we Americans still lack all sense for German music; the works of a Beethoven, Haydn, Mozart or Weber, when they are performed, are praised by all newspapers and magazines, because our model England pays them the proper recognition, and it is thus against good tone and would betray barbarism if one spoke otherwise. But we are mightily bored when we make this sacrifice to fashion. We are still a mercantile people; the head is our arbitrator in all relationships and appearances, and in matters of music only the heart, indeed only a feeling heart, can decide."

"I don't agree, Mr. Filson," old Zacharias retorted, "I have always been a businessman, but when I hear Yankee Doodle, my head and my heart are transported with enthusiasm."

"It is national pride, Mr. Stevens," Filson replied, "which swells your spirit with the playing of this song. Yankee Doodle is our Marseillaise, it helps drive away our enemies and thus these crude sounds of Basque Gypsies is a harmony which excites the ear of a patriot."

"You call our Yankee Doodle a crude Gypsy song?" *Master* Prescott spoke with a cutting tone.

"Yes, sir, the melody came from Spain to Cuba and Mexico, and from there we have derived our national hymn. We're very involved in taking over foreign melodies. You would be amazed if you traveled in Germany to hear all the tunes which here accompany the texts of our church hymns being used in student hangouts and the lowest bars as drinking songs and dirty ditties."

"We Americans also have our own original composers, sir," *Mistress* Morrell declared with dignity, "although their fame has not yet passed across the ocean. Only a few years ago I heard an enchanting opera in Philadelphia, composed by a native-born genius. Its name was 'Pocahontas.'"

"'Pocahontas!'" blurted Filson, biting back a smile.

"Do you know the opera?" asked *Mistress* Prescott in surprise.

"Do I know it, Madame? I was entrusted by the American minister in Paris to take it to the director of the Imperial Opera in Vienna."

"What, 'Pocahontas' has been performed in Vienna?" the enthused Prescott called.

"The composer," Filson began, "was a friend of our legation secretary in Paris, who did his best to get this American composition introduced to the European musical world at a grand opera as a new genre of music. Although supported by the total influence of the legation, these attempts remained without success. The score was returned to the secretary with numerous objections; first it was said that the scenery would present too many difficulties, and when this objection was removed, it was said that the repertory of the opera for that season had been closed.

"Tired of this fruitless effort, but determined to win my friend and my country laurels on this hitherto fallow field, I took the score to the Imperial Opera in Vienna, whose director was the famous Staudigl [a well-known German singer], who had made the friendship of the legation secretary during an art tour of England.

"Herr Staudigl received me in the friendliest manner, but when he learned the purpose of my visit, he declared his profound regret that he could not conform to the wishes of the Paris legation, since the opera company was involved in producing several Italian operas, the only new works which would be presented that winter.

"'But consider, sir,' I cried to him, 'leaving aside the zeal of the legation secretary for his friend's creation, who believes that I am really the bearer of a masterpiece, but consider the attractiveness which this opera would have for the German artistic world as an *American* opera. What is the oft-heard Italian cling-clang with its eternally returning, recast melodic frills against a richness of native, powerful, original harmonies which can challenge the soul from the trans-Atlantic world, with the power of its youthful nature, with the heroism of its settlers, with the resistance of the savage natives against European civilization?'

"'You are right, an American opera would be something new,' Staudigl responded, suddenly becoming attentive. 'We have often heard the sounds of many a European nightingale in the American forest primeval, we have Winter's 'Opernfest' and Spontini's 'Cortez,' but these works were poetic creations and not the concepts of what the composer had seen and experienced with his own spirit. You have genuinely awakened my interest, sir; a quick review will give me an idea of the character of your opera.'

"I happily complied with the desires of the great singer, who sat down quickly at his piano and ran through the composition.

"'You call that an *American* opera?' he called out. And sounding an *andante* which was not new to my ear, he continued:

"'That is *Donizetti!* Perhaps a bit more gracefully than we have it in 'Lucie.' And here, sounding a new tune, that's *Meyerbeer,* perhaps with a little more raw American spirit than the chevalier Bertram gives, and here, that's *Auber,* perhaps a little more imposing than we hear it in Pietro's barcarole. Do you call that an *American* opera?'" "The artist took the score from the stand and continued leafing through it, smiling as he went, while I wished I could sink into the earth on account of my nationalist pride.

"'Quite beautiful, quite clever," Staudigl continued. "Your composer picks pearls from all of our European masterpieces and gives them enhanced beauty in a novel setting. It is a true jewelry box of European tunes, illustrating the elevated taste of your countryman, sir; but as an *American* opera, this potpourri would only have interest in America.'

"You could only imagine the feelings with which I parted from the director of the Imperial Opera in Vienna, Madame," Filson concluded his narrative with a glance at *Mistress* Prescott. "I wished the legation secretary, his stupid friend and the American opera 'Pocahontas,' which had set me up for such a humiliation, were all on the upper fork of the Salt River. The adventure gave new confirmation to the old truth that we Americans must still be very modest pupils if we wish to collect laurels on the field of the arts."

Several pork packers wanted to make their protest against Filson's judgment and to break a lance for the honor of American art, but fortunately *Mistress* Ellen Steigerwald interrupted by inviting the company to the dining room, sparing the patriotic sentiments of the reader.

SOURCE: Emil Klauprecht, *Cincinnati; oder, die Geheimnisse des Westens (Cincinnati; or, The Mysteries of the West)*, trans. Steven Rowan (1854; reprint, New York: Lang, 1996): 485–89.

35

P. T. BARNUM AND THE JENNY LIND FEVER

The American promotion of the great soprano Jenny Lind (1820–1887) by Phineas T. Barnum (1810–1891) represents a watershed in the music business. Barnum transformed the admittedly already famous "Swedish Nightingale" into a celebrity, accompanied by endorsements, spin-off products, and fabulously successful concerts in many American cities. As the man who gave the American public such immortals as General Tom Thumb and the Fat Lady, Barnum applied his skills as a circus producer to the operatic stage and the diva. A risk taker, as shown in this selection, Barnum offered the Swedish Nightingale a huge contract for an American tour without hearing her sing.

From the beginning of the Lind adventure, Barnum understood the necessity for a persona of "true womanhood" to counteract suspicions about the morality of singers and actresses. Lind's repertoire not only included opera, but sentimental theater and parlor music, ranging from Bellini's prayerful "Casta Diva" to Bishop's "Home, Sweet Home." On her 1850 tour, Barnum and Lind together grossed more than $10,000 a night. Barnum exercised his genius in marketing and publicity as never before, foreshadowing the extent to which these would become industries unto themselves in the following century.

CHAPTER XVII. THE JENNY LIND ENTERPRISE

And now I come to speak of an undertaking which my worst enemy will admit was bold in its conception, complete in its development, and astounding in its success. It was an enterprise never before or since equaled in managerial annals. As I recall it now, I almost tremble at the seeming temerity of the attempt. That I am proud of it I freely confess. It placed me before the world in a new light; it gained me many warm friends in new circles; it was in itself a fortune to me—I risked much but I made more.

It was in October 1849, that I conceived the idea of bringing Jenny Lind to this country. I had never heard her sing, inasmuch as she arrived in London a few weeks after I left that city with General Tom Thumb. Her reputation, however, was sufficient for me. I usually jump at conclusions, and almost invariably find that my first impressions are correct. It struck me, when I first thought of this speculation, that if properly managed it must prove immensely profitable, provided I could engage the "Swedish Nightingale" on any terms within the range of reason. As it was a great undertaking, I considered the matter seriously for several days, and all my "cipherings" and calculations gave but one result—immense success.

Reflecting that very much would depend upon the manner in which she should be brought before the public, I saw that my task would be an exceedingly arduous one. It was possible, I knew, that circumstances might occur which would make the enterprise disastrous. "The public" is a very strange animal, and although a good knowledge of human nature will generally lead a caterer of amusements to hit the people, they are fickle, and ofttimes perverse. A slight misstep in the management of a public entertainment, frequently wrecks the most promising enterprise. But I had marked the "divine Jenny" as a sure card, and to secure the prize I began to cast about for a competent agent.

I found in Mr. John Hall Wilton, an Englishman who had visited this country with the Sax-Horn Players, the best man whom I knew for that purpose. A few minutes sufficed to make the arrangement with him, by which I was to pay but little more than his expenses if he failed in his mission, but by which also he was to be paid a large sum if he succeeded in bringing Jenny Lind to our shores, on any terms within a liberal schedule which I set forth to him in writing.

On the 6th of November, 1849, I furnished Wilton with the necessary documents, including a letter of general instructions which he was at liberty to exhibit to Jenny Lind and to any other musical notables whom he thought proper, and a private letter, containing hints and suggestions not embodied in the former. I also gave him letters of introduction to my bankers, Messrs. Baring Brothers & Co., of London, as well as to many friends in England and France.

The sum of all my instructions, public and private, to Wilton amounted to this: He was to engage her on shares, if possible. I, however, authorized him to engage her at any rate, not exceeding one thousand dollars a night, for any number of nights up to one hundred and fifty, with all her expenses, including servants, carriages, secretary, etc., besides also engaging such musical assistants, not exceeding three in number, as she should select, let the terms be what they might. If necessary, I should place the entire amount of money named in the engagement in the hands of London bankers before she sailed.

. . .

I was at my Museum in Philadelphia when Wilton arrived in New York, February 19, 1850. He immediately telegraphed to me, in the cipher we had agreed upon, that he had signed an engagement with Jenny Lind, by which she was to commence her concerts in America in the following

Picture of Jenny Lind dolls and locket holding an albumen photograph of Louis Moreau Gottschalk. Celebrity performers then as now had their images marketed and turned into products such as paper dolls and jewelry. Gottschalk's portrait was placed inside a locket or brooch made ca. 1860s.

September. I was somewhat startled by this sudden announcement; and feeling that the time to elapse before her arrival was so long that it would be [a good] policy to keep the engagement private for a few months, I immediately telegraphed him not to mention it to any person, and that I would meet him the next day in New York.

When we reflect how thoroughly Jenny Lind, her musical powers, her character, and wonderful successes, were subsequently known by all classes in this country as well as throughout the civilized world, it is difficult to realize that, at the time this engagement was made, she was comparatively unknown on this side [of] the water. We can hardly credit the fact, that millions of persons in America had never heard of her, that other millions had merely read her name, but had no distinct idea of who or what she was. Only a small portion of the public were really aware of her great musical triumphs in the Old World, and this portion was confined almost entirely to musical people, travellers who had visited the Old World, and the conductors of the press.

The next morning I started for New York. On arriving at Princeton we met the New York cars, and purchasing the morning papers, I was surprised to find in them a full account of my engagement with Jenny Lind. However, this premature announcement could not be recalled, and I put the best face on the matter. Anxious to learn how this communication would strike the public mind, I informed the conductor, whom I well knew, that I had made an engagement with Jenny Lind, and that she would surely visit this country in the following August.

"Jenny Lind! Is she a dancer?" asked the conductor.

I informed him who and what she was, but his question had chilled me as if his words were ice. Really, thought I, if this is all that a man in the capacity of a railroad conductor between Philadelphia and New York knows of the greatest songstress in the world, I am not sure that six months will be too long a time for me to occupy in enlightening the public in regard to her merits.

I had an interview with Wilton, and learned from him that, in accordance with the agreement, it would be requisite for me to place the entire amount stipulated, $187,500, in the hands of the London bankers. I at once resolved to ratify the agreement, and immediately sent the necessary documents to Miss Lind and Messrs. Benedict and Belletti.

I then began to prepare the public mind, through the newspapers, for the reception of the great songstress. How effectually this was done, is still within the remembrance of the American public. As a sample of the manner in which I accomplished my purpose, I present the following extract from my first letter, which appeared in the New York papers of February 22, 1850:

"Perhaps I may not make any money by this enterprise; but I assure you that if I knew I should not make a farthing profit, I would ratify the engagement, so anxious am I that the United States should be visited by a lady whose vocal powers have never been approached by any other human being, and whose character is charity, simplicity, and goodness personified.

"Miss Lind has great anxiety to visit America. She speaks of this country and its institutions in the highest terms of praise. In her engagement with me (which includes Havana), she expressly reserves the right to give charitable concerts whenever she thinks proper.

"Since her *début* in England, she has given to the poor from her own private purse more than the whole amount which I have engaged to pay her, and the proceeds of concerts for charitable purposes in Great Britain, where she has sung gratuitously, have realized more than ten times that amount."

CHAPTER XVIII. THE NIGHTINGALE IN NEW YORK

After the engagement with Miss Lind was consummated, she declined several liberal offers to sing in London, but, at my solicitation, gave two concerts in Liverpool, on the eve of her departure for America. My object in making this request was, to add the *éclat* of that side to the excitement on this side of the Atlantic, which was already nearly up to fever heat.

. . .

It was expected that the steamer would arrive on Sunday, September 1, but, determined to meet the songstress on her arrival whenever it might be, I went to Staten Island on Saturday, and slept at the hospitable residence of my friend, Dr. A. Sidney Doane, who was at that time the Health Officer of the Port of New York. A few minutes before twelve o'clock, on Sunday morning, the Atlantic hove in sight, and immediately afterwards, through the kindness of my friend Doane, I was on board the ship, and had taken Jenny Lind by the hand.

After a few moments' conversation, she asked me when and where I had heard her sing.

"I never had the pleasure of seeing you before in my life," I replied.

"How is it possible that you dared risk so much money on a person whom you never heard sing?" she asked in surprise.

"I risked it on your reputation, which in musical matters I would much rather trust than my own judgment," I replied.

I may as well state, that although I relied prominently upon Jenny Lind's reputation as a great musical *artiste,* I also took largely into my estimate of her success with all classes of the American public, her character for extraordinary benevolence and generosity. Without this peculiarity in her disposition, I never would have dared make the engagement which I did, as I felt sure that there were multitudes of individuals in America who would be prompted to attend her concerts by this feeling alone.

Thousands of persons covered the shipping [docks] and piers, and other thousands had congregated on the wharf at Canal Street, to see her. The wildest enthusiasm prevailed as the steamer approached the dock. So great was the rush on a sloop near the steamer's berth, that one man, in his zeal to obtain a good view, accidentally tumbled overboard, amid the shouts of those near him. Miss Lind witnessed this incident, and was much alarmed. He was, however, soon rescued, after taking to himself a cold duck instead of securing a view of the Nightingale.

. . .

A reference to the journals of that day will show, that never before had there been such enthusiasm in the City of New York, or indeed in America. Within ten minutes after our arrival at the Irving House, not less than twenty thousand persons had congregated around the entrance in Broadway, nor was the number diminished before nine o'clock in the evening. At her request, I dined with her that afternoon, and when, according to European custom, she prepared to pledge me in a glass of wine, she was somewhat surprised at my saying, "Miss Lind, I do not think you can ask any other favor on earth which I would not gladly grant; but I am a teetotaler, and must beg to be permitted to drink your health and happiness in a glass of cold water."

At twelve o'clock that night, she was serenaded by the New York Musical Fund Society, numbering, on that occasion, two hundred musicians. They were escorted to the Irving House by about three hundred firemen, in their red shirts, bearing torches. There was a far greater throng in the streets than there was even during the day. The calls for Jenny Lind were so vehement that I led her through a window to the balcony. The loud cheers from the crowds lasted for several minutes, before the serenade was permitted to proceed again.

I have given the merest sketch of but a portion of the incidents of Jenny Lind's first day in America. For weeks afterwards the excitement was unabated. Her rooms were thronged by visitors, including the magnates of the land in both Church and State. The carriages of the wealthiest citizens could be seen in front of her hotel at nearly all hours of the day, and it was with some difficulty that I prevented the "fashionables" from monopolizing her altogether, and thus, as I believed, sadly marring my interests by cutting her off from the warm sympathies she had awakened among the masses. Presents of all sorts were showered upon her. Milliners, mantua-makers, and shopkeepers vied with each other in calling her attention to their wares, of which they sent her many valuable specimens, delighted if, in return, they could receive her autograph acknowledgment. Songs, quadrilles and polkas were dedicated to her, and poets sung in her praise. We had Jenny Lind gloves, Jenny Lind bonnets, Jenny Lind riding hats, Jenny Lind shawls, mantillas, robes, chairs, sofas, pianos—in fact, every thing was Jenny Lind. Her movements were constantly watched, and the moment her carriage appeared at the door, it was surrounded by multitudes, eager to catch a glimpse of the Swedish Nightingale.

In looking over my "scrap-books" of extracts from the New York papers of that day, in which all accessible details concerning her were duly chronicled, it seems almost incredible that such a degree of enthusiasm should have existed. An abstract of the "sayings and doings" in regard to the Jenny Lind mania for the first ten days after her arrival, appeared in the London *Times* of Sept. 23, 1850, and although it was an ironical "showing up" of the American enthusiasm, filling several columns, it was nevertheless a faithful condensation of facts which at this late day seem even to myself more like a dream than reality.

SOURCE: P. T. Barnum, *Struggles and Triumphs; or, Forty Years' Recollections of P. T. Barnum* (Hartford: J. B. Burr, 1869): 271–73, 280–83, 286, 287–90.

36

MISKA HAUSER, HUNGARIAN VIOLINIST,

PANS FOR MUSICAL GOLD

These selections from *Aus dem Wanderbuche eines Oesterreichischen Virtuosen* [*From the Travel Diary of a Viennese Virtuoso*] by Miska Hauser (1822–1887) describe an extraordinary time in San Francisco, as seen through the eyes of a touring violinist. After a successful career in Europe, Hauser came to the United States in 1850. Initially sponsored and then exploited by P. T. Barnum (see chapter 35), a somewhat embittered Hauser soon took to the road as a freelancer. Miners were panning for gold in the streams and hill mines of El Dorado, and Hauser benefited from this entertainment-hungry clientele with nuggets in their pockets. He describes a staggering amount of music making. He includes in one letter the complete program of a special music festival which shows the popularity of contemporary opera transcriptions and arrangements. He also mentions German songs and choral music offered by local German singing societies. At his own concerts, Hauser pleased his Chinese listeners by interweaving Chinese songs into one of his compositions. This translation of selected letters from Hauser's memoir was underwritten by the federal government as part of the WPA in the 1930s, and the editor described the letters as "the richest single source of early San Francisco musical history."

EN ROUTE TO SAN FRANCISCO, JANUARY, 1853

Many years of touring Europe convinced me at last that there were no more opportunities left—at least not for the virtuoso. The Hesperian fields had been stripped of their golden fruit—so I packed my violin in a waterproof case, made a small package of my hopes, and sailed across the sea. America, I said to myself, is not yet spoiled and there perhaps I shall make my fortune.

I toured the States four times; I traveled to Canada and Havana; I played ten and twelve times in places. "What nice receipts you must have had!" you may be thinking—but not at all! I, an unbusinesslike novice, a greenhorn—made a trifle while my agent got it all. Such shrewd people as Barnum don't say, "You are an artist and you shall be paid according to your merits," but—"An artist? It is hard to market your talent. You must put yourself in my hands and permit me to squeeze your possibilities to the last drop!" In this country they do not limit the slave trade to negroes.

Suspecting my own worth, I tore loose from these dealers in souls. Since they had already done enough to make me hate the eastern part of the United States, I decided to go to California. Though Henrietta Sontag made me an offer to travel with her and a favorable contract to boot, I turned her down.[1]

With an idea of engaging a singer to accompany me on this journey, I went to Philadelphia and while there I ran across Ole Bull.[2] He told me of his own plans to go to California and make his violin draw to him a stream of California gold. He spoke of it with such an air of certainty, as if he had already accomplished it, so I hastened my departure. Since in my hurry I could not locate a singer, I decided instead to take Laveneau, a pianist.

We left New York harbor the first of January on board the *Baltic* and were swiftly borne out to the sea. . . .

SAN FRANCISCO, MARCH 15, 1853

(continuation)
The harbor of San Francisco is the most beautiful in the world. Nature has done so much for her that this city promises to become in a short time one of the greatest on earth. I was delighted on arriving to be received by a deputation of friends. I was taken to the same hotel where the singer, Katherine Hayes, was stopping; she was so glad to see an old acquaintance that she hugged and kissed me.[3] It was just seven years that we concertized together in Christiania and one year ago that we were in New York together.

During the past year Miss Hayes has earned with her singing half a million dollars; here she is overwhelmed with gold in the real sense of the word. But for her own personal intervention, it would have been impossible for me to secure a seat at her concert. The prices were $10, $5, and $3, and in Vienna they complain of having to pay three gulden.

The city is full of concertizing artists and all of the larger halls have long since been engaged, so I was forced to take a small theater for my first concert. The number of concert-givers, who all hope to become rich here, seem steadily to be increasing, like the Chinese, who already number 10,000 and have their own theater company. There are about 6,000 Germans here and the rest are English, French, Spaniards, etc. I even found five Hungarians, who honored me with a call; they arrived only recently but are already rich.

. . .

I went to see the opera *Martha*.[4] The composer would hardly have enjoyed the performance. I could bear it only one act. After that I went to a Chinese theater, where at least I understood nothing.

SAN FRANCISCO, APRIL 1, 1853

Without assisting artists, it is impossible to give a concert in San Francisco. The more variety programs contain and the more extreme the tastes shown, so much the better. But besides Miss Hayes and a Spanish woman there are no singers here. The unkind public has forced the rest of them to quit.

I shall recruit a quartet and, if possible, an entire orchestra. There is no shortage of musicians. They shoot up around us like mushrooms and thrive well in the hothouse atmosphere of the gambling dens. It is not uncommon for a lucky gambler to throw a lump of gold at the fiddler to get him to play "Yankee Doodle" or a Strauss waltz.

. . .

The receipts from my last concert were very satisfactory—more than $2500. I am proud of having assembled an orchestra which would do honor to the halls of a European nobleman. I collected musicians from the gambling houses, hired them and rehearsed them myself; and up to now we have given twenty-six concerts. I finally disciplined them to a point where we might dare to perform Beethoven's *Leonore Overture*. This concert took a full four hours because I had to give in to the audience—composed of Chinese, gringoes, adventurers from every country, etc.— and play three encores to each number. When I played a composition with Chinese melodies interwoven, "Die Kinder des Himmleichen Reiches" ["The Children of the Heavenly Kingdom"], [the Chinese] gave way suddenly to their enthusiasm. They let out inhuman howlings and set up such a racket that I finally hid in a corner of the hall until the Chinese triumph subsided.

The following day, May 16th, I travelled to the mining districts in company with the pianist Laveneau, the singer Gerold, the songstress Pattinos, and my agent. We went first to Sacramento, a trip of four days, and from there to Stockton and Novarra, newly-founded towns. My eyes popped at all the gold I beheld. Comparatively, our net receipts were not as large in the interior as in San Francisco, because expenses were so enormous. Each of my companions asked $60.00 a day! Since the people of the mines had little mind to go to the concerts, I played "Lieder ohne Gold"— "Songs for No Gold."

. . .

As I mentioned, there is an overabundance of concert performers and that dismal season, which recurs only once a year in Vienna is an all-the-year-round condition here. This brain-destroying season of virtuosi-concerts bears down on California's Capitol with the weight of the Alps causing her tortures like those of Tantalus. All the theaters and halls are engaged for weeks ahead by the modern followers of Apollo and Orpheus. Yet only a few of the sinning and playing adventurers here find the Golden Fleece. He who does not bring with him a name and reputation from Europe will have to make a firm stand. If such is the case, one must at once decide to pay homage to the low material tastes of the public and to give up the interests of true art for some time. This done, one cannot fail to achieve the most glittering success.

One banquet after another is given in my honor. These are expensive as everything else in the Land of Gold. The cost of the last banquet was more than $500. Besides this, the Chinese sent a special deputation to invite me to their quarter. I have already given sufficient mention of the methods by which I succeed in pleasing them.

But my better self still wants to escape from this turbulent, deceitful ocean of speculation and regain the health-bringing shore of true art.

While it lasted, the quartet which I brought together with such pains gave me more pleasure than if I had gained all the gold in California.

The quartet as Beethoven envisioned it—the mental discourse of four mutually attuned souls, embracing within itself a world of action, passion, and hope—has been the anchor of my soul. Whenever the Devil tried to entice my beloved bark, Art, toward the abyss, it kept me back. But now I am without this purest of all musical pleasures, and shall be for some time. My viola player has just died of indigestion—it is too bad.

Among the local artists is a pupil from the Vienna conservatory, who, in cooperation with other musicians, earns forty to fifty dollars daily. All the members of my orchestra have given a very commendable example—they have not asked for pay, except for one contrabass player, a Bohemian.

Ole Bull wrote me. His plans are as eccentric as ever. Since his last speculation failed he has taken it into his head to come to California on the next boat and make a million with his violin—just to recoup his fortunes a bit.

My wants are far more modest. I am already sick and tired of giving concerts. Soon I shall leave this most fortunate-yet-unfortunate country. When my goal is reached I'll return to England via South America.

This is the happiest land! A temperate climate, a miraculously vigorous vegetation, an over-abundant water supply, a surplus of the rarest metals, and a broad beautiful valley between the coast range and the Sierras, all rich resources, make California the true El Dorado.

SAN FRANCISCO, APRIL 15, 1853

The Local Governor Woodworth, a very cultured man with highly artistic tastes, gave a magnificent music festival at the French Theater. Here is the complete program:

1.   Mannerchor by Mendelssohn, sung by the German Liedertafel.

2.   Overture to *Tannhauser* by R. Wagner. Performed by the Societe Concordia.

3.   Grand Phantasy of *Lucretia Borgia* composed and played by Miska Hauser.

4.   The great aria from *Robert the Devil,* sung by Katherine Hayes.

5.   Spider Dance, by Senora Lola Montez, Countess of Landsfeldt.

6.   Polonaise by Meyerbeer, played by M. Hauser.

7.   Phantasy from the *Huguenots* by Thalberg, played by E. Pettinos.

8.   Trio by Mendelssohn in D-Minor, played by M. Hauser, Pettinos and Giraldo.

9.   Overture to the Opera, *Der Freischutz,* under direction of M. Hauser.

10. Italian Songs given by Katherine Hayes.

11. Solo from Yelva, the Russian Orphan, danced by Lola Montez.

12. Der Wanderer im Walde by Schubert, a chorale.

13. The Bird in the Tree, composed and played by M. Hauser.

14. Hail Columbia, sung by the German Liedertafel.

This was the most popular concert I ever saw. People got into brawls over seats. The net receipts were $5,000, and are to be used for charities, thus; $2,000 for the German and French hospitals; $1,000 for a fire engine and firemen; $1,000 for a Hebrew benevolent fund; and the remaining $1,000 to various other institutions.

SAN FRANCISCO, MAY 4, 1853

After the wonderful supper at the Governor's House, the German Liedertafel serenaded each of the artists who had been on the charity program. Half of the city was up and about to listen to their songs, and what a festival night it was! Of all the efforts of the Germans to band together in America, none has ever been so successful and such a source of pleasure as these German Mannergesangverein—Male Singers' Associations. They have been in existence only seven or eight years. The frequent repetitions [repeated performances] of their magnificent festivals are the true, and perhaps only, diversions in the life of Germans in California and are appreciated everywhere. . . .

It is a great task, for these singers, after the hard struggle for existence, to find so much time to plan and execute these festivals. But every beautiful chord will give fresh encouragement and permanent enthusiasm. It is these German singers, men living by the hard manual labor of gold digging, whom Germany has to thank for an otherwise little recognized folk life which [h]as won them a place of honor on the shores of the Pacific.

By torchlight with joyous music and flying flags, the singers marched through the streets of San Francisco, hailed from open windows by the fair sex who had donated many of the precious banners. Wreaths, flowers and other symbols of honor were showered on the marchers from many houses.

SOURCE: Miska Hauser, *Aus dem Wanderbuche Eines Oesterreichischen Virtuosen* (Leipzig, 1859); published in English as *The Letters of Miska Hauser: History of Music in San Francisco*, vol. 3, trans. Eric Benson, Donald Peet Cobb, and Horatio F. Stoll, Jr. (San Francisco, Calif.: Works Progress Administration, [1939]): 11–12, 21–22, 25, 28, 30–34, 45–49.

NOTES

1. Henrietta Sontag (1805–1854), a highly celebrated German singer.
2. Ole Bull (1810–1880) was a Norwegian violinist considered one of the greatest performers of the nineteenth century.
3. Katherine Hayes (1825–1861) was an Irish-born operatic soprano.
4. *Martha*, a comic opera composed by the German composer Friedrich von Flotow (1812–1883) in 1847.

37

Fʀᴏᴍ ᴛʜᴇ Jᴏᴜʀɴᴀʟꜱ ᴏꜰ

Lᴏᴜɪꜱ Mᴏʀᴇᴀᴜ Gᴏᴛᴛꜱᴄʜᴀʟᴋ

Born in New Orleans and shaped by its mix of French, African, and Spanish cultures, Louis Moreau Gottschalk (1829–1869) was the first American concert pianist and classical American composer to win recognition abroad. How exotic this "Lousianaise" composer seemed to the Paris elite when he played his piano compositions spiced with popular Afro-Latino melodies and syncopated dance tunes. At home, Gottschalk encouraged parlor-music tears with his flashy yet sentimental piano works. During the Civil War years, he wrote virtuosic paraphrases of Union tunes.

Gottschalk kept a journal, and after his death, his sister Clara Peterson organized the entries, enlisted her husband to translate them from French to English, and then published the whole in 1881. Filled with sardonic wit and lots of cultural gossip, Gottschalk's reporting vividly conveys the American scene in the 1850s and 1860s. He wrote one of the great diaries of his era.

Gottschalk's career fluctuated between extremes of glory and failure. After his glamorous adolescence in Paris in the 1840s, he returned to New York, expecting a hero's welcome. He quickly learned otherwise. A few years later, he was off again, this time to the West Indies. His second homecoming in 1862 reopened old wounds and led to this recollection of how this spoiled aristocrat was saved from financial ruin by the unexpected commercial success of his piano compositions.

~~~~~~~~~
~~~~~~~~~
~~~~~~~~~

NEW YORK 1862

When, in 1853, I returned to the United States, which I had left eleven years before (at eleven years of age),* my reputation, wholly Parisian, had not, so to speak, crossed the Atlantic. Two or three hundred concerts, given in Belgium, Italy, France, Spain, Switzerland, etc., had given me a name, but this name, so young, was not yet acclimated in America. My first concert in New York was a success, but the receipts did not amount to half the expenses. The second, given at Niblo's Theater, was a fiasco; in the two concerts I lost twenty-four hundred dollars.

. . .

From my birth I had always lived in affluence—thanks to the successful speculations entered into by my father. Certain of being able to rely upon him, I quietly permitted myself to follow those pursuits in which I anticipated only pleasure and enjoyment. Poorly prepared for the realities of American life by my long sojourn in the factitious and enervating atmosphere of Parisian salons (where I easily discounted the success that my youth, my independent position, the education I had received, and a certain originality in the compositions I already had published partly justified), I found myself taken unawares when one day, constrained by necessity and the death of my father, hastened by a series of financial disasters, I found myself without resources other than my talents to enable me to perform the sacred duties bequeathed to me by him. I was obliged to pay his debts, of which my concerts in New Orleans already had in part lightened the weight, and to sustain in Paris a numerous family, my mother and six brothers and sisters.

Of all misery, the saddest is not that which betrays itself by its rags. Poverty in a black coat, that poverty which, to save appearances, smiles with death at the heart, is certainly the most poignant; then I understood it. Nevertheless, my brilliant success in Europe was too recent for me not to perceive a near and easy escape from my sad troubles. I believed success still possible. I then undertook a tour in New England [1854–1855]. At Boston my first receipts exceeded one hundred dollars; at the second concert I made forty-nine dollars. I have not related that an hour before I was to begin a concert in Boston a dispatch from one of my uncles apprised me that my father was in the pangs of death and had just blessed me—a singular and touching wandering of his great intelligence at the moment of his dissolution—in seven languages, which he spoke admirably. I cannot describe to you my despair, but let those who comprehend it add to it the terrible necessity of appearing in public at such a moment. I might have put off the concert, but the expenses had been incurred; the least delay would have augmented my loss. I thought of those to whom I had become the only prop; I drove back my de[s]pair and played! I do not know what I did on that evening. H— thought it his duty, in view of my prostration, to make known to the public the circumstances in which I was placed. I need not say that Mr. X [John S. Dwight], who from my first appearance, had not ceased to disparage me in his musical journal, continued to attack me after this concert, not permitting the great affliction that had overwhelmed me to disarm him. Another newspaper had the melancholy courage to say that

*Gottschalk actually was thirteen when he left New Orleans for Paris.

doubtless it was unfortunate that I had lost my father, but that the public had paid a dollar for the purpose of receiving a dollar's worth of music, and had nothing to do with the personal affairs of Mr. Gottschalk—a logic more rigorous than Christian.

Throughout all New England (where, I am eager to say, some years later I found the most sympathetic reception), there was but a succession of losses; A. S., in a newspaper, devoted a whole column to my kid gloves; another to my handsome appearance and my French manners. At P., after my first concert, attended by seventeen persons, one editor gave a facetious account, in which he asserted that he hated music, but that mine was less insupportable to him because, in the noise that I drew from my piano, there was no music. Be it as it may, I lost sixteen hundred dollars in a few months.

Killed by the gross attacks of which I had been the object, discouraged by the injustice of self-styled musical judges, who denied me every species of merit; undeceived, disgusted with a career that even among my own countrymen did not promise the means of providing for the wants of my family and myself, I returned to New York.

My compositions continued to have a large sale in Paris. Then it was that I received a letter from one of my old friends and patrons, the respectable old Countess de Flavigny, who afterward was appointed lady in waiting to the Empress Eugénie. She exhorted me to return to Paris, and held out to me the probability of my soon being appointed pianist to the court. But I was held back by diffidence. It was painful to me to return to Paris, first theater of my great success, and confess that I had not succeeded in my own country, America, which at this time was the El Dorado, the dream of artists, especially as the exaggerated accounts of the money that Jenny Lind had made there rendered my ill success more striking.

. . .

At last one day I played some of my compositions for Mr. Hall, the publisher. "Why do you not give a concert to make them known?" he said to me. "*Ma foi*," I answered him, "it is a luxury that my means no longer permit me!" "Bah! I will pay you one hundred dollars for a piano concert at Dodsworth's Rooms."

Eight days later I played my new pieces in this small hall, (whose proportions are such that I should never wish to see them exceeded, as they are such that make the piano heard advantageously before a select audience): *The Banjo*, the *Marche de nuit*, the *Jota aragonesa*, and *Le Chant du soldat*. Its success surpassed my most brilliant expectations. During five months [December 1855 through June 1856] I continued, without interruption, a series of weekly concerts for the piano only, in the same place, without being forsaken by the public favor. *The Banjo, La Marche*, and many other pieces bought by Hall were published and sold with a rapidity that left no doubt as to the final result of Hall's speculation, which time has only corroborated. Everybody knows of the enormous edition that was published of *Banjo*, and *Marche de nuit*. I then concluded a contract that assured to Hall the exclusive rights to all my compositions for the United States. As Hall wished to possess my works written before those he had just published, and having faith in my talent as a composer, he addressed the publisher of the melancholy piece I have already spoken of, for the purpose of buying it. "Willingly," was the reply. "It does not sell at all; pay me the fifty dollars it has cost me, and it is yours." This little piece was *Last Hope*, of which more than thirty-five thousand copies have been published in America, and which still produces yearly to its publisher, after a run of more than twelve years, twenty times the amount that it cost him. I always have kept at the bottom of my heart a sentiment of gratitude for the house of Hall, who first discovered that I was worth something; and from that moment dates the friendship that unites me to his family, and that time has only ripened.

~~~~~~~

After three years in the United States, Gottschalk went to the West Indies (1857–
1862), where he composed his most important symphonic work, the two-movement
tone poem "Le Nuit des Tropiques," subtitled "Symphonie Romantique." Premiered
in Havana in 1860, not until 1955 did the work receive an American performance.
Here, Gottschalk recalls a sensuous experience that fills this still under-recognized
piece with Afro-Cuban colors.

1862

The house I lived in was an hour's distance from the first cabins of Caimito [in the interior of Cuba]. Throughout the vast plains and the fields of cane not a vestige of habitation, a true wilderness for a league around, with the mountains of Anafe on the horizon. Méry* and Théophile Gautier would have gone mad in contemplating this paradise, in which only an Eve was wanting. Unfortunately, the only company in my Eden was a very ugly Negress, who, every evening, after having roasted the coffee, crushed her maize in a hollow piece of wood, recited the Ave Maria before an old colored image of the Virgin, came and squatted down at my feet on the veranda, and there in the darkness, sang to me in a piercing, wild voice full of strange charm, the *canciones* [folk songs] of the country. I would light my cigar, extend myself in a *butaca* [armchair], and surrounded by this silent, primitive nature, plunge into a contemplative revery, which those in the midst of the everyday world can never understand. The moon rose over the Sierra de Anafe. The crickets chirped in the fields; the long avenue of palms, which extended from the *casa* to the entrance of the plantation, was separated into two black bands on the uniform ground of the fields. The phosphorescent arabesques of the fireflies flashed suddenly through the thick darkness that surrounded us. The distant noises of the savanna, borne softly by the breeze, struck my ears in drawn-out murmurs. The cadenced chant of some Negroes belated in the fields added one more attraction to all this poesy, which no one can ever imagine.

My thoughts flew away with the fumes of my cigar; my ideas were effaced, and I finished by feeling my brain benumbed by that delicious beatitude which is the extreme limit between sleep and life. I would have remained thus until the morning had it not been for the voice of the *sereno* [night watchman], who came to tell me that it was eleven o'clock—that is to say, the hour for retiring. Once more I threw a last look at all this marvelous nature and withdrew into my chamber.

~~~~~~~

Pressured by his manager, the famous Maurice Strakosch (1825–1887), Gottschalk
undertook a risky concert tour by train in the midst of the Civil War, which landed

*Joseph Méry (1798–1865) French *littérateur,* author of numerous poems, novels, and dramas. With Camille du Locle, he wrote the libretto of Verdi's *Don Carlos.*

him once near the front lines of battle. Early on, Gottschalk declared his allegiance to the Union cause, playing concerts in Washington, with Abraham Lincoln and his generals in the audience. Here, Gottschalk bears witness to a narrow escape and his musician's sense of priorities: what matters most are the grand pianos he calls "mastodons," symbols of the piano manufacturer Chickering and his big business.

IN THE CARS ON THE ROAD TO HARRISBURG
[PENNSYLVANIA, CA. JUNE 1863]

Hagerstown definitely is in [the] possession of the Confederates. The governor asks the people to put before their doors all the empty barrels that they may have to dispose of; they will use them on the fortifications to be thrown up at Harrisburg. All along the road we see farmers under arms, in battle array and doing military drill. They all seem to want to obey the command of the governor, who orders all able-bodied men to the field to meet the enemy, and to take the Susquehanna as the line for battle.

A traveler we picked up at the last station assures us that the Confederate Army is not more than thirty miles from Harrisburg. Everybody is frightened. Strakosch begins to see his mistake.

It is ten o'clock in the morning. The train continues to advance at full speed toward Harrisburg—that is to say, toward Jenkins, for the city must be attacked tonight, if it is not taken already. What shall we do? As for the concert, it is out of the question; but ourselves, our trunks—my pianos—what is to become of us in all this confusion?

I P.M. A mile this side of Harrisburg the road is completely obstructed by freight trains, wagons of all sorts, and in fine by all the immense mass of merchandise, etc., which for the last twelve hours has been concentrated near the town to avoid its capture or burning by the rebels. The train stops at the middle of the bridge over the Susquehanna—why? The anxiety increases. Can you conceive anything more terrible than the expectation of some vague, unknown danger? Some passengers have sat upon the floor so as to be sheltered from bullets in case the train should be fired upon.

One hour of anxiety, during which all the women, while pretending to be dead with fright, do not cease talking and making the most absurd conjectures. I myself am only slightly comforted, and the idea of a journey to the South at this time is not at all attractive. But the train standing in the middle of the bridge, the silence, the unknown, the solitude that surrounds us, the river whose deep and tremulous waves murmur beneath our feet, and, above all, our ignorance of what is taking place in front and what awaits us at the station—is not all this enough to worry us?

Tired of this suspense, I decide to get out of the car. Strakosch, Madame Amalia Patti, and I go toward the station, which we are assured is only a walk of twenty minutes. We find at the entrance to the depot piles, no, mountains of trunks blocking the way. One of the mountains has been tunneled by a frightened locomotive. Disemboweled trunks disgorge their contents, which charitable souls gather up with a zeal more or less disinterested. The conductor points out to me a pickpocket, an elegantly dressed young man moving quietly around with his hands behind his back.

What luck! I have just caught a glimpse of my two pianos—the cowardly mastodons (Chickering forgive me!) snugly lying in a corner and in perfect health. These two mastodons, which Chickering made expressly for me, follow me in all my peregrinations. The tails of these monster pianos measure three feet in width, their length is ten feet; they have seven and a half octaves, and despite all this formidable appearance possess a charming and obedient docility to the least movement of my fingers. The Chickering sons (Chickering, the father, founder of this great house, has been dead for some years) have given, by their labor and constructive talent, for some time past a great impetus to the manufacture of pianos. Their factories at Boston turn out forty-two pianos a week! Five hundred workmen are employed in them constantly. The later instruments, constructed on new models of their own invention, rival, if they do not surpass, the finest European pianos.

I acknowledge that my heart beat at the idea of leaving these two brave companions of my life exposed to the chances of a bombardment or an attack by assault. Poor pianos! Perhaps tomorrow you will have lived! You will probably serve to feed the fine bivouac fire of some obscure Confederate soldier, who will see your harmonious bowels consumed with an indifferent eye, having no regard for the three hundred concerts that you have survived and the fidelity with which you have followed me in my Western campaigns.

. . .

2 P.M. A battery of artillery passes at full gallop. We are crushed in the midst of the crowd. Jones's Hotel is a quarter of a mile away. Many groups stand before the telegraph office. The rebels, the dispatches announce, are eighteen miles away. All the shops are closed, and most of the houses from garret to cellar.

"Decidedly our concert is done for!" exclaims in a piteous voice my poor Strakosch, who has just returned from a voyage of discovery. The reflection is a rather late one and proves that my excellent friend and agent is a hopeful youth and trusts to the last, like Micawber, that something will "turn up."[1]

The hotel is overrun by a noisy crowd, in which I recognize many New York reporters sent in haste by the great newspapers in the hope of furnishing their readers with sensational news. Sensational news is a new synonym for "a canard." The three pretended captures of Charleston and that of Vicksburg, a year ago, the death of Jefferson Davis, and so many other canards have been very ingenious combinations by the newspapers, thanks to which, by causing the sale of many millions of "bulletins," they have realized enormous profits. Unfortunately everything wears out in this world, and credulity is so deadened that now everything is doubted.

. . .

Old men, women, and children are leaving the city. A train left this morning carrying off many thousand refugees. In a few hours our position has become very critical. We cannot advance, and I fear that our retreat will be cut off. A militia regiment passes at quickstep; it is going to the front. They are, for the most part, young men from fourteen to eighteen years old. They murmur greatly against Philadelphia, which, being the principal city in the state (numbering six hundred thousand inhabitants), has not yet sent one regiment of its National Guard to defend the seat of government, while the distant states of New Jersey, New York, and even Rhode Island already have fifteen or twenty thousand men on the road to Harrisburg and the valley of the Cumberland.

A train being announced to leave for Philadelphia in an hour, we run to the station. Strakosch will remain behind to search for our trunks, which have been missing these two hours. My tuner has lost his head; the two mastodons of Chickering's have disappeared, and the express company declines to be responsible for them. Too obstinate Strakosch, why in the world did he make us come to Harrisburg?

SOURCE: Louis Moreau Gottschalk, *Notes of a Pianist,* ed. Jeanne Behrend (New York: Knopf, 1964): 35–36, 46, 49–50, 133–34, 135, 137. With the first edition of *Notes of a Pianist* (1881) as her basic text, Behrend produced a landmark volume.

~~~~~~

NOTE

1.   Micawber is a character in the novel *David Copperfield* (1850) by Charles Dickens.

38

The "Four-part Blend"

OF THE HUTCHINSON FAMILY

The Hutchinson Family, a quartet of three New Hampshire–born brothers (John, Judson, Asa) and one sister (Abby), sang their way into fame and history through concerts of popular and topical songs in the 1840s and '50s. Songs about state pride like "The Old Granite State," which they sang at the White House for President John Tyler, nostalgic lyrics about "The Good Old Days of Yore," and sentimental homilies like "Kind Words Can Never Die" all had a wide appeal. But the way the Hutchinsons sang mattered just as much as the words themselves because audiences responded to them as "American" singers, praising their "natural" manner, "sweetness," "simplicity," and good diction.

The Hutchinson approach to part singing set precedents for commercial popular music that lasted well into the twentieth century. As the music historian Dale Cockrell writes, "In fact, the Hutchinsons, in the long-run, are probably most responsible for taking the four-part blend and bringing it into the mainstream of American popular song. Not only is the format of the various "family," "brother," and "sister" acts of the twentieth century—for example, the Osmonds, the Brothers Four, the Andrews Sisters—beholden to the Hutchinsons, but also very likely their sweet sound, one based on a rich vocal blend."[1]

The Hutchinsons' politics tied them to several reform movements. Appearing with Frederick Douglass at antislavery rallies, they popularized the abolitionist songs

"Get Off the Track" and "There's a Good Time Coming." They sang at a convention for women's rights in Akron, Ohio, in 1851. Their song "King Alcohol" promoted the temperance movement. These excerpts from brother John Hutchinson's history of the troupe begin with their early concerts.

NEW YORK, 1842

Bidding adieu to our Dutch and Yankee friends, we returned to fill our engagements in Albany. As before, the effort as far as finances were concerned, proved unsuccessful; a small surplus at the end of the week was handed us for our labor. We found a relative in the city who extended us some courtesy. Settling the hotel bill we had one shilling remaining, when up came the ever-importunate porter who pleaded for his usual perquisite. One of the brothers handed him our last shilling.

For a night or two we took cheaper quarters, twelve-and-a-half-cent lodgings on Broad Street, getting trusted for it, of course, and obtaining our food as best we might. Poverty stared us in the face. We seriously contemplated disbandment. A plan was devised to sell the team and take money enough to go home with Abby, for we had already kept her away from mother beyond the promised time. The lot fell upon me to go with her to New Hampshire, and leave Judson and Asa, who were to put off into the country and work their board until my return.

In the midst of these unsettled plans, there was a rap at the door and in stepped a tall gentleman, who introducing himself stated his errand. "Can you remain in the city till next Monday evening," said he; "I will give you a hundred dollars if you will sing for me that evening."

. . .

The neat, acceptable hall of the Albany Female Academy was the scene of much interest the night of the concert, August 29, 1842. The wealth and the fashion of that town were there, it being advertised as a complimentary concert. We were introduced to as large an audience as could be convened, while hundreds were crowded out. We were cheered, and every selection [we] sang elicited an encore. . . .

The programme consisted of selected and original songs and ballads, with humorous ditties, quartets, trios, duets, etc. "The Cot where we were Born," "The Grave of Bonaparte," "Snow-Storm," "The Irish Emigrant's Lament," "Crows in a Cornfield," "Indian Hunter," "Matrimonial Sweets," "The Land of Canaan," "The Angel's Invitation to the Pilgrim," "Alpine Hunter's Song," from the Swiss, "The Maniac," etc.

We did not attempt any performance that we could not master. At the suggestion of our amiable friend, Mr. Newland, we doffed the assumed name which we had sailed under, and resumed our own family name. "The Aeolian Vocalists" were no more, and the "Hutchinson Family" thereafter took all responsibility of praise and blame. He also suggested our giving up instrumental performances as a prominent feature in the progamme, and only using the stringed instruments as an accompaniment to the songs, thus making the instrumental music subordinate to the voices.

The leading characteristic in the "Hutchinson Family's" singing was then, as it always has been since, the exact balance of parts in their harmonies, each one striving to merge himself in the interest of the whole, forming a perfect quartet, which was rare in those early days. How often have we been questioned, "which of you boys sings bass, tenor or the air?" So united were we in our movements there could be no strife and neither's voice could be distinguished until he arose and sang a solo; then the characteristic features of each voice could be identified. Judson took the melody, John the tenor, Abby sang a rich contralto, while Asa gave deep bass; each being adapted by nature to the part necessary for perfect harmony.

Judson accompanied his own ballads with his violin, while Asa with 'cello and I with violin, played accompaniments for him also. Abby played no instrument and sang as did I, with Judson's and Asa's playing. The latter up to this time had not ventured any bass solos. Here we left our first original song to be published; and, not long after, we saw the "Vulture of the Alps," a descriptive song, issued in sheet form, displayed at the music-store of our ever-to-be-remembered friend, who, it should be added, extended us as the result of the concert one hundred and ten dollars, more being sent us after we reached our home in New Hampshire. So we bade adieu to the precious friendship so pleasantly formed, to see other climes and new relations. "Come home," said father in his letters, and all the household repeated the same beseeching words. So we started for New England once more.

. . .

~~~~~~~

On January 25, 1843, the Hutchinson Family sang at a meeting of the Massachusetts Anti-Slavery Society in Faneuil Hall, Boston. In the chapter called "Singing for Freedom," John Hutchinson reprinted an account of the meeting that had been published in the Herald of Freedom. *"Slavery would have died of that music," the writer proclaimed.*

SINGING FOR FREEDOM

The *Herald of Freedom*'s account was, of course, written by N. P. Rogers, who prided himself not a little on his success in enlisting our services for this and similar gatherings. He wrote as follows:

"The distinguishing incident of the anniversary was the co-operation of the New Hampshire Hutchinsons, aided by their brother from Lynn [Massachusetts]. These singers I have several times spoken of, and, as has been thought by those who had not heard them, with exaggeration. None, however, of those who heard their matchless strains at Faneuil Hall would have thought any degree of panegyric exaggeration, that language could bestow upon them. All those who have heard their modest concerts, in suitable sized rooms, and in tolerably clear atmosphere, would have said the people could get no idea of their enchanting powers amid the tumult and depraved air of that great, overgrown hall. But even there, it was a triumph for these 'New Hampshire Rainers,' as I have styled these unassuming young brothers (by this time a fourth brother, Jesse, had joined the group), though the celebrated Swiss minstrels, who wear that family name and have made it so famous in this country and in Europe, have more occasion to covet

for themselves the name of these singers from New Hampshire's Alps. They are not mere vocalists. They have hearts and minds as well as tuneful voices. They are not wandering, merce-
nary troubadors, who go about selling their strains for bread or for brandy. They are young
farmers. They work, *indoors* as well as out, in the noble kitchen as well as on the farm, and get
a sound and substantial living by their useful industry. The more entitled are they to the most
generous encouragement of their countrymen when they go forth occasionally to charm the
community by their music. That they are Abolitionists may engender prejudice against them in
the pro-slavery breast, but their lays will banish the demon from the meanest heart, as David's
harp played the devil out of King Saul.

"The Hutchinsons were present throughout the meetings, and it is probable contributed considerably to keeping up the unparalleled attendance that thronged the hall. They
were not there as mercenaries in an orchestra. They were not hired performers. They were there
as Garrison and Boyle were; as Douglass and Phillips, and the rest of us all, 'To help the cause
along'; and they helped it.[2] They were always in order, too, when they spoke; and it was what they
said, as well as how they said it, that sent anti-slavery like electricity to every heart. I never saw
such effect on human assemblies as these appeals produced. They made the vast multitudes
toss and heave and *clamor* like the roaring ocean. Orpheus is said to have made the trees dance
at his playing. The Hutchinsons made the thousands at Faneuil Hall spring to their feet simultaneously, 'as if in a dance,' and echo the anti-slavery appeal with a cheering that almost moved
the old Revolutionists from their stations on the wall. On one occasion it was absolutely amazing and sublime. Phillips had been speaking in his happiest vein. It was towards night. The old
hall was sombre in the *gloaming*. It was thronged to its vast extremities. Phillips closed his
speech at the highest pitch of his fine genius, and retired from the platform, when the four
brothers rushed to his place, and took up the argument where he had left it, on the very heights
of poetic declamation, and carried it off heavenwards on one of their boldest flights. Jesse had
framed a series of stanzas on the spot, while Phillips was speaking, embodying the leading arguments, and enforcing them, as mere oratory cannot, as music and poetry only can, and they
poured them forth with amazing spirit, in one of the maddening Second Advent tunes. The vast
multitude sprang to their feet, as one man, and at the close of the first strain, gave vent to their
enthusiasm in a thunder of unrestrained cheering. Three cheers, and three times three, and
ever so many more—for they could not count—they sent out, full-hearted and full-toned, till the
old roof rang again. And through-out the whole succeeding strains they repeated it, not allowing the singers to complete half the stanza before breaking out upon them in uncontrollable
emotion. Oh, it was glorious!

"And it was not the rude mobocratic shouting of the blind partisan, or the unearthly
glee of the religious maniac; it was Humanity's jubilee cry. And there was *music* in it. The multitude had caught the spirit and tone of the orator and the minstrel bards, and they exemplified
it in their humanized shoutings. There is grand music in this natural, generous uproar of the
mighty multitude, when it goes out spontaneously, as God made it to do. 'The sound of many
waters' is not more harmonious, nor a millionth part so expressive—for there is not a soul in
the unconscious waters. But I am exceeding my limits. I wish the whole city, and the entire
country could have been there—even all the people. Slavery would have died of that music and
the response of the multitude. If politics had been discountenanced altogether at the meetings—or suffered only to have their proportional attention—the whole tide of the proceedings
would have been as overwhelming as the bugle cries of the Hutchinsons."

The verses of which the writer speaks were improvised by Jesse, as Rogers says, to enforce the oratory of Phillips. They were sung to the tune of "The Old Granite State." I cannot now reproduce the words.

SOURCE: John Wallace Hutchinson, *Story of the Hutchinsons (Tribe of Jesse)*, 2 vols. (1896; reprint, New York: Da Capo, 1977): 1:60, 63–40; 2:75–77.

~~~~~~~~~~

NOTES

1.   Dale Cockrell, ed., *Excelsior: Journals of the Hutchinson Family Singers, 1842–1846* (Stuyvesant, N.Y.: Pendragon, 1989): 286.
2.   Named are leading figures in the Abolitionist movement, among them William Lloyd Garrison (1831–1865), Frederick Douglass (see chapter 41), and Wendell Phillips (1811–1884).

Walt Whitman's Conversion to Opera

The debates surrounding opera as an alien, elitist form in a democratic culture are displayed in this chapter, which includes examples of music criticism written by our great national poet Walt Whitman (1819–1892), who, in the mid-1840s, worked as a feature writer and critic for various New York journals and the newspaper the *Brooklyn Daily Eagle*. In early reviews, such as the first excerpt reprinted here, Whitman dismissed Italian opera in favor of popular music, as sung by such "family" groups as the Cheneys and the Hutchinsons. And then Whitman was reborn as an opera lover, converted by Bellini, Donizetti, and Verdi, whose operas were sung by a steady stream of dazzling Italian singers in New York during the 1840s and '50s (see chapter 40). The impact of opera on Whitman's art could not have been predicted, as it pushed him forward into free rather than rhymed verse forms. He later said, "But for the opera, I could never have written *Leaves of Grass*."[1] The selection following the review includes part of a long poem, "Proud Music of the Storm," in which Whitman provides a roster of some of the performances that helped him to change his mind about Italian opera.

December 4, 1846

MUSIC THAT *IS* MUSIC

A discriminating observer of the phases of humanity—particularly its affectations—propounded through his editorial voice, the other day, a query whether nineteen twentieths of those who *appear* to be enraptured at the N.Y. concerts with the florid Italian and French music, could really tell the difference, if they were blindfolded, between the playing of a tolerable amateur, and the "divine" execution of Sivori, De Meyer, and so on. We trow not! Four fifths of the enthusiasm at that sort of melody is unreal. We do not mean to say but what there *is* melody; but a man *here* might as well go into extatics at one of Cicero's orations, in its original Roman!

We do wish the good ladies and gentlemen of America would be truer to themselves and to legitimate refinement. With all honor and glory to the land of the olive and the vine, fair-skied Italy—with no turning up of noses at Germany, France, or England—we humbly demand whether we have not run after their beauties long enough. For nearly every nation has its peculiarities and its idioms which make its best intellectual efforts dearest to itself alone, so that hardly any thing which comes to us in the music and songs of the Old World, is strictly good and fitting to our nation. Except, indeed, that great scope of song which pictures love, hope, or mirth, in their most general aspect.

The music of feeling—heart music as distinguished from art music—is well exemplified in such singing as the Hutchinsons', and several other bands of American vocalists. With the richest physical power—with the guidance of discretion, and taste, and experience,—with the mellowing influence of discipline—it is marvellous that they do not *entirely* supplant the stale, second hand, foreign method, with its flourishes, its ridiculous sentimentality, its anti-republican spirit, and its sycophantic tainting the young taste of the nation! We allude to, and specially commend, all this school of singing—well exemplified as its beauty is in those "bands of brothers," whereof we have several now before the American public. Because whatever touches the heart is better than what is merely addressed to the ear. Elegant simplicity in manner is more judicious than the dancing school bows and curtsies, and inane smiles, and kissing of the tips of gloves *a la Pico*. Songs whose words you can hear and understand are preferable to a mass of unintelligible stuff, (for who makes out even the libretto of English opera, as now given on the stage?) which for all the sense you get out of it, might as well be Arabic. Sensible sweetness is better than sweetness all distorted by unnatural nonsense. . . .

Such hints as the above, however, we throw out rather as suggestive of a train of thought to other and more deliberate thinkers than we—and not as the criticisms of a musical connoisseur. If they have pith in them, well; if not, we at least know they are written in that true wish for benefitting the subject spoken of, which should characterize all such essays. We are absolutely sick to nausea of the patent-leather, curled hair, "japonicadom" [that is, the upper-class] style.—The *real* (not "artistes" but) singers are as much ahead of it as good real teeth are ahead of artificial ones. The sight of them, as they are, puts one in mind of health and fresh air in the country, at sunrise—the dewy, earthy fragrance that comes up then in the moisture, and touches the nostrils more gratefully than all the perfumes of the most ingenious chemist.

SOURCE: Walt Whitman, "Music That *IS* Music," *Brooklyn Daily Eagle*, December 4, 1846, reprinted in *The Collected Writings of Walt Whitman: The Journalism: vol. 2, 1846–1848*, ed. Herbert Bergman, Douglas A. Noverr, and Edward J. Recchia (New York: Peter Lang, 2003): 137–38.

～～～～

*These lines from Whitman's "Proud Music of the Storm" refer to many operas,
among them* Norma *and* La Sonnambula *by Bellini;* Lucia di Lammermoor *and*
La Favorita *by Donizetti;* Robert le Diable, Les Huguenots *and* Le Prophète *by
Meyerbeer; and* Ernani *by Verdi. Whitman also pays tribute to the Italian soprano
Marietta Alboni (1823–1894), a celebrity of her time.*

PROUD MUSIC OF THE STORM

1

*PROUD music of the storm,
Blast that careers so free, whistling across the prairies,
Strong hum of forest tree-tops—wind of the mountains,
Personified dim shapes—you hidden orchestras,
You serenades of phantoms with instruments alert,
Blending with Nature's rhythmus all the tongues of nations;
You chords left us by vast composers—you choruses,
You formless, free, religious dances—you from the Orient,
You undertone of rivers, roar of pouring cataracts,
You sounds from distant guns with galloping cavalry,
Echoes of camps with all the different bugle-calls,
Trooping tumultuous, filling the midnight late, bending me powerless,
Entering my lonesome slumber-chamber, why have you seiz'd me?*
. . .

3
. . .
*All songs of current lands come sounding round me,
The German airs of friendship, wine and love,
Irish ballads, merry jigs and dances, English warbles,
Chansons of France, Scotch tunes, and o'er the rest,
Italia's peerless compositions.*

*Across the stage with pallor on her face, yet lurid passion,
Stalks Norma brandishing the dagger in her hand.*

*I see poor crazed Lucia's eyes' unnatural gleam,
Her hair down her back falls loose and dishevel'd.*

*I see where Ernani walking the bridal garden,
Amid the scent of night-roses, radiant, holding his bride by the hand,
Hears the infernal call, the death-pledge of the horn.*

*To crossing swords and gray hairs bared to heaven,
The clear electric bass and baritone of the world,
The trombone duo, Libertad forever!*

From Spanish chestnut trees' dense shade,
By old and heavy convent walls a wailing song,
Song of lost love, the torch of youth and life quench'd in despair,
Song of the dying swan, Fernando's heart is breaking.

Awaking from her woes at last retriev'd Amina sings,
Copious as stars and glad as morning light the torrents of her joy.

(The teeming lady comes,
The lustrious orb, Venus contralto, the blooming mother,
Sister of loftiest gods, Alboni's self I hear.)

4
I hear those odes, symphonies, operas,
I hear in the William Tell the music of an arous'd and angry people,
I hear Meyerbeer's Huguenots, the Prophet, or Robert,
Gounod's Faust, or Mozart's Don Juan.

SOURCE: Walt Whitman, "Autumn Rivulets: Proud Music of the Storm," in *Leaves of Grass* (Philadelphia: David McKay 1891–1892). Available at http://www.princeton.edu/~batke/logr.

~~~~~~~~~~

NOTE

1.   John Townsend Trowbridge, "Reminiscences of Walt Whitman," *Atlantic Monthly*, February 1902, 166; cited in John Dizikes, *Opera in America: A Cultural History* (New Haven, Conn.: Yale University Press, 1993): 185.

40

CLARA KELLOGG AND THE MEMOIRS OF
AN AMERICAN PRIMA DONNA

Memoirs from the first few generations of American-born opera singers are filled with fascinating details about musical life that often contradict stereotypes about "elite" audiences for opera. The soprano Clara Louise Kellogg (1842–1916) began her climb to fame and fortune in New York in the 1850s. She ended up as the manager of her own touring-company specializing in translating the famous Italian and German operas into English. As the historian Katherine Preston writes, her company built on previous touring opera troupes in "the substantial English opera movement in the United States—a movement that espoused 'opera for the people' that featured fabulously successful companies headed by such American prima donnas as Emma Abbott and Clara Louise Kellogg."[1] These excerpts begin with anecdotes about courage.

FOREWORD BY ISABEL MOORE

When she came before her countrymen as a singer, she was several decades ahead of her musical public, for she was a lyric artist as well as a singer. America was not then producing lyric artists; and in fact we were, as a nation, just getting over the notion that America could not produce great voices.

. . . Nothing was so absolutely necessary for our self-respect as that some American woman should arise with sufficient American talent and bravery to prove beyond all cavil that the country was able to produce both singers and artists.

. . .

CHAPTER II   GIRLHOOD

In taking up vocal study, however, I had no fixed intention of going on the stage. All I decided was to make as much as I could of myself and of my voice. Many girls I knew studied singing merely as an accomplishment. In fact, the girl who aspired professionally was almost unknown.

I first studied under a Frenchman named Millet, a graduate of the Conservatory of Paris, who was teaching the daughters of Colonel Stebbins and, also, the daughter of the Baron de Trobriand. Later, I worked with Manzocchi, Rivarde, Errani, and Muzio, who was a great friend of Verdi.[2] . . . In those days the life of the theater was regarded as altogether outside the pale. One didn't know stage people; one couldn't speak to them, nor shake hands with them, nor even look at them except from a safe distance across the footlights. There were no "decent people on the stage"; how often did I hear that foolish thing said!

It is odd that in that most musical and artistic country, Italy, much the same prejudice exists to this day. I should never think of telling a really great Italian lady that I had been on the stage; she would immediately think that there was something queer about me. Of course in America all that was changed some time ago, after England had established the precedent. People are now pleased not only to meet artists socially, but to lionise them as well. But when I was a girl there was a gulf as deep as the Bottomless Pit between society and people of the theatre; and it was this gulf that I knew would open between myself and the friends of whom I was really fond as, in time, I realised that I was improving sufficiently to justify some definite ambitions. My work was steady and unremitting, and by the time I began study with Muzio my mind was pretty nearly made up.

A queer, nervous, brusque, red-headed man was Muzio, from the north of Italy, where the type always seems so curiously German. Besides being one of the conductors of the Opera, he organised concert tours, and promised to see that I should have my chance. It was said that he had fled from political disturbances in Italy, but this I never heard verified. Certainly he was quite a big man in the New York operatic world of his day, and was a most cultivated musician, with the "Italian traditions" of opera at his fingers' ends. It is to Muzio, incidentally, that I owe my trill.

. . .

It was almost time for my *début*, and there was still something I had to do. To my sheltered, puritanically brought up consciousness, there could be no two views among conventional people as to the life I was about to enter upon. I knew all about it. So, a few weeks before I was to make my professional bow to the public, I called my girl friends together, the companions of four years' study, and I said to them:

"Girls, I've made up my mind to go on the stage! I know just how your people feel about it, and I want to tell you now that you needn't know me any more. You needn't speak to me, nor bow to me if you meet me in the street. I shall quite understand, and I shan't feel a bit badly. Because I think the day will come when you will be proud to know me!"

CHAPTER III   "LIKE A PICKED CHICKEN"

Before my *début* in opera, Muzio took me out on a concert tour for a few weeks. Colson was the *prima donna*, Brignoli the tenor, Ferri the baritone, and Susini the basso. Susini had, I believe, distinguished himself in the Italian Revolution. His name means *plums* in Italian, and his voice as well as his name was rich and luscious.

I was a general utility member of the company, and sang to fill in the chinks. We sang four times a week, and I received twenty-five dollars each time—that is, one hundred dollars a week—not bad for inexperienced seventeen, although Muzio regarded the tour for me as merely educational and part of my training.

My mother travelled with me, for she never let me out of her sight. Yet, even with her along, the experience was very strange and new and rather terrifying. I had no knowledge of stage life, and that first *tournée* was comprised of a series of shocks and surprises, most of them disillusioning.

. . .

Our next stop was Cincinnati—*Cincinnata,* as it was called! I had there one of the shocks of my life. The leading newspaper of the city, in commenting on our concert, said of me that "this young girl's parents ought to remove her from public view, do her up in cotton wool, nourish her well, and not allow her to appear again until she looks less like a picked chicken"! No one said anything about my voice!

I *must* have been an odd, young creature—just five feet and four inches tall, and weighing only one hundred and four pounds. I was frail and big-eyed, and wrapped up in music (not cotton wool), and exceedingly childlike for my age. I knew nothing of life, for my puritanical surroundings and the way in which I had been brought up were developing my personality very slowly.

CHAPTER V   A YOUTHFUL REALIST

I was not popular with my fellow-artists and did not have a very pleasant time preparing and rehearsing for my first parts. The chorus was made up of Italians who never studied their music, merely learned it at rehearsal, and the rehearsals themselves were often farcical. The Italians of the chorus were always bitter against me for, up to that time, Italians had had the monopoly of music. It was not generally conceded that Americans could appreciate, much less interpret opera; and I, as the first American *prima donna*, was in the position of a foreigner in my own country. The chorus, indeed, could sometimes hardly contain themselves. "Who is she," they would demand indignantly, "to come and take the bread out of our mouths?"

. . .

My first season in Boston—from which I have strayed so far so many times—was destined to be a brief one, but also very strenuous, due to the fact that in the beginning I had only two operas in my répertoire, one of which [Verdi's *La Traviata*] Boston did not approve. After *Linda*, I was rushed on in Bellini's *I Puritani* and had to "get up in it" in three days. It went very

Portrait of Clara Louise Kellogg as Carmen.

well, and was followed with *La Sonnambula* by the same composer and after only one week's rehearsal.[3] I was a busy girl in those weeks; and I should have been still busier if opera in America had not received a sudden and tragic blow.

The "vacillating" Buchanan's reign was over. On March 4th Lincoln was inaugurated. A hush of suspense was in the air:—a hush broken on April 12th by the shot fired by South Carolina upon Fort Sumter. On April 14th Sumter capitulated and Abraham Lincoln called for volunteers. The Civil War had begun.

CHAPTER VI   WAR TIMES

At first the tremendous crisis filled everyone with a purely impersonal excitement and concern; but one fine morning we awoke to the fact that our opera season was paralysed.

The American people found the actual dramas of Bull Run, Big Bethel and Harpers Ferry more absorbing than any play or opera ever put upon the boards, and the airs of *Yankee Doodle* and *The Girl I Left Behind Me* more inspiring than the finest operatic *arias* in the world. They did not want to go to the theatres in the evening. They wanted to read the bulletin boards. Every move in the big game of war that was being played by the ruling powers of our country was of thrilling interest, and as fast as things happened they were "posted."

Maretzek "the Magnificent," so obstinate that he simply did not know how to give up a project merely because it was impossible, packed a few of us off to Philadelphia to produce the *Ballo in Maschera*.[4] We hoped against hope that it would be light enough to divert the public, at even that tragic moment. But the public refused to be diverted. . . . We could plainly see that opera was doomed for the time being in America.

Then Maretzek bethought himself of *La Figlia del Reggimento,* a military opera, very light and infectious, that might easily catch the wave of public sentiment at the moment. We put it on in a rush. I played the Daughter and we crowded into the performance every bit of martial feeling we could muster. I learned to play the drum, and we introduced all sorts of military business and bugle calls, and altogether contrived to create a warlike atmosphere. We were determined to make a success of it; but we were also genuinely moved by the contagious glow that pervaded the country and the times, and to this combined mood of patriotism and expediency we sacrificed many artistic details. For example, we were barbarous enough to put in sundry American national airs and we had the assistance of real Zouaves to lend colour; and this reminds me that about the same period Isabella Hinckley even sang "The Star Spangled Banner" in the middle of a performance of *Il Barbiere*.

Our attempt was a great success. We played Donizetti's little opera to houses of frantic enthusiasm, first in Baltimore, then in Washington on May the third, where naturally the war fever was at its highest heat. The audiences cheered and cried and let themselves go in the hysterical manner of people wrought up by great national excitements. Even on the stage we caught the feeling. I sang the Figlia better than I had ever sung anything yet, and I found myself wondering, as I sang, how many of my cadet friends of a few months earlier were already at the front.

. . .

Everybody went about singing Mrs. Howe's *Battle Hymn of the Republic* and it was then that I first learned that the air—the simple but rousing little melody of *John Brown's Body*—was in reality a melody by Felix Mendelssohn. Martial songs of all kinds were the order of the day and all more classic music was relegated to the background for the time being. It was not until the following winter that public sentiment subsided sufficiently for us to really consider another musical season.

CHAPTER VIII   MARGUERITE

As I have mentioned, we took wicked liberties with the operas, such as introducing the *Star Spangled Banner* and similar patriotic songs into the middle of Italian scores. . . . Nothing could give anyone so clear an idea of the universal acceptance of this custom of interpolation as the following criticism, printed during our second season:

> "The production of *Faust* last evening by the Maretzek troupe was excellent indeed. But why, O why, the eternal *Soldiers' Chorus?* Why this everlasting,

tedious march, when there are so many excellent band pieces on the market that would fit the occasion better?"

As a rule the public were quite satisfied with this chorus. It was whistled and sung all over the country and never failed to get eager applause.

CHAPTER XXIV   ENGLISH OPERA

THE idea of giving opera in English has always interested me. I never could understand why there were any more reasons against giving an English version of *Carmen* in New York than against giving a French version of *Die Freischütz* in Paris or a German version of *La Belle Helène* in Berlin. To be sure, it goes without saying, from a purist point of view it is a patent truth, that no libretto is ever so fine after it has been translated. Not only does the quality and spirit of the original evaporate in the process of translating, but, also, the syllables come wrong. Who has not suffered from the translations of foreign songs into which the translator has been obliged to introduce secondary notes to fit the extra syllables of the clumsily adapted English words? These are absolute objections to the performance of any operas or songs in a language other than the one to which the composer first set his music. Wagner in French is a joke; so is Goethe in Italian. . . .

My point is that such objections obtain not more stringently against English translations than against German, French, or Italian translations. Furthermore, after all is said that can be said against translations into whatsoever language, the fact remains that countries and races are not nearly so different as they pretend to be; and a human sentiment, a dramatic situation, or a lovely melody will permeate the consciousness of a Frenchman, an Englishman, or a German in approximately the same manner and in the same length of time. Adaptations and translations are merely different means, poorer or better as the case may be, of facilitating such assimilations; and, so soon as the idea reaches the audience, the audience is going to receive it joyfully, no matter what nation it comes from or through what medium:—that is, if it is a good idea to begin with.

Possibly this may be a little beside the point; but, at least, it serves to introduce the subject of English opera—or, rather, foreign grand opera given in English—the giving of which was an undertaking on which I embarked in 1873. I became my own manager and, with C. D. Hess, organised an English Opera Company that, by its success, brought the best music to the comprehension of the intelligent masses. I believe that the enterprise did much for the advancement of musical art in this country; and it, besides, gave employment to a large number of young Americans, several of whom began their careers in the chorus of the company and soon advanced to higher places in the musical world. . . .

During the three seasons of our English Opera Company, we put on a great number of operas of all schools, from *The Bohemian Girl* to *The Flying Dutchman*. The former is pretty poor stuff—cheap and insipid—I never liked to sing it.[5] But—the houses it drew! People loved it. I believe there would be a large and sentimental public ready for it to-day. Its extraneous matter, the two or three popular ballads that had been introduced, formed a part of its attraction, perhaps.

Unless the public can understand what is sung in opera or oratorio recital, song or ballad, no more than a passing interest can be awakened in the music-loving public. I do not agree with those who claim that language or thought is a secondary consideration to the enjoyment of vocal music. I believe that a superior writer of lyrics can fit words to the music of foreign operas that will not only be sensible but singable. I agree with *The Tribune* that opera in the English language has never had a fair show, but I claim that the reason for this is because of the bad translations that have been given to the artists to sing.

. . .

CHAPTER XXIX   TEACHING AND THE HALF-TALENTED

I have often and often received letters asking for advice and begging me to hear the voices of girls who have been told they have talent. It is a heart-breaking business. About one in sixty has had something resembling a voice and then, ten chances to one, she has not been in a position to cultivate herself.

. . .

There is something else which is very necessary for every girl to consider in going on the operatic stage. Has she the means for experimenting, or does she have to earn her living in some way meanwhile? If the former is the case, it will do no harm for her to play about with her voice, burn her fingers if need be, and come home to her mother and father not much the worse for the experience.

. . .

Yet, after all one's efforts to help, one can only let the young singers find out for themselves. If we could profit by each other's experience, there would be no need for the doctrine of reincarnation. But I wish—oh, how I wish—that I could save some foolish girls from embarking on the ocean of art as half of them do with neither chart or compass, nor even a seaworthy boat.

A better metaphor comes to me in my recollection of a famous lighthouse that I once visited. The rocks about were strewn with dead birds—pitiful, little, eager creatures that had broken their wings and beaten out their lives all night against the great revolving light. So the lighthouse of success lures the young, ambitious singers. And so they break their wings against it.

. . .

Herewith I say the same to four-fifths of all the girl singers who, in villages, in shops, in schools, everywhere, are all yearning to be great. They came to me in shoals in Paris and Milan, begging for just enough money to get home with. I have shipped many a failure back to America, and my soul has been sick for their disappointment and disillusionment. But they will *not* be guided by advice or warning. They have got to learn actually and bitterly.

SOURCE: Clara Louise Kellogg, *Memoirs of an American Prima Donna* (New York: Putnam's, 1913): 11–12, 21–22, 25, 27–28, 40–41, 54–57, 61, 88–89, 227, 256–58, 316, 319–20, 323.

~~~~~~~~

NOTES

1.   Katherine K. Preston, *Opera on the Road. Traveling Opera Troupes in the United States, 1825–1860* (Urbana: University of Illinois Press, 1993): 257.

2. Among the most prominent coaches named by Kellogg were the tenor Achille Errani (1824–1897) and the conductor and composer Emanuele Muzio (1825–1890), who was also a student and close associate of Verdi. For details about these figures, see chapter 32 for a reference to Vera Brodsky Lawrence's monumental editions of *Strong on Music*.

3. This excerpt refers to many bel canto operas in the standard popular repertory at this time, among them *Linda di Chamounix* and *La Figlia del Reggimento* (mentioned later by Kellogg), both by Donizetti; and *La Traviata* and *Un Ballo in Maschera* (*The Masked Ball*) by Verdi. Since its heroine was a "fallen woman," *La Traviata* occasionally was rejected for production in various cities, including Boston and Brooklyn.

4. Max Maretzek (1821–1897), dubbed "Max the Magnificent," was a powerful opera impresario and conductor/composer, who worked with the greatest musicians of his time.

5. Kellogg refers to operas at two ends of the spectrum, *The Bohemian Girl* (1843) by Michael Balfe (1808–1870) and *The Flying Dutchman* (*Der fliegende Holländer*, 1843) by Richard Wagner.

FREDERICK DOUGLASS FROM

MY BONDAGE AND MY FREEDOM

My Bondage and My Freedom (1855), the second of three autobiographies written by Frederick Douglass (1818?–1895) is not only a classic text of African-American enslavement, but a landmark for our understanding of black music in the United States before the twentieth century. Like Douglass's earlier autobiography, *Narrative of the Life of Frederick Douglass, an American Slave* (1845), sections of which Douglass reprised in this later book, these accounts of slave songs and music making are explicated as multilayered experiences, unknowable to the outsider and perhaps even to the insider. Ronald Radano writes, "More than any other single rhetorical aspect the slave song provides a marker of Douglass's authenticity. His words about song communicate a profound truth told, a story so powerful it has served for the past 150-odd years as the conceptual starting point for the history of modern African American culture."[1]

[ON WORK SONGS]

I have already referred to the business-like aspect of Col. Lloyd's plantation. This business-like appearance was much increased on the two days at the end of each month, when the slaves from the different farms came to get their monthly allowance of meal and meat. These were gala days for the slaves, and there was much rivalry among them as to *who* should be elected to go up to the great house farm for the allowance, and indeed, to attend to any business at this (for them) the capital. The beauty and grandeur of the place, its numerous slave population, and the fact that Harry, Peter and Jake the sailors of the sloop—almost always kept, privately, little trinkets which they bought at Baltimore, to sell, made it a privilege to come to the great house farm. Being selected, too, for this office, was deemed a high honor. It was taken as a proof of confidence and favor; but, probably, the chief motive of the competitors for the place, was, a desire to break the dull monotony of the field, and to get beyond the overseer's eye and lash. Once on the road with an ox team, and seated on the tongue of his cart, with no overseer to look after him, the slave was comparatively free; and, if thoughtful, he had time to think. Slaves are generally expected to sing as well as to work. A silent slave is not liked by masters or overseers. "*Make a noise,*" "*make a noise,*" and "*bear a hand,*" are the words usually addressed to the slaves when there is silence amongst them. This may account for the almost constant singing heard in the southern states. There was, generally, more or less singing among the teamsters, as it was one means of letting the overseer know where they were, and that they were moving on with the work. But, on allowance day, those who visited the great house farm were peculiarly excited and noisy. While on their way, they would make the dense old woods, for miles around, reverberate with their wild notes. These were not always merry because they were wild. On the contrary, they were mostly of a plaintive cast, and told a tale of grief and sorrow. In the most boisterous outbursts of rapturous sentiment, there was ever a tinge of deep melancholy. I have never heard any songs like those anywhere since I left slavery, except when in Ireland. There I heard the same *wailing notes,* and was much affected by them. It was during the famine of 1845–6. In all the songs of the slaves, there was ever some expression in praise of the great house farm; something which would flatter the pride of the owner, and, possibly, draw a favorable glance from him.

> *I am going away to the great house farm,*
>
>   *O yea! O yea! O yea!*
>
> *My old master is a good old master,*
>
>   *O yea! O yea! O yea!*

This they would sing, with other words of their own improvising—jargon to others, but full of meaning to themselves. I have sometimes thought, that the mere hearing of those songs would do more to impress truly spiritual-minded men and women with the soul-crushing and death-dealing character of slavery, than the reading of whole volumes of its mere physical cruelties. They speak to the heart and to the soul of the thoughtful. I cannot better express my sense of them now, than ten years ago, when, in sketching my life, I thus spoke of this feature of my plantation experience:

> I did not, when a slave, understand the deep meanings of those rude, and apparently incoherent songs. I was myself within the circle, so that I neither saw

or heard as those without might see and hear. They told a tale which was then altogether beyond my feeble comprehension; they were tones, loud, long and deep, breathing the prayer and complaint of souls boiling over with the bitterest anguish. Every tone was a testimony against slavery, and a prayer to God for deliverance from chains. The hearing of those wild notes always depressed my spirits, and filled my heart with ineffable sadness. The mere recurrence, even now, afflicts my spirit, and while I am writing these lines, my tears are falling. To those songs I trace my first glimmering conceptions of the dehumanizing character of slavery. I can never get rid of that conception. Those songs still follow me, to deepen my hatred of slavery, and quicken my sympathies for my brethren in bonds. If any one wishes to be impressed with a sense of the soul-killing power of slavery, let him go to Col. Lloyd's plantation, and, on allowance day, place himself in the deep, pine woods, and there let him, in silence, thoughtfully analyze the sounds that shall pass through the chambers of his soul, and if he is not thus impressed, it will only be because "there is no flesh in his obdurate heart."

The remark is not unfrequently made, that slaves are the most contended and happy laborers in the world. They dance and sing, and make all manner of joyful noises—so they do; but it is a great mistake to suppose them happy because they sing. The songs of the slave represent the sorrows, rather than the joys of his heart; and he is relieved by them, only as an aching heart is relieved by its tears. Such is the constitution of the human mind, that, when pressed to extremes, it often avails itself of the most opposite methods. Extremes meet in mind as in matter. When the slaves on board of the "Pearl" were overtaken, arrested, and carried to prison—their hopes for freedom blasted—as they marched in chains they sang, and found (as Emily Edmunson tells us) a melancholy relief in singing. The singing of a man cast away on a desolate island, might be as appropriately considered an evidence of his contentment and happiness, as the singing of a slave. Sorrow and desolation have their songs, as well as joy and peace. Slaves sing more to *make* themselves happy, than to express their happiness. . . .

[ON SLAVE SINGING AT HOLIDAYS]

The days between Christmas day and New Year's, [were] allowed the slaves as holidays. During these days, all regular work was suspended, and there was nothing to do but to keep fires, and look after the stock. This time was regarded as our own, by the grace of our masters, and we, therefore used it, or abused it, as we pleased. Those who had families at a distance, were now expected to visit them, and to spend with them the entire week. The younger slaves, or the unmarried ones, were expected to see to the cattle, and attend to incidental duties at home. The holidays were variously spent. The sober, thinking and industrious ones of our number, would employ themselves in manufacturing corn brooms, mats, horse collars and baskets, and some of these were very well made. Another class spent their time in hunting opossums, coons, rabbits, and other game. But the majority spent the holidays in sports, ball playing, wrestling, boxing, running foot races, dancing, and drinking whisky; and this latter mode of spending the time was generally most agreeable to their masters. A slave who would work during the holidays, was thought, by his master, undeserving of holidays. Such an one had rejected the favor of his master. There was, in this simple act of continued work, an accusation against slaves;

and a slave could not help thinking, that if he made three dollars during the holidays, he might make three hundred during the year. Not to be drunk during the holidays, was disgraceful; and he was esteemed a lazy and improvident man, who could not afford to drink whisky during Christmas.

The fiddling, dancing and *"jubilee beating,"* was going on in all directions. This latter performance is strictly southern. It supplies the place of a violin, or of other musical instruments, and is played so easily, that almost every farm has its "Juba" beater. The performer improvises as he beats, and sings his merry songs, so ordering the words as to have them fall pat with the movement of his hands. Among a mass of nonsense and wild frolic, once in a while a sharp hit is given to the meanness of slaveholders. Take the following, for an example:

> *We raise de wheat,*
>
> *Dey gib us de corn;*
>
> *We bake de bread,*
>
> *Dey gib us de cruss;*
>
> *We sif de meal,*
>
> *Dey gib us de huss;*
>
> *We peal de meat,*
>
> *Dey gib us de skin,*
>
> *And dat's de way*
>
> *Dey takes us in.*
>
> *We skim de pot,*
>
> *Dey gib us the liquor,*
>
> *And say dat's good enough for nigger.*
>
> *Walk over! walk over!*
>
> *Tom butter and de fat;*
>
> *Poor nigger you can't get over dat;*
>
> *Walk over!*

This is not a bad summary of the palpable injustice and fraud of slavery, giving—as it does—to the lazy and idle, the comforts which God designed should be given solely to the honest laborer. But to the holidays.

Judging from my own observation and experience, I believe these holidays to be among the most effective means, in the hands of slaveholders, of keeping down the spirit of insurrection among the slaves.

. . .

It is the interest and business of slaveholders to study human nature, with a view to practical results, and many of them attain astonishing proficiency in discerning the thoughts and emotions of slaves. They have to deal not with earth, wood, or stone, but with *men;* and, by every regard they have for their safety and prosperity, they must study to know the material on which they are at work. So much intellect as the slaveholder has around him, requires watching. Their safety depends upon their vigilance. Conscious of the injustice and wrong they are every hour perpetrating, and knowing what they themselves would do if made the victims of such wrongs, they are looking out for the first signs of the dread retribution of justice. They watch, therefore, with skilled and practiced eyes, and have learned to read, with great accuracy, the state of mind and heart of the slaves, through his sable face.

. . .

But with all our caution and studied reserve, I am not sure that Mr. Freeland did not suspect that all was not right with us. It *did* seem that he watched us more narrowly, after the plan of escape had been conceived and discussed amongst us. Men seldom see themselves as others see them; and while, to ourselves, everything connected with our contemplated escape appeared concealed, Mr. Freeland may have, with the peculiar prescience of a slaveholder, mastered the huge thought which was disturbing our peace in slavery.

I am the more inclined to think that he suspected us, because, prudent as we were, as I now look back, I can see that we did many silly things, very well calculated to awaken suspicion. We were, at times, remarkably buoyant, singing hymns and making joyous exclamations, almost as triumphant in their tone as if we [had] reached a land of freedom and safety. A keen observer might have detected in our repeated singing of

> *O Canaan, sweet Canaan,*
>
> *I am bound for the land of Canaan,*

something more than a hope of reaching heaven. We meant to reach the *north*—and the north was our Canaan.

> *I thought I heard them say,*
>
> *There were lions in the way,*
>
> *I don't expect to stay*
>
> *Much longer here.*
>
> *Run to Jesus—shun the danger—*
>
> *I don't expect to stay*
>
> *Much longer here,*

was a favorite air, and had a double meaning. In the lips of some, it meant the expectation of a speedy summons to a world of spirits; but, in the lips of *our* company, it simply meant, a speedy pilgrimage toward a free state, and deliverance from all the evils and dangers of slavery.

SOURCE: Frederick Douglass, *My Bondage and My Freedom* (New York and Auburn: Miller, Orton & Mulligan, 1855): 96–100, 251–53, 276–79. Available at http://etext.lib .virginia.edu/modeng/modengD.browse.html.

~~~~~~~~

NOTE

1.   Ronald A. Radano, *Lying Up a Nation: Race and Black Music* (Chicago: University of Chicago Press, 2003): 49.

HARRIET BEECHER STOWE AND

TWO SCENES FROM *UNCLE TOM'S CABIN*

Sometimes the critical vision of a writer can change the way her readers hear music. By filling her antislavery novel *Uncle Tom's Cabin* with spiritual drama and moral authority, Harriet Beecher Stowe (1811–1896) influenced the way her white audience experienced black hymnody. Writing before black spirituals were known as a distinctive genre, Stowe employed conventional Methodist hymns, which would have been familiar to her readership. In contrast to Frederick Douglass, who exposed the double meaning of Christian imagery as metaphors for liberation, Stowe dramatized the bonds among sanctified martyrdom, Christian guilt, and black singing under enslavement.

In this excerpt, which takes place on the shore of Lake Pontchartrain in New Orleans, Uncle Tom comes to recognize through a hymn text the imminent death of Little Eva.

At this time in our story, the whole St. Clare establishment is, for the time being, removed to their villa on Lake Pontchartrain. The heats of summer had driven all who were able to leave the sultry and unhealthy city, to seek the shores of the lake, and its cool sea-breezes.

St. Clare's villa was an East Indian cottage, surrounded by light verandahs of bamboo-work, and opening on all sides into gardens and pleasure-grounds. The common sitting-room opened on to a large garden, fragrant with every picturesque plant and flower of the tropics, where winding paths ran down to the very shores of the lake, whose silvery sheet of water lay there, rising and falling in the sunbeams,—a picture never for an hour the same, yet every hour more beautiful.

It is now one of those intensely golden sunsets which kindles the whole horizon into one blaze of glory, and makes the water another sky. The lake lay in rosy or golden streaks, save where white-winged vessels glided hither and thither, like so many spirits, and little golden stars twinkled through the glow, and looked down at themselves as they trembled in the water.

Tom and Eva were seated on a little mossy seat, in an arbor, at the foot of the garden. It was Sunday evening, and Eva's Bible lay open on her knee. She read,—"And I saw a sea of glass, mingled with fire."

"Tom," said Eva, suddenly stopping, and pointing to the lake, "there 't is."

"What, Miss Eva?"

"Don't you see,—there?" said the child, pointing to the glassy water, which, as it rose and fell, reflected the golden glow of the sky. "There's a 'sea of glass, mingled with fire.'"

"True enough, Miss Eva," said Tom; and Tom sang—

O, had I the wings of the morning,

I'd fly away to Canaan's shore;

Bright angels should convey me home,

To the new Jerusalem.

"Where do you suppose new Jerusalem is, Uncle Tom?" said Eva.

"O, up in the clouds, Miss Eva."

"Then I think I see it," said Eva. "Look in those clouds!—they look like great gates of pearl; and you can see beyond them—far, far off—it's all gold. Tom, sing about 'spirits bright.'"

Tom sung the words of a well-known Methodist hymn,

I see a band of spirits bright,

That taste the glories there;

They all are robed in spotless white,

And conquering palms they bear.

"Uncle Tom, I've seen *them*," said Eva.

Tom had no doubt of it at all; it did not surprise him in the least. If Eva had told him she had been to heaven, he would have thought it entirely probable.

"They come to me sometimes in my sleep, those spirits;" and Eva's eyes grew dreamy, and she hummed, in a low voice,

"They are all robed in spotless white, And conquering palms they bear."

"Uncle Tom," said Eva, "I'm going there."

"Where, Miss Eva?"

The child rose, and pointed her little hand to the sky; the glow of evening lit her golden hair and flushed cheek with a kind of unearthly radiance, and her eyes were bent earnestly on the skies.

"I'm going *there*," she said, "to the spirits bright, Tom; *I'm going, before long."*

The faithful old heart felt a sudden thrust; and Tom thought how often he had noticed, within six months, that Eva's little hands had grown thinner, and her skin more transparent, and her breath shorter; and how, when she ran or played in the garden, as she once could for hours, she became soon so tired and languid. He had heard Miss Ophelia speak often of a cough, that all her medicaments could not cure; and even now that fervent cheek and little hand were burning with hectic fever; and yet the thought that Eva's words suggested had never come to him till now.

~~~~~~~~

This second harrowing excerpt also uses hymns, but to a different end. Stowe contrasts virtue and sin in her depiction of a slave auction house, which will soon rip apart mother and child. The music of the Virgin mother, "Weeping Mary" symbolizes universal suffering as well as the suffering of black mothers. "Weeping Mary" is still found today in both black and white spiritual traditions. Here, Stowe also recognizes differences between white and black hymns; her comment on "wildness" was a typical way to describe African practices she did not understand.

And, Emmeline, if we shouldn't ever see each other again, after to-morrow,—if I'm sold way up on a plantation somewhere, and you somewhere else,—always remember how you've been brought up, and all Missis has told you; take your Bible with you, and your hymn-book; and if you're faithful to the Lord, he'll be faithful to you."

So speaks the poor soul, in sore discouragement; for she knows that to-morrow any man, however vile and brutal, however godless and merciless, if he only has money to pay for her, may become owner of her daughter, body and soul; and then, how is the child to be faithful? She thinks of all this, as she holds her daughter in her arms, and wishes that she were not handsome and attractive. It seems almost an aggravation to her to remember how purely and piously, how much above the ordinary lot, she has been brought up. But she has no resort but to *pray*; and many such prayers to God have gone up from those same trim, neatly-arranged, respectable slave-prisons,—prayers which God has not forgotten, as a coming day shall show; for it is written, "Who causeth one of these little ones to offend, it were better for him that a millstone were hanged about his neck, and that he were drowned in the depths of the sea."

The soft, earnest, quiet moonbeam looks in fixedly, marking the bars of the grated windows on the prostrate, sleeping forms. The mother and daughter are singing together a wild and melancholy dirge, common as a funeral hymn among the slaves:

> O, where is weeping Mary?
>
> O, where is weeping Mary?
>
> 'Rived in the goodly land.
>
> She is dead and gone to Heaven;
>
> She is dead and gone to Heaven;
>
> 'Rived in the goodly land.

These words, sung by voices of a peculiar and melancholy sweetness, in an air which seemed like the sighing of earthy despair after heavenly hope, floated through the dark prison rooms with a pathetic cadence, as verse after verse was breathed out:

> O, where are Paul and Silas?
>
> O, where are Paul and Silas?
>
> Gone to the goodly land.
>
> They are dead and gone to Heaven;
>
> They are dead and gone to Heaven;
>
> 'Rived in the goodly land.

Sing on poor souls! The night is short, and the morning will part you forever!

SOURCE: Harriet Beecher Stowe, *Uncle Tom's Cabin* (Boston: John P. Jewett, 1852): 380–83, 470–74. Available at http://etext.lib.virginia.edu/modeng/modengS.browse.html.

43

FROM *SLAVE SONGS OF THE UNITED STATES*

(1867)

In 1867, northern abolitionists William Francis Allen, Charles Pickard Ware, and Lucy McKim Garrison published a ground-breaking and now-classic collection of African-American folk music. "Roll, Jordan, Roll," "Nobody Knows the Trouble I've Had," "Michael, Row Your Boat Ashore," "No More Peck o' Corn for Me," "Jacob's Ladder," "The Good Old Way" ("I Went Down to the River to Pray"), and "Musieu Bainjo" are some of its many famous songs. Of the 136 tunes, 82 came from Port Royal, South Carolina—site of the "experimental free slave community"—as well as Georgia and the Sea Islands. In the mid-1900s, recordings of great folk artists from the Georgia Sea Islands, like Bessie Jones, testified to vibrant musical continuities.

Allen's long introduction raises many important, controversial issues. This opening excerpt confirms the difficulties in transcribing this music and, by describing singing styles, shows how oral practices defy notation. References to the "barbarity" of Africans expose the prejudice of the white ruling class. The spirituals and work songs support the idea of a distinctive black culture. Only partially accessible to the outsider's

understanding, they bear witness to the period of transition when one way that Africans learned how to survive as African Americans was through music.

The musical capacity of the negro race has been recognized for so many years that it is hard to explain why no systematic effort has hitherto been made to collect and preserve their melodies. More than thirty years ago those plantation songs made their appearance which were so extraordinarily popular for a while; and if "Coal-black Rose," "Zip Coon" and "Ole Virginny nebber tire" have been succeeded by spurious imitations, manufactured to suit the somewhat sentimental taste of our community, the fact that these were called "negro melodies" was itself a tribute to the musical genius of the race.*

The public had well-nigh forgotten these genuine slave songs, and with them the creative power from which they sprung, when a fresh interest was excited through the educational mission to the Port Royal islands, in 1861.[1] The agents of this mission were not long in discovering the rich vein of music that existed in these half-barbarous people, and when visitors from the North were on the islands, there was nothing that seemed better worth their while than to see a "shout" or hear the "people" sing their "sperichils." A few of these last, of special merit,** soon became established favorites among the whites, and hardly a Sunday passed at the church on St. Helena without "Gabriel's Trumpet," "I hear from Heaven to-day," or "Jehovah Hallelujah." The last time I myself heard these was at the Fourth of July celebration, at the church, in 1864. All of them were sung, and then the glorious shout, "I can't stay behind, my Lord," was struck up, and sung by the entire multitude with a zest and spirit, a swaying of the bodies and nodding of the heads and lighting of the countenances and rhythmical movement of the hands, which I think no one present will ever forget.

Attention was, I believe, first publicly directed to these songs in a letter from Miss McKim, of Philadelphia, to *Dwight's Journal of Music*, Nov. 8, 1862, from which some extracts will presently be given. At about the same time, Miss McKim arranged and published two of them, "Roll, Jordan" (No. 1) and "Poor Rosy" (No. 8)—probably on all accounts the two best specimens that could be selected. Mr. H. G. Spaulding not long after gave some well-chosen specimens of the music in an article entitled "Under the Palmetto," in the *Continental Monthly* for August, 1863, among them, "O Lord, remember me" (No. 15), and "The Lonesome Valley" (No. 7). Many other persons interested themselves in the collection of words and tunes, and it seems time at last that the partial collections in the possession of the editors, and known by them to be in the possession of others, should not be forgotten and lost, but that these relics of a state of society which has passed away should be preserved while it is still possible.***

The greater part of the music here presented has been taken down by the editors from the lips of the colored people themselves; when we have obtained it from other sources, we have

*It is not generally known that the beautiful air "Long time ago," or "Near the lake where drooped the willow," was borrowed from the negroes, by whom it was sung to words beginning, "Way down in Raccoon Hollow."

**The first seven spirituals in this collection, which were regularly sung at the church.

***Only this last spring a valuable collection of songs made at Richmond, Va., was lost in the *Wagner*. No copy had been made from the original manuscript, so that the labor of their collection was lost. We had hoped to have the use of them in preparing the present work.

given credit in the table of contents. The largest and most accurate single collection in existence is probably that made by Mr. Charles P. Ware, chiefly at Coffin's Point, St. Helena Island. We have thought it best to give this collection in its entirety, as the basis of the present work; it includes all the hymns as far as No. 43. Those which follow, as far as No. 55, were collected by myself on the Capt. John Fripp and neighboring plantations, on the same island. In all cases we have added words from other sources and other localities, when they could be obtained, as well as variations of the tunes wherever they were of sufficient importance to warrant it. Of the other hymns and songs we have given the locality whenever it could be ascertained.

The difficulty experienced in attaining absolute correctness is greater than might be supposed by those who have never tried the experiment, and we are far from claiming that we have made no mistakes. I have never felt quite sure of my notation without a fresh comparison with the singing, and have then often found that I had made some errors. I feel confident, however, that there are no mistakes of importance. What may appear to some to be an incorrect rendering is very likely to be a variation; for these variations are endless, and very entertaining and instructive.

Neither should any one be repelled by any difficulty in adapting the words to the tunes. The negroes keep exquisite time in singing, and do not suffer themselves to be daunted by any obstacle in the words. The most obstinate Scripture phrases or snatches from hymns they will force to do duty with any tune they please, and will dash heroically through a trochaic tune at the head of a column of iambs with wonderful skill. We have in all cases arranged one set of words carefully to each melody; for the rest, one must make them fit the best he can, as the negroes themselves do.

The best that we can do, however, with paper and types, or even with voices, will convey but a faint shadow of the original. The voices of the colored people have a peculiar quality that nothing can imitate; and the intonations and delicate variations of even one singer cannot be reproduced on paper. And I despair of conveying any notion of the effect of a number singing together, especially in a complicated shout, like "I can't stay behind, my Lord" (No. 8), or "Turn, sinner, turn O!" (No. 48). There is no singing in *parts*,* as we understand it, and yet no two appear to be singing the same thing—the leading singer starts the words of each verse, often improvising, and the others, who "base" him, as it is called, strike in with the refrain, or even join in the solo, when the words are familiar. When the "base" begins, the leader often stops, leaving the rest of his words to be guessed at, or it may be they are taken up by one of the other singers. And the "basers" themselves seem to follow their own whims, beginning when they please and leaving off when they please, striking an octave above or below (in case they have pitched the tune too low or too high), or hitting some other note that chords, so as to produce the effect of a marvellous complication and variety, and yet with the most perfect time, and rarely with any discord. And what makes it all the harder to unravel a thread of melody out of this strange network is that, like birds, they seem not infrequently to strike sounds that cannot be precisely

---

*"The high voices, all in unison, and the admirable time and true accent with which their responses are made, always make me wish that some great musical composer could hear these semi-savage performances. With a very little skilful adaptation and instrumentation, I think one or two barbaric chants and choruses might be evoked from them that would make the fortune of an opera." —Mrs. Kemble's "Life on a Georgian Plantation," p. 218. ["Journal of a Residence on a Georgian Plantation in 1833–1839" by Fanny Kemble (1863).]

represented by the gamut, and abound in "slides from one note to another, and turns and cadences not in articulated notes." "It is difficult," writes Miss McKim, "to express the entire character of these negro ballads by mere musical notes and signs. The odd turns made in the throat, and the curious rhythmic effect produced by single voices chiming in at different irregular intervals, seem almost as impossible to place on the score as the singing of birds or the tones of an Æolian Harp." There are also apparent irregularities in the time, which it is no less difficult to express accurately, and of which Nos. 10, 130, 131, and (eminently) 128, are examples.

Still, the chief part of the negro music is *civilized* in its character—partly composed under the influence of association with the whites, partly actually imitated from their music. In the main it appears to be original in the best sense of the word, and the more we examine the subject, the more genuine it appears to us to be. In a very few songs, as Nos. 19, 23, and 25, strains of familiar tunes are readily traced; and it may easily be that others contain strains of less familiar music, which the slaves heard their masters sing or play.*

On the other hand there are very few which are of an intrinsically barbaric character, and where this character does appear, it is chiefly in short passages, intermingled with others of a different character. Such passages may be found perhaps in Nos. 10, 12, and 18; and "Becky Lawton," for instance (No. 29), "Shall I die?" (No. 52), "Round the corn, Sally" (No. 87), and "O'er the crossing" (No. 93) may very well be purely African in origin. Indeed, it is very likely that if we had found it possible to get at more of their secular music, we should have come to another conclusion as to the proportion of the barbaric element. A gentleman in Delaware writes: "We must look among their non-religious songs for the purest specimens of negro minstrelsy. It is remarkable that they have themselves transferred the best of these to the uses of their churches—I suppose on Mr. Wesley's principle that 'it is not right the Devil should have all the good tunes.' Their leaders and preachers have not found this change difficult to effect; or at least they have taken so little pains about it that one often detects the profane *cropping out,* and revealing the origin of their most solemn 'hymns,' in spite of the best intentions of the poet and artist. Some of the best *pure negro* songs I have ever heard were those that used to be sung by the black stevedores, or perhaps the crews themselves, of the West India vessels, loading and unloading at the wharves in Philadelphia and Baltimore. I have stood for more than an hour, often, listening to them, as they hoisted and lowered the hogsheads and boxes of their cargoes; one man taking the burden of the song (and the slack of the rope) and the others striking in with the chorus. They would sing in this way more than a dozen different songs in an hour; most of which might indeed be warranted to contain 'nothing religious'—a few of them, 'on the contrary, quite the reverse'—but generally rather innocent and proper in their language, and strangely attractive in their music; and with a volume of voice that reached a square or two away. That plan of labor has now passed away, in Philadelphia at least, and the songs, I suppose, with it. So that these performances are to be heard only among black sailors on their vessels, or 'long-shore men' in out-of-the-way places, where opportunities for respectable persons to hear them are rather few."

These are the songs that are still heard upon the Mississippi steamboats—wild and strangely fascinating—one of which we have been so fortunate as to secure for this collection.

*We have rejected as spurious "Give me Jesus," "Climb Jacob's Ladder," (both sung at Port Royal), and "I'll take the wings of the morning," which we find in Methodist hymn-books. A few others, the character of which seemed somewhat suspicious, we have not felt at liberty to reject without direct evidence[.]

This, too, is no doubt the music of the colored firemen of Savannah, graphically described by Mr. Kane O'Donnel, in a letter to the Philadelphia *Press,* and one of which he was able to contribute for our use. Mr. E. S. Philbrick was struck with the resemblance of some of the rowing tunes at Port-Royal to the boatmen's songs he had heard upon the Nile.

The greater number of the songs which have come into our possession seem to be the natural and original production of a race of remarkable musical capacity and very teachable, which has been long enough associated with the more cultivated race to have become imbued with the mode and spirit of European music—often, nevertheless, retaining a distinct tinge of their native Africa.

~~~~~~~

The ring dance known as the "shout" accompanied the singing of some spirituals as part of a religious service. Demonstrating the persistence of African-based rituals, the shout represents a syncretic Afro-Protestant practice, mixing elements of African religion with Christianity.

The most peculiar and interesting of their customs is the "shout," an excellent description of which we are permitted to copy from the N.Y. *Nation* of May 30, 1867:

This is a ceremony which the white clergymen are inclined to discountenance, and even of the colored elders some of the more discreet try sometimes to put on a face of discouragement; and although, if pressed for Biblical warrant for the shout, they generally seem to think "he in de Book," or "he dere-da in Matchew," still it is not considered blasphemous or improper if "de chillen" and "dem young gal" carry it on in the evening for amusement's sake, and with no well-defined intention of "praise." But the true "shout" takes place on Sundays or on "praise"-nights through the week, and either in the praise-house or in some cabin in which a regular religious meeting has been held. Very likely more than half the population of the plantation is gathered together. Let it be the evening, and a light-wood fire burns red before the door of the house and on the hearth. For some time one can hear, though at a good distance, the vociferous exhortation or prayer of the presiding elder or of the brother who has a gift that way, and who is not "on the back seat,"—a phrase, the interpretation of which is, "under the censure of the church authorities for bad behavior;"— and at regular intervals one hears the elder "deaconing" a hymn-book hymn, which is sung two lines at a time, and whose wailing cadences, borne on the night air, are indescribably melancholy. But the benches are pushed back to the wall when the formal meeting is over, and old and young, men and women, sprucely-dressed young men, grotesquely half-clad field-hands—the women generally with gay handkerchiefs twisted about their heads and with short skirts—boys with tattered shirts and men's trousers, young girls barefooted, all stand up in the middle of the floor, and when the "sperichil" is struck up, begin first walking and by-and-by shuffling round, one after the other, in a ring. The foot is hardly taken from the floor, and the progression is mainly due to a jerking, hitching motion, which agitates the entire shouter, and soon brings out streams of perspiration. Sometimes they dance silently, sometimes as they shuffle they sing the chorus of the spiritual, and sometimes the song itself is also sung by the dancers. But more frequently a band, composed of some of the best singers and of tired shouters, stand at the side of the room to "base" the others, singing the body of the song and clapping their hands together or on the knees. Song and dance are alike extremely energetic, and often, when the shout lasts into the middle of the night, the monotonous thud, thud of the feet prevents sleep within half a mile of the praise-house.

In the form here described, the "shout" is probably confined to South Carolina and the States south of it. It appears to be found in Florida, but not in North Carolina or Virginia. It is, however, an interesting fact that the term "shouting" is used in Virginia in reference to a peculiar motion of the body not wholly unlike the Carolina shouting. It is not unlikely that this remarkable religious ceremony is a relic of some native African dance, as the Romaika is of the classical Pyrrhic. Dancing in the usual way is regarded with great horror by the people of Port Royal, but they enter with infinite zest into the movements of the "shout." It has its connoisseurs, too. "Jimmy great shouter," I was told; and Jimmy himself remarked to me, as he looked patronizingly on a ring of young people, "Dese yere worry deyseff—we don't worry weseff." And indeed, although the perspiration streamed copiously down his shiny face, he shuffled round the circle with great ease and grace.

The shouting may be to any tune, and perhaps all the Port Royal hymns here given are occasionally used for this purpose; so that our cook's classification into "sperichils" and "runnin' sperichils" (shouts), or the designation of certain ones as sung "just sittin' round, you know," will hardly hold in strictness. In practice, however, a distinction is generally observed. [signed] William Francis Allen,
Charles Pickard Ware,
Lucy McKim Garrison.

SOURCE: William Francis Allen, Charles Pickard Ware, and Lucy McKinn Garrison, eds. *Slave Songs of the United States* (New York: A. Simpson & Co., 1867): i–viii, xii–xix. Available at http://docsouth.unc.edu/church/allen/menu.htmh.

~~~~~~~~

NOTE

1.   During the Civil War, the War Department of the Union government initiated an education project to teach liberated ex-slaves who were left on plantations captured and controlled by the Union army. The first project began at Port Royal, South Carolina, and was known as the "Port Royal Experiment."

44

A SIDEBAR INTO MEMORY

Slave Narratives from the Federal Writers' Project

in the New Deal

Between 1936 and 1938, field workers of the Federal Writers' Project, a program under the auspices of Franklin D. Roosevelt's Music WPA (Works Progress Administration) conducted interviews with an aged population of former American slaves in the South and Southwest.[1] Music was one of many aspects of culture that concerned these field workers, and a rich repository of popular and folk songs and the persistence of African-American creativity in slavery and its immediate aftermath can be experienced through the words of one individual after another.[2] The selections here were chosen because of the references to many famous songs and a variety of song types, including blues ballads and hymns, popular songs and traditional lullabies, including some printed in *Slave Songs of the United States* (1867). The instruments mentioned include the banjo, which was, as is well known, an African import.

JIM DAVIS, PINE BLUFF, ARKANSAS, AGE 98

I used to be a banjo picker in Civil War times. I could pick a church song just as good as I could a reel.

Some of 'em I used to pick was "Amazing Grace," "Old Dan Tucker." Used to pick one went like this

> *Farewell, farewell, sweet Mary;*
>
> *I'm ruined forever*
>
> *By lovin' of you;*
>
> *Your parents don't like me,*
>
> *That I do know*
>
> *I am not worthy to enter your d[o].*[3]

I used to pick

> *Dark was the night*
>
> *Cold was the ground*
>
> *On which the Lord might lay.*[4]

I could pick anything.

> *Amazing grace*
>
> *How sweet it sounds*
>
> *To save a wretch like me.*
>
> *Go preach my Gospel*
>
> *Says the Lord,*
>
> *Bid this whole earth*
>
> *My grace receive;*
>
> *Oh trust my word*
>
> *Ye shall be saved.*

I used to talk that on my banjo just like I talked it there.

SOURCE: Slave Narratives: *A Folk History of Slavery in the United States from Interviews with Former Slaves:* vol. 2, *Arkansas Narratives* (Washington, D.C.: Federal Writers' Project, 1941), part 2. Available at *The Project Gutenberg EBook,* http://www.ibiblio.org/pub/docs/books/gutenberg/1/3/7/0/13700/13700-h/13700-h.htm#.

~~~~~~

W. L. BOST, ASHEVILLE, NORTH CAROLINA

Us niggers never have chance to go to Sunday School. The white folks feared for niggers to get any religion and education, but I reckon somethin' inside just told us about God and that there was a better place hereafter. We would sneak off and have prayer meetin'. Sometimes the paddyrollers catch us and beat us good but that didn't keep us from tryin'. I remember one old song we use to sing when we meet down in the woods back of the barn. My mother she sing an' pray to the Lord to deliver us out o' slavery. She always say she thankful she was never sold from her children, and that our Massa not so mean as some of the others. But the old song it went something like this:

> Oh, mother lets go down, lets go down, lets go down, lets go down.
>
> Oh, mother, lets go down, down in the valley to pray.
>
> As I went down in the valley to pray
>
> Studyin' about that good ole way
>
> Who shall wear that starry crown.
>
> Good Lord show me the way.[5]

Then the other part was just like that except it said "father" instead of "mother," and then "sister" and then "brother." Then they sing sometime:

> We camp a while in the wilderness, in the wilderness, in the wilderness.
>
> We camp a while in the wilderness, where the Lord makes me happy
>
> And then I'm a goin' home.

SOURCE: *Slave Narratives: A Folk History of Slavery in the United States from Interviews with Former Slaves:* vol. 11, *North Carolina Narratives* (Washington, D.C.: Federal Writers' Project, 1941), part 1. Available at http://memory.loc.gov/cgi-bin/query/D?mesnbib:1:./temp/~ammem_SQkW::.

~~~~~~

MOLLIE WILLIAMS, TERRY, MISSISSIPPI

Miss Margurite [the white mistress of the house] had a piany, a 'cordian, a flutena, an' a fiddle. She could play a fiddle good as a man. Law, I heerd many as three fiddles goin' in dat house many a time, an' I kin jes see her li'l old fair han's now, playin' jes as fast as lightnin' a chune [tune] 'bout

My father he cried, my mother she cried,

I wasn' cut out fer de army.

O, Capt'in Gink, my hoss me think,

But feed his hoss on co'n an' beans

An s'port de gals by any means!

'Cause I'm a Capt'in in de army.[6]

All us chullun begged ter play dat an' we all sing an' dance—*great goodness!*
One song I 'member mammy singin':

Let me nigh, by my cry,

Give me Jesus.

You may have all dis world,

But give me Jesus.[7]

Singin' an' shoutin', she had 'ligion all right. She b'longed to Old Farrett back in Missouri.

We didn' git sick much, but mammy made yeller top tea fer chills an' fever an' give us. Den iffen it didn' do no good, Miss Margurite called fer Dr. Hunt lak she done when her own chullun got sick.

None of de darkies on dat place could read an' write. Guess Miss Helen an' Miss Ann would'a learned me, but I was jes so bad an' didn' lak to set still no longer'n I had to.

I seen plenty of darkies whupped. Marse George buckled my mammy down an' whupped her 'cause she run off. Once when Marse George seen pappy stealin' a bucket of 'lasses an' totin' it to a gal on 'nother place, he whupped him but didn' stake him down. Pappy tol' him to whup him but not to stake him—he'd stan' fer it wid'out de stakin'—so I 'member he looked jes lak he was jumpin' a rope an' hollering, "*Pray Marser,*" ever time de strop hit 'im.

I heered 'bout some people whut nailed de darkies years [ears] to a tree an' beat 'em but I neber seen none whupped dat way.

I neber got no whuppins frum Marse George 'cause he didn' whup de chulluns none. Li'l darky chullun played 'long wid white chullun. Iffen de old house is still thar I 'spec you kin fin' mud cakes up under de house whut we made out'n eggs we stole frum de hen nests. Den we milked jes anybody's cows we could ketch, an' churned it. We's all time in ter some mischief.

Thar was plenty dancin' 'mong'st darkies on Marse George's place an' on ones nearby. Dey danced reels an' lak in de moonlight:

Mamma's got de whoopin' cough,

Daddy's got de measles,

Dat's whar de money goes,

Pop goes de weasel.

Buffalo gals, can't you come out tonight,

Come out tonight, an' dance by de light of de moon?[8]

Gennie, put de kettle on,

Sallie, boil de water strong,

Gennie, put de kittle on

An' le's have tea!

Run tell Coleman,

Run tell everbody

Dat de niggers is arisin'!

Run nigger run, de patterrollers ketch you—

Run nigger run, fer hits almos' day,

De nigger run; de nigger flew; de nigger los'

His big old shoe.[9]

SOURCE: *Slave Narratives: A Folk History of Slavery in the United States from Interviews with Former Slaves:* vol. 9, *Mississippi Narratives* (Washington, D.C.: Federal Writers' Project, 1941). Available at *The Project Gutenberg EBook,* http://www.gutenberg.org/dirs/1/2/0/5/12055/12055-h/12055-h.htm#WilliamsMollie.

JOANNA THOMPSON ISOM, LAFAYETTE COUNTY, MISSISSIPPI

I married Henry Isom when I wuz 15 years ole; we wuz married in de parlor of Mr. Macon Thompson's home; I'se had ten chillun; I didn't want but two; dat wuz 8 too many; my husban' died 19 years ago an' I wouldn't look at no man livin'; dere aint nuthin' to dese men nohow, I tells you.

I hav' been midwife, an' nuss, an' washerwoman; when I wuz little my granny taught me some ole, ole slave songs dat she sed had been used to sing babies to sleep ever since she wuz a chile. I used to sing dis one:

Little black sheep, where's yo' lam'

Way down yonder in de meado'

The bees an' de butterflies

A-peckin' out hiz eyes

The poor little black sheep

Cry Ma-a-a-my.[10]

Anudder one I sings to de chilluns goes lak dis:

I know, I know dese bones gwine rize agin

Dese bones gwine rize agin

I heared a big rumblin' in de sky

Hit mus' be Jesus cummin' by

Dese bones gwine rize agin

Dese bones gwine rize agin.

I know, I know dese bones gwine rise agen

Dese bones gwine rize agin

Mind my brothers how you step on de cross

Yo' rite foot's slippin' and yo' soul will be los'

Dese bones gwine rize agin

Dese bones gwine rize agin.

Dis is anudder ole one:

Preachin' time soon will be over all dis lan'

My Lord's callin' me an' I mus' go.

SOURCE: *Slave Narratives: A Folk History of Slavery in the United States from Interviews with Former Slaves:* vol. 9, *Mississippi Narratives* (Washington, D.C.: Federal Writers' Project, 1941). Available at http://mshistory.k12.ms.us/features/feature60/docs/JoannaIsom.doc.

~~~~~~~~~~

NOTES

1. In 1941, the interviews were assembled in 17 volumes under the title *Slave Narratives: A Folk History of Slavery in the United States from Interviews with Former Slaves.* These were re-edited and reorganized by George P. Rawick and published as *The American Slave: A Composite Autobiography* (Westport, Conn.: Greenwood, 1972). This collection contains more than twice

the number of narratives available through the Library of Congress website, *Born in Slavery: Slave Narratives from the Federal Writers' Project*, 1936–1938, http://www.loc.gov.; further supplements were published in 1979 and 1982.

2. For an annotated list of the contents of the slave narratives, see Eileen Southern and Josephine Wright, comps., *African-American Traditions in Song, Sermon, Tale, and Dance, 1600s–1920* (Westport, Conn.: Greenwood, 1990): 208–26.

3. The last two lines of this lyric can also be found in "The Wagoner's Lad," a traditional Anglo-American ballad.

4. A Protestant hymn by Haweis from before 1820. The opening two lines are associated with a famous blues performance by Blind Willie Johnson.

5. This song, included in the film *O Brother, Where Art Thou?* is printed in *Slave Songs of the United States* under the title "The Good Old Way."

6. This famous song, "Captain Jinks of the Horse Marines," was written for the stage, with words by William Horace, 1868.

7. A classic African-American spiritual.

8. "Buffalo Gals" was a minstrel song published in 1848 with a picture of the Ethiopian Serenaders on the cover.

9. This song is in *Slave Songs of the United States.*

10. This is related to the famous lullaby "Go to Sleepy, Little Baby," also known as "All the Pretty Little Horses."

45

GEORGE F. ROOT RECALLS HOW HE WROTE

A CLASSIC UNION SONG

George Root (1820–1895) wrote some of the most enduring songs of the Civil War. Master of many musical trades, Root gave music courses at teachers' conventions (inspired by the educational work of his hero Lowell Mason) and ran the music publishing firm of Root & Cady in Chicago. Root had the intuitions of a born popular-song writer for what he called the "people's song." His lyrics turned topical public issues into private moments of personal experience, and the melodies of his best songs have enough individuality to be memorable. Root's classic "The Battle-cry of Freedom" (1862) was a favorite of Charles Ives and was reputed to have sold 100,000 copies during the war years. These excerpts are from his autobiography.

THE STORY OF A MUSICAL LIFE

1851–1853, NEW YORK

. . .

My acquaintance with some of the best musicians of the day was such as to bring me into close contact with what they performed and liked, and in my family we were familiar with music of a grade considerably above that of the popular music of the day. The reservoir was, therefore, much better filled than it would have been if I had commenced when urged to do so by the friends of whom I have spoken, and the comparatively simple music that I have written from that time to this has included a greater variety of subjects, and has been better in quality in consequence.

I saw at once that mine must be the "people's song," still, I am ashamed to say, I shared the feeling that was around me in regard to that grade of music. When Stephen C. Foster's wonderful melodies (as I now see them) began to appear, and the famous Christy's Minstrels began to make them known, I "took a hand in" and wrote a few, but put "G. Friederich Wurzel" (the German for Root) to them instead of my own name. "Hazel Dell" and "Rosalie, the Prairie Flower" were the best known of those so written. It was not until I imbibed more of Dr. Mason's spirit, and went more among the people of the country, that I saw these things in a truer light, and respected myself, and was thankful when I could write something that all the people would sing.

"The Flower Queen" served an excellent purpose, both as an incentive to work on the part of the classes, and as an entertainment for the friends of the schools. I served in the double capacity of Recluse and stage manager in the first performances, and fear the latter character appeared sometimes during the performance of the former much to the detriment of that dignitary. However, we always rehearsed thoroughly, and the success of those first representations was all that could be desired.

1861–1870, CHICAGO

In common with my neighbors I felt strongly the gravity of the situation, and while waiting to see what would be done, wrote the first song of the war. It was entitled "The first gun is fired, may God protect the right." Then at every event, and in all the circumstances that followed, where I thought a song would be welcome, I wrote one. And here I found my fourteen years of extemporizing melodies on the blackboard, before classes that could be kept in order only by prompt and rapid movements, a great advantage. Such work as I could do at all I could do quickly. There was no waiting for a melody. Such as it was it came at once, as when I stood before the blackboard in the old school days.

I heard of President Lincoln's second call for troops one afternoon while reclining on a lounge in my brother's house. Immediately a song started in my mind, words and music together:

> *Yes, we'll rally round the flag, boys, we'll rally once again,*
>
> *Shouting the battle-cry of freedom!*

I thought it out that afternoon, and wrote it the next morning at the store. The ink was hardly dry when the Lumbard brothers—the great singers of the war—came in for something to sing at a war meeting that was to be holden immediately in the court-house square just opposite. They went through the new song once, and then hastened to the steps of the court-house, followed by a crowd that had gathered while the practice was going on. Then Jule's magnificent voice gave out the song, and Frank's trumpet tones led the refrain—

The Union forever, hurrah, boys, hurrah!

and at the fourth verse a thousand voices were joining in the chorus. From there the song went into the army, and the testimony in regard to its use in the camp and on the march, and even on the field of battle, from soldiers and officers, up to generals, and even to the good President himself, made me thankful that if I could not shoulder a musket in defense of my country I could serve her in this way.

Many interesting war incidents were connected with these songs. The one that moved me most was told by an officer who was in one of the battles during the siege of Vicksburg. He said an Iowa regiment went into the fight eight hundred strong, and came out with a terrible loss of more than half their number; but the brave fellows who remained were waving their torn and powder-stained banner, and singing

Yes, we'll rally round the flag, boys.

Some years after, at the closing concert of a musical convention in Anamosa, Iowa, I received a note, saying, "If the author of 'The Battle-cry of Freedom' would sing that song it would gratify several soldiers in the audience who used to sing it in the army." I read the request to the audience, and said I would willingly comply with it, but first would like to relate an incident concerning one of their Iowa regiments. Then I told the above about the battle near Vicksburg. When I finished I noticed a movement at the end of the hall, and an excited voice cried out, "Here is a soldier who lost his arm in that battle." I said, "Will he come forward and stand by me while I sing the song?" A tall, fine-looking man, with one empty sleeve, came immediately to my side, and I went through it, he joining in the chorus. But it was hard work. I had to choke a good deal, and there was hardly a dry eye in the house. He was teaching school a few miles from there, and was quite musical. I sent him some music after I returned to Chicago, and kept up the acquaintance by correspondence for some time.

SOURCE: George F. Root, *The Story of a Musical Life* (Cincinnati, Ohio: John Church, 1891): 83, 132–34.

46

A CONFEDERATE GIRL'S DIARY

DURING THE CIVIL WAR

Sarah Morgan (1872–1909), a young southern girl raised in Baton Rouge, Louisiana, wrote a diary that chronicles three years of her life during the Civil War from 1862 to 1865. Already regarded as a classic of its genre, and republished and scrupulously edited not that long ago, the Morgan diary begins in January, when no city in Louisiana has yet fallen to the Union Army. A few months later, the war comes home: New Orleans and then Baton Rouge are occupied by the enemy in late spring 1862. The Morgan diary reads like a documentary film on the one hand, filled with details of home invasions; on the other hand, it exudes the gentility of a privileged white urban household that owned seven slaves. It might seem blinkered to cull such a document for its references to music making were it not for the important role that music played in Sarah's family, and for her in particular, as a young girl who grew up fast on the Confederate home front in order to survive.

In the first selection, danger and the War seem remote. Sarah has time to reflect on her musical education.

BATON ROUGE, LOUISIANA, MARCH 9, 1862

HERE I am, at your service, Madame Idleness, waiting for any suggestion it may please you to put in my weary brain, as a means to pass this dull, cloudy Sunday afternoon; for the great Pike clock over the way has this instant struck only half-past three; and if a rain is added to the high wind that has been blowing ever since the month commenced, and prevents my going to Mrs. Brunot's before dark, I fear I shall fall a victim to "the blues" for the first time in my life. Indeed it is dull. Miriam went to Linewood with Lydia yesterday, and I miss them beyond all expression. . . .

I hold that every family has at heart one genius, in some line, no matter what—except in our family, where each is a genius, in his own way. [A]Hem! And Miriam has a genius for the piano. Now I never could bear to compete with any one, knowing that it is the law of my being to be inferior to others, consequently to fail, and failure is so humiliating to me. So it is, that people may force me to abandon any pursuit by competing with me; for knowing that failure is inevitable, rather than fight against destiny I give up *de bonne grâce*. Originally, I was said to have a talent for the piano, as well as Miriam. Sister and Miss Isabella said I would make a better musician than she, having more patience and perseverance. However, I took hardly six months' lessons to her ever so many years; heard how well she played, got disgusted with myself, and gave up the piano at fourteen, with spasmodic fits of playing every year or so. At sixteen, Harry gave me a guitar. Here was a new field where I would have no competitors. I knew no one who played on it; so I set to work, and taught myself to manage it, mother only teaching me how to tune it. But Miriam took a fancy to it, and I taught her all I knew; but as she gained, I lost my relish, and if she had not soon abandoned it, I would know nothing of it now. She does not know half that I do about it; they tell me I play much better than she; yet they let her play on it in company before me, and I cannot pretend to play after. Why is it? It is *not* vanity, or I would play, confident of excelling her. It is not jealousy, for I love to see her show her talents. It is not selfishness; I love her too much to be selfish to her. What is it then? "Simply lack of self-esteem" I would say if there was no phrenologist near to correct me, and point out that well-developed hump at the extreme southern and heavenward portion of my Morgan head. Self-esteem or not, Mr. Phrenologist, the result is, that Miriam is by far the best performer in Baton Rouge, and I would rank forty-third even in the delectable village of Jackson.

And yet I must have some ear for music. To "know as many songs as Sarah" is a family proverb; not very difficult songs, or very beautiful ones, to be sure, besides being very indifferently sung; but the tunes *will* run in my head, and it must take *some* ear to catch them. People say to me, "Of course you play?" to which I invariably respond, "Oh, no, but Miriam plays beautifully!" "You sing, I believe?" "Not at all—except for father" (that is what I used to say)—"and the children. But *Miriam* sings." "You are fond of dancing?" "Very; but I cannot dance as well as Miriam." "Of course, you are fond of society?" "No, indeed! Miriam is, and she goes to all the parties and returns all the visits for me." The consequence is, that if the person who questions is a stranger, he goes off satisfied that "that Miriam must be a great girl; but that little sister of hers—! Well! a *prig*, to say the least!"

So it is Miriam catches all my fish—and so it is, too, that it is not raining, and I'm off.

During the periods when Baton Rouge turned into a battlefront, Sarah and her family took shelter with friends outside the city, packing up possessions as best they could. In this account, Sarah returns to her home during a lull in the shelling to retrieve more items.

MAY 31, 1862

To return to my journal.

All the talk by the roadside was of burning homes, houses knocked to pieces by balls, famine, murder, desolation; so I comforted myself singing, "Better days are coming" and "I hope to die shouting, the Lord will provide"; while Lucy toiled through the sun and dust, and answered with a chorus of "I'm a-runnin', a-runnin' up to glo-ry!"

. . .

It was long after nine when we got there, and my first act was to look around the deserted house. What a scene of confusion! armoirs spread open, with clothes tumbled in every direction, inside and out; ribbons, laces on floors; chairs overturned; my desk wide open covered with letters, trinkets, etc.; bureau drawers half out, the bed filled with odds and ends of everything. I no longer recognized my little room. . . .

. . . For three hours I dreamed of rifled shells and battles, and at half-past six I was up and at work again. Mother came soon after, and after hard work we got safely off at three, saving nothing but our clothes and silver. All else is gone. It cost me a pang to leave my guitar, and Miriam's piano, but it seems there was no help for it, so I had to submit.

It was dark night when we reached here. A bright fire was blazing in front, but the house looked so desolate that I wanted to cry. Miriam cried when I told her her piano was left behind. . . .

Early yesterday morning, Miriam, Nettie, and Sophie, who did not then know of their brother's death, went to town in a cart, determined to save some things, Miriam to save her piano. As soon as they were halfway, news reached us that any one was allowed to enter, but none allowed to leave the town, and all vehicles confiscated as soon as they reached there. Alarmed for their safety, mother started off to find them, and we have heard of none of them since. What will happen next? I am not uneasy. They dare not harm them. It is glorious to shell a town full of women, but to kill four lone ones is not exciting enough.

WEDNESDAY, JULY 9, 1862

Poor Miriam! Poor Sarah! they are disgraced again! Last night we were all sitting on the balcony in the moonlight, singing as usual with our guitar. I have been so accustomed to hear father say in the evening, "Come, girls! where is my concert?" and he took so much pleasure in listening, that I could not think singing in the balcony was so very dreadful, since he encouraged us in it. But last night changed all my ideas. We noticed Federals, both officers and soldiers, pass singly, or by twos or threes at different times, but as we were not singing for their benefit, and they were evidently attending to their own affairs, there was no necessity of noticing them at all.

But about half-past nine, after we had sung two or three dozen others, we commenced "Mary of Argyle." As the last word died away, while the chords were still vibrating, came a sound of—clapping hands, in short! Down went every string of the guitar; Charlie cried, "I told you so!"

and ordered an immediate retreat; Miriam objected, as undignified, but renounced the guitar; mother sprang to her feet, and closed the front windows in an instant, whereupon, dignified or not, we all evacuated the gallery and fell back into the house. All this was done in a few minutes, and as quietly as possible; and while the gas was being turned off downstairs, Miriam and I flew upstairs,—I confess I was mortified to death, very, very much ashamed,—but we wanted to see the guilty party, for from below they were invisible. We stole out on the front balcony above, and in front of the house that used to be Gibbes's, we beheld one of the culprits. At the sight of the creature, my mortification vanished in intense compassion for his. He was standing under the tree, half in the moonlight, his hands in his pockets, looking at the extinction of light below, with the true state of affairs dawning on his astonished mind, and looking by no means satisfied with himself! Such an abashed creature! He looked just as though he had received a kick, that, conscious of deserving, he dared not return! While he yet gazed on the house in silent amazement and consternation, hands still forlornly searching his pockets, as though for a reason for our behavior, from under the dark shadow of the tree another slowly picked himself up from the ground—hope he was not knocked down by surprise—and joined the first. His hands sought his pockets, too, and, if possible, he looked more mortified than the other. After looking for some time at the house, satisfied that they had put an end to future singing from the gallery, they walked slowly away, turning back every now and then to be certain that it was a fact. If ever I saw two mortified, hangdog-looking men, they were these two as they took their way home. Was it not shocking?

But they could not have meant it merely to be insulting or they would have placed themselves in full view of us, rather than out of sight, under the trees. Perhaps they were thinking of their own homes, instead of us. Perhaps they came from Main[e], or Vermont, or some uncivilized people, and thought it a delicate manner of expressing their appreciation of our songs. Perhaps they just did it without thinking at all, and I really hope they are sorry for such a breech of decorum. But I can forget my mortification when I remember their exit from the scene of their exploit! Such crest fallen people!

O Yankees! Yankees! Why did you do such a thoughtless thing! It will prevent us from ever indulging in moonlight singing again. Yet if we sing in the parlor, they always stop in front of the house to listen, while if we are on the balcony, they always have the delicacy to stop just above or below, concealed under the shadows. What's the difference?

Must we give up music entirely, because some poor people debarred of female society by the state of affairs like to listen to old songs they may have heard their mothers sing when they were babies?

THURSDAY JULY 24, 1862

Soon, an exodus took place, in the direction of the Asylum, and we needs must follow the general example and run, too. In haste we packed a trunk with our remaining clothes,—what we could get in,—and the greatest confusion prevailed for an hour. Beatrice had commenced to cry early in the evening, and redoubled her screams when she saw the preparations; and Louis joining in, they cried in concert until eight o'clock, when we finally got off. What a din! Lilly looked perfectly exhausted; that look on her face made me heartsick. Miriam flew around everywhere; mother always had one more article to find, and the noise was dreadful, when white and black assembled in the hall ready at last. Charlie placed half of the trunks on the dray, leaving the rest for another trip; and we at last started off. Besides the inevitable running-bag, tied to my waist, on this stifling night I had my sunbonnet, veil, comb, toothbrush, cabas filled with dozens of small articles, and dagger to carry; and then my heart failed me when I thought of my guitar, so I caught it up in the case; and remembering father's heavy inkstand, I seized that, too, with two fans. If I was asked what I did with all these things, I could not answer. Certain it is I had every one in my hands, and was not *very* ridiculous to behold.

TUESDAY, MARCH 10, 1863

I had so many nice things to say—which now, alas, are knocked forever from my head—when news came that the Yankees were advancing on us, and were already within fifteen miles. The panic which followed reminded me forcibly of our running days in Baton Rouge. Each one rapidly threw into trunks all clothing worth saving, with silver and valuables, to send to the upper plantation. . . . My earthly possessions are all reposing by me on the bed at this instant, consisting of my guitar, a change of clothes, running-bag, cabas, and this book. . . . For in spite of their entreaties, I would not send it to Clinton, expecting those already there to meet with a fiery death—though I would like to preserve those of the most exciting year of my life. They tell me that this will be read aloud to me to torment me, but I am determined to burn it if there is any danger of that. Why I would die with out some means of expressing my feelings in the stirring hour so rapidly approaching. I shall keep it by me.

SOURCE: Sarah Morgan, *The Civil War Diary of a Southern Woman*, ed. Charles East (New York: Touchstone, 1991): 23–5, 93, 95, 158–60, 172–73, 436. East's annotations are not reproduced here. Also cited, partially quoted, and interpreted in Tim Brookes, *Guitar: An American Life* (New York: Grove, 2005): 43–4.

47

$\mathcal{S}$OLDIER-MUSICIANS FROM THE NORTH AND

THE SOUTH RECALL DUTIES ON THE FRONT

A vast literature reflects our fascination with the Civil War, and especially since the centennial commemorations of the Civil War in the 1960s, "re-enactors" along with scholars have focused on its music and related documents. These excerpts from the memoirs of soldier-musicians describe the roles that music played at the front. The fife-and-drum corps organized the daily operations of the troops. The regimental band marched with them, keeping spirits up and building morale. Sometimes, musicians took up arms; other times, they nursed the wounded. Given the number of regimental bands and the pervasiveness of fife-and-drum music, it is no wonder that after the war, bands played such prominent musical roles in civilian society.

The famous 26th North Carolina Regimental Band (from Winston-Salem) of the Confederate army recruited all of its members from the nearby village of Moravian-American Salem. Unique part books at the Moravian Music Foundation have preserved its repertoire, which has led to historically informed recordings of this band's

music making. The 26th included Moravian hymn tunes in its repertoire, along with the more usual marches, polkas, and arrangements from opera. The Trovatore quick-step, however, has no place in this eyewitness account of the battle of Gettysburg, penned by bandsman Julius Augustus Leinbach (1834–1930; the brother of well-known Moravian composer Edward Leinbach, 1823–1901). He remembers perhaps the most famous battle of the war, so ferocious that it earned his regiment the name "the bloody Twenty-sixth."

SCENES AT THE BATTLE OF GETTYSBURG: PAPER READ BEFORE THE WACHOVIA HISTORICAL SOCIETY, BY J. A. LEINBACH

I have been asked to give you an account of some of the experiences of the Twenty-sixth North Carolina Band during the Civil War, and the battle of Gettysburg was suggested as being the most notable. I am not sure that is just the kind of story you would care to listen to; if not, just place the responsibility for it on some one else, and call me down.

. . .

It so happened that immediately in front of Pettigrew's Brigade was the famous Iron Brigade, the finest in the Northern Army, that bore the proud boast of never having been defeated in any battle. In front of our troops lay a quarter-mile of nearly ripe wheat, then a branch, its banks thick with underbrush and briars, and beyond again an open field to a wooded hill, occupied by the Iron Brigade, and considered the key to the situation. Our men were resting, well knowing that a terrible struggle was before them.

Attention! Every man was up and ready and every officer at his post—Colonel Burgwyn in the center, Lieutenant-Colonel Lane on the right, Major Jones on the left, the color bearer six paces in advance of the line, proud of his position.

Forward!! All to a man, stepped off in perfect line, apparently as willingly and proudly as if on review.

The enemy opened fire at once, but this portion of the ground being descending, they mostly overshot our men. On across the wheat field moved the line of grey, until they came to the run, where there was some confusion in getting through the briars and underbrush. By this time Biddle's Brigade and Coper's Battery, on the right of [the] front, poured in a heavy enfilading fire that tore the Confederate line almost into fragments.

Our loss was frightful, but quickly reforming, the brave men surged up the hill, firing as they went. The engagement was becoming desperate. Lieutenant Colonel Lane, on the right, hurried to the center, anxious to know how things were going there. "It is all right in the center and on the left," Colonel Burgwyn informed him, "we have broken the first line of the enemy. We are all in line on the right, Colonel." By this time the colors had been cut down ten times. The second line of the enemy was encountered, when the fighting was the fiercest, and the killing the deadliest. Suddenly Captain McCreery, assistant-general of the brigade, rushed forward with a message from General Pettigrew to Colonel Burgwyn. "Tell him his regiment has covered itself with glory today." Then seizing the flag, he waved it aloft and advancing to the front was shot through the heart.

. . .

Just as the last shots were firing, a sergeant in the Twenty-fourth Michigan Regiment noticed the commanding figure of Colonel Lane carrying the colors and fired, just as Lane turned to see if his men were following him. The ball struck in the back of the neck, just below the brain, crashed through jaw and mouth, and, for the fourteenth and the last time, the colors were down. The fight was won, but at a fearful cost to victors as well as vanquished.

And where was the band all this time?

When the brigade had left the camp in the morning, after we had been on picket duty during the night, Colonel Burgwyn had told us we might stay with the wagons if we wanted to, and as the order had been for the men to leave their knapsacks and those not able to make a forced march to remain in camp, we thought that we wanted to stay back. When we heard the noise of battle, we went to an adjoining hill, from which we could see the smoke of the infantry firing, while the roar of the cannon was almost continuous. After a couple of hours, the firing ceased, and soon prisoners and our own wounded men began to come in, bringing sorrowful news from the fight and our hearts sickened from the harrowing details.

Our dear old Col. Burgwyn was killed. Lt. Col. Lane was seriously, if not mortally wounded, Major Jones hurt, we knew not how badly, as was Adjt. Jordan and nearly every captain in the regiment. Nearly or quite three-fourths of the men were either killed or wounded, but none taken prisoners. Our colors had been shot down fourteen times, both Col. Burgwyn and Lt. Col. Lane having fallen with the flag in their hands.

It was therefore with heavy hearts that we went about our duties of caring for the wounded. We worked until 11 o'clock that night, when I was so thoroughly worn out that I could do no more and lay down for some rest. At 3 o'clock I was up again and at work. The second day our regiment was not engaged, but we were busily occupied all day in our sad tasks. While thus engaged, in the afternoon, we were sent for to go to the right or what was left of it, and play for the men, and thus, perhaps, cheer them somewhat. Dr. Warren sent Sam with a note to the commanding officer of the brigade, that we could not be spared from attending to the wounded men. Some time later another order came for us, and this was peremptory. We accordingly went to the regiment and found the men much more cheerful than we were ourselves. We played for some time, the 11th N.C. Band playing with us, and the men cheered us lustily. Heavy cannonading was going on at the time, though not in our immediate front[.] we learned afterwards, from Northern papers, that our playing had been heard across the lines and caused wonder that we should play while fighting was going on around us. Some little while after we left, a bomb struck and exploded very close to the place where we had been standing, no doubt having been intended for us.

SOURCE: Julius August Leinbach, "Scenes at the Battle of Gettysburg" (undated speech, ca. early 1900s), in *The Salem Band*, ed. Bernard J. Pfohl (Winston-Salem, N.C.: privately published, 1953): 75, 77–80. For a recording, see *A Storm in the Land: Music from the 26th North Carolina Regiment Band* (New World Records, 80608-2). The date for the speech comes from Donald M. McCorkle, "Regiment Band of the Twenty-Sixth North Carolina," Civil War History 4 (1958): 226.

Concert flyer for a "Grand Military Concert" by Captain Collis's Zouaves d'Afrique Band, January 13, 1862.

This excerpt, written from the perspective of the North, lists some famous tunes of the war and ends with a reference to musicians nursing the wounded in the aftermath of battle.

Battle of Cold Harbor 1864, June 8 Wed.

This evening the Band of the Thirteenth goes into the trenches at the front, and indulges in a "competition concert" with a band that is playing over across in the enemy's trenches. The enemy's Band renders *Dixie, Bonnie Blue Flag, My Maryland,* and other airs dear to the Southerner's heart. Our Band replies with *America, Star Spangled Banner, Old John Brown,* etc. After a little time, the enemy's band introduces another class of music; only to be joined almost instantly by our Band with the same tune. All at once the band over there stops, and a rebel battery opens with grape. Very few of our men are exposed, so the enemy wastes his ammunition; while our Band continues its playing, all the more earnestly until all their shelling is over.

The Band of the Thirteenth becomes very proficient in its long term of service, and enlivens many a dreary and dragging hour with its cheering music, as our Regiment kills its weary time in camp or trenches, or plods along on its muddy, tiresome marches. "And then the Band played—and then the Thirteenth cheered," is the closing complimentary remark in many a story of camp, and march, and field. A good Band. In a battle the men of the bands and drum-corps are expected to help take care of the wounded, and our Band and young drum-corps are very efficient in that delicate and dangerous work.

SOURCE: S. Millett Thompson, *Thirteenth Regiment of New Hampshire Volunteer Infantry in the War of Rebellion, 1861–1865* (Boston and New York: Houghton Mifflin, 1888): 369–70.

~~~~~~

Frank Rauscher was bandmaster of the 114th Regiment P.V. (Pennsylvania Volunteers), led by Charles Henry Collis. Rauscher kept a diary of his duty with the main Union army in the field, the Army of the Potomac. The 114th Regiment adopted the uniforms of the "Zouave" troops, Algerian soldiers who were pressed into service in the Napoleonic Wars in the early 1800s. The Zouaves were known in both Europe and the United States for their bravery and their exotic uniforms; thus American soldiers who adopted their colorful uniforms advertised their elite status. Dressed in turbans and (initially) white leggings and sashes, the Zouave band of the 114th Pennsylvania Regiment marched thousands of miles and played on through the most famous battles of the Civil War. Rauscher's memoirs include the selections in a concert played for officers. On occasion the Zouaves appeared on stage in opera (see chapter 40).

. . .

[After Captain Collis was ordered to raise a full regiment of Zouaves d'Afrique, he] immediately returned to Philadelphia, and in a short time organized the 114th Regiment Pennsylvania Vol-

The Band of "Zouaves," 114th Pennsylvania Infantry, in front of Petersburg, Virginia, August 1864, photo from Library of Congress.

unteers. By this time President Lincoln, after the failure of General [George B.] McClellan on the Peninsula, called for the second instalment of 300,000 volunteers for three years, and under this call the regiment was enlisted. A camp was established in the lower part of Germantown, called Camp Banks, in honor of General [Nathaniel P.] Banks. The uniform adopted for the regiment was precisely like that of the original company—red pants, Zouave jacket, white leggings, blue sash around the waist, and white turban, which pricked up the pride of the new recruits, and gave the regiment an imposing and warlike appearance.

. . .

At the beginning of the war every regiment mustered into service for three months, and afterwards the three-year regiments, all had full brass bands, some of them numbering as high as fifty pieces. When it is considered that in every brigade there were from four to five regiments, three brigades in one division and three divisions in each corps, an aggregate of from thirty-six to forty bands is shown for every corps. When a division was encamped in a small space, which was frequently the case when on the march, and the band of each regiment performing at the same time at Regimental Headquarters, the effect of the confusion of sounds produced can hardly be imagined. Whilst this was an unnecessary arrangement and very expensive to the Government, it kept a host of non-combatants in the rear of the army. Congress, however, at an early day passed an act abolishing all regimental bands in the volunteer service, with the provision that each brigade should be entitled to a band at the headquarters. It so happened that when the order of disbandment reached the army, the bands had seen considerable and hard service on

the Peninsula, under General McClellan, and therefore the men gladly accepted their discharges and almost to a man went home. As a consequence the army was left with scarcely any music.
. . .

[FROM PART TWO]

July 22.—Remained in camp until 2 P.M., then packed up and went on the march again, passing through Upperville, the road we were on leading over Goose Creek. This significantly named stream we crossed and recrossed at least a dozen times during the day, fording the mud and water sometimes up to our knees; still, we persistently kept on marching into midnight, when with a sort of aristocratic feeling we encamped on a large and beautiful plantation. As a rule, our generals, when such opportunities were afforded, took possession of and put up at the plantation houses, where, during the evening, the band played for the entertainment of the ladies, who often appeared to enjoy the music quite as much as the officers. Toward the close of our serenade, how-ever, when "John Brown" or "Yankee Doodle" came in as an expected number on the programme, the sensitive fair ones would retire to the mansion, as if disgusted with that part of the performance. As these popular and patriotic selections seemed to annoy these Secesh [secession] ladies, we rarely failed to play our pranks, as it appeared to be particularly agreeable to the officers, who always enjoyed such innocent divertissement.
. . .

When the band arrived here for the first time, it was assigned a position in the centre of this circle. It was soon evident that our presence was very acceptable, for we were at once surrounded by most of the staff officers, who made themselves very sociable, and especially after we had played for them a few pieces. According to my diary, I find that on this occasion we rendered the following programme, the initial number having been selected just to introduce us and give the event a good send-off:

Headquarters Programme

1. Hell on the Rappahannock.

2. Potpourri from "Trovatore."
   (Introducing all the gems of that popular opera.)

3. Bild der Rose.

4. [Overture to Nebuchadnezzar.

5. Selections from Lucia.

6. Trap-Trap Galop.

Such a selection as the above had probably never been given at the Headquarters in the field by any of the army bands, and any musician familiar with this class of music for brass instruments will know precisely the difficulties our band of only fourteen pieces had to encounter, and at the same time do the intricate arrangements justice. And then, too, it should be considered that a few candles in the open air afforded all the light we had in reading difficult manuscript[s]. Our debut here, however, was regarded as quite a success, and the officers expressed themselves as highly pleased with the performance and the music, declaring that they had never had the pleasure of having such a musical treat in camp.

. . .

A response from a comrade of the 114th Regiment, in anticipation of the publication of the within reminiscent notes, is here given as an earnest of the love of and desire for music in the army during the Rebellion:

> Don't forget to put in the book how we boys used to yell at the band for music to cheer us up when we were tramping along so tired that we could hardly drag one foot after the other. Since the war I have often thought how cruel we were to do so; for, if we were tired, wasn't the band members equally so? and yet we wanted them to use up what little breath they had left to put spirit in us. But then, you know, that good old tune we called "Hell on the Rappahannock" had enough music in it to make a man who was just about dead brace up, throw his chest out, and take the step as if he had received a new lease of life. Those were hard days, but even after a long march, if we were only rested a little we could be as happy as the day was long, knowing that we were doing our duty to our country and the flag, and that was reward enough for tired limbs and blistered feet.

SOURCE: Frank Rauscher, *Music on the March, 1862–'65 with the Army of the Potomac: 114th Regt. P.V., Collis' Zouaves* (Philadelphia: Press of Wm. F. Fell, 1892): 12, 14, 109, 120, 265. Available at http://www.genealogysearch.org/free/bmilitary.html.

48

$\mathcal{E}$LLA SHEPPARD MOORE

A Fisk Jubilee Singer

After the Civil War, the Fisk Jubilee Singers made African-American spirituals internationally famous. Their legacy led to gospel quartets and concert spirituals, helping to explain, as the music historian Sandra Graham writes, "how the spiritual came to be embraced not merely as an exotic curiosity of black life but an American musical tradition."[1]

Ella Sheppard Moore (1851–1914), one of the original nine members of the first group of Fisk Jubilee Singers, also served as the group's accompanist and as assistant director to its leader, George White, for seven years, 1871–1878. Sheppard chronicles the rise from poverty to international fame on the strength of the "slave songs" which the group made famous—almost by accident, as she explains it. The troupe sang at Gilmore's famous Peace Jubilee, as she recounts here.

Historical Sketch of the Jubilee Singers

ELLA SHEPPARD MOORE
926 17TH AVENUE NORTH, NASHVILLE, TENN.

PART I. PERSONAL

Forty-five years ago the sudden death of my father in Cincinnati, Ohio, brought me to extreme poverty, without protection and with no chance to finish my education or to prepare myself for life's duties and responsibilities. Besides, I had been an invalid for nearly two years. Although frail, I tried every honorable opportunity to make a living. I took in washing and ironing, worked in a family, and had a few music pupils who paid me poorly. Finally I left Cincinnati and taught school in Gallatin, Tennessee. In five months I realized my deficiencies and came to Fisk School in September, 1868, with all my possessions in a trunk (which was not full) so small that the boys immediately called it [a] "Pie Box." I had six dollars, and when Mr. White, the Treasurer, said that this amount would keep me a little over three weeks, I asked for work. He said there were already many others waiting for a chance to work. I decided to stay until my money ran out.

Exceptional musical advantages then very rare for colored girls in the South secured me three pupils, who paid me four dollars each per month. Wednesdays and Saturdays I went to the city and taught each pupil one hour, which made it impossible for me, running all the way, over the rough, rocky hills and roads, to get back in time for the last tap of the bell for supper; so I went without supper those days and waited on the table one day and washed dishes the other day. The school was very poor and food was scarce, yet it filled one. . . .

There were no helpful "mission barrels" in those days; so many of us shivered through that first winter with not an inch of flannel upon our bodies. In spite of our poverty and hardships we were a jolly set of natural girlish girls, and when we had a chance romped and played with all the abandon of children. Once a month we were allowed to go to the city to church and once a month to an entertainment, usually at Baptist College (afterward Roger Williams University), occupying the oldest part of what is now Knowles Public School Building. Our girls and boys labored as strenuously then for the favorite ones to accompany them over the rough, muddy roads and hills, as now to entertainments.

ORGANIZING THE COMPANY

We were especially fond of music and gladly gave half of our noon hour and all spare time to study under Mr. George L. White. We made rapid progress, and soon began to help our school by sometimes going Fridays and Saturdays to neighboring towns and cities to give concerts. We always succeeded financially and left behind a thirst for education. Those were the days of the Ku Klux Klan and the Civil Rights Bill. The latter bill prevented our being put out of a ladies' coach if we once got in. Our trips often led into many hardships and real dangers. Sometimes after a concert we received private notice of such a nature that we wisely took the first train away.

Photograph of Fisk Jubilee Singers. In this photograph of the Fisk Jubilee Singers, ca. 1870s, Ella Sheppard Moore is the seated woman, fourth figure from the right.

A SAMPLE TRIP

Once we were *enroute* to a large city to give the "Cantata of Queen Esther," which we had already given most successfully in our own city. An accident ahead of us compelled us to stop all day at a station in the woods to await the night train. The only visible house was the hotel. It was election time. All day men gathered from far and near drinking at the hotel bar. Our presence attracted their attention, and seeing Mr. White among us and discovering our mission, word soon traveled that he was a "Yankee nigger school teacher."

Threatenings began near evening. Mr. White, anxious and fearful for us, had us stroll to the railway platform, and sitting on a pile of shingles we prayed through song for deliverance and protection. Mr. White stood between us and the men directing our singing. One by one the riotous crowd left off their jeering and swearing and slunk back, until only the leader stood near Mr. White, and finally took off his hat. Our hearts were fearful and tender and darkness was falling. We were softly finishing the last verse of "Beyond the smiling and the weeping I shall be soon," when we saw the bull's eye of the coming engine and knew that we were saved. The leader begged us with tears falling to sing the hymn again, which we did. As the train passed slowly by I heard him repeating, "Love, rest and home, sweet, sweet home."

SLAVE SONGS NOT IN REPERTOIRE

The slave songs were never used by us then in public. They were associated with slavery and the dark past, and represented the things to be forgotten. Then, too, they were sacred to our parents, who used them in their religious worship and shouted over them. We finally grew willing to sing them privately, usually in Professor Spence's sitting-room, and sitting upon the floor (there were but few chairs) we practiced softly, learning from each other the songs of our fathers. We did not dream of ever using them in public. Had Mr. White or Professor Spence suggested such a thing, we certainly [would have] rebelled. It was only after many months that gradually our hearts were opened to the influence of these friends and we began to appreciate the wonderful beauty and power of our songs; but we continued to sing in public the usual choruses, duets, solos, etc., learned at school.

FALLING BUILDINGS AND RESOURCES

The time came when the old hospital buildings must either be greatly repaired or torn down. Many a night in '68 and '69, while some of the girls occupied rooms in the back row of buildings, the wind whistled around and groaned so fearfully that we trembled in horror in our beds, thinking the sounds were the cries of lost spirits of the soldiers who had died in them. We dared not sleep for fear a ghost would grab us, and one night we were sure that a ghost cried out, "O Lordy, O Lordy." Our screams aroused the neighborhood as we fled in terror.

Our privations and limited food began to tell on the vitality of the students and some of our best pupils were sacrificed. There was no money even for food, much less for repairs. Many a time [a] special prayer was offered for the next meal. The American Missionary Association decided that the school must be given up. Teachers, pupils, and citizens felt that this would be an irreparable mistake and calamity, but no one could see how nor where to get the money even for our necessities, and our needs were growing.

When Mr. White proposed to take a company of students to the North to sing for the money, there was consternation at Fisk, and the city people began to object. Everywhere such a plan was looked upon as "a wild goose chase." Opposition developed and grew into vicious criticisms. Prayers for light, guidance and patience went up daily. His peace fell upon us, and while we waited for guidance Mr. White called for volunteers from his singing class and choir. More than enough volunteered and he selected eleven voices. He rehearsed us daily.

The American Missionary Association officers, having heard of Mr. White's plans and of the criticisms, and feeling no doubt the responsibility was too great to assume such a quixotic agency for raising funds, said we must not go. Mr. White wrote to a leading member of the Board and requested a loan to defray our expenses. He not only refused, but protested. Mr. White telegraphed him, "'Tis root, hog, or die; I'm depending on God, not you." Our teachers caught the vision and enthusiasm of Mr. White, and, although fearful of failure, set to and helped to get us ready, dividing their clothing with us. Our company's clothing represented Joseph's coat of many colors and styles. Not one of us had an overcoat or wrap. Mr. White had an old gray shawl.

THE SINGERS GO FORTH

Taking every cent he had, all the school treasury could spare, and all he could borrow, and leaving his invalid wife and two small children in the care of a faithful colored nurse, Mr. White started, in God's strength, October 6, 1871, with his little band of singers to sing the money out of the hearts and pockets of the people.

On our reaching Cincinnati, two Congregational ministers, the Reverend Messrs. Moore and Halley, opened their churches for us for praise meetings. On Sunday these meetings were crowded. On Monday we sang at Chillicothe, Ohio, realizing nearly $50.00. It was the Sunday and Monday of Chicago's awful fire. We gladly donated our first proceeds to the Chicago Relief Fund and left our needs and debts in God's hands. The mayor and citizens of Chillicothe took notice of our gift and in a public card cordially commended our cause. The two concerts which followed were well attended. In this city began the operation of caste prejudice which was to follow us, and which it was to be a part of our mission if not to remove at least to ameliorate.

There was no room for us at two leading hotels. A humane landlord of a third hotel took us in, serving our meals before the usual hour. Dense audiences met in Cincinnati on Sunday at Reverend Mr. Moore's church, but a slim audience greeted our paid concert in Mozart Hall. Evidently the concert was enjoyed and the morning papers said "the sweetness of the voices, the accuracy of the execution and the precision of the time carried the mind back to the early concerts of the Hutchinsons, the Gibsons and other famous families, who years ago delighted audiences and taught them with sentiment while they pleased them with melody."

THE NAME "JUBILEE SINGERS"

Realizing that we must have a name, we held a prayer meeting at Columbus, Ohio. Our Fisk pastor, Reverend H. S. Bennett, was present. Next morning Mr. White met us with a glowing face. He had remained in prayer all night alone with God. "Children," he said, "it shall be Jubilee Singers in memory of the Jewish year of Jubilee." The dignity of the name appealed to us. At our usual family worship that morning there was great rejoicing.

PROGRAMS

At first our programs had been made up wholly of what we called the white man's music. Occasionally two or three slave songs were sung at the close of the concert.

The following is a sample program sung at Mansfield, Ohio, November 29, 1871:

1. Holy Lord God of Sabaoth.

2. Friends, We Come with Hearts of Gladness.

3. There's Moonlight on the Lake.

4. Irish Ballad. Patrick McCuishla.

5. Recitation. Sheridan's Ride.

6. Gipsey Chorus.

7. Solo. The Loving Heart that Won Me.

8. Songs of Summer.

9. Temperance Medley.

10. Wine is a Mocker.

1. Hail America.

2. Merrily o'er the Calm Blue Sea.

3. Old Folks at Home.

4. Away to the Meadows.

5. Comin' Through the Rye.

6. Roll, *Jording* [Jordan], Roll.

7. Turn Back Pharaoh's Army.

8. Vocal Medley.

9. Home, Sweet Home.

But very soon our sufferings and the demand of the public changed this order. A program of nineteen numbers, only two or three of which were slave songs, was inverted. To recall and to learn of each other the slave songs demanded much mental labor, and to prepare them for public singing required much rehearsing. . . .

Our experiences repeated themselves from place to place on our journey toward New York. As the slave song says, "We were sometimes up and sometimes down, but still our souls kept heavenly bound." Arriving in New York we found "no room in the inn" and three of our American Missionary Association secretaries, the Reverends Cravath, Smith, and Pike, took us to their home in Brooklyn, where we remained for six weeks.

Through the interest and co-operation of the leading ministers of New York, led by that noble man, Henry Ward Beecher, our cause was soon before the public and we were received with the wildest enthusiasm. Our concerts were crowded. In each city where we appeared, a perfect furore of excitement prevailed. Varied and favorable criticisms filled the dailies of our ability as musicians, of the wonderful spiritual effect of the slave songs, now called Jubilee songs. We visited many of the principal cities and towns of New York, Pennsylvania and New Jersey. We went into New England, and everywhere the experience was the same. Hotels refused us, and families of the highest social prestige received us into their homes. We sang in halls where Negroes had never been allowed upon the platform. . . .

Success followed us to Washington, D.C. The President turned aside from pressing duties to receive us at the White House. Parson Brownlow, Tennessee's Senator, too ill to attend our concert, sent for us to visit him. He cried like a child as we sang our humble Southern slave melodies. Returning to New England we received a perfect ovation. Extra excursions were often run to our concerts. Our songs, which had been taken down by Professor Theodore F. Seward and published, were sold at our concerts during the intermission. Soon the land rang with our slave songs, sung in the homes of the people.

Our first campaign closed at Poughkeepsie, New York. We not only had paid the debts at home of nearly $1,500 and furnished other money for support of Fisk; but we carried home $20,000, with which was purchased the present site of twenty-five acres for our new school. At Louisville we were roughly turned out of the sitting-room at the railway station amid the jeers of about two thousand roughs, but the railroad superintendent put us in a first-class coach, in which we returned to Fisk amid great rejoicing.

PART II. AT THE WORLD'S PEACE JUBILEE

Remaining at home only one week we again took the road. That we might meet the greater demands for concerts, and also visit smaller places where it would be too expensive to go with a full company, our number had been increased. We had been invited to sing at the second World's Peace Jubilee in June. After a few concerts *enroute*, we stopped at Boston to rehearse and rest.

Mr. White had unusual taste and gifts. For weeks he trained our voices to sing the Battle Hymn of the Republic. He reasoned that the thousands of instruments to be used in the great building would very likely play it in E flat, the one key in which the various instruments could harmonize. Hence, in order to be heard satisfactorily by the vast audience, we must be able to enunciate with perfect accuracy of pitch and purity of tone every word and every part of a word in a key three half steps higher than usual. So, little by little, each day or two going a bit higher, using his violin, he trained us on those words from C to E flat until he was satisfied.

The day came when the Battle Hymn was to be sung. Two colored girls, sisters and beautiful singers, too, were to sing the first two verses, and we the last, "He hath sounded forth the trumpet." Evidently the sisters had not anticipated the change of key, and to their chagrin they found themselves obliged greatly to strain their voices and unable to sing their parts satisfactorily. The conductor told us to sing on the choruses, but we preferred to hold all our force in reserve until the time came for us to sing, though trembling like spirited race horses in our excitement to begin. Then with apparently one voice, pure, clear and distinct, we sang out,

> *He hath sounded forth the trumpet,*
>
> *Which shall never call retreat.*

The audience of forty thousand people was electrified. Men and women arose in their wild cheering, waving and throwing up handkerchiefs and hats. The twenty thousand musicians and singers behind us did likewise. One German raised his violincello and thwacked its back with the bow, crying, "Bravo, bravo!" and Strauss, the great composer, waved his violin excitedly. It was a triumph not to be forgotten. For days we sang; the people seemed never to tire of listening.

. . .

We felt that our first concert, which was to be given in the aristocratic Sing-Akademie, would be a test of our strength. Our interpreter, Mr. Kuistermaker, had said that a number of the greatest musical critics in the country, before whom all the great singers appeared, were to be present, and if we failed we would better pack our trunks and leave. So when we stood before these gentlemen (critics) all of them on the front seat, (the worst place from which to judge us) we trembled. One of our basses was absent, which left only one bass to balance nine voices. We labored hard to even up voices. We grouped as usual, leaned heads toward each other, and paused for a oneness of effort. Then everything else forgotten, in a musical whisper, "Steal Away" floated out so perfectly that one could not tell when it began. The astonishment upon the fixed, upturned faces of our critics told us that we had won; we were again at ease and did our best to maintain the good impression. Our concert was received with great enthusiasm. The audience, representing the greatest and best of the city, was in evening dress. We had never seen such an array of sparkling jewels as were worn that night. It was beautiful. After the concert many came up and congratulated us. The dailies gave us some of the finest criticisms we had received. Each piece was analyzed. One article was filled with such expressions as these: "What wealth of shading! What accuracy of declamation! Such a pianissimo, such a crescendo and a decrescendo as those at the close of 'Steal Away' might raise envy in the soul of any choir master." And further on: "Something may be learned from these Negro singers."

Our work and mission were the same in Germany as in other countries, with the same satisfying results. All the leading cities of Germany were visited. At Wittenburg we sang "Praise God from Whom all Blessings Flow" in Martin Luther's room in the old Monastery, and heard the wonderful chimes at sunrise. At Brunswick we met Franz Abt, the author and musician, and received a warm greeting. At Barmen we sang before one of the largest Sunday schools in the world, and they sang for us, the name of Jesus being the only familiar word in the songs. At Darmstadt the court theatre was placed at our disposal. We had the pleasure of meeting Princess Alice, Grand Duchess of Hessen, daughter of Queen Victoria, also her children. At another concert both the Duke and Duchess were present, also the Prince of Wales and his brother, the Duke of Connaught. After the concert we were summoned to the royal box and warmly greeted. At Dresden our successful concert was attended by the King and Queen of Saxony. At Leipzig our reception was delightful. The Gewandhaus, an aristocratic hall where only the best class of concerts was admitted, was placed at our disposal. The custom of cheaper admission fees and hard times made our tour financially less successful. After taking in a few other prominent cities and sights we prepared for disbanding and left the Continent, arriving home at Fisk in July, 1878.

SOURCE: Ella Sheppard Moore, "The Jubilee Singers," *Fisk University News* 2, no. 5 (1911): 41–58.

NOTE

1. Sandra J. Graham, "The Fisk Jubilee Singers and the Concert Spiritual: The Beginnings of an American Tradition" (Ph.D. diss., New York University, 2001): 361.

PATRICK S. GILMORE AND THE

GOLDEN AGE OF BANDS

(Newspaper Review, Herbert)

At the head of generations of band conductors stands the Irish-American musician Patrick S. Gilmore (1829–1892), who helped to establish the concert band as an American institution. In 1851, two years after arriving from Ireland, Gilmore was hired by P. T. Barnum to promote the Jenny Lind tour (see chapter 35). From the master showman himself, Gilmore learned the benefits of publicity and spectacle, which he later put to good use in his jubilee concerts.[1] By 1857, Gilmore had formed his own band, which later marched with the Massachusetts 24th Regiment in the Civil War. Under the pseudonym of Louis Lambert, Gilmore in 1863 published his famous patriotic song "When Johnny Comes Marching Home," with the tune based on an Irish folk song.

After the war, Gilmore and his band flourished. His most famous concert festival, the World Peace Jubilee (1872), featured a 2,000-piece orchestra, a 20,000-voice chorus, and a stirring musical moment by the Fisk Jubilee Singers (see chapter 48). In his later years, Gilmore presented summer concerts with the opera conductor and Wagnerian enthusiast Anton Seidl.

On April 11, 1875, Gilmore leased P. T. Barnum's Hippodrome, renaming it Gilmore's Garden, a site now called Madison Square Garden, where he continued to present oversized, "monster" jubilee concerts. Their popularity is recounted in a review from the *New York Times* of July 3, 1876, which documents the wide-ranging repertoire. In the second selection, composer Victor Herbert pays tribute to his mentor.

THE JUBILEE AT GILMORE'S GARDEN—GREAT THRONG PRESENT—THE CONCERT A TRIUMPH

The number of visitors at Gilmore's Garden last night was beyond computation. The spacious building was crowded in every part. The boxes were all filled, the tables rising in tiers about the vast space devoted to horticultural show[s] were all occupied, and an uneasy, moving, perspiring crowd crammed and crushed in the broad parterre in the vain effort to go through the usual exercise of the promenade. Outside of the building, too, crowds loitered, clustering on the stoops and railings, and testifying their genuine love of music by the eagerness with which they caught up the melodious sounds of chorus and orchestra that came to them gratis through the open windows of the "Garden." The 500 vocalists and Gilmore's Band occupied an enlarged platform in the middle of the parterre. The voices and the music, to the undisguised astonishment of most of the visitors, made comparatively little noise, but there was an adequate compensation in the quantity and quality of the melody afforded, for the singers were well trained as a body, and worked with mathematical precision under the baton of Dr. Damrosch.[2] The programme began with the overture to the "Freischutz," very well executed by Gilmore, followed by Schubert's Hymn, in which the chorus and orchestra came out in grand unison, Mme. Pappenheim followed with an aria from "Robert le Diable," which was so well treated—the lady being in good melodious voice, which easily and agreeably filled the vast and crowded building in every part, to the most remote corner—that an encore was enthusiastically demanded.[3] Hers was undoubtedly the success of the evening. Mr. Remmertz, in a baritone aria by Spohr, was not so successful[,] his voice being inaudible in the remote parts of the garden. The grand chorus attacked the "Bacchanalian Chorus," from Mendelssohn's "Antigone" with vigor and executed it with a dramatic shading that was triumphant.[4] "The song of 1876," enlisting the full orchestra, chorus and four male soloists, Messrs. Bischoff, Wagner, Remmertz and Trust, proved thrilling and brilliant, though too complicated in treatment to become popular if left to less skillful and well-trained combinations than the picked singers of the German societies, who last night, after having been rehearsed up to the very point of perfection, made it strike the popular and patriotic fancy. This memorable entertainment closed with the singing of the "Star Spangled Banner" by Mme. Pappennheim, with full grand orchestra and chorus aiding, and working up a fitting sensation climax to the suggestive musical features of the evening. . . .

SOURCE: "The Jubilee at Gilmore's Garden," *New York Times*, July 3, 1876, 8.

In 1893, the leadership of Gilmore's renowned band passed to composer Victor Herbert (1859–1924). In an article called "Artistic Bands," Herbert paid tribute to his predecessor.

The important part that military bands have taken in the development of musical knowledge in America cannot be overstated. In this land of the free a musician can seek engagements where he will, and is not compelled to accept enforced service. This freedom has drawn to our country the best musicians of the world, and has fostered native talent. In consequence of these conditions a band conductor has at his disposal artistic material, which has so stimulated public taste that to-day we have concert military bands bidding for the appreciation and support of music-lovers of every degree of culture. It would be interesting to analyze the popular preference for bands over orchestras, if space permitted, but the fact can be clearly demonstrated. There are to-day large and expensive concert bands which travel from State to State over the entire continent, while the orchestras have to limit their *tournées*. From the old bands which depended on the loud brasses and drums, all forced to their utmost to make the most noise possible, to the bands of the present day which interpret the works of the greatest so as to satisfy even the most exacting musician, has been a hard but glorious struggle up the steeps of Parnassus, and to Patrick Sarsfield Gilmore belongs most of the glory. Mr. Gilmore knew men and music, and through his knowledge of both he held the masses and led them. In each programme there was something that made each auditor a better man musically, and prepared him for another step ahead. The compositions of Wagner lend themselves readily to the transition from orchestra to band, a quality due to the prominence given the wood[s] and brasses in all his works. A remarkable example of this may be noted in "Elizabeth's Prayer," where the wood-winds are used alone; and in many of the most beautiful passages in the "Nibelungen" the strings are not used at all.[5] Wagner was the first composer to recognise the possibilities of these sections of the orchestra and to him is due the credit of enlarging them. For this reason, since Gilmore's time, every band conductor makes a feature of his great overtures, and a year's programmes will show many concerts exclusively devoted to Wagner. As the repertories of bands have increased, the demand for new tone-colour effects has caused new instruments to be made, so that to-day the composer or adapter has a wide range in registrating. The use of compositions originally written for orchestras has caused a great increase in the wood-wind section of the bands—flutes, oboes, clarinets, and saxophones—of which every band should have a quartet—bassoons, and contra-bassoons. These additions make the repertory of the band universal. The greater sustaining power of the wood-winds gives a beautiful richness of harmony, and relieves one from the torture of listening to the scratchiness of poorly played strings.

SOURCE: Victor Herbert, "Artistic Bands," in *Music of the Modern World*, ed. Anton Seidl (New York: Appleton, 1895): 120.

NOTES

1.   Information about Barnum and Gilmore is from an unsigned feature article, "Young Rugg Met Both Barnum and Gilmore in New York in 1858," *Salem Evening News*, January 30, 1931, 14.

2. Leopold Damrosch (1832–1885) was the German-born conductor of the Mannergesangverein Arion (a German male-singer society) as well as the conductor of the [New York] Philharmonic Society from 1876–1877.

3. "Freischutz" refers to Carl Maria Von Weber's opera *Der Freischutz* (1820). Eugenie Pappeheim (1849–1924) was an operatic soprano.

4. Mendelssohn's incidental music for Sophocles's play *Antigone* (1841) included this popular chorus. The German composer Giacomo Meyerbeer wrote the French grand opera, *Robert le Diable* (1831).

5. "Elizabeth's Prayer" refers to an aria from Wagner's opera *Tannhäuser;* "Nibelungen" refers to Wagner's cycle of four operas, known as *Der King des Nibelung.*

THEODORE THOMAS AND

HIS MUSICAL MANIFEST DESTINY

(Rose Fay Thomas, Theodore Thomas)

The career of the great conductor Theodore Thomas (1835–1905) exemplifies many issues that characterized American classical musical life after 1850: the transcontinental touring of large ensembles made possible by a transcontinental railroad, and a sense of mission fueled by territorial expansionism. Thomas believed in a cultural version of "manifest destiny" and did more than any other conductor in the nineteenth century to introduce European symphonic music (particularly Beethoven and Wagner) to novice American audiences. As a young boy, Thomas emigrated from Germany to New York with his family; he was on his own at 15 as a freelance musician in New York in the 1850s. That decade witnessed an influx of great Italian opera singers and also the arrival of the Germania Orchestra, both of which inspired Thomas to devote himself to classical music. Thomas was a legend in his own time, and in 1927 the journalist Charles Edward Russell's biography of Theodore Thomas won the only Pulitzer Prize ever awarded for the biography of a musician.

After establishing the Theodore Thomas Orchestra in New York in 1864, he soon took to the road in order to survive. His wife, Rose Fay Thomas, coined the phrase that became forevermore associated with her husband's travels: "the great musical highway of America."

The route which Thomas sketched out for his first tour with the orchestra in 1869, might be called the great musical highway of America, for it included all the large cities which Thomas thought might become musical centers in time. It was as follows:

Outward	Homeward
New York.	St. Louis.
New Haven.	Indianapolis.
Hartford.	Louisville.
Providence.	Cincinnati.
Boston.	Dayton.
Worcester.	Springfield, O.
Springfield, Mass.	Columbus.
Albany.	Pittsburg[h].
Schenectady.	Washington.
Utica.	Baltimore.
Syracuse.	Philadelphia.
Rochester.	New York.
Buffalo.	
Cleveland.	
Toledo.	
Detroit.	
Chicago.	

During the twenty-two years between 1869 and 1891, Thomas traveled over this "highway" a number of times every year. In the larger of its cities he gave concerts on every trip, arranging the intermediate stops in accordance with the engagements offered. But there was not a city on the list which was not visited more or less often, and given its own opportunity for musical culture. In addition to the regular route just specified, and which I have designated as the "highway," Thomas had a number of others over which he traveled at less frequent intervals. One of these led through the Southern States; another through New England to Montreal, and thence through Canada to the far Northwest; another straight across the continent to San Francisco, returning through Texas.

SOURCE: Rose Fay Thomas, "The Great Musical Highway of America," in *Memoirs of Theodore Thomas* (New York: Moffat, Yard, 1911): 52–53.

Drawing by Joseph Keppler (1838–1894), "At Steinway Hall," 1872. Source: R. Allen Lott, *From Paris to Peoria. How European Piano Virtuosos Brought Classical Music to the American Heartland* (New York: Oxford Univ. Press, 2003): 178. This caricature by Keppler (later a famous political cartoonist for *Punch*), surveys the season. Each musician responds to the cheers, whistles, clapping, and horn blowing of the audience with a slightly different emotion. In the center the temperamental pianist, Anton Rubinstein, listens to himself. From left to right: singers Giorgio Ronconi, Carlotta Patti, and Giovanni Mario. On the right, the violin virtuoso Henryk Wieniawski, then two more singers, Louise Leibhart, and Louise Ormeny. Theodore Thomas and his orchestra (under the word "Westward") and the Venezuelan concert pianist, Teresa Carreño, her glory days ahead, float up above.

Introducing Americans to Wagner became Thomas's cause, just as it was for Gilmore and for Seidl. In 1872, Thomas introduced the famous "Ride of the Valkyries" to New York audiences; their reaction is recorded in this excerpt. He also went on the road with the famous Anton Rubinstein, one of a group of European piano virtuosi doing nonstop concert tours all across the country, who in Thomas's view, helped to raise the standards of concert repertoires. Rubinstein played concertos by Schumann, Mendelssohn, and Liszt and his own Second and Fourth Concertos as well.

It was in response to the foregoing request [that he conduct summer concerts in New York] that I resumed my Symphony Concerts in New York during the season of 1872–73, but this time I gave six in place of five, and called them "Concerts" instead of "Soirees." Before the close of the Summer Night season, I gave, for the first time, at the one hundred and twenty-eighth concert, September 17, a Wagner programme, which met with tremendous success.* After the

*On that evening, September 17, 1872, Mr. Thomas laid before the members of his orchestra and other friends, assembled at his invitation, his project of founding a Richard

"Ritt der Walküren" ["The Ride of the Valkyries"], which was played that night for the first time (from manuscript), the people jumped on the chairs and shouted. After the concert a grand banquet took place, given to the orchestra by prominent citizens of New York, and that same night the New York Wagner *Verein* [society] was organized with great enthusiasm.

Our winter season, which opened as soon as that of the summer had closed, September 26, found us in Albany at the outset of our regular tour west to Chicago. We returned via St. Louis, Pittsburg[h], and the intermediate cities, to New York in time for the first Symphony Concert, Nov. 9. This season, 1872–73, was doubly memorable; first, because the Wagner programme, which I first gave at the Central Park Garden, I now repeated in many cities where I gave a series of concerts, thus familiarizing the public everywhere with Wagner's music, which at that time was unknown outside of New York; and second, because of the arrival of two great instrumentalists, Rubinstein and Wieniawski, who were brought to America by Maurice Grau.

These two famous artists gave many concerts and recitals in America, and afterwards in December, a "Grand Combination of the Rubinstein and Thomas Concert Companies," as they were advertised, was effected. The attraction was sufficient to justify for the first time in my life in making programmes without making allowance for ignorance or prejudice. Before the season closed, we had given many concerts in all the larger cities of the Eastern and Middle states. Programmes of works of the highest standard, rendered by such artists and such an orchestra, were a revelation everywhere, and made a lasting impression. They gave this country the great artistic impetus for which it seemed at least to be ripe.

~~~~~~

As his concert tours established his reputation, Thomas benefited from the local ambitions of urban elites. In Cincinnati, for example, Thomas inspired a choral festival which grew out of that city's German population and its own Saengerchor (singing society) traditions. An annual multiday May Festival, which continues today, is considered responsible for Cincinnati's development in classical music. The first Cincinnati May Festival took place on May 6–9, 1873. Thomas had just completed a grueling touring season of 85 concerts outside of New York. The emphasis on choral rather than symphonic music at the Cincinnati festivals illustrates the influence of the German Saengerchor. An audience of 5,000 heard music by Beethoven, Handel, and Haydn. The building which initially hosted meetings of the German singing societies turned into the civic center for music.

Wagner Union, on the plan of similar societies in Europe. His purpose was realized the same evening, and he was chosen president of the Union. Its immediate object was to raise a fund by subscription for the purchase of tickets to the Baireuth Festival in the summer of 1874 for the use of members of the orchestra and also to defray their travelling expenses. The fund was still further increased by the proceeds of two concerts given by the orchestra.—Edr.

Music Hall, a brick building constructed in 1878 for the Cincinnati Music Festivals (May Festivals).

Cincinnati, one of the oldest settlements in the West, not only possesses wealth and culture, but it also has sincere and capable musicians, who by their influence as teachers developed a genuine love and understanding of music in that community. About one-fourth of its population, thirty-five years ago [1870], was German, or of German descent, and while I, for one, do not believe that the German in America is necessarily musical, he nevertheless has a high respect for art. For many years music has been a large part of the daily life of the Cincinnati people, and the city at that time ranked second only to New York, Boston, or Philadelphia, in musical achievement. When I made my first visit to Cincinnati with my orchestra, in 1869, even at that early time I found excellent choral societies there, and an orchestra superior to that of any city west of New York. On my next visit, in 1871, a young married lady, who was a member of one of the leading families of the city, laid before me a plan for a large Musical Festival. She proposed that I should be the conductor of it, saying that if I would be responsible for the artistic side, she would find the men who would take charge of the business details.[1] I soon found out that this lady was not only very talented herself in many ways, but that her taste was not amateurish in anything, and I readily consented to undertake the work she wished me to do. Some of the programmes were sketched at her house, and the Festival took place, as planned, in May, 1873, and was a great success.

An advertisement for the "May Festival Music," *Cincinnati Daily Gazette*, May 8, 1878. Attendees are requested to study scores beforehand.

Here, in this famous discussion of strategic programming, Thomas reveals his understanding of the tensions between entertainment and art. He managed to survive waves of criticism in the press over his programming many times in his career.

The following pages have been written in response to a request for an account of the method I use in arranging my programmes.

In earlier years they always included a Beethoven number; first, because Beethoven is the nearest to us in spirit; second, because he expresses more than any other composer; and third, because he has reached the highest pinnacle in instrumental music, which became through him a language. Thus Beethoven answers a double purpose; he gives delight to the educated, and teaches the uneducated. His place was always in the first part of the programme.

I have always believed in climaxes, also in giving people the most recent musical productions, and Wagner is the composer who satisfies both these essentials. Like Beethoven, he
also answers a double purpose. He represents the modern spirit, and his effective scoring makes
the desired climax. Wagner excites his hearers, especially the younger generation, and interests
the less musical.

In this way Beethoven and Wagner became the pillars, so to speak, of my programmes.
The effect of these composers on the public was plainly apparent. So I placed them where they
belonged, and then filled out the rest of the programme so as to keep within a certain limit of
time, have each piece prepare for the one to follow, observe a steady *crescendo*, never allow an anti-
climax, and "keep a trump" for the last. I knew exactly the character of the pieces I needed for
filling up and completing the programme after I had selected my so-called pillars, and began to
hunt for them, but often I failed to find them. As I could not compose them, I finally had to give
up the search in such cases, and change my sketch.

The real trouble, however, was the one-sidedness of the public taste, which made it difficult in this scheme to meet the popular demand to any considerable extent and still preserve the
unity of the programme. Two numbers served this purpose well for many years—the "Träumerei"
by Schumann, and the "Blue Danube Waltz" by Johann Strauss. While I was in Europe, in the
spring of 1867, Mr. George Matzka had arranged the "Träumerei" for small orchestra at the request of some of the friends and patrons of the Summer Night Concerts at Terrace Garden, New
York. He added as a trio the well-known Romanza. For the following winter season I rearranged
the "Träumerei" for strings only, without the double basses, retained the trio, and then repeated
the "Träumerei," but this time with muted strings, making an effective *diminuendo* at the end,
finishing with a *piano, pianissimo, pianisissimo, à la* Ole Bull. This was altogether a new effect.
The tone colors created sufficient sensation to prove an attraction, but we remained in our places
after having reached the softest point of "*pianisissimo,*" while Ole Bull, in his performance of the
"Arkansas Traveller," would move slowly backward on the stage as he played softer and softer,
and finally only continue the movement of his bow, without touching the strings, leaving the listener to the illusions of his imagination.[2] About this time I brought over with me from Vienna,
where I had enjoyed hearing them as given by the composers, "The Blue Danube Waltz" and
many other dances, by the brothers Johann and Joseph Strauss, and the playing of these never
failed to make a popular sensation in the concert-room.

The greatest difficulty I have found in arranging programmes, until very recent times,
has been to interest the audience in other masters besides Beethoven and Wagner, and thereby
enlarge the *repertoire* of the public and broaden its conceptions. I have never wished to pose as
an educator or philanthropist, except in so far as I might help the public to get beyond certain
so-called "popular music"—which represents nothing more than sweet sentimentalism and
rhythm, on the level of the dime novel. Nor has it been a fad of mine, as some people have imagined, to persevere for half a century and insist upon preserving the unity of a programme. If
anything, it has been a fixed principle, and the determination to be associated with something
worthy and to represent something to which a man need not be ashamed of devoting his life,
which have actuated me. The practical question of "bread and butter" for the orchestra player
also entered into the problem. If the only aim of a musician were to amuse the people, the sub-
limest of all the arts would soon be lost to humanity.

SOURCE: Theodore Thomas, *A Musical Autobiography* Vol. 1, ed. George P. Upton
(Chicago: A. C. McClurg & Co., 1905):15–19, 62–64, 78–79.

NOTES

1. This is referring to Maria Longworth Nichols (1849–1932), who is credited as the founder of the May Festival. She was also a ceramics artist who founded the famous Rockwood Pottery Co.
2. For another reference to Ole Bull, see chapter 36.

1880–1920

51

JOHN PHILIP SOUSA

Excerpts from His Autobiography

The "March King," John Philip Sousa (1854–1932), influenced American music to an unprecedented degree. His life began when slavery was legal and ended after the invention of the phonograph and radio, which he regarded as harbingers of cultural decline. Sousa trained as a trombone player in the U.S. Marine Band and eventually became its leader in 1880. He founded his own band in 1892. Among the best known of his approximately 135 marches are "Semper Fidelis" (1888), the "Washington Post March" (1889), and "The Stars and Stripes Forever" (1897), which was declared the United States' national march in 1987. Sousa understood that the American public wanted to sing along at his concerts and toe-tap to his music.

These excerpts from Sousa's autobiography touch on important themes in his life and work. In the first part of the selection, Sousa compares himself to his hero Theodore Thomas (see chapter 50) and gives a touching account of their meeting at the World's Columbian Exposition in Chicago. It includes a famous succinct summary of their different goals, and explains why Sousa regularly programmed band arrangements of music by Wagner and hired classical musicians, such as violinist Maud Powell (1867–1920) and opera singer Estelle Liebling (1880–1970), as guest performers.

The second part of the selection includes the key to understanding Sousa's achievements as a composer. He writes that a good march must be "as free from padding as a marble statue."

In October, 1892, I had the honor to play in conjunction with Theodore Thomas' Orchestra at the dedication of the World's Fair Building in Chicago. The programme consisted, among other numbers, of *Columbus,* a march and hymn for orchestra, military band and chorus, written by John Knowles Paine of the Faculty of Harvard University. I had very thoroughly rehearsed the music we were to play in combination with the orchestra, and a general rehearsal was held in the Auditorium. Mr. Thomas stopped the orchestra in the middle of the number and turning to my band, said, "Sousa Band, start it from the beginning." He went through it, without once stopping them. Then he turned to me—I was sitting with Mr. Blakely in the front seat of the Auditorium—and smilingly said, "I thank you for the pains you have taken." After the rehearsal he came over to me and said, "Let's get some lunch." We sat in the Auditorium Hotel restaurant until after six. It was one of the happiest afternoons of my life. Thomas was one of the greatest conductors that ever lived.

It pleased my fancy to compare Thomas' career with my own, for they were very much alike. He had played second horn in a United States Navy Band stationed at Portsmouth, Virginia, when he was but thirteen; I had played second trombone in the Marine Band at Washington when I was thirteen. He had played the violin for dancing; so had I. He had become an orchestral violinist, and so had I. He was an American by adoption, coming from Essen, East Friesland, at the age of ten. I was an American by birth, but my parents were Portuguese and German. He had conducted an opera at sight without ever having seen the performance or score before; I had done the same thing for a German opera company in Washington. (The conductor missed the train, and I conducted *A Night in Granada* by Kreutzer, without ever having seen anything but the overture.)

I have heard it said of Thomas that a great violinist was side-tracked to become the greatest conductor in the world. No wonder I was thrilled to be with him! He ordered luncheon and then became reminiscent, and told me a number of interesting stories about his early career. He laughed especially over the memory of a concert in Terrace Garden, in New York. He had placed on the programme a piece entitled, *The Linnet Polka* for two piccolos, and he prevailed upon the piccolo players to get up into the trees. When the audience heard the sounds coming through the foliage above, they applauded so heartily that it was obvious that the performance was a real "hit."

I told Thomas that my early dream of heaven was his rendering of Schumann's *Träumerei* in Washington when I was a little fellow.

"That was some pianissimo," he commented. "But, speaking of concerts, you must be very careful about management. Managers will stick close when you are making money, but they'll desert you without a qualm when the first squall blows up. Beware of speculators, if only for art's sake. Barnum offered to undertake the management of my concerts years ago, but I declined because I had no faith in his artistic integrity, and felt that he would exploit me in much the same manner as he did the Siamese twins, the fat lady, or the skeleton."

We discussed many compositions I had heard him give, and when I became enthusiastic over some especially brilliant effect he had produced, he would inquire happily, "Do you really remember that?" adding, "I worked over that effect for hours but I finally got it." The afternoon sped by, and I only left when I had to get ready for my concert that evening.

Late that night, as I sat in my hotel room, musing over our conversation, I continued the parallel between Thomas and myself. Like him, I was tenacious of my rights, but more diplomatic and less given to irrevocable dicta. I would listen to advice, and if I knew it was no good, would quietly say, "I'll think that over," leaving the other fellow with no ammunition to discuss the matter further. If I thought the advice good, I'd make the other fellow advance more arguments in favor of it and thereby convince me of its practical worth. Thomas had a highly organized symphony orchestra with a traditional instrumentation; I a highly organized wind band with an instrumentation without precedent. Each of us was reaching an end, but through different methods. He gave Wagner, Liszt, and Tchaikowsky, in the belief that he was educating his public; I gave Wagner, Liszt and Tchaikowsky with the hope that I was entertaining my public.

. . .

Marches, of course, are well known to have a peculiar appeal for me. Although during a busy life I have written ten operas and a hundred other things—cantatas, symphonic poems, suites, waltzes, songs, dances and the like—marches are, in a sense, my musical children. I think Americans (and many other nationals for that matter) brighten at the tempo of a stirring march because it appeals to their fighting instincts. Like the beat of an African war drum, the march speaks to a fundamental rhythm in the human organization and it is answered. A march stimulates every center of vitality, wakens the imagination and spurs patriotic impulses which may have been dormant for years. I can speak with confidence because I have seen men profoundly moved by a few measures of a really inspired march.

But a march must be good. It must be as free from padding as a marble statue. Every line must be carved with unerring skill. Once padded, it ceases to be a march. There is no form of musical composition where the harmonic structure must be more clean-cut. The whole process is an exacting one. There must be a melody which appeals to the musical and unmusical alike. There must be no confusion in counterpoints. The composer must, to be sure, follow accepted harmonization; but that is not enough. He must be gifted with the ability to pick and choose here and there, to throw off the domination of any one tendency. If he is a so-called purist in music, that tendency will rule his marches and will limit their appeal.

How are marches written? I suppose every composer has a somewhat similar experience in his writing. With me the thought comes, sometimes slowly, sometimes with ease and rapidity. The idea gathers force in my brain and takes form not only melodically but harmonically at the same time. It must be complete before I commit it to paper. Then I instrument it according to the effects it requires. Often I fix my mind upon some objective—such as the broad spaces of the West, the languorous beauty of the South, the universal qualities of America as a whole. And then comes its musical expression—be it thunder or sunshine!

I do not, of course, manufacture my themes deliberately; the process isn't direct or arbitrary enough for that. It is not a nonchalant morning's work. I often dig for my themes. I practice a sort of self-hypnotism, by penetrating the inner chambers of my brain and *receiving* the themes. Any composer who is gloriously conscious that he *is* a composer must believe that he receives his inspiration from a source higher than himself. That is part of my life *credo*. Sincere composers believe in God.

Curiosity has often been expressed as to the building up of a musical background, of the whole complex orchestration. The process is difficult of description. In the fashioning of the orchestration the theme occupies somewhat the relation to the whole structure that a leader does to his orchestra—forever weaving in and out, emerging vividly here and subordinating itself there. Of course it is necessary to understand the science of music-making. I might say the theme sounds through the brain—it wakens vibrations from the memory chords of the brain and produces creative activity; the mind quickens, hovers intently about the suggested theme, and gradually the theme, the technique, and artistry of the composer all work together to build up the orchestration.

. . .

We were in Rome when news came of the election of Mr. McKinley to the Presidency. The bellboys, who for a few years had not received an abundance of tips, because of the shortage of opulent American tourists, had evidently heard some fervent Republican say that prosperity would accompany the election of McKinley, for on that night they shouted "McKinley and prosperity! Prosperity and McKinley."

Rome offered a thousand delights; for me there was the interest of observing a choir in the Vatican rehearsing from a large book of hymns whose notation differed absolutely from the Guidonian in use to-day; then there were the usual little contretemps with lazy sons of Italy anent "tipping"; Mrs. Sousa drank in avidly every beauty of the Holy City, and when we went on to Naples she seemed to find a sort of Earthly Paradise in the Madonnas of the National Museum, one of which is described in my novel, *The Fifth String*.

Our preparations to leave Naples and visit Sicily were abruptly ended when I chanced upon an item in the *Paris Herald*, cabled from New York, saying that David Blakely, the well-known musical manager, had dropped dead in his office the day before. The paper was four days old! I cabled at once, and Christianer replied that it was indeed our manager who had died so suddenly and that I must now be responsible for the next tour of the band. We sailed on the *Teutonic* for America the following Saturday.

Here came one of the most vivid incidents of my career. As the vessel steamed out of the harbor I was pacing the deck, absorbed in thoughts of my manager's death and the many duties and decisions which awaited me in New York. Suddenly, I began to sense the rhythmic beat of a band playing within my brain. It kept on ceaselessly, playing, playing, playing. Throughout the whole tense voyage, that imaginary band continued to unfold the same themes, echoing and re-echoing the most distinct melody. I did not transfer a note of that music to paper while I was on the steamer, but when we reached shore, I set down the measures that my brain-band had been playing for me, and not a note of it has ever been changed. The composition is known the world over as *The Stars and Stripes Forever!* and is probably my most popular march.

SOURCE: John Philip Sousa, *Marching Along: Recollections of Men, Women and Music*, rev. ed., ed. Paul Bierley (Boston, 1928; reprint, Westerville, Ohio: Integrity, 1994): 129–33, 156–57, 358–60.

52

WHY IS A GOOD MARCH LIKE A MARBLE STATUE?

(Pryor, Fennell)

John Philip Sousa's belief that a march "must be as free from padding as a marble statue" stands as a key to his compositions in particular and to the performance of classic American marches in general. In the first selection, Arthur Pryor (1870– 1942) explains how to perform marches up to Sousa's standard. One of the celebrity players in Sousa's band and a virtuoso trombonist, Pryor played with Sousa from the beginning of the band in 1892, then functioned as its assistant conductor from 1895 to 1903. In 1903 Pryor formed his own highly successful band. Here Pryor offers advice that passes on "historically informed" performance practice to new generations.

HOW TO PLAY A MARCH

There is one type of music in the playing of which the band has always been supreme—the march. No other musical ensemble can play a march with the zest, snap, and life as can a good band. For years the march has been the very backbone of the military band. And today the band still holds unquestioned supremacy as a marching unit and as an outdoor attraction.

Considering these facts it would seem that every band would have a group of irresistible marches in its repertory and play them so as to put new life into everyone within earshot. On the contrary, the way the march is played by the average band is nothing to get very excited about. Usually a march is not so difficult to play. Perhaps that is one of its disadvantages. At any rate, it is only the exceptional band that brings out the real possibilities of this movement. I have known professional bands to fail in this respect as well as amateurs.

Another reason may be that comparatively few of the present day composers score their marches as they wish them to be played.

They score a quarter note where they should have written an eighth note and rest. They write a string of notes apparently to be played legato, but which must be separated to give that bright, sparkling effect. I do not mean that one should take undue liberties with march music. But an experience of some forty years in playing marches has convinced me of the necessity of observing certain fundamentals and these I will explain in the examples to follow. There are certain values which should be applied to all parade marches, namely:

IN TWO-FOUR MARCHES

All quarter notes, dotted notes and half notes must be given full value. Each and every eighth note must be separated from the next note, unless tied over.

IN SIX-EIGHT MARCHES

All quarter notes and dotted notes must have full value. Eighth notes should be played short.

IN ALLA-BREVE

All quarter notes, unless tied, must be separated. All eighth notes as is. All dotted notes, half and whole notes, full value. This is the only way to play parade marches. Some examples will illustrate these points.

Example A. In two-four.

The eighth notes in Example A must be separated, the quarter notes given full value, else the effect will be dead and lifeless.

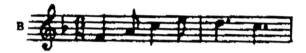

Example B. In six-eight.

In Example B, the eighth notes are played short, quarter and dotted quarter [notes] are played full.

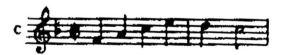

Example C. In alla-breve.

In Example C, quarter notes must be separated, as indicated in Example D.

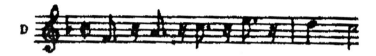

In Example D, half notes are always given full value.

When the trombone, baritone and basses find passages like that indicated in Example E,

they should be played as indicated in Example F.

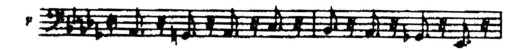

All band and orchestra performers should always give full values where indicated in Example G.

IN ALL COMPOSITIONS

In snapping up the quarter notes and giving full value to half notes in Alla-breve, snapping up the eighth notes, giving full value to quarter notes in two-four, you get the delightful effect of contrast. On parade, the band playing marches in this manner, will find it a great relief. That tired feeling will disappear completely.

You should not allow your reed section to separate the quarter notes in Alla-breve or the eighth notes in two-four, as much as your brass section.

Never allow your reed section to use a sharp attack. Let your brass do it. All notes should have a beauty and life of their own. Short notes, dotted notes, quarter notes, half dotted, half and full notes must be larger in the beginning than at the end. For example, all notes should be produced like

Measures as indicated in Example I,

should be played as shown in Example J.

A full note should be attacked and sustained as shown in Example K.

The beginning of the whole note should be louder than the last three-quarter values. There should be an attack [at] the beginning of the note, no matter how short or long the note is. *Never*, in parade marches, let it be broad all through the values of the note. Don't play it this way: Example L.

Play it this way: Example M.

Always begin the note with a sforzando. Short soft attack like striking a bell.

Allow the finish of the note to be less in volume. As I said before, never allow your reeds to attack any notes as forcefully as your brass.

Study Example N as written:

This example should be played as shown in Example O.

Be sure to give full value to the tied over half-tones as shown in Example P.

To continue—as written in Example Q,

Should be played as shown in Example R.

Now if the foregoing example is written as shown in Example[s] S–T

This measure

should be played

The notes should be given full value, first and second quarter notes in the example should be given full quarter value. If the measure reads as shown in Example U

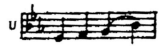

it should be played thus: Example V.

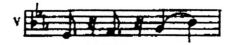

The first two quarters are played [missing word], the last two are given full value.

Here is a procedure you may not have noticed. Why do bands invariably get brighter effects from two-four marches than marches written in Alla-breve? This is the answer: Because quarter notes in Alla-breve marches are eighth notes in two-four marches. Naturally you play the eighth note in a two-four march shorter than a quarter note in an Alla-breve march, and strange to say, you will play a quarter note in a two-four march, longer than you will play a half note in an Alla-breve march.

As intimated previously bands are not solely to blame. Our bands would play much better if our composers were just a little more interested in their compositions when they score them. A quarter note should never appear in any composition unless it is supposed to receive full value.
. . .

The foregoing should prove of some assistance to leaders in getting better results with their marches. We learn to play a march after we have observed all the little details any one of which might not seem important in itself. During my experience I have played *Stars and Stripes Forever* at least 3,000 times and each time I usually see something I did not see before. The conductor who is through learning is through and had better retire.

SOURCE: Arthur Pryor, "How to Play a March," *Musical Courier* (September 26, 1931): 45, 56.

~~~~~~~

Inspired by Sousa as a young boy, the famous conductor Frederick Fennell (1914–2004) wrote a long tribute, which, like that of Pryor's above, includes many obser-

vations about performance practice. Belonging to the generation after Pryor, with a legacy still alive today, Fennell included along with his musical analyses a few recollections of what it was like to belong to a band in the twilight years of John Philip Sousa. In his own distinguished career, Fennell established a celebrated wind ensemble at the Eastman School of Music, which had a commercial recording career on the Mercury label in the 1950s and '60s. He is credited with the renaissance of interest in wind ensembles among American composers today.

THE SOUSA MARCH: A PERSONAL VIEW

I heard the first performance of John Philip Sousa's *The Black Horse Troop* when I was eleven years old. My father had taken me to a concert by Sousa's Band at the Public Auditorium in Cleveland, Ohio. At the end of the concert Sousa turned and faced the audience. This was obviously a signal, for the whole of Troop A of the Ohio National Guard Cavalry—The Black Horse Troop—walked their horses up the aisles and onto the stage. Standing at attention behind the Band, they faced the audience as Sousa led his musicians in the first performance of the march. Their reception as they made their way to the stage was wild enough, but the tumultuous applause for all at the conclusion of *The Black Horse Troop* was like nothing I had ever heard.

By the time that I—and about 699 other high school students—had the privilege of playing two concerts which he conducted with the National High School Band and Orchestra at the Bowl at Interlochen, Michigan, in July 1931, Mr. Sousa was no longer the exceptionally gifted physical conductor who had once ignited audiences everywhere to flaming acclaim and of whom no less a judge of performance than his contemporary, the distinguished actor Otis Skinner, declared that he was "the best actor America has ever produced."[*]

But the mere fact that he was John Philip Sousa was sufficient to mesmerize us all and draw the largest crowd imaginable to the National Music Camp's Interlochen bowl. Those of us there who did the playing at the rehearsals and concerts had not the slightest interest in, let alone any real ability to judge, his conducting technique. He made what we thought were the right motions, and when he did we played our hearts out for him. In this last summer of his life he was seventy-seven years old and comparatively frail, but he was "Our Sousa," the "King of the March."[**]

The youth of America became very involved with band performance during the last years of Sousa's life. He was their obvious idol. We young school musicians were beneficiaries

[*]Paul Bierley, *John Philip Sousa: American Phenomenon* (New York: Appleton, Century, Crofts, 1973), p. 133. Paul Bierley has assembled the most comprehensive overview of Sousa the conductor, and all who wish to know this in detail are referred to this book, particularly Chapter IV, "Sousa's Philosophy of Music."

[**]We did not know it then, and neither did his public, but Sousa had suffered a broken neck in 1921 when he was thrown from a horse. Recovery was limited and so, too, was his conducting style after his accident which immobilized his left arm for any action resembling the former colorful Sousa style; he could swing the arm but not lift it. At the outset of my career as a conductor well-meaning advisors always informed me that I should be much less active in my motions: "After all, Frederic, Sousa hardly moved at all!"

of the great band movement's desire to follow Sousa's example. We had the benefit of good instruction at public support, could play in a good group at an early age, and our instruments were provided by the school we attended—all of which did not exist when John Philip Sousa was a lad. But there it was, the great bursting forth of all those school bands as the result of the labors of so many.

Sousa was drawn inevitably into all of this as the honored guest conductor of enormous bands massed in his honor. He gave his name to causes that would enhance musical opportunities for young people. Among those exemplary leaders within music education who were drawn to him was the Director of Bands at the University of Illinois, Albert Austin Harding (1880–1958). He took what Sousa had done to make the indoor sit-down concert band artistically acceptable, expanded it, and eventually thrust that concept throughout schools in most of the forty-eight states. Sousa responded to Harding's devotion to bands and to his expertise and musicality by visiting the Urbana campus and guest conducting Harding's superb Illinois Concert Band.

Their friendship—together with the impact on music education that Joseph E. Maddy had made with the National High School Orchestra and the summer music camp that was built to house it at Interlochen, Michigan, where Harding was conductor of the band—led to two visits to Interlochen by Sousa. I was there for the second visit, described above, and for this occasion he honored all Interlochen campers with a march written just for us; number 136, his last. He called it *The Northern Pines* (1931). The preparation that preceded his arrival for dress rehearsals was done by Harding who was quick to notice several details in style, so well known to him, to be in need of adjustment, such as dynamic shadings and ensemble accents. These were subsequently approved by Sousa and incorporated into the printed edition. One time, Mr. Harding also suggested that it was more in the Sousa style to have the trombones join the solo cornets at the octave for the melody in the first half of the second strain rather than to play their inactive harmonic role. When he went back to the trombone section and picked up somebody's instrument and played the suggested change, Sousa smilingly approved. Sousa conducted the premiere of *The Northern Pines* on Sunday afternoon, July 27, 1931. Harding had assigned me the honor of playing bass drum for the occasion.

Such are my personal and youthful observations of Sousa.

SOURCE: Frederick Fennell, "The Sousa March: A Personal View," in *Perspectives on John Philip Sousa*, ed. Jon Newsom (Washington, D.C.: Library of Congress, 1983): 81–82.

53

WILLA CATHER MOURNS THE PASSING OF

THE SMALL-TOWN OPERA HOUSE

Opera played an essential (and still under-recognized) role in late nineteenth-century American cultural life. When two great sopranos, Lillian Nordica (1857–1914) and Adelina Patti (1843–1919), came to Omaha, Nebraska in 1890 to perform in, respectively, *Il Trovatore* and *The Barber of Seville,* "students in the Omaha schools were given half a day off to attend."[1] Almost 2,000 halls or spaces dubbed "opera houses" across the continent at that time offered many kinds of music, from opera to "opry."[2] In the 1890s, at least 37 Nebraska towns had opera houses, among them Red Cloud, home of the famous writer Willa Cather (1873–1947). In this selection, Cather writes nostalgic impressions of the touring opera and theater troupes she watched in her youth (see chapter 40). No wonder she frequently portrayed the transformational power of music and the stage in her novels and short stories.[3] Her lament involves the impact of movies on theater, but it could be applied to the impact of recorded sound on live music as well.

Dear Mr. Newbranch: It's a newspaper's business, is it not, to insist that everything is much better than it used to be? All the same we never gain anything without losing something—not even in Nebraska. When I go about among little Nebraska towns (and the little old towns, not the big cities, are the people), the thing I miss most is the opera house. No number of filling stations or moving picture houses can console me for the loss of the opera house. To be sure, the opera house was empty for most of the year, but that made its nights only the more exciting. Half a dozen times during each winter—in the larger towns much oftener—a traveling stock company settled down at the local hotel and thrilled and entertained us for a week.

That was a wonderful week for the children. The excitement began when the advance man came to town and posted the bills on the side of a barn, on the lumber yard fence, in the "plate glass" windows of drug stores and grocery stores. My playmates and I used to stand for an hour after school, studying every word on those posters; the names of the plays and the nights on which each would be given. After we had decided which were the most necessary to us, then there was always the question of how far we could prevail upon our parents. Would they let us go every night, or only on the opening and closing nights? None of us ever got to go every night, unless we had a father who owned stock in the opera house itself.

The company arrived on the night train. When we were not at school, my chums and I always walked a good half mile to the depot (I believe you call it "station" now) to see that train come in. Sometimes we pulled younger brothers or sisters along on a sled. We found it delightful to watch a theatrical company alight, pace the platform while their baggage was being sorted, and then drive off—the men in the hotel bus, the women [in] the "hack." If by any chance one of the show ladies carried a little dog with a blanket on, that simply doubled our pleasure. Our next concern was to invent some plausible pretext, some errand that would take us to the hotel. Several of my dearest playmates had perpetual entry to the hotel because they were favorites of the very unusual and interesting woman who owned it. But I, alas, had no such useful connection; so I never saw the leading lady breakfasting languidly at 9. Indeed, I never dared go near the hotel while the theatrical people were there—I suppose because I wanted to go so much.

How good some of those old traveling companies were, and how honestly they did their work and tried to put on a creditable performance. There was the Andrews Opera company, for example; they usually had a good voice or two among them, a small orchestra and a painstaking conductor, who was also the pianist. What good luck for a country child to hear those tuneful old operas sung by people who were doing their best: The Bohemian Girl,[4] The Chimes of Normandy,[5] Martha,[6] The Mikado.[7] Nothing takes hold of a child like living people. We got the old plays in the same day, done by living people, and often by people who were quite in earnest: "My Partner," "The Corsican Brothers," "Ingomar," "Damon and Pythias," "The Count of Monte Cristo."

I know that today I would rather hear James O'Neill, or even Frank Lindon, play The Count of Monte Cristo than see any moving picture, except three or four in which Charlie Chaplin is the whole thing. My preference would have been the same, though even stronger, when I was a child. Moving pictures may be very entertaining and amusing, and they may be, as they often claim to be, instructive; but what child ever cried at the movies, as we used to at East Lynne or The Two Orphans?

That is the heart of the matter; only living people can make us feel. Pictures of them, no matter how dazzling, do not make us feel anything more than interest or curiosity or astonishment. The "pity and terror" which the drama, even in its crudest form, can awaken in young people, is not to be found in the movies. Only a living human being, in some sort of rapport with us, speaking the lines, can make us forget who we are and where we are, can make us (especially children) actually live in the story that is going on before us, can make the dangers of that heroine and the desperation of that hero much more important to us, for the time much dearer to us, than our own lives.

That, after all, was the old glory of the drama in its great days; that is why its power was more searching than that of printed books or paintings because a story of human experience was given to us alive, given to us, not only by voice and attitude, but by all those unnamed ways in which an animal of any species makes known its terror or misery to other animals of its kind. And all the old-fashioned actors, even the poor ones, did "enter into the spirit" of their parts; it was the pleasure they got from this illusion that made them wish to be actors, despite the hardships of that profession. The extent to which they could enter into this illusion, much more than any physical attributes, measured their goodness or badness as actors. We heard the drama termed a thing in three dimensions; but it is really a thing in four dimensions, since it has two imaginative fires behind it, the playwright's and the actor's.

I am not lamenting the advent of the "screen drama" (there is a great deal to be said in its favor), but I do regret that it has put an end to the old-fashioned road companies which used to tour about in country towns and "cities of the second class." The "movie" and the play are two very different things; one is a play, and the other is a picture of a play. A movie, well done, may be very good indeed, may even appeal to what is called the artistic sense; but to the emotions, the deep feelings, never!

Never, that is, excepting Charlie Chaplin at his best—and his best—I have noticed, really gets through to very few people. Not to his enormous audience, but to actors and to people of great experience in the real drama. They admire and marvel. I go to the picture shows in the little towns I know, and I watch the audience, especially the children. I see easy, careless attention, amusement, occasionally a curiosity that amounts to mild excitement; but never that breathless, rapt attention and deep feeling that the old barnstorming companies were able to command. It was not only the "sob stuff" that we took hard; it was everything. When old Frank Lindon in a frilled shirt and a velvet coat blazing with diamonds, stood in the drawing room of Mme. Danglars' and revealed his identity to Mme. De Morcery, his faithless Mercedes, when she cowered and made excuses, and he took out a jeweled snuff box with a much powdered hand, raised his eyebrows, permitted his lip to curl, and said softly and bitterly, "A fidelity of six months!" then we children were not in the opera house in Red Cloud[;] we were in Mme. Danglars' salon in Paris, in the middle of lives so very different from our own.[8] Living people were making us feel things, and it is through the feelings, not at all through the eye, that one's imagination is fired.

Pictures of plots, unattended by the voice from the machine (which seems to me much worse than no voice), a rapid flow of scene and pageant, make a fine kind of "entertainment" and are an ideal diversion for the tired business man. But I am sorry that the old opera houses in the prairie towns are dark, because they really did give a

deeper thrill, at least to children. It did us good to weep at East Lynne, *even if the actress was fairly bad and the play absurd. Children have about a hundred years of unlived life wound up in them, and they want to be living some of it. Only real people speaking the lines can give us that feeling of living along with them, of participating in their existence. The poorest of the old road companies were at least made up of people who wanted to be actors and tried to be—that alone goes a long way. The very poorest of all were the* Uncle Tom's Cabin *companies, but even they had living bloodhounds. How the barking of these dogs behind the scenes used to make us catch our breath! That alone was worth the price of admission, as the star used to say, when he came before the curtain.*
Very cordially yours,
Willa Cather
Omaha World-Herald, *27 October 1929*

SOURCE: "Willa Cather Mourns Old Opera House," *Omaha World-Herald,* October 27, 1929, Sunday magazine section, 9. Also cited and partially quoted in Harlan Jennings, "Grand Opera in Nebraska in the 1890s," *Opera Quarterly* 11, no. 2 (1995): 98–118. Available at http://cather.unl.edu/writings/bohlke/letters/1929.html.

~~~~~~~~~~

NOTES

1. Harlan Jennings, "Grand Opera in Nebraska in the 1890s," *Opera Quarterly* 11, no. 2 (1995): 100.

2. Michael Broyles, "Art Music from 1860 to 1920," in *The Cambridge History of American Music,* ed. David Nicholls (Cambridge: Cambridge University Press, 1998): 224.

3. Two examples are the short story "A Wagner Matinee" (1905) and the novel *The Song of the Lark* (1915), whose heroine is modeled after the Swedish-American opera singer Olive Fremstad (1871–1951).

4. *The Bohemian Girl* (1843), an opera by the Irish composer Michael Balfe (1808–1870), was enormously popular in nineteenth-century America.

5. *The Chimes of Normandy* most likely was an English translation of the opéra comique *Les Cloches de Corneville* (1877) by Robert Planquette (1848–1903).

6. The German composer Friedrich von Flotow wrote the romantic comic opera *Martha* in 1847.

7. *The Mikado* (1885) is a famous operetta by the British team of W. S. Gilbert (1836–1911, libretto) and Arthur Sullivan (1842–1900, music).

8. Here, Cather refers to the characters and plot line of the play based on the novel *The Count of Monte Cristo* (1844) by the French writer Alexandre Dumas (1802–1870), who also wrote *The Three Musketeers.*

54

Henry Lee Higginson and the Founding of the Boston Symphony Orchestra

In one bold gesture, a Boston banker devoted to classical music single-handedly founded the Boston Symphony Orchestra in 1881. Henry Lee Higginson (1834–1918) explained how and why he did this in an open letter to the citizens of Boston, which was published in a local newspaper and is reprinted here. By that time, he had already chosen the BSO's first permanent conductor. With its long season and guarantee of a stable income for orchestral musicians, the Boston Symphony Orchestra established a national institutional model for other American cities. By 1900, ten more orchestras existed, including those in Chicago, Cincinnati, and Philadelphia.

There is no question that Higginson had enormous power. How wisely did he use it and where did it come from? As an enlightened philanthropist, Higginson believed that classical music could and should uplift all classes in society, and he instituted open rehearsal concerts with inexpensive ticket prices. But his relationship with the orchestra musicians soured somewhat over time. One social historian has written, "throughout his life Higginson fought to maintain control over the Orchestra's employees."[1]

The second selection in this chapter is a letter Higginson wrote to the BSO manager in 1906, when he was recruiting a new conductor. It reflects the interplay of sophisticated taste and cultural clout on an international scale, where no route of privilege is left unexplored.

HIGGINSON'S OPEN LETTER TO
THE CITIZENS OF BOSTON, 1881

IN THE INTEREST OF GOOD MUSIC

Notwithstanding the development of musical taste in Boston, we have never yet possessed a full and permanent orchestra, offering the best music at low prices, such as may be found in all the large European cities, or even in the smaller musical centres of Germany. The essential condition of such orchestras is their stability, whereas ours are necessarily shifting and uncertain, because we are dependent upon musicians whose work and time are largely pledged elsewhere.

To obviate this difficulty the following plan is offered. It is an effort made simply in the interest of good music, and though individual inasmuch as it is independent of societies or clubs, it is in no way antagonistic to any previously existing musical organization. Indeed, the first step as well as the natural impulse in announcing a new musical project, is to thank those who have brought us where we now stand. Whatever may be done in the future, to the Händel and Haydn Society and to the Harvard Musical Association, we all owe the greater part of our home education in music of a high character. Can we forget either how admirably their work has been supplemented by the taste and critical judgment of Mr. John S. Dwight, or by the artists who have identified themselves with the same cause in Boston? These have been our teachers. We build on foundations they have laid. Such details of this scheme as concern the public are stated below.

The orchestra is to number sixty selected musicians; their time, so far as required for careful training and for a given number of concerts, to be engaged in advance.

Mr. Georg Henschel will be the conductor for the coming season.

The concerts will be twenty in number, given in the Music Hall on Saturday evenings, from the middle of October to the middle of March.

The price of season tickets, with reserved seats, for the whole series of evening concerts will be either $10 or $5, according to position.

Single tickets, with reserved seats, will be seventy-five cents or twenty-five cents, according to position.

Besides the concerts, there will be a public rehearsal on one afternoon of every week, with single tickets at twenty-five cents, and no reserved seats.

The intention is that this orchestra shall be made permanent here, and shall be called "The Boston Symphony Orchestra."

Both as the condition and result of success the sympathy of the public is asked.
[signed] H. L. Higginson

SOURCE: Henry Lee Higginson, "The Boston Symphony Orchestra: In the Interest of Good Music," *Boston Herald* supplement, March 30, 1881, n.p. Also cited and reproduced in Joseph Horowitz, *Classical Music in America: A History of Its Rise and Fall* (New York: Norton, 2005): 43–44.

Higginson's letter written to Charles Ellis, the BSO's manager, discusses possible choices for a new conductor. Strategies involved appeals to the German emperor and king of Prussia, Wilhelm II, to release from his employ the musician Carl Muck (1859–1940), who since 1892 had been the conductor of the major state opera house in Berlin, the Staatsoper Unter den Linden. Diplomatic pressure as well as personal appeals to the emperor from noted Harvard University professors, among them the anthropologist George Peabody, who is mentioned in the letter, also aided this effort, which today reads a bit like a feudal document. The pressure succeeded, and Muck became the conductor of the BSO from 1906 to 1908, returning then to his post in Berlin. Muck again served as the BSO conductor in 1912–1918; his exit during an alleged spy scandal in the midst of anti-German war fever is another tale.

May 24, 1906
Dear Ellis,
We have passed a good many cables, and the other day it occurred to Lane that we might do something through the ambassador; therefore I telegraphed you about him.

Professor Peabody, who is in Berlin this winter to lecture (having been invited by the University of Berlin to do so), lectured before the Emperor, and afterwards saw His Majesty, and was most kindly treated. He recognizes the generous disposition of the Emperor, who has a very strong chivalric desire to do the handsome thing—more especially for this country. Other professors in the University will follow Professor Peabody, and other professors from Germany will come here—as they have already.

The Emperor has been very generous, indeed, in sending to the University various casts of great statues, etc., now in Europe, and there is a strong, warm feeling for him at Harvard University, as well as other places here. Professor Peabody thought that an appeal to His Majesty to do the handsome act by us might be successful, and he said that Ambassador Tower was so clever and tactful that he would know how to do it, if it should be done at all. That is the basis of our telegrams.

Professor Peabody said that money would not enter the Emperor's thought—money, I mean, to Dr. Muck—but that the other idea might appeal to him. I am now hoping that we will be able to accomplish our object in that way. We have nobody good enough to conduct the orchestra, and the Emperor has several distinguished men in Berlin, who will gladly conduct the Opera—Dr. Strauss being among them.[2] I do not ask for Dr. Muck during the rest of his life, but I ask him for a term of years, and then things will take care of themselves.

I also used the name of the University because of the Emperor's generosity toward the University, and because we were so glad to receive Prince Henry here, and do such honor to him as we could. As it so happened, I drove to Cambridge with Prince Henry (in the same carriage) and was the person who welcomed him (among others) to the Harvard Union, where a meeting was held, and where Prince Henry replied to us.[3]

All these things have a sentimental value, but that always appeals to the Emperor and is one of his strong holds on this nation and on the world.

It is needless to say that I shall be infinitely indebted to His Majesty if we are allowed to have Dr. Muck here, and I wish to thank our ambassador very much for

*the pains he has taken, whether he is successful or not. I shall do myself the pleasure
to write to him when I return from Chicago—where I go in an hour.*

*Now, in case we fail, I suppose you will turn either to Mengelberg or to Walther
[sic].⁴ Perhaps you may try both. Schroeder, by the way, was here yesterday, and he
asked to see you with regard to his own affairs, and then inquired about what he had
learned of Hausegger. He is still of the opinion that he is a valuable man, and I am of
the opinion that he is not.*

*If you see Walther or Mengelberg, you will have to say to them (what I wrote you
lately) that I do know something about music, and that I have very distinct ideas as
to how music should be played; that I shall not meddle with modern music, but that I
shall certainly ask them to play the classics as they were played. I was brought up in the
Vienna school (as you know) and there were plenty of men living then who had heard
Beethoven conduct, as well as Mendelssohn, and knew how he wished his music given.
I have known Brahms, myself, and heard his music. You know well enough what I
wish, and I shall not interfere unduly with any of these men, but I don't want crazy
work (such as sometimes even Nikish [sic] gave us, and Paur gave us too often), and
perhaps you had better tell them that I hate noise.⁵*

*I had given up hopes of Muck's coming here, but with this new lever I am in hopes
something may be accomplished. Thank you very much for all the trouble you are taking.*

*The Rolfe notes are paid, and the option for the Gauley runs out in a few days.
Thus far, we have no news in regard to it.*

Business is excellent throughout the country, but our kind of business is dull.

> *Good-by.*
> *Very truly yours,*
> *H. L. Higginson*

SOURCE: Letter from H. L. Higginson to Charles Ellis, May 24, 1906, Henry Lee Higginson Collection, Baker Library, Harvard Business School. A copy is in the Archives of the Boston Symphony Orchestra. Cited and partially quoted in Joseph Horowitz, *Classical Music in America: A History of Its Rise and Fall* (New York: Norton, 2005): 76–77.

NOTES

1. Paul DiMaggio, "Cultural Entrepreneurship in Boston: The Creation of an Organizational Base for High Culture in America," in *Rethinking Popular Culture: Contemporary Perspectives in Cultural Studies,* ed. Chandra Mukerji and Michael Schudson (Berkeley: University of California Press, 1991): 388–89.
2. He is referring to the opera composer and conductor Richard Strauss (1864–1949).
3. This refers to Wilhelm's brother, Prince Heinrich, who received an honorary doctorate from Harvard in 1912.
4. This refers to two conductors who achieved international fame, Bruno Walter (1876–1962) and Willem Mengelberg (1871–1951).
5. Arthur Nikisch (1855–1922) conducted the BSO from 1889 to 1893, followed by Emil Paur (1855–1932), who served 1893–1898.

55

AMERICAN CLASSICAL MUSIC GOES TO THE PARIS WORLD'S FAIR OF 1889

At the Exposition Universelle held at the Trocadéro in Paris in 1889, where the French composer Claude Debussy famously heard Javanese gamelan music, some of his compatriots also heard another novelty—a concert on July 12 devoted to classical music by living American composers. The Paris concert occurred as part of the efforts of an "American Music Movement," led by the activist-conductor Frank Van der Stucken (1858–1929), who sought to expand the audiences and opportunities for his generation. Although most reviewers reacted with mild enthusiasm or polite curiosity, one writer delivered what "may be the worst review ever published of a concert of American music," according to E. Douglas Bomberger, whose translation is used here. The opening sentence plays off the stereotypical view of the United States as a country whose genius showed only in its mechanical inventions and industrial efficiency. Could such a nation produce art? This question was typically asked rhetorically, as it is in this selection. The second point concerns the challenge of a national voice. Craft matters, but a national school of identifiable stylistic traits matters more. Only a few of the composers trashed here receive performances today, among them Edward MacDowell, who played his Second Piano Concerto at this concert, and George Chadwick (see chapters 56 and 61).

I was very curious to see how the country that has given the world such super-stupendous [*surabracadabrantes*] inventions as the telephone, suspenders, washing machines, and rich uncles would manage from an artistic point of view. I went to the Trocadéro—why should I hide it?—with defiance and a stupid prejudice, devoid in any case of a spirit that strains to be impartial. Well, for once, my defiance was not disappointed, and I spent there, in that *désert trocadéreux,* two of the worst hours I have spent—musically speaking, of course.

What I especially object to in some artists from over there who work conscientiously is that they are absolutely, oh! but absolutely impersonal. Not one of these gentlemen, neither MacDowell, nor Van der Stücken [*sic*] (a name precious little American, it should be said in passing), nor Huss,[1] nor Bird,[2] not one I say, had three measures that belonged to him, truly to him. There is some of everything in this music, a filet of Mendelssohn with a salmi of Schumann, some hors-d'oeuvres from here, from there, from Wagner or from Brahms, not a few nebulosities, and for dessert, boredom and monotony, a desperate monotony that left in the spirit of the hearer a spectral vision of a poor composer, or supposedly such, fanning the flames to make the ideas and notes come out. The notes come . . . but the ideas . . . !!!

The first number of the program was an overture by Goote [Arthur Foote][3] that I did not hear.

The Second Piano Concert[o] by MacDowell is made to disgust you forever with the instrument so dear to Reyer.* There is especially a *Presto giocoso* that has pretensions to grace and lightness but is nothing but irritating prattle. One asks oneself if it is really a piano playing or if it is not rather a mill for grinding out notes. God! it's annoying!!! Up to the end (two eighth notes on the fourth E-A) everything is pastiched, copied, repeated.

I refused to critique the *mélodies* [songs] which followed the concerto. One cannot critique them because they do not exist (I would willingly make an exception, however, for *Les Jours passés* by Chadwick). *La Chanson de la laitière* especially (A. Goote) is a nasty little song worthy at most of La Scala. Add to that the fact that Mme. Maude Starvetta,** who . . . presented the songs is less of a singer . . . than the *laitière* [milkmaid] in question, and you can judge with what circumspection I invite you to go to concerts called American.

The Tempest, by M. Van der Stücken, the conductor (an excellent conductor and a great musician) certainly merits more praise, but it is still not a work that is really worth the trouble of describing. There are care, research, and study, but also unpardonable errors in taste, an excessively vulgar phrase for trumpets, and ritards in the rhythms that are motivated by nothing and make the piece resemble an introduction to a German or Hungarian waltz. The "Chasse infernale" that ends this orchestral suite has good style, but it is not developed and the author remains short of breath.

*Ernest Reyer (1823–1909) was a French composer and critic. As a composer he was best known for his operas, while as the long-time critic of the *Journal des Débats* he enjoyed a position of unusual influence in France's musical life.

**According to Otto Floersheim, "The American Concert at the Tracedero, Paris," *Musical Courier* 19/5 (31 July 1889): 108, this was the stage name of Mrs. Starkweather of Boston, an American soprano studying with Mathilde Marchesi.

The only thing that I can really place beyond comparison in the American concert is the overture *Melpomene* by [George] Chadwick. That is grand, wisely and seriously conceived and it is art (very German art, to be sure) but it is art in every sense of the word.

I cannot refrain from speaking of M. Willis Nowell, who came to run his feeble fingers at random over a violin that is a marvel of sonority and instrumental workmanship. Under the pretext (is it really under that one?) that America has given us washing machines, M. Willis Nowell, American violinist, has soaped [away] all of his traits. He has neither attack, nor precision, nor virtuosity, but he has, I must confess, something that is half of a violinist . . . an incommensurable head of hair. If he wants to take a stroll to the Conservatoire and go hear only the students of the preparatory class led by M. Garcin, he will see that he is much more American but much less skillful than the least skillful of those urchins.

I left after the *Carnival Scene* by A. Bird. It is a polka (with an orgy of bassoon) in the middle of which one stops every now and then as if for a quadrille. It is not a carnival scene; it's a collection of dances.

Oh! American concerts (my excuses to Chadwick, the only one who interested me) but I won't be caught napping again!

SOURCE: Brument-Colleville, "Le concert américain au Trocadéro," *Le Monde Musical* 1, no. 6 (July 30, 1889): 7. Translated and annotated by Douglas Bomberger, University of Hawaii, and printed in the *Sonneck Society for American Music Bulletin* 24/1 (Spring 1998): 10.

~~~~~~~~~~~

NOTES

1. George Huss (1828–1904), composer and pianist.
2. Arthur Bird (1856–1923), composer, organist, and pianist.
3. Arthur Foote (1853–1937), a Boston-based composer and pianist.

56

GEORGE CHADWICK'S IDEALS

FOR COMPOSING CLASSICAL CONCERT MUSIC

With the establishment of an infrastructure for the performance of classical music came a center for American composers in late nineteenth-century Boston. Among the most notable, George Whitefield Chadwick (1854–1931) had a major national impact in his own time, as "the big celebrated man of American Music," to quote Charles Ives.[1] The Boston Symphony Orchestra played Chadwick's orchestral works more than 70 times before 1924, with Chadwick occasionally conducting. For many decades, Chadwick was treated like a Victorian collectible. But today his symphonies, symphonic poems, and overtures have been recorded and programmed—not often, but more than rarely—and they demonstrate his strong musical personality.

Two excerpts from his writings show aspects of Chadwick's attitudes toward his craft. His comments on musical ideas reflect his training in Germany, where he studied from 1877 to 1880: art reflects universal values of truth and beauty. His Symphonies nos. 2 and 3 realize these ideals.

The second selection indirectly comments on musical nationalism. Chadwick admired Dvořák, who, along with Beethoven, Mendelssohn, and Brahms, influenced his own composition, but both pride and prejudice made him initially reject Dvořák's view of American identity as linked to black or Indian folk tunes. Instead, he favored Anglo-American hymnody, folk-like pentatonic melodies, and Irish syncopated dance rhythms. Yet African-American idioms, which Chadwick calls "southern," surface in his *Symphonic Sketches* (1885–1904), which he deliberately set out to make "American in Style." The second selection is a set of previously unpublished program notes for this work, in which Chadwick describes the four movements.

HOW DO COMPOSERS THINK MUSIC

It is almost impossible to make a person not musical understand the mental process of composing music. It does not suffice to say that composers think music as others think words and ideas. It is incomprehensible to those "not in it" that music, which is dependent for its existence on audibility, can be thought out or heard in the mind before a key of the piano has sounded it, or a voice issued it forth, or even before a note of it has been written. But such is the fact. The composer not only hears his melodies, but their accompanying harmonies and most of the "effects" of orchestration or other coloring. The real composer does not sit down to the piano and coax or hammer out his music; he thinks it out, hearing every detail in his mind before a note has been struck. And like the poets who have never sung their sweetest songs, so the musician hears music he can never give utterance to in notes. The sweetest poems and the sweetest songs, as well as the loveliest conceptions of the sculptor and painter, must ever be sealed to the vulgar gaze, and from those who would not understand.

This fact is difficult, too, for people to understand who can not hear—i.e., who have no musical consciousness[,] says Mr. Chadwick, writing recently on the same subject:

> It is impossible for them to understand how the mind—the spiritual ear—may actually hear rhythm, pitch, quality, melody, and harmony, and may reduce it to black and white through the medium of musical notation without the aid of the physical ear. And how the composer can know how to make combinations of instruments and voices which he can not possibly have played and sung to him beforehand, is a problem which to them must remain forever unsolved. Nevertheless, the musical idea is a fact, and its function, like any other artistic or poetic idea, is the expression of truth and beauty. And just in proportion as it does express the beautiful and the true does it have life, health, and longevity. Every musical composition (if it be worthy of the name) is an art problem in which, with certain conditions given, and certain materials at hand, a certain result is to be obtained. Its perfection as a result depends on the effective adaptation of the means to the end—its unity of form and contents—the appropriate relation of its outside and inside. This is equally true of any other work of art, whether it be a painting or a poem, or a pile of buildings like those at Jackson Park.[2] The painter, with a burnt match and the paper his luncheon is wrapped in, gives you a man who breathes; the architect with a few laths, some plaster and swamp gives you at Chicago what Alladin saw when he put the light on his lamp; and Beethoven with four notes give us the fifth symphony.

SOURCE: Unsigned article, "How Do Composers Think Music," *Musical Leader* 22, no. 7 (July 1893): 181.

~~~~~~~

Chadwick's comments about the Symphonic Sketches *come from an undated handwritten manuscript on the letterhead of the New England Conservatory of Music, where Chadwick served as president from 1897 until his death. We preface them with a comment from Chadwick's unpublished memoirs. The* Symphonic Sketches *capture the idiom of light classical Americana, and here Chadwick sounds like a Boston Pops composer, even before that organization existed.*

1895: This winter I worked enthusiastically on my Symphonic Sketches. . . . I determined to make it American in style—as I understood the term.

SYMPHONIC SKETCHES: JUBILEE—NOEL—HOBGOBLIN—A VAGROM BALLAD

The symphonic sketches were composed in 1905 for the Boston Festival Orchestra which made an annual concert trip about the country playing at many choral festivals in the larger cities. The verses which precede the numbers are a sufficient indication of the character of the music viz.,

> *Jubilee* In simplified sonatina form. It expresses a generally optimistic view of life. One of the themes is quite southern in character.
>
> *Noel* The principle theme was originally improvised as a response in church.
>
> *Hobgoblin* Was added somewhat later to the original set of three pieces. It was suggested by "Puck's" description of his practical jokes in the "Midsummer Nights Dream."
>
> *a Vagrom Ballad* This word, now obsolete, is found in Shakespeare. The music represents an imaginary story told by a tramp to a group of hoboes who greet it with derisive laughter. This starts up a general fight which is interrupted by the police. They are all carried off to the court and sentenced to "do time." The last part may suggest their joy at being released.

This is program music. It does not make statements or state facts. But if you have sufficient imagination it may suggest a picture to you. Every one must make the picture for himself.

SOURCE: Manuscript in the possession of the pianist Virginia Eskin, given to her by Arthur Fiedler, conductor of the Boston Pops Orchestra.

NOTES

1.   Charles E. Ives, *Memos,* ed. John Kirkpatrick (New York: W. W. Norton & Co., 1973): 184.
2.   The wetlands or swamp of Jackson Park outside of Chicago was the site of the famous World's Columbian Exposition in 1893.

57

Late Nineteenth-Century

Cultural Nationalism

The Paradigm of Dvořák

(Creelman, Paine, Burleigh)

Cultural nationalism, which had earlier focused on professional advocacy for American composers and musicians, took a different turn in the 1890s when issues of musical style moved into the foreground. A serious and influential debate about national musical identity pivoted around the Czech composer Antonin Dvořák (1841–1904), who came to New York in 1892 to head the National Conservatory of Music at the invitation of its founder, Jeannette Thurber (1850–1946). Little did either of them foresee the impact of his three-year stay. His long American reach extended through his pupil Rubin Goldmark to Aaron Copland; and through his associations with Will Marion Cook to Duke Ellington; and through his influence on Harry T. Burleigh to the development of the concert spiritual. In his own country, Dvořák championed Slavonic folk songs and dances as source material for classical music. In the United States, in apparent innocence of American racism, Dvořák proclaimed the music of Indians and Negroes—by which he meant plantation songs along with spirituals—to be the American equivalent.

In the first selection, the journalist James Creelman (1859–1915) quotes Dvořák's controversial views on the importance of African-American music, also noting the new admissions policy and scholarship plan for black students at the National Conservatory of Music. Then follows a response to Dvořák's ideas from John Knowles Paine (1839–1906), representing an already established community of American classical composers, who want nothing more nor less than acceptance of their right to contribute to a universal tradition. Dvořák practiced what he preached so successfully in his Symphony no. 9, *From a New World*, that his model inspired the next generation, particularly African-American composers. Harry Burleigh's own career represents that achievement.

REAL VALUE OF NEGRO MELODIES

Dr. Dvořák Finds in Them the Basis for an American School of Music
RICH IN UNDEVELOPED THEMES
American Composers Urged to Study Plantation Songs and Build upon Them
USES OF NEGRO MINSTRELSY
Colored Students To Be Admitted to the National Conservatory—Prizes to Encourage Americans

It was [Anton] Rubinstein who bitterly said that the world would make no more progress in music until the controlling influence of Wagner, Berlioz and Liszt had passed away. Right on the heels of this anathema, Dr. Antonin Dvořák, the foremost figure among living composers, came to America, the acknowledged leader of the dramatic school and the chosen target for the arrows of the lyric school.

The great Bohemian composer has just ended his first season of musical exploration in New York and his opinion ought to stir the heart of every American who loves music.

"I am now satisfied," he said to me, "that the future music of this country must be founded upon what are called negro melodies. "This must be the real foundation of any serious and original school of composition to be developed in the United States. When I first came here last year I was impressed with this idea and it has developed into a settled conviction. These beautiful and varied themes are the product of the soil. They are American. I would like to trace out the traditional authorship of the negro melodies, for it would throw a great deal of light upon the question I am most deeply interested in at present.

"These are the folk songs of America and your composers must turn to them. All of the great musicians have borrowed from the songs of the common people. Beethoven's most charming scherzo is based upon what might now be considered a skillfully handled negro melody. I myself have gone to the simple, half forgotten tunes of the Bohemian peasants for hints in my most serious work. Only in this way can a musician express the true sentiment of his people. He gets into touch with the common humanity of his country."

POSSIBILITIES OF NEGRO MELODY

"In the negro melodies of America I discover all that is needed for a great and noble school of music. They are pathetic, tender, passionate, melancholy, solemn, religious, bold, merry, gay or what you will. It is music that suits itself to any mood or any purpose. There is nothing in the whole range of composition that cannot be supplied with themes from this source. The American musician understands these tunes and they move sentiment in him. They appeal to his imagination because of their associations.

"When I was in England one of the ablest musical critics in London complained to me that there was no distinctively English school of music, nothing that appealed particularly to the British mind and heart. I replied to him that the composers of England had turned their backs upon the fine melodies of Ireland and Scotland instead of making them the essence of an English school. It is a great pity that English musicians have not profited out of this rich store. Somehow the old Irish and Scotch ballads have not [been] seized upon or appealed to them.

"I hope it will not be so in this country, and I intend to do all in my power to call attention to the splendid treasure of melody which you have. Among my pupils in the National Conservatory of Music I have discovered strong talents. There is one young man upon whom I am building strong expectations. His compositions are based upon negro melodies, and I have encouraged him in this direction. The other members of the composition class seem to think that it is not in good taste to get ideas from the old plantation songs, but they are wrong, and I have tried to impress upon their minds the fact that the greatest composers have not considered it beneath their dignity to go to the humble folk songs for motifs.

"I did not come to America to interpret Beethoven or Wagner for the public. That is not my work and I would not waste any on it. I came to discover what young Americans had in them and to help them to express it. When the negro minstrels are here again I intend to take my young composers with me and have them comment on the melodies." And saying so[,] Dvořák sat down at his piano and ran his fingers lightly over the keys. It was his favorite pupil's adaptation of a Southern melody. Here, then, is a programme of musical growth, laid down by the most competent mind that has yet studied the American mold—a plan made without hesitation or reservation. It is the result of an almost microscopic examination and comes from a man who is always in earnest.

ELEMENTS TO CULTIVATE

The scheme outlined by Dr. Dvořák is in its very nature an utterance of the dramatic school. The land is full of melody. The countryside school echoes the songs of the working people. Take those simple themes and weave them into splendid and harmonious forms. Glorify them: give them breadth. So the Dutch painter talks to his pupils. Do not try to imagine the angel in heaven, but try to paint that wrinkled peasant woman at your side, that the angel in her may be seen by ordinary eyes. It is not what you paint that counts, but how you paint it. Dr. Dvořák takes a similar position. He cannot teach, nor can any one, a system of melody creation. Bacon asks:—

Who taught the raven in a drought to throw pebbles into a hollow tree, where she espied water so that the water might rise so as she might come to it? Who taught the bee to sail through such a vast sea of air and to find the way from a field in flower, a great way off, to her hive? Who taught the ant to find every grain of corn she buried in her hill, lest it should take root and grow?

Dr. Dvořák cannot cause melodies to bubble up in the minds of his pupils, but he can show them how to utter what is in them. And if it be granted that America teems with original songs, that the common people are tuneful, that their heads are properly formed by nature, that the creative faculty lies in them, is not method and style the most important thing in the formative period of a national school? Rubinstein told me that Wagner was a poor musician because he lacked the power of musical invention, and yet with a theme borrowed from the soil, as it were, Wagner accomplished more than the Russian master divinely endowed with the lyric quality. Many of the negro melodies—most of them, I believe—are the creations of negroes born and reared in America. That is the peculiar aspect of the problem. The negro does not produce music of that kind elsewhere. I have heard the black singers in Hayti [sic] for hours at the bamboola dances, and, as a rule, their songs are not unlike the monotonous and crude chantings of the Sioux tribes. It is so also in Africa. But the negro in America utters a new note, full of sweetness, and as characteristic as any music of any country.

TO ADMIT COLORED STUDENTS

This leads to an important announcement that the HERALD is authorized to make to-day, which is that the National Conservatory of Music, over which Dr. Dvořák presides, is to be thrown open free of charge to the negro race. Here is Mrs. Thurber's official announcement:—

The National Conservatory of Music of America, 126 and 128 East Seventeenth Street, New York, May 16, 1893

The National Conservatory of Music of America proposes to enlarge its sphere of usefulness by adding to its departments a branch for the instruction in music of colored pupils of talent, largely with the view of forming colored professors of merit. The aptitude of the colored race for music, vocal and instrumental, has long been recognized, but no definite steps have hitherto been taken to develop it, and it is believed that the decision of the Conservatory to move in this new direction will meet with general approval and be productive of prompt and encouraging results. Several of the trustees have shown special interest in the matter. Prominent among these is Mrs. Colus P. Huntington. Tuition will be furnished to students of exceptional talent free of charge. Two young but efficient colored pupils have already been encouraged as teachers and others will be secured as circumstances may require. Application for admission to the Conservatory classes is invited, and the assignment of pupils will be made to such instructors as may be deemed judicious. Dr. Antonin Dvořák, director of the Conservatory, expresses great pleasure at the decision of the

trustees, and will assist its fruition by sympathetic and active cooperation. May I ask you to place these facts before your readers and in favoring a worthy cause once again oblige yours, very truly.
[signed] JEANNETTE M. THURBER, President

The importance of this step can only be appreciated in the light of Dr. Dvořák's declaration that negro melody furnishes the only sure base for an American school of music. It is a bold innovation but those who have heard the Black Patti sing or "Blind" Tom play must have wondered why it was that no serious attempt was made to organize, train and refine, the musical talent of the negro race in the United States.[1] This institution has determined to add to the 800 white students as many negroes of positive talent as may apply. There will be absolutely no limit. I have the authority of Mrs. Thurber herself for that. After the expenditure of thousands of dollars the National Conservatory of Music is now beginning to see light. There is little doubt that the government will ever endow it, and Mrs. Thurber long ago gave that idea up. Dr. Dvořák, of course, cannot understand why the national authorities should not support such a broad educational enterprise out of the public Treasury. He looks back at the eighty years work done by the famous conservatory at Prague and recalls the long line of noble names that fostered it in conjunction with the government until all the arts were grouped together virtually under one roof.

But in America the wealthy citizens must do the work done by foreign governments. Already in the case of the grand opera, private subscriptions have been just as efficacious as public subsidies. But the ladies and gentlemen who parade their public spirit at the opera house must not forget the foundation of it all unless America is to remain forever a musical dependency of Europe. It requires a strong and pure interest to carry on the slow beginnings of a national school. People as a rule want to see the results at once when they contribute to a cause. A man will contribute to a hospital because the next day his self-esteem may be gratified by the grateful smile of a sick child, but would he as readily contribute to a bacteriological institute where the doctors who save the patient learn to grapple with disease. Americans vaunt their hospitals, and yet I have seen the most extensive and most perfectly equipped bacteriological institute in the world maintained by a few Russians without a word of boasting. Americans proudly proclaim the generosity that upholds a grand opera on a scale only equalled by Vienna, Dresden, Munich and Paris, but where is the serious spirit that supports the energy for producing operas and opera makers! So far the work of the National Conservatory of Music has been carried on under a charter from Congress by Mrs. Thurber and 111 friends scattered all over the country.

> SOURCE: [James Creelman], "Real Value of Negro Melodies," *New York Herald*, May 21, 1893. Available on Robert Winter's Web site, http://homepage.mac.com/rswinter/Direct Testimony/about.html.

〰〰〰〰〰

Several prominent musicians, including George Chadwick, Benjamin Lang, and Amy Beach, responded to Dvořák in a long article from which we reprint only the response of John Knowles Paine, the dean of the group. One of the first native-born composers to base his career on symphonic and choral music, Paine won widespread acclaim for such early works as his Mass in D Major (1865). As a professor of music at Harvard University, Paine exercised considerable influence in Boston. (One of his students was Henry Lee Higginson.) Trained mainly in Berlin and spending his formative years abroad, Paine represents the universal ideals of music transcending categories. His response clarifies issues of national style from the cosmopolitan perspective of an older generation.

"AMERICAN MUSIC: DR. ANTONIN DVOŘÁK EXPRESSES SOME RADICAL OPINIONS," *BOSTON HERALD,* MAY 28, 1893

His Advocacy of "Negro Melodies" as Regarded by Local Musicians Varied Views upon the Subject Interesting Ideas about the "Folk Songs" of This Country

If Dr. Dvořák has been correctly reported, he greatly overestimates the influence that national melodies and folk-songs have exercised on the higher forms of musical art. In the case of Haydn, Mozart, Beethoven, Schubert and other German masters, the old folk-songs have been used to a limited extent as motives; but movements founded on such themes are exceptional in comparison with the immense amount of entirely original thematic material that constitutes the bulk of their music. For instance, how much of folk-song melody is there in Bach's great organ toccatas and fugues, Handel's "Messiah," Beethoven's "Fifth Symphony," Mendelssohn's "Elijah," Wagner's "Lohengrin," Berlioz's "Romeo and Juliet"; in short, the vast majority of the works of the composers of different nationalities? But even if it be granted that musical style is formed to some extent on popular melodies, the time is past when composers are to be classed according to geographical limits.

It is not a question of nationality, but individuality, and individuality of style is not the result of limitation—whether of folk-songs, negro melodies, the tunes of the heathen Chine[s]e or Digger Indians, but of personal character and inborn originality. During the present century musical art has overstepped all national limits; it is no longer a mere question of Italian, German, French, English, Slavonic or American music, but of world music. Except in opera and church music, the prominent composers of the present day belong to this universal or cosmopolitan school of music, although most of them may express here and there certain characteristics of style, due in part to the influence of airs and dances of their respective countries. The music of Chopin, Grieg and Dvořák, for instance, is distinguished for strong local coloring; on the other hand, the works of Mozart, Mendelssohn, Berlioz, Liszt, Rubinstein and others are far less national than individual and universal in character and style.

Dr. Dvořák is probably unacquainted with what has already been accomplished in the higher forms of music by composers in America. In my estimation, it is a preposterous idea to say that in future American music will rest upon such an alien foundation as the melodies of a yet largely undeveloped race. No doubt some use may be made of the negro melodies as themes for musical compositions just as popular airs of any country may thus be used and, no doubt, symphonic poems, cantatas, operas, etc., will be composed on American musical subjects. But, as our civilization is a fusion of various European nationalities, so American music more than any other should be all-embracing and universal. American composers have not as rich a foundation for development of a national style or school of music as older countries, if we look at the subject only from [a] restricted national point of view. Dr. Dvořák is not the only one who holds this narrow view about the future of American musical art, but it is incomprehensible to me how any thoroughly cultivated musician or musical critic can have such limited and erroneous views of the true functions of American composers. It is more than probable that Dr. Dvořák's true ideas on [the] subject have not been fully expressed nor correctly reported; chance it may have been mere pleasantry on his part.

SOURCE: Reproduced in Adrienne Fried Block, "Boston Talks Back to Dvořák," *Institute for Studies in American Music Newsletter* 17, no. 2 (May 1989): 40.

~~~~~~~~~

Harry T. Burleigh (1866–1949) was a distinguished post–Civil War black composer who won national recognition. His choral arrangements of spirituals helped them to enter into the repertoire of white and mixed choirs as well as black performing troupes. Most important, the "runaway popularity" of Burleigh's arrangement of the great spiritual "Deep River" for solo voice and piano in 1916–1917, the historian Wayne Shirley writes, "made it thinkable for spirituals to appear on a mainstream vocal recital."[2] Even though black spirituals are rarely sung in concert by white singers today, on a print of this song from 1917, the names of 21 concert singers, including Alma Gluck, Louise Homer, and Marcella Sembrich, were listed as having performed Burleigh's arrangement.

THE NEGRO AND HIS SONG

Many of the songs [spirituals] are in the five-toned (pentatonic) scale which has been used by all races who have been in bondage, including the Hebrews. It is so old that no one knows its origin. The Scotch use it in their folk songs, and it has always been heard in music of the Orient. If one sings the common major scale, omitting the fourth and seventh tones, he has the pentatonic scale.

There is also a fondness in Negro song for use of either the major or minor scale with a flat seventh tone. This gives a peculiarly poignant quality. Dvořák, in his *New World Symphony*, made great use of the flat seventh in the minor. This great master literally saturated himself with Negro song[s] before he wrote the *New World*, and I myself, while never a student of Dvořák, not being far enough advanced at that time to be in his classes, was constantly associated with him during the two years that he taught in the National Conservatory in New York. I sang our Negro songs for him very often and, before he wrote his own themes, he filled himself with the spirit of the old Spirituals. I also helped to copy parts of the original score. A study of the musical material of which the *New World* is made will reveal the influence of Negro song upon it.

The introduction of the Symphony is pervaded with syncopation common to Negro song, and by a use of the flat seventh in the minor mode. This is suggestive of the strangeness of the new country. The syncopation is even more marked in the first theme of the opening movement which is followed by a four-measure subsidiary theme of real charm in which Dvořák employed the lowered, or flat, seventh. Then comes the second theme with its open reference to the beloved Spiritual "Swing Low, Sweet Chariot" of which Dvořák used the second and third measures almost note for note, as a comparison will show. The colorfulness of this entire movement, as well as that of the final movement, lies largely in the use of the flat seventh in the harmonization, this remark in no way belittling Dvořák's superb gift for instrumentation.

Negro Spirituals may be classified as narrative songs, songs of admonition, songs of inspiration, of tribulation, of death, and of play. Of the latter none is so gay as "Lil 'Liza Jane," of the Mississippi levees. The tribulation songs, strangely, are not all melancholy: Many of the Negro's best songs vacillate oddly, sometimes within a single phrase, between major and minor. But even when entirely in the minor, they are not always sad: poignant and appealing, yes, but never melancholy. No songs in the world have a greater or more deserved popularity than those Spirituals which tell of the universal striving and weariness of all men, not alone of the Negro race. There is the tender "Somebody's Knockin' at Yo' Door," and "I Bin in de Storm So Long," the imploring "I Want to Be Ready," and "Standin' in de Need of Prayer," this latter song being used, with modifications, by Louis Gruenberg, in his *Emperor Jones;* and the truly exquisite "Deep River."

In the narrative Spirituals, the Negro has translated the marvelous stories of the Old Testament into simple home language, each tale, in his telling, being colored by his own exaltation and understanding of the Scriptures. Here we find "De Gospel Train," "Didn't It Rain," "Who Built de Ark," and "Ezekiel Saw de Wheel."

Many modern composers see in the piquant rhythms of Negro song, and its simple but expressive melodies, material to use in a thematic way in the writing of great art works. The week that Dvořák sailed back to his Old World home, after two years spent as a teacher in New York, a prominent journal commented by saying that "no sum of money was large enough to keep Antonin Dvořák in the New World. He left us his *New World Symphony* and his *American Quartet,* but he took himself away." But even if he did he left behind a richer appreciation of the beauties of Negro song, of its peculiar flavor, its sometimes mystical atmosphere, its whimsical piquancy, and its individual idiom, from all of which many other splendid artists have already drawn inspiration.

SOURCE: Harry T. Burleigh, "The Negro and His Song," in *Music on the Air,* ed. Hazel Gertrude Kinscella (New York: Viking, 1934): 186–89.

~~~~~~~

NOTES

1. "Black Patti" was the nickname for the soprano Sissieretta Jones (1869–1933). Thomas "Blind Tom" Bethune (1849–1908) was a pianist-prodigy.
2. Wayne D. Shirley, "The Coming of 'Deep River,'" *American Music* 15, no. 4 (Winter 1997): 515.

58

H ENRY KREHBIEL EXPLAINS A CRITIC'S CRAFT
AND A LISTENER'S DUTY

Henry Krehbiel (1854–1923) was the preeminent music critic in the golden age of music journalism in the United States. This was the era when the premiere of Dvořák's *New World Symphony* received a 5,000-word review that began on the front page of the newspaper and included musical examples. The son of German immigrants, Krehbiel got his start writing music criticism for a newspaper in Cincinnati, a bastion of Austro-German classical music. At the *New York Tribune* from 1880 to 1923, he could make or break reputations overnight. In 1896, he published *How to Listen to Music,* the first music appreciation text for a general middle-class audience: it went through multiple editions in his lifetime.[1] Even these brief excerpts demonstrate Krehbiel's ethical convictions. However elaborate the prose style, Krehbiel's standards hold up and still guide many a music appreciation course. His distinction between "pedantic" and "rhapsodic" styles of music writing could apply to articles about popular as much as classical music.

INTRODUCTION

This book has a purpose, which is as simple as it is plain; and an unpretentious scope. It does not aim to edify either the musical professor or the musical scholar. It comes into the presence of the musical student with all becoming modesty. Its business is with those who love music and present themselves for its gracious ministrations in Concert-Room and Opera House, but have not studied it as professors and scholars are supposed to study. It is not for the careless unless they be willing to inquire whether it might not be well to yield the common conception of entertainment in favor of the higher enjoyment which springs from serious contemplation of beautiful things; but if they are willing so to inquire, they shall be accounted the class that the author is most anxious to reach. The reasons which prompted its writing and the laying out of its plan will presently appear. For the frankness of his disclosure the author might be willing to apologize were his reverence for music less and his consideration for popular affectations more; but because he is convinced that a love for music carries with it that which, so it be but awakened, shall speedily grow into an honest desire to know more about the beloved object, he is willing to seem unamiable to the amateur while arguing the need of even so mild a stimulant as his book, and ingenuous, maybe even childish, to the professional musician while trying to point a way in which better appreciation may be sought.

The capacity properly to listen to music is better proof of musical talent in the listener than skill to play upon an instrument or ability to sing acceptably when unaccompanied by that capacity. It makes more for that gentleness and refinement of emotion, thought, and action which, in the highest sense of the term, it is the province of music to promote. And it is a much rarer accomplishment.

. . .

It is not an exaggeration to say that one might listen for a lifetime to the polite conversation of our drawing-rooms (and I do not mean by this to refer to the United States alone) without hearing a symphony talked about in terms indicative of more than the most superficial knowledge of the outward form, that is, the dimensions and apparatus, of such a composition. No other art provides an exact analogy for this phenomenon. Everybody can say something containing a degree of appositeness about a poem, novel, painting, statue, or building. Nature failed to provide a model for this ethereal art. There is nothing in the natural world with which the simple man may compare it. If he can do no more he can go as far as Landseer's rural critic who objected to one of the artist's paintings on the ground that not one of the three pigs eating from a trough had a foot in it. It is the absence of the standard of judgment employed in this criticism which makes significant talk about music so difficult.

. . .

Ungracious as it may appear, it may yet not be amiss, therefore, at the very outset of an inquiry into the proper way in which to listen to music, to utter a warning against much that is written on the art. As a rule it will be found that writers on music are divided into two classes, and that neither of these classes can do much good. Too often they are either pedants or rhapsodists. This division is wholly natural. Music has many sides and is a science as well as an art. Its scientific side is that on which the pedant generally approaches it. He is concerned with forms and rules, with externals, to the forgetting of that which is expressibly nobler and higher. But the pedants are not harmful, because they are not interesting; strictly speaking, they do not write for the public at all, but only for their professional colleagues. The harmful men are the foolish rhapsodists who take advantage of the fact that the language of music is indeterminate and evanescent to talk about the art in such a way as to present themselves as persons of exquisite sensibilities rather than to direct attention to the real nature and beauty of music itself. To them I shall recur in a later chapter devoted to music criticism, and haply point out the difference between good and bad critics and commentators from the view-point of popular need and popular opportunity.

FROM CHAPTER IX, "MUSICIAN, CRITIC, AND PUBLIC"

The musician knows as well as anyone how impossible it is to escape the press, and it is, therefore, his plain duty to seek to raise the standard of its utterances by conceding the rights of the critic and encouraging honesty, fearlessness, impartiality, intelligence, and sympathy wherever he finds them. To this end he must cast away many antiquated and foolish prejudices. He must learn to confess with Wagner, the arch-enemy of criticism, that "blame is much more useful to the artist than praise," and that "the musician who goes to destruction because he is faulted, deserves destruction." He must stop the contention that only a musician is entitled to criticize a musician, and without abating one jot of his requirements as to knowledge, sympathy, liberality, broadmindedness, candor, and incorruptibility on the part of the critic, he must quit the foolish claim that to pronounce upon the excellence of a ragout one must be able to cook it; if he will not go farther he must, at least, go with the elder D'Israeli[2] [sic] to the extent of saying that "the talent of judgment may exist separately from the power of execution." One need not be a composer, but one must be able to feel with a composer before he can discuss his productions as they ought to be discussed. Not all the writers for the press are able to do this; many depend upon effrontery and a copious use of technical phrases to carry them through. The musician, alas! encourages this method whenever he gets a chance; nine times out of ten, when an opportunity to review a composition falls to him, he approaches it on its technical side. Yet music is of all the arts in the world the last that a mere pedant should discuss.

But if not a mere pedant, then neither a mere sentimentalist.

. . .

A critic's duty is to separate excellence from defect. . . . Much flows out of this conception of his duty. Holding it the critic will bring besides all needful knowledge a fullness of love into his work. "Where sympathy is lacking, correct judgment is also lacking," said Mendelssohn. The critic should be the mediator between the musician and the public. For all new works he should do what the symphonists of the Liszt school attempt to do by means of programmes; he should excite curiosity, arouse interest, and pave the way to popular comprehension. But for the old he should not fail to encourage reverence and admiration. To do both these things he must know his duty to the past, the present, and the future, and adjust each duty to the other. Such adjustment is only possible if he knows the music of the past and present, and is quick to perceive the bent and outcome of novel strivings. He should be catholic in taste, outspoken in judgment, unalterable in allegiance to his ideals, unswervable in integrity.

SOURCE: Henry Edward Krehbiel, *How to Listen to Music: Hints and Suggestions to Untaught Lovers of the Art* (New York: Scribner's, 1896: 11th ed., 1901): 3–5, 7–8, 13–14, 314–15, 322–23.

~~~~~~~~

NOTES

1. Five London editions appeared between 1900 and 1923.
2. Benjamin Disraeli (1804–1881) was the prime minister of England in 1868 and again from 1874 to 1880.

59

$\mathcal{A}$MY FAY TACKLES THE
"WOMAN QUESTION"

As the percentage of women in the musical professions in the United States between 1870 and 1910 increased from about 30 to 60 percent in that 40-year period, the "woman musician" became yet another incarnation of the "New Woman." In the articles and books that discussed the musical version of *her*, some depressingly familiar questions were posed: could women master the complexities of sophisticated musical structure? Did female instrumentalists have the stamina to play in professional "mixed" orchestras, competing with men? The concert pianist, lecturer, and critic Amy Fay (1844–1928) figured prominently in this debate at the turn of the twentieth century. After studying with Franz Liszt at Weimar in 1874, she returned home and wrote about her experiences in the book *Music Study in Germany* (1880), which unexpectedly made her famous. Here, she tackles the question of why there have been no great female composers.

WOMEN AND MUSIC

An article, which takes women to task for not being great musical composers, has recently appeared under the above caption, in the London "Musical News," and is being largely quoted in our papers.[1] . . .

Says the writer:

> It is impossible to find a single woman's name worthy to take rank with Beethoven, Handel, Mozart, Rossini, Brahms, Wagner, Schubert; we cannot even find one to place beside Balfe or Sir Arthur Sullivan. As a writer to the *Musical Times* remarked nearly twenty years since, "A few gifted members of the sex have been more or less fortunate in their emulation of men, and that is all. Not a single great work can be traced to a feminine pen." Nothing has been done since to lessen the truth of this remark. Year by year our great festivals produce new works; it is rare for even a minor production to be from the pen of a woman.

This is true, but when one reflects on the vast antiquity of the human race, which Professor John Fiske tells us in his "Discovery of America" may date back as far as 50,000 years, one is tempted to ask why the men have been so long about producing a Beethoven, a Schubert, or a Wagner? These great geniuses belong to the nineteenth century, and Beethoven's nine symphonies were composed during the first quarter of it, from 1802 to 1828, or thereabouts.

Music is the youngest of the arts, and is the most difficult of them all, since it creates something out of nothing. It has been developed within two hundred years, to its present height. Only towards the end of this century have women turned their attention to musical composition, and it is altogether premature to judge of what they may, and probably will, attain.

Women have been too much taken up with helping and encouraging men to place a proper value on their own talent, which they are too prone to underestimate and to think not worth making the most of. Their whole training, from time immemorial, has tended to make them take an intense interest in the work of men and to stimulate them to their best efforts. Ruskin was quite right when he so patronizingly said that "Woman's chief function is to praise." She has praised and praised, and kept herself in abeyance.

But now, all this is changed. Women are beginning to realize that they, too, have brains, and even musical ones. They are, at last, studying composition seriously, and will, ere long, feel out a path for themselves, instead of being "mere imitators of men."

For the matter of that, men have been imitators of each other at first. We all know that Mozart began to write like Haydn, and Beethoven began to write like Mozart, before each developed his own originality of style, and as for Wagner, he has furnished inspiration and ideas for all the composers who have succeeded him. Why, then, should we expect of women what men could not do (although Minerva was said to have sprung fully armed from the brain of Jove)? If it has required 50,000 years to produce a male Beethoven, surely one little century ought to be vouchsafed to create a female one!

It is a very shallow way of looking at the matter to say that "women have not been handicapped in music, because more girls than boys have been taught to play the piano or harpsichord." What does such teaching amount to? Really very little. To be a great creator in art, one must be trained to it from one's earliest years by a gifted parent or teacher. Mozart and Beethoven had fathers who fully realized the capacity of their sons, and they made them study early and late, "every day i' the hour," as Shakespeare says. No doubt, an hour of such work as these composers did in their youth, would be worth many days of the kind of musical preparation demanded of girls of this or any other period.

Edgar Poe, in his wonderful essay on the "Philosophy of Composition," in which he analyzes how he composed his own poem, "The Raven," makes the following remarkable statement:

> My first object (as usual) was originality. The extent to which this has been neglected, in versification, is one of the most unaccountable things in the world. Admitting that there is little possibility of variety in mere rhythm, it is still clear that the possible variety of metre and stanza are absolutely infinite; and yet, for centuries, no man, in verse, has ever done, or even seemed to think of doing, an original thing. The fact is, that originality (unless in minds of very unusual force) is by no means a matter, as some suppose, of impulse or intuition. In general, to be found, it must be elaborately sought, and although a positive merit of the highest class, demands in its attainment less of invention than negation.

When we read this marvelous analysis of Edgar Poe, we realize that he must have made the same exhaustive study of the art of poetry, that Beethoven did of the art of music, in order to be able to produce that masterpiece, "The Raven." This is the kind of mind training to which women have never been subjected, and it is idle to talk about their achieving great results in musical composition without it. To play the piano or the harpsichord is but one rung on the ladder which mounts to world-wide fame.

SOURCE: Amy Fay, "Women and Music," *Music* 18 (October 1900): 505–7.

~~~~~~~~

NOTE

1.   Fay is responding to the following article: A. L. S., "Women and Music," *Musical Courier* 41, no. 5 (August 1, 1900): 33.

60

AMY BEACH, COMPOSER, ON
"WHY I CHOSE MY PROFESSION"

Now considered a major figure in the Boston school of musicians, Amy Cheney Beach (1867–1944) was the first American woman to compose a symphony (1896) and a concerto (1900), thus succeeding in the "larger forms." Classical singers made her songs (such as "The Year's at the Spring" and "Ah but a Day") widely known standards. Because this article was published in a widely circulated magazine, one of many in the early 1900s aimed at women and the home (including the *Ladies Home Journal* and *Vogue*), Beach focused at length on her nineteenth-century upbringing. Her mother was determined to control the fate of her prodigy-daughter.

I had begun to coax to play on the piano before I could reach up and touch the ivory keys. My mother, who was a fine musician, and wanted to raise one, had no faith in the prodigy principle of forcing, or indulging. She believed rather in what Gerald Stanley Lee calls the "top bureau-drawer principle"—the principle of withholding.[1] I was not allowed to climb up on her lap, or on the music stool. I could only hear music, think music. I could not help thinking music. It was in my blood, it was the daily talk.

Though I had been singing and humming tunes before I could speak (my mother made a list of forty simple airs that I was humming when only a year old), it surprised her one day when she was singing to me, to have me join with her, taking not the air, but a small, but true alto. I cannot add my word to that feat, as I was not quite two. I imagine it was then that she decided that I was to be a musician and not a prodigy; that I was to be as carefully kept from music as later I would be helped to it.

I said I could not help thinking music. It was talked of at home as food and clothes are talked of in simpler homes. I was forbidden the piano; I had to think music—sing it. I was not three when I was first taken to a church or Sunday-school. I sang with the rest. I was lifted to the table, and gradually the singing stopped, and the congregation turned to see and listen to the infant singing to the accompaniment of the big organ.

At last, I was allowed to touch the piano. My mother was still opposed, but I can remember my aunt coming to the house, and putting me at the piano. I played at once the melodies I had been collecting, playing in my head, adding full harmonies to the simple, treble melodies. Then my aunt played a new air for me, and I reached up and picked out a harmonized bass accompaniment, as I had heard my mother do.

I can remember weaving my first compositions. I had been visiting at my grandfather's farm in Maine, one summer, and when I reached home, I told my mother that I had "made" three waltzes. She did not believe it at first, as there was no piano within miles of the farm. I explained that I had written them in my head, and proved it by playing them on her piano. The names betray the limitations of my experience. "Mamma's Waltz," the "Snowflake Waltz," and the third, the "Marlborough Waltz," because we were then living on Marlborough Street!

No more was made of the improvisations than there would have been had I exhibited a paper doll of my own cutting. I learned afterward from my mother herself, and her friends, that it was a part of her theory of education not to discuss before me my precocity; no one was permitted to make my accomplishments appear to me anything out of the expected, or normal. When I was in my sixth year, I went to play with the children of a friend of the family. When I came back, I related that I had been urged to play for the mother of the family.

"Did you play? What did you play?" demanded my mother.

"Beethoven's Spirit Waltz," I answered promptly, "but the piano was out of order, mother. It was a half-tone lower than ours. It sounded all wrong."

My mother was interested. "You did not finish it?"

"Oh, yes," I replied. "But I had to change it to a half-tone higher to bring it right."

It was the first suggestion to my mother of her later discovery. It helped her to patience later, when her child appeared only pert.

My father had been talking of Clara Louise Kellogg, and I remember my attention being caught by his saying that she had absolute pitch—that she could give or recognize any note away from the instrument.

My father rebuked me for pertness when I turned and said, "Oh, that's nothing. Anybody can do that. I can do that."

They continued their discussion. I was again reproved for interrupting. Then my mother, remembering, she said afterward, the "Spirit Waltz" incident, suggested that they would see if I knew what he was talking about. They made several experiments, and it was discovered that I really did have, untaught, absolute pitch.

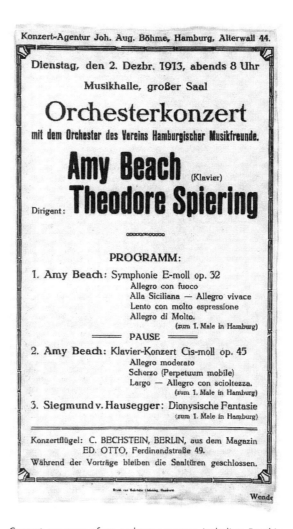

Concert program of an orchestra concert including Beach's Symphony in E Minor, Op. 32 and the Piano Concerto in C Sharp Minor, Op. 45, December 2, 1913 in Hamburg, Germany. Courtesy of Adrienne Fried Block.

My mother devoted all her time to my education. I was being given piano lessons, and other simple, regular instruction. I was not allowed to specialize on music. I was given an allot[t]ed time each day for practice. The piano was still, theoretically, in the top bureau drawer.

At seven, I was playing a Beethoven sonata, and a Chopin waltz. I was allowed to play in a few concerts—I imagine the consent was unwilling—and for encore, I used to play one of my own waltzes. Naturally, the child, who always looked younger than she was, because she was small for her age, and fair and slight, had several managerial offers, from men who wanted to advertise the child pianist. But my mother's good sense never considered an offer. I kept on studying, my mother herself teaching me music and the fundamental studies, until I was ten. Then my school world enlarged. I kept on studying music.

Amy Beach on her way to Europe, ca. 1929

When I was sixteen, I was allowed to make my début in Boston [in 1883]. I played the Moscheles G Minor concerto with a large orchestra. Life was beginning! I followed with a solo piece, a rondo by Chopin. From then, my concert work began. I gave recitals and played a good deal of chamber music, in concerts, and in the intervals worked at my composition. I had not then divided my enthusiasms; the work was complementary. It had not come to me that there was a choice to be made; that where many many people play music, few write music; that creation is higher than interpretation.

At seventeen [1885], I was invited to play with the Boston Symphony Orchestra. The same year, I was the soloist at a concert given by Theodore Thomas and his orchestra, playing the Mendelssohn concerto. I did not know that he was sparing me, but I did know that the tempo dragged, and I swung the orchestra into time. Mr. Thomas often laughed about it afterwards.

One of the sweetest of my recollections lies farther back. When I was ten, I was taken to California. In Berkeley, the university town, I met Edgar Rowland Sill, the poet. He was kind to me, and when he heard that I was the lucky possessor of a correct ear, of absolute pitch, he asked me to go out with him in the spring mornings, and steal from the birds! He told me that he was helping a friend, in the State University, who was writing a book on California bird songs. Professor Sill, whose ear was true, had been collecting bird melodies for him.

I shall always remember that first spring morning. The poet and I sat down behind a stone wall. It is a sweet memory of the kindly poet, of California, of the spring flowers, of the unconscious birds. With pencil and paper we took their melodies. We got twenty of their airs that morning.

I married at eighteen, but my husband, who was a physician and surgeon, was a keen amateur musician as well, and he insisted that my work was not to stop.[2] By that time, though I had not deliberately chosen, the work had chosen me. I continued to play at concerts, but my home life kept me in the neighborhood of Boston. My compositions gave me a larger field. From Boston, I could reach out to the world. The orders for special compositions kept increasing.

The Mass in E flat [1890] was begun when I was nineteen, but was not finished until later. It was given the first time by the Handel and Haydn Society of Boston. They wanted a tenor solo inserted for Campanini. I knew that a Mass had sometimes a *Graduali,* so I interpolated a *Graduali* as tenor solo. After the Mass, I was to play the piano solo in the Beethoven choral fantasy. I must have been excited over the production of the Mass, for I did not see that as I went out on the platform, the entire audience rose to its feet.

For the dedication of the Woman's Building at the Columbian Exposition at Chicago I was asked to compose a choral work. I took the hundredth Psalm for my text: "Oh, be joyful in the Lord, all ye lands!" [1893]. It was given by full orchestra and chorus under Theodore Thomas, the Apollo Club of Chicago uniting. The *Jubilate* was later performed by Walter Damrosch in New York.

The Boston Symphony Orchestra brought out my *Gaelic Symphony* [1896], and it was given afterwards by the Pittsburgh Orchestra and the Chicago, Kansas City and Buffalo Symphony Orchestras.

When the Trans-Mississippi Exposition was to be opened in Omaha, I was asked, three weeks before the opening, to write the music for an ode; for brass band and voices. I insisted [upon] seeing the verses before accepting the order, and my answer had to be learned before the committee could leave Boston. The ode was telegraphed on to me. Disguised as a telegram, it was not very inspiring, lacking punctuation and line arrangement, but after I had practically translated it, I saw that it would go. It was swift work, and after the music was done, I kept the printing office working overtime, but the ode reached Omaha in time for rehearsal.[3]

Many of my songs have been done swiftly, but they come with the sense of birth, not of conscious creation at such times. One of the best-known of my "lieder," is "The Year's at the Spring" [1900], which came so. I had been asked to write the music for the verses which had long been favorites of mine. The Browning Society of Boston was to give "Pippa Passes" on the anniversary of Browning's birthday. I was very busy at the time. There was a concert in New York to be got out of the way first. Going back to Boston from New York, it came to me suddenly that the celebration was to be that week. I decided to write the music the next day. The words, however, had been recalled, and I found that they were singing themselves into my consciousness. I listened to the melody—it was the only melody, after that, for that burst of joy and faith. I wrote it down as soon as I got home. Pleased as I was by its immediate adoption by the singers of the world, it gratified me more that the music was welcomed by the son of Robert Browning as the same impulse, artistically, which had prompted the verses.

<hr />

Beach's memoir concludes with a brief synopsis of her career by the writer-interviewer Ednah Aiken. It begins with a reference to the deaths of Beach's husband and mother in 1910–11 and Beach's move to Germany. Statements praising the composer alternate with pointed observations about cultural rivalry and the status of the American composer. The same year this article was published, the onset of World War I forced Beach's return to the United States.

A personal grief, two years ago, turned Mrs. H. H. A. Beach away from Boston where her work as composer and pianist had made for her a unique and enviable position. It was with no idea of broadening her usefulness, or of extending her reputation, that she went to Europe; that she made her temporary home in Germany. Yet both consequences were inevitable. A year ago, she began to find comfort again in her work. Her concerts, where she herself, at the piano, assists violin, or violin and cello, or voice, to interpret her compositions, are demanding and winning the recognition which an American, no matter how gifted, must here demand and win. It is acknowledged that the best music can be heard in America, as it is there, that the big prices are paid, but that anything prophetic can come out of Bethlehem, *"es ist zum lacheln"* [that is to be laughed at] and not always quietly!

It would not be necessary for Mrs. Beach, whose name rests on a firm foundation of distinguished achievement, to go to Europe, or Germany, to push her compositions into the *ultimate* appreciation of the public, or of the musical critics. Where her sonata for piano and violin has been played, or her quintette for piano and strings, they have been placed with dignity, in programs together with Schubert and Mozart, or Brahms and Tschaikowsky [sic]; and they have been enthusiastically received. For years, her name has been added to the programs of distinguished performers and singers whose liking they have claimed. But to enjoy the wide recognition she deserves, to conquer national prejudice; to get her compositions before many a virtuoso who might not open the score when he read that it was by an American composer, and a woman, required just the activity to which Mrs. Beach turned in her personal loss, and it is already bringing rich rewards.

Pugno, the pianist, tells the story that he and Ysaÿe had discovered the beauties of the sonata for piano and violin, and had played it during their concert tour in France, before discovering that it was by an American—least of all, that it was written by a woman.[4] It is to be wondered, though neither Pugno nor Ysaye would admit it, whether they would have gone farther than the cover had they read that it was the work of an American woman, no matter what her reputation in America might be. Boston means nothing to Germany. New York is the place where the German singers get their big pay. It is sad, but true, that the prejudice is deep and wide. It is based on national egotism. It is fed by the fact that music students come here to get their training. To achieve distinction in Germany or Austria, means winning it there; to be known to have obtained something there which can give a legitimate platform from which to rise. As Germany is the recognized music center, it is demanded that the composer who expects serious attention, storm that center, and win first from the Germans what Mrs. Beach is winning to-day—recognition, not as an American composer, but as a composer, regardless of sex or race, among composers of one race and sex.

It will [sic] not be long before her "Gaelic Symphony" will be heard in Europe, where it will undoubtedly receive the appreciation it was awarded in Boston when it was given by the Boston Symphony Orchestra, and later in Pittsburgh and Buffalo, in New York, Chicago and San Francisco. Her quintette has already made its place among programs of serious chamber music. Ysaye, [Teresa] Carreño, Pugno and many other distinguished performers have long included her compositions among their programs. Her songs are known and sung wherever English songs are known and sung. Given German words, they receive the applause awarded Brahms and Wolff. The best-known are her "June," "Ecstasy," and the world favorite "The Year's at the Spring." This last, which so delighted the son of Robert Browning that he declared it to be a spontaneous wedding of two artistic impulses, lends itself well to German words, and the result is an adoption in the land of national egotism of that Wagnerian burst of triumphant melody.

This season, Mrs. Beach is giving a series of concerts in Berlin, Breslau, Munich and other German cities. The sincerity of her work, the breadth of her understanding, the virility of her style have already challenged that prejudice against the land which is known as the place where good shoes are made, where good voices flourish, and where the best dance music comes from. Can anything good, meaning profound, original, come out of Bethlehem? American music is ragtime. "Ragtime" is, conversely, the American music. It is only Mrs. Beach and a few others who can, by challenging that prejudice, successfully do away with it.

[signed]—[Ednah Aiken.

> SOURCE: Amy Beach, "Why I Chose My Profession: The Autobiography of a Woman Composer: An Interview Written by Ednah Aiken," *Mother's Magazine* (February 1914): 7–8.

~~~~~~~~

NOTES

1. This refers to Gerald Stanley Lee, *The Lost Art of Reading* (New York, 1902): 77: "First. Decide what the owner of the mind most wants in the world. Second. Put this thing, whatever it may be, where the owner of the mind cannot get it unless he uses his mind. Take pains to put it where he can get it, if he does use his mind. Third. Lure him on. It is education." As cited and explained in Adrienne Fried Block, *Amy Beach, Passionate Victorian: The Life and Work of an American Composer, 1867–1944* (New York: Oxford University Press, 1998): 5, 314.
2. Henry Harris Aubrey Beach (1843–1910), 25 years older than Amy, did not approve of his wife performing for professional fees in public concerts. He did encourage her composition.
3. It was published as "Song of Welcome" (1898).
4. The Belgian violinist Eugène Ysaÿe and the pianist Raoul Pugno played the Violin Sonata in Paris in 1900. The title page of the score clearly attributes the work to "Mrs. H. H. A. Beach."

61

EDWARD MACDOWELL, POET-COMPOSER,

REMEMBERED

(Currier, Gilman)

Edward MacDowell (1860–1908) blazed a trail of glory for the American classical composer at the end of the nineteenth century. None of his contemporaries aroused the same kind of favorable comments from usually sober music critics and colleagues. The critic Henry Krehbiel waxed rhapsodic and so did the conductor Anton Seidl, who went on record as preferring MacDowell to Brahms. The praise lavished on such orchestral works as the Indian Suite hints at the eagerness and perhaps cultural anxiety of American critics to find a great American composer.

MacDowell began his career in music as a concert pianist, only slowly coming to recognize that, for him, composing mattered more. As a young boy, he took piano lessons with the great Venezuelan concert pianist Teresa Carreño (1853–1917). She remained his advocate throughout her long career, especially linked with one of his signature works, the Piano Concerto no. 2, which she performed more than 25 times between 1890 and 1908, both in the United States and abroad.

After 12 years in Europe, from 1876 on, studying composition mainly with Joachim Raff (1822–1882)—a then-famous figure—in Frankfurt, Germany, and then forging a career as a composer-pianist in that country, MacDowell and his wife, Marian, moved to Boston in 1888. The first excerpt reprinted here, from a memoir by his friend the pianist Thomas Parker Currier, describes MacDowell's musical home-coming, including an audacious after-dinner performance at the Harvard Musical Association with John S. Dwight in attendance.

The excerpt from Currier's memoir also includes his own assessment of Mac-Dowell's idiosyncratic performances of his piano music, describing a freedom that might be hard to replicate today. His intimate accounts evoke the poetic imagination that infuses MacDowell's best music.

In 1896, MacDowell moved to New York to join the faculty of Columbia University, which ended with his controversial departure in 1904. Soon after, he took ill with a brain disease—it is generally conceded that he had syphilis—and after a long decline, died. He left a legacy that included a famous artists' colony, the MacDowell Colony in Peterborough, New Hampshire, which was overseen by his devoted wife until her death and which still operates today.

The extent to which MacDowell was touted as the Great American Hope in music is hard to recapture today. Yet clearly he was received as a hero. Reprinted as the second selection is an excerpt from his biography by Lawrence Gilman, who glorifies the composer as a red-blooded, straight, white, Celtic male.

FROM T. P. CURRIER'S MEMOIR

During his last years in Germany [MacDowell] had become so absorbed in writing that his playing had suffered accordingly. He had renounced all idea of pursuing concert work, and, in spite of evidence to the contrary, he really adhered to his decision. For though circumstance compelled him the rest of his life into periodical appearances before the public, he always spoke of himself to intimates simply as a player of his own compositions. "I hate to practice," he said, "and if people think I don't play well,—well, I don't profess to;—I'm merely a composer-pianist."

The necessity for practicing and playing, however, was quickly forced upon him. Musical Boston was anxious to estimate for itself the ability of the young composer, whose music they liked. And the only way they could do so was through his public playing of the accepted repertory in general and his own compositions in particular.

The Kneisel Quartette offered an engagement. The Symphony audiences were ready to hear him interpret his concertos. The Harvard Musical Association asked him as an honored guest to their annual dinner, which meant that he would be expected to play. And the doors of private houses were open to him for their private musicales.

His first public appearance was at a Kneisel Quartette concert.[1] He played the piano part of a quartette, and movements from his first Suite. His performance met with polite friendliness. It was not notably good, though certainly to Boston's ears notably strange. And it was therefore scarcely calculated to arouse enthusiasm.

Mac Dowell had no love for the string quartette, which, he said to me, was to him like so much "cold veal." It may easily be guessed also that ensemble playing was no more to his taste.

At the Harvard Musical Association dinner, the venerable John S. Dwight's cordial introduction of the distinguished young musician ended with the question, "would he speak or play?" The bashful streak was in full possession of Mac Dowell as he, replying inaudibly "I'll play," slid quickly toward the piano. Once there, however, his spirit of aggressive determination asserted itself. Falling on the keys with a power he would have used to fill [the] old Music Hall, he launched into a performance which confounded the conservatives of the Association, and delighted the rest. Winding up with his "Czardas," which he rushed through with terrifying speed, he hastened to his seat amid amazed applause. Later in the evening he played with Mr. Lang a "Tone-Poem" for two pianos by his dear friend Templeton Strong.[2] By this time, the company, however pleased or displeased with his playing, was vibrantly aroused and interested. Like the "Czardas," this piece contained much rapid passage work, which fell largely to Mac Dowell. The performance, owing to the pace he set, together with the efforts of the elder pianist to keep up, was something the like of which the Association had perhaps never experienced.

Mac Dowell's playing that evening is dwelt upon because it largely influenced opinion regarding its merits in general. Soon it became apparent that the musical set then dominating Boston did not like his "method." The consensus was that his "scales" were extravagantly fast and blurred, his chord playing too loud, his effects too often vague and violent in contrast, and his use of the rubato and the soft pedal extreme.

It should be said, that at this time, at least, these opinions were not wholly astray. Mac Dowell was badly out of practice, and his hasty efforts at preparation were apparent. Moreover he was still wrathful over the necessity for playing at all, and still doggedly determined not to practice.

Gradually, nevertheless, compulsion had its due effect. By degrees he worked back into a state of technical efficiency, to the end that his performances of his Second Concerto with Thomas in New York, and the Boston Symphony Orchestra in Boston, in the spring of 1889, stamped his playing as distinctly virtuosic, even if it was universally liked.

. . .

IV

Mac Dowell's playing was not only virtuosic; it possessed marked original qualities. It had, in a sense, little in common with that of the virtuosi of those days. His scale and passage playing were decidedly hazy. As he told me, he hated scales and arpeggi for their own sake; and the sole use he had for them was for the purpose of creating effects,—waves and swirls and rushes of sound that should merely fill their place in the tone-picture he desired to portray. His octaves and chord playing, too were extremely powerful and often harsh in ff, and in pp hardly more clear than his passage playing. In accordance with his own viewpoint, he was always seeking for atmospheric and overtone effects, and to do so he made constant use of the "half-pedal" instead of the full pedal, which latter would have cut things out too clearly to suit him. Add to this his equally constant use of the "soft" pedal, his sudden and extreme contrasts, and his thundering fortissimi, (fff), and it is not difficult to realize why as a pianist in general he failed at first to satisfy the cultivated listener of that period.

It was not until Mac Dowell appeared in recitals containing a large proportion of his own works, that he won hearty recognition even from those who had been coldly critical, and enraptured those to whom his playing had been from the first more comprehensible.

He had been in Boston three years before he brought himself to the point of returning to the concert platform. In the autumn of 1891, he announced a series of three recitals, to take place in the old Chickering Hall on Tremont Street. I well recall the first drafts of the programmes. They contained that "old chestnut," as he called it, the "Moonlight" Sonata, and a miscellaneous collection of stock pieces, but included only small groups of his own music.

I may be pardoned for referring to my part in their rearrangement. On looking them over, "My dear man," I said, "why do you make programmes like these? What the public wants is to hear you play your own music. You ought to cut out about half of these things and put in much more of your own."

"Get out!" he replied, (a favorite expression of his whenever one opposed his own notions). A few days later, however, he acknowledged that he had "changed the programmes somewhat."

At one of these recitals I sat with Templeton Strong. Strong had been Mac Dowell's dearest friend in Wiesbaden, where the two had worked and tramped together; and Mac Dowell had no sooner got well settled in Boston before he began to urge Strong to return also. But the latter did not share Mac Dowell's enthusiasm for his own country, and was far more devoted to life in the old world. He finally, however, consented to try living in his native land again, and had come that autumn to Boston.

On this programme was what afterwards became the slow movement of the "Sonata Tragica." This was the first part of that work which Mac Dowell wrote. I am not sure that he had even sketched the remaining movements. After listening to it Strong said, "Well, that is about the finest thing Mac Dowell has done yet."

The recitals were successful. His would-be admirers were for the first time able to esti-mate Mac Dowell's playing at its true worth. They appreciated his exquisite and vivid presenta-tions of his own music and were made to realize that a poet-pianist lived among them, whose gifts were not paled even by those of Paderewski himself.

At these recitals, also, Mac Dowell's pianistic limitations were made plain. His treat-ment of [Beethoven's] Moonlight Sonata, for example, was erratic, and out of all proportion. For here he tried to create tonal effects to his own liking, with material that would not stand it. In spite of certain beautiful results attained by his radical interpretation, as a whole it lacked unity and Beethovenish feeling.

. . .

Mac Dowell's playing of his own music was a revelation of its possibilities, and, to play-ers who had studied it, unexpected and startling. It was as original as the pieces themselves. As Lawrence Gilman has said, Mac Dowell's music, in form and structure, with all its exquisite del-icacy and suggestion, is clarity itself. Yet other pianists who had tried their best to give it with commensurate delicacy, suggestion, and clarity, found themselves after hearing him far at sea.

Mac Dowell prided himself on his adherence to form. "Nobody," he remarked to me, "can say my pieces and my sonatas haven't form." His playing, nevertheless, far from emphasizing form, was distinctly impressionistic. When listening to him, thoughts of form one entirely for-got; the lingering impression was of a Monet-like tone-painting. It was mystifying. Melodies oth-ers loved and learned to play on conventional lines, with definite, singing tone, and correctly subordinated accompaniment, sounded under his hands vague, far off, floating in space. Pieces clearly written, and "splendid for practice," became streams of murmuring or rushing tone. Del-icate chord-groups, like his melodies, floated in air; while those in *fortissimi* resembled nothing so much as full orchestral bursts. Who that heard him can forget their first astonishment at his marvellously fascinating renderings of the "Hexentanz," over, almost before it had begun; of the "Shadow Dance," a vaporous mass of vanishing sound; of the ethereal "Water Lily"; of the surging rolling "To the Sea"; his impetuous, virtuosic playing of the "March wind"; and his great tone-massing in the Sonatas? And who can forget their subsequent conviction that these were the inevitable, the only true renderings?

At the piano Mac Dowell was a poet-musician. He was no mere note-player, and was not and never could have been a pianist in the conventional sense of the term. He was the same teller of exquisite poems, the same impressionistic tone-painter, that he was at his desk. He made his pieces suggest their title or story so vividly that notes and manner of sounding them were entirely lost sight of. For the moment he was an improviser. He had a command over technique, pedals, and especially the *rubato*, (which he used with infinite skill,) rarely attained. And back of all was his musical and poetic nature,—the real mainspring of his playing. Few pianists, it is safe to say, have, in this last respect, been so richly endowed.

SOURCE: T. P. Currier, "Edward MacDowell: As I Knew Him," *Musical Quarterly* 1, no. 1 (January 1915): 17–51; excerpts from 21–24, 29–30.

~~~~~~~~

The critic Lawrence Gilman (1878–1939), who was MacDowell's first biographer, championed MacDowell as artist and man. In this excerpt, Gilman discerns in Mac-Dowell's music an American masculinity and a Celtic race purity, which he opposes to the decadence of Wagner and Debussy. Gilman sounds a little bit like Charles Ives, whose Concord Sonata Gilman would later praise as a masterpiece at its premiere. Eight years later, in his essay "The American Composer," Paul Rosenfeld shoved MacDowell back into a Victorian easy chair (see chapter 62).

What are the distinguishing traits, after all, of MacDowell's music? The answer is not easily given. His music is characterised by great buoyancy and freshness, by an abounding vitality, by a constantly juxtaposed tenderness and strength, by a pervading nobility of tone and feeling. It is charged with emotion, yet it is not brooding or hectic, and it is seldom intricate or recondite in its psychology. It is music curiously free from the fevers of sex. And here I do not wish to be misunderstood. This music is anything but androgynous. It is always virile, often passionate, and, in its intensest moments, full of force and vigour. But the sexual impulse which underlies it is singularly fine, strong, and controlled. The strange and burdened winds, the subtle delirium, the disorder of sense, that stir at times in the music of Wagner, Tchaikovsky, Debussy, are not to be found here. In Wagner, in certain songs by Debussy, one often feels, as Pater felt in William Morris's "King Arthur's Tomb," the tyranny of a moon which is "not tender and far-off, but close down—the sorcerer's moon, large and feverish," and the presence of a colouring that is "as of scarlet lilies"; and there is the suggestion of poison, with "a sudden bewildered sickening of life and all things."[3] In the music of MacDowell there is no hint of these matters; there is rather the infinitely touching emotion of those rare beings who are in their interior lives both passionate and shy: they know desire and sorrow, supreme ardour and enamoured tenderness; but they do not know either the languor or the dementia of eroticism; they are haunted and swept by beauty, but they are not sickened or oppressed by it. Nor is their passion mystical and detached. MacDowell in his music is full-blooded, but he is never febrile: in this (though certainly in nothing else) he is like Brahms. The passion by which he is swayed is never, in its expression, ambiguous or exotic, his sensuousness is never luscious. It is difficult to think of a single passage from which that accent upon which I have dwelt—the accent of nobility, of a certain chivalry, a certain rare and spontaneous dignity—is absent. Yet he can be, withal, wonderfully tender and deeply impassioned, with a sharpness of emotion that is beyond denial. In such songs as "Deserted" (op. 9); "Menie" (op. 34); "The Robin Sings in the Apple Tree," "The West Wind Croons in the Cedar Trees" (op. 47); "The Swan Bent Low to the Lily," "As the Gloaming Shadows Creep" (op. 56); "Constancy" (op. 58); "Fair Springtide" (op. 60); in "Lancelot and Elaine"; in "Told at Sunset," from the "Woodland Sketches"; in "An Old Love Story," from "Fireside Tales": in this music the emotion is the distinctive emotion of sex; but it is the sexual emotion known to Burns rather than to Rossetti, to Schubert rather than to Wagner.

He had the rapt and transfiguring imagination, in the presence of nature, which is the special possession of the Celt. Yet he was more than a mere landscape painter. The human drama was for him a continually moving spectacle; he was most sensitively attuned to its tragedy and its comedy,—he was never more potent, more influential, indeed, than in celebrating its events. He is at the summit of his powers, for example, in the superb pageant of heroic grief and equally heroic love which is comprised within the four movements of the "Keltic" sonata, and in the piercing sadness and the transporting tenderness of the "Dirge" in the "Indian" suite.

In its general aspect his later music is not German, or French, or Italian—its spiritual antecedents are Northern, both Celtic and Scandinavian. MacDowell had not the Promethean imagination, the magniloquent passion, that are Strauss's; his art is far less elaborate and subtle than that of such typical moderns as Debussy and d'Indy. But it has an order of beauty that is not theirs, an order of eloquence that is not theirs, a kind of poetry whose secrets they do not know; and there speaks through it and out of it an individuality that is persuasive, lovable, unique.

There is no need to attempt, at this juncture, to speculate concerning his place among the company of the greater dead; it is enough to avow the conviction that he possessed genius of a rare order, that he wrought nobly and valuably for the art of the country which he loved.

SOURCE: Lawrence Gilman, *Edward MacDowell: A Study* (New York: John Lane, 1908). Available at http://www.gutenberg.org/files/14109/14109-8.txt.

~~~~~~~

NOTES

1. The concert on November 18, 1888 included Karl Goldmark's Piano Quintette in B-flat. See Margery Morgan Lowens, "The New York Years of Edward MacDowell" (Ph.D. diss., University of Michigan, 1971): 45ff.

2. The American expatriate composer George Templeton Strong II (1856–1948) wrote music in the style of the new German school and Wagner. See chapter 32 for information about Strong's father, George Templeton Strong.

3. This quotation comes from the essay "Aesthetic Poetry," in *Appreciations* (1889), by the famous literary critic, Walter Pater (1839–1894). Pater discusses the sensuality and eroticism in William Morris's poem, "King Arthur's Tomb."

62

PAUL ROSENFELD'S MANIFESTO

FOR AMERICAN COMPOSERS

Paul Rosenfeld (1890–1946) earned his place in American music history by championing American modernist art, music, and literature in the 1920s in the new "little" magazines such as *Seven Arts,* the *Dial,* and the *New Republic.* In this selection, written at the threshold of his career, this twenty-six-year-old critic issues a manifesto for the American classical-music composer. After dismissive comments about the current generation of established figures, ranging from the radical Leo Ornstein to the conservative Daniel Gregory Mason, Rosenfeld delivers a surprisingly mature statement about the need for a "vital relationship" between artist and community. Here, Rosenfeld—like the rest of his intellectual circle, which included Waldo Frank and Randolph Bourne—reflects the influence of the pragmatist-philosopher John Dewey. Aaron Copland admired Rosenfeld and called his *An Hour with American Music* (1929) "the first significant book on the American movement."[1]

THE AMERICAN COMPOSER

For the critic of the future remains the problem of estimating to what degree residence in America influenced the art of Charles Martin Loeffler[2] and of Leo Ornstein.[3] Patent enough to our own day is the fact that, however much Boston has imprinted its character on the composer of "A Pagan Poem" and New York given the genius of Ornstein its coloring, upon neither artist has the New World come as a process of actual assimilation. For both it has rather more been an experience shaping racial directions already present. Were their work shot through with America, could we, in consequence, claim it, there would doubtless exist in our hearts greater affection for American music. The moments would be less frequent when discussion of the art as it stands at present comes perilously near boring us. We would feel a thanksgiving for the American composer that even the presence among us of an Horatio Parker cannot stimulate to any heat. Above all, we should not have to look entirely to the future for the music we want.

Certainly, it is difficult to feel enthusiasm for American music as we know it today. But, however manifest this lack of cordiality, its origin still remains mysterious. Plentiful discussion has not succeeded in satisfactorily elucidating it. Of late, the blame has been laid to the American's lack of self-confidence that impels him to take his ideas and his art modestly and gratefully from Europe, and neglect his own. Whatever truth the suggestion contains, however much the failure of "Mona" can be explained in this fashion, one cannot ascribe to any such determinant the indifference of our public to the body of American music.[4] In spite of a persistent truckling to the aesthetic arbitration of foreign societies, there still perseveres among us a favorable predisposition to work just because "it's all of it home-brewed." There is continual agitation throughout the country for the production of American compositions, and among both the native and foreign musicians in control of the situation there exists a corresponding willingness to produce such works, although this impulse is scarcely ever rewarded. The Metropolitan has courted failure after failure by mounting operas recommended chiefly by their domestic origin. The orchestral conductors have been assiduous and unsuccessful in their search for American novelties that please their audiences. The repeated offering of huge money-prizes as incentives to composition, the frequent festivals and concerts devoted solely to native talent, the never-ending discussion in the public prints of questions pertaining to Americanism in music, of remedies suggested for the present conditions, bear witness to a general wish for a grand national expression. But the wish has remained unfulfilled, and it is evident that such methods of stimulating art are unavailing. The ineffectuality of the American composer cannot be laid to the absence of desire for an American music. The appetite may be groping enough, but it is sufficiently conscious to feel intense disappointment with the response encountered up to the present moment. If the community is not certain precisely what it demands of the American composer, it feels at least, that it gets from him nothing in any degree satisfying; that for solace and refreshment and inspiration it must go to the singers of other lands. It feels that his work, a pleasant enough diversion, is useless in the graver business of life, and with infallible practicality of instinct passes it over as something unrelatable to common experience.

And such it is. The fatal shortcoming of nine-tenths [of] the music produced in America is its utter innocence of any vital relationship to the community. We have heard long the complaint that the American composer suffers from an unfamiliarity with his tools from which the superior technical education of the Old World saves the European. And it is ignorance of the use of his tools that hampers him. But by the use of tools one does not understand greater proficiency in counterpoint and orchestration. Of that he has sufficient. It is rather the knowledge of how to handle his material. If there is anything he lacks, it is the ability to draw the substance of his art from out [of] the life that surges about him. For what else but the life that the artist shares in common with his compatriots is the material from which art is molded? Physical loneliness he may feel, spiritual never; for there is in him consciousness of what swells the breasts about him, a power of translating into personal terms the common experience, a sense of linked arms and of hearts beating together in one high purpose; and out of it he shapes his art, and with it he reveals man to himself and to his fellow, nation to nation, and age to age. It does not come through an intellectual attitude. It is rather the product of that emotional relationship to life, that openness by means of which the spirit of a community, of a nation, of whole continents and ages, comes into a man, and transforms him in its own image. To Shakespeare it came, to Balzac, to Whitman; to Bach and to Brahms; in our own day [to] Andreyev[5] and to Strawinsky [sic]. Who touches them, touches people, an age. Who touches the American composers, touches neither. Listen, if you will, to the clever and often erudite scores written here. Where for an instant do they speak of the proportions of our lives, of the energy in its myriad forms hurtling about us, of the vast hopes at stake, the vast dreams laboriously coming to birth, visible to any one with eyes half shut? Where for an instant is a ray cast into the chaos by which we can recognize ourselves, our fellows, our land, become conscious of health or evil, take new strength and courage and delight? Out of them all sounds one note, one common trait. A gulf separates the composer from the community for whom he would speak. The artist lives within himself, blind to what exists without, unacquainted with the very stuff of art. It is that unsubstantial contact that has lost the greater majority of our musicians the fruits of their efforts.

Present to some extent in practically every American musician, that divorce from life can be seen operating most purely in the tragic figure of Edward MacDowell. The story of this unfortunate composer is that of an engagingly talented man, formed in Lisztian Germany, who on contact with his own land retired further and further into himself, at last with shattering completeness. The quality of his work, at its best of a sweetness marred by an everpresent suggestion of chintz, is not of the sort to arouse antagonism. The weakness lies in the spiritual direction which it reveals. Joined sometimes with a warmer, sometimes with a duller talent, one perceives variation[s] of it in all his fellow-craftsmen. That turning-away from reality toward a pallid dream-world, that sense of experience largely aesthetic, that tendency to sentimentalize objects that have succeeded in entering consciousness—deserted farms, October sunsets, bricked fire-places, Indian legends—is characteristically repeated and modified. One feels it in the preciosity of a Hadley, a Chadwick, in the poetizings of a Converse, in the denaturization of a Daniel Gregory Mason or a David Stanley Smith.[6] The impulse that set John Alden Carpenter to writing fanciful little sketches about ideas of a baby's sensations,[7] the cold and almost cynical detachment displayed in Schelling's "Symphonic Variations", the attempt of a Stillman Kelley to resurrect in his "New England Symphony" the Pilgrim Father emotion, are easily recognizable variants. The exact quality of each talent may differ; the relationship to the life of the Republic, intellectual at best, never. One composer alone stands apart from the group. Were it not for Horatio Parker, one might suppose a divorce from reality the inalienable destiny of the American composer. It is from the viewpoint of the achievements of the creator of "Hora Novissima" and "Mona" that the want of the others becomes clear. For in Dr. Parker's work, an art that unites something of the brilliance of Richard Strauss with some of the turgidity of Max Reger, there speak[s] a strength and an intensity, a sense of the actual feel of life almost absent from other American music. That the attainment of a vital contact was something of a struggle for him, much of his work attests. But, whatever its limitations, there has gone into it much of the austerity and earnestness and idealism of the New England civilization out of which he comes; and with the folk-songs of Stephen Foster it remains the one musical expression of America. If it throws into bolder relief the ineffectuality of the rest of the art, it also constitutes an earnest [sic] of what glorious things lie with the future.

It is faith that, in the final test, is wanting [in] the American composer, as it is wanting [in] the rest of us—faith in the American destiny. So much have we lacked it that consciousness of our tepidity is but slow in reaching us. We have long turned our back on our land, content with being outposts of Europe, vouchsafing America only a half-hearted interest. From the cowardice of withholding ourselves we must now part. It is something more than an interest, half-hearted or full, that is demanded of us if we cherish our salvation, personal and common. From us there is now asked the surrender [of] ourselves to her life, the gift of ourselves to her future. There is asked of us supreme faith in her, love of her, belief that her highest good is the highest good of all [the] world.

That alone can save us from sterility and sentimentalism, that alone can enable us to throw ourselves, our energy, our dreams forward, give ourselves to the nature in which we live that she may fill us with her strength. It is faith alone that can let her come in on us and make us new. We must go on where Whitman led, casting from us our past, joyously sure that where the wizard power of faith goes, there life follows after. For all of us, it is the way to fruitfulness; for the artist, the way to his art. And for the composer, once he touches the life that nature spends so prodigally here, what power! It seems as if nature were prepared to deliver into his hands all the kingdoms of the world, if he but fulfil the conditions she demands. If we have already produced the staunch genius that reveals itself in the best of Dr. Parker's art, the promise shown in the fine sense of style, the feeling for form in the work of A. Walter Kramer, in the rapidly flowering talents of many of the new generation of musicians, what cannot be expected of saner conditions? The demolition of the old rules makes way for a musical expression as crude and powerful as American nature itself. The efflorescence of the new Russian, the new French art, music written out of a return to nature, music that sounds as if the national genius hurled itself into a Strawinsky or a Ravel, and poured itself out through their pens, comes as a trumpet-call to all [who] would dare afresh. The music of all races and all ages, from that of Asia to the songs of our negroes and aborigines, fierce rhythms of our rag-time, are before us, to teach, and to be used. Over the country, leaping from town to town, ramifying miraculously, spreads a love of music, blazing the path for the song of democracy. But let our composers write over their art the words in which Strawinsky made his proud apology for "Le Sacre du Printemps":—"I have performed an act of faith," and a great national music will be ours.

SOURCE: Paul L. Rosenfeld, "The American Composer," *Seven Arts* 1 (November 1916): 89–94.

~~~~~~~

NOTES

1.   Aaron Copland, "Conversation with Edward T. Cone" (1967), as cited in *Aaron Copland: A Reader: Selected Writings: 1923–1972*, ed. Richard Kostelanetz (New York: Routledge, 2004): 352.

2. Charles Martin Loeffler (1861–1935), an Alsatian-born composer, emigrated to the United States in 1881. He was a violinist for the Boston Symphony Orchestra.

3. Leo Ornstein (1893–2002) was a famous Russian-born pianist and the composer of a modernist piano piece, *Wild Men's Dance* (1913).

4. Horatio Parker (1863–1919) composed the opera *Mona* (1910).

5. Leonid Andreyev, a nineteenth-century Russian writer.

6. Here lumped together are a group of stylistically conservative composers: Henry Hadley (1871–1937) was a composer and founder of the San Francisco Symphony; for Chadwick, see chapter 56; Frederick Converse (1871–1940) was active in Boston; Daniel Gregory Mason (1873–1953), today the most prominent of this group, was on the faculty at Columbia University and was regarded as a stylistic and social conservative; David Stanley Smith (1877–1949) was on the faculty of Yale.

7. *Adventures in a Perambulator* (1914) was the first orchestral work of John Alden Carpenter (1876–1951).

63

$\mathcal{F}$ROM THE WRITINGS OF CHARLES IVES

The great composer Charles Ives (1874–1954) left a significant body of powerful writing. Commentaries on several works include a book to partner a piece: *Essays before a Sonata*, as a companion to *Sonata no. 2 for Piano: Concord, Mass., 1840–1860*. His autobiographical memoirs (*Memos*), which often describe the fascinating experiential origins of many of his compositions, also expose his psychological vulnerabilities and prejudices. Although he more or less stopped composing by 1920, Ives lived long enough to witness the remarkable shift in critical opinion about the merits of his work.

These excerpts represent recurrent themes in Ives's writing, including the composer's admiration for Ralph Waldo Emerson as a philosophical model for transcendental modernism. Ives plumbed everyday musical experience as a source for experimentation. He talked about the humanity of vernacular music making in a community, ranging from ragtime to gospel hymns. He used inflammatory, gendered language to express disapproval of almost anything or anybody—ranging from Bolsheviks to conventional musicians and critics around 1900–1920 who didn't like his work or wouldn't if they knew it, so he (for the most part, correctly) thought.

The first selection telescopes two portions from the long "Emerson" chapter in Essays
before a Sonata. *The first opens the essay, the second closes its second section. Ives
quotes Emerson's essay "Circles" and links Emerson to his own musical spirituality.
The comment about "substance" versus "manner" is an Ivesian motto, and the comparison between Emerson and Beethoven relates to Ives's quotations from Beethoven's*
Fifth Symphony in the Concord Sonata. *The selection also foreshadows certain words
and phrases that appear in other compositions, such as the chamber piece "The Seer"
and the song "Walking," whose words, which Ives wrote, include references to autumn colors and sumac. His description of a musical epiphany reads like an account
of a religious experience.*

It has seemed to the writer that Emerson is greater—his identity more complete, perhaps—in
the realms of revelation—natural disclosure—than in those of poetry, philosophy, or prophecy.
Though a great poet and prophet, he is greater, possibly, as an invader of the unknown—
America's deepest explorer of the spiritual immensities,—a seer painting his discoveries in
masses and with any color that may lie at hand—cosmic, religious, human, even sensuous; a
recorder freely describing the inevitable struggle in the soul's uprise—perceiving from this inward source alone that every "ultimate fact is only the first of a new series"; a discoverer, whose
heart knows, with Voltaire, "that man seriously reflects when left alone," and would then discover, if he can, that "wondrous chain which links the heavens with earth—the world of beings
subject to one law." In his reflections Emerson, unlike Plato, is not afraid to ride Arion's Dol-
phin, and to go wherever he is carried—to Parnassus or to "Musketaquid."[1]
. . .
Emerson seems to use the great definite interests of humanity to express the greater, indefinite,
spiritual values—to fulfill what he can in his realms of revelation. Thus, it seems that so close a
relation exists between his content and expression, his substance and manner, that if he were
more definite in the latter he would lose power in the former. Perhaps some of those occasional
flashes would have been unexpressed—flashes that have gone down through the world and will
flame on through the ages—flashes that approach as near the divine as Beethoven in his most
inspired moments—flashes of transcendent beauty, of such universal import, that they may
bring, of a sudden, some intimate personal experience, and produce the same indescribable
effect that comes in rare instances, to men, from some common sensation.

In the early morning of a Memorial Day, a boy is awakened by martial music—a village
band is marching down the street—and as the strains of Reeves' majestic Seventh Regiment
March[2] come nearer and nearer, he seems of a sudden translated—a moment of vivid power
comes, a consciousness of material nobility—an exultant something gleaming with the possibilities of this life—an assurance that nothing is impossible, and that the whole world lies at his
feet. But, as the band turns the corner, at the soldiers' monument, and the march steps of the
Grand Army become fainter and fainter, the boy's vision slowly vanishes—his "world" becomes
less and less probable—but the experience ever lies within him in its reality.

Later in life, the same boy hears the Sabbath morning bell ringing out from the white
steeple at the "[Danbury town] Center," and as it draws him to it, through the autumn fields of
sumac and asters, a Gospel hymn of simple devotion comes out to him—"There's a wideness in
God's mercy"[3]—an instant suggestion of that Memorial Day morning comes—but the moment
is of deeper import—there is no personal exultation—no intimate world vision—no magnified

personal hope—and in their place a profound sense of a spiritual truth—a sin within reach of forgiveness. And as the hymn voices die away, there lies at his feet—not the world, but the figure of the Saviour—he sees an unfathomable courage—an immortality for the lowest—the vastness in humility, the kindness of the human heart, man's noblest strength—and he knows that God is nothing—nothing but love!

Whence cometh the wonder of a moment? From sources we know not. But we do know that from obscurity, and from this higher Orpheus come measures of sphere melodies flowing in wild, native tones, ravaging the souls of men, flowing now with thousand-fold accompaniments and rich symphonies through all our hearts; modulating and divinely leading them.[4]

SOURCE: Charles Ives, *Essays Before a Sonata* in Howard Boatwright ed., *Essays Before a Sonata, The Majority, and Other Writings* (New York: W. W. Norton & Co., 1961. Paperback edition 1970): 11–12, 29–30.

~~~~~~~~~

This iconic passage from Memos *alludes to the many revival hymns that Ives used for quotations and paraphrases in his music. Ives's impressionistic portrait of music at a camp meeting fits into the nineteenth-century literary tradition of describing musical evangelism in similar scenes, and he subtitled the Symphony no. 3 "The Camp Meeting" (1901–1904; revised 1908–1911). Ives used hymn tunes in settings that function as his own idiosyncratic approach to the concert spiritual, which was just emerging as a separate genre in the early 1900s.*

Once a nice young man (his musical sense having been limited by three years' intensive study at the Boston Conservatory) said to Father, "How can you stand it to hear old John Bell (the best stone-mason in town) sing?" (as he used to at Camp Meetings) Father said, "He is a supreme musician." The young man (nice and educated) was horrified—"Why, he sings off the key, the wrong notes, and everything—and that horrible, raucous voice—and he bellows out and hits notes no one else does—it's awful!" Father said, "Watch him closely and reverently, look into his face and hear the music of the ages. Don't pay too much attention to the sounds—for if you do, you may miss the music. You won't get a wild, heroic ride to heaven on pretty little sounds."

I remember, when I was a boy—at the outdoor Camp Meeting services in Redding, all the farmers, their families, and field hands, for miles around, would come afoot or in their farm wagons. I remember how the great waves of sound used to come through the trees—when things like "Beulah Land," "Woodworth," "Nearer My God to Thee," "The Shining Shore," "Nettleton," "In the Sweet Bye and Bye" and the like were sung by thousands of "let out" souls. The music notes and words on paper were about as much like what they "were" (at those moments) as the monogram on a man's necktie may be like his face. Father, who led the singing, sometimes with his cornet or his voice, sometimes with both voice and arms, and sometimes in the quieter hymns with a French horn or violin, would always encourage the people to sing their own way. Most of them knew the words and music (theirs) by heart, and sang it that way. If they threw the poet or the composer around a bit, so much the better for the poetry and the music.

There was power and exaltation in these great enclaves of sound from humanity. I've heard the same hymns played by nice celebrated organists and sung by highly-known singers in beautifully upholstered churches, and in the process everything in the music was emasculated—precise (usually too fast) even time—"ta ta" down-left-right-up—pretty voices etc. They take a mountain and make a sponge cake [out] of it, and sometimes, as a result, one of these commercialized travelers gets a nice job at the Metropolitan. Today apparently even the Camp Meetings are getting easy-bodied and commercialized. There are not many more of them here in the east, and what is told of some of those that survive, such as [the evangelist] Amy McPherson & Co., seems but a form of easy entertainment and silk cushions—far different from the days of the "stone-fielders."

SOURCE: Charles E. Ives, *Memos* ed. John Kirkpatrick (New York: W. W. Norton & Co., 1972): 132–133. This selection and others following do not include Kirkpatrick's notes.

~~~~~~~~~

This description of "In the Inn," the second movement of Piano Sonata no. 1, points to the importance of ragtime as a source for Ives's rhythmic inventiveness.

The second movement ["In the Inn"] is one of the several ragtime dances which have been used in whole or in part in several things (and some of the same strains are used in part in several). Some of them started as far back as George Felsberg's reign in "Poli's." George could read a newspaper and play the piano better than some pianists could play the piano without any newspaper at all. When I was in college, I used to go down there and "spell him" a little if he wanted to go out for five minutes and get a glass of beer, or a dozen glasses. There were black-faced comedians then, ragging their songs. I had even heard the same thing at the Danbury Fair before coming to New Haven, which must have been before 1892. One song I remember hearing, while I was at the Hopkins Grammar School in 1893 and 94, and this is the song:[5]

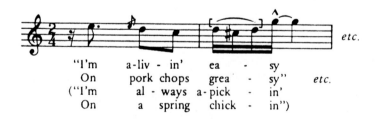

throwing the accent on the off-beat and holding over—a thing that so many people nowadays think was not done until jazz came along. I remember playing this at Poli's.

If one gets the feeling, or shall I say the bad habit, of these shifts and lilting accents, it seems to offer other basic things not used now (or used very little) in music of even beats and accents—(it will naturally start other rhythmic habits, perhaps leading into something of value)—at least it seems so to me. Even in the old brass-band days, there was a swinging into off-beats, shifted accents, etc.—and these ragtime pieces, written from about that time until ten or fifteen years ago, were but working out different combinations or rhythms that these began to suggest. For instance, if, in a few measures in a 2/4 time, the second beat is not struck and the 16th-note before the second beat is accented, other combinations of after-beats and beats and minus-beats etc. suggest themselves.

In one of the scherzo movements of the *First Piano Sonata,* ragging combinations of fives, twos, and sevens are tried out.

SOURCE: Charles E. Ives, *Memos* ed. John Kirkpatrick (New York: W. W. Norton & Co., 1972): 56–57.

Ives's Second String Quartet has many marginal notes in the manuscript corresponding to material in Memos. *The excerpt from* Memos *is followed by selected marginal notes transcribed from facsimile copies of the manuscript, thus connecting his words with his music.*

A better *Second String Quartet* was written in 1911, and is one of the best things I have, but the old ladies (male and female) don't like it anywhere at all. It makes them mad, etc. . . . About that time (after Bass Brigham's call at 70 West 11th Street), and even before, it used to come over me—especially after coming from some of those nice Kneisel Quartet concerts—that music had been, and still was, too much of an emasculated art.[6] Too much of what was easy and usual to play, and to hear was called beautiful, etc.—the same old even-vibration, Sybaritic apron strings, keeping music too much tied to the old ladies. The string quartet music got more and more weak, trite, and effeminate. After one of the Kneisel Quartet concerts in the old Mendelssohn Hall, I started a string quartet score, half mad, and half in fun, and half to try out, practice, and have some fun with making those men fiddlers get up and do something like men. The set of three pieces for string quartet called: I. Four Men Have Discussions, Conversations, II. Arguments and Fights, III. Contemplation—was done then. Only a part of a movement was copied out in parts and tried over (at Tam's one day)—it made all the men rather mad. I didn't blame them—it was very hard to play—but now it wouldn't cause so much trouble.

SOURCE: Charles E. Ives, *Memos* ed. John Kirkpatrick (New York: W. W. Norton & Co., 1972): 73–74.

Reproduced below are some notes inserted on margins and underneath sections of music in sketches for the Second String Quartet, ca. 1911–1914. "Rollo" is the name of a fictional little boy in a series of mid-nineteenth-century children's books by Jacob Abbott, and Ives adopted Rollo as a synonym for effeminacy and dutifulness.

CONVERSATIONS

I. DISCUSSIONS

[page 1, note on right side of the margin] 4 men have some discussions about some matters[,] what matters. Rollo? Not? Same Thing every time. Rollo Finck[7]

[note on the bottom of the page] SQ for 4 men—who converse, discuss, argue in re "Politick," fight, shake hands, shut up—then walk up the mountain side to view the firmament!

[page 5, note on right side of the margin] Hard Rollo This is music for men to play—not the Lady-bird Kneisel Q[uartet].

[mm. 99–100] "Keyes takes exception on that point" So do the others. Each has his say [mm. 102–4] But on this they all say Eyah!

[page 6, mm. 125–29] "I repeat again, what I, Sir, mean in those few words"

[m. 129] "enough discussions for us!"

II. ARGUMENTS

[page 7, mm. 17–19] saying the same thing over & over & louder & louder ain't arguing. DKE [Delta Kappa Epsilon].

[m. 32, a cadenza] Andante Emasculata, pretty tone, Ladies!

[m. 35] rit. ad sweetota

[m. 36] fff Allegro confisto Cut it out! Rollo!

[m. 37] andante emasculata

[m. 40] largo sweetota

[page 8, mm. 59–64] Prof. M. Stop. Too hard to play, *so it just can't* be good music, Rollo!

[m. 66] Beat time Rollo. D.L.R. up! Prof. M beat too.

[page 9, m. 73] Join us again Prof. M "all in key of C. you can? nice and pretty, Rollo"

[mm. 74–75] But my job is hard Rollo[.] frog? Jumps

[m. 77] now "when I started this argument, I said?["]

[m. 78] con fuoco (all mad!)

[page 10, m. 91] what's yours??

[m. 93] what's yours? B—?

[m. 109] Andante con?

[m. 110] Allegro confistaswat?

SOURCE: Sketches for the Second String Quartet, Yale Music Library, New Haven, Connecticut. Read with the help of but not entirely identical to John Kirkpatrick, ed., *A Temporary Mimeographed Catalogue of the Music Manuscripts and Related Materials of Charles Edward Ives 1874–1954* (New Haven, Conn.: Yale School of Music, 1960): 60.

~~~~~~~~~

NOTES

Notes 1–4 were adapted and modified from Howard Boatwright, ed., Charles E. Ives: Essays before a Sonata, The Majority, and Other Writings *(New York: Norton, 1970).*

1. "Musketaquid" refers to "Grass-ground River," an Indian name for the Concord River.
2. The piece in question is actually the "Second Connecticut National Guard March."
3. Text by Frederick William Faber, 1862; the tune is probably by John Zundel, 1870.
4. This is paraphrased from a passage in Thomas Carlyle's *Sartor Resartus; The Life and Opinions of Herr Teufelsdröckh,* a work mixing philosophical speculation with satire. Emerson's enthusiasm for the book helped its American reception.
5. Kirkpatrick notes that Ives did not go to Hopkins Grammar School until spring, 1893. Complicating this date, however, is the date of the "coon" song quoted here. "I'm livin' easy" was written by the African-American Composer Irving Jones (ca. 1874–1932) and published in New York: F. A. Mills, 1899.
6. The Kneisel String Quartet, formed in 1885 by the violinist Franz Kneisel (1865–1926), who became concertmaster of the Boston Symphony Orchestra, was the first important professional string quartet in the United States.
7. This refers to the well-known music critic for the *New York Evening Post,* Henry Finck (1854–1926).

64

Frédéric Louis Ritter Looks for the "People's Song"

Music in America (1883), the first full-length study of the subject, including folk, popular, and classical music, was written by the composer and Alsatian émigré Frédéric Louis Ritter (1834–1891) at the height of his career as a professor of music and the director of the School of Music at Vassar College. As a historian—and owner of a major musical library, which he brought with him from Strasbourg, France[1]—Ritter excelled in detailed accounts of the spread of European classical music through civic orchestras, touring opera companies, and German *Musikverein,* or choral societies. In contrast, he dismissed American popular songs, especially those composed for the minstrel stage or the parlor. His admiration for African-American spirituals notwithstanding, Ritter blamed the absence of the "people's song" on the dour culture of New England Puritans, a path that such future distinguished cultural critics as George Santayana, Alain Locke, and H. L. Mencken would follow. Mencken's famous description of Puritanism as "the haunting fear that someone, somewhere may be happy" fits right in with Ritter's diatribe against New Englanders' "gloom and repression."

CHAPTER XXII. "THE CULTIVATION OF POPULAR MUSIC"

The people's-song—"an outgrowth from the life of the people, the product of the innate artistic instinct of the people, seeking a more lofty expression than that of every-day speech for those feelings which are awakened in the soul by the varied events of life"[2]—is not to be found among the American people. The American farmer, mechanic, journeyman, stage-driver, shepherd, etc., does not sing,—unless he happens to belong to a church-choir or a singing-society: hence, the American landscape is silent and monotonous; it seems inanimate, and imparts a melancholy impression, though Nature has fashioned it beautifully. The sympathetic, refreshing, cheering, enlivening tones of the human voice are totally absent; the emotional life of the human being impressing his footprints upon the land he cultivates seems to be repressed within his bosom, or non-existent. The serious, industrious inhabitant of this beautiful land does not express his joys and sorrows in sounds; but for the bleating of sheep, the lowing of cattle, the barking of dogs, the crowing of cocks, the singing of birds,—the woods, the pastures, the farmyard, would be silent and gloomy. In an apparently taciturn, gloomy mood, the American farmer follows his plough, gathers his harvest, guards his cattle; or the mechanic sits in his shop; yet in their private life these people are not wanting in original humor and characteristic wit.

However, once in the year the landscape becomes enlivened by the sounds of human voices. Summer has come; and the "city boarder" appears on the scene, with his vulgar, arrogant, and frivolous rattle and shouting. Then the insipid, senseless, minstrel-ballad, with its ambiguous meaning and trivial musical strains, frightens the timid thrush—this sweetest of American woodland singers—from his favorite groves. If the landscape was silent and sad before, it now becomes loud and boisterous.

The American youth has no sweet, chaste, pathetic love ditties to sing in "doubtful hope" under the window of the adored one. He buys that article in the shape of a brass band: if this does not go directly to the heart, it, at any rate, can be heard for miles around. The American country girl is never caught singing during her work, happily and *naïvely*, her innocent blushes betraying the presence of the God that has put all those sweet thoughts and melodies into her heart. Such music she does not consider fashionable. She gets her father to buy her a "pianner" in order to be able to strum on it the ballads the city-folks sing.

It is astonishing how such shallow ware quickly finds its way to the remotest corners of this wide country. One summer, during the time Offenbach's "Grande Duchesse de Gerolstein"[3] was popular in New York, we went to spend the summer in one of the loveliest, most beautiful corners of the —— Mountains,—as far away from the piano or cabinet-organ as possible. Great was our astonishment when, on arriving at the place we had selected for our summer stay, we were greeted by a rustic laborer's little daughter about eight years old, who rushed out of the house singing incorrectly the melody of "Le Sabre de mon père."[4] The place, though one of the most romantic in the mountain range, at once lost half of its sylvan beauty for us. The vulgar "sabre de mon père" crossed the brook, climbed the trees, drove the cattle home, sat on the haywagon, chased the birds: in fine, it was in the air of the mountains. It needed little persuasion for us to leave the place at once; the only consideration that determined us to stay was the apprehension of possibly meeting at the next house, not only "Le Sabre," but also "Shoo fly, don't bother me,"[5] "The Babies in our Block,"[6] or "Let me kiss him for his Mother,"[7] etc. Thus it seems that the American country people are not in the possession of deep emotional power; at least, they seem to be too conscious to allow that natural element of human feeling any outward

Three musicians entertaining an outing at Skyland in 1895. Skyland was a summer resort now part of Shenandoah National Park, Virginia.

expression. A happy, pure song is the emanation of content and deep feeling: it beautifies and embellishes the most modest home; it impresses upon the human heart and mind, by means of a wonderful power of association, all that is sweetest, happiest, and purest during a child's life at home: and the cheerful or pathetic strains that may have struck the fancy of childhood impress upon the mind of the human wanderer a remembrance of home and its happy scenes, with stronger and clearer touches than the brush of the cleverest painter is able to convey to his canvas.

. . .

From the hearts of such people [the New England Puritans], in whose eyes an innocent smile, a merry laugh, was considered a sin, no *naïve*, cheerful, sweet melody could possibly spring. This gloom and repression, excluding all innocent cheer and joy from the hearts of the people, have remained the fundamental traits of the majority of New-Englanders up to our day. Documents are numerous, by means of which we are enabled to trace the historical steps of the American colonist's intellectual life. His emotional life was stifled and suppressed: therefore there are no folk-poetry and no folk-songs in America; unless we consider those little glees, sung to sacred words, written by psalm-tune composers since the time of W. Billings, as such. To be sure, during the War of Independence attempts were made at writing patriotic songs: Billings himself . . . tried his hand at it quite successfully; but none of these early attempts made any lasting impression on the people. When the war was over, the war-songs sunk into oblivion: the grotesque, foolishly skipping "Yankee Doodle"—and history designates this as of foreign growth—had jostled them all out of existence. The fact that a people of such innate, exasperating seriousness, at times bordering on gloom, has accepted a melody like "Yankee Doodle" as the emotional expression of their patriotic feeling, is a psychological problem. If a prize had been offered, open to competition among all the musicians of this globe, for the most melodiously insignificant, shallow, and trivial song, the author of "Yankee Doodle" surely would have received the distinguished award. The proverb "Les extrêmes se touchent" has never found a better application in the world's history.

SOURCE: Frédéric Louis Ritter, *Music in America* (New York: Scribner's, 1884): 385–90.

~~~~~~~~~

NOTES

1.   The contents of Ritter's library are available at www.library.tufts.edu/tisch/berger/Ritter.
2.   Ritter's *Student's History of Music.*
3.   In the summer of 1867, Jacques Offenbach's opéra bouffe *La Grande Duchesse de Gérolstein* was performed at the French Theatre in New York.
4.   "Voici le sabre de mon père" is from *La Grande Duchesse de Gérolstein.*
5.   A song popularized by Dan Bryant's Minstrels in the 1870s.
6.   An Irish ethnic song (words, Dave Braham; music, Edward Harrigan) which was introduced in the musical *The Mulligan Guard Ball* (1879).
7.   "Let Me Kiss Him for His Mother" was a parlor song published in 1859.

65

FRANCES DENSMORE AND THE DOCUMENTATION

OF AMERICAN INDIAN SONGS AND POETRY

Frances Densmore (1867–1957) represents the second generation of American folk-lorists and musical anthropologists, following those in the 1880s whose scholarship on Native American tribes founded American anthropology. With the formal establishment of the Bureau of American Ethnology (1879), the field gained a powerful institutional base.[1] Even so, the perspective of the bureau toward Indian "savages" reflected federal policies of control and management.[2] But individual researchers, such as Alice Fletcher and her Native American colleague Francis La Flesche, offered other models, and furthermore, by the time Densmore began her career, some policies had changed; the curriculum in federally controlled schools no longer excluded Indian culture. Densmore's cultural empathy is reflected in the sensitive commentaries in her scholarship as well as in her influential overview volume, *The American Indians and Their Music* (1926), written for the general public.

From 1907 through 1957, Densmore produced approximately 3,500 field recordings of traditional music from at least 76 different North American Indian tribes. In addition to the Frances Densmore Collection at the Smithsonian Institution, her field recordings are still available through the American Folklife Center and through a project at the Cognitive and Systematic Musicology Laboratory at Ohio State University, which is dedicated to making both transcriptions and music available online.

Densmore began her career working with the Chippewa, located in Minnesota, the state where she was born, publishing two books between 1910 and 1913 on their music. In the series Folk Recordings Selected from the Archive of Folk Culture, tape L22 contains six "dream songs," four "war songs," three "songs used in the treatment of the sick," six "songs of the Midewiwin," seven "love songs," and four "miscellaneous songs." Even the very small sample in this chapter of lyrics from two tribes reveals the power of Native American song.

DREAM SONG (L22 A1) "ONE WIND"

This is evidently a dream song, the words referring to the dream in which it was received. The song was recorded at Waba' ciñg, Minnesota, in 1909 by Ki' miwûn (Rainy), a [man] of middle age who was prominent in the tribal councils.

One

Wind,

I am master of it.

DREAM SONG (L22 A4) "SONG OF THE THUNDERS"

In this song the dreamer feels himself carried through the air. . . .
    "The second [of] three dream songs were recorded by Ga' gandac' (One whose sails are driven by the wind), who was commonly known by his English name, George Walters. He was a man of middle age, living at White Earth, Minnesota, and was a prominent singer at all tribal gatherings. His songs were recorded *circa* 1908."

Sometimes

I go about pitying

myself,

while I am carried by the wind

across the sky.

LOVE SONG (AFS L22, B11) "WORK STEADILY"

Many of the Chippewa love songs can be sung by either a man or a woman but this is a woman's song. It was recorded by Maiñ' gans (Little Wolf) at White Earth, about 1908. "The tempo is slow, as in a majority of Chippewa love songs, the fourth above the keynote is prominent and the melody has a peculiar, pleading quality."

Be very careful

to work steadily;

I am afraid they will take you

away from me.

SOURCE: *Songs of the Chippewa*, recorded and edited by Frances Densmore, AAFS L22 (Washington, D.C.: Archive of American Folk Song): 6–7, 17.

<hr>

SONGS OF THE SIOUX

INTRODUCTION

The 27 Sioux songs on this record were selected from a total of 340 songs recorded by the writer in a study of Sioux music conducted for the Bureau of American Ethnology. They represent the several classes of songs and show the connection between music and various tribal customs.

The study of Sioux music was begun in July 1911 on the Sisseton reservation in the northeastern part of South Dakota. Central Indians from this locality had recently attended a gathering of Chippewa in Minnesota where they had met the writer and had become acquainted with her work by talking with the Chippewa who had recorded songs. They were favorably impressed and commended the work to their friends on returning home. Thus she did not go among the Sioux as a stranger.

SONGS OF THE SUN DANCE

The element of physical pain which ennobled this ceremony in the mind of the Indian has over-shadowed the ceremony's significance in the mind of the white man. The Indian endured that pain in fulfillment of a vow made to Wakan'tanka (Great Spirit) in time of anxiety or danger, generally when on the warpath. The Sun Dance was held annually by the Sioux, and vows made during the year were fulfilled at that time. Chased-by-Bears, an informant on the subject, told of meeting a hostile Arikaree Indian far from home. He knew that his life was in danger and prayed to Wakan'tanka, saying, "If you will let me kill this man and capture his horse with this lariat, I will give you my flesh at the next Sun Dance." He returned safely and carried the lariat when suspended by the flesh of his right shoulder at the next Sun Dance. Such were the vows of all who took part in the Sun Dance.

OPENING PRAYER OF THE SUN DANCE (L23 A3)

After the opening dance the Intercessor sang the following prayer while all the people listened with reverence. This was recorded by Red Bird at Fort Yates, N[orth] Dak[ota], in 1911. At the age of 24 he took part in the Sun Dance, receiving 100 cuts on his arms in fulfillment of a vow.

Frances Densmore and Mountain Chief (Blackfoot), March 1916 at a recording session, Smithsonian Institution.

Grandfather,

a voice I am going to send,

hear me.

All over the universe

a voice I am going to send.

Hear me grandfather,

I will live,

I have said it.

SOURCE: *Songs of the Sioux from the Archive of Folk Song*, recorded and edited by Frances Densmore (Washington, D.C.: Library of Congress, 1951): 4–5. Also cited with commentary and a full transcription of the music in Victoria Lindsay Levine, *Writing American Indian Music: Historic Transcriptions, Notations, and Arrangements*, vol. 11 of *Music in the United States* (Middleton, Wis.: A-R Editions, 2002): 69–70.

~~~~~~~~

NOTES

1. The Bureau of American Ethnology published its first article on Native American music by 1887.
2. The perspective of the Bureau of American Ethnology includes this statement from the introductory section of the first annual report in 1881:

     In pursuing these ethnographic investigations it has been the endeavor as far as possible to produce results that would be of practical value in the administration of Indian affairs, and for this purpose especial attention has been paid to vital statistics, to the discovery of linguistic affinities, the progress made by Indians toward civilization, and the causes and remedies for the inevitable conflict that arises from the spread of civilization over a region previously inhabited by savages.

   See http://gallica.bnf.fr/Catalogue/noticesInd/FRBNF37572002.htm for copies of all annual reports of the Bureau of American Ethnology.

$\mathcal{A}$ SIDEBAR INTO NATIONAL CULTURAL POLICY

The Federal Cylinder Project

Many pioneering American folklorists and fledgling ethnographers produced cylinder recordings of Native American music. In 1979, the American Folklife Center began a special program to share its holdings with the people who created them. Alan Jabbour, who was the first director of the American Folklife Center from 1976 to 1999, discusses the Federal Cylinder Project/Documentary Cycle as an early example of "cultural repatriation." The term "cylinder" refers to the pre-disk recording object that was played on the earliest Edison recording machines; and "project" refers to more than 10,000 recordings of Native American music, the earliest from the 1800s, which were shared with the descendants of the original informants (both familial and tribal) many decades later.

THE FEDERAL CYLINDER PROJECT AND
THE DOCUMENTARY CYCLE

The Center began a third research project in 1979 that proved one of the most ambitious and challenging it has undertaken. Though all Center projects have increased the collections of the Archive of Folk Culture, the Federal Cylinder Project was the first to be based on existing Archive collections. The Archive over the decades had received many wax cylinder recordings of ethnographic material documented in the field from 1890 through the 1930s. Indeed, it had received so many that the Library's Recording Laboratory had developed a special expertise in the engineering challenge of copying them. Some had been copied onto disc in the 1930s and 1940s, and more were copied in the magnetic-tape era beginning in the 1950s.

But many of the over ten thousand wax cylinders and cylinder-based recordings in the Archive had never been copied for preservation and access. As the decades passed, it became apparent that the survival of the cylinders was imperiled. Not only were they extremely fragile, but they were made of emulsions that, in the fullness of time, tended to separate. Oils exuded into a film on the surface, where they attracted molds and other external perils. What was needed was an intensive and comprehensive effort to preserve them.

The time-consuming engineering required for preserving cylinders was going to be expensive. But equally time-consuming and expensive would be the cost of organizing and cataloging the collections to make them useful for research. In an extreme example of the cataloging challenge, one box of cylinders in the Archive contained absolutely no information except the large letters "ESKIMO" scrawled on the box; it turned out to contain the earliest field recordings made in central Africa.

The solution to the twin challenges of finding resources for preservation and cataloging lay in a third challenge. Sometime in the 1970s there was a sudden increase in American Indian visitors and correspondents attracted by the Archive's reputation as a national repository for American Indian music and lore. Most inquirers were of the younger generation; all were seeking their cultural heritage. Perhaps three-fourths of the cylinder recordings contained American Indian music and lore. Since they were recorded between 1890 (Jesse Walter Fewkes's cylinders of the Passamaquoddy Indians in Calais, Maine, the earliest field recordings anywhere) and the early 1940s, they represented the earliest recorded information about Indian tribal culture available from any source. More than that—they represented, for young Indian researchers, somebody's grandfather or great grandmother. The third challenge, then, was to return copies of these unique cultural resources to the tribal communities whence they came.

The Center devised a three-pronged plan for preserving, cataloging, and disseminating the cylinders; then it began to seek funding. Support came initially from the Bureau of Indian Affairs and the L. J. and Mary C. Skaggs Foundation. Then, as the project gained momentum and attention, the Ford Foundation weighed in with a generous grant of over $100,000. Project staff changed over a multi-year period, but Erika Brady, Judith A. Gray, Maria La Vigna, Dorothy Sara Lee, Edwin J. Schupman, and Ronald Walcott can be named as key contributors to the effort. Thomas Vennum of the Smithsonian Institution directed the project in its earlier stage, followed by Dorothy Sara Lee and Judith Gray. The early participation of the Smithsonian in planning and administering the project only partially accounts for the embracing title of the Federal Cylinder Project. Just as important in determining the title was the resolution to preserve and disseminate not only the Library's ethnographic cylinders but other smaller collections at the Smithsonian's National Anthropological Archives, the National Archives, and certain installations within the National Park Service.

The Federal Cylinder Project may have been the Center's most expensive project, and it was certainly among its most successful. Yet it is not finished. Though all the wax cylinders were preserved by duplicating them onto tape, only about three-fourths were cataloged, and copies of perhaps two-thirds were returned to Indian communities. Paradoxically, the interest generated by the project led to new batches of cylinder recordings being sent to the Library for copying. Thus it became a paradigm for those preservation projects for which the work is never done.

Yet it can fairly claim to have been a trail-blazing effort. A few other institutions with wax cylinder collections, notably the Lowie Museum of Anthropology (subsequently renamed the Hearst Museum) at the University of California-Berkeley and Indiana University's Archives of Traditional Music, emulated the design of the project in their own initiatives. The idea of sharing copies of collections with the originating communities led to many special successes.

It is noteworthy that the Center's experiment in sharing collections preceded by several years the Native American Graves Protection and Repatriation Act (NAGPRA), which has focused on museum collections. Whether because documents, unlike artifacts, can reside in more than one place through duplication, or because the Federal Cylinder Project embraced from the start the idea of cultural consultation with Indian communities, the Federal Cylinder Project was remarkably free of the controversy and turmoil that were to haunt some museums over the years.

THE DOCUMENTARY CYCLE

The return of the wax cylinder recordings to the communities whence they came dramatizes a process that underpins much of the Center's work with cultural documentation. Among the important cultural developments of the twentieth century has been the emergence of documentation, not only as a method of recording the cultural process, but as an actual part of the cultural process itself. We see this on every hand: photograph albums in the home, video documentation of weddings, recordings of baby's first word, the firefly effect of flashbulbs from the stadium during cultural events like the Olympics. The documentary process is an affirmation of the importance of the event, which calls forth the impulse to capture it for re-evocation later.

An important attendant feature of the documentary process is the emergence of the archive, not simply as a repository, but as a critical link in the "documentary cycle." That cycle begins with documentation, continues with preservation of the documentation, and concludes by recycling documents back into cultural use. The archive may function simply in the second stage—preserving the documents—but may also participate in the initial creation and again in the third-stage recycling. When it does this, the archive is not simply a way-station but a kind of cultural engine that can drive the documentary cycle through all its stages.

An event in the course of the Federal Cylinder Project illustrates the documentary cycle nicely. I traveled to Macy, Nebraska, to make a proposal to the Omaha Tribal Council. The Center had copied onto tape a large collection of wax cylinders recorded in the late nineteenth and early twentieth centuries by Alice Fletcher and Francis La Flesche, and wished to give a copy to the Omaha community. Since the acoustic quality of the cylinders was particularly good for the era, the Center also proposed to produce a published recording selected from the collection—the resulting publication was called OMAHA INDIAN MUSIC: HISTORIC RECORDINGS FROM THE FLETCHER/LA FLESCHE COLLECTION (1985).

The council was supportive but concerned that nothing regarded as secret or sacred be published. They referred me to an Omaha elder, John Turner, a singer familiar with the older traditions. We set up in the Tribal Administration Building, and I began playing cassette copies of the cylinder recordings, while recording his comments on another tape recorder. As he listened, explicated, cautioned, and offered a few of his own renditions, a crowd of young people quietly gathered to listen. Years later, as I listen to the tape we made, I hear Omaha singers from the turn of the century; John Turner, who was born about the time they sang, listening, talking, and singing in response; the younger generation of Omaha occasionally commenting or laughing in response to their elder guide; and myself—all speaking side by side on the same tape.

SOURCE: "The Federal Cylinder Project and the Documentary Cycle," in Alan Jabbour, "The American Folklife Center: A Twenty-Year Retrospective, Part 2," *American Folklife Center News* 18, nos. 3–4 (Summer–Fall 1996): 5–8. Available at http://www.loc.gov/folklife/news/Sum-Fall96.txt.

67

CHARLES K. HARRIS ON WRITING HITS

FOR TIN PAN ALLEY

During the 1880s and 1890s, the numerous publishing houses and music stores making, buying, and selling popular music in lower Manhattan were known collectively as Tin Pan Alley. In 1892, Charles K. Harris (1865–1930) conquered Tin Pan Alley with the success of a sentimental ballad (allegedly) based on an anecdote "from real life." "After the Ball" used the lilting rhythms of the waltz to dance its way into American parlors. Harris loved the music business, and his description of the action in Tin Pan Alley makes it sound like a racetrack. Publishers and their song pluggers (Irving Berlin and George Gershwin both paid their dues in this occupation) jockeyed for good professional singers or, even better, celebrity-singers who could get the material heard in New York and perhaps take it on the road. Harris himself was indebted to May Irwin, the vaudeville star who delivered "After the Ball" to the public in 1892, even before John Philip Sousa made an arrangement for his band.

Harris claims that profits from the song's sales brought him $25,000 a week in the mid-1890s. His list of hits from his rivals suggests his respect for their achievements, as well as his own.

My youngest sister, Ada, then about seventeen, had cultivated the friendship of a young girl living in Chicago, who often visited us in Milwaukee. It was on one of those occasions that my sister received an invitation to attend a ball to be given by a club presided over by her Chicago chum. The task of escorting my sister to Chicago was mine by assignment. Arriving two hours later in Chicago, we were put up in the home of Ada's friend. The ball was to take place that same evening. It was in the days when lamps dimly illuminated the paved streets, when surreys and carriages dotted the streets. It was the days of dancing before the great god Jazz had cracked his whip. The fox trot, two-step, tango and similar dances came some thirty years later. Couples then glided about the floor gracefully, executing the waltz, minuet, quadrille, and schottische. As a young man I had often attended balls, social soirées and the like; but that particular affair that night in Chicago will linger in my memory until I am laid away in the dreamless dust of silence. It was there that I got the inspiration for *After the Ball*, as the reader will see presently.

Let me return to it and live it over again. The ballroom was crowded, the majority of the dancers being members of the same club, all seeming to know one another. I was introduced by my hostess to a little dark-eyed Southern girl, who eventually became my wife—Miss Cora Lerhberg, of Owensboro, Kentucky—who, with her folks, had just moved to Chicago and was also a member of the club. Perhaps it was a case of love at first sight. We danced together all evening, much to my delight. Gathered in our group that night was a charming young couple, engaged to be married. Suddenly we learned that the engagement was broken. Just a lover's quarrel, I presumed at the time; but they were both too proud to acknowledge that they were in the wrong.

The ball lasted until early in the morning, and we were all leaving for our respective homes, when I noticed, just ahead of our party, waiting for his carriage, this young man escorting, not his fiancée, but another charming miss. Lover-like he probably felt that, by causing his sweetheart a pang of jealousy, she would be more willing to forgive and forget. Of course, she did not know this. She simply knew that her Harry was easily consoled and that her place was usurped by another. Tears came to her eyes, though she tried to hide them behind a smile and a careless toss of the head. On witnessing this little drama the thought came to me like a flash, "Many a heart is aching after the ball," and this was the inception of that well-known song.

When I returned to my small office the next day I was completely exhausted from the trip and the ball the previous evening, and lay down upon a sofa in my studio for relaxation before entering upon the day's work. I had rested only a few moments when an amateur singer, my tailor, Sam Doctor, rushed into my studio in great excitement and roused me from my peaceful slumber. He said he knew of a real honest-to-goodness job for me. The Wheelmen's Club, of which he was secretary, was getting up a minstrel show to be given within the next two weeks at the Academy of Music. This was due, I suppose, to Milwaukee being chosen that year as the scene of the club's annual convention, which was expected to bring to Milwaukee representatives of all other Wheelmen's Clubs throughout the United States.

Doctor told me that he would like to use in the minstrel show an entirely new song. I replied that I had just returned from Chicago, tired and sleepy, but that if he left me to myself for a few moments I would endeavor to think of an idea for him. After his departure I returned to the sofa, lay down upon it with my arms clasped behind my head, and gazed at the ceiling. There it was! It appeared as a mirage—the estranged couple of the previous night whose pride, for some reason or other, kept them apart. I immediately sprang from the sofa and in one hour's time wrote the complete lyric and music of *After the Ball*.

In doing this it was necessary for me to weave a complete story full of sentiment. I wrote of a little girl climbing upon her uncle's knee and, with child-like naïveté, asking for a story—"Why are you single, why live alone?" And then I created the situation where the uncle flashes back to the time when he saw his sweetheart in the arms of another. She tried to explain, but he would have nothing of her explanation, believing her faithless until years later, when he discovered that it was her brother who had held her. Of course, I capitalized the sentiment in the last four lines of the chorus, and out of its fabric were spun the three verses contained in that ballad.

I find that sentiment plays a large part in our lives. The most hardened character or the most cynical individual will succumb to sentiment sometime or other. In all my ballads I have purposely injected goodly doses of sentiment, and invariably the whole country paused.

So there I had my *After the Ball*. My next step was to send for my arranger, Joseph Clauder, who for the sum of ten dollars would make a piano and song orchestration so that a pianist or orchestra could play the melody by notes. Clauder came over immediately. I sat at the piano, playing by ear, with Clauder beside me. He had a blank sheet of manuscript paper and a pencil in his hand. First I sang the entire song over several times in order that he might catch the rhythm, after which he transcribed each note on paper. When he had finished this procedure, Clauder, who was an accomplished musician, played the piece over; if any of the notes were wrong, I would have him correct them. I did not ask my arranger whether he thought this new ballad would make a hit or not. He merely transcribed the notes, as a matter of course. I never dreamed that the song would be a success; I had simply promised the secretary of the Wheelmen's Club to write for him something different, and there it was.

. . .

In 1898 I visited my office in New York, on Twenty-eighth Street, and my memory will always cling around dear old Tin Pan Alley, whose soul-stirring times I often recall. It was only one block long, bounded on the East by Broadway and on the West by Sixth Avenue. What a lane of hilarious melody!—Tin-pan pianos working overtime, day and night, continuously, and I doubt if such a happy-go-lucky crowd of boys ever congregated on one block in any street before.

One of the earliest of the popular-song publishers on this street was the firm of M. Witmark & Sons. At that time the head of the firm was about twenty years of age, his brother Julius was about eighteen and Jay about fifteen. Talk about hustlers! They certainly were wonderful boys. M. Witmark, the dad of them all, had formerly been a printer owning a small printing establishment. The first song they published was *The Picture Turned To the Wall*, followed by *The Sunshine of Paradise Alley*, and many other popular songs of the day.

Just next door to this concern were two San Francisco boys who had opened up a publishing house and taken a chance in the big city. They were Broder & Schlam.

Sandwiched in between these two firms was the New York *Clipper*,[1] which was the means of bringing thousands of professional singers and actors to Tin Pan Alley.

F. A. Mills, known as Kerry Mills, a writer and publisher, was directly opposite the New York *Clipper*. He published *Rastus on Parade, Happy Days in Dixie, Whistling Rufus*, and *At a Georgia Camp Meeting*.

Next door to Mills was another song writer, Charles B. Ward, who had just gone into the publishing business with a big song-hit. There was a large canvas sign stretched across his building advertising the name of the song, *And the Band Played On*. Ward was very popular and a great many singers visited his office.

Opposite was the Harry Von Tilzer Music Publishing Company, announcing its big hit in large letters on its windows—*My Old New Hampshire Home*.

The Leo Feist Music Publishing Company also was located on that block and was plugging Abe Holzman's new instrumental hit, *Smoky Mokes*. While, not to be outdone, next door was Joseph Stern & Co., advertising *Sweet Rosy O'Grady* and *The Little Lost Child*.

Howley, Haviland & Dresser were publishing all of Paul Dresser's songs, among them *On the Banks of the Wabash*.

H. W. Petrie, too, was located in this block, publishing his own compositions, such as *I Don't Want to Play in Your Yard*.

Shapiro, Bernstein & Co. were hustling along, making a name for themselves.

Jerome Remick, the Detroit music publisher, also had an office located in Tin Pan Alley. Doty & Brill, two live young writers, were composing and publishing there.

My staff at that time consisted of Jules Ruby and Leo Wood, song pluggers; Al LaRue, arranger; Meyer Cohen, general manager and plugger.

Tin Pan Alley in those days always reminded me of Baxter Street, where the clothing men held forth and where, if a stranger happened to pass through the street, the puller-in saw to it that he did not leave without buying a suit of clothes or an overcoat. The same thing happened daily in Tin Pan Alley, where the song pluggers, from early morning until late at night, stood in front of their respective publishing houses waiting for singers to come along, when they would grab them by the arm and hoist them into the music studios. There was no escape. Once the singers entered the block, they left it with a dozen songs crammed into their pockets and the singers' promises ringing in the pluggers' ears,—promises to sing the newly acquired compositions. Each song plugger had his own clientele of friends who would stand by him through thick and thin, until some more enterprising plugger would offer them more money, which, naturally, would switch their allegiance. Keen rivalry existed among the publishing houses at that time, and publishers were continually hearing of scrapping among the pluggers on account of their stealing one another's pet singers.

Fourteenth Street was then the Mecca of the song pluggers as well as of the publishers. As soon as the lamps were lit, the pluggers would cluster around Tony Pastor's,[2] that being their headquarters, where, if not at their hotels and boarding houses close by, all the singers could usually be found. It was a common sight any night to see the pluggers, with pockets full of professional copies, stop the singers on the street and lead them to the first lamp-post, where the plugger would sing a song from a professional copy. It mattered not how many people were passing at the time. "Anything to land a singer" was their motto.

Tony Pastor was very lenient both to the popular-song pluggers, and to the publishers, allowing them back of the stage at all times to interview the singers, while old door-man Henderson, a fixture for more than twenty years, passed many of them into the theater through the front entrance.

But the song pluggers were not the only solicitors for their respective publishers; the heads of the concerns were also out doing their bit at the same time. Not only did they hustle in their respective publishing houses during the day, but as soon as they were through with their dinner, their work started all over again at night. On Fourteenth Street in those times you could see, walking nightly, such men as Ed Marks and his partner, Joe Stern; Kerry Mills; the Witmark boys; Pat Howley; Harry Von Tilzer; and Meyer Cohen. They all kept their eagle eyes open for a singer or an orchestra leader whom to induce to use their respective compositions.

The singers themselves were never neglected in those days. They certainly had a good time of it, as the pluggers and the publishers fed them up with cigars, drinks, and food of all kinds *gratis*. In order that a firm's song might be heard in different cities, many a singer's board bill was paid and many a new trunk, together with a railroad ticket, was purchased by the particular firm whose song the singer was exploiting. The publishers spent their money freely, their slogan being, "Anything and everything to land a hit." There was no system, no set rules, no combination of publishers, no music publishers' association; simply, do as you please, everybody for himself, and the devil take the hindmost.

No two publishers were friendly—very seldom even passed the time of day together. The rivalry was too keen. So it went on for several years. Hits came and hits went. New publishers came and some of the old publishers departed. Gradually they moved uptown, all of them locating in what is known as the Roaring Forties and as far up as Fifty-second Street and Broadway. If in the years to come, the theatrical district should move farther uptown, you will find the publishers located close by. As the vaudeville and musical-comedy theaters depend on the popular-song publishers for their music, it is only natural that they should wish to keep in close touch with each other.

SOURCE: Charles K. Harris, *After the Ball: Forty Years of Melody: An Autobiography* (New York: Frank Maurice, 1926): 54–62, 209–14.

~~~~~~~~~

NOTES

1.   This probably refers to the sporting and entertainment magazine.
2.   Tony Pastor's Opera House helped to establish early vaudeville, hosting the most famous entertainers of the era.

68

$\mathcal{S}$COTT JOPLIN, RAGTIME VISIONARY

(Scott Joplin, Lottie Joplin)

Scott Joplin (1867–1917) was the first great black composer in the history of American music. His ragtime compositions set the standard for the new popular songs and dances that swept the country after his "Maple Leaf Rag" (1899) became a bestseller. His life is "frustratingly elusive," according to his biographer, Edward A. Berlin. "He left no journal of his thoughts and activities, no personal letters are known to exist, and his associates' reminiscences have proven to be notoriously unreliable."[1]

The opening paragraph of his instruction book, *School of Ragtime* (1908), shows his tenacious approach to his art, while the meaning of his phrase "weird and intoxicating" is as elusive as his life. Joplin's defensive posture makes sense in light of the attacks on ragtime in this period. Just as 1950s rock provoked censorship, the American Federation of Musicians prohibited its members from playing ragtime in 1901. Eubie Blake once wrote, "The music itself is only part of it [experiencing ragtime]. You have to know about the backrooms of bars, the incredible prejudice we had to deal with, the hook shops, the beer and the sawdust all over the floor."[2]

In the second selection below, an interview with Joplin's third wife, Lottie, corroborates Joplin's ambitions for ragtime as well as his identification with the struggles of African Americans during Reconstruction. Her reference to a "ragtime symphony" reminds us of Joplin's many unfinished projects and lost scores. Joplin's opera

Treemonisha was performed in 1915, and its revival by the Houston Opera Company in 1975 proved revelatory. Joplin's rediscovered treasure was performed at the Prague State Opera in 2003.

FROM JOPLIN'S *SCHOOL OF RAGTIME*

Remarks—What is scurrilously called ragtime is an invention that is here to stay. That is now conceded by all classes of musicians. That all publications masquerading under the name of ragtime are not the genuine article will be better known when these exercises are studied. That real ragtime of the higher class is rather difficult to play is a painful truth which most pianists have discovered. Syncopations are no indication of light or trashy music, and to shy bricks at "hateful ragtime" no longer passes for musical culture. To assist amateur players in giving the "Joplin Rags" that weird and intoxicating effect intended by the composer is the object of this work.

> SOURCE: Scott Joplin, *School of Ragtime: Exercises for Piano* (New York, 1908), as reprinted in *The Collected Works of Scott Joplin*, vol. 1, *Works for Piano*, ed. Vera Brodsky Lawrence (New York: New York Public Library, 1971): 284.

INTERVIEW WITH LOTTIE JOPLIN

[Interviewer note by Kay Thompson] I first met Lottie Joplin—widow of the King of Ragtime Writers—through a mutual acquaintance, Hot Lips Page. That he should share my enthusiasm for the music of Scott Joplin is an altogether understandable circumstance, for Joplin has long been the admiration of trumpet-playing folk, from the days of Keppard, Perez, Johnson, Oliver, and Armstrong. The explanation is quite simple. In the early 1890's, some years before he turned to piano, Joplin himself played B flat cornet. Later, when he took up ragtime composition, he frequently incorporated trumpet-style passages. As a result, old-timers who played the lead regarded his compositions as embodying the real rudiments of jazz style, and thus they required younger men to master his works in order to win acceptance. This statement of the case may contradict the accounts of other writers. However, it is a fact that King Oliver collected just about every Joplin rag ever written, at one time having the entire lot bound in red leather.

Lottie and I have become good friends. Whenever I am weary of the picayune cats who infest the world of jazz, I find it a richly rewarding experience to call upon her. Since her husband's death in 1917, she has remained loyal to his memory with a devotion that is both singular and touching. For years—long years before any of the rest of us—she went forth almost daily, doing whatever a lone and courageous woman could to promote wider recognition for Scott's achievements in the field of American popular music. As she herself has expressed it to me many times: "Scott did it all, and he did it *first!*"

[answering the question "What was Joplin like?"]

"Well, I didn't know Scott when he was young. He came from out West, while I was raised down in Washington. We didn't meet until after he came to New York about 1904, when his publishers, John Stark & Son, opened an office here in town. We were married in 1907, and we lived together as man and wife for about ten years until he died. You might say he died of disappointments, his health broken mentally and physically. But he was a great man, a *great* man! He wanted to be a real leader. He wanted to free his people from poverty, ignorance, and superstition, just like the heroine of his ragtime opera, *Treemonisha*. That's why he was so ambitious; that's why he tackled major projects. In fact, that's why he was so far ahead of his time."

I asked Lottie for her recollections of the period when Joplin was at work on *Treemonisha*.

"What headaches that caused him! After Scott had finished writing it, and while he was showing it around, hoping to get it published, someone stole the theme, and made it into a popular song.[3] The number was quite a hit, too, but that didn't do Scott any good. To get his opera copyrighted, he had to re-write it, and later, to get it published, he had to have it printed at his own expense. I suppose one of these days, somebody will get around to producing it. I tried to get it on Broadway for years, and I remember that Earl Carroll once seemed really interested in the idea. If they were to adapt it to the present day theatre, with singers, dancers, and good musicians, it might be a bigger hit than *Green Pastures*. But things never materialize when you want them to, and next I knew, Earl Carroll had gotten into difficulties over some girl and that bathtub of champagne, and he told me, 'Lottie, I guess there's no chance now!'

"When Scott died, he was composing a ragtime symphony, which he believed would be his most important effort. Unfortunately, he died before he finished it completely, and up until now, I've never mentioned it, or showed it to any writer. I felt people wouldn't understand it. Besides, they would only pester me to death. As it is, every once in a while, someone comes around, wanting to know if Scott left any 'unfinished' manuscripts. Well, to get rid of them, I sometimes let them have a few scraps, but sooner or later, I always get after them, and make them bring them back. One reason I don't have more than I do is that Scott destroyed a lot of things before his last illness. He was afraid that, if anything happened to him, they might get stolen. In those days, there was a lot of that; more than you might think."

One question remained. Now that ragtime was beginning to receive a fuller measure of attention, how did Lottie feel about its future prospects? Would a Ragtime revival be just another short-lived episode, on the order of the recent Dixieland boom?

"I used to wonder sometimes whether Scott would ever receive recognition during my lifetime. You know, he would often say that he'd never be appreciated until after he was dead. But if anyone asked me, I would tell them that Louis Armstrong was right. Scott's music is still too hard for most modern youngsters. They've been raised on all that easy stuff. In fact, that was always my biggest problem, finding musicians who could play as much music as Scott could compose. Of course, today, I'm getting on, and it's really up to the next generation to discover Scott for themselves. When they do, this time it will be for keeps. You see, the numbers Scott wrote are *jazz* classics, and the classics never die—they live on forever!"

SOURCE: Kay C. Thompson, "Lottie Joplin: Scott's Widow Reminisces on the Ragtime King," *Record Changer* 9 (October 1950): 8, 18.

NOTES

1. See http://www.edwardaberlin.com/work4.htm.
2. Eubie Blake, foreword in Terry Waldo, *This Is Ragtime* (1976), as cited in Peter J. Rabinowitz, "Whiting the Wrongs of History: The Resurrection of Scott Joplin," *Black Music Research Journal* 11, no. 2 (Autumn 1991): 173.
3. The reference here is to Irving Berlin and is generally doubted. However, Joplin himself believed that Berlin had appropriated his tune.

"Le Cake Walk"—a French engraving from the 1920s. From a portfolio of original prints from André Hofer, Paris (ca. 1920–1930).

⒜ SIDEBAR INTO THE RAGTIME REVIVAL

OF THE 1970S

William Bolcom Reviews

The Collected Works of Scott Joplin

During the bicentennial decade of the 1970s, Scott Joplin's music experienced a surprising and widespread revival. The use of his music in such popular movies as *The Sting* (1973) gave it a national fan base. The publication of *The Collected Works of Scott Joplin,* edited by Vera Brodsky Lawrence for the New York Public Library, further validated his stature with the classically oriented music establishment. William Bolcom's (b. 1938) review of the first volume offers many insights into Joplin's style from the perspective of historically informed performance.

A distinguished composer and pianist, whose partnership with singer Joan Morris produced memorable recordings of late nineteenth-century popular music in the 1970s, Bolcom responded to the Joplin revival of that decade by immersing himself in Joplin's music and by writing new American piano rags. ("Graceful Ghost" is a classic from that decade.) Bolcom wrote this review fairly early in his career as a composer, and it foreshadows his sustained commitment to stylistic pluralism.

≈≈≈≈≈
≈≈≈≈≈
≈≈≈≈≈

This handsome and impressive edition is the first publication in "The Americana Collection Music Series" of the New York Public Library.[1] With the exception of one piano rag, *The Silver Swan,* attributed to Joplin and recently transcribed from a piano roll, it is essentially a reprint edition. It is not, however, one of those so-called "complete" reprint editions, such as we have seen lately, in which little or no editorial work has been done. Even though this is a compendium of photoengraved and republished original editions, much detailed editing was required because of the special conditions under which the music first appeared in print.

In Joplin's day popular music was often engraved carelessly and at great speed: one suspects that the composer was not often consulted even to read his own proofs, for the original editions were a welter of unmusical engraver's corruptions. Interestingly, the engraved editions carried many more errors of this kind than the far-less-elegant-looking editions set up in what looks like something similar to the steel-type process used by Novello in their nineteenth-century opera scores. Why this is so is uncertain; my guess is that the steel-type process may have been set up from left to right, like linotype, and one's mistakes thus were easier to see than in reversed intaglio engraving. To correct the manifold errors in these printed examples was almost purely an inductive task: there exist no known Joplin original manuscripts of any use to an editor. All I have seen in Joplin's hand are two examples: a few bars of *Euphonic Sounds* written out by way of an autograph for a friend, and some editorial revisions on one of the printed scores of *Treemonisha;* the latter were practically chiseled into the page, so heavy was Joplin's pressure on the pencil—he must have been in the last stages of the disease that was to kill him.

Thus internal evidence, and good musical sense, were the only editorial tools one could use in preparing this edition. However, as Joplin doubtless did not benefit or suffer from much editorial supervision, we can be fairly sure that, in the main—except for mistakes—Joplin's music was printed more or less as he wrote it. What we possess, therefore, is possibly more of an urtext than in most published editions of composers' works, for any editor would have taken exception to some of the things found especially in the printed rags.

To begin with, there is the matter of pedaling. Unlike most other popular piano composers, Joplin added phrasing, dynamics, and pedal indications in his scores. The phrase-markings hardly look like usual piano phrasing, consisting as they do mainly of short slurs with the main beats of the music, rather like standard violin-phrasing. (Does this mean, as it often did in Mozart's case, that Joplin might have expected a violin to play along sometimes with the tune in his rags? Such things happened in the *Hausmusik* of his day.) The dynamics are perfectly logical and follow standard march-music practice: e.g., "p-f" meant, in both marches and Joplin rags, to play a strain *p* the first time and *f* the second. Added to these bare indications is a fair number of *crescendos* and *diminuendos*—quite a refinement for popular sheet music in Joplin's day, and always effectively applied. In the two above-mentioned parameters there is every reason to believe that Joplin wrote down just what he wanted. But the pedal indications are another matter. Often Joplin will tell you to pedal right through a harmonic change in a measure, and it makes no musical sense at all. (When Beethoven did this, it was for a color effect; besides, his piano was far different from Joplin's modern instrument.) One can only assume that Joplin usually scribbled in his pedaling indications without much thought. One exception is the trio of *Eugenia;* but often as not I think it is wise to disregard them in his rags and other solo piano pieces.

In Joplin's favor, I must mention that in note-spelling he is far above most other popular piano-composers. In the rag field alone, one only has to compare his scores with those of Joseph Lamb and James Scott, often considered just below Joplin in quality. Lamb is especially remiss as regards orthography; one of his rags, *Sensation* (p. 288 in Volume I of the Joplin edition), included by virtue of the "Arr. by Scott Joplin" on the first page (which Joplin added to help Lamb sell his rag), is a case in point. Joplin's greater classical training shows through in every measure, not only in his correct orthography, but in his relatively copious phrasing, articulation (see especially the *Binks'* and *Bethena* waltzes) and fingering indications (see *Magnetic Rag,* published, like *Treemonisha,* at his own expense and carefully, though idiosyncratically, edited—doubtless by himself).

Thus it will be seen that Mrs. Lawrence's editorial policy did not include the correction of phrasings or pedalings that may have been musically questionable (though some obviously omitted ties were restored); to do so would have turned the present edition into something like one of those turn-of-the-century "over-editions," where one really has to plough through shrubbery to guess the composer's unadulterated meaning. I think her restraint in this regard is commendable and exactly right, allowing *The Collected Works of Scott Joplin* to stand as an excellent study edition as well as a performing edition (with the caveat as regards Joplin's pedaling that I have mentioned above).

. . .

Ragtime has for so long been considered a mechanical music, the province of the piano roll, that to encounter Joplin sheet-music is a revelation. To play Joplin properly requires all the *justesse* accorded the classical masters; the piano-writing is not *brillante,* and pyrotechnics of the speed-ragtime sort are just not to be found in Joplin's texture, even in such a showy rag as *Euphonic Sounds*—the performer's recourse is to use nuance in unfolding the melodic line. Classically trained pianists sense this, but they often go to the other extreme, at least in my experience of hearing them play Joplin: nuance is too often emphasized to the point of fussiness. Joplin's rags are *dance-pieces,* they were meant to be danced to. George Houle's excellent practice of teaching Renaissance-instrument players the Renaissance dance-steps could be just as instructive here: the cakewalk, two-step, and slow-drag steps are as generative of the piece in ragtime as the pavane and galliard steps are of their own period's dance-music. All in all, there is a tightrope to be walked here; Joplin's rags, his tango *Solace,* and the ragtime waltzes are all idealized dance-forms, and both the dance-aspect and the abstract musical idea-content must be satisfactorily dealt with in performance.

Whereas in Eastern, or urban, ragtime the emphasis is on brilliance and the dance-form is often left far behind, in the Missouri school (comprising Joplin, Arthur Marshall, Scott Hayden, Louis Chauvin, James Scott, and by adoption Joseph Lamb) the underlying dance is never totally let go of. Too, there is the gentler, pentatonic Missouri folksong style woven everywhere throughout the melodic line. In Joplin especially, other melodic influences prevail. One finds passages in his piano rags that are operatic in the extreme, as for example the A-flat strain in *A Breeze from Alabama;* snatches of march-like, quadrille-like, as well as song-like melody are synthesized in the Joplin melodic line throughout his rags and other works. It is, however, paramount to remember in playing Joplin that, while the Eastern rag composers—Lucky Roberts, Eubie Blake, and the rest—may sometimes want to dazzle, Joplin, like the Strausses, wanted always (as he put it) to "intoxicate."

. . .

An important factor to remember is that Joplin had financially no choice but to write music that would sell, and the publication of his *Maple Leaf Rag* in 1899 is important in that it did sell extremely well (to date more than a million copies). These were the days when everyone—or practically everyone—had a piano in the parlor, either for music-making or for looks, and to have *Maple Leaf* on one's music-stand looked good. It gave the piano's owner a "status symbol," as we would say today; even though few amateur pianists could master the intricacies of all four strains, everyone knew at least one tune from the rag (people still do, though they may not always know its name). Four tunes in one piece meant four possible hits if each tune could stand alone; but more important to Joplin was the fact that the four tunes should match well and flow easily one to another. In a way, his gift for matching and balancing musical statements is akin to John Philip Sousa's, but any comparison will show the greater subtlety of the Joplin rag structure. On the other hand, Joplin's march efforts are more curious than successful as marches: *Antoinette*'s trio section contains surprising modulations, very characteristic of Joplin, but the piece as a whole is uneven. *Maple Leaf* is, in fact, a study in balance: against pentatonic Missouri folksong is balanced a classical harmonic structure, flatted sixths, diminished sevenths and all; the bold opening of the first strain contrasts with the feminine cadence at its end; the dense third strain, with its jazzy, accacciatura [sic]-like right-hand chords, balances with the simplicity of the fourth and closing strain.

In its way, *Maple Leaf Rag* was the first real fusion of European and native American-Negro musical elements in our piano-music history. (Americanisms in Louis Moreau Gottschalk are more in the way of insertion than integration.) The new amalgam was to prove both irresistible and generative of a whole new attitude in American music: the need to fuse "classical" and popular elements into a more universal music, much in the way European music had often done, but here taking a different direction. Rag form is not dynamic, like European sonata-form; rather, it is static but inclusive, as any music seeking to encompass the huge panorama of American cultural heritages had to be. Joplin's accomplishment in *Maple Leaf* was to set in perfect balance all the popular culture he had absorbed, with his solid classical training—and to make the result work so well that it would appeal to a wide audience. It was the first real sheet-music hit in history, analogous for its time to the pop-record hits of our own era, and it could be said to be the first historical example of so wide a mass-media coverage in music.

SOURCE: William Bolcom, "Ragtime Revival: *The Collected Works of Scott Joplin*," *Anuario Interamericano de investigacion Musical* 8 (1972): 147–56.

~~~~~~

NOTE

1.   Vera Brodsky Lawrence, ed., *The Collected Works of Scott Joplin*, 2 vols., *Works for Piano* and *Works for Voice* (New York: New York Public Library, 1971).

70

JAMES REESE EUROPE ON THE ORIGIN OF "MODERN DANCES"

The decade of the 1910s, overshadowed by the Roaring Twenties, deserves to be celebrated as the moment when Americans began "steppin' out" into modernity through social dance. The ball of Charles K. Harris became the nightclub, and the waltz yielded to the fox-trot. Cities set the trends. In New York in the 1910s, before the Harlem Renaissance of the 1920s, there was Black Bohemia, a community of artists and intellectuals who lived uptown in what Manhattan now calls "midtown." Before Duke Ellington, there was James Reese Europe (1880–1919), who enjoyed fame and influence as a composer, conductor, and leader of the Clef Club, an early musicians' union of African-American musicians. Europe was a team player who gave credit where he thought it was due; and in this selection he extends his hand to many of his colleagues for their roles in creating modern American ballroom dance. His many acts as a good musical citizen were remembered decades later by the writer Ralph Ellison (see chapter 107).

Europe's collaboration with the white celebrity dance team of Vernon and Irene Castle gave him opportunities to make it big. He later achieved international fame as the band leader during World War I for the all-black 15th Infantry Regiment, nicknamed the Harlem Hellfighters Band, and as the jazz-band leader who brought American syncopated dance music to Paris.

The music of the negro like the music of the Indian has caused much ink to be spilled. Some enthusiastic souls have looked to the rhythms of the red man for the melody that is to create American music; in fact, some have gone so far as to declare that the only possible American music can be Indian music. Which is all very interesting and absolutely inconclusive. The fact remains that Indian composers, in any fair sense of the term, do not exist; while we have among us many talented and well-trained negro creative musicians. It was with one of these that a *Tribune* representative talked last week, with a man who has written a very large proportion of the so-called modern dances. The man was James Reese Europe; the composer of all the Castle dances, and the director of Europe's Orchestra, an organization which has all but secured complete control of the cabaret and dance field in the city. Mr. Europe is a well-trained musician and a man who has thought deeply on the musical possibilities of his race, and of these possibilities, he has firm and well defined opinions.

"I am striving at present to form an orchestra of negroes which will be able to take its place among the serious musical organizations of the country," said Mr. Europe.

"The Tempo Club now contains about two hundred members, all musicians, and from the body I supply at present a majority of the orchestras which play in the various cafés of the city and also at the private dances. Our negro musicians have nearly cleared the field of the so-called gypsy orchestras. The negro, while not generally equal to the demands of the more sophisticated forms of music, is peculiarly fitted for the modern dances. I don't think it too much to say that he plays this music better than the white man simply because all this music is indigenous with him. Rhythm is something that is born in the negro, and the modern dance requires rhythm above all else.

"I myself do not consider the modern dances a step backward. The one-step is more beautiful than the old two-step, and the fox trot than the schottische, of which it is a development. As to the so-called dance craze, it does not appear to be a 'craze.' I have had probably as good an opportunity to observe the various dances as anyone in this city, and I have found that dancing keeps husbands and wives together and eliminates much drinking, as no one can dance and drink to excess. However, these are questions for a philosopher and not for a musician.

"There is much interest in the growth of modern dances in the fact that they were all danced and played by us negroes long before the whites took them up. One of my own musicians, William Tyres [*sic*],[1] wrote the first tango in America as far back as the Spanish-American War. It was known as 'The Trocha,' and a few years later he wrote 'The Maori.' These two tangos are now most popular, yet who heard of them at the time they were written? They were essentially negro dances, played and danced by negroes alone. The same may be said of the fox trot, this season the most popular of all dances.

"The fox trot was created by a young negro of Memphis, Tenn., Mr. W. C. Handy, who five years ago wrote 'The Memphis Blues.' This dance was often played by me last season during the tour of the Castles, but never in public. Mr. Castle became interested in it, but did not believe it suitable for dancing. He thought the time too slow, the world of today demanding staccato music. Yet after a while he began to dance it at private entertainments in New York, and, to his astonishment, discovered that it was immediately taken up. It was not until then that Mr. and Mrs. Castle began to dance it in public, with the result that it is now danced as much as all the other dances put together. Mr. Castle has generously given me the credit for the fox trot, yet the credit, as I have said, really belongs to Mr. Handy. You see, then, that both the tango and the fox trot are really negro dances, as is the one-step. The one-step is the national dance of the negro, the negro always walking in his dances. I myself have written probably more of these new dances than any other composer, and one of my compositions, 'The Castle Lame Duck Waltz,' is perhaps the most widely known of any dance now before the public.

"Yet we negroes are under a great handicap. For 'The Castle Lame Duck' I receive only one cent a copy royalty and the phonograph royalties in like proportion. A white man would receive from six to twelve times the royalty I receive, and the compositions far less popular than mine, but written by white men, gain for their composers vastly greater rewards. I have done my best to put a stop to this discrimination, but I have found that it was no use. The music world is controlled by a trust, and the negro must submit to its demands or fail to have his compositions produced. I am not bitter about it. It is, after all, but a slight portion my race must pay in its at times almost hopeless fight for a place in the sun. Some day it will be different and justice will prevail.

"I firmly believe that there is a big field for the development of negro music in America. We already have a number of composers of great ability, the two foremost being Harry Burleigh and Will Marion Cook. Mr. Burleigh is remarkable for his development of negro themes and Mr. Cook is a true creative artist. Then, of course, there was Coleridge-Taylor,[2] the greatest composer of the negro race, although much of his music is not negro in character. What the negro needs is technical education, and this he is handicapped in acquiring. I myself have had to pick up my knowledge of music here and there, and the same holds true of my fellow composers. I do not believe that the negro at present should attempt music distinctively Caucasian in type. The symphony, for instance, he does not really feel as a white musician would feel it. I believe [the future] is in the creation of an entirely new school of music, a school developed from the basic negro rhythm and melodies. The negro is essentially a melodist, and his creation must be in the beautifying and enriching of the melodies which have become his.

"The negro's songs are the expression of the hopes and joys and fears of his race; [they] were before the [Civil] war the only method he possessed of answering back his boss. Into his songs he poured his heart, and while the boss did not understand, the negro's soul was calmed. These songs are the only folk music America possesses, and folk music being the basis of so much that is most beautiful in the world, there is indeed hope for the art product of our race."

SOURCE: Unsigned article, "Negro Composer on Race's Music: James Reese Europe Credits Men of His Blood with Introducing Modern Dances," *New York Tribune*, November 22, 1914. Cited and partially quoted in Reid Badger, *A Life in Ragtime: A Biography of James Reese Europe* (New York: Oxford University Press, 1995): 116; and reprinted in full in Robert Kimball and William Bolcom, *Reminiscing with Noble Sissle and Eubie Blake* (New York: Viking, 1973): 64.

NOTES

1.   William H. Tyers (1876–1924) was a successful Tin Pan Alley composer and a close associate of Europe's. Both *The Trocha* (1898?) and *Maori: A Samoan Dance* (1908) used Latin rhythms long before they were popularized in social dances.

2.   Samuel Coleridge-Taylor (1875–1912), an Afro-British composer, who was best known for his choral cantata, *Hiawatha's Wedding Feast* (1898).

71

Irving Berlin on "Love-Interest as a Commodity" in Popular Songs

Like many composers and publishers in Tin Pan Alley, Irving Berlin (1888–1989) was a refugee from Eastern Europe, who left behind pogroms to start a new life in a new country. In New York, where many Eastern European Jews settled, the popular-song business was available to accommodate their skills and ambitions. The historian Gerald Mast explains, "One reason Jews became so important to Tin Pan Alley was that the infant music business, like the infant movie business, had inherited no prejudices against hiring Jews and no hierarchical structures to impede the progress of talented immigrants or the sons of immigrants."[1]

Born Israel Baline in Russia, the son of a Jewish cantor, Berlin moved with his family to the Lower East Side of New York when he was five years old. At the time of his bar mitzvah, the 13-year-old boy was already supporting himself as a singing waiter and a song plugger in Tin Pan Alley. Part of the Berlin legend is his lack of formal training and his famous piano playing, which was restricted to the black-key scale of F-sharp major. And another part of the legend is the international popularity of his song "Alexander's Ragtime Band." Berlin produced over 1,000 songs for revues, stage musicals, and film musicals, among them "White Christmas" and "God Bless America." The excerpt below makes writing hits sound easy.

"LOVE-INTEREST" AS A COMMODITY

IT MAKES THE MUSIC WORLD GO ROUND
By Irving Berlin
Author of such popular song successes as "Alexander's Rag-Time Band," "Everybody's Doing It," "This Is the Life," "Snooky-Ookums," "When I Leave the World Behind," "Araby," and others
In collaboration with Justus Dickinson

It's the love-element that sells the song. It comes before everything else in popular music. America turns out between twenty-five thousand and fifty thousand songs a year. Every hamlet has two or three composers who grind out a dozen or two a season. Two-thirds of them strive for love-interest.

I do. Only recently, in writing a song, I found a rhyme I liked. It was:

> *Down in Texas,*
>
> *Where they brand the cattle with* X's.

It was too good to waste. I decided to write a song around it, and my first thought was—*love-interest*. Further, not so many popular song buyers would understand what I meant by the rhyme I had. The final version was "I Want to Go Back to Texas," and the rhyme ran:

> *Every letter I get from Texas*
>
> *Is covered with a lot of* X's.

While the first rhyme would, to the other song-writers, have been considered cleverer, cattle have no great sentimental interest; yet they might be more in the atmosphere of the theme. So I said to myself, "I'll have a fellow get letters, because every kid in school knows what *X's* on a letter mean. And it gives me a chance to go back to the old love interest."

That how things are twisted around until you develop a song.

We depend largely on tricks, we writers of songs. There's no such thing as a new melody. There has been a standing offer in Vienna, holding a large prize, to anyone who can write eight bars of original music. The offer has been up for more than twenty-five years. Thousands of composers have submitted, but all of them have been traced back to some other melody.

Our work is to connect the old phrases in a new way, so that they will sound like a new tune. Did you know that the public, when it hears a song, anticipates the next passage? Well the writers who do *not* give them *something they are expecting* are those who are successful.

I *fool* the auditor. The old idea was to follow the same theme throughout. The new idea is to change. Sometimes I have a half dozen different measures in one chorus. "Choo-choo from Alabam" was typical.

Every time the hearer begins to anticipate, fool him—give him something he isn't expecting. Work for surprises all the time. And never go back—never repeat.

Song writing is a game of new ideas. We always want the love-interest, but we want it served to us in a new way. And new ideas—*new* ones that are *popular* and not too *clever*—are as scarce as hen's teeth. No publisher has had a smashing success this season.

With the experience I have—or rather, with the knowledge of the game—I wouldn't, if I were choosing a career, start out as a writer of popular songs. It is too much of a gamble, and the rewards are not always what they might be. But at that, I believe the beginner has a better chance now than he ever had. The veterans, with two or three successes to their credit, have failed miserably. Where the public wants an entirely new order of songs, the writers are working to old standards.

Publishers, but not the public, estimate a song-writer on past performances. If a man has written four or five big hits and the publisher wants him badly enough, the writer can command almost his own figure. That is where the publisher is wrong. For there's no surefire song-writer in the business.

One of the reasons for this is interesting. After a song-writer has put out three or four "hits," he gets to know too much about popular songs. He begins to make his songs clever instead of popular. You'll often hear a publisher, when he is refusing a song, say, "It's a good song for song-writers, but it is no good for the public." He may have rhymes that other song-writers will say are immensely clever, but they won't mean anything to the public.

Being clever is as fatal in a popular song as being dull.

And another thing: after the writer has put out two or three successes, his past performances get the better of him; he is willing to sit back and consider the past.

But don't blame the song-writer for everything. There's the "follow-up" song, for instance. The publisher, not the song-writer, is usually at fault there.

Some company puts out a successful song, and the publishers rush to their song-writers and demand, "Give us a song like So-and-so." They don't seem to realize that the public won't stand for the same thing twice.

Still, the writer, being under orders and a guarantee, pounds out a song and gets all the discredit.

Another reason for this condition is that singers, having heard some one sing a popular song put out by another publisher, go to a rival and ask for "a song like So-and-so." And one is ground out.

For there's nothing much a publisher won't do for such artists as Eva Tanguay, Nora Bayes, Irene Franklin, Blanche Ring, Al Jolson, Kitty Gordon, Fritzi Scheff, Elizabeth Brice, Emma Caras and a few others. They are the best "pluggers"—the best *popularizers*, if I may use the word—a publisher can get. Now, excepting these names from all suspicion of being parties to such a thing, the stage singer and the vaudeville singer have come back into the "song-boosting" business that the publishers agreed a year ago to abolish.

Now,—I am getting to my point slowly,—remember that between twenty-five thousand and fifty thousand songs are turned out every year in the United States. Thousands of these are published. Yet if, out of this mass of published material, the market shows six natural song-hits (meaning songs selling a million or more copies), it has been a rarely successful season.

"TIME, GENTLEMEN, PLEASE!"

"Time, Gentlemen, Please!"—Reproduction of a drawing from an English newspaper, n.d. [ca. 1914–1920]. This drawing, which contains the titles of songs by Irving Berlin, depicts a variety of American performers seen harassing the Goddess of Music.

The publisher sells his songs to the jobber or "the trade" for six and a half cents a copy. He pays a cent a copy royalty to the men who have written the song. This leaves him a gross of five and a half cents a copy on a song. Out of this he must care for a tremendous over expense; the printing costs him a cent a copy; he has advertising he must keep up; he has branches and branch-staffs in a half-dozen cities; he maintains a staff of eight or nine piano players in his home office, and staffs of two or three in his branch offices; he keeps a force of "pluggers" or "song-boosters"—who go over the cities singing his songs in motion-picture theaters and cafes—at work; he employs a force of "outside men" whose duty it is to get his songs sung by stage people; and then, on top of it all, he (in the plural) has recommenced paying performers to sing his songs.

He does it on the chance that a song may be forced to success. I believe such a thing is impossible. Bad songs never can succeed; there have been times when a good song was made into a success by proper publicity. I know one publisher who has paid out more than fifty thousand dollars a year to vaudeville singers to have them put on his songs. And I know of several performers who have been paid one hundred dollars a week or more to put one song in their acts.

This cut throat competition, which has resulted recently in the failure of a number of publishing firms, operates in spite of the fact that it has become more and more difficult to make money out of the song-publishing business. Under present conditions a publisher loses money on a song unless he sells more than three hundred thousand copies. (I mean, by this, a song he has advertised and "plugged"—one he is betting on a success.) He must sell between five hundred thousand and six hundred thousand copies to make a fair profit.

There's persistent talk that the beginner has no chance in the song-writing business. Frankly, he has very little chance, though more now than before. First of all, the business is over-crowded; second, the amateur has no knowledge of the working of the trickiest game in the world.

And, not *living* song writing, he is not in the proper atmosphere.

Our publishing house has never received, from an amateur, a usable idea, either in lyrics or melody; and we have examined thousands of manuscripts. If we could find good ones, we'd be more than glad to pay for them. . . . Why, some of them even offer to let me put my name on their compositions.

Song-writers don't steal—at least, those of reputation don't. Why should they? But the public, by some freak of mind, would rather believe that the fellow who is getting the credit isn't the one who is doing the work. Two years or so ago, when "Alexander's Rag-Time Band" was a big hit, some one started the report among the publishers that I had paid a negro ten dollars for it and then published under my own name.[2]

When they told me about it, I asked them to tell me from whom I had bought my other successes—twenty-five or thirty of them. And I wanted to know, if a negro could write "Alexander," why couldn't I? Then I told them if they could produce the negro and he had another hit like "Alexander" in his system, I would choke it out of him and give him twenty thousand dollars in the bargain.

If the other fellow deserves credit, why doesn't he get it?

SOURCE: Irving Berlin in collaboration with Justus Dickinson, "'Love-Interest' as a Commodity," *Green Book Magazine*, February 1915, 695–98.

NOTES

1. Gerald Mast, *Can't Help Singin': The American Musical on Stage and Screen* (New York: Oxford University Press): 35.
2. Berlin is alluding to the charges of plagiarism raised by Lottie Joplin in chapter 68.

72

CAROLINE CAFFIN ON THE "MUSIC AND NEAR-MUSIC" OF VAUDEVILLE

By 1900 Vaudeville was big business, and music played a major role in making its fortunes. The excerpts from one of the earliest books about Vaudeville show how by the early 1900s coon songs and striptease competed with family fare, at least some of the time. A modernist critic in the arts, as well as a playwright, Caroline Caffin wrote ironic yet affectionate observations about everybody, including the audience. New immigrants made their voices heard as Italian opera stars, Russian balalaika players, blackface tent-show veterans, and Tin Pan Alley singers. Vaudeville offered American composers a new range of possibilities for whatever kind of music they dreamed of writing.

MUSIC AND NEAR-MUSIC

We, of the Vaudeville Audience, all love music. Individually we may differ as to what particular variety of noise we honor with the name of music, but our own brand we each love fervently.

In Vaudeville we are offered a gorgeous variety of brands: from melody extracted from the unwilling material of xylophones and musical glasses through the varying offerings of singers and instrumentalists, both comic and serious, to the performance of high class chamber-music or the singing of an operatic diva.

For the purposes of this chapter we will eliminate the singers who use the song simply as a medium to get over to the audience some amusing patter. We have looked at some of these in other chapters and our Vaudeville sense will not allow us to give too much attention to any one form of amusement. So now let us listen to music as music.

Let it be admitted that the Vaudeville house is not the place in which the musical connoisseur looks for music of the highest rank. There is no aim to compete with the Philharmonic Society or the Boston Symphony Orchestra. But for all that there are some good music and fine musicians and no lack of appreciation for them. Perhaps it is not to be denied that the strange and curious are as highly favored as the artistic; and a violinist may excite as much applause by playing "Suwanee River" on one string as by the most exquisite rendering of a violin Fantasia by Brahms. But there are always some in the audience who are grateful for the best, even if they are not so noisy in their acknowledgment of it. There has been from time to time a large array of talent, musicians of repute, both instrumentalists and singers, who have found their way on to the Vaudeville stage for a longer or shorter period.

The stars of Musical Comedy and Light Opera drift with apparent indifference from one sphere to the other and sooner or later they are likely to be heard in Vaudeville. In the heyday of her vocal triumphs Lillian Russell[1] sang for a short time in Vaudeville, where her crisp, well-assured individuality and her familiarity with the technique of her craft, quite apart from her well advertised beauty, would always make her welcome.

...

But while these luminaries flash across the horizon from time to time like splendid comets, the constellation of Vaudeville numbers stars of its own which belong to it by right. There is "The East side Caruso," a young Italian whose voice has tones which are not unlike those of the famous tenor; while his ingenuous gratification at the favor he wins is much more charming in its naivete than the sophistication of the better known artist.

...

There is, too, some delightful singing, included in a little drama which presents a real human problem. It is enacted by Sophye Barnard, Lou Anger and Company and is entitled, "The Song of the Heart." It introduces to us a young prima-donna about to make her debut in the opera of "Thais."[2] Her husband and family, although opposed to her career, are to witness her triumph from a box. But just as she is prepared to make her first entrance the husband appears, imploring her to come with him to their child who lies at the point of death and is calling for her. The impresario pleads with her through the arduous years of study and begs her not to abandon her purpose now that its achievement is within her grasp. The overture has already begun and the distracted woman is hurried on to the stage. She has sung the first part and returned to her dressing-room to sing the aria offstage before she realizes the agony of her position, but as she again comes before the public her distress unnerves her. She falters, hesitates, her voice breaks and she is unable to proceed. Hisses and hoots from the audience drive her from the stage. Horrified at the cruelty and heartlessness of the public she throws herself into her husband's arms, imploring him to take her back to their child and determining to devote herself to them henceforth.

Sophye Barnard has made a great impression not only with her rendering of the music but also with her acting of the part of the heroine. But it is the singing which gives to the performance its distinction and which remains in the memory as especially enjoyable.

Meanwhile, besides the instrumentalists who delight us with the one instrument of their choice we have versatile artists who play with equal facility any instrument from violin to saxophone. There is Charles F. Seamon, who seems to be equally familiar with every instrument one can name. Wood, brass, strings,—so long as it is an instrument of music he is its master. Of each he seems to be not only the facile manipulator, but the diviner of its special capability of expression and to be able to wring from it its special quality of vibrant tone.

Not only the acknowledged instruments of the orchestra have their exponents but we have wizards who wring sweetness from accordions, ocarinas or other weird instruments. Unnumbered effects are obtained from the piano by performers who play a different melody with each hand, or change the key every few bars or play complicated settings using one hand only. Or "Violinsky" executes for us the most complicated of exercises on the violin, winding up with a piano-cello duet which he performs alone. The bow of the 'cello is strapped to his right knee while the right hand manipulates the strings as he plays the air on it. The left hand, meanwhile, plays on the piano an elaborate accompaniment. Of course we do not look for a great deal of soul in such performances, the exhibition is much more a thing of skill and ingenuity.

There are quartettes and sextettes that play with considerable charm. . . . I call to mind a group of clever instrumentalists who after playing cornets, trombones and other better known instruments gave an excellent performance on some huge, strange-looking tubas, during which all the lights in the house were extinguished except rings of electric light around the mouths of their instruments. There was something very uncanny in those rings of light emitting deep, full-diapasoned tones, seemingly of their own volition, for the performers were quite invisible.

I don't know that this evident necessity for something over and above the music pleases me. It seems to betoken an inability on the part of the audience to give itself sympathetically to the deeper enjoyment of music and smacks too much of mere restless craving for novelty. It would seem as if the audience will take no step toward the entertainer but must not only be entertained but coaxed into allowing itself to be entertained. In the old days when the singer sat with the audience and was not above sharing a mug of beer with an ardent admirer he might be asked for this or that favorite ditty and the audience joined in the chorus. But it seems that this divorce which has put the footlights permanently between them has cut so deep as to paralyze the desire of the audience to cooperate even mentally with the performer.

And so the audience is losing the full enjoyment of music because it insists on having it combined with some more obvious form of amusement. The beauty of a song well sung is not really enhanced by being combined with feats of horsemanship nor are we really receiving increased pleasure by mixing the two. There is much to be desired in the sympathetic appreciation of an audience that demands the combination. It is not doing its share.

Therein lies the trouble. The audience is inclined to become inert and to rely on the performer not only for "delight" but for the creation of the mood in which to accept it.

As for joining in a chorus it is seldom that the audience can be induced to make more than a very half-hearted attempt at it. Sometimes, as was very cleverly done by Emma Carus,[3] a singer is "planted" in a remote part of the house who takes up the strain, not too noticeably at first, but just enough to encourage others to join. Gradually this one trained voice overtops all the rest, who are usually doing little more than hum shamefacedly at best, and then stop to listen to him until he is left singing alone. Of course, with an experienced actress like Miss Carus on the stage, who knows how to work up the interest by the first expression of pleased surprise, followed by the questioning look, the effort to locate the singer, then the confirming approval, and at last the congratulatory delight, this is very effective. But, after all, this is only one more effort to capture the audience by novelty and does not really make any demand on their cooperation.

But still, as I have said before, the Vaudeville audience does love music, provided it happens to be of its own peculiar brand, Witness its devotion to the Male Quartette. This particular brand flourishes perpetually in its bald simplicity. And "flourishes" seems a peculiarly appropriate word. For, though I have not been able to substantiate it as a scientific fact, it would seem that Quartette singing has a magical effect in increasing the singer's girth, especially toward what might be called the equatorial zone. Occasionally a Quartette will comprise one thin singer and he is the basso profondo. For the rest, the higher the voice the greater the circumference. And Oh! the oozing sentimentality of these fat men! "If you should go away" they will "kneel down and pray." If they do, it seems only too probable that a derrick would have to be rigged in order to raise them to their feet again. Those well padded knees, however, show no signs of abrasions on cold, hard floors. Still, in mellifluous numbers, they regret that they "lost the angel that guides" them when they "lost you!" It is sad, it is heart-breaking! But it does not seem to have worried them to the extent of growing thin about it. Why should they, when they can sing and grow fat?

Perhaps I do them injustice in doubting their agility. Anyhow, they always run quite quickly off the stage. That is one of the regulations,—Run off—Walk on.

...

Every now and then we find on our programme an item of rare musical distinction. Such is the performance of Theodore Bendix's ensemble players. This Quartette of players contrives very happily to give us real music while not entirely ignoring that personal appeal which their audience craves. Their playing is manifestly for the audience. There is none of the aloofness and impersonality that marks the high gods of Olympus. The players do not disdain to look into the faces of their audience and gain fresh inspiration as they see the answering response to the throb of the elemental stir of their music. They give free play to the temperament and abandon with which the response fills them. Listen to the playing of Sarasate's *Gypsy Fantasy*,[4] by Michael Bernstein and give yourself up to the pulsing beat of life which stirs through the out-of-door world.

Such organizations, too, as the Russian Balalaika Orchestra, are a genuine pleasure from a purely musical standpoint. They feed the imagination instead of stunting it, and by the charm of their rendering of their characteristic music call up pictures to the mind, fraught with an atmosphere strange and convincing. Hear them play the folk song of the Volga boatmen. At first it is monotonous and heavy, timed to their laborious breathing as they pull their long strokes, against the stream. Then it swells into the passionate cry of yearning for some better lot, some longed-for rest from labor. Then once again it settles down into the monotonous dirge-like chant, dying away in the far distance as the boat disappears up the misty river.

These are the things which weave the real spell of music and lift us for the moment above the commonplace and personal. But they call for a co-operation on the part of the imagination of the bearer. And if a touch of the dramatic in the bearing of the performers can awaken that imagination, we need have no quarrel with it. But sometimes this dramatic bearing usurps the throne which should be occupied by the music itself and we find our audience intent on the peculiarities of the performer instead of yielding themselves to the sway of his music. So, when Francesco Creatore's orchestra plays, fully one-half of his audience are absorbed in watching the antics and eccentricities of the conductor. The wild flap of hair over his forehead, which, as he waves his head in crazy excitement, threatens to blind him—the crouching grasp with which he seems to be plucking a melody from the atmosphere, or the defiant rage with which he flings it at the performers—the beckoning, the nodding and all the capers in which he indulges, become so engrossing that the actual music passes unheeded. It is true that he can stimulate his audience to a thrilled enthusiasm; yet the spell is not that of music but of his own excitable, effervescent personality.

And while we are speaking of the music we must not forget the Vaudeville orchestra which does such gallant work in augmenting our delight in each and every one of the many turns. It is no light responsibility that rests on the head of the leader of a Vaudeville orchestra and his company of musicians. They can mar if they cannot actually make a turn successful. Notwithstanding a bill that changes completely at least once a week, the leader must be always perfectly familiar with entrances, exits, cues and effects desired by each individual performer. Besides playing for all the song and dances with their special peculiarities of pause or acceleration of the time, supplying accompaniment for instrumentalists, introducing each turn and playing overture and exit march there are many other numbers which look to the orchestra for assistance.

There is the "thrilly" music for the sensational play; the specially accentuated accompaniments, to animal acts. Then the acrobats, trapeze and wire acts and other daring feats must have their own particular variety of accompaniment, and the long whirring roll of the drum with its clash of cymbals to mark exactly the climax of some notable feature, and the sudden silence, as though the orchestra itself were too amazed to play for the hair-raising episode which caps the whole performance. Each and every one of these must be timed to the exact second or the effect will be spoiled. Moreover, the leader of the orchestra will often be expected to join in some dialogue with the comedian or to interrupt some specialty, or "fill in," in one way or another, in the many efforts to bring actor and audience into personal relation.

And by no means the least of his requirements—the leader of the orchestra must not allow himself the indulgence of looking bored. He may be wearied of hearing the same joke repeated twelve times in a week, the same song with the same emphasis occurring twelve times, the same surprise which he has seen eleven times before, but his face must not betray him. The first violinist or even the drummer, though a person of tremendous importance, may look as they feel. I have even seen them yawn discreetly, but the leader must keep up a semblance of geniality even if inwardly boredom reigns supreme.

His is the position of the commanding officer who marshals the forces in battle, keeping the ranks in line and filling up the gaps made by those who fall. He must observe a tradition like that of the British army, that though the rank and file may lie down under cover, the commanding officer must remain in full view, bearing the brunt of the enemies' fire with unflinching mien, regardless of praise or blame. We are his debtors, we of the sheltered onlookers who may leave the field, if so inclined, without a spot on our honor. Here is our salute to him and the brave battalion under his command. We dare not refuse it, for have I not said already that we, of the Vaudeville audience, all love music?

SOURCE: Caroline Caffin, *Vaudeville* (New York: M. Kennerley, 1914): 76–95.

~~~~~~~~

NOTES

1. Lillian Russell (1861–1922), American soprano and actress.
2. Jules Massenet's (1842–1912) *Thais* premiered in 1894.
3. Emma Carus (1879–1927), American vaudeville and musical comedy actress and singer, who in 1911 introduced Irving Berlin's famous "Alexander's Ragtime Band."
4. Pablo de Sarasate (1844–1908), Spanish violinist and composer.

73

FERDINAND "JELLY ROLL" MORTON DESCRIBES

NEW ORLEANS AND THE DISCIPLINE OF JAZZ

Jelly Roll Morton (1890–1941) was born Ferdinand LaMenthe, a socially privileged
Creole de couleur. He later took his mother's name, "Mouton," and then Anglicized
it to "Morton." These excerpts make several different points about his career and
his sense of jazz as discipline and practice. Frequent references to opera remind us
of its popularity (particularly Verdi) in New Orleans. The famous phrase "the Spanish tinge" acknowledges the Hispanic influence in his music; his description of the
"right seasoning" sounds like gumbo or salsa. Morton explains how to achieve a
balance between collective improvisation and sophisticated form. Although the
foundation of Morton's historical reputation is the great recordings he and his
group, the Red Hot Peppers, made in Chicago in the 1920s, these selections evoke
his formative years in New Orleans.

Of course, my folks never had the idea they wanted a musician in the family. They always
had it in their minds that a musician was a tramp, trying to duck work, with the exception
of the French Opera House players which they patronized. As a matter of fact, I, myself, was

inspired to play piano by going to a recital at the French Opera House. There was a gentleman who rendered a selection on the piano, very marvelous music that made me want to play the piano very, very much. The only trouble was that this gentleman had long bushy hair, and, because the piano was known in our circle as an instrument for a lady, this confirmed me in my idea that if I played the piano I would be misunderstood.

I didn't want to be called a sissy. I wanted to marry and raise a family and be known as a man among men when I became of age. So I studied various other instruments, such as violin, drums and guitar, until one day at a party I saw a gentleman sit down at the piano and play a very good piece of ragtime. This particular gentleman had short hair and I decided then that the instrument was good for a gentleman same as it was for a lady. I must have been about ten years old at the time.

. . .

So in the year of 1902 when I was about seventeen years old I happened to invade one of the sections where the birth of jazz originated from. Some friends took me to The Frenchman's on the corner of Villery and Bienville, which was at that time the most famous nightspot after everything was closed. It was only a back room, but it was where all the greatest pianists frequented after they got off from work in the sportinghouses. About four A.M., unless plenty of money was involved on their jobs, they would go to The Frenchman's and there would be everything in the line of hilarity there.

All the girls that could get out of their houses was there. The millionaires would come to listen to their favorite pianists. There weren't any discrimination of any kind. They all sat at different tables or anywhere they felt like sitting. They all mingled together just as they wished to and everyone was just like one big happy family. People came from all over the country and most times you couldn't get in. So this place would go on at a tremendous rate of speed—plenty [of] money, drinks of all kinds—from four o'clock in the morning until maybe twelve, one, two, or three o'clock in the daytime. Then, when the great pianists used to leave, the crowds would leave.

New Orleans was the stomping grounds for all the greatest pianists in the country. We had Spanish, we had colored, we had white, we had Frenchmens, we had Americans, we had them from all parts of the world, because there were more jobs for pianists than any other ten places in the world. The sporting-houses needed professors, and we had so many different styles that whenever you came to New Orleans, it wouldn't make any difference that you just came from Paris or any part of England, Europe, or any place—whatever your tunes were over there, we played them in New Orleans.

. . .

I might name some of the other great hot men operating around New Orleans at this period and a little later. There was Emmanuel Perez, played strictly ragtime, who was maybe the best trumpet in New Orleans till Freddie Keppard came along. John Robechaux probably had the best band in New Orleans at the time, a strictly all-reading, legitimate bunch. Before him, there was Happy Galloway. Both men had the same type [of] seven-piece orchestra—cornet, clarinet, trombone, drums, mandolin, guitar, and bass. A guy named Payton had a band that played a very lowdown type of quadrille for the lowclass dance halls. Also a lot of bad bands that we used to call "spasm" bands, played any jobs they could get in the streets. They did a lot of ad-libbing in ragtime style with different solos in succession, not in a regular routine, but just as one guy would get tired and let another musician have the lead.

None of these men made much money—maybe a dollar a night or a couple of bucks for a funeral, but still they didn't like to leave New Orleans. They used to say, "This is the best town in the world. What's the use for me to go any other place?" So the town was full of the best musicians you ever heard. Even the rags-bottles-and-bones men would advertise their trade by playing the blues on the wooden mouthpieces of Christmas horns—yes sir, play more lowdown, dirty blues on those Kress horns than the rest of the country ever thought of.

All of these people played ragtime in a hot style, but man, you can play hot all you want to, and you still won't be playing jazz. Hot means some-thing spicy. Ragtime is a certain type of syncopation and only certain tunes can be played in that idea. But jazz is a style that can be applied to any type of tune. I started using the word in 1902 to show people the difference between jazz and ragtime.

Jazz music came from New Orleans and New Orleans was inhabited with maybe every race on the face of the globe and, of course, plenty of French people. Many of the earliest tunes in New Orleans was from French origin. Then we had Spanish people there. I heard a lot of Spanish tunes and I tried to play them in correct tempo, but I personally didn't believe they were really perfected in the tempos. Now take *La Paloma*, which I transformed in New Orleans style.[1] You leave the left hand just the same. The difference comes in the right hand—in the syncopation, which gives it an entirely different color that really changes the color from red to blue.

Now in one of my earliest tunes, *New Orleans Blues,* you can notice the Spanish tinge. In fact, if you can't manage to put tinges of Spanish in your tunes, you will never be able to get the right seasoning, I call it, for jazz. This *New Orleans Blues* comes from around 1902. I wrote it with the help of Frank Richards, a great piano player in the ragtime style. All the bands in the city played it at that time.

. . .

About harmony, my theory is never to discard the melody. Always have a melody going some kind of way against a background of perfect harmony with plenty of riffs—meaning figures. A riff is something that gives an orchestra a great background and is the main idea in playing jazz. No jazz piano player can really play good jazz unless they try to give an imitation of a band, that is, by providing a basis of riffs. I've seen riffs blundered up so many times it has give me heart failure, because most of these modern guys don't regard the harmony or the rules of the system of music at all. They just play anything, their main idea being to keep the bass going. They think by keeping the bass going and getting a set rhythm, they are doing the right thing, which is wrong. Of all the pianists today, I know of only one that has a tendency to be on the right track and that's Bob Zurke of the Bob Crosby Band. Far as the rest of them, all I can see is ragtime pianists in very fine form.

Now the riff is what we call a foundation, like something that you walk on. It's standard. But without breaks and without clean breaks and without beautiful ideas in breaks, you don't even need to think about doing anything else, you haven't got a jazz band and you can't play jazz. Even if a tune haven't got a break in it, it's always necessary to arrange some kind of a spot to make a break.

A break, itself, is like a musical surprise which didn't come in until I originated the idea of jazz, as I told you. We New Orleans musicians were always looking for novelty effects to attract the public, and many of the most important things in jazz originated in some guy's crazy idea that we tried out for a laugh or just to surprise the folks.

Most people don't understand the novelty side of jazz. Vibrato—which is all right for one instrument but the worst thing that ever happened when a whole bunch of instruments use it—was nothing at the beginning but an imitation of a jackass hollering. There were many other imitations of animal sounds we used—such as the wah-wahs on trumpets and trombones.

Mutes came in with King Oliver, who first just stuck bottles into his trumpet so he could play softer, but then began to use all sorts of mutes to give his instrument a different flavor. And I, myself, by accident, discovered the swats on drums. Out in Los Angeles I had a drummer that hit his snares so loud that one night I gave him a couple of fly swatters for a gag. This drummer fell in with the joke and used them, but they worked so smooth he kept right on using them. So we have "the swats" today—a nice soft way to keep your rhythm going.

A lot of people have a wrong conception of jazz. Somehow it got into the dictionary that jazz was considered a lot of blatant noises and discordant tones, something that would be even harmful to the ears. The fact of it is that every musician in America had the wrong understanding of jazz music. I know many times that I'd be playing against different orchestras and I would notice some of the patrons get near an orchestra and put their hands over their ears. (Of course, I wouldn't permit mine to play that way.) Anyhow, I heard a funny fellow say once: "If that fellow blows any louder, he'll knock my ear drums down." Even Germany and Italy don't want this discordant type of jazz, because of the noise.

Jazz music is to be played sweet, soft, plenty rhythm. When you have your plenty rhythm with your plenty swing, it becomes beautiful. To start with, you can't make crescendos and diminuendos when one is playing triple forte. You got to be able to come down in order to go up. If a glass of water is full, you can't fill it any more; but if you have half a glass, you have the opportunity to put more water in it. Jazz music is based on the same principles, because jazz is based on strictly music. You have the finest ideas from the greatest operas, symphonies, and overtures in jazz music. There is nothing finer than jazz because it comes from everything of the finest-class music. Take the *Sextet* from *Lucia* and the *Miserere* from *Il Trovatore,* that they used to play in the French Opera House, tunes that have always lived in my mind as the great favorites of the opera singers; I transformed a lot of those numbers into jazz time, using different little variations and ideas to masquerade the tunes.

The *Tiger Rag,* for an instance, I happened to transform from an old quadrille, which was originally in many different tempos. First there was an introduction, "Everybody get your partners!" and the people would be rushing around the hall getting their partners. After a five-minute lapse of time, the next strain would be the waltz strain . . . then another strain that comes right beside the waltz strain in mazooka [mazurka] time.

We had two other strains in two-four time. Then I transformed these strains into the *Tiger Rag* which I also named, from the way I made the "tiger" roar with my elbow. A person said once, "That sounds like a tiger hollering." I said to myself, "That's the name." All this happened back in the early days before the Dixieland Band was ever heard of.

ABOUT 1912

It was along about that time that the first hot arrangements came into existence. Up until then, everything had been in the heads of the men who played jazz out of New Orleans. Nowadays they talk about these jam sessions. Well, that is something I never permitted. Most guys, they improvise and they'll go wrong. Most of the so-called jazz musicians still don't know how to play jazz until this day; they don't understand the principles of jazz music. In all my recording sessions and in all my band work, I always wrote out the arrangements in advance. When it was a New Orleans man, that wasn't so much trouble, because those boys know a lot of my breaks; but in traveling from place to place I found other musicians had to be taught. So around 1912, I began to write down this peculiar form of mathematics and harmonics that was strange to all the world.

For a time I had been working with McCabe's Minstrel Show and, when that folded in St. Louis, I began looking around for a job. My goodness, the snow was piled up till you couldn't see the streetcars. I was afraid that I'd meet some piano player that could top me a whole lot, so I wouldn't admit that I could play. I claimed that I was a singer. At that time I kinda figured I was a pretty good singer, which was way out of the way, but I figured it anyhow. Well, I was hired at the Democratic Club where they had a piano player named George Reynolds. He was a brick-layer trying to play piano. He couldn't even read music. In fact, none of the boys couldn't [sic] read much and so it was very tough for them to get those tough tunes. They bought sheet music just to learn the words of the songs. . . .

They brought me all Scott Joplin's tunes—he was the great St. Louis ragtime composer —and I knew them all by heart and played them right off. They brought me James Scott's tunes and Louis Chauvin's and I knew them all. Then Artie Matthews (the best reader in the whole bunch) brought me his *Pastimes* and I played it. So he decided to find out whether I could really read and play piano and he brought me different light operas like *Humoresque*, the *Overture* from *Martha*, the *Miserere* from *Il Trovatore* and, of course, I knowed them all.

Finally they brought me *The Poet and the Peasant*.[2] It seems like in St. Louis, if you was able to play this piece correctly, you was really considered the tops. The man that brought it was the best musician in town and he hadn't been able to master this piece. Well, I had played this thing in recitals for years, but I started looking at it like I hadn't ever seen it before. Then I started in. I got to a very fast passage where I also had to turn the page over. I couldn't turn the page, due to the fact that I had to manipulate this passage so fast. I went right on. Artie Matthews grabbed the tune from in front of me and said, "Hell, don't be messing with this guy. This guy is a shark!" I told them, "Boys, I been kidding you all along. I knew all these tunes anyhow. Just listen." Then I swung the *Miserere* and combined it with the *Anvil Chorus*.

You find, though, that people act very savage in this world. From then on it was George Reynolds's object to try to crush me. He couldn't do this, but he made things so unpleasant that I finally took a job out in the German section of town. The manager wanted a band, so I got some men together, although there wasn't many to pick from—clarinet, trumpet, man-dolin, drums, and myself. These were not hot men, but they were Negroes and they could read. They didn't play to suit me, but I told them if they played exactly what I put down on paper, they would be playing exactly as I wanted. Then I arranged all the popular tunes of that time—I even made a jazz arrangement of *Schnitzelbank*—and we made some pretty fair jazz for St. Louis in 1912.

St. Louis had been a great town for ragtime for years because Stark and Company spe-cialized in publishing Negro music. Among the composers the Starks published were: Scott Joplin (the greatest ragtime writer who ever lived and composer of *Maple Leaf Rag*), Tom Turpin, Louis Chauvin, Artie Matthews, and James Scott. But St. Louis wasn't like New Orleans; it was prejudiced. I moved on to Kansas City and found it was like St. Louis, except it did not have one decent pianist and didn't want any. That was why I went on to Chicago. In Chicago at that time you could go anywhere you wanted regardless of creed or color. So Chicago came to be one of the earliest places that jazz arrived, because of nice treatment—and we folks from New Orleans were used to nice treatment.

SOURCE: Alan Lomax, ed., *Mister Jelly Roll: The Fortunes of Jelly Roll Morton, New Orleans Creole and "Inventor of Jazz"* (Berkeley, CA: University of California Press, 1950). 2nd ed. 1973: 6–7, 42–43, 61–64, 66, 147–50.

~~~~~~~~

NOTES

1.   "La Paloma," ("The Dove") is a Spanish folk melody often attributed to the composer Sebastían Yradien (1809–1865). It is a standard, used by dance bands even today.

2.   This probably refers to a piano transcription of the overture to the operetta *The Poet and the Peasant* by the Viennese composer Franz von Suppé (1819–1895).

1920–1950

74

BESSIE SMITH, ARTIST AND BLUES SINGER

(Press Notice, Bailey, Schuller)

Considered the greatest of the classic blues singers, Bessie Smith (1894–1937) was a big woman—about six feet tall—with a voice to match. She was known as a "shouter," and sometimes critics labeled her "primitive" and crude, but she sang with hypnotic finesse. Her career, which began in southern tent shows and vaude-ville, changed dramatically after she signed with Columbia Records in 1923 and reached a national audience. When her career ended in the early '30s, an estimated six to ten million of her records had been sold and about 160 sides had been recorded and hence preserved; they are treasured today.

Frank Walker, the A&R (artist and repertoire) man for Columbia, sent his talent scout, clarinet player Clarence Williams, down to Atlanta to bring Smith back to New York. This notice appeared not long after in Music Trades, *an industry magazine.*

Bessie Smith has signed a contract to record Columbia new process records. Her singing of "Gulf Coast Blues" has made that selection deservedly popular among the younger set of her race in nearly every city.

Miss Smith draws capacity houses in every city where she appears in vaudeville. North or South, it makes no difference, for wherever there are colored folks, there is a strong demand for Bessie Smith's blues. The size of the crowds that hear her seems to be limited only [by] the sitting and standing room of the houses in which she appears.

The sale of negro records is becoming more and more of a volume proposition for phonograph dealers all over the country. Dealers who can offer the latest blues by the most important of all colored singers of blues selections, are in a strategic position to dominate the sale of records to the colored population of their locality. That is just what Bessie Smith's Columbia new process records mean to Columbia dealers.

It is interesting to note that although Bessie Smith sings selections written especially for the colored trade and generally written by colored composers, her records enjoy a considerable demand among white people. This has been specially noted among professional white entertainers, all of whom seem to recognize and appreciate her unique artistry.

Bessie Smith possesses a voice of that peculiarly desirable quality for which the old fashioned colored folks of the South were so noted. She recognizes the value of this gift—and strives constantly to retain those qualities which many a colored entertainer has lost beyond recall through a mistaken desire to take on a so-called metropolitan polish.

A consummate actress, Bessie Smith throws her whole personality into [the] characters of her songs. To hear the records is to realize this. Columbia dealers all over the country have learned, to their profit, the value of Bessie Smith's records as a drawing card.

SOURCE: "Dealers Expect Big Sale of Blues Records by Bessie Smith, Who Has Joined Columbia Artists," *Music Trades*, February 16, 1924, as quoted in Chris Albertson, *Bessie*, rev. ed. (New Haven, Conn.: Yale University Press, 2003): 64.

~~~~~~~

One of Bessie Smith's studio musicians was William "Buster" Bailey (1902–1967), a highly respected clarinetist who worked with many leading musicians, including a stint with Fletcher Henderson's band from 1924 through 1927. His Columbia sessions with Bessie Smith include "The Yellow Dog Blues" (1925) and "After You've Gone" (1927).

Bessie Smith was a kind of roughish sort of woman. She was good-hearted and big-hearted, and she liked to juice, and she liked to sing her blues slow. She didn't want no fast stuff. She had a style of phrasing, what they used to call swing—she had a certain way she used to sing. I hear a lot of singers now trying to sing something like that. Like this record that came out a few years ago—*Why Don't You Do Right?*—they're trying to imitate her.

We didn't have any rehearsals for Bessie's records. She'd just go with us to the studio around Columbus Circle. None of us rehearsed the things we recorded with her. We'd just go to the studio; Fletcher [Henderson] would get the key. This, by the way, applied not only to Bessie but to almost all the blues singers. The singers might have something written out to remind them what the verse was but there was no music written on it. On a lot of the records by Bessie you'll see lyrics by Bessie Smith and music by George Brooks. That was Fletcher.

We recorded by the horn. You know the way they used to record in those days. We'd monkey around until we had a good balance and we'd make two or three takes but we never made more than two masters on a tune. We'd make only two sides in a session and at that time we got more money for that than we do now.

For Bessie, singing was just a living. She didn't consider it anything special. She was certainly recognized among blues singers—a shouter, they called her. They all respected her because she had a powerful pair of lungs. There were no microphones in those days. She could fill up Carnegie Hall, Madison Square Garden, or a cabaret. She could fill it up from her muscle and she could last all night. There was none of this whispering jive.

SOURCE: Undated interview with William "Buster" Bailey in Nat Shapiro and Nat Hentoff, eds., *Hear Me Talkin' to Ya: The Story of Jazz as Told by the Men Who Made It* (1955; reprint, Dover, 1966): 244–45.

~~~~~~~~~

Smith's techniques of nuanced ornamentation were honored by the composer and educator Gunther Schuller (b. 1925) in his classic study, Early Jazz. *His sensitive "formalist" analysis prefigured the revival of interest in women's blues in general and Smith in particular, which occurred in the 1970s with the emergence of black feminism, women's studies, and African-American studies.*

In the hierarchy of jazz royalty, Bessie Smith was called "the Empress of the Blues." Probably the greatest "classic blues" singer, she certainly deserved the title not only because she was pre-eminent in the field but also because she was the first great professional urban-blues singer,[1] and therefore the first important *jazz* singer.

. . .

John Hammond's often quoted 1937 statement on Bessie Smith, "I'm not sure that her art did not reach beyond the limits of the term *jazz*," is another way of saying that Bessie's singing represented the ultimate fusion of technical perfection with a profound depth of expression that "penetrated"—to complete Hammond's thought—"the inner recesses of the listener." Much has been written about Bessie's depth of expression—a quality canonized by her premature, tragic death—but little has been written about her technical perfection. What, in a musician's terms, made Bessie Smith such a superior singer? Again it is a combination of elements: a remarkable ear for and control of intonation, in all its subtlest functions; a perfectly centered, naturally produced voice (in her prime); an extreme sensitivity to word meaning and the sensory, almost physical, feeling of a word; and, related to this, superb diction and what singers call projection. She was certainly the first singer on jazz records to value diction, not for itself, but as a vehicle for conveying emotional states. Most of Bessie's rivals, including Ma Rainey,[2] sang with a slurry pronunciation, vocally oriented to be sure. But the miracle of Bessie was that her careful diction was never achieved at the expense of musical flow or swing. I believe that much of her great commercial success was based on the fact that her audience really could understand every word and thus identify with her, especially in her many narrative "representational" blues.

Perhaps even more remarkable was her pitch control. She handled this with such ease and naturalness that one is apt to take it for granted. Bessie's fine microtonal shadings, the various "flatnesses" with which she could color a pitch in relation to a particular word or vowel, the way she could move into the center of a pitch with a short, beautifully executed scoop or "fall" out of it with a little moaning slide; or the way she could hit a note square in the middle—these are all part of a personal, masterful technique of great subtlety, despite the frequently boisterous mood or language. I am not saying that she knew these things in the learned "conservatory" sense, but simply that she knew how to do them at will, by whatever combination of instincts, musicality, and physical equipment she possessed.

Unlike instrumentalists, singers have an extra burden to cope with: they must delineate words. For the singer[,] vowels carry the pitch, while opening and closing consonants (if any) or glottal attacks specify the attack and decay pattern of a note. Here again Bessie Smith instinctively used these acoustical "components" in a musical way that almost defies analysis. Because she was never overtly spectacular in her vocal delivery, seemingly effortless style being the key to her art, we are apt to overlook the unique way in which she used consonants or glottal attacks to help delineate rhythmic ideas, to inflect them in a *jazz* manner—in short to *swing*.

. . .

As early as *Jailhouse Blues* (September 1923) we can hear the embellishment traits that form the essence of Bessie's style. In the first line (after the scene-setting introduction), "Thirty days in jail with my back turned to the wall," the importance of the words in the sentence determines the degree of embellishment each receives. Almost every word is emphasized by an upward scoop or slide, but each one differently. The words "thirty," "jail," and "wall"—the three main words of the sentence—are also those most modified by slides. "Thirty" starts with a relatively fast upward slur from approximately *e* flat to *g* flat. "Days" slides more slowly from the blue flat third to the major third, *g*. The next word, "in," is a slightly flat *g*, in preparation for a large major-third upward scoop on "jail": the most important word, *ergo* the strongest embellishment.

These four elements are now reused, but with different words, of course, and in a different sequence: a flat *g* for "with," and *e* flat for "my," a minor-third slide on "back" (similar to "thirty"), and a longer *g* flat to *g* slur on the word "turned." In the sense that "with my" is similar to "in jail"—the only difference being that the final return to *g* on "jail" is not consummated on "my"—we have here a reshuffling of four degrees of slides from the initial order of 1, 2, 3, 4 to 3, 4, 1, 2. The next two words, "to the," transitional and less important, are appropriately unembellished *g*'s, rhythmically short and connective.

So far all embellishments have been upward slides. Now, on "wall" Bessie uses one of her other frequently employed ornamental devices, a double slide which at first descends and then ascends to a final pitch. Here, in *Jailhouse Blues*, because Bessie is heading for the tonic, the the approximate sliding pitches are (Bessie used two other variants of this embellishment. Another one, also on the tonic, was , a quick downward dip to the sixth of the chord and up again. It is used, for example, on the word "wall" in the repeat of the first line of *Jailhouse Blues*. But her most frequently used double-note ornament was reserved for the third of the chord . This latter ornament appears with great consistency starting around 1925, and can be heard on any number of recordings: *Reckless Blues, Sobbin' Hearted Blues, Cold in Hand Blues,* and many others.)

On the word "wall" in the repeat line, we encounter another of Bessie's favorite devices, a phrase-ending "drop-off" or "fall-off." It is usually associated with the tonic and drops quickly to the sixth of the scale ♪ . But occasionally she did similar "drop-offs" on the third and even on the fifth of the key, as in *Cold in Hand Blues,* where the "fall-off" drops to the flat third ♪ .

Two further phrase idiosyncrasies appear in *Jailhouse Blues.* The one is a variant of the "drop-off," longer and more pitch-inflected. We hear it here on the word "turned," an interpolated phrase repeating the last half of the first line as a fill-in. (This two-bar "fill-in" would normally have been an instrumental response to the singer's first line, but since *Jailhouse Blues* was accompanied only by a pianist, Clarence Williams, Bessie occasionally decided to fill in the two bars herself.) On the word "turned" she sings ♪ , thus turning the word into a blues moan. Here, although the pitches are still connected by slides, they are nevertheless more articulated than in her other ornaments so that an actual melodic motive emerges.

Bessie also had a unique ability to break phrases into unexpected segments and to breathe at such phrase interruptions without in the slightest impairing over-all continuity, textual or melodic. In the repeat of the "Thirty days" line, Bessie breathes twice at unexpected places: between the words "my" and "back" for a real break in the phrase; then again between "turned" and "to the wall," a smaller interruption. The reason for these breath breaks is the previously mentioned interpolated half-phrase, "turned to the wall," which prevented her from going to the end of the second repeat line without breathing. Thus the over-all partitioning of both lines is as follows (' is an incidental breath mark, ˇ is a more pronounced interruption):

Thirty days in jail ' with my back turned ' to the wall '

Turned ˇ to the wall **x**

Thirty days in jail with my ˇ back turned ' to the wall.

Note that in the one place where one might have expected a breath, marked **x,** Bessie goes right on, bridging the natural division of the sentence.

SOURCE: Gunther Schuller, *Early Jazz: Its Roots and Musical Development* (New York: Oxford University Press, 1968): 226, 229–30, 231–33.

~~~~~~~

NOTES

1.   Actually, Bessie Smith was far from being the first to record vocal blues. That distinction falls to Mamie Smith (no relation). Though Mamie was more of a show and ballad singer than a blues singer, she delivered her songs with a reckless abandon and a wide-open shouting style that was worlds removed from the whimpering balladeers of the day.

2.   Gertrude "Ma" Rainey (1886–1939).

75

THOMAS ANDREW DORSEY "BRINGS THE
PEOPLE UP" AND CARRIES HIMSELF ALONG

Modern gospel music emerged as a distinctive genre within the African-American
church through the pioneering efforts of a generation of composers led by Thomas
A. Dorsey[1] (1899–1993), today widely recognized as the "father" of African-American
gospel music. His most famous composition, "Take My Hand, Precious Lord"—
which he wrote in 1932 after the tragedy of both his wife and child dying in childbirth—
is so successful that it has now been incorporated into many church hymnals.

A pianist as well as a singer, Dorsey began his career as a pianist and the director of the back-up band for the famous blues singer, Gertrude "Ma" Rainey. Thus
he was at the top of his game even before he surfaced in the church circuit. He combined both keyboard and vocal techniques from the blues to develop a new dynamic
style of musical worship. Despite resistance from those who associated the blues
with "devil's music" and those who remained dedicated to the spirituals and hymns,
Dorsey persevered and survived because of his ability to understand the various
musical expressions of community within the black church.

In the 1970s Dorsey gave a series of remarkable interviews to his biographer
Michael Harris from which these selections are taken. They concern vocal and instrumental improvisational techniques which still define contemporary mainstream
American vernacular performance practice. Following these excerpts are two transcriptions of "Amazing Grace," the first in the "moaning" style Harris calls "the

dominant musical source for Dorsey's gospel blues"[2] and the second in Dorsey's embellished keyboard style.

(a) That moan . . . is just about known only to the black folk. Now I've heard them sing like this when I was a boy in churches, and that kind of singing would stir the churches up more so than one of those fast hymns or one of those hymns they sang out of the book. . . . They'd get more shouts out of the moans than they did sometime out of the words, for the people, they didn't, everybody couldn't read back there, see? But it kind of brings the people up, puts them on their feet, starts them to thinking. After a while it hits the heart and they start to holler, hollering "hallelujah" or something like that. I don't know what it is, but there's something to it that nobody knows what it is; I don't know. . . . I'd hear my mother and other folk get together, get around and get to talking and then start moaning.

(b) Every singer who performs, speaker also, preacher, anybody, you don't stick exactly to your script. You got to have something that comes from inside of you that Providence or something gives to you while you are performing. Well, now, we call that, religiously, you call that the voice of God speaking through you. See you got to always be—everybody who performs or does anything, even talk—susceptible, openly susceptible to whatever comes in the heart or the mind or your ear.

(c) Blues is as important to a person feeling bad as "Nearer My God to Thee." I'm not talking about popularity; I'm talking about inside the individual. This moan gets into a person where there is some secret down there that they didn't bring out. See this stuff to come out is in you. When you cry out, that is something down there that should have come out a long time ago. Whether it's blues or gospel, there is a vehicle that comes along to take it away or push it away. A man or woman singing the blues in the church will cry out, "Holy, holy, holy."

(d) Blue notes are on the piano; been on the piano just like opera and its trills and things. A blues note? There's no such thing as a blue note. Blues don't own no notes. The world of music owns the notes and sounds on the piano. You're talking about the old blue seventh. We gave the blues that seventh. But it can be in anything. It's up to the individual to know how and when to bring it out.

(e) Now, I didn't originate the word gospel, I want you to know. I didn't originate that world. Gospel, the word "gospel" has been used down through the ages. But I took the word, took a group of singers, or one singer, as far as that's concerned, and I embellished [gospel], made it beautiful, more noticeable, more susceptible with runs and trills and moans in it. That's really one of the reasons my folk called it gospel music.

(f) I wouldn't have been as successful in gospel songs if I hadn't known some of these things, trills, turns, movements in blues. It's the trills and turns in it that you can't get into anything else but blues and gospel songs. There are moans that you can't get into anything else but blues and gospel songs. Now you take some of the gospel singers—some of the best ones were good blues singers.

Amazing Grace ("moaning style")

mm. 1-3

mm. 4-5

mm. 6-7

mm. 8-10

mm. 11-13

mm. 14-16

Amazing Grace in two styles, the "Moaning Style," and in Thomas Dorsey's style for piano and voice. Transcribed by Michael J. Harris.

Amazing Grace (Dorsey's style—2)

mm. 1-2

mm. 3-4

mm. 5-6

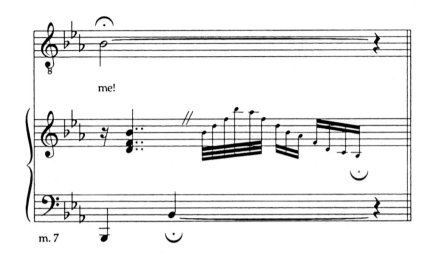

me!

m. 7

SOURCE: Interviews with Thomas A. Dorsey as follows: (a) February 2, 1976, (b) and (c) January 19, 1977; (d) no date given; and (e), January 22, 1977, conducted by and as quoted in Michael W. Harris, *The Rise of Gospel Blues: The Music of Thomas Andrew Dorsey in the Urban Church* (New York: Oxford University Press, 1992); 22, 100–101, 97, 209. The interviews are not available outside of this book. The introductory headnote was written in collaboration with Emmett Price.

~~~~~~~~~~~~

NOTES

1.   Not to be confused with the trombonist and swing band leader, Tommy Dorsey (1905–1956).
2.   Harris, *The Rise of Gospel Blues*, 24.

76

LOUIS ARMSTRONG IN HIS OWN WORDS

The great artist Louis Armstrong (1901–1971) left a written legacy that is matched by few other jazz musicians of his historical significance. He published not one but two autobiographies in his lifetime, and a recent collection of new writings adds to these life stories. The first selection reprinted here pertains to his Chicago years, his early marriage to Lillian Hardin, and working with King Oliver. It follows the original editor's policy of retaining the spellings, italics, and punctuation of the original. The subsequent excerpt comes from a magazine article, in which Armstrong succinctly describes some of his most famous music.

There were *lots of* the musicians from Downtown Chicago—hurrying from their Jobs—to *Dig* us every night that we played at the Lincoln Gardens on *31st* Street, near the Cottage Grove Avenue. When Joe Oliver's contract was finished at the Gardens, we sure did hate to leave. In fact—that happens to most musicians. They stay at a place for a long time. And they get so used to the joint, until—it *seems* a *Drag* to leave. But—we finally did. We toured all through Iowa—Pennsylvania—Maryland—Illinois—etc. A very nice tour, I thought. King Oliver's Band was the first, All Colored Band to sign up with the M.C.A. Corporation. I used to do my little Dance with the band, when they hit the road. Although I was a Singer when I joined the King's outfit, and he knew that I could sing. But, he didn't seem to bother. And I did not feel that I should—*force* the issue. Maybe "Pappa Joe"—that's the name I used to call King Oliver—felt the same way that Fletcher Henderson *did* concerning my singing with the Band. Not that they weren't for it. It was just the idea that there never was a *trumpet* player, or, any *instrument* player at that time—way back in the olden days the instrumentalists just weren't singing, that's all. So, I gathered that those two Big shot Boys, Joe + Fletcher, just was afraid to let me sing, thinking maybe, I'd sort of ruin their reputations, with their musical public. They not *knowing* that I had been singing, all of my life. In *Churches, etc.* I had one of the finest All Boys Quartets that ever walked the streets of New Orleans. So you see? Singing was more *into* my Blood, than the trumpet. Anyway, we forgot about the singing—All together. But, as I've said before, Fletcher did manage to let me sing, a vocal chorus to the tune of—"Everybody Loves My Baby," on a Banner Label. And—my goodness—the compliments Fletcher received, when the recording was released. And still Fletcher, or King Oliver, never did *pick up* on my *vocalizings*, which until this day was nothing to write home about. *But. It was Different.*

. . .

    After the Lincoln Gardens let out—the first night *Lil and I* got *married*—we made the 'Rounds to all of the After Hour *spots*. And Everywhere we went, everybody *commenced* throwing a lot of *Rice* on us. *My my*—I often wondered—where on earth did they find so much *Rice. Why*—every place that we would leave—in front of the door was real white—the same as if there had been a real heavy *snow* on the ground—from so much Rice lying thrown around. *Lillian* and myself, we did not take a Honeymoon, or anything like that. We both thought—it would be a better idea to save all the money we could and try and buy ourselves a nice little *pad* (a home)—kinda look out for a rainy day. It is—an old saying, and it has been around for Generations. Instead of a Honeymoon, we went on tour with King Oliver + his Band. We saved our money together. And, we accumulated quite a bit of *Loot* (money) together. And—sure enough—we really did save enough money to buy a very nice family house, in Chicago of course—at 421 East 44th St. We were both lucky in buying this house. Because the people who had it in front of us certainly did leave it in real fine—good shape. We didn't have to do a thing but *move* in with our furniture. At the same time Lil + I got married, she was living with her mother, Dempsey Miller. Of course, Dempsey's *nick* name, was "*Deecie*." Deecie was a Christian woman and very nice. She treated me swell from the first day we were married, and even after we all moved in our home together. Deecie was from Memphis, Tennessee. She raised *Lil,* to be a real smart gal. Lil, was so smart, until, when she attended *Fisk* University—She was Valedictorian of the class. When Deecie + her husband came to Chicago she brought *Lil* with her.

    By that time *Lil* had turned out to be a fine piano player. She was *so* good, until all the Jazz Bands on the South Side, were Dickering for her to join their Bands. But she settle[d] for King Oliver's Band, which I personally think she made the right move. Lil was in Joe's Band when I came to Chicago. She was the best. She would give out with that good 'ol' New Orleans 4 Beat, which a lot of Northern piano players couldn't do, to save their lives. *Ol Lil,* would make my "Boy" King Oliver, really *Give* out, when she would Commence to *Lay* that good 4 beat under *Papa Joe. Yessir*—Between Lil and Baby Dodds, Ol Joe Oliver would create more New Riffs and Ideas, than *any* musician I *know* of. And—for a "woman" there are very few *men* piano players, who can Swing a Band as good as *Lil.* And I am not just saying this because I was married to her. If you'll notice—you'll find a lot of good piano players ruined their beautiful Dixieland style—

fooling around that old "Bop Slop" Music. *Lil* had, the best jobs *Sewed up* when I first came to Chicago to join King Oliver.

. . .

Out of all of the After hour Joints that were running in Chicago at that time (1922–1923), I kinda liked the Edelweiss Gardens the best. Later on—during my stay in Chicago, there was another After hour *Joint*—very pretty—opened up at 35th and State Street, called the Fume (or Fieum or Fiume—one of these) [Fiume]. The *Fiume* was a Black + Tan place, which means Colored (of course) and they had an *All White,* Dixieland Combo playing there Nightly. Which was Something (at that time) very rare. Of course, there wasn't, no particular reason why that I was a *little bit* surprised to see White Boys, playing music on the South Side of Chicago. It's just that I had never seen such a beautiful picture before. I had just come up from the South, where there weren't anything as near beautiful as that happening. *White* musicians, playing all of that good "Jump" music,—making those Colored people (mostly colored) *Swing like Mad.* The Fiume and the Edelweiss Gardens became a toss *up* with me as to *which* one of the places that I should *hang* out, in the mornings after I finish work with my *man*—Joe King Oliver.

Sometimes I'd persuade *Papa* Joe (I calls *him*) to make the Rounds with me, after work, which would be—two o'clock in the A.M. It was real "*Kicks*—listening to music, *Diggin'* his thoughts—comments *etc*. His Conception of *things*—life—Music, people in general, were really wonderful. It is really too bad that the world did not have a chance to *Dig* the real Joe King Oliver and his greatness. His human interest in things was really something to think about. All Joe Oliver had to do—was just to talk to me, and I'd feel just like I had one of those good old music lessons of his. It was a *solid gassuh* the way he would explain things.

SOURCE: *Louis Armstrong in His Own Words: Selected Writings,* ed. Thomas Brothers (New York: Oxford University Press, 1999): 63–64, 67.

~~~~~~~~

In 1951, Esquire magazine asked Armstrong to comment on some of his best-known recordings. These included material from the Hot Five and Hot Seven recordings made during the 1920s. Even if there were precedents for scat before "Heebie Jeebies," Armstrong made it famous.

"POTATO HEAD BLUES." LOUIS ARMSTRONG AND HIS HOT SEVEN

Kid Ory, trombone—Johnny Dodds, clarinet—Johnny St. Cyr, banjo—Baby Dodds, drums—Pete Briggs, tuba—Lil Hardin, piano—Louis Armstrong, trumpet. . . . This particular recording really "gassed me" because of the perfect phrasing that was done by Johnny and Ory. . . . I could look direct into the Pelican Dance Hall, at Gravier and Rampart Streets in New Orleans, during the days of the First World War. . . . That was in the years of 1918–1919. . . . And their bandstand was built in the left-hand corner of the hall. . . . And the stand was up over everybody's head. . . . in order to say hello to any member of the band, you had to look up. . . . And all of that good music was pouring out of those instruments—making you want to just dance and listen and wishing they'd never stop. . . . "Potato Head Blues" was a tune they really did swing out with. . . . My man, Joe Oliver, bless [his] heart. . . . Papa Joe (I used to call him) he really used to blow the kind of cornet I used to just love to hear. . . . His playing still lingers in my mind. . . . There never was a creator of cornet any greater than Joe Oliver. . . . I've never heard anyone to come up to him as yet. . . . And he's been dead since 1938. . . . "Potato Head Blues" . . . Hmm . . . Every note that I blew in this recording, I thought of Papa Joe . . . "Yass Lawd."

. . .

"HEEBIE JEEBIES." LOUIS ARMSTRONG'S HOT FIVE

"Heebie Jeebies" was another recording, was another incident that I shall not ever forget. . . . This time the laugh was on me. . . . When everybody heard about this record was made they all got a big laugh out of it. . . . They also said that this particular recording was the beginning of Scat Singing. . . . Because the day we recorded "Heebie Jeebies," I dropped the paper with the lyrics—right in the middle of the tune. . . . And I did not want to stop and spoil the record which was moving along so wonderfully. . . . So when I dropped the paper, I immediately turned back into the horn and started to Scatting. . . . Just as nothing had happened. . . . When I finished the record I just knew the recording people would throw it out. . . . And to my surprise they all came running out of the controlling booth and said—"Leave That In." . . .

My, my . . . I gave a big sigh of relief. . . . And sure enough—they did publish "Heebie Jeebies" the same way it was mistakenly recorded. . . . Kid Ory—John A. St. Cyr—Johnny Dodds—Lil Hardin—and myself on this recording. . . . Boyd Atkins who used to play the violin in my band at the Sunset Cafe wrote the tune. . . . He must have made a nice little "taste" (meaning) the tune made a quite a bit of "loot" (meaning) they sold lots of records and made lots of "dough" (meaning) "money." . . . On this record the players were—Kid Ory, trombone—Lil Hardin, piano—John A. St. Cyr—Johnny Dodds, clarinet—oh yes—St. Cyr, banjo . . . Louis Armstrong, trumpet.

. . .

"CORNET CHOP SUEY." LOUIS ARMSTRONG'S HOT FIVE

Written by Satchmo Louis Armstrong . . . On the steps (back steps) of his second wife Lillian Hardin Armstrong['s house]. . . . "Cornet Chop Suey" turned out to be a very popular tune—especially among the musicians & actors and music lovers. . . . Kid Ory—Lil Hardin—Johnny Dodds—Johnny St. Cyr and myself played on the recording date also. . . . Those variations in this recording remind me of the days when we played the tail gate (advertisings) in New Orleans. . . . We kids, including Henry Rena—Buddy Petit—Joe Johnson and myself, we all were very fast on our cornets . . . And had some of the fastest fingers anyone could ever imagine a cornet player could have. . . . And to us—we did not pay any attention to the idea that we were fingering our horns so terribly fast. . . . And all of those boys had good tones . . . And when I say tone, I'm speaking of tones that blend with the tone that a trumpet man should have when playing a swing tune—And you'll hear a lot of them blowing like mad . . . But they never lost essence and the mellow fragrance of the tune. "Cornet Chop Suey" could be played as a trumpet solo, or with a symphony orchestra.

. . .

"BASIN STREET BLUES." LOUIS ARMSTRONG AND HIS SAVOY BALLROOM FIVE—FEATURING EARL HINES

This is another recording date that was a real "Gassuh" . . . with Earl Hines, piano—Mancy Cara, banjo guitar—Jimmy Strong, clarinet—Fred Robinson, trombone—Louis Armstrong, cornet. . . . "Basin Street Blues" was also a tune written from the good old days of Storyville. . . . In fact, there's a street named Basin Street in New Orleans. . . . Lulu White, the Octoroon Chick, had a very famous house on that street in those days, called "Mahogany Hall" . . . Jelly Roll Morton, the great jazz man at the piano, played for Lulu . . . In the days when money was flowing like wine, down there. . . . Basin Street is what travelers call a "landmark" nowadays.

SOURCE: Louis Armstrong, "Jazz on a High Note," *Esquire*, December 1951, as reprinted in *Louis Armstrong in His Own Words: Selected Writings*, ed. Thomas Brothers (New York: Oxford University Press, 1999): 127–35.

77

GILBERT SELDES WAVES THE FLAG OF POP

At just the right time—the 1920s—the critic Gilbert Seldes (1893–1970) took popular culture more seriously than had any of his contemporary colleagues. His brave book *The Seven Lively Arts* crushes the "high" and raises the "low" to new heights of aesthetic virtue. Seldes was one of the first modern critics to treat as artists pop-culture icons, among them the film star Charlie Chaplin, the vaudeville entertainers Al Jolson and Fanny Brice, and the song composer Irving Berlin, whom George Gershwin extolled. This miniature manifesto, which looks backward to the writings of the critic Van Wyck Brooks, who began what might be called the "terminology of the brow"—as in "high," low," and "middle"—also anticipates the second half of the twentieth century, when critics had no trouble applying intellectual history to rock or political philosophy to MTV (see chapters 114 and 153).

M ost of the great works of art have reference to our time only indirectly—as they and we are related to eternity. And we require arts which specifically refer to our moment, which create the image of our lives. There are some twenty workers in literature, music, painting, sculpture, architecture, and the dance who are doing this for us now—and doing it in such a manner as to associate our modern existence with that extraordinary march of mankind which we like to call the progress of humanity. It is not enough. In addition to them—in addition, not in place of them—we must have arts which, we feel, are for ourselves alone, which no one before us could have cared for so much, which no one after us will wholly understand. The picture by Picasso could have been admired by an unprejudiced critic a thousand years ago, and will be a thousand years hence. We require, for nourishment, something fresh and transient. It is this which makes jazz so much the characteristic art of our time and Jolson a more typical figure than Chaplin, who, also is outside of time. There must be ephemera. Let us see to it that they are good.

The characteristic of the great arts is high seriousness—it occurs in Mozart and Aristophanes and Rabelais and Molière as surely as in Æschylus and Racine. And the essence of the minor arts is high levity which existed in the *commedia dell'arte* and exists in Chaplin, which you find in the music of Berlin and Kern (not "funny" in any case). It is a question of exaltation, of carrying a given theme to the "high" point. The reference in a great work of art is to something more profound; and no trivial theme has ever required, or had, or been able to bear, a high seriousness in treatment. Avoiding the question of creative genius, what impresses us in a work of art is the intensity or the pressure with which the theme, emotion, sentiment, even "idea" is rendered. Assuming that a blow from the butt of a revolver is not exactly artistic presentation, that "effectiveness" is not the only criterion, we have the beginning of a criticism of aesthetics. We know that the method does count, the creativeness, the construction, the form. We know also that while the part of humanity which is fully civilized will always care for high seriousness, it will be quick to appreciate the high levity of the minor arts. There is no conflict. The battle is only against solemnity which is not high, against ill-rendered profundity, against the shoddy and the dull.

I have allowed myself to catalogue my preferences; it is possible to set the basis of them down in impersonal terms, in propositions:

That there is no opposition between the great and the lively arts.

That both are opposed in the spirit to the middle or bogus arts.

That the bogus arts are easier to appreciate, appeal to low and mixed emotions, and jeopardize the purity of both the great and the minor arts.

That except in a period when the major arts flourish with exceptional vigour, the lively arts are likely to be the most intelligent phenomena of their day.

That the lively arts as they exist in America to-day are entertaining, interesting, and important.

That with a few exceptions these same arts are more interesting to the adult cultivated intelligence than most of the things which pass for art in cultured society.

That there exists a "genteel tradition" about the arts which has prevented any just appreciation of the popular arts, and that these have therefore missed the corrective criticism given to the serious arts, receiving instead only abuse.

That therefore the pretentious intellectual is as much responsible as any one for what is actually absurd and vulgar in the lively arts.

That the simple practitioners and simple admirers of the lively arts being un-corrupted by the bogus preserve a sure instinct for what is artistic in America.

SOURCE: Gilbert Seldes, *The Seven Lively Arts* (New York: Harper, 1924): 347–350.

78

$\mathcal{A}$L JOLSON AND *THE JAZZ SINGER*

If not the first "talking film," *The Jazz Singer* (1927) was the first film musical in which real-time spoken dialogue (as opposed to prerecorded, synchronized sound) occurred. Its star, Al Jolson (1886–1950), was the most famous entertainer of his time, and the film *The Jazz Singer* stands as a landmark for its Vitaphone song synchronizations and Jolson's impromptu film conversations. Providing a log of American pop-music styles, Jolson performed seven songs which track the 1890s–1920s—from Paul Dresser's "My Gal Sal" to Irving Berlin's "Blue Skies."

The fact that none of these songs are considered "jazz" today only heightens the incongruity of a white singer in blackface singing them. As a Jewish minstrel, Al Jolson wore blackface and specialized in the genre of "Mammy" songs so popular in the early 1900s. In *The Jazz Singer,* Jolson's character "blacks up," a convention which remained widely accepted even into the 1930s and '40s. Still, the story line is not about race, but rather about immigration and cultural conflicts, as seen through the eyes of the Jewish experience in particular.

The title card which opens the film reads, "The New York Ghetto, throbbing to that rhythm of music which is older than civilization." That music belonged to the *Ostjuden,* the Eastern European Jews who emigrated in great numbers to the United States from the 1890s through 1924, when restrictive immigration laws were passed. After initial footage from the Lower East Side, the camera moves inside an Orthodox Jewish synagogue; a service is in progress, enabling many Christian Americans to hear for the first time the "exotic," "Oriental" sounds of Jewish liturgy, in particular the "Kol Nidre," a chant sung on the Day of Atonement. Music makes explicit the movie's central themes of guilt and forgiveness.

The film was adapted from a play by Samson Raphaelson (1894–1983), which reached a mainly Jewish audience in New York City in 1925. Raphaelson's preface, which is reprinted here, is a theatrical conceit, linking jazz with prayer. He paints a portrait of social desperation symbolized by musical conflict. A few of Raphaelson's dramatic hooks had general currency, particularly his acceptance of jazz as a symbol of urban modernity. However, he took the idea of jazz defined as a Tin Pan Alley song—one widely accepted in the 1920s—to naïve extremes.

First- and second-generation Jewish Americans understood the theme of conflicted identity, both collective and personal: can one leave the ghetto and still be authentic? Should a *yeshiva bocher*—the Yiddish phrase meaning a Jewish boy student, one in this case destined to be a cantor in a synagogue—go on stage like a *goy*, a non-Jew? The play's ambiguous ending does not answer these questions, but the film did. Jolson's character gets his big career and forgiveness.

Following Raphaelson's preface is an article about the commercial potential of Jolson's personality.

American life, in this year 1925, consists essentially of surfaces. You may point out New England communities and say here is depth, and I will answer, true, but New England is dead so far as the America of now is concerned. You may show me an integrity in the West where a century ago pioneers came, and I will answer, that integrity resides with the elders and not with the mightier young ones. He who wishes to picture today's America must do it kaleidoscopically; he must show you a vivid contrast of surfaces, raucous, sentimental, egotistical, vulgar, ineffably busy—surfaces whirling in a dance which is sometimes a dance to Aphrodite and more frequently a dance to Jehovah.

In seeking a symbol of the vital chaos of America's soul, I find no more adequate one than jazz. Here you have the rhythm of frenzy staggering against a symphonic background—a background composed of lewdness, heart's delight, soul-racked madness, monumental boldness, exquisite humility, but principally prayer.

I hear jazz, and I am given a vision of cathedrals and temples collapsing and, silhouetted against the setting sun, a solitary figure, a lost soul, dancing grotesquely on the ruins. . . . Thus do I see the jazz singer.

Jazz is prayer. It is too passionate to be anything else. It is prayer distorted, sick, unconscious of its destination. The singer of jazz is what Matthew Arnold said of the Jew, "lost between two worlds, one dead, the other powerless to be born." In this, my first play, I have tried to crystallize the ironic truth that one of the Americas of 1925—the one which packs to overflowing our cabarets, musical revues and dance halls—is praying with a fervor as intense as that of the America which goes sedately to church and synagogue. The jazz American is different from the dancing dervish, from the Zulu medicine man, from the negro evangelist only in that he doesn't know he is praying.

I have used a Jewish youth as my protagonist because the Jews are determining the nature and scope of jazz more than any other race—more than the negroes, from whom they have stolen jazz and given it a new color and meaning. Jazz is Irving Berlin, Al Jolson, George Gershwin, Sophie Tucker. These are Jews with their roots in the synagogue. And these are expressing in evangelical terms the nature of our chaos today.

You find the soul of a people in the songs they sing. You find the meaning of the songs in the souls of the minstrels who create and interpret them. In "The Jazz Singer" I have attempted an exploration of the soul of one of these minstrels.

SOURCE: Samson Raphaelson, *The Jazz Singer* (New York: Brentano, 1925): 9–10.

~~~~~~~~~~

In The Jazz Singer, *Jolson's voice throbbed with emotion, mixing operatic vibrato and Jewish cantorial passion. His sense of rhythmic timing echoed his manic energy. And he moved like a 1920s Elvis. This review from* Variety *magazine displays the power of personality as well as the impact of the Vitaphone synchronized score.*

SID SILVERMAN PRAISES VITAPHONE AND ITS STAR

Undoubtedly the best thing Vitaphone has ever put on the screen. The combination of the religious heart interest story and Jolson's singing "Kol Nidre" in a synagog while his father is dying and two "Mammy" lyrics as his mother stands in the wings of the theatre, and later as she sits in the first row, carries abundant power and appeal. Besides which the finish of the "Mammy" melody (the one that goes "The sun shines east, the sun shines west")[1] is also the end of the picture with Jolson supposedly on a stage and a closeup on the screen as his voice pours through the amplifiers.

To a first night Broadway [audience] that finale was a whale and resulted in a tumultuous ovation. Jolson, personally, has never been more warmly greeted than at this premiere. He was there, in person, also.

But "The Jazz Singer" minus Vitaphone is something else again. There's really no love interest in the script, except between mother and son. It's doubtful if the general public will take to the Jewish boy's problem of becoming a cantor or a stage luminary as told on celluloid. On the other hand, with Vitaphone it can't miss. It is understood that W[arner] B[rothers] has prepared two versions of the film, with and without Vitaphone, for the exhibition angle.

Jolson, when singing, is Jolson. There are six instances of this, each running from two to three minutes. When he's without that instrumental spur Jolson is camera conscious. Yet for his first picture the Shubert ace does exceptionally well. Plus [with] his camera makeup[,] this holder of a $17,500 check for one week in a picture house isn't quite the Al his vast audience knows. But as soon as he gets under cork [blackface] the lens picks up that spark of individual personality solely identified with him. That much goes with or without Vitaphone.

The picture is all Jolson, although Alan Crosland, directing, has creditably dodged the hazard of over-emphasizing the star as well as refraining from laying it on too thick in the scenes between the mother and boy. The film dovetails splendidly, which speaks well for those component parts of the technical staff. Cast support stands out in the persons of Eugenie Besserer, as the mother; Otto Lederer, as a friend of the family; and Warner Oland as the father. Oland recently left this theatre as a Chinese dastard in "Old San Francisco" and comes back as a Jewish cantor, so if his performance isn't what it might be, it's excusable on the territory he covers.

May McAvoy is pretty well smothered on footage with no love theme to help, but being instrumental in getting Jakie, nee Jack Robin, his chance in a Broadway show. She is also a performer in the story.

Heavy heart interest in the film and some comedy, plus adept titling, which helps both these ingredients. Tho[ugh] pathos makes the picture a contender for Jewish neighborhoods, minus the voice feature. With Jolson's audible rendering of "Kol Nidre" this bit will likely make a tremendous impression in such houses. Or any audience for that matter as, after all, anybody's religion demands respect and consideration and when as seriously presented as here, the genuineness of the effort will make everybody listen. Besides which the story has the father dying as his son sings for him with the boy's voice coming through a window as the parent passes on.

By script it tells of young Jakie running away from home to eventually become a vaudevillian. Bobbie Gordon plays this early sequence with Jolson's entrance in Coffee Dan's cellar restaurant in 'Frisco, where he gets up and does two songs, "Dirty Hands, Dirty Face" and "Toot, Toot, Tootsie, Goodbye."

. . .

George Jessel originally did the show and was supposed to have done this picture. Jessel is still out in the play and doing big business. When the show first opened on Broadway last year talk was that the story was based on Jolson, so now with Jolson actually doing it the psychology is perfect.

Louis Silvers gets credit for having arranged the Vita-synchronization with the projection booth switching machines for Jolson's songs, the change over generally coming on a title. An odd factor is that the orchestral accompaniment to the story is scratchy, but when Jolson sings it's about the best recording Vitaphone has turned out to date.

Jolson in "The Jazz Singer" is surefire for Broadway. With his songs that holds good for any town or street. Exclude Vitaphone and there crops up the problem that it amounts to a Jewish mother-son religious story with Jolson not yet enough the screen actor to carry it. It's running for a consecutive 88 minutes at the Warner and will have totaled a lot of screen hours by the time it reaches the end of its stay.

As presented with Vitaphone, it's a credit to everybody concerned.

[signed] Sid [Silverman]

SOURCE: Sid Silverman, original review from *Variety*, October 12, 1927. Available at *Variety 100: Film Reviews through the Years.* http://www.variety.com/index.asp.

NOTE

1.   "My Mammy," W. Joe Young and Sam Lewis, M. Walter Donaldson, 1921.

CARL STALLING, MASTER OF CARTOON MUSIC

An Interview

The advent of sound film brought with it sound animation and cartoon music. One of the outstanding composers in this genre, Carl Stalling (1891–1972), scored Walt Disney's cartoons in the late 1920s, and then moved in 1936 to Warner Brothers, where he stayed for the rest of his career. He composed soundtracks for its popular cartoon characters such as Bugs Bunny, Porky Pig, Sylvester, Daffy Duck, and the Road Runner. Because of his early background playing and improvising music at the organ for the silent films in movie houses, Stalling knew how to cannibalize classical music with flair and imagination. Even if we were unaware, many of us heard Liszt, Rossini, and Wagner through cartoons. Stalling also wrote original scores, which are increasingly appreciated for their artistry today. This selection is taken from "the *only* extensive interview of any kind ever conducted" with Stalling, which took place in 1971.

MILTON GRAY:[1]   How did you become a composer of music for cartoons?

CARL STALLING: As I recall, I first met Walt Disney in the early twenties. He used to come to the Isis Theater, where I played the organ and had my own orchestra. This was music to accompany silent movies, and I played the whole afternoon and evening. When I wasn't at the organ, I'd be conducting, or playing the piano and conducting. I had a pianist for a number of years, and then I just conducted. Walt was making short commercials at that time, and he'd have us run them for him. We got acquainted, and I had him make several song films. *The End of a Perfect Day*,[2] showing sunset . . . Victor Herbert's "A Kiss in the Dark." The words would come on one at a time, with the music. This was before sound, of course.

Walt left for Hollywood shortly after that time, and I didn't see him again until 1928. I started writing him when sound pictures came in, and in our correspondence back and forth, we just agreed that there would be a position for a musical director at his studio. He came through Kansas City on his way to New York to record the music for *Steamboat Willie* (1928).[3] I didn't go with him, since he already had that all set up. I had nothing to do with that. Walt took a taxi to my home, and we talked principally of how sound pictures were causing a revolution in Hollywood. He had two silent pictures—*Gallopin' Gaucho* and *Plane Crazy*—already made, and he left those with me. I wrote most of the music for them at home in Kansas City. I met Walt in New York to record that music and we shared the same hotel room; we both washed out our socks in the same bathroom sink. I was with Walt when *Steamboat Willie* was previewed at the Colony Theater, down on Broadway, and we got the audience reaction. The reaction was very good. We sat in almost the last row and heard laughs and snickers all around us.

. . .

BILL SPICER: Had you done any composing before your first cartoon work for Walt?

CS: No. I improvised at the theaters, and that's composing, but it's not writing it down.

BS: Could you tell us about the music you did for *The Skeleton Dance* (1929), the first of the Silly Symphonies?

CS: It was mostly original; that was forty years ago, and I can't remember if I used anything else or not. But it wasn't Saint-Saëns' *Danse Macabre*, although some writers [have] said it was.

MG: I've read that Walt wanted to use that music, but couldn't get copyright clearance, so he asked you to compose something similar.

CS: That's what he usually did when something was copyrighted, but my music wasn't similar at all to the *Danse Macabre*. It was mostly a fox trot, in a minor key.

MIKE BARRIER: I've been told that you used some of the music from Grieg's *Peer Gynt Suite* in *The Skeleton Dance*. Do you remember using that music?

CS: No. When we were working out a story, usually for the Silly Symphonies, I would sometimes use a musical number as a pattern, suggesting a certain style or mood. I would play it on the piano for the director, and then write something similar, but original, for recording.

Walt never wanted to pay for music; he wanted me to just make up something. In one picture, he wanted to use the song "School Days," but he would have had to pay for it. So he said, "Carl, can't you write something that sounds like 'School Days' but isn't?"

The Skeleton Dance goes way back to my kid days. When I was eight or ten years old, I saw an ad in The American Boy magazine of a dancing skeleton, and I got my dad to give me a quarter so I could send for it. It turned out to be a pasteboard cut-out of a loose-jointed skeleton, slung over a six-foot cord under the arm pits. It would "dance" when kids pulled and jerked at each end of the string.

. . .

MG: So the idea for The Skeleton Dance was really yours. And the story, too?

CS: If you call it a story. We'd all get together on gags, in what they called a gag meeting.

MG: What did Walt say when you brought up the idea for The Skeleton Dance? Did he like it right away?

CS: He was interested right away. After two or three of the Mickeys had been completed and were being run in theaters, Walt talked with me on getting started on the musical series that I had in mind. He thought I meant illustrated songs, but I didn't have that in mind at all. When I told him that I was thinking of inanimate figures, like skeletons, trees, flowers, etc., coming to life and dancing and doing other animated actions fitted to music more or less in [a] humorous and rhythmic mood, he became very much interested. I gave him the idea of using the four seasons, and he made a cartoon on each one of those. I scored one of them [Springtime (1930)] before I left.

For a name or title for the series, I suggested not using the word "music" or "musical," as it sounded too commonplace, but to use the word "Symphony" together with a humorous word. At the next gag meeting, I don't know who suggested it, but Walt asked me: "Carl, how would 'Silly Symphony' sound to you?" I said, "Perfect!" Then I suggested the first subject, The Skeleton Dance, because ever since I was a kid I had wanted to see real skeletons dancing and had always enjoyed seeing skeleton-dancing acts in vaudeville. As kids, we all like spooky pictures and stories, I think.

That's how the Silly Symphonies got started. Of course, everyone knows that if it had not been for Walt Disney, then in all probability there would never have been a Mickey Mouse. This makes me wonder sometimes, would there ever have been a Silly Symphony or who would have suggested The Skeleton Dance—if?

. . .

MG: How was Walt as a boss? Was he demanding, or easy to work for?

CS: Well, he couldn't explain just what he wanted, at times. We'd go crazy trying to figure out what he wanted. But he inspired us that way. We wanted to help him, we wanted to do it, and we all worked together in that respect. That was his genius, I think, inspiring people who worked for him to come up with new ideas.

MB: Did Walt tell you what he wanted in the way of music?

CS: He had definite ideas sometimes, and sometimes it'd be the other way around.
        . . .

MB: You invented the "tick" system of recording music for animated cartoons, didn't you? Do you recall the circumstances that led to that?

CS: The "tick" system was not really an invention, since it was not patentable. Perfect synchronization of music for cartoons was a problem, since there were so many quick changes and actions that the music had to match. The thought struck me that if each member of the orchestra had a steady beat in his ear, from a telephone receiver, this would solve the problem. I had exposure sheets for the films, with the picture broken down frame by frame, sort of like a script, and twelve of the film frames went through the projector in a half second. That gave us a beat.
        . . .

MB: How large an orchestra did they use at the Disney and Iwerks studios?

CS: Eight to twelve players. At Warner's we had as many as fifty or so, their main studio orchestra. We had a vocal group, too, once in a while. The chorus director wrote the music for them.
        . . .

MB: Now, after you went to work for Schlesinger,[4] you were the only composer Warner's had until you retired?

CS: For the cartoons, yes, for twenty-two years. I retired in 1958.

MB: Did your music differ much at Warner's from what it had been at Disney's and Iwerks?

CS: Yes, because at Warner's, I could use popular music. That opened up a new field so far as the kind of music we could use. At Disney's, we had to go back to the nineteenth century, to classical music, to "My Old Kentucky Home."
        When I came out here, there was no law that cartoon music was copyrightable. That went into effect in the late forties. Then they started paying royalties retroactive from the day I started with Warner Bros. They're still paying, on the television reruns. Royalties are paid to composers whose music I used, and also to me for my original music.

MG: Apart from the increased use of popular songs, did you notice much of a change in your music over the years, as you composed it?

CS: It depended on the picture. When we had a very modern picture, I used as much music in the modern style as I could think up—augmented intervals, and so forth. But other than that, my style didn't change much.

MB: Of your music for cartoons, how much was other composers' music that you reworked and how much was original?

CS: Eighty to ninety per cent was original. It had to be, because you had to match the music to the action, unless it was singing or something like that.

        . . .

MB: Were there ever any cartoons that you had trouble writing music for, where the music didn't seem to suggest itself naturally?

CS: No. You see, I had played in theaters for about twenty years before sound came in. We improvised all the time, on the organ. I'd have to put music out for the orchestra, for features, but for comedies and newsreels we just improvised at the organ. So I really was used to composing for films before I started writing for cartoons. I just imagined myself playing for a cartoon in the theater, improvising, and it came easier.

MB: Did you have certain instruments that you liked to use more than others in your cartoon scores?

CS: The bassoon . . . the trombone, the slides on the trombone . . . the violin, with the glissandos, for comic effects. The viola is very good for mysterious effects.

        . . .

MB: Playing for a cartoon score would be hard for many musicians to get used to, wouldn't it?

CS: The musicians said they enjoyed the cartoons more than anything else. They looked forward to coming down to record the cartoon. It was screwy stuff, you know. A cartoon score was usually made up of about ten sections. We'd run through a section once or twice—usually just once—and then record it. We had a wonderful orchestra at Warner's. It took about three hours to record a cartoon score.

MG: Did the directors show you the storyboards, and you then decided from that what music would be most suitable?

CS: That's right.

MB: Did the directors tell you what they wanted in the way of music? Did they want a certain kind of music for particular scenes?

CS: As a rule, no. Sometimes they'd just want something with a twelve-beat for one sequence, and then maybe an eight-beat for the next sequence, and so on. Sometimes they'd build a whole picture around a song like "What's Up, Doc," which I wrote, but many popular songs were treated likewise, using the song title as the cartoon title. . . .

MB: Were there any cartoon characters that it was especially enjoyable to write scores for, or did it make any difference?

CS: Each character had a different feeling, enjoyable, and, of course, very original, but there weren't any that were especially enjoyable to work with, unless it would be Bugs Bunny. He was the standout.

BS: Did you ever get tired of doing music for cartoons with "funny animals"?

CS: No, there were several directors at Warner's, and when you got through with one there was another one waiting for you. There was plenty of variety.

MG: Many times, you used the music to tell the story. In *Catch as Cats Can* (1947), Sylvester the Cat swallowed a bar of soap and was hiccupping bubbles, and the music was "I'm forever blowing bubbles." Did you make up those gags yourself, or did the directors help?

CS: It happened both ways.

MB: You worked closely with the sound effects men, didn't you, to keep the music and sound effects coordinated?

CS: Yes. Treg Brown handled all the sound effects. Treg had thousands of sound effects on short reels, and he would make up a whole soundtrack out of these, as well as adding new ones for each cartoon. He had been there for three or four years when I came to Warner's. His room was next to mine.

MG: Did you ever actually write your music so that a sound effect came out as part of the music?

CS: Yes, and sometimes I'd just lay out altogether and let the sound effect stand alone.

MB: In some of Chuck Jones's *Road Runner* cartoons, there are long involved gags for which there's no music; nothing is heard except the sound effects. Was this something Chuck wanted to do, or was this your idea?

CS: I don't remember, but I do remember that if the sound effect called for it, we'd stop the music altogether. And, of course, for a lot of the dialogue we would stop the music or we'd cut it down to just a few strings.

      . . .

MG: What was your schooling before you went to work in the theaters?

CS: I had a private teacher; I started when I was six years old. My dad was a carpenter, and he found a broken toy piano. It was all broken to pieces and had little metal keys, like xylophone keys. One of them was missing, so he had to make one himself. He gave me a little frame box, and put the keys on that, and made some little hammers, and I started picking out tunes on that. That's how they started me studying piano.

MB: So then you started formal study of the piano after that, when you were six, and really learned how to play it.

cs:	Yes. I couldn't reach the pedal when I started playing; somebody had to pedal for me. I couldn't do the pedaling on the old church organs, either. I started playing them when I was eight or ten years old.
mb:	How old were you when you started playing in theaters?
cs:	Seventeen or eighteen. I didn't finish high school; I only went two years. My ear gave me trouble and I couldn't hear the teachers, so I had to quit.
mg:	So you couldn't hear too well even while you were composing all that music for Disney and Warner Bros.?
cs:	I had trouble there, but the trouble was only talking with the boys, not with the music.
mg:	What was your very first job as a musician?
cs:	I played the piano at a theater about a block from former President [Harry S.] Truman's house in Independence, Missouri, around 1910. That was my first job in the Kansas City area, but I'd played the piano in 1904 at Lexington, where I was born. Lexington is forty miles east of Independence. In those days, they just wanted a piano going while the operator was changing reels. In the cities, they had two machines, so you didn't have to wait for the next reel, but in little towns like Lexington they hadn't gotten that far yet.
mb:	Do you remember when you saw your first movie?
cs:	The first movie I ever saw was *The Great Train Robbery*. I saw it in a tent at a street fair in Lexington, around 1903. It made such an impression on me that from then on I had only one desire in life: to be connected with the movies in *some way*.

SOURCE: Mike Barrier, "An Interview with Carl Stalling," *Funnyworld* 13 (Spring 1971): 21–27, as reprinted in *The Cartoon Music Book*, ed. Daniel Goldmark and Yuval Taylor (Chicago: A Capella Books, 2002): 38–39, 40–41, 42, 48, 50–51, 52–53, 55–56.

~~~~~~~~~

NOTES

1. Mike Barrier, "An Interview with Carl Stallings" in *The Cartoon Music Book*, p. 38. The interview as printed combines material from two separate recorded interviews, the first with Milton Gray and Barrier on June 4, 1969 and the second with Gray and Bill Spicer on November 25, 1969. Gray is a professional animator and Spicer a writer about animation history.

2. Carrie Jacobs-Bond's (1862–1946) song "The Perfect Day" (1910) was a standard of the era.

3. *Steamboat Willie* was Disney's first animated feature with sound and thus is a historic milestone.

4. Leon Schlesinger (1884–1949) was the producer of Warner Bros. cartoons between 1930 and 1944.

80

A SIDEBAR INTO POSTMODERNISM

John Zorn Turns Carl Stalling

into a Prophet

With the advent of postmodernism, some composers who came of age in TV-land recognized that cartoon music affected them without their quite knowing how. The general interest in referential borrowings and collage and in fragmentation and quotation led to their adaptations and reinventions of the cartoon as a defining musical experience. In the following essay, the composer John Zorn (b. 1953) pays tribute to Carl Stalling and the power of the cartoon's long reach into the musical "subconscious." Zorn draws on the archetype of the musical cartoon soundtrack in such compositions as *Carny* and *Forbidden Fruit*.

CARL STALLING: AN APPRECIATION

When I was too young to talk, but old enough to scream, the "tube" was the only thing that would shut me up. Maybe that's why they called me "bottle-bottoms" in grammar school. Next best thing to those Indian Head test patterns were Warner Bros.' MERRIE MELODIES. As I got older (and started getting paid to scream), like many other hard core Stalling freaks, I treasured my tapes of Stalling's Road Runner scores dubbed straight off the TV.

Separating his music from the images it was created to support, it becomes clear that Stalling was one of the most revolutionary visionaries in American music—especially in his conception of time. In following the visual logic of screen action rather than the traditional rules of musical form (*development, theme and variations, etc.*), Stalling created a radical compositional arc unprecedented in the history of music. On first hearing, Stalling's immense musical talents are immediately apparent, and certainly all these basic musical elements are there—but they are broken into shards: a constantly changing kaleidoscope of styles, forms, melodies, quotations, and of course the "Mickey Mousing" (*sonic descriptions of visual events*). Stalling developed this technique while playing piano for silent films in Kansas City, honed it to a science with Disney and elevated it to an art with Warner Bros.

Set against the historical happenings in American music in the 30's and 40's, Stalling's achievements become even more impressive. Copland's pan-tonality; Cage beginning to explore the sonic possibilities of the prepared piano with quiet, Satie-inspired music; [Harry] Partch freaking out and building his own instruments based on his own 46-tone tuning theories; Ellington balancing improvisation and composition with his swinging, harmonically lush big band; the beginning of a new music by Charlie Parker and Dizzy Gillespie; [Edgard] Varèse basically in retirement—it was a period of basically conservative American impressionism invaded by the search for new sonic resources.

Stalling was easily one of the most extreme composers of the period. A maverick who brought us to a new all-encompassing universe filled with a humor ranging from the subtlest musical reference to side-splitting slapstick. No musical style seemed beyond his reach—and his willingness to include them, any and all, whenever necessary (and *never* gratuitously, I might add) implies an openness—a non-hierarchical musical overview—typical of today's younger composers, but all too rare before the mid-1960's. All genres of music are *equal*—no *one* is inherently better than the other—and with Stalling, all are embraced, chewed up and spit out in a format closer to [William] Burroughs' cut ups, or [Jean-Luc] Godard's film editing of the 60's, than to anything happening in the 40's.

To this day, Stalling is considered a nine-to-fiver. A craftsman. A company man. A square. His colleagues love to slight him, but anyone who would create music of this violent and passionate originality deserves more.

Although much should be said for the collaborative nature of the team he worked with—the brilliant orchestrator Milt Franklyn and the comic genius/sound effects wizard Treg Brown—the fact of the matter is that when Stalling stopped composing music for animation in the late 50's, the quality of cartoon music and eventually of American animation itself plummeted. The Golden Age was over.

Stallings's scores for Warner Bros.' cartoons were as essential an element to their visual counterpart as [Nino] Rota's music for [Federico] Fellini, [Bernard] Herrmann's music for

[Alfred] Hitchcock, [John] Barry's scores for the James Bond series, [Ernie] Morricone's work with [Sergio] Leone. But also like these masters, his music stands tall on its own.

The first album of Stalling's music, and the volumes to come, will go a long way in raising Stalling to his rightful position as one of America's great composers. Like Charles Ives, Carl Stalling is a true original. A visionary who created the music most of us were *weaned* on—the music of our subconscious.

[signed] John Zorn, NYC

April 1990

SOURCE: John Zorn, liner notes for *The Carl Stalling Project: Music from Warner Bros. Cartoons 1936–1958* (Warner Bros. 26027-2, 1990).

81

ALEC WILDER WRITES LOVINGLY

ABOUT JEROME KERN

Alec Wilder (1907–1980) wrote about American popular songs from the point of view of a composer, whose own songs were performed and written for such singers as Mildred Bailey, Cab Calloway, Bing Crosby, Ethel Waters, Mabel Mercer, and, in the 1940s, Frank Sinatra. A witty writer who gave titles like "Sea Fugue Mama" and "Neurotic Goldfish" to octets for harpsichord, woodwinds, double bass, and drums in 1939, Wilder also wrote "lovingly" about the songs of his contemporaries—to quote the composer Gunther Schuller.[1]

In his classic book, *American Popular Song,* Wilder writes with an expert's insight about craft and history that tempers his occasional sharp critique. The selection comes from Wilder's discussion of the songs of Jerome Kern (1885–1945) and focuses on two stylistically contrasting classics: "Ol' Man River" from the musical *Show Boat* represents Kern at his most folk-like; "Smoke Gets in Your Eyes" from *Roberta* approaches operetta.

In 1927 came "Show Boat," and with it the best-known of all Kern scores. Kern was now at the top of his form. There remained very little to perfect in his personal style. He had learned to move about in the American musical milieu with relative freedom, even though his best songs in the native idiom lay well ahead. Immediately at hand was a curious period in his career when he would seem to go forward and sideways almost simultaneously, when he would plunge into the problems of "Show Boat," with its ambience of pure Americana, and then abandon the native implications of a realistic American theater and devote himself to a succession of romantic musicals which, while not a complete reversion, were a return in spirit to operetta. Kern strove to create a new kind of musically sophisticated theater, but always, it seems to me, the vision of a new kind of American operetta, freed perhaps of the traditional plots and machinery, tempted him away from the implications of "Show Boat." All the while the Kern melodies flowed forth, some of them suggesting new directions, some of them betraying his inner urge to impose art songs on Broadway, many of them suggesting he was slowly losing touch with the world of music around him in American life. It was for him a strange time of searching and pomposity.

Frankly, I don't believe that "Show Boat" best exemplifies Kern's work. *Ol' Man River* is, of course, the big song in the score. It is one of the best known of all American songs. The expression, "tote dat barge, lif' dat bale," is part of the language. The song is a singer's delight, having a wide range, drama, and no difficult melodic hurdles to jump. Since it does have a very wide range, an octave and a sixth, it requires a true singer to perform it. Paul Robeson of the second production of "Show Boat" could scarcely make a public appearance without singing it, and later, Frank Sinatra, though in no way associated with any of its productions, considered it an essential song in his repertory.

Its extended verse of an odd twenty-five measures contains an eight-measure section which, with almost identical notes, is the release of the chorus. And the principal theme of the verse is rhythmically so like what one says of banjo music, "plink-a-plink," that the legend has grown in England that the sound of a banjo player idly noodling at a break in a rehearsal gave Kern the notion for the song. This is pleasant enough, considering the association in most minds of the banjo with the South, but like most such tales, it is unsubstantiated, and, of course, though it could apply to the verse, fails completely to explain the chorus.

The close musical and lyrical relationship of verse and chorus is proven by the fact that all singers I've ever heard perform the song always start with the verse.

The conventional A-A-B-A structure (main strain: its virtual repetition: a release,[2] almost always new material: and finally, a literal, varied, or extended restatement of the main strain) was used in *Ol' Man River*. Many people, including song writers who should know better, assume that this form goes back much further than it actually does. There were few instances of it in any type of popular music until the late teens. And it didn't become the principal form until 1925–1926.

Ol' Man River is not a complex song, melodically or harmonically. Its principal characteristics are the rhythmic devices of the second half of each measure (except in the release), and the extremely high ending. Undoubtedly the lyric accounts for half of the song's acceptance, though it is frowned on by the society of the [nineteen] seventies.

. . .

The Hollywood phase of Kern's career begins with the filming of "Roberta," which was released in 1935. It was, one must immediately observe, an extraordinarily happy debut, but at the same time it should be remembered that the score had been one of Kern's finest on Broadway. The movie was, of course, leavened with new songs, one of which had been brought over from London and dressed in newer, sprightlier lyrics.

"Roberta," originally called "Gowns By Roberta," was produced as a Broadway musical in 1933. And because there are no songs to be discussed from the years between the stage and film versions, I'll discuss both scores together.

In the stage version there was a marvelous rhythm song, *Let's Begin*. Every bit of it works—verse, chorus, and lyric—even if one's eyebrows rise slightly at the rhyme of "exempting" and "preempting" as being a bit high-flown for a popular song. Well, no matter. The same lyricist, Otto Harbach, used the word "chaffed" in *Smoke Gets In Your Eyes*.

. . .

Mr. Harbach, a very pleasant gentleman, once told me, a virtual stranger, that in looking through discarded, or un-set, Kern manuscripts, he came across one which he was told by the composer had been written, I gathered, in order to make a scene change in "Show Boat." It was an "instrumental" composed for a tap routine "in one" as they say; that is, in front of the curtain while the scenery is being changed. It looked like this.

The short notes were used, obviously, to allow the taps to be heard. Mr. Harbach told me that he asked Kern if these short notes might be made long notes and that, might it not make an attractive ballad? Kern agreed, and the result was *Smoke Gets In Your Eyes*. I have no idea what the length of the original piece was; whether or not, for example, it included the release of the later song. I do know that the song was one of Kern's biggest hits and most popular standard songs. It is also without a verse. In this instance, unlike *Yesterdays,* I feel that it might well have had one. Probably the situation didn't call for one, and it is true that the lyric begins almost as casually as the words of a verse. It is a superb lyric, whether or not "chaffed" comes as a shock. The song itself has never been one of my favorites, though I can't deny its inventiveness and its very daring release. For me it's always on the edge of artiness; in fact, the tempo marking for the release is "*un poco piu mosso,*" which really does move us back into the world of the operetta.

The five sets of four eighth-note phrases, each eight measures long, keep the melody from flowing. Many will disagree with this opinion, for this song is usually one of the most dramatically and ornately orchestrated of all Kern songs—that is, when the occasion includes an orchestra capable of making very opulent and elaborate sounds. It is unlike any other song, certainly honest and professional and containing a passage of extreme adroitness in the return from the out-of-key release back into (the printed) key of E flat.

There is also in this song an accompanimental figure which has become an essential element of any performance—no arranger would ever dream of leaving it out.

SOURCE: Alec Wilder, *American Popular Song: The Great Innovators 1900–1950* (New York: Oxford University Press, 1972): 55–56, 65–66, 71–72.

~~~~~~~~~

NOTES

1.   Gunther Schuller, entry on "Alec Wilder" in *Grove Music Online,* ed. L. Macy. Available at http://www.grovemusic.com.

2.   Connecting section of a song between the principal sections, or strains. Thus, in the most familiar song structure—A-A-B-A—the B section. (A.W.)

82

GEORGE GERSHWIN EXPLAINS THAT "JAZZ IS THE VOICE OF THE AMERICAN SOUL"

During the 1920s, the coalescing decade for jazz, a new term, "symphonic jazz," was coined in order to describe attempts to fuse this new music with European classical forms. George Gershwin's *Rhapsody in Blue,* which premiered on Lincoln's Birthday, 1924 as an "experiment in modern music," still endures as the most famous example. Even so, the term "symphonic jazz" among music historians can still recall the condescension of the classical-music establishment, which then treated jazz as a kind of "folk"—or worse, "primitive"—music waiting to be civilized into "art." But music often transcends the limits of the words around it. And so do composers like Gershwin (1989–1937), who challenged the limits of confining categories by writing his *Rhapsody* and the piece which spurred this article on—his *Concerto in F* for piano and orchestra. Writing prophetically about the centrality of jazz for American music in 1927, at a time when white vaudeville singers still "blacked up," Gershwin describes his own journey towards an American sound. First came "intensive listening," then an awareness of his musical environment. He catalogues the resources for his musical experiences with a broad sweep evocative of Walt Whitman.

The editors of *Theatre Magazine,* which published Gershwin's article, provided this lead-in: "Hailed by Musicians and Critics as the Outstanding Figure Among Native Composers, the Author of This Article Defends and Glorifies Syncopation."

~~~~~~~~~
~~~~~~~~~
~~~~~~~~~

The peak of my career was not, as my friends and the public think, when I played in my own "Concerto in F" in Carnegie Hall with the New York Symphony Orchestra, Walter Damrosch conducting. That was an event which amiable contemporary biographers are recording as notable. And I may say, with gratitude and humility, it was.

But there are invisible peaks that anticipate the visible. There are spiritual fulfillments that precede the physical. The peak of my highest joy in completed work was when I listened to that concerto played by the fifty thorough musicians I had engaged for it. Two weeks before the evening when the concerto was heard in Carnegie Hall there was a reading of it on an afternoon in the Globe Theatre. Charles Dillingham had permitted the reading in his playhouse. I enjoyed it, not as one of my fair and mischievous friends said, as the mad king Ludwig enjoyed Wagner, being the sole audience in his theatre, for Mr. Damrosch[1] was there, and about a dozen others who I wished to hear it. Four of these were music critics. The rest were personal friends. That was the time I heard my most serious work with my own ears. On this occasion I played the piano myself, and was listening, as it were, with the multiple ears of the audience. Another peak will be the evening of this day in which I am preparing these impressions for the *Theatre Magazine* when I play my biggest composition with the New York Symphony Orchestra, for the radio and a million listeners.

When, last year at Carnegie Hall, I played my first concerto I was twenty-seven years old. For eight years I had been writing compositions, so I was not totally surprised when great musicians came to the piano and paid me compliments upon my efforts as a composer. What caused a surprised smile, however, was that all of them, Rachmaninoff, Heifetz, Hoffman, complimented me upon my piano execution. For I had had but four years of piano study and those not with teachers of celebrity. My facility had come, not from tuition but from a habit I had consciously cultivated since I was in my early teens. I mean my habit of intensive listening. I had gone to concerts and listened not only with my ears, but with my nerves, my mind, my heart. I had listened so earnestly that I became saturated with the music.

Then I went home and listened in memory. I sat at the piano and repeated the *motifs*. I was becoming acquainted with that which later I was to interpret—the soul of the American people.

Having been born in New York, and grown up among New Yorkers, I have heard the voice of that soul. It spoke to me on the streets, in school, at the theatre, In the chorus of city sounds I heard it. Though of Russian parentage I owed no sensitiveness to melodious sounds from that source. My father was a business man. No one in my family save my brother Ira and myself had an interest in music.

Wherever I went I heard a concourse of sounds. Many of them were not audible to my companions, for I was hearing them in memory. Strains from the latest concert, the cracked tones of a hurdy gurdy, the wail of a street singer to the obligato of a broken violin, past or present music, I was hearing within me.

Old music and new music, forgotten melodies and the craze of the moment, bits of opera, Russian folk songs, Spanish ballads, chansons, ragtime ditties, combined in a mighty chorus in my inner ear. And through and over it all I heard, faint at first, loud at last, the soul of this great America of ours.

And what is the voice of the American soul? It is jazz developed out of rag-time, jazz that is the plantation song improved and transformed into finer, bigger harmonies.

Does the American spirit voice itself in "coon songs"? I note the sneer. Oh, I hear the highbrow derision. I answer that it includes them. But it is more. I do not assert that the American soul is negroid. But it is a combination that includes the wail, the whine and the exultant note of the old mammy songs of the South. It is black and white. It is all colors and all souls unified in the great melting-pot of the world. Its dominant note is vibrant syncopation.

If I were an Asiatic or a European, suddenly set down by an aeroplane on this soil and listening with fresh ear to the American chorus of sounds, I should say that American life is nervous, hurried, syncopated, ever accelerando, and slightly vulgar. I should use the word vulgar without intent of offense. There is a vulgarity that is newness. It is essential. The Charleston is vulgar. But it has a strength, an earthiness, that is an essential part of symphonic sound.

When I realized beyond any possibility of error, or need of recantation, that the voice of America, the expression of its soul, is jazz, a determination to do the best possible in that idiom filled me.

Jazz is young. It is not more than ten years old. Ragtime is dead. It was dying when my ear began to be attuned to the voice of the spirit of America. I began to write songs. My first published one had the singular and unabbreviated title "When You Want 'Em, You Can't Get 'Em." I was seventeen when I offered it to an indifferent world. The publishing house for which I was working showed its estimation of the merits of the song by deciding to publish it. But the house of Von Tilzer was willing also to print my second song with the title "You, Just You." The first that pleased the sweetheart we all woo, that coy damsel, Miss Public, was, "I Was So Young—You Were So Beautiful." The melodious brother and sister, Mollie and Charles King sang it in a musical version of *The Magistrate,* called "Good Morning Judge." When I was twenty my first 'show,' *La La Lucile,* was produced. It was at Henry Miller's Theatre.

The best song I have written measured by its reception was "Suwanee" sung by Al Jolson. Mr. Jolson interpolated it in *Sinbad.* I have written the music for twenty-two musical comedies, the next to the last, now in its third year, being *Lady Be Good,* and the last and most popular, *Oh Kay.* Of my record for industry I am not ashamed. My average is about three musical comedies a year.

I shall go on writing them. They make it possible to flit away as I shall do after writing this, to Lake Placid in the Adirondacks for a rest. My work is agreeable and remunerable. But to my compositions that most gratify the inward seeking, they are as numbers sung by Al Jolson and by a Caruso. That statement does not decry Mr. Jolson. In his realm he is a king. But the creator longs to write what is worthy [of] the voice of a master vocal musician.

My best works therefore are my "Rhapsody in Blue" and my "Concerto in F." The "Rhapsody in Blue" represents what I had been striving for since my earliest composition. I wanted to show that jazz is an idiom not to be limited to a mere song and chorus that consumed three minutes in presentation. The "Rhapsody" was a longer work. It required fifteen minutes for the playing. It included more than a dance medium. I succeeded in showing that jazz is not merely a dance, it comprises bigger themes and purposes. It may have the quality of an epic. I wrote it in ten days. It has lived for three years and is healthfully growing.

I do not know what the next decade will disclose in music. No composer knows. But to be true music it must repeat the thoughts and aspirations of the people and the time. My people are Americans. My time is today. Of tomorrow and of my tomorrow, as an interpreter of American life in music, I am sure of but one thing: That the essence of future music will hold enough of the melody and harmony of today to reveal its origin. It will be sure to have a tincture of the derided yesterday, which has been accepted today and which perhaps tomorrow will be exalted—jazz.

SOURCE: George Gershwin, "Jazz is the Voice of the American Soul." *Theatre Magazine* 45/3 (March 1927): 14, 52B.

~~~~~~~~~~~~

NOTE

1. Walter Damrosch (1862–1950), the conductor of the New York Symphony, which merged with the New York Philharmonic in 1928, commissioned Gershwin to write the Concerto in F.

83

W̶ILLIAM GRANT STILL, PIONEERING AFRICAN-

AMERICAN COMPOSER

(Still, Locke, Still)

William Grant Still (1895–1978) is remembered today as the "dean" of African-American classical composers. His *Afro-American Symphony* was the first such work to be performed by a major American orchestra, when it was premiered by Howard Hanson's Rochester Philharmonic Orchestra in 1931. Initially raised with classical music and only later moving into the pop world, Still had an eclectic career. In the 1920s, he made a living as an arranger for the blues bandmaster and composer W. C. Handy and as a pit musician in Noble Sissle and Eubie Blake's famous musical revue, *Shuffle Along*. He pursued his broad ambitions to be a classical composer by refusing to stay in his place, so to speak, studying classical composition first, in 1922, with a traditionalist, the Boston composer George Chadwick—whom he acknowledged as a mentor—and then subsequently with the radical Edgard Varèse.

In 1933, responding to a request for information from a friend and potential biographer, Harold Bruce Forsythe, Still supplied a set of "Personal Notes," which include the sometimes condescending commentary reprinted here on his most famous work, the *Afro-American Symphony*. Like Ellington's suite *Black, Brown, and Beige* (1943), Still's symphony offers a panoramic view of blacks' cultural character, as he explained in the descriptive program he wrote for the work. Yet later Still tempered the extent to which program mattered. His musical program still embodied the ideals of the Harlem Renaissance and the courageous spirit of the "New Negro," to use the phrase popularized by Alain Locke (1886–1954), a leading intellectual of the movement and Still's friend and occasional collaborator.

In works like *The Negro and His Music,* Locke used the arts to vindicate black people's equality. His comments about Still's music, reprinted here in the third selection, also suggest the continuing influence of Dvořák's model and the idealistic belief in "universal" music.

In the final selection, Still's letter to Locke, written shortly after the premiere of his second symphony, Symphony in G Minor (*Song of a New Race,* 1937), wryly comments on the risks posed by his musical ambitions.

PERSONAL NOTES

AFRO-AMERICAN SYMPHONY—MODERATO ASSAI; ADAGIO; ANIMATO; LENTO CON RESOLUZIONE
Completed 1931.
First Performance—Rochester Symphony, Oct. 28, 1931.

The entire work is based on a simple little blues theme. This theme plays an important part in each movement except the scherzo, where it appears merely as an accompanying figure. The four movements present successively the pathetic, sorrowful, humorous and sincere (or noble) sides of the American Negro.

Press Comments (1st performance):—

This headline appeared in the *Rochester Evening Journal,* "NEW SYMPHONIC WORK ACCLAIMED AT FIRST PLAYING IN AMERICAN COMPOSER'S CONCERT." Following are excerpts from the article under the above headline.

Interest in the program, however, centered chiefly in Arthur Farwell's "Gods of the Mountain" Suite and William Grant Still's "Afro-American Symphony." Both rank among the best constructed and most provocative compositions heard in the history of these concerts. Mr. Still's symphony was especially intriguing. . . . Throughout the symphony has life and sparkle when needed and a deep haunting beauty that aids in conveying a picture of the mercurial temperament of the Negro. The symphony sometimes shuffles its feet, at other times dances. It laughs unrestrainedly, it mourns dolefully and sways often in the barbaric rhythm of its subject. And always it sings. . . . Finally, Mr. Still has succeeded in being original without any self conscious effort.

[signed]—David Kessler

Mr. Still's symphony is by far the most direct in appeal to a general audience of any of his music heard here. . . . Mr. Still has done his work well in this new composition, but to some extent he has replaced that arresting vigor one has admired by deft sophistications.

[signed]—Stewart R. Sabin

Mr. Still's *Afro-American Symphony* is built up from a "Blues" theme which he develops into a composition of poignant beauty through which one feels intense . . . emotion held within bounds by a fine intelligence. There is not a cheap or banal passage in the entire composition, and none which impresses one as having been set down merely for the sake of keeping the instruments busy or covering a set amount of manuscript paper. To give one such composer as Mr. Still an opportunity to have his compositions heard and to hear them himself would justify the entire American Composers' Movement.

[signed]—Amy H. Croughton

2nd performance—Rochester Symphony—Mar. 3, 1932.
Press Comments (2nd performance):—

It is honest, sincere music . . . etc . . . Mr. Still and his music were given an ovation by the audience.

[signed]—Amy H. Croughton

(Let me explain here that I was present at this concert. I missed the first because Dr. Hanson's[1] secretary failed to notify me in time. As is characteristic of Dr. Hanson, when he discovered that it would be too late for me to get there in time by train he wired me to come by airplane at the expense of the school. But the day was so bad that the companies operating planes would not take passengers. . . . When *Sahdji*[2] was produced I was broke, and did not have the money to get to Rochester. Dr. Hanson sent me $100.00 to make the trip. Do you see now why I admire him so much when, in addition to encouraging [me] as [he] does, he offers me material aid of that sort?)

Let's get back to the subject.

He has written a symphonic piece that will be heard with pleasure by audiences at large.

[signed]—Stewart R. Sabin

The *Afro-American Symphony* seemed a much more important work on second hearing than it did the first time it was played in this series.

[signed]—David Kessler

Press Comments (3rd performance):—

Some explanation is necessary here. After this second performance the Scherzo of the symphony was broadcast in a special broadcast to Germany. Now to get to the third performance. In December Dr. Hanson sailed to Germany to conduct the Berlin Philharmonic in a special concert of American music. The Scherzo of the symphony was included on the program.

The following is an excerpt from an article that appeared in the *New York Times* concerning the concert: "The audience demanded a repetition of Still's scherzo."

My Opinion: This symphony approaches but does not attain to the profound symphonic work I hope to write; a work presenting a great truth that will be of value to mankind in general. I have good reasons to expect its performance in Switzerland soon, and probably in England.

SOURCE: Typescript published in Catherine Parsons Smith, *William Grant Still: A Study in Contradictions* (Berkeley: University of California Press, 2000): 231–32.

~~~~~~~~

FURTHER COMMENTS BY STILL ON THE *AFRO-AMERICAN SYMPHONY* (1939)

At the time it was written, no thought was given to a program for the *Afro-American Symphony*, the program being added after the completion of the work. I have regretted this step because in this particular instance a program is decidedly inadequate.

The program devised at that time stated that the music portrayed the "songs of the soil," that is[,] that it offered a composite musical portrait of those Afro-Americans who have not responded completely to the cultural influences of today. It is true that an interpretation of that sort may be read into the music. Nevertheless, one who hears it is quite sure to discover other meanings, which are probably broader in their scope. He may find that the piece portrays four distinct types of Afro-Americans whose sole relationship is the physical one of dark skins. On the other hand, he may find that the music offers the sorrows and joys, the struggles and achievements of an individual Afro-American. Also it is quite probable that the music will speak to him of moods peculiar to colored Americans. Unquestionably, various other interpretations may be read into the music.

Each movement of this Symphony presents a definite emotion, excerpts from poems of Paul Laurence Dunbar being included in the score for the purpose of explaining these emotions. Each movement has a suggestive title: the first is Longing, the second Sorrow, the third (or the Scherzo) Humor, and the fourth Sincerity. In it, I have stressed an original motif in the blues idiom, employed as the principal theme of the first movement, and appearing in various forms in the succeeding movements, where I have tried to present it in a characteristic manner.

When judged by the laws of musical forms the Symphony is somewhat irregular. This irregularity is in my estimation justified since it has no ill effect on the proportional balance of the composition. Moreover, when one considers that an architect is free to design new forms of buildings, and [when one] bears in mind the freedom permitted creators in other fields of art, he can hardly deny a composer the privilege of altering established forms as long as the sense of proportion is justified.

SOURCE: From Verna Arvey, *William Grant Still* (New York: Fischer, 1939), as reprinted in Catherine Parsons Smith, *William Grant Still: A Study in Contradictions* (Berkeley: University of California Press, 2000): 318–19.

~~~~~~~~

In one of the first textbooks on the history of African-American music, Alain Locke included a chapter on "Classical Jazz and Modern American Music." Locke discusses Still and other black symphonists of the period, among them the obscure Edmund Jenkins and the more well-known William Dawson and Florence Price.

By coincidence America's entry into the World War took jazz to Europe in the knapsacks of the Negro soldiers, most particularly in the kit of Jim Europe's Fifteenth New York Regiment Band. [There follows a list of European compositions influenced by jazz.]

. . .

Meanwhile, the younger Negro musicians were tossing off anonymously impromptu jazz creations that could have established musical fame and fortune, if more deliberately handled. Edmund Jenkins had the training and the foresight to write his "Charlestonia: A Negro Rhapsody for Full Orchestra," which was played in Brussels and Paris in 1924; and under the inspiration of Edgard Varèse, Wm. Grant Still began presenting his serious classical compositions on the programs of the International League of Composers. Thus New York heard in 1927 "From the Land of Dreams," for chamber orchestra; in 1929 "Levee Land," a suite for voice and orchestra,—a vehicle, by the way, for Florence Mills's one and only serious concert engagement; *Africa: A Symphonic Poem* in 1930, and parts of the now completed "Afro-American Symphony." The latter and other works in classical form have been presented often under the patronage of Howard Hanson, of the Eastman School of Music, Rochester, where seldom a year passes without some new work by Mr. Still on the annual festival program. Both Jenkins and Still are graduates of the jazz ranks, and while many of their anonymous "arrangements" have made the reputation and fortune of others in commercial jazz, the fruits of that apprenticeship have deepened the skill and racial character of their more formal music.

. . .

The American School.—Classical jazz, however, is still a somewhat unstable and anaemic hybrid. In many cases, the effort to lift jazz to the level and form of the classics has devitalized it. Often it has been too evident where the jazz idiom left off and the superimposed Liszt, Puccini, Stravinsky, or Wagner began. George Gershwin has, of course, been associated in the public mind with this movement, and must be given credit for his bold pioneering and firm faith in the future of "symphonic jazz." From the *Rhapsody in Blue* in 1923 up to last year's American folk opera, *Porgy and Bess*, he has feverishly experimented, with increasing but not fully complete success. Discerning critics detect too much Liszt in the *Rhapsody* and too much Puccini and Wagner in *Porgy*; and it is not yet certain how well such musical oil and water can be made to mix.

. . .

However, much remains to be done, and one has a right to expect a large share of it from the Negro composer. The death of Edmund Jenkins, just a week or so before his "Rhapsody No. 2" was scheduled for performance in Paris by the Pasdeloup Orchestra, was one of the tragic losses of our racial and national art. Jenkins grew up as a juvenile member of his father's famous Charleston, S.C. Orphanage Band, and never lost his hold on Negro idioms and the jazz accents even after years abroad following his graduation from the London Royal College of

Music. No composition of maturity and genius equal to his appeared from Negro sources until the rather recent work of Wm. Grant Still and William Dawson. But with the successful presentation of symphonies based on folk themes from each of these young composers in the last year, the hope for symphonic music in Negro idiom has risen notably.

. . .

After several performances by the Rochester Symphony Orchestra, under Howard Hanson, Wm. Grant Still's *Afro-American Symphony* had its New York premiere with the Philharmonic under the baton of Hans Lange, in December, 1935. Much of this composer's work, especially his *Sahdji: An African Ballet* and his *Eben Chronicle*, are ultra-modernistic and too sophisticated for the laity, though startling bits of musicianship. The "Symphony," however, has a moving simplicity and directness of musical speech. It, too, has a folk theme, treated in contrasting moods with corresponding rhythms, making for a combined symphony and tone poem of Negro experience. This work, is, however, less programistic [*sic*] than [William] Dawson's, and gains by its nearer approach to pure music. An interesting third contribution from the pen of a Negro composer is the *Symphony in E Minor* by Florence E. Price of Chicago, presented several times by the Chicago Orchestra under Frederick Stock, with whom Mrs. Price has also had the honor of playing her own *Piano Concerto*. In the straight classical idiom and form, Mrs. Price's work vindicates the Negro's right, at choice, to go up Parnassus by the broad high road of classicism rather than the narrower, more hazardous, but often more rewarding path of racialism. At the pinnacle, the paths converge, and the attainment becomes, in the last analysis, neither racial nor national, but universal music.

SOURCE: Alain Locke, *The Negro and His Music and Negro Art: Past and Present* (1936; reprint, New York: Arno, 1969): 109–15.

In this letter to Alain Locke, Still complains about the lack of critical sympathy for his chosen path of symphonic jazz. Probably the recent premiere of his Symphony in G Minor by the Philadelphia Orchestra under the direction of Leopold Stokowski just a few weeks earlier was on his mind. As was the future. Still refers to a grand opera in progress, Troubled Island, *a work he took over ten years to complete. Despite the negative reviews,* Troubled Island *retains its landmark status as the first grand opera by an African-American composer to be staged by a major American opera company; it was produced by the New York City Opera in 1949.*

December 31, 1937
Dear Alain,

On this last day of the old year, I am writing to wish you all possible happiness and prosperity and artistic accomplishment in the New Year.

I want to tell you, too, that your comment on my new Symphony in G minor was, to me, the most apt that has yet been made. I thoroughly disapprove of following tradition—just because it is the thing to do. As a matter of fact, if I had done so in any *of my compositions, I believe that the critics would have accused me of slavishly adhering to the methods and treatments developed by others. Imitation is, in their eyes, the worst fault that a colored man can possess. Yet we find them criticizing when he does <u>not</u> possess it!*

It also seems strange to me that when I write short compositions I am roundly censured for not developing my thematic material to the fullest possible extent, whereas when I <u>do</u> develop it, they say my compositions are too long.

Did you notice that Lawrence Gilman has twice accused me of imitating Delius? When I wrote the first composition of which he said that, I had not heard a note of Delius' music in my life. Moreover, recently I was reading a book about Delius, wherein it was said that Delius received his first inspiration to compose from hearing the Negroes sing on his Florida plantation.

Well, I guess that no matter what we do we will be criticized or accused of something. We must just keep doing things: that's the important thing.

You ask what I am working on now. It is an opera on a Haitian subject, to Langston Hughes' libretto. What are you working on? I wish that you would write to me and tell me what you are doing whenever you have the time. You know that I am interested.

Thanks again for your letter, and—a very splendid New Year to you!
Sincerely,
Still

SOURCE: The Still-Locke Correspondence 1937 in the collection of the Spingarn Library, Howard University, with copyright also owned by the William Grant Still Estate. A copy of this letter is available through a digital exhibition about Still at Duke University, posted at: http://scriptorium.lib.duke.edu/sgo/exhibit/captions/caption39aa.html.

~~~~~~~~~~

NOTES

1. Howard Hanson (1896–1981), a composer and director of the Eastman School of Music, was a mentor of Still's.
2. Still composed the ballet *Sahdji* in 1929–30.

84

THE INIMITABLE HENRY COWELL AS DESCRIBED

BY THE IRREPRESSIBLE NICOLAS SLONIMSKY

The composer-pianist Henry Cowell (1897–1965) won his reputation as a radical modernist in the 1920s. Soon after his New York debut recital in 1924, Cowell launched himself into a leadership role by founding the New Music Society in Los Angeles and, as editor of its companion journal, the *New Music Quarterly,* he published scores by his American contemporaries. During his career, he composed over 1,000 musical works.

Cowell's bold piano music established him as a fearless experimenter. He exploited every possible way to make sounds from, on, and in the piano, most infamously by hammering the keyboard with his elbows and fists. In 1933, Cowell edited *American Composers on American Music,* a book of short biographical essays written by composers about one another. He entrusted the writing of his own entry to the composer, conductor, critic, lexicographer, and intellectual prodigy Nicolas Slonimsky (1894–1995).

A champion of Ives in the 1920s and a maverick at heart, Slonimsky published *Lexicon of Musical Invective* (1952), which included some outrageous reviews of Ives's music in concerts that Slonimsky himself conducted. Many musicians, among them John Adams and John Coltrane, knew Slonimsky as the author of the *Thesaurus of Scales and Melodic Patterns* (1947). Slonimsky loved playing with language, as shown in this witty portrait of his friend Henry.

It is rare to find a crusader in a big cause whose intellect is as strong as his battle-ax. Not all crusaders are more interested in their cause than in themselves. Few are creators of original work in a field of art. Henry Cowell is the exceptional type who possesses all of these qualities. In Pushkin's fantastic tale of Mozart and Salieri,[1] there are these amazing lines:

> And I dissected music as a corpse,
>
> By algebra I tested harmony of sounds.

This scientific procedure Henry Cowell unashamedly resumes. If there is one rule in his creative work, it consists in taking nothing for granted. Harmony, rhythm, tone-color—Henry Cowell submits them to a test as if they were mere human beliefs, not divine laws.

Henry Cowell's life-story includes many adventurous chapters—born in California, of intellectual parents, he lived in the freedom of the hospitable country, without benefit of an estate or even as much property as would insure safe transition from infancy into adulthood. Having had no compulsory education, he conjectured and speculated by himself, unaided and unhindered. Musical sounds around him fascinated him as suitable material for synthetical experiments. When he first got hold of a decrepit upright piano, he discovered new possibilities on it. Considerably later, when he revealed to astonished audiences gathered in New York, San Francisco, London, Berlin, Paris, Warsaw, and Moscow what could be done with the grand piano, he was merely developing his first-hand knowledge derived from these earlier experiences. At some intervening date he thought up a convenient terminology. He was scientific as well as pictorial when he named a group of keys struck with the forearm a "tone-cluster"; a compound fairly threatening to break into the sacrosanct pages of *Grove's Dictionary of Music,* for the lack of another descriptive name and from the necessity of designating a musical phenomenon which, however unpalatable to purists, is forcing itself irrepressibly into musical existence. Cowell had many years of conventional study, but only after he had already created, developed, and scientifically systematized an individual style of his own. When the first shock resulting from the exterior appearance of his piano-playing passed, intelligent people found that there is sound harmonic sense in the use of complete blocks of sounds, diatonically or chromatically arranged, treated as indivisible units. Our musical generation saw the use of triads in parallel construction, as if they were unisons or octaves; and, in polytonal writing, still bulkier entities were liberally handled. Apart from the question of using one's antebrachia for the production of "tone-clusters," there is nothing unacceptable in the idea to the seasoned musician; on the other hand, it is a logical development of modern harmonic resources.

Thus, from innocent experimenting with the acoustical possibilities latent in an ordinary piano, Cowell came to conclusions of harmonic order. Experimenting with the sound-board of the grand piano led him to discoveries in the field of tone-color. Everyone who has heard his weird glissandos, interpretive of the ghost of his Irish ancestors, "The Banshee" [1925], rendered directly on the piano strings, will admit that as a new orchestral color it is an undeniable acquisition. Pizzicato on the piano strings, as well as the entire gamut of percussion, conjured up from the pianistic entrails, make the piano a richer instrument without impinging on its historical dignity. As an orchestral instrument, Cowell's string and percussion piano (that is, the ordinary piano enriched by extraordinary applications) ought to be used whenever a masculine harp tone is required, and for new battery sounds not obtainable on drums or cymbals.

Henry Cowell, as a composer, made an early start. Before he was twenty, in the midst of distracting activities in rural and pastoral life around the paternal shack in which he was born and which is still his only sedentary home-sweet-home, he had composed music of all descriptions, including a symphony and an opera. At the same vigesimal calendas he delved for the first time into the problems of notation. This latter, not having been taught him as an established religion, he examined without fear—and dissented from its inadequacies. The duple system of rhythmical designations, giving adequate representation of only halves, quarters, eighths, etc., was the particular beam in the eye which Henry Cowell endeavored to extricate. He proposed a special notation for other fractions, so as to avoid the annoying and unscientific methods of setting down triplets, quintuplets, etc. This lore, nurtured by Cowell at Stanford University, where he worked as a free lance, was later embodied in a book, *New Musical Resources,* published in 1930 by Knopf. In 1931 Cowell, annoyed by the wistful realization that, no matter what notation we may decree, human players will still be human—that is, inaccurate, physiologically limited, rhythmically crippled, and unwilling to reform—hit upon the idea of an instrument which would faithfully produce all kinds of rhythms and cross-rhythms, as the tempered piano faithfully produces a given intonation for which a player on a string-instrument has to fumble by ear. He spoke to Professor Leon Theremin, builder of acoustical instruments, expounded his ideas, and secured the inventor's valued collaboration. As a result, a new musical wonder, provisionally christened "rhythmicon," was presented to the world for the first time on January 19, 1932, at the New School for Social Research, where Cowell is in charge of musical activities. The rhythmicon can play triplets against quintuplets, or any other combinations up to sixteen notes in a group. The metrical index is associated, in accordance with Henry Cowell's scheme as expounded in *New Musical Resources,* with the corresponding frequenc[y] of vibrations. In other words, quintuplets are of necessity sounded on the fifth harmonic, nonuplets on the ninth harmonic, and so forth. A complete chord of sixteen notes presents sixteen rhythmical figures in sixteen harmonics within the range of four octaves. All sixteen notes coincide, with the beginning of each period, thus producing a synthetic harmonic series of tones.

. . .

Henry Cowell edits a unique quarterly publishing ultra-modern music, under the title, *New Music.* As publisher, he demands no preconceived qualifications from his composers, and anyone with anything new to say engages his interest. He bars no one except himself—not a note of Cowell's music has been published in Cowell's edition. He specializes on American composers of the non-conformist type, but welcomes occasional Europeans. He publishes piano pieces, chamber music, and even full scores when finances permit. *New Music* has distribution all over the habitable globe, from Japan over both Americas to all of Europe.

Henry Cowell, in managing various non-lucrative enterprises, is as much of an innovator as he is in composing his own and administering other contemporaries' music. As director of the North American section of the Pan-American Association of Composers, he has organized every activity which this organization has had, including concerts in New York, San Francisco, Havana, Paris, Berlin, Madrid, Vienna, Prague, Budapest, and other places. He works with determination unlessened by the realization that the world, even that part of the world that goes by the name of musical, is little flexible. But Henry Cowell would not be himself if he did not follow the path of most resistance.

Henry Cowell attacks the grand piano, from *Punch Magazine*, 1930s.

SOURCE: Nicolas Slonimsky, "Henry Cowell," in *American Composers on American Music: A Symposium,* ed. Henry Cowell (1933; reprint, New York: Ungar, 1962): 57–63.

NOTE

1. The Russian playwright Alexander Pushkin (1799–1837) wrote in 1828 the verse play *Mozart and Salieri,* which inspired Peter Shaffer's play *Amadeus* (1984).

85

RUTH CRAWFORD SEEGER AND HER "ASTONISHING JUXTAPOSITIONS"

Pete Seeger (see chapter 116) once told me that his stepmother Ruth Crawford Seeger (1901–1953) appreciated "astonishing juxtapositions."[1] This phrase applies to her own life and work: on the one hand, an avant garde composer looking for individuality and uniqueness, and on the other, a pioneering folk-music specialist, embracing the "nice and common" (her phrase) just as fiercely.

Crawford, the composer, put her faith in music based on an expanded concept of dissonance. Just at the time that Arnold Schoenberg was working out his 12-tone practice, she and other colleagues (among them Carl Ruggles and Henry Cowell) were developing approaches to "dissonant counterpoint." Was it possible to write dissonant music that nevertheless remained grounded in some sense of tonal center? Yes, according to her mentor, the composer-theorist most responsible for dissonant counterpoint as a distinctive practice—Charles Seeger (1886–1979), whom she later married. In a letter to her protégée, the composer Vivian Fine (1913–2000) reprinted here in full for the first time, Crawford envisages a great composer who will release the emotional potential in dissonant music and link it to the people.

By the end of the 1930s, Ruth Seeger was working for another version of music for the people by collaborating with John and Alan Lomax on the folk-music book *Our Singing Country*. Out of this came her remarkable transcriptions of field recordings and a long monograph called *the Music of American Folk Song,* in which she meticulously described the challenges of that process. The second selection in this chapter reproduces a small section from this monograph, which has only recently been published, along with two musical examples. Its editor, Larry Polansky, writes, "When RCS made these transcriptions, and wrote *The Music of American Folk Song,* the recordings of these songs had not yet been publicly released. The Library of Congress decided to do this only in 1941. RCS's transcriptions, when she made them, were the *only* way that these songs were described for the public. She noted that nothing would replace the experience of listening to them [the field recordings], but in 1939–41, that opportunity was available only to a few fortunate musicians and scholars. . . . Her transcriptions were to become the way a nation would *see* its folk music."[2] Little did she suspect then, nor did she live long enough to witness, how one of her transcriptions turned into a 20th-century American musical signature (see chapter 92).

〰〰〰〰
〰〰〰〰

Berlin W. 56
January 26, 1931

Dear lovable Vivian,

    Yes, I understand very well your not "being in the spirit" for a Christmas letter two weeks ahead of time. I was not only in the spirit, but also in the midst of much copying and composing which had to be finished very quickly, and which kept me intensely busy til the 24th.

    You are busy. I am glad you are learning German,—you will not, then, arrive as I did in Aachen with my tongue tied. Such an experience teaches one to understand why wars can be: the wall of uncomprehension between two human beings who speak different languages is appalling. Although, underneath the words, the two are very much alike. And although with a smile and a light in the eyes, the wall often falls far lower.

    No, I am working with no one,—quite alone. Late works of Hindemith have not encouraged me. As for Schönberg, I feel clearly that Seeger can give the value of discipline which might come from working with Schönberg, yet with Seeger the discipline is constructive and far-seeing. To me, Schönberg is not. He is to me leaves without a tree, without a root,—as I may perhaps have said to you before. One can learn much from him, however, and from studying his intricately co-ordinate[d] works, constructed with unbelievable thematic cohesion. He comes near being great, but has just missed his path.

    Bela Bartók's last [fourth] quartet is to me very fine, vigorous, lacking the watery and weak neoclassic inanities of so much modern music. Get it, if you can. Heller of Universal should have it. The Pro Arte Quartet played it in Bruxelles [Brussels] at the Liege festival, with a vigor and poesy that only the Pro Arte possess.

    Perhaps Imre Weisshaus[3] has mentioned it to you in one of his letters (yes, he is a dear, rare person, a friend to treasure)—the present condition and tendency regarding

Ruth Crawford, ca. 1929–1930.

*modern music,—that is, dissonant music. The Europeans seem to feel more and more
that they have passed through a kind of poisonous gas-belt of dissonance, that now
they can breathe again in the pure air of Chopin-Bach-Strauss imitations, and sit
down again in easy chairs to enjoy music instead of perspiring over it. Though it is
increasingly easy to become depressed by this strong tendency, my feeling (I think not
blinded by having gotten in a "rut" of dissonance) is still unshaken: that dissonant
music, having rushed to the extreme of dissonance as a reaction from romanticism, will
yet find the great composer who will mould from a mixture of consonance and dissonance a great music which is not only dryly intellectual, as most dissonant music has
been so far, but carrying also a deep simplicity—emotion, if we want to use the word—
which will link it with the people as with the intellectuals. This may happen very far in*

the future. But I can't believe, as many do, that a medium in which so few of the possi-
bilities have been touched, can be lost, dropped, after fifteen years of trial.

You have happened on two books to which I too reacted deeply: "The Dance of
Life," and glorious Robinson Jeffers. Get "Cawdor" too, and the "Loving Shepherdess,"
a direct contrast to it.[4]

Not having heard from the Sandburgs,[5] *I took the liberty tonight of writing again,*
telling Mrs. Sandburg this: that I have told you to write a little note asking if you may
come to see them, and if she is too busy to see you, she is not to answer. I hope you will
hear from her. I told her you would play for her and for Sandburg my songs and yours:
this was mainly an excuse for getting you there! They are people who live very much in
their own family, needing few outside interests. Mrs. Sandburg is an exquisite person
with fine strands of poetry. You may feel her cool, indifferent. If you learn to know her,
you will find that this indifference has in it a quality of the east, of the Tao of Laotzu,
and that the coolness has depths. And perhaps you may strange enough find the cool
depths warm after all.

My love to your mother, and to you in the midst of your anstregend Arbeit [stress-
ful work]. Please give my love also to Rose, and send me her address in your next letter.

Affectionately
Ruth

(Mrs. Carl Sandburg, Harbert, Michigan. You must ask Mrs. Sandburg to let you know
how to come—bus or train.)

SOURCE: Letter from Ruth Crawford to Vivian Fine. Unpublished and in the collection of
the editor.

～～～～～

RUTH CRAWFORD SEEGER, *THE MUSIC OF AMERICAN FOLK SONG*, "MUSIC NOTATION AS A BRIDGE"

Music notations of folk songs serve, then, as a bridge between, mainly, two different types of singers. Over this bridge a vital heritage of culture can pass, from the rural people who, for the most part, have preserved it, to the urban people who have more or less lost it and wish to recapture it.

A great deal depends upon just how this bridge is built. It must compensate not only for the gap between the types of singers, but also for as many as possible of the technical short-comings of the system of notation itself, which, as has been shown above, are especially apparent when we try to use it in connection with an idiom with which it has not customarily been associated.

The manner of its building must be determined, for the most part, by the specific use to which the notations will be put. If they are to be used for strictly scientific study rather than for singing, the transcriber will wish to include in them all details—rhythmic, tonal and formal, perceptible to him. If they are to be published in song books for school or community use, he will no doubt feel constrained to indicate only the outline, the bare skeleton of the song. *It has been the aim, in transcribing this collection of songs, to follow a course midway between these extremes: to catch a just balance which will convey as much as possible of the rich complexity of the folk singer's art, yet in simple enough terms to allow ready grasp by the amateur.*

EXAMPLE 1

EXAMPLE 2

SOURCE: Ruth Crawford Seeger, The *Music of American Folk Song*, ed. Larry Polansky with Judith Tick (Rochester: University of Rochester Press, 2000): 13, 51; For the complete transcription of Example 2, see John and Alan Lomax, eds. *Our Singing Country. Folk Songs and Ballads*. (1941; reprinted Mineola, New York: Dover Publications, Inc., 2000): 352.

NOTES

1. Pete Seeger in conversation with the author, ca. 1990, in relation to her biography, *Ruth Crawford Seeger. A Composer's Search for American Music* (New York: Oxford University Press, 1997).
2. Ruth Crawford Seeger, *The Music of American Folk Song and Selected Other Writings on American Folk Music*. Ed. Larry Polansky with Judith Tick (Rochester, N.Y.: University of Rochester Press, 2001): xliv; xxxii.
3. Imre Weisshaus (1905–1987) was a Hungarian pianist and composer who eventually settled in France and changed his name to Paul Arma.
4. "Cawdor" and "The Loving Shepherdess" are poems by the pantheistic California poet Robinson Jeffers (1887–1962).
5. This refers to her friend Carl Sandburg (1878–1967), the famous Chicago poet, and his family.

86

"RIVER SIRENS, LION ROARS,

ALL MUSIC TO VARÈSE"

An Interview in Santa Fe

Edgard Varèse (1883–1965) was a pioneer of twentieth-century modernism. Born in Paris, Varèse studied composition with Vincent D'Indy, among others, but after the outbreak of World War I, he moved to New York City, where his charismatic personality immediately won him support from the patrons of ultramodern, or radical modernist, American music. Varèse was the twentieth century's "foremost genius of timbre."[1] The title of this chapter, which comes from an interview given in Santa Fe, New Mexico, refers exactly to that aspect of Varèse's style. It was his credo that any sound, whether made by machine or nature, could be turned into a musical event. Varèse used sirens in his landmark work for percussion, *Ionisation* (1929–31). "Lion's roar" is an actual instrument used in *Hyperprism* (1922–23)—it is a bucket with a hole in the bottom through which a rope or cord is drawn.

These acoustic compositions were followed by compositions for electronic music. Varèse stood for freedom of thought and process, but more important, he had the musical gifts to turn his seductive calls for sonic revolution into enduring music. His *Poème électronique* for electronic tape (1958) is a masterpiece of the genre.

Interviewing Edgar[d] Varèse is like trying to nail down a typhoon, but the result is a firm conviction that the composer knows more of the history of music than any of his contemporaries, that he can give the layman a new knowledge of how music was notated, that from such as he will come new electrical instruments to enlarge the horizon of sound, and that experience will be incomplete until his symphonies have been heard in the west as they have been in the great centers of music.

Varèse will speak on "Music and the Times" at the Mary Austin house at 8:30 o'clock Sunday night in the Indian Affairs Association benefit series. It will not be a casual lecture, for when music is the subject, Varèse cannot be casual. It will be illustrated with blackboard charts showing [the] notation of music as in the beginning and survived to present times. It will be thorough insight into the past of music leading up to the wide fields of the future which Varèse sees with the intensity of a prophet, which he has anticipated with [an] emphasis on noise in his ultramodern symphonies. Between "noise" and "sounds," he finds no difference for "noise is sound in the making." When asked, "Are you a musician?" his reply is "No, I am a worker in rhythm, frequencies and intensities."

It was for a certain sound that Varèse came to America, "dreamed as a kid" of coming here as he dreamed of "certain sounds, certain vibrations." The sound he dreamed he found on arrival: "A C-sharp that is heard in a river siren, on some factory whistles. I would stop and listen," he says, and he has since incorporated this peculiar form of "music" into his compositions.

Mrs. Varèse[2] says that the composer has "innocent ears" even as George Moore believed that art should be viewed with "innocent eyes." It is this quality that makes sounds mean something more to him than to the average musician. He tells the story of standing attentive listening to the noise of drilling and riveting on a new building in New York. Someone asked him what he was doing and Varèse answered truthfully that he was "practicing."

It was 21 years ago that Varèse arrived in America to find the sounds he had heard in his "inner ear." "In that time," he explains, "I have acquired American citizenship but unfortunately not the accent." His native French language is still easier for him and when he finds himself stuck for adequate expression in English, he and Mrs. Varèse explode to each other in rapid French until the right term is worked out.

BACH AND BEETHOVEN

To Varèse the two colossal geniuses of past music composition are "Bach, who closed a gate, and Beethoven, who opened the horizon."

"It was really a blessing that Beethoven was deaf and being so isolated himself from the world," he says. "He heard with his inner ear . . . and really wanted the effects that can be had today. I believe he returned to the quartet because he imagined beyond the physical possibilities of his time." Varèse returns time and again to the Beethoven ninth symphony in illustration of various points, referring to its "colossal majesty" and calling it "the greatest choral work."

All the contradictions of music are felt by this composer, who says, "Music is the most abstract of the arts and also the most physical and quoting, music is under two signs, the stars and wine." He gives three principles at the base of all composition, "inertia, force and rhythm," with their further contradictions.

In sound masses he finds that "people confuse melodies with tunes." In his own work, these "organized masses of sound move against each other, varying in radiance and volume." He seeks the third dimensional quality in sound projection in which "the beams of sound are akin to beams of light played by a searchlight . . . a prolongation, a journey into space."

USES NEW INSTRUMENTS

It is natural that the old mediums do not entirely satisfy such a composer, especially when his formula for composers is "Write what you want, and it is up to the engineers to transmit what you want." He feels it stupid of composers to write for any certain medium, for instance "when you broadcast, to write for the microphone." In the development of science there should be new instruments to fit the conception, and Varèse is one who has worked in new laboratories on this problem.

Of the new instruments he uses in his symphony "Equatorial," [he chose] the theremin for its pitch and intensity. "It has a high tone that has never been heard before and the posses-sion of all power," he says. "[It] has been used a lot in concerts in France. The trouble is they try to play the old music and thus make it sound like any other instrument."

Two other new developments in mediums he mentions, the Martenot "with its thread of steadiness on and on to an end," and the Bertrand dynaphone. All are of the electric magnetic field—"You either interfere or you don't" to produce the sound. A fingerboard control on one the size of a small table, a needle control, or merely a hand and presence, "play" these instru-ments. The nearest comparison to them found locally is the principle of the Hammond electric organ.

"Equatorial" in which the theremin is used is described by its composer as "an incan-tation and vociferation at the same time." He has taken the text of the Papal Vuh [sic], the sacred bible of the Maya-Quiche, Guatemalan Indians, a fragment of the book, a prayer and invocation of a tribe lost in the interior after leaving the city of abundance. He uses a voice with amplifier, as if in a trance, and a few instruments for this symphony, percussion first as always with Varèse, the trombones and trumpets for the human element, the declamatory voice, and finally the organ "that reservoir of power to which all feeds."

"Ionisation" is his symphony for percussion instruments only, his "work with so-called unpitched instruments, although that is stupid for everything is pitched if but relatively." Of it he says: "I worked with percussion because I did not want other instruments to give me an anecdote of melody when I was speculating purely on rhythm. I wanted the pure differentia-tion of rhythm given by different densities." Following the New York performance of this sym-phony, Paul Rosenfeld wrote in the *New Republic* that the "forty-one percussion and friction pianos for which it is cast—triangles, Chinese blocks, rattles, snare drums, cymbals, lion-roars, gongs, tom-toms, bells, piano tone clusters, and the rest (including two sirens, capable of running con-tinuous ascending and descending scales)—in themselves do suggest the life of the inanimate universe. . . . *That music,* written, like *Ionisation,* for the non-melodic components of the percus-sion choir alone, can be satisfactory, will not seem incomprehensible to those who realize that the battery, as it has been augmented and diversified by the new composers, is perfectly capable of functioning as a sonorous unit. . . . there exist definite soprano, also [alto], tenor and bass groups, susceptible of combination in four-part harmonies."

MASTER OF HIS MEDIUM

"The composer must be a master of his medium, not [its] slave," says Varèse. "This is the difference between artists and artisans. The artisan is good, honest, but never goes beyond the craftsmanship and tools at his disposal."

By going beyond these tools, Rosenfeld says of Varèse's *Integrales* . . . "In quality of sound it is entirely Varèse; the piercing screams, sudden stops, extremely rapid crescendo and diminuendi are his own. . . . Varèse's polyphony is very different from the fundamentally linear polyphony of Strawinsky [*sic*]. The music is built more vertically, moved more in solid masses of sound, and is held very rigorously in them. Even the climaxes do not break the cubism of the form. . . . The whole brought an amazing feeling of weighty power, much as though the overwhelming bulks of over-organization, institutionalization, herd-repression, unkultur, which crush the American individual beneath them, suddenly start swinging in obedience to a strength greater than theirs, and began glowing with wonderful new life."[3]

MISUNDERSTAND NEW MUSIC?

Varèse finds a misunderstanding between new music and the public and feels that it is unfair to composer, conductor and audience for orchestras to "give one work once." Until it has been played 20 or 30 times, "there is not the spirit," he says, "just the notes." He emphasizes the "greater the knowledge, the greater the love" in the musical field, and that it is the "emotional contact that counts in a work of art . . . art is not to prove a formula or dogma."

The Varèse symphonies have been played more than once, and by Stokowski more than once in one evening when they have been presented in New York in a hissing, cheering riot. Stokowski has stated that "Varèse, with Schoenberg, constitutes the actual forefront of musical advance."

The composer is entirely satisfied with his works conducted by Stokowski, [Otto] Klemperer, or [Eugene] Goossens and has no desire to conduct them himself, as he hates to be seen in public. Varèse has, however, conducted orchestras in Berlin, Prague, Paris, New York and Cincinnati.

Varèse is president of the Pan-American Association of Composers, member of the Beethoven Association, Acoustical Society of America, director of the new American Grand Rights Association of America in which all serious composers are eligible for membership. He founded the International Composers' Guild in 1921; with the purpose of fighting for the contemporary composer, to help him, to produce him.

MOST MAGNIFICENT PUBLIC

In America Varèse finds "the most magnificent public, for it is the one with the most healthy curiosity." He feels a "spiritual wave coming, coming and it will come first to America." His New York interviews, as the one in Santa Fe, have left reporters groping with a maze of advanced ideas, impossible to present fully in newspaper space, if one were capable at all of presenting them. And in New York he learned that the final formula for a newspaper interview is an expression of views on American life. No wonder one reporter breathed easier when after two hours of intense music education the composer answered one question: "What do you like best in America?" Although the tone was of disgust, the answer could be understood: "Your girls' legs and grapefruits."

SOURCE: "River Sirens, Lion Roars, All Music to Varèse," *Santa Fe New Mexican,* August 21, 1936, 2.

~~~~~~~~~

NOTES

1. Kyle Gann, *American Music in the Twentieth Century* (New York: Schirmer, 1997): 38.
2. Louise Varèse (1890–1989) was a translator of French and the author of a biography of her husband, *Varèse: A Looking-Glass Diary* (1972).
3. This is a loose paraphrase from Paul Rosenfeld's *An Hour with American Music* (Philadelphia: Lippincott, 1929): 173–74.

LEOPOLD STOKOWSKI AND "DEBATABLE MUSIC"

The stock market crash of 1929 and the onset of the Great Depression stifled the risk-taking, modernist artistic movements of the previous decade. The conductor of the Philadelphia Orchestra, Leopold Stokowski (1882–1977), felt the impact of the cultural weather change. Known as a champion of the avant-garde, Stokowski was a celebrity. In 1926, he had experimented with concert-hall lighting: he turned out all the house lights and left just enough small lights on the music stands to produce a massive spotlight underneath the conductor—leaving him in silhouette. In 1940, when he "costarred" with Mickey Mouse in Walt Disney's classic animation *Fantasia,* the silhouette image defined his screen presence.

Stokowski conducted many important premieres, including the world premieres of Rachmaninoff's Third Symphony and Arnold Schoenberg's Violin Concerto and the American premieres of Stravinsky's *Le Sacre du Printemps,* Mahler's Eighth Symphony, Alban Berg's *Wozzeck,* and Schoenberg's *Pierrot lunaire.* However, in 1932, the board of the Philadelphia Orchestra Association forced a policy change upon his programming by declaring that no more "debatable music" would be played, as explained in the newspaper notice reprinted here. Stokowski resigned as artistic director three years later but remained as co-conductor when Eugene Ormandy assumed the position of artistic director of the Philadelphia Orchestra.

ORCHESTRA AVOIDS "DEBATABLE MUSIC"
Philadelphia Programs to Consist Almost Wholly of Standard Works

PHILADELPHIA, Sept. 10. "Debatable music" will be missing from the programs of the Philadelphia Orchestra in the coming season.

The Orchestra Association has made this decision, in its preliminary announcement to subscribers. "The programs will be devoted almost entirely to the acknowledged masterpieces. The directors feel in times such as the present, that audiences prefer music which they know and love and that the performance of debatable music should be postponed until a more suitable time. With these opinions the conductors fully concur." The orchestra has been notable in recent seasons for sponsoring extreme modernistic works.

Drastic economies have been made wherever possible, but owing to the fact that the income producing endowment funds are not bringing in as high a percentage as formerly, it has not been possible to reduce the price of tickets, even at a time of falling prices in most activities.

The season will run for thirty consecutive weeks, beginning Oct. 7–8–10. All the concerts will be given in the Academy of Music—an announcement which indicates that there will be none of the elaborate and expensive stage productions of recent years at the Metropolitan Opera House.

Leopold Stokowski will start the season and will conduct seventeen weeks in all. He will, however, take only one long recess, from Jan. 13 to Feb. 27, when the conductor will be Issay Dobrowen, of the San Francisco Symphony Orchestra. Other conductors will be Alexander Smallens, Eugene Ormandy and Artur Rodzinski.

A new scenic setting has been devised according to the plans and suggestions of Leopold Stokowski for the Academy of Music stage. Not only will the scenery built for the orchestra provide a pleasant variation from the color background of the sets used in former seasons, but also it has the value of improving the acoustics.

In addition to the regular weekly series and the twelve Monday evening series of symphony concerts, there will be two series of Young People's Concerts of five each with Dr. Ernest Schelling as lecturer and conductor.

[signed] W. R. MURPHY

SOURCE: "Orchestra Avoids 'Debatable Music,'" *Musical America* (September 1932); reproduced in facsimile in *American Mavericks: Visionaries, Pioneers, Iconoclasts*, ed. Susan Key and Larry Rothe (Berkeley: University of California Press, 2001): 14.

88

Henry Leland Clarke on
The Composers Collective

In the early 1930s, American communism had an official political party to which few belonged and an unofficial culture that touched many. One large political issue—opposition to fascism, which was then sweeping Europe—and one large cultural issue—the value attached to collectivism rather than individualism—came together in the Composers Collective. A New York–based group of composers formed this collective in order to write militant, or "mass" songs. These songs were intended to reach out to working-class people and to be sung by them at political demonstrations and rallies. A number of distinguished American composers moved in and out of the collective, subjecting their songs to group critique. From one point of view, the collective was a fascinating byway in the intersections between American Marxist ideas and American music; from another, it had more influence than one might suspect. One of its members, composer Henry Leland Clarke (1907–1992) links its musical social conscience to later works in American musical theater. This brief, musically perceptive memoir, published here for the first time, is by a true believer in the virtues of the group approach to creativity.

The Composers Collective of 1935 was a rare institution. It was a club. It was a camerata. It was a Society for the Propagation of the Good News. Rarely have creative artists worked for a common cause with sufficient dedication to make them WANT criticism from each other. Without the Composers Collective there would have been no "Abe Lincoln Song" by Earl Robinson, and without his "Lincoln Song" there would have been no *Lincoln Portrait* by Aaron Copland. Without the Composers Collective there would have been no *Cradle Will Rock* by Marc Blitzstein, and without his *Cradle Will Rock* there would have been no *West Side Story* by Leonard Bernstein.

The Collective was all set up and busily working on its second *Workers Song Book* when Hanns Eisler[1] arrived to give it his encouragement. Among the reasons why Berthold Brecht turned from Kurt Weill to Hanns Eisler as the man to set his words to music are these: Weil [*sic*] wanted his music to be important; Eisler wanted his to be instructive. Weill was a Walt Whitman; Eisler was a Tom Paine. The one proclaimed liberty; the other, fraternity, [that] is, not the individual, but the collective.

Eisler was a great teacher. He insisted on métier, craftsmanship, as much as Nadia Boulanger; on composing what is really needed as much as Gustav Holst. He never deviated from common sense. When one of the collective was pounced on by his peers for composing too much like Schumann, Eisler said, "But the point is, is it good Schumann?" Eisler had some special words for Earl Robinson on the subject of simplicity. Earl has to be simple; won't be complex. (Just as Elliott Carter must be complicated; won't be simple.) But Eisler pointed out that simplicity is not enough. Even an ordinary pop song to be successful has to have some special twist or trick. This is why Earl Robinson's "Joe Hill" has reached tens of thousands of people all over the globe. It is that extra repeat of the last line at the end going up to the high octave.

There were reasons why my own "United Front Song" was chosen to be the first song in the *Workers Song Book No. 2*, which we were then preparing. It was not just because I was a bright boy. There is no doubt that Aaron Copland was a bright boy, too. But his "Into the Streets May First" never got anywhere. The chief reason is that my song went through the entire *collective process*. First, it was the only one of mine to be accepted at all; some had been rejected with near derision. Second, it summed up the one thing we all really agreed upon, the danger of fascism. The fascists under Hitler were wiping out all resistance in Germany. The one thing we were all absolutely correct about was that the fascists were threatening the world with a second world war. Third, my text was edited (some would say censored) by V. J. Jerome, the Yale man then recognized by the left as the arbiter of all things aesthetic and ideological.[2] By altering a single sound in my verse he redirected the entire thrust of [the] message from a Platonic meditation to a call for action. I had written

> *Fascists want our blood and sweat*
>
> *That's what they will never get.*
>
> *Once we KNOW we are one,*
>
> *They must go—their day is done.*

The revised third line reads, "Once we SHOW we are one."

As a matter of fact any creative artist anywhere is always censored—often more drastically than he realizes. I was fortunate in having so constructive a critic. And finally, I had a constructive critic for my music as well: Hanns Eisler. By altering a note or two in my left hand, he effectively added an augmentation of the main motive to the bass line.

Twenty years later I had the privilege of belonging to another words-and-music collective, the Hymnbook Commission that put together *Hymns for the Celebration of Life*. The same collective process had the same beneficial results. But it was not quite the same. The Composers Collective of 1935 was on fire with something both urgent and inspiring. Recalling it brings to mind the lines,

> *Bliss was it in that dawn to be alive,*
>
> *But to be young was very heaven.*[3]

SOURCE: Unpublished typescript of a "Response (slightly revised)" by Henry Leland Clarke to Steven Gilbert's "In Seventy-Six the Sky was Red: A Profile of Earl Robinson," a paper presented to the American Musicological Society annual meeting in Washington, D.C., November 7, 1976.

~~~~~~~~~~

NOTES

1. Eisler (1898–1962) was a German composer whose life and work were strongly shaped by his communist beliefs.
2. Victor Jerome (1896–1965) was "cultural commissioner" of the Communist Party USA in the 1930s. He was not a "Yale man," but educated at City College, New York.
3. A famous quotation from "The French Revolution As It Appeared At Its Commencement," 1804, by the English poet William Wordsworth.

$\mathcal{M}$ARC BLITZSTEIN IN AND OUT OF

THE TREETOPS OF *THE CRADLE WILL ROCK*

The musical theater piece *The Cradle Will Rock* by Marc Blitzstein (1905–1964) famously embraced what the liberal 1930s called "social significance" or "social conscience": so much so that it enjoyed a politically charged *succés de scandal* (success through scandal) not often seen in American musical life. The show was initially scheduled to be produced by theater people employed under a new deal W.P.A. program called the Federal Theater Project, conceived under Roosevelt's White House and funded by Congress. Just as today, when Congress appropriates money to run the National Endowment of the Arts, back then in the 1930s, Congress also determined the WPA FTP budget. And just as today, when political values affect funding, so back then, the Republicans and Democrats, Congress and the White House tussled in and through the arts. Blitzstein stood at the threshold of success—when a cut in the FTP budget, aimed directly at the New York and its left-wing theater, stopped the show, or was supposed to. As this memoir explains, members of the Federal Theatre Project carried on in surprising, defiant ways.

Even so, *Cradle* was largely spurned after the premiere. In the 1940s Blitzstein's work became a sort of cult show with no chance of hitting the mainstream. Yet in the 1950s and 60s, various revivals rewrote the musical into history. New audiences recognized its innovative approaches to musical theater that made its dated topical satire seem relevant. Thus *The Cradle Will Rock* lives on through a fascinating performance history that shows how shifts in the larger political climate revitalize controversial works of art to fit new times. Not that long ago the actor-activist Tim Robbins produced a film adaptation *Cradle Will Rock* (1999). Blitzstein's *The Cradle Will Rock* simultaneously symbolizes art as agit-prop and art as free speech. Here, standing at the threshold of the first full-fledged revival of the work as it was supposed to be done, Blitzstein reminisces about that legendary night in the theater that gave his baby a special birthright.

OUT OF THE CRADLE

I wrote *The Cradle Will Rock,* both words and music, at white heat during five weeks in 1936. When I played it for Orson Welles, he was just twenty-one but already an extravagantly brilliant and magnetic theatre man. He fell in love straight off and made me promise that no matter who should produce it, he would do the staging. I was glad to agree. Many producers then toyed with the notion of putting it on; all of them dropped it. It was considered controversial, since it dealt with the rising struggle for unionism in the American steel industry, at a time when the combine known as "Little Steel" was all over the newspapers with its union problems.[1] Finally, Welles and John Houseman decided to produce the work as part of the Federal Theatre Project, which they had joined. We had unlimited time to prepare the production, and quite extraordinary talent in every department at our disposal. Rehearsals moved toward a quality rarely achieved by any company. But as our opening date began to loom, there were rumors that *Cradle* might not be permitted to rock publicly at all. On the chance that we might never really open, Welles and Houseman invited to our dress rehearsal the most elite New York audience imaginable. That rehearsal was the first, and at this writing the last, time the work has ever been fully performed exactly as I wrote it; and it seemed a success. This was June 1937.

The next day we waited with some impatience for the traditional telegram from Washington authorizing us to go ahead with our premiere. It was not forthcoming. Instead, the "military" appeared; the box-office personnel were instructed to turn away ticket-buyers; the sets and the costumes were placed out of reach. Now the irrepressible energy and lightning drive of Orson Welles revealed themselves. He called the entire company together in the theatre's greenroom (actually the ladies' powder room downstairs). Welles said to us, "We have a production ready, we have a fully paid audience outside [it was true: many people had arrived early in the afternoon, having heard the rumors and scenting excitement] and we will have our premiere—tonight."

But how? And where? The main thing was to find a theatre; but there were a dozen jobs to do in the meantime. What was the contractual situation of the actors, of the musicians? Could they leave this theatre, perform the work elsewhere? Actors Equity told us by telephone that the actors could not perform *Cradle* on another stage, under different auspices, without losing their status in the Project. (The information turned out to be false.) Then we were told by the Musicians' Local that moving our orchestra into another theatre pit would set us in competition with regular Broadway musicals, and that not only must the men be paid Broadway salaries but their number increased. However, said this informant, if we called ourselves a "concert" and put our musicians onstage, then we could use as many or as few as we wished. There we were in the position of having a production without a theatre, actors who could not appear onstage, musicians who could appear nowhere else—enough to make the stoutest enthusiast admit utter defeat. But Welles proceeded to solve problems with an ingenuity, a speed and a daring I can hardly believe as I tell it. To the actors he said, "You may not appear onstage; but there is nothing to prevent you from buying your way into whatever theatre we find, and then getting up in your seats to speak your piece when your cue comes." As to the music: Welles, consulting Houseman, decided that we could afford only one musician, which would be myself, at a piano on-stage. I had indeed played and sung the work so often for prospective producers (we used to call it my "Essex House run") and done so many rehearsals with the actors that I felt quite confident. At once we all began to catch fire; the ladies' powder room of the Maxine Elliot Theatre became a beehive of activity, an arsenal of planning. Newspaper reporters and photographers were summoned with the word that something was up.

We were by now collectively tearing our hair with frustration at the lack of a theatre, when a little man who had been with us for several hours sighed and said, "All right: you'll have to take my house, I guess." It was the Venice Theatre (now Videotape Center), some twenty blocks away. A stage manager was phoned and promptly brought an old upright piano to a sleepy caretaker, who woke up on cue and managed to get four stalwart neighboring firemen to help lift the instrument onto the new stage.

The theatre's address was now announced to the audience outside the Maxine Elliot. Then commenced a parade up Broadway and Seventh Avenue to Fifty-eighth Street, with taxis containing Welles, Houseman, Abe Feder (our lighting man), myself and reporters, all followed by an entire audience on foot, marching to witness an opera. By the time we reached the Venice, as the word spread, our original audience of less than a thousand had doubled. Onstage at the theatre, with the curtains closed, we pulled the front off the piano so that its guts showed, since in so large a house we needed a considerable volume of tone, and Feder arranged a spotlight for it. I could hear an enormous buzz of talk in the house; when the curtains parted, I saw the place jammed to the rafters. The side aisles were lined with standing camera men and reporters. And there was I, alone on a bare stage, perched before the naked piano in my shirt sleeves (it was a hot night): myself, produced by Houseman, directed by Welles, lit by Feder and conducted by Lehman Engel, who had rushed home, got his heavy winter overcoat and returned, sweating, to smuggle my orchestra score out of one theatre and into another.

I couldn't know which or how many actors had elected to take Welles' "suggestion," or where they were in the audience. But I began ready to do the whole work myself. I started singing the Moll's first song and heard the words taken from my mouth by the Moll herself, seated in a right loge; clever Feder instantly switched the spot to her. Then occurs a dialogue between the Moll and the Gent; again I heard an actor take over from me, this time from mid-center in the down-stairs hall. Flash bulbs began to pop. The audience seethed with excitement; as the play progressed, it turned as at a tennis match from one actor to another, while Feder caught as many performers as he could with his spotlight, and musical conversations took place across the house. The cast had studied the work so thoroughly that they could have done it in their sleep. Not a hitch occurred in the continuity. The work itself held up astonishingly under this brutal manhandling.

Theatre managers rushed to us within minutes and begged to be allowed to put us on Broadway in the exact form our opera had taken that night. Later, Houseman and Welles presented *The Cradle Will Rock* as part of their Mercury Theatre season; critics were invited and gave us rave notices. There have been some twenty-five other productions of the piece in the United States and England. In 1947 Leonard Bernstein revived it in concert form with his City Symphony, this time with the cast seated onstage in rows, oratorio-style, and this time conducting an orchestra in my original orchestration. Again it was moved to Broadway and had two successive producers. And now, in the good year 1960, for the first time I shall see *The Cradle Will Rock* in a full-scale production with sets, costumes, lights and all the trimmings, thanks to the New York City Opera Company and the Ford Foundation.

SOURCE: Marc Blitzstein, "Out of the Cradle," *Opera News* (February 13, 1960): 10–11.

~~~~~~~~

NOTE

1. This refers to the struggle between the CIO, an emerging labor union, and the steel industry over the right to unionize workers. Big Steel, dominated by U.S. Steel, recognized the CIO, but the smaller steel producing companies, known as "Little Steel," would not. This led to the infamous "Memorial Day Massacre" of 1937 in Chicago, when several striking workers were killed by police.

SAMUEL BARBER AND THE CONTROVERSY AROUND THE PREMIERE OF ADAGIO FOR STRINGS

(Downes, Pettis, Menotti, Harris)

During the middle decades of the twentieth century, not only were concerts of classical music routinely broadcast live on radio to national audiences, but the networks supported their own orchestras as well. The most famous radio celebrity, Arturo Toscanini (1867–1957), the conductor of the NBC Symphony Orchestra, had his concerts broadcast from 1937 through 1954; David Sarnoff, the head of NBC, built Studio 8H and assembled the orchestra just for him. In this era, Toscanini's power as the standard-bearer of classical music should not be underestimated: the maestro's voice carried across the continent.

On November 5, 1938, the select audience invited to Studio 8H heard and watched Toscanini conduct Samuel Barber's (1910–1981) Adagio for Strings, an adaptation of the second movement of Barber's String Quartet. The adagio has since become Barber's most famous work and one of the most popular pieces of American classical music.

The initial critical reception of Barber's adagio points to historical rivalries over musical style. A favorable review by Olin Downes, critic for the *New York Times,* sparked an unusual controversy. Downes was reproached for overpraising a work that some readers felt was weak and, more important, stylistically reactionary. This response ignited a miniature critical scandal argued in the "Letters to the Editor" column. Some of the letters from prominent respondents, including composers, are reprinted here.

~~~~~~~~~~~~
~~~~~~~~

TOSCANINI PLAYS TWO NEW WORKS
Two by Barber, American Composer, "Adagio for Strings" and "Essay for Orchestra"
THIRD BY PAUL GRAENER
Dvorak's "New World" Symphony and Debussy's "Iberia" Also on the NBC Program
By OLIN DOWNES

The audience assembled last night for the Toscanini concert of the NBC Symphony Orchestra with the same eagerness, and listened and applauded with the same intensity which is customary at this series of events. There was the same almost laughable silence and solemnity as the orchestra ceased tuning and the gathering waited for seconds for the conductor to step silently through the door that opens on the stage. And there was the same highly privileged sensation of listening to performances which had almost the clarity and purity of chamber music, and finally, of hearing some interesting new scores.

Two works by Samuel Barber, the young American composer, twenty-eight years old, were performed for the first time anywhere. They are an "Adagio for Strings" and an "Essay for Orchestra." It goes without saying that Toscanini conducted these scores as if his reputation rested upon the results. He does that with whatever he undertakes.

Mr. Barber had reason for thankfulness for a premier[e] under such leadership. And the music proved eminently worth playing. The Adagio for Strings, particularly, is the work of a young musician of true talent, rapidly increasing skill, and, one would infer, capacity for self-criticism. It is not pretentious music. Its author does not pose and posture in his score. He writes with a definite purpose, a clear objective and a sense of structure.

ARCH OF MELODY AND FORM

A long line, in the Adagio, is well sustained. There is an arch of melody and form. The composition is most simple at the climaxes, when it develops that the simplest chord, or figure, is the one most significant. That is because we have here honest music, by a musician not striving for pretentious effect, not behaving as a writer would who, having a clear, short, popular word handy for his purpose, got the dictionary and fished out a long one.

This is the product of a musically creative nature, and an earnest student who leaves nothing undone to achieve something as perfect in mass and detail as his craftsmanship permits. A young man who has so genuine a talent and purpose should go far.

The "Essay for Orchestra," modestly named, is well integrated, with clear instrumentation, and with development of the ideas that unifies the music in spite of changes of tempo and marked contrasts of orchestration. The Adagio impressed this chronicler, at the first hearing, as the better composition of the two, but it would be premature to put this down as a definite conclusion, and it is a matter of secondary importance. Of the first importance is the fact of a composer who is attempting no more than he can do, and doing that genuinely, and well.

SOURCE: Olin Downes, "Toscanini Plays Two New Works," New York Times, November 6, 1938, 1A.

~~~~~~

Debate over the meaning of a contemporary idiom in new American music began with a letter from Ashley Pettis, music critic for New Masses *magazine and a coordinator of the WPA-sponsored Composers Forum Laboratory concerts. It provoked rebuttals and counterrebuttals from important figures in American classical music across the country, among them Gian Carlo Menotti, the opera composer and Barber's life partner, and Roy Harris, a well-known composer.*

FROM THE MAIL POUCH
"Important" American Music

To the Music Editor:
When an artist of the enormous reputation and equally great ability of Arturo Toscanini decides to present a composition by an American the announcement of such an event possesses the accepted attributes of "news." Potentially it is an event of great significance and might easily have an enormous influence upon our musical life, both in acquainting a wide public with the fact that there are serious, contemporary works and to provide fresh impetus and incentive to our musical craftsmen.

The term "might easily have an enormous influence" is used advisedly when one considers the most recent and rare gesture of Maestro Toscanini in performing two works by an American, young Samuel Barber, on his NBC broadcast Nov. 5.

There are important American composers and important American compositions of every type of thought and tendency. But from "at least one listener's point of view" neither Mr. Barber nor his works may be justly so termed. One listened in vain for evidences of youthful vigor, freshness or fire, for use of a contemporary idiom (which was characteristic of every composer whose works have withstood the vicissitudes of time). Mr. Barber's was "authentic," "dull," "serious," music—utterly anachronistic as the utterance of a young man of 28, A.D. 1938!

Such a choice by the great musical Messiah in our midst can only have a retarding influence on the advance of our creative musicians. They realize only too well that they have small chance of performance by the greatest musical organization[s] and conductors (not to mention individual artists of the first magnitude) unless they write music for people who listen with ears of the nineteenth and early twentieth centuries at latest—whose criteria are that "new" music shall have the familiar melodic, harmonic and rhythmic characteristics of the past, that it be a hodge-podge of clichés, that it presupposes no spirit of musical adventure on the part of either performer or public.

We have music by Americans, legitimately redolent of other days, both by composers living and dead. Off hand one thinks of [Edward] MacDowell, [Charles] Griffes, and our own living youngster, the octogenarian Edgar Stillman Kelley of the New England Symphony. Of a later date, living, writing in and of the present, come to mind the names of Aaron Copland, Roy Harris, Roger Sessions, the always mentioned but almost never played Charles Ives. What chance, if any, have they and many others one should mention in the forward march of the followers of David against the Philistines?

[signed] Ashley Pettis

New York, Nov. 8, 1938.

DRAWN FROM THE MAIL POUCH
Which Is "Modern Music"?

To the Music Editor:

In regard to Ashley Pettis's letter of last week, will Mr. Pettis please give his meaning of "modern idiom"? Must there be in art one "modern idiom"? Because there is Gertrude Stein, must we condemn a Thomas Mann? Isn't the field of music vast enough for opposing currents to flow together?

I am afraid Mr. Pettis is very passé and still accepts as the modern idiom the Parisian style of twenty years ago. If Mr. Barber dares to defy the servile imitation of that style (which has been called American music) and experiments successfully with melodic line and new form, is he not to be praised for his courage?

Mr. Pettis doesn't realize that this is a fast-moving world. Music must go on, and it is time for some one to make a reaction against a school of composition that has bored concert audiences for twenty years. All through Europe there are signs of this healthy reaction among the younger generations. Mr. Pettis is behind the times.

If Mr. Barber's music is not startlingly original, surely that is not to his discredit. He is young. The early Michelangelo accepted the influence of Signorelli, Beethoven that of Mozart, and some of Leonardo's early work is scarcely distinguishable from Verrocchio.

It was very amusing to Mr. Pettis's artistic generation to be revolutionists. But now let them recognize that the younger generation is left with the thankless job of building on their ruins.

Finally, adopting Mr. Pettis's metaphor, isn't it high time that a young David appeared and struck on the forehead that inflated monster which still parades under the anachronistic name of modern music?

[signed] Gian-Carlo Menotti

New York, Nov. 16, 1938

FROM THE MAIL POUCH
The Old and the New

To the Music Editor:

For years there has been a cultural storm gathering in our land. The old and the new are digging up the time-worn battleaxe again. The old was ever venerable—the new ever vulnerable. The venerable dwell on their solid Parnassus, secure in the well-being of having done the right thing by us. In the spirit of good citizenship they contributed to our cultural perspective by patronizing the best of European traditions and bringing them into our midst. They built our halls, stocked our libraries, imported the finest European musicians to play for, and teach us.

The vulnerable? A handful of improvidents with nothing but their talents, energies and ambitions. They have everything to win. A whole new world is theirs for the taking— if they can serve it. Young America's savage vitality and profound searching hopes await their articulate expression. Thousands of young musicians who memorized the standard repertory are looking for something new; radio, recording, choruses, orchestras, wearing the proved past thin with repetition; the public—many and various publics—waiting.

What can the venerable do? They can only continue to offer the past. The vulnerable contemporary composer will have to create whatever is added. And Time, who is no respecter of persons, will call his own court of appraisal to order and render final judgement on what is offered. No amount of wish-thinking on the part of either party will alter the real stature of what we do.

[signed] Roy Harris

New York, Nov. 22, 1938

SOURCE: *The New York Times* as follows: letter from Pettis, November 13, 1938, letter from Menotti, November 20, 1938, letter from Harris, November 27, 1938. See also Barbara Heyman, *Samuel Barber: The Composer and His Music* (New York: Oxford University Press, 1992): 168–73.

V IRGIL THOMSON, COMPOSER AND CRITIC

The opera *Four Saints in Three Acts* by Virgil Thomson (1896–1989) was born during the unlikely decade of the Great Depression. At a time when values of "social conscience" and documentary realism dominated art, Thomson's opera rejoiced in subversive whimsy. His sensibility, which has affinities for what later critics described as "camp"—perhaps related to the fact that he was gay, or perhaps not—delighted in covert critiques of mainstream middle-class culture. Thomson hired the painter Florine Stettheimer to design the opera's famous rococo cellophane sets. He used hymn tunes and folk-based melodies to play off the surrealistic libretto, written by the avant-garde writer Gertrude Stein (1874–1946). Would the expatriate poet of such lines as "Pigeons on the grass alas, pigeons on the grass" actually come to the Hartford premiere of their opera? In the letter reprinted here, written shortly before the premiere in February 1934, Thomson hopes to entice Stein there. She heard the opera later in Chicago.

Thomson supported himself primarily as a music critic; his reviews are still read today for their insight and wit. Reigning supreme at the *New York Herald Tribune* from 1940 through 1954, just as the late nineteenth-century critic Henry Krehbiel shaped his influence by championing the European classical canon, so Thomson defined his own by resisting it. He hated the cults surrounding celebrity performers and was famous in particular for bravely criticizing the conductor Arturo Toscanini. His essay "Conducting Modern Music," reprinted as the second selection below, insists on a genuine relationship between the public and contemporary music.

~~~~~~~~~
~~~~~~~~~

LETTER TO GERTRUDE STEIN

[Hartford]
December 6 [1933]
Dear Gertrude

Here is a newspaper article that will amuse you from the Hartford Times. The cast of the opera is hired and rehearsals begun. I have a chorus of 32 & six soloists, very, very fine ones indeed. Miss Stettheimer's[1] sets are of a beauty incredible, with trees made out of feathers and a sea-wall at Barcelona made out of shells and for the procession a baldachino of black chiffon & branches of black ostrich plumes just like a Spanish funeral. St. Teresa comes to the picnic in the 2nd act on a cart drawn by a real white donkey & brings her tent with her and sets it up & sits in the doorway of it. It is made of white gauze with gold fringe and has a most elegant shape. My singers, as I have wanted, are Negros [sic], & you can't imagine how beautifully they sing.[2] Frederick Ashton is arriving from London this week to make choreography for us all.[3] Not only for the dance numbers but for the whole show, so that all the movements will be regulated to the music, measure by measure, and all our complicated stage action made into a controllable spectacle. Houseman is a playwright, friend, & collaborator of Lewis Galantière.[4] He "understands" the opera too if you know what I mean by that word. Everything about the opera is shaping up so beautifully, even the raising of money (it's going to cost $10,000), that the press is chomping at the bit and the New York ladies already ordering dresses & engaging hotel rooms. Carl [Van Vechten]'s niece has taken a Hartford house for the opera week. Rumors of your arrival are floating about and everybody asks me if she is really coming and I always answer that it wouldn't surprise me. Certainly, if everything goes off as fancy as it looks now, you would be very happy to be here and see your opera on the stage and I would be very happy to see it with you and your presence would be all we need to make the opera perfect in every way. (February 7th is the opening date, I believe.) Many people, seeing my copy, have asked me where Operas and Plays *can be bought here and those who have tried tell me it isn't to be had. Couldn't you send a consignment to several of the good bookstores? Big stores are best now. Nobody goes to little ones anymore & they've mostly gone out of business anyway.*

Always affectionately,

SOURCE: Tim Page and Vanessa Weeks Page, eds., *Selected Letters of Virgil Thomson* (New York: Simon & Schuster, 1988): 112–13. Also cited and partially quoted in Anthony Tommasini, *Virgil Thomson: Composer on the Aisle* (New York: Norton, 1997): 249–50.

~~~~~~~~

CONDUCTING MODERN MUSIC

The prime consideration in interpreting new musical works is to avoid doing anything that might possibly make these appear to be emulating the music of the past. Such emulation may or may not have been a part of the composer's intention, but playing it up in presentation produces a false relation between a work and its own time that is fatal to the comprehension of the work by its own time. Dressing and directing *Hamlet* as if it were a modern play is a piquant procedure. Treating a modern play as if it were Shakespeare's *Hamlet* can only make for pretentiousness and obscurity.

There is a prestige attached to any art work that has survived the death of its author which no work by a living hand can enjoy. This fact of survival is correctly called immortality, and that immortality surrounds the surviving work with a white light. In that radiance all becomes beautiful. Obscurities disappear too, or at least they cease to bother. When I refer, as not infrequently I do, to live music and dead music, I mean that there is the same difference between the two that there is between live persons and dead ones. The spirit and influence of the dead are often far more powerful than those of the living. But they are not the same thing, because you can only argue *about* them, never *with*. The dead have glory and a magnificent weight. The living have nothing but life.

The glorification of the dead is a perfectly good thing. Indeed, the greater civilizations have always done it more than the lesser. But a clear separation of the dead from the living is also a mark of the higher cultures. That is the fecundating drama between tradition and spontaneity that keeps people and empires alive. Consequently no good is accomplished by pretending, or seeming to pretend, that a work by Igor Stravinsky or Aaron Copland is a museum piece, because it isn't and won't be till they are dead, if then. And framing such a work among museum pieces in such a way that it appears to be subsidiary to them invariably makes the living work seem deader than a doornail. Its lack of white-light immortality makes it appear gravely inferior to the works on the same program that have such an aura and glamour.

The moral of this explanation is that new works must be played alone, in company with other new works, or surrounded by old ones carefully chosen, if one wishes to bring out their resemblances to the traditional past as well as their essential differences from the past. A new work may not be the most important piece on the program; but unless it is the determining item in the choice of the whole program, it will always sound like second-rate music, because it is pretty certain to be placed in unfair glamour competition with the classics of repertory. Modern music indiscriminately programmed, no matter what kind of music it is, is framed to flop.

Neither can it be interpreted in the same style as older music. Insufficient rehearsal often works to a new piece's advantage. When there isn't time to do much but read the notes and observe the author's tempos, it gets a neutral reading that is at least better than a false interpretation. If the conductor has time to work it up into an imitation of all his favorite war-horses or to streamline it into a faint reminder of Beethoven and Tchaikovsky, it is very difficult for the listener to hear anything in it but a memory of these authors, or at most a feeble attempt to dethrone them by being arbitrarily different.

The best international style for playing the classics is one which reduces them to a common denominator of clarity and elegance. That was always Toscanini's force as a conductor of standard repertory. He was never very effective as a conductor of modern music (and he avoided it whenever possible, for that reason, I imagine), because he knew no other way of conducting anything. Characteristic national differences, which are of minor importance in standard repertory but which are the very essence of modern stylistic comprehension, seem to have escaped him. And being a musician of too high temperament to be satisfied with a merely neutral reading of anything, he wisely refrained from taking on a job in which neither he nor the living composer was likely to do much shining.

The conductors who do best by the music of our century are seldom equally good at interpreting all the kinds of it. Koussevitzky does well by anything Russian and fair by the English and the Americans, provided these last are not too local in flavor. He is not bad with German music, adds to it a Slavic elegance that is sometimes advantageous. French music escapes him utterly, in spite of his many years' residence in Paris. Mitropoulos is at his best with the central-European styles. Beecham is fine for English music, for all Slavic, for some German, for anything that has lyric afflatus or rhythmic punch. The Germans are rather messy when they play German music—always were, as Richard Wagner pointed out. Some are excellent with French music, however—Furtwängler, for instance, and Stock of Chicago.[5] Italians do not always do their best by Italian works, especially those of strong French influence, though they do beautifully by anything Germanic, even Brahms. Only the French (and a few Germans) make sense with French music. Nobody, literally nobody, who has not passed his formative adolescent years in this country ever conducts American music with complete intelligibility.

The basis of American musical thought is a special approach to rhythm. Underneath everything is a continuity of short quantities all equal in length and in percussive articulation. These are not always articulated, but they must always be understood. If for any expressive reason one alters the flow of them temporarily, they must start up again exactly as before, once the expressive alteration is terminated. In order to make the whole thing clear, all instruments, string and wind, must play with a clean, slightly percussive attack. This attack must never be sacrificed for the sake of a beautiful tone or even for pitch accuracy, because it is more important than either. Besides, once a steady rhythm is established, the music plays itself; pitch and sonorities adjust themselves automatically; as in a good jazz band the whole takes on an air of completeness.

French music is the nearest thing in Europe to our music, because French rhythm, like ours, is less accentual than quantitative. Keeping downbeats out of a Debussy rendition, for instance, is virtually impossible to anybody but a Frenchman. Steady quantities, a little longer than ours and requiring no percussive definition at all, are its rhythmic foundation. Definition is achieved by a leisurely breathing between phrases and an almost imperceptible wait before attacking, with no added force, what in any other music would be played as a downbeat. As with American music, a proper rhythm is cardinal and must be achieved before the pitch and the tone production can be polished up.

Modern German music is not very interesting rhythmically. It needs no exact quantities, only a thwacking downbeat. Even that can be advanced or held back, as is the Viennese custom, to express sentiment. What is most important is to get the harmony right and don't go *too* sentimental. Nothing else counts, provided care for the harmony includes a clear plotting out of the key relations in the whole piece. This means being sure there is always plenty of bass at the piece's joints.

Russian music is an alteration of very free rhythms with rigid and insistent ones. The latter are easy to render. But few conductors ever take enough liberties with the sentimental passages. English formulas are always closely related to the Russian (*vide* the English novel and the English church). In music, both peoples conceive of rhythm as either nonexistent or quite inflexible. Both observe beat rhythms too, not quantities. And both alternate speech inflections with footwork, as in a song-and-dance. The chief difference between them is that the Russian mind dramatizes itself with a grandiloquent simplicity, whereas the English tradition values a more intimate and personal kind of forthrightness in the expression of tender thought. The grander passages of both repertories may be rendered with the utmost of pomp and of panache.

Matters like these seem to me more important to restate than international [a]esthetic principles. All conductors know nowadays what the neo-classic style is all about. Also the neo-Romantic style and the twelve-tone syntax. And certainly the survivals of late Romanticism are not difficult to decipher. But these are the stylistic elements that underlie all modern music; they have been written about ad infinitum and ad nauseam. What I am pointing out is that underneath these international tendencies and observances there are ethnic differences that must be taken account of. Also to remind my readers that these ethnic differences preclude the possibility that conductors of foreign upbringing now resident among us will play a leading role in our present musical expansion. They render great service by their constant acts of good will toward homemade music. But they have only the vaguest idea of what it's all about. And so has that part of our musical public that hears it only through their well-intentioned but unconvincing renditions.

SOURCE: Virgil Thomson, "Conducting Modern Music," *New York Herald Tribune*, January 25, 1942, as reprinted in Virgil Thomson, *A Virgil Thomson Reader* (Boston: Houghton Mifflin, 1981): 222–25.

NOTES

1.   Florine Stettheimer (1871–1944) was an American painter.
2.   *Four Saints in Three Acts* had an African-American cast, including a chorus directed by Eva Jessye (1895–1992), who later worked on Gershwin's *Porgy and Bess*.
3.   Frederick Ashton (1904–1988) was the major choreographer for the Royal Ballet in the 1930s.
4.   John Houseman (1902–1988) was a director and later a successful film actor. Lewis Galantière (1895–1977) was a French-American writer and translator.
5.   The list of conductors with their orchestras ca. 1942 named here are Sergey Koussevitsky (1874–1951), Boston Symphony Orchestra; Dmitri Mitropoulos (1896–1960), Minneapolis Symphony Orchestra; Thomas Beecham (1879–1971), Metropolitan Opera Orchestra and the Seattle Symphony Orchestra; Wilhelm Furtwängler (1886–1954), Berlin Philharmonic; and Frederick Stock (1872–1942), Chicago Symphony Orchestra.

92

ARTHUR BERGER DIVIDES AARON COPLAND INTO TWO STYLES, AND COPLAND PUTS HIMSELF BACK TOGETHER AGAIN

The composer Arthur Berger (1912–2003) shaped an influential framework for understanding the music of Aaron Copland through his critical loyalty to the music itself. A member of the Young Composers Group, an informal New York–based collective led by Copland in the 1930s, Berger wrote assessments of Copland's major works when many of them were premiered.

This review of Copland's Piano Sonata reveals much more about Copland's music than just a focus on one piece. Berger describes other works, such Copland's earlier Piano Variations, to explain Copland's "severe" style. In addition, Berger criticizes Copland's goal of writing "accessible" music. Berger's approach endured—and perhaps still does—as a staple of the Copland literature partly because it encodes a larger debate over elitism and populism.

Berger's rhetorical engine was fueled by an article that Copland published in the journal *Modern Music,* which included this statement:

> But the radio and phonograph have given us listeners whose sheer numbers in themselves create a special problem. They can't be ignored if musical creation is to flourish. More and more

we shall have to find a musical style and language which satisfies both us and them. That is the job of the forties. I have seldom advanced this point of view without being misinterpreted. I can only repeat that I do not advocate "writing down" to the public.[1]

Following this selection are documents which show Copland offering rebuttals and resistance in theory and in practice.

MUSIC CHRONICLE

COPLAND'S PIANO SONATA

About nine years ago, Aaron Copland added to an "austere," somewhat uncompromising style of musical composition, an alternate style appropriate to "music for use"—music for cinema, radio, schools, and the picket-line. This new preoccupation was not to exclude other "more serious" work, but some of us were apprehensive of the effect on the future of the remarkable idiom expressed by the *Piano Variations* (1930) and the *Short Symphony* (1933) which indicated so many possibilities as yet but partially fulfilled. The *Piano Sonata* (1941), which has finally been presented in New York,* is, however, reassurance of the fact that the other Copland not only continues to function, but assumes further significance. If anything is to be deplored, it is that the demands for "occasional" music stand in the way of the completion of more than one work like the *Sonata* in the course of several years. But this condition may be altered. An obliging forecaster of his musical intentions, Copland now advocates a musical language which would realize the implications of radio and phonograph by addressing a larger audience without "writing down" and after the manner of Shostakovich when his "obvious weaknesses" have been discounted, without sacrificing seriousness. The *Sonata* may thus be a step towards concentrating in one form what Copland has been accomplishing separately in two fairly discrete series of efforts (to the partial exclusion of one of them.) For while the allegedly "very severe" style of the *Variations* is much in evidence to discourage many listeners of their first acquaintance, there is also an admixture of the wholesome atmosphere of the music for the movie *Our Town* to soften the effect.

The exaggerated determinism of a certain glib school of "sociological" criticism is recalled when Copland insists: "More and more we shall have to find a musical style and language which satisfies both us and them"—i.e., the composers who now constitute one another's audience, and the radio-phonograph public. Nevertheless, it is interesting in this regard to consider Mozart's confession (in one of his letters) that he put certain effects into his music to please his patrons (and he expected approval of these effects to be manifested in a way, moreover,

*The Sonata was performed by John Kirkpatrick at Town Hall in January and by Leonard Bernstein at the concert given in February by the Town Hall Forum.

that would certainly be considered barbaric anywhere but at the ballet—namely by applause *during the music* as each effect is heard, just as we now applaud a pirouette). The merely ingratiating figures in Mozart's profounder works do not, however, stand apart from [the rest] as superimposed elements which aim at quick response. If we knew more about the music he might have composed without such concessions, we might even find that it profited from their inclusion.

In Copland's case, it would seem that his more immediately appealing efforts have actually exerted a favorable influence on the *Sonata* in return for the sensitivity and ingenuity which invest the "workaday" music as a residue of the "serious" style. For example, the *Sonata* has some tunes which are like those we normally whistle or hum. That is, the tunes do not exceed average vocal range, nor are the skips too eccentric. The ease with which a tune may be reproduced or retained or merely apprehended depends upon its resemblance to ordinary nonmusical, vocal experience (speech, sighs, shouts). A means is thus provided for touching upon commonly felt emotions; for one way in which music imitates feeling is by analogy with vocal inflection, and the commonly felt emotions are obviously embodied in inflections experienced in daily life. And, provided with this means, Copland has caught intensely human attitudes to animate the "tonal edifices" which Paul Rosenfeld once found to "resemble nothing so much as steel cranes, bridges, and the frames of skyscrapers."

There is still another aspect in which the *Sonata* reflects Copland's recent concern with what psychologists would call "audience preference": the sonorous texture. Listeners like to abandon themselves in an aura of sound and in the *Our Town* music, *Quiet City,* and the *Lincoln Portrait,* Copland shows an awareness of this. At the other extreme is the *Variations* with its sparse chords, the gaunt exposed dissonances, its theme starkly disengaged from the quickly released harmonies (except in the fifth variation and the closing section). The *Sonata* lies somewhere in between. There is still the pervading gloom of the *Variations,* the same bleakness in the constricted theme and its unvoluptuous harmonies; but there is an alleviating warmth and at times a cozy resonance. The chords do not leave us abruptly, but linger as if to plead a sorrowful case to evoke pity, or as if partly content in a certain resignation. This makes for an important difference between the two piano works which touches seriously upon their performance. There is a tendency of pianists to approach and leave the chords of the *Sonata* with a percussive sharpness appropriate for their treatment in the *Variations.* When Copland plays the *Sonata,* however, he has a way of resting in the keys as if to urge the maximum resonance out of them, and he encourages the listener to make much of the sonorous moment between the striking of one chord and the next.

I do not think the *Sonata* achieves a "language which satisfies both us and them," nor do I think Copland consciously sought it. The tunes are far from obvious enough for your "average listener," and while he will prefer the protracted chords to the ascetic single tones prolonged in the *Variations,* he will crave a prettiness to relieve the gloom. (And your average listener is also likely to lose patience at the extension of certain attitudes, unless he is sensitive to the subtle harmonies through which the attitudes are projected.) But more lyricism and greater sonority were needed to balance Copland's idiom of the *Variations;* and the impetus to acquire these attributes in a music to satisfy a more popular demand may have transferred itself in a modified form to the separate plane of his serious music where they are represented in quite a different way. Thus, while the *Variations* remains an admirable work, the *Sonata* surpasses it precisely in this new resonance and melodic warmth which now offset the dark atmosphere of prophecy and the contrasting nervous athleticism which are common to both works.

If, like Stravinsky, Copland is capable of absorbing so much of what in literature would correspond to the colloquial, without the music itself losing dignity or sophistication,* it is because of that early concern with purification and structure which gave him the reputation for severity. Platitude is not simply paraphrased (as in the Roy Harris *Folk Song Symphony*) but recast to fit into a significant form (even in *El Salón México* and the new *Piece on Cuban Themes*). Whatever cliché he seizes upon—a cowboy ditty, a Spanish turn, a New England hymn—is transformed into an unmistakably Coplandesque configuration.

. . .

Copland's and a still older generation had accomplished the leveling off of the effusive remnants of Wagnerian hysteria and Impressionist revery. But [David] Diamond and [Harold] Shapero (as represented in a *Concerto for Two Solo Pianos* and a *Violin Sonata*) show an awareness of a necessity for building up the thinned-out musical medium with more genuine substance.[2] Once Copland had arrived at a skeletonized music he remained fairly faithful to it since it satisfied a certain romantic desire for a highly personalized expression in which so many notes had to be excluded because they were not completely his own—even the common stock of useful ornaments, like *arpeggios* and scales. (It is a mistake to attribute Copland's sifting out of coloristic material to purely "neo-classic" motives.) The result is a music which often lacks enough matter with which to achieve long undulating lines and various levels of significance, though the personality comes through excellently. There is, however, so much solidity and precision in what is given, that an ultimate evaluation should properly set the *Piano Sonata* among the best contemporary works that have been written in that form.

SOURCE: Arthur Berger, "Music Chronicle: Copland's Piano Sonata," *Partisan Review* 10, no. 2 (March–April 1943): 187–90.

~~~~~~~~

Copland's response to Berger, reprinted here, shows his strategies of resistance. In addition to tempering Berger's division of styles, Copland poked at Stravinsky, Berger's idol, and praised a new book by an Americanist literary critic, Alfred Kazin. Coincidentally, six weeks later one of Copland's most successful "simple" pieces was heard in a concert hall for the first time, with the premiere of Four Dance Episodes *from the ballet* Rodeo. *Its much-loved last movement, "Hoe-Down," has since evolved into a musical signature of Americana. The transcription of the "fiddle-picture" tune Copland borrowed for "Hoe-Down," which is reprinted here, allows us to mull over Berger's later description of Copland's piece as "virtually photographic"—an example of Copland resorting to "disarming extremes of simplicity."[3]*

*It is, of course, to be admitted that Copland does, in rare instances, fail to go beyond mere uncritical reproduction, as in the slow middle part of *El Salon Mexico* where one passage creates the illusion of listening to almost any competent Mexican band—as if the composer were saving his ideas for the brilliant long line of the fast closing section. This is not true of Stravinsky. Compare, for example, *Jeu de Cartes* where the only instance of almost exact repetition of the object alluded to (a reference to Rossini) has an obviously ironic intent.

Hollywood, April 10, 1943

Dear Arthur:

The other night, while walking down Hollywood Blvd., I happened on a copy of the Partisan Review. Imagine my surprise when I came upon your piece on the Sonata. I wonder what made you not tell me about it—just neglect? Or was it "fright" at my reaction? Anyhow it was lots of fun to be surprised like that. Subsequently Victor [Kraft] wrote me that you had mentioned it to him.

I don't know what others will think, but I liked it. My one objection is that it came to a rather sudden end, just as things were getting along. Were you cramped for space? It gives that impression.

There are a few things I'd like to comment upon. One is the meaning of my articles and "pronunciamentos." When I call for a "style that satisfies both us and them," I am mostly trying to goad composers on toward what I think is a healthy direction. I am emphatically not laying out an a priori plan for my own future compositions. I reserve the right always to practice not what I preach, but what the muse dictates.

I think also that for the sake of drawing sharp distinctions you rather overdo the dichotomy between my "severe" and "simple" styles. The inference is that only the severe style is really serious. I don't believe that. What I was trying for in the simpler works was only partly a larger audience; they also gave me a chance to try for a home-spun musical idiom, similar to what I was trying for in a more hectic fashion in the earlier jazz works. In other words, it was not only musical functionalism that was in question, but also musical language. I like to think that in Billy [the Kid] and Our Town, and somewhat in Lincoln [Portrait], I have touched off for myself and others a kind of musical naturalness that we have badly needed—along with "great" works.

The reference to David [Diamond]'s and Harold [Shapero]'s building up the "thinned out musical substance" needs to be expanded to be clear. I didn't understand it myself. But I'm sure they were pleased with the plug!

Did Victor tell you Stravinsky had me and Antheil[4] to dinner? (After reading Kazin's book,[5] I've come to the conclusion that Stravinsky is the Henry James of composers. Same "exile" psychology, same exquisite perfection, same hold on certain temperaments, same lack of immediacy of contact with the world around him.) He was extremely cordial with us. We played the Symphony from off-the-air records, and S. complained bitterly about some of Stokowski's tempi.[6] I don't think he's in a very good period. He copies himself unashamedly, and therefore one rarely comes upon a really fresh page—for him, I mean. I know this is blasphemy in the Berger household, but there it is—so make the most of it.

I hear glamorous reports of parties at the Berger household that make my mouth water. Apparently the Guggenheim fiasco didn't completely floor you. And everyone speaks of seeing you both at all the concerts there are, so you must have a lot to write me about. Please do, because I'm homesick like hell!

Love to Esther,
[signed] Aaron

SOURCE: Wayne Shirley, ed., "Aaron Copland and Arthur Berger in Correspondence," in *Aaron Copland and His World*, ed. Carol J. Oja and Judith Tick (Princeton, N.J.: Princeton University Press, 2005): 191–92.

BONYPARTE

d, d'. No. 1568. W. M. Stepp, Salyersville, Ky., 1937.
Known sometimes as "Bonaparte's Retreat Across the Rocky
Mountains." The piece is descriptive—marching, wind
howling, etc.

"Bonyparte," transcribed by Ruth Crawford Seeger for *Our Singing Country* (1941). From a performance by W. M. Stepp, 1937, Salyersville, Kentucky (available on Rounder Records). This fiddle tune is used by Aaron Copland for the "Hoedown" movement of his suite, *Rodeo*.

~~~~~~~

NOTES

1.   Aaron Copland, "From the '20s to the '40s and Beyond," *Modern Music* 20 (January–February 1943): 78–82.

2.   David Diamond (1915–2005) and Harold Shapero (1920–), American composers, were associated with American neoclassicism.

3.   Arthur Berger, *Aaron Copland* (New York: Oxford University Press, 1953): 57. "Hoe-Down" was premiered on May 28, 1943, by the Boston Pops Orchestra, conducted by Arthur Fiedler. Ira Ford, in *Traditional Music of America* (1940; New York: Da Capo Press, 1978): 129, offers another version of "Bonaparte's Retreat," which is described as a "'fiddle-picture' of Napoleon at the battle of Waterloo."

4.   George Antheil (1900–1959), an American composer most famous for his score to the film *Ballet Mécanique*.

5.   Alfred Kazin's (1915–1998) now-classic *On Native Grounds* (1942) was a critical study of American writers and thinkers from ca. 1890 to 1940.

6.   This is referring to Stravinsky's Symphony in C as conducted by Leopold Stokowski.

93

AARON COPLAND ON THE

"PERSONALITY OF STRAVINSKY"

Aaron Copland's brief tribute, which was written for a special collection devoted to Stravinsky and published in 1949, tells us as much about Copland as it does about its subject. Copland's emphasis on "personality" recurs frequently in his own writings, where it stands for a composer's distinctive musical voice and artistic orientation (see chapter 143 for more comments on "personality"). The comment about Stravinsky's musical remoteness from "everyday events" also sounds a familiar leitmotif because Copland made paying attention to them a centerpiece of his own music and cultural theory.

For almost thirty years I have wondered about the exact nature of the personality of Stravinsky. Everyone agrees that Stravinsky possesses one of the most individual natures of our time. But to get at the essence of it is another matter.

Certain composers are literally drenched in their own personal atmosphere. One thinks immediately of Chopin, or of the later Beethoven, or the mature Wagner. On the other hand, if you don't listen closely, there are times when you might mistake Mozart for Haydn, or Bach for

Handel, or even Ravel for Debussy. I cannot ever remember being fooled by the music of Stravinsky. It invariably sounds like music that only he could have written.

Why? I'm sure I don't know . . . but I keep wondering about it. Musicians will tell you that you must take the music apart, see how it is made, then put it together again, and you will have the answer. I've tried it, but it really doesn't work. Knowing Stravinsky the man helps a little, but not enough. At home he is a charming host, a man with clearly defined ideas and a sharp tongue . . . but the music seems to exist on a supra-personal plane, in an aural world of its own.

It is his work of the last few years that holds the mystery tightest. One thinks of the Ode, the Mass, the ballet Orpheus . . . these works, in some curious way, seem strangely removed from everyday "events"—and yet they remain profoundly human. Sobriety is the keynote—it seems hardly possible to create a music of less sensuous appeal. Nevertheless, there are moments of enriched texture—all the more rare and precious because they are measured out so carefully. In these works thought and instinct are inextricably wedded, as they should be.

These few remarks hardly touch the surface of the problem. Perhaps it is just because the secret cannot be extracted that the fascination of Stravinsky's personality continues to hold us.

SOURCE: Aaron Copland, "The Personality of Stravinsky," in *Igor Stravinsky: A Merle Armitage Book*, ed. Edwin Corle (New York: Duell, Sloan and Pearce, 1949): 121–22.

94

THE AMERICAN PERIOD OF
ARNOLD SCHOENBERG
(Sessions, Newlin)

Arnold Schoenbeg (1874–1951) arrived in New York in 1933 as a political refugee from Hitler's Nazi regime. Although he did not leave Europe at a high point in his career, he grew more isolated in the United States. Among the few Americans who never doubted the magnitude of Schoenberg was the composer, teacher, and writer Roger Sessions (1896–1985). In the 1930s and '40s, when simplicity was exalted as an American musical virtue, Sessions remained fundamentally committed to the complexities he felt were necessary to and for his own musical language.

Reprinted here is a tribute Sessions published when Schoenberg turned 70. When revising this article in 1972, Sessions added a footnote explaining his own adoption of Schoenberg's 12-tone methods in the early 1950s, which is reprinted here as well. How much was Sessions describing himself in this portrait of a hero?

This chapter concludes with an intimate account of Schoenberg in an American classroom in Los Angeles in 1939. Dika Newlin studied with him for a few years in the late 1930s. She also worked with Roger Sessions after that as well.

In any survey of Schoenberg's work one fact must be emphasized above all: that no younger composer writes quite the same music as he would have written, had Schoenberg's music not existed. The influence of an artist is not, even during his life time, confined to his disciples or even to those who have felt the direct impact of his work. It is filtered through to the humblest participant, first in the work of other original artists who have absorbed and re-interpreted it for their own purposes; then through the work of hundreds of lesser individuals, who unconsciously reflect the new tendencies even when they are opposed to them. For genuinely new ideas determine the battlegrounds on which their opponents are forced to attack. In the very process of combat the latter undergo decisive experiences which help to carry the new ideas forward.

. . .

In 1933 Schoenberg came to the United States and ten years later became an American citizen. In the country to which he came, musical activity is intense on many levels, and despite many necessary reservations the development within the last generation has been phenomenal. Musical education has penetrated everywhere; both the general level and the quality of instruction available on the highest level of all have risen to a degree amazing to all who confronted the musical conditions of thirty-five years ago. American composers of serious intent have begun to appear in considerable numbers, and to achieve an influence and recognition undreamed by their predecessors; moreover, they have become aware of themselves, of their inner and outer problems, and better equipped to face these. Above all it has become evident that musical talent, the raw material from which musical culture grows, is strikingly abundant.

It is however clear that the institutional structure of music in the United States has not yet been established in definitive outlines. The relationship between the art and the business of music, and of both of these with the 'public'; the role and direction of musical education; the influence of radio, gramophone, and amateur musical activities—these are questions which in the United States are still fundamentally unsettled. There is similar confusion as to what we may call the structure of musical effort: the respective roles in musical culture and production of the composer, performer, critic, and scholar.

These latter observations are true of course not only of the United States but of modern civilization in general. But conditions here differ from those elsewhere in the fact that whereas elsewhere the forces of opposition are those of established cultural tradition, here there is a perceptible undertow in the growing musical consciousness of a culture still in the making. It is this which keeps the musical life of the country in a state of constant change and flux, and which makes the situation chaotic but far from hopeless.

It is not surprising therefore that Schoenberg should have found himself in a quite new relationship to his environment and that his impact should have taken on a new significance. I do not mean to minimize the importance of either the revolutionary or the specifically Viennese Schoenberg. The former has already affected the course of music in a profound sense, and though possibly the first full impact of a composer's work is the most immediately powerful one—think of the 'Eroica,' or 'Tristan,' in contrast to the last quartets or 'Parsifal'—nevertheless with the constant ripening of his art, the latter imposes itself in another, more gradual and more definitely constructive, sense. But that is a task for the composer's successors, and is even independent of his purely historical importance.

As for Vienna, Schoenberg has outlived it as he has outlived Alban Berg. Had he not done so his position might be today less evident than it is. There are other musicians from Central, also from Western and Eastern, Europe, whose impact has been purely provincial; they have conceived their mission as that of winning spheres of influence for their own native background;

and have found—by an inexorable law of human polarization—the most sympathetic acclaim often in circles most tenacious in the pursuit of an American "national" style. Undeniably Schoenberg is a product of Vienna, and of a Viennese tradition with which he is as deeply imbued as anyone living. But it is characteristic of the man, the situation, and possibly of the Viennese tradition itself that his impact on the United States has been that of a third Schoenberg—one by no means unknown in Europe nor difficult to find for those who sought him, but one often obscured in the heat of controversy and the battle positions which his followers were led to assume in his behalf. For in coming to the United States, he left the scene of his most bitter struggles, he came with the prestige of a fighter of distant and only dimly understood battles, with the respect and admiration of a few to whom the battles were neither so distant nor so dimly understood. Others recognized the achievement of the composer of "Verklaerte Nacht" and other early works, and were ready to acclaim him as at least an asset to American musical life.

He taught and lectured in Boston and New York and finally was appointed Professor of Music, first at the University of Southern California, later at the University of California in Los Angeles. His music received sporadic performances; he found himself frequently quoted, frequently in demand as a writer and lecturer. His main influence, however, has been exerted through his teaching, the musicians with whom he has come in contact, and finally the series of works composed in the years since he has lived in the United States, works which in my opinion represent a separate phase and a new level in his music as a whole.

These works include a suite for strings, written in 1934; the fourth string quartet, written in 1936 and performed by the Kolisch Quartet in 1937; the violin concerto, performed in 1940 by Louis Krasner with the Philadelphia Orchestra; a second chamber symphony; a setting of the Kol Nidrei for chorus and orchestra; 'Variations on a Recitative' for organ, first performed by Carl Weinrich for the United States section of the I.S.C.M. [International Society for Contemporary Music] in March, 1944; the Concerto for Piano first performed by Edward Steuermann and the Philadelphia Orchestra in the spring of this year; finally two works shortly to be performed, the 'Ode to Napoleon,' after Byron, for *sprechstimme*, piano and strings, and a theme and variations, written originally for band and later arranged for orchestra.

Of these works, the suite is consciously in an 'old style,' and the second chamber symphony is the completion of a work left unfinished some forty years earlier. With the latter, the organ variations have given rise to rumors of a 'conservative' trend in Schoenberg's music—a 'return' at least to 'tonality' and to a more 'consonant' style. No doubt, the new variations and possibly the Ode, both shortly to receive their world premieres, will add to these rumors which purport to herald a 'capitulation' on Schoenberg's part. The organ variations are extremely freely but none the less unmistakably, in the key of D minor, though also in the twelve-tone system; the orchestral variations are in G minor, signature and all, and definitely in a simpler style. The 'Ode to Napoleon,' though still in the twelve-tone system, is superficially more 'consonant' than many of Schoenberg's earlier works in that, to a very large extent, its style is characterized by the superimposition of triads and their derivatives. It is however doubtful if either the Ode or the organ variations will prove comforting to those who pretend to see any reversal on Schoenberg's part. They are presumably quite as 'forbidding' as any of his reputedly 'atonal' works.

. . .

Perhaps it will be seen from this what I meant in speaking at the beginning of this paper of a 'third Schoenberg.' In his educational tenets he has not, of course, changed through living in the United States. But he has brought these tenets from the principal stronghold of a great and old tradition to a fresh land which is beginning slowly and even cautiously to feel its musical strength. He has given to many young musicians by direct influence, and to others through his disciples, a renewed sense of all that music is and has been, and it is hardly over-bold to foresee that this is going to play its role, perhaps a mighty one, in the musical development of the United States. [A] small testimony to what this new contact may produce may be seen in a very valuable little book—"Models for Beginners in Composition"—which Schoenberg prepared for students in a six-weeks' summer course in California. Certainly the eagerly-awaited treatise on counterpoint and the one also planned on the principles of composition, based on Beethoven's practice, will furnish deeper insights; they cannot fail to prove to be works of capital value. But the little book has for me a special significance as a moving testimony to Schoenberg's relationship to the American musical scene and his brilliantly successful efforts to come to grips with certain of its problems.

. . .

What is essential now is to recognize the need our world has for the qualities that Schoenberg possesses and how admirably he supplies our need. In a world-wide condition in which the rewards of facile mediocrity and of compromise are greater than ever, and in which one hears an ever-insistent demand that music and the other arts devote themselves to the task of furnishing bread and circuses to an economically or politically pliable multitude, the musical world yet celebrates in sincere homage the seventieth birthday of an artist who not only, in the face of the most bitter and persistent opposition, scorn and neglect, has always gone his own way in uncompromising integrity and independence, but who has been and is still the most dangerous enemy of the musical *status quo*. This takes place in spite of the fact that his work is all too seldom performed, that it is exacting in the extreme, and is virtually unknown except to a very few who have made the attempt really to penetrate its secrets. It is in the last analysis an act of gratitude to one who has, so much more than any other individual, been one of the masculine forces that have shaped the music of our time, even that music which seems farthest from his own. It is not only a tribute to a truly great musician, but a hopeful sign that art on the highest level may still survive the bewilderments and the terrors of a mighty world crisis, of which so much is still ahead of us, and which contains so many imponderables.

SOURCE: Roger Sessions, "Schoenberg in the United States," *Tempo* 9 (December 1944): 2–7.

~~~~~~~

SESSIONS ADOPTS TWELVE-TONE PRACTICES

I used the twelve-tone principle for the first time in 1953, in my Sonata for Violin Solo, and have used it to various degrees and in various ways ever since—always, of course, in my own terms. My first use of it was, at the beginning, quite involuntary. I had at various times, for my own self-enlightenment, carried out quite small-scale exercises with the technique, but I still envisaged it as not applicable to my own musical ideas. It was therefore a surprise to me when I found the composition of the Sonata flowing easily and without constraint in its terms. I used it consistently in several well-defined sections of the piece; but on several grounds I decided not to mention this to anyone. However, a colleague to whom I showed the piece immediately recognized the twelve-tone procedures, and afterwards observed, with some surprise, "But it's still your music." This of course is the crux of the matter; I would not have adopted the principle had it been otherwise. It is a mistake to regard the adoption by an artist of a new technical procedure, or even a new "manner," as in any way changing his essential artistic nature.

Once—in 1948, I believe—in the course of a long conversation with Schoenberg, I told him of my opinion that the "twelve-tone method" had been over-publicized and, in the process itself as well as in the controversy which resulted, had become grossly distorted in the minds of many people; and that this had led to strained and artificial attitudes towards the music itself. He replied, somewhat glumly, "Yes, you are right, and I have to admit that it's partly my fault." After a pause he recovered his animation and added, "But it's still more the fault of some of my disciples."

I cite these incidents not in order to play down the importance of the twelve-tone principle—or "method" as Schoenberg insisted on calling it—but rather to place it in its proper perspective as a means and not an end or—above all, at this late date—a "cause." Obviously it is a fact relevant to the music of composers who adopt it—one fact among others, after all. But in no sense does it determine musical value, still less can it be regarded as a quasi-historical end to be pursued for its own sake. In my view it is an all too common error of our times to invoke a facile historicism as a valid basis for both musical effort and musical judgment. One should never forget that it is music, and music alone, that determines musical history; in Schoenberg's case, *Moses und Aron* and the String Trio and many other works are more important facts, historically as well as musically, than the discovery of the twelve-tone method. The same is of course true of the music of [Alban] Berg and [Anton] Webern, not to mention Stravinsky and many others.

SOURCE: Roger Sessions, revision of the original "Schoenberg in the United States," *Tempo*, new ser., 103 (1972): n. 6.

~~~~~~

SCHOENBERG REMEMBERED BY A STUDENT
IN LOS ANGELES

Dika Newlin (1923–2006) was a composer as well as a musicologist, whose training with Arnold Schoenberg began in Los Angeles when she was in her teens. A pioneer in research about Schoenberg, Newlin also studied with Roger Sessions as well, and her own music reflects the impact of twelve-tone modernism. The diaries Newlin kept during these years, which were published much later, reveal Schoenberg's personality in the classroom. Late in life, Newlin cut loose as a cult figure in punk-rock indie movies! Perhaps her maverick temperament comes through even here. This sixteen-year-old treats the famous maestro with total candor. More importantly, this anecdote highlights not only the droll humor that probably helped Schoenberg deal with novice composers, but also the pleasure he took in the craftsmanship of counterpoint—and

even further, his rivalry with Igor Stravinsky, who was the butt of the satirical pieces
for chorus mentioned as models (Drei Satiren, 1925).

I'd half hoped that he might glance over my new sonata theme today. He didn't though; for, in the composition class, he took all the time to discuss the nature of transitions, and spared only about five minutes at the end for looking at the themes of those who hadn't shown him anything the last time. But he did look at my set of imitations in the double counterpoint class; admitted they were "not so bad," but couldn't let me go without the usual quota of sarcastic remarks. Best one, in reference to a spot where the two voices were almost rubbing noses: "So, so, I hope they do not have corns, because if they do, they will step on them and it will hurt, no?" At least, however, I did not relapse into the more flagrant sin of crossing-parts, which practically everyone else did. Every time he came to one of these passages, he would stick one hand over the other with a show of great effort, look sadly at the hands thus intertwined, wiggle his fingers ineffectually in a mock attempt to loose them, and finally remark, "Oh dear, oh dear, I will never get them uncrossed again, never!"; all this to the accompaniment of facial grimaces so pathetic that, unless you were gifted with the special sense of humor which you infallibly develop in a year spent with him, you would hardly know whether to cry with him or laugh at him. After he'd finished looking over our papers, he spent the rest of the two hours talking about and writing inversions, except for a short time at the close of the class when he showed us a few of the innumerable contrapuntal finesses of his *Drei Satiren*. He doesn't like them a bit less now than he did then, either; his face was all wrinkled up with childish glee as he pointed out to us one wonder after another. But these, he called after us as we were leaving the room, these are not the best I ever wrote! There are better ones yet, finer ones. I will show you!

SOURCE: Dika Newlin, *Schoenberg Remembered. Diaries and Recollections (1938–76)*. New York (Pendragon Press, 1980): 105–06. Cited and partially quoted in http://www .schoenberg.at/1_as/schueler/usa/Newlin3.htm.

THE BRISTOL SESSIONS AND COUNTRY MUSIC

During the 1920s, the recording industry found niche markets in ethnic and regional musics and also a new way of doing business. Enter the talent scouts, as entrepreneurial session producers made expeditions to the South and throughout Appalachia in search of musicians to record on location rather than in the studio. One of the greatest figures in the field, Ralph Peer (1892–1960) invented the marketing label "hillbilly," a term carrying humor and stigma simultaneously. On a trip to Atlanta in 1923, Peer made the first country music recording with Fiddlin' John Carson for Okeh Records (see chapter 97).[1]

After moving to Victor Records, Peer undertook a similar mission in Bristol, Tennessee, in July 1927. Within two weeks of running recording auditions at a local furniture store, the Victor team left with pressings of 19 acts—among them two future legends, the singer Jimmie Rodgers and the Carter Family, and others like Ernest Stoneman, and Blind Alfred Reed, with long reaches in the country-music industry and the folk revival.[2] Reprinted here is a complete list of the 35 sides released by Victor. The repertoire includes a novelty fiddling tune, gospel tunes, nineteenth-century sentimental songs, and ballads. The whole operation of the Bristol sessions is often described as a history-making moment, the big bang of country music.

Such success was a combination of luck and foresight. Bristol, the largest city in the Appalachian Mountains, already had a musical reputation. Peer brought sophisticated Western Electric microphones with his crew and started scouting ahead of time. At the end of the summer, local newspapers took stock in a feature article reprinted in the second selection. Neither the Carter Family nor Jimmie Rodgers is mentioned because they had not yet found their publics. The following summer, Peer returned, and by then Jimmie Rodgers was making $15,000 a year, so the newspaper reported.

RECORDINGS MADE JULY 27–AUGUST 4, 1927, AT THE BRISTOL SESSIONS

Skip to Ma Lou, My Darling: Uncle Eck Dunford

O Molly Dear: B. F. Shelton

Walking in the Way with Jesus: Blind Alfred Reed

The Newmarket Wreck: Mr. and Mrs. J. W. Baker

The Soldier's Sweetheart: Jimmie Rodgers

Greasy String: West Virginia Coon Hunters

Are You Washed in the Blood? Ernest V. Stoneman & His Dixie
    Mountaineers

Henry Whitter's Fox Chase

Bury Me under the Weeping Willow Tree: Carter Family

The Jealous Sweetheart: Johnson Brothers

When They Ring the Golden Bells: Alfred G. Karnes

Sandy River Belle: Dad Blackard's Moonshiners

Sleep, Baby, Sleep: Jimmie Rodgers

Johnny Goodwin: Bull Mountain Moonshiners

I'm Redeemed: Alcoa Quartet

Little Log Cabin by the Sea: Carter Family

Old Time Corn Shuckin' (Parts 1 and 2): Blue Ridge Corn Shuckers

I Want to Go Where Jesus Is: Ernest Phipps & His Holiness Quartet

Midnight on the Stormy Deep: Ernest Stoneman, Irma Frost, and Eck
    Dunford

The Wandering Boy: Carter Family

To the Work: Alfred G. Karnes

Black-Eyed Susie: J. P. Nestor

A Passing Policeman: Johnson Brothers

Tell Mother I Will Meet Her: Ernest Stoneman, K. Brewer, and M. Mooney

Single Girl, Married Girl: Carter Family

Pot Licker Blues: El Watson

The Longest Train I Ever Saw: Tenneva Ramblers

The Resurrection: Ernest Stoneman & His Dixie Mountaineers

The Storms Are on the Ocean: Carter Family

The Wreck of the Virginian: Blind Alfred Reed

Billy Grimes, the Rover: Shelor Family

Standing on the Promises: Tennessee Mountaineers

The Mountaineer's Courtship: Ernest Stoneman, Irma Frost, and Eck Dunford

The Poor Orphan Child: Carter Family

I Am Bound for the Promised Land: Alfred G. Karnes

SOURCE: *The Bristol Sessions: Historic Recordings from Bristol, Tennessee* (Country Music Foundation Records, 1991).

FROM THE *BRISTOL HERALD-COURIER* (1927)

MANY PHONOGRAPH RECORDS MADE OF LOCAL TALENT DURING PAST SUMMERS

Musical talent from this section is rapidly winning favor with the leading phonograph record producing companies. Three times since the first of January companies who are recognized as leaders in the recording field have utilized talent from this section in the production of their records. The latest company to secure the services of talent from this section is the Okay [*sic*] Record Company of New York City, recognized along with Columbia and Victor as the biggest record producer in the world.

Tobe S. McNeil, local dealer for the Okay Company, induced F. B. Brockman . . . to come here early in August to hear local talent in a tryout arranged at the McNeil Furniture Company. Approximately 30 persons tried out before Mr. Brockman and after hearing them he finally selected the male quartet of Avoca Tennessee Methodist Church. Composed of O. M. Hunt, K. T. Hunt, W. R. Stidman, and W. H. Bowers, the quartet went to Asheville, North Carolina on September 12 and made six records for world distribution and probably 100,000 of them will be made.

Columbia was first to utilize local talent, H. W. Dolton coming here early in the year to hear talent recommended by Miss Margaret Owen, in charge of the Music Dept. at Boggs-Rice Company. Among those heard were Fred and Henry Roe, with Lewis Morrell. Dutton sent this trio to Atlanta in April, where they made three records, with Morrell doing the vocals.

Following this, Peer, Eckhart, and Lynch of Victor came here in July and set up a regular recording station on State Street in the building at one time occupied by the Buchanan Furniture Company. The record station was kept open for approximately two weeks, during which time talent from all parts of these sections had try-outs.

Among the talent was: The Tennessee Mountaineers, Tenneva Ramblers, West Virginia Coon Hunters, Blue Ridge Corn Shuckers, Ernest Phipps, Ernest Stoneman, B. F. Shelton, Mr. and Mrs. Baker, and Mr. and Mrs. Carter of Gate City, Virginia.

All three companies are planning tryouts in the near future, and Brunswick plans one as well.

SOURCE: Bristol Herald-Courier, September 25, 1927, as quoted in Charles K. Wolfe, "The Legend That Peer Built: Reappraising the Bristol Sessions," Journal of Country Music 12, no. 2 (1989): 24–35, as reprinted in The Country Reader: Twenty-five Years of the Journal of Country Music, ed. Paul Kingsbury (Nashville, Tenn.: Country Music Foundation Press and Vanderbilt University Press, 1996): 6–7.

~~~~~~

VICTOR MACHINE COMPANY'S RECORDING CREW ARRIVES IN BRISTOL TO MAKE RECORDS (1928)

The Victor Talking Machine Company's recording crew which will make records of the musical talent of Bristol and the immediate section arrived in the city Friday with approximately half a car load of equipment. Last year when the same crew was working in Bristol, they ran across some very fortunate material which during the last year has been developed into leading characters.

Ralph S. Peer who is directing the workings of the crew explained that only 75 records would be made this year, and that these had already been booked since their coming here.

Referring to one of the characters which he ran into last year, Mr. Peer said that Jimmie Rodgers, one of his exceptions, had been running around in the mountains playing at most any place where music would be accepted, and that one day Jimmie happened to pick up one of the Bristol papers and saw where the recording crew was working in Bristol. Bumming his way here, he asked for a try out to see what he could do, he was laughed at but being an exceptional singer and yodeler, he was given a chance. He combined these two together and produced his first record the "Blue Yodel."[3] He was paid his share for the performance and went back into the mountains.

Later when the record was published the public went wild over the piece and Jimmie was called to the factory to work regularly for the company.

Now he is drawing over $15,000 a year, and is on a circuit booked for twelve weeks, making over half a thousand a week. He produces a record every month for the Victor company and is Gene Austin's keenest rival.

The crew will continue their stay here for ten days, and during the time will be producing records in the studio located in the Peter's building back of the City Bank.

The records which are made here will be published and on sale within a month and can be secured from the Clark Jones Sheeley Company who will handle the entire line.

SOURCE: "Victor Machine Company's Recording Crew Arrives in Bristol to Make Records," *Bristol Herald-Courier,* October 28, 1928, as reprinted in Charles K. Wolfe, "The Discovery of Jimmie Rodgers: A Further Note," *Old Time Music* 9 (Summer 1973): 24.

~~~~~~~~~

NOTES

1. Fiddlin' John Carson (1868–1949) confounded Peer's expectations with big sales of the recording of "Little Old Log Cabin" and "The Old Hen Cackled and the Rooster's Going to Crow."
2. Jimmie Rodgers (1897–1933) is often called "The Father of Country Music." The famous Carter Family consisted of A. P. Carter (1891–1960), his wife Sara Carter (1898–1979), and his sister-in-law Maybelle Addington Carter (1909–1978), whose guitar style became famous. Ernest Stoneman (1893–1968) and Blind Alfred Reed (1880–1976) were classic "old-time" musicians.
3. Rodgers recorded the "Blue Yodel" at the Victor Studio in Camden, New Jersey, in November 1927.

96

UNCLE DAVE MACON, BANJO TRICKSTER,

AT THE GRAND OLE OPRY

Uncle Dave Macon (1870–1952) started his career when he was 50 years old. He became famous as a beloved fixture on the stage of the Grand Ole Opry in Nashville. Macon claims a special place in American pop music history through his virtuoso banjo playing—in which one can clearly hear the roots of bluegrass—and his unusually broad repertoire of songs. He knew everything: minstrel numbers written before the Civil War, Tin Pan Alley ditties, vaudeville routines, gospel hymns, and fresh material too, such as the roustabouts' river-boat song "Rock about My Saro Jane," or "Sail Away Ladies," the latter complete with a clog accompaniment, fiddle, and guitar, captured on a recording with his group, the Fruit Jar Drinkers. Bob Hyland, the author of this reminiscence, was a radio producer of country music and a pioneering record collector known especially for his love of Uncle Dave.

Uncle Dave used to play piano and often did so on the Grand Ole Opry in the early '30s. I remember many times of hearing Judge Hay say "Let's have Uncle Dave give us a number on the old three-legged piano," whatever kind of piano that is, and he would play "Eli Green's

Cake Walk" or "The Girl I Left Behind Me," the only tunes I remember him playing. It seems to me as I recall it that it was usually late at night when he was called on for his performance, probably to fill in, or maybe just to be different. I used to think to myself "Well, Uncle Dave, I thought you had gone home for the night" when here all along he was back there "whoopin' it up" with some of the other performers. Sometimes a late recall would net something on the banjo that was out of this world and almost impossible to describe, but I will attempt it, having heard it a number of times on the air, and saw it performed once in person.

To begin with, in addition to being one of the greatest banjo players of all time, he was a showman and trick banjoist. When he had just wowed the audience with a magnificent grand finale number and it seemed they just had to have some more, the Judge or Uncle Dave would say "Well now we'll just show you how 'Uncle Dave Handles a Banjo Like a Monkey Handles a Peanut'" then a few chords on the banjo, the feet would start, and he would say "Clean gone now, ah," spin back to his hands as he says "got to get behind the plow," then in a clock like motion the banjo, still plunking all the while went under one leg, under the other, then behind him, back to the front, up in the air again, with more verses and stomping which by then had brought the house down. He had knocked them cold: he knew and the audience knew there were no toppers.

Over the years Macon would latch on to the latest Country or Western hit tune and present his own rendition on the air or [at a] personal appearance. Such tunes as "Candy Kisses," "Deep in the Heart of Texas" and "Pistol Packin' Mama." This reminds me of the last time I saw him here in Springfield in 1950. He had been featuring Eddy Arnold's hit of about that time titled "I'll Hold You in My Heart." When [it was] announced that he was going to sing it, two teen-age girls, obviously Eddy Arnold fans, exclaimed "Oh no!" as if revulsed at the idea of an old man singing a beautiful love song. At the conclusion they were as loud in their applause as anyone there.

The show that night finished with a whirlwind performance of "Take Me Back To My Old Carolina Home" in which he jumped from his chair on the last chorus, took his hat from his head, and fanning it against the strings of the banjo placed on the floor and held high on the neck, and did a clog around it, bringing the rendition to a grand climactic conclusion. And this was done only about a year and a half before his death, with the same agility and precision as when I first saw him do it fourteen years before.

His sacred song for the evening was "Rock of Ages," and after the show I went backstage to try to have a brief chat. Behind me came an elderly gentleman to see and compliment him on his performance. The man walked over and says "Uncle Dave, whenever I hear you sing 'Rock of Ages' like you did tonight I can just feel the POWER!" Looking very pleased, Uncle Dave stood up and shaking hands, said, "Thank you, Brother."

SOURCE: "Reminiscences of Uncle Dave by Bob Hyland," in *Uncle Dave Macon: A Bio-Discography*, ed. Ralph Rinzler and Norm Cohen (Los Angeles: John Edwards Memorial Foundation, 1970): 50.

97

A SIDEBAR INTO THE FOLK REVIVAL

Harry Smith's Canon of Old-Time Recordings

In 1952, obscure hillbilly and race records from the late 1920s turned into vintage classics when Moses Asch (1905–1986), head of Folkways Records, issued Harry Smith's *Anthology of American Folk Music,* an eccentric compendium of "old-time music." Smith (1923–1991) was a film artist and amateur folklorist. Because of his impeccable taste and the prophetic reach of his musical curiosity, the *Anthology* turned into a main resource for the folk-revival generation of the 1950s and beyond. In 1997, the Smithsonian Institution, which bought the Folkways catalog, reissued the *Anthology* in CD format, accompanied by a "booklet of essays, appreciations, and annotations" in tribute to Smith's achievement.

FOREWORD BY HARRY SMITH

By 1888 many important recordings of folk song had been cut on cylinders, but it was not until that year and the perfection of the gramophone disc by Emile Berliner that inexpensive records were made available to the public. Out of about thirty folk song titles issued by Berliner between 1885 and 1899 the most important were no. 3012, an exciting banjo and vocal version of "Who Broke the Lock" by Cousins and Demoss (recorded November 14, 1885); no. 942, "Dixie," with partisan lyrics, by George G. Gaskin (Washington, D.C., October 14, 1896); no. 670, "Virginia Camp Meeting" by George Graham and Billy Golden (Washington, D.C., March 8, 1897) containing the first authentic American religious music on records; and no. 0730, "A Day in a Country School" by George Graham (New York, November 15, 1899) which includes a recording of chanted mathematical problems.

During the early 1900's a number of releases were made, the most famous being Uncle John's unaccompanied "Frog Went a Courting" on the Columbia, Victor and Edison versions of "A Meeting of the School Directors," also Billy Golden's several cuttings made at that time of "Roll on the Ground" and "Rabbit Hash" have very full texts of these well known songs.

The modern era of folk music recording began shortly after World War I when Ralph Peer, of Okeh Records, went to Atlanta with portable equipment and a record dealer there offered to buy 1000 copies if Peer would record the singing of circus barker "Fiddling" John Carson. "The Little Old Log Cabin in the Lane" and "The Old Hen Cackled and the Rooster's Going to Crow" were cut, and according to Peer, "It was so bad that we didn't even put a serial number on the records, thinking that when the local dealer got his supply that would be the end of it. We sent him 1,000 records which he got on Thursday. That night he called New York on the phone and ordered 5,000 more sent by express and 10,000 by freight. When the national sales got to 500,000 we were so ashamed we had 'Fiddling' John come up to New York and do a re-recording of the numbers." Mr. Peer invented the terms "hillbilly" records and "race" records. Concerning the latter he says: "We had records by all foreign groups: German records, Swedish records, Polish records, but we were afraid to advertise Negro records, so I listed them as 'race' records and they are still known as that." Unfortunately these unpleasant terms are still used by some manufacturers.

Only through recordings is it possible to learn of those developments that have been so characteristic of American music, but which are unknowable through written transcriptions alone. Then too, records of the type found in the present set played a large part in stimulating these historic changes by making easily available to each other the rhythmically and verbally specialized musics of groups living in mutual social and cultural isolation.

The eighty-four recordings in this set were made between 1927, when electronic recording made possible accurate music reproduction, and 1932, when the depression halted folk music sales. During this five year period American music still retained some of the regional qualities evident in the days before the phonograph, radio and talking picture had tended to integrate local types. Volumes 4, 5, and 6, of this series will be devoted to examples of rhythm changes between 1890 and 1950.

~~~~~~~~

Smith leavened his scholarship, which emphasizes what musicologists call "concordances," with whimsy and daffy graphics. These four examples show off Smith's foresight and taste. Sometimes his descriptions, notes written as newspaper headlines, helped listeners to understand the text of the songs as well. Smith's internal references to the discography and bibliography have been omitted here.

SELECTED ANNOTATIONS BY HARRY SMITH

No. 21 "Frankie" by Mississippi John Hurt
vocal solo with guitar
recorded in 1928
original issue Okeh 8560 (w40022)

ALBERT DIES PREFERRING ALICE FRY, BUT JUDGE FINDS FRANKIE CHARMING AT LATTER'S TRIAL

Allen Britt shot Frankie Baker of 212 Targee Street, St. Louis, Missouri, October 25, 1899. This song was first sung by, and probably written by, "Mammy Lou," a singer at Babe Conner's famous cabaret in that city.

No. 53 "Little Moses" (A. P. Carter) by the Carter Family
vocal trio with autoharp, guitar
recorded in 1932
original issue Victor 2364/B

PHARO'S DAUGHTER OPENED ARK, SENT FOR NURSE. INFANT SAD, THEN GLAD, CARRIED TO MOTHER; BY SEA RED, LIFTED ROD, JEWS CROSS, HOST LOST. ON MOUNTAIN HIGH, LABORS CEASE, DEPART IN PEACE

According to Sara Carter, she and her former husband, Alonzo Pleasant, and Cousin Maybelle, made over 300 sides for various companies. Their 1927 records made by Victor in Maces Springs, Virginia, are among the very first electrical recordings. Using autoharp chords, played by Sara (who usually leads the singing), and a guitar melodic line (Maybelle), their instantly recognizable rhythm has influenced every folk musician for the past 25 years.

No. 76 "See That My Grave Is Kept Green"
by Blind Lemon Jefferson
vocal solo with guitar
recorded in 1928
original issue Paramount 12608B (20374-1)

FAVOR I ASK YOU; SEE MY GRAVE KEPT GREEN. LONG LANE, NO END, BEAR AWAY WITH SILVER CHAIN. TWO WHITE HORSES IN LINE, TAKE ME TO BURYING GROUND. HEART STOPPED, HANDS COLD. YOU HEARD COFFIN SOUND? POOR BOY IN GROUND. DIG GRAVE WITH SILVER SPADE, LEAD DOWN WITH GOLDEN CHAIN. YOU HEARD CHURCH BELL? POOR BOY'S DEAD AND GONE

In Walter and Byrd's *Wasn't It Sad about Lemon* (Paramount 12945 [20374-1]), after mentioning that Jefferson was born in Texas and died "on the streets of Chicago," they sing that the last tune he recorded was "see that my grave is kept green." The master numbers of this record also seem to indicate it was made at his last session. On the other side (of Paramount 12945) Rev. Emmet Dickenson parallels the life of Jefferson with that of Christ. "See that my grave is kept green" is often known as "Two White Horses in a Line" and almost always, as here, imitates the tone of a church bell at one point.

SOURCE: Harry Smith, ed., *Handbook for American Folk Music:* vol. 1, *Ballads;* vol. 2, *Social Music;* vol. 3, *Songs* (New York: Folkways Records & Service, 1952): n.p. Updated concordances as well as a list of artists and titles are available at http://www.folkways .si.edu/learn_discover/anthology/anthology.html.

98

ZORA NEALE HURSTON ON

"SPIRITUALS AND NEO-SPIRITUALS"

Zora Neale Hurston (1891–1960), the famous author of *Their Eyes Were Watching God,* trained in anthropology at Columbia University and then did field work in Florida, where she grew up. Grounded in her personal experience, this provocative article challenged many then-prevailing assumptions about black spirituals. First, Hurston rejected the equation of spirituals as "sorrow songs," a label used by the great cultural critic and African-American writer W. E. B. Du Bois in his classic *The Souls of Black Folk* (1903). Second, she disputed the authenticity of concert practice and art-song arrangements of spirituals from the Fisk University Jubilee Singers onward just at the time when Harlem Renaissance writers like Alain Locke were praising singers like Paul Robeson and Roland Hayes. In her mind, these transformations of spirituals into concert pieces subverted their folk roots. Hurston's discussion of the poetry of black preaching which, along with music, stands at the center of black expressive culture, foreshadows the emergence of later speech-based genres such as rap.

The real spirituals are not really just songs. They are unceasing variations around a theme.

Contrary to popular belief their creation is not confined to the slavery period. Like the folk-tales, the spirituals are being made and forgotten everyday. There is this difference: the makers of the songs of the present go about from town to town and church to church singing their songs. Some are printed and called ballads, and offered for sale after the services at ten and fifteen cents each. Others just go about singing them in competition with other religious minstrels. The lifting of the collection is the time for the song battles. Quite a bit of rivalry develops.

These songs, even the printed ones, do not remain long in their original form. Every congregation that takes it up alters it considerably. For instance, *The Dying Bed Maker,* which is easily the most popular of the recent compositions, has been changed to *He's a Mind Regulator* by a Baptist church in New Orleans.

The idea that the whole body of spirituals are "sorrow songs" is ridiculous. They cover a wide range of subjects from a peeve at gossipers to Death and Judgment.

The nearest thing to a description one can reach is that they are Negro religious songs, sung by a group, and a group bent on expression of feelings and not on sound effects.

There never has been a presentation of genuine Negro spirituals to any audience anywhere. What is being sung by the concert artists and glee clubs are the works of Negro composers or adaptors *based* on the spirituals. Under this head come the works of Harry T. Burleigh, Rosamond Johnson, Lawrence Brown, Nathaniel Dett, Hall Johnson and [John W.] Work. All good work and beautiful, but *not* the spirituals. These neo-spirituals are the outgrowth of the glee clubs. Fisk University boasts perhaps the oldest and certainly the most famous of these. They have spread their interpretation over America and Europe. Hampton and Tuskegee have not been unheard. But with all the glee clubs and soloists, there has not been one genuine spiritual presented.

To begin with, Negro spirituals are not solo or quartette material. The jagged harmony is what makes it, and it ceases to be what it was when this is absent. Neither can any group be trained to reproduce it. Its truth dies under training like flowers under hot water. The harmony of the true spiritual is not regular. The dissonances are important and not to be ironed out by the trained musician. The various parts break in at any old time. Falsetto often takes the place of regular voices for short periods. Keys change. Moreover, each singing of the piece is a new creation. The congregation is bound by no rules. No two times singing is alike, so that we must consider the rendition of a song not as a final thing, but as a mood. It won't be the same thing next Sunday.

Negro songs to be heard truly must be sung by a group, and a group bent on expression of feelings and not on sound effects.

Glee clubs and concert singers put on their tuxedoes, bow prettily to the audience, get the pitch and burst into magnificent song—but not *Negro* song. The real Negro singer cares nothing about pitch. The first notes just burst out and the rest of the church join in—fired by the same inner urge. Every man trying to express himself through song. Every man for himself. Hence the harmony and disharmony, the shifting keys and broken time that make up the spiritual.

I have noticed that whenever an untampered-with congregation attempts the renovated spirituals, the people grow self-conscious. They sing sheepishly in unison. None of the glorious individualistic flights that make up their own songs. Perhaps they feel on strange ground. Like the unlettered parent before his child just home from college. At any rate they are not very popular.

This is no condemnation of the neo-spirituals. They are a valuable contribution to the music and literature of the world. But let no one imagine that they are the songs of the people, as sung by them.

The lack of dialect in the religious expression—particularly in the prayers—will seem irregular.

The truth is, that the religious service is a conscious art expression. The artist is consciously creating—carefully choosing every syllable and every breath. The dialect breaks through only when the speaker has reached the emotional pitch where he loses self-consciousness.

In the mouth of the Negro the English language loses its stiffness, yet conveys its meaning accurately. "The booming bounderries of this whirling world" conveys just as accurate a picture as mere "boundaries," and a little music is gained besides. "The rim bones of nothing" is just as truthful as "limitless space."

Negro singing and formal speech are breathy. The audible breathing is part of the performance and various devices are resorted to adorn the breath taking. Even the lack of breath is embellished with syllables. This is, of course, the very antithesis of white vocal art. European singing is considered good when each syllable floats out on a column of air, seeming not to have any mechanics at all. Breathing must be hidden. Negro song ornaments both the song and the mechanics. It is said of a popular preacher, "He's got a good straining voice." I will make a parable to illustrate the difference between Negro and European.

A white man built a house. So he got it built and he told the man: "Plaster it good so that nobody can see the beams and uprights." So he did. Then he had it papered with beautiful paper, and painted the outside. And a Negro built him a house. So when he got the beams and all in, he carved beautiful grotesques over all the sills and stanchions, and beams and rafters. So both went to live in their houses and were happy.

The well known "ha!" of the Negro preacher is a breathing device. It is the tail end of the expulsion just before inhalation. Instead of permitting the breath to drain out, when the wind gets too low for words, the remnant is expelled violently. Example: (inhalation) "And oh!"; (full breath) "my Father and my wonder-working God"; (explosive exhalation) "ha!"

Chants and hums are not used indiscriminately as it would appear to a casual listener. They have a definite place and time. They are used to "bear up" the speaker. As Mama Jane of Second Zion Baptist Church, New Orleans, explained to me: "What point they come out on, you bear 'em up."

For instance, if the preacher should say: "Jesus will lead us," the congregation would bear him up with: "I'm got my ha-hands in my Jesus' hands." If in prayer or sermon, the mention is made of nailing Christ to the cross: "Didn't Calvary tremble when they nailed Him down."

There is no definite post-prayer chant. One may follow, however, because of intense emotion. A song immediately follows prayer. There is a pre-prayer hum which depends for its material upon the song just sung. It is usually a pianissimo continuation of the song without words. If some of the people use the words it is done so indistinctly that they would be hard to catch by a person unfamiliar with the song.

As indefinite as hums sound, they also are formal and can be found unchanged all over the South. The Negroised white hymns are not exactly sung. They are converted into a barbaric chant that is not a chant. It is a sort of liquefying of words. These songs are always used at funerals and on any solemn occasion. The Negro has created no songs for death and burials, in spite of the sombre subject matter contained in some of the spirituals. Negro songs are one and all based on a dance-possible rhythm. The heavy interpretations have been added by the more cultured singers. So for funerals fitting white hymns are used.

Beneath the seeming informality of religious worship there is a set formality. Sermons, prayers, moans and testimonies have their definite forms. The individual may hang as many new ornaments upon the traditional form as he likes, but the audience would be disagreeably surprised if the form were abandoned. Any new and original elaboration is welcomed, however, and this brings out the fact that all religious expression among Negroes is regarded as art, and ability is recognised as definitely as in any other art. The beautiful prayer receives the accolade as well as the beautiful song. It is merely a form of expression which people generally are not accustomed to think of as art. Nothing outside of the Old Testament is as rich in figure as a Negro prayer. Some instances are unsurpassed anywhere in literature.

There is a lively rivalry in the technical artistry of all of these fields. It is a special honor to be called upon to pray over the covered communion table, for the greatest prayer-artist present is chosen by the pastor for this, a lively something spreads over the church as he kneels, and the "bearing up" hum precedes him. It continues sometimes through the introduction, but ceases as he makes the complimentary salutation to the deity. This consists in giving to God all the titles that form allows.

The introduction to the prayer usually consists of one or two verses of some well known hymn. "O, that I knew a secret place" seems to be the favorite. There is a definite pause after this, then follows an elaboration of all or parts of the Lord's Prayer. Follows after that what I call the setting, that is, the artist calling attention to the physical situation of himself and the church. After the dramatic setting, the action begins.

There are certain rhythmic breaks throughout the prayer, and the church "bears him up" at every one of these. There is in the body of the prayer an accelerando passage where the audience takes no part. It would be like applauding in the middle of a solo at the Metropolitan. It is here that the artist comes forth. He adorns the prayer with every sparkle of earth, water and sky, and nobody wants to miss a syllable. He comes down from this height to a slower tempo and is borne up again. The last few sentences are unaccompanied, for here again one listens to the individual's closing peroration. Several may join in the final amen. The best figure that I can think of is that the prayer is an obligato [sic] over and above the harmony of the assembly.

SOURCE: Zora Neale Hurston, "Spirituals and Neo-Spirituals," in *Negro: An Anthology,* ed. *Nancy Cunard* (1934; reprint, New York: Continuum, 1996): 223–25.

THE HARD TIMES OF EMMA DUSENBURY,

SOURCE SINGER

Emma Dusenbury (1862–1941), an Arkansas woman who lived in poverty, is remembered today for her contributions to American folk music. She was a folk collector's treasure—a "source singer," or especially invaluable folk artist, who knew and could sing special versions of classic songs. Dusenbury's repertoire contained a large number of Child ballads, so prized in the early days of folk-music collecting (see chapter 12). So often when people turn into abstractions like "source singers," we know little about them or the circumstances in which they were "discovered." Emma Dusenbury met up with John Lomax in 1936 (see chapter 100). In his memoir *Adventures of a Ballad Hunter,* Lomax states that he recorded about 82 songs from her in two days.

Handicapped by blindness, Dusenbury lived hand-to-mouth with her daughter in Mena, Arkansas. A few months before her mother died, Nora Dusenbury wrote Lomax about her hard times in the letter reproduced here. She wanted more money for her work, which Lomax did give to her. Also mentioned are other musicians who collected songs from Emma and then disappeared into their own lives. Field work often raises difficult questions of responsibility and copyright, for which there are few easy answers. This letter shows the hardships of the life of the rural poor, standing out against the background of musical encounters with folklorists from different worlds.

March 2 1941 dear mr lomax i was glad to here from you i thout you for got us by this time we not got no rado nar clost to one we never herd on yet a nuf to no what thar lik hardly we not able to by on mother only get a very small pencen thay cut it down to five a mont for a whyle then raised it to seven and a haf for 2 years the last 3 bin 10 soe you se we to pore to have iney then met[?] mother not got but one five dollars from po[w]ell yet that was last year we don't know whare he at i rote to flether[1] a yere and haf a go to tri to find out about him and if he don iney thang with the songs then flether sent five that he got from powell[2] we not herd from po[w]ell in over 3 yers i wis (wns?) he do somtin with them songs if he can and send us out part for we hadda (badda?) need it as mother[3] bin helth for over a year and bin bad sick now over 2 moonce and i nede to by medcen for her and thang to tri to get her to eat we kant get a doctor tha wont com for les then 10 dollars and we not got it i don't know that is the mater with her she proid of what you sent for we nee it we bin told that mothers songs was a bin brodkst over the rado but if ther ar we not got nothin out of it yet hop you do come to see us we like to see you we live under the hill from whare we ded live when you was here strat rod from the male box just com rit down the fence over well I clos hopen to here from you a gin soon hop this will find ever bidy well thankin you for the check I remain as ever a frend mrs dusnberry and nora mena ark r 2[4]

well you rember that fat prity cow we had when you was here well she did a yere a go now

SOURCE: Letter from Nora Dusenbury to John A. Lomax in the John A. Lomax Collection, Eugene C. Barker Texas History Center, University of Texas, Austin. This typed transcription of the letter is marked "(copy)" and was probably made from a letter written by hand. All original spellings and punctuation are preserved here.

NOTES

1. "Flether" refers to the poet John Gould Fletcher (1886–1950), who wrote a fictionalized account of his meeting Dusenbury in "The Ozark Singer," *Criterion* 16, no. 52 (October 1936): 1–13.
2. "Powell" refers to Laurence Powell, director of the Arkansas Symphony, who used some of Dusenbury's songs in his compositions.
3. These "mothers' songs" were written by Nora for Emma Dusenbury.
4. Mena, Arkansas, Route 2.

JOHN AND ALAN LOMAX PROPOSE A
"CANON FOR AMERICAN FOLK SONG"

John Lomax (1867–1948) and his son Alan Lomax (1915–2002) were the most important documenters of American folk music in the twentieth century—legends in a field crowded with legends. Their prodigious collecting formed the backbone of the Archive of American Folk Song at the Library of Congress for decades. Using their own field recordings, they published two anthologies with transcriptions of single-line melodies, *American Ballads and Folk Songs* (1934) and *Our Singing Country* (1941). As folk music spread into the urban middle classes, and other competitors produced books of folk songs with piano accompaniments, the Lomaxes followed suit. They hired Charles Seeger and Ruth Crawford Seeger to make piano arrangements of quality and simplicity for their third book, *Folk Song USA: 111 Best American Ballads* (1947). As the title suggests, they set out to establish what Alan described as a "canon for American folk song."

As in the other Lomax collections, the music was enhanced by the literary gifts of both father and son. In *Folk Song USA*, each song is partnered with "collecting anecdotes," which often include oral histories from the Lomaxes' informants. Two samples of these anecdotes are included here.

Alan wrote the preface in the spirit of Walt Whitman. A passionate advocate for that New Deal icon, the "common man," he could make political policy sound like Romantic idealism and music the most important thing in the world.

PREFACE

So many are the folk songs, so various are the themes, tunes, types, and styles of folk music found in the United States that one may well say . . .

These forty-eight states came singing out the wilderness many long years ago. . . .

A people made a three-thousand-mile march between the eastern and western oceans. Songs traveled with them; songs were born along the way. Every hamlet produced its crop of local ballads of murders, disasters, and scandals. Every occupation had its specialized poesy. Every fiddler put his own twists on the tunes he learned from his pappy. Every child had its own skipping jingle, a little different from the next child. . . . Songs flowered up out of the lives of the people as liberally as wildflowers on the West Texas plains in April, and most of them vanished as quickly, sowing the land with seed for the next springtime crop of songs. Those songs that lived to walk the long, lonesome road with the people have been largely written down by folklorists during the past fifty years. The "best" of these, the "most representative"—our favorites after years of collecting and singing—we have chosen for *Folk Songs: U.S.A.* For beauty, variety, strength, and singability these 111 songs will, we believe, stand alongside any songs from any nation or level of culture.

You may not like them all at first. Folk song, as all art of serious intent, improves on acquaintance. Sing your way through this book. It was designed to be crooned and lilted, moaned and shouted through, not contemplated. Join your sin-ridden forefather as he bellows and thrashes all over the camp-meeting ground. Stomp and yell the lines of the hell-for-leather breakdown tunes. Raise up your head and howl with the cowboy over the lonesomeness and wonder of the Big West. Rock your own child to sleep with a tune that has lulled babies in log cabins and shanties. Only then will you feel how close these songs lie to your own and your country's marrow. Only then will you feel the surging life and the violent passions that lie hidden at times beneath the surface of these poker-faced songs. Only then will you feel the invigorating strength of this powerful folk art, the quality that sets it apart from popular song with its surface emotion and its cloying sweetness.

This is a sampling of America's folk songs—homemade hand-me-downs in words and music, songs accepted by whole communities, songs voted good by generations of singers and passed on by word of mouth to succeeding generations, a tradition quite distinct from popular song (made to sell and sell quickly) and cultivated art (made, so much of it, to conform to prestige patterns). If these songs had composers at first, they have been largely forgotten, and rightly so, since folk composers are adapters of old material rather than creators of original set pieces. The folk ballad-maker prefers to change an old song slightly to fit a new situation, making use of a tried tune and a well-loved plot formula and thus assuring himself of the favor of his audience. Every singer may then make his own emendations, to be accepted and passed on or rejected and forgotten by *his* audiences. So the *mass* of a people participate in folk song's growth, forever reweaving old materials to create new versions, much as an old lady creates a new quilt out of an old by adding, year by year, new scraps and patches. So folk song grows in small steps, with every slight change tested for audience reaction, thereby achieving a permanence in man's affection matched only by the greatest art. This art lives upon the lips of the multitude and is transmitted by the grapevine, surviving sometimes for centuries because it reflects so well the deepest emotional convictions of the common man. This is a truly democratic art, painting a portrait of the people, unmatched for honesty and validity in any other record.

Examine the American record. This is not calendar art, not escape literature (although there is much fantasy), or yet propaganda put out by some boost-America group advertising ours as the best of all possible lands and our people as generous and gay, well fed and genteel. Folk song, like any serious art, deals with realities—with poor boys, a long way from home, with workers killed on the job, with bloody-handed murderers, with children dancing and fighting in the back yards, and with the dreams of all of these folk. There are deep shadows on this landscape, the shadows of poverty and graceless toil. There are bitter hard lines in these faces, lines of violence and cruelty. . . . What lies in the minds of the gentle grandmothers we have heard, hour upon hour, chanting as their "favorite love songs" the old ballads in which love so often leads to bloodshed? What of the continual brooding over death in the spirituals?

> *O lovely appearance of death,*
>
> *No sight upon earth is so fair,*
>
> *Not all the gay pageants that breathe*
>
> *Can with a dead body compare . . .*

Yet, like Lincoln's, the somber face of the people suddenly splits with a sunburst of laughter. . . .

> *Old Dan Tucker was a fine old man,*
>
> *Washed his face in a frying pan.*
>
> *Combed his head with a wagon wheel*
>
> *And died with a toothache in his heel.*

This awkward and melancholic American could kick up his heels and hooraw the world. . . .

> *What'll we do with the baby-o,*
>
> *Take him to his mammy-o,*
>
> *Wrap him up in a tablecloth,*
>
> *Throw him up in the old hay loft.*

. . .

The amazing popularity of "John Henry," "Frankie," and other Negro ballads among white singers, the tremendous enthusiasm of all Americans, no matter what their prejudices, for Negro folk music, and the profound influence of this music on American culture—all this denies the effect of Jim Crow at this level of human communication. From the beginning, Negroes and whites have swapped tunes, tales, dances, and religious ideas. And in the even more basic areas of speech and motor behavior this meeting of minds between the two groups is clearer still. White Americans, perhaps at first attracted by the exotic rhythms and earthy poesy of Negro song, have been deeply stirred by the poignant sorrow, the biting irony, and the noble yearning for a better world implicit there. And with every passing year American music becomes more definitely an Anglo-African blend. In American folk song, indeed—*A man ain't nothin' but a man*. . . .

Certainly this is what the folklorist has to say to *his* audience. He goes where book-learning is not. He lives with the underprivileged. He brings back the proof in their songs and stories and dances that these folks are expressive and concerned about the beautiful and the good. In doing so, he continually denies the validity of caste lines and class barriers. [Bronislaw] Malinowski says of the anthropologist, "He also has the duty to speak as the native's advocate." Just so, the folklorist has the duty to speak as the advocate of the common man.

When my father collected and published the songs of the cowboy and the other pioneers of the great West, he became their advocate, just as a half century earlier Major [Thomas Wentworth] Higginson had championed the Negro slave in publishing the spirituals and declaring them beautiful. In the final analysis, it is our identification with the common man that has carried my father and myself on our ballad hunt across this continent—into work camps and honky-tonks, into a thousand small houses, into the little churches, up back-country roads, and through the still horror of a score of penitentiaries. It is this enthusiasm that laid the basis for the Archive of American Folk Song in the Library of Congress, where we added the voice of the common man to the written record of America.

Our work and that of all other American folklorists now begins to bear fruit. When the people of this country, under the impact of the war against fascism, looked about them for songs which reflected their equalitarian and democratic political principles, there came a sudden rise in popularity of American folk music. Every passing day indicates that this quickening of interest in homemade songs is no temporary fad, but the advance ground swell of an important cultural movement.

This treasury is the first attempt to set up a canon for American folk song, defining this world of people's music in terms of examples, and placing the songs in their historical, social, and psychological backgrounds. Alongside the songs themselves, we have set down our impressions of various types of singers and song-making communities. This continuity, with its illustrative folk-tales and anecdotes will, we hope, serve to make the American folk singer more real and understandable to those who have not been privileged to know him. When you come to know him, you will be well prepared to meet his kinfolk in Russia, China, Spain, Ireland, or wherever oral song lives, for in song and folklore one encounters ancient bonds that link the races and the nations into the big family of humanity.

. . .

We feel most deeply indebted, however, to the hundreds of Americans who took us in out of the cold and sang for us when we went visiting around the country. We found them "common" in the folk sense, that is, generous and hospitable. We knew that, in allowing a pair of strangers to record their ballads, these singers were giving us their dearest possessions; for to them the songs are not part of the public domain, but treasured family heirlooms, mementos of adventures in the big world of tales of dearly bought experience. Typical of the attitudes of the many singers we met along the road is this statement of a Virginia mountain ballad singer.

This old house where we lived had big wide planks for a floor. There wasn't any carpet and you could look down and see the chickens walking underneath the house, and in the wintertime the snow would blow up through the cracks. We had a fireplace, but there were so many of us kids and we had so many cousins to visit us, we used to wonder how we were all gonna get near it. That's why we all tried to learn songs just as perfect as we could, because when you was the one doin' the singin' you'd get to stand close to the fire and warm.

Father would usually suggest singin' hymns and all us children would join in. Then he'd pick up his banjo and play "Boats a-Whistlin'" or "Sourwood Mountain" or "John Henry." By the time I was four or five, I was trying to mock him. I'd grab hold of our old fire shovel and pick it for a banjo. When they'd ask me what I was playin', I'd tell 'em "Sour Colic." . . .

Then there was an old colored man used to come in of an evening with his fiddle. Seem like to me my hair would raise right up on my head when he'd be fiddlin', just settin' there as close to that fire as he could get. When it would begin to sort of scorch him, he wouldn't move, he'd just rare back in his chair and keep on fiddlin'.

Then my momma, a-singin' all those beautiful old love songs like "Barbara Allen" and "Fair Ellender" and "Careless Love," she taught me all the best songs I know—and how to sing. She had a knack of puttin' little twists and quavers into a note that would send cold chills runnin' through you. I can see her right now, settin' across the fireplace from my dad and us children crowdin' in as close as we could get, with her head thrown back and her eyes closed, singin' like a mocking bird.

May these songs bring you closer to the fire that burns on the hearth of the people. May you keep on "fiddlin'" with these tunes until, when you sing them, you can "raise the hair right up on the heads" of your listeners.
[signed]—Alan Lomax
New York City

~~~~~~~~

COLLECTING ANECDOTES

63. GOODBY, OLD PAINT [WRITTEN BY JOHN A. LOMAX]

July Fourth in 1910 I sat in the grandstand at the Cheyenne, Wyoming, Frontier Day Wild West Show and watched the most thrilling bull-dogging and the wildest bronco-busting that can be found anywhere in the world. Teddy Roosevelt had put on the first act, dashing by a cheering crowd of 30,000 people astride a snow-white horse and waving a ten-gallon hat. That night as I went into a saloon looking for frontier songs I came face to face with a University of Texas friend.

Boothe Merrill expressed surprise at meeting a former YMCA leader going into a saloon and I replied that I was downright astonished to find Boothe Merrill coming out of one. He joined me in one of the back rooms of the place to argue the question. There, later, he sang "Goodby Old Paint" (Version I), which he said had replaced "Home Sweet Home" as the last dance of the evening at cowboy shindigs in western Oklahoma. It was a slow waltz and told about the kind of horse variously described by the cowboy as paint, pinto, spotted, or calico—calico not because of the color of the horse, but because, mounted on his paint pony, the cowboy rode to see his best girl, his calico.

Boothe Merrill scorned the clumsy horn of my Ediphone and I failed to record the song. However, he amiably sang it over and over until I held the tune safely in my mind. In my Austin home it became a family favorite. I passed it on to Oscar J. Fox of San Antonio, who issued "Goodby Old Paint" in sheet music. Only recently at a West Texas play party on Orville Bullington's ranch in Wheeler County, I heard the song used as the farewell dance of the evening.

Carl Sandburg picked up a different melody for this song from Margaret Larkin (Version II). Perhaps better than any other cowboy creation, this song captures the bigness of the West and the love of the Westerner for his wide horizon.

95. ANOTHER MAN DONE GONE [WRITTEN BY ALAN LOMAX]

Some of them are chained. Some of them work under the eye of a riding boss with a Winchester across the pommel of his saddle. There is always a pack of bloodhounds ready to strike out on their trail. But still they keep running, zigzagging till they're out of range of the rifle, laying a crooked trail through the bottoms for the hounds. They're brought back, whipped, put in solitary, deprived [of] their few privileges and then, once back in the field or on the road, they'll make a break as soon as they get the chance. Some men are built like that.

Long John—they sing about him in Texas—had a pair of shoes:

With a heel in front and a heel behind,

Till you couldn't tell where that boy was gwine.

Then there was Riley, another Texas escape artist, who made it to the river, when it was on a rise and the water was boiling with whirlpools and floating timber. Riley swam that river, when the captain said no man could. Now the convicts tell how Riley "walked the water like Jesus." A prisoner named Lightning told us, proudly, in the presence of the guards, that he could leave Darrington State Farm anytime he got ready to go. There was no horse on the place that could outrun him nor dog that could follow his trail.

Like every underprivileged Negro in the South, Vera Hall knew all about the county farm and the state pen. She had heard about them from people who were close to her. Although Vera Hall was a peaceloving cook and washerwoman and the pillar of the choir in her Baptist church, she knew about these things and she knew, as well, a song from the prison, a song about escape. Her song, "Another Man Done Gone" can be a blues or a work-song, but mostly it is enigmatic, full of silent spaces, speaking of the night and of a man slipping by in the night. You see his face, you know him, but at the same time you put him out of your mind, so that when the white man asks after him, you can say:

I didn't know his name,

I didn't know his name.

I don't know where he's gone,

I don't know where he's gone.

SOURCE: John A. Lomax and Alan Lomax, eds., *Folk Song USA: 111 Best American Ballads* (1947; reprint, New York: Signet, 1966): vii–xiii, 254, 376–77.

101

<W>OODY GUTHRIE PRAISES THE
"SPUNKFIRE" ATTITUDE OF A FOLK SONG

Woody Guthrie (1912–1967) left a legacy of words and music that continues to inspire folk singers and singer-songwriters to this day. Many of his songs have entered
into the historical tradition of the urban folk revival, among them "This Land Is Your
Land," "This Train Is Bound for Glory," and "Tom Joad." Guthrie also handed down
his attitude—a fusion of rural outsider-artist, modernist poet, and left-wing political
activist. Guthrie's whole way of being—his personality, his literary style, and his
musical commitments—had a profound influence on the urban folk revival and its
most prominent musicians, among them Bob Dylan and Bruce Springsteen.

This selection prints for the first time a letter that Guthrie wrote to the Lomaxes
and the Seegers when their book *Folk Song USA* was published. In it, Guthrie rejects
the commercial sweetness of pop music—it is "sissified," he writes, sounding more
than a little like Charles Ives (see chapter 63). The letter captures his imaginative
use of language as well as his politics.

3520 MERMAID AVENUE, BROOKLYN 24, NEW YORK, SATURDAY APRIL 10TH, 1948, 9[:]47

DEAR LOMAXES, & DEAR SEEGERS:
ALL OF YOU FOLKS HAVE DONE YOURSELF PROUD ON THIS BOOK OF A HUNDRED AND ELEVEN BEST AMERICAN BALLADS. I CAN THINK UP A SHORT LIST OF OLD GOODUNS I'D HAVE SHOVED IN AND A FEW OF THESE I MIGHT HAVE SHOVELED OUT. BUT, I HAVE TO SAY SUCH THINGS AS THIS TO GIVE ME THE PETEREEMUS TO KEEP ON CHOPPING AND WEEDING AROUND MY OWN BOOK OF BALLADS. THE WAY YOUR BOOK IS DONE IS WHAT COUNTS, AND NOT THE GOODNESS OR BADNESS OF ANY OF THE BALLADS OR SONGS, LORD KNOWS, NO BOOK OF TEN HUNDRED AND LEVENTY LEVEN CAN THROW UP A VERY GOOD FENCE AROUND A PASTURE OF OUR BEST BALLADS. YOUR BOOK MAKES ME GLAD THAT I'VE ALWAYS HAD SUCH A FAITH IN THESE KINDS OF AMERICAN SONGS AND BALLADS, WHICH FAITH HAS BURNT FAIRLY DIM AT TIMES WHEN I SET AND LISTEN TO THE BACKBONELESS SISSIFIED CRAP WHICH IS NOWADAYS GETTING ANNOUNCED OVER THE AIR WAVES AS A BALLAD OR AS A FOLK SONG. YOUR BOOK VERY PLAINLY SHOWS, AT LEAST, JUST WHAT SPUNKFIRE IT TAKES TO MAKE A BALLAD A BALLAD, OR A FOLK SONG A FOLK SONG. EVERY SONG I HEAR OVER THE AIR THESE DAYS OR ON FONOGRAF RECORDS SING OUT THAT THE DAY'S A FINE DAY WITHOUT NO NICKELS RUBBING TOGETHER IN MY POCKET, NO HOUSE TO LOVE IN, NO MONEY TO WORRY WITH, NO MEDICINE NOR NO HOSPITAL TO CURE ME, NO JOB AT A FAIR SALARY TO PIDDLE WITH, NO ROOM TO RAISE MY KIDS TO PESTER ABOUT, NO CLEAN PRETTY WIDE STREETS TO FESTER NOR TO BOTHER MY EYES, NO CHILLS NO FEVERS, NO MALARIA, NO PALEGRA, NOTHING, NOTHING, WRONG NOR DIRTY, MEAN NOR FILTHY, NOR ANY CHAIN GANGS FULL, NOR ANY OVERLOADED JAILS AND PRISONS, NOR ANY BELLEVUE INSANE ASYLUMS CRYING AND HOWLING AT THE ROACHES, SPIDERS, AND HAIRYLEG BUGS, NOT ANY RUNNING GANGS WITH BURN-ING CROSSES, NOT ANY BLUBBERING MOBS WITH A LYNCHING ROPE IN ITS HANDS, NOT ANY CROOKS, NOT ANY THIEVES, NOT ANY REPUBLICANS AND NOT ANY MORE TRUMAN AND TAFT DEMOCRATS, NOT ANYTHING TO BE ASCARED NOR AFRAID OF, NOTHING TO THINK ABOUT NOR TO GO AROUND WORRYING ABOUT. EVERY POP SONG SINGS DOWN INTO YOUR BRAIN AND IT ASKS YOUR BRAIN TO QUIT ITS VERY THINKING. POP TUNES TELL YOUR EYE TO STOP ITS LOOKING, TELL YOUR HAND TO STOP REACH-ING, YOUR NOSE TO SMELL THINGS THAT AREN'T THERE, AND YOUR MOUTH TO STOP ITS TASTING AND ITS YELLING AND ITS CUSSING. POP TUNES ARE BOUGHT AND PAID FOR TO KEEP DOWN THE MOST NATURAL AND NATIVE GIFTS AND TALENTS OF YOUR HUMAN N[sic] MIND, TO KEEP YOU FROM LOOKING UNDER THE HOOD OF YOUR OWN CAR AND SINGING OUT WHAT'S WRONG WITH THE ENGINE. YOUR BOOK, FOLKSONG USA, SHOWS THAT OUR BEST SONGS HAVE ALWAYS COME FROM MEN, WOMEN, AND KIDS OF ALL AGES, ALIVE AND ON THE BALL AND SINGING ABOUT

WHAT THEY SEE WRONG WITH THE WORLD AND HOW TO FIX IT UP BY
HARD WORK, HARD FIGHT, AND HARD SWEAT, LONG VISIONING AND TALL
TALKING, MIXED IN WITH A HATFUL OF SALTY SWEATING, GOOD FUNNY
JOSHING, KIDDING, TOPPING AND FRIENDLY COMPETITION IN THE AF-
FAIRS OF WORK, LOVE, ETC., ETC., BUT, ALL OF THE FOLK BALLADS THAT
ARE WORTH THEIR WEIGHT IN SALT, DON'T LOOK AROUND A CROWDED
HOUSE FULL OF DIRTY AND BITING PEOPLE, RAGGED AND DIRTY KIDS,
AND FAIL ENTIRELY TO SEE ANYTHING THE LEAST BIT WRONG: NO, IT'S
MORE LIKELY TO CAUSE THE LADY IN THE SALTIEST APRON TO WIPE HER
HAIR BACK OUT OF HER EYES AND TO SET HERSELF DOWN WITH AN OLD
PENCIL AT HER TABLE, THEN TO SCRIBBLE DOWN, "THREE LITTLE CHIL-
DREN LYIN' IN THEIR BED. ALL OF THEM SO HUNGRY, LORD, THEY CAIN'T
RAISE UP THEIR HEAD." . . . NO, SHE'LL NOT LET HER PENCIL WRITE A SONG
TO SAY, "I GOT PLENTY OF NUTHIN AN' NUTHIN'S PLENTY FOR ME." . . .[1]
BUT THIS VERY SAME LADY IN THE TEAR WARSHED APRON WILL OUTSHINE
AND OUT DANCE ALL OF US FOR TWO OR THREE HOURS AT THE WHANG-
DOWN ANKLE JUMP WHEN WE ALL GET OVER AND GET THE FLOOR
WARMED UP. I LIKE THIS WHOLE TONE OF YOUR NEW BOOK, AMERICAN
BALLADS, I MEAN, FOLK SONG USA. I LIKE THE LITTLE JIGS AND JAGS OF
ROCKY POETRY YOU'VE MADE UP TO TELL US ABOUT EVERY BALLAD. . . .
YOU'VE POUNDED OUT A SINGYDANCY HISTORY POEM HERE FOUR HUN-
DRED AND SEVEN PAGES LONG. I GUESS, IN ALL, BY NOW, I'VE SCANNED
THROUGH ONLY A DOZEN OR TWO PAGES, BUT SO FAR, I LIKE EVERY-
THING I'VE SEEN. IT WOULD BE A BIG LIE IF I BUZZED MY THUMB DOWN
THROUGH SUCH A BOOK AS THIS IN SOMETHING LESS THAN AN HOUR
AND KNOCKED YOU OUT A TERT PARAGRAF TO LET YOU KNOW HOW ALL
OF IT REGISTERED IN MY WHOLE MIND. MARJORIE[2] SAYS SHE LIKES THE
LOOKS OF THE BIG NICE CLEAR PIANO NOTES AND PLAIN PRINT OF THE
WORDS. I NEVER COULD EVEN MAKE USE OF THE GUITAR CHORDS WHICH
YOU SHOW HERE IN YOUR DIAGRAMS, SINCE I ALWAYS PLAY BY EAR, IN-
STINCT, FEELING, AND GUESSYGRABS.

JOHN A. MIGHT LIKE THIS BOOK BETTER THAN THE WORDS THAT GOT
SAID AT HIS FUNERAL. I KNOW THAT A FEW BOOKS AS GOOD AS THIS
WOULD BE ALL OF THE TOMB STONE THAT I'D EVER WANT. I KEEP ON
WONDERING WHAT IN THE WORLD YOU LOMAXES AND YOU SEEGERS ARE
GOING TO RIDE OUT NEXT. IF YOUR NEXT BOOK IS MUCH BETTER THAN
THIS ONE, IT'S GOING TO KNOCK ME FOR A BIG LOOP. I'M GLAD TO SEE
MY VERSION OF "900 MILES" GOT IN LIKE IT DID. I'M THINKING, TOO THAT
PETE SEEGER AND HIS CRANEY NECK BANJO DONE THIS FOLKSONG USA
BOOK A HEAP OF GOOD. PETE SEEGER IS A WHOLE LOT LIKE ONE OF
THESE OLD DEALERS IN ANTIQUES, I MEAN, HE CAN PICK ANY OLD THING
UP AND SAY A FEW WORDS, SING UP A LITTLE SONG ABOUT IT, AND GIVE IT
A NEW SHOT OF LIFE. I FEEL LIKE HALLY WOOD[3] DOES THIS SAME THING
TO OLD SONGS, BE THEY HIGHJUMPS OR PROTESTS, OR COURTING AT THE
RIGHT AND PROPER SPEED. HALLY KNOWS MORE ABOUT FOLKSONGS AND
ABOUT HUMANLY PEOPLE THAN MOST ANY TWO OTHER WOMEN I CAN

CALL TO MY MIND. WITH ANNY'S POKINGS AND ELIZABETH'S FIDDLE-
STRING FOR LIVING POETRY, AND WITH ALAN'S WILD CANYON OF HAR-
NESSING POWERS LIGHTING THINGS UP ALONG, WELL, YOU LOMAXS, YOU
SEEGERS, YOU BANJERS, YOU KID BRINGERS, YOU HALLY WOOD AND YOU
PAYFARING FAREPAYING FOLKS, ALL OF YOU MAKE SUCH A GOOD TEAM,
THAT I'D SAY AMERICA'S WAKINGUP, SHAKINGUP, LOOKING UP FOLK-
SONGS AND BALLADS.
    [signed] WOODY GUTHRIE

SOURCE: Letter to the Lomaxes and the Seegers, typescript written in uppercase on the
backside of a cover of the book *Folk Song USA*, in the Ruth Crawford Seeger Collection,
Library of Congress (see chapter 100).

~~~~~~~

NOTES

1.   This lyric comes from a song sung by Porgy in Gershwin's opera *Porgy and Bess*.
2.   Guthrie's second wife, Marjorie Mazia Guthrie (1917–1983).
3.   Harriet "Hally" Wood (1922–1988) was a folksinger and folklorist from Texas and an active
      collaborator with many leading folk-revival singers.

$\overset{\text{F}}{}$RED ASTAIRE DANCES LIKE A

TWENTIETH-CENTURY AMERICAN

(Williams)

Fred Astaire (1899–1987) defined dance in film musicals for decades. He treated American popular songs like a banquet of choreographic possibilities; sometimes he sang them as snacks in his films, but most often he treated them as haute cuisine in his unique approach to American movement. This homage to his originality was written by a famous jazz critic, Martin Williams (1924–1992). Like Gilbert Seldes (see chapter 77), Williams recognized art in entertainment. His take on Astaire draws on his jazz expertise. Best known as the mind behind the canonical Smithsonian Collection of Classic Jazz, Williams frames Astaire's achievement in dance as an expression of supremely democratic art—not unlike jazz in that respect. Williams opens with the typical strategy of having popular artists "vetted" by classical authorities. But by the end of the essay, he leaves that cliché far behind and delves into what John Dewey would have called "the collective individuality" of a great artist.

When Mikhail Baryshnikov[1] defected in 1974, he granted several interviews in which he seemed to find the right moment to praise Fred Astaire. Baryshnikov's "he is great dancer" was perhaps the least of the many things he said in praise of Astaire the performer and Astaire the choreographer, and it would probably be no exaggeration to say that Baryshnikov considers Fred Astaire one of the great figures in the twentieth-century dance.

Such recognition was not the first Astaire had received from other "classic" dancers, to be sure. George Balanchine[2] had praised him often and had reputedly shocked his first American sponsors when he said that he too would like to work with Ginger Rogers. Merce Cunningham[3] had praised Astaire. Jerome Robbins had praised him and modeled some of his early work on him—or had tried to until he discovered that his classically trained dancers could not execute Astaire-inspired movements.[4] But with our dance critics, and with the traditional guardians of our culture—perhaps with most of us—the story seems a bit different. As a people, if we praise Astaire it is usually with the reservation that, yes, he was wonderful but surely his work was not in the class with "serious" dance, with truly artistic choreography.

What Fred Astaire accomplished is more significant than it may seem. When Baryshnikov decides he wants to become a dancer, he goes to a teacher and he is told, well, yes, you must learn this movement and that one; and learn this and the other technique; and if you learn them all well enough you will be a dancer. And that means—let us be clear about this—you will learn to dance in the tradition of eighteenth-century French courtly dance, a highly stylized craft to say the least.

Astaire, in his totally unpretentious way, obviously did not want to dance like an eighteenth-century European. He undertook to dance like a twentieth-century American; he wanted to put our lives, our feelings, our experiences into dance. Who was to teach him how to do that? No one of course. He had to find out for himself what that meant, and that was a large and—if we admit it—culturally significant task. Astaire took the then-young traditions of American vaudeville and musical comedy dance in which he had grown up as his point of departure. And from bits of ballroom and ballroom-driven "specialty" dance, from black tap dancing and (yes) some bits of classical ballet—from any sources that seemed appropriate to him—he fashioned his art.

Furthermore, Astaire had to learn what it meant to dance like an American named Fred Astaire, and there I think is where the truly democratic element entered. For an artist of his potential range and depth, learning to dance like Fred Astaire was, again, a sizeable task. It was also a task which he clearly undertook with seriousness and discipline and with an unpretentious spirit of discovery and delight that always showed in the results.

If I could imitate Mikhail Baryshnikov I could have quite a career in classic ballet. Indeed, in classic ballet imitating Baryshnikov is in a sense what I would be asked to do. But if I could imitate Fred Astaire, I could probably have only a small career as a dancer. If Gene Kelly had based his work directly on Astaire's, it would have meant very little. Kelly, stocky, boyish, had to learn to dance like Kelly, and Kelly's elaborations of the hornpipe and the waltz clog, and his clownish acrobatics would have had as little place in Astaire's choreography as Astaire's elegantly romantic *pas de deux* might have had in Kelly's.

To draw a parallel for a moment, I have had the experience of playing a Sarah Vaughan record or two for opera aficionados and had them respond—once they were past their initial astonishment at her range and technique—"Why doesn't she study?" "Study what?" one may ask about a woman who had Vaughan's vocal resources and vocal discipline. But more seriously, vocal study would have meant that she would have to learn to sing like a nineteenth-century Italian contralto. Sarah Vaughan wanted to sing like a mid-twentieth-century contralto. She also had the privilege (and the responsibility) of discovering what it meant to sing like a twentieth-century American. And to sing like a twentieth-century American named Sarah Vaughan. And that meant, among other things, that she had the high privilege of turning almost any piece of music into an artistic experience.

Do I suggest that perhaps Americans ask of their performing artists that they have an individuality, that they exercise a self-discovery, even beyond that which Europe has traditionally asked only of her poets?

If Fred Astaire had been any less modest and a lot more pretentious about himself and his work—as pretentious, and as self important let us say, as one or two of our "modern" dancers—he would have been written up regularly in our major newspapers and magazines as a great American artist. Astaire simply became a great American artist not by announcing that he was one but by becoming one, and by leading and instructing his audiences, if not always his critics.

In making such comparisons and distinctions as I make here, I hope I will not seem to be praising Astaire at the expense of classic ballet. A young country like ours particularly needs the presence of ballet, not only for its intrinsic merit, but as a challenge and an example of the value and meaning of artistic stylization, discipline and tradition. We also need the pioneering example of a Martha Graham, whose sheer theatricality might challenge any performer, and whose best dances have a mythic profundity unequaled in our drama, even in [Eugene] O'Neill.
. . .

Astaire had natural elegance. He was a democratic aristocrat, to use an apparent oxymoron. Rogers, with her growing accomplishments as an actress, serious as well as comic, seemed more and more to play the grand lady. Astaire's innately modest yet confident nature was naturally elegant, and never seemed capable of putting on airs. We are apt to think first of Astaire's great specialty solo dances, from the controlled virtuosity of, say, "Don't Let It Bother You" from *The Gay Divorcee* (1934) and "I Won't Dance" from *Roberta* (1935) through the drunken bar-room dance of "One for My Baby" from *The Sky's the Limit* (1943), and including the top-hat-and-tails masterpiece of "Puttin' on the Ritz" from *Blue Skies* (1946), and the ad lib[bed] chair and piano dance from *Let's Dance* (1950). But a fascinating study might be done on the progression of Astaire's great romantic *pas de deux*, the seduction of "Night and Day" (*The Gay Divorcee*); the teasing, joyous, mutual self-discovery of "I'll Be Hard to Handle" (*Roberta*); the amorous awakening [of] "Isn't This a Lovely Day?" (*Top Hat*, 1935); the poignant farewell of "Never Gonna Dance" (*Swing Time*, 1936); the guarded affection of "I'm Old Fashioned" (*You Were Never Lovelier*, 1942); and the beautiful falling-in-love of two former antagonists of "Dancing in the Dark" (*The Band Wagon*, 1953).

He was an unlikely romantic dancer, and an even more unlikely movie star, this man. Not only shy and modest, he was long of face almost to the point of being horse-faced. He was in his mid-thirties and balding when he made his first movie. He was loose limbed almost to the point of being gangly. He was thin and had large hands. No, not thin, Astaire was skinny, and his skinny frame was even used as a gag in the army induction scene in *You'll Never Get Rich* (1941). He was also graceful, elegant, and flexibly controlled. But Astaire in his greatness was made possible by the movies; he found himself and the true size of his talent when he entered Hollywood films. He discovered what he could do as a dancer and designer of dances, and what film could do with dance.

One hears rumbles nowadays that particularly in the early films, the dances are fine but the plots are silly and trivial. The plots are as standard as the scenarios of *commedia dell'arte*, of

Plautus and Terence, as standard as the plots of Molière. As much as Molière's lines give the stuff of life to his plots, much as Shakespeare's lines and insights give life and depth to his borrowed plots and their characters, much as Verdi's and Puccini's music gives dimension and art to their plot lines and their sometimes banal libretti, so do Astaire's dances give life and depth to his films. It is through the dances that the stuff of character, conflict, and relationships is defined and made joyous and universal. And it is through them that we learn that a light-hearted view of the human condition can be a wise one, even a profound one.

SOURCE: Martin Williams, *Hidden in Plain Sight: An Examination of the American Arts* (New York: Oxford University Press, 1992): 9–14.

~~~~~~~~~

NOTES

1. Mikhail Baryshnikov (b. 1948) is a classically trained, Russian-born dancer who defected to the United States in 1974 while touring with the Bolshoi Ballet. He has since gone on to a career as a choreographer and an actor in film and television.
2. George Balanchine (1904–1983), a dancer and Russian émigré, founded the New York City Ballet and is also famous for his collaborations with the composer Igor Stravinsky.
3. Cunningham (b. 1919) is a modernist master choreographer, famous for his collaborations with his life partner, the composer John Cage.
4. In fact, Robbins did use a film sequence from *You Were Never Lovelier,* starring Fred Astaire and Rita Hayworth, in the ballet *I'm Old-Fashioned* with music by Morton Gould, based on a theme by Jerome Kern. In this ballet, premiered at the New York City Ballet in 1983, the dancers mimic the choreography by Astaire in the film sequence.

103

THE INNOVATIONS OF *OKLAHOMA!*

(de Mille, Engel)

Oklahoma! remains a watershed for American musical theater. An unexpected success, it arrived in 1943 on the cultural front of World War II, when the time was just right for innocent farm girls and homespun western optimism.

Historians tout *Oklahoma!* as a landmark in the development of the "integrated musical." This "musical play"—the term that the composer, Richard Rodgers (1902–1979), and lyricist, Oscar Hammerstein II (1895–1960), used for the work—challenged theatrical conventions. Chorus-line production numbers yielded to modern dance sequences, and songs outshone dialogue in furthering character and plot development.

The modernity of *Oklahoma!* rests partly on its innovative approach to dance. The choreographer, Agnes de Mille (1905–1993), came to the show directly from her success with the western ballet *Rodeo* (1942), set to Aaron Copland's now iconic score. In *Rodeo*, de Mille used American vernacular movements to tell a story about the American heartland through the genre of concert dance. One could argue that the story line of *Rodeo*, which centers around a heroine discovering true love, moved right into *Oklahoma!*.

Excerpts from de Mille's memoir of that period convey the interplay between the concept of "integration" and the necessities of theatrical collaboration. She evokes the climate on the set that allowed her to create the sequence known as the "Dream

Ballet," which ends act 1. This moment in particular foreshadows the later contributions of the choreographer Jerome Robbins to a string of subsequent musicals, including *On the Town*, *The King and I*, and *West Side Story*.

The circumstances which governed the creation of *Rodeo* were not unusual; nearly all ballets are composed just this way—with the company in full motion. If there were difficulties there were also enormous advantages not to be found in other forms of the musical theater. In the first place the company was a unit and had worked together for years. Furthermore, they were all dancers with a uniform training and discipline. The cast of a musical play on the other hand I knew would be made up of a heterogeneous group, dancers from various schools, actors, singers, acrobats, of all ages and sizes. If I did the new Rodgers-Hammerstein show I was going to have to face this situation. And there would be other problems as well. In a ballet company choreography is the essential element and the choreographer complete, total boss toward whom all artists bend their will in the interest of a common success. The drawbacks, not enough money, not enough rehearsal time, and always exhaustion, do not overbalance the advantages of scope and power.

In a musical play all would be different: the dancers would have to suit the book; they would have to build the author's line and develop his action, adding an element not obtainable through acting or singing and necessary if for no other reason than their dynamic effect. The problem of preserving character, period atmosphere and style would be a tough one since the bulk of the play would be performed realistically in a style as divorced from dance gesture as speaking is from singing. Transition was accordingly going to have to become a fine art, for if the audience could not be swung from dramatic dialogue through song into dance and back again without [a] hitch, the dance would be destroyed. The choreographer was going to have to learn surgery, to graft and splice.

Furthermore in this medium the dance director was no longer boss or anything like. By tradition the composer was tyrant although Oscar Hammerstein was to prove shortly that the author of the book might be equally important. The director had some say and also the producer, but the dance director not much. The designers were never charged to protect the dancing. They were told only to fill the stage with color, to see that girls looked lovely whether they could move or not, to favor the star and to do something sufficiently splashy to get more shows to design. If the dancing was hobbled or overweighted, it never reflected on anyone but the choreographer. The duration of numbers would be strictly limited—because of course for every minute of dancing there would be one less minute of singing or acting, something the composer, author and director never forgot. Besides it had long since, had it not, been established that the general public was less interested in dancing than in anything else?

. . .

But every aspect was challenging. If I had to fit the dances to the story, the story itself might suggest much. If the score were good and the songs witty, they might help further and the music would be composed to the dancing right in the rehearsal hall and orchestrated only after the dance was completed. I could order exactly what I wanted right on the spot. The other members of the creative staff might be more powerful but they were not ungifted. One did not have to take full responsibility alone. One had great collaborators. And there was money for anything reasonable one needed and one could pick one's cast at will. And last and most wonderfully, the curtain would not go up in New York until all had been brought to shining, lustrous perfection. Not a single risk would be tolerated. Not one.

. . .

But even after the success of *Rodeo,* I just barely succeeded in getting the new Rodgers and Hammerstein show. Indeed, I heard nothing official until I met Oscar Hammerstein by chance in a New York drugstore and knocked a plate off the counter in my haste to speak to him. Dick had qualms, he said. I continued pressing until Dick capitulated.

When I started my tour with the Ballet Russe I had the promise of the dances for the musical version of Lynn Riggs' play *Green Grow the Lilacs* [the original play from which *Oklahoma!* was adapted]. For I was to tour with the Ballet Russe de Monte Carlo as a guest star.

. . .

So, on the tour in my suitcase went a blank copybook labeled *Lilacs* with pages entitled "Ballet," "Many a New Day," "Cowmen and the Farmer," "Kansas City," "Jud's Postcards," and as I sat happily in hotel bedrooms, I made notes—

"Laurie [sic] sits under a tree thinking. She is worried. Downstage left she appears to herself dressed in her own dress, but with a wreath on her head. The music changes to 'Beautiful Morning.' She is moving about in her morning and taking possession of her world. She is to be a bride."

. . .

I heard the enchanting music. At these auditions, Oscar always read the role of Aunt Eller. Certainly it has never been played so well since. I remember the gasp that went around the room after "Beautiful Morning." Dick looked up from the keyboard and smiled abstractedly. He and his assistant, Margot Hopkins, together at double pianos, always accompanied auditions. They played very many these days. They were having a dreadful time raising money. I advised them to drop from the score "People Will Say We're in Love," a song shortly to become one of the most lucrative hits of the century.

There were conferences and casting. My contract with the [Theater] Guild called for a meager cash payment and no royalties, and I was to get no further rights of any kind. After all costs were paid off, they promised I should receive an additional five hundred dollars.

. . .

The Guild was on the verge of bankruptcy. We worked in their old theater on 52nd Street which they did not clean for economic reasons. [The director Rouben] Mamoulian took the stage. I worked below in what had been the foyer and way above in what had been costume and rehearsal rooms, and with the assistance of Marc Platt and Ray Harrison I kept three rehearsals going at once. I was like a pitcher that had been overfilled; the dances simply spilled out of me. I had girls and boys in every spare corner of the theater sliding, riding, tapping, ruffling skirts, kicking. We worked with tremendous excitement, but always under great strain. For the first three days Richard Rodgers never left my side. He sat fixed with surgical attention watching everything. This made the dancers nervous, but it was I who really sweated. He did not relax until the third afternoon, when smiling and patting me on the shoulder he gave the first intimation that on this show I would not be fired.

Rodgers is not only a very great song writer, he is one of the most astute theater men in the world. He concerns himself zestfully and relentlessly with every detail of production. Nothing escapes his attention and he takes vigorous and instant action. This might be interfering if he were not sensitive, sensible, and greatly experienced. He knows also when to keep his hands off. Mamoulian and the Guild frequently said, "It can't be done." It was always Rodgers who urged, "Let's see."

. . .

The first night was by no means sold out. The Guild subscription had fallen very low. I had ten front-row balcony seats and I didn't know whom to give them to. I think a couple remained empty. I stood at the back beside Rodgers and the staff. Oscar, who was calm, sat with his wife.

Marc's foot was very bad, but he said if he lost his leg he would dance the opening so a doctor anesthetized it. He danced on a frozen leg and foot. He had to be cut out of his boot afterwards.

I stood at the back in Margaret's black evening dress. Rodgers held my hand. The curtain went up on a woman churning butter; a very fine baritone came on stage singing the closest thing to lieder our theater has produced. He sang exquisitely with his whole heart about what a morning in our Southwest is like. At the end, people gave an audible sigh and looked at one another—this had seldom happened before. It was music. They sat right back and opened their hearts. The show rolled.

SOURCE: Agnes de Mille, *Dance to the Piper* (Boston: Little, Brown, 1951): 242–44, 247–48, 254.

~~~~~~

This selection comments briefly on other theatrical aspects of Oklahoma! including the celebrated moment of the opening song, "Oh, What a Beautiful Morning," which is performed as a soliloquy by the male lead in the show, Curly. The revolutionary nature of this gesture is recognized by Lehman Engel (1910–1982), who explains how it flouted the convention of the grand chorus number which typically opened a Broadway stage show.

Engel conducted many of the major musicals of the era plus their original-cast albums. In 1943, Oklahoma! was the first musical recorded for such an album, kicking off the still-current practice of recording, archiving, and making money from American stage musicals. Engel was a prolific chronicler of the theater as well, and ran musical theater workshops sponsored by BMI (Broadcast Music, Inc.), where he trained several generations of American composers, dramatists, and lyricists.

Out of the [many] longest lasting musicals, six were based on plays, seven on collections of short stories, three on motion pictures, three on biographies, three on novels, one on a single short story, and one on history. I would like to examine first five of the six that were converted from plays to note the changes that were made.

. . .

Oklahoma! followed its parent play closely. The major change in the scenes was near the end. In the play, after the hero has accidentally killed the villain on the hero's wedding night, there is one subsequent scene. The hero has been arrested at the end of the penultimate scene, and the final one takes place at Laurey's farmhouse a few nights later. Curly appears, having broken out of jail. A group of neighbors who have been deputized come to take [him] back to jail. As in the musical, Aunt Eller coyly "blackmails" the men into allowing Curly to spend the night with his bride.

Rodgers and Hammerstein also created one character not in Riggs's play, Will Parker, a young man who becomes Ado Annie's opposite number. With him and Ali Hakim, there is a full subplot and a considerable amount of comedy which is not in the original. In *Green Grow the Lilacs* Ado's character had been dull. She existed only as a friend of the heroine's. In *Oklahoma!* she was infused with a mischievous life of her own. The villain Jud (Jeeter in the original), through his one song (soliloquy), "Lonely Room," is made into an understandable human being without any loss of repugnance.

The libretto's sequence follows that of the play. At the very opening of the show (Riggs's idea, but unheard of in a musical), the hero enters singing a folklike ballad *unaccompanied* and begun off stage! How revolutionary can one musical be? One song establishes him more thoroughly than ten pages of dialogue might have done. The songs are fresh and tuneful, the lyrics are vivid and precise, and an enormous amount of humor that was oddly lacking in the original play is injected into the musical.

SOURCE: Lehman Engel, *Words with Music* (New York: Macmillan, 1972): 231–32.

ＤUKE ELLINGTON ON SWING AS A WAY OF LIFE

Edward Kennedy "Duke" Ellington (1899–1974) changed the course of American music through his pioneering compositional approaches to jazz. His legacy has been reevaluated after his death. His historical stature has risen to new heights, entering him into what the cultural critic Albert Murray describes (somewhat ironically) as the "hallowing halls" of the musical pantheon.[1]

Both of the selections reflect Ellington's double consciousness of race pride and cultural nationalism. In the first article, "My Hunt for Song Titles," Ellington explains how he finds musical inspiration in "the life of Harlem." Ellington launched his career during the Harlem Renaissance, embodying its cultural aspirations of dignity and equality through art. In the second article, Ellington describes his way of composing, which combined a sensitivity to the individuals in his band—on his scores, he wrote their names, rather than the names of their instruments—and the ability to fuse improvisation with larger forms. His magical synthesis still challenges and inspires contemporary jazz practitioners.

MY HUNT FOR SONG TITLES

The question is always being asked whether jazz music will ever be accepted seriously. I think so; and it has to be accepted as serious music because it is the only type which describes this age. As an illustration of what I mean, I must repeat what I said on the radio on the Friday I arrived in England [June 9, 1933]. If an artist wanted to paint a picture of a sunset, he would have to use some tone of red to describe it. Similarly, if serious music is supposed to be descriptive of a period, then jazz will have to be used to describe this, the jazz age. Since I think jazz is a serious thing, I must be serious in my choice of song titles.

But originality in this matter is always difficult, particularly in these times when the trite sentimental caption is a popular way of naming dance tunes. Our aim as a dance orchestra is not so much to reproduce "hot" or "jazz" music as to describe emotions, moods, and activities which have a wide range, leading from the very gay to the sombre. It will not, therefore, surprise the public to know that every one of my song titles is taken from, and naturally principally from, the life of Harlem.

The first big tune I ever used was *East St. Louis Toddle-O,* a number that I still use as my radio theme song. But since that time, I have advanced far from my song titles, looking to the everyday life and customs of the Negro, to supply my inspiration. Of all people, the Negro is most given to leg-pulling, this word has been added to my vocabulary since I have been here— a very pleasant way of passing the time. In local dialect this is known as "jive," and from this I derived *Jive Stomp. Send Me* comes from an expression used only to show the heights of ecstasy.

You have in England a very old proverb which runs "Every man for himself," and we have a saying just as old, "Every tub must stand on its own bottom"—which means the same thing. I have [had] a great success with *Every Tub,* taken from this source.

A "swanky" person is known in America as "ritzy," in Harlem as "dicty," and this was the basis of my *Dicty Glide.* Of course, a large part of the meaning is conveyed not only by the music and singing, but by the dance itself, for which certain steps fitting to the rhythm should be used. A lofty carriage is needed for this particular dance. The word "moocher" became familiar to you some time ago through a popular dance tune,* but I doubt whether many people knew the real meaning of it, which is "swindler." From the same basis I named a song, *The Mooch,* but here the meaning is slightly different, representing a certain lazy gait peculiar to some of the folk of Harlem.

Those old Negroes who work in the fields for year upon year, and are tired at the end of their day's labour, may be seen walking home at night with a broken, limping step locally known as the "toddle-O," with the accent on the last syllable. I was able to get a new rhythm from this, and what better title could I find than the original?

Another of my tunes, *The Birmingham Break-down,* may seem easy enough to understand, but here the word "break-down" typifies a fast, unrestrained dance in which all the dancers are out to do their hottest work. It is nothing less than a race. But there are other negro moods which are quieter.

We have affectionate terms. I took the title *Ducky Wucky,* equivalent in affectionate value to the English "my darling," from [the] "Amos 'n' Andy" hour on the American radio.

---

*Cab Calloway's "Minnie the Moocher," recorded in 1931.

I have been told that in England the words "black and tan" recall memories of the voluntary force that went to Ireland during the rebellion immediately after the war, and that it can also mean a familiar term for the Manchester terrier. But in *Black and Tan Fantasy* the words have a very different meaning. There are in Harlem certain places after the style of night clubs patronised by both white and coloured amusement seekers, and these are colloquially known as "black and tans."

Another custom is the *Breakfast Dance* which commences about four in the morning and continues until about nine o'clock, with intervals for breakfast. And what a time they have! From these impromptu dances taking place solely in Harlem I have derived much inspiration. There are *Rent Party Blues, Parlour Social Stomp*, and *Saturday Nite Function*, all of which mean more or less the same thing. The Negro who owes his rent does not run the risk of being thrown out by his landlord. He merely organises one of these gatherings. The neighbours all come, pay a standard rate for their tickets of admission and have a swell time. You can imagine how pleased the unfortunate host is to be able to pay his rent. He stands with a happy grin on his face watching the proceedings. The party spirit is not allowed to flag. Owing the rent is here more a case for rejoicing than for despair, and is as much an excuse for a party as it is a means for raising money. It really is a source of income as pleasant as it is novel. You have the basis of the idea when you give "bottle parties."

The first tune I ever wrote specially for microphone transmission was *Mood Indigo*, a title which explains itself. But my latest composition *Sophisticated Lady* may not be so obvious in its meaning, for my idea of sophistication may differ from yours. My conception of the word is the blasé type.

You are all familiar with the word "swing," but in *It Don't Mean a Thing If It Ain't Got That Swing*, there is a slight difference. Here the swing does not influence the rhythm, for the rhythm is still there without it, nor does it wholly describe the step. It is a subtle combination of the two, best described as a buoyant rhythm.

Since I have been in England I have composed a new number entitled *Best Wishes*, which was played and broadcast on June 14, [1933] for the first time. The lyric is by Ted Koehler, one of the writers of *Stormy Weather*. I have dedicated this song to Britain—the title, not the lyrics—and I hope that the visit of my orchestra has given you a better insight into the Negro mind. For it is through the medium of my music that I want to give you a better understanding of my race.

SOURCE: Duke Ellington, "My Hunt for Song Titles," *Rhythm* (August 1933): 22–23. This selection and the next are reprinted in Mark Tucker, ed., *The Duke Ellington Reader* (New York: Oxford University Press, 1993): 87–89.

~~~~~~~~

In 1944, Ellington published an essay on swing and the blurring lines between "concert hall" music and jazz in the Canadian magazine New Advance. *Of particular note in this essay is a brief discussion of his composing methods—a topic he usually avoided.*

SWING IS MY BEAT!

Americans have always listened to music, when they aren't busy making it. This is part of our culture. For some, hearing "live" music is a luxury. For others it's part of the daily diet. Everything depends on how the budget stacks up against the price of admission to Carnegie Hall or the cover charge at nightclubs giving out with the "hot" brand of music.

Well, when the war came along, a few years back, people wondered whether music was going to be one of the casualties. Would it have to take a back seat for a while? Would we have to sacrifice it at a time when bombs and bullets have an A-1 priority over Boogie-Woogie and Bach? I think these last few years have proved that music doesn't kick up its heels and call it quits under crisis. Music is staying by popular request of the fighting men and the folks they left behind. And that goes for all music.

Ours is a country of two major types of music—the concert hall variety and what goes under the general heading of "jazz." It wouldn't be right to draw too thick a line between them because nowadays we are beginning to see "jazz" moving into the Concert Hall—into the scores played by symphony orchestras, and the other way around. My own Carnegie Hall concert, recently, is an example of what I mean.

Swing is my beat. Not jazz in the popular sense of the word, which usually means a chatty combination of instruments knocking out a tune. Swing, as I like to make it and play it, is an expression of sentiment and ideas—modern ideas. It's the kind of music that catches the rhythm of the way people feel and live today. It's American music because it grew out of our folk music, picking up a little from every section of the country as it traveled from New Orleans to Chicago to Kansas City to New York.

Swing came along as a new brand of jazz. It wasn't the "hot" type, the "sweet" style and the so-called popular music that the boy friend was singing to his girl on a park bench. At the start people said it was a fad and scheduled for a short life—if a happy one. But it fooled them, as any real style will. It didn't date but instead has become a brand of music in which people are creating as hardily as pioneers in any new field.

What swings? Rhythm. A few notes, a chord combination, a simple musical phrase is developed into a series of rhythm patterns which creates a form that is listened to as seriously as a concert hall piece. Part of the reason is that this rhythm hits home to the people who hear it. It speaks their language and tells their story. It's the musician and his audience talking things over.

When I get an idea, I write the melody and often work out the arrangement, too. But sometimes the band and I collaborate on the arrangement. I write the melody down and play it at rehearsal. Then the boys will start making suggestions in a "free-for-all." One of them might get up and demonstrate his idea of what a measure should be like. Then another one of the boys will pick it up and maybe fix it a little. Sometimes we'll all argue back and forth with our instruments, each one playing a couple of bars his own way.

Still other times I might just sit down at the piano and start composing a little melody, telling a story about it at the same time to give the mood of the piece. I'll play eight bars, talk a bit, then play another eight and soon the melody is finished. Then the boys go to work on it, improvising, adding a phrase here and there. We don't write like this very often and when we do it's usually three o'clock in the morning after we've finished a date.

The Duke Ellington Orchestra at New York's Fulton Street Theater, 1930; (left to right) Freddie Jenkins, Cootie Williams, Sonny Greer, Duke Ellington, Arthur Whetsol, Juan Tizol, Wellman Braud, Johnny Hodges, Harry Carney, Joe "Tricky Sam" Nanton, Freddy Guy, and Barney Bigard.

Duke Ellington and his orchestra, ca. 1930.

But this is a little off the point. What I am trying to get across is that music for me is a language. It expresses more than just sound. I often think of tones as colors or memories, and all that helps in composing.

I said that swing is my beat. But because of all the confusion about what swing is and isn't, I prefer to say that I am carrying on the tradition of American folk music, particularly the folk music of my people. In my tone poem "Black, Brown and Beige" I tried to parallel the history of the Negro in music. My opera, "Boola," which is still unproduced, tells the story of the Negro in America.

What's the future of swing?

It has been said that it has no future because it's too narrow in its form. I don't think that's right. Swing at its best is "free" within the form itself. Take, for example, the lyrical "Stardust" and then take the more recent "Your Socks Don't Match." The two are completely opposite in sentiment, mood, and character, but they are both a product of swing.

A number of composers have been experimenting with these new musical ideas on a large scale. I spoke of my own tone poem and opera. Then there's the work of Gershwin which is not the same but moves in the same general direction. There are others, too, and I am convinced that still others will come along and their music will stick. For swing is a product of the time. Whether it's a jam session brand which is its purest state, or music written down on paper for a market, it's alive, creative and that's what gives it its future.

SOURCE: Duke Ellington, "Swing Is My Beat!" *New Advance* (October 1944): 14.

The cover of *The Kingdom of Swing*. Benny Goodman was so popular and so identified with the Home Front that the Armed Services issued his biography in a pocket edition for soldiers to carry with them.

~~~~~~~~~

NOTE

1.   Albert Murray, "The Ellington Synthesis," in Albert Murray, *The Blue Devils of Nada: A Contemporary American Approach to Aesthetic Statement* (New York: Pantheon, 1996): 77.

MALCOLM X RECALLS THE YEARS OF SWING

Malcolm X (1925–1965) was the most prominent political leader of the Black Muslim movement in the 1960s. After the murder of Martin Luther King, Jr., in 1968, Malcolm's greater militancy moved onto center stage. His controversial ideas about black nationalism encompassed cultural as well as economic autonomy.

Few know how much Malcolm X loved jazz and swing—and what a fantastic dancer he evidently was. He spent his youth in the Roxbury section of Boston and became an expert Lindy dancer. In these excerpts from his famous *Autobiography*, he recalls his encounters with many great musicians of the swing decade, the hits of the era, and the energy of youth.

CHAPTER 2: "MASCOT"

I was growing up to be even bigger than Wilfred and Philbert, who had begun to meet girls at the school dances, and other places, and introduced me to a few. But the ones who seemed to like me, I didn't go for—vice versa. I couldn't dance a lick, anyway, and I couldn't see squandering my few dimes on girls. So mostly, I pleasured myself these Saturday nights by gawking around the Negro bars and restaurants. The jukeboxes were wailing Erskine Hawkins' "Tuxedo Junction," Slim and Slam's "Flatfoot Floogie," things like that. Sometimes, big bands from New York, out touring the one-night stands in the sticks, would play for big dances in Lansing. Everybody with legs would come out to see any performer who bore the magic name "New York." Which is how I first heard Lucky Thompson and Milt Jackson, both of whom I later got to know well in Harlem.

. . .

CHAPTER 3: "HOMEBOY"

Most of Roseland's dances were for whites only, and they had white bands only. But the only white band ever to play there at a Negro dance, to my recollection, was Charlie Barnet's. The fact is that very few white bands could have satisfied the Negro dancers. But I know that Charlie Barnet's "Cherokee" and his "Redskin Rhumba" drove those Negroes wild. They'd jampack that ballroom, the black girls in way-out silk and satin dresses and shoes, their hair done in all kinds of styles, the men sharp in their zoot suits and crazy conks, and everybody grinning and greased and gassed.

Some of the bandsmen would come up to the men's room at about eight o'clock and get shoeshines before they went to work. Duke Ellington, Count Basie, Lionel Hampton, Cootie Williams, Jimmie Lunceford were just a few of those who sat in my chair. I would really make my shine rag sound like someone had set off Chinese firecrackers. Duke's great alto saxman, Johnny Hodges—he was Shorty's idol—still owes me for a shoeshine I gave him. He was in the chair one night, having a friendly argument with the drummer, Sonny Greer, who was standing there, when I tapped the bottom of his shoes to signal that I was finished. Hodges stepped down, reaching his hand in his pocket to pay me, but then snatched his hand out to gesture, and just forgot me, and walked away. I wouldn't have dared to bother the man who could do what he did with "Daydream" by asking him for fifteen cents.

I remember that I struck up a little shoeshine-stand conversation with Count Basie's great blues singer, Jimmie Rushing. (He's the one famous for "Sent for You Yesterday, Here You Come Today" and things like that.) Rushing's feet, I remember, were big and funny-shaped—not long like most big feet, but they were round and roly-poly like Rushing. Anyhow, he even introduced me to some of the other Basie cats, like Lester Young, Harry Edison, Buddy Tate, Don Byas, Dickie Wells, and Buck Clayton. They'd walk in the rest room later, by themselves. "Hi, Red." They'd be up there in my chair, and my shine rag was popping to the beat of all of their records, spinning in my head. Musicians never have had, anywhere, a greater shoeshine-boy fan than I was. I would write to Wilfred and Hilda and Philbert and Reginald back in Lansing, trying to describe it. "*Showtime!*" people would start hollering about the last hour of the dance. Then a couple of dozen really wild couples would stay on the floor, the girls changing to low white sneakers. The band now would really be blasting, and all the other dancers would form a clapping, shouting circle to watch that wild competition as it began, covering only a quarter or so of the ballroom floor. The band, the spectators, and the dancers would be making the Roseland Ballroom feel like a big, rocking, ship. The spotlight would be turning, pink, yellow, green, and blue, picking up the couples lindy-hopping as if they had gone mad. "*Wail, man, wail!*" people would be shouting at the band: and it *would* be wailing, until first one and then another couple just ran out of strength and stumbled off toward the crowd, exhausted and soaked with sweat. Sometimes I would be down there standing inside the door jumping up and down in my gray jacket with the whiskbroom in the pocket, and the manager would have to come and shout at me that I had customers upstairs.

. . .

I'd been lindying previously only in cramped little apartment living rooms, and now I had room to maneuver. Once I really got myself warmed and loosened up, I was snatching partners from among the hundreds of unattached, free-lancing girls along the sidelines—almost every one of them could really dance—and I just about went wild! Hamp's band wailing. I was whirling girls so fast their skirts were snapping. Black girls, brownskins, high yellows, even a couple of white girls there. Boosting them over my hips, my shoulders, into the air. Though I wasn't quite sixteen then, I was tall and rawboned and looked like twenty-one; I was also pretty strong for my age. Circling, tapdancing, I was underneath them when they landed—doing the "flapping eagle," "the kangaroo" and the "split." After that, I never missed a Roseland lindy-hop as long as I stayed in Boston.

. . .

A third of the way or so through the evening the main vocalizing and instrumental stylings would come—and then showtime, when only the greatest lindy-hoppers would stay on the floor, to try and eliminate each other. All the other dancers would form a big "U" with the band at the open end. . . .

Now Count Basie turned on the showtime blast, and the other dancers moved off the floor, shifting for good watching positions, and began their hollering for their favorites. "All right now, Red!" they shouted to me, "Go get 'em, Red." And then a free-lancing lindy-girl I'd danced with before, Mamie Bevels, a waitress and a wild dancer, ran up to me, with Laura standing right there. I wasn't sure what to do. But Laura started backing away toward the crowd, still looking at me.

The Count's band was wailing. I grabbed Mamie and we started to work. She was a big, rough, strong gal, and she lindied like a bucking horse. I remember the very night that she became known as one of the showtime favorites there at the Roseland. A band was screaming when she kicked off her shoes and got barefooted, and shouted, and shook herself as if she were in some African jungle frenzy, and then she let loose with some dancing, shouting with every step, until the guy that was out there with her nearly had to fight to control her. The crowd loved any way-out lindying style that made a colorful show like that. It was how Mamie had become known.

. . .

CHAPTER 5: "HARLEMITE"

I went along with the railroad job for my own reasons. For a long time I'd wanted to visit New York City. Since I had been in Roxbury, I had heard a lot about "the Big Apple," as it was called by the well-traveled musicians, merchant mariners, salesmen, chauffeurs for white families, and various kinds of hustlers I ran into. . . . Later on, even later that night, I would find out that Harlem contained hundreds of thousands of my people who were just as loud and gaudy as Negroes anywhere else. . . .

From Small's, I taxied over to the Apollo Theater. (I remember so well that Jay McShann's band was playing, because his vocalist was later my close friend, Walter Brown, the one who used to sing "Hooty Hooty Blues.") From there, on the other side of 125th Street, at Seventh Avenue, I saw the big, tall, gray Theresa Hotel. It was the finest in New York City where Negroes could then stay, years before the downtown hotels would accept the black man. . . .

Professional Lindy dancers. Whitey's International Hoppers in Hollywood.

The Braddock Hotel was just up 126th Street, near the Apollo's backstage entrance. I knew its bar was famous as a Negro celebrity hang-out. I walked in and saw, along that jam-packed bar, such famous stars as Dizzy Gillespie, Billy Eckstine, Billie Holiday, Ella Fitzgerald, and Dinah Washington.

As Dinah Washington was leaving with some friend, I overheard someone say she was on her way to the Savoy Ballroom where Lionel Hampton was appearing that night—she was then Hamp's vocalist. The ballroom made the Roseland in Boston look small and shabby by comparison. And the lindy-hopping there matched the size and elegance of the place. Hampton's hard-driving outfit kept a red-hot pace with his greats such as Arnett Cobb, Illinois Jacquet, Dexter Gordon, Alvin Hayse, Joe Newman, and George Jenkins. I went a couple of rounds on the floor with girls from the sidelines.

Probably a third of the sideline booths were filled with white people, mostly just watching the Negroes dance; but some of them danced together, and, as in Boston, a few white women were with Negroes. The people kept shouting for Hamp's "Flyin' Home," and finally he did it. (I could believe the story I'd heard in Boston about this number—that once in the Apollo, Hamp's "Flyin' Home" had made some reefer-smoking Negro in the second balcony believe he could fly, so he tried—and jumped—and broke his leg, an event later immortalized in song when Earl

Posters from the Savoy Ballroom, ca. 1920s–1950s.

Hines wrote a hit tune called "Second Balcony Jump.") I had never seen such fever-heat dancing. After a couple of slow numbers cooled the place off, they brought on Dinah Washington. When she did her "Salty Papa Blues," those people just about tore the Savoy roof off. (Poor Dinah's funeral was held not long ago in Chicago. I read that over twenty thousand people viewed her body, and I should have been there myself. Poor Dinah! We became great friends, back in those days.)

. . .

SOURCE: Malcolm X with the assistance of Alex Haley, *The Autobiography of Malcolm X* (New York: Ballantine, 1964): 32, 56–58, 64–67, 72–73.

THE MANY FACES OF BILLIE HOLIDAY

(Holiday, Wilson, Bennett)

"This is a book about the greatest jazz singer in history," writes Robert O'Meally in his study of Billie Holiday (1915–1959). This chapter follows his goal of "charting Billie Holiday's rise not as a social phenomenon but as the story of an artist."[1] As with many great artists, the literature surrounding her life and work abounds with myth and controversy. These excerpts begin with a section from her autobiography, *Lady Sings the Blues*, that concerns the tenor saxophonist Lester Young (1909–1959). Known as Holiday's musical soulmate, Young shared her understated approach to tone and timbre. Holiday turned the song "Strange Fruit" (with words and music by Lewis Allan, often mistakenly attributed to her) into a signature song. The section on "Strange Fruit" reveals the cost of grieving in public.

Then follow two excerpts by other musicians. The first is an account from a pianist who worked and played alongside Holiday: Teddy Wilson (1912–1986), who organized the famous recording sessions on the Brunswick label in the late 1930s. In the final selection, the composer Richard Rodney Bennett (b. 1936) offers a succinct profile of Holiday's approach to melodic improvisation.

FROM *LADY SINGS THE BLUES*

For my money Lester was one of the world's greatest. I loved his music, and some of my favorite recordings are the ones with Lester's pretty solos.

I remember how the late Herschel Evans used to hate me. Whenever Basie had an arranger work out something for me, I'd tell him I wanted Lester to solo behind me. That always made Herschel salty. It wasn't that I didn't love his playing. It was just that I liked Lester's more.

Lester sings with his horn; you listen to him and can almost hear the words. People think he's cocky and secure, but you can hurt his feelings in two seconds. I know, because I found out once that I had. We've been hungry together, and I'll always love him and his horn.

I often think about how we used to record in those days. We'd get off a bus after a five-hundred-mile trip, go into the studio with no music, nothing to eat but coffee and sandwiches. Me and Lester would drink what we called top and bottom, half gin and half port wine.

I'd say, "What'll we do, two-bar or four-bar intro?"

Somebody'd say make it four and a chorus—one, one and a half.

Then I'd say, "You play behind me the first eight, Lester," and then Harry Edison would come in or Buck Clayton and take the next eight bars. "Jo, you just brush and don't hit the cymbals too much."

Now with all their damn preparation, complicated arrangements, you've got to kiss everybody's behind to get ten minutes to do eight sides in.

When I did "Night and Day" I had never seen that song before in my life. I don't read music either. I just walked in, Teddy Wilson played it for me, and I did it.

With artists like Lester, Don Byas, Benny Carter, and Coleman Hawkins, something was always happening. No amount of preparation today is a match for them.

. . .

It's only five miles—thirty-five minutes by the IRT—from Pod's and Jerry's at 133rd Street off Seventh Avenue to Sheridan Square, near Fourth Street on the same avenue. But the places were worlds apart and it took about seven years to make the trip.

The next big thing that happened to me was at Café Society Downtown. It was just a basement full of people mopping, cleaning, dusting, painting murals, and a hopeful notion of a Jersey shoe manufacturer named Barney Josephson when I first went down there. I met him through John Hammond.

Barney and his wife, a really wonderful girl, told me this was to be one club where there was going to be no segregation, no racial prejudice. "Everybody's going to be for real in here."

This was what I'd been waiting for. I was so happy. The opening bill included Meade Lux Lewis, the two-piano boogie-woogie team of Albert Ammons and Pete Johnson, Joe Turner, and Frank Newton had the band.

I'll never forget that opening night. There must have been six hundred people in the joint, celebrities, artists, rich society people. And a big hitch. Barney had his liquor license, but nobody could go on until we had the cabaret license—and it hadn't arrived. It got to be eleven o'clock, and we were getting panicky. The cops were standing by. I couldn't stand the suspense any longer. "Come on, let's take a chance," I told Barney. "One night in jail isn't going to hurt anybody."

We had already decided to take the chance and go on at eleven-thirty, when the license arrived at the last minute, like the Marines. So with the cops standing by, we went on. Meade

Lux Lewis knocked them out; Ammons and Johnson flipped them; Joe Turner killed them; Newton's band sent them; and then I came on. This was an audience.

It was during my stint at Café Society that a song was born which became my personal protest—"Strange Fruit." The germ of the song was in a poem written by Lewis Allan. I first met him at Café Society. When he showed me that poem, I dug it right off. It seemed to spell out all the things that had killed Pop.[2]

Allen, too, had heard how Pop died and of course was interested in my singing. He suggested that Sonny White, who had been my accompanist, and I turn it into music. So the three of us got together and did the job in about three weeks. I also got a wonderful assist from Danny Mendelsohn, another writer who had done arrangements for me. He helped me with arranging the song and rehearsing it patiently. I worked like the devil on it because I was never sure I could put it across or that I could get across to a plush night-club audience the things that it meant to me.

I was scared people would hate it. The first time I sang it I thought it was a mistake and I had been right being scared. There wasn't even a patter of applause when I finished. Then a lone person began to clap nervously. Then suddenly everyone was clapping.

It caught on after a while and people began to ask for it. The version I recorded for Commodore became my biggest-selling record. It still depresses me every time I sing it, though. It reminds me of how Pop died. But I have to keep singing it, not only because people ask for it but because twenty years after Pop died the things that killed him are still happening in the South.

Over the years I've had a lot of weird experiences as a result of that song. It has a way of separating the straight people from the squares and cripples. One night in Los Angeles a bitch stood right up in the club where I was singing and said, "Billie, why don't you sing that sexy song you're so famous for? You know, the one about the naked bodies swinging in the trees."

Needless to say, I didn't.

But another time, on 52nd Street, I finished a set with "Strange Fruit" and headed, as usual, for the bathroom. I always do. When I sing it, it affects me so much I get sick. It takes all the strength out of me.

This woman came in the ladies' room at the Down-beat Club and found me all broken up from crying. I had come off the floor running, hot and cold, miserable and happy. She looked at me, and the tears started coming to her eyes. "My God," she said, "I never heard anything so beautiful in my life. You can still hear a pin drop out there."

Just a few months ago in a club in Miami I had run through an entire two-week date without ever doing "Strange Fruit." I was in no mood to be bothered with the scenes that always come on when I do that number in the South. I didn't want to start anything I couldn't finish. But one night after everybody had asked me twenty times to do it, I finally gave in. There was a special character who had haunted the club for days, always asking for "Strange Fruit" and "Gloomy Sunday." I don't know why he wanted to hear either one. He looked like Gloomy Sunday to me. But I finally gave them what they asked for as an encore.

When I came to the final phrase of the lyrics I was in the angriest and strongest voice I had been in for months. My piano player was in the same kind of form. When I said, ". . . for the sun to rot," and then a piano punctuation, ". . . for the wind to suck," I pounced on those words like they had never been hit before.

I was flailing the audience, but the applause was like nothing I'd ever heard. I came off, went upstairs, changed into street clothes, and when I came down they were still applauding.

Not many other singers ever tried to do "Strange Fruit." I never tried to discourage them, but audiences did. Years after me at Café Society, Josh White came on with his guitar and his shirt front split down to here and did it. The audience shouted for him to leave the song alone.

A few years later Lillian Smith told me the song inspired her to write the novel and the play about a lynching. You know what she called it.

. . .

You can be up to your boobies in white satin, with gardenias in your hair and no sugar cane for miles, but you can still be working on a plantation.

Take 52nd Street in the late thirties and early forties. It was supposed to be a big deal. "Swing Street," they called it. Joint after joint was jumping. It was this "new" kind of music. They could get away with calling it new because millions of squares hadn't taken a trip to 131st Street. If they had they could have dug swing for twenty years.

By the time the ofays got around to copping "swing" a new-style music was already breaking out all over uptown. Ten years later that became the newest thing when the white boys downtown figured out how to cop it.

Anyway, white musicians were "swinging" from one end of 52nd Street to the other, but there wasn't a black face in sight on the street except Teddy Wilson and me. Teddy played intermission piano at the Famous Door and I sang. There was no cotton to be picked between Leon and Eddie's and the East River, but man, it was a plantation any way you looked at it. And we had to not only look at it, we lived in it. We were not allowed to mingle any kind of way. The minute we were finished with our intermission stint we had to scoot out back to the alley or go out and sit in the street.

Teddy had an old beat-up Ford he used to drive to work in. Sometimes we'd just go out and sit in it parked at the curb.

There was a wild cat who used to come around the joint all the time and he drove a crazy foreign car. Every time he got in it to take off, it sounded like a B-29, and the Famous Door management didn't like that. Anyway, we got friendly with him, and he got friendly with us, and it cost both Teddy and me our first jobs on 52nd Street. We got our asses fraternized right off the street.

He was a young millionaire living it up and nobody was going to tell him what to do, who to drink with and who not to drink with. He'd come in the joint and listen to me and Teddy and always wanted to buy us drinks. He insisted we ball with him. And as much as they wanted to please a big spender, both the boss and the headwaiter insisted we didn't.

We told him we were under orders not to socialize with the customers, but he'd insist back that nobody was going to give him orders. Finally one night after he'd bugged me so and practically made me feel like a Tom for not sitting down with him, I got fed up and did.

We had a couple drinks together, and they were my last ones in that joint for a while. When I got up, the boss told me to go pick up my papers, I was fired. He was nasty enough to fire Teddy, too, although Teddy hadn't done a thing. After this big scandal which might ruin him on the street, he said he didn't want any Negroes in the place at all.

I burned. I had to get out, but I hated like hell to go home and tell Mom I'd been bounced again—over something as silly as this. So our millionaire friend tried to cheer us up. We went off with him in his fancy foreign car and drove uptown through Central Park in that crazy-assed wagon in three minutes.

He told us not to worry, he had plenty of money and there were plenty of jobs. And besides, he was a musician and going to have his own damn dance band soon and everything would be fine.

"Yeah," I told him, "big deal. You've got plenty of money, but in the meantime you've ruined my life so I don't even dare go home. What's going to happen to Teddy and me?"

So he said, "Don't go home, let's ball a little." We wound up back at the Uptown House. Everyone insisted I get up and sing. So I did. And they offered me a regular job again back at the old stand.

Our millionaire friend kept his word, too. He pulled a few wires and got Teddy a job in a radio studio band. He also kept his word and ended up with his own band—and a good one. He was Charlie Barnet.

But 52nd Street couldn't hold the line against Negroes forever. Something had to give. And eventually it was the plantation owners. They found they could make money off Negro artists and they couldn't afford their old prejudices. So the barriers went down, and it gave jobs to a lot of great musicians.

I went into Ralph Watkins' Kelly's Stables as a headliner—no more intermission stuff. The typical bill I appeared with in those days would cost plenty today. One time there was Coleman Hawkins' band, me and Stuff Smith, and for intermission Nat Cole and his trio. Nobody in the joint got two hundred a week. I was there for two years at a top of $175 and I was the star. Then there was Roy Eldridge's band, Una Mae Carlisle, Lips Page and his group, and the great Art Tatum playing intermission piano.

Working on the street seemed like a homecoming every night. People I'd met in Harlem, Hollywood, and Café Society used to come in and there was always some kind of re-union. I was getting a little billing and publicity, so my old friends and acquaintances knew where to find me.

SOURCE: Billie Holiday with William Dufty, *Lady Sings the Blues* (New York: Penguin, 1956; reprint, 1992): 59–60, 83–86, 91, 97–102.

───∼∼∼∼───

The recordings that Billie Holiday made with the pianist Teddy Wilson form a principal part of her legacy. Even today's jazz singers return to them as foundational examples of the art of ensemble music making. In this excerpt, from a book based on interviews given in the mid 1970s, Wilson pays tribute to the art and craft of the various virtuoso musicians who contributed to the recordings.

TEDDY WILSON ON HIS BRUNSWICK SESSIONS

At that time John Hammond knew every bar in New York where there was any good music. He introduced me to Billie Holiday—Lady Day as she later got to be known—when she was still obscure and was singing in Harlem. John said to me: "Teddy, there's a young lady I want you to hear sing. Her name is Billie Holiday and she's singing in a club called Jerry's in Harlem." So off we went and listened to Billie singing by turns with another girl called Beverley "Baby" White, and a piano accompanist named Bobby Henderson. The two girls were both singing. That was the whole show. "Baby" did a lovely job of the ballads, and Billie was just incomparable with her rhythm singing. Later, when Bobby Henderson left, Garnet Clark was the accompanist.

When Billie and I were introduced we hit it off extremely well and Hammond decided to set up the recording series which I did with Billie for Brunswick, beginning in 1935, and which later made jazz history and is now so famous. I organized the bands—mostly seven-piece—and helped Billie select the songs she was to sing. I would do sketch orchestrations that could be easily geared to the three-minute duration of the 78 rpm records of those days. I would sketch the main body of the music, leaving the rest to be improvised, aside from the vocal chorus. By the time the Brunswick contract was over in 1939 I reckon we must have made some 200 sides together.

Billie was in her prime then: you only have to think of such numbers as *What a Little Moonlight Can Do* and *Miss Brown to You*, with Benny Goodman on clarinet, Ben Webster on tenor sax, Roy Eldridge on trumpet, John Kirby on bass, and Cozy Cole on drums. Later it was tenor sax player Lester Young who accompanied Billie over the years, although Johnny Hodges, Duke Ellington's star alto player, did a lot too. I think those were among the first recordings Johnny ever made outside the Ellington band. We were recording about four tunes a month for Brunswick, which later became Columbia.

People have often asked me how I ever managed to get together such a collection of star musicians to accompany Billie Holiday on those records. In retrospect I suppose it is astonishing that I succeeded in getting together that quantity of top-flight talent! They were all big names and it was natural to think it must have cost a fortune to get them together. Looking back I realize that, great as they were, no recording company would have put up the money for such a dazzling show of talent on a purely commercial basis. What actually happened was that I would just get on the phone and call whoever was in town, and I was extremely lucky to hit the jackpot so often. Johnny Hodges did a lot on alto sax, Benny Carter did a lot, Ben Webster did a lot on tenor, also Chu Berry and Bud Freeman, but Lester Young did most of the tenor. On one or two dates we had Prince Robinson from the old McKinney's Cotton Pickers band playing clarinet or tenor sax. Our trumpets were Buck Clayton and Roy Eldridge, Charlie Shavers, Bobby Hackett and Jonah Jones. Benny Goodman himself did quite a few, and a lot of the men from his band are on those records, people like Gene Krupa and Harry James. On clarinet, aside from Benny, we had some with Pee Wee Russell. We had some of the men from the Basie and Ellington outfits, and some from Chick Webb's band. The cream of the crop, just the best in New York I could get. Moreover, I succeeded in getting them on the recordings at rates which, to put it mildly, were only a pittance compared with what they were earning outside.

I can only explain the mystery by saying that it was only in those sessions that those artists could play with a group which was at their own level. In their own bands they were the number one soloist, but at my recording sessions they themselves were one of seven top soloists. You simply could not pay these groups to keep them together on a steady basis; imagine trying to get together a reed section line-up like Johnny Hodges, Lester Young, Ben Webster, Benny Carter and Benny Goodman on an economic basis! The series was named "Teddy Wilson and his Orchestra." Besides Billie Holiday, vocalists included Ella Fitzgerald, Midge Williams and Frances Hunt.

So the Teddy Wilson small group sessions were the only chance these men had to play with their peers instead of being the best in the whole band. The result was that nobody really cared about the money they were getting; they were more interested in the excitement of playing with seven men who were all as good as they were. The music that was produced was a rare monthly event—art for art's sake, if you want to use a high-sounding term. Many sides featured the musicians alone with no vocals at all.

In these sessions Benny Goodman, for example, made four tunes for twenty dollars—five dollars a side. Can you imagine Benny Goodman recording for five dollars a tune? I guess it would be 5000, or 10,000 dollars a tune now. Johnny Hodges and Gene Krupa did the same, and so did the others. So you can truly say it was a band of "All Stars," a frequently abused term.

As far as Billie Holiday herself was concerned, she was very popular with the musicians. You might call her a musician's singer, and she was in the company of soloists who were on par with herself.

The two girl singers in those days who were giants of the jazz scene were Billie Holiday and Ella Fitzgerald. Ella did one of those dates I am talking about because Billie couldn't make it. If I remember rightly, I got Ella, who wasn't famous then, to sing *All My Life* and *Melancholy Baby*. Those two girls dominated the jazz scene in Harlem before they were really known among the white population of America. Nevertheless, there were records of Billie Holiday and of Ella Fitzgerald with Chick Webb's band in all the juke boxes in the Negro ghettoes. Billie was singing well then, with no trouble with narcotics, as there were later. She was very good to work with, extremely cooperative, and no trouble at all.

At our sessions we did four songs in three hours. The musicians had no rehearsal—they were such fine artists they didn't need it. Most of the songs the musicians never saw before we recorded them. They'd just run over the tune once to get the balance. I'd have the sketch arrangements with me for those tunes they'd never seen before. My little sketches would be to the length of a 78 rpm record, three minutes, and I would plan the tempo and give each man a part so he would know what was to happen: when he would solo, when Billie was to sing, whether one of the players was to improvise softly in the background behind her, or when he would be featured in the foreground. They would read the melody I'd written for them and they would improvise in between on the chord tones I had put down for them. This was because, when you improvise, you throw the melody out and make your own melody based on the chord structure underneath the original melody. You might compare it to a guitar part: there's a chord line and a melody line. All this made it easy to say: "Lester [Young], you take the first sixteen bars of this chorus and we'll do three choruses all together, and then partition it all out easily."

Billie Holiday had to do her own rehearsing and had to get familiar with the lyric and the music. But most of the time she was singing with the sheet music in front of her, although she had been over the tune several times between dates with me—just the two of us at the piano.

SOURCE: Teddy Wilson with Arie Ligthart and Humphrey Van Loo, *Teddy Wilson Talks Jazz* (New York and London: Continuum, 1996): 22–25.

~~~~~~~

An English composer-arranger of concert music and film scores and a cabaret pianist, Richard Rodney Bennett wrote about American jazz singing with an appealing matter-of-factness and an acknowledgment of the dignity of the profession at a time when scholarship about jazz singing was sparse. This excerpt from a long article on jazz singing includes Bennett's transcription of an example of Holiday's "minimalist" approach to jazz improvisation.

The first true *jazz* singer (as opposed to blues singer) who comes immediately to mind is
Billie Holiday. She was never a blues singer in that she always sang the music of her own time
and was not concerned with the heritage of American negro folk music and the blues, although
Bessie Smith the blues singer was, with Louis Armstrong, her strongest influence. The tragic
life of Billie Holiday has been often described—in any case the voice, as one listens chronologically to her recordings, provides sufficient documentation. It turned from the almost mocking
lightness of many of her early performances—the voice touching deftly on the notes of the
melody, sketching curves and slides between them, the more serious emotions half-disguised,
a marvelous combination of cynicism and warmth—to the terrible dragging sadness of the late
recordings. The vibrato became uncontrolled, the typical glides and scoops became almost a parody, and the emotions were too naked for comfortable listening. Nevertheless she always had the
ability to turn the most thin and frivolous song into a quite unique statement, full of emotional
depths which the song itself does not necessarily reveal. She was without doubt the strongest
single influence on almost all of the singers who were to follow her. A purely musical examination of her art only skates across the surface, but it is perhaps the most fruitful approach.

The basic qualities of all the best jazz singing were present in Billie Holiday's voice. Certainly a great voice is not essential—indeed it can often obscure the spontaneous, mercurial
quality of the performance. Her voice was always limited in range, slightly raw and edgy, and
she seemed to use it with total unconcern for its limitations. Her performances were as free and
(in the best sense) unrepeatable as those of any good jazz instrumentalist. It is impossible to
think that her delicate shadings, glides and half-sung tones could be either calculated or reduced
to a "standard" performance, to be repeated even once again. . . . However many times Billie Holiday recorded—let alone performed—the same song, there were always different nuances and
new variations. In the same way that a good jazz player always gives a feeling of improvisation,
of invention, even when merely stating a melody, so I believe that a true jazz singer is constantly
improvising, even if this involves only a rethinking of the rhythmic structure of a song. Later
singers, such as the technically amazing Sarah Vaughan, based their improvisations largely on
embellishment; Billie Holiday's great strength was that she almost always simplified. A typical
example of this technique of "pruning" is given in her 1936 recording of Kern's *A Fine Romance*.
(. . . in all the following transcriptions I have tried to notate something of the singer's rhythmic
quality as well as a suggestion of the vocal devices employed. Notes in brackets are "ghost-notes,"
which are implied rather than fully sung.) The lagging rhythm and "flattened-out" melody, together with her plaintive insistence on the upper notes of each phrase are an elegant equivalent
of the gentle cynicism of the lyrics.

Even Billie Holiday's most deeply rooted mannerisms were entirely personal, and
stemmed from her emotional attitude to the material rather than from a self-consciously "styl-
ish" manner. She began more and more to slide wearily towards and away from each note,
almost dragging her voice up to the next, and even to start a phrase with a fall to the "right" note
from a half-sounded higher note, giving a touchingly poignant quality to her singing. Her harmonic sense was excellent: all these inflections touched instinctively on other notes which were
essential parts of the harmonic structure of the song, as though she were sketching out the supporting chords. This is, of course, an essential part of jazz improvisation, and all the more improvisatory jazz singers—[Ella] Fitzgerald, [Anita] O'Day, [Sarah] Vaughan and [Carmen] McRae,
[Cleo] Laine, [Chris] Connor and [Sheila] Jordan—have a well developed ear for harmony. The
rhythm depends typically on speech rhythms, the voice floating freely over the solid pulse of the
accompaniment, sometimes slipping behind it, sometimes moving ahead, occasionally landing

right on the beat, and altogether producing complex and subtle patterns which create the inde-finable "swing." Her highly inflected vocal lines made the simplest phrase extraordinarily ex-pressive [see the musical example]. Her last recordings have a tragic intensity beyond anything else in jazz.

SOURCE: Richard Rodney Bennett, "The Technique of the Jazz Singer," *Music and Musi-cians* (February 1972): 30–31. The complete essay is reprinted in Lewis Porter, ed., *Jazz: A Century of Change: Readings and New Essays* (New York: Schirmer, 1997): 57–67.

~~~~~~~~

NOTES

1.   Robert O'Meally, *Lady Day: The Many Faces of Billie Holiday* (New York: Arcade, 1991): 9.
2.   Pop refers to Holiday's father, Clarence Holiday (1898–1937), who died from pneumonia while on tour with Don Redman's band in Texas.

107

RALPH ELLISON ON THE
BIRTH OF BEBOP AT MINTON'S

The novelist Ralph Ellison (1914–1994) wrote some of the most perceptive and elegant jazz criticism of the twentieth century. His taste was formed in the era of swing, and he admired Louis Armstrong and Duke Ellington above all others. His profound understanding of American culture and his empathy for the creative imaginations of artists touched whatever he wrote, even if he was wary of their music. These excerpts, which open with a vignette capturing the atmosphere at Minton's, a legendary jazz club at 210 West 118th Street in Harlem, highlight the importance of place, symbolizing tradition and community.

When asked how it was back then, back in the forties, they will smile: then, frowning with the puzzlement of one attempting to recall the details of a pleasant but elusive dream, they'll say: "Oh, man, it was a hell of a time! A wailing time! Things were jumping, you couldn't get in here for the people. The place was packed with celebrities. Park Avenue, man! Big people in show business, college professors along with the pimps and their women. And college boys and girls. Everybody came. You know how the old words to 'Basin Street Blues' used to go before

Sinatra got hold of it? *Basin Street is the street where the dark and light folks meet*—that's what I'm talking about. That was Minton's, man. It was a place where everybody could be entertained because it was a place that was jumping with good times."

Or some will tell you that it was here that Dizzy Gillespie found his own trumpet voice; that here Kenny Clarke worked out the patterns of his drumming style; where Charlie Christian played out the last creative and truly satisfying moments of his brief life, his New York home; where Charlie Parker built the monument of his art; where Thelonious Monk formulated his contribution to the chordal progressions and the hide-and-seek melodic methods of modern jazz. And they'll call such famous names as Lester Young, Ben Webster and Coleman Hawkins, or Fats Waller, who came here in the after-hours stillness of the early morning to compose. They'll tell you that Benny Goodman, Art Tatum, Count Basie, and Lena Horne would drop in to join in the fun; that it was here that George Shearing played on his first night in the United States; or of Tony Scott's great love of the place; and they'll repeat all the stories of how, when, and by whom the word "bebop" was coined here—but withal, few actually remember, and these leave much unresolved.

Usually music gives resonance to memory (and Minton's was a hotbed of jazz), but not the music in the making here. It was itself a texture of fragments, repetitive, nervous, not fully formed; its melodic lines underground, secret and taunting; its riffs jeering—"Salt peanuts! Salt peanuts!"—its timbres flat or shrill, with a minimum of thrilling vibrato.[1] Its rhythms were out of stride and seemingly arbitrary, its drummers frozen-faced introverts dedicated to chaos. And in it the steady flow of memory, desire and defined experience summed up by the traditional jazz beat and blues mood seemed swept like a great river from its old, deep bed. We know better now, and recognize the old moods in the new sounds, but what we know is that which was then becoming. For most of those who gathered here, the enduring meaning of the great moment at Minton's took place off to the side beyond the range of attention, like a death blow glimpsed from the corner of the eye, the revolutionary rumpus sounding like a series of flubbed notes blasting the talk with discord. So that the events which made Minton's *Minton's* arrived in conflict and ran their course; then the heat was gone and all that is left to mark its passage is the controlled fury of the music itself, sealed pure and irrevocable, banalities and excellencies alike, in the early recordings, or swept along by our restless quest for the new, to be diluted in more recent styles, the best of it absorbed like drops of fully distilled technique, mood and emotions into the great stream of jazz.

. . .

Jazz, for all the insistence on legends, has been far more closely associated with cabarets and dance halls than with brothels, and it was these which provided both the employment for the musicians and an audience initiated and aware of the overtones of the music; which knew the language of the riffs, the unstated meanings of the blues idiom, and the dance steps developed from, and complementary to, its rhythms. And in the beginning it was in the Negro dance hall and night club that jazz was most completely a part of a total cultural expression, and in which it was freest and most satisfying, both for the musicians and for those in whose lives it played a major role. As a night club in a Negro community, then, Minton's was part of a national pattern.

But in the old days Minton's was far more than this; it was also a rendezvous for musicians. As such, and although it was not formally organized, it goes back historically to the first New York center of Negro musicians, the Clef Club. Organized in 1910, during the start of the great migration of Negroes northward, by James Reese Europe, the director whom Irene Castle credits with having invented the fox trot, the Clef Club was set up on West 53rd Street to serve as a meeting place and booking office for Negro musicians and entertainers. Here wage scales were regulated, musical styles and techniques worked out, and entertainment was supplied for such establishments as Rector's and Delmonico's, and for such producers as Florenz Ziegfeld and Oscar Hammerstein. Later, when Harlem evolved into a Negro section, a similar function was served by the Rhythm Club, located then in the old Lafayette Theatre building on 132nd Street and Seventh Avenue. Henry Minton, a former saxophonist and officer of the Rhythm Club, became the first local delegate to Local 802 of the American Federation of Musicians, and was thus doubly aware of the needs, artistic as well as economic, of jazzmen. He was generous with loans, was fond of food himself and, as an old acquaintance recalled, "loved to put a pot on the range" to share with unemployed friends. Naturally when he opened Minton's Playhouse many musicians made it their own.

Henry Minton also provided, as did the Clef and Rhythm Clubs, a necessity more important to jazz musicians than food: a place in which to hold their interminable jam sessions. And it is here that Minton's becomes most important in the development of modern jazz. It is here, too, that it joins up with all the other countless rooms, private and public, in which jazzmen have worked out the secrets of their craft. Today jam sessions are offered as entertainment by night clubs and on radio and television, and some are quite exciting, but what is seen and heard is only one aspect of the true jam session: the "cutting session," or contest of improvisational skill and physical endurance between two or more musicians. But the jam session is far more than this, and when carried out by musicians in the privacy of small rooms (as in the mural at Minton's), or in such places as Halley Richardson's shoeshine parlor in Oklahoma City, where I first heard Lester Young jamming in a shine chair, his head thrown back, his horn even then outthrust, his feet working on the footrests, as he played with and against Lem Johnson, Ben Webster, and other members of the old Blue Devils Orchestra (this was 1929) or during the after hours in Piney Brown's old Sunset Club in Kansas City; in such places as these, with only musicians and jazzmen present, then the jam session is revealed as the jazzman's true academy.

It is here that he learns tradition, group techniques and style. For although since the twenties many jazzmen have had conservatory training and are well grounded in formal theory and instrumental technique, when we approach jazz we are entering quite a different sphere of training. Here it is more meaningful to speak not of courses of study, of grades and degrees, but of apprenticeship, ordeals, initiation ceremonies, of rebirth. For after the jazzman has learned the fundamentals of his instrument and the traditional techniques of jazz—the intonations, the mute work, manipulation of timbre, the body of traditional styles—he must then "find himself," must be reborn, must find, as it were, his soul. All this through achieving that subtle identification between his instrument and his deepest drives which will allow him to express his own unique ideas and his own unique voice. He must achieve, in short, his self-determined identity.

In this his instructors are his fellow musicians, especially the acknowledged masters, and his recognition of manhood depends upon their acceptance of his ability as having reached a standard which is all the more difficult for not having been rigidly codified. This does not depend upon his ability to simply hold a job, but upon his power to express an individuality in tone. Nor is his status ever unquestioned, for the health of jazz and the unceasing attraction which it holds for the musicians themselves lies in the ceaseless warfare for mastery and recognition— not among the general public, though commercial success is not spurned, but among their artistic peers. And even the greatest can never rest on past accomplishments, for, as with the fast guns of the Old West, there is always someone waiting in a jam session to blow him literally, not only down, but into shame and discouragement.

By making his club hospitable to jam sessions even to the point that customers who were not musicians were crowded out, Henry Minton provided a retreat, a homogenous community where a collectivity of common experience could find continuity and meaningful expression. Thus the stage was set for the birth of bop.

In 1941 Mr. Minton handed over the management to Teddy Hill, the saxophonist and former band leader, and Hill turned the Playhouse into a musical dueling ground. Not only did he continue Minton's policies, he expanded them. It was Hill who established the Monday Celebrity Nights, the house band which included such members from his own disbanded orchestra, such as Kenny Clarke, Dizzy Gillespie, Thelonious Monk, sometimes Joe Guy, and later Charlie Christian and Charlie Parker, and it was Hill who allowed the musicians free rein to play whatever they liked. Perhaps no other club except Clarke Monroe's Uptown House was so permissive, and with the hospitality extended to musicians of all schools the news spread swiftly. Minton's became the focal point for musicians all over the country.

Herman Pritchard, who presided over the bar in the old days, tells us that every time they came, "Lester Young and Ben Webster used to tie up in battle like dogs in the road. They'd fight on those saxophones until they were tired out; then they'd put in long distance calls to their mothers, both of whom lived in Kansas City, and tell them about it."

And most of the jazz masters came either to observe or to participate and be influenced and listen to their own discoveries transformed, and the aspiring stars sought to win their approval, as the younger tenor men tried to win the esteem of Coleman Hawkins. Or they tried to vanquish them in jamming contests as [Dizzy] Gillespie is said to have outblown his idol, Roy Eldridge. It was during this period that Eddie "Lockjaw" Davis went through an ordeal of jeering rejection until finally he came through as an admired tenor man.

In the perspective of the time we now see that what was happening at Minton's was a continuing symposium of jazz, a summation of all the styles, personal and traditional, of jazz. Here it was possible to hear its resources of technique, ideas, harmonic structure, melodic phrasing and rhythmical possibilities explored more thoroughly than ever before. It was also possible to hear the first attempts toward a conscious statement of the sensibility of the younger generation of musicians as they worked out the techniques, structures and rhythmical patterns with which to express themselves. Part of this was arbitrary, a revolt of the younger against the established jazz stylists; part of it was inevitable. For jazz had reached a crisis, and new paths were certain to be searched for and found. An increasing number of the younger men were formally trained, and the post-Depression developments in the country had made for quite a break between their experience and that of the older men. Many were even of a different physical build. Often they were quiet and of a reserve which contrasted sharply with the exuberant and outgoing lyricism of the older men, and they were intensely concerned that their identity as Negroes place no restriction upon the music they played or the manner in which they used their talent. They were concerned, they said, with art, not entertainment. Especially were they resentful of Louis Armstrong, whom (confusing the spirit of his music with his clowning) they considered an Uncle Tom.

But they too, some of them, had their own myths and misconceptions: that theirs was the only generation of Negro musicians who listened [to] or enjoyed the classics; that to be truly free they must act exactly the opposite of what white people might believe, rightly or wrongly, a

Negro to be; that the performing artist can be completely and absolutely free of the obligations of the entertainer, and that they could play jazz with dignity only by frowning and treating the audience with aggressive contempt; and that to be in control, artistically and personally, one must be so cool as to quench one's own human fire.

Nor should we overlook the despair which must have swept Minton's before the technical mastery, the tonal authenticity, the authority and fecundity of imagination of such men as Hawkins, Young, Goodman, Tatum, Teagarden, Ellington and Waller. Despair, after all, is ever an important force in revolutions.

They were also responding to the nonmusical pressures affecting jazz. It was a time of big bands, and the greatest prestige and economic returns were falling outside the Negro community—often to leaders whose popularity grew from the compositions and arrangements of Negroes—to white instrumentalists whose originality lay in the enterprise with which they rushed to market with some Negro musician's hard-won style. Still there was no policy of racial discrimination at Minton's. Indeed, it was very much like those Negro cabarets of the twenties and thirties in which a megaphone was placed on the piano so that anyone with the urge could sing a blues. Nevertheless, the inside-dopesters will tell you that the "changes" or chord progressions and melodic inversions worked out by the creators of bop sprang partially from their desire to create a jazz which could not be so easily imitated and exploited by white musicians to whom the market was more open simply *because* of their whiteness. They wished to receive credit for what they created; besides, it was easier to "get rid of the trash" who crowded the bandstand with inept playing and thus make room for the real musicians, whether white or black. Nevertheless, white musicians like Tony Scott, Remo Palmieri and Al Haig who were part of the development at Minton's became so by passing a test of musicianship, sincerity, and temperament. Later, it is said, the boppers became engrossed in solving the musical problems which they set themselves. Except for a few sympathetic older musicians, it was they who best knew the promise of the Minton moment, and it was they, caught like the rest of us in all the complex forces of American life which comes to focus in jazz, who made the most of it. Now the tall tales told as history must feed on the results of their efforts.

SOURCE: Ralph Ellison, "The Golden Age, Time Past," *Esquire*, January 1959; reprinted in Ralph Ellison, *Living with Music: Ralph Ellison's Jazz Writings*, ed. Robert G. O'Meally (New York: Modern Library, 2001): 50–64; excerpts from 54–56, 59–64.

NOTE

1.   Ellison is referring to a famous novelty bop tune, "Salt Peanuts," written by Dizzy Gillespie and recorded in 1945 with Charlie Parker and Gillespie, which became identified with the bebop style.

1950–1975

$\mathcal{E}$LLA FITZGERALD ON STAGE

(Peterson)

One of the most celebrated singers in the twentieth century, Ella Fitzgerald (1917–1996) applied her prodigious gifts to jazz and popular music. In control of jazz techniques such as scatting and instrumental mimicry, Fitzgerald became best known as a solo interpreter of popular standards, where she often muted these gifts. The deceptive simplicity of her approach [as well as her vocal charisma] made her *Songbook* albums, which were produced by Norman Granz (1918–2001), stand as classics. Along with her contemporary partner in swing, Frank Sinatra, Fitzgerald helped to establish the historical framework for what (since the 1970s) has been called the "great American songbook."

Oscar Peterson (1925–2007), the legendary jazz pianist, worked with Ella Fitzgerald and often performed with her in the Jazz at the Philharmonic concerts (called JATP in these excerpts) in New York, which were produced by Granz in the 1950s. Mentioned also are the pianist Hank Jones (b. 1918) and the bass player, Ray Brown (1926–2002), then married to Fitzgerald. In this selection from his autobiography, Peterson remembers "Lady Fitz" and gives us an insider's view of jazz as the art of musical conversation.

S he loved to walk up to you and ask what you thought about a certain song. If you asked her why, she'd shyly say that she thought that she would like to include it in her repertoire, and that it more than likely would sound good with a big band. It wasn't hard to work out the proper key for her, mainly because she would often make herself stretch rather than saying it's either too high or too low for her. I never understood this quirk within her. Perhaps it was some sort of test that she felt that she had to run on herself.

There were many parts to Lady Fitz (as I affectionately named her in 1951) that I still don't claim to know, although I knew her for over 40 years and worked with her on and off throughout. She was innately shy and insecure, a very private person who remained somewhat enigmatic to even her closest friends.

After we'd met in 1950, I got to know her fairly well. I used to stand in the wings almost every night not only to listen to her sing, but also to hear how Hank Jones played for her. The early trio on JATP was Hank on piano, Ray on bass, and Buddy Rich on drums. These were dream nights for me. Here was Ella doing at least a one-hour show, accompanied by these three masters of their instruments. Were someone to ask me to choose my favourite Ella period, I would have to name the early 1950s as one of the strongest contenders. Those nights of awed listening are as fresh in my memory as yesterday—and remember that Ella in the early 1950s was not even close to being the worldwide international star that she was to become. She was just beginning to enjoy the musical challenge of Jazz At The Philharmonic.

At the outset, Ella's set would follow the intermission; but later developments—my trio's slot and guest appearances by other groups (e.g. the Gene Krupa Quartet and the Modern Jazz Quartet)—led to her batting in the "clean-up spot." If one thinks about all the heavy traffic that preceded her on stage, one begins to realize how much music Ella and her group had to produce to survive, never mind break it up (which she did almost nightly). It always amazed me how this woman could sit in her dressing-room from the start of the concert—she was invariably one of the first to arrive—joke and chat with the guys, the press, and the hangers-on who didn't know when to leave, and then when the moment arrived, go out on stage and rip up the concert!

What was it she had that earned not only the love, but also the musical respect of these heavy players around her? Lester Young used to sidle up to me in the wings with his taste in one hand, the other holding his bottom lip with an aghast stare on his face, listen for a couple of choruses, take my arm, grunt, and say, "Sis is kicking ass out there tonight, ain't she, Lady F? Lester better go get his horn and get ready for the finale and things." No one could have put it better.

When Ella reached her own cruising speed or comfort zone, she would make it awfully hard for you to be out there with her, regardless of the instrument that you played. Hank would feed her just enough to cause her to react to his phrasing and harmonic lead. Ella would respond to this and instinctively tack on her own linear answer while retaining the shape and cadence of the particular song. Ray would intercede with a bass figure, and Fitz would come across him, almost pre-thinking him with her response. Buddy would lay in some kind of drum figure that was still appropriate, and she would knead and mould the lyric and line within the same rhythmic structure that Buddy used. They would then often take off on flights of almost impossible key changes, which Fitz would sail through like a Ferrari going through a simple S-curve.

All through those days I had the feeling that Fitz was musically happier than at any other time before or since. She had an unbridled zest for musical investigation and exploration; at times, some prearranged things would go out of whack, and Fitz would take over and lead the group out of its confusion via a totally transformed version that vied for inclusion in the books as a new arrangement. "What about that, fellas?" Fitz would laughingly ask as she walked to her dressing-room. "I kinda like it like that. Shall I leave it that way? What do you think, OP?" Everyone would usually nod assent because to us Lady Fitz could do no wrong. It wasn't a case of giving in to the great lady: it was simply that we all sensed that she was on an undeniable musical roll, and none of us even cared to guess when it would come to an end.

Fitz continued on her merry way unperturbed by anything or anyone. She sauntered through her show each evening with that same imperturbable musical confidence. On the finale each night, she courageously took on the front line horns, regardless of who they were—Pres [Lester Young, Roy Eldridge, Coleman Hawkins], Benny Carter, Ben Webster, and so on. Ella traded fours, eights, sixteens, or whatever they wanted with them and never got hurt. As a matter of fact, on various nights when some of the horns got a smidgen careless, Fitz would run over them and keep right on going.

"I told you about getting too sporty out there with Lady Fitz," Pres reminded Flip Phillips one night when he decided to stay at the mike and "fairground" as Pres put it.

"Geez," muttered Flip in disbelief, "I didn't think she'd get that rough!"

"Rough?" repeated Pres in sarcasm. "You stay out there long enough and Lady Fitz will really lay waste to your ass! Lester knows better. Lester lets Lady Fitz sing her little four-bar song, then Lester plays his four-bar song, and then Goodnight Irene. Lester's through!"

None of this was said with any vehemence: Pres was merely stating an honest musical credo—that he never played games on the challenges with Ella. Wise man.

I got the opportunity to play for Ella quite unexpectedly. It was in 1952 and Norman was taking JATP to Europe for its debut over there. We were all assembled excitedly at the New York airport, chattering away, when someone suddenly asked, "Say, where's Hank?" The whole atmosphere immediately changed from one of excited clamour to one of anxious curiosity. Norman remained placid and carried on his business at the counter as before. Finally, departure time arrived, and we all boarded the plane for Stockholm. It took some time for the group to realize that Hank had in fact missed the plane, but after it struck home, everyone settled down to enjoy our first European jaunt.

After our arrival and reception in Stockholm, I asked Norman what was going to happen. He calmly looked at me and said, "You'll have to play for her, that's all." After delivering his bombshell, he left as was normal for him, and I sat there much like a condemned man, wondering exactly how I had managed to come to grief at such an early stage of the tour, considering the fact that we hadn't even struck a single note as yet. I had subbed for Hank on a couple of earlier tours in America, but that was different. Those occasions simply meant substituting for him for one single night, not a whole tour, let alone the first European tour. I knew that Ella would naturally want to do some of her arrangements, and that would normally have meant some quick rehearsals and memorizing on my part; however, with opening night staring us all in the face, there would be no time for any of that.

I searched out Ray Brown, whom I did not know well at this stage: he was working with Ella and I was using Major Holley, and we had not yet teamed up as a duo. I told him what Norman had said, and he was very nonchalant about the whole thing, tossing it off with a "Just listen to and watch me, and everything will be OK." Given that he had not only been playing Ella's arrangements nightly, but had also been responsible for some of them, in part at least, I considered his response to my concern rather cavalier.

Opening night arrived as opening nights must, and throughout the first half of the concert I could only focus on that impending set with Lady Fitz. Finally, the intermission arrived and I nervously followed Ray into Ella's dressing-room along with Norman to discuss her set. They chucked out and installed songs one after the other; it didn't really matter much to me what they called, for I knew that I was in foreign territory whichever way they went. Then, as I nervously stood in the wings with Ella, Norman, and Ray, I said to myself, "Peterson, you screw this one up, and they're going to hear this one all the way back to Montreal, including Pop!" It's strange how we tend to relate to someone in particular whenever we find ourselves in any kind of jeopardy. At this moment, it was Dad who came to mind—not out of fear, but more out of what I imagined would be his total disappointment at my failure. I can remember straightening myself up, and deciding that I wasn't going to quit before I was beaten, which would have been Dad's philosophy.

As Ella walked on to thunderous applause and cheers, Ray set the first tempo with the snap of his fingers and by slapping the inside shell of the piano (a trademark of his). It was an easy loping tempo, and I found it to be quite easy to cope with once the primary flush of apprehension had passed. In fact, it felt good, and I decided to make the most of it. Fortunately, the magic worked and the night was a success. Ella came off smiling and happy, and I thanked the powers-that-be for getting me through that first important concert. I felt that if we succeeded in having a good first shot, things would roll from then on. I am still grateful to Ray for virtually conducting me through the various tempi that were needed in order to make Fitz's set work: he hadn't been so cavalier after all!

I grew to know practically all the little signs and mannerisms that telegraphed exactly what Ella was feeling.

1. The first slight side glance accompanied by a sort of half-laugh.
   Meaning: What was that change or that line that you played behind me?

2. The left hand cupped to her ear.
   Meaning: Something is out of tune. Is it me or the piano? (Note: Bet on it being the piano!)

3. The head tilts slightly to the side; the left hand starts snapping with a vengeance.
   Meaning: The time pulsation is not reaching her the way she wants it to. Tighten up the time, fellas!

4. The left foot is tapping the time along with a natural snap of the left hand.
   Meaning: All's well up front, guys. She's cruising with it.

5. The handkerchief is nervously being switched from hand to hand.
   Meaning: She's not comfortable. The dynamic level is too high or the tempo is not what she wanted from the outset.

6. The left hand is slapping the hip.
   Meaning: This reaction is gauged by the intensity of the slap, or what accompanies it. If it is a normal tap, she is perhaps trying to raise or lower the tempo. Experiment. If the intensity is much deeper, look out, she's getting ready to go for it and wants to make sure that you go with her.

These are but a few of the vital signs that I learned to use as a guide when playing for Ella.

SOURCE: Oscar Peterson, *A Jazz Odyssey: An Autobiography* (New York: Continuum International, 2002): 155–65.

LEONARD BERNSTEIN CHARTS AN

EPIC ROLE FOR MUSICAL THEATER

The multifaceted gifts of Leonard Bernstein (1918–1990) sometimes challenged his artistic peace of mind. Which road should he take: the conductor of the great tradition or the composer of a new tradition? Today, his Broadway musicals are considered his chief legacy. His commitment to American musical theater was thoughtful and deeply experienced. It symbolized his sense of national ambition as a composer, and he believed that by the 1950s, the golden age of the American musical had arrived. These excerpts represent turning points from the beginning of his career in 1938 to one of its great highlights, *West Side Story* in 1957, and then onward to his Mass in 1971.

This first letter is from Bernstein to his new friend and mentor, the composer Aaron Copland. The letter dates from the beginning of their relationship, and Copland would eventually become Bernstein's teacher, lover, colleague, "rival," and, ultimately, musical father. Then at Harvard University, Bernstein undertook an undergraduate thesis that prefigured his compositional directions. The thesis includes sections on the

importance of African-American music and penetrating analyses of music by Copland and George Gershwin.[1]

FROM A LETTER OF LEONARD BERNSTEIN
TO AARON COPLAND, NOVEMBER 19, 1938

In the midst of ten million other things I'm writing a thesis for honors. . . . the subject is Nationalism in American music—presumably a nonentity but on the whole a vital problem. We've talked about it once or twice. You said, "Don't worry—just write it—it will come out American—"

The thesis tries to show how the stuff that the old boys turned out (Chadwick, Converse, Shepherd-Gilbert-MacD.-Cadman (!), etc.) failed utterly to develop an American style or school or music at all, because their material (Negro, American Indian, etc.) was not common—the old problem of America the melting pot. . . . I will try to show that there is something American in the newer music, which relies not on folk material, but on a native spirit (like your music, and maybe Harris & Session's [*sic*]—I don't know), or which relies on a new American form, like Blitzstein's. Whether this is tenable or not, it is my thesis, and I'm sticking to it.

Now how to go about it? It means going through recent American things, finding those that sound for some reason, American and translate that American sound into musical terms. I feel convinced that there is such a thing or else why is it that the Variations sound fresh and vital and not stale and European and dry?[2]

This is why you can help, if you would. What music of what other composers in America would support my point, and where can I get hold of it? Would the music of Harris? Or Ives? Or Schuman? Or Piston? Or Berezowsky?

SOURCE: Vivian Perlis, "Dear Aaron, Dear Lenny: A Friendship in Letters," in *Aaron Copland and His World*, ed. Carol J. Oja and Judith Tick (Princeton, N.J.: Princeton University Press, 2005): 161–62.

This intimate letter, written by Bernstein to his wife, the Chilean actress Felicia Montealegre, affords a special glimpse into the intensity and precision with which Bernstein approached the musical realization of a theatrical character. The letter concerns a new song for Tony, the leading male character in West Side Story. *How to communicate Tony's character in music as well as lyrics? The song was most likely "Something's Coming."*

FROM LEONARD BERNSTEIN TO FELICIA,
AUGUST 8, 1957

8 Aug already!

Darling: I had a real scare with the news of Asian flu—& when your letter came about how you were all down with it I got scareder—But your cable made me feel better— please be careful! I can't bear the thought of you all sick.

I missed you terribly yesterday—We wrote a new song for Tony that's a killer, & it just wasn't the same not playing it first for you—It's really going to save his character— a driving 2/4 in the great tradition (but of course fucked up by me with the 3/4s and what not)—but it gives Tony balls—so that he doesn't emerge as just a euphoric dreamer—

These days have flown so—I don't sleep much; I work every—literally every— second (since I'm doing four jobs on this show—composing, lyric-writing, orchestrating, & rehearsing the cast). It's murder, but I'm excited. It may be something extraordinary. We're having our first run thru for PEOPLE on Friday—Please may they dig it! And fi- jate,[3] I leave for Washington on Tues. the 13th—so soon, so soon. It's all rushed by like a cyclone. Of course, we're way behind on orchestration, etc.—but that's the usual hassle.

How are you? You don't say. Are you fatter from eating? (me; I'm a bit skinnier.) Do you smoke? (I do, lots.) Have you skied? (I haven't). Do you love me?

Bless you & be well.

Love,

L

I adored Jamies letter.[4] Especially the lentils.

SOURCE: Leonard Bernstein, Letter to wife, Felicia, August 8, 1957, available at http:// memory.loc.gov/music/lbcorr/0062/001.gif.

~~~~~~~

This interview with a critic for the New York Times *took place at the height of Bern- stein's popularity as a conductor and influence as a public intellectual. The inter- view recapitulates running themes in Bernstein's writings, mainly the still unreal- ized potential of American musical theater and the need for a democratically viable aesthetic of contemporary engagement. Could borders between pop music and clas- sical music be erased? Could one specific religious tradition stand for many? Four years later Bernstein premiered his Mass, "A Theatre Piece for Singers, Players, and Dancers," at the opening of the Kennedy Center in Washington D.C. in 1971. In this Mass, Catholic liturgy is expanded by meditations and arias; Latin is complemented with English, a pit orchestra meets up with a rock band, and not one but two cho- ruses, along with a boy's choir, are supplemented by many individual soloists and dancers.*

Leonard Bernstein had just finished conducting a new recording of Mendelssohn's "Reformation" Symphony for Columbia Records and he invited me to sit with him in the control room backstage at Philharmonic Hall to listen to the playback. He insisted on hearing the exquisite little andante first, and as the New York Philharmonic sang enamoringly, he murmured his admiration. "Aren't they playing with freedom and love." They were.

The movement ended and Mr. Bernstein sat quietly, as if awed by the music's ineffable simplicity and purity. "Can you believe," he finally said with a sigh, "that Mendelssohn wrote that when he was not much more than 20?"

To a world-famous musician like Leonard Bernstein such a fact could be inhibiting. For he apparently wants, more than anything in music, to compose. In 1969 he will become the Philharmonic's conductor laureate, which means that he will lead several weeks of concerts, continue his justly admired TV programs and join the orchestra on an occasional tour. Although he may conduct another orchestra or an opera here and there, the bulk of his time will be devoted to composing.

But to a man who knows, loves and interprets the great masters, isn't the prospect of composing intimidating? It might well be if he lacked ideas and a sense of direction. Mr. Bernstein, who will be 50 years old in 1969, has both.

He may write in other forms, but the theater, not the opera house, is foremost in his mind. He regards the opera and the symphony orchestra as all but impossible to encompass for the contemporary composer. In the theater, he feels it is possible, at least for him, to be true to himself and the spirit of his time.

A FRESH SYNTHESIS

Does this mean creating a new form? Mr. Bernstein disclaims an ambition so grandiose, but there is no doubt that he is thinking about a fresh, modern synthesis of music and drama. He has been searching eagerly for a subject because he has a commission to write a theater piece for the opening of the Kennedy Center in Washington in several years. He has listened to suggestions like Hawthorne's "Scarlet Letter," but they don't ring a bell. The trouble is that in his inner ear he hears sounds different from those that would be suitable for Hawthorne.

He hears modern sounds—believe it or not, the beat and exuberant bounce of pop music. In the introduction to his new book, *The Infinite Variety of Music*, he wrote that "right now, on the 21st of June, 1966, I feel (that) pop music seems to me to be the only area where there is to be found unabashed vitality, the fun of invention, the feeling of fresh air." When we talked the other day, his attitude was unchanged.

He would like to find a subject to which he could bring his special feeling about this kind of music. He wants to help tell a story about this kind of music. He wants to help tell a story on the stage in the vernacular. In the telling, music must play an indispensable role and must function on many levels. He is eager to take on such a challenge; he has had nothing in the theater since *West Side Story* opened a decade ago.

He wondered why there had not been more originality in Broadway's musical theater in recent years. Was it lack of talent? Had composers failed to live up to their promise? When I suggested that some of America's most literate composers had not had much welcome or opportunity in the commercial theater, he agreed that this was possible. But, he demanded, didn't Broadway's imperative—the need to fill the house every night—have a lot to do with it?

CONFRONTING BROADWAY

He was not fretting, however, about whether the forms he envisaged would find a place on Broadway. Probably he doesn't have to. Broadway is eager for his next work, and one would predict that its public will be ready for it. If not, he surely will find another forum.

No one knows better than he the history of the *Singspiel,* the 18th-century form so popular in German-speaking lands. It was a loose, often careless amalgam of spoken scenes and musical numbers. Then Mozart came along, accepting the vernacular and investing it with his genius; the result, a masterpiece like *The Magic Flute.*

Lenny is not so presumptuous as to equate himself with Wolfgang Amadeus. But he believes it is time to take a step—then another and another—toward a marriage of our vernacular and music that reflects our time and place. With his talents, he may well be the composer to lead the way.

> *SOURCE:* Howard Taubman, "Bernstein as Composer. Maestro Contemplates Stage Synthesis of Vernacular and Music of Our Time," *New York Times,* January 13, 1967: 19.

~~~~~~~

NOTES

1. It is published in Leonard Bernstein, *Findings* (New York: Simon & Schuster, 1982): 36–102.
2. Copland's *Piano Variations* (1930).
3. In Spanish, *fíjate* means "listen up" or "pay attention."
4. Bernstein's daughter.

STEPHEN SONDHEIM

ON WRITING THEATER LYRICS

Stephen Sondheim (b. 1930) is a student and master of the American musical. Steeped in its traditions, he moved beyond them when he wrote the music as well as the lyrics for his own shows, beginning with *Company* (1970), which was followed by *A Little Night Music* (1973), *Sweeney Todd* (1979), and *Sunday in the Park with George* (1984), among others. Yet that classic division between "lyrics" and "music" misses the point of his gifts because his best songs are fusions, almost like Broadway "text-sound" pieces—where language shapes melody, and rhythm shapes words, and sometimes the sounds of words matter more than their meanings. These excerpts, which come from a long essay that Sondheim wrote, "Theater Lyrics," often refer to *Company*.

In retrospect, the theme and book of *Company*—a cynical yet heartfelt look at the fault lines in marriage—anticipated the ironic sensibility of the '90s. Its hero, Bobby, behaves like the modern-day TV sitcom character and star, Jerry Seinfeld. So fragmented is the plot line of the show that *Company*'s postmodernity derives from its being "really about nothing" (to paraphrase a Seinfeld theme)—except relationships—which are "everything." The absence of a conventional plot line, which gave rise to the genre term "concept musical," frames Sondheim's achievement all the more.

That point is made, perhaps inadvertently, by a documentary film about the production of the cast recording in 1970, which was released under the title *Original Cast Album: Company*. The 18-hour marathon studio session that produced the cast recording was filmed in cinema vérité style by D. A. Pennebaker. Screened to critical acclaim at the New York Film Festival in 1970 and then released in 2001 on DVD, Pennebaker's film makes the live "drama" in the recording studio the surrogate plot. This *Company* has no script, no set, no stage movement, no dancing—and Sondheim's version of musical marriage, where words and notes merge in a harmony of purpose, sounds more dazzling than ever.

〜〜〜〜〜〜
〜〜〜〜〜〜

I am just going to talk and I am just going to ramble. Some of the thoughts will be incomplete, some will be pontifical. And contentious and dogmatic and opinionated.

I'm going to talk only about theater lyrics, lyrics in a dramatic situation on a stage in terms of character—not pop lyrics. Most of the examples are going to be from my own work simply because I know it best; and from Oscar Hammerstein II and Cole Porter because they are among the few lyricists who have been deemed worthy of having their lyrics published in book form. I'll quote some others, but a lot will be from Hammerstein and Porter also because I like them a lot. Many of the examples from my own work will be songs you've never heard, cutouts from shows. Generally they are songs I like, and I seldom get a chance like this to lay them on people.

. . .

TWO PRINCIPLES

It's hard to talk about lyrics independently of music, but I will try. Obviously, all the principles of writing apply to lyrics: grace, affinity for words, a feeling for the weight of words, resonances, tone, all of that. But there are two basic differences between lyric writing and all other forms, and they dictate what you have to do as a lyric writer. They are not even rules, they are just principles. First, lyrics exist in time—as opposed to poetry, for example. You can read a poem at your own speed. I find most poetry very difficult, and there are a few poets I like very much. Wallace Stevens is one, but it takes me a good twenty minutes to get through a medium-length Wallace Stevens poem, and even then I don't understand a lot of it, yet I enjoy it and can read it at my own speed. That's the point. On the stage, the lyrics come at you and you hear them once. If there's a reprise you hear them twice, if there are two reprises you hear them three times, but that's all. Quite often you've had the experience, or you've heard friends say, "Gee, I didn't get the lyric until I heard the record." Well that's the problem, you only get it once. The music is a relentless engine and keeps the lyrics going.

This leads to the second principle. Lyrics go with music, and music is very rich, in my opinion the richest form of art. It's also abstract and does very strange things to your emotions. So not only do you have that going, but you also have lights, costumes, scenery, characters, performers. There's a great deal to hear and get. Lyrics therefore have to be underwritten. They have to be very simple in essence. That doesn't mean you can't do convoluted lyrics, but essentially the thought is what counts and you have to stretch the thought out enough so that the listener has a fair chance to get it. Many lyrics suffer from being much too packed.

I'll give you some samples of my own later, but my favorite example is "Oh, what a beautiful mornin' / Oh, what a beautiful day."[1] I would be ashamed to put it down on paper, it would look silly. What Hammerstein knew was that set to music it was going to have an enormous richness. It did, it's a *beautiful* lyric—but not on paper.

I have a book of Hammerstein's lyrics and one of Cole Porter's. Hammerstein's you fall asleep reading, while Porter's is an absolute delight, like reading light verse. "Oh what a beautiful mornin'" is not anywhere near as much fun to read as to hear. An imitation Hammerstein lyric that I did is "Maria" in *West Side Story*, a lyric I am not terribly fond of except for one good line: "Maria, I've just kissed a girl named Maria." I remember when I wrote that I thought, "I can't do that bland and banal but I'll fix it later." Of course when it went with the music it just soared, it was perfect. The fancier part of the lyric "Say it loud and there's music playing / Say it soft . . ." etc. etc. (I'm too embarrassed to quote it) is a very fruity lyric, too much, overripe.

Serious poets make very bad lyric writers. Auden, for example; his lyrics for [Stravinsky's opera] *The Rake's Progress* read brilliantly, they are sharp and witty but so packed and so full of reverberations and resonances that they are impossible to get, they are wearying, they are exhausting. It's an opera that should be read—or as with most operas, you can hear it without having to hear the words anyway because of the singers—but *the* point is that the lyrics are too packed.

I've always thought of lyric writing as a craft rather than an art. It's so small. There are how many words in an average lyric? I'm tending to write long songs these days, but the average lyric has maybe 60 to 80 words, so each word counts for a great deal. Now, any novelist or short story writer takes as much pains as he can over each individual word, but they are not as important as in a lyric, not even as important to a playwright because each lyric line is practically a scene in itself. If there are 12 lines in a song, this is like 12 scenes in a play, and if one word is off it's like an entire section of the scene.

The opening line of *Porgy and Bess* by DuBose Heyward, who wrote all the lyrics for the first act, is "Summertime and the livin' is easy"—and that "and" is worth a great deal of attention. I would write "Summertime when" but that "and" sets up a tone, a whole poetic tone, not to mention a whole kind of diction that is going to be used in the play; an informal, uneducated diction and a stream of consciousness, as in many of the songs like "My Man's Gone Now." It's the exact right word and that word is worth its weight in gold. "Summertime, *when* the livin' is easy" is a boring line compared to "Summertime *and*." The choices of "ands" and "buts" become almost traumatic as you are writing a lyric—or should, anyway—because each one weighs so much.

Oscar Hammerstein once told me how astonished he was to learn that the sculptor of the Statue of Liberty had carved the top of the head as carefully as the rest of the statue, even though he couldn't possible have known that one day there would be airplanes. That's what you have to do in a lyric, too—every word counts, whether the audience hears it specifically or not. In "Everything's Coming Up Roses" there was very little to say in the lyric after the title was over, so I decided that I would give it its feeling by restricting myself to images of traveling, children and show business, because the scene was in a railroad station and was about a mother pushing her child into show business. Now that may be of no interest except to somebody doing a doctorate in 200 years on the use of traveling images in *Gypsy*. But the point is, it's there, and it informs the whole song.

On one level, I suppose, lyric writing is an elegant form of puzzle, and I am a great puzzle fan. There's a great deal of joy for me in the sweat involved in the working out of lyrics, but it can lead to bloodlessness, and I've often been capable of writing bloodless lyrics (there are a number of them in *West Side Story*).

Anyway, all the principles extend from this one, which is lyrics existing in time. They also help shape the music, just as the music shapes them. The rigidity of lyric writing is like sonnets, and onstage this rigidity makes creating characters difficult, because characters, if they are to be alive, don't tend to talk in well-rounded phrases. But on the other hand, the power that is packed into the rigid form can give it enormous punch and make the characters splat out at you. An example from my own work is "The Ladies Who Lunch" in *Company* which is so packed that it gives out a ferocity, mainly because I chose a fairly rigid form, full of inner rhymes and with the lines in the music almost square—not that it's sung square, I mean the lines are very formed.

. . .

"THE GENESIS OF SONGS"

To illustrate another thing I do, I remember I played "Maria" for Jerome Robbins, and he liked the song just fine but got very angry about the pauses. He said, "'Maria, I've just met a girl named Maria, and suddenly that name will never be the same to me,' and then there's this bar-and-a-half pause. What am I supposed to do there?" I said, "Well, he's just standing there on the stage." Jerry said, "But how am I supposed to direct him?" I said, "Well, can't he just stand there?" Jerry said, "You've got to give me something for him to do, or do you want to stage it?" Choreographers and many directors don't like pauses, but he had a point there that's very important. You should stage your numbers when you are writing them. Never just write a love song and give it to the director and the choreographer, expecting them to invent. That's not their job. That's their job *after* you've invented. When you've invented the staging, they can do anything they want with it, completely change it, but they have to have at least a blueprint, some idea of the theatrical use of the song. "Company" I staged in my own head all the way through to the second chorus including the use of the long word "love," which was to get the cast off the elevators and down to the main level. I wanted that to be the first time the elevators moved, but we couldn't work that out specifically. I knew where Bobby was standing. I knew in *my* head where all the people were. This had nothing to do with what Michael Bennett [the director] eventually did with it, except that he was delighted to receive a general blueprint which helped him over certain hurdles. He was able to invent freely because he never felt he would be hung the next day in rehearsal by having to wonder what to do about a blank space.

. . .

In the genesis of a song, another important principle that I've always believed in is: content dictates form. There's a song in *Company* called "Getting Married Today." In content, it is about this hysterical girl who doesn't want to get married except that she's forced to in her own head, so it suggested the counterpoint and the contrast between a serene choir and a hysterical lady, between the slow and the fast and the serene and the hysterical.

Looking back at the first page of notes I ever made about *Company*, I see that we sat around and talked about how to turn these one-act plays into a musical. We talked about the central character, and Hal Prince said it would be nice to have a number called "Company." Well, "company" is a word you can't rhyme—except Lorenz Hart rhymed it with "bump a knee," which is not my kind of rhyme—so it would be a little hard to do it as a title refrain. Then Hal said, "And also I would like it to introduce the various styles of the show, the way we are going to cut back and forth; also I would like to introduce the main character and include all the other characters; also I would like it to use the set . . ." So I replied in my usual grudging way, "Well, I am not sure if I can, well, let me see if I can do it, and maybe I can write the score, I don't know."

I have my sketch sheets here. Let me read you some of the notes I put down: "Everybody loves Robert (Bob, Bobby) . . ." the idea of nicknames had already occurred to me. Then I had Robert say, "I've got the best friends in the world," and then the line occurred to me, "You I love and you I love and you I love," and then, talking about marriage, "A country I've never been to," and "Who wants vine-covered cottages, marriage is for children." It's all Bob's attitude: "Companion for life, who wants that?" And then he says, "I've got company, love is company, three is company, friends are company," and I started a list of what's company. Then I started to expand the lines: "Love is what you need is company. What I've got as friends is company. Good friends, weird friends, married friends, days go, years go, full of company." I started to spin free associations, and I got to "Phones ring, bells buzz, door clicks, company, call back, get a bite," and the whole notion of short phrases, staccato phrases, occurred to me. By the time I got through just listing general thoughts, I had a smell of the rhythm of the vocal line, so that when I was able to turn to the next page and start expanding it I got into the whole lists of things: "No ties, small lies. So much, too much. Easy, comfy, hearts pour, the nets descend, private jokes," all short phrases—but what came out of it eventually was the form of that song, which worked out better than I had expected.

SOURCE: From Otis L. Guernsey, Jr., ed., *Playwrights, Lyricists, Composers on Theater* (New York: Dodd, Mead, 1974): 61, 64–66, 72–74.

~~~~~~~~~~

NOTE

1.   This is the first line of the song which opens Rodgers and Hammerstein's *Oklahoma!* (1943). See chapter 103.

MUDDY WATERS EXPLAINS WHY
"IT DOESN'T PAY TO RUN FROM TROUBLE"

Muddy Waters (1915–1983), who was born McKinley A. Morganfield, used bottle-neck slide guitar and Delta blues as his bridge to cross over into electric guitar, amplified music, and Chess Records in Chicago. He was famously "discovered" by Alan Lomax in Mississippi, soon after recording blues sides for the Library of Congress. Waters learned his craft from some legendary bluesmen like Robert Johnson and Son House. In Chicago, he added rhythm and switched to the electric guitar, collaborating with Jimmy Rogers (1924–1997), another electric guitarist, and working out a high-voltage way of delivering musical energy. It took Waters a while to find his Chicago style; city people initially rejected his country musical manners. By the 1960s, Waters had inspired countless musicians, including the Rolling Stones, who adopted their name from a 1950 release, emulated his dynamic style, and made him internationally renowned.

In this interview, he has yet to become the famous icon for British blues fans. On the contrary, he is validating the psychological truth and integrity of his music to the readers of the *Chicago Defender*—the leading African-American news weekly of the time—explaining why his kind of blues still matters. On the same page in the adjacent column to this feature, the newspaper reported the death of Charlie Parker, the jazz genius of bebop.

≈≈≈
≈≈≈
≈≈≈

When I was a kid, growing up in Rollingfork, Miss., there were a lot of things happening around me to make me sad.

People talk about Negroes in the South having trouble, but in my lifetime, I've seen a lot of progress made and a lot of Southerners getting to learn to appreciate my people as human beings.

I'm not up on a platform preaching. I make my living recording blues which sell to millions of people all over the country and appearing in night clubs which, fortunately for me, are usually jammed with people who want to hear my music.

I'm grateful to the Lord for giving me the talent and the opportunity to become successful with my music. But even if I couldn't make a great deal of money at it, I'd be playing the blues in somebody's place where somebody could hear me play them.

Somebody once asked me what my blues meant. I answered in one word—"trouble." I don't know whether they got the message but what I meant was that the blues—from the gutbucket, alley blues which I can offer right straight up to the sophisticated, drawing room lament fashioned by that master musician, Duke Ellington—the blues belong to my people. The blues are an expression of trouble in mind, trouble in body, trouble in soul. And when a man has trouble, it helps him to express it, to let it be known.

TROUBLE THE DEVIL

Some people like to try to run from trouble. To go off in a corner somewhere and mourn about their problems. Trouble ain't nothin' but the devil operating. And as long as there's a God in the skies—a God merciful enough to give you a prayerbook or a hymn, or a banjo or a guitar with which to express yourself and defy the devil, there's no sense in getting lost in a corner and giving the devil a victory.

I can hear some of my friends right now. "Muddy," they'll say, "How you gonna connect God up with a guitar—with jazz—with playing in a night club or cutting a blues record?" All I've got to answer is that the devil put everything on earth that is destructive and God gave us everything possible to be a Christian in the way you do whatever you do. The devil can quote scripture, they say, so I guess it's fair for good people to take the devil's tools and use them to live a good and decent life.

Back in Rollingfork, Miss., I made up my mind when I was pretty young that I was going to live a good life. My name wasn't Muddy Waters then. It was McKinley Morganfield. But my folks called me Muddy—and don't ask me why. After I got into show business, the public added the "Waters." Lots of people think I wrote the tune "Id Rather Drink Muddy Water." Sorry to say I can't claim that one. Fact is, I was hearing that tune when I was a youngster.

In those boyhood days I always had an ear for the blues. I loved the blues. I guess I was born with two things—trouble and love for the blues. The music of Big Bill, Lonnie Johnson, Leroy Cobb and others fascinated me. My daddy played a guitar in his day. But it was a good buddy of mine, Scott Bohanna, who taught me guitar after I'd been fooling around with the harmonica for a few years. My uncle, Joe Grant, gave me a chance to get some real kicks out of the songs I was writing—alley blues, country blues—what people call gut-bucket. People down home appreciated and like[d] my music. They understood it.

But it was a different story when I came to big time Chicago. I found out that my people who had left the South, even though they still weren't really free, wanted to run off in a corner and escape their troubles. They wanted to make believe trouble didn't exist. The way I felt, that's the best way to let trouble beat you. The way to defeat trouble is to look it straight in the eye. That's what I was doing when I sang the blues.

DIDN'T LIKE BLUES

The blues didn't move anybody in the big city. They called it sharecropper music. They said I was a square and would never get anywhere trying to sell the public that kind of stuff. They laughed at me when I wailed the blues. I had every reason to believe they had a right to laugh. For quite a while I didn't get anywhere with my music. I was working but only because I wanted to work— not because anyone wanted me. People let me appear in their places because I would work almost for nothing. If I had been forced to depend on my income as a musician, I would have starved to death. But I didn't intend to starve. And I didn't intend to give up my determination to play the blues. So I sold venetian blinds whenever I could get a chance.

My big break came when a talent scout for Leonard Chess of Chess Records heard me in a club. He understood. And he believed that what I was doing could be commercial in a big way. He took me to Leonard. To Leonard my music was a big joke. He didn't believe in my blues. He thought it was a waste of money to invest in my career. But he didn't want to let the talent scout down and he took an immediate liking to me. My first record for Chess Records was "Feel Like Goin' Home." It went over like mad. Then the talent scout knew he had been right. Leonard knew that he had played a good hunch even if he hadn't wanted to. And I knew that I had been right to stick to my guns in spite of everything.

After that, I had it made. People began to listen to the blues they had laughed at. They began to realize that these blues expressed their own feelings when they were low or discouraged. It's a funny thing about people and trouble. When a person thinks he's the only one in hot water, he's miserable. But when he gets to realize that others have the same kind of trouble— or even worse—he understands that life isn't just picking on him alone.

I had lots of records that sold in the hundreds of thousands. My most successful ones— the ones that sold a half million or more—were "Screamin' and Cryin'," "Rollin' Stone," and "Still a Fool," "Hootchie Kootchie Man," "I'm Ready" and "Just Make Love to Me."

Wonderful things happened to me because of my success on records. The first was that a friendship developed between Leonard Chess and myself for which I wouldn't take a million dollars. Here was a guy who had blind faith. He didn't believe in my blues but he believed in me as a person when we started out. I got more of a kick [proving myself to him as a performer] out of the fact that we had become more than business associates—real intimate friends. I tell everyone who asks that the one person responsible for my success is Leonard.

DEEJAYS HELPED

But there are other factors which helped to make my career an important one. The second thing that happened was that disc jockeys all over the nation gave me a break. If it hadn't been for them, I would still be playing for people as a favor. I wouldn't dare to begin [to] name the radio

Bluesmen as heroes in the community. Photograph by Ernest C. Withers. Identifications left to right: unidentified, B. B. King, Howlin' Wolf, Muddy Waters, Ivory Joe Hunter, and WDIA Little Leaguers, Memphis, ca. 1960.

people who have helped me. It would take all the pages in the *Defender*. But I couldn't sleep if I didn't say that among them, Sam Evans, of Chicago, went out of his way to push me and my music.

There was a third wonderful thing that happened to me. Success in recording brought me engagements all over the nation. During my travels, I met and married a wonderful girl. Her name was Geneva Wade. She is from Lexington, Miss. I'd come across many, many women but it seems like you know immediately when you find the one who's exactly right for you. Geneva was and she is today. When I met her, even though I was a recording success, there were still people who scorned my music. Geneva encouraged me to ignore them and fight for what I wanted to accomplish. I'll never be able to put into words the way I feel about her, her love and support. Maybe some day I'll write a song and do it. We have a wonderful life together. We have a 19-year-old daughter, Azine, and a 14-year-old son, Charles. We have just bought a home in Chicago.

Somebody once wrote that a whole school of blues has come about in imitation of Muddy Waters. I don't agree that it is imitation. No one can duplicate the blues I create and play. And neither can I imitate the ones who came after me. What makes me proud is that, in making a success for myself in Chicago, I was able to open the doors for other blues artists to come up. Maybe that happened in other parts of the country too.

My daddy, Ollie Morganfield, who still lives in Rollingfork, is proud of my success. But he is more proud that I remember what he once told me. He advised me to forget about the folks who laughed at me. But, he warned, if I ever got to be big, I should never feel like saying "I told you so."

I don't feel like that. I feel as though these folks should know now that it doesn't pay to run from trouble. Like Joe Louis said, you can run, but you can't hide. Long as we're Negroes, we got a right to sing the blues—and long as we sing them, we ought to be proud of them.

SOURCE: Muddy Waters interviewed by Alfred Duckett, "'Got a Right to Sing Blues'—Muddy Waters: Something That Troubles Gets Needed Airing," *Chicago Defender,* March 26, 1955, 6.

ℰLVIS PRESLEY IN THE EYE OF A MUSICAL TWISTER

(Newspaper Reviews, Gould, Lewis)

Elvis Presley (1935–1977), the great entertainer who led the rock–and-roll revolution in the mid-1950s, was trapped by his sudden rise to fame. Presley's flight to and from celebrity was jet-fueled by television and the unexpected charisma of his stage persona. Yet his gifts and musicality have only recently received their full due in a two-volume biography by Peter Guralnick. The documents in this chapter focus on Presley's beginnings and perhaps help to humanize the star of Graceland.

The first selection comes from a northern music magazine appalled at the racist actions of local authorities in Memphis in 1948, the year Presley's family moved there from Tupelo, Mississippi.

MEMPHIS GESTAPO SMASHES RECORDS,
EYES RADIO-FLICKS

Memphis—"Home-of-the-Blues." Censorship, already firmly established as official for movies and stage shows, reached into a new category this week when Vice-Mayor Joe Boyle ordered police smashing of 400 copies of three blues records, labeled "obscene" by the police department, of which Boyle is commissioner. Sale or jukebox use of the platters has been forbidden in Memphis.

"Banned-by-Boyle" were "Move Your Hand, Baby" by Crown Prince Waterford, "Take Your Hand Off of It" by Billy Hughes, and "Operation Blues" featuring Amos Milburn.

Boyle said an anonymous caller had complained to police about one of the discs which he heard on a local jukebox. The complainant said the record had already been banned in Dallas. Memphis police confiscated all copies of the platter in question, smashed them, and ordered juke ops to bring other such records to police headquarters. Police Chief Seabrook then called in Boyle to hear the other two, and the absolute ban is the result of his audition.

CENSOR COMMENDED

The commissioner took advantage of the situation to commend highly Lloyd Binford, head of the Memphis censorship board, whose action in banning [the film] *New Orleans* because of Louis Armstrong's prominent role, and other motion picture deletions of Pearl Bailey, Lena Horne, Rochester, and Farina of "Our Gang" have resulted in nation-wide publicity. Binford also prohibited the local showing of [the film] *Annie Get Your Gun* because of Negroes in the cast. Boyle said "Binford deserves a monument . . . for trying to clean up the picture show business."

The Freedom Train's scheduled Memphis stop was cancelled by its sponsors, the American Heritage Foundation, because of insistence upon segregation by Memphis Mayor Pleasants, although other non-segregated showings in the South have occurred without notable incident.[1]

RADIO NEXT

Possible censorship of radio programs in Memphis was forecast by Boyle's condemnation of "supposed-to-be comedians," who he said were "pulling some stuff they couldn't have gotten by with in the old shooting days of the wild and woolly West." He declined to name the programs involved "but when I have to I will do it." He said national programs were out of his jurisdiction, implying otherwise as to local shows.

Asked by interviewers under what law the platters were banned, Boyle replied "Police power! That goes a long way. It covers a multitude of sins."

Which should rank as the understatement of the year.—bee

SOURCE: "Memphis Gestapo Smashes Records, Eyes Radio-Flicks," *Down Beat* (February 25, 1948): 3. Reproduced in facsimile in Colin Escott with Martin Hawkins, *Good Rockin' Tonight: Sun Records and the Birth of Rock 'n' Roll* (New York: St. Martin's, 1991): 84.

After Presley signed with RCA, he was booked on national network television. On the variety show hosted by the veteran comic Milton Berle on June 5, 1956, Presley sang "Hound Dog," written by Jerry Leiber and Mike Stoller, which had been previously recorded by blues singer Big Mama Thornton. Immediately, a rhythm-and-blues number geared to a black adult audience became a rock-and-roll hit for white teenagers. Presley's sexual charisma made him a target for social anxiety about "juvenile delinquency." Jack Gould, a respected journalist and media critic, slammed him after Presley's now-legendary second appearance on the Ed Sullivan Show *on September 9, 1956.*

ELVIS PRESLEY: LACK OF RESPONSIBILITY IS SHOWN BY TV IN EXPLOITING TEENAGERS

Television broadcasters cannot be asked to solve life's problems. But they can be expected to display adult leadership and responsibility in areas where they do have some significant influence. This they have hardly done in the case of Elvis Presley, entertainer and phenomenon.

Last Sunday on the Ed Sullivan show Mr. Presley made another of his appearances and attracted a record audience. In some ways it was perhaps the most unpleasant of his recent three performances.

Mr. Presley initially disturbed adult viewers—and instantly became a martyr in the eyes of his teen-age following—for his striptease behavior on last spring's Milton Berle program. Then with Steve Allen he was much more sedate. On the Sullivan program he injected movements of the tongue and indulged in wordless singing that were singularly distasteful.

At least some parents are puzzled or confused by Presley's almost hypnotic power; others are concerned; perhaps most are a shade disgusted and content to permit the Presley fad to play itself out.

Neither criticism of Presley nor of the teen-agers who admire him is particularly to the point. Presley has fallen into a fortune with a routine that in one form or another has always existed on the fringe of show business; in his gyrating figure and suggestive gestures the teen-agers have found something that for the moment seems exciting or important.

VOID

Quite possibly Presley just happened to move in where society has failed the teen-ager. Certainly, modern youngsters have been subjected to a great deal of censure and perhaps too little understanding. Greater in their numbers than ever before, they may have found in Presley a rallying point, a nationally prominent figure who seems to be on their side. And, just as surely, there are limitless teen-agers who cannot put up with the boy, either vocally or calisthenically.

Family counselors have wisely noted that ours is still a culture in a stage of frantic and tense transition. With even 16-year-olds capable of commanding $20 or $30 a week in their spare time, with access to automobiles at an early age, with communications media of all kinds exposing them to new thoughts very early in life, theirs indeed is a high degree of independence. Inevitably it has been accompanied by a lessening of parental control.

Small wonder, therefore, that the teen-ager is susceptible to overstimulation from the outside. He is at the age when an awareness of sex is both thoroughly natural and normal, when latent rebellion is to be expected. But what is new and a little discouraging is the willingness and indeed eagerness of reputable business men to exploit those critical factors beyond all reasonable grounds.

Television surely is not the only culprit. Exposé magazines, which once were more or less bootleg items, are now carried openly on the best newsstands. The music-publishing business—as Variety most courageously has pointed out—has all but disgraced itself with some of the "rock 'n' roll" songs it has issued. Some of the finest recording companies have been willing to go right along with the trend, too.

DISTINCTIVE

Of all these businesses, however, television is in a unique position. First and foremost, it has access directly to the home and its wares are free. Second, the broadcasters are not only addressing themselves to the teen-agers but, much more importantly, also to the lower age groups. When Presley executes his bumps and grinds, it must be remembered by the Columbia Broadcasting System that even the 12-year-old's curiosity may be overstimulated. It is on this score that the adult viewer has every right to expect sympathetic understanding and cooperation from a broadcaster.

A perennial weakness in the executive echelons of the networks is their opportunistic rationalization of television's function. The industry lives fundamentally by the code of giving the public what it wants. This is not the place to argue the artistic foolishness of such a standard; in the case of situation comedies and other escapist diversions it is relatively unimportant.

But when this code is applied to teen-agers just becoming conscious of life's processes, not only is it manifestly without validity but it also is perilous. Catering to the interests of the younger generation is one of television's main jobs; because those interests do not always coincide with parental tastes should not deter the broadcasters. But selfish exploitation and commercialized overstimulation of youth's physical impulses is certainly a gross national disservice.

SENSIBLE

The issue is not one of censorship, which solves nothing; it is one of common sense. It is no impingement on the medium's artistic freedom to ask the broadcaster merely to exercise good sense and display responsibility. It is no blue-nosed suppression of the proper way of depicting life in the theatre to expect stage manners somewhat above the level of the carnival sideshow.

In the long run, perhaps Presley will do everyone a favor by pointing up the need for earlier sex education so that neither his successors nor TV can capitalize on the idea that his type of routine is somehow highly tempting yet forbidden fruit. But that takes time, and meanwhile the broadcasters at least can employ a measure of mature and helpful thoughtfulness in not contributing further to the exploitation of the teenager.

With congested schools, early dating, the appeals of the car, military service, acceptance by the right crowd, sex and the normal parental pressures, the teen-ager has all the problems he needs.

MERCENARY

To resort to the world's oldest theatrical come-on just to make a fast buck from such a sensitive individual is cheap and tawdry stuff. At least Presley is honest in what he is doing. That the teen-ager sometimes finds it difficult to feel respect for the moralizing older generation may of itself be an encouraging sign of his intelligence. If the profiteering hypocrite is above reproach and Presley isn't, today's youngsters might well ask what God do adults worship.

> SOURCE: Jack Gould, "Elvis Presley: Lack of Responsibility Is Shown by TV in Exploiting Teen-agers," *New York Times*, September 16, 1956.

~~~~~~

Reacting to the obscenity and indecency charges growing in the press, Presley defended himself in an interview with a reporter in Charlotte, North Carolina, who was already both amused and cynical about the publicity hype. According to his biographer, Peter Guralnick, Presley rarely exploded at the press quite so baldly. The interview also contains an important statement by Presley of his admiration for the meaning as well as the music of the blues.

ELVIS DEFENDS LOW-DOWN STYLE

Elvis Presley is a worried man. Some, that is, for a man with four Cadillacs and a $40,000 weekly pay check. Critics are saying bad things about him. It has been especially rough during the past three weeks. And that is why he bucked his manager's orders to stay away from newsmen in Charlotte, Tuesday until show time. That is why he refused to stay in the seclusion of his hotel room. At 4:10 p.m. he couldn't stand it any longer and, with "Cousin Junior," left the room.

He walked quickly to a restaurant a few doors away for a barbecue, flirtation with a few women and a 30-minute round of pool next door.

"Sure, I'll talk. Sit down. Most of you guys, though, been writin' bad things about me, man!"

His knees bounced while he sat. His hands drummed a tattoo on the table top. Eyes, under long lashes, darted from booth to booth, firing rapid winks at the girls who stared at him.

"Hi ya baby," he breathed. And she flopped back in the booth like she'd been pole-axed.

"This Crosby guy, whoever he is. He says I'm obscene on the Berle show. Nasty. What does he know?"[2]

"Did you see the show? This Debra Paget is on the same show. She wore a tight thing with feathers on the behind where they wiggle the most. And I never saw anything like it. Sex? Man, she bumped and pooshed out all over the place. I'm like Little Boy Blue. And who do they say is obscene? Me!

"It's because I make more money than Debra. Them critics don't like to see nobody win doing any kind of music they don't know nothin' about!"

And he started to eat. The waitress brought his coffee.

Elvis reached down and fingered the lace on her slip.

"Aren't you the one!"

"I'm the one, baby!"

Presley says he does what he does because this is what is making money. And it is music that was around before he was born.

"The colored folks been singing it and playing it just like I'm doin' now, man, for more years than I know. They played it like that in the shanties and in their juke joints and nobody paid it no mind 'til I goose[d] it up. I got it from them. Down in Tupelo, Mississippi, I used to hear old Arthur Crudup bang his box the way I do now, and I said if I ever got to the place I could feel all old Arthur felt, I'd be a music man like nobody ever saw."

Yep, some of the music is low-down.

"But not like Crosby means. There is low-down people and high-up people but all of them get the kind of feeling this rock 'n' roll music tells about."

Elvis says he doesn't know how long rock and roll will last.

"When it's gone, I'll switch to something else. I like to sing ballads the way Eddie Fisher does and the way Perry Como does. But the way I'm singing now is what makes the money. Would you change if you was me?"

Investments?

"I haven't got to the place for investments. I put it in the bank, man, because I don't know how long it will last."

How about the Cadillacs?

"Yeh, that's right. I got me four Cadillacs. I keep two at home and two with me. One pink and white."

He never reads his fan mail. "I got nine secretaries in Madison, Tenn., to do that. If I meet somebody on the road I want to keep on knowing I give 'em my home address."

Little Rosie Tatsis walked up to the booth and held out a trembling hand.

Elvis gave her the autograph.

"Look, I'm shaking all over," she tittered.

And the grown-up girls in the next booth and Elvis swapped long, searching looks.

Elvis fingered the collar of his shirt, opened half-way down his chest.

"Some people like me. There's more people than critics."

The people who like him, he said, include Eddie Fisher, Como, Liberace, Kate Smith, Bob Hope and Guy Lombardo. And there are more. Lots more.

"When I sang hymns back home with Mom and Pop I stood still and I looked like you feel when you sing a hymn. When I sing this rock and roll, my eyes won't stay open and my legs won't stand still. I don't care what they say, it ain't nasty."

SOURCE: Kays Gary, "Elvis Defends Low-Down Style," *Charlotte Observer*, June 26, 1956, B1. Partially quoted in Peter Guralnick, *Last Train to Memphis: The Rise of Elvis Presley* (Boston: Little, Brown, 1994): 289–90.

In this selection, Presley's friend Jerry Lee Lewis (b. 1935) offers a glimpse of the an-
tics of the Sun Records crowd and some insight into the influence of white gospel
music on rockabilly.

In this business, whatever you do you answer to the public. The public has a right to demand answers from you, and I don't care what it is, if you do something that is even semiwrong in any kind of way, you are going to pay for it.

When I married my cousin, I paid. God, I didn't know the hole could be that deep. She was a good ole gal. We were married for fourteen years, but it didn't work out. But I knew even before I married her that I was going to pay for it. Everybody warned me—Sam Philips, Judd Philips. They said, "Oh, Jerry Lee, you are going to ruin the greatest career in the world if you marry her."

Even Elvis. He laughed. Elvis Presley said, "You're not going to marry this little girl, are you? This is a joke, isn't it?"

I said, "No, I'm going to marry her."

And he said, "Well, God bless you, Jerry Lee. You just saved my career."

We were just cutting up, joking. But he knew what he was talking about because I did pay.

I remember the first time I met Elvis. He came up to Sun Records to meet me, and I wanted to meet him. Carl Perkins was doing a session, which was a flop, as usual, and Johnny Cash just happened to be there, too.

Elvis started in '53, and I started in '56. Elvis was something else. He was my main man. First time I heard an Elvis Presley record I was living in Louisiana, eighteen miles out of Monroe, where I met my first wife. I married her when I was fifteen. Shows you what sense I had. But I heard Elvis singing, "Blue moon of Kentucky, keep on shining," and I said, "Wow, looka right here. I don't know who this dude is, but somebody done opened the door."

Success for me started with "Crazy Arms," my first record. "Whole Lotta Shakin' Goin' On" was my second record, and it was banned for eight months. No one would have any part of it. Then we got it on the Steve Allen show, and it broke nationwide.

That's right around the time when I met Alan Freed. Looking back, I didn't know how to deal with success. I was a kid. I didn't really know what was going on. Probably I still don't. I never was the smartest person in the world. I just played my piano and sang my songs and left the business to people like Sam and Judd and Alan Freed. Brainy people. Without the disc jockeys, people like me couldn't have made it. We created payola through Alan Freed and Dick Clark by giving them money. They did it. I was only a kid.

I was raised Pentecostal, and I guess it's how you are raised that determines how you grow up. You learn that God is a big God. You don't put him in one corner. He spreads himself out.

I got a cousin, you know, Jimmy Swaggart [a popular media evangelist]. I was at his house recently, and he wants to know why I don't do what he's doing. And I tell him real quick, I don't do what he's doing because he can't do what I do. I was a preacher before he was. But I started growing up and realizing that I couldn't carry the whole world on my shoulders and tell everybody they had to be exactly like me, or otherwise they were going to hell. That is not right.

I went to Bible college in Waxahatchie, Texas, and I preached for three years. I was probably one of the best. A lot of people were saved under my missionary [sic]. A lot of people are missionaries now who were saved under my missionary. They come to see my shows, and they knew me when. But I don't try to tell Jimmy Swaggart what to do. What he's doing is right for him.

All my life I've tried to open doors. I was a stylist, and no matter what I did people related. They took notice of what I did. Whether they liked it or not, accepted it or not, dismissed it or not, it was all OK. Of course, if they dismissed it, they lost.

You make your bed, and then you have to lay in it. We learn from our mistakes. We're not perfect. I don't believe that Jerry Lee Lewis was a stupid enough person to have gotten married as many times as he did, but there had to be some reason for it. It's nobody's fault but mine.

I was lucky to have great people around me like Sam and Judd, and Jack Clement, who made the records. Jack's still in Nashville. Great ole boy. Sure could drink. Still can. I once went to a party at Jack Clement's house, me and Elvis, and we got naked and rode our motorcycles down the street. Buck naked. And this policeman on a horse sees us. It was two-thirty, three o'clock in the morning. It was awful. If anybody would have seen us, they never would have bought another record. If that cop would have arrested us, we never would have gotten out of jail.

Back then, down South where me and Elvis came from, that time of the morning all the lights are out. We didn't know there'd be a policeman on a horse. Otherwise we wouldn't have done it. It was only for thirty-five or forty seconds, 'round the corner and back. How it ever happened I will never know. We were just kids. Jack was a kid. Me and Elvis were kids. Actually, I think Elvis had shorts on. You could say Elvis was nearly naked. But it was funny.

I was very honored to be the first performer inducted into the Rock 'n' Roll Hall of Fame. Rock 'n' roll went through a lot of hell, man. People have put it through a lot of pain. But it's carried its own load, and it's come through. You are not going to beat it.

SOURCE: Joe Smith, ed., *Off the Record: An Oral History of Popular Music* (New York: Warner, 1988): 97–99.

~~~~~~~~

NOTES

1. The Freedom Train was a traveling exhibition of historical documents from the National Archives related to democracy and civil liberties. No segregation by race was allowed in visitor lines or inside the train itself, which caused the Memphis actions. The exhibition visited many other southern cities without incident.

2. John Crosby (1912–1991) was a well-known columnist and radio and television critic for the *New York Herald Tribune* from 1946–1965.

113

CHUCK BERRY IN HIS OWN WORDS

Chuck Berry (b. 1926) made the electric guitar his partner on the stage of rock and roll: his inimitable guitar openings became his still immediately recognizable musical fingerprints. Born in St. Louis, he eventually moved to Chicago where he signed with Chess Records. Berry single-handedly shifted Chess away from rhythm and blues into rock and roll. He listened and learned from many styles of popular music, including gospel, blues, commercial swing, jazz, and country music. His hometown audiences called him a "black hillbilly," but Berry aimed at a new generation of teenagers, both white and black. A gifted storyteller, he wrote songs with lyrics aimed at adolescent lives, and his movements on stage spelled freedom. So many of his songs have turned into classics, revived by one generation of bands after another, that a list of "covered Berries" includes songs by Count Basie, the Ramones, the Beatles, the Grateful Dead, Linda Ronstadt, the Animals, Bruce Springsteen, and Jimi Hendrix.[1]

Mother and Daddy were of the Baptist Faith and sang in the Antioch Church Choir. The choir rehearsed in our home around the upright piano in the front room. My very first memories, while still in my baby crib, are of musical sounds—the assembled pure harmonies of the Baptist hymns, dominated by my mother's soprano and supported by my father's bass blending with the stirring rhythms of the true Baptist soul.

. . .

Around this time [early 1940s] Lucy [Berry's sister] took seriously to singing and her voice was said to be comparable to Marian Anderson's. The rest of us had started sneaking in records of blues singers like St. Louis Jimmy doing his "Going Down Slow," "Worried Life Blues" by Big Maceo, "In the Dark" by Lil Green, "C.C. Rider" by Bea Boo, "Please, Mr. Johnson" by Buddy and Ella Johnson, "A Tisket a Tasket" by Ella Fitzgerald, and you name it, but Lucy stuck with stuff like "Ave Maria" and "God Bless America." . . .

When I began to listen to boogie woogie and swing my desire to hear anything without a beat diminished. I became a fan of Tampa Red, Big Maceo, Lonnie Johnson, Arthur Crudup, Muddy Waters, Lil Green, Bea Boo, Rosetta Tharp[e], and later Louis Jordan, T-Bone Walker, Buddy Johnson, Nat Cole, and Charles Brown, all of whom were black artists whose songs were only played by the black radio station in East St. Louis [Illinois]. Whenever Thelma [Berry's sister], Henry [Berry's father], and Lucy bought any records they favored Duke Ellington, Count Basie, and Tommy Dorsey, whose recording "Tommy Dorsey's Boogie Woogie" was the tune that launched my determination to produce such music. The music of Harry James, Glenn Miller, and a lot of the white bands were beginning to "get down" then and show up on the jukeboxes and black radio programs.

. . .

It [the electric guitar] was my first really good-looking instrument to have and hold. From the inspiration of it, I began really searching at every chance I got for opportunities to play music.

During the summer of '51 I bought a secondhand reel-to-reel magnetic wire recorder from a friend who recorded me singing on it at his house. I think I would have stolen it if he hadn't sold it as I was completely fascinated by its reproduction qualities. It was that inspiration that started me to record the first of my original improvisations, both poetical and melodical.

With the recorder, I started hanging around more with Ira Harris. I picked up a lot of new swing riffs and ideas from Ira's playing, which was similar to the style of Charlie Christian's. Ira showed me many licks and riffs on the guitar that came to be the foundation of the style that is said to be Chuck Berry's. Carl Hogan, the guitarist in Louis Jordan's Tympany Five, was another idol of mine. I buckled down and started taking seriously the task of learning to play the guitar. I studied a book of guitar chords by Nick Mannaloft [Manoloff] and practiced daily. The chord book led to my getting a textbook explaining the basics of theory and harmony and the fundamental functions of notes, staff, and scale. It's amazing how much you can learn if your intentions are truly earnest.

On June 13, 1952, Tommy Stevens phoned me to ask if I could sing with his three-piece combo at Huff's Garden. It was to be our first time to play together since the All Men's Review yet we had seen each other at many intervals. My heart leaped as I answered, "When?" We squared away the address, agreed on the finances, and I showed up shouting that Saturday and every Saturday thereafter on through to December, earning six dollars a night. It was my first paid night-club appearance.

The combo, a small group, consisted of Tommy on lead guitar, Pee Wee (I can't remember his last name) was on alto sax, and I was on guitar singing the blues. Muddy Waters, Elmore James, and Joe Turner with his "Chains of Love" were the favorites of all the black disk jockeys' turntables while Nat Cole sang love songs and Harry Belafonte was popular also on the tropical scene. These were the types of songs that made up our selections, along with the backbone of our program, which was always the blues. . . . As Christmas approached, a rumor was out that a good band was at Huff's Garden and Tommy was telling us that we were being sought by larger nightclubs for jobs.

On December 30, a piano player named Johnnie Johnson phoned me, asking me to join his Sir John's Trio for a gig on the eve of the year of 1953. The nightclub he mentioned was four times as big as Huff's Garden, six times as plush, and ten times as popular. It had been renovated from a supermarket and named the Cosmopolitan Club, which is still located on the corner of 17th and Bond Street in East St. Louis, Illinois. It was on New Year's Eve of 1953 that my career took its first firm step. . . .

. . . The music played most around St. Louis was country-western, which was usually called hillbilly music, and swing. Curiosity provoked me to lay a lot of the country stuff on our predominantly black audience and some of the clubgoers started whispering, "Who is that black hillbilly at the Cosmo?" After they laughed at me a few times, they began requesting the hillbilly stuff and enjoyed trying to dance to it. If you ever want to see something that is far out, watch a crowd of colored folk, half high, wholeheartedly doing the hoedown barefooted.

Toddy [Berry's wife] would get the biggest kick out of our rehearsals around the house, hearing me sing the country stuff. She cared less for country music, being a blues lover, and saw only the fictitious impressions I would insert in a tune to impress the audience with my hilarious hilly and basic billy delivery of the song. It could have been because of my country-western songs that the white spectators showed up in greater numbers as we continued playing at the Cosmo Club, bringing the fairly crowded showplace to a full house. Sometimes nearly forty percent of the clients were Caucasian, causing the event to be worthy of publicity across the river in St. Louis.

The state of Illinois in the beginning of the 1950s was a bit more liberal than Missouri in regards to relations between blacks and whites. A traveler might notice a considerable difference in the community just across the Mississippi in East St. Louis. For one thing, if a black and white couple were stopped by a squad car there they did not have to go to a police station and get a mandatory shot for venereal disease, as was the custom across the river in St. Louis. Nightclub people were known to flock across the river to the east side, where they could escape the bounds of Missouri's early-closing blue laws and continue their enjoyment.

Over half of the songs I was singing at the Cosmo Club were directly from the recordings of Nat "King" Cole and Muddy Waters. They are the major chords in the staff of music I have composed. Listening to my idol Nat Cole prompted me to sing sentimental songs with distinct diction. The songs of Muddy Waters impelled me to deliver the down-home blues in the language they came from, the Negro dialect. When I played hillbilly songs, I stressed my diction so that it was harder and whiter. All in all it was my intention to hold both the black and white clientele by voicing the different kinds of songs in their customary tongues.

. . .

During this period, there were only two black disk jockeys in St. Louis, and the many small record companies had problems getting major white stations to spin records by black artists. There were great songs by black performers that were still seldom played on stations listened to by the white population. In some of the larger cities where black disk jockeys had gotten a foothold in a major radio station, many of the white kids were lending an ear and picking up on the black sounds, often against family traditions. Some of the kids in well-integrated cities heard black artists performing firsthand and would have to sneak to buy the songs they had heard and liked. . . .

It seems to me that the white teenagers of the forties and fifties helped launch black artists nationally into the main line of popular music. Like in the sixties, when the white teenagers who became known as hippies brought the entire world into so many changes, these transistor-radio teenagers exercised great liberty in following their musical tastes.

~~~~~~~~~

Chuck Berry's first hit, "Maybelline," had its origins at the Cosmo Club. His account makes clear its relationship to the blues-ballad tradition. He added a classic three-line blues refrain to a ballad stanza structure.

"Maybelline" [1955] was my effort to sing country-western, which I had always liked. The Cosmo clubgoers didn't know any of the words to those songs, which gave me a chance to improvise and add comical lines to the lyrics. "Mountain Dew," "Jambalaya," and "Ida Red" were the favorites of the Cosmo audience, mainly because of the honky-tonk gestures I inserted while singing the songs.

"Maybelline" was written from the inspiration that grew out of the country song, "Ida Red." I'd heard it sung long before when I was a teenager and thought it was rhythmic and amusing to hear. I'd sung it in the yard gatherings and parties around home when I was first learning to strum the guitar in my high-school days. Later in life, at the Cosmo Club, I added my bit to the song and still enjoyed a good response so I coined it a good one to sing. . . . When I wrote "Maybelline" I had originally titled it "Ida May," but when I took the song to Chess Records I was advised to change its title. That was simple because the rhythmic swing of the three syllables fit with many other names.

. . .

"Roll over Beethoven" [1956] was written based on the feelings I had when my sister would monopolize the piano at home during our youthful school years. In fact most of the words were aimed at Lucy instead of the Maestro Ludwig Van Beethoven. Thelma also took lessons in classical music but Lucy was the culprit that delayed rock 'n' roll music twenty years.

. . .

"Johnny B. Goode" [1958]: Leonard Chess took an instant liking to this song and stayed in the studio coaching us the whole time we were cutting it. . . . I'd guess my mother has as much right to be declared the source of "Johnny B. Goode" as any other contender in that she was the one who repeatedly commented that I would be a millionaire someday. . . . "Johnny" in the song is more or less myself although I wrote it intending it to be a song for Johnnie Johnson. . . . It seems easy, now that it's been around so long, that it took only a period of about two weeks of periodic application to put the lyrics together when I worked on "Drifting Heart" almost four months and it sold scarcely twenty copies.

It is obvious that a story that brings a subject from out of the boondocks to fame and fortune is more dramatic than one out of midtown to somewhere crosstown. "Rags to riches" even sounds more attractive than "fortune to fame." It was with this in mind that I wrote of a boy with an ambition to become a guitar player, who came from the least of luxury to be seen by many, practicing until the listener believes he has all but made it to the top as the chorus prompts him like his mother's encouraging voice, "Go Johnny Go."

The gateway from freedom, I was led to understand, was somewhere "close to New Orleans" where most Africans were sorted through and sold. I had driven through New Orleans on tour and I'd been told my great grandfather lived "way back up in the woods among the evergreens" in a log cabin. I revived the era with a story about a "colored boy named Johnny B. Goode." My first thought was to make his life follow as my own had come along, but I thought it would seem biased to white fans to say "colored boy" and changed it to "country boy."

As it turned out, my name was in lights and it is a fact that "Johnny B. Goode" is most instrumental in causing it to B[e].

SOURCE: Chuck Berry, *The Autobiography* (New York: Harmony, 1987): 1–2, 25, 87–91, 94, 143, 150, 155.

~~~~~~~~~

NOTE

1.   For this list, see "Covered Berries" at Berry's Web site, http://www.chuckberry.com/music/covers.htm.

THE FIVE-STRING BANJO

Hints from the 1960s Speed Master, Earl Scruggs

In the 1940s, a new genre of country music emerged that by the early 1950s was identified by the evocative term "bluegrass." "Mountain music bluegrass style," as described by Mike Seeger, the noted folk-revival musician and banjo authority, meant
a distinctive combination of "high pitched, emotional singing," and dazzling syncopated instrumental music, with the banjo as the lead melody instrument.[1] Although
initially understood as a white style, more recent scholarship has stressed the influence of black fiddle and banjo playing as well. The major innovator of bluegrass, Bill
Monroe, built his Blue Grass Boys around his mandolin, plus fiddle, guitar, string
bass, and banjo. When Earl Scruggs (b. 1924) joined Monroe's group in 1945, his
high-speed banjo claimed the spotlight. His "three-finger" style set new standards
for virtuosity within bluegrass and country music and in the folk revival as well.

In 1968, Scruggs published a banjo manual. In the excerpt included here,
Scruggs describes his early years and his home-grown training. He honors his influences (particularly Uncle Dave Macon; see chapter 96) and describes the background for the banjo-picking technique which still bears his name. His partnership
with Lester Flatt, a consummate guitarist and singer, led to their mainstream popularity, particularly through the use of bluegrass themes on television shows such
as *The Beverly Hillbillies* and in films in the 1970s (*Bonnie and Clyde* and *Deliverance*).
Scruggs's manual includes many of his famous tunes in tab and in musical notation.

"Foggy Mountain Breakdown" is reprinted here as it appears in musical notation. In the banjo's current "newgrass" generation, Scruggs's influence extends into the present through such musicians as Tony Trischka and his star pupil, Béla Fleck.

~~~~~~~~~~~
~~~~~~~~~~~

EARL SCRUGGS, BIOGRAPHICAL NOTES

I would like to add hints and information on banjo playing. When I first began playing the banjo, I used the thumb and index finger. This is referred to as two-finger picking. However, I found that my rhythm was choppy and not as syncopated as I wanted it to be. My three-finger style of picking began when I was around the age of ten. I recall that my brother and I had gotten into an argument and I took my banjo and went into a room by myself. I was picking away, and suddenly discovered I was using the thumb, index, and middle finger rather than the usual two. The number I was playing at the time was "Reuben." For an entire week I played that tune and nothing else. I kept playing it over and over in order to become accustomed to using the middle finger on the notes. Soon after that, I was able to use the same technique on other songs.

At the time I first began playing the three-finger style, I still wasn't completely happy with the sound I was getting because the way I was picking didn't sound exactly like the other three-finger banjo pickers I had admired so much. However, I was very careful with my picking and learned later the style was much more versatile than the style I had previously been using. I could play slower songs as well as the faster tunes.

My dear old mother must have had nerves of steel and a built-in system of not hearing the noise because she never discouraged me about my playing. I do recall that one time when I was picking some kind of wild banjo runs she said to me, "If you are going to play, then play so the tune can be recognized."

I now realize how right she was, and I am a firm believer that the melody should be played so as to be recognized over the other picking. For this reason, I prefer [to pick] the melody notes as much as possible with my thumb since it is most capable of bringing out the strong melody notes.

I went through several stages during the years when I was learning to play the banjo. One was a tendency to become disgusted with my banjo playing. Then, I also went through a stage of trying to play any tune I heard. I soon realized that every tune can't be played on the banjo. You may be able to accompany someone else very nicely, or accompany yourself when you sing, but you may have to leave out a banjo solo on some numbers. I would also like to mention that it is best to not become alarmed if you sometimes become disgusted with your playing. (If you do reach this point, lay your banjo aside for awhile and perhaps when you pick it up again you may find you have come up with a new idea.) This is normal and your progress comes in small bits but you will have quite a bit of knowledge adding up.

Looking back over my childhood days, I can't remember anything more satisfying and more pleasurable than the banjo. I remember looking forward to getting up early to build a fire in the fireplace and in our wood cook stove, just to sit before it and pick a few numbers before it was time to go to school or to work on the farm.

Some days I might be picking away on a song and some new run or pattern might spring up. Then, sometimes, I would go for several days and seemed to be at a complete stand-still as far as my playing was concerned. This may sound slightly unbelievable but I have actually dreamed about a certain run or a tune and I could get up the next morning and play it all the way through even though I had never played the song before. Occasionally, I would hear some other artist play or sing a song and I could adapt portions of that into my work.

In the late 30's and early 40's, I was greatly inspired by Roy Acuff and his Smoky Mountain Boys. Roy has carried a very professional show all down through the years. The act of Rachel and Oswald really gave me many enjoyable moments. They worked mainly as a comedy, brother and sister act and both of them played a fine old time frail 5 string banjo. Oswald was the first person I remember to do such fine work with the old un-amplified steel Hawaiian guitar. His solo playing was outstanding and he had a number of great fill-in licks he used when he was backing Roy's solo parts. I don't suppose his tenor singing with Roy has ever been topped, as well as his solo singing on such a song as "Well, I Am A Going Down The Road Feeling Bad."

There were other groups who also inspired me and I suppose every musician has been similarly inspired by various groups.

One of my favorite people I had occasion to work with while on the Grand Ole Opry in the 40's was Uncle Dave Macon. There was probably never a musician before and chances are none since who enjoyed entertaining people more than Uncle Dave. In my travels with him, I remember a few goodies with which I was impressed. With all his fame and the money he made on shows, he never got away from his earthy or simple way of living. Fame, I think, is an understatement in his case, because it was my first experience of seeing a man so well loved by so many. People would walk, ride horse-back, you name it, just to see him perform, and I don't think he ever let them down. His slogan was, "I don't put on, I put out," and this he did. He didn't have an interest in a fancy or a society way of living, and he didn't try to impress anyone with his hotel address or fancy dinners.

He never ceased to drop a bit of enjoyment whenever possible. Due to his age and running the risk of taking a cold, he would ride at night in the automobile with a cap tied around his head. He never ate a meal without using a bib to protect his clothing. I never heard him complain about tiring, even though many of our trips were in excess of 1,000 miles and made in a 1941 Chevrolet.

. . .

He had a great tendency to call people by the wrong name, or to give them a nick-name. He called me Ernest. A couple of classics to me were, "Ernest, you play good in a band but you're not a bit funny, are you?" Meaning of course, I had no comedy routine. Another was, "You pick good in a band but you don't sing a lick, do you?" The comedy and singing remarks were true since I had devoted all my attention to playing the banjo. I suppose all these talents, the singing, comedy, and banjo playing combined, that Uncle Dave had, added to my admiration of him. But, for him to say he admired my banjo playing was as satisfying as "writing home for five and getting ten."

It will take a considerable amount of practice and time to accomplish playing the banjo. This probably applies to anything that requires coordination. My first playing dated back to when I was four or five years old. However, I do not feel that starting at an early age will make one a better banjo player than starting ten or fifteen years later. The effort you put forth will determine how quickly and smoothly you progress. As I have often said, don't try to learn too much at once; if you are a beginner, learn a small portion and do that over and over until you have accomplished

Earl Scruggs
FOGGY MOUNTAIN BREAKDOWN
(Featured in the film "BONNIE AND CLYDE")
(G tuning)

Earl Scruggs, "Foggy Mountain Breakdown," pitch notation only, from Earl Scruggs, "*Earl Scruggs and the 5-String Banjo* (New York: Peer International Corporation, 1968): 84–85.

it with ease. I am also of the opinion that everyone who learns to play will come up with some original sound of his own.

It has been a great pleasure to me to hear the many fine banjo players who have started playing from my style, and, encouraging too, to hear their own ideas and talents added into their playing. It could probably be correctly stated that I was the first person to expose this style nationally. I would honestly like to say "Thank you" personally to all of you who have learned from my playing.

One of the greatest honors I have received comes from the people who, since about 1946, have referred to three-finger banjo picking as "Scruggs-Style."

SOURCE: Earl Scruggs, "The Anatomy of Scruggs-Style Picking," in his *Earl Scruggs and the 5-String Banjo* (New York: Peer International, 1968): 84–85, 155–56.

~~~~~~~~~~

NOTE

1. Mike Seeger, "Mountain Music Bluegrass Style: Liner Notes for *Mountain Music Bluegrass Style*, Folkways 2318," as reprinted in *The Bluegrass Reader*, ed. Thomas Goldsmith (Urbana: University of Illinois Press, 2004): 101.

115

PETE SEEGER, A TCUSAPSS, SINGS OUT!

Pete Seeger (b. 1919) stands tall as one of the most important folk-based performer-composers of our time. Is he a "folksinger"? He says technically not, explaining in one of the excerpts reprinted here that he is a "TCUSAPSS (pronounced 'Tikoosaps'— a Twentieth-Century USA professional singer-songwriter)." His career intertwines politics and music in both obvious and subtle ways, including powerful protest songs such as "Where Have All the Flowers Gone?" and "Waist Deep in the Big Muddy." In a sense, Seeger is an American hybrid—part urban-educated intellectual, part social-justice singer, and part descendant of the New England singing-school movement. As the son of Charles Seeger and the stepson of Ruth Crawford Seeger, he grew up with singing and playing folk music as a way of life. Seeger believes that the cultural health of a nation depends on the way its people make music together.

For more than half a century Seeger has been contributing a column for the "folk song magazine" *Sing Out!* from which these selections are taken. Initially titled "Johnny Appleseed, Jr.," and then in the mid-1970s retitled simply "Appleseeds," the column's tagline reads, "Since 1954 Pete Seeger has used this column to spread ideas so that some of them can grow." Officially, Seeger contributed his last column in 2004, but he has continued—and likely will continue—to publish occasional pieces.

VIVE LA COMPAGNIE

One and one equal four. Two and two equal fifty. How come?

When two people get together their ideas multiply geometrically. Ten ideas plus ten ideas equal not twenty but one hundred.

In traveling this continent I have observed that the greatest music has been in those communities not where a few talented individuals compete for the limelight, but where young people have pooled their repertoire[s], talent, ideas and energies, and formed folk-singing groups.

They are not choruses or quartets in the strict sense of the terms. They work out their own arrangements and harmonies in their heads, and have no rigid requirements for voices.

The Weavers were a good example. Two low baritones, one brilliant alto, and a split tenor. What more unlikely combination could you have for a quartet? Yet the Weavers produced a solidity of tone that every recording company on Tin Pan Alley tried to copy.

As our knowledge of the folk traditions of the world deepens and broadens, we realize that the best music will come from a group. How can fewer than two sing many songs from Latin America? How can fewer than four really enjoy the harmonies and counterrhythms of a South African choral chant? We need a small chorus to know the full power of some Slavic folk tunes. And a roomful must rock and swell if we are to sing "Saints Go Marching In" or "We Shall Overcome."

How to start? In your family, school, camp, college, or club. Don't demand a large group. Two or three can start. Don't feel you have to have harmony. Start singing all in unison and gradually work out one or two extra parts.

(The Weavers' song arrangements were seldom written down at first. They were what musicians call "head arrangements": one person might scribble out an idea, others would try it, amend it, even swap parts; the song was worked out in rehearsal and ironed out in performance.)

By thus improvising their parts, groups can create the subtle variations in melody, rhythm, tempo, harmony and accompaniment, to bring out the true meaning and purpose of a song.

Set a date to put on a program for your friends. Pool your ideas. Be firm in criticism and self-criticism until you are all happy with the result.

Down with the star system!

SOURCE: Pete Seeger, "Johnny Appleseed, Jr." column, *Sing Out!* (Spring 1955), as reprinted in Pete Seeger, *The Incompleat Folksinger* (New York: Simon and Schuster, 1972): 155–56.

THE THEORY OF CULTURAL GUERRILLA TACTICS

When the Nazis overran the other nations of Europe, those who opposed them had several possible choices of action. Some foolhardy young ones said:

"I'm going down and throw a hand grenade at the very first Nazi truck I see. I may get killed, but I'll do something. I won't stand by and let them take over our country."

And they did this, and they were killed, and it was the last of their contribution against Nazism. Certain more cautious citizens took the opposite stand:

"The thing to do is get some groceries and hole up somewhere. There is no sense in getting killed yet. When the liberating armies appear, we'll emerge to help them."

But rarely did these live to see liberation either. Because they stayed in the same place, they were sooner or later discovered by the Nazis, captured, and executed.

Those who not only stood the best chance of living to see liberation, as well as consistently doing the most to harass the Nazis, were those who kept *mobility*. It took coolness and self control. They picked their own battles, and always selected limited engagements which they would win. Since they had no reserves to call upon, they could not capture a town and hold it for more than a very short while. But over the country as a whole, these thousands of [isolated] guerrillas did tremendous damage to the Nazis. In Yugoslavia alone a whole division of Nazi troops, which Hitler badly needed elsewhere, was tied down.

It may seem a farfetched comparison, but for many years I figured I pursued a theory of cultural guerrilla tactics. I could not hold a steady job on a single radio or TV station. But I could appear as a guest on a thousand and one disc jokey [sic] shows, say a few words while they played a few records. I could not hold down a job at the average college or University, but I could appear to sing some songs, and then be on my way. I kept as home base this one sector of our society which refused most courageously to knuckle under to the witch hunters: the college students. Now, I figure my job is done. The young people who have learned songs from me are taking them to thousands of places where I myself could never expect to go. Though I cannot get on network TV, many of my friends do. Though I cannot get a job in a university, those whom I have helped get interested in folk music are getting them.

But even more important are the literally hundreds of thousands of amateur guitar pickers and banjo pickers—and each has an important job. Like fireflies they light up the night. Or maybe I should compare them to a more potent insect. Once a white politician told Sojourner Truth, the Negro abolitionist leader:

"Woman, I care no more for you than a mosquito."

"Mebbe so," said she. "But, praise God, I'll keep you scratching."

SOURCE: Pete Seeger, "Johnny Appleseed, Jr." column, *Sing Out!* 11, no. 4 (October–November 1961): 60.

~~~~~~

A thought for the holiday season: in spite of all the commercial business, this is still a season for singing. In many corners of our country, readers of this magazine have tuned up their guitars and banjoes, rehearsed briefly, and sallied forth into the cold air, to bring songs of peace and good will, old and new, near and far, to their neighbors. Have you tried it? There's a sound to friendly, raw voices that no loudspeaker can ever match.

. . .

If any reader is thinking of starting a chorus, here again is an idea: try a family chorus, open only to two or more members of families. No adult allowed without a child, and vice versa. Keep the arrangements in two or three parts, so that they can be rehearsed over the supper dishes, or driving home in the car. Mother might be alto, son or daughter a soprano, father a bass of some sort, or else double on the melody.

SOURCE: Pete Seeger, "Johnny Appleseed, Jr." column, *Sing Out!* 12, no. 5 (December–January 1962): 67.

I wrote Ian Robb that I was glad to see him struggling to keep folk festivals from going the way of all commerce. But he should broaden the use of the F-word to cover people who sing in languages other than English. Strictly speaking, I'm not a folksinger. I'm a TCUSAPSS (pronounced "Ti*koo*saps"—a Twentieth Century USA professional singer-songwriter). The Québecois folksingers and Ukrainian folksingers you have at your festivals are more folksingers than I am, who learns songs mainly out of books or from records. And when you have a gospel singing group, do you take pains to point out that they are singing religious folk music?

If you don't use the word "folk music" for people like them, don't use it for people like me. If "TCUSAPSS" is too unwieldy, find a better word. But not "folksinger." Because we're not. (Except perhaps when we're offstage, when anyone can be one.)

I admit that we're loused up by the whole modern approach to "professionalism." I built my house but I don't call myself a carpenter.

Words, words. "The wolf's definition of freedom is quite different from that of the shepherd." *(A. Lincoln)*

. . .

I think that *Broadside* and *Sing Out!* and other "folk" magazines make a mistake not to print the best new rap songs. If they are listened to and imitated by new rap singers, they are important parts of this swiftly flowing stream we call the folk process.

I'm thinking of such lines as "Junkies in the alleys with baseball bats" and "pushers drive big cars, spending twenties and tens, and you just want to grow up to be just like them."

"But we're folk music magazines," some of their editors will tell me. "If somebody wants to put out a rap magazine, let them do it."

This is a too-narrow definition of folk music. It is like the Christians calling Native Americans unreligious because their rites and words were different.

SOURCE: Pete Seeger, "Appleseeds" column, *Sing Out!* 33, no. 2 (Spring 1989): 25, 26.

The "folksong revival" will be a success when more people sing in the bathtub, before and after meals, in meetings and gatherings, and standing in queues.

SOURCE: Pete Seeger, "Appleseeds" column, *Sing Out!* 36, no. 1 (Spring 1991): 58.

116

Bob Dylan Turns Liner Notes Into Poetry

Bob Dylan (b. 1941) used his prodigious gifts as a poet and songwriter to reshape folk-based popular song in the 1960s and '70s. In retrospect, he followed the path of a number of great American songwriters by integrating many strands of American culture, and—like Stephen Foster and Irving Berlin—he writes melodies of deceptive simplicity. In his formative years, Dylan combined different aspects within the Anglo-American ballad tradition (exemplified by Woody Guthrie, Jimmie Rodgers, Hank Williams) with a literary aesthetic indebted partly to Walt Whitman. He owed even more to the rebellious Beat Generation poets, particularly Allen Ginsberg, who became a friend. Dylan's powerful poetry reached a mass audience. Later, his turn to electric guitar brought both rock and stylistic controversy into his music. Bob Dylan's impact is marked in part by the number and diversity of the fellow musicians who have covered his songs. As of 2002, there were 5,870 interpretations of 350 different Dylan songs by 2,791 artists.[1]

In his album Bringing It All Back Home *(1965), which includes the famous "Mr. Tambourine Man" and "Subterranean Homesick Blues," Dylan turned the liner notes*

into a poem, and with that act set an important precedent for the manifestos and
artistic credos that accompanied many later rock albums.

BRINGING IT ALL BACK HOME

i'm standing there watching the parade
feeling combination of sleepy john estes.
jayne mansfield. humphry bogart / morti-
mer snerd. murph the surf and so forth
erotic hitchhiker wearing japanese
blanket. gets my attention by asking didn't
he see me at this hootenanny down in
puerto vallarta, mexico / i say no you must
be mistaken. i happen to be one of the
Supremes / then he rips off his blanket
an' suddenly becomes a middle-aged druggist.
up for district attorney. he starts screaming at me you're the one. you're the one
that's been causing all them riots over in
vietnam. immediately turns t' a bunch of
people an' says if elected, he'll have me
electrocuted publicly on the next fourth
of july. i look around an' all these people
he's talking to are carrying blowtorches
needless t' say, i split fast go back t' the
nice quiet country. am standing there writing
WHAAT? on my favorite wall when who should
pass by in a jet plane but my recording
engineer "i'm here t' pick up you and your
latest works of art. do you need any help
with anything?"
        (pause)
my songs're written with the kettledrum
in mind / a touch of any anxious color. un-
mentionable. obvious. an' people perhaps
like a soft brazilian singer . . . i have
given up at making any attempt at perfection
the fact that the white house is filled with
leaders that've never been t' the apollo
theater amazes me. why allen ginsberg was
not chosen t' read poetry at the inauguration
boggles my mind / if someone thinks norman
mailer is more important than hank williams
that's fine. i have no arguments an' i

never drink milk. i would rather model har-
monica holders than discuss aztec anthropology
english literature. or history of the united
nations. i accept chaos. I am not sure whether
it accepts me. i know there're some people terrified
of the bomb. but there are other people terrified
t' be seen carrying a modern screen magazine.
experience teaches that silence terrifies people
the most . . . i am convinced that all souls have
some superior t' deal with / like the school
system, an invisible circle of which no one
can think without consulting someone / in the
face of this, responsibility / security, success
mean absolutely nothing . . . i would not want
t' be bach. mozart. tolstoy. joe hill. gertrude
stein or james dean / they are all dead. the
Great books've been written. the Great sayings
have all been said / i am about t' sketch You
a picture of what goes on around here some-
times. tho i don't understand too well
myself what's really happening. i do know
that we're all gonna die someday an' that no
death has ever stopped the world. my poems
are written in a rhythm of unpoetic distortion
divided by pierced ears. false eyelashes / sub-
tracted by people constantly torturing each
other. with a melodic purring line of descriptive
hollowness—seen at times through dark sunglasses
an' other forms of psychic explosion. a song is
anything that can walk by itself / i am called
a songwriter. a poem is a naked person . . . some
people say that i am a poet
　　(end of pause)
an' so i answer my recording engineer
"yes. well i could use some help in getting
this wall in the plane"

SOURCE: http://bobdylan.com/linernotes/bringing.html. Also reprinted in William McKeen, ed., *Rock and Roll: An Anthology* (New York: Norton, 2000): 31–32.

~~~~~~~

NOTE

1.　This list, called "'It Ain't Me Babe': The Bob Dylan Cover List," is available at http://www.bjorner.com/covers.htm.

JANIS JOPLIN GRABS PIECES OF OUR HEARTS

(Joplin, Graham)

Texas-born and -raised Janis Joplin (1943–1970) burst like a musical comet into the San Francisco rock scene of the 1960s, which was centered in the neighborhood known as Haight Ashbury—a West Coast counterpart to Greenwich Village. In 1967, Joplin stunned audiences at the Monterey Pop Festival with her performance of "Ball and Chain"—a blues ballad earlier recorded by Big Mama Thornton. Then followed a string of hits with her first band, Big Brother and the Holding Company, including "Piece of My Heart."[1] Joplin molded interpretations of African-American blues into vehicles for a modern white woman of reckless ambition and hippie defiance.

Living and working in the "boys' world" of outlaw rock, Joplin was dealing with an often ruthless music business. These selections show the vulnerabilities and mythologies that she mined in her art. In the first, a dutiful daughter writes to her family in a starstruck tone. In the second, a famous producer who opened the venues of Fillmore West and Fillmore East in the mid-1960s describes a lonely diva both oppressed and empowered by the persona of the classic African-American female blues singer.

April 1967

Dear Mother, family

Things are going so good for us & me personally I can't quite believe it! I never ever thought things could be so wonderful! Allow me to explain. First of all, the group— we're better than ever (please see enclosed review from S.F. Examiner) and working all the time. Just finished 3 weeks straight engagements, 6 nights a week & we're booked up week-ends for well over a month. And we're making a thousand or over for a week- end. For single nights we're getting from $500–$900. Not bad for a bunch of beatniks, eh? And our reputation is still going uphill. It's funny to watch—you can tell where you are by the people that are on your side. Y'know, the scene-followers, the people "with the finger on the pulse of the public." One of the merchants on Haight St. has given all of us free clothes (I got a beautiful blue leather skirt) just because 1) she really digs us & 2) she thinks we're going to make it & it'll be good publicity. Our record is enjoying a fair reception—much better than our first one which was much, much better. We made #29 in Detroit but we don't really know what's happening because we never hear from Mainstream. It's a long & involved story but we really feel like we've been used & abused by our record co[mpany] & we'd like to get out of the contract but don't know whether we can. We talked to a lawyer about it & he seemed fairly negative & we can't even get ahold of our record co. to talk about it. So until further news, we're hung up. There's a slim possibility we might go to Europe & play this summer. There's a hippie boat going back and forth & rock bands get free passage if they play on the way over. And Chet, head of the Family Dog, is trying to organize dances over there & if he does, we'd have a place to work. Probably won't work but it sure would be groovey [sic]. Speaking of England, guess who was in town last week—Paul McCartney!!! (he's a Beatle). And he came to see us!!! SIGH Honest to God! He came to the Matrix & saw us & told some people that he dug us. Isn't that exciting!!!! Gawd, I was so thrilled—I still am! Imagine—Paul!!!! If it could only have been George. . . . Oh, well. I didn't get to see him anyway—we heard about it afterwards. Why, if I'd known that he was out there, I would have jumped right off the stage & made a fool of myself.

Now earlier, I spoke of how well things are going for me personally—it's really true. I'm becoming quite a celebrity among the hippies & everyone who goes to the dances. Why, last Sunday we played a Spring Mobilization for Peace benefit & a simply amazing thing happened. As the boys were tuning, I walked up to the front of the stage to set up the microphones & as I raised the middle mike up to my mouth, the whole audience applauded!! Too much! And then as we're getting ready to play, a girl yelled out "Janis Joplin lives!" Now you can't argue with that, and they clapped again. Also, a rock publication named World Countdown *had a collage on its cover using photo- graphs of important personages in & about the scene & I'm in there. Also they're bring- ing out a poster of me! Maybe you've read in* Time *magazine about the personality posters. They're big, very big photographs, Jean Harlow, Einstein, Belmondo, Dylan, & Joplin. Yes, folks, it's me wearing a sequined cape, thousands of strings of beads & top- less. But it barely shows because of the beads. Very dramatic photograph & [I] look re- ally beautiful!! If it wouldn't embarrass you, I'll send you one. I'm thrilled! I can be Haight-Ashbury's first pin-up.*

Speaking of the Haight-Ashbury, read the enclosed article from LOOK *magazine. There've been lots of articles written about the scene here.* Newsweek *has had two &*

this new one. And even the Chronicle—they've all had articles with more understanding than the one in Time. As a matter of fact, I just plain quit reading it because of that article—not because I was mad. Because I was aware of how distorted they were & I figured they were probably that wrong about everything. I really am not social critic enough to know/discuss what is going on, but in answer to your question—Yes, they are our audience & we're hoping they can turn on the rest of the country because then we'd be nation-wide. We'd be the Monkees! Well, at any rate, a good article.

Okay, on to news: For one thing we've gotten a raise—the guys with wives were feeling constrained, so now we get $100 a week! Good heavens.

Second in importance, I have a new apartment. Really fine!! Two big rooms, kitchen, bathroom & balcony. And I'm right across the street from the park! You can't really understand living there with a yard, but here you can go 10–20 blocks without ever seeing a living plant and I just look out my window or step out on my balcony & I've got fresh air & trees & grass!! So wonderful, sigh. My new address is 123 Cole St., S.F. Still in the Haight-Ashbury. Have lots of plans for the place—two rooms need painting but I may just end up hanging stuff up on the walls. I've sort of got the front room fixed up now & it's really nice to live in. SIGH! See what I mean, about things going my way? Also, I have a boyfriend. Really nice. He's head of Country Joe and the Fish, a band from Berkeley. Named Joe McDonald, he's a Capricorn like me, & is 25 & so far we're getting along fine. Everyone in the rock scene just thinks it's the cutest thing they've ever seen. It is rather cute actually. Speaking of boyfriends, I've been hearing from John again. He's written several letters. For some reason I get the feeling he's planning on coming out here & is sort of putting out feelers.

Next, guess what (special for Dad) I've done—I've quit smoking!!! Still want one now & then but it's been about a month now. I felt it was just too hard on my voice. I'd been smoking for 10 yrs! I got a real bad cold & bronchitis & I just couldn't smoke for about a week & when I got well, I refused to start again. I may break down but I hope not. This is really better for me.

More news, George is really getting to be a fine dog. Learning things every day. Today he learned the hard way not to run across the street to the park by himself—he got hit by a car. But the vet said he wasn't hurt very badly—bruised & scared. Poor thing, he's just moping around with a very paranoid look on his face.

I'm having a few clothes made for me now—had a beautiful dress made out of a madras bed spread & now she's working on one out of green crepe with a very low V neckline. I've been making things out of leather lately. Made a beautiful blue & green Garbo hat & pair of green shoes.

I'm also sending our new promo picture. Not very flattering of me but a very strong picture. Pretty good looking group, eh?

Really enjoyed seeing the pictures of all of you. Looking beautiful, Mother. And Laura looks really cute! Is her dress white or silver? And I've never seen Mike look so charming. Must be the Big Brother T shirt.

Now, please let me know when you are coming. Oh, I have so many places to take you to & show you! But we'll be working so let me know as soon as you can your plans. Well, I guess that's it for now. Write me.

LoveXXX

Janis

SOURCE: Laura Joplin, *Love XX Janis* (New York: Villard, 1992): 191–94. The chapter introduction was written by Rachel Gillett.

~~~~~~~~

BILL GRAHAM'S SNAPSHOT OF JANIS JOPLIN

BILL: Janis Joplin's talent was that you believed she was singing her guts out every night. In that sense she was like Piaf.[2] You were watching a candle burn, with no wax to replace what had already been used up.

Janis was a feel, an emotion, a spur. Janis was not a song. Janis was the first white singer of that era who sounded like she had come from the world of black blues. I don't think men found her that attractive. I think men found her an awesome female. Not necessarily sexually but sensually. She aroused something in men. She aroused desire but was not the object of that desire. And I think she was never able to deal with that reality.

At the beginning of the scene there were no stars. The bands just played. But then it started to happen. The instant acceptance by so many other people as the goddess. It *had* to have an effect on her. She had no choice in the matter really. She became an involuntary leader. People wanted to dress like her and wear their hair like her. It wasn't like it had been for Judy Garland or Billie Holiday. Because they played mostly clubs. Look at the scope of the audience that the sixties wound up creating. As a result of that era, a girl from Port Arthur, Texas, became an international sociological queen. But still just the same person she had always been. Janis was one of the few who really didn't want to make it just for the sake of making it. She wanted to be a star on the stage. Not a commercial asset star. Not, "I'll get bigger, I'll buy things. I'll be more respected in the world." She was a street blues singer who lived in fear of something. My guess would be when she put all her talent, adulation, and financial security on one side of the scale, what did she have on the other? When she woke up at home on Sunday morning after being on the road, what did she really have to call her own and balance out her success?

In the case of Janis, the private side was *not* happy. The balance wasn't there.

CHET HELMS[3]:   I think the Albert Grossman organization[4] tried to mold Janis in this white Billie Holiday role. The blues singer. Down and out and junked out. I think emotionally she got wrapped up in that image. She felt she *had* to pay her dues to sing the blues. She felt in some sense that she had *not* suffered enough. Therefore, she *had* to suffer. I think she had probably already suffered enough, as it was.

JOHN MORRIS[5]:   I remember a scene in the Pan Am Building in New York. Janis wanted Bill to manage her. We were in two pay phones and he was saying, "No, no, no, I can't do it!" and I was standing there saying, "You're out of your mind!" And he was saying, "No, no, no. I'm going to give her to Albert." And I was saying, "You're crazy!"

We had this screaming, yelling, argument and he *did* give her to Albert. When I say he gave her to Albert, I mean he convinced her to go with Albert. And he could have done it himself. Because at that time, Bill's respect for Albert was *immense*. Albert was like a *god*.

BILL: I remember saying that if they wanted somebody of strength, they should go with Albert. If he was shifty, it was justified because he always tried to do the best for his artist. He maneuvered very well in the big game. I wasn't qualified to manage Janis at that time. I wasn't qualified because of time. I knew who Janis was. I knew she was not a sometime thing. She needed full-time management or she would go astray. She needed somebody to really lock her into her career and her life. She would've been a whole life for someone. And I couldn't give my life over to her. Because I felt that what I was doing was bigger and more important than dealing with one single artist.

The two or three times that Janis and I spent a lot of time together were flukes. They were never planned. One night at Winterland when she was still with Big Brother but already a star, we got together after the show. She mumbled something to me about, "Do you want to get something to eat?" We went to her car, a psychedelic painted Porsche but she said she didn't feel like driving. She said, "Let's get something to eat somewhere we can sit outside." It was one of those nights that come so seldom to San Francisco and are so rare. When you can drive in an open car and sit outside. So I drove.

We went to Mel's on Geary and got a bunch of hamburgers and fries and milkshakes. She also had some booze with her. We went out by the bunkers across the Golden Gate Bridge on the Marin Headlands. We sat out there and ate and she started talking. She was a little loaded. Her life was not going so well. She had some personal problems. Mainly, she wanted a new relationship with a man. She talked about her life on the road. She said, "I go on the road and I'm in the Holiday Inn in Toronto. After the gig, all the guys go upstairs and freshen up. Then they come down and score chicks." There was this long pause. Then she said, "What does a woman do?" That always explained it for me.

Janis was among the very few who on a given night could be an erupting volcano on stage. She'd give the kind of performance that you could *never* capture on record. Like the Dead. Very few artists have the talent and the hunger to *go* for it every night. To convince the audience that their performance is as important and meaningful to them as it is to those who watch them perform. For an entertainer, that's the ultimate challenge. To put it out there every night. The very best they can.

On certain nights when she paced herself on stage, Janis would get you feeling great through the middle section. Then she would go to the big finale and she would get onto a *higher* level. Otis [Redding] had that. Then she would come back for an encore and say, "You think you've had it all? You're *wrong*."

On a personal level, what she said to me that night always stayed in my mind. I know a lot of happy men who can be on the road for weeks and be with women and then come home to a wife.

But what does a *woman* do?

SOURCE: Bill Graham and Robert Greenfield, *Bill Graham Presents: My Life Inside Rock and Out* (Garden City, N.Y.: Doubleday, 1992): 204–6.

~~~~~~~

NOTES

1. This song was originally recorded in the rhythm-and-blues category by Erma Franklin in 1967.
2. Edith Piaf (1915–1963) was a popular Parisian singer, also called the "Little Sparrow."
3. Chet Helms (1942–2005) managed Big Brother and the Holding Company, recruiting Joplin for the group.
4. Albert Grossman (1926–1986) managed the superstars of the era, including Bob Dylan.
5. John Morris worked in the music business and managed rock venues such as Fillmore East in New York.

Wes Wilson poster. Translation of print: Otis Rush and His Chicago
Blues Band. Grateful Dead. The Canned Heat Blues Band. Fri: Sat:
Sun. February 24:25:26. Fri: Sat: 9 pm: $3.00. Sun: 2–7 pm: $2.00.
At the Fillmore. Poster art from the Psychedelic Era, capturing a
musical style and a way of life.

118

"HANDCRAFTING THE GROOVES"

IN THE STUDIO

Aretha Franklin at Muscle Shoals

(Wexler)

When Aretha Franklin (b. 1942) moved from Columbia Records to Atlantic Records in 1966, she launched herself into stardom. Between 1967 and 1973, Franklin produced 13 million-sellers and 13 top-ten hits on the Atlantic label. Her producer, Jerry Wexler (b. 1917), helped her to find what Aaron Copland would call her "personality"— her unique voice as a recording artist.

Wexler brought to the task decades of immersion in black music. In 1949, as a staff writer for *Billboard* magazine, he coined the term "rhythm and blues." In 1953, he joined Atlantic Records and began producing Ray Charles, who released the energies of gospel into his rock-and-roll music. Working with southern musicians at Stax Studios in Memphis, Wexler learned what he described as the southern way of making records. When he took Aretha Franklin from urban Detroit down to Fame Studios at Muscle Shoals to play with white musicians who knew little about her, she taught them her way with soul.

Because soul is a style rooted in African American gospel and its vocal and keyboard improvisational practices, the creative atmosphere at Muscle Shoals proved catalytic for Franklin's talents as a singer, pianist, and arranger. The dynamic collaboration between Franklin and the session musicians is one theme of these excerpts, which are taken from Wexler's autobiography. It could stand as an example of the trend in the 1960s to establish recording studios as creative centers of signature sounds made by virtuoso session musicians: Detroit and Motown had the Funk Brothers; Nashville and the "Nashville sound" had Chet Atkins and Floyd Cramer.

It was a respite in a turbulent time. Franklin's performance of "Respect" linked black pride with the women's movement, and with black feminism in particular. Unfortunately, the vaunted collaborative harmony between black and white musicians got derailed in the aftermath of the assassination of Martin Luther King, Jr. Aretha Franklin sang Thomas Dorsey's "Precious Lord" at his funeral.

SOUL MEN

The musical integration was a joy to hear and behold. The racial mix was serendipitous. For the past decade, musicians in the Memphis–Muscle Shoals axis, black and white, had found a ready market in the fraternity parties of the great Southern universities. Ever since those early pre–rock 'n' roll "beach" recordings emerging from the Carolina coast in the fifties, I could see that Southern whites liked their music uncompromisingly black. Despite the ugly legacy of Jim Crow, their white hearts and minds were gripped, it would seem, forevermore.

Credit the reach and power of [radio station] WLAC in Nashville, which broadcast clear-channel nondirectional in twenty-two states. The white deejays—John R. [Richbourg], Gene Nobles, and Hoss Allen—were black-talking, blues-loving stars. The records they played influenced at least two generations of fans. From a sales point of view, they were marvelous. The ad spots cost a buck apiece late at night, and in conjunction with mail-order operations like Ernie's and Randy's, we got fantastic sales results throughout the country.

First came the fans, and not long after, the musicians. As Al Bell, later Stax's promo director, pointed out, the collision between openly integrated music and a tightly segregated society created a new kind of energy. You can hear a subtle defiance in the songs. White Southern musicians—unlike their British counterparts, who learned the blues off records—lived the blues themselves, saw them, tasted them, were rooted in the same soil as their black teachers.

I was in my early fifties; the Muscle Shoals players were in their early twenties, a couple of generations younger. Later on, a real bonding took place—we became family. But in the beginning it took some real getting used to.

"I remember the first time Jerry called me into the control room," says David Hood, the bassist in what would become the basic Shoals rhythm section of drummer Roger Hawkins, guitarist Jimmy Johnson, and keyboardist Barry Beckett. "Wexler's loud voice—his New York accent—just boomed all over the room. He could stun you with that voice. Man, I was petrified. Later on, we became so tight I asked him to officiate at my wedding. He began the ceremony by saying, 'I have no power vested in me whatsoever . . .'"

"After a while," says Jimmy Johnson, "we became Jerry's second set of kids."

"Before Wexler," Hawkins remembers, "things were pretty quiet around the Shoals. Spooner Oldham and Dan Penn had written 'I'm Your Puppet,' which became a big hit for James and Bobby Purify, and there were a couple of other items, but not many. Jerry put the national spotlight on us. When Wexler said he liked my playing, well, that was a big moment in my life."

No bigger than it was for me, because it was the boys in Muscle Shoals who taught me a new way of making records, spontaneously, synergistically. I'd hit town on the weekend. I'd get together with the singer and Barry Beckett, who ultimately evolved into the de facto leader of the group, and we'd rough out the songs which we'd already selected. We'd set the layout and the keys, then Barry would write a bare-bones chart by the numbers. The Muscle Shoals method of arrangements involved numbering—not naming chords. It was simple—one through six, which might sound musically illiterate but worked like a charm, making it easy to change keys and leaving lots of room for variations.

When the boys came in Monday afternoon, they'd copy the chord chart and would start to pick. They'd play around, maybe lock into a lick, find a nourishing groove, feel their way into the structure. Someone might develop an especially tasty rhythm line—maybe a two-bar syncopated pattern, an outstanding turnaround, or a provocative fill. The arrangement would build communally and organically. The ideas could come from anyone. Pete Carr, for example, another tremendous Muscle Shoals lead guitarist, made marvelous contributions to dozens of sessions. Pete's thinking was not conventional; his two-bar patterns formed the basis of many a rhythm arrangement.

The bottom line was rhythm. Horns and strings—the icing on the cake—might be added afterwards, or not. The trick was to keep the session open, the creative juices flowing, the improvisatory feeling of on-the-spot, here-and-now creation vital and fresh.

. . .

"LISTEN AT HER . . . LISTEN AT HER!"

When she was fourteen, Aretha Franklin sang "Precious Lord" in her father's church. The Reverend C. L. Franklin was spiritual leader of the New Bethel Baptist Church, one of Detroit's biggest congregations. The live recording, a favorite of mine, came out on Chess in 1956. The voice was not that of a child but rather of an ecstatic hierophant. Since the days of covering Mahalia Jackson and Sister Rosetta Tharpe for Billboard, I'd been a fan of gospel, realizing that the church, along with the raw blues, was the foundation of the music that moved me so much. On Aretha's first recording, her singing was informed with her genius. From the congregation, a man cried out, "Listen at her . . . listen at her!" And I did.

From 1961 through 1967, Aretha made over a dozen albums for Columbia. She'd been signed by John Hammond, who called hers the greatest voice since Billie Holiday's. John cut superb sides on her, including "Today I Sing the Blues." Eventually she became the ward of the pop department, which turned out gems like "If Ever I Should Lose You." But as producer Clyde Otis said, "No one really knew what to do with her." There were minor hits, such as "Running Out of Fools," but mostly Aretha languished.

I always had my eye on her, although in 1967 there were a million other matters that seemed more important. . . .

Because I was always doing twelve things at once, I was also always on the lookout for producers with my artists. In Aretha's case, fate, fortune, or the pull of my own passion led me into the studio with her to work in a more involving way than I had ever worked before. John Hammond, more friend than competitor, had encouraged me from the outset. "You'll do good things with Aretha," he assured me. "You understand her musically." Personally, John tipped me, she was enigmatic and withdrawn.

I knew that her preacher father was respected by his community as a civil rights leader and early advocate of black pride. He was a close friend of Martin Luther King, whom he brought to Detroit for the famous 1963 march up Woodward Avenue. He had recorded dozens of sermons for Chess which were rhetorical and metaphorical masterpieces, "The Eagle Stirreth Her Nest" being a classic of the genre. He had the gift of Good Book storytelling, never failing to rouse his church to fevered pitch. Franklin was a national leader, a charismatic character who reputedly occasionally took a walk on the wild side. He'd been busted for pot possession and liked to party. Under unexplained circumstances, his wife had left him and their five children—Vaughn, Erma, Cecil, Aretha, and baby Carolyn—when Aretha was six. When Aretha was ten, her mother died. Some say the preacher used his children, especially the precocious Aretha, as props and pawns; others called him a devoted father. Aretha generally avoided the subject.

She started touring as a teenager, an opening act on her father's gospel show along with Lucy Branch and Sammy Bryant. C.L. also sang. In addition to loving religious song, Reverend Franklin loved jazz and R&B. Aretha's early education was formed by both the gospel greats of her day—Clara Ward, the Staple Singers, the Soul Stirrers, James Cleveland, the Mighty Clouds of Joy—and the secular stars as well. On the road and in his spacious mansion in Detroit, Reverend Franklin entertained artists like Art Tatum and Dinah Washington, R&B luminaries like Sam Cooke, Fats Domino, and Bobby Bland. In a world filled with musical and sexual excitement, Aretha heard and saw everything at an early age. By age seventeen, she herself had given birth to two children. And in a twist on the old myth where the preacher wants his child to sing only for the Lord, C.L. helped Aretha go pop. After all, he was something of a pop preacher himself and lived the pop life to the hilt. When members of his congregation objected to Aretha's secular songs, the Reverend set them straight in a hurry.

John Hammond signed her in 1960. "Sam Cooke was desperately trying to get Aretha for RCA," Hammond remembered. "I'm glad I prevailed. I cherish the records we made together, but, finally, Columbia was a white company who misunderstood her genius."

"Genius" is the word. Clearly Aretha was continuing what Ray Charles had begun—the secularization of gospel, turning church rhythms, church patterns, and especially church feelings into personalized love songs. Like Ray, Aretha was a hands-on performer, a two-fisted pianist plugged into the main circuit of Holy Ghost power. Even though we produced Aretha in a way that we never produced Ray, she remained the central orchestrator of her own sound, the essential contributor and final arbiter of what fit or did not fit her musical persona.

Writing at the start of the nineties, it's easy to forget that a quarter-century ago there was no one else like Aretha Franklin. Pop music today is rich with glorious gospel voices and women singers in the mold cast by Aretha. As Bird [Charlie Parker] gave birth to decades of altoists, Aretha became a model for people like Chaka Khan, Natalie Cole, Donna Summer, Martha Washington, Whitney Houston, Miki Howard, Marva Hicks, Vesta [Williams], Sharon Bryant. The list of her disciples is long. From the start—at least after our first experiences in the studio—I saw she had raised the ante and upgraded the art form.

After Jim Stewart declined the opportunity, my instinct was to take her south anyway and bring her to Muscle Shoals, where I was still in the first flush of exhilaration with that wonderful rhythm section of Alabama white boys who took a left turn at the blues.

Before the trip we naturally mapped out a strategy. I had no lofty notions of correcting Columbia's mistakes or making her into a Mount Rushmore monument. My idea was to make good tracks, use the best players, put Aretha back on piano, and let the lady wail. Aretha, like Ray, was an inner-directed singer—as opposed, let's say, to Mary Wells, who came to us after her Motown successes. We soon realized that we could do nothing with Mary. The fault wasn't hers, nor was it ours; she was an artist who required the idiosyncratic Motown production, which was simply out of our ken. There was something unique about that little Detroit studio—the attitude, the vibes, the energy—that couldn't be duplicated elsewhere. The same is true of Memphis and Muscle Shoals.

It's interesting to consider why Aretha, a Detroiter, never signed with Motown herself, especially given that she was of the same generation as such Motown friends as Smokey Robinson, Diana Ross, and Martha Reeves—you'd think the connection inevitable. It's important to remember, though, that Berry Gordy's empire was built on a new phenomenon. In the early sixties, when his records started hitting, he had expanded the market. Like Phil Spector before him, Gordy was selling to white teenagers. This was a new formula—black music, produced by a black man and sold to white youth—and it became the backbone of Gordy's fortune.

Even though Atlantic and Motown were the only labels where the owners made the records, our approach was entirely different. I've never been interested in confecting teenage music. Ever since Ahmet [Ertegun] began recording Stick McGhee in 1949, the gut of the Atlantic R&B catalogue was pointed at black adults. If white people went for it, fine; if not, we'd survive. But I've always been amazed by Berry Gordy. His music was incredible—the ethereal Smokey Robinson songs, the Temps, the Tops, Marvin Gaye, the Marvelettes, the Supremes, Stevie Wonder. And he pulled off a miracle of marketing that never occurred to me: he made his music acceptable, carefully covering it with gloss and glamour that enabled his artists to become fixtures on the *Ed Sullivan Show*. The sons and daughters of white-bread America became the children of Motown, and even today that generation, now middle-aged, remains loyal to the sound of Gordy's energetic sexuality, a mixture of charm and innocence.

When Aretha arrived at Atlantic, she was not innocent. She was a twenty-five-year-old woman with the sound, feelings, and experience of someone much older. She fit into the matrix of music I had always worked with—songs expressing adult emotions. Aretha didn't come to us to be made over or refashioned; she was searching for herself, not for gimmicks, and in that regard I might have helped. I urged Aretha to be Aretha.

I was happy with the songs for the first album, most of which she either selected or wrote herself. Preproduction went smoothly. Aretha worked on her Fender Rhodes at home, doing a rough outline of the songs. I would never dream of starting tracks without Aretha at the piano; that's what made her material organic. She'd find the key, devise the rhythm pattern, and work out the background vocals with either her sisters, Carolyn and Erma, or the Sweet Inspirations.

The Sweet Inspirations became one of the pillars of the Atlantic Church of Sixties Soul. Led by Cissy Houston (Whitney's mom), Estelle Brown, Sylvia Shemwell, and Myrna Smith were fabulous background singers who, like Aretha, instinctively understood harmonies; they could match vibratos, switch parts, and turn on a dime. And like the great King Curtis—our sax man, arranger, and in-house bandleader—they were always relaxed, fun, and ready to offer a suggestion or innovative passage. Ultimately, it was only a matter of common decency to put them under contract as a featured group. I suggested the name Inspirations, which unfortunately turned out to be already registered (to a group of acrobats!), so I added the "Sweet." In 1968, they had a top twenty hit, the eponymous "Sweet Inspirations," produced by Tom Dowd and Chips Moman in Memphis. They spread soul all over the album *From Elvis in Memphis.*

Aretha was a natural for the Southern style of recording. Once she had the basics—rhythm groove and vocal patterns—I knew she'd get off on the spontaneity of the studio. I took her to Muscle Shoals with only a modicum of doubt. I was a little anxious about presenting Aretha and Ted[1] with a wall-to-wall white band, and consequently I asked Rick Hall to hire a basic black horn section—either the Memphis Horns or a section led by Bowlegs Miller. In addition to the racial mix, I also wanted a certain sonority that the brothers would bring to the horn section. Hall goofed and hired an all-white section. Aretha's response was no response. I never should have worried—about her. She just sat down at the piano and played the music.

. . .

The minute Aretha touched the piano and sang one note, the musicians were captivated. They caught the fever and raced for their instruments. "I've never experienced so much feeling coming out of one human being," says drummer Roger Hawkins. "When she hit that first chord," adds Dan Penn, "we knew everything was gonna be all right."

. . .

If the first release, "I Never Loved a Man," was a success—Aretha's first million-selling record—the second single was a rocket to the moon. She took Otis Redding's "Respect" and turned it inside out, making it deeper, stronger, loading it with double entendres. She and her sister Carolyn (who, along with Erma, sang background vocals) came up with the famous "sock it to me" line. For Otis, "respect" had the traditional connotation, the more abstract meaning of esteem. The fervor in Aretha's magnificent voice demanded that respect and more: respect also involved sexual attention of the highest order. What else could "sock it to me" mean? Given the political climate, respect became a touchstone of an era of emerging ethnic and feminist pride. Aretha's "Respect" resonates on a number of levels and lives on.

For the rest of her debut Atlantic album, *I Never Loved a Man (the Way I Love You)*, Aretha rode the same track. When she arrived at the studio, she had already worked out her piano part, the lead and background vocal arrangements, set the keys, and hand-crafted the grooves. The songs were close to Aretha's heart. This was true not only of her own compositions ("Don't Let Me Lose This Dream," "Baby, Baby, Baby," and "Dr. Feelgood," which is straight from the Bessie Smith–Dinah Washington lineage of lay-it-on-the-line sexual celebrations) but also of tunes linked with artists who had moved her most—Sam Cooke's "A Change Is Gonna Come" and the Ray Charles–associated "Drown in My Own Tears." King Curtis contributed "Soul Serenade" and wrote "Save Me" along with Aretha and Carolyn. (Rick Hall was such a fan of "Save Me" that he used it to shape Etta James's "Tell Mama.")

This formula served for the majority of Aretha's albums, which tumbled out at the rate of two a year. The follow-up *Aretha Arrives* included "Baby I Love You" by Ronnie Shannon, writer of "I Never Loved a Man."

Next came *Lady Soul,* which yielded four hits. The first was the biggest. Songwriter Ellie Greenwich dropped by my office while I was listening to an acetate of Aretha busting up Don Covay's combustible "Chain of Fools." I'd brought Joe South up from Atlanta to play a special guitar part; we went for the Pops Staple sound by tuning the guitar down four or five steps and turning up the vibrato to the max, creating a deep, mysterious tremolo. For me the record couldn't be improved. But Ellie knew better; she loved the song, but insisted she heard another background part. "Sing it for me," I urged. She did, and it was perfect, so right then and there I whisked her into the studio and had her overdub the part on the final master, thickening the already extra-thick harmony.

"(You Make Me Feel Like) A Natural Woman" was a title I suggested to Carole King and Gerry Goffin, who brilliantly wrote it to order, a prime example of custom-made composition. The song has become part of Aretha's own persona, a product of her own soul. Aretha (along with Ted White) wrote "Since You Been Gone." Two other guitarists made significant contributions to the album—Bobby Womack and Eric Clapton. Ahmet brought Eric into the control room one day while we were doing a vocal with Aretha on "Good to Me as I Am to You." There was a spot for guitar obbligato. Eric didn't quite hear it that day, but he came back the next afternoon and killed it.

SOURCE: Jerry Wexler and David Ritz, *Rhythm and the Blues: A Life in American Music* (New York: Knopf, 1993): 192–94, 206–10, 213–16.

~~~~~~~~~~~

NOTE

1.   Ted White was Franklin's ex-husband and manager at the time.

Jimi Hendrix, Virtuoso of Electricity

(Hendrix, Bloomfield)

Jimi Hendrix (1942–1970) changed the history of twentieth-century rock through his virtuosity on the electric guitar as a composer/improviser and performer. Any number of his performances are anthems of a remarkable era: "Wild Thing," performed at the Monterey Pop Festival (captured on video); "All Along the Watchtower," an improvisatory exploration of the Bob Dylan classic; and his solo rumination on "The Star Spangled Banner" at the Woodstock rock festival.

The first selection, an interview with Hendrix for the photo magazine *Life*, reads like a psychedelic sermon on the idea of the "electric church." Its flamboyant incoherence makes it sound like Hendrix is "tripping"—to use the slang of the era— rather than thinking. But in fact, he repeated his spiritual credo in many other interviews. The second excerpt comes from an issue of *Guitar Player* in 1975 devoted to Hendrix and written by one of the earliest white blues guitar players to command international respect in the blues revival of the 1960s.

FROM "AN INFINITI OF JIMIS"

Introduction] Jimi Hendrix is a rock demigod whose onstage ecstasies have sometimes, to square eyes, seemed to border on the berserk. In his frenzy he would make love to his guitar, then conclude his carryings-on by dousing it with lighter fluid and burning it up. The Jimi Hendrix Experience, "a shock treatment kind of thing," he says, made him famous but did not hide his enormous talents as a musician. Today he wants to abandon the excesses for the more spiritual, quiet region of life and music he describes below, in an interview with *Life* Reporter Robin Richman.

[Hendrix transcript begins here.]
Pretend your mind is a big muddy bowl and the silt is very slowly settling down—but remember your mind's still muddy and you can't possibly grasp all I'm saying.

Music is going to break the way. There'll be a day when houses will be made of diamonds and emeralds which won't have any value anymore and they'd last longer in a rainstorm than a wooden house. Bullets'll be fairy tales. There'll be a renaissance from bad to completely clear and pure and good—from lost to found.

The everyday mud world we're living in today compared to the spiritual world is like a parasite compared to the ocean and the ocean is the biggest living thing you know about. One way to approach the spiritual side is facing the truth. People who make a lot of money—they are sadder and sadder 'cause deep down they have a hurt. So they go and buy a prostitute on Saturday and go to church on Sunday and pray down on the ground in a little salt box, hearing another man who has the same problems preach—and the collection plate keeps going around and around. That man thinks he's found religion but he gets hurt more and more because he's not going towards the spiritual side which is the way the atmosphere is.

Atmospheres are going to come through music because music is in a spiritual thing of its own. It's like the waves of the ocean. You can't just cut out the perfect wave and take it home with you. It's constantly moving all the time. It is the biggest thing electrifying the earth. Music and motion are all part of the race of man.

I don't think what I say is abstract. It's reality. What's unreal is all those people living in cement beehives with no color and making themselves look like their gig and slaving themselves for that one last dollar and crying with millions in their pockets and constantly playing war games and making bets. They're losing themselves in big ego scenes and being above another man in some kind of form. Look at the pimps and congressmen.

But I can explain everything better through music. You hypnotize people to where they go right back to their natural state which is pure positive—like in childhood when you got natural highs. And when you get people at that weakest point, you can preach into the subconscious what we want to say. That's why the name "electric church" flashes in and out.

People want release any kind of way nowadays. The idea is to release in the proper form. Then they'll feel like going into another world, a clearer world. The music flows from the air; that's why I can connect with a spirit, and when they come down off this natural high, they see clearer, feel different things—don't think of pain and hurting the next person. You think of getting your own thing together. You can't be lazy. You have to look at all the faults you have.

There's no telling how many lives your spirit will go through—die and be reborn. Like my mind will be back in the days when I was a flying horse. Before I can remember anything, I can remember music and stars and planets. I could go to sleep and write 15 symphonies. I had very strange feelings that I was here for something and I was going to get a chance to be heard. I got the guitar together 'cause that was all I had. I used to be really lonely.

A musician, if he's a messenger, is like a child who hasn't been handled too many times by man, hasn't had too many fingerprints across his brain. That's why music is so much heavier than anything you ever felt.

SOURCE: Jimi Hendrix in an interview with Robin Richman, "An Infiniti of Jimis," *Life,* October 3, 1969, 72–75.

~~~~~~~~~

Michael Bloomfield (1943–1981) was an important blues guitarist, known for his work with the Paul Butterfield Blues Band. In this selection, Bloomfield writes about Hendrix's work with a scholarly depth of knowledge about the tradition they shared.

The first time I saw Jimi play he was Jimmy James with the Blue Flames. I was performing with Paul Butterfield, and I was the hot shot guitarist on the block—I thought I was *it*. I'd never heard of Hendrix. Then someone said, "You got to see the guitar player with John Hammond." I was at the Cafe Au Go Go and he was at the Nite Owl or the Cafe Wha?—I went right across the street and saw him. Hendrix knew who I was, and that day, in front of my eyes, he burned me to death. I didn't even get my guitar out. H bombs were going off, guided missiles were flying—I can't tell you the sounds he was getting out of his instrument. He was getting every sound I was ever to hear him get right there in that room with a Stratocaster, a Twin (amplifier), a Maestro fuzz tone, and that was all—he was doing it mainly through extreme volume. How he did this, I wish I understood. He just got right up in my face with that axe, and I didn't even want to pick up a guitar for the next year.

I was awed. I'd never heard anything like it. I didn't even know where he was coming from musically, because he wasn't playing any of his own tunes. He was doing things like "Like a Rolling Stone," but in the most unusual way. He wasn't a singer, he wasn't even particularly a player. That day, Jimi Hendrix was laying things on me that were more sounds than they were licks. But I found, that after hearing him two or three more times, that he was into pure melodic playing and lyricism as much as he was into sounds. In fact, he had melded them into a perfect blend.

Jimi told me that he'd been playing the chitlin circuit, and he hadn't heard guitarists doing anything new—he was bored out of his mind. He was a real shy talker, and often spoke in riddles, though he could be quite lucid if pinned down. He explained that he could do more than play backup guitar in the chitlin circuit, and though he was a rotten singer, he knew that he had a lot going on electric guitar. Jimi said he had never heard anyone play in his style.

. . .

There was no great electric guitarist in rock and roll that Jimi didn't know of. I could ask him about records that I knew had real fancy guitar parts, where the performer was ahead of his time or playing funky on a record that wasn't particularly funky. For example, Jimi knew all about a very early Righteous Brothers record on which there's a guitarist who plays very advanced rock and roll guitar for that time. There's another record by Robert Parker, who made "Barefootin'," called, "You Better Watch Yourself," that has a real hot guitar player with a style more like Hendrix than most session players. Jimi said it wasn't him, but that he knew the guy—somebody named Big Tom Collins. He knew every hot guitarist on record.

When *Are You Experienced* came out, it was fantastic, but I was even more impressed with Jimi's second LP, *Axis: Bold as Love*. It was fabulous, utterly funky. I'd heard the Who and Cream and much loud electric power music, but I had never heard a trio that really worked and was so danceable. Hendrix defined how a trio should sound. He had such an orchestral concept that *Are You Experienced* negated everything I had heard in the English lead guitar power trio field.

Jimi had been fooling around with feedback, but when he heard the Yardbirds, he realized its huge potential. Hendrix would sustain a note and add vibrato so that it sounded just like a human voice. He used an immense vocabulary of controlled sounds, not just hoping to get those sounds, but actually controlling them as soon as he produced them. I have never heard such controlled frenzy, especially in electric music. Jimi said that he went to England to wipe them out, and he did.

When he came back to the U.S., he jammed a lot. He was in the habit, around 1968 or '69, of carrying two very good home recorders with him, and every time he jammed he would set these up so that, with the two four-track machines, he was getting eight tracks of recording. God knows who has these tapes, but Jimi was a massive chronicler of his own and other people's jams, and I personally saw at least ten jams that he recorded. The Cafe Au Go Go in New York also had extremely good recording facilities, and I believe they recorded every time Hendrix jammed there—he did that countless times.

. . .

I never saw anything customized on any of his guitars, except he told me that his whang [tremolo] bar was customized on all of his guitars, so he could pull it back much farther than a whole step. He wanted to be able to lower it three steps. He had no favorite guitar—they were all expendable. Buddy Miles has some of his Strats, and all the ones that I've tried are hard to play—heavy strings and heavy action. I'm amazed that he could play them as facilely as he did.

Jimi's musical approach, as he explained it to me, was to lay out the entire song and decide how it should be—horns, strings, the way it would wind up. He would play the drum beat on a damp wah-wah pedal, the bass part on the bass strings of his guitar, and the pattern of the song with just the wah-wah pedal. Then he would flesh the pattern out by playing it with chords and syncopation. He was extremely interested in form—in a few seconds of playing, he'd let you know about the entire structure. That's why he liked rhythm guitar playing so much—the rhythm guitar could lay out the structure for the whole song. He would always say, "This is a world of lead guitar players, but the most essential thing to learn is the time, the rhythm." He once told me he wanted to burn Clapton to death because he didn't play rhythm.

Jimi would play a bass pattern, and then fill it up with chords, and at the exact same time he would play lead by making a high note ring out while using very unorthodox chord positions. He had a massive thumb, which he used like an additional finger, so his hand positions were unconventional for every chord.

Once we played a gig at The Shrine in Los Angeles, and we were backstage fooling around with our guitars. Hendrix was playing with his toggle switch—he was taking the toggle switch of the guitar, tapping the back of the neck, and using vibrato, and it came out sounding like a sirocco, a wind coming up from the desert. I have never heard a sound on a Hendrix record that I have not seen him create in front of my eyes.

I don't know how he kept the guitar in tune. If you jerk a whang bar, your guitar goes out of tune. But his didn't apparently. He could bend it in tune.

Somehow, by tapping the back of his guitar neck (which he constantly did) and by using the bar, Jimi could control feedback. You would hear a rumbling start—he knew which note would feed back and what harmonic he was shooting for, and then he controlled it. Somehow, when he had all the notes open, he would raise the pitch level by using the bar and he'd get a higher note to feed back, or he would make the bass note feed back harmonically. He was listening for such things, and I believe he heard them on the English records, particularly by the Yardbirds and Jeff Beck. He was very modest. He never said he took feedback further than the Yardbirds. He said, "I fool with it, and what I'm doing now is the fruits of my fooling around."

You couldn't even tell what Hendrix was doing with his body. He moved with all those tricks that black guitarists had been using since T-Bone Walker and Guitar Slim—playing behind his head and with his teeth. He took exhibitionism to a new degree. He used to crash his guitar against his hip. It was a bold gesture, and he would get a roaring, fuzzy, feedback sound. His body motion was so integrated with his playing that you couldn't tell where one started and the other left off.

Many of his sounds were things that Jimi stumbled on and a lot he shopped for. They became part of his musical language. It wasn't something he could just tell you how to do. You had to understand the whole way he heard sound, the way he wanted to feel sound and get it out to create music.

. . .

Melodically, he used two basic scales: The blues minor scale and its relative major. If he was playing *A* minor, he would go to *C* major and make it a major seventh scale. "All Along the Watchtower" is a perfect vehicle for minor or blues scale improvisation, while "Bold as Love," "Little Wing," and "The Wind Cries Mary" were perfect for major key explorations.

But it was no big thing for Hendrix to play melodies—he wanted to play like an orchestra. This is the crux of his music—it's not just lead guitar, it's orchestral guitar, like Segovia, Chet Atkins, Wilburn Burchette, Ry Cooder, and George Van Eps. Jimi Hendrix was the most orchestral of all. Have you ever heard "The Star Spangled Banner" on *Rainbow Bridge?* That's recorded like a huge symphony.

. . .

Hendrix was by far the greatest expert I've ever heard at playing rhythm and blues, the style of playing developed by Bobby Womack, Curtis Mayfield, Eric Gale[s], and others. I got the feeling there was no guitaring of any kind that he hadn't heard or studied, including steel guitar, Hawaiian, and dobro.

In his playing I can really hear Curtis Mayfield, Wes Montgomery, Albert King, B. B. King, and Muddy Waters. Jimi was the blackest guitarist I ever heard. His music was deeply rooted in pre-blues, the oldest musical forms, like field hollers and gospel melodies. From what I can garner, there was no form of black music that he hadn't listened to or studied, but he especially loved the real old black music forms, and they poured out in his playing. We often talked about Son House and the old blues guys. But what really did it to him was early Muddy Waters and John Lee Hooker records—that early guitar music where the guitar was hugely amplified, and boosted by the studio to give it the effect of more presence than it really had. He knew that stuff backwards—you can hear every old John Lee Hooker and Muddy Waters thing that ever was on that one long version of "Voodoo Chile" [on *Electric Ladyland*].

. . .

I feel that Hendrix was one of the most innovative guitar players who ever lived. He was the man that took electric music and defined it. He turned sounds from devices into wah-wahs into music. They weren't gimmicks when he used them. In fact, they were beyond music, they were in the realm of pure sound and music combined. Every time I saw Jimi play, I felt that he was an object lesson for everything that I should be and wasn't. But I could never say something like that to him, because he was a super-modest guy.

SOURCE: Excerpts from "Michael Bloomfield Reminisces," *Guitar Player* (September 19, 1975): 22–30. Partially quoted in Steve Waksman, *Instruments of Desire: The Electric Guitar and the Shaping of Musical Experience* (Cambridge, Mass.: Harvard University Press, 1999): 197, 200.

120

$\mathcal{A}$MIRI BARAKA THEORIZES A

BLACK NATIONALIST AESTHETIC

Amiri Baraka (b. 1934 as LeRoi Jones) uses his formidable creative gifts to shape a context through which the expressive culture of African-American people can be understood as a unified whole. Emerging as an intellectual force in the 1960s, Baraka foretold the shifts in consciousness (that '60s keyword) toward intellectual and artistic autonomy and "black power." Baraka contributed significantly to the development of the black aesthetic movement (or black arts movement) in the 1960s. His cultural politics reflects debates over integration and separatist strategies in politics at the time when black nationalism and the Black Muslim movement challenged the strategies of Martin Luther King Jr.'s civil rights movement.

In the landmark *Blues People,* Baraka treated black blues and jazz as the crucible for the black experience in America. For him, by the end of the twentieth century, the blues had supplanted the spiritual as the most important artistic representation of black identity. The first excerpt from *Blues People* reprinted here explains Baraka's critical angle of vision; the second, its powerful reach.

Here (as well as in his second book, *Black Music*), Baraka argues for the relevance of consciousness in understanding the common ground of all black music, be it rhythm and blues or the "new black music"—the avant-garde jazz pioneered by Ornette Coleman, John Coltrane, and Sun Ra, among others.

~~~~~~~~
~~~~~~~~
~~~~~~~~

FROM *BLUES PEOPLE*

INTRODUCTION

I am trying in this book, by means of analogy and some attention to historical example, to establish certain general conclusions about a particular segment of American society.

This book should be taken as a strictly *theoretical* endeavor. Theoretical, in that none of the questions it poses can be said to have been answered definitively or for all time, etc. In fact, the book proposes more questions than it will answer. The only questions it will properly move to answer have, I think, been answered already within the patterns of American life. We need only [to] give these patterns serious scrutiny and draw certain permissible conclusions.

The Negro as slave is one thing. The Negro as American is quite another. But the *path* the slave took to "citizenship" is what I want to look at. And I make my analogy through the slave citizen's music—through the music that is most closely associated with him: blues and a later, but parallel development, jazz. And it seems to me that if the Negro represents, or is symbolic of, something in and about the nature of American culture, this certainly should be revealed by his characteristic music.

In other words, I am saying that if the music of the Negro in America, in all its permutations, is subjected to a socio-anthropological as well as musical scrutiny, something about the essential nature of the Negro's existence in this country ought to be revealed, as well as something about the essential nature of this country, i.e., society as a whole.

Blues, had, and still has, a certain *weight* in the psyches of its inventors. What I am proposing is that the alteration or repositioning of this weight in those same psyches indicates changes in the Negro that are manifested externally. I am proposing that the weight of the blues for the slave, for the completely disenfranchised individual, differs radically from the weight of the same music in the psyches of most contemporary American Negroes. I mean, we know certain definite things about the lives of the Negro slaves. We also, with even more certainty, know things about the lives of the contemporary American Negros. The one peculiar referent to the drastic change in the Negro from slavery to "citizenship" is his music.

There are definite *stages* in the Negro's transmutation from African to American: or, at least, there are certain very apparent changes in the Negro's reactions to America from the time of his first importation as slave until the present that can, I think, be seen—and again, I insist that these changes are most graphic in his music. I have tried to scrutinize each one of these stages as closely as I could, with a musical as well as a sociological and anthropological emphasis.

If we take 1619, twelve years after the settling of Jamestown in 1607, as the date of the first importation of Negroes into this country to *stay* (not merely brought here for a time to do odd jobs, etc., and then be bumped off, as was very often the case), we have a good point in history to move from. First, we know that West Africans, who are the peoples most modern scholarship has cited as contributing almost 85 per cent of the slaves finally brought to the United States, did not sing blues. Undoubtedly, none of the African prisoners broke out into *St. James*

Infirmary the minute the first of them was herded off the ship. We also know that [the] first African slaves, when they worked in those fields, if they sang or shouted at all, sang or shouted in some pure African dialect (either from the parent Bantu or Sudanic, with maybe even the Hamitic as a subbase, which would include Coptic, Berber, or Cushitic). But there are no records of 12-bar AAB songs in those languages—at least none that would show a direct interest in social and agricultural problems in the Southern U.S., although, it should be noted here, and I will go into it further in the chapter on Africanisms, the most salient characteristic of African, or at least West African, music is a type of song in which there is a leader and a chorus; the leading lines of the song sung by a single voice, the leader's, alternating with a refrain sung by the chorus. It is easy enough to see the definite analogy between a kind of song in which there is a simple A-B response and a kind of song that could be developed out of it to be sung by one person, where the first line of the song is repeated twice (leader), followed by a third line (chorus), sometimes rhymed but usually dissimilar, and always a direct comment on the first two lines. And then we know of the patois-type languages and the other half-African languages that sprang up through the South, which must, after a time, have been what those various laments, chants, stories, etc. were told and sung in.

But what I am most anxious about here is the American Negro. When did he merge? Out of what strange incunabula did the peculiar heritage and attitudes of the American Negro arise? I suppose it is technically correct to call any African who was brought here and had no chance of ever leaving, from that very minute when his residence and his life had been changed irrevocably, an American Negro. But it is imperative to realize that the first slaves did not believe they would be here forever. Or even if they did, they thought of themselves merely as *captives*. This, America, was a foreign land. These people were foreigners, they spoke in a language which was not colonial American; and the only Western customs or mores of which they had any idea at all were that every morning at a certain time certain work had to be done and that they would probably be asked to do it.

And the point I want to make most evident here is that I cite the beginning of the blues as one beginning of American Negroes. Or, let me say, the reaction and subsequent relation of the Negro's experience in this country in *his* English is one beginning of the Negro's *conscious* appearance on the American scene. If you are taken to Mongolia as a slave and work there for seventy-five years and learn twenty words of Mongolian and live in a small house from which you leave only to work, I don't think we can call you a Mongolian. It is only when you begin to accept the idea that you *are* part of that country that you can be said to be a permanent resident. I mean, that until the time when you have sufficient ideas about this new country to begin making some lasting *moral* generalizations about it—relating your experience, in some lasting form, *in the language* of that country, with whatever subtleties and obliqueness you bring to it—you are merely a transient. There were no formal stories about the Negro's existence in America passed down in any pure African tongue. The stories, myths, moral examples, etc., given in African were *about* Africa. When America became important enough to the African to be passed on, in those *formal* renditions, to the young, those renditions were in some kind of Afro-American language. And finally, when a man looked up in some anonymous field and shouted, "Oh, Ahm tired a dis mess, / Oh, yes, Ahm tired a dis mess," you can be sure he was an American.

FROM CHAPTER 10: "SWING—FROM VERB TO NOUN"

. . .

Music, as paradoxical as it may seem, is the result of thought. It is the result of thought perfected at its most empirical, i.e., as *attitude*, or *stance*. Thought is largely conditioned by reference; it is the result of consideration or speculation against reference, which is largely arbitrary. There is no one way of thinking, since reference (hence value) is as scattered and dissimilar as men themselves. If Negro music can be seen to be [the] result of certain attitudes, certain specific ways of thinking about the world (and only ultimately about the *ways* in which music is made), then the basic hypothesis of this book is understood. The Negro's music changed as he changed, reflecting shifting attitudes or (and this is equally important), *consistent attitudes within changed contexts*. And it is *why* the music changed that seems most important to me.

When jazz first began to appear during the twenties on the American scene, in one form or another, it was introduced in a great many instances into that scene by white Americans. Jazz as it was originally conceived and in most instances of its most vital development was the result of certain attitudes, or empirical ideas, attributable to the Afro-American culture. Jazz as played by white musicians was not the same as that played by black musicians, nor was there any reason for it to be. The music of the white jazz musician did not issue from the same cultural circumstance; it was, at its most profound instance, a learned art. The blues, for example, which I take to be an autonomous black music, had very little weight at all in pre-jazz white American culture. But blues is an extremely important part of jazz. However, the way in which jazz utilizes the blues "attitude" provided a musical analogy the white musician could understand and thus utilize in his music to arrive at a style of jazz music. The white musician understood the blues first as music, but seldom as an attitude, since the attitude, or world-view, the white musician was responsible to was necessarily quite a different one. And in many cases, this attitude, or world-view, was one that was not consistent with the making of jazz.

There should be no cause for wonder that the trumpets of Bix Beiderbecke and Louis Armstrong were so dissimilar. The white middle-class boy from Iowa was the product of a culture which could place Louis Armstrong, but could never understand him. Beiderbecke was also the product of a subculture that most nearly emulates the "official" or formal culture of North America. He was an instinctive intellectual who had a taste for Stravinsky, Schoenberg, and Debussy, and had an emotional life that, as it turned out, was based on his conscious or unconscious disapproval of most of the sacraments of his culture. On the other hand, Armstrong was, in terms of emotional archetypes, an honored priest of his culture—one of the most impressive products of his society. Armstrong was not *rebelling* against anything with his music. In fact, his music was one of the most beautiful refinements of Afro-American musical tradition, and it was immediately recognized as such by those Negroes who were not trying to pretend that they had issued from Beiderbecke's culture. The incredible irony of the situation was that both stood in similar places in the superstructure of American society: Beiderbecke, because of the isolation any deviation from mass culture imposed upon its bearer; and Armstrong, because of the socio-historical estrangement of the Negro from the rest of America. Nevertheless, the music the two made was as dissimilar as is possible within jazz. Beiderbecke's slight reflective tone and impressionistic lyricism was the most impressive example of the "artifact given expression" in jazz. He played "white jazz" in the sense I am trying to convey, that is, as a music that is the product of attitudes expressive of a peculiar culture. Armstrong, of course, played jazz that was securely within the traditions of Afro-

American music. His tone was brassy, broad, and aggressively dramatic. He also relied heavily on the vocal blues tradition in his playing to amplify the expressiveness of his instrumental technique.

I am using these two men as examples because they were two early masters of a developing *American* music, though they expressed antithetical versions of it. The point is that Afro-American music did not become a completely American expression until the white man could play it! Bix Beiderbecke, more than any of the early white jazzmen, signified this development because he was the first white musician who brought to the jazz he created any of the ultimate concern Negro musicians brought to it as a casual attitude of their culture. This development signified also that jazz would someday have to contend with the idea of its being an art (since that *was* the white man's only way into it). The emergence of the white player meant that Afro-American culture had already become the expression of a particular kind of American experience, and what is most important, that this experience was available intellectually, that it could be learned.

SOURCE: LeRoi Jones [Amiri Baraka], *Blues People: Negro Music in White America* (New York: Morrow, 1963): ix–xii, 152–55.

GREIL MARCUS AND THE NEW ROCK CRITICISM

In the 1950s, rock and roll was treated as the popular passion of a peculiarly susceptible generation of rebellious (spoiled) teenagers. When, in the late 1960s, rock turned into "art" as well, a new kind of rock criticism followed in its wake. Written by a new generation of writers—most of them mavericks reared on the rhythms of television news, the rhetoric of advertising, and the permissive prose of the Beat Generation—rock criticism gave the music a history and an ideology by the 1970s. The process did not take all that much time: between 1967 and 1975, the magazine *Rolling Stone* changed from "just a little rock 'n' roll newspaper from San Francisco" to a "biweekly general interest magazine covering contemporary American culture, politics, and arts, with a special interest in music."[1] One of its most celebrated contributing critics, Greil Marcus (b. 1945) published his first book, *Mystery Train,* in 1975; a fifth, revised, twenty-fifth anniversary edition published in 2000 acknowledged its stature.

Even these few excerpts from *Mystery Train* show how Marcus treats rock as a symbolic representation of American experience. The first selection makes its point slowly as we wade through a now-dated account of an exchange between a serious critic and a popular romance novelist. Nevertheless, as the 1950s rock 'n' roll star Little Richard (Richard Penniman, b. 1932) emerges from the prose in capital letters, Marcus steel-drives home the message about the black roots of rock. Following that, other selections embellish the enterprise of writing about rock the way American studies scholars treated literature.

One could argue that Marcus and his colleagues shaped the ways in which the current generation still responds to the meanings of popular music. Rock is no longer mere entertainment, or even art—it is heritage.

AUTHOR'S NOTE AND THE PROLOGUE

Writing these opening notes reminds me of the prefaces to the American history books that were written during World War II, when the authors, looking back for the meaning of the Revolution or the Civil War or whatever, drew modest but determined parallels between their work and the struggle; that an attempt to understand America took on a special meaning when America was up for grabs. Those writers were also saying—at least, this is what they say to me—that to do one's most personal work in a time of public crisis is an honest, legitimate, paradoxically democratic act of common faith; that one keeps faith with one's community by offering whatever it is that one has to say. I mean those writers were exhilarated, thirty years ago, by something we can only call patriotism, and humbled by it too. Well, I feel some kinship with those writers. I began this book in the fall of 1972, and finished it late in the summer of 1974. Inevitably, it reflects, and I hope contains, the peculiar moods of those times, when the country came face to face with an obscene perversion of itself that could be neither accepted nor destroyed: moods of rage, excitement, loneliness, fatalism, desire.

. . .

PROLOGUE

Our story begins just after midnight, not so long ago. The *Dick Cavett Show* is in full swing.

Seated on Cavett's left is John Simon, the New York Critic. On Cavett's right, in order of distance from him, are Little Richard, Rock 'n' Roll Singer and Weirdo; Rita Moreno, Actress; and Erich Segal, Yale Professor of Classics and Author of *Love Story*. Miss Moreno and Mr. Segal adored *Love Story*. Mr. Simon did not. Little Richard has not read it.

Cavett is finishing a commercial. Mr. Simon is mentally rehearsing his opening thrust against Mr. Segal, who is very nervous. Miss Moreno seems to be falling asleep. Little Richard is looking for an opening.

Mr. Simon has attacked Mr. Segal. Mr. Segal attempts a reply, but he is too nervous to be coherent. Mr. Simon attacks a second time. Little Richard is about to jump out of his seat and jam his face in front of the camera but Mr. Simon beats him out. He attacks Mr. Segal again.

"NEGATIVE! NEGATIVE NEGATIVE NEGATIVE!" screams Mr. Segal. He and Simon are debating a fine point in the history of Greek tragedy, to which Mr. Simon has compared *Love Story* unfavorably.

"Neg-a-tive," muses Mr. Simon. "Does that mean 'no'?"

Mr. Segal attempts, unsuccessfully, to ignore Mr. Simon's contempt for his odd patois, and claims that the critics were wrong about Aeschylus. He implies that Simon would have walked out on the *Oresteia*. Backed by the audience, which sounds like a Philadelphia baseball crowd that has somehow mistaken Mr. Simon for Richie Allen, Segal presses his advantage. Little Richard sits back in his chair, momentarily intimidated.

"MILLIONS OF PEOPLE WERE DEEPLY MOVED by my book," cries Segal, forgetting to sit up straight and slumping in his chair until his body is near parallel with the floor. "AND IF ALL THOSE PEOPLE LIKED IT—" (Segal's voice has now achieved a curious tremolo) "*I MUST BE DOING SOMETHING RIGHT!*"

The effort has exhausted Mr. Segal, and as he takes a deep breath Little Richard begins to rise from his seat. Again, Simon is too fast for him. Simon attempts to make Segal understand that he is amazed that anyone, especially Segal, takes this trash to be anything more than, well, trash.

"I have read it and reread it many times," counters Segal with great honesty. "I am always moved."

"Mr. Segal," says Simon, having confused the bull with his cape and now moving in for the kill, "you had the choice of acting the knave or the fool. You have chosen the latter."

Segal is stunned. Cavett is stunned. He calls for a commercial. Little Richard considers the situation.

The battle resumes. Segal has now slumped even lower in his chair, if that is possible, and seems to be arguing with the ceiling. "*You're* only a critic," he says as if to Simon. "What have *you* ever written? What do you know about art? Never in the history of art . . . "

"WHY, NEVER IN THE HISTORY!"

The time has come. Little Richard makes his move. Leaping from his seat, he takes the floor, arms waving, hair coming undone, eyes wild, mouth working. He advances on Segal, Cavett, and Simon, who cringe as one man. The camera cuts to a close-up of Segal, who looks miserable, then to Simon, who is attempting to compose the sort of bemused expression he would have if, say, someone were to defecate on the floor. Little Richard is audible off-camera, and then his face quickly fills the screen.

"WHY, YES, IN THE WHOLE HISTORY OF AAAART! THAT'S RIGHT! SHUT UP! SHUT UP! WHAT DO YOU KNOW, MR. CRITIC? WHY, WHEN THE CREEDENCE CLEARWATER PUT OUT WITH THEIR 'TRAVELIN' BAND' EVERYBODY SAY WHEEE-OOO BUT I KNOW IT CAUSE THEY ONLY DOING 'LONG TALL SALLY' JUST LIKE THE BEATLES ANDTHESTONESANDTOMJONESANDELVIS—I AM ALL OF IT, LITTLE RICHARD HIMSELF, VERY TRULY THE GREATEST, THE HANDSOMEST, AND NOW TO YOU (to Segal, who now appears to be *on* the floor) AND TO YOU (to Simon, who looks to Cavett as if to say, really old man, this *has* been fun, but this, ah, *fellow* is becoming a bit much, perhaps a commercial is in order?), I HAVE WRITTEN A BOOK, MYSELF, I AM A WRITER, I HAVE WRITTEN A BOOK AND IT'S CALLED—

"'HE GOT WHAT HE WANTED BUT HE LOST WHAT HE HAD'! THAT'S IT! SHUT UP! SHUT UP! SHUT UP! HE GOT WHAT HE WANTED BUT HE LOST WHAT HE HAD! THE STORY OF MY LIFE. CAN YOU DIG IT? THAT'S MY BOY LITTLE RICHARD, SURE IS. OO MAH SOUL!"

Little Richard flies back to his chair and slams down into it. "WHEEEEE-OO! OOO MAH SOUL! OO mah soul . . ."

Little Richard sits with the arbiters of taste, oblivious to their bitter stares, savoring his moment. He is Little Richard. Who are they? Who will remember Erich Segal, John Simon, Dick Cavett? Who will care? Ah, but Little Richard, Little Richard *himself!* There is a man who matters. He knows how to rock.

A phrase that Little Richard snatched off Erich Segal stays in my mind: "Never in the history—*in the whole history of art . . .*" And that was it. Little Richard was the only artist on the set that night, the only one who disrupted an era, the only one with a claim to immortality. The one who broke the rules, created a form; the one who gave shape to a vitality that wailed silently in each of us until he found a voice for it.

He is the rock, the jive bomber, the savant. "Tutti Frutti" was his first hit, breaking off the radio in 1955 to shuffle the bland expectations of white youth; fifteen years later the Weirdo on the *Cavett Show* reached back for whatever he had left and busted up an argument about the meaning of art with a spirit that recalled the absurd promise of his glory days. "I HAVE WRITTEN A BOOK, MYSELF, AND IT'S CALLED . . ."

Listening now to Little Richard, to Elvis, to Jerry Lee Lewis, the Monotones, the Drifters, Chuck Berry, and dozens of others, I feel a sense of awe at how fine their music was. I can only marvel at their arrogance, their humor, their delight. They were so sure of themselves. They sang as if they knew they were destined to survive not only a few weeks on the charts but to make history; to displace the dreary events of the fifties in the memories of those who heard their records; and to anchor a music that twenty years later would be struggling to keep the promises they made. Naturally, they sound as if they could care less, so long as their little black 45's hit number one and made them rich and famous. But they delivered a new version of America with their music, and more people than anyone can count are still trying to figure out how to live in it.

Well, then, this is a book about rock 'n' roll—some of it—and America. It is not a history, or a purely musical analysis, or a set of personality profiles. It is an attempt to broaden the context in which the music is heard; to deal with rock 'n' roll not as youth culture, or counterculture, but simply as American culture.

The performers that I have written about appeal to me partly because they are more ambitious and because they take more risks than most. They risk artistic disaster (in rock['s] term, pretentiousness), or the alienation of an audience that can be soothed far more easily than it can be provoked; their ambitions have a good deal to do with Robbie Robertson's statement of his ambitions for the Band: "Music should never be harmless."

What attracts me even more to the Band, Sly Stone, Randy Newman, and Elvis, is that I think these men tend to see themselves as symbolic Americans; I think their music is an attempt to live up to that role. Their records—the Band's *Big Pink,* Sly's *There's a Riot Goin' On,* a few of Randy Newman's tunes, Elvis Presley's very first Tennessee singles—dramatize a sense of what it is to be an American; what it means, what it's worth, what the stakes of life in America might be. This book, then, is an exploration of a few artists, all of whom seem to me to have found their own voices; it is rooted in the idea that these artists can illuminate those American questions and that the questions can add resonance to their work.

The two men whose tales begin the book—white country hokum singer Harmonica Frank and black Mississippi blues singer Robert Johnson—came and went before the words "rock 'n' roll" had any cultural meaning at all. Both men represent traditions crucial to rock 'n' roll, and both are unique. They worked at the frontiers of the music, and they can give us an idea of what the country has to give the music to work with—a sense of how far the music can go. Harmonica Frank sang with a simple joy and a fool's pride; he caught a spirit the earliest rock 'n' roll mastered effortlessly, a mood the music is always losing and trying to win back. Robert Johnson was very different. He was a brooding man who did his work on the darker side of American life; his songs deal with terrors and fears that few American artists have ever expressed so directly. In this book, Frank and Johnson figure as metaphors more than musical influences. Their chapters are meant to form a backdrop against which the later chapters can take shape, a framework for the images the other artists have made.

The Band, Sly Stone, Randy Newman, and Elvis Presley share unique musical and public personalities, enough ambition to make even their failures interesting, and a lack of critical commentary extensive or committed enough to do their work justice. In their music and in their careers, they share a range and a depth that seem to crystallize naturally in visions and versions of America; its possibilities, limits, openings, traps. Their stories are hardly the whole story, but they can tell us how much the story matters. That is what this book is about.

> . . . to be an American (unlike being English or French or whatever) is precisely
> to *imagine* a destiny rather than to inherit one; since we have always been, in-
> sofar as we are Americans at all, inhabitants of myth rather than history. . . .
> —Leslie Fiedler, "Cross the Border, Close the Gap"

It's easy to forget how young this country is; how little distance really separates us from the beginnings of the myths, like that of Lincoln, that still haunt the national imagination. It's easy to forget how much remains to be settled. Since roots are sought out and seized as well as simply accepted, cultural history is never a straight line; along with the artists we care about we fill in the gaps ourselves. When we do, we reclaim, rework, or invent America, or a piece of it, all over again. We make choices (or are caught by the choices others have made) about what is worth keeping and what isn't, trying to create a world where we feel alive, risky, ambitious, and free (or merely safe), dispensing with the rest of the American reality if we can. We make the oldest stories new when we succeed, and we are trapped by the old stories when we fail.

This is as close as I can come to a simple description of what I think the performers in this book have done—but of course what they have done is more complex than that.

. . .

The best popular artists create immediate links between people who might have nothing in common but a response to their work, but the best popular artists never stop trying to understand the impact of their work on their audiences. That means their ideal images must change as their understanding grows. One may find horror where one expected only pleasure; one may find that the truth one told has become a lie. If the audience demands only more of what it has already accepted, the artist has a choice. He can move on, and perhaps cut himself off from his audience; if he does, his work will lose all the vitality and strength it had when he knew it mattered to other people. Or the artist can accept the audience's image of himself, pretend that his audience is his shadowy ideal, and lose himself in his audience. Then he will only be able to confirm; he will never be able to create.

The most interesting rock 'n' rollers sometimes go to these extremes; most don't, because these are contradictions they struggle with more than resolve. The tension between community and self-reliance; between distance from one's audience and affection for it; between the shared experience of popular culture and the special talents of artists who both draw on that shared experience and change it—these things are what make rock 'n' roll at its best a democratic art, at least in the American meaning of the word democracy. I think that is true because our democracy is nothing if not a contradiction: the creed of every man and woman for themselves, and thus the loneliness of separation, and thus the yearning for harmony, and for community. The performers in this book, in their different ways, all trace that line.

If they are in touch with their audiences and with the images of community their songs hint at, rock 'n' rollers get to see their myths and parables in action, and ultimately they may even find out what they are worth. When the story is a long one—a career—they find the story coming back to them in pieces, which of course is how it was received.

Here is where a critic might count. Putting the pieces together, trying to understand what is novel and adventurous, what is enervated and complacent, can give us an idea of how much room there is in this musical culture, and in American culture—an idea of what a singer and a band can do with a set of songs mixed into the uncertainty that is the pop audience. Looking back into the corners, we might discover whose America we are living in at any moment, and where it came from. With luck, we might even touch that spirit of place Americans have always sought, and in the seeking have created.

SOURCE: Greil Marcus, *Mystery Train: Images of America in Rock 'n' Roll Music*, rev. ed. (1975; reprint, New York: Dutton, 1982): ix, 1–7.

~~~~~~~

NOTE

1. Jann Wenner, the founder of *Rolling Stone,* in Robert Draper, *Rolling Stone Magazine: The Uncensored History* (New York: Doubleday, 1990), as quoted by Mark Mazzulo, "Greil Marcus's Mystery Train as Rock 'n' Roll History," *Musical Quarterly* 81, no. 2 (Summer 1997): 149.

CHARLES REICH ON THE MUSIC OF "CONSCIOUSNESS III"

When Charles Reich (b. 1928), a law professor at Yale University, published *The Greening of America* in 1970, he celebrated what is now widely labeled as the "counterculture," discerning in it a political expression of an enlightened consciousness— a keyword of the 1960s. He distinguished three stages of consciousness. The first was self-reliance fostered in rural societies; the second, the corporate conformism of advanced capitalism; and finally, the transformative consciousness III, whose ideals and values were expressed through 1960s rock.

While Reich's utopian claims for rock in this era seem inflated today, his heady prose captures the musical exhilaration of that decade, and his discussion of key pieces, bands, and soloists have held up. Reich's sense of politicized culture as well as his prescient emphasis on "self" foreshadow the "culture wars" of the 1980s. His extravagant views capture the ideology of the decade when rock became a way of life.

There is a revolution coming. It will not be like revolutions of the past. It will originate with the individual and with culture, and it will change the political structure only as its final act. It will not require violence to succeed, and it cannot be successfully resisted by violence. It is now spreading with amazing rapidity, and already our laws, institutions and social structure are changing in consequence. It promises a higher reason, a more human community, and a new and liberated individual. Its ultimate creation will be a new and enduring wholeness and beauty—a renewed relationship of man to himself, to other men, to society, to nature, and to land.

This is the revolution of the new generation. Their protest and rebellion, their culture, clothes, music, drugs, ways of thought, and liberated life-style are not a passing fad or a form of dissent and refusal, nor are they in any sense irrational. The whole emerging pattern, from ideals to campus demonstrations to beads and bell bottoms to the Woodstock Festival, makes sense and is part of a consistent philosophy. It is both necessary and inevitable, and in time it will include not only youth, but all people in America.

. . .

When we turn to the music of Consciousness III, we come to the chief medium of expression, the chief means by which inner feelings are communicated. Consciousness III has not yet developed a widely accepted written poetry, literature, or theatre; the functions of all of these have so far been assumed by music and the lyrics that go with it.

The new music was built out of materials already in existence: blues, rock 'n' roll, folk music. But although the forms remained, something wholly new and original was made out of these older elements—more original, perhaps, than even the new musicians themselves yet realize. The transformation took place in 1966–1967. Up to that time, the blues had been an essentially black medium. Rock 'n' roll, a blues derivative, was rhythmic, raunchy, teen-age dance music. Folk music, old and modern, was popular among college students. The three forms remained musically and culturally distinct, and even as late as 1965, none of them were expressing any radically new states of consciousness. Blues expressed black soul; rock, as made famous by Elvis Presley, was the beat of youthful sensuality; and folk music, with such singers as Joan Baez, expressed antiwar sentiments as well as the universal themes of love and disillusionment.

In 1966–1967 there was a spontaneous transformation. In the United States, it originated with youthful rock groups playing in San Francisco. In England, it was led by the Beatles, who were already established as an extremely fine and highly individual rock group. What happened, as well as it can be put into words, was this. First, the separate musical traditions were brought together. Bob Dylan and the Jefferson Airplane played folk rock, folk ideas with a rock beat. White rock groups began experimenting with the blues. Of course, white musicians had always played the blues, but essentially as imitators of the Negro style; now it began to be the white bands' own music. And all of the groups moved toward a broader eclecticism and synthesis. They freely took over elements from Indian ragas, from jazz, from American country music, and as time went on from even more diverse sources (one group seems recently to have been trying out Gregorian chants).[1] What developed was a protean music, capable of an almost limitless range of expression.

The second thing that happened was that all the musical groups began using the full range of electric instruments and the technology of electronic amplifiers. The twangy electric guitar was an old country-western standby, but the new electronic effects were altogether different— so different that a new listener in 1967 might well feel that there had never been any sounds like that in the world before. The high, piercing, unearthly sounds of the guitar seemed to come from other realms. Electronics did, in fact, make possible sounds that no instrument up to that time could produce. And in studio recordings, multiple tracking, feedback, and other devices made possible effects that not even an electronic band could produce live. Electronic amplification also made possible a fantastic increase in volume, the music becoming as loud and penetrating as the human ear could stand, and thereby achieving a "total" effect, so that instead of an audience of passive listeners, there were now audiences of total participants, feeling the music in all of their senses and all of their bones.

Third, the music [became] a multimedia experience; a part of a total environment. In the Bay Area ballrooms, the Fillmore, the Avalon, or Pauley Ballroom at the University of California, the walls were covered with fantastic changing patterns of light, the beginning of the new art of the light show. And the audience did not sit, it danced. With records at home, listeners imitated these lighting effects as best they could, and heightened the whole experience by using drugs. Often music was played out of doors, where nature—the sea or tall redwoods—provided the environment.

Fourth, each band began to develop a personality; often they lived together as a commune, and their music expressed their group life. The names of the groups, while often chosen rather casually and for the public effect, nevertheless expressed the anti-Establishment, "outsider" identity of the groups. One way to gauge this is to imagine congressmen from the House Internal Security Committee (formerly HUAC) trying to grasp the derivations and nuances of such names as Notes From Underground, Loading Zone, Steppenwolf, the Cleanliness and Godliness Skiffle band. A name such as the Grateful Dead, with its implication of atomic holocaust, Hiroshima, bitter alienation from society, and playful, joking, don't-give-a-damness, would baffle the security investigators for a long time. The name may have been chosen for the band's own esoteric reasons. But it suggests the idea that in our society the living are really dead, and only the "dead" are really alive; this idea would probably escape the investigators altogether. In short, the bands, by achieving a high degree of individual identity, and being clearly "outsiders," members of the youth culture themselves, became groups with which young audiences could feel a great closeness and rapport. By contrast, Consciousness II people have little identification with band members or the musicians in a symphony orchestra.

Fifth, musician-listener rapport has been heightened by two other kinds of participation: an enormous number of the young listeners had instruments or even bands and played the new music themselves, and both bands and listeners considered drugs to be an integral part of the musical experience. Consciousness II people may love Mozart, or jazz, but comparatively few of them spend much time playing an instrument. The use of drugs, especially because they are illegal, establishes a blood-brotherhood before the musicians even begin to play. And drugs, as we shall point out later, add a whole new dimension to creativity and to experience.

Sixth, a pulsing new energy entered into all the forms of music. Not even the turbulent fury of Beethoven's Ninth Symphony can compete for sheer energy with the Rolling Stones. Compared to the new music, earlier popular songs seem escapist and soft, jazz seems cerebral, classical music seems dainty or mushy; these epithets are surely undeserved but the driving, screaming, crying, bitter-happy-sad heights and depths and motion of the new music adds a dimension unknown in any earlier western music. The older music was essentially intellectual; it was located in the mind and in the feelings known to the mind; the new music rocks the whole body, and penetrates the soul.

Seventh, the new music, despite its apparently simple form and beat, gradually evolved a remarkably complex texture. It has a complexity unknown to classical music, even to symphonies written for full orchestra. Beethoven seems like a series of parallel lines, sometimes vertical, sometimes diagonal; Mozart a flow of rounded forms, but as few as three rock musicians, such as the Cream, or Crosby, Stills & Nash can set up a texture of rhythms, timbres, kinds of sounds, emotions that create a world by contrast to which the classical composers seem to have lived in a world of simple verities, straightforward emotions, and established, reassuring conventions. It is no criticism of the eighteenth- or nineteenth-century geniuses to say that today's music has found a world they never knew.

Eighth, not only did many young people play the new music in one form or another, a great many, amateur and professional alike, began composing it. Nearly all of the successful rock groups of today write most of their own words and music. The distinction between composer and performer as professions has virtually disappeared. Thus songs are highly personal to the singer, not a mere "interpretation" of someone else's thought. Also, what is undeniably a mass culture is at the same time a genuine folk culture, because it is not imposed upon the people but written by them. And the writing is not limited to professional musicians; amateur and casual groups also compose some of their own material. And when one group does play another person's song, the group freely adds to it. There is no such thing then, as the musician who tries in all things to be faithful to some remote composer, reserving for himself a display of skill and subtlety, spirit and nuance. The new music is a music of unrestrained creativity and self-expression.

Ninth, the new music, most notably through the poetry of its songs, has succeeded in expressing an understanding of the world, and of people's feelings, incredibly far in advance of what other media have been able to express. Journalists, writers for opinion journals, social scientists, novelists have all tried their hand at discussing the issues of the day. But almost without exception, they have been far more superficial than writers of rock poetry, and what is even more striking, several years behind the musicians. Compare a writer for the *New York Times,* or for the *New Republic,* talking about contemporary political and social ills, with Dylan's "It's All Right Ma (I'm Only Bleeding)" or "Subterranean Homesick Blues." Compare a sociologist talking about alienation with the Beatles' "Eleanor Rigby" or "Strawberry Fields Forever." But more important than comparisons is the fact that rock music has been able to give critiques of society at a profound level ("Draft Morning," by the Byrds, "Tommy," by the Who) and at the same time express the longings and aspirations of the new generation ("I Feel Free," by the Cream, "Wooden Ships," by Crosby, Stills & Nash, "Stand," by Sly and the Family Stone). The music has achieved a relevance, an ability to penetrate to the essence of what is wrong with society, a power to speak to man "in his condition" that is perhaps the deepest source of its power.

If we combine all of these aspects of the transformation we can begin to see how vastly different the new music is from the older forms that it seems superficially to resemble. The blues offers an example. The essence of blues' radical subjectivity [is that] the singer follows a form, but he cannot help but express his own personality, his own life experiences, his own encounters with his world. When Janis Joplin, a white girl, sang "Ball and Chain" to a pulsing, communal audience of middle-class young white people, it was not the same as a black singer in the classic blues tradition. It was contemporary American white "soul," and it spoke of the bomb, and the war, drugs, and the cops as well as the intense sexuality of the blues and the yearnings and mysteries of black soul. A similar transformation takes place when the new groups play jazz, early rock, folk songs, or even classical music. Procol Harum's "Salty Dog" sounds like an ordinary folk song about a sea voyage when it is first heard. But when one listens more closely there is much more: classical music is blended into a folk style; the song has an almost unbearable tension; drums build up powerful climaxes; gulls' cries and a bosun's pipe give an eerie feeling; the words do not quite make sense; the captain is apparently mad; death is in the air; the ship goes to places unknown to man; the simple sea song has become an awesome, mysterious and frightening "trip" to some place beyond man's experience. Happy, sad, or spiritual, the new music transforms older forms into "trips" that enter a dimension which the original forms never reached.

What the new music has become is a medium that expresses the whole range of the new generation's experiences and feelings. The complex, frantic, disjointed machinelike experiences of modern urban existence were presented, with piercing notes of pain, and dark notes of anger, by the Cream. The mystical transcendence of ordinary experience achieved by the hippies, the drug world, and the spiritual realm, soaring fantasy and brilliant patterns of rhythm and sound, are the domain of the San Francisco acid rock of the Jefferson Airplane, and the psychedelic meditations of the early music of Country Joe and the Fish. Irony, satire, mockery of the Establishment and of rational thought were the specialty of the Mothers of Invention. A uniquely personal but universal view of the world has been achieved by the Beatles, gentle, unearthy [sic], the world transformed. Another highly personal view of the world, but one close to the experiences of young listeners, is that of Bob Dylan. Dylan has gone through a whole cycle of experience, from folk music to social protest and commentary, next to folk rock, then to the extraordinary personal world of the ballad "Sad-Eyed Lady of the Lowlands," and finally to the serene, but achieved, innocence of the country music of the album "Nashville Skyline." Perhaps more than any other individual in the field of music, Dylan has been, from the very beginning, a true prophet of the new consciousness.

Among the most important forms of the new music is the blues, for it expresses what is common to all the individual types of music we have discussed—experience coming from the self, coming deeply, honestly, and searchingly from the self, expressing thoughts and feelings that most people conceal from their own view and from others. For the black man in the South, the blues expressed his identity, an identity oppressed, forbidden, and denied in other ways. So long as whites in America did not realize that their own identity was also oppressed and denied, so long as whites failed to search for their own selves, there could be no white "soul," no white blues to sing. The white man could be sentimental or romantic, but he had no knowledge of himself, and therefore no words of his own for the blues. The new generation, in its discovery of self, in its discovery of oppression, also discovered white "soul," and that is what its music is starting to tell about. The new music is uniquely and deeply personal, allowing individuals and groups to express their special vision of the world to all their brothers and sisters; it deals with the entire world as seen and felt by the new consciousness, and it takes listeners to places they have never been before.

But no single form of music can really claim preeminence. It is the richness and variety and continually changing quality of the new music that is its essence. It defies analysis and explication by critics because it never stands still to be analyzed; it ranges from the mystic expressiveness of Procol Harum, the emotional intensity of the Who's rock opera, "Tommy," the heavy sounds of Led Zeppelin, to anywhere else the heads of the new generation have been. Its essence is the total scene: a huge and happy noontime crowd in Lower Sproul Plaza at Berkeley, some standing, some sitting, some dancing; every variety of clothes and costume, knapsacks and rolled-up sleeping bags; piled-up Afro hair and shoulder-length golden-blond hair; a sense of everyone's sharing the values and experience that the scene represents; music by the Crabs, a local group, mostly soaring, ecstatic, earthly rock that shakes the crowd, the buildings, and the heavens themselves with joy; and above the scene presiding over it, those benevolent deities, the sungod, the ocean breeze, the brown-green Berkeley hills.

> SOURCE: Charles Reich, *The Greening of America* (New York: Random House, 1970): 4–5, 242–50.

~~~~~~~~~~

NOTE

1.   The author may be referring to the English band, the Yardbirds.

123

Mccoy Tyner on the Jubilant Experience of
John Coltrane's Classic Quartet

From 1960 until 1965, the pianist McCoy Tyner (b. 1938) formed an integral part of one of jazz history's great ensembles led by saxophonist John Coltrane (1926–1967). The group recorded about 66 tracks for several albums on the Impulse! label, including *A Love Supreme,* and *My Favorite Things.* In this interview, the musician and Coltrane discographer David Wild encourages Tyner to range freely over his musical and personal relationships within the quartet. They touch on some important topics, including Tyner's characteristic "quartal harmonies," his summary comments about other jazz pianists and their harmonic orientations, and finally, what might be called the apprenticeship system in jazz—that is to say, the way education and training is passed on from mentors to students.

[David Wild's introductory remarks to the interview]

The four piece group John Coltrane led from 1961 through 1965 has been called the "Classic Quartet." Its instrumentation was the common saxophone-plus-rhythm, but the exceptional interplay of its members—Coltrane on soprano and tenor, pianist McCoy Tyner, bassist Jimmy Garrison and drummer Elvin Jones—created something special within the familiar framework. The group's sound (preserved in a series of seminal recordings) is instantly identifiable; its evolving stylistic approach exerted a dominant influence on the development of the music. And Tyner's experiments with modes and chord voicings taught a generation of pianists how to create in the increasingly free idiom of Coltrane.

Born in Philadelphia on December 11, 1938, Tyner grew up in a rich musical environment (pianists Bud and Richie Powell were neighbors). After gigging around the city in the late '50s, he left in 1959 to tour with saxophonist Benny Golson and soon joined the newly formed Jazztet co-led by Golson and Art Farmer. He left that band in June, 1960 to join Coltrane, beginning an association that lasted until December, 1965.

After some lean years in the late '60s, Tyner began to receive well deserved recognition with the release of his album *Sahara* (Milestone) in '72, and his successful relationship with that record label continues—he collaborated with Ron Carter, Sonny Rollins and Al Foster in the Milestone Jazzstars. His most recent release is *Together*, featuring Stanley Clarke, Jack DeJohnette, Freddie Hubbard, Bobby Hutcherson, Hubert Laws, Bennie Maupinn [*sic*] and Bill Summers. Tyner also continues to tour and has added violinist John Blair to his entourage.

I talked to Tyner this spring over lunch at Detroit's Plaza Hotel; the pianist was in the middle of a week-long engagement at Baker's Keyboard Lounge.

WILD: Did you find it interesting working with Sonny Rollins on the tour?

TYNER: Yeah, it was interesting, quite different. Of course I had played with Sonny before, when I was 18, the first time. That was with Clifford Brown and Richie Powell. They came through Philadelphia with Sonny, George Morrow on bass, and Kenny Dorham. I worked with that band, and I was 18 and I had just got out of school or something like that, I'd just met my wife, and I said I'm not going any place right now, and so I stayed home. But Max Roach wanted me to come on the road with them, you know. But I was real young. And then of course I'd met John prior to that and I was working quite a bit around the city.

WILD: You were also with trumpeter Cal Massey's band at that time, right?

TYNER: Yeah, Cal and John were pals, used to practice together when they were teenagers, used to hang out together. And that's how I met John, the summer of '55, one afternoon during the matinee.

WILD: Was there a lot of music around when you were growing up?

TYNER: Yeah, a lot of musical activity. I guess there must have been about three or four guys that I'd really owe a lot to, because I was a younger guy and they saw something there and they really tried to help me. I remember when I worked with Max, when I was 18, they were down there on pay night to make sure he paid me [laughs].

That was a very fruitful period. At the time my mother had a beauty shop and we would have sessions in the shop. Sometimes a lady would be sitting having her hair done with a saxophone player right next to her [laughs]. Sometimes it developed into a big band.

I used to go to John's house and sit on the porch and talk about music—about a lot of things that he eventually began to get into. So I think theoretically I was sort of involved in his way of thinking quite early, from those conversations. It's funny, it wasn't a thing where we were convinced by him. It just seemed that it naturally happened that we had sort of a consistency there, we coincided.

WILD: Your minds went in the same direction.

TYNER: Same direction, yeah. And then after he went back with Miles, he told me that he would come back to Philly sometimes when Miles wasn't working; I would work with him, and he said that whenever he got his own group he would definitely want for me to join the group.[1]

WILD: But you went with the Jazztet first.[2]

TYNER: Yeah. Every time John would leave Miles, Miles encouraged him to stay. It wasn't the Jazztet then, it was just Benny Golson, who asked me to go to San Francisco with him. Then a little later he said that Art Farmer and he had been talking about this group, and he wondered if I wanted to be involved. I said that John told me that whenever he left Miles, that we have sort of a verbal commitment, that I'd like to work with him, that's really where my heart is. But I didn't know when John was going to leave Miles, so I had to do something. Consequently we went to New York and the Jazztet was formed. A very uniform group, but not quite as inventive, it wasn't really the type of creative environment that I was looking for. But it was interesting and it was the first real professional band I had ever been with.

So I stayed with them about six months, and the latter part of that six months, the last few weeks of it, John left Miles. But John didn't want to ask me to leave the Jazztet, because Benny and John grew up in the same area, and he didn't want to steal me. And I was just young, you know, 20 years old, I couldn't go up to these guys and tell them "I quit!" I had to be prodded a little bit, even though I wanted to go. So John's wife said that if he wanted me to quit he'd better ask me.

So, I came in, trying to learn. I had my own ear, I knew what I wanted to hear out of my instrument, my own style and feeling, but I think that I had a chance to really grow there. It was a tremendous learning experience for me and it reached the point where it was actually a *jubilant* experience, being on stage with them. It was like going to a university when Elvin first joined the band—it was just tremendous between him and John. Both of these guys taught me so much—Elvin from the rhythmic point of view. They played so well together, after a while there seemed to be almost an automatic communication.

WILD: One thing that's always interested me as a piano player—looking back, the changes you were playing behind John, those very open quartal voicings, seemed to fit so well. Where did they come from? I know [Paul] Hindemith uses that kind of voicing.

TYNER: I don't know where. I think I was hearing his style. I had a collection of Debussy records when I was real young—I don't know where these records came from—but I liked his sound, his open whole-tone system. I don't think I was trying to copy that, though, it just interested me.

WILD: I know the way Bill Evans was playing just after he left Miles has some of that same approach. It's almost as if it just was in the air, because you hear Wynton Kelly using the same kind of voicings. But those particular very wide-interval chords seemed to fit so well with what Trane was doing, because they gave him the room to go in any direction he wanted.

TYNER: That's true, too. It's a funny thing, though. Bill was out here before I was, so I think that a lot of people probably thought—because Bill writes as well— that he was the source. You do hear a similar thing. But it came to me so naturally, it wasn't a thing where I actually copied. You cannot develop anything you copy from somebody else, there's no way you can really do that. I had heard this sound a long time, when I was real young, and it just took me a while to develop it out. I had to work with somebody and that group was the natural vehicle.

Another person is Richard Powell. He used the sustaining pedal sometimes when he was playing with Max, and I heard this sound. The voicing wasn't the same, but he would use the sustaining pedal to get a flowing type of thing, because he wasn't really technically that proficient a piano player. And then Bill came along and a couple of other people.

That type of sound was really prevalent at that time because there was a lot of experimentation going on. I've always thought I could play with Ornette [Coleman], although I never did anything with him. But I always felt that I could do something with him or any other horn player. Even now I feel as though I could go in either direction, because I've done things like that, it's not an alien area for me. I think that I could really just experiment with different material. Because some of the things that I did with John in the late '60s were like that.

WILD: Impulse put out a version of the *Meditations* suite done by the quartet which is really interesting, really experimental, because you can see that transition between the sound when Elvin was playing and the sound after Rashied came in.[3] There are three or four levels of rhythm going on at once, and you're playing chords that were getting away from any one tonality. One of those chords—it's a nice sound, it's got like a tritone in there somewhere, it's not straight fourths, it's got a nice bit to it. I'm going to sit down at the piano one day and figure out what the hell it was.

TYNER: When you find out, let me know, will you? [laughs] No it's . . . I found out that a lot of it is intuitive, in the sense that when you're in a situation like that, you're sort of indoctrinated into the sound. You don't think about "What am I playing," you just play a chord that fits with whatever the sound is. I really feel very comfortable doing things like that.

WILD: In the early '60s the music that you were playing with John was changing and growing in different directions. Did you find any difficulty taking the audience along with you?

TYNER: No, because I learned something from John's approach which was very interesting. He always worked from a very fundamental foundation or element. He never lost sight of the nucleus of what we were trying to do. What made it such a vital force and also truly part of the lineage of the music was that it maintained certain elements; there was this firm foundation present. You could break it down to its bare fundamental elements—it wasn't just complex. It was something that built from simplistics, it was very simple but yet complex at the same time. Which kind of reminds me of life in itself [laughs]. Being made up of simple elements but yet very complex in many ways.

I've found that music for complexity's sake doesn't seem like it really works. So therefore sometimes we'd play things that really would appeal to people of all age brackets, like *My Favorite Things*. We had people of 65, 70 come in to hear the music, it's funny, and they would say, "Play *My Favorite Things*." I think that was very important in the group, its forms were very simple basically but lent themselves to more complex work.

Flexibility too was another thing I learned from playing with John and Elvin, flexibility of time and form. [short silence] Learned a lot of things [laughs]. Yeah, it was an education, it really was.

WILD: When you said lineage, I was thinking that you can almost trace a master/ pupil relationship all the way back through the music. You see John with Miles, you see Miles with Parker, you see Parker listening to Lester Young outside places in Kansas City. It's like it goes all the way back.

TYNER: Yes, it does.

WILD: I suppose there are guys playing with you now that are getting the same kind of experience.

TYNER: Yeah, I hope so. I think George Adams, I hope that he is. But we'll see what happens.

WILD: It's interesting that some of the players who have worked with you, like George, seem to have assimilated a lot of Coltrane. But I would imagine that's natural, because after all a lot of it is your music, too.

TYNER: Yeah. It's a funny thing, the John Coltrane Quartet was actually four elements. We had one guy who led the whole team, but it was really a compounding of personalities, like four personalities contributing. Whenever any of us were missing . . . when Roy [Haynes] was with the band it was interesting, but when Elvin came back it was a glorious situation. And Roy was very interesting, I enjoyed him, he's a very good musician, a good performer. But I think that Elvin was really a missed part of that, because it was just his spot, you know.

One time, when my son was born, I took a couple of weeks off, Eric Dolphy was with the band, and John didn't hire a piano player for those weeks—he played without a piano player.

When you're a part of something like that you can't really ascertain how strong it is. We knew that we were doing something different, that it was fresh, timely. We knew that it had come from something that had happened before. At the same time, you're swept up in that force—you're not cognizant of how different it is. When something is good, timely, it has a lasting quality.

I still haven't actually brought out everything that I learned from that experience. I've digested a lot of that music over the years. That was a very interesting period of my life, because I think I was growing at that time, and at the same time I was there absorbing what was happening, assimilating it. After leaving John, of course, I realized that I couldn't do the same thing. I was very strongly influenced by that group, but then at the same time I realized that I had to go on in a direction that I felt would be extremely personal, even though I had given a lot to that group. It offered the freedom to express yourself so that whatever was done was purely and rawly us. It wasn't a situation where John said "do this" or "do that." We more or less were able to play together and we felt very comfortable. I think that what I was faced with was the need to relate to what was happening, what I felt was interesting from today's period, or what I was feeling in terms of the music. It was an outgrowth of a particular period of my experience with John.

That's *another* point. I found it was very difficult at one point for me to find musicians to play with, because of my tenure with John. With John we could come in, he would give us two notes and we could play a *whole* composition on two notes. We really could. I mean, sometimes he wouldn't bring in a tune, he'd bring in a scale, and we'd play the scale and everything would be right there. We were familiar with each other, the musicianship was high. But then I ran into a situation where it was very difficult to find sidemen with the sort of experience and understanding to play like that. So I said, well how can you allow that kind of freedom to someone who's not disciplined enough and not knowledgeable enough to handle it?

WILD: You have to go through that before you can create with so few guidelines.

TYNER: Exactly. You have to go through the stages of discipline before you can reach the point where you can assume the responsibility of freedom. And that's the reason why I think you find a lot of groups try for something and it all seems to get locked into one area. It's like a tree that doesn't have the roots; it can't really grow that high. It's the same thing—it'll always be a midget tree. When the roots are deep you can approach music from that level and be able to create a lot of different things. But it was hard to find people that really had that kind of background.

I'm glad I went through all the phases of playing, with the blues bands and r&b groups when I was a teenager, and then to bebop, and Bud Powell was living around the corner, that kind of thing. I'm glad I went through that because it was like stepping stones. And then—working with John was the greatest musical experience of my life.

SOURCE: McCoy Tyner interview by David Wild, "The Jubilant Experience of the Classic Quartet," *Down Beat* 46, no. 13 (July 12, 1979): 18, 48, 54.

~~~~~~~~~~

NOTES

1. John Coltrane worked with Miles Davis as part of his quintet in 1955–1956, 1958–1959, and 1961.
2. The Jazztet was a sextet known for its hard bop style.
3. Tyner is referring to the drummer Rashied Ali (b. 1935), who was the second drummer, along with Elvin Jones, with Coltrane on *Meditations* (1965).

MILES DAVIS

Excerpts from His Autobiography

The influential and innovative trumpeter Miles Davis (1926–1991) reinvented himself by reinventing tradition in jazz. Two albums define watershed moments in his career, whose stylistic unpredictability continues to provoke controversy and admiration. The first selection discusses the birth of *The Birth of the Cool* (1948–1950) and his collaboration with the composer and arranger, Gil Evans (1912–1988). The second selection focuses on the equally transformative rock–infused album *Bitches Brew* (1969). Davis comments candidly on many aspects of making music, with comments about details that occupy musicians bent on perfection right alongside assessments of industry pressure. Contemporary jazz is still absorbing his legacy.

Gil [Evans] and I had already started doing things together and everything was going real well for us. I was looking for a vehicle where I could solo more in the style that I was hearing. My music was a little slower and not as intense as Bird's. My conversations with Gil about experimenting with more subtle voicing and shit were exciting to me. Gerry Mulligan, Gil, and I started talking about forming this group. We thought nine pieces would be the right amount of musicians to be in the band. Gil and Gerry had decided what the instruments in the band would be before I really came into the discussions. But the theory, the musical interpretation and what the band would play, was my idea.

I remember when we started to get the nonet together that I wanted Sonny Stitt on alto saxophone. Sonny sounded a lot like Bird, so I thought of him right away. But Gerry Mulligan wanted Lee Konitz because he had a light sound rather than a hard bebop sound. He felt that this kind of sound was going to make the album and the band different.

Max [Roach] was hanging out with Gil and Gerry and me over at Gil's and so was John Lewis, so they knew what we wanted to do. Al McKibbon too. We also wanted J.J. Johnson, but he was traveling with Illinois Jacquet's band, so I thought about Ted Kelly, who was playing trombone with Dizzy's band. But he was busy and couldn't make it. So we settled on a white guy, Michael Zwerin, who was younger than me. I had met him up at Minton's one night when he was sitting in and asked him if he could rehearse the next day with us at Nola's Studio. He made it and was in the band.

See, this whole idea started out just as an experiment, a collaborative experiment. Then a lot of black musicians came down on my case about their not having work, and here I was hiring white guys in my band. So I just told them that if a guy could play as good as Lee Konitz played—that's who they were mad about most, because there were a lot of black alto players around—I would hire him every time, and I wouldn't give a damn if he was green with red breath. I'm hiring a motherfucker to play, not for what color he is. When I told them that, a lot of them got off my case. But a few of them stayed mad with me.

. . .

But around this time, Gil went into a musical writing slump. It would take him a week to write eight bars. He finally got it together though, and wrote a tune called "Moon Dreams" and some thing for "Boplicity" for *Birth of the Cool*. The *Birth of the Cool* album came from some of the sessions we did trying to sound like Claude Thornhill's band. We wanted that sound, but the difference was that we wanted it as small as possible. I said it had to be the voicing of a quartet, with soprano, alto, baritone, and bass voices. We had to have tenor, half-alto, and half-bass. I was the soprano voice, Lee Konitz was the alto. We had another voice in a French horn and a baritone voice, which was a bass tuba. We had alto and soprano up to me and Lee Konitz. We also used the French horn for the alto voicing and the baritone sax for baritone voicing and bass tuba for bass voicing. I looked at the group like it was a choir, a choir that was a quartet. A lot of people put the baritone sax on the bottom, but's it not a bottom instrument, like a tuba is. The tuba is a bass instrument. I wanted the instruments to sound like human voices, and they did.

. . .

Birth of the Cool became a collector's item, I think, out of a reaction to Bird and Dizzy's music. Bird and Dizzy played this hip, real fast thing, and if you weren't a fast listener, you couldn't catch the humor or the feeling in their music. Their musical sound wasn't sweet, and it didn't have harmonic lines that you could easily hum out on the street with your girlfriend trying to get over with a kiss. Bebop didn't have the humanity of Duke Ellington. It didn't even have that recognizable thing. Bird and Diz were great, fantastic, challenging—but they weren't sweet. But *Birth of the Cool* was different because you could hear everything and hum it also.

Birth of the Cool came from black musical roots. It came from Duke Ellington. We were trying to sound like Claude Thornhill, but he had gotten his shit from Duke Ellington and Fletcher Henderson. Gil Evens himself was a big fan of Duke's and Billy Strayhorn's, and Gil was the arranger for *Birth of the Cool*. Duke and Billy used to use that doubling thing up in the chords like we did on *Birth*. You always hear Duke doing that and he would always get guys with a sound that you could recognize. If they played alone in Duke's band, you could always tell who they were by their sound. If they played in a section thing, then you could still tell who they were in the section by voicing. They put their own personality on certain chords.

So that's what we did in *Birth*. And that's why I think it got over like it did. White people back then liked music they could understand, that they could *hear* without straining. Bebop didn't come out of them and so it was hard for many of them to hear what was going on in the music. It was an all-black thing. But *Birth* was not only hummable but it had white people playing the music and serving in prominent roles. The white critics liked that. They liked the fact that *they* seemed to have something to do with what was going on. It was just like somebody shaking your hand just a little extra. We shook people's ears a little softer than Bird or Diz did, took the music more mainstream. That's all it was.

BITCHES BREW AND THE BACKGROUND OF FUSION

Nineteen sixty-nine was the year rock and funk were selling like hotcakes and all this was put on display at Woodstock. There were over 400,000 people at the concert. That many people at a concert makes everybody go crazy, and especially people who make records. The only thing on their minds is, How can we sell records to that many people all the time? If we haven't been doing that, then how can we do it?

That was the atmosphere all around the record companies. At the same time, people were packing stadiums to hear and see stars in person. And jazz music seemed to be withering on the vine, in record sales and live performances. It was the first time in a long time that I didn't sell out crowds everywhere I played. In Europe I always had sellouts, but in the United States, we played to a lot of half-empty clubs in 1969. That told me something. Compared to what my records used to sell, when you put them beside what Bob Dylan or Sly Stone sold, it was no contest. Their sales had gone through the roof. Clive Davis was the president of Columbia Records and he signed Blood, Sweat and Tears in 1968 and a group called Chicago in 1969. He was trying to take Columbia into the future and pull in all those young record buyers. After a rough start he and I got along well, because he thinks like an artist instead of a straight businessman. He had a good sense for what was happening; I thought he was a great man.

He started talking to me about trying to reach this younger market and about changing. He suggested that the way for me to reach this new audience was to play my music where they went, places like the Fillmore. The first time we had a conversation I got mad with him because I thought he was putting down me and all the things I had done for Columbia. I hung up on him after telling him I was going to find another record company to record for. But they wouldn't give me a release. After we went back and forth in these arguments for a while, everything finally cooled down and we got all right again. For a while, I was thinking about going over to Motown Records, because I liked what they were doing and figured that they could understand what I was trying to do better.

What Clive really didn't like was that the agreement I had with Columbia allowed me to get advances against royalties earned, so whenever I needed money, I would call up and get an advance. Clive felt that I wasn't making enough money for the company to be giving me this type of treatment. Maybe he was right, now that I'm looking back on all of it, but right from a strictly business position, not an artistic one. I felt that Columbia should live up to what they had agreed to. They thought that since I sold around 60,000 albums every time I put out a record—

which was enough for them before the new thing came around—that wasn't enough to keep on giving me money.

So this was the climate with Columbia and me just before I went into the studio to record *Bitches Brew*. What they didn't understand was that I wasn't prepared to be a memory yet, wasn't prepared to be listed only on Columbia's so-called classical list. I had seen the way to the future with my music, and I was going for it like I had always done. Not for Columbia and their record sales, and not for trying to get to some young white record buyers. I was going for it for myself, for what I wanted and needed in my own music. *I* wanted to change course, *had* to change course for me to continue to believe in and love what I was playing.

When I went into the studio in August 1969, besides listening to rock music and funk, I had been listening to Joe Zawinul and Cannonball [Adderley] playing shit like "Country Joe and the Preacher." And I had met another English guy, named Paul Buckmaster, in London. I asked him to come over sometime and help me put an album together. I liked what he was doing then. I had been experimenting with writing a few simple chord changes for three pianos. Simple shit, and it was funny because I used to think when I was doing them how Stravinsky went back to simple forms. So I had been writing these things down, like one beat chord and a bass line, and I found out that the more we played it, it was always different. I would write a chord, a rest, maybe another chord, and it turned out that the more it was played, the more it just kept getting different. This started happening in 1968 when I had Chick [Corea], Joe [Zawinul], and Herbie [Hancock] for those studio dates. It went on into the sessions we had for *In a Silent Way*. Then I started thinking about something larger, a skeleton of a piece. I would write a chord on two beats and they'd have two beats out. So they would do one, two, three, da-dum, right? Then I put the accent on the fourth beat. Maybe I had three chords on the first bar. Anyway, I told the musicians that they could do anything they wanted, play anything they heard but that I had to have this, what they did, as a chord. Then they knew what they could do, so that's what they did. Played off that chord, and it made it sound like a whole lot of stuff.

I told them that at rehearsals and then I brought in these musical sketches that nobody had seen, just like I did on *Kind of Blue* and *In a Silent Way*. We started early in the day in Columbia's studio on 52nd Street and recorded all day for three days in August. I had told Teo Macero, who was producing the record, to just let the tapes run and get everything we played, told him to get *everything* and not to be coming in interrupting, asking questions. "Just stay in the booth and worry about getting down the sound," is what I told him. And he did, didn't fuck with us once and got down everything, got it down real good.

So I would direct, like a conductor, once we started to play, and I would either write down some music for somebody or I would tell him to play different things I was hearing, as the music was growing, coming together. It was loose and tight at the same time. It was casual but alert, everybody was alert to different possibilities that were coming up in the music. While the music was developing I would hear something that I thought could be extended or cut back. So that recording was a development of the creative process, a living composition. It was like a fugue, or motif, that we all bounced off of. After it had developed to a certain point, I would tell a certain musician to come in and play something else, like Benny Maupin on bass clarinet. I wish I had thought of video taping that whole session because it must have been something and I would have liked to have been able to see just what went down, like a football or basketball instant replay. Sometimes, instead of just letting the tape run, I would tell Teo to back it up so I could hear what we had done. If I wanted something else in a certain spot, I would just bring the musician in, and we would just do it.

That was a great recording session, man, and we didn't have any problems as I can re-member. It was just like one of them old-time jam sessions we used to have up at Minton's back in the old bebop days. Everybody was excited when we all left there each day.

Some people have written that doing *Bitches Brew* was Clive Davis's or Teo Macero's idea. That's a lie, because they didn't have nothing to do with none of it. Again, it was white people trying to give some credit to other white people where it wasn't deserved because the record be-came a break-through concept, very innovative. They were going to rewrite history after the fact like they always do.

What we did on *Bitches Brew* you couldn't ever write down for an orchestra to play. That's why I didn't write it all out, not because I didn't know what I wanted; I knew that what I wanted would come out of a process and not some prearranged shit. This session was about im-provisation, and that's what makes jazz so fabulous. Any time the weather changes it's going to change your whole attitude about something, and so a musician will play differently, especially if everything is not put in front of him. A musician's attitude is the music he plays. Like in Cal-ifornia, out by the beach, you have silence and the sound of waves crashing against the shore. In New York you're dealing with the sounds of cars honking their horns and people on the streets running their mouths and shit like that. Hardly ever in California do you hear people talk-ing on the streets. California is mellow, it's about sunshine and exercise and beautiful women on the beaches showing off their bad-ass bodies and fine, long legs. People there have color in their skin because they go out in the sun all the time. People in New York go out but it's a dif-ferent thing, it's an inside thing. California is an outside thing and the music that comes out of there reflects that open space and freeways, shit you don't hear in music that comes out of New York, which is usually more intense and energetic.

After I finished *Bitches Brew,* Clive Davis put me in touch with Bill Graham, who owned the Fillmore in San Francisco and the Fillmore East in downtown New York. Bill wanted me to play San Francisco first, with the Grateful Dead, and so we did. That was an eye-opening concert for me, because there were about five thousand people there that night, mostly young, white hippies, and they hadn't hardly heard of me if they had heard of me at all. We opened for the Grateful Dead, but another group came on before us. The place was packed with these real spacy, high white people, and when we first started playing, people were walking around and talking. But after a while they got all quiet and really got into the music. I played a little of something like *Sketches of Spain* and then we went into the *Bitches Brew* shit and that really blew them out. After that concert, every time I would play out there in San Francisco, a lot of young white people showed up at the gigs.

SOURCE: Miles Davis with Quincy Troupe, *Miles: The Autobiography* (New York: Simon and Schuster, 1989):116–19, 297–301. These selections are also reprinted in Robert Walser, ed. *Keeping Time: Readings in Jazz History* (New York: Oxford University Press, 1999): 365–76.

125

A VIETNAM VET REMEMBERS

ROCKING AND ROLLING IN THE MUD OF WAR

Music serves many functions in war, ranging from propaganda to nostalgia for home. The role of music in the Vietnam War, which has already entered popular memory through such films as *Good Morning, Vietnam* (1987), is movingly recounted here by the writer Michael W. Rodriguez, who served in the U.S. Marine Corps from 1965 to 1970. This memoir, which Rodriguez contributed to a documentary project of the Second Battalion, First Marine Regiment (Vietnam), in 1989, brings us onto the Vietnam battlefield—where the term "rock 'n' roll" meant everybody shooting at once. Since 1984, Rodriguez has advocated for the rights of Vietnam veterans.

In the Fall of 1967, the Second Battalion, First Marine Regiment (2/1) had just come off what too many Grunts—infantrymen fighting the war in Vietnam—believed was a disastrous combat operation called Medina. Hotel Company had had *beaucoup* hurt and killed, so we returned to our mountain, licking our wounds, seeing that our new people got into the routine of a Marine rifle company in the field, drawing fresh ammo and gear, and waited for the orders that would send us back in the jungles of Vietnam near the Demilitarized Zone (DMZ). Into this chaos came my man, Luis Alejandro Parker.

Parker was returning to us from R&R [rest and relaxation, or rest and recuperation] in Hong Kong where, he told us, he'd come down with malaria. He had this portable record player—the kind powered by 10 D-cell batteries—and a red vinyl record album tucked under his arm, the sort of album we bought overseas.

So we said, "What you got there, Louie?"

He said, "It's a new album by the Beatles." He showed us the album jacket. "It's called *Sergeant Pepper's Lonely Hearts Club Band.*"

Huh?

Now, just days before Parker came back, we'd welcomed into the Company a couple of Fucking New Guys (FNGs). We'd naturally asked them what was hot back in The World, besides mini-skirts (we'd already seen pictures of those), and this one kid said, "A record by the Boxtops called 'The Letter' is pretty hot right now, and it's good, too."

Not too long after that, but before Parker came diddy-bopping back to the Bush, we'd heard "The Letter" on Armed Forces Radio Vietnam (AFRVN), the radio station from down in Saigon. We heard it and thought, "Yeah, there it is! Get me a ticket on an airplane. *I heard that.*"

We lost track of the number of times in Vietnam we went *rock 'n' roll* and not mean[ing] the Rolling Stones or the Who or the Four Tops. Rock 'N' Roll was full automatic rifle and machine-gun fire, everybody shooting at once, adrenaline running through the body like a runaway truck.

Although not warfare's first generation to go to war to the sound of music (pun intended), we were certainly the first of America's fighting men to go off to war in a foreign land listening to rock and folk artists with such names as the Beatles, the Boxtops, the Midnighters, the Dell-Kings, and Sam & Dave. The music was loud and raucous, music guaranteed to piss off our folks. It was music that proclaimed, "This is ours. *This is us.*"

We went off to war having grown up listening to Jerry Lee Lewis (remember his 13-year-old bride?), Fats Domino, Elvis, the Rolling Stones (they didn't want to hold your hand, they wanted to spend the night together), the Kinks (some folks maintain "Louie, Louie" was the dirtiest song ever performed; it was definitely one of the best party songs ever recorded), and Doug Sahm (remember the Sir Douglas Quintet?). We listened, too, to those that sang of young love: the Flamingos, the Shirelles ("Soldier Boy" anticipated Jody but by a few years), and the anthem to junior high school's often-unrequited love, the Five Satins' "In the Still of the Night."

We fought that war digging the Animals, the Doors ("Light My Fire" remains a classic of the period), Bob Dylan (you don't need a weatherman to know which [way] the wind blows), Janis Joplin, and Credence Clearwater Revival's "You Better Run Through the Jungle." Country Joe McDonald's "I-Feel-Like-I'm-Fixin'-to-Die Rag" became for many of us the song for Vietnam: "[Uncle Sam's] got himself in a terrible jam, way down yonder in Vietnam . . ." Bitter, disillusioned, and angry with a government we felt had betrayed us, the "Rag" became the battle hymn of the Grunt in Vietnam.

I can't leave out Gracie Slick, the Grateful Dead, Iron Butterfly ("In-a-Gadda-Da-Vida" has a permanent home on my iPod), and the ubiquitous Four Seasons ("Walk Like a Man" but sing like a girl), and, for Gary Reinhardt (wherever you are), the Beach Boys' "Surfer Girl." We got drunk and moody to Barry McGuire's "Eve of Destruction" (I left not long before 1968's Tet Offensive; I didn't miss a thing, not a thing), and we thought about and longed for our loves— our babysans—back in The World while listening to Aaron Neville's "Tell It Like It Is."

Hey, hey, my, my, rock 'n' roll will never die. My man Parker, along with his 10 D-cell portable record player and Beatles album, introduced culture-starved 18- and 19-year-old Marines to an entirely new concept in music: album rock, even as our government was introducing [an] *accounting war* to us (so many bullets fired by us should equal so many enemy dead).

Vietnam and rock 'n' roll belong together. I cannot think of Vietnam without recalling those songs to which I listened and what they meant, and continue to mean, to me. Remember the television series, "Tour of Duty"?[1] The opening scene has helicopters flying low in a valley as the Stones' "Paint It Black" plays as soundtrack. Producer Zev Braun could not have selected a more fitting song to define his vision of the American war in Vietnam.

I am certain [that] current American music in general and rock 'n' roll in particular remain important, but I have no direct empirical knowledge of that. As Kevin Kline's character remarks in the movie "The Big Chill," there is no other music in my house.

"My baby, she wrote me a letter . . ."

Hey, hey, my, my. Yo, Parker. This one's for you.

SOURCE: Michael Rodriguez, *Run through the Jungle,* available at http://www.vietvet .org/rockroll.htm, accessed April 11, 2005. Since this article was accessed, it has been modified online, as of April 10, 2006.

~~~~~~~

In an e-mail exchange with the assistant editor of this volume, Paul Beaudoin, in May–June 2005, Michael Rodriguez added some details to the memoir above.

A POSTSCRIPT

PB: While I know you were in Vietnam from 1965 until 1970 I don't know how old you were during those years—I imagine getting inducted at 18 but could you let me know for sure.

MR: I was 17 years old when I enlisted in the United States Marine Corps in 1965, but 19 years old when I arrived in Vietnam in September 1966. You must understand, in those days, that young Chicano males would most definitely be drafted into the Army unless said Chicano had connections (no one I knew had any) or had been accepted into a major university (like we could afford that).

Military service was a given. Our choices, then, were be drafted into the Army or enlist in the service of your choice; I chose the Marine Corps. I thought I'd look silly in Navy whites and even sillier in Air Force blues.

I was born in 1947 in San Antonio and enlisted here. Hell, I'd never even seen an airplane until I boarded the one that would take me (and 74 other recruits) to Marine Corps Recruit Depot (MCRD), San Diego in 1965.

PB: It seems confusing that you wrote this for the oral history project of the Second Battalion, First Marine Regiment (Vietnam), in 1989. Is it more a written archive or one where people are telling of their experiences on tape—also is there a place where someone can go to hear these histories (aside from the documents on the web)?

MR: I used the term "oral history" because the idea was presented to me as such in the original pitch for what became the book. As far as I know, no recordings were made of what any of us might have said; all was written and submitted to the editors—one of whom, incidentally, had been my platoon commander in Vietnam, David Novak, and the other was his wife, author and essayist Marian Faye Novak (my hero and mentor, whose seminal work, "Lonely Girls with Burning Eyes," is out of print).

PB: Michael, in your writing music seems very important to you—does it take a larger role in your life than what this piece suggests?

MR: I could tell you of playing tenor saxophone in the local rock 'n' roll bands of the 60s, or of performing with the house band at the Tiffany Lounge on Houston Street. I took the music of my time with me to Vietnam. It was what I knew. It was familiar where familiar was often bizarre.

I could tell you of coming off watch at Marine Barracks, Naval Weapons Station, Concord, California, and tuning my SONY portable radio to KMPX-FM San Francisco (106.7 I think) to listen to Credence Clearwater Revival's "Susie Q" at one o'clock in the morning.

PB: These memories seem as vivid as yesterday—how do you explain that?

MR: True story:

"So," says the Vet Center counselor to the anonymous Grunt, "You were in Vietnam?"

The anonymous Grunt says, "Yeah."

The Vet Center counselor says, "Yeah? When were you there?"

The Anonymous Grunt says, "Last night."

PB: Michael, thank you for sharing your experiences and for the courage you showed then as now.

~~~~~~~~~~

NOTE

1.   The TV series *Tour of Duty* ran 1987–1990.

GEORGE CRUMB AND *BLACK ANGELS*

A Quartet in Time of War

(Crumb, Harrington)

George Crumb (b. 1929) helped to define a stylistic path in American music that owed little to serial composition. In the 1960s and early '70s, Crumb explored new sonorities on conventional instruments and embedded quotations from historical Western classical music into new compositions. These techniques, along with his use of the concert stage as theater, come together in one of Crumb's best-known works—the string quartet *Black Angels,* initially titled *A Quartet in Time of War.*

And what a time it was! The piece was commissioned and then premiered on October 23, 1970, by the Stanley Quartet, in residence at the University of Michigan's School of Music, Crumb's alma mater. During the previous spring, the nation had witnessed several devastating events surrounding the Vietnam War: the exposure of the My Lai massacre, the invasion of Cambodia, the Kent State University protests during which four students were shot and killed by the National Guard, and the subsequent spread of student strikes to about 500 universities nationwide. When Crumb completed *Black Angels,* he inscribed it "finished on Friday the Thirteenth, March 1970 (*in tempore belli*)."

Within two years, the first recording of *Black Angels* was made by the New York String Quartet for a small independent label, Composers Recordings Inc. (CRI), for which Crumb wrote the liner notes reprinted here. So powerfully did Crumb merge ritual with fear that, in 1973, one of the 13 movements from the piece was used in the soundtrack of a classic horror film, *The Exorcist*.

Since then, several major ensembles have taken up the work. Thus, following Crumb's own program notes for *Black Angels* is a testimonial to its impact from the founding member of the famous Kronos String Quartet, whose recording of the work is the standard one today.

BLACK ANGELS (IMAGES I)

THIRTEEN IMAGES FROM THE DARK LAND

*B*lack Angels was conceived as a kind of parable on our troubled contemporary world. The numerous quasi-programmatic allusions in the work are therefore symbolic, although the essential polarity—God versus Devil—implies more than a purely metaphysical reality. The image of the "black angel" was a conventional device used by early painters to symbolize the fallen angel.

The underlying structure of *Black Angels* is a huge arch-like design which is suspended from the three "Threnody" pieces. The work portrays a voyage of the soul. The three stages of this voyage are Departure (fall from grace), Absence (spiritual annihilation) and Return (redemption).

The numerological symbolism of *Black Angels,* while perhaps not immediately perceptible to the ear, is nonetheless quite faithfully reflected in the musical structure. These "magical" relationships are variously expressed; e.g., in terms of phrase length, groupings for single tones, durations, patterns of repetition, etc. An important pitch element in the work—ascending D-sharp, A, and E—also symbolizes the fateful numbers 7–13. At certain points in the score there occurs a kind of ritualistic counting in various languages, including German, French, Russian, Hungarian, Japanese and Swahili.

There are several allusions to tonal music in *Black Angels:* a quotation from Schubert's "Death and the Maiden" quartet (in the *Pavana Lachrymae* and also faintly echoed on the last page of the work); an original *Sarabanda,* which is stylistically synthetic; the sustained B major tonality of *God-Music;* and several references to the Latin sequence *Dies Irae* ("Day of Wrath"). The work abounds in conventional musical symbolisms such as the *Diabolus in Musica* (the interval of the tritone) and the *Trillo di Diavolo* (the "Devil's Trill," after Tartini).

The amplification of the stringed instruments in *Black Angels* is intended to produce a highly surrealistic effect. This surrealism is heightened by the use of certain unusual string effects, e.g., pedal tones (the intensely obscene sounds of the *Devil-Music*); bowing on the "wrong" side of the strings (to produce the viol-consort effect); trilling on the strings with thimble-capped fingers. The performers also play maracas, tam-tams and water-tuned crystal goblets, the latter played with the bow for the "glass-harmonica" effect in *God-Music.*

Black Angels was commissioned by the University of Michigan and first performed by the Stanley Quartet. The score is inscribed: "finished on Friday, the Thirteenth, March 1970 (*in tempore belli*)."

SOURCE: George Crumb, liner notes to New York String Quartet, *Black Angels* (Composers Recordings Inc., 1972 CRI SD 283), which also included a diagram showing the formal symmetry in the work. Excerpts from these notes were also used for the later recording of the work by the Kronos String Quartet (Nonesuch, 1990).

~~~~~~~~~~

The interview excerpted here was conducted when the Kronos Quartet had been together for 22 years. It opens with violinist David Harrington answering a question about the formation of the ensemble.

Well, in 1973 I was living in Seattle, and I had grown up playing quartet music. When I was in high school that was the major passion of my life at that point, and [I] began to get to know some of the major recent composers, and then when I was about sixteen a composer in Seattle named Ken Benchoff, whose music we're going to play tonight, by the way, wrote a piece for the group I was in, and that was my first involvement with the newest music, and music that was written especially for me.

. . .

And then in 1973, during the summertime late one night, I heard this music called *Black Angels* by George Crumb. It was a startling, scary experience to hear that music, and it was a kind of experience that maybe you have once in a lifetime where all of a sudden I knew—exactly—what I was going to do, and what I wanted to do was play that music.

. . .

We recorded it in 1989, it came out in 1990. That's really what got me started and gave me the propulsion and the energy to form Kronos, was hearing that piece, live on the radio, late one night.

. . .

Our first recording on Nonesuch came out in '85 and it wasn't until 1990 that we released *Black Angels*. Sometimes it just takes a long time to find out how you really want to present something, and for me, that piece was so much a part of the early reasons for wanting to have Kronos, you know, as a way of life, that I wanted to be sure that we did it exactly the way we all wanted it, and that just took about seventeen years.

SOURCE: Interview conducted by radio station KUCI at the University of California, Irvine, in May 1995, available at http://www.kuci.org/~dany/philharmonic/kronos.html.

Milton Babbitt on Electronic Music

(Babbitt, Brody and Miller)

Before the years of MIDI (musical instrument digital interface) and other software interfaces for music making, electronic music synthesis demanded the tenacity of a bull terrier from composers wishing to work with processed sound. One of the earliest resources for such projects, the RCA Mark II synthesizer, captured the interest of the composer Milton Babbitt (b. 1916). In 1959, Babbitt, with his musician colleague Roger Sessions and his Columbia University colleagues Vladimir Ussachevsky (1911–1990) and Otto Luening (1900–1996), helped to relocate the RCA Mark II synthesizer to Columbia. They established the Columbia-Princeton Electronic Music Center—the most technologically complete and advanced electronic music center in the world at that time.

In the first article reprinted here, in which Babbitt writes for a general university community, he explains the significance of the event not only for him as an individual artist but for music as a whole. During the 1960s, perhaps inspired by the pioneering challenges of his new medium, Babbitt composed works such as *Philomel, Phonemena, Vision and Prayer* (all with voice), and *Ensembles for Synthesizer*, which are considered masterpieces of early American electronic music.

In the selection following, he describes his commuting pilgrimages to the Mark II in New Jersey. Both excerpts are written in a less formal style than the dense prose of a composer-philosopher-theorist.

~~~~~~~
~~~~~~~
~~~~~~~

MILTON BABBITT DESCRIBES THE REVOLUTION IN
SOUND: ELECTRONIC MUSIC (1960)

There exists today a music which is produced entirely without performers and musical instruments. Indeed it cannot be produced by performers on musical instruments, and can
be presented to the listener only through the medium of a loudspeaker. This should be a matter
of little surprise to anyone who has ever thoughtfully placed a phonograph needle in a record
groove. For, contained in the varying side to side undulations of these grooves is all of the
"sound" that eventually reaches the listeners' ears as the complex musical phenomenon of, let
us say, a seventy-five piece symphony orchestra. Therefore, it follows—ghosts in the machine
aside—that this same music could be created merely by mechanically, even manually, cutting
the grooves directly on a blank record, thus dispensing with the actual orchestra. This is a con-
ceivable, if not highly recommended, way of creating purely electronic music.

Electronic music is just what its name suggests: music produced by means of "instructed" electronic oscillations. Music is, of course, sound. To produce it electronically should
be no more alarming than producing it with that oddly shaped wooden box equipped with taut
strings which we call a violin.

Furthermore the idea, although perhaps startling, is hardly new. Instruments for the
electronic production of sound emerged full-blown and as efficient as the technology of the time
allowed only a few years after *the first* successful attempts at recording sound, and, indeed, before the invention of the vacuum tube itself. The American [Thaddeus] Cahill, [in] 1895, and the
Englishman [William] Duddell, in 1899, began the construction of instruments which were, in
principle, the precursors of such familiar "direct performance" electronic instruments as the
Hammond organ and the Theremin.

PRIMITIVE ELECTRONICS

To be sure, most of the electronic instruments of the first half of this century offered little beyond limited sonic novelty, primarily because they were "instruments," to be performed on in
the usual sense. But the "handwritten sound-track" of the movies where the "instructions" were
provided by wave forms directly drawn on film, possessed—potentially, at least—all of the properties of today's totally electronic media. There were technical problems, certainly, but the absence of a widespread, intensive attack on the problems was a reflection of the almost total lack
of interest in and knowledge of this medium on the part of composers. There was, apparently,
little incentive to expend valuable time and energy on the merely possible.

Now, for many composers, such possibilities have become necessities. Surely it is not
surprising that there is music written in the twentieth century which makes demands that cannot be fulfilled by musical instruments designed in the eighteenth and nineteenth centuries for
the performance of eighteenth- and nineteenth-century music.

The twentieth century has produced what, in all circumspection, must be termed a
revolution in musical thought. And this revolution has affected profoundly not only the pitch

organization of music, but the rhythmic, dynamic, and timbral organization, creating the need for precision in these domains which cannot be satisfied by conventional musical instruments, which possess automatic or semiautomatic means of pitch control, but no comparable means of rhythmic and dynamic control, and are limited timbrally by their inherent physical structure. On the contrary, contemporary electronic media, whatever the particular artifact, are characterized minimally by the regulability [sic] and measurability of the frequency, the temporal duration, the intensity, the growth and decay characteristics of a note, and the spectrum of a musical tone. And these media are not "real-time media"; they are not direct performance instruments. The performance "instructions" are prepared prior to and independent of actual performance, which involves human participation to no greater extent than does the playing of a phonograph record.

The strategic stimulus to the new era of electronic music was the emergence of magnetic tape recording and reproduction of sound after World War II. For the new possibility of manually splicing together electronically produced individual sounds eliminated the complex necessity of providing instructions for sound succession. Although this splicing procedure is laborious and tedious, and imposes severe and undesirable limitations on the characteristics of sound succession, precise frequency control is provided by the electronic oscillator, control of temporal duration is provided by the measurement of tape length, loudness is controlled by electronic amplification of the individual sound, and spectrum is determined by the particular combination of oscillators employed to produce the individual sound.

This, basically, is the method employed at the first and most widely publicized electronic music studio, that of the Cologne radio station, and the later studios at Milan, Tokyo, Stockholm, Warsaw, and Brussels. Even earlier, in Paris, the properties of the tape recorder were exploited to produce "*musique concrète*," which, however, is not "purely" electronic music insofar as the signal itself is not necessarily electronically produced, but may be merely a recorded musical or naturalistic sound, which then undergoes electronic mutation and modification before being spliced into a succession of such sounds.

In the United States, comparable activity was confined to individuals working with extremely limited technological means. The only studio, in any sense, was a small one at Columbia University, where Professors Otto Luening and Vladimir Ussachevsky created "tape music" employing procedures related to those of both *musique concrète* and the Cologne studio; for all that the physical resources were decidedly less than luxurious, unique and ingenious technical devices were constructed under the direction of Peter Mauzey of Columbia.

These studios were founded by and for composers, whose musical demands and desires had led them to the electronic medium as the only foreseeable answer to their compositional requirements. Meanwhile, far removed from such considerations—indeed, totally unaware of them—a group of scientists at the Radio Corporation of America were designing and constructing the most sophisticated electronic sound producer yet conceived: the Olson-Belar Electronic Music Synthesizer, named after Dr. Harry Olson and Mr. Herbert Belar of RCA. This elaborate apparatus eliminated entirely the laborious techniques of tape splicing and similar procedures by providing efficient and precise means of supplying instructions to—that is, of "programming"—the electronic components, not only instructions for the precise description of each musical event, but for the manner of progression of each such event to the following event. The Synthesizer was revealed publicly in 1955, but very soon thereafter work was begun, at RCA, on a second, much improved and enlarged version of the Synthesizer, whose construction was completed some two years later.

OPERATION SIMPLIFIES

This elaborate device cannot be fully understood and its tremendous range of musical implication appreciated without an extended technical discussion. Put in simple terms what happens is this:

> The operator sits before a keyboard, not unlike a typewriter, and conveys to the machine his instructions in the form of holes punched on a paper roll fifteen inches wide. These holes represent binary decimal code numbers which determine the resultant pitch class, octave, envelope (growth and decay characteristics), spectrum (broadly speaking: timbre), and intensity of the musical event. For pitch class and octave, the complete frequency continuum is available including what is known as "white" noise. This noise—which sounds much like the thermal noise of steam—contains every frequency in the range of sound audible to the human ear. It is, in other words, the full spectrum of sound and is called "white" as an analogy to white light, which contains the full visual spectrum (the analogy holds when one or more frequency bands are damped out, the result being called "colored" noise). For envelope, any time-rate of growth and decay can be specified; for spectrum, there is—measured with regard to human life span—an "infinity" of possible spectra; for intensity, the only limitations imposed are those of the recording medium which is to be the permanent record of the Synthesizer output.

It must be understood that these code numbers have no permanent denotation, but denote whatever the composer-operator has wired the machine for. The composer, having made such correlations for a particular composition or part of a composition, may hear—at once—the result of these choices by flipping switches on the panel above the keyboard; these switches operate the same relays which will be activated by the punched holes passing under contact brushes. Then, after punching the corresponding holes on the paper roll, the composer can hear the complete succession at any desired speed; any changes can be made immediately by further punching. When the composer is satisfied that he has achieved what he desired, the roll is driven under the brushes by [the] machine at a chosen speed, and the music is simultaneously heard and recorded. Such aural luxury and immediacy is not available on any other electronic medium, where the final result can be heard only after recording. The composer, in punching his instructions onto the paper roll, is—at once and in one single act—composing, copying his score and parts, rehearsing, performing, and recording his composition.

In January 1957, RCA generously allowed Professors Luening, Ussachevsky, and myself to begin a series of visits to the Sarnoff Research Center for the purpose of acquainting ourselves with this second Synthesizer. Professor Luening was obliged to leave for Europe soon after these visits began, but Ussachevsky and I continued to spend, for the next four months, one or two days a week with the machine, under the instructive supervision of Herbert Belar. Active mastery, or even passive understanding of the total possibilities of this complex machine, was not and could not have been the goal of such a limited number of visits.

Rather, our desire was to acquaint ourselves with the machine to the extent necessary for us to be able to speak and demonstrate with first-hand authority its value and importance to the composer of serious contemporary music, and to apply this authority to the task of securing the necessary funds to acquire such a machine for our universities, where it could be made freely available to qualified composers and researchers.

MUSIC CENTER ESTABLISHED

In early 1959, electronic music in this country received a tremendous boost when the Rockefeller Foundation announced a grant of $175,000 to cover a five-year period to establish the Electronic Music Center under the joint control of Columbia and Princeton Universities. The Committee of Direction of the Center, Professors Luening and Ussachevsky of Columbia, and Professor Roger Sessions and myself of Princeton, was empowered to secure and have constructed the necessary equipment for the production of electronic music. Obviously, the size of the available funds eliminated the possibility of acquiring a Synthesizer, but RCA offered us a lease-maintenance arrangement for this one and only existing model of the second Synthesizer, which was thereby installed in the Center at Columbia University in early July 1959. With this, albeit temporary, acquisition, the Center is assured of being the most technologically complete and advanced electronic music center in the world and, since in resources begin responsibilities, it was particularly significant that these resources were entrusted to the first electronic studio associated with [a] university. (Subsequently, a studio has been founded at the University of Toronto.)

It represents the all too rare recognition that the most complex, advanced, and "problematical" activities in music, as in science, belong properly in the university. For it is not too much to say that the Electronic Music Center is, in the scope of its implications and its strategic nature—if not in its budget—the "Matterhorn" of contemporary music. This research requires the cooperation of the musician, the electrical engineer, the psychologist, and even the mathematician: the community of diverse and specialized knowledge available uniquely at the university.

Too, the very novelty of the electronic medium makes it the easy vehicle of sensationalism, which can—at best—create distrust with and misunderstanding of the whole domain of activity. The university, it is hoped, provides the means of resistance to such temptation.

Again, the difficult and unprecedented task of equipping the composer to work with electronic media can be undertaken only by a university. For the composer must not anticipate reliance upon an engineer-technician, who will communicate for him to the machine; to do so would be to return to his dependence upon a "performer," a "performer" with whom communication will be much more difficult and constrained than it has been even with conventional music and the difficulties inherent in the imprecision of normal notation. The composer must attain, at least, full descriptive mastery of the new media, and, preferably, complete active mastery. To achieve this is to admit the necessity of additional and demanding educational preparation: acoustics, electronics, computer theory, and the mathematics necessary for an understanding of the literature of these fields. Assuming a presentation of these materials designed specifically to equip the composer for his electronic task, it is estimated that four one-year university courses would be necessary. If this appears an excessive expenditure of time, let it be recalled that a comparable expenditure spent on the study of the piano would fall very short of that required for mastery.

In any case, many of our young composers are willing, able, and—waiting. For, although musical necessity, primarily, has motivated the extension to the electronic realm, practical—one might say hesitatingly "socioeconomic"—considerations are of almost equal weight. All factors militate against the composition of complex contemporary music: the uncompensated time involved in its composition, the crushing costs of preparing materials, the inadequate number of rehearsals, and the consequent, usually unsatisfactory, always ephemeral performance. The electronic medium discriminates not at all against such complexity; rather, it is most appropriate to it. Such music can now remove itself entirely from the inapposite milieu of the public concert hall; it exists, in any case, only in recorded form, and is so available to anyone who is interested, to be played and replayed at the listener's convenience.

What of the music that has been produced and may be expected to be produced by electronic means? I shall make no attempt to answer this question, not only because of the gross inadequacy of any summary description of a musical work, but because—at this chronological point—it is of the most fundamental importance that the nature and potentialities of the medium not be confused with specific instances of its use. This most vast and flexible of media imposes no limitations of "styles" or "idiom" upon the music created with its use, but few composers have had access to this medium, and many of the available examples employ technologically limited electronic apparatus. The music can be, and will be, whatever the composer wills it to be within the almost unconfined joys of the electronic realm.

In attempting to anticipate some of the nontechnical questions which might come to mind, let it first be emphasized that no one anticipates or hopes that electronic music will supplant instrumentally and vocally produced music; it is intended to supplement these resources, not supplant them. There is certainly no desire to produce a purely electronic version of the *Eroica* Symphony. Such a version would be but one possible version chosen from all the versions legitimately inferable from Beethoven's score, and the use of the electronic medium for music not requiring it is, at least, inefficient.

Certainly, it is assumed that the performer who enjoys playing the instrument will continue to do so, both for pleasure and profit, since the listener who demands the presence of live musicians participating in performances to be seen as well as heard will not have, at least, both of these desires fulfilled by electronic music. To the unfortunately often heard question: "What of the human element?" one is tempted to turn one's back, and should, to the extent that it originates in the notion that, somehow, an instrument constructed of steel wire, felt, and wood is more "human" than one constructed of copper wire, vacuum tubes, and switches. But, if the question arises—as it often does—from a profound misunderstanding, then it should be answered to dispel such misunderstanding. I am not speaking of machines that "compose," but of machines that carry out only the instructions of the, we assume, "human" composer. They can and will do nothing more and nothing less. And, if the question carries the further burden of querying the loss of "human" performance, it must be emphasized that to speak of the "performance" of electronic music is meaningless: performance and composition are here an indissoluble act; one may as justifiably speak of the "performance" of a painting. If the question emanates from a composer, he may add that he welcomes the performer as "collaborator." This, naturally, is his prerogative, a matter of personal disposition. But ask such a composer whether the deviations from the score which he is willing to allow the performer in rhythm, tempo, dynamics, and phrasing extend to the realm of pitch, and he will, unless he is a "chance" composer, demur violently. Then, he must be made to realize that there are composers who structure those aspects of the work as precisely as they structure pitch; perceptible deviations would produce a new and, probably, unintelligible total structure.

One can understand sympathetically two possible extreme reactions to [the] first confrontation by the fact of electronic music: (1) we are entering the worst of musical times; (2) we are entering the best of musical times. But it is difficult to see how anyone should feel other than that we are entering the most exciting of musical times.

SOURCE: Milton Babbitt, "The Revolution in Sound: Electronic Music," *Music Journal* 18, no. 7 (1965): 34–37. An earlier version appeared in *Columbia University Magazine* (Spring 1960): 4–8.

~~~~~~~~~

In this excerpt, Babbitt talks to two composers of the younger generation. The tone of the previous selection here yields to nostalgia. Babbitt gets on the train to New Jersey and discusses the development of computer-generated sound.

FROM AN INTERVIEW WITH MILTON BABBITT

INTERVIEWERS MARTIN BRODY AND DENNIS MILLER: Perhaps the single most dramatic development in the long stretch of his career from the late 1940s to the present has been the development of electronic music synthesis, a medium that has had particularly important consequences for Babbitt.

MILTON BABBITT: Forgetting the PhDs and whatnot, what happened in the fifties was that we went to RCA [to develop one of the first major electronic music synthesizers], and then of course opened a studio. That was really in the late fifties. The first piece came in 1961. That dominated the whole period. Vladimir [Ussachevsky] and I had to do it on our own with a little help from the department. We had to do this really on our own. . . . We spent years out of our lives.

MB AND DM: In all his electronic works, Babbitt has used the same sound-synthesis device, the RCA synthesizer. When the instrument was first developed, he quickly recognized its importance and announced the potential of the new medium to composers in a series of important theoretical articles. But the engineers who developed the synthesizer were less aware of its compositional significance.

MILTON BABBITT: The engineers at RCA gave the first synthesizer to [David] Sarnoff. . . . They turned out a commercial record. I don't know whether it was sold or not, but it was certainly distributed, and it was called the "Voice of the RCA Synthesizer." They did a version of *Nola* à la Vincent Lopez. They did Stephen Foster. For example, they did a military polonaise. It wasn't bad, you know, but it was awful.

MB AND DM: When the synthesizer was first developed, Babbitt and his colleague, Vladimir Ussachevsky, would commute from New York City to the RCA laboratory in New Jersey to use the new machine.

MILTON BABBITT: Vladimir and I would get on the train at six o'clock, and he would eat a chocolate bar and go to sleep. Vladimir quickly discovered that it wasn't his cup of tea. He was interested in getting some of the sounds out of it, but it wasn't for him. I stuck with it, and suddenly came that fateful day when they said, "We don't know what to do with the synthesizer. If you guys want it, just pay a service fee." We paid a service fee for a while, but we stopped doing that, because we were servicing it ourselves.

MB AND DM: Thus, the RCA synthesizer moved to the Columbia-Princeton Electronic Music Studio in uptown Manhattan. As Babbitt recognized, the new electronic medium had profound consequences for composition. . . . "In an electronic piece, let's face it, anything that can be perceived can be differentiated [and] can be structured."

SOURCE: Martin Brody and Dennis Miller, "Milton Babbitt: An Appreciation," in *Essays on Modern Music*, ed. Martin Brody (for the League International Society for Contemporary Music, 1985): 3–10; excerpt on 7.

128

EDWARD T. CONE SATIRIZES

MUSIC THEORY'S NEW VOCABULARY

In the 1950s and '60s, American composers virtually invented post-tonal music theory as a specialized discourse. Using as models the serial music of Arnold Schoenberg, Alban Berg, and Anton Webern, they produced a formidable analytical vocabulary, as represented in the new journals of the era such as the *Journal of Music Theory* (1957) and *Perspectives of New Music* (1962).

Princeton University was home to leaders of this movement, particularly one member of its faculty, Milton Babbitt, who, for over 50 years, has wrestled with theoretical questions surrounding the emancipation of dissonance. Using ideas from philosophy and mathematics, he constructed meta-theories to deal with the absence of compositional norms in post-tonal music. The vocabulary he helped to invent initially daunted even such formidable colleagues as the music theorist Edward Cone (1917–2004), who satirized it with insider skill in this supposed spin-off from *The Grove Dictionary of Music*. Today, this language has triumphed as the lingua franca of contemporary theory and is routinely used in music theory textbooks.

A BUDDING GROVE

The following short dictionary is designed both as an aid to the reader of up-to-date articles on contemporary music, such as are to be found in the pages of PERSPECTIVES OF NEW MUSIC, and as a guide to the prospective writer thereof. It makes no pretense to comprehensiveness: it deals with only a few of the most interesting and troublesome terms in current use. The discussions are as simple and as non-technical as possible. Precisely systematic definitions in many cases would have had to be couched in terms even less intelligible to the lay reader than those being defined. In such instances, I have resorted to explanation by example, or to homely analogy—without, I trust, sacrificing accuracy.

Like all other dictionary-makers, I confess to certain prejudices, most of which will become evident to anyone taking the trouble to read through the following discussions. Some unkind readers may even come to the conclusion that I have undertaken this task simply in order to air them. Nothing could be further from the truth: my aim has been solely that of clarification.

All page references are to PERSPECTIVES OF NEW MUSIC. Quotations without reference are my own.

ADJACENCY

(a) Nearest neighbor, often used in the plural to indicate a reciprocal relation; e.g., "North Carolina and Virginia are adjacencies," or "C and E are adjacencies in the original statement of the row of *Threni*." This form is considered much more elegant than the simple adjective adjacent.

(b) An instance of such a relationship; e.g., "This transposition preserves one adjacency of the original row-form."

Note: Each of the above uses of this word is an example of what I call "transferred concretion"—the use of an abstract noun as a common noun. It is a usage that, although deplored by some conservative stylists, seems to be increasingly in vogue (see density and simultaneity), no doubt because it subtly suggests that the writer is at ease among abstractions.

AGGREGATE

By definition, the totality of any number of notes (or of anything else under discussion) can be considered as an aggregate. It is chic, however, to speak of "an aggregate," with no further qualification, as referring to the total note-content of the chromatic scale, as if it were the only kind of aggregate possible.

ALEATORY

Derived from the Latin *aleator* (dice-thrower), this is a euphemistic honorific which is applied to composition by methods of chance, and to the results thereof. It is properly an adjective but often appears as a noun. While this usage may displease some purists, it has had the estimable result of calling forth yet another word to serve as the adjective: "aleatoric." This form, which would otherwise be superfluous, has recently found favor among many writers.

ARCHITECTONIC

Architectural, structural. The word has a pleasing sound, since it seems to unite architecture and tone. For this reason it is often taken to mean "pertaining to the architecture of tone" or "pertaining to the structure of tonality." Although it means neither, it is nevertheless a great favorite, especially with those who use "structure" as a verb.

COMPOSING-OUT

(a) An anglicization of Heinrich Schenker's *Auskomponierung,* for a discussion of which see his works *passim.*

(b) Writing music al fresco (cf. camping out).

(c) Especially in the passive voice, the idiom may be used to indicate that a composer has reached the end of his creative rope: "Strauss was composed-out by the time he got to *Ariadne.*"

COMBINATORIAL

It would be perhaps presumptuous, and anyway unnecessary, for me to attempt to explain this term, together with a few others such as *secondary set, derived set,* etc., since they have been rigorously defined in articles by Milton Babbitt, who is responsible for their introduction into twelve-tone theory. And Mr. Babbitt's practice of referring to these articles when he has occasion to use the terms is a model of the correct scholarly use of words and phrases not yet to be found in standard dictionaries.

Many of his followers, however, consider this practice old-fashioned and academic; they use the words freely, with neither definition nor footnote reference. Two advantages accrue: the writer thus establishes himself as a member of a select group, and the reader has the fun of trying to find out for himself just what is meant.

CONTOUR INVERSION

There are so many kinds of inversion under discussion nowadays that it seems necessary to specify in this way that plain old melodic inversion is meant—the kind that Bach applied to fugue-subjects.

DEGENERATE

Not, as one might think, a term of opprobrium or of psycho-pathological diagnosis (indeed, I believe the word has passed out of medical usage, although it is still to be encountered in the daily press). It characterizes certain twelve-tone rows that, under normal transformations, fail to produce 48 distinct forms. (In some of Webern's rows, for example, the retrograde inversions are identical with the prime forms.) Since, in the minds of many, *all* twelve-tone rows are degenerate, I suggest, as a less loaded word, "reductive."

DENSITY

A chord, especially one with a lot of notes. An example of transferred concretion (see *adjacency*).

DERIVED SET

See *combinatorial.*

DERANGEMENT

Not, as one might suspect, a characterization of the mental state of certain composers and critics; but:

(a) variation from the original order of the elements of a series, or

(b) the measure of such variation.

Again, I suggest a less highly connotative substitute: "disarrangement."

DODECAPHONIC

Properly, characterized by twelve-voiced texture (cf. "monophonic," "polyphonic"), but almost universally used whenever a Greek-derived polysyllable for "twelve-tone" is desired. The fact that one almost never encounters the correct "dodecatonic" in this country indicates that the sound of the Greek, with its concomitant scholarly aura, is the desideratum, rather than linguistic accuracy. Actually, there is no case of adjectival use where the locution "twelve-tone" (in British parlance, "twelve-note") will not be just as clear; but this term is by no means so satisfyingly mouth-filling.

Unfortunately there is no convenient standard abstract noun form. "Dodecaphony," sometimes seen, if accented on the antepenult, strongly suggests "cacophony"; if on the penult, "phony" (see the writings of Hans Keller). "Dodecatony," and native forms such as "twelve-tonism," "twelve-tonishness," "twelve-tonality," and "twelve-tonery," have somehow never caught on. (But see Godfrey Winham's use of the last, Vol. 1, No. 2, p. 143.)

DYAD

A unit of two tones. See *hexachord.*

EVENT

Anything that happens (but not a "happening," q.v.). It is a conveniently loose way of referring to a chord, a motif, a measure, a theme, etc., without bothering to specify just what (or how much) is meant.

Query: Is a rest an event? If so, then the definition must be extended to include something that doesn't happen, or the failure of something to happen. Perhaps rests should be called "non-events."

"HAPPENING"

Since writers on serious music will hardly have occasion to refer to "happenings," this word is here only in order to make sure that it is not confused with *event*, although a "happening" may indeed be an Event.

HEXACHORD

Another term that attests the grecophilia of those responsible for the new musical terminology. Reactionaries wring their hands, because its current meaning—six consecutive elements of a tone-row (usually the first or the last six) used as a structural unit—is at odds with its traditional meaning of six successive tones of a mode (as in "Guidonian hexachord"); and also because for one unaware of the traditional meaning, the word seems to refer to "chord" in the modern sense (viz., to mean "six-note chord"). Similar difficulties apply, they say, to the current use of *trichord, tetrachord, pentachord,* etc., but not of course, to *dyad.* Why then cannot the last be taken as the model for a new terminology? Obviously because at the very next step—*triad*—a new confusion would arise, since this term, too, is preempted by classical use.

For the die-hard conservative, then, the best way out of the difficulty would be complete anglicization. What is wanted, of course, are short, convenient terms for "two-note sub-set," "three-note sub-set," etc. I suggest "two-noter," "three-noter," etc.; or, if those seem too jaunty, "two-set," "three-set," etc. But these have, of course, the disadvantage of all terms derived from ordinary language: they do not immediately impart to one's discourse that ponderousness of style that predisposes the reader to take for granted a scientific exactitude of content.

INTERSECTION

Element or elements in common; most often common tones, or *pitch-classes* (q.v.). To be used whenever an effect of geometrical precision is desired.

INTERVAL-CLASS

A locution derived, like *pitch-class* (q.v.), from the notion of residue-classes, and credited to the same author. It is so useful in twelve-tone theory that one suspects that it was coined expressly for the purpose; for just those intervals treated as equivalent for most twelve-tone purposes conveniently form a single interval-class. For example, all ascending perfect fifths, twelfths, and other compound perfect fifths, plus all descending perfect fourths and compounds thereof, form one interval-class. Some fear that confusion may arise from the fact that there are many other ways of classifying intervals: e.g., the class of imperfect consonances, the class of non-tritones, etc.; and in this case there is not even a British word to fall back on (see *pitch-class*). Perhaps, following the clever suggestion of Michael Kassler, who uses *lyne* to stand for a refined and precise version of what is more generally referred to as *line* (see Vol. 1, No. 2, p. 93), one might use *ynterval;* but this, I fear, will need a lot of propaganda before it achieves general acceptance. I see no immediate way out for the timid; so I suppose they are stuck with "interval-class," at least for the time being.

ORDER-NUMBER PITCH-NUMBER COUPLE

A systematic way of indicating an element of a tone-row by two numbers, the first of which indicates its position in the row and the second of which indicates its *pitch-class* (q.v.). Although some will no doubt cavil at what they call the cumbersomeness of the expression, others will not fail to recognize it for what it is: sheer poetry, with a rhythm all its own. Listen, for example, to the subtle repetition of the word "number," and to the way the whole is brought up short by the final "couple."

No doubt, in this workaday world of ours, analysts, like others, will find themselves increasingly pressed for time and space; so I suppose we shall have to resign ourselves to reading about "o.n.p.n.c.'s."

PARAMETER

A word with several precise technical meanings, and therefore often used in discussions of serial methods as a means of assuring the reader's confidence in the writer's mathematical knowledgeability. In such contexts it is to be preferred even to "variable" and is far superior to "component." (For an example of its use in this way, see *serial*.)

PARTITION

Partition theory is a branch of modern mathematics that has been applied to certain aspects of twelve-tone theory. But the word itself, quite apart from the theory, has proved endlessly useful as an elegant synonym for "divide" or "division" or "section."

P.C.

(a) Panama Canal, Patres Conscripti, per cent, Perpetual Curate, Philippine Constabulary, Privy Council.

(b) In juvenile parlance, "privileged character."

(c) See *pitch-class*.

PENTACHORD

See *hexachord*.

PRE-COMPOSITIONAL

Properly, pertaining to, or taking place during, the time preceding actual composition. Thus one might speak of eating a pre-compositional meal, or of taking a pre-compositional nap. In actual use, it often means *proto-compositional*: pertaining to the earliest planning or gestating stages of composition, as in "pre-compositional sketches." Someone has surely slipped up here. The chance to popularize the scientific, Greek-derived prefix *proto* should not have been lost. Perhaps it is not too late.

PITCH-CLASS

A useful term credited to Milton Babbitt, and derived from the mathematical notion of residue-classes. All C's, for example, form one pitch-class; all C#'s another (provided, of course, that we refer to a single system of tuning). But precisely because it is so useful, it is already beginning to seem unwieldy to some—at least to J. K. Randall, who has introduced the abbreviation "p.c." (Vol. 2, No. 1, p. 103). Furthermore, some timid souls (see *interval-class*) fearfully suggest that one might wish to refer to pitch-classes of a different kind.

For these reasons, it is unfortunate that Americans cannot use the admirably simple and concise term available to the English: "note." For us, alas, that refers to marks on paper. Therefore, following the lead of Michael Kassler (see *interval-class*), I venture to suggest "pytch" (pronounced *peitsch*) as a possibly viable substitute.

PITCH FIELD

A metaphor, possibly from mathematics, possibly from physics, possibly from baseball. It means the totality of pitches in use in any given context.

PITCH-TIME EVENT

A specific pitch heard at a specific time (see *event*). In other words, a tone.

ROW

See *series*.

SECONDARY SET

See *combinatorial*.

SEGMENT

Section; continuous portion; especially from 2 to 11 consecutive notes of a row. It is especially popular in its adjectival form, as in "segmental generator," "segmental adjacency," "segmental invariance," etc. In this form, it should be followed wherever possible (as in the foregoing examples) by a noun of at least four syllables.

SERIAL

An interesting word with two contrary meanings:

(a) Characterizing a work based on a tone-row, but not necessarily twelve-tone perhaps even historically pre-twelve-tone: "Schoenberg's Piano Pieces Opus 23 are serial."

(b) Characterizing works in which not only the *pitch-classes* (q.v.) but also other *parameters* (q.v.) of composition, such as temporal values, dynamics, and registers, are determined by one or more *pre-compositional* (q.v.) numerical *series* (q.v.): "Schoenberg's Piano Pieces Opus 23 are not serial."

SERIES

See *set*.

SET

See *row*.

SIMULTANEITY

Two or more tones attacked at the same time (see *density*). An example of transferred concretion (see *adjacency*). The word is especially powerful in combination with what might be called the "segmental adjectives," as in "dyadic simultaneity," "trichordal simultaneity," etc.

SOURCE-SET

A twelve-tone set considered not as completely ordered, but as consisting of two or more unordered collections, especially two unordered *hexachords* (q.v.). I should like to enter a plea here for substituting the word "trope" (of good Greek derivation), in honor of Josef Matthias Hauer, whose tropes were indeed very similar to what are now called source-sets.[1] True, "trope" already has a lot of other meanings, both musical and non-musical; but a glance through this dictionary will convince one that this difficulty need not be taken seriously. And Hauer gets little enough credit these days.

SONORITY

An old-fashioned, nay, almost obsolete term. The preferred form is now *density* (q.v.).

TETRACHORD

See *hexachord*.

TRICHORD

See *hexachord*.

WHITE-NOTE COLLECTION

An unfortunately ambiguous locution. It could have two distinct meanings (aside from further possible confusion with "white noise"):

(a) A collection of half-notes and whole-notes, since in normal modern notation these are white in contrast to the black quarters, eighths, and smaller values. (On a blackboard, I suppose, the latter should be called the white notes.)

(b) The tones of the C-major scale, since these are white keys on most modern keyboard instruments. In this case the proper term should be "white-key collection."

No doubt two distinct expressions, preferably Greek derivatives, will be coined to take care of these two senses.

As an appendix, I present a short paragraph in (a) ordinary language, and (b) up-to-date musical parlance. This can be used in either of two ways: a reader, wishing to test his knowledge of the new terminology, can begin with (b) and check his own translation with (a); or a writer, wishing to practice the new style for himself, can try rewriting (a) and compare his own results with (b).

(a) The composer apparently chose his transpositions carefully. The composition begins with three four-note chords that are later stated melodically in such a way as to make clear the exact order of the twelve-tone row that they imply. The first four notes of the original form of the row are Bb, F, C, and B; one will readily observe that the first two intervals are, from a twelve-tone point of view, equivalent, each being a perfect (ascending) fifth. When the composer later transposes the entire row by this interval, he thus ensures that the notes F and C will continue to be neighbors, although now at the beginning of the row. In the case of the only other transposition used, that of two semitones up, the inversion exhibits an important interval in common with the prime of the original; for the first two notes of the former are F and Bb—the same, in reverse order, as the corresponding notes of the latter. This identity is musically emphasized through common register and similar attack—these components thus exhibiting a structural function even though they are not serially organized.

(b) Aleatory factors were apparently at a minimum in determining the composer's choice of transpositions. The opening densities of the composition, three tetrachordal simultaneities, are subsequently linearized in such a way as to clarify the total ordering of the twelve-pitch-class set of which they represent the three disjunct tetrachordal partitions. The first segmental partition may be represented by the order-number pitch-number couple-succession (0,0), (1,7), (2,2), (3,1), from which one will immediately be struck by the identity of interval-class observable between the first and second conjunct dyadic segments, each belonging to the interval-class 7. When the composer later employs a transposition of the same interval-class, he thereby ensures the preservation of the adjacency (1,7), (2,2), now appearing, slightly deranged, as (0,7), (1,2). The only other transposition used, that of interval-class 2, exhibits an interesting intersection between its inversion and the prime of the original: the initial dyad of the former, (0,7), (1,0), preserves the pitch-class content of the opening dyad of the latter, although of course in reverse order. This intersection is compositionally exploited in contiguous events through the use of other parameters such as register and attack. Thus, although the latter are not serially structured, they nonetheless play an important architectonic role.

> SOURCE: Edward T. Cone, "A Budding Grove," *Perspectives of New Music* 3, no. 2 (Spring–Summer 1965): 38–46. Reference to this article was found in Arthur Berger, *Reflections of an American Composer* (Berkeley: University of California Press, 2002): 88–89.

NOTE

1.   George Perle, too, has long been eager to give Hauer his due (see *Serial Composition and Atonality*).

129

MARIO DAVIDOVSKY

An Introduction

(Chasalow)

Argentinean-American composer Mario Davidovsky (b. 1934) finds ingenious ways to blend electroacoustic sound with conventional instruments. In 1960, Davidovsky joined the Columbia-Princeton Electronic Music Center, where he remained until 1993. In his series of *Synchronisms*, Davidovsky combined different solo instruments and ensembles with processed sound, putting a speaker on stage with a player to engage in musical conversations. The relationship between live and electronic music makes for a subtle dynamic, and sometimes the electronic sound seems like an extension of a live instrument. This perceptive tribute by the composer Eric Chasalow was written when Davidovsky received the major international award in music, the Siemens Prize.[1]

In the context of a decidedly anti-intellectual and market-driven climate for the arts in the United States, Mario Davidovsky's sustained contributions over a career of more than 35 years, are both admirable and remarkable. A consummate musician who always focuses on core musical issues, he has never been concerned with superficial aspects of career. Nor, recognizing the necessity of artistic risk-taking, has he ever taken the easy path. Of late, Mario has become fond of explaining his approach this way: "I always enjoyed the challenge of being left in the desert for a few days with a knife and a jug of water. . . . I thought it would be important to try to do the opposite of what came naturally to me." In the 1960s, that "desert" was the emerging world of electroacoustic music, and the "knife and jug" the classic tape studio—the Columbia-Princeton Electronic Music Center. Together with his close friend, Turkish composer, Bulent Arel,[2] Davidovsky invented an approach to electroacoustic music that uses electronic sounds to enrich the art-music tradition, not to replace it. He has shown a whole generation of younger composers that it is not necessary to throw away the musical past in order to embrace the resources of new technology. While many others, then as now, have been seduced by the novelty of electronic sounds, Davidovsky has continuously discovered how to use new sounds in musically motivated ways. The handmade tape sounds in a Davidovsky piece are just as sensitive and convincing as those made by any virtuoso instrumentalist. Further, the musical ideas seem so completely motivated by the electronic materials, that they could only be expressed in the studio and not by any other instrument. Davidovsky has emerged from his desert looking like he must have been born there.

In the 1950s and 1960s, much electronic music consisted of dense layers or successions of sounds whose placement in time was of little consequence. Composers of the period were often satisfied with "discovering" sensuous sounds and few would go any further to build these into a musical architecture. A lack of musicality in electronic music composition pervaded the profession then as it does today. Poor composition hides behind the seductive idol of the machine, enabled by the twentieth-century habit of blindly valuing technological innovation above all else. Beginning almost fifty years ago, the profession of composer became artificially fractured into several specialties. On one hand, there are those who continue to write for traditional instruments, on the other, those who specialize in electroacoustic composition. Electroacoustic composers who work with the computer often insist on arrogantly dividing the profession further, between digital or computer composers and everyone else, which in the 1960s meant those working in the analog studio. These divisions have allowed the claim (most often by those with more technical than musical training and ability) that because we have new models for creating and controlling sound, that we should ignore the most central realities of music. These are that it unfolds in time and that to follow a musical argument, one must have and use memory. If we discard these tenets, then it is enough for a composer to "invent" sounds and simply expose them without any attention to ordering. Such an approach can, in some hands generate mildly interesting sound environments, but more often it is an excuse for a disengaged, mindless activity that reveals nothing and produces little that resembles art.

When Davidovsky came to the Columbia-Princeton Electronic Music Center in 1960, he became a central part of a community of composers seeking new expressive means and willing to use their highly developed musicianship as the point of departure. His development at that time of a new mode of phrase articulation, which builds upon his history of successful instrumental writing, can be followed through a series of ever more masterful pieces for tape, *Electronic Study I, II,* and *III* (1960, 1962, and 1964). In these pieces, Davidovsky finds ways of making every aspect of each sound count. When first confronted with electronic sounds, Davidovsky heard, not something exciting and new, but something very crude, especially when compared to the highly refined, two hundred plus year old tradition of western instruments that was already in his ear. To begin to approach the sensitivity of traditional instruments, Davidovsky spent count-less hours listening to each sound. He painstakingly constructed phrases made up mostly of short articulated events, accepting nothing that did not have a convincing dramatic shape. If this was all he had done, however, the music would have been no more than a kind of synthesized traditional music—a pale imitation, for example, of music for solo violin. Instead, he invented ways to use aspects of each sound that, in older music, had been less prominent in shaping musical ideas. The envelope (attack, sustain, and decay) characteristics of each sound became especially useful. A phrase could now open up or find closure not just through a series of hier-archically related pitches, but also through a succession of different attacks, from very hard and abrupt to ones so gradual and soft that notes gently appear out of silence. Of course, traditional instruments also have a range of articulations, but these are usually only a detail of the musical surface, lending a general character to a passage of music.

In Davidovsky's electronic works, control of articulation becomes more significant. A succession of widely varying articulations can shape an event, a gesture, a motive that can be developed in the course of a piece. The control of articulation also allows the composer to choose what, if anything, feels like a downbeat and the sense of pacing of each episode. This is no small matter. When a live musician performs a piece of music in concert, there are many cues, visual as well as aural, that project the sense of phrasing and pacing to the audience. We take this for granted, and many tape pieces fail to take the need for these cues into account. As he worked in the studio, Davidovsky cannily realized not only that he was creating the actual performance, but also that he needed to find new ways of compensating for the loss of the live musician.

Still, composers primarily write music for concert performance, and tape pieces played back through loudspeakers, no matter how brilliantly made, make for a dull concert. It was nat-ural for composers to begin to think about combining electronic sounds with live instruments. It is for his work in this area that Davidovsky is certainly best known. His series of *Synchronisms* pieces, beginning with *Synchronisms #1* for flute and electronic sounds in 1962, had an imme-diate impact. Here is music in which live and electronic forces reinvigorate one another in sur-prising ways. In these pieces he achieved the first true "hyper-instruments" where the live and electronic modulate one another and become something totally new, joined in one expanded acoustical space; a kind of musical virtual reality.

The key to the *Synchronisms* pieces, from *#1* (1962) through *#10* (1992), is that each takes into account the most basic acoustical properties of the live instrument employed. While today computer tools make it possible to do sophisticated acoustical analysis of instruments, Davidovsky's approach has always been to use the most sensitive tool of all, his musician's ear. Every detail of a sound becomes an important part of the basic material for a piece. As in the tape pieces, envelopes, overall tone color, even individual overtones are each considered and used. Here, we also have the reality of the live instrument's limitations to contend with. It is Davi-dovsky's ability to exploit our expectations about the instrument in front of us—to manipulate the instrument's normal limitations with wit and sophistication, that make[s] these pieces so compelling. To this day he remains the acknowledged master of the medium of electronically manipulated instruments and these pieces [are] the touchstones for anyone trying to work in this area.

In *Synchronisms #6,* for piano and electronic sounds (awarded the Pulitzer Prize for Music in 1971), the natural envelope of the piano, which has a limited range of attack possibilities—mostly fast and fairly hard, is the point of departure. The piece opens with a single G from the piano, which, as it naturally dies away, is surreptitiously picked up by the tape, which then crescendos and leads to the next attack point in the piano part. The net effect sounds like a piano making a crescendo—a decidedly "unnatural act." This is surprising, delightful, and potentially a gimmick. In Davidovsky's hands however, something more profound takes place. In addition to the attractive, but mostly superficial sleight of hand, the composer has focused our attention on something musically generative—a motive from which every aspect can and will be exploited. The listener is given an important pitch, the G (which remains static, controlling the harmonic pacing), two different registers (that of the high G and the midrange E that follows), and a sparse texture in which piano and electronic sounds seamlessly mix to make a single gesture. The motive is also defined by envelope type—the long crescendo followed by the staccato attack. The simplicity of texture allows us to focus on these sonic details—hard, bright, short attacks and longer, mellower sustained and crescendoing sounds. So strong is this opening motif, that when it returns much later, at pitch, it creates one of the most significant structural landmarks in the piece. From the first, we know that this is music of great economy; nothing is wasted, every detail is rich with possibility.

. . .

Many composers would have done everything possible to capitalize on the success of the first *Synchronisms* pieces. Davidovsky could have easily written nothing but electronic music for the remainder of his career. He eschewed this approach, finding it limiting and rejecting the idea that a composer needs to specialize in either electronic music or music for instruments. His achievements as composer, teacher, and mentor have proven the wisdom of this view. Following *Synchronisms #8* in 1974, he focused on a series of purely instrumental pieces which exploit many of the lessons learned in the studio. The sound-world and sense of continuity Davidovsky invented in the studio is translated to various chamber ensembles in a long list of compositions that includes *Inflexions* (1965) (perhaps the most electronic sounding chamber piece ever written), *Pennplay* (1979), five string quartets, a flute quartet, *Quartetto* (1987), and many others.

Commenting on an early example of Davidovsky's electronic music in the 1960s, Karlheinz Stockhausen declared, "I feel that after hearing this piece I am no longer the same person as before." Dozens of students (including this author) have felt much the same and have flocked to study with Davidovsky, first at the City University of New York and Columbia University, now at Harvard University [since 1993]. A whole generation of composers is now working at studios throughout the United States, extending Davidovsky's tradition and the standard he has set by steadfastly pursuing musical clarity, inventiveness, and wit in the face of ever-greater pressure to conform to the latest stylistic trend. His primary lesson for us is to take the work and not ourselves seriously.

SOURCE: Eric Chasalow, "Mario Davidovsky: An Introduction," *AGNI Magazine* 50 (1999). Available at https://www.bu.edu/agni/miscellany/print/1999/50-chasalow.html.

~~~~~~~~~

NOTES

1.   Siemens is a German electrical engineering corporation.
2.   Bulent Arel (1919–1990) was a Turkish composer who worked at the Columbia-Princeton Electronic Music Studio from 1959 on.

130

ELLIOTT CARTER ON THE
"DIFFERENT TIME WORLDS" IN
STRING QUARTETS NOS. 1 AND 2

The individual voice of Elliott Carter (b. 1908) emerged in the 1950s, as he enriched neoclassicism with the experimental modernism of the 1920s. In 1951, his String Quartet no. 1, as described by the Carter specialist David Schiff, was a "break-through" work; his String Quartet no. 2 (1959) approached the four instruments as different personalities, evoking Charles Ives's Second String Quartet (see chapter 63), but representing Carter's own interest in metric experimentation as well. Both quartets contain many of Carter's stylistic traits from this formative period, especially fragmentation and complex dissonant counterpoint. In 1960, Carter was awarded the Pulitzer Prize for his contributions to string quartet literature.

In this chapter, Carter looks back on these compositions in liner notes for a CD produced in 1970. There is little doubt about the importance of the shifts chronicled here. Carter has continued composing into his 90s, resisting an easy cataloging of his style.

Hearing these two quartets now, I get the impression of their living in different time worlds, the first an expanded one, the second in a condensed and concentrated one—although this was hardly a conscious opposition at the times of their composition. Each presents a different version of humanly experienced time as the two imagined by Thomas Mann in "By the Ocean of Time," a chapter in *The Magic Mountain,* where he writes: "It would not be hard to imagine the existence of creatures, perhaps upon smaller planets than ours, practicing a miniature time-economy. . . . And, contrariwise, one can conceive of a world so spacious that its time system too has a majestic stride."

Although both quartets are concerned with motion, change, progression in which literal or mechanical repetition finds little place, yet the development of musical expression and thought during the eight years that separate them seems to me far-reaching. The difference, aside from that of their time-scales, might be compared to the types of continuities found in Mann's own writings, where in the earlier ones, characters maintain their characterized identities with some revelatory changes throughout a work, while in the Joseph novels, each character is an exemplification of an archetype whose various other incarnations are constantly referred to (as Joyce does in another way in *Finnegans Wake*). Recurrence of idea in the *First Quartet* is, then, more nearly literal than in the *Second,* where recall brings back only certain traits of expression—"behavior patterns," speeds, and interval-sounds—that form the basis of an ever-changing series of incarnations but link these together as a group. The musical language of the *Second Quartet* emerged almost unconsciously through working during the '50s with ideas the *First* gave rise to.

The *First Quartet* was "written largely for my own satisfaction and grew out of an effort to understand myself," as the late Joseph Wood Krutch (a neighbor during the 1950–51 year of this quartet) wrote of his book *The Modern Temper.* For there were so many emotional and expressive experiences that I kept having, and so many notions of processes and continuities, especially musical ones—fragments I could find no ways to use in my compositions—that I decided to leave my usual New York activities to seek the undisturbed quiet to work these out. The decision to stay in a place in the Lower Sonoran Desert near Tucson, Arizona, brought me by chance into contact with that superb naturalist Joe Krutch, who was then writing *The Desert Year.* Our almost daily meetings led to fascinating talks about the ecology of the region—how birds, animals, insects, and plants had adapted to the heat and the limited water supply, which consists of infrequent, spectacular but brief cloudbursts that for an hour seem about to wash everything away, and then very long droughts. There were trips to remote places such as Carr Canyon, the wild-bird paradise, but mainly it was right around the house that exotica (for an Easterner) could be seen—comic road runners, giant suguaros, flowering ocatillos, all sharing this special, dry world. It was indeed a kind of "magic mountain," and its specialness (for me) certainly encouraged the specialness (for me at that time) of the quartet as I worked on it during the fall and winter of '50 and the spring of '51.

Among the lessons this piece taught me was one about my relationship with performers and audiences. For as I wrote, an increasing number of musical difficulties arose for prospective performers and listeners, which the musical conception seemed to demand. I often wondered whether the quartet would ever have any performers or listeners. Yet within a few years of its composition it won an important prize and was played (always with a great deal of rehearsal) more than any work I had written up to that time. It even received praise from admired colleagues. Up to this time, I had quite consciously been trying to write for a certain audience—not that which frequented concerts of traditional music, nor that which had supported the avant-garde of the '20s (which in the '40s had come to seem elitist) but a new, more progressive and more popular audience. I had felt that it was my professional and social responsibility to write interesting, direct, easily understood music.

With this quartet, however, I decided to focus on what had always been one of my own musical interests, that of "advanced" music, and to follow out, with a minimal concern for their reception, my own musical thoughts along these lines. Now, in 1970, I think there is every reason to assume that if a composer has been well taught and has had experience (as was true of me in 1950), then his private judgment of comprehensibility and quality is what he must rely on if he is to communicate importantly.

Like the desert horizons I saw daily while it was being written, the *First Quartet* presents a continuous unfolding and changing of expressive characters—one woven into the other or emerging from it—on a large scale. The general plan was suggested by Jean Cocteau's film *Le Sang d'un poète,* in which the entire dream-like action is framed by an interrupted slow-motion shot of a tall brick chimney in an empty lot being dynamited. Just as the chimney begins to fall apart, the shot is broken off and the entire movie follows, after which the shot of the chimney is resumed at the point it left off, showing its disintegration in mid-air, and closing the film with its collapse on the ground. A similar interrupted continuity is employed in this quartet's starting with a cadenza for cello alone that is continued by the first violin alone at the very end. On one level, I interpret Cocteau's idea (and my own) as establishing the difference between external time (measured by the falling chimney, or the cadenza) and internal dream time (the main body of the work)—the dream time lasting but a moment of external time but from the dreamer's point of view, a long stretch. In the *First Quartet,* the opening cadenza also acts as an introduction to the rest, and when it reappears at the end, it forms the last variation in a set of variations. Not only is this plan like that of many "circular" works of modern literature, but the interlocked presentation of ideas parallels many characteristic devices found in Joyce and others—the controlled "stream of consciousness," the "epiphany," the many uses of punctuation, of grammatical ambiguities, including the use of quotation. This quartet, for instance, quotes the opening theme of Ives's *First Violin Sonata,* first played by the cello in its lowest register after each of the other instruments has come in near the beginning. A rhythmic idea from Conlon Nancarrow's *First Rhythmic Study* is quoted at the beginning of the *Variations.* These two composers, through both their music and their conversation, had been a great help to me in imagining this work and were quoted in homage.

Since both these quartets are made up of many-layered contrasts of character—hence of theme or motive, rhythm, and styles of playing—they are hard to describe without adding to their apparent complication. Briefly, the *First* is in four large sections: *Fantasia, Allegro scorrevole, Adagio,* and *Variations.* This scheme is broken by two pauses, one in the middle of the *Allegro scorrevole* and the other just after the *Variations* have been started by the cello, while the other instruments were concluding the *Adagio.* The first section, *Fantasia,* contrasts many themes of different character frequently counterpointed against each other. It concludes with the four main ideas being heard together, fading in and out of prominence. This leads directly to a rapid *Allegro scorrevole,* a sound-mosaic of brief fragments, interrupted once by a dramatic outburst, then resumed, again interrupted by a pause, again resumed, and finally interrupted by another outburst that forms the beginning of the *Adagio.*

During this extended slow movement, the two muted violins play soft, contemplative music answered by an impassioned, rough recitative of the viola and cello. This *Adagio* forms the extreme point of divergence between simultaneous ideas in the quartet and has been led up to and is led away from by many lesser degrees of differentiation. The last section, *Variations*, consists of a series of different themes repeated faster at each successive recurrence, some reaching their speed vanishing point sooner than others. One that persists almost throughout is the slow motive heard in separated notes played by the cello just before and after the pause that precedes the *Variations*. This motive passes through many stages of acceleration until it reaches a rapid tremolo near the end.

Written in 1959, the *Second Quartet* represents quite a contrast to the *First*. In it, as mentioned previously, there is little dependence on thematic recurrence, which is replaced by an ever-changing series of motives and figures having certain internal relationships with each other. To a certain extent, the instruments are typecast, for each fairly consistently invents its material out of its own special expressive attitude and its own repertory of musical speeds and intervals. In a certain sense each instrument is like a character in an opera made up primarily of "quartets." The separation of the instrumental characters is kept quite distinct throughout the first half of the work but becomes increasingly homogenized up to the *Conclusion*, at which point the separation reemerges. The musical contrasts of behavior and material associated with each instrument can be brought to the listener's attention by a special stereophonic placement which helps to sort them out—as accomplished in this recording—although this is not absolutely necessary, since the total effect at any given moment is the primary consideration, the contribution of each instrument secondary.

The form of the quartet itself helps to make the elements of this four-way conversation clear. The individuals of this group are related to each other in what might be metaphorically termed three forms of responsiveness: discipleship, companionship, and confrontation. The *Introduction* and *Conclusion* present in aphoristic form and in "companionate" manner the repertory of each instrument. The *Allegro fantastico* is led by the first violin, whose whimsical, ornate part is "imitated" by the other three, each according to his own individuality; the same occurs in the *Presto scherzando* led by the second violin and the *Andante espressivo* led by the viola. The final *Allegro*, although partially led by the cello—which eventually draws the others into one of its characteristic accelerations—tends to stress the "companionship" rather than the "discipleship" pattern.

In between these movements are cadenzas of instrumental "confrontation" or opposition: after the *Allegro fantastico*, the viola plays its expressive, almost lamenting cadenza to be confronted with explosions of what may be anger or ridicule by the other three; after the *Presto scherzando*, the cello, playing in its romantically free way, is confronted by the others' insistence on strict time; finally, after the *Andante espressivo*, the first violin carries on like a virtuoso, to be confronted by the silence of the others, who, before this cadenza is over, commence the final *Allegro*. Throughout the entire quartet, the second violin acts as a moderating influence, using its *pizzicato* and *arco* notes to mark regular time, its half, or double always at the same speed.

On this record, Anahid Ajemian plays the second violin part with fascinating wit and humor where needed and with refined expressivity or robust vigor elsewhere. Indeed, all the members of the Composers Quartet—Matthew Raimondi, Jean Dupouy, and Michael Rudiakov as well as Miss Ajemian, accomplishing the difficult and unprecedented feat of maintaining both quartets in their repertory simultaneously—play their parts as if they meant what they were doing, as if it were very important, in order to reveal what both pieces are about, to play them accurately and musically. What more could a composer want of performers?

SOURCE: Elliott Carter, liner notes for *String Quartets No. 1* (1951) and *No. 2* (1959) (Nonesuch Records, 1970; Nonesuch CD H-71249).

JOHN CAGE

Words and *Music of Changes*

(Cage, Anderson)

The revolutionary composer John Cage (1912–1992) lived long enough to see the scorn he endured for many decades transform into admiration. Cage's aesthetic practice drew on a miscellany of sources: Arnold Schoenberg's 12-tone composition, Henry Cowell's string piano, Ananda Coomaraswamy's metaphysical teachings, Ralph Waldo Emerson and Henry David Thoreau's transcendentalism, Marcel Duchamp's aesthetics of indifference—the list could go on—and finally, the *I Ching*, a book of Chinese divination, which yielded "indeterminacy" as a musical process. Cage's constantly evolving body of thought worked in tandem with his remarkable musical compositions, which balance risk with control.

Cage left an important literary legacy as well, particularly through the collection of writings *Silence* (1961), which includes a transcript of a lecture titled "Composition as Process" (1958). This excerpt from the lecture concerns two of Cage's most important works: the *Sonatas and Interludes for Prepared Piano*, his masterpiece of 1946–1948, and *Music of Changes* (1951), another landmark.

In 1958, Cage presented the lecture at Darmstadt, Germany, site of the famous summer program for contemporary music. The lecture was a stop-and-go duet between Cage and the pianist David Tudor, performing *Music of Changes*. Cage spoke a paragraph or two; Tudor then played a section of the music lasting exactly the same number of seconds as the talk. Cage's appearance at Darmstadt was not a success, and decades passed until the music (in the 1980s) and the man (1990) would return.

In the second selection, which is from an interview conducted by the performance artist Laurie Anderson just a few months before his death, Cage talks about how he practiced chance as a way of life.

COMPOSITION AS PROCESS

I. CHANGES

Having been asked by Dr. Wolfgang Steinecke, Director of Internationale Ferienkurse für Neue Musik [International Summer Course for New Music] at Darmstadt, to discuss in particular my Music of Changes, *I decided to make a lecture within the time length of the* Music of Changes *(each line of the text whether speech or silence requiring one second for its performance), so that whenever I would stop speaking, the corresponding part of the* Music of Changes *itself would be played. The music is not superimposed on the speech but is heard only in the interruptions of the speech—which, like the lengths of the paragraphs themselves, were the result of chance operations.*

This is a lecture on changes that have taken place in my composition means, with particular reference to what, a decade ago, I termed "structure" and "method." By "structure" was meant the division of a whole into parts; by "method" the note-to-note procedure. Both structure and method (and also "material"— the sounds and silences of a composition)

were, it seemed to me then, the proper concern of the mind (as opposed to the heart) (one's ideas of order as opposed to one's spontaneous actions); whereas the two last of these, namely method and material, together with form (the morphology of a continuity) were equally the proper concern of the heart. Composition, then, I viewed, ten years ago, as an activity integrating the opposites, the rational and the irrational, bringing about, i-

deally, a freely moving continuity within a strict division of parts, the sounds, their combination and succession being either logically related or arbitrarily chosen. ¶The strict division of parts, the structure, was a function of the duration aspect of sound, since, of all the aspects of sound including frequency, amplitude, and timbre, duration, alone, was also a characteristic of silence. The structure, then, was a division of actual time by conventional metrical means, meter taken as simply the measurement of quantity. ¶In the case of the *Sonatas and Interludes* (which I finished in nineteen forty-eight), only structure was organized, quite roughly for the work as a whole, exactly, however, within each single piece. The method was that of considered improvisation (mainly at the piano, though ideas came to me at some moments away from the instrument).

The materials, the piano preparations, were chosen as one chooses shells while walking along a beach. The form was as natural as my taste permitted: so that where, as in all of the *Sonatas* and two of the *Interludes*, parts were to be repeated, the formal concern was to make the progress from the end of a section to its beginning seem inevitable. ¶The structure of one of the *Sonatas*, the fourth, was one hundred measures of two-two time, divided into ten units of ten measures each. These units were combined in the proportion three, three, two, two, to give the piece large parts, and they were subdivided in the same proportion to give small parts to each unit. In contrast to a structure based on the frequency aspect of sound, tonality, that is, this rhythmic structure was as hospitable to non-musical sounds, noises, as it was to those of the conventional scales and instruments. For nothing about the structure was determined by the materials which were to occur in it; it was conceived, in fact, so that it could be as well expressed by the

absence of these
materials
as by their pres-
ence. ¶In terms
of the oppo-
sition of free-
dom and law, a
piece written ten
years before the
*Sonatas and
Interludes, Con-
struction in Met-
al,* presents the
same relation-
ship, but reversed:
structure, method,
and materi-
als were all of
them subjected
to organi-
zation. The mor-
phology of
the continu-
ity, form, a-
lone was free. Draw-
ing a straight line
between this sit-
uation and
that presented

by the later
work, the deduc-
tion might be made
that there is a
tendency in
my composi-
tion means away
from ideas
of order towards
no ideas
of order. And
though when exam-
ined histo-
ry would probab-
ly not read as
a straight line, re-
cent works, begin-
ning with the *Mu-
sic of Changes,*
support the ac-
curacy of

this deduction.
¶For, in the *Mu-
sic of Changes,*
the note-to-note
procedure, the
method, is the
function of chance
operations.
And the structure,
though planned precise-
ly as those of
the *Sonatas
and Interludes,*
and more thorough-
ly since it en-
compassed the whole
span of the com-
position, was
only a se-
ries of numbers,
three, five, six, and
three quarters, six,
and three quarters,
five, three and one
eighth, which became,
on the one hand,
the number of
units within
each section, and,
on the other,
number of meas-
ures of four-four
within each u-
nit. At each small
structural di-
vision in the

*Music of Chan-
ges,* at the be-
ginning, for ex-
ample, and a-

gain at the fourth
and ninth measures
and so on, chance
operations
determined sta-
bility or
change of tempo.
Thus, by intro-
ducing the ac-
tion of method
into the bod-
y of the struc-
ture, and these two
opposed in terms
of order and
freedom, that struc-
ture became in-
determinate:
it was not pos-
sible to know the
total time-length
of the piece un-
til the final
chance opera-
tion, the last toss
of coins af-
fecting the rate
of tempo, had
been made. Being

indetermi-
nate, though still pres-
ent, it became
apparent that
structure was not
necessary,
even though it had
certain uses.
¶One of these u-
ses was the de-
termination
of density,
the determi-
nation, that is,
of how many
of the poten-
tially present
eight lines, each com-
posed of sounds and
silences, were
actually
to be present
within a giv-
en small structur-
al part. ¶Anoth-
er use of the
structure affect-
ed the charts of
sounds and silen-
ces, amplitudes,
durations, po-
tentially ac-
tive in the con-
tinuity.
These twenty-four
charts, eight for sounds

and silences,
eight for ampli-
tudes, eight for du-
rations, were, through-
out the course of
a single struc-
tural unit, half
of them mobile
and half of them
immobile. Mo-
bile meant that once
any of these
elements in
a chart was used,

two, four, six and
eight, were mobile
and which of the
charts were immo-
bile—not changing.

it disappeared
to be replaced
by a new one.
Immobile meant
that though an el-
ement in a
chart had been used,
it remained to
be used again.
At each unit
structural point,
a chance oper-
ation deter-
mined which of the
charts, number one,
three, five, and sev-
en or numbers

SOURCE: John Cage, "Composition as Process," in his *Silence: Lectures and Writings by John Cage* (Middletown, Conn.: Wesleyan University Press, 1961): 18–21.

~~~~~~~~

Laurie Anderson interviewed John Cage for a Buddhist magazine in March 1992, just a few months before he died in August of that year.

ANDERSON: In using chance operations, did you ever feel that something didn't work as well as you wanted?

CAGE: No. In such circumstances I thought the thing that needs changing is me— you know—the thinking through. If it was something I didn't like, it was clearly a situation in which I could change toward the liking rather than getting rid of it.

ANDERSON: Would you think of it as a kind of design whose rules you just couldn't understand?

CAGE: I was already thinking of one rather than two, so that I wasn't involved in that relationship. And that what was actually annoying me was the cropping up of an old relationship, which seemed at first to be out of place. But then, once it was accepted, it was extraordinarily productive of space. A kind of emptiness that invites, not what you are doing, but all that you're not doing into your awareness and your enjoyment.

ANDERSON: So you did, in fact, make a kind of judgment on yourself.

CAGE: Yes, instead of wiping out what I didn't like, I tried to change myself so that I could use it. I keep manuscripts that are clearly no good because they must have some reason for existing too.

ANDERSON: In what sense do you mean no good?

CAGE: Not interesting. Where the ideas aren't radical, where they don't have likeliness or—what Bob Rauschenberg says—"they don't change you." And I think that the idea of change, or the ego itself changing direction, is implicit in Suzuki's understanding of the effect of Buddhism on the structure of the mind. I use chance operations instead of operating according to my likes and dislikes. I use my work to change myself and I accept what the chance operations say. The *I Ching* says that if you don't accept the chance operations you have no right to use them. Which is very clear, so that's what I do.

SOURCE: Laurie Anderson and John Cage, "Taking Chances," *Tricycle: The Buddhist Review* 1, no. 4 (Summer 1992): 52–57; excerpts on 56–57. Available at http://www.tricycle .com/cage2.html.

HAROLD SCHONBERG ON "ART AND BUNK, MATTER AND ANTI-MATTER"

Composer-experimenters made easy targets for the combative *New York Times* music critic Harold Schonberg (1915–2003). He spent years lambasting the new styles, new composers, and new aesthetics that emerged in the 1950s and '60s, including Cage and the New York school and the bicoastal "minimalists," who had yet to be labeled such when this review was written. Here, Schonberg reviews the first issue of a new journal, *Source: Music of the Avant-Garde*, edited by the California-based composer Larry Austin (b. 1930). A pioneering publication, *Source*, which lasted from 1967 to 1974, printed scores and articles from an emerging generation of composers, among them Alvin Lucier, Steve Reich, Anthony Braxton, Cornelius Cardew, and Pauline Oliveros. Schonberg linked the "unethical" aesthetic of the avant-garde to pop art and its guru, Andy Warhol, whom he dismissed. Following the review is the table of contents for volume 1 of *Source*, which gave crucial support to an important school of composers at just the right time. (Two articles from *Source* are reprinted in chapters 133 and 134.)

ART AND BUNK, MATTER AND ANTI-MATTER

Art, they used to say, mirrors life, and I kept repeating that to myself at the U.S. Pavilion in Expo 67 while looking at the enormous paintings hanging in that equally enormous structure. But are they paintings, or sociology, or social commentary, those works by Jim Dine, Andy Warhol and the others? Certainly the brush work is not very accomplished (brush work? or electric paint sprayers?), the compositions not very interesting, the draftsmanship distinctly minor-league. But all that really is beside the point. It is the message that counts, and the message comes through loud and clear: Art (as the old Dadaists so loudly proclaimed) is bunk, values are bunk, beauty is bunk. Pop art, like so many artistic manifestations today, is a cosmic thumb of the nose to the old values—values that apparently did not work, that have been discarded with none to take their place.

And so to New York, to find on my desk the new issue of "Source," the publication (twice yearly) dedicated to the music of the avant-garde. This is a publication quite different from "Perspectives of New Music," which is the Establishment organ of the post-serial group, with Elliott Carter the Father, Milton Babbitt the Son and Igor Stravinsky the Holy Ghost. To the staff of "Source"—the editor is Larry Austin, a composer who is one of the more convulsive experimenters of the avant-garde—the great hero, Father, Son and Holy Ghost combined, is John Cage.

Austin speaks for a very strong segment of the international avant-garde, and it is a segment that is beginning to take control of the younger generation, The older [Pierre] Boulez-Babbitt axis, around which revolved so much activity after World War II, has been declining as the younger composers become increasingly impatient with the serial movement. Where the great Boulez-Babbitt progenitor was Anton Webern, the new line goes back to Cage, Earle Brown and Morton Feldman, who were the pioneers in a kind of music that later was enthusiastically adopted and refined by such composers as Karlheinz Stockhausen.

. . .

"Source" is primarily an organ that prints music of the avant-garde. Those who visualize printed music as a collection of five-line staffs, G clefs and bass clefs, quarter notes and flags, are in for a shock as they leaf through the pages of "Source." The magazine also publishes essays and discussions, one of which (a discussion) opens the current issue. Austin and a group of composers go into the role of the composer today, and there seems great doubt about the role of that once preeminent musical figure. Pauline Oliveros and Toshi Ichiyanagi will have nothing to do with it. "I think we ought to obscure the composer," says Oliveros. "It doesn't matter whether my name appears or not," says Ichiyanagi. Both of those—er, composers, even if they do not like the word—represent a position in which the performer is at the very least equally as important as the composer.

It is not the printed note or the score that is important. The score, says Austin, is merely a "subjective motivation to play." It is only a symbol of the act of making music, often not referred to at all. Instead of the score we now have what should be called "process-perception." It is the performer who realizes the message of the creator, not as the baroque composers used to "realize" a figured bass, but with a freedom, a generosity, a lack of inhibition that puts him on an equal pedestal. "I want to reintegrate the figure of the interpreter," says Mario Bertoncini. "I only want to make him *free*." As Austin puts it: "Composer-to-performer: one-to-one."

By performer is not meant only an instrumentalist or singer, but also a technician, as electronic music comes to play an increasingly greater part in the avant-garde. The great majority of the young avant-garde is entirely willing to cede incredible liberties to the interpreter/ technician. He can start in the middle of a composition or at the end. He can make the score-symbol a five-minute work or run it to three hours. He may, within the parameters of the piece, play as soft or loud as he wishes, use his fists or fingers.

. . .

A typical instruction comes in Stanley Lunetta's "Piano Music," published in this issue of "Source." "Put both hands on the lowest keys of the piano, make tight fists. Viciously move hands as if you were playing a fast roll on a conga drum. Then you should move your fingers in the normal manner on the piano's lower (but not lowest) keys. Gradually restrict the number of keys from ten to four. Now you are trying to play, as rapidly as possible, the same four notes with all ten fingers." Later on, Lunetta gives detailed instructions about aping an old-fashioned virtuoso pianist.

It's all very funny, the way pop art is funny. Of course, it leaves conventional ideas about music far behind, and there is one amusing irony in the section of "Source" where Austin speaks with the composers. Morton Feldman is one. Feldman was experimenting with graphed music and with dynamics pushed to the point of inaudibility when most of the young composers today were in diapers. Now Feldman is considered by them an old master, a relic of the pioneer days, and he himself has something to say about it. The poor guy, after all, actually deals with notes, of a kind. He waggles his finger at the younger generation and talks plaintively:

> In the early fifties, when Cage, Brown,[1] and I were discovering so many exciting things, it was very difficult to set aside my composer's ego. It was painful. I had to step aside to see how beautiful the music was. Some of the kids writing music today only see the gesture. They don't hear the music. For me, the medium is the hero, not the composer. The kids make an anti-hero stance, wear a cape, and say "I'm not a composer," the dramatic gesture. To them, John Cage, the person, has become a hero, not his music. When John and I were working together, there wasn't that feeling. We suppressed our egos in favor of the music!

. . .

But in the early fifties life was less complicated. If it is any comfort to Feldman, he and his group were among the apostles in what has developed into a new religion. They were among the first, along with some of the abstract expressionists, neo-symbolist poets, existentialists, and—yes—nuclear physicists to question eternal verities. From them and allied thinkers came the subsequent developments—pop art, the theater of the absurd, the concept of the non-hero, the psychedelics, the neo-Dadaists. Perhaps, indirectly, even television, the greatest of pop-art forms and the very exponent of Camp itself, even though television does not know it.

Basically the entire avant-garde manifestation is revolt, unease, a profound dissatisfaction with current social, religious and cultural standards. At [its] basis is the feeling that nothing means anything, certainly not when the Bomb has taken the place of God in so many minds as the ultimate disposer of the earth. The avant-garde in the arts, deriding the romantic concept of "beauty," has deliberately substituted an anti-ethical concept that is intended to demolish the grand ethos upon which all art of the past was based.

What they do, whether or not you like it, remains art, in that it uses materials for expressive effect, even if the expression is intended to be anti-expressive. (But have we not been told by the scientists that anti-matter is indistinguishable from matter?) It is not art in the Robert

Browning sense, of infinite passion and the pain of finite hearts that yearn. It is art in the [Arthur] Rimbaud sense, in the style of a bad dream. And, in a funny, delirious, black-is-white upheaval, it turns out that the avant-gardists in their way are as romantic, as much poseurs (in the romantic sense of the word), unconsciously as sentimental, as the Byron[s], Schumann[s] and Delacroixes of the early 19th century. Only, unfortunately, none of them seems to have their genius.

SOURCE: Harold Schonberg, "Art and Bunk, Matter and Anti-Matter," *New York Times*, September 24, 1967.

<hr />

TABLE OF CONTENTS FOR *SOURCE*, VOL. 1, NO. 1 (1967)

1. Preface

2. Larry Austin, The Maze [electronic piece]

3. Giuseppe Chiari, Quel che Volete [composition]

4. Robert Ashley, In Memoriam [composition]

5. Earle Brown, Form in New Music [essay]

6. Barney Childs, Jack's New Bag [composition]

7. Bertram Turetzky, Notes on the Bass [article]

8. David Reck, Blues and Screamer [composition]

9. David Freund, Harry Partch [photo essay]

10. Harry Partch, Lecture

11. Robert Ashley, Larry Austin, Karlheinz Stockhausen, Conversation

<hr />

NOTE

1. Earle Brown (1926–2002), composer.

133

Pauline Oliveros, Composer and Teacher

Pauline Oliveros (b. 1932) is a classic American maverick. Shaped by the various cultural and artistic revolutions of the late '60s and early '70s, Oliveros creates work with an outsider's art sensibility that belies her own impeccable professional credentials as a major force in the avant-garde. Born in Houston, Oliveros acquired a lifelong devotion to the accordion, that Texas conjunto instrument, and continues to explore its possibilities. Associated with the San Francisco Tape Music Center from its initial founding in 1961, Oliveros directed the center when it moved to Mills College in 1966. By that time, Oliveros had composed *Bye Bye Butterfly*, one of her major early electronic works. Reprinted here is Oliveros's succinct description from the program of the piece, which is an important feminist statement made at an early moment in the women's movement. Oliveros has taken public stands against gender discrimination in music and in society at large throughout her career. She has courageously championed gay rights, publicly identifying herself as a lesbian in the early 1970s.

The 1960s also guided Oliveros to what the composer Heidi Von Gunden—an astute critic of Oliveros's work—calls "consciousness studies." These in turn led to *Sonic Meditations*, which Oliveros composed in the early 1970s. Oliveros published the scores for these meditations, some of which are reprinted here, in *Source*, preceding them with some remarks designed to initiate participants into the discipline required to realize them. After a long stint on the faculty of the University of California at San Diego from 1967 to 1981, Oliveros resigned her position to devote herself to the next phase of practice associated with *Sonic Meditations,* which she calls "deep listening."

OLIVEROS DESCRIBES *BYE BYE BUTTERFLY*

It] bids farewell not only to the music of the 19th century but also to the system of polite morality of that age and its attendant institutionalized oppression of the female sex. The title refers to the operatic disc, *Madame Butterfly* by Giacomo Puccini, which was at hand in the studio at the time and which was spontaneously incorporated into the ongoing compositional mix.

> SOURCE: Notes to Bye Bye Butterfly by Pauline Oliveros, in *The Transparent Tape Music Festival Program* (concert given January 11, 2002). Available at http://sfsound.org/tape/oliveros.html.

SONIC MEDITATIONS

DEDICATION TO THE ♀ ENSEMBLE AND AMELIA EARHART
PAULINE OLIVEROS, MARCH–NOVEMBER 1971

Sonic Meditations are intended for group work over a long period of time with regular meetings. No special skills are necessary. Any persons who are willing to commit themselves can participate. The ♀ ensemble to whom these meditations are dedicated has found that non-verbal meetings intensify the results of these meditations and help provide an atmosphere which is conducive to such activity. With continuous work some of the following becomes possible with sonic meditations: heightened states of awareness or expanded consciousness, changes in physiology and psychology from known and unknown tensions to relaxations which gradually become permanent. These changes represent the tuning of mind and body. The group develops positive energy which can influence others who are less experienced. Members of the group achieve greater awareness and sensitivity to each other. Music is a welcome by-product of this activity.

I. TEACH YOURSELF TO FLY

Any number of persons sit in a circle facing the center. Illuminate the space with dim blue light. Begin by simply observing your own breathing. Always be an observer. Gradually observe your breathing become audible. Then gradually introduce your voice. Color your breathing very softly at first with sound. Let the intensity increase very slowly as you observe it. Continue as long as possible and until all others are quiet.

Variation: Translate voice to an instrument.

. . .

V. NATIVE

Take a walk at night. Walk so silently that the bottoms of your feet become ears.

. . .

VIII. ENVIRONMENTAL DIALOGUE

Each person finds a place to be, either near to or distant from the others, either indoors or out-of-doors. Begin the meditation by observing your own breathing. As you become aware of sounds from the environment, gradually begin to reinforce the pitch of the sound source. Reinforce either vocally, mentally, or with an instrument. If you lose touch with the source, wait quietly for another. Reinforce means to strengthen or sustain.

. . .

[ENVIRONMENTAL DIALOGUE NO. 3]: THE FLAMING INDIAN
FOR GERALD SHAPIRO AND MARGOT BLUM

Tape record a selected environment alone or with a group. Place the microphone carefully in one location. Do the environmental dialogue mentally while you are recording. Reinforce everything you hear mentally. When the meditation is complete, make a translation of the environmental dialogue in the following way:

Reinforce the pitches of the recorded sounds with vocal, instrumental, electronic or a combination of these sources. The resulting translation may exist in one or more channels as the translated sounds only or a combination of the translation and original dialogue. A new dialogue is then performed in the same or different environment with the recorded translation and a soloist or a group, either vocal, instrumental, or electronic or any combination. The live dialogue should include the sounds of the live environment as well as the recorded translation.

SOURCE: Pauline Oliveros, "Sonic Meditations," *Source: Music of the Avant-Garde* 5, no. 2 (1971): 103–8; excerpts on 104, 108–9.

134

$\mathcal{S}$TEVE REICH ON

"MUSIC AS A GRADUAL PROCESS"

Steve Reich (b. 1936) wrote this now-famous essay in October 1968, and it was published as his biographical statement for an exhibition at the Whitney Museum of American Art in 1969 titled "Anti-Illusion: Procedures/Materials." (The exhibition included works by minimalist artists, among them Lynda Benglis, Eva Hesse, Robert Ryman, and Richard Serra.) Here, Reich rejects serial music and indeterminacy (as practiced by Babbitt and Cage) as processes which cannot be heard and therefore exist only as *theoretical* rather than *experiential* musical constructs. Reich helped to launch a new musical movement which critics eventually called "minimalism," because of its shared aesthetic affinities with artists like those in the Whitney show. Despite resistance to the term "minimalism" from Reich and some of his contemporaries, among them Philip Glass and Terry Riley, the branding has stuck. Other names for this new music at the time included "trance music" and "pulse music."

Reich reprinted "Music as a Gradual Process" in several places, including *Source* magazine in 1971 and then as liner notes for the album *Drumming*—his most important music from his first stylistic period. Each version of the essay differs slightly. For *Drumming*, he added some additional remarks about his ensemble, which are included here as well.

By 1976, Reich had moved beyond his self-imposed limitations of compositional transparency in a more complex work of extended length—*Music for 18 Instruments,* which is now regarded as a late twentieth-century masterpiece. Despite its relatively greater complexity, Reich's reliance on phase shifting, evolving canons, and pulse still relate to the aesthetic defined so austerely and so powerfully here.

I do not mean the process of composition, but rather pieces of music that are, literally, processes.

The distinctive thing about musical processes is that they determine the note-to-note (sound-to-sound) details and the overall formal morphology simultaneously. (Think of a round or an infinite canon in traditional music.)

I am interested in perceptible processes. I want to be able to hear the process happening throughout the sounding music.

To facilitate closely detailed listening, a musical process should happen very gradually. Performing and listening to a gradual musical process resembles:

turning over an hourglass and watching the sand slowly run through to the bottom; pulling back a swing, releasing it, and observing it gradually come to rest;

placing your feet in the sand by the ocean's edge and watching, feeling, and listening to the waves gradually bury them.

Though I may have the pleasure of discovering musical processes and composing the musical material to run through them, once the process is set up and loaded, it runs by itself.

Material may suggest what sort of process it should be run through (content suggests form), and processes may suggest what sort of material should be run through them (form suggests content). If the shoe fits, wear it.

Whether a musical process is realized through live human performance, or through some electro-mechanical means is not finally very important. One of the most beautiful concerts I ever heard consisted of four composers playing their tapes in a dark hall. (A tape is interesting when it's an interesting tape.)

It's quite natural to think about musical processes if one is frequently working with electro-mechanical sound equipment. (All music turns out to be ethnic music.)

Musical processes can give one a direct contact with the impersonal and also a kind of complete control, and one doesn't always think of the impersonal and complete control as going together. By "a kind" of complete control I mean: by running this material through this process I completely control all that results, but also I accept all that results without changes.

John Cage has used processes and has certainly accepted their results, but the processes he used were more compositional ones that could not be heard when the piece was performed. The process of using the *I Ching* or imperfections in a sheet of paper to determine musical parameters can't be heard when listening to music composed that way. The compositional processes and the sounding music have no audible connection. Similarly, in serial music, the series itself is seldom audible. (This is a basic difference between serial [basically European] music and serial [basically American] art, where, in the latter, the perceived series is usually the focal point of the work.)

What I'm interested in is a compositional process and a sounding music that are one and the same thing.

James Tenney said in conversation, "then the composer isn't privy to anything." I don't know any secrets of structure that you can't hear. We all listen to the process together, since it's quite audible, and one of the reasons it's quite audible, is because it's happening extremely gradually.

The use of hidden structural devices in music never appealed to me. Even when all the cards are on the table and everyone hears what is gradually happening in a musical process, there are still enough mysteries to satisfy all. These mysteries are the impersonal, unintended, psycho-acoustic by-products of the intended process. These might include sub-melodies heard within repeated melodic patterns, stereophonic effects due to loudspeaker or listener location, slight irregularities in performance etc.

I begin to perceive these minute details when I can sustain close attention, and a gradual process invites my sustained attention. By "gradual" I mean extremely gradual; a process happening so slowly and gradually that listening to it resembles watching the minute hand on a watch—you can perceive it moving after you stay with it a little while.

Many modal musics, such as Indian Classical, John Coltrane's during the early 1960s, some recent rock and roll and other new musics may make us aware of minute sound details; because in being modal (constant key center, hypnotically droning) they naturally focus on these details rather than on key modulation, counterpoint, and other peculiarly western devices. Nevertheless, these modal musics remain more or less strict frameworks for improvisation and/or for expression. They are not processes.

While performing and listening to gradual musical processes one can participate in a particularly liberating and impersonal kind of ritual. Focusing in on the musical process makes possible that shift of attention away from *he* and *she* and *you* and *me* outwards towards *it*.

SOURCE: Steve Reich, "Music as a Gradual Process," in *Anti-Illusion: Procedures/Materials*, ed. James Monte and Marcia Tucker (catalog for exhibition at the Whitney Museum of American Art, New York, May 19–July 6, 1969) (New York: Whitney Museum of American Art, 1969): 56–57. Reprinted in *Source: Music of the Avant-Garde* 2, no. 10 (1971): 30.

A slightly modified version of the above essay appears as liner notes in Steve Reich's Drumming, Music for Mallet Instruments, Voices and Organ, Six Pianos. *It includes the following new material.*

NOTES ON THE ENSEMBLE 12/73

Since 1966 I have been rehearsing and performing my music with my own ensemble. A few years earlier I decided that despite my limitations as a performer I had to play in all my compositions. It seemed clear that a healthy musical situation would only result when the functions of composer and performer were united. This ensemble began in 1966 with three musicians, grew in 1970 to five, and in 1971, with the composition of DRUMMING, grew to twelve musicians and singers. This is a repertory ensemble. Each new composition is added to the repertoire and our concerts present a selection of new and/or older works.

The question often arises as to what contribution the performers make to the music? The answer is that they select the resulting patterns in all compositions that have resulting patterns, and that certain details of the music are worked out by members of the ensemble during rehearsals. Resulting patterns are melodic patterns that result from the combination of two or more identical instruments playing the same repeating pattern one or more beats out of phase with each other. During the selection of resulting patterns to be sung in the second part of DRUMMING, Joan La Barbara, Jay Clayton and myself all contributed various patterns we heard resulting from the combination of three marimbas. These patterns were selected, and an order for singing them worked out, with the help of tape loops of the various marimba combinations played over and over again at my studio in New York during rehearsals held throughout the summer of 1971. The resulting patterns in MUSIC FOR MALLET INSTRUMENTS, VOICES AND ORGAN were selected by Jay Clayton and myself in a similar way, two years later. In SIX PIANOS, Steve Chambers, James Preiss and myself worked out the resulting patterns and the order in which to play them during evening rehearsals at the Baldwin Piano store in New York during the fall and winter of 1972–73.

Selecting resulting patterns is not improvising; it is actually filling in the details of the composition itself. It offers the performer the opportunity to listen to minute details and to sing or play the ones he or she finds most musical.

There's a certain idea that's been in the air, particularly since the 1960s, and I think it is an extremely misleading idea. It is that the only pleasure a performer can get while performing is to improvise, or in some way be free to express his or her momentary state of mind. If a composer gives them a fixed musical score, or specific instructions to work with this is equated with political control and it means the performer is going to be unhappy about it. But if you work with musicians you will see that what gives them joy is playing music they love, and whether that music is improvised or completely worked out is really not the main issue. The main issue is what's happening *musically*; is this beautiful, is this sending chills up and down my spine, or isn't it?

The musicians play in this ensemble, usually for periods of three to five years or more, because, presumably, they like playing the music, or at least because they find it of some musical interest. They do not make all their income from playing in this ensemble. Some are Doctoral candidates in the study of African, Indonesian and Indian music, some teach percussion, and all perform professionally in a variety of musical ensembles including orchestras, chamber groups, Medieval music ensembles, South Indian, African and Indonesian classical ensembles, free improvisation and jazz groups. It is precisely the sort of musician who starts with a strong Western classical background and then later gravitates towards these other types of music that I find ideally suited for this ensemble.

SOURCE: Steve Reich, liner notes for *Drumming, Music for Mallet Instruments, Voices and Organ, Six Pianos* (Hamburg: Deutscher Grammophon; Polydor, 1974).

1975–2000

135

STAR WARS MEETS WAGNER

(Dyer, Tomlinson)

John Williams (b. 1932), who has earned great success as the premier American film composer of the last half of the twentieth century, is often justly credited with reviving the art of the independent film score. Typically crafted through late-Romantic symphonic and operatic techniques, William's scores lead independent lives apart from the films themselves. Those associated with the double trilogy of films known as *Star Wars,* in particular, have themes that have entered popular culture. The description of these films as "space operas," so named by their director George Lucas, only heightens the prominence of Williams's adoption of the famous "leitmotif" process of the great German opera composer, Richard Wagner (1813–1883). In Wagner's cycle of four operas known as *The Ring of the Nibelung (1848–1874),* gods and goddesses, and heroic men and women have musical calling cards. So do Princess Leia and the ultimate evildoer, Darth Vader. Between the release of the first *Star Wars* trilogy (1977–1983) and the second (1999–2005), which began with the film *The Phantom Menace,* Williams had a lexicon of musical themes behind him, some of which he reasonably expected —given the global success of *Star Wars* as a mass-culture phenomenon—viewers and listeners might remember. Like Wagner, he could work on their collective emotional memories, adding nuanced psychological and dramatic depth to the experience of the music.

The first selection, taken from a feature article written by Richard Dyer, a sophisticated music critic and journalist, offers up sensitive musical details about the craft of film scoring and the musical resources available to Williams as he shapes the music for *The Phantom Menace*. Dyer pays attention to Williams's scores and the musicianship demanded by the production process. Additional references beyond Wagner to other classical composers further demonstrate the stature this neo-Romantic revivalist composer enjoys. Never mind Wagner; Dyer brings in Schubert and Stravinsky.

Following this are the more skeptical judgments of the musicologist Gary Tomlinson, who continues to take *Star Wars* and its musical power just as seriously.

MAKING "STAR WARS" SING AGAIN

LONDON—"John Williams communicates so beautifully," says George Lucas, "that I can make a silent movie."

"The Phantom Menace," the eagerly awaited first film in Lucas's new prequel trilogy to "Star Wars," isn't a silent movie. But neither were films of the "silent" era, which depended on musical accompaniment to make their full effect. Lucas knows his film history, and will quote the great Russian filmmaker Sergei Eisenstein's dictum that "film is music."[1]

No one can think of the "Star Wars" movies without hearing John Williams's music. Williams's score has even gone beyond the films to become part of the soundtrack to people's lives. In February, Williams and the London Symphony Orchestra were back in EMI's Abbey Road Studios to record the music for "The Phantom Menace"; Lucas was there to hear his new movie for the first time.

Lucas says he loves music, and it's clear he does. He remembers the music in the films he grew up with—Liszt's "Les Preludes" introduced the old Flash Gordon serials, which were a primal source for "Star Wars." He calls the trilogy his "space opera," and there are many narrative and mythic parallels to Wagner's "Ring" cycle. He writes his scripts while he's listening to music; he listens to music when he's filming; he edits to a dummy track of existing music that gives each sequence the emotional charge he's looking for.

"You have no idea what John's music contributes to the films," says actor Anthony Daniels, who plays the golden tin man, C3-PO. "The first time I saw any of 'Star Wars,' Ravel's 'Bolero' was still on the soundtrack."

It is easy to believe Daniels. In the first trilogy, Carrie Fisher's Princess Leia was flat-voiced, as plain, prosaic, and practical as a can opener, but from the moment the flute begins to intone her theme, she becomes pure romantic enchantment. The success of the film, and of Williams's music, helped restore the romantic symphonic movie score to popularity. The gadgetry in the film, and the technology that makes it possible, are futuristic, but the story is built on classic patterns–and, the scroll at the opening reminds us, takes place "long ago" in a galaxy far away.

Now there is an even older story to be told in image and music. Most of the time, Williams meets with the directors of the films he's going to score to "spot" the scenes that are going to need music; with Lucas, he knows, "we are going to play through everything." There were 16 three-hour recording sessions to set down 900 pages of score, two full hours of music. The sessions were intense, exhausting, and utterly professional. As in every business, time means money, even though music represents only a modest proportion of the film's $115 million budget.

. . .

There's another special visitor. Williams introduces him to the orchestra—"Look who's here—the man who tamed dinosaurs and taught them to speak and act"—and the players applaud Steven Spielberg, whom they have already recognized with a gasp. Lucas cracks a joke at the expense of his friend since film-school days: "I just know he's going to take over . . ."

Spielberg has helped Lucas make these weeks a difficult time for their old friend, whom both filmmakers address as "Johnny." Williams had completed his score to an earlier cut of the film. After consultation with Spielberg, though, Lucas had recently reedited the sixth and final reel, the last 20 minutes of the film, which present simultaneous actions converging on the climax.

Williams tries to be philosophical about the pickle this has dropped him into. "If I hit the ground running," he says, "I can write two minutes of music a day. If I were to have started all over again on the last reel, I would be ready to record in July—with the picture already in the theaters! So I've been making the music fit as we go along. That's why I'm constantly telling the players to drop measures 7 to 14."

. . .

From the start, Lucas had a conception of the big story he wanted to tell. Williams, on the other hand, says that back in 1977 he had no idea that he was beginning the score for a trilogy—let alone a sextet. "I'm afraid I thought of it as a Saturday-afternoon movie," he says. "A good one, though." Richard Wagner wrote the text to his "Ring" cycle rather the way Lucas wrote the "Star Wars" films, working backward, but he did have the advantage of composing the operas in order, an advantage that Williams has lacked.

"The Phantom Menace" contains many of the familiar "Star Wars" themes—it was a thrill to hear the most famous of them all appear in the trumpets again—but there are also new themes for new characters. The old themes and the new ones combine as they range across the spectrum of cinematic experience. There is scary music, exciting music, tenderhearted music, comic music, noble funeral music, and music of heroic resolve.

The 8-year-old Anakin has a theme that Williams says "is the sweetest and most innocent thing you've ever heard." That's how it sounds, though alert ears will be uneasy when they realize it is built on a chromatically unstable 12-tone row. But wait a minute—isn't there something familiar about this? The principal horn player voices the question: "Isn't this Darth Vader's music?" Later in the film there is a big celebration in some kind of coliseum. There's some funny music, a children's chorus, a march. "It's struggling to be the Imperial March," Williams says.[2] Then he shoots a rare grin. "And it's going to get there."

As it happens, not many "Phantom Menace" secrets were revealed during close observation of four days of recording sessions. Scenes from the film were projected out of sequence and without dialogue; the color registration was off; and most of the special effects were not in the work print yet (and music editor Wannberg points out that there are 2,000 special effects in this film, which works out to an average of almost 17 special effects per minute). More often than not the images were incomplete, with a live actor appearing in front of what looked like an architectural drawing, or an old print by Piranesi. These drawings, or just plain squiggles, represented what computers and special-effects wizards will fill in.

One of the new alien creatures in "The Phantom Menace" is called Jar Jar Binks, who looks like a friendly cross between a horse and a kangaroo; Jar Jar has eyes in the middle of his (or her) ears. (Lucas says he imagines his new species, then keeps on describing them to artists until they are able to draw what he has in mind; the process sounds a little like what police artists do in trying to create a suspect's portrait.) This may be a bit of a subconscious tribute to Williams, whose superiority as a film composer lies not only in his musical ability but in his skill at reading an image and at sensing the rhythmic and emotional relationships images create in movement. Williams reads a piece of film and feels the music in it the way Schubert or Benjamin Britten heard music when they read poetry.

The condition of the work print may have been responsible for Williams's one misjudgment—about 4 seconds into the first hour of music he recorded.

The young Queen Amidala (Natalie Portman) stares out of a palace window; she sees a tower with spacecraft circling around it. Everything looks red, and when we see the tower, Williams's music surges triumphantly. Lucas doesn't cry "Cut!" the way directors do in the movies. But he does speak quietly to Williams in the control booth. He is quite clear about the emotional texture he wants. "I thought of this as a quieter, more romantic moment," Lucas says. "She's very sad. Sad and romantic—the story of my life, the story of everyone's life. The actual color here is not as red as that—it's more blue." Williams listens thoughtfully. "I was too red," he admits, "when I should have been blue. I'll fix it tonight."

Lucas is full of praise for William's versatility and skill. "John's music tells the story. Each character has a theme that develops and interacts with the themes of the other characters; the musical themes connect the themes of the stories and make them resonate. He also creates an emotional context for each scene. In fact you can have it both ways, because you can play a scene against the emotions that are in it because the music is there to tell you the truth. The music can communicate nuances you can't see; it says things the film doesn't say."

And Williams is confident enough with Lucas to spring some surprises of his own. Unlike Spielberg, who enjoys coming into Williams's studio at Amblin Productions in California to sit on the piano bench and listen to the music as it emerges, Lucas usually doesn't hear Williams's score until it's being recorded.

One day 88 professional singers from London Voices arrive to record two episodes with chorus.[3] One is funeral music for one of the film's emotional climaxes; the other is for the closing credits, a terrifying, primitive pagan rite that makes even Stravinsky's "Les Noces" sound tame. Lucas loves this dark, driven music so much he shows off the recording for Spielberg when he arrives. Spielberg says to Williams, "I'm glad I didn't drop around for a cigar on the day you wrote that." Lucas says Williams doesn't know it yet, but this music will accompany a crucial scene in the third new film.

The words the chorus is singing in this dark, demonic cue are clear, but the language is unfamiliar. It turns out it's Sanskrit. ("Sanskrit!" Lucas exclaims when Williams tells him. "That'll give the fans something to figure out.") Williams had been strongly affected by a phrase from an old Welsh poem by Taliesin, "The Battle of the Trees," that the poet Robert Graves had cited and translated in "The White Goddess." "Under the tongue root, a fight most dread, / And another rages behind in the head" seemed to fit the evil ritual. Williams arranged to have these

English words translated back into the original Celtic and into other ancient languages. "I chose the Sanskrit," he says, "because I loved the sound of it. I condensed this into 'most dread / inside the head,' which seemed both cryptic and appropriate. For the funeral scene, I had my own words, 'Death's long sweet sleep,' translated into Sanskrit too."

. . .

The process for each musical cue is the same. The orchestra reads the passage through —and the LSO is famed above all other orchestras for its sight-reading. Then Williams rehearses the music, sometimes repeatedly. When it is ready, the passage is recorded, sometimes several times; Williams and the orchestra listen to the advice of the producer. Williams goes into the control room to listen to the takes, often accompanied by key members of the orchestra. Then they go out again and work until they get it the way they want it. And then they move on to the next cue. It's an exhilarating and exhausting process.

Nothing seems to ruffle Williams's composure or the old-fashioned courtesy that seems fundamental to his nature—not even 10 successive takes of the same passage. "Thank you," he says to the players after a problematic reading. "I have learned some more things that I needed to know. I think we can get it together better, and I know I can conduct it better." "Let's see if we can make a more noble sound," he will say to the brass and percussion, including himself in the equation. His experience shows in everything. "It's not too loud," he says, "but the sound is too close; it will obscure the dialogue." "Could you menace without getting louder?" he asks. "The audience should feel this rather than hear it." "Let me ask the harp not to play here—I think the sound of the harp will take the eye away from what it needs to see right here." "I'd love to take it that slowly," he says, looking at the screen, "but I can't."

Williams cannot conceal his delight, however, at how some things are turning out. He will deftly sidestep a compliment: "That's my homage to old man Korngold," he says, paying tribute to the great Viennese prodigy Erich Wolfgang Korngold, who fled from Hitler and wound up in Hollywood writing the scores to classic Warner Bros. adventure movies like "The Adventures of Robin Hood [1938]," "The Sea Hawk [1940]," and "Captain Blood [1935]." After the tremendous, charging rhythmic excitement of one cue, Williams jokes, "That ought to be enough to scare the children of the world."

When the music soars, Williams seems to soar a little too. "I'm a very lucky man," he says, smiling. "If it weren't for the movies, no one would be able to write this kind of music anymore."

SOURCE: Richard Dyer, "Making 'Star Wars' Sing Again in a London Studio. John Williams Puts Together the Soundtrack of George Lucas's Next Adventure," *Boston Globe*, March 28, 1999.

~~~~~~

STAR WARS AND THE "ENDGAME OF WAGNERISM"

When Adorno pronounced film to be the telos of Wagnerian music drama, it is improbable that he had anything quite like George Lucas's *Star Wars* series in mind. Nevertheless, the films—"space operas," as Lucas himself has called them—show enough points of contact with the *Ring* to amount to something of a late-twentieth-century *reductio* of it under the aegis of full-blown mass-commodification (toy tie-ins included; might Siegfried action figures be soon to follow?). Like the *Ring*, the *Star Wars* films rely on leveling myth—in this case, a generalized but heavy-handed and immensely approachable mythical ethos—to portray their struggle of titanic forces of good and evil. The films, like the music dramas, play out across a cosmic scale where little less than the fate of the universe hangs in the balance. The corrosive evils they portray are such that even the noblest of characters may be twisted by them: like the ever-more-deeply implicated Wotan, Darth Vader (once a Jedi knight with a less menacing name and wardrobe) can be "seduced by the dark side of the Force."

The films are accompanied by a score that trucks in the straightforward leitmotivism and brassily heroic orchestration that were always lurking in Wagner's style. These features became, largely by force of John Williams's *Star Wars* scores, the coin of the musical realm for the epic film fantasies that conveyed the simplified moralism and U.S. self-confidence of the Reagan era: *E.T.* (though this enduring children's fable shines with an innocence, musical also, lacking in the rest), the *Raiders of the Lost Ark* series, the *Superman* series, and so forth. Indeed a climactic scene of *Superman II* cinches the Wagnerian connection. It echoes exactly the musico-dramatic techniques of Siegmund's discovery of the sword in the tree in Hunding's house: to the accompaniment of the fanfare motive the superhero spies, shining in the gloom, the lone surviving shard from which he will rebuild his crystal palace at the North Pole and reacquire his powers. Here the film closes a circle, unsettlingly: to portray a superhero invented in the 1930s as an American answer to the Fascist *Übermensch,* it returns to Wagnerian gestures that had defined the *Übermensch* in the first place.[4]

The *Star Wars* films also have involved their creator Lucas in a back-and-fill maneuver that eerily reproduces the genesis of the *Ring.* Just as Wagner started with a drama concerning Siegfried's death and gradually expanded his conception to tell the story of heroic and divine generations before Siegfried, so Lucas now promises three *Star Wars* "prequels," across the turn of the millennium, that will trace the prehistory of Luke Skywalker's adventures in the youths of Obi-Wan Kenobi and Darth Vader. The forward progress of each narrative seems to call for deeper and deeper immersion in mythic prehistory.

The most significant resemblance of all, however, is also the most general: *Star Wars* continues the tradition inaugurated by the *Ring* of an unchallenging packaging of mysticism, myth, and religion whose very ease or digestibility, as Adorno saw in related varieties of modern occultism, encourages its alliance with the commodity form. Indeed such pablum–mysticism in recent film not only resembles Wagnerian myth but is derived from it. It looks back to Wagnerian fantasy along a straight path that includes fiction as well as film: the religio-mystical epics of such writers as J. R. [R.] Tolkien and C. S. Lewis, distant sources for *Star Wars* alongside more direct influences such as Edgar Rice Burroughs's Martian series and Frank Herbert's *Dune* novels, sprang from the Wageromania that seized Britain already in the 1890s. The coordinator of the re-release of the *Star Wars* trilogy in 1997 (expected to gross more than $600 million in worldwide ticket sales alone) was referring to the movies' original release when he remarked, grandly, "It's like we're . . . part of a cultural phenomenon that after all these years has never lost its impact on mankind." But he could just as well have been thinking back all the way to the *Ring.*

SOURCE: Gary Tomlinson, "Excursis 6. Film Fantasy, Endgame of Wagnerism," *Metaphysical Song: An Essay on Opera* (Princeton, N.J.: Princeton University Press, 1999): 145–46.

~~~~~~~~~

NOTES

1. Sergei Eisenstein (1898–1948), who left notes on the importance of music in his films, is well-known in particular for his collaborations with the Russian composer Sergei Prokofiev.

2. "The Imperial March," associated with the character Darth Vader, was used in the second film of the first trilogy, *The Empire Strikes Back* (1980). It is often referenced for its thematic associations of authoritarian tyranny.

3. London Voices is the name of a booking agency for professional singers for solo, chamber and choral music in a wide range of venues and needs, including classical concerts and film scores.

4. *Übermensch* refers to the philosophical concept of the "superior man," a term coined and explained by the German philosopher, Friedrich Nietzsche (1844–1900). Here, the author refers to the appropriation of this idea by the Nazis and fascists in the era of World War II.

136

TOM JOHNSON DEMONSTRATES

WHAT MINIMALISM IS REALLY ABOUT

Tom Johnson (b. 1939), a composer and critic for the *Village Voice,* covered the downtown music scene in New York from 1971 to 1981. He wrote about concerts in SoHo and in Greenwich Village, thus documenting the rise of a new avant-garde—minimalism. A student of Morton Feldman, Johnson defines his critical approach: "I always used to say, when I was doing criticism, that I should do first description, second interpretation, and only third evaluation. I didn't always achieve that. Sometimes evaluations got up front."[1] In this selection, description melds with interpretation as Johnson mimics the minimalist strategy of small changes over time, using words instead of notes.

Just as I was getting ready to leave a loft concert, an inquisitive young man, perhaps 20 years old, approached me. Apparently someone had told him I was a critic, and he figured I might be able to understand the music he had just heard. "Why are so many people playing minimal music these days? What is it all about?"

I thought for a moment about what I ought to say and settled for a brief generalization. "It has a lot to do with repetition." It was not a complete answer, of course, but I thought I'd settle for it for the time being and see how he responded.

Through a nearby window one could hear a truck passing by. At the other side of the room one of the musicians was talking to a friend who had come to the concert. In front of me, the young man was looking into my eyes, intent on the subject of minimalism and trying to work it all out.

He talked a little about how he didn't think repetition was very interesting and about how he didn't think anyone could be seriously concerned with that, and decided to try me again. "So what is it really about?"

I thought for a moment about what I ought to say this time, and settled for another generalization. "It has a lot to do with tiny variations." It was not a complete answer, of course, but I thought I'd settle for it for the time being and see how he responded.

Through the nearby window one could hear another truck passing by. At the other side of the room one of the musicians was disconnecting his electronic equipment. In front of me, the young man was staring at the floor, intent on the subject of minimalism and trying to work it all out.

He talked a little about how he didn't think tiny variations were very interesting and about how he didn't think anyone could be seriously concerned with that, and tried again. "So what is it really about?" I thought for a moment about what I ought to say this time, and settled for another generalization. "It has something to do with hyper-clarity." It was not a complete answer, of course, but I thought I'd settle for it for the time being and see how he responded.

Through the nearby window one could hear a car passing by. At the other side of the room one of the musicians was beginning to pack his electronic equipment into cases. In front of me, the young man was staring at a loudspeaker, intent on the subject of minimalism and trying to work it all out.

He talked a little about how he didn't think hyper-clarity was very interesting and about how he didn't think anyone could be seriously concerned with that, and tried me again. "So what is it really about?" I thought for a moment about what I ought to say to him this time, and settled for another generalization. "It has something to do with encouraging more subtle perceptions." It was not a complete answer, of course, but I thought I'd settle for it for the time being and see how he responded.

Through the nearby window one could hear a car passing by. At the other side of the room one of the musicians was packing his electronic equipment into cases. In front of me, the young man was staring at the floor, intent on the subject of minimalism and trying to work it all out.

He talked a little about how he didn't think encouraging more subtle perceptions was very interesting and about how he didn't think anyone could be seriously concerned with that, and tried me again. "So what is it really about?"

I thought for a moment about what I ought to say this time, and settled for another generalization. "It has something to do with making music less dramatic." It was not a complete answer, of course, but I thought I'd settle for it for the time being and see how he responded.

Through the nearby window one could hear another car passing by. At the other side of the room one of the musicians was packing his electronic equipment into cases. In front of me, the young man was looking me in the eye, intent on the subject of minimalism and trying to work it all out.

He talked a little about how he didn't think nondramatic qualities were very interesting and about how he didn't think anyone could be seriously concerned with that, and tried me again. "So what is it really about?"

I thought for a moment about what I ought to say this time, and settled for another generalization. "It stems partly from certain Asian and African attitudes." It was not a complete answer, of course, but I thought I'd settle for it for the time being and see how he responded.

Through the nearby window one could hear a group of teenagers talking and laughing. At the other side of the room one of the musicians was buckling straps around the cases that contained his electronic equipment. In front of me the young man was staring at a loudspeaker, intent on the subject of minimalism and trying to work it all out.

He talked a little about how he didn't see that Asian and African attitudes were very relevant and about how he didn't think anyone could be seriously concerned about such things, and tried me again. "So what is it really about?"

I thought for a moment about what I ought to say this time, and tried another approach. "Well, like any kind of music, it isn't really about ideas, and it can't really be explained in words. It can only be demonstrated. And even then, every demonstration is going to be a little different, and no one demonstration will ever be definitive." It was not a complete answer, but it seemed to make more sense than the others.

Through the nearby window one could hear another truck passing by. At the other side of the room one of the musicians was carrying his loaded electronic equipment toward the exit.

SOURCE: Tom Johnson, "What Is Minimalism Really About?" *Village Voice*, June 13, 1977; reprinted in Tom Johnson, *The Voice of New Music: New York City 1972–1982: A Collection of Articles Originally Published in the Village Voice* (Eindhoven, Netherlands: Het Apollo-huis, 1989): 296–98. Now in the public domain, it is available at www.tom .johnson.org.

⁓⁓⁓⁓⁓

NOTE

1.   "Problems Facing Music Criticism," *New Music Box*, September 1, 2002. Available at http:// www.newmusicbox.org/article.nmbx?id=1865.

137

Morton Feldman and His
West German Fan Base
(Feldman, Post)

In the 1950s, Morton Feldman (1926–1987) was known primarily as a member of the New York school of composers, so named for their affinities and relationships with the New York school of abstract expressionist painters. After his appointment in 1973 to the faculty at the State University of New York, Buffalo—a campus oasis for avant-garde music—Feldman wrote increasingly long works for acoustic instruments in a more accessible style. As described by the critic-composer Kyle Gann, Feldman's music has "a quiet, delicately introverted, almost mournful aesthetic."[1]

During the mid-1980s, interest in Feldman's music grew in the unlikely environment of West German new-music circles. In February 1984, Frankfurt hosted Feldman in a week-long seminar with two concerts. That summer, the European premiere of his String Quartet no. 2 (lasting over three hours) was played by the Kronos Quartet at the famous Internationale Ferienkurse für Neue Musik (International Summer Course for New Music) in Darmstadt. In 1985, the German composer and friend of American experimental music Walter Zimmermann edited and published the first book devoted to Feldman's work—a bilingual volume of Feldman's writings. After another Darmstadt premiere in 1986, Feldman had become, in the words of a West German critic, "music-historically relevant."[2] This level of critical acclaim marked a crucial turning point in Feldman's career.

The excerpts reprinted below from Feldman's Frankfurt lecture allude to re-current themes surrounding his music and thought, including his compositional approach, his sense of difference from his contemporaries, and his self-conscious journey toward a purity of sonic experience. The other selections relate to his West German reception. Here, the genuine belief about national identity and the individ-ualism of an American artist reinforce cultural interpretations.

EXCERPTS FROM "XXX ANECDOTES AND DRAWINGS"

IV

I think what really makes a composer distinguished from another composer, except for Stock-hausen, is one's instrumentation. And this is something that I know my most sophisticated stu-dents never talk about, no one ever thinks about. They feel it's an ad hoc thing, any instruments; it's the notes given to them from god, the ideas in a sense that give the work a certain distinc-tion, naturally. You see, I feel that orchestration is another gift. And Varèse once said to me, "or-chestrators are born." He never said composers are born, he used the word orchestrators are born. And I really feel it's another gift and very few people have that gift. Maybe that's why it's not considered a parameter. I mean, Messiaen is not an orchestrator. That's not orchestration you hear, I don't know what the hell it is. It's Disney, it's Disneyland. It's technicolor, you know like from the forties when they first came out, like a Doris Day movie, those crazy colors, you know how crazy people look in the old technicolor, that's Messiaen, just something is wrong someplace.

Somebody, an old man in Berlin, two days ago, he was about 84, 86, he told me he was the only composer alive in Berlin that was born in the nineteenth century. That was *his* distinc-tion. He asked me what I thought composition was, he heard my piece, he liked it, though he thought it was too "colorful." And I said, "I am not interested in color." I said, "My definition of composition is: the right note in the right place with the right instrument!"

Schoenberg in his Harmony book talks about the relationship between pitch and timbre. And he says that timbre is the prince of the domain, that the resulting timbre is to some degree more important than the pitch itself, as we think of pitch. That's a very important idea. That's why I feel a lot of Webern's subsequent orchestration and many people feel this, that his or-chestration was somewhat arbitrary. That you just can't take a row and give it to a piccolo and then give the other segment to the double bass. You can't be insensitive to the pitches here, you see, how they speak and go on. So, that's the whole Darmstadt world, or the Webern influence is that essentially instruments were used just as another denominator of variation. And very few were sensitive to the instruments playing those notes. They associate pitch as tonal music. I don't, you see. In other words, something happened to pitch that was terrible. It was like these people get sex changes, it's as if pitch went to Scandinavia and came back an interval, had a sex change. It had to come back an interval. It's like in my early piano pieces in 1951, I would have a chromatic field and I introduced an octave. No one was doing that. Very beautiful, it worked. But even Webern had octaves. You are not supposed to hear anything out of the context.

A very funny incident happened to me many years ago. I was in a Chinese restaurant in New York and in came a group, a very strong group, like the Darmstadt group in New York, from Princeton University, Milton Babbitt and all these people, they all came in, they had some kind of meeting and they were in New York and they went into this Chinese restaurant and I was there with my wife. And I grew up with these people, I went to school with them. And they waved and I waved and then, I was getting up, I paid the check and I passed their table and I shook hands and they were all looking at me and I said, "Boys, forgive me for speaking in broken music."

V

. . .

I work with the pen and that's a very interesting phenomen[on] because when I work with the pen everything is crossed out. Some pages there is nothing crossed out and it's usually those pages when there is something in a continuity, you see. Many times I make my continuity later, which essentially is the way Tolstoy worked. I don't necessarily work in a continuity.

Usually my pieces began maybe on the tenth measure, kind of getting into it. And then I would look at it and throw away the first ten measures. And that's why my music has always that opening, you see, because I borrow from all different things. I'll tell you how I get my opening. I got it from Kafka. I read an article once on Kafka, and I was very fond of Kafka. You'll notice Kafka's first sentences: "Someone has been telling lies about Joseph K." You know that's Kafka, you are in the world of Kafka. We were all reading Kafka in New York at about twenty, twenty-one, fantastic thing. I took that idea and I put it in my own music. Kafka definitely influenced my feeling of how to begin a piece. Immediately in the atmosphere. Not like Bartók, *mesto* or something, another *mesto*.[3]

I work every day, more in terms of feeling that I have done a day's work. Now it could be two hours, it could be sixteen hours, it could be two days going into each other without sleep. Unless I feel that the day's work is completed, I'm not counting how much work I do, I just psychologically feel that I have to do a day's work. By day's work I don't mean, you know, seven hours, it could be any time. Sometimes a day's work is waiting. Stravinsky worked that way. Stravinsky talks about waiting, and he would sit around and wait. I clean my *teppich*,[4] read books on *teppich*, I clean the house, always waiting. I learned from painter friends. I have one friend, he became very successful, he had three houses, he had one in Florida, he had one in Woodstock, and he had another studio in New York. Everything was waiting, all different sizes of canvases were already stretched, well, he was a millionaire, already. All the paints are there, anything, in case he might want to use acrylic even though he didn't have it, it was all there, all the possibilities, all the parameters of work, not of art, but of work was ready for him, so that if he comes in he doesn't waste any time with the preparation. I'm very much the same, it's very important for me to have all the types of paper waiting, I'm very sensitive to paper. Pens are very important for a lot of reasons, because of my eyes.

. . .

VII

When you hear my new string quartet, there is a section that appears to be tonal. And I had an idea which is to take something and then finally have it disintegrate. And so finally what I did was that the beginning is presented straight, then [I] make other connections, say from A-Z I do

C-A-B-F. It's all constructed so I could place anything against anything else and it would seem normal because the design of that little module is perfect, the whole thing is a nightmare, it's like a giant jigsaw puzzle that every piece you put in fits. And then when you finish it, you see that it's not the picture. That was the idea. The jigsaw puzzle, everything finishes and it's not the picture. Then you do another version and it's not the picture. Finally you realize that you are not gonna get the picture. It goes on for an hour. It's very beautiful. The only thing I don't like about it: it was idea-oriented. Because I knew as a priori by the nature of the material that it's gonna have stages of disintegration. Now what was interesting only about its disintegration was that only the process of disintegration was variation. Do it in different degrees of abstraction and various degrees of its literaryness [sic].

. . .

XIV

I did one lesson on the street with Varèse, one lesson on the street, it lasted half a minute, it made me an orchestrator. He said, "what are you writing now, Morton?" I told him. He says, "make sure you think about the time it takes from the stage to go out there [into the audience]. Let me know when you get a performance, I'd like to hear it." And he walked away. That was my one lesson, it became like instant, one lesson and I started out. I was about 17 when I knew him, and from then on, I started to listen.

. . .

XXIII

What I picked up from painting is what every art student knows. And it's called the picture plane. I substituted for my ears the aural plane and it's a kind of balance but it has nothing to do with foreground and background. It has to do with, how do I keep it on the plane, from falling off, from having the sound fall on the floor. Most people have a sound that doesn't fall on the floor by giving it a system. Harmony or twelve tone, you see. Without the system it falls on the floor. That young fellow that was just improvising that stupid piece, he didn't know that he was just falling on the floor every two minutes off his chair. Now, this could be an element of the aural plane, where I'm trying to balance, a kind of coexistence between the chromatic field and those notes selected from the chromatic field that are not in the chromatic series. And so I'm involved like a painter, involved with gradations within the chromatic world. And the reason I do this is to have the ear make those trips. Back and forth, and it gets more and more saturated. But I work very much like a painter, insofar as I'm watching the phenomena and I'm thickening and I'm thinning and I'm working in that way and just watching what it needs. I mean, I have the skill to hear it. I don't know what the skill is to think it, I was never involved with the skills to think it.

I'm the only one that works this way. But it's like Rothko, just a question of keeping that tension or that stasis. You find it in Matisse, the whole idea of stasis. That's the word. I'm involved with stasis. It's frozen, at the same time it's vibrating.

XXIV

So essentially I am working with three notes and of course we have to use the other notes. But the other notes are like shadows of the basic notes. So then all I have to decide is where I [am] gonna start on the three notes, chromatic, you know. After a few years I added another one . . .

because the four notes then would give me the relationship of either two minor seconds or two major seconds. And also in a sense give me a minor second, a major second, a minor third and a major third. In other words, at least I have a little more texture if I want to isolate. Essentially a piece of about three or four minutes is just orchestrating the four notes.

You can either do two things with music, you could be involved with variation, which in simple terms means only vary it, or you could be in repetition. Reiterative. What my work is, is a synthesis between variation and repetition. However, I might repeat [a] thing that, as it's going around, is varying itself on one aspect. Or I could vary repetition. But again, it's a performance, I see it as I'm doing it. Very important concept in my work.

XXV

I'm defining, it's a redefinition of *Kunst* [art] not society. It's not a redefining of *Kunst* in society or society into *Kunst*. It's redefining of how free one can think and still have all the wonderful things: notation, instruments, the making of things, the unmaking of things, see. It still has to do with that. The other has to do with its aspect in society, philosophy, psychology, to make a relation between the one and the other. I cannot make a relationship between music and society. I don't know what society is because it is *alles,* everything. My teacher [Stefan] Wolpe was a marxist and he felt my music was too esoteric at the time. And he had his studio on a proletarian street on 14th Street and 6th Ave., and at that time I just became involved, I was 20 years old, I became involved with the artists in Greenwich Village, all these people. And he was on the second floor and we were looking out the window, and he said "what about the man on the street?" At that moment he said what about the man in the street, Jackson Pollack was crossing the street, the crazy artist of my generation was crossing the street at that moment.

> SOURCE: Morton Feldman, "XXX Anecdotes and Drawings," from the transcript by Gerhard Westerath of the seminar "The Future of Local Music," given at the Theater am Turm (Theater at the Tower) in Frankfurt, February 1984, translated by Hanfried Blume in Essays, ed. Walter Zimmerman (Kerpen, Germany: Beginner Press, 1985): 146–48, 151, 156, 166, 168, 169, 170. Also reprinted in Morton Feldman, *Give My Regards to Eighth Street: Collected Writings of Morton Feldman* (Cambridge, Mass.: Exact Change Press, 2000): 157–95.

Feldman's career displays the impact of an American experimental tradition (from Edgard Varèse to John Cage and the New York school) on twentieth-century European musical modernism. In this selection, Nora Post, a noted American oboist, records memories from that crucial 1984 Darmstadt conference. Both stories—one about the revisionist director Friedrich Hommel and the other about an encounter between Feldman and Walter Zimmermann—show how stereotypes about "the American character" shaped critical language about Feldman's music.

Beginning with his first Darmstadt course in 1982 (the two and a half week festival is held every second year), the new director, Friedrich Hommel, began to create a new Darmstadt, a truly international contemporary music festival. To the amazement of all, especially the "old guard"—some of whom traveled to Darmstadt in 1982 to see for themselves what had happened —a sweeping transformation occurred and, somewhere along the line, the famed post-war German serialist stronghold known as the Darmstadt School rolled over and quietly died. Of neglect, I suspect.

. . .

One hardly need mention that there are still wide cultural and musical differences between Europe and North America. Discussing Morton Feldman as a case in point, Hommel told this story:

> Since you mentioned Morton Feldman, I'd like to tell you a wonderful remark he made, which really shows the difference between America and Europe. During one discussion, Walter Zimmermann, who is a great promoter and connoisseur of American music here in Germany, and a friend of Feldman, made a comment. One assumed that he and Feldman would be in full agreement when Zimmermann spoke to Feldman, apologizing for the schedule and structure of the Darmstadt courses, saying, "What I would really like would be to behave like a nomad, to roam freely." He was sure he would have Morton Feldman's full agreement. Instead, Feldman said, "My dear Walter Zimmermann, what you have just stated is pure German Romanticism. Let me remind you that nomads don't roam. They just move their positions in order to seek better food for their sheep." THIS was American realism, and this was the greatest symbolic encounter between friends of two different countries.

> SOURCE: Nora Post, "Survivor from Darmstadt," *Symposium: Journal of the College Music Society* (1985). Available at http://symposium.music.org/cgi-bin/m_symp_show .pl?id=169.

This advertisement accompanied the showing of a video in 1997 of Feldman's lecture at Darmstadt in 1986. The video was released by Universal Edition.

Morton Feldman and Darmstadt . . . the very idea of lecturing to all those Europeans must have amused him! For Feldman, one of the New York group of composers, was acutely aware of being an American and was just as aware—critically, ironically, even sarcastically aware— that his fellow composers were European.

Feldman equated being American with being open, unfettered by tradition. For him, serialists (and Darmstadt was *the* serialist stronghold) were typical Europeans, blinkered fellows unable to think freely about music.

In the video Feldman is smiling, having a good time, making jokes—but all the while he is making provocative remarks, right under the watchful eyes of the elder composers and musicologists—and to the amusement of quite a few young people.

Feldman's music was performed in Darmstadt since 1956, but in 1986, a year before his death, Feldman still could not have foreseen that less than ten years later his oeuvre would

John Cage and Morton Feldman at the Summer Olympics, Munich, 1972.

enjoy tremendous prestige in Europe, where recognition for him, along with his open, free-thinking American compatriots, has become unquestioned.

The video is a valuable document showing this American composer on the eve of his conquest of the old world.

> *SOURCE:* Advertisement for the video of Feldman's lecture in Darmstadt in 1986, as quoted in Amy Beal, *New Music, New Allies: American Experimental Music in West Germany from the Zero Hour to Reunification* (Berkeley: University of California Press, 2006): 244–45.

NOTES

1. Kyle Gann, *American Music in the Twentieth Century* (New York: Schirmer, 1997): 142.
2. Bernd Leukert, as quoted and translated in Amy C. Beal, *New Music, New Allies: American Experimental Music in West Germany from the Zero Hour to Reunification* (Berkeley: University of California Press, 2006): 244.
3. *Mesto* is an indication to play the music sorrowfully.
4. *Teppich* is the Yiddish word for carpet.

138

PHILIP GLASS AND THE ROOTS OF REFORM OPERA

Philip Glass (b. 1937) brought minimalism into the cultural spotlight with his marathon opera *Einstein on the Beach* (1976). This opera was a collaborative triumph for Glass and the theater director-designer-artist Robert Wilson (b. 1941), in tandem with the choreographer Lucinda Childs (b. 1940). Glass's list of theatrical models deserves close attention as it is the artistic tradition which gave him the tools to "reform" narrative opera.

   In the second excerpt, which is taken from an interview for a Buddhist magazine, Glass rebuffs the interviewer's repeated attempts to contextualize his music through the practice of meditation. One can understand why the attempt was made. Glass's music, like Robert Wilson's art, can be "cool, distant, and often hypnotic."[1] Glass's account of his work with Nadia Boulanger also acknowledges the disciplines of craft in an artist's sense of self.

I have often said that I became an opera composer by accident. I never set out to become one, and even today I use the word "opera" with reluctance. In the 1950s, when I was a music student, I dutifully studied the standards of the opera repertory, and I made regular visits to the old Metropolitan Opera House on Broadway at 39th Street where, for fifty cents, one could use a score desk near the top of the house. You could hear the operas perfectly from up there, but you could see them only by stretching forward and peering straight down, a posture not only uncomfortable but positively life-threatening. From this extreme perspective I heard—and, in a fashion, "saw"—any number of the old warhorses as well as the extremely modern (or what seemed modern in those days) *Wozzeck*. These were "duty" visits, undertaken to round out my education. Not in a million years would it have occurred to me that I might someday write an opera myself, let alone spend the greater part of my adult working life in the theater.

As it turned out, I was thirty-nine years old when, with *Einstein on the Beach,* I suddenly found myself actually working in opera houses. *Einstein* was soon followed by two more operas (*Satyagraha* and *Akhnaten*), forming a trilogy of what I regard as "portrait" operas—musical dramatic portraits of powerful personalities who have engaged my attention at particular times. By then, clearly, I had become a composer of operas.

I find now in writing about these first three "portrait" operas that some of the most interesting aspects of their creation are the chains of "accidents" that led me to opera in the first place. Therefore, though I began this book with the intention of writing only about my own operas, I find I must start a full ten years before, during the time of my first theater work in Paris in the mid-1960s. Those were the years in which my music work and theater music became closely intertwined. No doubt it was the particular kind of theater I was drawn to, and the somewhat unusual theater music I began to write, that has led to the highly personal approach to theater music (opera, if you will) that marks this trilogy of portrait operas. This is how it came about.

The first theater of which I, like most people, was aware was the "traditional kind." This was narrative theater, that which starts from a literary base. This does not imply that literary theater is necessarily conservative. Several decades ago writers such as Bertolt Brecht, Samuel Beckett, Jean Genet and Harold Pinter were all developing new attitudes to material and audience, attitudes requiring new techniques of performance and presentation. At the same time, and continuing right up to the present, there exists a modern theater rooted in the conservative mode known as "naturalism." Beginning in the nineteenth century with [Anton] Chekhov, it continued into the twentieth with such American writers as Eugene O'Neill, Arthur Miller and Tennessee Williams.

For a great many people, this latter type *is* theater. But this kind of theater never interested me very much, and it has played almost no part at all in my own working life. Growing up in the world of "progressive" theater as I did, and experiencing it in the ways I have, theater has always meant to me something quite different: a kind of experience that even today is viewed as anything *but* traditional. The kinds of theater which spin familiar stories, moralizing, sometimes satirizing, occasionally comforting us about our lives, have never meant much to me. What has always stirred me is theater that challenges one's ideas of society, one's notions of order.

When I was living in Europe in the early 1960s, I was very much in touch with theater that represented these ideals. Jean-Louis Barrault's Théâtre Odéon in Paris regularly presented new works by Beckett and Genet, and I particularly remember a stunning production of Genet's *The Screens,* directed by Roger Blin.[2] Also, I saw the unforgettable Madeleine Renaud playing the Woman in what may have been one of the very first productions of Beckett's *Happy Days*. At about the same time, I made a pilgrimage to East Berlin with JoAnne Akalaitis (whom I had recently married) to spend more than a week watching the Berliner Ensemble in productions of Brecht that were fairly close to their originals. Brecht also was regular fare at the Théâtre Nationale Populaire in Paris. In this way I was able to see two very different versions of this great playwright's work, both unlike anything I had encountered at home.

During this period I made regular trips to London as well. We were students then and, not having much money, we often hitchhiked to London, managing somehow to pay the boat fare across the Channel, queuing all night to buy balcony seats for the National Theater, where we might see Lawrence [sic] Olivier in *Othello* or perhaps [August] Strindberg's *Dance of Death*.

It was in the Paris of the early 1960s, though, that I became associated with the group of people who, in a few years, would become known as Mabou Mines, an experimental theater collective that has become well known in New York since the 1970s. This initial group included JoAnne Akalaitis, Lee Breuer, Ruth Maleczech, David Warrilow and, sometime later, Fred Neumann, Bill Raymond and Terry O'Reilly (not to be confused with composer Terry Riley). JoAnne, Breuer and Maleczech had worked together previously at the Actors Workshop in San Francisco with Herb Blau and Jules Irving, and at the San Francisco Tape Center with Morton Subotnick and Ramone Sender. From their Paris beginnings, however, they functioned as a unit, though they were not yet formally organized as a theater, and I soon began working with them as their resident musician.

At first our work began with the kinds of progressive European theater to which we all were attracted. In fact, the first two pieces that emerged from this association were stagings of Brecht and Beckett. Lee Breuer directed a production of Brecht's *Mother Courage,* for which I acted as music director, coaching the actors/singers in the wonderful Paul Dessau score. Then came a production of *Play* by Beckett, also directed by Breuer, with the first original score I wrote for this company.

We soon discovered, though, that there simply wasn't a large enough audience for an English-speaking theater company in Paris. Furthermore, I was beginning to encounter the stiff resistance to my new music that would pursue me for years to come. As a result, by 1967 we had all left Paris to settle in New York (although JoAnne and I first took a detour through Central Asia and India, the first of many visits to that part of the world).

Though we had our beginnings together in the progressive "literary" theater of Europe, in New York we soon began presenting theater pieces originating within the group itself. As was normal with many of the new theater groups at this time, our finished pieces were the result of an intense, protracted work period. An image, a movement, sometimes a title could provide the initial inspiration for a work. After that came a long period of improvising, selecting, discarding and refining before it began to take its final shape. Invariably, the text itself was a result of this shaping process; it was hardly ever a point of origin. Much of this was what came to be called nonnarrative theater. This was hardly our own invention, since its roots can be found in a still earlier period—specifically in the works of Antonin Artaud, who attempted to transcend words by creating a theater of pure expression in Paris during the 1920s. Another important influence was Jerzey Grotowski and the Polish Lab Theater. JoAnne and Ruth had studied with him in France in 1969, and they were among the first Americans who brought his ideas back to New York.

After the late 1960s, there came a progressive proliferation of these "new theater" ensembles, all working, generally speaking, toward a similar goal. In New York I saw the work of Joe Chaikin's Open Theater and Richard Schechner's Performance Group, as well as the theater work of Meredith Monk, Richard Foreman and Robert Wilson. By the early 1970s there had developed a lively community of innovative theater people intensely involved in their own work and equally supportive, if often critical, of the efforts of their colleagues.

In all of this activity, the Living Theater served as inspiration and, at least to many young theater people like ourselves, standard-bearer for the new theater. I remember the "Living," as it was often called, from the late 1950s, when they performed in a downtown New York theater on Seventh Avenue. These were the days of Kenneth Brown's *The Brig* and Jack Gelber's *The Connection*. In my New York student days, they were part of the general avant-garde mix of the time, a mix that included the Beats (Jack Kerouac, Gregory Corso and Allen Ginsberg), the hard bop of John Coltrane, and Claes Oldenberg's [sic] "Store Days."[3]

I don't think I had any clearer sense of who or what the "Living" was than that. It had originated with Julian Beck and his wife, Judith Malina, who, in the early 1960s, had taken their theater collective for an extended stay in Europe, where their social/political anarchy was taken seriously. It was in the south of France, in a little festival outside Marseilles, where I saw them again in the summer of 1964, and this time the "Living" made an enormous impression on me.

The work was *Frankenstein,* and we saw its premiere performance. The weight of the work was in images and movement. Further, it was the first theater work I had seen that so radically extended the accepted sense of theater time: The performance began around eight in the evening and went on until sometime around three in the morning. I don't know to what extent, if any, *Frankenstein*'s time scale was modeled on that of Eastern theater, but I saw this same kind of scale used some years later in South India by the Khatikali theater. I encountered it again in New York in the early work of Robert Wilson. But what later came to be called Wilson's "theater of images"[4] I saw for the first time with the "Living" in the early 1960s.

. . .

At first the Soho audiences at these music, dance and theater events were made up almost entirely of other performers, musicians, painters, sculptors, filmmakers, poets, writers, etc. Very often, theater, dance and music events took place in the art galleries that were just beginning to appear in what was by then the center of an almost unprecedented scene.

We accepted all this at the time rather matter of factly. But, in reality, in the early 1970s we were witnessing and participating in a scene of tremendous vitality, one probably unparalleled since the Paris of the 1920s. Gallery collectives such as 112 Greene Street, The Kitchen (which, a few years later, became one of the centers for a totally new kind of performance art) and galleries like those of Leo Castelli and Paula Cooper encouraged and vigorously supported a whole range of events. This was the gestation period, as well as the place, when and where the "performance art" of the late 1970s and early 1980s began. And it was in these places that collaborative work could be practiced; where the technical skills were acquired which made possible the music theater pieces in which I became involved a few years later. At the same time there were people like Laurie Anderson, Julia Heyward, Stuart Sherman, Vito Acconci, artists who blurred the lines between art and the *performance* of art until the distinction finally disappeared and performance art emerged.

This was a very lively, very large and highly varied bunch of people. There could have been two hundred, or even two thousand, artists involved in these various movements. I don't think anybody knows because in those days everybody was simply too busy to stop and count. And if the arts were becoming more theatrical, then it was possible that the theater also was tending, if somewhat reluctantly, to become more involved with making art.

SOURCE: Philip Glass, *Music by Philip Glass.* New York: Harper and Row, 1987: 3–10.

Glass practices Buddhism, and many critics have linked his musical aesthetic not only to the influence of sitarist Ravi Shankar and Indian rhythmic techniques, but also to meditation. In this interview, Glass disputes these interpretations. Some anecdotes about his training with the famous Nadia Boulanger underscore the importance of discipline as the foundation of craft. In her own way, Boulanger followed the practice of devotional discipline.

Introduction by *Tricycle*'s editor. In 1966, Philip Glass made the first of many trips to India. His Buddhist study and meditation practice began at that time. This interview was conducted for *Tricycle* by Helen Tworkov together with Robert Coe, author, critic, and playwright.

TRICYCLE: As your Buddhist studies followed an interest in yoga, let's start there. That puts us back in 1962, when even a yoga teacher was hard to come by.

PG: I found one in the Yellow Pages, under the Y's. For the next three years I studied with Indian yoga teachers, including one who started me being a vegetarian.

TRICYCLE: And did yoga put you under some kind of Eastern umbrella that extended to Buddhism?

PG: I never heard anything about Buddhism through my yoga teachers. It was through John Cage that I knew anything at all, through his book *Silence*. And just a year or two before that, the first really good edition of the *I Ching* came out, which I knew about through an English painter who had joined the Native American Church and was a peyote eater. . . So it's not surprising that I would know of the *I Ching* through a painter. And then John Cage. I certainly did not learn about him at music school. He was not considered a serious musical influence at that time. Certainly not by the people at Juilliard. Then in *Silence* there were all these references to Zen koans. But the big explosion in the culture happened in 1968 when the Beatles went to India to study with the Maharishi. They brought back Indian culture. Only after that did people like Ravi Shankar begin performing in large concert halls—and filling them. George Harrison made Ravi Shankar a household name. But when I started out, any kind of Eastern interest was still pretty marginal. . . But I didn't get to India until 1965.

TRICYCLE: After working with Ravi Shankar in Paris?

PG: Yes. I had received a fellowship to study in Paris with Nadia Boulanger in 1964. For extra money, I took a job transcribing music for Ravi Shankar. He had been invited to Paris by Conrad Rook to write the score for the film *Chappaqua*.

TRICYCLE: Had you worked with Indian music before?

PG: I had never even *heard* Indian music before! Funny, isn't it?

TRICYCLE: Yes. Because in another two years it was on everybody's transistor radios.

PG: It seemed to have happened overnight. But in order to find a way of notating the music, I made my first on-the-spot analysis of how Indian music was put together.

TRICYCLE: How did you notate it?

PG: The trick, of course, was to take a medium that was based on a different principle of organization and to write it in a language developed for Western music. Western notation was developed for music that is organized along Western lines.

TRICYCLE: There has been criticism of the interpretation you made of Indian music at that time. And haven't you yourself referred to your own music of the late Sixties as having grown from mistakes that you made about the structure of Indian music?

PG: I'm not sure it was a mistake. But it was a very narrow reading.

TRICYCLE: Wasn't there a real misunderstanding of the structure? That the central technique of Indian music is additive?

PG: That's what I thought it was. And that was a misapprehension. I thought I was listening to music that was built in an additive way, but it turned out it really wasn't. It is built in a cyclic way. And that turned out to be very useful, because the misunderstanding, the use of an additive process, became, in fact, the way I began to write music. . . .

TRICYCLE: By 1967 you were back in New York, fresh from India and doing beginning meditation practices; and your minimalist compositions of the years 1967, 1968, and 1969 to some extent evolved out of the work you did with Ravi Shankar. Yet you have denied a common assumption that this music was influenced by meditation practice, and you have also been quick to disclaim any association between your work and so-called meditation music.

PG: At the time, there were a lot of composers doing similar experiments with composition, and they hadn't been to India. They didn't have Buddhist teachers, and they hadn't been studying yoga since 1961.

TRICYCLE: By around 1968, there were articles on the "new meditation music" that referred to you, Terry Riley, La Monte Young, and Steve Reich.

PG: I have always considered that a misconception.

TRICYCLE: Let's clarify something: meditation music does not imply that meditation is the inspiration for the music, or that the music comes from the experience of meditation, but that the music itself promotes—or induces—a contemplative state of mind. A mind that is encouraged to find its own resting place rather than get jerked around by auditory emotive buttons.

PG: If you go to any of these float tanks or new-age spas, what's the music that they play? They don't play Terry or La Monte or me. They have "new-age" music, which doesn't sound the same. The music that the critics thought was that music hadn't even been written yet. It came later.

TRICYCLE: Was there no common source for the minimal music that was written in the late Sixties?

PG: What's confusing here is that by 1968 North America was awash with ideas of a new culture, and the associations are inescapable.

TRICYCLE: Is it completely coincidental that at the same time as meditation practice enters North America in a big way, a movement in music appears with obvious parallels to meditation—music that, for example, denies habitual patterns of expectations, breaks the convention of beginnings and endings, eliminates crescendos, and dissolves the dualities of peaks and valleys?

PG: There are other sources.

TRICYCLE: Such as?

PG: Samuel Beckett. Don't forget that I was working with the Mabou Mines Theater at the time. And in those days we were all completely involved with Beckett.

TRICYCLE: How does Beckett's influence translate in musical terms?

PG: Nonnarrative theater or nonnarrative art is not based on theme and development but on a different structure. The influences are not Indian alone. Beckett was a big influence. So was Brecht. Genet, too.

TRICYCLE: Can you say something about the parallels to the dharma?

PG: These writers took the subject out of the narrative. They broke the pattern of the reader identifying with the main character.

TRICYCLE: How is that accomplished?

PG: Brecht does it with irony, as in *Mother Courage*. Beckett does it through fragmentation, as in the theater piece *Play*. And Genet does it through transcendent vision. *Miracle of the Rose* is an example.

TRICYCLE: Is it the detachment from character identification that apprehends a dharmic sensibility?

PG: It has to do with the self-grasping or self-cherishing mind. Brecht is the obvious example of trying to go beyond the self-cherishing mind. But in each case, the attempt is the basis for defining the artist as avant-garde.

TRICYCLE: What accounts for this?

PG: World War I saw the end of a nineteenth-century Romantic idealism. These men came after that. They had lived through that disillusionment, and it produced an attitude that was freshly and newly critical of the Western tradition that landed the world in such a mess. Then, of course, it is even more intense for the generation after World War II. That's us. By the Sixties, coincidences of cultural ideas were going on. On the one hand, you have an explosion of Indian culture, and on the other, a reaction to nineteenth- and twentieth-century narrative art. These two cross-currents tended to reinforce each other. When I came back from that first trip to India, I started looking at paintings by Frank Stella and Jasper Johns, and again I saw work based on a different kind of thinking, work that was as different from abstract expressionism as abstract art was from the post-Dadaists. Genet and Beckett were two of the most important people in this respect, and you can trace that back to [Marcel] Duchamp, if you like.

TRICYCLE: That's an interesting crossroad, because the Duchamp-Cage-Zen connection is probably both the quietest and the most effective Buddhist influence in this culture. And if you really want to get into Western Buddhist genealogies, you can connect Cage and Genet to Artaud and to Bali.

PG: I'm not trying to deny the Indian connection. But the base of it was much broader.

TRICYCLE: Well, it's curious. At a certain point there is the Indian explosion and what the press is calling "minimal meditation music." Yet throughout all of your interviews you have always said, "No, they've got it all wrong." Yet the parallel remains; but unlike your contemporaries, there has been an aspect of your music—that obsessive, compulsive, driven dimension—that, shall we say, is even "Faustian." This seems to be about a Western sense of control. And one could see, in retrospect, how that would lead you back to a Western tradition.

PG: I think that's accurate. And another dimension to this is that the word *minimalist* was originally applied to visual artists that I knew quite well—Sol LeWitt, Don Judd, and Robert Morris. If you spoke to them, they would probably not make any reference to the Indian influence at all. There was a cultural change of mind that was happening in the Sixties that embraced all of these art forms and drew from many sources: European as well as Far Eastern, Indian as well as American. Yet within all these influences and changes, it never occurred to me that my music was about meditation. The theater was an important source for me. A lot of my work came out of a need to evolve a musical language that could be married to the theatrical language that was going on around me.

TRICYCLE: And this musical language had no concrete reference.

PG: That's right. It was a self-referential musical language that was, in essence, abstract.

TRICYCLE: Did that commitment to an abstract language also set you apart from your peers at the time?

PG: In the late Sixties, any number of people were doing music based directly or indirectly on Indian influences. It was not uncommon to see Western musicians dressed in Indian clothes and lighting incense on stage. What I was doing was far, far away from that. I was quite content to let other people light the incense. . .

TRICYCLE: Even though certain aspects of the Buddhist path may have unexpectedly routed you from the exotic to the mundane, other aspects of Buddhist meditation practice complement the classical training of a Western musician: discipline, rigor, the relationship between formal structure and personal creativity, between discipline and playfulness.

PG: That's what you learned from a teacher like Nadia Boulanger. Though actually, I was already pretty disciplined by the time I got to her. Ane Pema Chodron (from Gampo Abbey) gave me a pin with the abbey's motto, which is the Tibetan word for "discipline." And I said, "Pema, this is the pin I don't need!"

TRICYCLE: The late Zen teacher Maurine Stuart studied piano with Boulanger some fifteen years before you did, and she often spoke of Boulanger in the same terms that one might speak of a spiritual teacher.

PG: I can understand that. Before I went to Paris I had acquired very good work habits, which in itself is a discipline. But Boulanger carried the idea of discipline to another level. She added something that I became familiar with later through Tibetan practice, something that I can only describe as a devotional aspect of musical study, and anyone who studied with her could talk about that.

TRICYCLE: Were you inspired by Boulanger's devotion?

PG: Boulanger set herself up as an incomparable model of discipline and dedication, and she expected you to be just like her. And that was almost impossible, because she seemed beyond what any human being could really hope to be. Yet, she did it in a very simple way—I would not say gracious, no one ever said that Boulanger was gracious—but she did it in a simple, clear way. When I studied with her, for example, the only way to live up to her standards and to turn out the amount of work she expected every week was to get up between 6 and 7 in the morning and work all day long. And, if I did that every day, I would turn up at my lesson and Boulanger gave me the impression that I had done just about the very minimum.

TRICYCLE: You have also referred to Boulanger as a monster.

PG: In the sense that she was a relentless, unwavering example that she expected you to follow. One day I came to a harmony lesson. She saw an error in something called "hidden parallel fifths." She studied the page in silence and then turned toward me. With a look of understanding and compassion she asked how I was feeling. I said, "I'm feeling fine, Mademoiselle." She asked, "Do you have a fever? Do you have a headache?" And I didn't get what was going on. "I know of a good psychiatrist. Seeing a therapist can be very confidential, and one need not be embarrassed at all." I explained that I didn't need that kind of help. Finally, she said, "Well I don't understand." And I said, "You don't understand what?" And she said, "*This!*" Then she wheeled around and pointed at the mistake I had made. "How else do you explain the state of mind that produced this error? You're so distracted, so out of touch with reality; if you were really conscious of what you were doing, this could not have happened. How can you live such a distracted, unconscious life that you would bring this in here?" That was Mademoiselle Boulanger.

TRICYCLE: What effect did that have?

PG: I decided to find a way of guaranteeing without fail that the lessons would be perfect. I devised a system that entailed a mathematical analysis for each notation so that visually the page took on a completely different look. For the next year and a half every exercise that I brought to her had that analysis, and she never made any comment about it. Amazing.

TRICYCLE: What were the aspects of her teaching that became more clear to you through Buddhist practice?

PG: Her insistence on conscious living, on what you might call "self-remembering," though she certainly did not use that term. Her conviction that attention to detail was not just an exercise but a state of mind that reflected the quality of your life. . .

TRICYCLE: And then, too, you did a series of operas with overt social themes.

PG: I did three operas about social change through nonviolence. It started with *Einstein on the Beach,* which I did with Bob Wilson, though at the time I didn't know what I was doing and would not have seen it that way. But with the next one, *Satyagraha* (in which Mahatma Gandhi was the main character), I was consciously thinking about a religious revolutionary. Again with Akhnaten and with his impact on the social order—in terms of the society as a whole or the individual in society. In my own work, those polarities went from *The Making of the Representative for Planet Eight* by Doris Lessing, which is about the transcendence of a whole society, to a personal hallucination such as [Edgar Allan] Poe's *The Fall of the House of Usher.* That's the range, and the concern reflects Buddhist practice.

TRICYCLE: How deliberately did that enter your music?

PG: At a certain point, I wanted the music to reflect my feelings of social responsibility. Take the image of the artist as someone cut off from society. We learn from dharma teachers that this separateness is an illusion, and things begin to shift—we begin to see ourselves as connected.

SOURCE: Philip Glass, Helen Tworkov, and Robert Coe, "First Lesson, Best Lesson," *Tricycle* Vol. 1 no. 2 (Winter 1991): 8–18. Also reprinted in *Writings on Glass: Essays, Interviews, Criticism,* ed. Richard Kostelanetz; assist. ed. Robert Flemming (Berkeley: University of California Press, 1997): 316–27.

~~~~~~~~~

NOTES

1. Arnold Aronson, *American Avant Garde Theater: A History* (New York: Routledge, 2000): 111.
2. *The Screens* by Jean Genet (1910–1986) is a five-hour-long play.
3. Claes Oldenburg (b. 1929) is a sculptor associated with pop art.
4. The term "theater of images" was coined by Barbara Marranca in *The Theater of Images* (New York: Drama Book Specialists, 1977): xii.

LAURIE ANDERSON DOES "STAND-UP" PERFORMANCE ART

(Anderson, Gordon)

Laurie Anderson (b. 1947) began her career in SoHo, a neighborhood south of Houston Street in Manhattan. As artists settled into what had been an industrial district in the late 1960s and early '70s, they turned derelict cast-iron buildings into galleries and lofts with performance spaces for installations and theater. They collaborated in experimental multimedia work. Even if Anderson parodied SoHo's solemnity about work in the satirical song "New York Social Life," she too produced some of her best work on its urban stage. She reached a new audience in 1981 when a song released as a single, "O Superman," made the pop charts in England.

Anderson's work combines several key trends of the 1970s and '80s, among them the exploration of new timbres and electronic technology. Inventing and playing the tape-bow violin and demonstrating theatrical as well as musical showmanship, Anderson also brought politically charged humor into her performance art. She took on big issues, including American foreign policy, sexuality, and gender relationships, in her own inimitable fashion.*

*In recognition of her "futurist" originality, NASA appointed Anderson as an artist-in-residence in 2004.

The first excerpt is Anderson's statement for an art magazine where she offers a surprising angle of vision for her work in her comments about the American comic Andy Kaufman (1949–1984). Best known for his surrealistic approach to stand-up comedy routines, Kaufman typically manipulated audience expectations about reality and theater, destabilizing his stage persona through elaborate subterfuges. In one routine from the late '70s, Kaufman anointed himself "Inter Gender Wrestling Champion of the World," and planted women in the audience who would agree to wrestle with him on stage. Anderson played that role. She turned her experiences with this unlikely muse into material for her own music. Since his death, Kaufman has occasionally been described as a postmodern performance artist, so perhaps it is not inappropriate to think of Anderson, in her early work, as a performance artist doing "stand-up" multimedia.

In the second selection, a theater historian and director astutely analyzes Anderson's work through the juxtapositions of opposites, providing a transcript of one of her performances, a part of which is reproduced here.

LAURIE ANDERSON'S STATEMENT ABOUT PERFORMANCE ART, 1980

[Laurie Anderson's words follow this opening statement by the editor of the article, Nancy Foote] At the end of the 1970s many artists are dissatisfied with the exclusive posture of the traditional avant-garde and seem to be seeking ways to extend the art audience without compromising their work. It could be argued that '70s, as distinct from '60s, art is characterized more by this change in attitude toward the audience than by a change in actual forms, or even content. The increase in the '70s of "project," performance, film and video art, all of which have their origins in the '60s, would seem to bear this out.

(1)   How has the artist's perception of his/her audience changed in the '70s?

(2)   What shifts in emphasis, esthetic and otherwise, have the impermanence and specificity of project and performance art brought about?

I asked a number of artists who seem to be exploring this territory to comment on these questions. Not all replied, but those who did offer some provocative, if conflicting, speculations.

•

When I began doing public performances, I tried to imagine that no one was there. I stared into the lights and talked to myself. My idea of the perfect performance was analogous to a bad movie. At a bad movie you notice the popcorn under your feet, the height of the armrests, placement of the exit signs, etc. throughout the film. At a good movie you fall away . . . and at the end it's a mild surprise to find yourself sitting there.

In performance I tried to emphasize the flat-footed local effect—the physical aspects of the room—by sending sound waves through the room so people in the audience could physically feel the space they displaced . . . so that space could exist (as for the blind) in back of the body as well as the visually informed front; also by using images of architecture that commented on the volume and scale of the room rather than competing with it. I suspect now that spatial aspects of my work evolved as much from doing it in museum/gallery '60s architecture space as from my own ideas about space.

My attempts to engineer "real space" turned out, however, to be diagrammatic. I was doing a performance in Berlin when I suddenly heard a loud "z-z-z-z-z." It didn't sound like feedback and I knew it wasn't on tape. I looked out at an angle and saw several rows of Germans, arms linked, swaying from side to side and singing along to the tape. I wasn't sure whether they were making fun of me or not. I never found out. But it was the first time I realized the audience was capable of changing the scale.

A few years ago I was in a night club and saw Andy Kaufman, the comedian, actually shrink a room. He seemed to understand space in a way I have never considered. He was an expert at letting the energy level in the room drop off disastrously—to the point where people suddenly become aware that they are part of a half-drunk clientele crowded in a room waiting to laugh. The walls start to close in.

I learned a lot about space from Andy. For a while I was straight/woman/audience plant for him. I was an angry women's libber and my job was to heckle him until he said, "Yeah, well, I'll only respect you when you come up here and wrestle me down." Andy never just pretended to wrestle. We used to go out to Coney Island and ride the Roto-Whirl—the cylinder that plasters you against the wall, stretching mouths into grotesque smiles, and then the bottom drops out. As soon as everybody is inside, the door is locked and about three minutes pass while the cylinder is checked. It was this time frame that Andy understood. The moment the door was locked he began to look panicked. "I don't think I want to be here. I don't think this ride is safe. Let me out. Get me out of here." Suddenly the other riders' mood changed, and they began to act like hijack victims. The bottom dropped out.

I have received and continue to receive psychological and intellectual support from the art world and believe that the structure and intentions of my work are best understood by other artists. However, in the past two years I have found myself doing as many things for nonart audiences as for art audiences. I don't change the work according to the audience. As a result, it is now possible for me to think of American art as something that can enter culture in other ways, unescorted by institutional art intermediaries. Radio, TV and a variety of spaces—old movie houses, rock clubs, bars, V.F.W.s and amphitheatres—have become more accessible to artists who work in live situations. Using these channels makes it possible as well as necessary continually to revise my ideas about the flexibility of space—physical, electronic, and psychological—and finally to learn to look at people. The art audience appears to be expanding and although I'm not *that* enthusiastic about going uptown to Ticketron to get tickets to something I used to just be able to go around the corner (at the last minute) to see, I think it's interesting that there's so much enthusiasm. It's hard to tell who's coming to these things, but I know that *something's* different because now I receive fan mail. Nobody used to ask me what my favorite color is, what I like for breakfast, what I do in my spare time. Strangely, a few of the letters appear to be form letters, with multiple-choice questions.

I'm also interested in wider audiences because it takes performance art out of slightly ingrown situations (twice a year for the same three hundred people) and because it pays better to do things sponsored by Schlitz than the Museum of Modern Art. Besides, I have only one year left of declaring business failure before the I.R.S. changes my category from "profession" to "hobby!"

SOURCE: Nancy Foote, ed., "Situation Esthetics: Impermanent Art and the Seventies Audience," *Artforum* (18/5 January 1980): 22–23.

〜〜〜〜〜

Mel Gordon's discussion of Anderson's techniques pierces the shell of Anderson's verbal games. His transcription of a performance, part of which is reprinted here, shows how skillfully she plays havoc with the conversational conventions of everyday life.

Since her first performance work in 1974, Laurie Anderson has found herself concerned with a basic esthetic dilemma that has troubled a number of other performance artists: how to create an intensely personal art that is not just simple autobiography. How can the performer/author bring raw, unmediated materials from his/her life and structure them to strike a balance between his/her own needs and those of the audience? For Anderson, the resolution is not only intellectual but technical; it is one that leads to a new performance style.

What Anderson calls a "system of pairing," of placing polar opposites side-by-side or before one another, of incorporating and transposing a kind of spiraling dialectic of styles and frames of reference pattern her productions like an electrical grid. Her performance methodologies revolve around a network of dualities: artist as person/character, language/sound, private/public activity, memory/fantasy, audio/visual space, male/female, nineteenth/twentieth century musical instrumentation, history/prophecy, filmic/live presentation.

Even Anderson's reception as a performance artist has a dual aspect to it. Despite the dense theatricality of her work, her support and renown seem to come almost exclusively from the art world, where she has an enthusiastic following. Although a *Life* magazine photo-essay (January 1980) described her as "a former teacher and critic, who may be the most popular performance artist," relatively few individuals in experimental theatre are aware of her work. Possibly, the difficulty in actually seeing Anderson's presentations—she normally performs only once or twice a year in New York, where she lives—and her tendency to mount her productions in art galleries and museums may also explain why she has been generally overlooked in theatre circles.

Born in 1947 and raised in northern Illinois, Laurie Anderson feels her early childhood may have had a lasting influence on her artistic thinking. One of eight children, she remembers a family ritual where everyone sat around the table telling stories about what happened to him that day. Amidst this mob scene, she quickly learned that the simple narration of interesting experiences did not always lead to interesting stories. Reports had to be tailored in places, expanded in others, points of view sometimes had to be altered, occasionally missing details or more dramatic conclusions had to be supplied. Besides stories, family members played musical instruments, composed private songs, did voice imitations. Anderson also discovered at this time, like may tellers of yarns, that one often forgets what reportage is factual and what is invented. This sometimes leads to a certain artistic confusion or complexity. (For example, during a piece she presented at the Whitney Museum in 1976, where she related a personal story, her father was heard relating another version of it in the audience.)

During the 1960s, Anderson studied at Barnard College where she graduated with honors in art history. Later she took a master's degree at Columbia in sculpture and began teaching

"Principles of Art History," which she subtitled "Skrooples," at City College in New York. Both in and out of the classroom, Anderson found herself fascinated with the perceptual contrasts of words—whether handwritten, printed, or spoken—and visual imagery. The notion of students filling notebooks in the colored light of projected slide transparencies while she lectured struck Anderson as a bizarre esthetic relationship.

It was just at this time, around 1972, that Anderson's interest in paper sculpture and in art generally began to fade. Instead, she turned to writing, a kind of conceptual writing that consisted of one-sentence books, diary entries, even a dream series that resulted from the mixing of daydreams, memories, real dreams, and paintings that were projected on the screen during an art history class.

During the summer of 1972, Anderson and a friend organized a performance event in a small Vermont town. Every Sunday evening, residents of Rochester would drive up to their park in automobiles, trucks, and motorcycles to hear music played by a local band. Without ever leaving their car seats, the spectators would sit and honk their horns to show approval at the end of each section. Enthralled by the naiveté and sophistication of the situation, Anderson managed to reverse the audience/entertainer relationship by forming an orchestra of the same vehicles. This time the people in the driver's seats made the music with their horns and spectators sat in the park's gazebo.

Laurie Anderson's first major performance piece, *As: If,* was mounted at the Artists Space in Soho in 1974. Encouraged by Vito Acconci, she attempted to structurally blend different personal stories with oversized projections of words. On one side of the screen was a word concerned with language, and on the other, separated by a colon, was a word related to water. (For example, "SOUND:DROWN.") The slides were used as a subtext to both highlight and diagram the narration.

In the summers of 1974 and 1975, Anderson performed *Duets on Ice* in various outdoor locations in New York City. Standing on ice skates, whose blades were embedded in blocks of ice, she played a violin that contained a built-in speaker. Wired to a hidden tape recorder, the violin could produce prerecorded sound as well as live music. In this way, Anderson was able to perform a duet with herself.

More than a simple Dada-type escapade, *Duets on Ice* revealed a number of central features in Anderson's ethos—notably a deep concern with performance time and objects. Possibly influenced by her storytelling and teaching experiences, Anderson tries to keep the length of her performances within set limits, usually less than 60 or 75 minutes. In *Duets on Ice,* the melting of the ice regulated the performance time in an obvious, graphic fashion.

For Anderson, certain personal objects play a significant part in the production. Unlike standard stage props, these special items, or what Anderson calls "dense objects," signify a whole range of private memories or emotions, while remaining entirely functional to the piece. The ice and the skates take on personal and metaphysical expressions of time passing, of internal and outer balance, of musical and anatomical rhythms. Of all the "dense objects" in Anderson's repertoire, none is so readily associated with her as the violin. Used as an instrument, a partner, a piece of machinery, a screen, a weapon, the violin and bow (or symbolically, wood and horsehair) have undergone dozens of technical incarnations in Anderson's work. Sometimes electrified, at other times played naturally, Anderson's most innovative violin-creation has consisted of an instrument whose strings have been replaced with an audio head from a tape-recorder and whose horsehair on the bow has been replaced with recording tape. This "tape-bow violin" can create a sound-speech that has never existed before. As the bow is passed across the audio bridge, a totally reversible music-language is heard: "no" on the up-bow becomes "one," on the down-bow, "yes" becomes "say." All a demonstration of the liquid nature of language.

. . .

Laurie Anderson's longest and most complex piece, *Americans on the Move*, was presented at the Carnegie Recital Hall and at The Kitchen in the spring of 1979.

LIFE IN LOS ANGELES FROM AMERICANS ON THE MOVE: PARTS 1 & 2 BY LAURIE ANDERSON

(This text was compiled from Anderson's notes and a transcription made from a recording of her performance at The Kitchen in New York in April 1979.)

ANDERSON: *Facing the audience, she speaks in a sincere, presentational voice. Behind her is a crude outline of the U.S. projected on a screen.* A certain American sect has been looking at conditions of the world during the Flood. According to their calculations, during the Flood, the winds, tides, and currents were in an overall southeasterly direction. [*Purple arrows appear.*] This would then mean that in order for the Ark to have landed on Mt. Ararat it would had to have started several thousand miles to the west. [*A red arrow leaves map on right, and the projection of the arrow advances left.*] This would then locate pre-Flood history in Upstate New York, and the Garden of Eden somewhere, roughly, in Genesee County. [*Red arrow projection points on map.*] Now in order to get from one place to another, something must move, so the question here is . . . did we move or did the Ark move? [*Red arrows move in a circular direction away from each other.*] Now no one here remembers moving, and there are no traces of Biblical history in this area, so we are led to the only available conclusion in this time warp . . . and that is: The Ark has simply not left yet.

Let's compare this situation to a familiar occurrence: You're driving alone [*hypnotically*] at night on a dark road and it's raining and you can't see where you're going. . . . you took a turn back there, but you're not sure it was a right turn, but you took the turn and just kept going that way and eventually it starts to get [*She waves a violin bow like a windshield wiper. When flagged quickly enough, the bow reflects projected images like a screen.*] light and you look out and you realize you have absolutely no idea where you are. You're not even sure whether you've been driving all night over a great distance . . . or whether you only went a few feet and just forgot where you started from. So you get out at the next gas station and you say . . .

Hello excuse me can you tell me where I am?

[*In a slow, distorted voice that is electronically dropped one octave.*] You can read the signs. [*Word "rut" projected on bow-screen.*] You've been on this road before. [*Word "route."*] Do you want to go home? Do you want to go home now? [*Normal voice.*] Hello excuse me, can you tell me where I am? [*With each "hello" an image of a waving hand is projected.*]

[*Distorted voice.*] You can read this sign language. In our country, goodbye looks just like hello. Say hello.

[*Normal voice.*] Hello, excuse me, can you tell me where I am?

[*Distorted voice.*] In our country, this is the way we say hello. It is a diagram of movement between two points. It is shorthand for you were here last night, but when I woke up in the morning you were gone. In our country, goodbye looks just like hello. Say hello.

[*Normal voice.*] Hello, excuse me, can you tell me where I am?

[*Distorted voice.*] In our country, sometimes you don't know when you've really arrived. You don't even know if you've left yet. In our country, this is the way we say hello. It is a diagram of movement between two points. It is a sweep on the dial. In our country, goodbye looks just like hello. Say hello.

[*Normal voice.*] Hello, excuse me, can you tell me where I am?

[*Distorted voice.*] In our country, we send pictures of people speaking our sign language into outer space. [*Diagram of a man and a woman from Pioneer 11 image is projected onto bow.*] We are speaking our sign language in these pictures. Do you think his arm is permanently attached in this position? [*Negative image.*] Or do you think they will read our signs? In our country, goodbye looks just like hello. Say hello. Say hello. [*Positive image again.*]

Sounds of highway traffic. Her humming merges with that sound.

[*Provocatively.*] Say, you're an American aren't you? I can tell by the way you move that you're an American.

Slides of columns are projected on screen; these are synchronized with the bow movements of the violin. Sounds of water, traffic, birds, airplanes, and ship horns are heard in succession. A film of trees is projected on the slides of columns. Tree film dims.

Strumming a violin like a ukulele and entoning in a warbled, mad way like an Apache, she sing-speaks the following:

Well, I saw a lot of trees today, and they were all made of wood. They were wooden trees, and they were made entirely of wood.

Well, I came home today, and you were all on fire—your shirt was on fire, and your hair was on fire, and flames were licking all around your feet. . . . And I did not know what to do. . . . And then a thousand violins began to play, and I really did not know what to do then. So I just decided to go out, and walk the . . . dog.

Well, I went to the movies, and I saw a dog 30 feet high. And this dog was made entirely of light. And he filled up the whole screen. And his eyes were long hallways. He had those long echoing hallway eyes. . . .

Well, I turned on the radio and I head a song by Dolly Parton, and she was singing [*in sarcastic, garbled voice*] "Oh! I feel so sad, I feel so bad . . . I left my mom and I left my dad . . . and I just want to go back home now . . . I just want to go back up to my Tennessee mountain home. . . . " Well, you know she's not gonna go back home. . . . I know she's not gonna go back home . . . and she knows she's never gonna go back there . . . and I just want to know who's gonna walk *that* dog.

Well, I feel so sad, I feel so bad . . . but not as bad as the night I wrote this song.

[*Satirical, commercial voice.*] Close your eyes. Okay. Now imagine you're at the most wonderful party. Okay. Great people, mmm. Delicious food, mmm.

Terrific music, mmm. Now open them! Oh no! I just want to go back home now. I just want to go back home and walk the dog.
Red light. Violin-ukulele is played at reduced level.

SOURCE: Mel Gordon, "Laurie Anderson: Performance Artist," *The Drama Review* (June 1980): 51–53, 54–56.

MEREDITH MONK AND THE

REVELATION OF VOICE

The composer and multimedia artist Meredith Monk (b. 1942), has roots in the avant-garde New York scene of the 1960s and '70s. Although she resists the term "minimalism" as a label for her compositions, she employs its techniques of harmonic repetition and evolving ostinati as the foundation for her expanded vocal techniques. Monk explores the voice as a kind of body language through which to explore sonic freedom, and her work takes an artistic stance which appealed to a number of women composing music in the 1970s, including Pauline Oliveros, Joan La Barbara, and Laurie Anderson.

This chapter begins with excerpts from interviews. Monk's own mission statement is then supplemented by excerpts from her notes on *Atlas: An Opera in Three Parts for 18 Voices and Large Ensemble* (1991), her most important work to date.

One day in 1965, while sitting at the piano, I had a revelation. I realized that the voice could be as fluid as the spine, that it could have the flexibility and range of the body. And that I could work with my voice to develop my own instrument and my own vocabulary, just as I might do choreography for my body. That same day I realized that the voice has all these characters and landscapes within it—and in a flash I saw where I would go from that point on.

SOURCE: Uncited interview in K. Robert Schwarz, *Minimalists* (London: Phaidon, 1996): 189.

~~~~~~~

I come from a folk music tradition. I was a folk singer with a guitar. The repetition in my music I think of as being like folk music: you have your chorus and verse. I'm more interested in how the voice digs down into emotional reality. It's like the freedom of a jazz singer, it's not a patterning impulse. The minimalist thing is about reduction. Vocally, I have always thought about magnification, expansion. The repetitions are just a layer for the voice to take off from and go somewhere, and also to land on again.

SOURCE: Interview with Kyle Gann, September 21, 1996, as quoted in Kyle Gann, *American Music in the Twentieth Century* (New York: Schirmer, 1997): 209.

~~~~~~~

MISSION STATEMENT, 1983, REVISED 1996

MY GOALS

To create an art that breaks down boundaries between the disciplines, an art which in turn becomes a metaphor for opening up thought, perception, experience.

An art that is inclusive, rather than exclusive; that is expansive, whole, human, multidimensional.

An art that cleanses the senses, that offers insight, feeling, magic. That allows the public to perhaps see familiar things in a new, fresh way—that gives them the possibility of feeling more alive.

An art that seeks to reestablish the unity existing between music, theater, and dance—the wholeness that is found in cultures where performing arts practice is considered a spiritual discipline with healing and transformative power.

An art that reaches toward emotion we have no words for, that we barely remember—an art that affirms the world of feeling in a time and society where feelings are in danger of being eliminated.

SOURCE: Meredith Monk, "Mission Statement, 1983, Revised 1996," in *Meredith Monk*, ed. Deborah Jowitt (Baltimore, Md.: Johns Hopkins University Press, 1997): 17.

141

RECAPTURING THE SOUL OF

THE AMERICAN ORCHESTRA

(Duffy, Tower)

In the 1970s and '80s, composers, musicians, conductors, teachers, critics—in short, the classical-music community—frequently expressed concern that their world was falling apart. They believed that they were living through a period of cultural atrophy, many finger-pointing the stagnant repertoire of American symphony orchestras. Neither American orchestral players nor their audiences associated the institution of the orchestra with living composers. The more that symphony orchestras programmed primarily old European music, the more they left contemporary composers in limbo, shutting them out of opportunities for indispensable practical experience.

As the program director of an early outreach organization in New York called Meet the Composer, John Duffy (b. 1926) helped to found and to lead the Orchestra Residencies Program, which was designed to "recapture the soul of the American orchestra." The program selected individual American composers to live with a particular orchestra, so to speak, by moving to its community, getting to know its players, and writing an orchestral work which it would premiere. Over the next ten years, the CRP amassed an impressive track record and in its wake came many vital and important new symphonic compositions. Among the participant composers were John Adams, John Corigliano, David Del Tredici, Aaron J. Kernis, and Joan Tower.

JOHN DUFFY ON THE
ORCHESTRA RESIDENCIES PROGRAM

The Orchestra Residencies Program began with people bonding together in the belief that we could heal the breach between American composers, American orchestras, and symphony audiences. This noble goal was blessed by an exceptional spirit of cooperation that fueled our energies for nearly two years as our efforts took shape. When the Program was officially launched, our collaborative accord caught fire; it swept over inertia and mistrust as it advanced living music—embodied in our pioneer composers—as the means to recapture the soul of the American orchestra.

With the variables each residency involved—the intricate coordination, divergent opinions, human frailties—it was natural that each mirrored the teamwork and dynamism of the program's genesis. Composer, music director, musicians, orchestra board, staff, funders—all were called upon to examine their pasts, envision their futures, and rethink their relationships to the music of our time. Each residency was handcrafted with such commitment; each was a labor of love. "Our Composer in Residence," was proudly said by musicians, volunteers, board members, and orchestra staff. The resident composers, as musical evangelists and public servants, reached out to everyone from fifth graders to corporate executives, from nurses and firefighters to poets, from debutantes to college professors. They created extraordinary opportunities for other composers where none had existed before. Dedicated to the art and craft of composition, they spoke eloquently with their music. Without any narrow sense of entitlement, they claimed their birthright as America's twentieth-century composers. They are why the program succeeded.

Equally crucial was the participation of the funding community, whose members contributed so much more than money. Full of grit and vision, they asked tough questions, gave honest opinions, and spent generously of their own inspiration and integrity. The Program would not have begun in 1982 without Howard Klein at The Rockefeller Foundation, Leonard Fleischer at Exxon, and Ezra Laderman at the National Endowment for the Arts. Their model leadership was emulated and surpassed by those who followed: Alberta Arthurs at the Rockefeller Foundation; Barbara Barclay at the William and Flora Hewlett Foundation; Marian Godfrey at The Pew Charitable Trusts; Antoinette Handy at the National Endowment for the Arts; Gayle Morgan at the Mary Flagler Cary Charitable Trust; Carlos Moseley at the Eleanor Naylor Dana Charitable Trust; and Arlene Shuler, formerly of the Lila Wallace-Reader's Digest Fund. I deeply thank them all.

Twelve years ago, it seemed the symphony world had largely forgotten that music that was written by living composers. Now we look to the number of residencies, commissions, performances, recordings, and premieres, and see how this has changed. Hearts and minds sprung open in appreciation and respect as living composers returned to the concert hall. The creative, humanistic spirit returned home to the heart of the orchestra where it belonged. This is the remarkable accomplishment of the past ten years. And now a new day dawns. There is no turning back.

SOURCE: John Duffy, "Preface," in *Meet the Composers' Residency Program, 1982–92,* ed. Theodore Wiprud and Joyce Lawler (New York: Meet the Composer, 1995).

~~~~~~~~

A founding member in 1969 and pianist in the Da Capo Chamber Players, Joan Tower (b. 1938) left the group in 1984, joined the faculty at Bard College, and focused mainly on composing rather than performing. At that point in her career, Tower had composed mainly chamber music. In this selection, Tower recounts the benefits of her experience as a composer-in-residence with the St. Louis Symphony Orchestra, 1985–1988. The orchestral piece Silver Ladders, *which she wrote during her residency, won the prestigious Grawemeyer Award in 1990 and has been recorded by the St. Louis Orchestra.* Silver Ladders *has since become one of her best-known works, and Tower has continued to write fine symphonic music.*

MOVING IN WITH THE ORCHESTRA:
JOAN TOWER, COMPOSER-IN-RESIDENCE,
SAINT LOUIS SYMPHONY ORCHESTRA, 1985–1987

Bringing a new piece of music to life is most productive and exciting in a serious, creative, and friendly environment. The symphonic world needs to improve on the last of these qualities. Pre-hearing resistance to new compositions still runs deep in both the audience and the orchestra. I recently asked a pre-concert audience of around 1500 people how many of them expected to dislike my piece, and about 90 percent of the hands went up. I then asked how many thought that was unfair. The same hands went up! With orchestra players, it's a little better, but not much. Most orchestra players avoid you, at least at first, and privately complain either about the way the parts are copied, or about the idiomatic (or less than idiomatic) nature of the writing. Occasionally they might even tell you directly. For the longest time I blamed myself or my piece. I have learned to wait for them to get to know my piece in the event that they may grow to like it and play it with more intensity, and to take the initiative at being friendly.

Until Leonard Slatkin asked me to become composer in residence with the Saint Louis Symphony, I had been almost exclusively involved in chamber music, where there is more time to prepare, to digest a piece and try out changes in the score. Interacting with the composer is a much less pressurized process, therefore a more creative and less mechanical one. I am still adjusting to the orchestra's approach. One thing I have learned is to stay away from the first rehearsal—too painful.

Because of the economics of the symphonic world, bringing a new piece of music to life is a fast process. Time to digest and live with a new piece is very short. Changes can be made

Meet the Composer Residency Project: The Residency Composers at Midpoint, 1986–1987.
From left, back row: John Harbison, Charles Wuorinen, John Adams, Christopher Rouse, Alvin Singleton.
Middle row: Jacob Druckman, Joan Tower, William Kraft, Libby Larsen, Robert Xavier Rodriguez, Tobias Picker.
Front row: Stephen Paulus, Joseph Schwantner, Stephen Albert.

only on the cosmetic level of dynamics and articulation, resulting in enormous pressure for the composer to produce a "perfect" blueprint in the notated score. Corrections take up too much precious time, and the composer is put in the precarious position of making fast changes that may backfire. Should he or she wait for the orchestra to adjust balances and dynamics, or immediately make a change that may be wrong? I remember sitting next to a player during a rehearsal of Brahms' Symphony No. 1, and asking him why he wasn't playing the dynamics indicated. He replied rather angrily that if he played the dynamics on the page, he would be totally out of balance with the rest of our orchestra. "Now you might understand and sympathize with some of our problems," I replied.

As a composer, you are often considered an outsider by the orchestra. Composers have the "authority" to tell the conductor and the players what to do. Soloists, as fellow players, are treated more as colleagues, but composers are viewed as more like management. This can be a major problem for some conductors and even more for many soloists, and may be one of the reasons some of them never play the music of our time. I once asked Radu Lupu whether he ever played the music of a live composer. "I did once," he said, "but he died." I remember one famous conductor asking me seven times in a rehearsal whether his *tempi* were right, and all seven times I said they were either a little too fast or a little too slow. To me and to him, it was a simple discussion. But to several players in the orchestra, who later spoke to me in private, we were having a *major* confrontation. They congratulated me on "standing my ground."[1]

Most of what I have said here applies less to my experiences in Saint Louis. I grew to love that orchestra. They have integrity and are willing to work to make music as best they can. I tried hard to become a colleague: I played piano with them, I conducted, I gave dinners, I took a tour bus ride with them, drank at the bars, and told jokes. They treated me very well after a while, and we did a lot of wonderful things together, things I will always treasure. I remember one performance that made me feel particularly close to them: we were on a West Coast tour and they performed my *Silver Ladders* on the last concert in San Francisco. It was their twelfth performance of the piece, and a loving and beautiful one. Leonard [Slatkin] had developed an overall pacing that gave the piece a strong continuity, and the orchestra was in great shape that night. All the balances, phrasing, and articulations were there. Tears were rolling down my cheeks. We had made music together. It felt almost as though I was back in my chamber group.

SOURCE: Joan Tower, "Moving in with the Orchestra," in *Meet the Composers' Residency Program, 1982–92*, ed. Theodore Wiprud and Joyce Lawler (New York: Meet the Composer, 1995): 13.

~~~~~~~~~

NOTE

1.   In an e-mail communication from Tower to the editor, October 5, 2006, the composer added the name of the conductor and orchestra described here: Zubin Mehta and the New York Philharmonic. She also notes today that conductors' "fear of programming new works stems from the fact that they have to stand alone with their musical choices of new pieces and that is a musical risk that most conductors and soloists are not always willing to take."

142

Two Economists Measure
the Impact of Blind Auditions

Equal access to professional opportunities was an important objective of the civil rights movements for women and minorities during the 1960s and 1970s. Along with new laws came the threat of litigation against performing institutions through allegations of gender bias in their practices. New goals included democratizing not only avenues for professional recognition, which affected composers above all (hence the new societies for "women composers"), but also job opportunities for performers in classical music. The practice of holding "blind auditions" for prestigious jobs in orchestras slowly became the rule rather than the exception during the 1970s and '80s. Such practices provided economists Claudia Goldin and Cecilia Rouse with what they describe as the opportunity to "test for sex-biased hiring." The excerpts here are from a much longer study presenting their key data and conclusions.

FROM "ORCHESTRATING IMPARTIALITY: THE IMPACT OF 'BLIND' AUDITIONS ON FEMALE MUSICIANS"

Until recently, the great symphony orchestras in the United States consisted of members who were largely handpicked by the music director. Although virtually all had auditioned for the position, most of the contenders would have been the (male) students of a select group of teachers. In an attempt to overcome this seeming bias in the hiring of musicians, most major U.S. orchestras changed their audition policies in the 1970's and 1980's making them more open and routinized. Openings became widely advertised in the union papers, and many positions attracted more than 100 applicants where fewer than 20 would have been considered before. Audition committees were restructured to consist of members of the orchestra, not just the conductor and section principal. The audition procedure became democratized at a time when many other institutions in America did as well.

But democratization did not guarantee impartiality, because favorites could still be identified by sight and through resumes. Another set of procedures was adopted to ensure, or at least give the impression of, impartiality. These procedures involve hiding the identity of the player from the jury. Although they take several forms, we use the terms "blind" and "screen" to describe the group.* The question we pose is whether the hiring process became more impartial through the use of blind auditions. Because we are able to identify sex, but no other characteristics for a large sample, we focus on the impact of the screen on the employment of women.**

Screens were not adopted by all orchestras at once. Among the major orchestras, one still does not have any blind round to their audition procedure (Cleveland) and one adopted the screen in 1952 for the preliminary round (Boston Symphony Orchestra), decades before the others. Most other orchestras shifted to blind preliminaries from the early 1970's to the late 1980's. The variation in screen adoption at various rounds in the audition process allows us to assess its use as a treatment.***

The change in audition procedures with the adoption of the screen allows us to test whether bias exists in its absence. In both our study and studies using audits, the issue is whether sex (or race or ethnicity), apart from objective criteria (e.g., the sound of a musical performance, the content of a resume), is considered in the hiring process. Why sex might make a difference is another matter.

Our data come from two sources: rosters and audition records. Rosters are simply lists of orchestra personnel, together with instrument and position (e.g., principal), found in orchestra programs. The audition records are the actual accounts of the hiring process kept by the personnel manager of the orchestra. Both are described in more detail below.

*For an article about the blind audition process see *The Economist* (1996).

**The screen may also have opened opportunities for individuals from less well-known orchestras, those trained outside mainstream institutions, and those from minority groups.

***The blind audition procedures bear some resemblance to "double-blind" refereeing in academic journals. See Rebecca Blank (1991) for an assessment of the treatment effect of such refereeing in the *American Economic Review*.

The audition records we have collected form an uncommon data set. Our sample includes who was advanced and hired from an initial group of contestants and also what happened to approximately two-thirds of the individuals in our data set who competed in other auditions in the sample. There are, to be certain, various data sets containing information on applicant pools and hiring practices. . . .* But our data set is unique because it has the complete applicant pool for each of the auditions and links individuals across auditions. Most important for our study is that audition procedures differed across orchestras in known ways and that the majority of the orchestras in our sample changed [their] audition procedure during the period of study.**

We find, using our audition sample in an individual fixed-effects framework, that the screen increases the probability that a woman will be advanced out of a preliminary round when there is no semifinal round. The screen also greatly enhances the likelihood that a female contestant will be the winner in a final round. Using both the roster and audition samples, and reasonable assumptions, the switch to blind auditions can explain about one-third of the increase in the proportion [of] female[s] among new hires (whereas another one-third is the result of the increased pool of female candidates). Estimates based on the roster sample indicate that blind auditions may account for 25 percent of the increase in the percentage of orchestra musicians who are female.

I. SEX COMPOSITION OF ORCHESTRAS

Symphony orchestras consist of about 100 musicians and, although the number has varied between 90 [and] 105, it is rarely lower or higher. The positions, moreover, are nearly identical between orchestras and over time. As opposed to firms, symphony orchestras do not vary much in size and have virtually identical numbers and types of jobs. Thus we can easily look at the proportion [of] women in an orchestra without being concerned about changes in the composition of occupations and the number of workers. An increase in the number of women from, say 1 to 10, cannot arise because the number of harpists (a female-dominated instrument), has greatly expanded. It must be because the proportion [of] female[s] within many groups has increased.

Among the five highest-ranked orchestras in the nation (known as the "Big Five")—the Boston Symphony Orchestra (BSO), the Chicago Symphony Orchestra, the Cleveland Symphony Orchestra, the New York Philharmonic (NYPhil), and the Philadelphia Orchestra—none contained more than 12 percent women until about 1980.*** As can be seen in Figure 1A, each of the five lines (giving the proportion [of] female[s]) greatly increases after some point. For the NYPhil, the line steeply ascends in the early 1970's. For the BSO, the turning point appears to be a bit earlier. The percentage [of] female[s] in the NYPhil is currently 35 percent, the highest among all 11 orchestras in our sample after being the lowest (generally at zero) for decades. Thus the increase of women in the nation's finest orchestras has been extraordinary. The increase is even more remarkable because, as we discuss below, turnover in these orchestras is exceedingly low. The proportion of new players who were women must have been, and indeed was, exceedingly high.

*Harry Holzer and David Neumark, 1996.

**This statement is true for the roster sample. There are only a few orchestras that changed audition procedures during the years of our audition data.

***The date referred to, and used in Figures 1 to 3, are from orchestral rosters, described in more detail below.

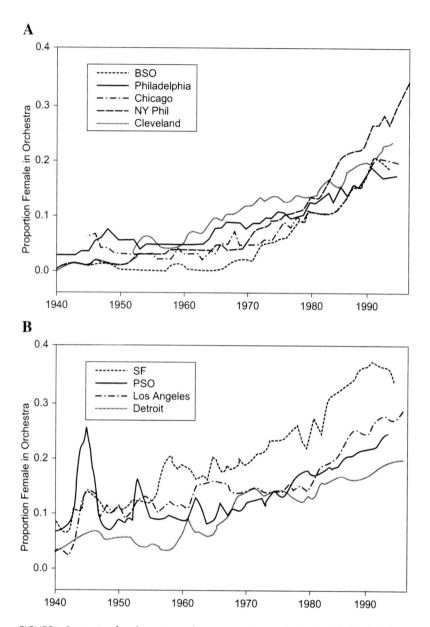

FIGURE 1 Proportion female in nine orchestras, 1940 to 1990's. A: The "Big Five"; B: Four others. *Source:* Roster sample. See text.

Similar trends can be discerned for four other orchestras—the Los Angeles Symphony Orchestra (LA), the San Francisco Philharmonic (SF), the Detroit Symphony Orchestra, and the Pittsburgh Symphony Orchestra (PSO)—given in Figure 1B.* The upward trend in the proportion [of] female[s] is also obvious in Figure 1B, although initial levels are higher than in Figure 1A.

*Our roster sample also includes the Metropolitan Opera Orchestra and the St. Louis Symphony.

There is somewhat more choppiness to the graph, particularly during the 1940's. Although we have tried to eliminate all substitute, temporary, and guest musicians, especially during World War II and the Korean War, this was not always possible.

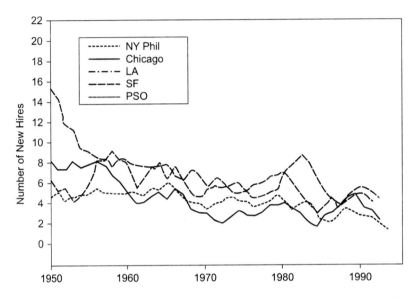

FIGURE 2 Number of new hires in five orchestras, 1950 to 1990's. *Source:* Roster sample. See text.

The only way to increase the proportion [of] women is to hire more female musicians and turnover during most periods was low. The number of new hires is graphed in Figure 2 for five orchestras. Because "new hires" is a volatile construct, we use a centered five-year moving average. In most years after the late 1950's, the top-ranked orchestras in the group (Chicago and NYPhil) hired about four musicians a year, whereas the other three hired about six. Prior to 1960 the numbers are extremely high for LA and the PSO, because, it has been claimed, their music directors exercised their power to terminate, at will, the employment of musicians. Also of interest is that the number of new hires trends down, even excluding years prior to 1960. The important points to take from Figure 2 are that the number of new hires was small after 1960 and that it declined over time.

The proportion [of] female[s] among the new hires must have been sizable to increase the proportion [of] female[s] in the orchestras. Figure 3 shows the trend in the share of women among new hires for four of the "Big Five" (Figure 3A) and four other orchestras (Figure 3B).* In both groups the female share of new hires rose over time, at a somewhat steeper rate for the more prestigious orchestras. Since the early 1980's the share [of] female[s] among new hires has been about 35 percent for the BSO and Chicago, and about 50 percent for the NYPhil, whereas before 1970 less than 10 percent of new hires were women.**

*A centered five-year moving average is also used for this variable.

**In virtually all cases the share of women among new hires has decreased in the 1990's.

A

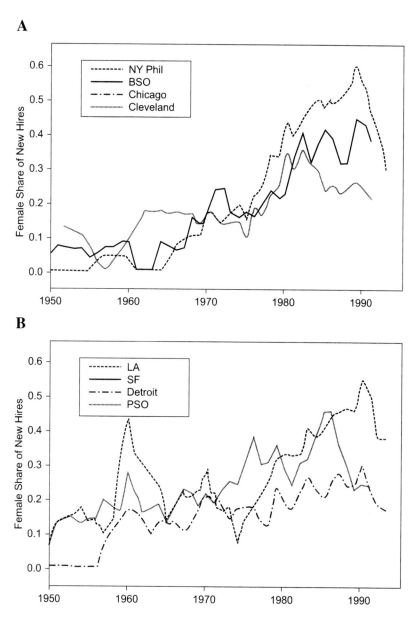

FIGURE 3 Female share of new hires in eight orchestras, 1950 to 1990's. A: Four of the "Big Five"; B: Four others. *Source:* Roster sample. See text.

But why would changes in audition procedures alter the sex mix of those hired? Many of the most renowned conductors have, at one time or another, asserted that female musicians are not the equal of male musicians. Claims abound in the world of music that "women have smaller techniques than men," "are more temperamental and more likely to demand special attention or treatment," and that "the more women [in an orchestra], the poorer the sound."*

*Seltzer (1989), p. 215

Zubin Mehta, conductor of the Los Angeles Symphony from 1964 to 1978 and of the New York Philharmonic from 1978 to 1990, is credited with saying, "I just don't think women should be in an orchestra."* Many European orchestras had, and some continue to have, stated policies not to hire women. The Vienna Philharmonic has only recently admitted its first female member (a harpist).** Female musicians, it can be convincingly argued, have historically faced considerable discrimination.*** Thus a blind hiring procedure, such as a screen that conceals the identity of the musician auditioning, could eliminate the possibility of discrimination and increase the number of women in orchestras.

. . .

IV. CONCLUSION

The audition procedures of the great U.S. symphony orchestras began to change sometime in the 1970's. The changes included increasing the number of candidates at auditions—a democratization of the process—and using a physical screen during the audition to conceal the candidate's identity and ensure impartiality. We analyze what difference blind auditions have meant for female musicians.

We have collected, from orchestral management files and archives, a sample of auditions for eight major orchestras. These records contain the names of all candidates and identify those advanced to the next round, including the ultimate winner of the competition. The data provide a unique means of testing whether discrimination existed in the various rounds of a hiring process and even allow the linkage of individuals across auditions. A strong presumption exists that discrimination has limited the employment of female musicians, especially by the great symphony orchestras. Not only were their numbers extremely low until the 1970's, but many music directors, ultimately in charge of hiring new musicians, publicly disclosed their belief that female players had lower musical talent.

The question is whether hard evidence can support an impact of discrimination on hiring. Our analysis of the audition and roster data indicates that it can, although we mention various caveats before we summarize the reasons. Even though our sample size is large, we identify the coefficients of interest from a much smaller sample. Some of our coefficients of interest, therefore, do not pass standard tests of statistical significance and there is, in addition, one persistent result that goes in the opposite direction. The weight of the evidence, however, is what we find most persuasive and what we have emphasized. The point estimates, moreover, are almost all economically significant.

*Seltzer (1989), p. 215. According to Seltzer, the fact that new hires at the NYPhil were about 45 percent female during Mehta's tenure as conductor suggests that Mehta's views may have changed.

**In comparison with the United Kingdom and the two Germanys, the United States in 1990 had the highest percentage female among its regional symphony orchestras and was a close second to the United Kingdom in the major orchestras category. (Jutta J. Allmendinger et al., 1996).

***In addition, an African-American cellist (Earl Madison) brought a civil suit against the NYPhil in 1968 alleging that their audition procedures were discriminatory because they did not use a screen. The orchestra was found not guilty of discriminating in hiring permanent musicians, but it was found to discriminate in the hiring of substitutes.

Using the audition data, we find that the screen increases—by 50 percent—the probability that a woman will be advanced from certain preliminary rounds and increases by several-fold the likelihood that a woman will be selected in the final round. By the use of the roster data, the switch to blind auditions can explain 30 percent of the increase in the proportion female[s] among new hires and possibly 25 percent of the increase in the percentage [of] female[s] in the orchestras from 1970 to 1996.* As in research in economics and other fields on double-blind refereeing . . . , the impact of a blind procedure is toward impartiality and the costs to the journal (here to the orchestra) are relatively small. We conclude that the adoption of the screen and blind auditions served to help female musicians in their quest for orchestral positions.

SOURCE: Claudia Goldin and Cecilia Rouse, "Orchestrating Impartiality: The Impact of 'Blind' Auditions on Female Musicians," *American Economic Review* 90, no. 4 (September 2000): 715–41; excerpts on 715–20, 737–38; nn. 9, 12, 13, 57.

~~~~~~~~~~~

REFERENCES CITED IN THESE EXCERPTS

Allmendinger, Jutta and Hackman, J. Richard and Lehman, Erin V. "Life and Work in Symphony Orchestras." *Music[al] Quarterly,* Summer 1996, 80/2, pp. 194–219.

Blank, Rebecca. "The Effects of Double-Blind versus Single-Blind Refereeing: Experimental Evidence from the *American Economic Review.*" *American Economic Review.* December 1991, 81/5, pp. 1041–67.

Economist, The. "'American Orchestras' All Ears." (November 30, 1996).

Holzer, Harry and Neumark, David. "Are Affirmative Action Hires Less Qualified? Evidence from Employer-Employee Data on New Hires," National Bureau of Economic Research (Cambridge, MA) Working Paper No. 5603, June 1996.

Seltzer, George. *Music Matters: The Performer and the American Federation of Musicians.* Metuchen, NJ: Scarecrow Press, 1989.

*The [percentage] point estimate for the increased likelihood [that] a woman would be a new hire, as a result of the adoption of blind auditions, is 7.5 percentage points using the roster data. . . Because the percentage [of] female[s] among new hires increased from 10 to 35 percent from before 1970 to the 1990's, our estimate implies that 30 percent of the 25 percentage-point increase can be explained by the adoption of the screen. How this increase affected the percentage [of] female[s] in the orchestra depends on the sex composition of the orchestra, retirement (or turnover), and the time frame. We assume a 25-year time frame (from 1970 to 1995) and two retirements (thus two hires) per year. An increase in the percentage [of] female[s] among new hires from 10 percent (its level pre-1970) to 17.5 percent (10 + 7.5%) implies that in 25 years, 13.75 women (out of 100) will be in the orchestra, or an increase of 3.75. The actual increase was 15 women, meaning 25 percent of the increase can be explained by the adoption of the screen. We assume in this example that the age distribution of the 100 players in 1970 is uniform between ages 25 and 74, that all hires occur at age 25, and that men and women are drawn from the same age distribution.

JOHN HARBISON ON MODES OF COMPOSING

Both the music and writings of the Boston-based composer John Harbison (b. 1938) reflect a strong sense of tradition. He has contributed important works to the mainstream acoustic genres of oratorio, chamber music, and symphonic works. As an American composer, he acknowledges both Bach and jazz as important guideposts for his own idiom. One of his most memorable works, the opera *The Great Gatsby* (1999) is infused with sophisticated transformations of popular music from the 1920s within a rich contrapuntal fabric.

In the summer of 1984, as composer-in-residence at the Boston Symphony Orchestra's Berkshire Music Center, Harbison addressed the young composers of the Tanglewood Music Center. The two lectures reprinted below deal with two aspects of his historicist[1] orientation, the first dealing with classical music, the second with popular song. Harbison's discussion of "personality" among composers recalls Aaron Copland's comments about Stravinsky in chapter 93. In the first lecture, Harbison supplemented this written text with recordings of music by John Adams, Peter Maxwell Davies, Roger Sessions, Michael Tippett, and Yehudi Wyner.

LECTURE 1. HISTORY

Recent research with songbirds has shown that when they are raised from infancy away from other birds they make only a weak semblance of their song, without fantasy, variety, or confidence. But when they are placed among other mature singers they develop their own individualities, progressing from imitation to subtle but intense variants of the *ur-song* [basic song] of their species variants too subtle for *our* species to detect without long training.

The story of the songbirds meant something to me, though I do not know whether we have any right to an analogy: it seems to support the proposition as we begin to work together at Tanglewood—that *some* things about our art might be taught, and learned. But even if we do teach and learn something, or by some other means discover ways to write music, we are destined to produce, even in full maturity, only subtle variants imperceptible to those on other planets, ringing small and momentarily momentous changes in the great collective song on which our civilization has worked for centuries.

This suggests a fascination with history, and a respect for its force. My father was a historian. I answered this in the usual way, by being very poor on the subject, even uninterested, until he died. Then nothing seemed *more* interesting: I have come to believe that a composer begins early constructing his own history of music, one which has nothing to do with the official hierarchies. The writings of Wagner, Debussy, and Stravinsky attest to the efficacy of this practice and, increasingly in modern times, composers from Boulez to Rochberg have also written history to lead inexorably to them.

We must do this.

We must begin with the standard version. We can't intentionally omit Haydn or Beethoven or Wagner or Berg from our studies because they don't appeal to us. We must study and learn "the classics" on faith. Not to do so means that our eventual, personal history will be too parochial to be useful.

But very soon, as we go along, our appetites take more and more initiative. At each stage of life the hierarchy seems inviolate; then, lo and behold, a few years later it has shifted. At each moment we must mobilize our versions of the past behind us like support troops.

Here is how it went for me: in adolescence Mozart *String Quintets* and Bach *Cantatas*, Stravinsky *Symphony of Psalms*, Bartók *Concerto for Orchestra*. With jazz groups: [Jerome] Kern and [George] Gershwin songs, Oscar Peterson, later Horace Silver. And I freely admit the Four Freshmen, Nat King Cole. This is the most impressionable time. Everything from these years is indelible. If we really cared about teaching music we'd do it then, and before, and then leave people alone.

During college: more Stravinsky, some Hindemith and Dallapiccola. Bach and Mozart even more preponderant. Discovery of Monk and Parker. Against my teachers' will—suspicion that Wagner might be *both* corrupting *and* great.

After college: Schütz, a revelation of five hundred more things music can do. Schoenberg likewise but the price higher. Verdi, from complete misunderstanding to adoration, triggered by Sessions' remark "one scene of *Falstaff* is worth the whole *Ring* to me" (this from a lifelong Wagnerian). Bach still central, due to my performances of over forty of his cantatas, Mozart in a state of estrangement due to a discovery that I couldn't perform him convincingly.

Out of school, on my own: forbidden fruits like Varèse, Cage, Bellini, D. Scarlatti; none challenge Bach or Schumann or Stravinsky as a daily diet, but they suggest I may not be who I think I am.

Early maturity: finally ready for Schubert, who wrote the best piece in every genre he really tackled. English music, especially [Sir Michael] Tippett, suddenly speaks. Finally grown up to Sessions. Demanding more and more linguistic density, but paradoxically hearing something in some of the minimal music of the 70's.

Along with bearing witness to these changing appetites comes the need for a potential theoretical framework. My first important redrawn historical boundary places the Second Viennese School at the end of an era, not at the beginning. (This harmonizes with an astrological conclusion of Yeats in *A Vision*,[2] as well as with Toynbee.)[3] This done, Monteverdi also shifts into a similar role. The compositional task becomes one of rebuilding and reconnecting, rather than following a dialectic line.

The full availability of four centuries of history, plus music from other cultures and from popular culture, is a recent resource for composers, but it slows and confuses our development. We must early and ruthlessly begin understanding what is for *us,* and what is distracting. The older we get the more we must telescope and distort it for our own purposes. It should be used as we use texts for setting; freely, lovingly, and brutally.

With this in mind I have examined my own changing but oddly consistent hierarchies and found in them a broad unifying bias.

I prefer what I would call the Philosophic Mode to Voice (or Personality).

Early in our careers as composers we are urged or we urge ourselves to find our own voice. That self-conscious position is favorable to some, damaging to many more. I would prefer that *voice* be a by-product of maturity and wholeness, rather than a heightening of idiosyncrasies which can make a piece or two "striking" but will diminish range and staying power. The luxury of imitating, vegetating, and stealing must be granted to all young composers. If they don't seize it they will have to do it later, when it carries fatal risks. The following comparisons will illustrate my two categories.

Personality	*The Philosophic Mode*
Monteverdi	Schütz
Handel	Bach
Telemann	Rameau
Liszt	Schumann
Copland	Sessions
Britten	Tippett
Messiaen	Carter
Webern	Schoenberg
Davies	Birtwistle

No quality difference is meant here, only sympathy. The "voice" composers tend to be recognizable early and always. They devote much energy to the making of the imprint. The philosophers tend to "sound like themselves" only gradually, and to place little priority on when or how they arrive. The first group engrosses more as we are hearing their music, the second more after we have heard it.

I want to be a composer of the philosophic mode, which I think requires a sophisticated harmonic language, an ability to re-imagine melody as a guiding force, an inventive formal sense, a willingness to be misunderstood, and much patience. As such I will say just about anything to justify the category.

But after we choose lineage, our colleagues past, present, and future, via appetite, whim, and involuntary reflex, and justify it by schemes like this one, we have only begun; we have to transmute what we have chosen into something we can't find anywhere else.

To do that we need maturity. That doesn't mean we have to be old. Mozart and Mendelssohn had it as teenagers. But in our era it is harder to imagine that again; we are too protected from birth, death, filth, and discomfort. The baffling availability of four hundred years of musical materials throws up its own barriers.

So we must *mature ourselves*. This, more than our musical development, is where we need mentors. And we need contact with a cultural heritage hardly breathing in the society at large. Although all composers should be able to sight-read a Bach fugue, conduct Varèse's *Octandre*, write down complex chords in dictation, it may be even more determining that they read *War and Peace*, the Bible, all of Shakespeare, and today's best poetry. The history of music simply doesn't contain any major figures who lack this intellectual curiosity, and I believe I can hear in a new piece whether its composer experiences a pressing inner life, or whether he is merely successful at projecting individuality or "musicality."

Nor would I exclude from this characterization an attachment to popular culture as long as it is avid and not passive. My own penchant for [the television shows] *All My Children* and *Rockford Files* is attached somewhere to my pursuing of Dickens' novels; if you love serial narration, and want music to have it, you have to take it where you can find it.

Music cannot teach music without the help of a complicated woven life fabric. In the one talk I had with Luigi Dallapiccola he spoke of his discovery of a kinship with Webern in the early forties and his joy at that feeling of community. But I remember even more clearly his illustration of that feeling with a long quote from the *Divine Comedy*, delivered without hesitation or effort, and remember thinking then, this must be what a composer is.

LECTURE 2. USES OF POPULAR MUSIC

Concert music makes up only a tiny percentage of the music played and heard today, and accounts for an even smaller percentage of the revenues earned by music. To most of the people in the world, *music* is TV music, movie music, and above all pop music (the latter recently having also taken on a visual form). These musics are elective—someone has caused them to begin by buying a ticket or turning on a [television] set or record player. There is also a great deal of non-elective music, played in supermarkets, airports, hotel lobbies, and even outdoor public spaces. It is clear now that most people regard music as an accompaniment to something: at best an enhancer, like a wine at a meal, at worst an environmental accident which can create habits and dependencies of a passive kind.

Although ambient music is an important sociological subject, I want to address here that "vernacular" music which is *experienced* and retained, and which becomes an important part of people's lives. Such music is major competition for concert music. It is also a potential nourishment for concert music.

All the most vital forms of pop music stemmed from jazz originally, but pure jazz has now become relatively limited in public appeal. The jazz public resembles, even overlaps with the concert music public; it is even much like the new music public, gradually emerging from years in the ghetto underground.

Early in the century jazz was *not* esoteric: it gave birth to the first unimported American popular music. This popular music was created by two symbiotic forces, the musical comedy and Tin Pan Alley writers, and the nightclub, radio, and phonograph record performers. The unit of currency was the "tune," the best of which originated as theater songs. A tune became a "hit" when many interpreters played and sang it, each in their own way, and many copies of the sheet music were sold. (The sheet music represented the original, authoritative version of the tune, rendered in the exact detail the composer wanted, and requiring an advanced performer to play it at home.) A tune became a "standard" when this process continued over many years, through generations, until the tune literally entered the popular subconscious. Each era was proud to contribute a few standards, hardy emblems of the vitality of their times.

It is these standards that I began playing, solo and in groups, around 1950, an inheritance I took for granted, though I was very aware of the quality of some of these perennials. They were often as demanding as any "art" music. I remember working hard to make sure that all the harmonies were right in the bridge of *Body and Soul*, that the common tones which brought about the fabulous transitions back to the A sections of *The Song Is You* and *All the Things You Are* were given enough weight, that the second chord of *Foggy Day* was *not* a diminished chord but a minor sixth (I was shocked and grateful to be corrected on that by a fastidious trumpet player). It was a hard exhilarating school, harder and more exhilarating than the learning and performance of baroque continuo parts ten years later, because it was a living language. What my colleagues and I were fortunate to be sharing was a late flowering of a disciplined, linguistically-demanding improviser's art, based on the melodic and harmonic inventions of some of America's greatest musicians—Kern, Gershwin, [Richard] Rodgers, [Irving] Berlin, [Harry] Warren, [Jimmy] Van Heusen, and many others. To this day I'm told, by composers who experienced the same kind of background, that we are still "composing out those changes."

The late fifties were the last time this was a culturally central activity. Those who later became composers of concert music—[William] Kraft, Schuman, [André] Previn, [Gunther] Schuller, [Salvatore] Martirano, and countless others—were still close to the public pulse when they went out to play those standards on their jazz jobs.

I remember sensing the presence of a powerful interloper around 1956, when the first rockers began moving us out of our club! About the same time the musical comedy, the fountainhead of the best songs, began to founder. As a teenager I was already aware that "the standards" I carried in my head were becoming less a shared common "melos," more the property of buffs. I listened among the Hit Parade tunes for something I thought had that quality. I found *Too Late Now!*

But it *was* too late, that song was by Burton Lane, survivor from a different age.

The tunes were gradually being replaced by the groups, or the hero performers, who were bigger than their tunes. It isn't *Heartbreak Hotel* or *Hound Dog* that survive as cultural artifacts, it is *Elvis Presley* or his posthumous doubles singing them. Sheet music disappeared or became hopelessly primitive. The *song* became the *record*: few tunes circulated among performers, they were instead identified definitely with a single recorded performance, which that performer tried to duplicate exactly in live performance or lip-synched to the record. The beat, the harmonies, and the forms emphasized clear reiterated shapes ("hooks"), root position chords, and hypnotic, crushing pulsations, physicality and presence above all.

Partly through this drastic grammatical simplification, partly through new marketing techniques, pop music found a wider public than ever before. In spite of the anachronistic presence of some actual tune-writers, like the Beatles, I became aware of a steadily-narrowing vocabulary as I taught, through many years, a course called Practical Harmony for nonclassical musicians. I shall never forget the response to one of my assignments—the writing out of a lead-sheet for *Nice Work If You Can Get It*, giving the melody only. I was glad none of the class had ever heard Gershwin's version. I thought they would be thrilled by his evasive, dapper strategies. Their versions were unanimous, firmly rooted in the mid-seventies root position cut. I then played Gershwin for them; they were deeply unimpressed, found him "complicated," "weird," and "wrong." I knew I was in alien country.

Soon after, I was asked by a very gifted composition student and "crossover" pianist to show him what I heard in "all that grey music" I like—Bach cantatas, thirties Stravinsky, etc. He was himself already an accomplished handler of "gesture," "areas," and "colors," and was asking out of genuine curiosity and good humor that will eventually carry him over all obstacles. I chose Cantata 23, one of the greatest, and greyest, and we went virtually bar by bar. Then the Stravinsky *Symphony of Psalms*—I think it stayed grey for him, while it glowed for me.

Am I making too much of these and other encounters if I begin asking wild questions?

1. Does the root position, static harmony, the modal triadic droning in Duran Duran songs mean I should worry about an atrophy of purposeful harmonic progression among young concert composers?

2. Does the young pianist who rides roughshod over the deceptive cadence at the end of the Mozart G Minor Piano Quartet do so because Kiss has a repertoire of four chords and that isn't one of them?

3. Is the young cellist whose choreography is better than her timing, who does not *feel* the drop to E flat early in the Schubert Quintet, mesmerized by the gestural, exaggerated monotone of David Bowie?

4. Does the distance from *For All We Know* to *Beat It* signify the approaching end of structural hearing?

Each generation believes deep down that the other generation's music is somehow wrong—maybe good but unnatural, unfaithful to experience. This perception finds double force with popular music. Pop music is above all the music of adolescence, sometimes prolonged adolescence. Every generation feels their pop music was the last good pop music, because they feel their early years were the last good early years. Adults nurse their generation's hits in their memories to their dying day because their most irreversible moments danced to that pulse. But then on their dying day it all dies, all except the standards and the few things that have achieved an artistic life, because for the most part they are associations with events and emotions, not durable free-standing musical objects. This is the poignancy of pop to each generation: its mortality and frailty. This is why pop music dates so comically and touchingly, so even the *beat* of the last decade seems so quaint and unhip.

This is why I will always believe *Teach Me Tonight* is a wonderful song (I hope it is); it is a blonde in forty crinolines and extra makeup who refused to be taught. This is why the only popular music we can honestly and viably incorporate into our compositional style is that of our own adolescence. It is the perishable icon we seek to enshrine in something more durable, to find its essence, to strip it of its nostalgia and trap only its vitality.

It is up to you to find out what to do with yours, and me with mine, it could take us the rest of our lives.

SOURCE: John Harbison, "Six Tanglewood Talks (1, 2, 3)," *Perspectives of New Music* 23, no. 2 (Spring–Summer 1985): 12–19.

~~~~~~~~~~~

NOTES

1. For a definition of that term, in relation to jazz, see chapter 144.
2. From 1917 on, English poet W. B. Yeats (1865–1939) worked with his wife on a project involving "automatic writing." *A Vision*, as the work became known, shows what Yeats believes to be the meaning of life, death, and time.
3. British historian and philosopher of history Arnold Toynbee (1889–1975).

WYNTON MARSALIS ON LEARNING FROM THE PAST FOR THE SAKE OF THE PRESENT

As musical director of the Lincoln Center Jazz Orchestra, the New Orleans–born trumpet virtuoso, composer, and educator Wynton Marsalis (b. 1961) is a major force in contemporary jazz. Like John Harbison (see chapter 143), Marsalis has a historicist aesthetic. That is, Marsalis believes in history as enabling freedom of the imagination, autonomy and growth. Often, Marsalis is called a "neoclassicist." That term has the advantage of linking Marsalis to the larger context of twentieth-century music as a whole. In fact, an earlier wave of American neoclassicism in the 1920s and '30s, as practiced by Copland and Stravinsky, informs Marsalis's lengthier works for voices and instrumental ensemble, such as *Blood on the Fields* (1997) and the symphonic choral work, *All Rise* (2002). Gershwin's influence in symphonic jazz is there as well, as is Ellington's, above all. Marsalis embraces Ellington as his teacher, which he makes clear in the interview reprinted below. And the blues, with its patterns of call and response, its traditions of meeting adversity with elegance, and with its long reach from enslavement to bebop, serves as Marsalis's defining trope for American experience.

    This chapter includes lengthy excerpts from an interview between Marsalis and Lolis Eric Elie, who served as road manager for the Wynton Marsalis Septet in the late 1980s and collaborated with Marsalis on the book, *Sweet Swing Blues on the Road*

(1994). These excerpts also reveal Marsalis's rejection of fusion at this point in his career.

～～～～～～
～～～～～～
～～～～～～

ELIE: You keep talking about writing for the musicians in the band, which is some-
           thing Ellington is known for. Is that where you got that concept from?

MARSALIS: Not really. At that time [the 1970s] especially I wasn't even on a high enough
           level to deal with anything Ellington was doing. I was just trying to do what
           seemed logical to me. Now I know a lot more of Duke's music than I knew
           then. By then I was listening to Duke, but I never thought of anything that I
           did in terms of anything he did. His music is so great and it's so intimidating
           for a musician, especially when philosophically you have big holes in your
           conception. It's really hard to understand Duke Ellington's music because
           his music illuminates all of what jazz is. So, whatever percentage of jazz you
           don't understand, you can't recognize that in Duke's music.

ELIE: Elaborate on that when you say it illuminates all of what jazz is.

MARSALIS: His music is not a style of music, it's jazz music. It's not bebop; it's not swing;
           it's not New Orleans–style jazz; it's not Latin jazz; it's not fusion. It's just
           jazz. Be it bebop tunes, swing, standards, blue mood pieces, songs with
           vocalists, thousands of different blues with different grooves on them, tone
           poems, suites, adaptations of European music. Anything you want to call on
           in music, Duke Ellington has done it.

ELIE: Is there anyone else in the history of the music that is as comprehensive as
           Duke?

MARSALIS: No, no one is even close. At least they didn't make records. Maybe they were
           comprehensive at home. Well, maybe Bach. But Duke's achievement is truly
           remarkable. . . .

ELIE: You mentioned earlier that there has been a New Orleans influence through-
           out your music, particularly in terms of bass, for example taking "Hey Pock-
           oway," a black New Orleans folk tune, and using influences from it. What
           made you take the leap to doing a record that sounds much like the guys
           used to make years and years ago, that sounds more firmly in the tradition?

MARSALIS: This album was just an idea I had on an airplane. I was trying to make a
           statement about the continuity of the music. And actually I wrote some of
           the tunes on the plane also. Stanley Crouch agreed to write a sermon about
           the music, and I conceived of the structure, which would be a funeral dirge—
           a minor blues—and a dominant blues that would use the same theme. I call
           the dominant blues, "Oh, But on the Third Day," so it has three choruses.
           The minor blues has one chorus. I thought of this idea and who to get on the

album about two years ago—Danny Barker [banjoist] and Michael White [clarinet player]. I also just wanted to pay homage to the New Orleans style because at that time, by listening to Duke Ellington, I could really see the power of the New Orleans style. We were talking before about sophistication— I think that the problem with what happened to the music after 1940 was that a lot of the sophistication was cut out, because you have a genius like Charlie Parker who mastered single-line playing. So single-line playing be- came elevated over the mastery and genius of somebody like Duke Ellington, who had control over many lines.

ELIE: That's a hell of a statement.

MARSALIS: But it's true. If you compare anything that Charlie Parker played in 1945 to "Diminuendo and Crescendo in Blue," which was written in 193[7], it's defi- nitely not more sophisticated in any way, shape or form. It might make people mad, but I'm sorry. If you give any musician in the world a pen and paper, play those two records and say which one you would rather transcribe, they'd definitely pick Bird's [Charlie Parker's] music. The first thing is that "Dimin- uendo and Crescendo in Blue" goes through all kinds of keys. It also has a suite-type of form. It uses the New Orleans polyphony, and it expands on that conception.

ELIE: Has jazz progressed since the 1930s, when Duke was writing those things?

MARSALIS: Yes, it's progressed. Certainly, for example, the work of people like Coltrane, and some of Miles's work. What Miles Davis did was take the music back in the direction of Duke Ellington, not nearly as sophisticated as Duke of course, but in his small group he tried to go back in that direction. He was playing melodies and using different grooves behind different soloists, using the album as a whole form, and using different sounds—playing more melodic passages in his solos, and playing a wider range of music. I think Coltrane was really successful with doing that. And he is a really important link in modern music. He really links the modern music back to the heritage of the music in terms of a small group conception. And in a small group there's only so much that you really can deal with. Even Max Roach's playing with Bird is an extension of the New Orleans call and response. So is Ed Blackwell's playing with Ornette Coleman. . . .

ELIE: Is a small group by definition less sophisticated than a group like the Duke Ellington Orchestra?

MARSALIS: Well, unless it's Duke Ellington with a small group. All I'm saying is that the small group conception became popular, playing the head, then the solo, then the head again. I mean that form in itself is not as sophisticated as the form of something like *Such Sweet Thunder*.

ELIE: Is that in part why on "Puheeman Strut" on the *Majesty of the Blues* album you have composed different interludes between each of the solos? Is that an attempt to get back to the orchestral concept?

MARSALIS: Yes, I was trying to understand Ellington's approach myself and also to get back to Jelly Roll Morton's music. In fact, Jelly Roll Morton was the first great intellectual in jazz.

ELIE: Specify what his contribution was. Elaborate on that.

MARSALIS: He codified the New Orleans music, and he had a definite concept of what it was. He could express what it was verbally and that is always important in terms of the dissemination of knowledge and information. If you listen to the Library of Congress recordings or get the book *Mr. Jelly Lord*, then you can really see that the things that he says about what jazz is are still pertinent today. Duke Ellington added a lot to that, of course, but you can see how a lot of Duke Ellington's own development is based on things that Jelly Roll said. Not necessarily saying that Duke followed these things exactly. Jelly Roll's conception was universal in that it encompassed things like the 4/4, the Latin tinge, swing—things that Trane addressed. Also, Jelly Roll said the piano player should always play like a big band when he's comping. If you can't accompany like a big band would accompany, then you're not playing. He also stressed the importance of understanding all the parts. He could demonstrate how jazz took European songs and marches and light opera tunes and turned them into jazz, how jazz became jazz coming out of rag-time. And he had a group conception of thematic improvisation, and a way to construct forms, like composing little interludes. He also said that he thought it was important for jazz musicians to learn how to play on medium-slow tunes, because you can deal with playing the rhythms that help you learn how to swing better at those tempos.

ELIE: After Duke Ellington, is there still a clear New Orleans influence in the music?

MARSALIS: Well, you have a clear New Orleans influence in some of the songs Charlie Parker wrote like "A-Leu-Cha," and "Chasin' the Bird," and also the dialogue that Charlie Parker and Max Roach used to have. Also Ornette Coleman's and Charles Mingus's music. That's clearly New Orleans, because that's the type of call and response that's in a lot of Jelly Roll's music. There is the influence of New Orleans in the music of John Coltrane. His decision to start playing the soprano saxophone was influenced by Sidney Bechet. When you really get into that music, it's such a deep and rich music and it addresses so much of the mythology of America that you will find that most of what we hear in music has its roots in that music. Also, just the joy of swinging on any in-strument has the sound of freedom that's in the early New Orleans music.

    . . .

ELIE: Why is fusion not jazz?

MARSALIS: What makes fusion not jazz is that certain key elements of jazz are not ad-dressed. First and foremost the blues. If you aren't addressing the blues you can't be playing jazz. Then the second thing is that [fusion] music in its 20-something years of existence has become just what it always wanted to be—

pop music. And one example of that would be the development of its major figure, Miles Davis. He went from some esoteric imitation of rock music, a combination of jazz and rock, to what he does today, Cyndi Lauper tunes and just blatant attempts to be R&B. Actually, it's not R&B because there's not really R&B anymore. But just blatant attempts to be what the pop form of the day is. What fusion does is it relieves us, our country, of the problem of dealing with jazz and the contribution of the Negro to the mythology of America. The question in jazz has always been: is it pop music or is it a classical music? And I don't mean classical in terms of European music, but I mean does it have formal aspects that make it worthy of study, and does it carry pertinent mythic information about being American? The thing that these musicians did in the 1970s is they relieved all of the cultural pressure that Duke Ellington placed on our nation to address the music seriously and teach it, which would make us deal with ourselves and our racism, which everyone knows is our greatest problem, even more so than dope. So what they did is just become rock musicians. This is the most popular form of "jazz" today. If you ask most people what jazz is they are not going to say John Coltrane. They're going to say Kenny G or any of a whole host of other people whose names change day by day. And the thing that Marcus Roberts pointed out is the reason that these musicians want to be called jazz artists is for longevity. So what they can do is constantly play these jazz festivals for 15, 20 years, playing basically pop music. Whereas in pop music, gigs are almost always based on a steady stream of hits, especially for black groups. You can't name a black group like the Rolling Stones or the Who who can sell out [a] stadium 20 years after their most potent hits. You go to jazz festivals in Europe and there's almost nobody playing jazz. And part of the problem is the whole conception of new and old. As Americans we have a tragic problem with that, because great art is always new. If you could sit down tonight and write "Diminuendo and Crescendo in Blue," you'd be a great musician. Nobody would say, "Boy, that sure is some great old music." If someone could paint the Sistine Chapel today, they would be heavy in terms of today's art. Instead, we look for innovative properties in reductions of art like graffiti. The production of masterpieces takes a concentrated effort and the desire to elevate rather than to exploit.

ELIE: People are constantly asking of you and other young jazz musicians what new ideas you have contributed to the music. Are you saying that is not a fair criteria by which to judge you?

MARSALIS: No, I think it's fair to judge us against the history of the music. But I'm saying that our emergence itself was new. And we've contributed so many things that are new to the music that have not been addressed because the level of sophistication and [of] critiquing something is so low. Critics have accepted new as being some pop music or the use of a synthesizer to make something new. We've contributed a whole other way to interpret a call-and-response conception. We're now formulating another way to interpret the blues. We haven't done that yet. But we're formulating that at this time. We brought into existence another conception of what the music is. And in terms of our generation, we certainly have been a major influence on any type of cultural movement that's going on, if any is happening. Certainly we would have to be considered in the forefront of increasing public awareness of the music. I feel that our way of interpreting harmony and form is different from the way that it's been done before. Also our attempt to articulate the holistic understanding of the music is a new conception. Also our conception of ourselves as musicians in this society is new.

ELIE: What's the holistic approach to the music? What do you mean by that?

MARSALIS: In other words, we don't want to fall into an era. We don't want to fall into a style that can be identified and called the "new style." We want to address all of the music. That is what we've been doing. We are not allied to any style of the music because we didn't grow up in any particular style. . . .

ELIE: All of the American musicians that you talk about, and all the jazz musicians you talk about being influenced by are black, yet you don't like the notion of calling it black music. You prefer to call it American music.

MARSALIS: That's because there are many other musicians that are black that are not Duke Ellington. And also I have the question of at which point somebody becomes black. For instance, Duke Ellington's skin was very light. Louis Armstrong's skin was real dark. So I guess somebody decides that if a Negro has one drop of Negro blood, then he's black. But I think that the statement that these individual men made are universal statements. Also, they didn't refer to their music as black. Even John Coltrane didn't do that.

. . .

ELIE: You keep mentioning the blues over and over again. And most people when they think about jazz don't necessarily realize that much of what people like John Coltrane and Miles Davis played was the blues. Why is it you say you cannot play jazz until you deal with the blues?

MARSALIS: Not just jazz. You can't even deal with American music if you don't deal with the blues, because that's what our country is about. That sound, the sound of the blues, is America. First of all, the blues addresses all of the centers of Western harmony. And technically it's a perfect form. And it has a bittersweet quality. It expresses a 360-degree range of human experience. And the curious thing is that you can use the blues idiom and really see where our country has gone wrong. For instance, how the racism allows people in our country to accept third- and fourth-rate imitations of blues from English artists and not accept an American artist. So what we end up doing is cheating ourselves out of our own experience. It's as if the British had never lost the war. But then we don't want to address the sophistication of European music.

ELIE: The sophistication of European classical music?

MARSALIS: Exactly. That won't be addressed. That's viewed as something corny for people who are stodgy and uptight. If you want to be hip you have to address some

European imitation of U.S. Negroes or some white American imitation of U.S. Negroes. Whereas by this time we could have been producing people, black and white, who could play authentically in these styles had there been an attempt to actually deal with this, with our mythology and our nation. But in order for us to produce these types of musicians that means that these two groups of people would have to come together and clichés would have to be abandoned. But we don't want to abandon those clichés. So we end up constantly exploiting ourselves. . . .

ELIE: A lot of African-American scholars have argued for the creation of a black aesthetic, saying that we need some criteria to evaluate cultural and artistic achievement that is ours. Do you support that call?

MARSALIS: No. I think that the question is how can we incorporate the achievement of Afro-Americans into the American aesthetic. Just because somebody else is going to define you doesn't mean that you have to accept it. A lot of that is Al Murray's argument, but I agree with it. For example, I went to school with a lot of white Americans and I know for a fact that culturally what I was thinking was much more advanced and much more important for them to know. See, what I'm saying, it's not just for me to know. They need to try to figure out what Duke Ellington was dealing with.

ELIE: Why is that? Why do they need to know that?

MARSALIS: Because it will make them more American. But maybe they want to be more European. I don't know. It will make them more American. And that's the reason any group of people should know their own art anyway. It makes them more of themselves, the best part of themselves.

ELIE: What type of stuff do you read and what has been its influence on your music or on your philosophy?

MARSALIS: Well, the main things that I read that have influenced my philosophy will be Al Murray's books *Stompin' the Blues* and *The Omni-Americans*. *Stompin' the Blues* is like the poetics of jazz. But I read a lot of the jazz books, autobiographies, books on classical musicians, Martin Luther King's writings and letters, Ernest Hemingway, Ralph Ellison, historical books and books about folklore. Also, I've learned a lot from reading Stanley Crouch's essays and just talking with him. . . .

ELIE: What was Louis Armstrong's contribution to the music? Why is he so great?

MARSALIS: First of all, as a trumpet player he was better than anybody who has ever played, at least anybody who's documented. The nuance and the shading of his tone, the majesty in his sound; he actually was playing three different instruments. He had that clarion sound when he wanted to go in the upper register and make a call. He had the real melodic purity in the middle register when he just wanted to sing a simple song. And he had the real gravity and profundity of the lower register when he wanted to end the phrase with a real depth and profound emotion. So just the fact that he could do that alone is an incredible achievement in terms of trumpet playing. And his singing. All of the great American singers have imitated something in his singing. . . .

ELIE: What's your quest?

MARSALIS: Well, mainly it's just an attempt to make the country deal with its own mythology and with the music. That's what I would consider a quest. But for me personally, as a musician, it's to really learn. I mean I feel so grateful I had the opportunity to play music and discover the music had so many wonders. It's such a wondrous art form. It's just like being a tinker or something. It's my hobby, too. I can play with it, figure out different things.

ELIE: Do you still play classical music?

MARSALIS: No.

ELIE: Why not?

MARSALIS: There aren't that many pieces, and I just don't have the time. It's too hard to develop as a jazz musician, and that's really what I want to do.

ELIE: Why be a jazz musician instead of a classical musician?

MARSALIS: Well, classical music is good but it's not as difficult to play as jazz. It's not as challenging. It's just not as hard to play classical music as a performer. In composition it might be different, but to be a jazz performer is much more difficult because you are confronted with many more variables.

SOURCE: Lolis Eric Elie, "An Interview with Wynton Marsalis," *Callaloo* 13, no. 2 (Spring 1990): 270–90.

JOHN ADAMS, AN AMERICAN MASTER

The composer John Adams (b. 1947) is recognized as one of the most distinguished American composers of classical music today. In 2003, honoring his 50th-birthday year, Lincoln Center in New York City mounted a festival entitled John Adams: An American Master, one of the largest retrospectives ever organized for a living American composer.

After rejecting his academic training in serial composition, Adams encountered minimalist music. He later stated that hearing Steve Reich's major work, *Drumming,* in San Francisco in 1974 was a turning point in his own career. By 1978, Adams had written the brilliant orchestral work for strings *Shaker Loops.* In this work, as in others, Adams adopted minimalism as a style, to be distinguished from minimalism as an aesthetic ideology. It became one option among many, and Adams soon found his own "post-minimalist" path. He introduced more harmonic and contrapuntal complexity into his compositions, modifying what he later described as minimalism's "endless prairies of non-event."[1]

The second crucial direction in Adams's work has involved opera as a genre of living theater and social relevance. Here, Philip Glass and Robert Wilson's success with the opera *Einstein on the Beach* provided an important precedent. In 1983, Adams also met the avant-garde director Peter Sellars (b. 1957), then producing his famous revisionist versions of Mozart's operas. Sellars charted a course which Adams has followed for many years by suggesting a contemporary political event as an operatic subject. With a lyrical libretto by the poet Alice Goodman and staging by Sellars, Adams premiered the opera *Nixon in China* in 1987. Other operas, among them the still-controversial *The Death of Klinghoffer* (1991) discussed in this excerpt, and *Dr. Atomic* (2005), have followed.

~~~~~~~~
~~~~~~~~

FROM AN INTERVIEW OF JOHN ADAMS
BY DAVID BEVERLY (1995)

This interview was conducted on the campus of the University of Louisville after John Adams accepted the Grawemeyer Award for his Violin Concerto on October 25, 1995.

DB: I've been very interested in your comments on "Tricksters" and serious works, and I saw in a recent interview you seem to be distancing yourself from some of this. Do you see "Tricksters" as influenced more by American music and serious works as more European?

JA: It's possible. I think it's quite possibly true, but I'm trying to distance myself from these facile characterizations. You know what happens frequently is that you say something in passing and it gets picked up by a writer or a fan and eventually gets into common usage and becomes impossible to shed. Milton Babbitt, for example—he could never ever get free of the phrase "Who Cares if You Listen?" which he claims he never said anyway. Apparently an editor for *High Fidelity* magazine had added that phrase as a title for an article that Milton had written. Milton was doubtless appalled by it, but it's curious that the phrase did stick. Perhaps it has lingered for so long in the public's mind because that is the emotion many listeners have when they are confronted by his music. But the "trickster" term applied to my own work probably came about as a result of that one which paired *Fearful Symmetries* and *Wound [The Wound Dresser]*—I myself may have been responsible for introducing the idea in a desperate attempt to put a bracket around these two wildly different pieces. And I did perceive that about myself from time to time—that there were pieces that seemed to be very brash and had a Mark Twain tone to them, and then other pieces that were much more serious and contemplative. But you know, now that I look back on it, I see that in every supposedly serious piece, even in *Klinghoffer* there's almost always a moment or two of my own brand of levity. There's the British Dancing Girl scene in *Klinghoffer*, which briefly relaxes some of the tension. And of course, there is *Grand Pianola*, which, despite all its reputation for roguishness and vulgarity, is in fact a piece that is largely quite serene and sublimated. So, I acknowledge the bipolar nature of my music, but I am not anxious to make too much of it. I don't want people to always listen to John Adams's work and decide whether it's black or white, green or blue.

DB: Do you think too maybe you're starting to integrate these styles?

JA: I don't think it's really any different than it ever has been. What I notice in recent pieces is that I've become even more openly embracing of a certain ambiance or tonality in American music. And I don't mean a tonality like B minor, I'm talking about a tonality of mood. I'm very deeply attached to American art, painting, literature, poetry, and, for sure, American music. Lately I've been reading a lot of contemporary American works of fiction. You know for years I read fiction from the nineteenth century or eighteenth century—a lot of German literature and French literature, but lately I've been reading works by novelists like Russell Banks (I read his *Continental Drift* [1985]), Paul Auster, Cormac McCarthy. Right now I'm reading Ralph Ellison's *Invisible Man*. These things always have a way of finding a route into my music, no matter how subliminal the influence or the reference may be. So I think I'm going through a very strong, possibly even self-consciously American phase right now.

DB: I've noticed you've mentioned a lot of writers, especially nineteenth-century writers. So you take quite a bit of time to study literature?

JA: Well, I do it also just out of pure pleasure, you know—the pleasure principle. And it also defines my being in the culture as an artist. As you begin to gray and get older you begin to start thinking, "How do I really fit into this whole scene?"

DB: Could you ever write an opera about your heroes? Or are [Richard] Nixon and [Leon] Klinghoffer heroes?

JA: No, they're not my heroes in the sense of archetypes that I'd like to model myself after. But as dramatic figures they are very appealing. Nixon was a fantastically complex and unpredictable figure, and I found it a real adventure to go "under his skin" in writing the opera. And the same goes for all the other characters in that opera. We know very little about the real Leon Klinghoffer. He was not a particularly interesting figure in himself in the way that Nixon and Mao [Zedong] were. But he was a symbol. He was a symbol of an American tourist, a modestly affluent American tourist, a modestly affluent Jewish-American tourist, and, last but not least, a modestly affluent handicapped Jewish-American tourist who was caught in the wrong place at the wrong time. All of these identities that he stood for made him an ideal target for a young Palestinian fanatic. It made him an archetype, especially when set up against a young Palestinian who had grown up in a horrible refugee camp in Lebanon hearing nothing from his parents or from his contemporaries except how Israel and America were the great Satans and that there was nothing nobler than to die for one's beliefs and for Allah. So to put these two packets of energy together on the stage was an irresistible dramatic impulse.

DB: I always thought he seemed to represent everything we feared with these kinds of random acts of violence.

JA: I suppose that's true.

DB: I guess Leon Klinghoffer was just on the *Achille Lauro* to have a good time.

JA: He was an unfortunate man caught arbitrarily in the middle of huge historical forces that collided momentarily, and he may well have been powerless to
do anything about them. But in Act II, in his confrontation with the terrorist
called "Rambo," Alice Goodman gave him a kind of dignified anger, which,
while it may have felt good to vent, may also have brought about his demise.

DB: I was struck by the vocal parts in both [of] the operas, how, not all the time,
but a lot of the time they seem to [mirror] the rhythms of speech very closely.
Do you grant your performers a little latitude as long as they come out on the
downbeat with the interpretation of these rhythms?

JA: Well actually, my approach to setting the English language, and particularly
the American language, is one of almost no embellishment at all. I work very
hard to make the musical setting of a text reflect its exact inflection. And I
would say in general I give very little leeway to the performers. One of the reasons I like working with singers like James Maddalena and Sanford Sylvan is
that they are supremely accurate rhythmically. My guess is that they're probably more accurate than most opera singers. Now in the case of the *Ceiling/
Sky* [*I was Looking at the Ceiling and Then I Saw the Sky*], my last piece, I was
working in a more popular genre, it's expected of the singers that they use
the typical improvisatory leeway that's granted a good pop singer.

DB: I've heard you've said that the first and second movements of the Violin Concerto [is] one of your most rigorous works. Were your methods this rigorous
in *Death of Klinghoffer*? I ask this because of your comments saying the *Chamber Symphony* uses a "post-Klinghoffer" musical language.

JA: No, the use of the term rigor applying to the Violin Concerto had to do with
what for me is a kind of extreme organic integrity of the material. Motives
and little cells of material were recycled and used in an extremely economical
fashion. I would say I got an enormous amount of mileage out of a very small
number of ideas in the concerto, which pleases me. I think it creates a sort of
subliminal sense of unity in the work. In the case of *Klinghoffer,* the answer's
no. I certainly used my intuitive sense of organization, but I didn't use motives, and scale forms, and received forms as I did in the case of the Violin
Concerto. You know the concerto itself is a "received form," and particularly
the chaconne is an archaic form. My use of it was a rare example of neo-
classic behavior on my part. But *Klinghoffer* is more intuitive and less self-
consciously organized, although I do think that it's very obvious that the
parallel between the Bach *Passions* and any number of sacred oratorios is
quite evident to anybody that takes the time to look at it. . . .

DB: Why did you want couplets in both *Nixon in China* and *The Death of Klinghoffer*?

JA: I liked the idea of setting couplets because their use in poetry creates a very
tight internal structure. Of course nowadays hardly any poets write verse like

that. That's what made Alice so special: she could write in any style, but she could also write couplets, and I think part of the brilliance of her librettos is due to the fact that she placed this rigor on herself. Of course, what I like to do is work against the rhythm of the couplet, upsetting it, so to speak.

DB: I never thought your settings emphasized them.

JA: No, they don't emphasize it, but somehow the urgency of the couplet, the symmetry of it seems to force the poet into a very concise and, for me, very rhythmically organized speech. I certainly had lots of moments of frustration and confusion working with Alice Goodman's work, as any composer working with great poetry would have. I mean there are moments when the rhythms just can't be harnessed. But I will say that after working twice with Alice Goodman, I worked with June Jordan [librettist for *I Was Looking at the Ceiling and Then I Saw the Sky*]. June did not like to work in couplets and wrote a much structurally freer form of poetry, and I found that even more difficult to work with. Even now I think I still would prefer working with couplets. Certainly in the cases of *Nixon in China* and *Klinghoffer* we're talking about an event that came to us over the contemporary media in all its banal and deadly unpoetic manner. You know how the news sounds when it comes over the TV or the radio. The language of the media has that ugly, loud, aggressive tone that is so devoid of feeling and emotion. So to express these stories in this archaic form of the couplet gave it a wonderfully mythic quality, a mythology that was flavored with an "only in America" kind of irony. I mean one could make a satiric version of the O. J. Simpson trial and do it in neat little couplets that would be quite devastating, in the manner of Alexander Pope. But Alice and I weren't looking for satire. We were looking for a treatment that brought the entire experience, even Nixon's most foolish comments, up to a much higher level of discourse.

DB: Both operas strike me as very neutral.

JA: Politically neutral?

DB: Politically neutral. Maybe not *Nixon* as much but *Klinghoffer* was really neutral.

JA: Well, it for sure didn't strike some people as neutral. You know *The Death of Klinghoffer* was picketed by the Jewish Information League when it was done in San Francisco and I don't know if you've seen any of the reviews that came out like the one in the *Wall Street Journal*.

DB: I think they didn't understand.

JA: Well, I hope I can speak for my collaborators. We weren't making an overly conscious attempt to be neutral, but on the other hand, after reading about the background it was impossible not to have strong feelings. All of us did a lot of research. I read the Old Testament for the first time since I was in Sunday school, and read many books on the history of the Middle East, the foundations of Zionism, the Balfour Declaration, Theodore Herzl, etc. And I read a great deal of Edward Said's writing. I know Alice Goodman read most of the Koran. And I think we all felt independently of one another that the situation like any complicated political situation in the world is much too complex to fall into one easy answer or another. Clearly his death was a kind of a crucifixion. He was crucified for the class of people that he happened to fall into.

. . .

DB: What was the function of the choruses in *Klinghoffer*? Did they bring multiple perspectives or give a historical perspective?

JA: In some cases the choruses provide a historical setting, and they do so in what I think is a very ceremonial way. To me the sound of a chorus is a very archaic sound. They are [a] bracket, so to speak—isolated from the action. When I hear them they make me feel as if the camera has suddenly moved way, way, way back as if looking at all this action through the reverse end of a telescope. Suddenly we are allowed to see this event as part of a vast historical perspective. In the "Ocean Chorus" we go back, not just to Adam and Eve, but to pre-history. Alice's imagery in the "Ocean" is of paramecium, primordial cells dividing—the very beginnings of life, a wonderful image for what goes on in the darkness of those depths. The ocean, into which Leon Klinghoffer's body returns, is the same ocean that was the source of the very first stirrings of biological life. So this chorus gives a sense of perspective and depth to this otherwise strident and glaringly contemporary event.

. . .

DB: Are the titles themselves *Ocean/Desert Chorus [Night/Day]* biblical references?

JA: The entire opera is about symmetries and polarities. It may be that the first symmetry was suggested by the Israelis and Palestinians [referring to the *Chorus of Exiled Palestinians* and the *Chorus of Exiled Jews* from the prologue]. And then it followed that there would be a *Night* and *Day*, and *Ocean* and *Desert*. The *Hagar Chorus* contains its own symmetry within the story, which is of course the story of Abraham and his two sons, Ishmael and Isaac. So everything has its little built-in symmetry. . . .

DB: What is the significance of the term "gates" in your music? Do they take you to a vastly different place? Or are they evolutionary?

JA: It's more the first meaning. I don't use the term anymore. It was a term that I started using in the late '70s when I was very much preoccupied with electronic music, particularly analogue electronic music. A gate is a module in an electronic synthesizer which changes the state of a waveform radically and immediately. If you look at those early pieces of mine, particularly a piano piece called *Phrygian Gates*, you can see how the music is its own kind of "analogue" of waveforms. I viewed the two hands playing different waveforms, each constantly modulating the wave. The major changes of mode and of energy levels were analogues of the "gate" principle. This technique is also the case, although to a lesser extent, with *Harmonium*, the big choral piece, and *Shaker Loops*. They all have in common a kind of irreversible modulations that take place [claps] in a split second which transform the *affekt,* the sensibility, the tonality and so on. Most often they happen suddenly, like an immediate shifting of gears.

DB: I think in a lot of your works there is this sense of continuity.

JA: Well, they exist within a continuity. Certainly *Phrygian Gates* or *Harmonium* give the feeling of being very continuous pieces, and the gates provide those all-important moments of transformation of the material. Nowadays, I do that less, partly because my harmonic language has, I suppose one could say, been "compromised" by increasing dissonance. So that a gate doesn't have quite the shock value that it did fifteen years ago when I used to write very, very purely modal or diatonic music. . . .

DB: From your Grawemeyer lecture yesterday, what do you feel your social re-sponsibilities are as a composer, and in particular, an opera composer?

JA: Well, it's hard and quite possibly dangerous to think as an artist in terms of social responsibilities. We had a big ceremony last night at the art museum, and everybody got their awards, all the other people and I. I had to say I felt very humbled and insignificant next to people who were genuinely doing things to change the world. You know these two women who worked with inner-city kids and the Australian foreign minister who's been instrumental in bringing about a peace settlement in Cambodia. And here I am—all I do is push little black dots around all day long. [Adams is speaking of events at the University of Louisville campus when he and others accepted the Grawe-meyer Award.] And I try not to think about my work as being prompted by a sense of social responsibility. I think that great poetry and great music, and great poetry set to great music, can sensitize people. In some cases I suppose it can educate them, but more importantly it can sensitize them. Which is something that any kind of ceremony can make happen, whether it's a reli-gious ceremony or a performance of a great work of art. It focuses the mind on let's say a higher level of consciousness or awareness. And, you know, whether it's the *Goldberg Variations* or *Götterdämmerung* one can come out of an experience with possibly an elevated moral awareness. But art's a funny thing. It can't be pinned down. A great work of art can conceivably have no moral impact whatsoever, and yet it can delight, it can do anything. It might simply just exist to give pleasure, any kind of pleasure from the purely sen-sual to most intellectual. So fortunately its potential is so vast that one can't really assign a function to it.

        . . .

DB: You said in 1985, "It's difficult to write a good tonal piece with real integrity that sounds fresh." Is this true ten years later?

JA: Sure. [laughing] It's difficult to write anything that sounds fresh. But tonal music is especially hard because so much of the language's possibilities have been covered before, and covered extremely well. What I've noticed about my

style in the last year is that I'm moving away from the contrapuntal and harmonic density of pieces like the *Chamber Symphony* and *Klinghoffer* and now
I am tending to work with more clearly tonal palettes. And we'll see what this
produces.

SOURCE: Excerpts from the interview with John Adams by David B. Beverly, "John
Adams on Klinghoffer and the Art of Composing," October 25, 1995, at the University of
Louisville, Kentucky. Available at http://www.earbox.com/sub-html/interviews/ja-on-kling-
low.html.

~~~~~~~

NOTE

1.   This quotation and context comes from Robert Fink, "(Post-)minimalisms 1970–2000, the
Search for a New Mainstream," in *The Cambridge History of Twentieth-Century Music,* ed.
Nicholas Cook and Anthony Pople (Cambridge: Cambridge University Press, 2004): 544.

THE INCORPORATION OF THE
AMERICAN FOLKLIFE CENTER

The American Folklife Center, established in 1976 by the U.S. Congress, expanded the mandate for a national center for folk culture. Initially, the collecting of folk music at the Library of Congress was centered in the Archive of American Folk Song, established in 1928 as part of the Music Division at the Library of Congress. This archive was renamed the Archive of Folk Culture when it was integrated into the American Folklife Center. The public law creating the American Folklife Center responded to the revival of interest in ethnic heritage that coalesced around the ideas of "multiculturalism" in the 1970s. The act responded to the spirit of the '70s, with its heightened awareness of and sensitivity to the cultural legacies of non-English-speaking populations in the United States. The Federal Cylinder Project (see chapter 66), as well as a major conference and a bibliographical project on ethnic recordings, soon followed.

EXCERPTS FROM PUBLIC LAW 94-201, 94TH CONGRESS, H.R. 6673, JANUARY 2, 1976.

The Creation of the American Folklife Center

AN ACT

To provide for the establishment of an American Folklife Center in the Library of Congress, and for other purposes.

Be it enacted by the Senate and House of Representatives of the United States of America in Congress assembled, That this Act may be cited as the "American Folklife Preservation Act."

DECLARATION OF FINDINGS AND PURPOSE
Sec. 2.

(a)   The Congress hereby finds and declares—

(1)   that the diversity inherent in American folklife has contributed greatly to the cultural richness of the Nation and has fostered a sense of individuality and identity among the American people;

(2)   that the history of the United States effectively demonstrates that building a strong nation does not require the sacrifice of cultural differences;

(3)   that American folklife has a fundamental influence on the desires, beliefs, values, and character of the American people;

(4)   that it is appropriate and necessary for the Federal Government to support research and scholarship in American folklife in order to contribute to an understanding of the complex problems of the basic desires, beliefs, and values of the American people in both rural and urban areas;

(5)   that the encouragement and support of American folklife, while primarily a matter for private and local initiative, is also an appropriate matter of concern to the Federal Government; and

(6)   that it is in the interest of the general welfare of the Nation to preserve, support, revitalize, and disseminate American folklife traditions and arts.

(b)   It is therefore the purpose of this Act to establish in the Library of Congress an American Folklife Center to preserve and present American folklife.

DEFINITIONS
Sec. 3. As used in this Act—

(1)   the term "American folklife" means the traditional expressive culture shared within the various groups in the United States: familial,

ethnic, occupational, religious, regional; expressive culture includes a wide range of creative and symbolic forms such as custom, belief, technical skill, language, literature, art, architecture, music, play, dance, drama, ritual, pageantry, handicraft; these expressions are mainly learned orally, by imitation, or in performance, and are generally maintained without benefit of formal instruction or institutional direction.

. . .

SOURCE: http://www.loc.gov/folklife/public_law.html.

147

$\mathcal{D}$ANIEL J. BOORSTIN'S WELCOMING REMARKS

AT THE CONFERENCE ON

ETHNIC RECORDINGS IN AMERICA

The famous American historian and the official librarian of Congress from 1975 to 1987, Daniel J. Boorstin (1914–2004), delivered these remarks at the opening of a groundbreaking Conference on Ethnic Recordings in America sponsored by the American Folklife Center in 1977. (See chapter 66 for another AFC project.) The conference concerned popular and folk musics associated with ethnic minorities living in the United States as people in "diaspora": "a people living outside their historic homeland who maintain memories of and attachments to their place of origin."[1] It focused on the American recording industry, which recognized early on that it had an untapped market out there among first- and second-generation Americans. In the "golden age of ethnic recording," ca. 1900–1930, American companies recorded musicians living in the United States in the following languages: Albanian, Arabic, Armenian, Bulgarian, Cajun, Chinese (several dialects), Croatian, Czech, Danish, Dutch, Finnish, French (from France and Canada), German, Greek, Hawaiian, Hebrew, Hungarian, Irish, Italian, Lithuanian, Norwegian, Polish, Portuguese, Rumanian, Russian, Serbian, Slovak, Slovenian, Spanish, Spanish-Hebrew (Ladino), Swedish, Syrian, Turkish, Ukrainian, and Yiddish. (Available now through the scholarship of one of the conference organizers is a seven-volume discography.)[2] These recordings are a relatively unexplored source of information about music that now may be historically extinct in the host countries;[3] music that later had significant revivals (Cajun, Mexican-American, Yiddish via klezmer); and from a theoretical point of view, music that expresses the shifting meanings of "home."

In his overview, Boorstin focuses on "the American experience"—an ideological cornerstone of his scholarship; Boorstin won the Pulitzer Prize in 1974 for his book *The Americans: The Democratic Experience*. Here, Boorstin discusses cultural achievement as an aspect of experience. His comments on the historical relevance of various kinds of American music belong to the ongoing national debate involving hierarchies of high and low style and their connection to national character.

This is a historic as well as a historical occasion, because it is the first conference to be held by the new American Folklife Center in the Library of Congress. The Library has of course been a pioneer in enlarging our concept of American civilization and in bringing together all the materials that are related to it. Our collection of folksongs goes back to 1928, and in some respects earlier. We hope that the Folklife Center will make it possible for us to be even more active, more wide-ranging, more imaginative in the exploration of the folk cultural aspects of American civilization.

I should like briefly to put this meeting in the perspective of American civilization. The title of the conference is "Ethnic Recordings in America: A Neglected Heritage." In that title and in the purpose of our meeting there are three distinctive features of American civilization: music, technology, and ethnicity.

Music in this country has had a quite distinct character. The American achievement has not been expressed in chamber music, or in symphony, or in grand opera, but in popular music. The line between popular music and folk music is a difficult one, and I shall leave its definition to more competent hands, but there is certainly some connection between the special character of its folk music and the spectacular success of popular music in the United States. Wherever you go in the world, whatever you may hear said about American civilization, you will find juxtaposed to those comments performances of American popular music, usually from phonograph recordings.

But we ourselves have found it hard to come to terms with popular music. We have found it hard to give musical comedy the dignity which seems to come with grand opera or music of high culture. Our most articulate wits and pundits have had trouble finding the proper place for music in our civilization. This puzzlement was perhaps best expressed by Mark Twain when he observed that Wagner's music is better than it sounds. The assumption that somehow there is a cultural measure or standard for music which is different from the way it sounds has, of course, plagued all of us.

Popular music has been a special feature of American life, and it has had a special relationship to technology. The phonograph is as good a symbol as any of the peculiar intrusion of technology in America into the traditional categories of culture. I think perhaps someone should compile an anthology of the comments about the phonograph when it was first invented. It was treated primarily as a threat; in *The Americans: The Democratic Experience* I have explored

A recording by Ukrainian-American musicians made in 1927 of a skit about the customs associated with a Christmas feast called "Jordan's Eve," from *Ethnic Recordings in America. A Neglected Heritage* (Library of Congress: American Folklife Center, 1982): xii.

some of the consequences of John Philip Sousa's attack on what he called "the menace of mechanical music."[4] We forget now that, just as when movable type was introduced people preferred hand-made Bibles to the machine-made Bibles, so when the phonograph came in people tended to prefer hand-made music to machine-made music. There were many quips by more witty people than John Philip Sousa. Ambrose Bierce, for example, defined the phonograph as "an irritating toy that restores life to dead noises."[5]

The phonograph asserted itself in American life largely because it was a democratic instrument. It was a machine which not only repeated experience but democratized it. While Ambrose Bierce and Sousa could indicate their fears of the phonograph around 1906, within a decade or two it was one of the primary sources for reaching everybody with music—including the high-brow music that so aroused the suspicion of Mark Twain and others.

Finally, let me mention the third element which is brought together in our conference—ethnicity. We have heard again and again—in fact so often that perhaps our ears have become immune to the message—that this is a nation of nations, that we were comprised of many peoples. That multiplicity is expressed in our language, in the fact that the real American language is broken English, familiar to many of us as it was spoken by our parents or grandparents. One of the reasons, perhaps, why foreign language study has not been popular in the United States, is that so many Americans already speak another language. We are interested in this pluralism of American life. It is interesting to note that the cover of our conference program reproduces a Victor record label for a Ukrainian-American recording which uses the Cyrillic alphabet. We are here celebrating the multiplicity of American life, the manyness of it, the subtlety of it.

This conference is significant because it serves the large purpose of the Library of Congress, which is not only to celebrate but to understand and reach deep into American civilization —to discover how it has been limited, how it has been fulfilled and how we can make it more fulfilling. We here bring together these three elements which have been characteristic of American civilization: the popularity and democratic character of our music, the speed and effectiveness of our technology, and the vividness and richness of our ethnicity. We have high hopes for this, our debut for the Folklife Center. We trust it is a signal and a symbol of much more to come.

> SOURCE: Daniel J. Boorstin, "Welcoming Remarks to the Conference on Ethnic Recordings in America," in *Ethnic Recordings in America: A Neglected Heritage* (Washington, D.C.: American Folklife Center, Library of Congress, 1982): xi–xiii.

NOTES

1. Kay Kaufman Shelemay, *Soundspaces: Exploring Music in a Changing World*, 2nd ed. (New York: Norton, 2006): 210.

2. Richard Spottswood, "Commercial Ethnic Recordings in the United States," in ibid., 51–66. See Spottswood, *Ethnic Music on Records: A Discography of Ethnic Recordings Produced in the United States, 1893 to 1942* (Urbana: University of Illinois Press, 1990).

3. See Pekka Gronow, "Ethnic Recordings: An Introduction," in *Ethnic Recordings in America: A Neglected Heritage* (Washington, D.C.: American Folklife Center, Library of Congress, 1982): 1–50.

4. John Philip Sousa, "The Menace of Mechanical Music," *Appleton's Magazine*, September 1906.

5. Ambrose Bierce (1842–1914?) was a journalist and writer known for his sharp wit.

148

WILLIE COLÓN ON "CONSCIOUS SALSA"

In the 1950s and '60s, the urban dance music known as "salsa" developed as a Latino hybrid of the Cuban *son* and Puerto Rican timbres, flavored with other elements from jazz and rock. Born in the South Bronx, New York, the Puerto-Rican American musician Willie Colón (b. 1950) has been a leader in the salsa movement for over 40 years. Both as a musician and a citizen, Colón is political, writing social critiques in his songs, advocating "conscious salsa," and even running for the U.S. Congress in 1994. In this interview by the Cuban writer, Leonardo Padura Fuentes, Colón discusses the interplay between music and the global marketplace. He pays tribute to such legendary greats as the singer Celia Cruz. His sense of musical tradition will, he hopes, be sustained by future generations of Latino-American musicians.

LPF: Willie, if you look back at the 1960s and 1970s, would you say that the best days of salsa have come and gone?

WC: I don't know why you're asking me that, because from what I can see, salsa is still very much alive and well. Salsa is becoming more popular all the time: it's listened to in Latin America, it's winning over Europe, and it continues to evolve. And that evolution provokes transformations, passing fashions, which by no means signify exhaustion, such as erotic salsa, which has been the most recent wave. The same thing happens with musicians: new stars are appearing all the time, and among the newest and the best are Juan Luis Guerra, Frankie Ruiz, and Eddie Santiago. So, I would describe salsa as a sort of Latin American rock because of its ability to evolve, but like rock, it's here to stay.

LPF: You were always a typical barrio guy. What's the significance of the barrio in the birth and character of salsa?

WC: Look, for many reasons Latinos in the United States don't assimilate well; they don't have confidence, and the barrio is a refuge, a ghetto for Latin Americans. In the United States, Latinos are a minority living in a context of discrimination, and only in the barrio are they able to reproduce their original environment. And that very environment creates a necessity: in the barrios a social formation takes place, which is the expression of a little piece of the homeland of each immigrant, and in that environment all things Latin American are valued as important and indispensable; without them one can't live (or one refuses to do so). I think that in those spiritual necessities and the lack of communication beyond the borders of the barrio, we can find the profound psychological and cultural factors that give rise to salsa precisely in the Latino neighborhoods of New York, where it emerges as a manifestation of cultural resistance. After all, if we know we're still not completely accepted by U.S. culture, why not follow the lead of rock and roll or another type of music? And salsa emerges as something of our own, which is why it's full of politics and stories from the street. It's a music of the city, and its melodies are essentially urban.

LPF: And for you personally, what has the barrio meant to your musical formation?

WC: I was born in the South Bronx, the son of two Latinos also born in New York and the grandson of a Puerto Rican woman who left the island in 1923 and who still doesn't speak English. The woman who took care of me as a child was Panamanian, and on our block there were also Cubans, Dominicans, Venezuelans, Chicanos, people from all over the Caribbean, and all you heard was music in Spanish. So you're formed in that social and musical environment, absorbing all the folklore, mannerisms, music—*son, cumbia, el aguinaldo*—and suddenly all those roots begin to meld very naturally inside of you, with no contradictions. . . . That's the story of salsa itself: a harmonic blend of all the Latin music of New York, expressed in a new way through a completely mestizo type of music.

LPF: Whenever you talk about your roots, you mention your grandmother.

WC: That's because she's been an important person in my life: she's my blood link with Puerto Rico and was the person who bought me my first trumpet when I was ten years old. That's pretty important, don't you think?

LPF: And does your "bad boy" image, which was your calling card in the 1960s, come from that barrio where you were born?

WC: For a lot of people, I'm still the "bad boy" [*el malo*] but at one time I really was. In my barrio, if I wanted to keep the trumpet my grandmother bought me, I had to defend it. . . . Even so, it was stolen twice. I think that's why I changed to the trombone: it's a lot bigger and more difficult to run off with.

LPF: One hears a lot of talk about certain limitations of Latin music in the United States. There's even talk of censorship. Is there any truth to all this?

WC: There's really no censorship per se. . . . It's just that within the commercial scheme of things, the creative space for working and experimenting is always shrinking, for the simple reason that one must obey the market forces, and that's a limitation. An example from my own perspective is the length of the songs, which are usually around four minutes, and for me it's very difficult to write an important work if I have to think about time constraints. Can you imagine if jazz were created in a similar format? Well, it's the same for us, and that's why many of my best pieces haven't been hits in the United States and Puerto Rico, even though they have been in Latin America. On the other hand, the control of the media by the large multinationals means that one cannot escape certain restrictions, and merely holding liberal views—especially when you're a Latino—is already dangerous from a commercial standpoint.

And on the other hand, you have the lyrics of our songs. Lyrics that are a bit harsh can always scare off a sponsor. Luckily, the ultraright doesn't worry too much about our lyrics because, fortunately, they don't understand Spanish. But in any case, it's always easier for musicians who write softer lyrics and less complicated melodies that can easily penetrate the market, and this reality limits the artistic elaboration of our music.

LPF: But in your case, the lyrics seem as important as the music, because you're one of the founders of "conscious salsa."

WC: Yes, that's right. I've never stopped writing music with a message. At the beginning I did it with Héctor Lavoe, and later with Rubén Blades, and now I'm still doing it on my own because I think it's useful and necessary. And that type of composition caused us a lot of trouble, so much so that at one point when we were doing "Pedro Navaja" [1978] or "Tiburón" [1980] with Rubén, we had to perform in bulletproof vests.

But I also try to assure that my lyrics have positive messages for our people, and I complement my role as an artist by participating in lots of programs for youth. I go to schools and give speeches, I do ads on TV, I attend cultural events that help give Latinos pride and help raise their self-esteem because a good number of them, most of all the young people, suffer a cultural schizophrenia that makes them reject their values since they're not allowed to participate fully in the society in which they live. I think we should help them recover the pride in their roots and the idea that their culture is as valuable as any other. In the same vein, it's not a coincidence that I've just recorded an album titled *Honra y cultura* [*Honor and Culture*].

LPF: Why do you feel that need to give salsa a social content?

WC: Salsa is like a newspaper, a chronicle of our lives in the big city, and that's why it talks about topics like crime, drugs, prostitution, pain, uprootedness, and even about our history of exploitation and underdevelopment. We no longer talk about cutting sugarcane or the life of the *campesino*—although that's still possible—but rather about the social problems of Latinos living in the modern world and the causes of these problems.

LPF: But you also sing love songs.

WC: None of that means that songs about love, music, or happiness have to be excluded. But as a significant cultural movement, I don't believe salsa can renounce the possibility of exploring social themes. That's why, to paraphrase Oscar Hijuelos, "the salsa kings don't just play songs of love."

LPF: What's your definition of salsa?

WC: I don't believe salsa is a rhythm or a genre that can be identified or classified: salsa is an idea, a concept, the result of a way of approaching music from the Latin American cultural perspective.

LPF: Around 1975 the first great salsa boom occurred. To what extent did it help to consolidate this new music?

WC: The boom was a double-edged sword: it helped us get exposure, but it definitely introduced commercial interests. When salsa began to become popular among the Latin public of the United States and the Caribbean, it became part of a business, and soon the record labels started looking for formulas to take advantage of that success. One of those formulas was the most typical of all: to ride certain talented singers and create a repertoire for them, give them some arrangements, a band, and even a style, and then launch them. Another of the ideas was to dust off the old Cuban hits from the 1950s—the music of Benny Moré, Arsenio Rodríguez, and Celia Cruz and the Sonora Matancera—and "salsify" it a bit with new arrangements and melodies. These songs were sure to be hits all over again. So the boom became an obstacle for experimentation, and it has affected me personally quite a bit because I've always tried to improve with every new record. As far as I know, the only way to do so is to unleash your creativity, without worrying too much about whether or not you're going to sell a lot of records. That was a risk we took with Rubén, and you see, *Siembra* is still the best-selling salsa record of all time.

LPF: In my view, it's no coincidence that when the labels went back to the Cuban music of the 1950s they chose Benny Moré, Arsenio Rodríguez, and Celia Cruz and Sonora Matancera. What do you think of these artists?

WC: Without a shadow of a doubt, I think Cuban music has been my teacher and the teacher of many *salseros*. It's clear that salsa has its deepest roots in Cuban *son* and that due to the blockade and the political climate of the 1960s, less information started to come out of Cuba. That break was a decisive factor in the birth of salsa, which emerges as a grafting of the musical folklore of other Latin American countries onto *son*. And it's precisely this element that distinguishes *son* from salsa: while *son* has a specific structure, salsa is pure freedom, which means it can start with *a guaguancó* and finish with a Puerto Rican *aguinaldo,* with a dash of Brazilian *batucada* or a passage from Mozart.

But that root has names, and Benny, Arsenio, and Celia were the most important and the best known. Benny is freedom and talent, so much so that even today there are people making a good living singing his tunes the same way he did, or almost the same. So if he were alive today, he'd still be on top. I remember having seen Arsenio two or three times in New York; I was quite young, but I always listened to his records and he was our number-one teacher. We learned the feeling of Cuban music from him, orthodox *son,* so to speak. And Celia Cruz and Sonora Matancera were the models of fidelity to Cuban music. I always dreamed of working with Celia—she was the living image of the greatness that came from Cuba—and thank God I was able to do so. And we are also indebted to Celia because she always fought for Afro-Caribbean music, often in the face of great adversity. It's fair to say that without her and her determination, salsa might not have come to be in New York.

LPF: What do you know about the Cuban music of today?

WC: I've had the opportunity to share the stage with great orchestras like Los Van Van and Irakere, and I've heard a lot of what's being recorded in Cuba because fortunately we can get music from there now. And what makes me the happiest when I hear them is that the Cubans also prove we were right when we opposed the purists who refused to change a few things. They were trying to make music like putting on a Shakespearean play, which is staged time and again with the same text. And now, with the new Cuban groups that have started to emerge, the purists have seen that music cannot be reined in by a static model. The fact is that salsa also helped the Cubans to evolve; they nurtured their own music through salsa. There's no doubt about that.

SOURCE: Leonardo Padura Fuentes, "Willie Colon: The Salsa Kings Don't Just Play Songs of Love," in *Faces of Salsa: A Spoken History of the Music,* trans. Stephen J. Clark (Washington, D.C.: Smithsonian Books, 2003): 26–33.

THE ACCORDION TRAVELS THROUGH

"ROOTS MUSIC"

(Savoy)

The accordion speaks many musical languages, from Polish polkas in Illinois, to zydeco breakdowns and Cajun waltzes in Louisiana, to tejano and conjunto in Texas. Its American history reflects the impact of German immigration in the 1800s to the South and Southwest. Accordion virtuosos past and present abound in American ethnic musics, from Joe Falcon, who with his wife, Cleoma Breaux, made the first Cajun recording in 1928, to Clifton Chenier in zydeco, to the progressive conjunto innovators Flaco Jiménez and Esteban "Steve" Jordan.

On most Saturday mornings at the Savoy Music Center near Eunice, Louisiana, local musicians get together to make Cajun music. A noted accordion player and Cajun music activist, Marc Savoy (b. 1940) and his wife, Ann Savoy, a musician and folklorist, preside over a vibrant scene. A small area in their store, not far away from the cabinets selling CDs, books, and instruments, seats about 30 musicians. Locals are well aware of the Savoys' open house. For others, directions on the Web site invite you in:

> The Center hosts an *acoustic* jam session every Saturday morning, beginning at 9 in the A.M., and jamming until noon. All

are invited to join in, no permission or approval is needed, but we ask only one thing. . . . Please, no more than ONE triangle player at a time. If you're wondering how to find the music center, just look for thirty cars lined up Hwy. 190 between Eunice and Lawtell.

We are open for business, and admission is free, but a small box of boudin or cracklins would make you the most popular guy in there for about 2–3 minutes.

Marc Savoy's skillful summary of the history of the regional accordion reflects the patterns of immigration, adaptation, mobility, and hybridization that characterize distinctive American ethnic musics. The sentence in this summary concerning the impact of discovering oil makes the geographic leap from Texas to Louisiana come alive.

ACCORDIONS IN LOUISIANA

The mother of all accordions was a Chinese invention called a Sheng which consisted of a mouth piece connected to a bowl from which protruded a series of bamboo cane pipes internally implanted with vibrating steel reeds. To make the reeds vibrate, the player would blow into the mouth piece creating an ancient music of reed tonality. From this primitive beginning came many adaptations of the free reed. In around 1830, Europeans came forth with a refined and playable free reed instrument eventually modifying this concept to incorporate a set of bellows to drive the reeds instead of blowing into a mouth piece. The cane pipes were replaced with a right hand keyboard having buttons arranged in various configurations. Since the only function of the left hand was to pump the bellows providing an air source to drive the reeds, a system of buttons was also added to the left side for the bass/chord accompaniment. Such an instrument could now play a melody on the right side and play the bass chord accompaniment on the left side. Since the air source was no longer generated by the lungs, this made it possible for the player to sing to his own accompaniment. Here was an instrument that could make a lot of music even in the hands of a beginner. It was very easy to play, and just about anyone could pick it up and play a simple tune. For these reasons alone, the mid-1800s saw the popularity of this instrument mushroom in Germany to the extent that an accordion having ten treble buttons playing a major scale, two bass chord accompaniments along with the voices or stops placed on the top side of the instrument became internationally known as a "German style" accordion or "Melodeon." It became popular in regional music on a world-wide scale, and it appears in early Daguerreotype in Japan, Alaska, Africa, Cuba, and throughout the United States. It arrived in Louisiana with the immigration of German farmers and its popularity in the mid-1850s soon created such a demand on the local business establishments that music companies such as C. Bruno and Sons (est. 1834) in San Antonio, Texas, began supplying a variety of retail outlets. Louisiana stores that sold clothing carried "German style" accordions. Stores that sold farm implements sold them also. Almost every business place had accordions for sale. The accordion was found not in the fishing and trapping communities of the bayou country but rather in the flat, fertile rice farms around Crowley, considered today as the Rice Capital of the World. The German immigrants, besides introducing the accordion in the Louisiana prairies, are also credited by many with introducing rice farming to Louisiana. This may be disputed, but one factor remains undisputed—wherever you find rice farming, you will also find Cajun music with the accordion.

Nero is reported to have played the violin while Rome burned. But whether or not this point is fact, it is a fact that violins have been around for much longer than accordions. The exiled Acadians undoubtedly arrived in Louisiana either with violins or the knowledge of how to play them. It is immediately evident by listening to the early repertoire of Dennis McGee (which is a window into what early Cajun music was like) that this early fiddle music was very complex in its structure, requiring more than the seven note major scale available on the "German style" accordion. Not only did many of the melodies require the twelve note chromatic scale, but also many of the tunes required the fiddle to be "cross tuned" in open tunings. The newly arrived "German style" accordion had many limitations as to what could be played on it, but the advantages it did possess very soon propelled it forward to surpass the popularity of the fiddle. Regardless of the limitations of the newly arrived German Accordion, it did have many other advantages. Compared to string instruments, here was an instrument that, because of the steel reeds, had tremendous volume, did not need to be tuned each time it was played, did not incorporate the "sound board principle" of the string family which, because of its fragility, is very susceptible to humidity, temperature variations and very easily damaged. These advantages quickly caused the accordion to gain popularity to the point where accordion players outnumbered fiddle players ten to one.

Initially the accordion did not find favor with the fiddlers. Unfortunately the first accordions to arrive from Germany were in the keys of A, B, and G. The fiddlers' concept of the violin was that it was a diatonic instrument, one that could play in only one key and had to be tuned to whatever key it desired to play in. The concept of tuning to concert pitch and playing in whatever key was necessary to match up with the accordion had not yet developed and actually did not develop in Louisiana until 1960. Therefore, in attempting to tune violins with accordions in the key of A, B, and G, the strings were either so loose that they would not respond or so tight that they would break. It was not until the early 1900s that accordions began arriving from Germany in the key of C and D, making it possible at last for the fiddle to tune to the accordion. That, for the Louisiana Acadians, was a historical moment of great importance because it made it possible for the two instruments to play together rather than each instrument playing solo. However, it virtually destroyed most of the early Acadian fiddle music which required a twelve note chromatic scale instead of the seven notes offered by the accordion. Along with the availability of accordions in the right key enabling fiddles and accordions to play together, recording companies became interested in recording the vernacular music of America—reaching as far as the little isolated communities of Louisiana.

In 1928, Columbia Recording Company came to Crowley and recorded "Allons à Lafayette" by Joe and Cleoma Falcon. Cajun music was now and forever afterwards a part of American folk music—legitimate but not yet important. However this importance would eventually happen also. This first recording of Cajun music had a tremendous impact on the Cajun people. Here was this group of French-speaking Americans, who by the year 1928 had slowly begun to realize that they were quite different from the rest of America. Deeply rooted to their music and the role it played in their life, they were very impressed that the Columbia Recording

Company from "way up north" had come down to Crowley to record their music. Due to the impact of the first recordings, Cajun bands were now in big demand. Musicians could make more money playing a Saturday night dance than they could make all week long working in the fields from sun up to sun down. Accordions were everywhere, and every town had a store of some type that also sold accordions. Apparently Columbia's recording adventure was successful (especially since many Cajuns who didn't even own a Victrola would buy two or three copies just [to] have them in their possession). Because of Columbia's success, other companies followed in their footsteps and began recording material that would become the bulk of the repertoire that would endure into the next millennium.

The phenomenal growth of the popularity of the accordion continued until the outbreak of World War II. Trade was terminated with Germany, and new accordions were no longer to be found on the shelves of any stores. By this time, oil had been discovered in Louisiana which brought in many oil field workers from Texas who in turn introduced swing band music to the Cajuns. Accordion players soon found themselves to be no longer in demand. People's taste in music was changing and the accordion did not have the same connotation it once did. Accordion players had two options—either learn another instrument, or quit playing and let the old accordions collect dust in the attic. After the war, young men who had survived the horrors they had witnessed, returned home to reconnect with all the things they had longed for while they were so far away in a strange land. They wanted their families, their food, their lifestyles, and, yes, their music. It was back to the attic to get the old accordion down, clean the cobwebs off, and crank up the Cajun band. The problem however was that these instruments were becoming old now—reeds had either broken or gone out of tune, mice and moths had cut holes in the bellows, springs were weak or broken, etc. Replacement parts were not available, the technology to repair and service an accordion was not available, and worst of all, the new instruments themselves were no longer available. All the factories that had been producing these instruments were located in Saxony (which was in East Germany) and all trade with the U.S. was terminated.

The first known attempts (late 40s) at minor repairs and tuning is credited to a black man in Cecilia, Louisiana. The simple repairs which he performed were accomplished by replacing the damaged part with the same but undamaged part from another accordion. The repair or replacement of a worn or damaged part by actually fabricating a new replacement part did not occur until about 1955 when a very fine musician and woodworker in Lake Charles by the name of Sidney Brown set himself up as a tuner and repairer of accordions. Eventually, after realizing that he was fabricating a variety of replacement parts, he had the intuition to realize that it was possible to build an entire instrument with a minimum of shop tools. The only German style accordion around at that time was the "Hohner," made in West Germany, which, by as early as 1930, had been stream-lined and retuned to the point that no self respecting Cajun would be caught dead playing one. Nevertheless, this stream-lined Hohner did contain parts such as reeds (which could be retuned), bellows, buttons, stops, reed mounts, straps, etc. that were needed to build an accordion. All that was needed to imitate the famed prewar Sterlings and Monarchs was to fabricate the keyboard, bass section, and frame work based upon the measurements of the old pre-war accordions, use the parts from the Hohner which couldn't easily be manufactured without very expensive tooling and technology and voilà [sic]—a handmade accordion resembling the famed pre-war Sterlings and Monarchs was created. The fact that it was pretty much built around parts from a rather inexpensive accordion didn't really matter to anyone. It was retuned to sound like the Cajuns wanted, it looked like the old prewar accordions, and best of all, it was available.

If Cajun music exists today, it can thank the talent, efforts, and intuition of Sidney Brown. Without better accordions, Cajun music would probably have faded into obscurity and following in its footsteps would have been all other aspects of the culture because the music always was, and still is, the glue that holds the culture together. Today there are over one hundred people in Louisiana building accordions using imported reeds and bellows of the highest quality. With so many accordion factories today in Europe, China, and Brazil, it would seem that this type of accordion could be mass produced in large quantities, making a handmade instrument too costly and not competitive on the world market. What prevents this from happening is that this "German style" accordion employed a system of building the interior which is very labor intensive and does not lend itself easily to a mass production assembly line. This is still the same system used by accordion builders in Louisiana today. The popularity of handmade accordions is based upon the fact that the tone and response resulting from this labor-intensive system is not to be compared with the mass produced production line model.

The instrument which long ago was so very popular in Germany is no longer in demand in Germany today. The popularity of this accordion in Louisiana has become such that the old name "German style" has now become internationally known as "Cajun style." Cajun accordions today are being shipped back to Germany not for the purpose of playing German folk music, but rather to supply German musicians interested in playing Cajun music.

[signed] Marc Savoy

SOURCE: http://www.savoymusiccenter.com.

CONJUNTO MUSIC—"A VERY BEAUTIFUL ACCORDIONATE FLOWER"

(Santiago Jiménez, Flaco Jiménez, Jordán)

Conjunto, which literally means dance ensemble, generically refers to a Mexican-American dance music that emerged in the Southwest at the turn of the twentieth century. As this selection explains, conjunto merges German dance music with a Latino sensibility and, as with other ethnic musics, began as a regional style on regional radio through recordings geared to a regional market. Conjunto changes over time through the genius of its innovators and the preservers of its traditions. While accordion is its principal instrument, a typical conjunto includes the baja sexto (a twelve-string bass guitar), drums, and an electric bass.

Excerpts from three interviews show style as process changing musical choices and values. A patriarch of the tradition, Santiago Jiménez (b. 1913) stresses his exposure to German-American social dance music. His descriptions of dances—most of which originated in the 1800s—bring an otherwise distant social world into the present. Santiago's son Flaco Jiménez (b. 1939), who has continued to seek out new stylistic fusions for "progressive conjunto," bridges old and new worlds. The style and approach of Esteban (Steve) Jordán (b. 1939) registers the impact and attitude of popular music, particularly rock and jazz, on the tradition.

FROM AN INTERVIEW WITH SANTIAGO JIMÉNEZ, 1982

SANTIAGO: I am Santiago Jiménez, one of the first accordionists to play norteño [conjunto] music here in San Antonio. I was born in 1913 and I am now seventy . . . no, excuse me, I am now sixty-seven years old.

. . .

JUAN: When did you learn to play the accordion?

SANTIAGO: Well, I learned to play the accordion at the age of twelve. Back then, my father played at dances and I, watching him, started to learn the polkas, redowas, and schottishes. And then, some time later, well, maybe at the age of twenty, I began to make the first recordings here in San Antonio.

. . .

JUAN: And the polkas, then of *mexicanos* here and different from German polkas?

SANTIAGO: Well, they are a little different, but as I've told you, that music always came from Germany. Because, well, my father learned it from the Germans, and then other accordionists, hearing my father play, started to play the same ones, with the same rhythm, right? But I think the music came from Germany.

JUAN: Your father, what was his name?

SANTIAGO: Patricio Jiménez.

JUAN: And before him, did you know of anyone, a *mexicano*, who also played the accordion?

SANTIAGO: No. There in the *barrio* where I was born, he was the only accordionist there was.

JUAN: Here in San Antonio?

SANTIAGO: Yes, here in San Antonio. They called it the *barrio* of La Piedrera [the Quarry]. That is precisely why I composed that polka "La Piedrera." And in those days dances were just held in people's homes. There weren't any microphones, there weren't any amplifiers, nothing like that. Just the accordion and guitar. In the way they held those dances, back in those days, it would've been about 1920 or 1925, when I was barely ten years old. . . . My father played in the *barrio* of La Piedrera every eight days, every Saturday. The young people from there in the same *barrio* would all get together, and the way they did the dances, they would move the furniture into another room and they'd leave one room clear for dancing. And then the dances would last, oftentimes, from eight at night until seven in the morning.

. . .

JUAN: What was the first record?

SANTIAGO: Well, I'm not certain, I'm not too sure, but it seems that it was a polka that
                   we called "El aguacero polca." [*He later remembered that it was the polka "Dices
                   pescao."*]

. . .

JUAN: And what did you record with? The instruments: accordion, and what else?

SANTIAGO: Accordion, *bajo sexto,* and the contrabass, which they call the *tololoche.*

. . .

JUAN: With whom did you make those first records?

SANTIAGO: The first recordings I made were with the Decca company.

JUAN: From here, in San Antonio?

SANTIAGO: No, they were, I believe, from California. They came here to San Antonio to
                   record me.

. . .

JUAN: Then you hit it pretty big in those days, right?

SANTIAGO: Yes, well, those first records were . . . well, it was really something because
                   in those times, there weren't many who played or made records. The first
                   records that I made became hits right away. And since I was very well known
                   here in San Antonio, well . . . people always gave me a lot of support, and
                   they started to buy records. And even to this day, the last album that Flaco
                   Jiménez and I recorded has sold very well.

. . .

[Which polkas did his band make popular on recordings]

SANTIAGO: Well, the one that I made very popular and which is still heard a lot is "Viva
                   Seguín," "La Piedrera," and "El aguacero," which I recorded first. That one
                   has never died either, it's still heard a lot around here. But, one of the most
                   famous that is still heard everywhere, and which has been recorded by many
                   artists, *orquestas* too, is "Viva Seguín,"

. . .

JUAN: So, here the Chicano has taken the Germans' music and made something
                   different out of it, right?

SANTIAGO: Yes, something different, but that music has always come from there. I've
                   always said it, I don't know if I'm right or if I'm wrong, but that music comes
                   from Germany. It's just that here we've arranged it in another way, right? But
                   it still comes from over there.

JUAN: Have you written any new songs lately?

SANTIAGO: Yes, I wrote a few that will be coming out in an album. I gave them to Flaco
                Jiménez so that he could record them, and you'll be hearing them very soon.
                They're four or five songs of mine that are going to come out on a record.
                Joey recorded them. Joey López recorded them for Flaco, and I think that
                perhaps this month, that new album by Flaco Jiménez will be out. It will
                include my songs, which I wrote.

                . . .

JUAN: I read in a study about accordion music that early on accordion music was
                kind of for common people, or it was for low-class people, as opposed to
                orquesta music. What do you think? Was that attitude there, something like
                that?

SANTIAGO: Well, I never thought about it that way, but a lot of people, let's say, who
                wrote a lot music, as there still are today, they would say that accordion
                music, no . . . to them, well, it was nothing, it was just a very ordinary sound.
                But I never thought of it that way, because from the very beginning I thought
                that I liked all kinds of music. But the joy of the accordion was greater, it was
                greater all the time, more than any other music that was being played, like
                rock and roll, in those days, for instance . . . the Charleston. But a lot of horn
                blowing over here and horn blowing over there and, to me, it was just like
                they used to say, that it was monotonous.
                    Now, the accordion, I always thought, not just because I played it and my
                father did too, but I thought that accordion music had a very happy rhythm,
                simple though it might have been, but very happy—which is the thing in
                music that makes people happy: happiness. Because what good is it to be
                able to play really, really well and not . . . if it doesn't come from here, right,
                from the heart, right, whether it's the singer or whether the one who's play-
                ing. And what you say is indeed true. I heard many things like that said. But
                for me, I never thought it would be that way. And now today, all the people
                are seeing it, and they're hearing it, listening to it day after day, that accordion
                music is very happy music, and no one can say that it isn't.

                . . .

JUAN: The schottische, where does that kind of music come from?

SANTIAGO: The schottische, to be exact, comes from Germany. Yes, sir. The schottische,
                polkas, redowas, also come [from there], waltzes.

JUAN: So then, isn't there any music that comes more from here and not from
                Germany, with the accordion, right? The *huapango*?

SANTIAGO: Well the *huapango*, I believe, comes from Mexico, with the *mariachis*. *Corri-
                dos* also come from over there. But as to very old music, it comes, as far as I
                know, it comes from over there, from Germany.

JUAN: I thought that the schottische had something else, because the way it's danced is Indian, very Indian.

SANTIAGO: Well, now there are different ways to dance the schottische, but when I saw my father playing the schottische, and the people danced it very different from how they dance them today. Today they dance them real loosely, but not back then. The woman and the man would hold each other, and take two, three steps forward, and two, three steps back, and then the turns on tiptoe, on the tips of their feet. Waltzes, too, they danced on tiptoe. They didn't put their heels down or on the floor, never. The waltz . . .

JUAN: It must have been very hard, right?

SANTIAGO: It was very beautiful, the way they did it. And now, well, it is danced in all kinds of ways. And now to me, well, many *cumbias* out there today—I never in my life even knew what a *cumbia* was or anything, in those days you didn't hear any of that—well, now I see that the same rhythm . . . there are some, some *cumbias* that are very fast, and there are some *cumbias* that are slower, and you can see it as a polka. The *cumbia,* too, can be danced the same way, it's just that they have other names that they've come out with there. But as far as I know about old music, I only know like the schottisches, waltzes, re-dowas, and polkas. And the *huapangos,* well, the *huapangos* come from around Mexico, from over there. Those are the dances from long ago.

        . . .

SANTIAGO: Yes, [the dance the "Paul Jones"] came from the Germans, because I remember that I would see them in Brackenridge Park, they had dances there sometimes, and many Germans from here in New Braunfels would come there. All of them would come here to Brackenridge Park to the dances, and that's the way they danced it.[1]

JUAN: And why did they call it the "Paul Jones"?

SANTIAGO: I have no idea where that came from, "Paul Jones."

JUAN: Who knows who "Paul Jones" was! And they say that the German didn't care much for the *mexicano.*

SANTIAGO: No, not at that time. My father had, I believe, many German friends here in New Braunfels, and all that. That is precisely where he learned to play the accordion. He had many German friends, so that some didn't like them, and others did. But yes it's true that the Germans didn't like the Mexicans very much.

        . . .

JUAN: Well, I am very pleased to have had the opportunity to be here, talking with you, since you are one of the greats in conjunto music here in Texas, and, well, all of the United States. And I believe that there'll still be many fine things that you will leave to those of us who are following this tradition of conjunto music. I wish you luck.

SANTIAGO: Thank you very much. Let it be so.

SOURCE: Juan Jiménez, "Santiago Jiménez, Sr.," an interview conducted on February 26, 1982 (translated by Max Martínez with Victor Guera and Martha Vogel); in *Puro conjunto: An Album in Words and Pictures*, ed. Juan Tejeda and Avelardo Valdez (Austin, Tex: Center for Mexican American Studies/Guadalupe Cultural Arts Center, 2001):267–78.

~~~~~~~~

FROM AN INTERVIEW WITH FLACO JIMÉNEZ, 1988

Styles—starting with the legitimate style of my father, Don Santiago Jiménez, who was the pioneer of accordion-sound, *tejano* music—a lot of styles have been developed.

. . .

My style came from listening to various styles. When I began, I had to start with the style of my father, Don Santiago Jiménez, a style. . . . I won't say [of] long ago, but when that particular accordion-sound began. Then I started to listen to [other] accordionists. After my father it was Salvador García Torres, "El Pavo" of Los Pavos Reales. I listened a lot to Narciso [Martinez], I listened a lot to Paulino [Bernal], to Valerio [Longoria]. I listened to a lot of them. Manuel Guerrero, with Daniel Garcés's Los Tres Reyes. So I combined all of that and perhaps from here, from there, from all those friends in accordion music. . . . suddenly my style emerged.

Actually, there is a difference between [between *norteño* and *tejano*]. Because, without wishing to offend anyone, the truth is, the original music was explored, and the cradle of that accordion that came from over there from Europe, the pioneer was my father, Don Santiago Jiménez. From then on, different styles were developed. But there is a difference in a certain sense, but in knowledge of the accordion, there are as many good ones here as there are in Mexico. But in my view, it's in Texas where a different style originated, everything that's style in general.

We [Mexicans and *tejanos*] have the same feeling, the same feeling, be it *tejano* or *mexicano*. Naturally, there is a little bit of difference in the fact that the Mexican included—that is, *norteño* type and all that—the Mexican included the saxophone combined with the accordion, which is what followed the original from here in Texas.

I believe it is the brotherhood, the relationships among accordionists, that we're in agreement and we're in harmony, to talk with each other, and to say and to feel what one feels in the [Rio Grande} Valley, in Mexico, here in the United States, Texas, wherever. It all becomes a beautiful, very accordion-ate flower that blooms, and each one has his style. But then, it closes up with all of us united on that point.

A poster for the first Tejano Conjunto Festival, San Antonio, Texas, 1982.

In each region it's the same thing. If you happen to speak with a certain accent, and you go somewhere else and the language sounds different, be it the rhythm of how we talk, it's the same thing as with the accordion. We have our different accents to convey that musical message. . . .

. . .

Style—from Don Santiago Jiménez, which was really simple but beautiful, up to the very top, like Esteban Jordán and Valerio Longoria—I don't think it's going to change. Everything will remain enclosed in a certain atmosphere.

There is going to be something new in the exposure. There's going to be exposure in not just a local breakthrough, working just like we've worked over the years. No, the matter of the accordion, accordionists, youngsters, young accordionists who are about to make their debut. . . . we're going to see them on the international scene. It's not going to be just here, local.

The feeling should always be there. It's like the particular feeling in country-western when the Hank Williams sound comes along. Country-western and all that has never disappeared, and it will never disappear. Conjunto is here to stay! Of course, with the accordian!

FROM AN INTERVIEW WITH ESTEBAN JORDÁN, 1988

In each region, the musician's tempo is very important. . . . like if you go to Corpus [Christi], brother, there's the same polka that I play in Houston. I play it different in Corpus. . . . not different, except just the tempo, the tempo slows down. I know where, and where not to. In the Valley, I pick it up a little more. I do know about the dances. In Houston, it is the *tacuachito,* in San Antonio it's the *serruchito,* in West Texas it's the *tiezo* [he laughs], the *tiezo,* dude! I know all of them, man.

. . .

Today there are many people who hear a bit of this, a bit of that and the other, and they create a style. But those people are opportunists, those people aren't stylists any more. . . . Right now, there are false stylists. . . . My thing, very few can copy it, that's why they haven't copied it.

. . .

I like to play everything, that's what I like to do, but sometimes, you mix it up too much. If you're in the Valley, you can't be playing jazz, rock, and then turn around and play them some real tasty *salsa,* and a good solid *bolero,* like a *danzón,* and then a polka, because they'll kill you! There's no such thing as that. But in California, yes. Now, in Califas [California], one or two polkas a night and that's it. . . .

. . .

Tito Puente, Machito, Tito Rodríguez, Count Basie, in the big bands, you known, arrangements, like I'm saying, Buddy Rich, man. Son of a, he was bad! Since he's a drummer, man, the horns would sound, and he'd do the same on the drums as the horns. That influenced me, bro.

I mix it into the polka, I mix it into the redowa, wherever I fucking feel like it. I do whatever I want. Okay, for soul, Ray Charles. For drummer, Buddy Rich. For wild, Jimmy Smith. Get with it. Henry Mancini, I learn from there, I learn from anywhere, Dixieland.

Bro, I'm a universal stylist. Me, right now, wherever I want to go, I go, brother. I have a very crazy freedom. . . . It's so hard for me to follow one style. I'm very much a stylist of everything. And I never stop learning.

The only new style you're gonna see is me. I'm coming out with a new style, for me—not for the musicians, only for me. See, I'm bringing out the style that I did in the fifties, sixties, okay?

Conjunto is going to continue, bro. Polkas and the whole thing will go on. All they're gonna do is recycle mainly what they did. It's not going to end. It's not going to stop. Right now they're using combination, violins and all that stuff, with the accordion. It's cool. They're using little pieces of it.

It's our time to move it! To learn from ourselves. Find out what you got. Find out about your own self. How much have you got inside your head? You think just because you got a pocketful of money, you think you're it. And it's not where it's at, at all. If you're going to create, it doesn't take money to create. Just go out and grab a hook, or go to the mountains, man. Do something, go break your head, you'll find it. Look for it, you'll find it.

SOURCE: Juan Tejeda, "Conjunto! Style and Class. Narciso Martinez, Valerio Longoria, Tony de la Rosa, Paulino Bernal, Flaco Jiménez, and Esteban Jordán." In Spanish with English translation. *Puro Conjunto: An Album in Words and Pictures*, ed. Juan Tejeda and Avelardo Valdez (Austin, Tex.: Center for Mexican American Studies/Guadalupe Cultural Arts Center, 2001): 346–51. Poster reproduction, p. 163.

NOTE

1. The "Paul Jones" was a social dance popular in the early 1900s. See Charles J. Coll and Gabrielle Rosiere, "Dancing Made Easy" (1919) online in *American Ballroom Companion, Dance Instruction Manuals ca. 1490–1920,* <lcweb2.loc.gov/ammem/dihtml/dihome.html>.

GLORIA ANZALDÚA ON *VISTAS Y CORRIDOS*

My Native Tongue

Gloria Anzaldúa (1942–2004), a leader in Chicano studies and a political intellectual, helped to make the idea of "border studies" and *la frontera* an important part of cultural studies through her writings. In a selection from her first and probably best-known book, Anzaldúa describes the tensions in "Tex-Mex" identity, sometimes expressed through music. A noted activist for Latinas and for gay rights, Anzaldúa deliberately wrote in two languages at once, sometimes more English, sometimes less.

In this bilingual excerpt, she refers to the music of Lydia Mendoza (b. 1916) and her performance of the *corrido* "El Tango Negro."

In the 1960s, I read my first Chicano novel. It was *City of Night* by John Rechy, a gay Texan, son of a Scottish father and a Mexican mother. For days I walked around in stunned amazement that a Chicano could write and could get published. When I read *I Am Joaquín** I was

---

*Rodolfo Gonzales, *I Am Joaquín/Yo Soy Joaquín* (New York: Bantam Books, 1972).

surprised to see a bilingual book by a Chicano in print. When I saw poetry written in Tex-Mex for the first time, a feeling of pure joy flashed through me. I felt like we really existed as a people. In 1971, when I started teaching High School English to Chicano students, I tried to supplement the required texts with works by Chicanos, only to be reprimanded and forbidden to do so by the principal. He claimed that I was supposed to teach "American" and English literature. At the risk of being fired, I swore my students to secrecy and slipped in Chicano short stories, poems, a play. In graduate school, while working toward a Ph.D., I had to "argue" with one advisor after the other, semester after semester, before I was allowed to make Chicano literature an area of focus.

Even before I read books by Chicanos or Mexicans, it was the Mexican movies I saw at the drive-in—the Thursday night special of $1.00 a carload—that gave me a sense of belonging. "*Vámanos a la vistas,*" my mother would call out and we'd all—grandmother, brothers, sister and cousins—squeeze into the car. We'd wolf down cheese and bologna white bread sandwiches while watching Pedro Infante in melodramatic tear-jerkers like *Nosotros los pobres,* the first "real" Mexican movie (that was not an imitation of European movies).[1] I remember seeing *Cuando los hijos se van*[2] and surmising that all Mexican movies played up the love a mother has for her children and what ungrateful sons and daughters suffer when they are not devoted to their mothers. I remember the singing-type "westerns" of Jorge Negrete and Miguel Aceves Mejía. When watching Mexican movies, I felt a sense of homecoming as well as alienation. People who were to amount to something didn't go to Mexican movies, or *bailes* or tune their radios to *bolero,* *rancherita,* and *corrido* music.

The whole time I was growing up, there was *norteño* music sometimes called North Mexican border music, or Tex-Mex music, or Chicano music, or *cantina* (bar) music. I grew up listening to conjuntos, three- or four-piece bands made up of folk musicians playing guitar, *bajo sexto,* drums and button accordion, which Chicanos had borrowed from the German immigrants who had come to Central Texas and Mexico to farm and build breweries. In the Rio Grande Valley, Steve Jordan and Little Joe Hernández were popular, and Flaco Jiménez was the accordion king. The rhythms of Tex-Mex music are those of the polka, also adapted from the Germans, who in turn had borrowed the polka from the Czechs and Bohemians.

I remember the hot, sultry evenings when *corridos*—songs of love and death on the Texas-Mexican borderlands—reverberated out of cheap amplifiers from the local *cantinas* and wafted in through my bedroom window.

Corridos first became widely used along the South Texas/Mexican border during the early conflict between the Chicanos and Anglos. The *corridos* are usually about Mexican heroes who do valiant deeds against the Anglo oppressors. Pancho Villa's song, "*La cucaracha,*" is still the most famous one. *Corridos* of John F. Kennedy and his death are still very popular in the Valley. Older Chicanos remember Lydia Mendoza, one of the great border *corrido* singers who was called *la Gloria de Tejás.* Her "*El Tango Negro,*" sung during the Great Depression, made her a singer of the people.[3] The everpresent *corridos* narrated one hundred years of border history, bringing news of events as well as entertaining. These folk musicians and folk songs are our chief cultural mythmakers, and they made our hard lives seem bearable.

I grew up feeling ambivalent about our music. Country-western and rock-and-roll had more status. In the 50s and 60s, for the slightly educated and *agrinagado* Chicanos, there existed a sense of shame at being caught listening to our music. Yet I couldn't stop my feet from thumping to the music, could not stop humming the words, nor hide from myself the exhilaration I felt when I heard it.

SOURCE: Gloria Anzaldúa, *Borderlands/La Frontera: The New Mestiza* (1987; 2nd ed., San Francisco, Calif.: Aunt Lute Books, 1999): 81–83.

~~~~~~~~~~

NOTES

1. Ismael Rodriguez (b. 1917), a Mexican director, made this film (*We the Poor*) in 1948.

2. *When Children Leave Home* was made in Mexico in 1941 and released in the United States in 1943.

3. Lydia Mendoza (1916–2007) was a legendary Tejano singer and guitarist, who was often called "la alondra de la frontera" ("the lark of the border"). Among her signature songs was the "Tango Negro," a popular song by Belisario de Jesús Garcia. A recording is available on the album *La Alondra de la Frontera*—Live! (Arwhoolie Productions, 2001, CD 490).

152

CONTEMPORARY NATIVE AMERICAN MUSIC AND THE PINE RIDGE RESERVATION

(Porcupine Singers, Frazier)

Tradition and modernity intermingle in Native American powwows—gatherings, as Tara Browner describes them, where "Native North Americans come together to celebrate their cultures through the medium of music and dance."[1] Powwows can be pantribal or local events. Through their encouragement of new kinds of songs and dances, including many categories for competition, they have stimulated a modern renaissance of Indian music and dance. "Native American music" was designated a separate category for the Grammy Awards in 1999.

The Porcupine Singers travel on the powwow trail. Named for the Porcupine District on the Pine Ridge Reservation in South Dakota, the Porcupine Singers trace their roots back to the 1860s. They gained recognition through road tours in the 1970s and '80s, and in the first selection, song texts from a current CD offer samples of their traditional songs.

The second selection describes the making of a heroine. The well-known essayist and journalist Ian Frazier (b. 1951) offers a fuller account of the Pine Ridge Reservation in his book *On the Rez,* a study of contemporary Indian life. He writes about tensions between life on and outside of the reservation, sometimes embedded in musical culture and politics. The heroine was SuAnne Big Crow; her stage was a basketball court, and her moves, a fancy dance typically performed on the powwow circuit.

A few years after this triumphant moment, SuAnne Big Crow died as the result of injuries sustained in an automobile accident. She was awarded a heroine's funeral and her name has since become legend.

TEXTS FOR TRADITIONAL LAKOTA SONGS FROM THE REPERTOIRE OF THE PORCUPINE SINGERS

A. LAKOTA NATIONAL ANTHEM (FLAG SONG) AND VETERANS' SONG

*Tunkaśila yapi, tawapaha ki han
oihankesni (he) nanjin kte lo.
Iyohilateya oyate ki han wicicaġin kte ca.
Iecamun welo.*

*[The President's Flag will stand forever.
Under it, the people will grow: so I do this.]*

B. LITTLE BIG HORN BATTLE SONG: A SONG MADE FOR THE BATTLE OF LITTLE BIG HORN (1876)

*Kola tokile, kola tokile, kola ceyapelo.
Waziyata ki cizape.
Kola tokile, kola tokile, kola ceyapelo.*

*[Friend, where are you?
Friend, they are crying.
They are fighting up north.
Friend, where are you?
Friend, they are crying.]*

C. WORLD WAR I VETERANS' SONG

*Lakota hokśila iya śica tamakoce ki ota
iyacuca ekta wicaceyahe.*

*[The Lakota soldiers took the Germans'
land so they are still crying.]*

D. THE JEALOUS WOMAN

*Iyuśkinyan waunci yunkan winyanla ki
nawizina iśikcin amakinape.*

*[We were having a good time dancing, so
my little woman got jealous and took me
out of the dance hall.]*

E. SONG OF THE DANCERS

*Lakol wicoh'an kin tohanl abluśtan ki
    Oiokipi wani cin kte lo.
Waci wicasa heya yaun ca tamunka śni
yelo.*

*[Whenever I quit my Native ways, there will be no more happiness.
The dancers are saying this.
It is difficult to take.]*

SOURCE: Porcupine Singers, *Traditional Lakota Songs* (Canyon Records, 1997; CR-8007).

〜〜〜〜〜

A young basketball player named SuAnne Big Crow (1974–1992) led her local high-school team, the Pine Ridge Lady Thorpes, to a state championship in 1989, the first Native American girls' team to achieve this level of success. These two selections portray before-and-after events related to that victory and the role played by music and dance in them. The first selection from 1988 portrays a test of nerve and a psychological turning point, all embedded in music and dance. The Fancy Shawl dance described here most likely originated with the Lakota Sioux in the 1940s. One of the dances for soloists on the powwow circuit, it requires improvisation within limits. The Fancy Shawl reflects the showmanship and skill encouraged by public powwow competitions. Beginning in the 1920s and '30s with large powwows in Oklahoma, dancers "fancied up" their movements, adding spins and steps not found in the traditional dances.

Some people who live in the cities and towns near reservations treat their Indian neighbors decently; some don't. In cities like Denver and Minneapolis and Rapid City, police have been known to harass Indian teenagers and rough up Indian drunks and needlessly stop and search Indian cars. Local banks whose deposits include millions in tribal funds sometimes charge Indians higher loan interest rates than they charge whites. Gift shops near reservations sell junky caricature Indian pictures and dolls, and until not long ago, beer coolers had signs on them that said, INDIAN POWER. In a big discount store in a reservation border town, a white clerk observes a lot of Indians waiting at the checkout and remarks, "Oh, they're Indians—they're used to standing in line." Some people in South Dakota hate Indians, unapologetically, and will tell you why; in their voices you can hear a particular American meanness that is centuries old.

When teams from Pine Ridge play non-Indian teams, the question of race is always there. When Pine Ridge is the visiting team, usually their hosts are courteous, and the players and fans have a good time. But Pine Ridge coaches know that occasionally at away games their kids will be insulted, their fans will not feel welcome, the host gym will be dense with hostility, and the referees will call fouls on Indian players every chance they get. Sometimes in a game between Indian and non-Indian teams, the difference in race becomes an important and distracting part of the event.

One place where Pine Ridge teams used to get harassed regularly was in the high school gymnasium in Lead, South Dakota. Lead is a town of about 3,200 northwest of the reservation, in the Black Hills. It is laid out among the mines that are its main industry, and low, wooded mountains hedge it round. The brick high school building is set into a hillside. The school's only gym in those days was small, with tiers of gray-painted concrete on which the spectator benches descended from just below the steel-beamed roof to the very edge of the basketball court—an arrangement that greatly magnified the interior noise.

In the fall of 1988, the Pine Ridge Lady Thorpes went to Lead to play a basketball game. SuAnne was a full member of the team by then. She was a freshman, fourteen years old. Getting ready in the locker room, the Pine Ridge girls could hear the din from the fans. They were yelling fake-Indian war cries, a "woo-woo-woo" sound. The usual plan for the pre-game warm-up was for the visiting team to run onto the court in a line, take a lap or two around the floor, shoot some baskets, and then go to their bench at courtside. After that, the home team would come out and do the same, and then the game would begin. Usually the Thorpes lined up for their entry more or less according to height, which meant that senior Doni De Cory, one of the tallest, went first. As the team waited in the hallway leading from the locker room, the heckling got louder. The Lead fans were yelling epithets like "squaw" and "gut-eater." Some were waving food stamps, a reference to the reservation's receiving federal aid. Others yelled, "Where's the cheese?"—the joke being that if Indians were lining up, it must be to get commodity cheese. The Lead high school band had joined in, with fake-Indian drumming and a fake-Indian tune. Doni De Cory looked out the door and told her teammates, "I can't handle this." SuAnne quickly offered to go first in her place. She was so eager that Doni became suspicious. "Don't embarrass us," Doni told her. SuAnne said, "I won't. I won't embarrass you." Doni gave her the ball, and SuAnne stood first in line.

She came running onto the court dribbling the basketball, with her teammates running behind. On the court, the noise was deafeningly loud. SuAnne went right down the middle; but instead of running a full lap, she suddenly stopped when she got to center court. Her teammates were taken by surprise, and some bumped into one another. Coach Zimiga at the rear of the line did not know why they had stopped. SuAnne turned to Doni De Cory and tossed her the ball. Then she stepped into the jump-ball circle at center court, in front of the Lead fans. She unbuttoned her warm-up jacket, took it off, draped it over her shoulders, and began to do the Lakota shawl dance. SuAnne knew all the traditional dances—she had competed in many powwows as a little girl—and the dance she chose is a young woman's dance, graceful and modest and show-offy all at the same time. "I couldn't believe it—she was powwowin', like, 'get down!'" Doni De Cory recalled. "And then she started to sing." SuAnne began to sing in Lakota, swaying back and forth in the jump-ball circle, doing the shawl dance, using her warm-up jacket for a shawl. The crowd went completely silent. "All that stuff the Lead fans were yelling—it was like she *reversed* it somehow," a teammate said. In the sudden quiet, all you could hear was her Lakota song. SuAnne stood up, dropped her jacket, took the ball from Doni De Cory, and ran a lap around the court dribbling expertly and fast. The fans began to cheer and applaud. She sprinted to the basket, went up in the air, and laid the ball through the hoop, with the fans cheering loudly now. Of course, Pine Ridge went on to win the game. *The celebration of the state championship in 1989 won by the Pine Ridge Lady Thorpes, would be the high point of SuAnne Crow's life. Through powwow drumming, dance, and song, which affirmed community pride and joy, everybody found a way to belong.*

Next morning they got on the bus for the long drive back to Pine Ridge. Most of the girls finally slept then. The bus stopped at a McDonald's someplace for a lunch break, and Jeanne Horse and the girls decorated the outside of the bus with streamers and slogans. The whole reservation knew about the victory by that time. In the most remote places, in houses and trailers scattered across the prairie, people had listened to the game on KILI radio, and at the end of it they had thrown open their doors and cheered themselves hoarse into the night. Rosebud Sioux police cars escorted the bus across the Rosebud Reservation. As soon as the bus crossed the eastern edge of the Pine Ridge Reservation at the Bennett County line (still over fifty miles from Pine Ridge village) carloads of fans began to fall into line behind. By the time the bus reached the Wounded Knee turnoff, hundreds of cars were waiting for it. Parents and kids and grandparents stood by the intersection peering east to catch the first glimpse of it. As the bus went by, they waved and cheered and ran to their cars to honk the horns, and then they joined the lengthening train. The cars had their headlights on in the late-autumn twilight, and the line of lights stretched behind the bus for miles. SuAnne and Coach [Charley] Zimiga were standing by the front door of the bus on the steps looking out the window. At a place in the road where it curved, far into the distance she could see the line of lights following them. She said to Zimiga, "Oh, Char! Oh, Char! Oh, Char!"

Along the road approaching Pine Ridge village people had pulled their cars onto the shoulder on both sides facing perpendicular, and their headlights made a lit-up aisle. Hastily painted welcoming signboards lined the route. Horns were honking; pedestrians everywhere caused the bus and its entourage to go slower and slower. By the time the bus reached the four-way intersection in the middle of town, the crowds were too thick for it to move anymore. The sun had just gone down. SuAnne and the others came from the bus to loud cheering, and then several climbed onto the bus roof. They had promised each other that when they got to the four-way they would twirl on the streetlight, but now that they saw it they decided it was too high. A drum group had set up by the intersection and was drumming at top powwow volume as the singers' voices rose in a Lakota victory song. On the roof of the bus, SuAnne and the other girls danced.

People later said that it seemed as if everybody on the reservation was there. "It was the festival of festivals," recalled Dennis Banks, who had flown home early from a conference when he heard about the victory and had joined the procession behind the bus with his limousine. "Those girls *owned* that town," he said. People were carrying SuAnne and Rita and Mary and Darla and the other girls on their shoulders. As the drumbeats sounded, people threw their arms around each other's shoulders and formed a big circle and began a dance called the round dance. People outside the ring danced, too, stepping now this way, now that, shouting and singing. Kids from Pine Ridge High School and their rivals from Red Cloud, political enemies who hadn't spoken to each other in decades, country people who had supported AIM [the American Indian Movement] and village guys who had been goons, Dennis Banks and men who in 1973 might have been proud to shoot Dennis Banks[2]—there on the pavement beneath the single streetlight at the four-way, everybody danced.

SOURCE: Ian Frazier, *On the Rez* (New York: Farrar, Straus, and Giroux, 2000): 207–9; 234–35.

~~~~~~~

NOTES

1.   Tara Browner, "Contemporary Native American Pow-wow Dancing," in *I See America Dancing: Selected Readings, 1685–2000*, ed. Maureen Needham (Urbana: University of Illinois Press, 2002): 47.
2.   Dennis Banks helped to found AIM, the American Indian Movement, in 1968. The site Wounded Knee, South Dakota, played an important role in the political activism surrounding AIM because of both its historic associations with a massacre of Lakota Sioux in the 1890s and its contemporary associations with militant action by AIM in the 1970s, which again resulted in bloodshed between Lakota Sioux and the U.S. government.

MTV AND THE MUSIC VIDEO

(MoMA, Hoberman)

The introduction of Music Television (MTV) in 1980 changed the balance between sight and sound in the popular music world. The evolution of what had been promotional videos for individual songs into a significant genre in its own right has had a deep impact on the music industry. In 1985, the Museum of Modern Art (MoMA) in New York held its first exhibition of music videos, demonstrating the synergy between the avant-garde and technology, as its press release, reprinted here, explains. Then follows excerpts from a sophisticated critique of the exhibition by the notable film critic for the *Village Voice*, J. Hoberman. Along the way, Hoberman exposes the reader to postmodernist debates about what we now call "media culture."

MUSEUM OF MODERN ART
MUSIC VIDEO: THE INDUSTRY AND ITS FRINGES
September 6–30, 1985
PRESS SCREENING ANNOUNCEMENT

Equally striking in sound and image, music video is the subject of the exhibition *MUSIC VIDEO: THE INDUSTRY AND ITS FRINGES,* opening at the Museum of Modern Art on September 6. Including more than thirty video tapes, the 90-minute program runs chronologically from 1967 to the present. The survey includes such early tapes as *Penny Lane* and *Strawberry Fields Forever* by the Beatles and such recent works as *Road to Nowhere,* directed by David Byrne and Stephen Johnson with music by The Talking Heads, and *Decoy,* directed by Annabel Jankel and Rocky Morton with music by Miles Davis.

Promotional tools of the music industry, music videos have brought to public attention some of the experimental image process techniques, such as kaleidoscopic and analog video synthesizer effects, developed by independent artists in the sixties, such as Woody and Steina Vasulkas, Nam June Paik, and Ed Emschwiller. The music video artists have polished the techniques, shaping them into a cohesive medium that is a major force in popular culture.

Popular tapes such as *Beat It* (1983), directed by Bob Giraldi with music by Michael Jackson, will be shown in the exhibition with more experimental works such as *Sharkey's Day* (1984), with music and direction by Laurie Anderson, and the rarely seen *Frankie Teardrop* (1978), produced by Paul Dougherty, Walter Robinson, and Edit de Ak with music by Suicide. The program also includes such strongly self-reflexive works as *(Modern Industry)* (1985), directed by David Hogan, produced by Steve Buck with music by Fishbone, and *Lick My Decals Off, Baby* (1970), directed by Don Van Vliet with music by Captain Beefheart. A highlight of the exhibition is the surrealistic work *One Minute Movies* (1980) by Graeme Whifler, with music by the Residents.

MUSIC VIDEO: THE INDUSTRY AND ITS FRINGES has been organized by Barbara London, assistant curator of video in the Department of Film, with the assistance of Keith Johnson, assistant in the video program. The program is part of the fiftieth anniversary celebration of the Department of Film. The tapes will be shown in the Video Gallery on the first floor.

SOURCE: Museum of Modern Art Archives, New York City.

~~~~~~~

Hoberman used the occasion of the MoMA exhibition to survey styles of music-video making. In these excerpts from his essay, he refers to several landmark videos, making brief but insightful comments about historic precedents in the Beatles' promotional videos and a sly reference to the commodification of image represented by Madonna. (Just at this time Madonna became a superstar, and Macy's introduced a boutique named "Madonnaland" into its stores. Through music videos, Madonna reached an ever-widening public, who stopped, looked, listened, and bought.) Hoberman's sophisticated analysis treats a music video director as an "auteur," the French word for "author," which was popularized by French film critics in the 1960s to acknowledge the influence and artistic control of the film director. What music video makers deserve to be called "auteurs"?

WHAT'S ART GOT TO DO WITH IT?

The music video is the quintessential postmodern form—this week, anyway. Friday night, the Second Annual MTV Video Awards will be handed out at Radio City. Simultaneously, three and a half blocks uptown, the same mode (if not the same program) is being exhibited at the Museum of Modern Art. That the marketplace celebration promises to be less entertaining and more sanctimonious than the museum installation is a reversal inherent to the age.

"The erosion of the older distinction between high culture and so-called mass or popular culture," Frederic Jameson has suggested, is a hallmark of postmodernism.[1] So is the acceleration of this process: It took nearly half a century and a technological upheaval for movies to become culturally respectable; it's taken music videos the relative equivalent of half a minute.

For MTV's target audience, videos are pop songs, movies, sitcoms, pulp novels, and comic books all rolled into one. At their very least, mainstream videos are the prime show biz fossils of the future—packed with incidents and privileged moments. (Bette Midler's unsuccessful "Beast of Burden" [dir. Allan Arkush, 1983] is a rich example, complete with Mick Jagger cameo.) But superior "marginal" work notwithstanding, are they ever anything more?

For the past few years, many of the hippest film buffs I know have been fascinated by videos—as well they might be. For one thing, music videos reverse the customary relationship between sound and image. For another, they challenge the tyranny of the feature-length film. (I would rather watch a great five-minute video like Cyndi Lauper's "Girls Just Want to Have Fun" or Billy Idol's "Dancing by Myself" 15 times than sit, even once, through three-quarters of the movies that open in New York.) And, although most videos are panderingly puerile, when not monotonously parasitic—lifting from *Casablanca* and Cocteau alike—the form is basically nonnarrative and theoretically open to anything.

If the marriage of television and rock 'n' roll was consummated with Elvis Presley's epochal appearance on the *Ed Sullivan Show*, the offspring was slow to arrive. Only gradually building momentum from the mid-'70s on, video promos didn't truly emerge as a cultural force until Warner Amex's MTV went online in 1981. Within two years, however, rock videos rejuvenated the moribund record industry (fending off the threat of video games) and made the leap to network television. Since then, the oft-derided MTV aesthetic inexorably has invaded prime time (from *West 57th Street* to *Miami Vice*) and inspired several Hollywood blockbusters, as well as more than a few clinkers. Music video promos are now all but de rigueur for commercial movies.

While a number of rock video's more flamboyant directing talents, notably Russell Mulcahy and Steve Barron, have gone on to make commercial features, the traffic has been thicker the other way—Brian De Palma, Tobe Hooper, Bob Rafelson, Jonathan Demme, Allan Arkush, John Sayles, Paul Schrader, and John Landis having all made videos that can be compared usefully to their other work. But as hypnotic as the spectacle of MTV-inspired movies and TV shows may be, what's really interesting about rock videos isn't their impact on Hollywood feature-making; it's the videos themselves.

•

Perhaps because its blatant commercialism is one more affront to the utopian rock consciousness of the counterculture, rock video seems to have come in for more analysis from film critics than [from] the rock intelligentsia. *Film Comment, Film Quarterly,* and *Jump Cut* all have published major pieces on the form; music videos have been featured at film festivals on three continents; and papers on individual videos are beginning to crop up at academic film conferences.

As yet, there's no consensus about what makes a good, let alone a great, music video. (USA for Africa's "We Are the World," for example, seems destined to win MTV's Best Video award for reasons that have nothing to do with the quality of the direction, performances, or original material.) Nor is there a critical strategy by which the form can be politically redeemed.

Last year in *Film Quarterly,* Marsha Kinder pointed out that "everything on MTV is a commercial—advertising, news, station IDs, interviews, and, of course, the music videos themselves."[2] The videos are again characteristically postmodern in that, to paraphrase Jameson, they tend to reproduce and reinforce the logic of consumer capitalism. (Indeed, another Jameson account of the postmodern condition is a virtual description of MTV: "the transformation of reality into images, the fragmentation of time into a series of perceptual presents.")[3] Still, the left has a sorry history of rejecting mass culture out of hand—like any popular entertainment, music videos express utopian yearnings all their own.

If MTV is the most fully realized example of one-dimensional culture we have, there should be a special place accorded the videos that either address this directly, e.g., Bowie's "Let's Dance" (dir. David Mallet, 1982), in which the video subverts the positivist "message" of the song, or, alternately, those that hyperbolize their commercial nature, e.g., Madonna's "Material Girl," an MTV nominee for "Best Female Video." Similarly, "Dancing in the Dark," directed with sinister cool by Brian De Palma and nominated for two MTV awards, including "Best Stage Performance," presents Bruce Springsteen as the sweatless Stakhanovite[4] of rock and roll, a heroic model worker whose infinitely repeatable—and here artfully synthetic—rite climaxes with the dramatic selection of a partner out of the front row.

The perversely radical realism of this approach seems preferable, for example, to Springsteen's subsequent video—the affirmatively patriotic beer commercial montage of "Born in the USA" (dir. John Sayles, 1985). As for "Dancing with Myself" (dir. Tobe Hooper, 1983), Billy Idol dramatizes his blatant narcissism, romantic solipsism, desire to obliterate the world, and love-hate relation with his fans (visualized as implacable zombies who try to consume him) with such panache it's impossible not to get the joke. The song's title even mirrors the situation of the adolescent viewer.

•

As far as art history goes, it's telling that the first 10 videos in the MoMA show (assembled by video curator Barbara London) all were produced in the form's pre-MTV stone age, and have been inducted into Michael Shore's Rock-Video Hall of Fame. Published late last year, Shore's indispensable *Rolling Stone Book of Rock Video* is, partly for lack of anything else, the standard work on the subject. (Shore combines at least a reading acquaintance with relevant film history, a fan's enthusiasm, and an insider's knowledge of the music industry.) Taking the Hall of Fame/MoMA 10 as a basis of sorts, it's possible to establish some genres and pose a few useful juxtapositions.

Advertisements for Myself: "Penny Lane"/"Strawberry Fields Forever" versus "Lick My Decals Off, Baby." At their worst (which is not infrequent), music videos are tediously literal illustrations of banal songs, with a generic resemblance to television commercials. When not straight performance documentary, they attempt to reinforce product familiarity with shtick, be it narrative mini-melodramas or the worst clichés of a denatured pop surrealism. The product they sell, however, is far more ethereal than an automobile, a credit card, or a roll of bathroom tissue. Music videos are meta-showbiz; they're entertainment in the same sense that photorealist paintings were images of images. Thinking about them, you have to wonder just what "entertainment" is. It's as though movie trailers developed into, first, a sort of free-associative meditation on the movies they promoted and then, [into] things unto themselves.

Because music videos are even more steeped in the cult of personality than Hollywood movies, the easiest videos to theorize about are those in which the performing artist is also the auteur. (For the highbrow aesthete, this is something akin to recognizing what Levi-Strauss felicitously termed "the thinking of savages.") Rightly or wrongly, the first rock stars to be taken seriously by intellectuals and middlebrow pundits were the Beatles. In this sense, they resemble Charlie Chaplin—the first movie icon perceived as an artist. Canonized as meaningful pop, the Beatles were thus the most visible members of the first wave of postmodernist rock, and it's fitting that both MoMA and Shore recognize them as pioneers of video.

If the films the Beatles made with Richard Lester remain among rock video's most enduring sources, the Beatles were the first to tap them—with their 1967 promos for "Penny Lane" and "Strawberry Fields Forever" and then, the following year, *Magical Mystery Tour*. Yet, nostalgic cult value aside, "Penny Lane" and "Strawberry Fields Forever" are relatively weak videos, all jolly self-indulgence and cute self-satisfaction. Bigger than Jesus, freer than any pop artists had been before (or have been since), the Beatles could do little more with their image than coat it with a treacly surrealism: Like we're not morons, we have inner lives too, y'know? (The "Penny Lane"/"Strawberry Fields Forever" tendency to mimic surrealism rather than embody it reaches a grotesque apotheosis with Paul Simon's solemnly idiotic "Rene and Georgette Magritte with Their Dog after the War" [dir. John Logue, 1984], arguably the most abusively postmodern video in the MoMA retro.)

. . .

The ultimate magpie form, rock videos are crammed with media allusions even more than the films of hard-core movie brats like [Steven] Spielberg and [Martin] Scorsese. Still, for all the Hollywood iconography they purvey, they're far closer (as cinema) to avant-garde films and animated cartoons than to commercial genres. That's one reason narrative-bound critics have a hard time dealing with them—and also why more avant-garde types find them anathema.

. . .

The MoMA show is pointedly subtitled "the industry and its fringes," and, the presence of the Beatles, David Bowie, and Michael Jackson notwithstanding, its emphasis is less on the industry than on the margins. This is as it should be, but it presents a skewed image of music videos as a medium: Art aside, the two most prevalent genres are the mini-movie and the performance documentary. And, with the exception of Jackson's compelling "Beat It" (dir. Bob Giraldi, 1983)—a rousing paean to the power of show biz, as well as the '80s equivalent of Frank Sinatra's socially responsible "The House I Live In"—and Thomas Dolby's ambitious "Field Work" (dir. Thomas Dolby, 1985), a quasi-*Taxi Driver* with Ryuichi Sakamoto playing an embittered Japanese war veteran, the MOMA show de-emphasizes narrative. (Completely absent is the English director Julian [sic] Temple, whose 1983 "Come Dancing" and "Undercover"—with the Kinks and Rolling Stones, respectively—are models of dramatic compression and dreamlike layering.)

Curator London is further inclined to demonstrate music video's affinities with video art rather than with film. For all the name directors who have made videos, MoMA's movie auteurs are both underground: Beth B and Andy Warhol, neither of whom is shown to spectacular advantage. (B's cheerfully kinky "The Dominatrix Sleeps Tonight" [1984] is a pale reflection of her super-8 *Black Box* while Warhol's "Hello Again," made for the Cars, is basically a factory second—not even as kicky as the Cars' "You Might Think" [dir. Jeff Stein, Alex Weil, and Charlie Levi, 1984], which MTV viewers last year voted their favorite video.) The MoMA show acknowledges many of the most talented video-makers but here, as much as on MTV, the strongest auteurs are the performer-artists: Laurie Anderson, Toni Basil, David Bowie, David Byrne.

From the mega-pop realm of Michael Jackson, Madonna, and Bruce Springsteen, moving (toward the front line of aesthetic self-consciousness) through the artier domains of Bowie, Byrne, and Anderson, to the far side of clubland where, for example, Michael Smith has just completed a mock video, "Go for It, Mike," the most interesting current rock stars are primarily the authors of their own image[s]. In this sense, Bowie, particularly, is a prophetic figure.

Clearly, music video has induced the convergence of pop and performance art, crystallizing the element of psychodrama that always has been latent in rock 'n' roll. The fascination Michael Jackson exerts has as much to do with his self-presentation as show biz messiah, misunderstood elf, and werewolf-in-disguise as with his dancing, while Madonna and Cyndi Lauper are closer to Yvonne Rainer than to Little Eva.[5] (Lauper's "Girls Just Want to Have Fun" [dir. Ken Walz, 1983] can be construed as an answer song—to Sigmund Freud, no less. "There is so much pathos and desire secreted in this piece of squeaky blippy frou-frou sexism that it calls for a redefinition of the word 'fun,' if not 'girls,' if not 'just,'" Greil Marcus observed—and he wasn't even referring to the astonishing display of anarchic energy, neither sexually nor socially sublimated, that Lauper packs into the video.)

. . .

The ability to construct, project, and market a persona has become the *sine qua non* of '80s pop as well as '80s politics. Only the most fanatical Springsteen purists would insist that it was not his capitulation to music video that sent his career into the stratosphere. Who knows? MTV may well supplant Hollywood as the new spawning ground of the stars—or worse.

SOURCE: J. Hoberman, "What's Art Got to Do with It?" *Village Voice*, September 17, 1985, 39–40, 43, 65.

NOTES

1. Hoberman is quoting Frederic Jameson, "Postmodernism and Consumer Society," in *The Anti-Aesthetic: Essays on Postmodern Culture,* ed. Hal Foster (Port Townsend, Wash.: Bay, 1983): 128.

2. Marsha Kinder, "Music Video and the Spectator: Television, Ideology and Dream," *Film Quarterly* 38/1 (Oct. 1984): 2–15.

3. Ibid., 144.

4. "Stakhanovite" refers to Aleksei Grigorievich Stakhanov (1906–1977), a Soviet worker honored and rewarded for his exceptional diligence in increasing production.

5. Rainer (b. 1934) is an avant-garde dancer and choreographer. "Little Eva" was the stage name of the pop singer Eva Boyd (1943–2003).

154

TURNING POINTS IN THE CAREER OF

MICHAEL JACKSON

(Jackson, Jones)

It is open to question whether Michael Jackson (b. 1958) has survived his own celebrity. The scandals as well as the enormous publicity surrounding his way of life have, at least at this moment, eclipsed his gifts. Yet Jackson legitimately claims the position of a superstar entertainer as a singer, dancer, songwriter, and video creator.

These selections deal with turning points in his career during the 1980s, the decade of his greatest accomplishments. The first excerpt from Jackson's autobiography discusses his performance on the special telecast honoring the 25th anniversary of Motown Records in 1983, including a telling reference to Fred Astaire. (A portrait of the two artists side by side appeared in Jackson's book.) This is followed by a short statement about his ambitions in 1983 for the video *Thriller*, which not only challenged the racist policies of MTV, which had deliberately excluded black artists from its playlists, but also brought new production values and artistic direction to the genre as a whole. Then an excerpt from the autobiography of Jackson's collaborator, the musician and producer Quincy Jones (b. 1933), brings us into the record studio where the album *Thriller* was conceived and produced.

The theme of the changing relationship of Jackson to black culture runs through these excerpts. In reaching a mass audience, how much of the "street" did Jackson retain in his work? The excerpt by Jones shows just how much Jackson valued his identity as a black artist, trusting more than anything else "smelly jelly"—slang for funky black music—just at the time that he moved into mainstream pop.

FROM MICHAEL JACKSON'S *MOONWALK*

On May 16, 1983, I performed "Billie Jean" on a network telecast in honor of Motown's twenty-fifth anniversary. Almost fifty million people saw that show. After that, many things changed.

. . .

But the night before the taping, I still had no idea what I was going to do with my solo number. So I went down to the kitchen of our house and played "Billie Jean." Loud. I was in there by myself, the night before the show, and I pretty much stood there and let the song tell me what to do. I kind of let the dance create itself. I really let it *talk* to me; I heard the beat come in, and I took this spy's hat and started to pose and step, letting the "Billie Jean" rhythm create the movements. I felt almost compelled to let it create itself. I couldn't help it. And that—being able to "step back" and let the dance come through—was a lot of fun.

I had also been practicing certain steps and movements, although most of the performance was actually spontaneous. I had been practicing the Moonwalk for some time, and it dawned on me in our kitchen that I would finally do the Moonwalk in public on *Motown 25*.

Now the Moonwalk was already out on the street by this time, but I enhanced it a little when I did it. It was born as a break-dance step, a "popping" type of thing that black kids had created dancing on street corners in the ghetto. Black people are truly innovative dancers; they create many of the new dances, pure and simple. So I said, "This is my chance to do it," and I did it. These three kids taught it to me. They gave me the basics—and I had been doing it a lot in private. I had practiced it together with certain other steps. All I was really sure of was that on the bridge to "Billie Jean" I was going to walk backward and forward at the same time, like walking on the moon.

. . .

The day after the *Motown 25* show, Fred Astaire called me on the telephone. He said—these are his exact words—"You're a hell of a mover. Man, you really put them on their asses last night." That's what Fred Astaire said to me. I thanked him. Then he said, "You're an angry dancer. I'm the same way. I used to do the same thing with my cane."

. . .

It was the greatest compliment I had ever received in my life, and the only one I had ever wanted to believe. For Fred Astaire to tell me that meant more to me than anything. Later my performance was nominated for an Emmy award in a musical category, but I lost to Leontyne Price. It didn't matter. Fred Astaire had told me things I would never forget—*that* was my reward. Later he invited me to his house, and there were more compliments from him until I really blushed. He went over my "Billie Jean" performance step by step. The great choreographer Hermes Pan, who had choreographed Fred's dances in the movies, came over, and I showed them how to Moonwalk and demonstrated some other steps that really interested them.

Not long after that Gene Kelly came by my house to visit and also said he liked my danc-ing. It was a fantastic experience, that show, because I felt I had been inducted into an informal fraternity of dancers, and I felt so honored because these were the people I admired most in the world.

. . .

The three videos that came out of *Thriller*—"Billie Jean," "Beat It," and "Thriller"—were all part of my original concept for the album. I was determined to present this music as visually as possible. At the time I would look at what people were doing with video, and I couldn't un-derstand why so much of it seemed so primitive and weak. I saw kids watching and accepting boring videos because they had no alternatives. My goal is to do the best I can in every area, so why work hard on an album and then produce a terrible video? I wanted something that would glue you to the set, something you'd watch over and over. The idea from the beginning was to give people quality. So I wanted to be a pioneer in this relatively new medium and make the best short music movies we could make. I don't even like to call them videos. On the set I explained that we were doing a *film,* and that was how I approached it. I wanted the most talented people in the business—the best cinematographer, the best director, the best lighting people we could get. We weren't shooting on videotape; it was 35mm film. We were serious.

SOURCE: Michael Jackson, *Moonwalk* (Garden City, N.Y.: Doubleday, 1988): 200, 207, 209, 213.

~~~~~~

QUINCY JONES ON RECORDING *THRILLER*

The making of *Thriller* in a little more than two months was like riding a rocket. Everything about it was done at hyperspeed. Rod Temperton, who also co-wrote several of the album's songs, and I listened to nearly 600 songs before picking out a dozen we liked. Rod would then submit to me about thirty-three of his own songs on totally complete demos with bass lines, counter lines, and all, recorded on the Temperton high-tech system of bouncing the sound of two cassette recordings between ghetto blasters, and ten to twenty-five alternate titles for each song, with the beginnings of lyric schemes. He was absolutely the best to work with—always totally prepared, not one drop of b.s. We have always kept it very real with each other, exchang-ing strong opinions and comments without ever "throwing a wobbly"—British slang for "losing it." He's the kind of warrior you want at your side on the battlefield.

Michael was also writing music like a machine. He could really crank it up. In the time I worked with him he wrote three of the songs on *Off the Wall,* four on *Thriller,* and six on *Bad.* At this point on *Thriller* I'd been bugging him for months to write a Michael Jackson version of "My Sharona."[1] One day I went to his house and said, "Smelly, give it up. The train is leaving the station." He said, "Quincy, I got this thing I want you to hear, but it's not finished yet. I don't have any vocals on it."

I called Michael "Smelly" because when he liked a piece of music or a certain beat, in-stead of calling it funky, he'd call it "smelly jelly."[2] When it was really good, he'd say, "That's some smelly jelly." I said, "Smelly, it's getting late. Let's do it."

I took him to the studio inside his house. He called his engineer and we stacked the vocals on then and there. Michael sang his heart out. The song was "Beat It."

We knew the music was hot. On "Beat It" the level was literally so hot that at one point in the studio [the audio engineer] Bruce Swedien called us over and the right speaker burst into flames.[3] We'd never seen anything like that in forty years in the business. That was the first time I began to see the wildness that was in Michael's life during the *Thriller* sessions. One time we were working in the Westlake studio and a healthy California girl walked by the front window of the studio, which was a one-way mirror facing the street, and pulled her dress up over her head. She was wearing absolutely nothing underneath. Rod and Bruce and I got an eyeful. It was right on time in the middle of intense deadline pressure. We stood there gawking. We turned around and saw Michael, devoted Jehovah's Witness that he was, hiding behind the console.

We did the final mixes and fixes and overdubs up until nine o'clock in the morning of the deadline for the reference copy. We had three studios going at once. We put final touches on Michael's vocals on "Billie Jean," which he sang through six-foot cardboard tubes. Then Bruce put his magic on the final overdub of Ndugu Chancler's live drums, replacing the drum machine. I took Eddie Van Halen to another small studio with two huge Gibson speakers and two six-packs of beer to do his classic guitar solo, dubbing the bass line on "Beat It" with Greg on mini Moog. Bruce liked to record our rhythm tracks on sixteen-track tape, then go to digital to get that fat, analog rhythm sound that we all loved and called "big legs and tight skirts."[4] He left with the tape to go to Bernie Grundman's studio to master the record: Bernie's the absolute best in the business. In the meantime I took Michael to my place, laid him out on the couch in my den, and covered him with a blanket for a three-hour nap at 9 A.M. By twelve o'clock we had to be back to hear the test pressing that was going out to the world. I couldn't sleep myself; the anticipation was tremendous. We'd all worked ourselves into a near-frenzy. Meanwhile, back at the studio, Larkin Arnold, the head honcho of black music at Epic, was popping champagne, anxiously waiting to hear the final mix.

This was it, the big moment: Rod, Bruce, Michael, his managers Freddie DeMann and Ron Weisner, and myself sat down and listened to the final test pressing of a record that was to be the follow-up to *Off the Wall*. It was a disaster. After all the great songs and the great performances and great mixes and a great tune stack, we had 24-karat sonic doo-doo. There was total silence in the studio. One by one we crept across the hall for some privacy: more silence ensued.

We'd put too much material on the record. To be really competitive on the radio, you need big fat grooves to make a big fat sound. If you squeeze it into thin grooves, you get tinny sound.[5] We had twenty-eight minutes of sound on each side; we knew there was nothing to discuss. Smelly would say, "Oh, no, that's the jelly, that's what makes me want to dance," which would end the conversation every time. With vinyl, you had to be realistic; it had to be under nineteen minutes of music per side. This was now all about physics first, then music. On CDs it doesn't matter, because it's digital. Deep down inside we must have all known this all along as we were working, but chose not to deal with reality in our fatigue and musical euphoria.

We were in trouble and tears were streaming down Michael's face. He said, "What do we do now?" "The Girl Is Mine" single was already out in the marketplace and charting at number 2 with a bullet; the album was late. The record company wanted the masters that afternoon.

We told Larkin Arnold, "In its present state, this record is unreleasable."

We took two days off and in the next eight days we put it dead in the pocket, mixing one tune per day. Rod cut one verse from "The Lady in My Life," and Smelly finally agreed to give up some of the jelly in the long, long, long intro to "Billie Jean." Something clicked after that, and it wasn't just the album. One prominent performer was reported to have said of "The Girl Is Mine," "After all this time, this is all they've got?" Hell no—that song was our lead-in, our red herring. On the trail of each other "Billie Jean" and "Beat It" hit the charts and inhaled them. Both went to number 1, providing me with the unique experience of having three number 1 hits in a row replacing each other, since Michael's two songs followed Patti Austin and James Ingram's "Baby, Come to Me." Michael was splashed all over the globe visually as well as musically: Michael, the MTV videos, and the music all rode each other in glory. The single "Thriller," which came out a year and a half after the album, was the first fourteen-minute video ever made and was treated like the premiere of a feature film around the world. The truth is, many of the videos that became trademarks of MTV imitate "Beat It," "Thriller," and "Billie Jean"—it's Michael's choreography all over the screen, even today. His videos made a sensation in tandem with the rise of the video as an art form. He helped define the music video in terms of style, dance ensembles, and overall performances. CBS likes to claim the credit, but it was Steve Ross who insisted that MTV air Michael's videos, because of the channel's policy to focus on "just rock 'n' roll," not black artists. Rick James and Motown were ballistic over the boycott of "Super Freak." I love that—third-generation rockers are thoroughly convinced that rock music was born in Idaho.

Like everyone else in the world, I always go into the studio to make a number 1 record, but the ones that really get my attention are the ones that don't do what you thought they were going to do, like go to number 1. You put a million dollars cash in front of a singer or a songwriter, it doesn't correlate to the music; it doesn't speak one word to the creative process. We just strive to give ourselves goose bumps, and if we do, there's a good chance that the audience will feel the same vibe.

The fans couldn't keep clear of Michael after *Thriller* took over the world.

Michael was a different kind of entertainer. Completely dedicated. He practiced his dancing for hours. Every lick, every gesture, every movement was carefully conceived and considered. He lived in a fantasyland because that's what worked for him. At his place in Havenhurst, he used to have a mouthy parrot with a lot of attitude as well as a boa constrictor named Muscles. One day Muscles was missing. They looked all over the property, inside and out, and after two days they finally found him dangling from the parrot's cage, with the parrot's beak sticking out his mouth. He'd swallowed that sucker whole and couldn't back his head out the bars because he hadn't digested the bird yet. In a way, that's a metaphor for Michael's life after *Thriller*, because at a certain point, he couldn't back out of the cage. It all became overwhelming for him.

You have to remember that in the music business every decade produced a monster, screaming-groupies phenomenon: in the forties it was Frank Sinatra, in the fifties Elvis Presley, in the sixties the Beatles. In the seventies Stevie Wonder and the introduction of the full-range Dolby sound for films had a big impact. In the eighties Michael took it home, because no matter what anyone thought music was before, he was light-years ahead. *Thriller* sold 50 million copies all over the world, more than any other album in the history of the record business. Let's get real: Michael was the biggest entertainer on the planet Earth. We made history together. This was the first time a young black performer had won the hearts of everyone from eight years old to eighty, all over the world. This was breaking major barriers.

SOURCE: Quincy Jones, *Q: The Autobiography of Quincy Jones* (Garden City, N.Y.: Doubleday, 2001): 236–41.

NOTES

1. Released on June 11, 1979, "My Sharona" by the Knack was a successful teenage rock-and-roll tune that went gold in 13 days.
2. "Smelly jelly," means some black music idiom that really sticks in your head.
3. "Burst into flames" is slang for an overheated speaker.
4. This means overdubbing in unison with different low textures.
5. A "fat" groove typically has bass and a syncopated drum beat; a "thin" groove typically is less syncopated and uses more cymbals.

155

$\mathcal{S}$ALLY BANES EXPLAINS WHY

"BREAKING IS HARD TO DO"

In one of the first articles to focus on break-dancing—and occasionally credited with putting the term itself into print—the author, dance scholar, and critic Sally Banes reports and interprets this new vernacular art form. Occasionally, Banes uses terminology from classical dance, perhaps to suggest that while it comes from "the street," in this case from the black neighborhoods of New York, and is celebrated as an authentic cultural expression, break-dancing is also about making the body into an instrument of wonder. At the time Banes wrote this article, rap was finding its mainstream audience.

PHYSICAL GRAFFITI

C hico and Tee and their friends from 175th street in the High Times crew were breaking in the subway and the cops busted them for fighting.

"We're not fighting. We're dancing!" they claimed. At the precinct station, one kid demonstrated certain moves: a head spin, ass spin, swipe, chin freeze, "the Helicopter," "the Baby."

An officer called in the other members of the crew, one by one. "Do a head spin," he would command as he consulted a clipboard full of notes. "Do 'the Baby.'" As each kid complied, performing on cue as unhesitatingly as a ballet dancer might toss off an enchainement,[1] the cops scratched their heads in bewildered defeat.

Or so the story goes. But then, like ballet and like great battles (it shares elements of both), breaking is wreathed in legends. "This guy in Queens does a whole bunch of head spins in a row, more than ten; he spins, stops real quick, spins . . ."

"Yeah, but he stops. Left just goes right into seven spins, he never stops."

"There's a ten-year-old kid on my block learned to break in three days."

"The best is Spy, Ronnie Don, Drago, me [Crazy Legs], Freeze, Mongo, Mr. Freeze, Lace, Track Two, Weevil . . ."

"Spy, he's called the man with the thousand moves, he had a girl and he taught her how to break. She did it good. She looked like a guy."

"Spy, man, in '78—he was breaking at Mom and Pop's on Katonah Avenue in the Bronx, he did his footwork so fast you could hardly see his feet."

"I saw Spy doing something wild in a garage where all the old-timers used to break. They had a priest judging a contest, and Spy was doing some kind of Indian dance. All of a sudden, he threw himself in the air, his hat flew up, he spun on his back, and the hat landed right on his chest. And everyone said, 'That was luck.' So he did it once more for the priest, and the hat landed right on his chest. If I didn't see it, I would never have believed it."

The heroes of these legends are the Break Kids, the B Boys, the Puerto Rican and black teenagers who invent and endlessly elaborate this exquisite, heady blend of dancing, acrobatics, and martial spectacle. Like other forms of ghetto street culture—graffiti, verbal dueling, rapping—breaking is a public arena for the flamboyant triumph of virility, wit, and skill. In short, of style. Breaking is a way of using your body to inscribe your identity on streets and trains, in parks and high school gyms. It is a physical version of two favorite modes of street rhetoric, the taunt and the boast. It is a celebration of the flexibility and budding sexuality of the gangly male adolescent body. It is a subjunctive expression of bodily states, testing things that might be or are not, contrasting masculine vitality with its range of opposites: women, babies, animals; and death. It is a way of claiming territory and status, for yourself and for your group, your crew. But most of all, breaking is a competitive display of physical and imaginative virtuosity, a codified dance-form-cum-warfare that cracks open to flaunt personal inventiveness.

For the current generation of B Boys, it doesn't really matter that the Breakdown is an old name in Afro-American dance for both rapid, complex foot work and a competitive format. Or that a break in jazz means a soloist's improvised bridge between melodies. For the B Boys, the history of breaking started six or seven years ago, maybe in the Bronx, maybe in Harlem. It started with the Zulus. Or with Charlie Rock. Or with Joe, from the Casanovas, from the Bronx, who taught Charlie Rock. "Breaking means going crazy on the floor. It means making a style for yourself." In Manhattan, kids call it rocking. A dancer in the center of a ring of onlookers drops to the floor, circles around his own axis with a flurry of slashing steps, then spins, flips, gesticulates, and poses in a flood of rhythmic motion and fleeting imagery that prompts the next guy to top him. To burn him, as the B Boys put it.

Fab 5 Freddy Love, a graffiti-based artist and rapper from Bedford-Stuyvesant, remembers that breaking began around the same time as rapping, as a physical analogue for a musical impulse. "Everybody would be at a party in the park in the summer, jamming. Guys would get together and dance with each other, sort of a macho thing where they would show each other who could do the best moves." They started going wild when the music got real funky—music by groups like Super Sperm and Apache. As the beat of the drummer came to the fore, the music let you know it was time to break down, to free style. The cadenced, rhyming, fast-talking epic mode of rapping, with its smooth surface of sexual braggadocio, provides a perfect base for a dance style that is cool, swift, and intricate.

But breaking isn't just an urgent response to pulsating music. It is also a ritual combat that transmutes aggression into art. "In the summer of '78," Tee remembers, "when you got mad at someone, instead of saying, 'Hey, man, you want to fight?' you'd say, 'Hey, man, you want to rock?'" Inside the ritual frame, burgeoning adolescent anxieties, hostilities, and powers are symbolically manipulated and controlled.

Each segment in breaking is short, from ten to thirty seconds—but packed with action and meaning. The dancing always follows a specific format: the *entry*, a stylized walk into the ring for four or five beats to the music; the *footwork*, a rapid, circular scan of the floor by sneakered feet while the hands support the body's weight and the head and torso revolve slowly—a kind of syncopated pirouette; the *freeze*, or stylized signature pose, usually preceded by a spin; the *exit*, a return to verticality and to the outside of the circle. The length of the "combination" can be extended by adding on more footwork-spin-freeze sequences. The entry, the footwork, and the exit are pretty much the same from dancer to dancer—although some do variations, like Freeze from the Breakmasters crew, who stuffs a Charleston into his entry, and then exits on pointe. But it is largely in the freeze that each dancer's originality shines forth, in configurations that are as intricate, witty, obscene, or insulting as possible. A dancer will twist himself into a pretzel. Or he will quote the poses of a pinup girl. He might graphically hump the floor, or arch up grabbing his crotch. Someone else might mime rowing a boat or swimming or emphasize acrobatic stunts like backflips and fish dives. Sometimes two breakers team up for a stunt: imitating a dog on a leash, or a dead person brought back to life by a healthy thump on the chest. According to Rammelzee, a DJ who's gotten too tall to break, the set of sequences adds up to a continuing pantomimic narrative. It is each dancer's responsibility to create a new chapter in the story. "Like if you see a guy acting like he's dead, the brother who went before him probably shot him."

When you choose your moves, you not only try to look good; you try to make your successor look bad by upping the ante. That's one way to win points from the crowd, which collectively judges. Going first is a way to score a point, but so is coming up with a cool response, chilling out. Through the freeze, you insult, challenge, and humiliate the next person. You stick your ass in his direction. You hold your nose to your spine, signaling a move so good it hurts. But the elegant abstract dancing that couches these messages counts, too. B Boys from the Bronx and Manhattan look down on the "up rock" prevalent in Brooklyn, a mere string of scatological and sexual affronts without the aesthetic glue of spinning and getting down on the floor.

Naming and performing the freezes you invent are ways of laying claim to them, though some poses are in the public domain. A lot of breakers are also graffiti artists, and one way to announce a new freeze is to write it as graffiti. Speed and smoothness are essential to the entire dance, but in the freeze humor and difficulty are prized above all. "You try to put your head on your arm and your toenails on your ears," says Ken of the Breakmasters. "Hard stuff, like when I made up my elbow walk," says Kip Dee of Rock Steady. "When you spin on your head. When you take your legs and put them in back of your head out of the spin."

During the summers the B Boys gravitate to the parks, where DJs and rappers hang out. Younger kids learn to break by imitating the older kids, who tend to outgrow it when they're about sixteen. Concrete provides the best surface for the feet and hands to grip, but the jamming is the thickest in the parks, where the DJs can bring their mikes and amplifiers. During the winters, breakers devise new moves. Crazy Legs, of Rock Steady, claims the "W," in which he sits on doubled-back legs, was an accident.

"Once I was laying on the floor and I kicked my leg and I started spinning," says Mr. Freeze, of Breakmasters. But inventing freezes also demands the hard daily work of conscious experiment. "You got to sweat it out." You don't stop, even when you sleep. "I have breaking dreams," several B Boys have told me. "I wake up and try to do it like I saw it." Kip Dee dreamed he spun on his chin, "but I woke up and tried it and almost broke my face."

Part of the macho quality of breaking comes from the physical risk involved. It's not only the bruises, scratches, cuts, and scrapes. As the rivalry between the crews heats up, ritual combat sometimes erupts into fighting for real. And part of it is impressing the girls. "They go crazy over it," says Ken. "When you're in front of a girl, you like to show off. You want to burn the public eye, because then she might like you."

Some people claim that breaking is played out. Freddy Love disagrees. "The younger kids keep developing it, doing more wild things and more new stuff. We never used to spin or do acrobatics. The people who started it just laid down the foundations. Just like in graffiti—you make a new style. That's what life in the street is all about, just being you, being who you are around your friends. What's at stake is a guy's honor and his position in the street. Which is all you have. That's what makes it feel so important, that's what makes it feel so good—that pressure on you to be the best. Or try to be the best. To develop a new style nobody can deal with. If it's true that this stuff reflects life, it's a fast life."

SOURCE: Sally Banes, "Physical Graffiti: Breaking Is Hard to Do," *Village Voice*, April 22, 1981; reprinted in *And It Don't Stop! The Best American Hip-Hop Journalism of the Last 25 Years*, ed. Raquel Cepeda (New York: Faber & Faber, Inc., 2004) 7–11.

~~~~~~~~

NOTE

1. *Enchaînement* is a connected series of moves and steps in a ballet dance sequence.

156

TWO MEMBERS OF PUBLIC ENEMY DISCUSS

SAMPLING AND COPYRIGHT LAW

This composite interview with two members of the rap group Public Enemy high-lights many important themes in hip-hop.[1] Spreading far beyond its roots in black neighborhoods and street dancing (discussed in chapter 155), during the 1980s hip-hop spawned a multifaceted movement, embracing dance, music, rap, and art. Groups such as Run-DMC and Public Enemy expanded hip-hop's domain into protest music and black nationalism.

Developing musical styles also reflected the creative energy of this movement, with the wordplay of the lyrics matched by inventive instrumental backgrounds of processed sound. In this excerpt, the key instrumental technique of "sampling"[2] is discussed both by rap artist Chuck D (b. 1960) and the producer of Public Enemy's rhythm tracks, Hank Shocklee. They talk about being "crafty," that is to say, practic-ing the craft of sample-based hip-hop. Then unsurpassed in its ferocious political agenda and confrontational lyrics, the landmark album *It Takes a Nation of Millions to Hold Us Back* used samples from many artists, including James Brown, George Clinton, the Beastie Boys, and Bob Marley.

In the 1990s, new copyright laws and increased industry vigilance in enforcing them challenged sampling as a stylistic resource. The conflict between "ownership" and "freedom"—a battle between right and right, one might say—is often at the cen-ter of current cultural debates. The interview was published in *Stay Free!* a Brooklyn-based magazine that offers sharp critiques of intellectual property laws and con-sumer culture.

When Public Enemy released *It Takes a Nation of Millions to Hold Us Back,* in 1988, it was as if the album had landed from another planet. Nothing sounded like it at the time. *It Takes a Nation* came frontloaded with sirens, squeals, and squawks that augmented the chaotic, collaged backing tracks over which P.E. [Public Enemy] frontman Chuck D laid his politically and poetically radical rhymes. He rapped about white supremacy, capitalism, the music industry, black nationalism, and—in the case of "Caught, Can I Get a Witness?"—digital sampling: "CAUGHT, NOW IN COURT 'CAUSE I STOLE A BEAT / THIS IS A SAMPLING SPORT / MAIL FROM THE COURTS AND JAIL / CLAIMS I STOLE THE BEATS THAT I RAIL . . . I FOUND THIS MINERAL THAT I CALL A BEAT / I PAID ZERO."

In the mid- to late 1980s, hip-hop artists had a very small window of opportunity to run wild with the newly emerging sampling technologies before the record labels and lawyers started paying attention. No one took advantage of these technologies more effectively than Public Enemy, who put hundreds of sampled aural fragments into *It Takes a Nation* and stirred them up to create a new, radical sound that changed the way we hear music. But by 1991, no one paid zero for the records they sampled without getting sued. They had to pay a lot.

Stay Free! talked to the two major architects of P.E.'s sound, Chuck D and Hank Shocklee, about hip-hop, sampling, and how copyright law altered the way P.E. and other hip-hop artists made their music. The following is a combination of two interviews conducted separately with Chuck D and Hank Shocklee. [signed]—Kembrew McLeod

. . .

STAY FREE!:   What are the origins of sampling in hip-hop?

CHUCK D: Sampling basically comes from the fact that rap music is not music. It's rap over music. So vocals were used over records in the very beginning stages of hip-hop in the 70s to the early '80s. In the late 1980s, rappers were recording over live bands who were basically emulating the sounds off of the records. Eventually, you had synthesizers and samplers, which would take sounds that would then get arranged or looped, so rappers can still do their thing over it. The arrangement of sounds taken from recordings came around 1984 to 1989.

STAY FREE!:   Those synthesizers and samplers were expensive back then, especially in 1984. How did hip-hop artists get them if they didn't have a lot of money?

CHUCK D: Not only were they expensive, but they were limited in what they could do— they could only sample two seconds at a time. But people were able to get ahold of equipment by renting time out in studios.

STAY FREE!:   How did the Bomb Squad [Public Enemy's production team, led by Shocklee] use samplers and other recording technologies to put together the tracks on *It Takes a Nation of Millions.*

HANK SHOCKLEE: The first thing we would do is the beat, the skeleton of the track. The beat would actually have bits and pieces of samples already in it, but it would only be rhythm sections. Chuck would start writing and trying different ideas to see what worked. Once he got an idea, we would look at it and see where the track was going. Then we would just start adding on whatever it needed, depending on the lyrics. I kind of architected the whole idea. The sound has a look to me, and Public Enemy was all about having a sound that had its own distinct vision. We didn't want to use anything we considered traditional R&B stuff—bass lines and melodies and chord structures and things of that nature.

STAY FREE!:   How did you use samplers as instruments?

CHUCK D: We thought sampling was just another way of arranging sounds. Just like a musician would take the sounds off of an instrument and arrange them their own particular way. So we thought we was quite crafty with it.

SHOCKLEE: "Don't Believe the Hype," for example—that was basically played with the turntable and transformed and then sampled. Some of the manipulation we was doing was more on the turntable, live end of it.

STAY FREE!:   When you were sampling from many different sources during the making of It Takes a Nation, were you at all worried about copyright clearance?

SHOCKLEE: No. Nobody did. At the time, it wasn't even an issue. The only time copyright was an issue was if you actually took the entire rhythm of a song, as in looping, which a lot of people are doing today. You're going to take a track, loop the entire thing, and then that becomes the basic track for the song. They just paperclip a backbeat to it. But we were taking a horn hit here, a guitar riff there, we might take a little speech, a kicking snare from somewhere else. It was all bits and pieces.

STAY FREE!:   Did you have to license the samples in It Takes a Nation of Millions before it was released?

SHOCKLEE: No, it was cleared afterwards. A lot of stuff was cleared afterwards. Back in the day, things was different. The copyright laws didn't really extend into sampling until the hip-hop artists started getting sued. As a matter of fact, copyright didn't start catching up with us until Fear of a Black Planet [1990]. That's when the copyrights and everything started becoming stricter because you had a lot of groups doing it and people were taking whole songs. It got so widespread that the record companies started policing the releases before they got out.

STAY FREE!:   With its hundreds of samples, is it possible to make a record like It Takes a Nation of Millions today? Would it be possible to clear every sample?

SHOCKLEE: It wouldn't be impossible. It would just be very, very costly. The first thing that was starting to happen by the late 1980s was that the people were doing buyouts. You could have a buyout—meaning you could purchase the rights to sample a sound—for around $1,500. Then it started creeping up to $3,000, $3,500, $5,000, $7,500. Then they threw in this thing called rollover rates. If your rollover rate is every 100,000 units, then for every 100,000 units you sell, you have to pay an additional $7,500. A record that sells two million copies would kick that cost up twenty times. Now you're looking at one song costing you more than half of what you would make on your album.

CHUCK D: Corporations found that hip-hop music was viable. It sold albums, which was the bread and butter of corporations. Since the corporations owned all the sounds, their lawyers began to search out people who illegally infringed upon their records. All the rap artists were on the big six record companies, so you might have some lawyers from Sony looking at some lawyers from BMG and some lawyers from BMG saying, "Your artist is doing this," so it was a tit for tat that usually made money for the lawyers, garnering money for the company. Very little went to the original artist or the publishing company.

SHOCKLEE: By 1990, all the publishers and their lawyers started making moves. One big one was Bridgeport, the publishing house that owns all the George Clinton stuff. Once all the little guys started realizing you can get paid from rappers if they use your sample, it prompted the record companies to start investigating because now the people that they publish are getting paid.

STAY FREE!:   There's a noticeable difference in Public Enemy's sound between 1988 and 1991. Did this have to do with the lawsuits and enforcement of copyright laws at the turn of the decade?

CHUCK D: Public Enemy's music was affected more than anybody's because we were taking thousands of sounds. If you separated the sounds, they wouldn't have been anything—they were unrecognizable. The sounds were all collaged together to make a sonic wall. Public Enemy was affected because it is too expensive to defend against a claim. So we had to change our whole style, the style of *It Takes a Nation* and *Fear of a Black Planet*, by 1991.

SHOCKLEE: We were forced to start using different organic instruments, but you can't really get the right kind of compression that way. A guitar sampled off a record is going to hit differently than a guitar sampled in the studio. The guitar that's sampled off a record is going to have all the compression that they put on the recording, the equalization. It's going to hit the tape harder. It's going to slap at you. Something that's organic is almost going to have a powder effect. It hits more like a pillow than a piece of wood. So those things change your mood, the feeling you can get off of a record. If you notice that by the early 1990s, the sound has gotten a lot softer.

CHUCK D: Copyright laws pretty much led people like Dr. Dre to replay the sounds that were on records, then sample musicians imitating those records. That way you could get by the master clearance, but you still had to pay a publishing note.

SHOCKLEE: See, there's two different copyrights: publishing and master recording. The publishing copyright is of the written music, the song structure. And the master recording is the song as it is played on a particular recording.

Sampling violates both of these copyrights. Whereas if I record my own version of someone else's song, I only have to pay the publishing copyright. When you violate the master recording, the money just goes to the record company.

CHUCK D: Putting a hundred small fragments into a song meant that you had a hundred different people to answer to. Whereas someone like EPMD might have taken an entire loop and stuck with it, which meant that they only had to pay one artist.

STAY FREE!:   So is that one reason why a lot of popular hip-hop songs today just use one hook, one primary sample, instead of a collage of different sounds?

CHUCK D: Exactly. There's only one person to answer to. Dr. Dre changed things when he did *The Chronic* and took something like Leon Haywood's "I Want'a Do Something Freaky to You" and revamped it in his own way but basically kept the rhythm and instrumental hook intact. It's easier to sample a groove than it is to create a whole new collage. That entire collage element is out the window.

SHOCKLEE: We're not really privy to all the laws and everything that the record company creates within the company. From our standpoint, it was looking like the record company was spying on us, so to speak.

CHUCK D: The lawyers didn't seem to differentiate between the craftiness of it and what was blatantly taken.

STAY FREE!:   Switching from the past to the present, on the new Public Enemy album, *Revolverlution* [2002], you had fans remix a few old Public Enemy tracks. How did you get this idea?

CHUCK D: We have a powerful online community through Rapstation.com, PublicEnemy .com, Slamjams.com, and Bringthenoise.com. My thing was just looking at the community and being able to say, "Can we actually make them involved in the creative process?" Why not see if we can connect all these bedroom and basement studios, and the ocean of producers, and expand the Bomb Squad to a worldwide concept?

STAY FREE!:   As you probably know, some music fans are now sampling and mashing together two or more songs and trading the results online. There's one track by Evolution Control Committee that uses a Herb Alpert instrumental as the backing track for your "By the Time I Get to Arizona." It sounds like you're rapping over a Herb Alpert and the Tijuana Brass song. How do you feel about other people remixing your tracks without permission?

CHUCK D: I think my feelings are obvious. I think it's great.

SOURCE: Kembrew McLeod, "How Copyright Law Changed Hip Hop: An Interview with Public Enemy's Chuck D and Hank Shocklee," *Stay Free! Magazine* 20 (Fall 2002). Available at http://www.stayfreemagazine.org/archives/20/public_enemy.html.

NOTES

1. In an e-mail communication to the editor (December 1, 2006), McLeod wrote that this published article combined two telephone interviews he conducted, the first with Hank Shocklee on August 5, 2002, and the second with Chuck D on August 23, 2002.

2. As defined by Larry Starr and Christopher Waterman, *American Popular Music: From Minstrelsy to MTV* (New York: Oxford University Press, 2003): 466, "sampling" is "a digital recording process wherein a sound source is recorded or 'sampled' with a microphone, converted into a stream of binary numbers that represent the profile of the sound, quantized, and stored in computer memory."

$\mathcal{D}$J QBERT, MASTER OF TURNTABLE MUSIC

Richard Quitevis (b. 1969), known professionally as DJ Qbert or simply Qbert, is an acknowledged virtuoso of "scratch music"—a genre of turntable music which grew out of the earlier hip-hop innovations of Kool DJ Herc and other rap-based musicians in the 1970s and '80s. Acknowledging the impact of jazz and electronic music in his work, Qbert in this interview shows just how far a style can travel from its original roots; in contrast to the social realism of most hip-hop, Qbert talks about nature and space. This excerpt also alludes to the popularity of turntable-music making among Filipino-Americans living in or around San Francisco, focusing on the West Coast as an innovative site and further registering the impact of what has been called "Pacific Rim" culture. It is likely that another Pacific Rim artist, Henry Cowell (see chapter 84), would have admired DJ Qbert's ensemble, the Invisibl Skratch Piklz, which dominated DJ competitions in the 1990s. This interview coincided with the release of a fine video documentary by Doug Pray called *Scratch,* which focuses on technical wizardry and features Qbert's predecessors, among them Kool DJ Herc and Grandmaster Flash.

"SCRATCH" AND SNIFF WITH DJ QBERT

For many, DJs, hip hop and turntables probably seem like a pure product of a hard-knock urban life. That's where DJ Qbert, former member of the Invisibl Skratch Piklz, begs to differ. The Bay Area turntablist finds inspiration in the city and the natural beauty that surrounds it.

"I'm a very nature person," says the DJ from his Daly City home. "And from there, I get concepts of music that are natural, like the way, say, a scratch would sound. Say I would be at the ocean—I would emulate that hypnotic way the waves would sound. Or—this is corny—but looking at clouds, you see how they naturally move in any way, like water. How it's formless. So I try to make the sound formless but at the same time have form."

Qbert, otherwise known as Richard Quitevis, is something of a philosopher, as *Scratch,* a new documentary, demonstrates. The film by Doug Pray (who covered the Seattle grunge scene in *Hype*) opens March 8 in San Francisco and Berkeley, and Qbert appears with Pray at Lumiere Theatre on opening night, before departing on the film's spin-off DJ tour with Mix Master Mike, Dilated Peoples, Afrika Bambaataa and Z-Trip.

Scratch will give scratch culture newcomers a dose of Qbert and Mix Master Mike's out-there perspective. The film captures them talking at length about their interests in intergalactic travel and extraterrestrials.

"We'd always talk about how music would sound on other worlds and stuff. Our imaginations just exploded, thinking about all these imaginary sounds, and I guess that was the big inspiration, sure," the 32-year-old DJ says enthusiastically. "Invisibl Skratch Piklz were definitely a sci-fi thing. A lot of it had to do as well with the sounds you can play with a turntable. You can just pick the weirdest sounds, and of course, that's going to sound alien."

Those otherworldly sounds are the sole focus of *Scratch* which, unlike *Wild Style* and other films about hip hop culture, concentrates completely on DJs and the art of scratching. With that premise in mind, Pray turns a lens on an outpost apart from L.A. and New York—the Bay Area, home of Qbert, Mix Master Mike and Yoga Frog, who were all members of the madly adept, influential turntablist crew Invisibl Skratch Piklz. The film also includes David Paul, the owner of Bomb Records, which broke ground with its "Return of the DJ" compilations, and DJ Shadow, the innovative Marin County-via-Davis, Calif., turntablist.

"L.A. and New York got a lot of coverage on their sound, and San Francisco was like on the same trip but there was just no one filming before," theorizes Qbert. "By the time they got to San Francisco, which was really recently in the mid-'90s, they discovered, 'Wow, look at this style that was brewing out here.' So I guess it became very interesting to people who hadn't seen this elevated type of scratching type of music going on."

Invisibl Skratch Piklz were definitely on another level in terms of scratching. The ensemble included Qbert, a two-time DMC turntablist competition world champion and considered by some to be one of the most technically adept DJs around, as well as Mix Master Mike (who went on to join the Beastie Boys), DJ Apollo, DJ Disk and DJ Shortkut. The group was known for their amazing skill at eking out all kinds of sounds from a turntable, performing together with superhuman synchronicity and influencing turntablist groups such as the X-ecutioners. In fact, Pray concentrates so extensively on the Filipino American Piklz crew in *Scratch* that he ends up excluding earlier innovators, a flaw in an otherwise informative and inspired film.

The Invisibl Skratch Piklz were just doing what came naturally, says Qbert today. "Everyone in the group pretty much did their own thing, let their own personality come out in the group and everyone had multiple personalities," he notes. "Say in a band, you have a drummer, guitarist and bass player, that type of thing. With turntables, one guy could be drumming one section, then the next guy right after could take the drums and the other guy can play . . . chickens on the record and the next guy can play . . . [laughs] sheep. Another guy can play bass out of nowhere and take turns doing whatever. You can play all the instruments on vinyl. Whatever someone's doing, you got to play something that would blend with that and not clash with that guy's sounds."

Was it any coincidence that the Piklz were all Filipino American? "Ha, I think there's a lot of every nationality in DJing," Qbert says, but he concedes, "A lot of the entertainers are Filipino. I think that's just in the blood. Say you go to a Chinese party, you play some music, everybody goes home. But at a Filipino party, you're eating and everyone's waiting for the music."

The Piklz broke up two years ago with a final performance at Skratchcon 2000 at the Fillmore in San Francisco, and since then, Qbert has been concentrating on refining his style and learning even more turntable tricks. He limbers up for practice with back and arm exercises designed for violinists, whose motions resemble turntablists', and likes to guzzle plenty of "clear fluids." Practice happens at least two hours a day in his "Lair of the Octagon," named after the eight-sided table of turntables, which his carpenter father, Larry, built.

"The turntable is a musical instrument in that sense," Qbert says. "How many different things can you do on a guitar? It's just infinity. Your imagination is your limit to how many tricks or how many ways you have of doing things."

It's a lesson Qbert learned from his mother, Ninda, whom he describes as the "queen of recruiting for Mary Kay for four years in a row in the whole United States."

"She had taught me that you can do anything," he says. "You know all the positive affirmations—growing up listening to all that, that just totally sunk in, that there's no boundaries. Whatever you dream is possible. Follow your dreams. Invent your life. Things like that." He also applies that business sense to the Thug Rumble, a company he runs with Yoga Frog, which is currently putting out his animated sci-fi film, *Wave Twisters,* on DVD as well as DJ records. An instructional video is in the works in addition to *Wave Twisters II.*

First the earth's turntable, next the universe's flying disks, from the sound of the stories the energetic DJ tells. "One time with DJ Disk, I was looking up at the sky in San Francisco, and a dot just went across the sky, and it wasn't a shooting star because it was kind of moving a little slow and that just *tripped* us out. It was like the coolest thing. Like, hey, look at that dot in the sky. It looked like a star, not a bright star, but a dim star. All of a sudden it started moving across the sky—it was like wwwwwhoooo, that is *fresh.*"

SOURCE: Kimberly Chun, "'Scratch' and Sniff with DJ Qbert," *Asian Week* (March 8–14, 2002). Available at www.asianweek.com/2002_03_08/arts_hotnsour.html.

158

A PRESS RELEASE FROM

THE COUNTRY MUSIC ASSOCIATION

This news release from the Country Music Association is reprinted here partly because the CMA was the first music lobby group to organize on behalf of a specific regional style with the explicit function of increasing its share in the American music market. From that perspective, the CMA represents the trajectory of growth in the music industry as a whole as well as the corporate investment in cultural demographics. Here, it hardly stands alone. Probably no one in 1958, when the CMA was founded, anticipated the popularity of country music as a national style. How should we interpret this growth? From the perspective of national politics, the popularity of country music also coincides with what some have called the "southernization" of the American mainstream. Yet, as this chapter demonstrates, the global market for country music has grown as well, with audiences in England, Thailand, and Germany listening to Garth Brooks and Shania Twain.

The rise of country music has served sociologists of culture well, and its expansion is considered a classical model for understanding what is called "the production of culture." Left out in that model, however, is basic musical appeal.[1] In short, what is there in the music itself that explains the extraordinary success demonstrated here? What do the songs of Willie Nelson and Reba McEntire mean to various people and why?

≈≈≈≈
≈≈≈≈
≈≈≈≈

FOR IMMEDIATE RELEASE
December 17, 1997
1997 Wrap-Up: Country Music Industry Stable
Country Music Growing in the International Marketplace,
Corporate America

NASHVILLE—In addition to the CMA consumer survey recently released in which 51 percent of Country Music listeners said they are listening to the music more in the last year, there are further indications that Country is alive and well.

- According to AMUSEMENT BUSINESS, three Country artists ranked among the overall top 10 U.S. touring acts of the year (Garth Brooks, Reba McEntire and Brooks & Dunn).

- Country remains the leading radio format in number of stations. As of November 1997, there are 2,505 primary Country stations, followed by News/ Talk with 1,567 and Adult Contemporary with 917. (M Street Corporation)

- Each week, over 45 million Americans listen to Country Radio stations nationwide, leading the second-largest listenership format (Adult Contemporary) by over 7 million. (SMRB)

- Garth Brooks' album, SEVENS, sold 896,932 units in its first week. Only Pearl Jam's 1993 release, VS., sold more albums in its first week with 950,000, and only five albums have sold more than 700,000 in the first week since Soundscan began reporting in 1991. SEVENS is the fourth album of Brooks to debut at No. 1 on BILLBOARD magazine's "Billboard 200" pop album chart.

- Shania Twain [became] one of four female recording artists to hit the 10 million mark with sales of a single album in the U.S. The other women to share this distinction are Carole King, Whitney Houston and Alanis Morissette. To date, Twain's Mercury Records 1995 release, THE WOMAN IN ME, has sold 12 million copies worldwide. Her third album, COME ON OVER, was released in November and has already sold over 1 million albums according to Soundscan.

- George Strait's box set, STRAIT OUT OF THE BOX, has been certified multi-platinum with sales of 5 million, making it the third biggest selling box set of all time trailing only BRUCE SPRINGSTEEN & THE E STREET BAND LIVE / 1977–85 (12 million) and Led Zeppelin's self-titled set (6 million).

- LeAnn Rimes is the top recording artist in all genres in 1997, according to the RIAA, with combined certified sales of 12.5 million units. This includes 2 million copies of her single, "How Do I Live." Her success and appeal across all musical genres was further evidenced with her Grammy win as best new artist and when she won artist of the year at the 1997 Billboard Music Awards.

- Garth Brooks' now legendary August concert in New York's Central Park was broadcast by HBO and was the most watched special on cable TV in 1997.

- Going head-to-head against season premiere night on ABC and NBC, "The 31st Annual CMA Awards," telecast live September 24 on the CBS Television Network, placed first for the night in households, viewers and all adult demographics. The annual live CBS special broadcast 8–11 PM (EDT) won every half-hour among households and adults 25–54.

- Hollywood has tapped Country Music again in 1997. Soundtracks such as Steven Seagal's "Fire Down Below," Dennis Quaide [sic] and Danny Glover's "Switchback," the animated film "Annabelle's Wish" and Robert Duvall's "The Apostle" all feature Country Music. In addition, Deana Carter released a video for her song "Once Upon A December" off the soundtrack for the animated movie "Anastasia." Trisha Yearwood's track of "How Do I Live" is featured on the soundtrack of "Con Air," while Mary Chapin Carpenter covered Dionne Warwick's classic "What Do You Get When You Fall in Love" on the soundtrack of the popular summer movie "My Best Friend's Wedding," starring Julia Roberts.

- This year, the CMA debuted its first-ever CMA Awards webcast to coincide with the popular televised special taking cybersurfers behind-the-scenes during pre-event rehearsals, backstage activities, as well as the post-awards party. The webcast included artist photos, chats, backstage interviews, and a trivia contest. The CMA Awards webcast was proven a huge success with 11 million hits.

- Movie moguls Steven Spielberg, David Geffen and Jeffrey Katzenberg invested in the Country Music industry opening Dreamworks Records, while the world's number-one entertainment company, Disney, opened its first Country Music label, Lyric Street Records. Both are based in Nashville.

- The 26th Annual International Country Music Fan Fair sold out in advance for the seventh consecutive year.

- The sold-out "Music Industry & New Technologies" (MINT) conference developed by the Country Music Association was the first Nashville conference to explore the Internet, websites, multimedia, hardware and other applications to market Country Music.

Corporate America further strengthened its ties with Country Music in 1997:

- Once again, over 200 registrants including representatives from American Airlines, Blockbuster, Coca-Cola, Lifestyle Marketing Group, Nabisco, Time Warner Cable Direct and UniRoyal Tire, attended the second annual Marketing With Country Music conference presented by the CMA to familiarize marketing and advertising industry decision-makers on opportunities available with Country Music to meet brand marketing objectives.

- During 1997, Country artists have been involved in a wide variety of national ads and corporate promotions including Coca-Cola, Chevy Trucks, Justin Boots, Ford, 1-800-COLLECT, Folgers Coffee, Discover Card, the GAP, Southwest Airlines and Wrangler.

- Mobil 1 sponsored the Reba McEntire/Brooks & Dunn tour, marking the first time a major petroleum company has backed a musical event.

- Primestar, one of the nation's leading providers of satellite television and entertainment, will continue its 1997 sponsorship with Clay Walker throughout 1998. For the second straight year, Alison Krauss & Union Station have linked up with Martha White Foods. For his first-ever sponsored tour, Vince Gill joined forces with Kraft this year for the Kraft Country Tour '97.

- Target and Capitol Nashville recently enlisted John Berry to help promote "Club Wedd," the retail chain's in-store, computerized bridal registry. The sweepstakes was promoted via in-store promotions, point-of-sale and print advertising.

- Billed as the largest single-day ticket event in music history, Fruit of the Loom, Inc. drew an estimated 220,000 Country Music fans to the Dallas Motor Speedway in Fort Worth, Texas.

The international marketplace's interest in Country Music is evident in 1997:

- Since 1982 when CMA's first international office opened in the U.K., Country Music has grown significantly in the international marketplace. In 1997, CMA appointed new full-time representatives for the U.K./Ireland, as well as Germany/Switzerland/Austria joining CMA's Benelux representative. CMA's first representative for Australia was also appointed.

- A high-profile retail and media campaign surrounding BBC-2's telecast of the 1997 CMA Awards on September 28 resulted in a significant increase in Country Music sales in the U.K. and Ireland according to retailers there. Trisha Yearwood's SONGBOOK: A COLLECTION OF HITS garnered an 84-percent increase over the previous week's sales, while works by LeAnn Rimes, Deana Carter and George Strait earned significant increases as well. Over 2.5 million viewers tuned in to at least part of the Awards program.

- "The 31st Annual CMA Awards" were televised in more countries than ever before including the United Kingdom, Germany, Switzerland, Thailand, Holland, Ireland, Sweden, Denmark and Finland.

- Nationally networked BBC Radio 2 launched the first-ever Country Music Week, which included a live broadcast of the CMA Awards.

- Trisha Yearwood's "How Do I Live" has become a huge radio hit in Australia, Ireland and Asia Pacific regions.

- Alan Jackson, Trisha Yearwood and Shania Twain all scored gold albums in Australia while LeAnn Rimes has been certified Triple Platinum for sales of over 210,000.

- Over 560 radio programs outside North America feature Country Music, reaching over 30 million listeners in 32 countries.

Founded in 1958, the Country Music Association was the first trade organization formed to promote a type of music. More than 7,000 music industry professionals and companies from 41 countries around the world are members of CMA. The organization's objectives are to guide and enhance the development of Country Music and to demonstrate it as a viable medium to advertisers, consumers and media throughout the world.

SOURCE: CMA World, accessed http://cmaworld.com/news_publications/pr_archive/ pr_97_dec17.asp.

NOTE

1. As one cultural sociologist explains, this approach "focuses on the production of culture, rather than the cultural objects themselves. It does not purport to explain the 'statement' itself, to uncover what cultural objects/statements mean." Laura Desfor Edles, *Cultural Sociology in Practice* (Malden, Mass.: Blackwell, 2002): 13.

159

ℰPHEMERAL MUSIC

Napster's Congressional Testimony

The business model currently used by the recorded-music industry has been in place since the late nineteenth century. In this model, a record label identifies musical artists worthy of recording. Music, under the constitutional protection of copyright law and with the cooperation of authors and publishers, is selected. The recording artist completes a suitable master recording, usually at the expense of the label. The label mass-produces the final master recording and sets about to create a desire for the recording in the marketplace. Access to the market is provided by a network of distribution companies, which also participate in the promotion of the recording. Retailers sell the recording for consideration to a network of consumers. In this model, everyone gets paid: the label, the distributor, the authors and publishers, the retailers, and, after the label has been repaid for the investment in the production of the recording, even the recording artist.

At the end of the twentieth century, a convergence of technologies, and the synergy of their application, undermined this traditional business model. Widespread access to high-speed Internet connections; data compression algorithms, based on human perception for the transmission of smaller and smaller high-quality digital renderings of sound recordings; and the creative application of computer software to allow access to music over the Internet have contributed to an environment where music may be distributed outside of the traditional system.

The owners of the recordings have sought to prevent the use of these data files, claiming their rights of ownership, protected by the Constitution, in the federal courts and in many highly publicized lawsuits. The invention of Napster is probably the most famous example of the challenges posed by such new technology. In this selection, its inventor testifies before Congress. At the beginning of the twenty-first century, a number of ephemeral "music stores," selling properly licensed recordings, have achieved wide acceptance in the marketplace.[1]

〜〜〜〜〜
〜〜〜〜〜
〜〜〜〜〜

TESTIMONY OF SHAWN FANNING, FOUNDER, NAPSTER, INC., BEFORE THE SENATE JUDICIARY COMMITTEE, PROVO, UTAH

October 9, 2000

Good morning, Senator Hatch. Thank you for inviting me for my first visit to Utah and my first appearance before a Congressional committee. Napster has broadened my own horizons in many ways that I never expected, and these are two examples. I also want to introduce Hank Barry, Napster's CEO, who is here with me today.

I am very happy to have this opportunity to tell you about Napster's origins, describe how the technology works and discuss the future potential of peer-to-peer file sharing and distributed computing.

NAPSTER'S BEGINNINGS IN A NORTHEASTERN DORM ROOM

You may have heard or read that I started working on Napster in my dorm room at Northeastern University; while that's true, the story is a little more complicated than that.

I grew up in Massachusetts and during my high school years lived in Harwich. In 1996, between my sophomore and junior years in high school, my uncle, John Fanning, gave me a computer and access to the Internet. That was my first real experience with computers. I was a good student and focused a lot of attention on school, but my real love at that time was sports: I played baseball, basketball and tennis. The computer and the Internet fascinated me totally, and before long I gave up sports so I could spend more of my spare time at the computer learning about programming.

I started my freshman year at Northeastern University in the fall of 1998 intending to major in computer science. Looking for a challenge beyond the entry-level courses, I decided to start writing a Windows-based program on my own. I spent a lot of time in Internet Relay Chat (IRC) rooms getting advice and information from the experienced developers and programmers who hang out there. IRC is a network of people organized into communities, through real-time channels on various topics including programming and Internet security. "Napster" was my nickname, and I used it for my e-mail address and as my user name in IRC rooms.

One of my college roommates loved listening to MP3s and used Internet sites such as MP3.lycos.com to find them. He often complained about the unreliability of those sites, finding links to sites that were often dead ends, and indexes that were out of date because they were updated infrequently. I started thinking about ways to solve the reliability problems my roommate was experiencing.

I began designing and programming a real-time system for locating MP3 files of other users on the Internet. I designed the Napster software to find MP3s because they are the most compressed format (in consideration of bandwidth) and they were very popular at the time. The system I had in mind was unlike ordinary search engines at that time.

A traditional search engine sends out "robots" to roam the Internet periodically, updating itself every hour or more to remove sites that are down or unavailable. The database created is entirely driven by what the central computer finds by "crawling" the Internet. The indexes become outdated as sites go up or down, a significant problem when looking for MP3s because most of the files were housed on people's home computers.

My idea was to have users list the files they were willing to share on a computer that they all could access. That list would then be updated each time a person logged on to and off of that computer. The index computer would at all times have an up-to-date list of the files people were willing to share, and the list would be voluntarily made by the users as they logged on and off the system. A user searching the index would see all the files shared by users on the network and available to others on the network at that moment.

In contrast to traditional search engines, I envisioned a system that would be affirmatively powered by the users, who would select what information they wanted to list on the index. Then, when the user exited the application, their portion of the list (their files) would automatically drop from the index. The index was only one part of participating in the community. I also wanted users to be able to chat with each other and share information about their favorite music, so I added these functions to the application.

I very quickly became totally absorbed in this project. It was more compelling than my classes and more meaningful than socializing at school. I wrote a small design for this real-time search engine, and then began the implementation. I first wrote the server software. I next worked on writing the client application, i.e., the user interface. I ordered a Windows programming book over Amazon.com to learn what I needed and wrote the client software.

The Napster system I designed combined a real-time system for finding MP3s with chat rooms and instant messaging (functionality similar to IRC). The chat rooms and instant messaging are integral to creating the community experience; I imagined that they would be used similarly to how people use IRC—as a means for people to learn from each other and develop ongoing relationships. I also added a "hot list" function that enables people to see others' musical preferences by viewing the files they have chosen to share. This synergy of technologies created a platform for a community of users interested in music with different channels organized by genres of music (again, similar to IRC), and with genuine opportunity for participation, interaction and individual involvement by the members' sharing files together.

During the winter, I made the decision to leave school—I found I couldn't concentrate on developing the program and deal with my classes and life on campus. I was driven to figure out if I could make the program actually work. Initially, I didn't intend to even build it out; I was focused purely on establishing a "proof of concept." I figured that if I could make it work, others could too, and someone else would take it from there. There were many unknowns. The design required a networking infrastructure of servers and bandwidth in order to maintain large numbers of user connections. I didn't know if enough users had access to sufficient bandwidth. Other people were skeptical about whether users would be willing to share their files.

After developing the software prototype, I started sending it to friends, who sent it to other friends. A few early adopters provided feedback and helped track down bugs in the software. The consistently supportive and enthusiastic responses I got convinced me to try to build out the system. My uncle and I incorporated the company in May 1999 and he raised some money from angel investors. I released an early beta version of the Napster software during the summer and it spread quickly by word of mouth.

In September 1999 Napster, Inc. obtained office space and I moved to California. Download.com featured Napster in its Download Spotlight in early fall 1999, and the user community grew significantly.

It hasn't stopped growing since. Today the Napster community numbers over thirty-two million; for the past four months, it has been growing at the rate of one million new users each week. There are consistently over 800,000 people using the system simultaneously, limited only by our network resources. Napster users are in all corners of the world, and while I think it was initially adopted mostly by college students, a significant portion of our users are now over 30 (we received e-mail just last Friday from one 91-year-old man).

The underlying principle of the technology and the service is that people determine entirely for themselves how they are going to use the system and participate in the community—Napster provides the tools, but has no ability to impose limitations or exercise control. The music people are sharing and discussing ranges from the rock music you might expect to classical, opera, country, gospel, jazz, you name it. I receive thousands of e-mails personally and the company receives hundreds of thousands. People tell us that they use Napster to sample new music before deciding what to buy, find new artists, and house music in their computers that they already own on CD, cassette, vinyl and sometimes 8-track. We hear regularly from mothers who say they use Napster to screen the music their children are listening to and parents who say that Napster is a shared activity that helps them communicate with their teenagers.

I am an avid music fan myself and it is important to me that Napster benefit artists. Many users have told us that using Napster has led them to buy more CDs. Napster has implemented a range of features, most notably our New Artist and Featured Music programs, that help users find out about new and emerging artists and help artists promote their music throughout the Napster community, making it possible for them to reach a broad audience. And artists, both new and established, will be financially compensated when Napster is able to implement a business model.

HOW NAPSTER WORKS

Napster is a throwback to the original structure of the Internet. Rather than build large servers that house information, Napster relies on communication between the personal computers of the members of the Napster community. The information is distributed all across the Internet, allowing for a depth and scale of information that is virtually limitless.

Napster does not post, host, or serve MP3 files. The Napster software allows users to connect with each other, in order that they may share MP3 files stored on their individual hard drives. The number of song files available at any given time depends on the number of song files that active users choose to share from their hard drives. Users need not share any or all of their files—they can choose which ones to make available to others. MP3 files do not pass through a centralized server. The transfer is directly from computer to computer, known as "peer to peer." The "peer to peer" or decentralized nature of the technology means that the users, and only the users, determine what is shared.

Unlike ordinary web-based search engines, the Napster system cannot index files based on their content and organize them in a meaningful way for the users. MP3 and Windows Media Audio (WMA) files are not currently designed for such content-based indexing. Instead, such files can only be located and organized based on the file names assigned by the users, specific information in the MPEG header, bandwidth or ping time of the source (such as T1, cable DSL, 35 milliseconds) or by manually opening each file, listening to the file and then categorizing the file based on a personal judgment about what the file contains. Napster provides a directory through which users may find files, by file name, residing on the computers of other Napster users. The Napster service also provides location information allowing a computer to connect to the other user and transfer the file from its location.

THE UNLIMITED POTENTIAL OF PEER-TO-PEER TECHNOLOGY

I believe that the peer-to-peer technology on which Napster is based has the potential to be adopted for many different uses. People generally speak about the ability to share other kinds of files in addition to music, and indeed, Napster has been contacted by entities such as the Human Genome Project that are interested in sharing information among specific communities of interest. But peer-to-peer, or distributed computing also has tremendous opportunity for sharing resources or computing power, lowering information and transaction costs. Peer-to-peer could be used to create a pool of resources in aggregate to solve a range of complex problems.

Peer-to-peer also has the potential to change today's understanding of the relationship between source and site. Think how much faster and more efficient the Internet could be if instead of always connecting you to a central server every time you click on to a website, your computer would find the source that housed that information nearest to you—if it's already on the computer of the kid down the hall, why travel halfway around the world to retrieve it? A number of companies, from Intel on down to small start-ups, are looking at ways to develop peer-to-peer technology, and I believe that many of them will succeed. The result will be not just a better use of computing resources, but also the development of a myriad of communities and super-communities fulfilling the promise of the Internet that its founders envisioned.

SOURCE: Available at http://judiciary.senate.gov/oldsite/1092000_sf.htm.

~~~~~~~~~~

NOTE

1.   This introduction was written by Leon Janikian.

Index

Note: Page numbers in **boldface** indicate authorship of a selection. Page numbers in *italic* indicate illustrations.

Williams, Tennessee, 723
Williams, Vesta, 615
Williamsburg, Virginia, 36–40, 43, 44, 45
Willis, Richard Storrs, **128**, 163
Wilson, Robert, 722, 724, 731, 771
Wilson, Teddy, 544, 545, 547–48, **548–50**
Wilson, Wes, *611*
Wilton, John Hall, 186–88
"Wind Cries Mary, The," 623
Winterland (San Francisco), 609
Witmark family, 364
Wolpe, Stefan, 719
Womack, Bobby, 618, 623
women
    as blues singers, 399–403
    as composers, 320–29, 427n2, 443–44,
        450–55, 493–94, 512, 696–98, 725, 733–42,
        745–47
    as concert artists, 185–89, 191–92, 258–65,
        326, 328, 330
    diaries and letters of, 93–94, 245–49, 293–96
    enslaved African American, 237–40
    as jazz singers, 544–52, 561–64
    music education for nineteenth-century girls,
        155–59, 212–13, 217, 246, 259, 321–22,
        323–25
    Native American, 9–10
    as opera singers, 129–30, 191, 211–18
    as orchestral musicians, 748–58
    as organizers/leaders, 274, 277n1, 308, 311–12,
        810–13
    as rock musicians, 605–10
    as soul singers, 612–18
    as source singers, 510–11
    as writers, 506–9, 805–7, 826–29
women's rights movement, 203. *See also* feminism
Wonder, Stevie, 616, 824
Wood, Harriet "Hally," 521, 522n3
Wood, Leo, 364
Wood, William, **9–10**
Woodbridge, William C., 147
"Wooden Ships," 639
"Woodland Sketches," 335
Woodstock Festival, 619
"Woodworth," 343
Wooldridge, George B., 117
Wordsworth, William, 465n3
Work, John W., 507
work songs, 220–21, 229–33, 308, 627
Workers Song Book, 464
Works Progress Administration, 134, 190,
    235–41, 466–69, 472

World's Columbian Exposition (Chicago), 281,
    282, 307n1, 327
World's Peace Jubilee (Boston), 258, 264–65,
    266–69
"Worried Life Blues," 589
Wound Dresser, The (Adams), 772
Wozzeck (Berg), 461
Wuorinen, Charles, 746
Wyandot Indians, 101–4
Wyeth, John, 101–4
Wyner, Yehudi, 756
Wynton Marsalis Septet, 763

"Yankee Doodle," 180, 182, 215, 256, 350–51
Yardbirds, the, 622, 623, 641n1
"Year's at the Spring, The," 323, 327, 329
Yeats, William B., 758, 762n2
"Yellow Dog Blues, The," 400
"Yesterdays," 433
yodeling, 498
Yoga Frog, 837, 838
"You, Just You," 437
"(You Make Me Feel Like) A Natural Woman,"
    618
"You Better Run Through the Jungle," 655
"You Better Watch Yourself," 622
You Might Think video, 819
You Were Never Lovelier (film), 525, 526n4
You'll Never Get Rich (film), 525
Young, La Monte, 727
Young, Lester, 539, 544, 545, 549, 550, 554, 555,
    556, 557, 562, 563
Young Composers Group, 480
Young Ladies' Choir, The (anthology), 155
"Your Socks Don't Match," 536
Yradien, Sebastián, 395n1
Ysaÿe, Eugène, 328, 329n2

Z-Trip, 837
Zawinul, Joe, 652
Ziegfeld, Florenz, 555
Zimiga, Charley, 812
Zimmermann, Walter, 715, 719–20
zingari, I (Paisiello), 152
"Zion's Walls," 133
Zorn, John, **428–30**
Zouaves, 215, *253, 255*
Zundel, John, 347n3
Zuni Indians, 3–4
Zurke, Bob, 392
Zwerin, Michael, 650
zydeco, 791

CPSIA information can be obtained at www.ICGtesting.com
Printed in the USA
269889BV00004B/1-32/P